Arnould on the law
insurance and average
(Volume I)

Edward Louis De Hart,
Ralph Iliff Simey

Alpha Editions

This edition published in 2019

ISBN : 9789353896522

Design and Setting By
Alpha Editions
email - alphaedis@gmail.com

As per information held with us this book is in Public Domain.
This book is a reproduction of an important historical work. Alpha Editions uses the best technology to reproduce historical work in the same manner it was first published to preserve its original nature. Any marks or number seen are left intentionally to preserve its true form.

Joseph **ARNOULD**

ON THE LAW OF

MARINE INSURANCE
AND AVERAGE.

NINTH EDITION

BY

EDWARD LOUIS DE HART, M.A., LL.B. (Cantab.)

AND

RALPH ILIFF SIMEY, B.A. (Oxon.)

JOINT EDITORS OF "SMITH'S MERCANTILE LAW";
BOTH OF THE INNER TEMPLE AND NORTH-EASTERN CIRCUIT, BARRISTERS-AT-LAW.

IN TWO VOLUMES.

VOL. I.

LONDON:

STEVENS & SONS, LTD., | SWEET & MAXWELL, LTD.,
119 & 120, CHANCERY LANE. | 3, CHANCERY LANE.

1914.

PREFACE
TO THE NINTH EDITION.

THE eighth edition of this work followed the passing of the Marine Insurance Act, 1906. In that edition the editors adhered to the arrangement of the seventh edition (which was itself based on that of the second), introducing and explaining the provisions of the statute on all appropriate occasions. They feel justified in saying that this method of treating the subject has met with the general approval of the legal profession, and they have made no new departure in this edition.

All the cases decided before the Long Vacation of this year have been cited, and the changes in the law effected by the Marine Insurance (Gambling Policies) Act, 1909, have been duly noticed.

The Law of Naval Prize has an important bearing on some branches of marine insurance law, and has always been discussed at some length in this treatise. The law as stated in its pages is chiefly based on the decisions of the British Prize Courts; but it was considered advisable when this edition was prepared to indicate all essential difference between the British rules and those of the Declaration of London, although this instrument has not been ratified. Since this edition was in type, the British Government have announced, by Order in Council of August 20th, 1914, that during the present war the Declaration of London will be put in force with the following additions and modifications:—

(1) The lists of contraband contained in the Proclamation dated August 4th, 1914 (see *post*, Vol. II., App. E.), shall be substituted for the lists contained in Arts. 22 and 24.

(2) A neutral vessel which succeeded in carrying contraband to the enemy with false papers may be detained for having carried such contraband if she is encountered before she has completed her return voyage.

(3) The destination referred to in Art. 33 may be inferred from any sufficient evidence, and (in addition to the presumption laid down in Art. 34) shall be presumed to exist if the goods are consigned to or for an agent of the Enemy State or to or for a merchant or other person under the control of the authorities of the Enemy State.

(4) The existence of a blockade shall be presumed to be known—

    (a) to all ships which sailed from or touched at an enemy port a sufficient time after the notification of the blockade to the local authorities to have enabled the enemy Government to make known the existence of the blockade,

    (b) to all ships which sailed from or touched at a British or allied port after the publication of the declaration of blockade.

(5) Notwithstanding the provisions of Art. 35, conditional contraband, if shown to have the destination referred to in Art. 33, is liable to capture to whatever port the vessel is bound and at whatever port the cargo is to be discharged.

(6) The General Report of the Drafting Committee on the Declaration adopted by the Naval Conference at the eleventh plenary meeting on February 25th, 1909, shall be considered by all Prize Courts as an authoritative statement of the meaning of the Declaration, and such Courts shall construe and interpret the provisions of the Declaration by the light of the commentary given therein.

The Editors wish to acknowledge their indebtedness to Mr. G. R. Rudolph, Member of the Association of Average Adjusters, for some valuable suggestions, and once more to Mr. Charles Wright, of Lloyd's, for much useful information relating to the course of insurance business.

E. L. DE H.
R. I. S.

11, KING'S BENCH WALK, TEMPLE,
    August, 1914.

The following Editions of Treatises have been used for the references in this work.

ABBOTT on Shipping; 5th and 14th. Lond. 1827 and 1901.
Baily on General Average; 2nd. Lond. 1856.
—— on Perils of the Sea. Liverpool, 1860.
Beawes' Lex Mercatoria; 6th. Lond. 1813.
Benecke, Principles of Indemnity. Lond. 1824.
————, System des Assekuranz und Bodmereiwesens. Lond. 1810.
———————————————————— par Nolte. Hamburg, 1851—2.
Boulay-Paty, Droit Commercial Maritime. Paris, 1834.
Bynkershoek, Opera Omnia a Vicat. Col. Allob. 1761.
Carver on Carriage by Sea; 4th and 5th. Lond. 1905 and 1909.
Casaregis, Discursus Legales de Commercio; 2nd. Venetiis, 1740.
Cleirac, Us et Coutumes de la Mer. Bordeaux, 1661.
Dicey, Conflict of Laws; 2nd. Lond. 1908.
Duer on Marine Insurance. New York, 1845—6.
—— on Representations in Marine Insurance. New York, 1844.
Emerigon, Des Assurances et des Contrats à la Grosse par Boulay-Paty. Rennes, 1827.
Gow on Marine Insurance; 4th. Lond. 1913.
Grotius, de Jure Belli et Pacis, by Whewell. Cambridge, 1853.
Joyce on Insurance. San Francisco, 1897.
Kent, Commentaries on American Law; 10th. New York, 1860.
Kuricke, de Assecurationibus, in the Fasciculus Scriptorum de Jur. Naut. et Marit. of J. G. Heinneccius. Halae Magd. 1740.
Lampredi, del Commercio de Popoli Neutrali in tempo di guerra. Milano, 1831.
Loccenius, de Jure Maritimo, in the Fasciculus Scriptorum de Jur. Naut. et Marit. of J. G. Heinneccius. Halae Magd. 1740.
Lowndes, R., on General Average; 5th. Lond. 1912.
——————— on Marine Insurance; 2nd. Lond. 1885.
McArthur on the Contract of Marine Insurance; 2nd. Lond. 1890.
Maclachlan on the Law of Merchant Shipping; 5th. Lond. 1911.
Magens on Insurances. Lond. 1755.
Malyne's Lex Mercatoria; 3rd. Lond. 1686.

Marquardus de Jure Mercatorum. Francf. 1662.
Marshall on Insurance, by Chas. Marshall; 3rd. Lond. 1823.
Maude and Pollock on Merchant Shipping; 4th. Lond. 1881.
Molloy de Jure Maritimo. Lond. 1682.
Paley on Principal and Agent, by Lloyd; 3rd. Lond. 1833.
Pardessus, de Droit Commercial; 5th. Paris, 1840.
―――――, Lois Maritimes ant. au XVIIIe siècle (*cited* Pardess.). Paris, 1828—45.
Park on Insurance, by Hildyard; 8th. Lond. 1842.
Parsons on Insurance. Boston, U.S. 1868.
Phillips on Insurance; 4th. Boston, U.S. 1854.
Pothier des Assurances, du Charte-partie, vol. 5 of his Œuvres par M. Bugnet. Paris, 1845—48.
――――――――――――― par Estrangin. Paris, 1810.
Roccus de Navibus, etc.; ed. nova. Amst. 1708.
Rutherforth, Institutes of National Law. Cambridge, 1754—6.
Santerna, de Assecurationibus. Col. Agripp. 1599.
Stevens on Average; 5th. Lond. 1835.
Story on Agency. Lond. 1839.
―――― on the Conflict of Laws; 2nd. Lond. 1841.
Straccha, de Mercaturâ et Assecurationibus. Amst. 1669.
Temperley, Merchant Shipping Acts; 2nd. Lond. 1907.
Valin, Nouveau Commentaire sur l'Ordonnance de 1681. Rochelle, 1766.
―――――――――――――――par Becanne. Poitiers, 1829.
Vattel, Droit des Gens, par Pradier-Fodéré. Paris, 1863.
Vinnius in Peckium, ad Rem Nauticam. Ludg. 1647.

CONTENTS.

	PAGE
PREFACE	v
EDITIONS OF WORKS OF REFERENCE	vii
TABLE OF CASES CITED	xiii

PART I.

OF THE NATURE, FORMATION AND SUBJECT-MATTER OF THE CONTRACT OF MARINE INSURANCE.

CHAPTER I.
The Contract of Marine Insurance generally 1

CHAPTER II.
The Form and Contents of Sea Policies 8

CHAPTER III.
Of the Construction of Sea Policies 74

CHAPTER IV.
Different Classes of Insurers on Sea Policies 101

CHAPTER V.
Of the Assured: who may be insured 120

CHAPTER VI.
Course of Business in Sea Insurance—Relations between Assured, Broker and Underwriter 141

CHAPTER VII.

Insurance Agents generally: their Rights, Duties and Liabilities 188

CHAPTER VIII.

Description of the Assured in the Policy—Assignment of the Policy 229

CHAPTER IX.

Of the Ship 246

CHAPTER X.

Of the Master 262

CHAPTER XI.

The Subjects of Marine Insurance 288

CHAPTER XII.

Of the Interest that gives the Title to Insure—*i.e.*, Insurable Interest 339

CHAPTER XIII.

Valuation of Insurable Interests 457

CHAPTER XIV.

The Voyage Insured 504

CHAPTER XV.

Deviation and Change of Risk 511

CHAPTER XVI.

Nature and Duration of the Risk in Time Policies 588

CHAPTER XVII.

Duration of the Risk in Voyage Policies 600

PART II.

OF CERTAIN MATTERS THAT RENDER THE CONTRACT OF INSURANCE VOID OR UNAVAILABLE.

CHAPTER I.

	PAGE
Misrepresentation	685

CHAPTER II.

Concealment 737

CHAPTER III.

Express Warranties 807

CHAPTER IV.

Implied Warranties 871

CHAPTER V.

Illegality of the Risk 925

PART III.

OF LOSSES AND THE RELATIONS OF THE ASSURED AND UNDERWRITER THENCE ARISING.

CHAPTER I.

Losses not covered by the Policy 967

CHAPTER II.

Losses by the Perils insured against 1016

CHAPTER III.

Excepted Risks and Losses 1103

CHAPTER IV.

Of General Average 1129

CHAPTER V

Of Particular Average 1260

CONTENTS.

CHAPTER VI.
Actual or Absolute Total Loss 1306

CHAPTER VII.
Constructive Total Loss 1358

CHAPTER VIII.
Abandonment 1472

CHAPTER IX.
Subrogation 1522

CHAPTER X.
Settlement of Losses 1542

CHAPTER XI.
Return of Premium 1550

PART IV.

Procedure and Evidence 1585

APPENDICES.

A. Statutes 1607
B. Specimen Slip, Institute Clauses, Club Policy 1647
C. York-Antwerp Rules 1669
D. Rules of Practice of the Association of Average Adjusters 1676
E. List of Contraband Articles (August, 1914) 1693

TABLE OF CASES CITED.

[*The sections in which a case is particularly referred to in the text, and is not merely cited, are printed in* **black type.**]

A.

	SECT.
ABBOTT *v.* Sebor, 3 Johns. Cas. 39	288, 1203
Abel *v.* Potts, 3 Esp. 242; 6 R. R. 826	1192, 1283
Abo, The, Spinks' Prize Cas. 42	93, 657
Acanthus, The, [1902] P. 17; 71 L. J. P. 14; 85 L. T. 696	1039
Acatos *v.* Burns, 3 Ex. D. 282; 47 L. J. Ex. 566; 26 W. R. 624	205, 206, 689
Achard *v.* Ring, 31 L. T. (N. S.) 647; 2 Asp. M. C. 422	936
Adam SS. Co. *v.* London Ass. Corp., W. N. 1st Aug. 1914	1272
Adams *v.* Bankart, 4 L. J. Ex. 69; 1 C. M. & R. 681; 5 Tyr. 425; 1 Gale, 48; 40 R. R. 670	168
Adams *v.* Delaware Ins. Co., 3 Binn. 287	1138
Adams *v.* McKenzie, 32 L. J. C. P. 92; 13 C. B. (N. S.) 442; 9 Jur. (N. S.) 849; 7 L. T. 711; 11 W. R. 342; 134 R. R. 593...884, 902, 1091	
Adams *v.* Saunders, 4 C. & P. 25; M. & Malk. 373	1241
Adelaide, The, 2 C. Rob. 111, n.	768
Adelaide, The, 3 C. Rob. 281	766
Adonis, The, 5 C. Rob. 256	765
African Co. *v.* Bull, 1 Show. 132	331
African SS. Co. *v.* Swanzy, 2 K. & J. 660; 25 L. J. Ch. 870; 4 W. R. 210, 692	1135
Agenoria SS. Co., Ltd. *v.* Merchants' Mar. Ins. Co., Ltd., 8 Com. Cas. 212	1022, 1023, 1127
Aguilar *v.* Rodgers, 7 T. R. 421; 4 R. R. 478	1263
Aikshaw, The, 9 Times L. R. 605	41
Aina, The, Spinks' Prize Cas. 8	93
Airy *v.* Bland, 2 Park, Ins. 811	107
Aitchison *v.* Lohre, 2 Q. B. D. 501; 3 Q. B. D. 558; 4 App. Cas. 755, 764; 49 L. J. Q. B. 123; 41 L. T. 323; 28 W. R. 1; 4 Asp. M. C. 168...22, 863, **864**, 865, 870, 871, 902, 964, 1023, 1024, **1033**, 1092, 1107, 1184	
Ajum Goolam Hossen *v.* Union Marine Ins. Co., [1901] A. C. 362; 70 L. J. P. C. 34; 84 L. T. 366; 9 Asp. M. C. 167; 17 Times L. R. 376	725, 812
Albert Average Assn., In re, Blyth's Case, L. R. 13 Eq. 529; 20 W. R. 504	81

TABLE OF CASES.

	SECT.

Albion Life and Fire Ins. Co. v. Mills. (*See* Patterson v. Mills.)
Alcenius v. Nygren, 23 L. J. Q. B. 287; 24 L. J. Q. B. 19; 4 E. & B.
    217; 1 Jur. (N. S.) 16; 3 W. R. 25; 90 R. R. 435 89
Alcock v. Royal Exch. Ass. Corp., 13 Q. B. 292; 18 L. J. Q. B. 121;
    13 Jur. 445; 78 R. R. 364 203
Aldridge v. Bell, 1 Stark. 498 ....1193, 1274
Alers v. Tobin, Abbott on Shipping, 14th ed. 551 ....200, 1031
Alexander v. Baltimore Ins. Co., 4 Cranch, S. C. R. 370 1104
Alexander v. Campbell, 41 L. J. Ch. 478; 27 L. T. 25, 462; 1 Asp.
    M. C. 447 ....82, 559
Allegre v. Maryland Ins. Co., 2 Gill & Johns. R. 136 543
Allemannia Ins. Co. v. Firemen's Ins. Co., 209 U. S. 326 437
Allen v. Long, 2 Marsh. Ins. 668 1256
Allen v. Sugrue, Dans. & Ll. 188; 3 Man. & Ry. 9; 8 B. & C. 561; 7
    L. J. (O. S.) K. B. 53; 32 R. R. 483 ......348, 1054, 1058, 1064, 1111,
        1123, 1133, 1203
Allison v. Bristol Marine Ins. Co., L. R. 9 C. P. 559; 1 App. Cas. 209;
    34 L. T. 809; 24 W. R. 1039; 3 Asp. M. C. 178...232, 233, 252b, 263, 264
Allkins v. Jupe, 2 C. P. D. 375; 46 L. J. C. P. 824; 36 L. T. 851 ...241, 313,
        313a, 315, 1253
Allwood v. Henckell, 1 Park, Ins. 399 ....1052, 1059, 1192, 1197
Alps, The, [1893] P. 109; 62 L. J. Adm. 59; 68 L. T. 624; 41 W. R.
    527; 7 Asp. M. C. 337 ....608, 786
Alsace Lorraine, The, [1893] P. 209; 62 L. J. Adm. 107; 1 R. 632; 69
    L. T. 261; 42 W. R. 112; 7 Asp. M. C. 362 887
Alsop v. Coit, 12 Mass. R. 40 ....161, 543
Alsop v. Commercial Ins. Co., 1 Sumner, R. 451 617
Alston v. Campbell, 4 Bro. P. C. 476 (Tomlin's ed.) 179, 299
Alston v. Mechanics' Ins. Co., 4 Hill, 329 543
Amalia, The, 1 Moo. P. C. (N. S.) 471; Br. & Lush. 151; 2 N. R. 533;
    32 L. J. Adm. 191; 9 Jur. (N. S.) 1111; 8 L. T. 805; 12 W. R.
    24; 138 R. R. 591 802
America Ins. Co. v. Gossler, 96 U. S. 643 ....1137, 1217
American Ins. Co. v. Center, 4 Wend. S. C. R. 45 ....204, 1030
American Ins. Co. v. Ogden, 15 Wend. 532 1116
American Steamship Co. v. Indemnity Mut. Ins. Co., 108 Fed. R. 421. 75
American Surety Co. v. Wrightson, 16 Com. Cas. 37; 103 L. T. 663;
    27 Times L. R. 91 ....330, 331, 354
Amery v. Rodgers, 1 Esp. 207; 5 R. R. 731 ....361, 1185, 1278
Andersen v. Marten, [1907] 2 K. B. 248; [1908] 1 K. B. 601; [1908]
    A. C. 334; 76 L. J. K. B. 674; 77 L. J. K. B. 569, 950; 97 L. T.
    375; 98 L. T. 146; 99 L. T. 254; 10 Asp. M. C. 494, 605; 12 Com.
    Cas. 309; 13 Com. Cas. 205, 321; 24 Times L. R. 775 ......247, 790,
        801, **820**, 829, 830
Anderson v. Morice, L. R. 10 C. P. 58, 609; 1 App. Cas. 713; 44 L. J.
    C. P. 341; 46 L. J. C. P. 11; 35 L. T. 566; 25 W. R. 14 ...241, 255a,
        258, 282, **283**, 285, 725
Anderson v. Ocean Steamship Co., 13 Q. B. D. 651; 10 App. Cas. 107;
    54 L. J. Q. B. 192; 52 L. T. 441; 33 W. R. 433; 5 Asp. M. C.
    401 ....965, 1004, 1005

TABLE OF CASES. XV

SECT.

Anderson v. Pacific Fire and Mar. Ins. Co., L. R. 7 C. P. 65; 26 L. T. 130; 20 W. R. 280; 1 Asp. M. C. 220 ....535, **549**, 575
Anderson v. Pitcher, 2 B. & P. 164; 3 Esp. 134; Stark. 262; 5 R. R. 565 654
Anderson v. Royal Exchange Ass. Co., 7 East, 38; 3 Smith, 48; 8 R. R. 589............................165, 1048, **1072, 1149,** 1158, 1197, 1274
Anderson v. Thornton, 8 Exch. 425; 20 L. T. (O. S.) 250; 91 R. R. 565. 555, 1256
Anderson v. Wallis, 2 M. & S. 240; 3 Camp. 440; 14 R. R. 642 ...206, 1093, 1143, 1144, **1147**, 1184
André Théodore, The, 10 Asp. M. C. 94 101
Andree v. Fletcher, 3 T. R. 266 ....313a, 1255
Andrew v. Robinson, 3 Camp. 199; 13 R. R. 788 ....119, 125
Andrews v. Essex Fire and Marine Ins. Co., 3 Mason, 6 41
Andrews v. Mellish (see Mellish v. Andrews), 5 Taunt. 496; 2 M. & S. 27; 16 East, 312 ....393, 403
Angel v. Merchants' Mar. Ins. Co., [1903] 1 K. B. 811; 72 L. J. K. B. 498; 88 L. T. 717; 51 W. R. 530; 8 Com. Cas. 179 1124
Angerstein v. Bell, 1 Park, Ins. 54 491
Anglo-Argentine Live Stock and Produce Agency v. Temperley Shipping Co., [1899] 2 Q. B. 356; 68 L. J. Q. B. 1021; 81 L. T. 231; 48 W. R. 48; 4 Com. Cas. 281 944
Ann Green, The, 1 Gall. Adm. Rep. 274 ....91, 92
Anna Catherina, The, 4 C. Rob. 107 ....93, 98, 657, 659
Annen v. Woodman, 3 Taunt. 299; 12 R. R. 663 ......475, 478, 634, 687, 698, 710, 1251, 1256
Anon. v. Westmore, 6 Esp. 109 508
Anon., 1 Chit. 49 ....756, 1285
Anon., cited Paley's Principal & Agent, 20 161
Anon., 2 Show. 283 263
Anon., Skinner's R. 243 493
Anon., Skinner's R. 327; 1 Marsh. Ins. 452; 1 Park, Ins. (8th ed.) 405. 537
Anstey v. Ocean Mar. Ins. Co., 19 Com. Cas. 8; 83 L. J. K. B. 218; 109 L. T. 854; 58 S. J. 49; 30 Times L. R. 5 ....245, 367
Antonia Johanna, The, 1 Wheaton, 159 ....93, 658
Apollinaris Co. v. Nord-Deutsche Ins. Co., [1904] 1 K. B. 252; 73 L. J. K. B. 62; 89 L. T. 670; 52 W. R. 174; 9 Com. Cas. 91; 9 Asp. M. C. 526; 20 Times L. R. 79 ....60, 225, 921
Apollo, The, 4 C. Rob. 158 763
Arcangelo v. Thompson, 2 Camp. 620; 12 R. R. 758 ...784, 829, 859, 1277
Armett v. Innes, 4 J. B. Moore, 150; 21 R. R. 737 ....404, 405
Arnot v. Stewart, 5 Dow, 274; 16 R. R. 123 ....555, 560
Arrow Shipping Co. v. Tyne Commissioners. (See Crystal, The.)
Arthur, The, Edw. Adm. R. 202 770
Arthur Average Assn., In re The, L. R. 10 Ch. 542; 44 L. J. Ch. 509; 32 L. T. 713; 23 W. R. 939; 2 Asp. M. C. 570 ....8, 26, 80
Asfar v. Blundell, [1895] 2 Q. B. 196; [1896] 1 Q. B. 123; 65 L. J. Q. B. 138; 15 R. 481; 73 L. T. 648; 44 W. R. 130; 8 Asp. M. C. 106; 1 Com. Cas. 71, 185 ...20, 239, 339, 591, 608, 611, 1067, 1072, 1074, **1076**, 1080

TABLE OF CASES.

SECT.

Ashbury Railway Carriage, &c. Co. *v.* Riche, L. R. 9 Ex. 224; L. R. 7 H. L. 653; 44 L. J. Ex. 185; 33 L. T. 451; 24 W. R. 794 79
Ashley *v.* Pratt, 16 M. & W. 471; 17 L. J. Ex. 135; 1 Ex. 257; 73 R. R. 575 ....**396**, 401
Aspinwall *v.* Merchants' Shipping Co., cited 45 L. J. Q. B. 646 936
Assicurazioni Generali de Trieste *v.* Empress Ass. Corpn., [1904] 2 K. B. 814; 76 L. J. K. B. 980; 97 L. T. 785; 10 Asp. M. C. 577; 13 Com. Cas. 37; 23 Times L. R. 700 1225
Assieviedo *v.* Cambridge, 10 Mod. 77 ....**311**, 1104
Astor *v.* Union Ins. Co., 7 Cowen, 202 ....**68**, 883
Atalanta, The, 6 C. Rob. 440 ....**669**, 760
Atkinson *v.* Abbott, 11 East, 135; 1 Camp. 535; 3 Drew. 251...96, **751**, 758
Atkinson *v.* Stephens, 21 L. J. Ex. 329; 7 Exch. 567; 86 R. R. 739 ... 200, 927, 978, 982, 1031
Atlantic Ins. Co. *v.* Storrow, 5 Paige, 293 837
Atlantic Mutual Ins. Co. *v.* Huth, 16 Ch. D. 474, 481; 44 L. T. 67; 29 W. R. 387; 4 Asp. M. C. 369 206
Atlas, The, 3 C. Rob. 299 659
Attorney-General *v.* Great Eastern Ry., 11 Ch. D. 449; 5 A. C. 473; 49 L. J. Ch. 545; 42 L. T. 810; 28 W. R. 769 79
Atty *v.* Lindo, 1 B. & P. (N. R.) 236; 8 R. R. 788 ......266, 272, **274**, 513, 520, 1087, 1089
Atwood *v.* Sellar, 4 Q. B. D. 342; 5 Q. B. D. 286; 49 L. J. Q. B. 515; 42 L. T. 644; 28 W. R. 604; 4 Asp. M. C. 283 ...212, 947, **949**, 955, 957, 959, 960, 961, 991
Aubert *v.* Gray, 32 L. J. Q. B. 50; 3 B. & S. 163; 9 Jur. (N. S.) 714; 7 L. T. 469; 11 W. R. 27; 129 R. R. 281 ....295, 803, 832, **833**, 834
Aubert *v.* Walsh, 3 Taunt. 277; 12 R. R. 651 1254
Audley *v.* Duff, 2 B. & P. 111; 5 R. R. 549 1266
Australasian Ins. Co. *v.* Jackson, 33 L. T. (N. S.) 286; 3 Asp. M. C. 26 ....745, 829, 842
Australian Agricultural Co. *v.* Saunders, L. R. 10 C. P. 668; 44 L. J. C. P. 391; 33 L. T. 447; 3 Asp. M. C. 63 ....460, 461, 468
Australian Steam Nav. Co. *v.* Morse, L. R. 4 P. C. 222; 8 Moo. P. C. (N. S.) 482; 27 L. T. 357; 20 W. R. 728 ....195, 203, 205, 1055, 1058

B.

Backhouse *v.* Ripley, 1 Park, Ins. (8th ed.) 24 ....225, 801
Baillie *v.* Moudigliani, 1 Park, Ins. (8th ed.) 116 ......214, 811, 877, 1211
Bain *v.* Case, 3 C. & P. 496; M. & M. 262 ....416, 1284
Bainbridge *v.* Neilson, 1 Camp. 240; 10 East, 329; 10 R. R. 316...1094, 1095, 1096, 1100, **1101**, 1102, 1138, 1183
Baines *v.* Ewing, L. R. 1 Ex. 320; 35 L. J. Ex. 194; 4 H. & C. 511; 14 L. T. 733; 14 W. R. 732 168
Baines *v.* Holland, 24 L. J. Ex. 204; 10 Exch. 802; 3 C. L. R. 593; 102 R. R. 841 653

TABLE OF CASES. xvii

SECT.

Baines v. Woodfall, 6 C. B. (N. S.) 657; 28 L. J. C. P. 338; 6 Jur.
(N. S.) 19; 120 R. R. 328 54
Baker v. Adam, 15 Com. Cas. 227; 102 L. T. 248; 11 Asp. M. C. 368...175, 176, 177
Baker v. Langhorn, 6 Taunt. 519; 2 Marsh. 216; 4 Camp. 396; 16 R. R.
662 ....112, 115, 118
Baker v. Ludlow, 2 Johns. Cas. 289 883
Baker v. Towry, 1 Stark. 436; 18 R. R. 803 888
Baker-Whiteley Coal Co. v. Marten, 26 Times L. R. 314 ....816, 888
Bakewell v. United Ins. Co., 2 Johns. Cas. 246 883
Ballantyne v. Mackinnon, [1896] 2 Q. B. 455; 65 L. J. Q. B. 616; 75
L. T. 95; 45 W. R. 70; 8 Asp. M. C. 173; 1 Com. Cas. 339—424 ......678, 682, 726, 729, 778, 799, 863
Balmoral Steamship Co. v. Marten, [1900] 2 Q. B. 748; [1901] 2 K. B.
896; [1902] A. C. 511; 71 L. J. K. B. 819; 87 L. T. 247; 51 W. R.
175; 7 Com. Cas. 292; 9 Asp. M. C. 321 ....339, 1006
Baltazzi v. Ryder, 12 Moo. P. C. 168 766
Baltica, The, Spinks' Prize Cases, 264 ....93, 95
Bangor and North Wales Mutual, &c. Assn., *In re* Baird's Case, 68
L. J. Ch. 521; [1899] 2 Ch. 593; 80 L. T. 870; 47 W. R. 695...... 80
Bank of England v. Vagliano, [1891] A. C. 107; 60 L. J. Q. B. 145; 64
L. T. 353; 39 W. R. 657; 55 J. P. 676 1
Barber v. Fleming, L. R. 5 Q. B. 59; 39 L. J. Q. B. 25; 10 B. & S. 879;
18 W. R. 254 ....270, 271, **275**, 276, 279, **513**
Barber v. Fletcher, 1 Dougl. 306; Campbell's Ruling Cases, vol. xiii.
pp. 536—539 ....543, 546, 571, 1256
Barclay v. Cousins, 2 East, 544; 6 R. R. 505 ....236, 240, 249, 254, 287
Barclay v. Pearson, [1893] 2 Ch. 154; 62 L. J. Ch. 636; 3 R. 388; 68
L. T. 709; 42 W. R. 74 1254
Barclay v. Stirling, 5 M. & S. 6; 17 R. R. 245 ...402, **452**, 519, 880, 1089,
1166, 1167, 1178, **1181**, 1211
Baring v. Claggett or Christie, 3 B. & P. 201; 5 East, 398; 6 R. R. 759;
7 R. R. 719 ....630, 655, 656, 661, **662**, 683
Baring v. Henckle, 1 Marsh. Ins. 232 888
Baring v. Royal Exchange Ass. Co., 5 East, 99; 7 R. R. 657 ....680, 685
Baring v. Stanton, 3 Ch. D. 502; 35 L. T. 652; 25 W. R. 237; 3
Asp. M. C. 294 104
Baring v. Vaux, 2 Camp. 541; 11 R. R. 791 905
Barker v. Baltimore and Ohio Railroad Co., 22 Ohio St. 45 961
Barker v. Blakes, 9 East, 283; 9 R. R. 558 ....613, 658, 667, 772, 832,
1138, **1143**, 1197
Barker v. Janson, L. R. 3 C. P. 303; 37 L. J. C. P. 105; 17 L. T. 473;
16 W. R. 399 ....20, **339**, 342, 1032b, 1049, 1115
Barker v. Marine Ins. Co., 2 Mason, 369 308
Barker v. Phœnix Ins. Co., 8 Johns. R. 237 661
Barlow v. Leckie, 4 J. B. Moore, 8 ....140, 142, 171
Barnett v. Brandao, 6 M. & Gr. 630 1273
Barnewall v. Church, 1 Caines, 217 610
Barque Robert S. Besnard Co., Ltd. v. Murton. (*See* Robert
S. Besnard Co., Ltd. v. Murton.)

A.—VOL. I.   b

xviii   TABLE OF CASES.

SECT.

Barraclough v. Brown, [1897] A. C. 615; 66 L. J. Q. B. 672; 76 L. T.
    797; 8 Asp. M. C. 290; 1 Com. Cas. 262, 329; 2 Com. Cas. 249 1212
Barrass v. London Ass. Co., 1 Park, Ins. 74 ....464, 496
Barrow v. Bell, 4 L. J. (O. S.) K. B. 47; 7 D. & R. 244; 4 B. & C. 736;
    28 R. R. 468 890
Barrow-in-Furness Mutual Ship Ins. Co. v. Ashburner, 54 L. J. Q. B.
    377; 54 L. T. 58; 5 Asp. M. C. 527 ....36, 82
Barry v. Louisiana Ins. Co., 11 Martin (N. S.) 630 852
Bartlett v. Pentland, 10 B. & C. 760; 8 L. J. (O. S.) K. B. 264; 34
    R. R. 560 ....62, 64, 65, 66, 125, **127**
Barzillai v. Lewis, 3 Dougl. 126 ....597, 663, 683
Bates v. Hewitt, L. R. 2 Q. B. 595; 36 L. J. Q. B. 282; 15 W. R.
    1172 ....183, 598, **609**, 614, 616, 625
Bauduy v. Union Ins. Co., 2 Wash. C. C. R. 391 598
Bayard v. Massachusetts Fire and Mar. Ins. Co., 4 Mason, 256 658
Bazett v. Meyer, 5 Taunt. 824 ....803, 833
Beacon Fire and Life Ass. Co. v. Gibb, 1 Moo. P. C. (N. S.) 73; 1 N. R.
    110; 9 Jur. (N. S.) 185; 7 L. T. 574; 11 W. R. 194 70
Bean v. Stupart, 1 Dougl. 11 ....29, 637
Beatson v. Haworth, 6 T. R. 531; 3 R. R. 258 394
Beattie v. Lord Ebury, L. R. 7 Ch. 777; 41 L. J. Ch. 804; 27 L. T.
    398; 20 W. R. 994 542
Beaver, The, 3 C. Rob. 292 434
Beckett v. West of England Ins. Co., 25 L. T. (N. S.) 739; 1 Asp. M. C.
    185 516
Beckwaite v. Nalgrove, cited 3 Taunt. 41 600
Beckwith v. Sydebotham, 1 Camp. 116; 10 R. R. 652 ....618, 619, 641, 726
Bedouin, The, [1894] P. 1; 63 L. J. Adm. 30; 6 R. 693; 69 L. T. 782;
    42 W. R. 292; 7 Asp. M. C. 391 ....233, 536, 555, 608, 611, **786**
Beeston v. Beeston, 1 Ex. D. 13; 45 L. J. Ex. 230; 33 L. T. 700; 24
    W. R. 96 .... 313a
Bell v. Bell, 2 Camp. 475; 11 R. R. 769 ....478, 515, 596, **623**
Bell v. Bromfield, 15 East, 364 ....666, 729, **730**, 732
Bell v. Buller, 1 M. & S. 726; 14 R. R. 557 755
Bell v. Carstairs, 2 Camp. 543; 14 East, 374; 11 R. R. 593; 12 R. R.
    557 ....571, 680, 727, **729**, 731, **801**
Bell v. Gilson, 1 B. & P. 345; 4 R. R. 823 ....85, 170, 754
Bell v. Hobson, 16 East, 240; 3 Camp. 272; 14 R. R. 337.................. 450
Bell v. Humphries, 2 Stark. 345 136
Bell v. Janson, 1 M. & S. 201 ....142, 171, 1275
Bell v. Jutting, 1 J. B. Moore, 155; 19 R. R. 533 122
Bell v. Nixon, Holt, N. P. R. 423 ....1047, 1053, **1060**
Bell v. Reed, 4 Binn. 127 700
Bell v. Reid, 1 M. & S. 726; 14 R. R. 557 ....93, 95, 98, 755
Bell v. Smith, 2 Johns. R. 98 984
Bempdé v. Johnstone, 3 Ves. 198 90
Bennett SS. Co., Ltd. v. Hull Mutual SS. Protecting Soc., Ltd., [1913]
    3 K. B. 372; [1914] 3 K. B. 57; 82 L. J. K. B. 1003; 109 L. T.
    213; 18 Com. Cas. 274; 58 S. J. 14; 29 Times L. R. 645; 30
    Times L. R. 515 795

TABLE OF CASES. xix

	SECT.
Bennett v. Brumfield, L. R. 3 C. P. 28	26

Bensaude v. Thames and Mersey Mar. Ins. Co., [1897] 1 Q. B. 25;
[1897] A. C. 609; 66 L. J. Q. B. 666; 77 L. T. 282; 46 W. R. 78;
8 Asp. M. C. 315; 2 Com. Cas. 33, 238 ....629, 787
Benson v. Chapman, 6 M. & Gr. 792; 2 H. L. Cas. 696; 5 C. B. 330;
8 C. B. 950; 13 Jur. 969; 81 R. R. 346.........195, 1106, 1123, 1136, 1164,
1165, 1167, 1169, 1174
Benson v. Duncan, 17 L. J. Ex. 238; 18 L. J. Ex. 169; 1 Exch. 537;
3 Exch. 655; 12 Jur. 218; 14 Jur. 218; 74 R. R. 754; 77 R. R.
776 ....195, 196, **197**, 200, 877, 978
Bentzon v. Boyle, 9 Cranch, 191 97
Berens v. Rucker, 1 W. Bl. 313 ....98, 660, 664, 771, 830
Bermon v. Woodbridge, 2 Dougl. 781........................375, **691**, 1249, **1251**
Bermuda, The, 3 Wallace, 514 763
Bernardi v. Motteux, 2 Dougl. 575 ....666, 680, 684
Bernìna, The, 12 P. D. 36; 56 L. J. Adm. 38; 55 L. T. 781; 56 L. T.
450; 35 W. R. 214; 6 Asp. M. C. 65, 112 213
Bernon, The, 1 C. Rob. 102 90
Berridge v. Man On Ins. Co., 18 Q. B. D. 346; 56 L. J. Q. B. 223; 56
L. T. 375; 35 W. R. 343; 6 Asp. M. C. 104 ....241, 313, 317
Bertbon v. Loughman, 2 Stark. 229 626
Betsey, The, 1 C. Rob. 93 ....767, 769
Betsey, The, 2 C. Rob. 210, n. 676
Bhugwandass v. Netherlands Indian Sea and Fire Ins. Co. of Batavia,
14 App. Cas. 83 39
Biccard v. Shepherd, 14 Moo. P. C. 471; 5 L. T. 504; 10 W. R. 136;
134 R. R. 74 ....**691**, 692, 698, 699, 717
Bilbie v. Lumley, 2 East, 469; 6 R. R. 479 1244
Bird v. Appleton, 8 T. R. 562; 5 R. R. 468 ....663, 684, 737, 738, 746
Bird v. Pigou, 2 Selw. N. P. (13th ed.) 932 735
Birkley v. Presgrave, 1 East, 220; 6 R. R. 256..907, 914, 931, **932**, 952, 1004
Birrell v. Dryer, 9 App. Cas. 345; 51 L. T. 130; 5 Asp. M. C. 267
(see also Dryer v. Birrell) 70, 75, 436, 639
Bishop v. Pentland, 7 B. & C. 219; 1 M. & Ry. 49; 6 L. J. (O. S.)
K. B. 6; 31 R. R. 177 ....692, 723, **798**, 890
Bize v. Fletcher, 1 Dougl. 12, n. (4), 284 ....529, 535, 560, 629
Blaauwpot v. Da Costa, 1 Eden, 130 ....1209, 1234, 1235, 1245
Blackburn v. Haslam, 21 Q. B. D. 144; 57 L. J. Q. B. 479; 59 L. T.
407; 36 W. R. 855; 6 Asp. M. C. 326 ....587, 588
Blackburn v. Liverpool Steam Navign. Co., [1902] 1 K. B. 290; 71
L. J. K. B. 177; 85 L. T. 783; 50 W. R. 272; 7 Com. Cas. 10;
9 Asp. M. C. 263 812
Blackburn v. Thompson, 3 Camp. 61; 13 R. R. 382 ....96, 756, 758
Blackburn v. Vigors, 17 Q. B. D. 553, 561; 12 A. C. 531; 57 L. J.
Q. B. 114; 57 L. T. 730; 36 W. R. 449; 6 Asp. M. C. 216...535, 553, 578,
579, **580**, 581, 583, 585, 587
Blackenhagen v. London Ass. Co., 1 Camp. 454; 10 R. R. 729 ....431, 432,
504, 804, **806**
Blackett v. Royal Exch. Ass. Co., 2 C. & J. 244; 2 Tyr. 266; 1 L. J. Ex.
101; 37 R. R. 695 ....57, 60, 71, **72**, 75, 221, 225, 893, 936, 1032a

b 2

TABLE OF CASES.

| | SECT. |

Blackhurst v. Cockell, 3 T. R. 360; 1 R. R. 717 ....29, 629, **640**
Blagge v. New York Ins. Co., 1 Caines, 549 598
Blairmore v. Macredie. (*See* Sailing Ship "Blairmore" Co. v. Macredie.)
Blaize v. Paris General Ass. Co., 4 Boulay-Paty, Droit Mar. 397......... 1180
Blakey v. Dixon, 2 B. & P. 321 233
Blankenhagen v. London Ass. Co., 1 Camp. 453 ....431, 432
Blasco v. Fletcher, 32 L. J. C. P. 284; 14 C. B. (N. S.) 147; 9 Jur.
   (N. S.) 1105; 9 L. T. 169; 11 W. R. 997; 135 R. R. 633 207
Blyth v. Shepherd, 9 M. & W. 763; 1 Dowl. (N. S.) 880; 11 L. J. Ex.
   293; 6 Jur. 489; 60 R. R. 877 .... 822, 859
Bodo, The, 156 Fed. R. 981 1233
Boedes Lust, The, 5 C. Rob. 238 833
Boehm v. Bell, 8 T. R. 154; 4 R. R. 620 ....303, 1258
Boehm v. Combe, 2 M. & S. 172; 17 R. R. 611 860
Bold v. Rotherham, 8 Q. B. 781; 1 Car. & K. 360; 15 L. J. Q. B. 279;
   10 Jur. 875; 70 R. R. 655..467, 468
Bolivia, Republic of, v. Indemnity Mut. Mar. Ins. Co., Ltd. (*See*
   Republic of Olivia v. Indemnity Mut. Mar. Ins. Co.)
Bolton v. Dobree, 2 Camp. 163...89, 753
Bolton v. Gladstone, 5 East, 155; 2 Taunt. 85; 7 R. R. 674; 11
   R. R. 532..678, 680, 682
Bona, The, [1895] P. 125; 64 L. J. Adm. 64; 11 R. 707; 71 L. T. 870;
   43 W. R. 290; 7 Asp. M. C. 557 ....932, 936
Bond v. Gonzales, 2 Salk. 445; Holt, 469.. 433
Bond v. Nutt, 2 Cowp. 601; 1 Dougl. 367, n. 433, 644, 649
Bondrett v. Hentigg, Holt, N. P. 149; 17 R. R. 625 ....837, 1049
Bone v. Ekless, 5 H. & N. 925; 29 L. J. Ex. 438; 120 R. R. 896......... 1254
Bonita, The, 30 L. J. Adm. 145; Lush, 252; 5 L. T. 141 202
Booth v. Gair, 33 L. J. C. P. 99; 15 C. B. (N. S.) 291; 9 Jur. (N. S.)
   1326; 9 L. T. 286; 12 W. R. 106 ....22, 214, 869, **870**, 1156
Boseley v. Chesapeake Ins. Co., 3 Gill & Johnson, 450 1094
Boston Fruit Co. v. British & Foreign Mar. Ins. Co., [1905] 1 K. B. 637;
   [1906] A. C. 336; 74 L. J. K. B. 273; 75 L. J. K. B. 537; 92 L. T.
   514; 94 L. T. 806; 53 W. R. 420; 54 W. R. 557; 10 Asp. M. C. 37,
   260; 11 Com. Cas. 196; 21 Times L. R. 248; 22 Times L. R. 571...140, 172,
   173, 1275
Bottomley v. Bovill, 7 D. & R. 702; 5 B. & C. 210; 4 L. J. (O. S.) K. B.
   237; 29 R. R. 221 ....384, **406**, 840, **846**
Bouillon v. Lupton, 33 L. J. C. P. 37; 15 C. B. (N. S.) 113; 10 Jur.
   (N. S.) 422; 8 L. T. 575; 11 W. R. 966; 137 R. R. 422...424a, 428, 647,
   648, 687, 698, **701**, 710, 723
Boulton v. Houlder, [1904] 1 K. B. 784; 73 L. J. K. B. 493; 90 L. T. 621;
   52 W. R. 388; 9 Com. Cas. 182; 20 Times L. R. 328 1272
Bourne v. Gatliffe (*see* Gatliffe v. Bourne), 11 Cl. & F. 45; 8 Scott
   (N. R.) 604; 3 M. & Gr. 643; 7 M. & G. R. 850; 44 R. R. 723...... 456
Bousfield v. Barnes, 4 Camp. 228; 16 R. R. 780 ....350, 1023
Bousfield v. Cresswell, 2 Camp. 545; 11 R. R. 794 ....119, 164
Bousfield v. Wilson, 16 L. J. Ex. 44 1255
Boutflower v. Wilmer, cited Selw. N. P. 976, 9th ed. 851
Bowden v. Vaughan, 10 East, 415; 10 R. R. 340 ....543, 548
Bowring v. Elmslie, cited 7 T. R. 216 886

	SECT.
Bowring v. Thibaud, 42 Fed. R. 794	948
Boyd v. Dubois, 3 Camp. 133	621, 778, 828
Boydell v. Drummond, 11 East, 142; 2 Camp. 157; 10 R. R. 450	629
Boyfield v. Brown, 2 Str. 1065	882, 1074
Bradford v. Levy, 2 C. & P. 137; Ry. & M. 331; 31 R. R. 657	800, 811, 847
Bradford v. Symondson, 7 Q. B. D. 456, 463; 50 L. J. Q. B. 582; 45 L. T. 364; 30 W. R. 27; 4 Asp. M. C. 455	13, **1248**, 1257
Bradhurst v. Columbian Ins. Co., 9 Johns. 9	937, 940, 1172
Bradlie v. Maryland Ins. Co., 12 Peters, 378	1030, 1104, 1129, 1134
Bradstreet v. Neptune Ins. Co., 3 Sumn. 600	678
Bragg v. Anderson, 4 Taunt. 229; 13 R. R. 584	396, 402
Bramhall v. Sun Ins. Co., 104 Mass. R. 510	492
Brandon v. Curling, 4 East, 410; 1 Smith, 85; 7 R. R. 592	85, 86, 753, 831
Brandon v. Nesbitt, 6 T. R. 23; 3 R. R. 109	85, 86, 753
Brankelow Steamship Co. v. Canton Ins. Office, [1899] 2 Q. B. 178; 68 L. J. Q. B. 811; 81 L. T. 6; 47 W. R. 611; 4 Com. Cas. 239	789, 879
Brett v. Beckwith, 26 L. J. Ch. 130; 3 Jur. (N. S.) 31; 5 W. R. 112	26, 79
Brewster v. Kitchell or Kitchin, 1 Ld. Raym. 321; 1 Salk. 198	636
Bridge v. Niagara Ins. Co., 1 Hall, 247	142
Bridger v. Savage, 15 Q. B. D. 363; 54 L. J. Q. B. 464; 53 L. T. 129; 33 W. R. 891; 49 J. P. 725	313a
Bridges v. Hunter, 1 M. & S. 15; 14 R. R. 380	546, 556, **593**, 626
Brigella, The, [1893] P. 189; 62 L. J. Adm. 81; 1 R. 616; 69 L. T. 834; 7 Asp. M. C. 337	908, 985, 1001, 1005
Briggs v. Merchant Traders' Assn., 18 L. J. Q. B. 178; 13 Q. B. 167; 13 Jur. 787; 78 R. R. 341	280
Brine v. Featherstone, 4 Taunt. 869; 14 R. R. 689	**549**, 565, 573
Bristol Steam Navigation Co. v. Indemnity Mutual Mar. Ins. Co., 57 L. T. 101; 6 Asp. M. C. 173	1034
Bristow v. Towers, 6 T. R. 23, 35; 3 R. R. 113, n.	85, 86, 753
British and Foreign Mar. Ins. Co. v. Sturge, 77 L. T. 208; 2 Com. Cas. 204; 8 Asp. M. C. 303	576
British Dominions Gen. Ins. Co. v. Duder, [1914] W. N. 311; 30 Times L. R. 636	324, 1091
British Marine Mutual Ins. Co. v. Jenkins, [1900] 1 Q. B. 299; 5 Com. Cas. 143	83
British S. Africa Co. v. De Beers Consolidated Mines, Ltd., [1910] 1 Ch. 354; 2 Ch. 502; [1912] A. C. 52; 79 L. J. Ch. 345; 80 L. J. Ch. 65; 81 L. J. Ch. 137; 102 L. T. 95; 103 L. T. 4; 105 L. T. 683; 54 S. J. 289, 679; 56 S. J. 175; 17 Manson, 190; 26 Times L. R. 591; 28 Times L. R. 114	744
Brocklebank v. Sugrue, 1 B. & Ad. 81; 1 M. & Rob. 102; 5 C. & P. 21; 8 L. J. (O. S.) K. B. 371	46, 47, 166, 878, 880, 1089, 1167, 1172, 1209
Bromley v. Hesseltine, 1 Camp. 75; 10 R. R. 635	90, 95, 96, 757
Bromley v. Williams, 32 L. J. Ch. 716; 1 N. R. 413; 32 Beav. 177; 8 Jur. (N. S.) 240; 8 L. T. 78; 11 W. R. 392; 138 R. R. 694	80
Brook v. Louisiana Ins. Co., 4 Martin (N. S.) 640—681	346
Brooking v. Maudslay, 38 Ch. D. 636; 57 L. J. Ch. 1001; 51 L. T. 852; 36 W. R. 664; 6 Asp. M. C. 296	526, 689
Brooks v. M'Donnell, 1 Y. & C. 500; 41 R. R. 336	1210, 1245, 1246

xxii   TABLE OF CASES.

                                                                          SECT.
Brooks v. Oriental Ins. Co., 7 Pick. 259 ....893, 900, 1031
Broomfield v. Southern Ins. Co., L. R. 5 Ex. 192; 39 L. J. Ex. 186; 22
  L. T. 371; 18 W. R. 801 ....199, 290, 1137
Brotherston v. Barber, 5 M. & S. 418; 17 R. R. 378 ....1096, 1102
Brough v. Whitmore, 4 T. R. 206; 2 R. R. 361 ....58, 219, 460, 507
Brown v. Byrne, 3 E. & B. 703; 23 L. J. Q. B. 313; 2 C. L. R. 1599;
  18 Jur. 700; 2 W. R. 471; 97 R. R. 715 71
Brown v. Carstairs, 3 Camp. 161 ....59, 460
Brown v. Fleming, 7 Com. Cas. 245 ....228, 784, 811, 1018
Brown v. Hartford Ins. Co., 3 Day's R. 58 331
Brown v. Mayor of London, 9 C. B. (N. S.) 726; 13 C. B. (N. S.) 828;
  30 L. J. C. P. 225; 31 L. J. C. P. 280; 7 Jur. (N. S.) 755; 8 Jur.
  (N. S.) 1103; 3 L. T. (N. S.) 813; 9 W. R. 336; 10 W. R. 522;
  127 R. R. 853 636
Brown v. Merchants' Mar. Ins. Co., 152 Fed. R. 411 ....247, 321
Brown v. Neilson, 1 Caines, 525 442
Brown v. North, 8 Exch. 1; 22 L. J. Ex. 49; 91 R. R. 348 1178
Brown v. Smith, 1 Dow. P. C. 349; 14 R. R. 78 ...836, 844, 1104, 1106, 1203
Brown v. Stapyleton, 5 L. J. (O. S.) C. P. 121; 12 J. B. Moore, 334;
  4 Bing. 119; 29 R. R. 524 ....224, 227, 972
Brown v. Tayleur, 5 L. J. K. B. 57; 4 A. & E. 241; 5 N. & M. 472;
  1 Hurls. & Walms. 578; 43 R. R. 331 ....69, 397, 485, 486
Brown v. Tierney, 1 Taunt. 517; 10 R. R. 599 905
Browne v. Vigne, 12 East, 283; 11 R .R. 375....................467, 502, 504
Brown v. Wilkinson, 16 L. J. Ex. 34; 15 M. & W. 391 802
Browning v. Provincial Ins. Co. of Canada, L. R. 5 P. C. 263; 28 L. T.
  853; 21 W. R. 587 ....12, 1273
Brownlie v. Campbell, 5 App. Cas. 925 1244
Bruce v. Bruce, 2 B. & P. 229, n. 90
Bruce v. Jones, 32 L. J. Ex. 132; 1 H. & C. 769; 9 Jur. (N. S.) 628;
  7 L. T. 748; 11 W. R. 371; 130 R. R. 768.........339, 351, 353, 1023
Bryan v. American Ins. Co., 5 Paige, 842 837
Bryant v. Commonwealth Ins. Co., 13 Pick. 543 468
Bryant v. Ocean Ins. Co., 22 Pick. 200 543
Bryant & May v. London Ass. Co., 2 Times L. R. 591 891
Brymer v. Atkins, 1 H. Bl. 165, 191 98
Buchanan v. Faber, 4 Com. Cas. 223 ......240, 241, 246, 257, 297, 315, 698
Buchanan v. London and Provincial Mar. Ins. Co., 65 L. J. Q. B. 92;
  1 Com. Cas. 165 867
Buchanan v. Ocean Ins. Co., 6 Cowen, 318 310
Buck v. Chesapeake Ins. Co., 1 Peters, S. C. R. 151 598
Buller v. Christie, cited 2 M. & S. 374; 15 R. R. 277 1076
Buller v. Fisher, 3 Esp. 67; Peake's Add. Cas. 183; 4 R. R. 902 ...... 827a
Buller v. Harrison, 2 Cowp. 565 ....109, 1246
Burge v. Ashley & Smith, [1900] 1 Q. B. 744; 69 L. J. Q. B. 538; 82
  L. T. 518; 48 W. R. 438 ....121, 1255
Burger v. Indemnity Mut. Mar. Ins. Co., [1900] 2 Q. B. 348; 69 L. J.
  Q. B. 838; 82 L. T. 831; 48 W. R. 643; 5 Com. Cas. 315; 9 Asp.
  M. C. 85 795
Burges & Stock's case, 31 L. J. Ch. 749; 2 J. & H. 441; 2 Jur. (N. S.)
  15; 7 L. T. 191; 10 W. R. 816; 134 R. R. 297 79

TABLE OF CASES. xxiii

SECT.

Burges v. Wickham, 33 L. J. Q. B. 17; 3 B. & S. 669; 8 L. T. 47;
11 W. R. 992; 129 R. R. 506 ....57, 696, 709, 710, 711
Burnand, In re, [1904] 2 K. B. 68; 73 L. J. K. B. 413; 91 L. T. 46;
52 W. R. 437; 11 Manson, 113; 20 Times L. R. 377 77
Burnand v. Rodocanachi, 5 C. P. D. 424; 6 Q. B. D. 633; 7 App. Cas.
333; 51 L. J. Q. B. 548; 47 L. T. 277; 31 W. R. 65; 4 Asp. M. C.
576..............................339, 345, 1209, 1214, 1225, 1230, **1234**, 1235
Burnett v. Kensington, 7 T. R. 210; 1 Esp. 416; Peake's Add. Cas. 71;
4 R. R. 424 ....886, 1067
Burnham v. China Mut. Ins. Co., 189 Mass. R. 100 795
Burton v. English, 12 Q. B. D. 218; 53 L. J. Q. B. 133; 49 L. T. 768;
32 W. R. 655; 5 Asp. M. C. 187 ....908, 923
Busk v. Royal Exch. Ass. Co., 2 B. & Ald. 73; 20 R. R. 350 ...692, 723, 784,
798, 828
Butler v. Allnutt, 1 Stark. 222 750
Butler v. Wildman, 3 B. & Ald. 398; 22 R. R. 435 ....860, 911
Byas v. Miller, 3 Com. Cas. 39..**143**, 172, 173
Byrne v. Schiller, L. R. 6 Ex. 20, 319; 40 L. J. Ex. 177; 25 L. T. 211;
19 W. R. 1114; 1 Asp. M. C. 111 264
Byrnes v. National Ins. Co., 1 Cowen, 265 1030

C.

Cahill v. Dawson, 26 L. J. C. P. 253; 3 C. B. (N. S.) 106; 3 Jur. (N. S)
1128; 111 R. R. 565 ....131, 132, 134
Cahn v. Pockett's Bristol Channel Steam Packet Co., [1899] 1 Q. B.
643; 68 L. J. Q. B. 515; 80 L. T. 269; 47 W. R. 422; 8 Asp. M. C.
516; 4 Com. Cas. 168 282
Caine v. Palace SS. Co., [1907] 1 K. B. 679; [1907] A. C. 386; 76
L. J. K. B. 292, 1079; 96 L. T. 587; 13 Com. Cas. 51; 23 Times
L. R. 731; 10 Asp. M. C. 380 760
Calbreath v. Gracy, 1 Wash. C. C. R. 219 ....658, 1190
Calcutta and Burmah Steam Nav. Co. v. De Matthos, 32 L. J. Q. B.
322; 11 W. R. 1024; 139 R. R. 752 284
Caldwell v. Ball, 1 T. R. 205; 1 R. R. 87 1279
Caledonia, The, 157 U. S. (50 Davis) 174................................688, 689
Callander v. Oelrichs, 8 L. J. C. P. 25; 5 Bing. (N. C.) 58; 6 Scott,
761; 50 R. R. 602 149
Calvert v. Bovill, 7 T. R. 523; 4 R. R. 517 680
Calypso, The, 2 C. Rob. 298 768
Cambridge v. Anderton, 2 L. J. (O. S.) K. B. 141; 2 B. & Cr. 691;
4 D. & R. 203; 1 Car. & P. 213; 1 Ry. & M. 60; 26 R. R.
517 ....202, 203, 348, 1047, **1054**, 1055, 1111
Camden v. Anderson, 5 T. R. 709; 6 T. R. 723; 1 B. & P. 272 266
Camden v. Cowley, 1 W. Bl. 417 ....59, 455, 475, **486**, 496
Camelo v. Britten, 4 B. & Ald. 184 750
Campbell v. Bordieu, 2 Str. 1265 433
Campbell v. Christie, 2 Stark. 64 ....42, 43
Campbell v. Innes, 4 B. & Ald. 423; 23 R. R. 238 ....**598**, 803, 833

TABLE OF CASES.

	SECT.
Campbell v. Rickards, 2 L. J. K. B. 204; 5 B. & Ad. 840, 845; 2 N. & M. 542; 39 R. R. 679	152, 159, 626
Campbell v. Thompson, 1 Stark. 490	200
Canada Shipping Co. v. British Shipowners' Mutual Protection Assn., 23 Q. B. D. 342; 58 L. J. Q. B. 462; 61 L. T. 312; 38 W. R. 87; 6 Asp. M. C. 422	81
Canham v. Barry, 15 C. B. 597; 3 C. L. R. 487; 24 L. J. C. P. 100; 1 Jur. (N. S.) 402	536
Cannan v. Meaburn, 1 Bing. 243; 8 Moore, 127; 2 L. J. (O. S.) C. P. 60	1120, 1128, 1158
Cantiere Meccanico Brindisino v. Constant, 17 Com. Cas. 182, 332; 12 Asp. M. C. 186	181
Cantiere Meccanico Brindisino v. Janson, [1912] 2 K. B. 112; 3 K. B. 452, 463; 81 L. J. K. B. 1043; 107 L. T. 281; 17 Com. Cas. 182, 332; 12 Asp. M. C. 246; 57 S. J. 62; 28 Times L. R. 564	522, 555, 591, 598, 618, 622, 623, 694, 710
Cantillon v. London Ass. Co., cited 3 Burr. 1553	886
Cargo ex Schiller, The, 2 P. D. 145; 46 L. J. Adm. 9; 36 L. T. 714; 3 Asp. M. C. 439	868
Carisbrook SS. Co. v. London & Provincial Marine Ins. Co., [1901] 2 K. B. 861; [1902] 2 K. B. 681; 70 L. J. K. B. 930; 71 L. J. K. B. 978; 50 W. R. 42, 691; 87 L. T. 418; 6 Com. Cas. 291; 7 Com. Cas. 235	986
Carlton SS. Co., Ltd. v. Castle Mail Packets Co., Ltd., [1898] A. C. 486; 67 L. J. Q. B. 795; 78 L. T. 661; 47 W. R. 65	480
Carmichael v. Liverpool Sailing Ship Owners' Mutual Indemnity Assn., 19 Q. B. D. 242; 56 L. J. Q. B. 428; 57 L. T. 550; 35 W. R. 793; 6 Asp. M. C. 184	81
Caroline, The, 6 C. Rob. 461	669, 760
Carpenters' Case,-The Year Books, XI. H. IV. p. 33, ed. 1679	145
Carr v. Montefiore, 33 L. J. Q. B. 57, 256; 34 L. J. Q. B. 21; 5 B. & S. 408, 425; 10 Jur. (N. S.) 1069; 11 L. T. 157; 12 W. R. 870; 136 R. R. 618	56, 448, 449, 450, 451, 1268
Carr v. Royal Exch. Ass. Co., 31 L. J. Q. B. 93; 33 L. J. Q. B. 63; 34 L. J. Q. B. 21; 1 B. & S. 956; 5 B. & S. 433; 8 Jur. (N. S.) 384; 10 Jur. (N. S.) 316; 6 L. T. 105; 10 L. T. 265; 10 W. R. 352; 12 W. R. 127; 136 R. R. 618	78, 1268
Carrere v. Union Ins. Co., 3 Har. & Johns. 324; 2 Hall's Law J. 197	666
Carrington v. Merchants' Ins. Co., 8 Peters, 495	763
Carron v. Marine Ins. Co., 2 Wash. C. C. R. 468	365
Carron Park, The, 15 P. D. 203; 59 L. J. Adm. 74; 63 L. T. 356; 29 W. R. 191; 6 Asp. M. C. 543	918
Carruthers v. Gray, 3 Camp. 142; 15 East, 35; 31 R. R. 658, n.	731, 1283
Carruthers v. Sheddon, 6 Taunt. 14; 1 Marsh. R. 416	138, **252**, 295, 298, 1274
Carruthers v. Sydebotham, 4 M. & S. 77; 16 R. R. 392	798, 890
Carstairs v. Allnutt, 3 Camp. 497	745, 801
Carter v. Boehm, 3 Burr. 1905; 1 W. Bl. 593; 1 Smith's L. C.	160, 522, 561, 575, 609, 618, 624, 626, 1256
Carter v. Royal Exch. Ass. Co., cited 2 Str. 1249	381

TABLE OF CASES. XXV

	SECT.
Caruthers v. Graham, 14 East, 578	105
Cary v. King, Cas. temp. Hardwicke, 304	863, 865
Case v. Davidson, 8 Price, 542; 5 Moore, 116; 2 Br. & B. 379; 5 M. & S. 79; 17 R. R. 280	358, **1175**, 1206
Casseres v. Bell, 8 T. R. 166	89
Castellain v. Preston, 11 Q. B. D. 380; 52 L. J. Q. B. 366; 49 L. T. 29; 31 W. R. 557	292, 1225, 1230, 1231, 1234, 1236
Castelli v. Boddington, 1 E. & B. 66, 879; 1 C. L. R. 281; 22 L. J. Q. B. 5; 23 L. J. Q. B. 31; 17 Jur. 781; 1 W. R. 359; 93 R. R. 21, 457	110, 176
Castle v. Playford, L. R. 7 Ex. 98; 41 L. J. Ex. 44; 26 L. T. 315; 20 W. R. 440; 1 Asp. M. C. 255	282, 284
Castrique v. Imrie, L. R. 4 H. L. 414; 30 L. J. C. P. 177; 39 L. J. C. P. 350; 8 C. B. (N. S.) 405; 7 Jur. (N. S.) 1076; 4 L. T. 143; 23 L. T. 48; 9 W. R. 455; 19 W. R. 1; 125 R. R. 705	310, 678, 681, 682
Cator v. Gt. Western Ins. Co. of New York, L. R. 8 C. P. 552; 42 L. J. C. P. 266; 29 L. T. 136; 21 W. R. 850; 2 Asp. M. C. 90	359, 784, 811, 1018
Cazalet v. St. Barbe, 1 T. R. 187; 1 R. R. 178	1093, 1104, 1184
Chandler v. Blogg, [1898] 1 Q. B. 32; 67 L. J. Q. B. 336; 77 L. T. 524; 8 Asp. M. C. 349; 3 Com. Cas. 18	795, 826
Chapman v. Benson. (*See* Benson v. Chapman.)	
Chapman v. Fisher, 20 Times L. R. 319	795
Chapman v. Fraser, 1 Park. Ins. (8th ed.) 456	1256
Chapman v. Royal Netherlands Steam Navigation Co., 4 P. D. 157; 48 L. J. Ch. 449; 40 L. T. 433; 27 W. R. 554; 4 Asp. M. C. 107	793
Chapman v. Walton, 2 L. J. C. P. 210; 10 Bing. 57; 3 M. & Scott, 389; 38 R. R. 396	152, 160, 626
Charlesworth v. Faber, 5 Com. Cas. 408	53, 328, 440, 611
Charlotte, The, [1908] P. 206; 77 L. J. P. 132; 99 L. T. 380; 11 Asp. M. C. 87; 24 Times L. R. 416	1226
Chatenay v. Brazilian Submarine Telegraph Co., [1891] 1 Q. B. 79; 60 L. J. Q. B. 295; 63 L. T. 739; 39 W. R. 65	744
Chaurand v. Angerstein, Peake, N. P. 43	560, 566, 626
Chavasse, Ex parte, Grazebrook, In re, 34 L. J. Bank. 17; 6 N. R. 6; 11 Jur. (N. S.) 400; 12 L. T. 249; 13 W. R. 627	760
Cheraw and Salisbury Railroad Co. v. Broadnax, 109 Penn. St. 432	918
China Transpacific SS. Co. v. Commercial Union Ass. Co., 8 Q. B. D. 142; 51 L. J. Q. B. 132; 45 L. T. 647; 30 W. R. 224	1271, 1272
China Traders' Ins. Co. v. Royal Exchange Ass. Co., [1898] 2 Q. B. 187; 67 L. J. Q. B. 736; 78 L. T. 783; 46 W. R. 497; 3 Com. Cas. 189	324, 1272
Chippendale v. Holt, 65 L. J. Q. B. 104; 73 L. T. 472; 44 W. R. 128; 8 Asp. M. C. 78; 1 Com. Cas. 197	324, 327, 328
Chitty v. Selwyn, 2 Atkyns, 359	413, 474, 482
Chope v. Reynolds, 5 C. B. (N. S.) 642; 28 L. J. C. P. 194; 5 Jur. (N. S.) 822; 7 W. R. 208; 116 R. R. 808	805
Christian v. Coombe, 2 Esp. 489; 4 R. R. 887, n.	1242
Christian v. Ditchell, Peake's Add. Cases, 141; 4 R. R. 898	559
Christie v. Secretan, 8 T. R. 192	680, 686, 728

TABLE OF CASES.

SECT.

Christopher, The, 2 C. Rob. 209 ....676, 677
Cincinnati Ins. Co. v. Bakewell, 4 B. Munroe R. (Ken.) 541............ 1200
Citizens' Bank of Louisiana v. First National Bank of New Orleans,
   L. R. 6 H. L. 352; 43 L. J. Ch. 269; 22 W. R. 194 542
Clapham v. Cologan, 3 Camp. 382 ....44, 182, 517, 630, 727
Clapham v. Langton, 34 L. J. Q. B. 46; 10 L. T. 875; 12 W. R. 1011..696, 710
Clark v. Ocean Ins. Co., 16 Pick. R. 289 233
Clarke v. Westmore, cited in Selw. N. P. 939 (13th ed.) 640
Clason v. Simmonds, cited 6 T. R. 533; 3 R. R. 260 ....390, 393, 500
Clason v. Smith, 3 Wash. C. C. R. 156 623
Clifford v. Hunter, M. & M. 103; 3 Car. & P. 16 722
Clough v. London & N. W. Ry. Co., L. R. 7 Ex. 26; 41 L. J. Ex. 17;
   25 L. T. 708; 20 W. R. 189 525
Coast Wrecking Co. v. Phœnix Ins. Co., 7 Fed. R. 236 969
Cobequid Marine Ins. Co. v. Barteaux, L. R. 6 P. C. 319; 32 L. T. 510;
   23 W. R. 892; 2 Asp. M. C. 536 ....203, 1055, 1116
Cock v. Townson, 2 Park. Ins. (8th ed.) 630 419
Cockey v. Atkinson, 2 B. & Ald. 460; 21 R. R. 357 ....69, 485, 1274
Cocking v. Fraser, 4 Dougl. 295 1067
Cocking v. Ward, 1 C. B. 858; 15 L. J. C. P. 245; 68 R. R. 831 36
Cockran v. Retberg, 3 Esp. 121 29
Cockrane v. Fisher, 2 Cr. & M. 581; 4 Tyr. 424; 5 Tyr. 496; 1
   C. M. & R. 809; 4 L. J. Ex. 328; 3 L. J. Ex. 185; 39 R. R. 854;
   40 R. R. 730 651
Coffin v. Newburyport Mar. Ins. Co., 9 Mass. R. 436 365
Coffin v. Storer, 5 Mass. R. 252 1041
Coggs v. Bernard, Smith's Leading Cases 145
Cohen v. Hinckley, 2 Camp. 51; 1 Taunt. 249; 11 R. R. 660 ....814, 1281
Coit v. Commercial Ins. Co., 7 Johns. 385 ....68, 883
Coker v. Bolton, [1912] 3 K. B. 315; 82 L. J. K. B. 91; 107 L. T. 54;
   12 Asp. M. C. 231; 17 Com. Cas. 313; 56 S. J. 751 ......81, 317, 1165,
                                                      1176, 1206
Colby v. Hunter, 1 Moo. & M. 81; 3 Car. & P. 7; 33 R. R. 634 ...640, 1256
Cole v. Parkin, 12 East, 471 50
Coles v. Mar. Ins. Co., 3 Wash. C. C. R. 159 379
Colledge v. Harty, 20 L. J. Ex. 146; 6 Exch. 205; 86 R. R. 240..84, 629, 639
Cologan v. London Ass. Co., 5 M. & S. 447; 17 R. R. 390 ...1066, 1067, **1069**,
                                                         1080, 1082, **1141**, 1202
Colonial Ins. Co. of New Zealand v. Adelaide Mar. Ins. Co., 12 App.
   Cas. 128; 56 L. J. P. C. 19; 56 L. T. 173; 35 W. R. 636; 6 Asp.
   M. C. 94 ....255a, 282, **283**
Columbia, The, 1 C. Rob. 154 ....767, 770
Columbia Ins. Co. v. Laurence, 10 Peters, S. C. R. 517 828
Columbian Ins. Co. v. Ashby, 4 Peters, S. C. R. 139 ....799a, 1202, 1220
Columbian Ins. Co. v. Ashby, 13 Peters, S. C. R. 331 ....914, 940, 979
Columbian Ins. Co. v. Catlett, 12 Wheat. 383 ....367, 415, 417, 1211
Comber v. Anderson, 1 Camp. 523 ....157, 176
Comet, The, 1 Edw. 32 769
Commercen, The, 1 Wheat. 382 764

TABLE OF CASES. xxvii

SECT.

Commonwealth, The, [1907] P. 216; 76 L. J. P. 106; 97 L. T. 625; 10 Asp. M. C. 538; 23 Times L. R. 420 ....1187, 1215
Company of African Merchants v. British and Foreign Mar. Ins. Co., L. R. 8 Ex. 154; 42 L. J. Ex. 60; 28 L. T. 233; 21 W. R. 484; 1 Asp. M. C. 588 ....376, 405, 409
Constable v. Noble, 2 Taunt. 403; 11 R. R. 617 ......69, 454, 485, 1274
Constancia, The, 2 W. Rob. 404; 10 Jur. 845 198
Conway v. Forbes, 10 East, 539 803
Conway v. Gray, 10 East, 536 ....88, 260, **295**, 803, 833, 1188
Cook v. Commercial Ins. Co., 11 Johns. 40 852
Coolidge v. Gloucester Marine Ins. Co., 15 Mass. 341 ....358, 879
Coolidge v. Gray, 8 Mass. 527 ....498, 500
Cope v. Miller, 1 Com. Cas. 296 ....26, 27, 166
Copeland v. Mercantile Ins. Co., 6 Pick. 198 308
Copenhagen, The, 1 C. Rob. 289 772
Copernicus, The, [1896] P. 237; 65 L. J. Adm. 108; 74 L. T. 757; 8 Asp. M. C. 166 510
Corcoran v. Gurney, 1 E. & B. 456; 22 L. J. Q. B. 113; 17 Jur. 1152; 1 W. R. 129; 93 R. R. 232 ....888, 890
Corfield v. Buchanan, 29 Times L. R. 258 ....80, 83
Corlett v. Gordon, 3 Camp. 472; 14 R. R. 813 148
Cormack v. Gladstone, 11 East, 347; 10 R. R. 518.............391, 407
Cornfoot v. Fowke, 6 M. & W. 358; 9 L. J. Ex. 297; 4 Jur. 919; 55 R. R. 655 ....529, 535
Cornfoot v. Royal Exchange Ass. Corpn., [1903] 2 K. B. 363; [1904] 1 K. B. 40; 73 L. J. K. B. 22; 89 L. T. 490; 52 W. R. 49; 8 Com. Cas. 204 495
Cornwall v. Wilson, 1 Ves. sen. 214 139
Cory v. Burr, 8 Q. B. D. 313; 9 Q. B. D. 463; 8 A. C. 393; 52 L. J. Q. B. 657; 49 L. T. 78; 31 W. R. 894; 5 Asp. M. C. 109......829, 858, 905
Cory v. Patton, L. R. 7 Q. B. 304; L. R. 9 Q. B. 577; 41 L. J. Q. B. 195; 43 L. J. Q. B. 181; 26 L. T. 161; 30 L. T. 758; 20 W. R. 364; 23 W. R. 46; 1 Asp. M. C. 225; 2 Asp. M. C. 302......34, 37, 568, 576
Cossman v. West, 13 App. Cas. 160; 57 L. J. P. C. 17; 58 L. T. 122; 6 Asp. M. C. 233 ....1049, 1055, 1056
Courier, The, 1 Edw. 249 768
Court v. Martineau, 3 Dougl. 161 ....556, 617, 622
Courteen v. Touse, 1 Camp. 43, n.; 10 R. R. 627............ 166
Cousins v. Nantes, 3 Taunt. 513; 12 R. R. 696 ....9, 311, 314
Couston v. Chapman, L. R. 2 H. L. Sc. 250.................. 139
Couturier v. Hastie, 8 Exch. 40; 9 Exch. 109; 5 H. L. Cas. 673; 22 L. J. Ex. 97, 299; 25 L. J. Ex. 253; 17 Jur. 1127; 2 Jur. (N. S.) 1241; 96 R. R. 584, 598 ....13, 105
Covington v. Roberts, 2 B. & P. (N. R.) 378; 9 R. R. 669.........776, 822, 934
Cowie v. Barber, 4 M. & S. 16; 16 R. R. 368 1255
Cox v. May, 4 M. & S. 159; 16 R. R. 422 985
Cox v. Parry, 1 T. R. 464 169
Cox v. Prentice, 3 M. & S. 344; 16 R. R. 288 1246

xxviii TABLE OF CASES.

SECT.

Cox *v.* Troy, 5 B. & Ald. 474; 1 D. & R. 38; 24 R. R. 460................ 27
Coxe *v.* Harden, 4 East, 211; 1 Smith, 20; 7 R. R. 570................ 282
Craufurd *v.* Hunter, 8 T. R. 13, 23; 4 R. R. 576;........**138, 139, 188, 266,**
304, 311, 360
Crocker *v.* General Ins. Co. of Trieste, 2 Com. Cas. 233; 3 Com. Cas. 22... 503
Crocker *v.* Jackson, Sprague, R. 141... 434
Crocker *v.* Sturge, [1897] 1 Q. B. 330; 66 L. J. Q. B. 514; 75 L. T. 549;
45 W. R. 271; 8 Asp. M. C. 208; 2 Com. Cas. 43........................ 503
Crofts *v.* Marshall, 7 Car. & P. 597; 48 R. R. 828.......................72, 779
Crooks *v.* Allan, 5 Q. B. D. 38; 49 L. J. Q. B. 201; 41 L. T. 800; 28
W. R. 304; 4 Asp. M. C. 216...923, 1004
Crouan *v.* Stanier, [1904] 1 K. B. 87; 73 L. J. K. B. 102; 52 W. R. 75;
9 Com. Cas. 27 ....874, 902
Croudson *v.* Leonard, 4 Cranch, 434 678
Crowley *v.* Cohen, 1 L. J. K. B. 158; 3 B. & Ad. 478; 37 R. R. 472......251,
252, 254, 257, 309, **367,** 1021
Cruickshank *v.* Janson, 2 Taunt. 301; 11 R. R. 584.........486, 496, 642, 644
Crystal, The, [1894] A. C. 508; 63 L. J. Adm. 146; 6 R. 258; 71 L. T.
346; 7 Asp. M. C. 513 1212
Cullen *v.* Butler, 5 M. & S. 461; 4 Camp. 289; 17 R. R. 400......823, 860, 861
Cumming *v.* Forrester, 1 M. & S. 498; 14 R. R. 531..................... 112
Cunard *v.* Hyde, E. B. & E. 670; 2 E. & E. 1; 27 L. J. Q. B. 408;
29 L. J. Q. B. 6; 5 Jur. (N. S.) 40; 113 R. R. 824..................... 745
Cunard SS. Co. *v.* Marten, [1902] 2 K. B. 624; [1903] 2 K. B. 511;
71 L. J. K. B. 968; 72 L. J. K. B. 754; 89 L. T. 152; 52 W. R. 39;
9 Com. Cas. 9; 9 Asp. 452 ....73, 252, **368,** 872
Cunningham *v.* Maritime Ins. Co., [1899] 2 Ir. R. 257 1072
Curling *v.* Long, 1 B. & P. 636; 4 R. R. 747 266
Currie *v.* Bombay Native Ins. Co., 6 Moo. P. C. (N. S.) 302; L. R.
3 P. C. 72; 39 L. J. P. C. 1; 22 L. T. 317; 18 W. R. 296...233, 246, 799a,
1189, 1196

D.

Da Costa *v.* Edmunds, 4 Camp. 142; 2 Chit. 227; 16 R. R. 763...57, 60, 225,
610, 801
Da Costa *v.* Firth, 4 Burr. 1966 ....224, 1214, 1245
Da Costa *v.* Newnham, 2 T. R. 407; 2 Burr. 407...961, 1024, 1028, 1052, 1136
Da Costa *v.* Scandaret, 2 P. Wms. 179 ....600, 1256
Dagleish *v.* Davidson, 5 D. & Ry. 6; 27 R. R. 519..................... 993
D'Aguilar *v.* Tobin, Holt, N. P. 185; 2 Marsh. R. 265.............433, 1285
Daintrey, In re, Ex parte Mant, [1900] 1 Q. B. 546................110, 134
Dakin *v.* Oxley, 15 C. B. (N. S.) 646; 33 L. J. C. P. 115; 10 Jur. (N. S.)
655; 12 W. R. 557; 137 R. R. 698....................................... 1213
Dalgleish *v.* Brooke, 15 East, 295; 13 R. R. 476 ....903, 1265
Dalgleish *v.* Hodgson, 5 M. & P. 407; 7 Bing. 495; 9 L. J. (O. S.) C. P.
138; 33 R. R. 546 ....680, 770
Dalzell *v.* Mair, 1 Camp. 532 ....24, 106, 107
Danaöus, The, cited 4 C. Rob. 255 ....93, 95, 755
Daniels *v.* Harris, L. R. 10 C. P. 1; 44 L. J. C. P. 1; 31 L. T. 408; 28
W. R. 86; 2 Asp. M. C. 413 ....710, 712, 717

	SECT.
Darrell v. Tibbitts, 5 Q. B. D. 560; 50 L. J. Q. B. 33; 42 L. T. 797; 29 W. R. 66; 44 J. P. 695 1226
Dart, The, cited Edw. Adm. R. 1 96
Davidson v. Burnand, L. R. 4 C. P. 117; 38 L. J. C. P. 73; 19 L. T. 782; 17 W. R. 121 ....725, **798**, 822, 861
Davidson v. Case. (*See* Case v. Davidson.)
Davidson v. Cooper, 11 M. & W. 778; 13 M. & W. 343; 1 D. & L. 377; 12 L. J. Ex. 467; 63 R. R. 756 40
Davidson v. Willasey, 1 M. & S. 312; 14 R. R. 438...266, 267, 272, **274**, 513
Davies v. National Fire Co. of New Zealand, [1891] A. C. 485; 60 L. J. P. C. 73; 65 L. T. 560 185
Davies v. Reynolds, 1 Stark. 115 1279
Davies v. Wilkinson, 6 L. J. (O. S.) C. P. 121; 4 Bing. 573; 1 M. & P. 502; 29 R. R. 634 .... 114, 118
Davis v. Cary, 15 Q. B. 418; 20 L. J. Q. B. 48; 15 Jur. 310 636
Davis v. Garrett, 6 Bing. 716; 4 M. & P. 540; 8 L. J. (O. S.) C. P. 253; 31 R. R. 524 377
Davis v. Gildart, cited 1 Marsh. Ins. 140; 2 Park, 601 331
Davy v. Milford, 15 East, 559; 15 R. R. 279, n 1082
Dawson v. Atty, 7 East, 367 ....561, 567, 728, **731**, 801
Dean v. Dicker, 2 Str. 1250 ....311, 320, 1104
Dean v. Hornby, 3 E. & B. 180; 2 C. L. R. 1519; 23 L. J. Q. B. 129; 18 Jur. 623; 2 W. R. 156; 97 R. R. 439 ....829, 1105, 1106, 1141
De Beers Consolidated Mines, Ltd. v. Howe, [1906] A. C. 455; 75 L. J. K. B. 858; 95 L. T. 221; 22 Times L. R. 756 99
Deblois v. Ocean Ins. Co., 16 Pick. 303 ....395, 496
De Cuadra v. Swann, 16 C. B. (N. S.) 772; 139 R. R. 699............207, 468
Dederer v. Delaware Ins. Co., 2 Wash. C. C. R. 61 842
De Farconnet v. Western Ins. Co., 122 Fed. R. 448 1190
De Feise v. Stephens, cited Marsh. Ins. 523, n. (*b*) 848
De Forest v. Fulton Ins. Co., 1 Hall, 84................................139, 295
De Gaminde v. Pigou, 4 Taunt. 246 ....24, 106
De Garron v. Galbraith, 1 Park, Ins. 267; 2 Peake, 37; 4 R. R. 886... 1242
De Ghetoff v. London Ass. Co., 4 Bro. P. C. 436 174
D'Egnino v. Bewicke, 2 H. Bl. 551; 3 R. R. 503 654
De Hahn v. Hartley, 1 T. R. 343; 2 T. R. 186, n.; 1 R. R. 221...29, 559, 632, **633**
De Hart v. Compania Anonima, "Aurora," [1903] 1 K. B. 109; 2 K. B. 503; 72 L. J. K. B. 818; 89 L. T. 154; 52 W. R. 36; 8 Com. Cas. 314; 9 Asp. M. C. 345 ....994, 997, **1000**
Deidericks v. Commercial Ins. Co. of New York, 10 Johns. 234......... 1186
Delaney v. Stoddart, 1 T. R. 22; 1 R. R. 139........................161, 178, 431
Delmada v. Motteux, 1 T. R. 85, n. 752
Delonguemere v. Firemen's Ins. Co., 10 Johns. R. 126..................... 485
De Mattos v. Benjamin, 63 L. J. Q. B. 248; 10 R. 103; 70 L. T. 560; 42 W. R. 284..109, 121, 315, 1255
De Mattos v. North, L. R. 3 Ex. 185; 37 L. J. Ex. 116; 18 L. T. 797... 313
De Mattos v. Saunders, L. R. 7 C. P. 570; 27 L. T. 120; 20 W. R. 801; 1 Asp. M. C. 377...176, 177, 890
Dennis v. Home Ins. Co., 136 Fed. R. 481.................................58, 221
Dennison v. Modigliani, 5 T. R. 580 418

TABLE OF CASES.

SECT.

Dennistoun v. Lillie, 3 Bligh, 202; 1 Shaw's App. Cas. 22; 22 R. R.
13 ....535, 540, **541**, 543, 555
Denoon v. Home & Colonial Ins. Co., L. R. 7 C. P. 341; 41 L. J. C. P.
162; 26 L. T. 628; 20 W. R. 970; 1 Asp. M. C. 309...235, 252b, **346**, 1041
Dent v. Smith, L. R. 4 Q. B. 414; 38 L. J. Q. B. 144; 20 L. T. 868;
17 W. R. 646 ....630, 727, 863, 996
Depaba v. Ludlow, 1 Comyns R. 360 ....311, 1104
Depau v. Ocean Ins. Co., 5 Cowen, 63 ....982, 1131
Depeyster v. Columbian Ins. Co., 2 Caines, 85 1131
De Pothonier v. De Mattos, 27 L. J. Q. B. 260; E. B. & E. 461; 4 Jur.
(N. S.) 1034 176
Derry v. Peek, 37 Ch. D. 541; 14 A. C. 337; 57 L. J. Ch. 347; 58
L. J. Ch. 864; 59 L. T. 78; 61 L. T. 265; 36 W. R. 899; 38 W. R.
33; 1 Meg. 292; 54 J. P. 148 546
De Silvale v. Kendall, 4 M. & S. 37; 16 R. R. 373 ....232, 263, **264**
De Symonds v. Shedden, 2 B. & P. 153 228
De Tastet v. Taylor, 4 Taunt. 233; 13 R. R. 585 88
Deutsch-Australische Dampfschiffsgesellschaft v. Sturge, 30 Times
L. R. 137; 109 L. T. 905 470
Devaux v. J'Anson, 8 L. J. C. P. 284; 5 Bing. (N. C.) 519; 7 Scott, 507;
2 Arn. 82; 3 Jur. 678; 50 R. R. 786...229, 233, 262, 266, **268**, 269, 270,
271, 277, 511, **512**, 860
De Vaux v. Salvador, 4 A. & E. 420; 6 N. & M. 713; 1 H. & W. 751;
5 L. J. K. B. 134; 43 R. R. 374 ....10, 784, 791, 792, 821, 827a, 961
Devaux v. Steele, 6 Bing. (N. C.) 358; 8 Scott, 637; 54 R. R. 818...302, 303
De Vignier v. Swanson, 1 B. & P. 346, n.; 4 R. R. 825, n. 170
Devitt v. Providence Washington Ins. Co., 173 N. Y. 18.................. 1145
Dewa Gungadhui Sailing Ship Co. v. United Kingdom Mar. Mut. Ins.
Assn. (See Sailing Ship "Dewa Gunghadhui" Co. v. United
Kingdom Mar. Mut. Ins. Assn.)
De Wolf v. Archangel Marit. Bank & Ins. Co., L. R. 9 Q. B. 451; 43
L. J. Q. B. 147; 39 L. T. 605; 22 W. R. 801; 2 Asp. M. C. 273 ... 479,
480, **483**
De Wolf v. New York Firemen's Ins. Co., 20 Johns. R. 214; 2 Cowen,
56 ....620, 659
Diana, The, 5 C. Rob. 60, 67 ....90, 91, 92, 773
Dickenson v. Commercial Ins. Co. of New York, Anthon's N. P. R. 92 ... 617
Dickenson v. Jardine, L. R. 3 C. P. 639; 37 L. J. C. P. 321; 18 L. T.
717; 16 W. R. 1169 ....976, 1001, 1004, 1005
Dickey v. American Ins. Co., 3 Wend. 658 1203
Dickey v. United Ins. Co., 11 Johns. 358 ....491, 493
Dickson v. Lodge, 1 Stark. 226; 18 R. R. 764 1279
Difiori v. Adams, 53 L. J. Q. B. 437; 1 Cab. & E. 228 443
Dispatch, The, 3 C. Rob. 278 674
D'Israeli v. Jowett, 1 Esp. 427 1277
Dixon v. Hamond, 2 B. & Ald. 310 ....121, 1278
Dixon v. Hovill, 6 L. J. (O. S.) C. P. 155; 4 Bing. 665; 1 M. & P. 656;
29 R. R. 680 123
Dixon v. Reid, 5 B. & Ald. 597; 1 D. & R. 207; 24 R. R. 481..836, 844, **1140**

TABLE OF CASES. xxxi

	SECT.

Dixon v. Sadler (see Sadler v. Dixon), 5 M. & W. 405; 8 M. & W.
 895; 9 L. J. Ex. 48; 11 L. J. Ex. 435; 52 R. R. 774, 784 ...686, 687,
  691, 692, 693, 697, 698, 699, 702, 703, 710, 723, **798**
Dixon v. Sea Ins. Co., 4 Asp. M. C. 327 902
Dixon v. Stanfield, 10 C. B. 398; 84 R. R. 631 134
Dixon v. Whitworth, 4 C. P. D. 371; 4 Asp. M. C. 11, 327 ...863, 865, 871, 884
Dobell v. SS. Rossmore Co., [1895] 2 Q. B. 408; 64 L. J. Q. B. 777;
 14 R. 558; 73 L. T. 74; 44 W. R. 37; 8 Asp. M. C. 83 918
Dobson v. Bolton, 1 Park, Ins. (8th ed.) 239 888
Dobson v. Wilson, 3 Camp. 479; 14 R. R. 817 926
Doelwijk, The. (See Ruys v. Royal Exchange Ass. Corpn.)
Dodwell v. Munich Ass. Co., 123 Fed. R. 841; 128 Fed. R. 410 ......280, 309
Dollar v. La Fonciere Co., 162 Fed. R. 563; 181 Fed. R. 945 1005
Domett v. Young, Car. & M. 465 1121
Donaldson, J. P., The, 167 U. S. 599 933
Donaldson v. Thompson, 1 Camp. 429; 10 R. R. 717 ....96, 676, 678, 757
Donath v. Ins. Co. of North America, 4 Dall. 463 1252
Donnell v. Columbian Ins. Co., 2 Sumn. 366 893
Dora Forster, The, [1900] P. 241; 69 L. J. P. 85; 49 W. R. 271 1032
Dos Hermanos, The, 2 Wheat. 76 ....95, 657, 665, 755
Douglas v. Moody, 9 Mass. R. 518 977
Douglas v. Scougall, 4 Dow. 269; 16 R. R. 69 ....686, 688, 716, 725
Dowdall v. Allan, 19 L. J. Q. B. 41 ....26, 79
Dowell v. Moon, 4 Camp. 166 ....26, 80
Doyle v. Dallas, 1 M. & Rob. 48; 42 R. R. 758 ...203, 1048, 1055, 1057, 1058,
  1104, 1117, **1121**, 1122, 1127, 1129
Doyle v. Powell, 4 B. & Ad. 267; 1 N. & M. 678; 38 R. R. 248 414
Drake v. Marryatt, 1 L. J. (O. S.) K. B. 161; 1 B. & C. 473; 2 D. & R.
 696; 25 R. R. 46 168
Dree Gebroeders, 4 C. Rob. 232 ....97, 98
Driefontein Consolidated Mines v. Janson. (See Janson v. Driefontein.)
Driscol v. Bovil, 1 B. & P. 313 ....427, 432
Driscol v. Passmore, 1 B. & P. 200; 4 R. R. 782 ....383, 432
Dryer v. Birrell, 10 Ct. of Sess. Cas. (4th Ser.) 585 (see also Birrell
 v. Dryer) 639
Duchess of Kingston's Case; see notes, 2 Smith's L. C. 682
Dudgeon v. Pembroke, L. R. 9 Q. B. 581; 1 Q. B. D. 96; 2 App. Cas.
 284; 43 L. J. Q. B. 220; 46 L. J. Q. B. 409; 31 L. T. 31; 36 L. T.
 382; 22 W. R. 914; 25 W. R. 499; 3 Asp. M. C. 393 ...15, 73, 194, 436,
  692, 693, 694, 695, 697, 745, 777, 778, 799, 918
Duff v. Mackenzie, 26 L. J. C. P. 313; 3 C. B. (N. S.) 16; 3 Jur. (N. S.)
 1025; 111 R. R. 524 ....224, 245, 359, 1021, 1086
Duffell v. Wilson, 1 Camp. 401 1256
Dufourcet v. Bishop, 18 Q. B. D. 373; 56 L. J. Q. B. 497; 56 L. T.
 633; 6 Asp. M. C. 109 1226
Dugnet v. Rhinelander, 2 Johns. R. 476 95
Duncan v. Benson. (See Benson v. Duncan.)
Dundee, The, 1 Hag. Ad. R. 109, 123; 2 Hag. Ad. R. 137 219
Dunham v. Commercial Ins. Co., 11 Johns. 315 986

xxxii TABLE OF CASES.

SECT.

Durant v. Roberts, [1900] 1 Q. B. 629; [1901] A. C. 240; 70 L. J. K. B. 662; 84 L. T. 777; 17 Times L. R. 527 143
Durrell v. Bederley, Holt, N. P. 283; 17 R. R. 639 ....600, 602, 626
Duus, Brown & Co. v. Binning, 11 Com. Cas. 190; 22 Times L. R. 529 ... 1215
Dyson v. Rowcroft, 3 B. & P. 474; 7 R. R. 809......882, 884, 1066, 1067, **1069**

E.

Earle v. Harris, 1 Dougl. 357 ....645, 649
Earle v. Rowcroft, 8 East, 126; 9 R. R. 385 ...838, 839, 841, **842**, 845, 852, 858
Ebsworth v. Alliance Mar. Ins. Co., L. R. 8 C. P. 596; 42 L. J. C. P. 305; 29 L. T. 479; 2 Asp. M. C. 125 ....292, 300, 305
Eddystone Mar. Ins. Co., In re, [1892] 2 Ch. 423; 61 L. J. Ch. 326; 66 L. T. 70; 40 W. R. 441; 7 Asp. M. C. 167 324
Eden v. Parkinson, 2 Dougl. 732 ....656, 691
Eden v. Poole, 1 T. R. 132, n. 784, 835, 876, 880, 961
Edgar v. Bumstead, 1 Camp. 411; 10 R. R. 713 120
Edgar v. Fowler, 3 East, 222; 7 R. R. 433 ....109, 121
Edgington v. Fitzmaurice, 29 Ch. D. 459; 55 L. J. Ch. 650; 53 L. T. 369; 33 W. R. 911; 50 J. P. 52 545
Edward, The, 4 C. Rob. 68 763
Edwards v. Aberayron Mutual Ship Ins. Soc., 1 Q. B. D. 563; 34 L. T. 457 ....8, 18, 38, 82, 629
Edwards v. Footner, 1 Camp. 530 ....540, 541, 543, 555, 561
Eenrom, The, 2 C. Rob. 1 746
Elbers v. United Ins. Co., 16 Johns. 128 91
Elgood v. Harris, [1896] 2 Q. B. 491; 66 L. J. Q. B. 53; 75 L. T. 419; 45 W. R. 158; 3 Manson, 332; 8 Asp. M. C. 206 ....117, 118
Eliza Ann, The, 1 Dod. 244 831
Elizabeth, The, Edw. 198 770
Eliza Cornish, The, 1 Spinks, 36; 17 Jur. 738 ....726, 1158
Eliza Lines, The, 61 Fed. R. 308 908
Eliza Lines, The, 102 Fed. R. 184; 114 Fed. R. 307 990
Elkin v. Jansen, 13 M. & W. 655; 14 L. J. Ex. 201; 9 Jur. 353; 67 R. R. 771 ....535, 594, **595**, 627
Ellery v. New England Ins. Co., 8 Pickering, R. 14 417
Ellinger v. Mutual Life Ins. Co. of New York, [1905] 1 K. B. 31; 74 L. J. K. B. 39; 91 L. T. 733; 10 Com. Cas. 22; 21 Times L. R. 20. 56
Elliot v. Wilson, 4 Bro. P. C. 470 ....377, 392
Ellis v. Lafone, 22 L. J. Ex. 124; 8 Exch. 546; 17 Jur. 213; 1 W. R. 200; 91 R. R. 615...272, **274**, 276, 513, **517**
Elting v. Scott, 2 Johnson's R. 157 728
Elton v. Brogden, 2 Str. 1264 ....427, 848
Elton v. Larkins, 8 Bing. 198; 1 M. & Scott, 323; 5 Car. & P. 86, 385; 34 R. R. 676 ....575, 592, **594**, 614, 626
Ely v. Hallett, 2 Caines, 57 603
Emanuel v. Weir, 30 Times L. R. 518 41
Emanuel, The, 1 C. Rob. 296, 302 ....95, 657
Embiricos v. Sydney Reid & Co., [1914] 3 K. B. 45; 30 Times L. R. 451. 1089

SECT.

Empress Ass. Corp. v. Bowring & Co., 11 Com. Cas. 107 ......37, 41, 101, 145
Enderby v. Fletcher, 2 Park, Ins. 646 433
Entwistle v. Ellis, 27 L. J. Ex. 105; 2 H. & N. 549; 6 W. R. 76; 115
   R. R. 685 ....359, 1085
Erasmus v. Banks, cited 2 East, 113 340
Esposito v. Bowden, 24 L. J. Q. B. 210; 27 L. J. Q. B. 17; 4 E. & B.
   963; 7 E. & B. 763; 3 C. L. R. 1167; 1 Jur. (N. S.) 729; 3 Jur.
   (N. S.) 1209; 3 W. R. 451; 5 W. R. 732; 110 R. R. 816, 822 94
Essex, The, cited 5 C. Rob. 368 ....660, 665
Estrella, The, 4 Wheat. 298 676
Etches v. Aldan, 6 L. J. (O. S.) K. B. 65; 1 M. & R. 157; 31 R. R. 309.. 233
Etherington & Lancashire & Yorkshire Accident Ins. Co., In re, [1909]
   1 K. B. 591; 78 L. J. K. B. 684; 100 L. T. 568; 53 S. J. 266; 25
   Times L. R. 287 75
Etrusco, The, cited 3 C. Rob. 11 100
Ettrick, The, 6 P. D. 127; 45 L. T. 399; 4 Asp. M. C. 465; 50 L. J.
   Adm. 65 918
Evans v. Edmonds, 13 C. B. 777; 1 C. L. R. 653; 22 L. J. C. P. 211;
   17 Jur. 883; 1 W. R. 412; 93 R. R. 732 546
Everth v. Hannam, 2 Marsh. R. 74; 6 Taunt. 375 ....822, 841, 859
Everth v. Smith, 2 M. & S. 278; 5 M. & S. 6; 15 R. R. 246 ....252b, 876,
   880, 1089, **1166**, 1209
Eyre v. Glover, 3 Camp. 276; 16 East, 218; 13 R. R. 801...237, 241, 287, 1259

F.

Fairfield Shipbuilding Co. v. Gardner, Mountain & Co., 104 L. T. 288;
   11 Asp. M. C. 594; 27 Times L. R. 281...............................131, 134
Fairlie v. Christie, 7 Taunt. 416; 1 Moore, 114; Holt, 331; 18 R. R. 515... 40,
   42, 43
Falkner v. Ritchie, 2 M. & S. 290; 15 R. R. 253.........844, 1095, 1104, 1105
Fanny, The, 1 Dodson's Adm. R. 443.....................................667, 773
Fanny and Elmira, The, Edw. 117......................................202, 203, 1116
Farmer v. Legg, 7 T. R. 186 745
Farmer v. Russell, 1 B. & P. 298 ....121, 1255
Farnworth v. Hyde, L. R. 2 C. P. 204; 34 L. J. C. P. 207; 36 L. J.
   C. P. 33; 18 C. B. (N. S.) 835; 11 Jur. (N. S.) 349; 12 L. T. 231;
   13 W. R. 613 ....203, 206, 214, **1056**, 1144, 1145, 1152,
   1153, 1157, 1158, 1191
Farquharson v. Hunter, 1 Park, Ins. 105 ....58, 391, 505
Farquharson v. King, [1902] A. C. 325; 71 L. J. K. B. 667; 86 L. T.
   810; 51 W. R. 94 581
Fawcus v. Sarsfield, 6 E. & B. 192; 25 L. J. Q. B. 249; 2 Jur. (N. S.)
   665; 106 R. R. 559 ....694, 697, 777, 778, 799
Fawkes v. Lamb, 31 L. J. Q. B. 98; 8 Jur. (N. S.) 385; 10 W. R. 348;
   136 R. R. 846 ....57, 696
Feise v. Aguilar, 3 Taunt. 506; 12 R. R. 695...........................252b, 355
Feise v. Parkinson, 4 Taunt. 640; 13 R. R. 710.................535, 571, 1256

TABLE OF CASES.

SECT.

Fenwick v. Merchants' Mar. Ins. Co., [1914] W. N. 296; 30 Times
L. R. 609 795
Fenwick v. Robinson, Dans. & Ll. 8; 3 C. & P. 323; 33 R. R. 675...1024, 1026
Fernandez v. Da Costa, Beawes, 314 680
Field SS. Co. v. Burr, [1898] 1 Q. B. 821; [1899] 1 Q. B. 579; 68 L. J.
Q. B. 426; 80 L. T. 445; 47 W. R. 341; 8 Asp. M. C. 529; 4 Com.
Cas. 106 ....218, 784, 811, 835, 876
Fielden v. Morley Corp., [1899] 1 Ch. 1; 67 L. J. Ch. 611; 79 L. T.
231; 47 W. R. 295 1
Fillis v. Brutton, 1 Park, Ins. (8th ed.) 414..................... 535, 555, 560
Finlay v. Liverpool & G. W. SS. Co., 23 L. T. (N. S.) 251................ 832
First Nat. Bank of Kansas City v. Hartford F. Ins. Co., 95 U. S. 678... 75
Fisher v. Liverpool Marine Ins. Co., L. R. 8 Q. B. 469, 474; L. R. 9
Q. B. 418; 43 L. J. Q. B. 114; 30 L. T. 501; 22 W. R. 951; 2 Asp.
M. C. 454 ....34, 35
Fisher v. Ogle, 1 Camp. 418 ....678, 680
Fisher v. Smith, 4 App. Cas. 12; 48 L. J. Ex. 411; 39 L. T. 430;
27 W. R. 113 130
Fisk v. Masterman, 10 L. J. Ex. 306; 8 M. & W. 165; 58 R. R. 657 ... 332,
1259, 1261, **1262**
Fiske v. New England Ins. Co., 15 Pick. 310 603
Fitch v. Jones, 5 E. & B. 238; 24 L. J. Q. B. 293; 25 L. T. (O. S.) 160;
1 Jur. (N. S.) 854; 3 W. R. 507; 103 R. R. 455 .... 313a.
Fitzgerald v. Pole. (*See* Pole v. Fitzgerald.)
Fitzherbert v. Mather, 1 T. R. 12; 1 R. R. 134...**534**, 535, **553**, 570, 579, 581
Flad Oyen, The, 1 C. Rob. 135 676
Fleming v. Smith, 1 H. L. Cas. 513; 73 R. R. 139.......216, 1061, 1063, 1106,
1184, 1192, **1194**, 1197, 1202
Fletcher v. Alexander, L. R. 3 C. P. 375; 37 L. J. C. P. 193; 18 L. T.
432; 16 W. R. 803..975, 980, 981, 986, 990, 992
Fletcher v. Inglis, 2 B. & Ald. 315; 20 R. R. 448........................816, 890
Fletcher v. Poole, 1 Park, Ins. (8th ed.) 115............................784, 876
Flindt v. Atkins, 3 Camp. 215, n. 675
Flindt v. Crokatt, 15 East, 522; 5 Taunt. 674; 15 R. R. 615............ 803
Flindt v. Scott, 15 East, 525; 5 Taunt. 674; 15 R. R. 615............... 803
Flindt v. Waters, 15 East, 260; 13 R. R. 457..............................89, 753
Flinn v. Headlam, 9 B. & C. 693; 7 L. J. (O. S.) K. B. 307; 33 R. R.
291 ....539, 555
Flinn v. Tobin, Moo. & M. 367; 31 R. R. 789 ....535, 539, 555
Flint v. Flemyng, 8 L. J. (O. S.) K. B. 350; 1 B. & Ad. 45; Ll. &
Wels. 257; 35 R. R. 205......229, 233, 262, 266, **268**, 269, 271, 277, 511,
512, 1282
Flint v. Le Mesurier, 2 Park, Ins. 563 ....240, 297
Foley v. Moline, 5 Taunt. 430; 1 Marsh. R. 117; 15 R. R. 541......... 594
Foley v. Tabor, 2 F. & F. 663 ....556, **614**, 717
Foley v. United Fire and Mar. Ins. Co. of Sydney, L. R. 5 C. P. 155;
39 L. J. C. P. 206; 22 L. T. 108; 18 W. R. 437...270, 272, **273**, 275, 279,
475, 513, 514
Folsom v. Mercantile Mutual Ins. Co., 8 Blatchford, 170; 9 Blatchford,
201; 18 Wallace, 237 ....13, 583
Fomin v. Oswell, 3 Camp. 357; 1 M. & S. 393.............................. 155
Fontaine v. Phœnix Ins. Co., 10 Johns. 58..................................... 719

TABLE OF CASES. XXXV

	SECT.
Fontaine v. Phœnix Ins. Co., 11 Johns. 293	1122
Forbes v. Aspinall, 13 East, 323; 12 R. R. 352......219, 229, 252b, 266, **269**,	
270, 271, 340, 343, 345, **346**, 365, 455, 878, 1041, 1259	
Forbes v. Cowie, 1 Camp. 520	269, 878, 1041
Forbes v. Wilson, 1 Park, Ins. (8th ed.) 472; 1 Marshall, Ins, 148...374, 475,	
	478, 698
Forester v. Pigou, 1 M. & S. 9; 3 Camp. 380	571, 573
Forshaw v. Chabert, 3 Br. & B. 158; 6 J. B. Moore, 369; 23 R. R.	
596 ......42, 43, 430, 688, 700, **723**, 799	
Forster v. Christie, 11 East, 205; 10 R. R. 470 ......804, **806**, 1108	
Forster v. Wilson, 13 L. J. Ex. 209; 12 M.& W. 203; 67 R. R. 298	110
Fort v. Lee, 3 Taunt. 381; 12 R. R. 670	618
Fortitude, The Ship, 3 Sumn. 228	1122, 1136
Fortuna, The, 4 C. Rob. 278	773
Forwood v. North Wales Mutual Mar. Ins. Co., 9 Q. B. D. 732; 49 L. J.	
Q. B. 593; 42 L. T. 837; 28 W. R. 938; 4 Asp. M. C. 293	1134
Foster v. Alvez, 3 Bing. (N. C.) 896; 4 Scott, 535	726
Foster v. Steele, 3 Bing. (N. C.) 892; 5 Scott, 25; 6 L. J. C. P. 265...725, 726	
Foster v. Wilmer, 2 Str. 1249	381
Foundling Hospital v. Crane [1911] 2 K. B. 367; 80 L. J. K. B. 853;	
105 L. T. 187	1213
Fowler v. English and Scottish Marine Ins. Co., 34 L. J. C. P. 253; 18	
C. B. (N. S.) 919; 11 Jur. (N. S.) 411; 12 L. T. 381; 13 W. R. 658;	
144 R. R. 691	77, 1109
Fox v. Black, 2 Park, Ins. (8th ed.) 620	390
Foy v. Bell, 3 Taunt. 493; 12 R. R. 691	24, 107
Fracis v. Sea Ins. Co., 3 Com. Cas. 229; 79 L. T. 28; 47 W. R. 119...597, 774	
Fragano v. Long, 3 L. J. (O. S.) K. B. 177; 4 B. & C. 219; 6 D. & R.	
283; 28 R. R. 226	282
Frances, The, 8 Cranch, S. C. R. 363	93
Francis v. Boulton, 65 L. J. Q. B. 153; 73 L. T. 578; 44 W. R. 222;	
8 Asp. M. C. 79; 1 Com. Cas. 217	1015, 1023
Franco-Hungarian Ins. Co. v. Merchants' Mar. Ins. Co., Shipping	
Gazette Weekly Summary, 15th June, 1888	328
Franklin, The, 6 C. Rob. 127, 132	97
Franklin, The, 3 C. Rob. 217	763
Frayes v. Worms. (See Trayes v. Worms.)	
Frederick Molke, The, 1 C. Rob. 86	767, 769
Freeland v. Glover, 7 East, 457; 3 Smith, 426; 6 Esp. 14; 9 R. R. 803...	
	565, 621
Freeman v. East India Co., 5 B. & Ald. 617; 1 D. & R. 234; 24 R. R.	
497	200, 206, 1158
French v. Backhouse, 5 Burr. 2727	136, 140, 141
French v. Patten, 9 East, 351; 1 Camp. 180; 9 R. R. 571	51
Frey, The, 92 Fed. R. 667	717
Friendschaft, The, 3 Wheat. 14, 51; 4 Wheat. 105	91, 92, 93
Friendship, The, 6 C. Rob. 420	760
Friere v. Woodhouse, 1 Holt, N. P. 572; 17 R. R. 679	614
Fuller v. McCall, 1 Yeates, 464	1117
Furneaux v. Bradley, 1 Park, Ins. (8th ed.) 365	203, 1093
Furtado v. Rogers, 3 B. & P. 191; 6 R. R. 752 ......85, 86, 87, 753, 831	

c 2

G.

SECT.

Gabarron v. Kreeft, L. R. 10 Ex. 274; 44 L. J. Ex. 238; 33 L. T. 365;
24 W. R. 146; 3 Asp. M. C. 36.. 282
Gabay v. Lloyd, 3 L. J. (O. S.) K. B. 116; 3 B. & C. 793; 5 D. & R.
641; 27 R. R. 486 ....65, 227, **782**, 824, 1273
Gaetano and Maria, The, 7 P. D. 137; 51 L. J. P. 67; 46 L. T. 835; 30
W. R. 766; 4 Asp. M. C. 535 195
Gairdner v. Senhouse, 3 Taunt. 16; 12 R. R. 573 ....394, 395, 401
Gale v. Laurie, 4 L. J. (O. S.) K. B. 149; 5 B. & C. 156; 7 D. & R. 711;
29 R. R. 199 ....219, 802
Gale v. Machell, 2 Marsh. Ins. 667; 2 Park, Ins. 797................... 1250
Galloway v. Morris, 3 Yeates, 445 ....244, 308
Gamba v. Le Mesurier, 4 East, 407; 1 Smith, 81; 7 R. R. 590......85, 86, 89,
753, 831
Gambles v. Ocean Mar. Ins. Co. of Bombay, 1 Ex. D. 141; 45 L. J. Ex.
366; 34 L. T. 198; 24 W. R. 384; 3 Asp. M. C. 180.................. 495
Gammon v. Beverley, 1 Moore, 563; 8 Taunt. 119........................ 1224
Gandy v. Adelaide Ins. Co., L. R. 6 Q. B. 746; 40 L. J. Q. B. 239;
25 L. T. 742; 1 Asp. M. C. 188........................614, 619, **625**, 626
Gardiner v. Croasdale, 2 Burr. 904; 1 W. Bl. 198....................1280, 1284
Gardiner v. Smith, 1 Johns. 142 1117
Gardner v. Salvador, 1 M. & Rob. 116; 42 R. R. 767......203, 1055, 1057,.
1113, 1121, 1129
Garrels v. Kensington, 8 T. R. 230; 4 R. R. 635...................674, 842
Garron v. Galbraith. (*See* De Garron v. Galbraith.)
Garston Sailing Ship Co. v. Hickie. (*See* Sailing Ship Garston Co.
v. Hickie.)
Gatliffe v. Bourne, 4 Bing. (N. C.) 314; 7 M. & Gr. 850; 5 Scott, 667;
7 L. J. C. P. 172; 44 R. R. 714; 456, 460
Gedge v. Royal Exchange Ass. Corp.; [1900] 2 Q. B. 214, 223; 5 Com.
Cas. 229 ....313a, 315, 316
Geipel v. Smith, L. R. 7 Q. B. 404; 41 L. J. Q. B. 153; 26 L. T. 361;
20 W. R. 332; 1 Asp. M. C. 268 807
General Hamilton, The, 6 C. Rob. 61 769
General Ins. Co. of Trieste v. Cory, [1897] 1 Q. B. 335; 66 L. J. Q. B.
313; 2 Com. Cas. 58 ....637, 797
General Mut. Ins. Co. v. Sherwood, 14 Howard's R. 352 791
Genforsikrings Aktieselskabet v. Da Costa, [1911] 1 K. B. 137; 80 L. J.
K. B. 236; 103 L. T. 767; 16 Com. Cas. 1; 11 Asp. M. C. 548;
27 Times L. R. 43 ....31, 39
Gernon v. Royal Exchange Ass. Co., 2 Marsh. 88; 6 Taunt. 383; Holt,
N. P. 49; 16 R. R. 630....................**1159**, 1192, 1196, 1197, 1274
Geyer v. Aguilar, 7 T. R. 681; 4 R. R. 543 681
Gibson v. Bell, 4 L. J. C. P. 242; 1 Bing. N. C. 743, 754; 1 Scott, 712;
1 Hodges, 136; 41 R. R. 660 110
Gibson v. Bradford, 24 L. J. Q. B. 159; 4 E. & B. 586; 1 Jur. (N. S.)
520; 3 W. R. 183; 99 R. R. 633 ....235, 280
Gibson v. Mair, 1 Marsh. R. 39; 15 R. R. 668 750
Gibson v. Service, 5 Taunt. 433; 1 Marsh. R. 119; 15 R. R. 541 ...750, 765
Gibson v. Small, 4 H. L. Cas. 353; 1 C. L. R. 363; 17 Jur. 1131; 94
R. R. 138 ....687, 697, 702, 708, 709, 710, 799

TABLE OF CASES. xxxvii

	SECT.
Gibson v. Winter, 5 B. & Ad. 96; 2 N. & M. 737; 2 L. J. (N. S.) K. B. 130; 39 R. R. 411	129, 176
Gilchrist v. Chicago Ins. Co., 104 Fed. R. 566	216, 1211, 1220
Gillan v. Simpkin, 4 Camp. 241; 16 R. R. 784	235
Gilroy v. Price, [1893] A. C. 56; 18 Ct. of Sess. Cas. (4th Ser.) 569; 1 R. 76; 68 L. T. 302; 7 Asp. M. C. 314	720
Gipsy, The, 33 L. J. Adm. 195; 11 L. T. 351	195
Gist v. Mason, 1 T. R. 88; 1 R. R. 154	85
Gladstone v. Clay, 1 M. & S. 418; 14 R. R. 479	448, 450
Gladstone v. King, 1 M. & S. 35; 14 R. R. 392	553, 579, 581, **584**, 585, 606
Glaser v. Cowie, 1 M. & S. 52	154, 161
Glasgow Ass. Corp. v. Symondson, 16 Com. Cas. 109; 104 L. T. 254; 11 Asp. M. C. 583; 27 Times L. R. 245	11, 101, 104, 145, 589, 607, 618, 623
Glasgow, The, Swabey, 145; 12 Moo. P. C. 355, n.; 2 Jur. (N. S.) 1147; 5 W. R. 10	202
Gledstanes v. Royal Exch. Ass. Co., 34 L. J. Q. B. 30; 5 B. & S. 797; 11 Jur. (N. S.) 108; 11 L. T. 305; 13 W. R. 71	13, **188**, 360
Glenfruin, The, 10 P. D. 103; 54 L. J. Adm. 49; 52 L. T. 769; 33 W. R. 826; 5 Asp. M. C. 413	688
Glenlivet, The, [1893] P. 164; [1894] P. 48; 63 L. J. Adm. 45; 6 R. 665; 69 L. T. 706; 42 W. R. 97; 7 Asp. M. C. 395	882, 891
Glennie v. London Ass. Co., 2 M. & S. 371; 15 R. R. 275	1076
Glover v. Black, 3 Burr. 1394; 1 W. Bl. 396, 399, 405, 422	242, 243, 252, 252a, 1279
Glynn v. Margetson, [1892] 1 Q. B. 337; [1893] A. C. 351; 62 L. J. Q. B. 466; 1 R. 193; 69 L. T. 1; 7 Asp. M. C. 366	401
Godard v. Gray, L. R. 6 Q. B. 139; 40 L. J. Q. B. 62; 24 L. T. 89; 19 W. R. 348	678, 682
Goddard v. East Texas Fire Ins. Co., 67 Texas, 69; 60 American R. 1	629
Godin v. London Ass. Co., 1 Burr. 489; 1 Ld. Ken. 254; 1 W. Bl. 103	133, 292, **334**
Goeben, The	972
Goldschmidt v. Lyon, 4 Taunt. 534; 13 R. R. 670	116, 117, 118
Goldschmidt v. Marryat, 1 Camp. 562; 53 R. R. 268	1271
Goldschmidt v. Whitmore, 3 Taunt. 508	841, 859
Goldsmid v. Gillies, 4 Taunt. 803; 14 R. R. 671	340, **1051**, 1097a, 1138, 1214, 1245
Good v. London SS. Owners Mut. Prot. Assn., L. R. 6 C. P. 563; 20 W. R. 33	81
Goodbody v. Balfour, 5 Com. Cas. 59; 82 L. T. 484; 9 Asp. M. C. 69	485
Gooding v. White, 29 Times L. R. 312	589
Goodson v. Brooke, 4 Camp. 163	119, 168
Goodwin v. Roberts, L. R. 10 Ex. 337, 346; 1 App. Cas. 476; 45 L. J. Ex. 748; 35 L. T. 179; 24 W. R. 987	63
Gordon v. Massachusetts Fire and Mar. Ins. Co., 2 Pick. 249	204, 1188
Gordon v. Morley, 2 Str. 1265	433, 654
Gordon v. Rimmington, 1 Camp. 123; 10 R. R. 656	828
Gordon v. Street, [1899] 2 Q. B. 641; 69 L. J. Q. B 45; 81 L. T. 237; 48 W. R. 158	536, 589

xxxviii   TABLE OF CASES.

                                                                              SECT.
Gorsedd SS. Co. v. Forbes, 5 Com. Cas. 413 1267
Goss v. Withers, 2 Burr. 683, 694; 2 Ld. Ken. 325 ....829, 1104, 1183
Gould v. Oliver, 4 Bing. (N. C.) 134; 7 L. J. C. P. 68; 5 Scott, 445;
    3 Hodges, 307; 2 Scott (N. R.), 241; 2 Man. & Gr. 208; 44 R. R.
    674; 58 R. R. 622 ....60, 225, 801, 920
Gracie v. Maryland Ins. Co., 8 Cranch, S. C. R. 75 59
Gracie v. New York Ins. Co., 8 Johns. 237 1234
Graham v. Barras, 5 B. & Ad. 1011; 3 N. & M. 125; 39 R. R. 723 ...629, 647
Graham v. Commercial Ins. Co., 11 Johns. 352 431
Grainger v. Martin, 2 B. & S. 456; 4 B. & S. 9; 31 L. J. Q. B. 186;
    8 L. T. 796; 11 W. R. 758; 8 Jur. (N. S.) 995; 127 R. R. 438 ... 984,
                                                                         1123, **1135**
Grand Saint Antoine, The 828
Grant v. Ætna Ins. Co., 15 Moo. P. C. 516; 8 Jur. (N. S.) 705; 6 L. T.
    735; 10 W. R. 772; 137 R. R. 123 509
Grant v. Delacour, cited 1 Taunt. 466 ....452, 453
Grant v. Hill, 4 Taunt. 380 173
Grant v. King, 4 Esp. 175; 6 R. R. 849 ....415, 481
Grant v. Norway, 10 C. B. 665; 20 L. J. C. P. 93; 15 Jur. 296; 84
    R. R. 747 1279
Grant v. Parkinson, 3 Dougl. 16; 6 T. R. 483; 3 B. & P. 85, n. ...287, 317
Grant v. Paxton, 1 Taunt. 463; 2 Chit. 319; 10 R. R. 583 ......452, 453, 610
Gratitudine, The, 3 C. Rob. 240, 259 ....196, 200, 205, 926
Great Britain 100 A1 SS. Ins. Assn. v. Wyllie, 22 Q. B. D. 710; 58
    L. J. Q. B. 614; 60 L. T. 916; 37 W. R. 407; 6 Asp. M. C. 398 ... 83
Great Britain SS. Premium Assn. v. White, 19 Ct. of Sess. Cas.
    (4th Ser.) 109; [1896] W. N. 91 31
Great Indian Peninsular Ry. Co. v. Saunders, 1 B. & S. 41; 2 B. & S.
    266; 30 L. J. Q. B. 218; 31 L. J. Q. B. 206; 9 Jur. (N. S.) 198; 6
    L. T. 297; 10 W. R. 520; 124 R. R. 446; 127 R. R. 363 22,
                                                                         214, **870**, 1156
Great Pacific, The, 6 Moo. P. C. (N. S.) 151; L. R. 2 A. & E. 383;
    L. R. 2 P. C. 516; 38 L. J. Adm. 45; 21 L. T. 38; 17 W. R. 933 ... 199
Great Western Ins. Co. v. Cunliffe, L. R. 9 Ch. 525; 43 L. J. Ch. 741
    30 L. T. 661 104
Green v. Browne, 2 Strange, 1199 814
Green v. Elmslie, 1 Peake, N. P. 212; 3 R. R. 693..........784, 819, 829, 905
Green v. Royal Exch. Ass. Co., 1 Marshall, R. 447; 6 Taunt. 68; 16
    R. R. 571 ....1122, 1164, 1167, **1170**, 1209
Green v. Tughan, 30 Times L. R. 64 104
Green v. Young, 2 Lord Raym. 840; 2 Salk. 444 ....378, 803, 834
Greene v. Merchants Ins. Co., 10 Pick. 402 ....570, 617
Greenock SS. Co. v. Maritime Ins. Co., [1903] 1 K. B. 367; 2 K. B.
    657; 72 L. J. K. B. 868; 89 L. T. 200; 9 Com. Cas. 41; 51 W. R.
    447; 9 Asp. M. C. 364 ....376, 686, 699, 705, 707, 719
Greenshields, Cowie & Co. v. Stephens, [1908] 1 K. B. 51; [1908] A. C.
    431; 77 L. J. K. B. 124, 985; 98 L. T. 89; 18 Com. Cas. 91; 10
    Asp. M. C. 597 ....**918**, 923, 936
Greer v. Poole, 5 Q. B. D. 272; 49 L. J. Q. B. 463; 42 L. T. 687; 28
    W. R. 582; 4 Asp. M. C. 300 ....784, 999

TABLE OF CASES. xxxix

SECT.
Gregory v. Christie, 3 Dougl. 419 ....58, 243, 391, 505, 610, 1279
Gregson v. Gilbert, 3 Dougl. 232 ....781, 799, 824
Grieve v. Young, Millar, Ins. 65 577
Griffiths v. Bramley-Moore, 4 Q. B. D. 70; 48 L. J. Q. B. 201; 40 L. T.
    149; 27 W. R. 480; 4 Asp. M. C. 66 232
Grill v. General Iron Screw Co., L. R. 3 C. P. 476; 37 L. J. C. P. 205;
    18 L. T. 485; 16 W. R. 796 845
Grimoldby v. Wells, L. R. 10 C. P. 391; 44 L. J. C. P. 203; 32 L. T.
    490; 23 W. R. 524 139
Griswold v. New York Ins. Co., 1 Johns. R. 205 1172
Grove v. Dubois, 1 T. R. 112; 16 R. R. 664, n. 111, 112, 118
Grover v. Mathews, [1910] 2 K. B. 401; 79 L. J. K. B. 1025; 102 L. T.
    650; 15 Com. Cas. 249; 26 Times L. R. 411 142
Guerlain v. Col. Ins. Co., 7 Johns. 527 1185
Guibert v. Readshaw, 2 Park, Ins. (8th ed.) 637 429
Gumm v. Tyrie, 33 L. J. Q. B. 97; 34 L. J. Q. B. 124; 13 W. R. 436 ... 73
Gunford Ship Co. v. Thames and Mersey Mar. Ins. Co., [1910] Sess.
    Cas. 1072; [1911] A. C. 533; 80 L. J. P. C. 146; 105 L. T. 312; 16
    Com. Cas. 270; 12 Asp. M. C. 49; 55 S. J. 631; 27 Times L. R.
    518 ....17, 20, 246, 247, 315, 315a, 319, 330, 339, 342,
                                      343, **589**, 607, 626, 637, 721, 797
Guthrie v. Armstrong, 1 Dow. & Ry. 248; 5 B. & Ald. 628 167
Guthrie v. North China Ins. Co., 6 Com. Cas. 25; 7 Com. Cas. 130 ... 1163,
                                                                            1164, 1165

H.

Haabet, The, [1899] P. 295; 68 L. J. P. 121; 81 L. T. 463......199, 243, 289
Haddow v. Parry, 3 Taunt. 303; 12 R. R. 666 1279
Hadkinson v. Robinson, 3 B. & P. 388; 7 R. R. 786 ....784, 804, **805**
Hadley v. Clarke, 8 T. R. 259; 4 R. R. 641 876
Hagan v. Scottish Ins. Co., 186 U. S. 423 ....73, 75
Hagedorn v. Bazett, 2 M. & S. 100 ....749, 753
Hagedorn v. Bell, 1 M. & S. 450; 14 R. R. 497 ....96, 676, 757, 759
Hagedorn v. Oliverson, 2 M. & S. 485; 15 R. R. 317 ......140, 142, 171, 1275
Hagedorn v. Whitmore, 1 Stark. 157 ....822, 834, 900
Hahn v. Corbett, 9 Moore, 390; 2 Bing. 205; 3 L. J. (O. S.) C. P. 253;
    27 R. R. 590 ....784, **820**, 905
Haigh v. De la Cour, 3 Camp. 319; 13 R. R. 813 ....20, 342
Haigh v. Sheffield Town Council, L. R. 10 Q. B. 102; 44 L. J. M. C.
    17; 31 L. T. 536; 23 W. R. 547 ....313a, 1124
Halhead v. Young, 25 L. J. Q. B. 290; 6 E. & B. 312; 2 Jur. (N. S.)
    970; 4 W. R. 530; 106 R. R. 615 ....**238**, 288, 805
Hall v. Brown, 2 Dow. 367 ....232, 385, 518
Hall v. Franklin Ins. Co., 9 Pick. 466 ....204, 429
Hall v. Hayman, [1912] 2 K. B. 5; 81 L. J. K. B. 509; 106 L. T. 142;
    17 Com. Cas. 80, 88; 12 Asp. M. C. 158; 56 S. J. 205; 28 Times
    L. R. 171 ....1091, 1189
Hall v. Janson, 4 E. & B. 500; 24 L. J. Q. B. 97; 3 C. L. R. 737; 1
    Jur. (N. S.) 571; 3 W. R. 213; 99 R. R. 578 ....71, 72, 233, **248**, 958

TABLE OF CASES.

	SECT.
Hall v. Ocean Ins. Co., 21 Pick. 472	221
Hallett v. Dowdall, 21 L. J. Q. B. 98; 18 Q. B. 2; 16 Jur. 462	79
Hallett v. Wigram, 19 L. J. C. P. 281; 9 C. B. 580; 82 R. R. 450...200, 924, 926, 927, 944, 948	
Hambro v. Burnand, [1904] 2 K. B. 10; 73 L. J. K. B. 669; 90 L. T. 803; 52 W. R. 583; 9 Com. Cas. 251; 20 Times L. R. 398	329
Hambro v. Hull and London Fire Ass. Co., 3 H. & N. 789; 28 L. J. Ex. 62	79
Hamburg, The, 33 L. J. Adm. 116; 2 Moo. P. C. (N. S.) 289; Br. & Lush. 253; 10 Jur. (N. S.) 600; 10 L. T. 206; 12 W. R. 628; 141 R. R. 77	207
Hamel v. Peninsular and Oriental Steam Nav. Co., [1908] 2 K. B. 298; 77 L. J. K. B. 637; 13 Com. Cas. 270	958
Hamilton, Fraser & Co. v. Pandorf & Co., 16 Q. B. D. 629; 12 App. Cas. 518; 57 L. J. Q. B. 24; 57 L. T. 726; 36 W. R. 369; 52 J. P. 196; 6 Asp. M. C. 212 ...777, 812, 825, 827a	
Hamilton, Fraser & Co. v. Thames and Mersey Mar. Ins. Co. (See Thames and Mersey Mar. Ins. Co. v. Hamilton, Fraser & Co.)	
Hamilton v. Mendes, 2 Burr. 1198; 1 W. Bl. 276 ......831, 1099, **1100**, 1104, 1138, 1183	
Hamilton v. Sheddon, 3 M. & W. 49; M. & H. 334; 7 L. J. Ex. 1; 49 R. R. 707 ...384, **406**, 414	
Hammond v. Allen, 2 Sumn. 397	13
Hammond v. Reid, 4 B. & Ald. 72; 22 R. R. 629 ...405, 410	
Hansen v. Dunn, 11 Com. Cas. 100; 22 Times L. R. 458 ...195, 207, 212, 1168	
Happy Couple, The, cited Edw. Adm. R. 1	96
Harburg India Rubber Comb Co. v. Martin, [1902] 1 K. B. 778; 71 L. J. K. B. 529; 86 L. T. 505; 50 W. R. 449 ...105, 307	
Harding v. Bussell, [1905] 2 K. B. 83; 74 L. J. K. B. 500; 92 L. T. 531; 10 Com. Cas. 184; 10 Asp. M. C. 50; 21 Times L. R. 401	1272
Harding v. Carter, 1 Park, Ins. 5; 1 Marshall, 309 ...130, 161	
Hardy v. Innes, 6 Moore, 574; 23 R. R. 630	1224
Hare v. Travis, 7 B. & C. 14; 9 D. & R. 748; 5 L. J. (O. S.) K. B. 348; 31 R. R. 139 ...378, 381	
Harford v. Maynard, cited 1 Park, Ins. (8th ed.) 36	837
Harland v. Burstall, 6 Com. Cas. 113; 84 L. T. 324; 9 Asp. M. C. 184; 17 Times L. R. 338	181
Harman v. Kingston, 3 Camp. 150, 152; 13 R. R. 775...89, 186, 188, 360, 753	
Harman v. Vaux, 3 Camp. 429; 14 R. R. 773	888
Harmonides, The, [1903] P. 1; 72 L. J. P. 9; 87 L. T. 448; 51 W. R. 303; 9 Asp. M. C. 354	1135
Harmony, The, 2 C. Rob. 322 ...90, 91	
Harratt v. Wise, 4 M. & Ry. 521; 9 B. & C. 712; 7 L. J. (O. S.) K. B. 309; Dan. & Ll. 234; 33 R. R. 300 ...760, 768, 1274	
Harrington v. Halkeld, 2 Park, Ins. (8th ed.) 639	431
Harris v. Scaramanga, L. R. 7 C. P. 481; 41 L. J. C. P. 170; 26 L. T. 797; 20 W. R. 777; 1 Asp. M. C. 339......994, 996, 997, **998**, 999, 1000, 1003	
Harrison v. Bank of Australasia, L. R. 7 Ex. 39; 41 L. J. Ex. 36; 25 L. T. 944; 20 W. R. 385; 1 Asp. M. C. 198......916, 932, 948, 952	

TABLE OF CASES. xli

	SECT.

Harrison v. Douglas, 3 A. & E. 396; 5 N. & M. 180; 1 H. & W. 380;
  42 R. R. 417 ....84, 629
Harrison v. Ellis, 26 L. J. Q. B. 239; 7 E. & B. 465; 3 Jur. (N. S.) 908;
  5 W. R. 494; 110 R. R. 679 ....455, 460
Harrison v. Millar, 7 T. R. 340, n.; 2 Esp. 513, n. 80
Harrison v. Universal Mar. Ins. Co., 3 F. & F. 190. 777
Harrower v. Hutchinson, 10 B. & S. 469; L. R. 4 Q. B. 523; L. R. 5
  Q. B. 584; 39 L. J. Q. B. 229; 22 L. T. 684............................397, 605
Hart v. Standard Mar. Ins. Co., 22 Q. B. D. 499; 58 L. J. Q. B. 284; 60
  L. T. 649; 37 W. R. 366; 6 Asp. M. C. 368...............56, 68, 228, 637
Hartley v. Buggin, 3 Dougl. 39 ....376, 377, 414
Harvey v. Beckwith, 2 H. & M. 429; 4 N. R. 258; 10 L. T. 632; 12
  W. R. 896 80
Harvey v. Seligman, 10 Ct. of Sess. Cas. (4th Ser.) 680..................... 555
Hastie v. Couturier, 9 Exch. Ch. 109; 22 L. J. Ex. 299; 96 R. R. 598
  (see Couturier v. Hastie).. 13
Hastie v. De Peyster, 3 Caines, 190 326
Hathaway v. St. Paul Fire and Mar. Ins. Co., 1 Fed. R. 197............722, 724
Hatton v. Royle, 27 L. J. Ex. 486; 3 H. & N. 500; 117 R. R. 821......... 168
Haughton v. Empire Mar. Ins. Co., 4 H. & C. 41; L. R. 1 Ex. 206;
  35 L. J. Ex. 117; 12 Jur. (N. S.) 376; 15 L. T. 80; 14 W. R. 645;
  143 R. R. 476 ....477, **478**, 486, 499
Haughton v. Ewbank, 4 Camp. 88.................................15, 73, 166, 218
Havelock v. Hancill, 3 T. R. 277; 1 R. R. 703.....................635, 637, 844
Havelock v. Rockwood, 8 T. R. 268 ....676, 831, 1187
Haven v. Gray, 12 Mass. 71 ....360, 455
Haven v. Holland, 2 Mason, 230 421
Hawkins v. Twizell, 25 L. J. Q. B. 160; 5 E. & B. 883; 2 Jur. (N. S.)
  302; 4 W. R. 242 ....245, 308
Hayman v. Moulton, 5 Esp. 65; 8 R. R. 837 203
Haywood v. Rodgers, 4 East, 590; 7 R. R. 638.........555, 600, 619, 620, 626
Hazard v. New England Mar. Ins. Co., 8 Peters, S. C. R. 557.........564, 825
Hearne v. Edmunds, 1 Br. & B. 388; 4 Moore, 15; 21 R. R. 660......... 889
Heckenrath v. American Mutual Ins. Co., 3 Barb. Ch. N. Y. 63...324, 325
Hedburgh v. Pearson, 7 Taunt. 154 1073
Hedley v. Pinkney & Sons SS. Co., [1892] 1 Q. B. 58; 61 L. J. Q. B.
  179; 66 L. T. 71; 40 W. R. 113; 7 Asp. M. C. 135; 56 J. P. 308... 720
Helen, The, L. R. 1 A. & E. 1; 35 L. J. Adm. 2; 11 Jur. (N. S.) 1025;
  13 L. T. 305; 14 W. R. 136 760
Henchman v. Offley, 2 H. Bl. 345, n.; 3 Dougl. 139; 3 R. R. 408, 413... 189
Henderson v. Shankland, [1896] 1 Q. B. 525; 65 L. J. Q. B. 340; 74
  L. T. 238; 44 W. R. 401; 8 Asp. M. C. 136; 1 Com. Cas. 252, 333......982,
    984, **1025**, 1129
Henderson v. Stevenson, L. R. 2 H. L. (Sc.) 470; 32 L. T. 709......45, 629
Henderson v. The Underwriting, &c. Assn., [1891] 1 Q. B. 557; 60 L. J.
  Q. B. 406; 64 L. T. 774; 39 W. R. 528.................................... 1272
Hendricks v. Australasian Ins. Co., L. R. 9 C. P. 460; 43 L. J. C. P.
  188; 30 L. T. 419; 22 W. R. 947; 2 Asp. M. C. 44...................... 996
Henkle v. Royal Exch. Ass. Co., 1 Ves. sen. 317, 320.........41, 85, 388, 1256
Henrich Björn, The, 11 App. Cas. 270. 55 L. J. Adm. 80; 55 L. T. 66;
  6 Asp. M. C. 1 ....255a, 257a

TABLE OF CASES.

	SECT.
Henrick and Maria, The, 4 C. Rob. 43; 6 C. Rob. 138, n.	677
Henry v. Staniforth, 4 Camp. 270; 17 R. R. 293	1255
Hentig v. Staniforth, 5 M. & S. 122; 17 R. R. 293	87, 740, 1255
Herbert v. Champion, 1 Camp. 133; 10 R. R. 657	1242, 1243

Herckenrath v. American Mutual Ins. Co., 3 Barb. Ch. N. Y. 63;
 1 Parsons, Ins. 301; 2 Phillips, Ins. s. 1751..................324, 325
Herman, The, 4 C. Rob. 228 ....97, 658
Herman v. Jeuchner, 15 Q. B. D. 561; 54 L. J. Q. B. 340; 53 L. T. 94;
 33 W. R. 606; 49 J. P. 502 1254
Hermann v. Charlesworth, [1905] 2 K. B. 123; 74 L. J. K. B. 620; 93
 L. T. 284; 54 W. R. 22; 21 Times L. R. 368 1254
Herring v. Janson, 1 Com. Cas. 177..................20, 319, 342, 589, 626
Herstelder, The, 1 C. Rob. 114, 119, n. 677, 833
Heselton v. Allnutt, 1 M. & S. 45 ....381, 382, 433
Hewit v. Flexney, Beawes, Lex Mercator. 458 1242
Hewitt v. Wilson, 30 Times L. R. 619 ....228, 604
Heye v. North German Lloyd, 33 Fed. R. 60; 36 Fed. R. 705..................972
Heyman v. Parish, 2 Camp. 149; 11 R. R. 688..................784, 821, 838, 845, 859
Hibbert v. Carter, 1 T. R. 745; 1 R. R. 388..................178, 179, 292, 299, 1279
Hibbert v. Halliday, 2 Taunt. 428; 11 R. R. 633..................423
Hibbert v. Martin, 1 Camp. 538..................698, 844
Hibbert v. Pigou, 1 Marsh. Ins. 375; 2 Park, Ins. 694, 700......632, 633, 654
Hick v. London Ass. Co., 1 Com. Cas. 244..................918, 1001, 1003
Hick v. Raymond, [1893] A. C. 22; 62 L. J. Q. B. 98; 1 R. 125; 68
 L. T. 175; 41 W. R. 384; 7 Asp. M. C. 233..................480
Hickie v. Rodocanachi, 4 H. & N. 455; 28 L. J. Ex. 273; 5 Jur. (N. S.)
 550; 7 W. R. 545; 118 R. R. 551..................1178, 1206, 1209, 1220, 1278
Hicks v. Palington, Moore, Q. B. 297 925
Hicks v. Shield, 26 L. J. Q. B. 205; 7 E. & B. 633; 3 Jur. (N. S.) 715;
 5 W. R. 536; 110 R. R. 762..................232, 264
Higgins v. Sargent, 3 D. & R. 613; 2 B. & C. 348; 2 L. J. (O. S.) K. B.
 33; 26 R. R. 379 1284
Higginson v. Dall, 13 Mass. 96 ....299, 629, 1188
Hill v. Patten, 8 East, 373; 1 Camp. 72; 9 R. R. 469 ......48, 51, 219, 222, 224, 226
Hill v. Scott, [1895] 2 Q. B. 713; 65 L. J. Q. B. 87; 73 L. T. 458; 1
 Com. Cas. 140, 200 ....173, 309
Hill v. Secretan, 1 B. & P. 315; 4 R. R. 806 293
Hill v. Wilson, 4 C. P. D. 329; 48 L. J. C. P. 764; 41 L. T. 412; 4
 Asp. M. C. 198 ....981, 992, 995
Hills v. London Ass. Co., 5 M. & W. 569; 9 L. J. Ex. 25; 52 R. R.
 843 ....1083, 1085
Hine v. Steamship Ins. Syndicate, 72 L. T. 79; 11 R. 777; 7 Asp.
 M. C. 558 ....119, 125
Hingston v. Wendt, 1 Q. B. D. 367; 45 L. J. Q. B. 440; 34 L. T. 181;
 24 W. R. 664; 3 Asp. M. C. 126 910
Hiram, The, 3 C. Rob. 180 876
Hobart v. Norton, 8 Pick. 159 381
Hobbs v. Hannam, 3 Camp. 93; 13 R. R. 764 ....261, 309, 851
Hobbs v. Henning, 17 C. B. (N. S.) 791; 34 L. J. C. P. 117; 11 Jur.
 (N. S.) 223; 12 L. T. 205; 13 W. R. 431 ....731, 745, 764, 1285

	SECT.
Hobson v. Lord, 92 U. S. 397	948, 961
Hodgson v. Blakiston, 1 Park, Ins. (8th ed.) 400, n.	1059
Hodgson v. Glover, 6 East, 316; 8 R. R. 495	237, 287
Hodgson v. Malcolm, 2 B. & P. (N. R.) 336; 9 R. R. 656	798
Hodgson v. Richardson, 1 W. Bl. 463	533, 605, 618
Hoffman v. Marshall, 2 Bing. (N. C.) 383; 2 Scott, 559; 1 Hodges, 330; 5 L. J. C. P. 70; 42 R. R. 626	887
Hoffnung, The, 6 C. Rob. 112	767
Hogarth v. Walker, [1899] 2 Q. B. 401; [1900] 2 Q. B. 283; 68 L. J. Q. B. 888; 69 L. J. Q. B. 634; 48 W. R. 47, 545; 5 Com. Cas. 280; 82 L. T. 744; 9 Asp. M. C. 84	219
Hogg v. Gouldney, Beawes, Lex Mercator. 310	1242
Hogg v. Horner, 2 Park, Ins. 626	401, 1251
Holbrook v. Brown, 2 Mass. 280	241
Holdsworth v. Wise, 1 M. & Ry. 673; 7 B. & C. 794; 6 L. J. (O. S.) K. B. 134; 31 R. R. 299	691, 692, **798**, 1105, **1106**, 1141, 1285
Holland v. Russell, 1 B. & S. 424; 4 B. & S. 14; 30 L. J. Q. B. 308; 32 L. J. Q. B. 297; 8 L. T. 468; 11 W. R. 757; 7 Jur. (N. S.) 842; 129 R. R. 629, 635	109, 1246
Hollingworth v. Brodrick, 7 A. & E. 40; 2 N. & P. 608; 8 L. J. Q. B. 80; 1 Jur. 430	699, 702, 703
Holman v. Johnson, 1 Cowp. 343	740
Home Mar. Ins. Co. v. Smith, [1898] 1 Q. B. 829; [1898] 2 Q. B. 351; 67 L. J. Q. B. 777; 78 L. T. 734; 46 W. R. 661; 3 Com. Cas. 172	7, 8, 26, 32, 35, 37
Hooper v. Lusby, 4 Camp. 66	136
Hooper v. Robinson, 98 U. S. 528	172
Hopper No. 66, The, [1907] P. 254; [1908] A. C. 126; 76 L. J. P. 110; 77 L. J. P. 84; 97 L. T. 360; 98 L. T. 464; 23 Times L. R. 414	802
Hopper v. Burness, 1 C. P. D. 137; 45 L. J. C. P. 377; 34 L. T. 528; 24 W. R. 612; 3 Asp. M. C. 149	200, 206, 927, 978, 982
Hopper v. Wear Mar. Ins. Co., 46 L. T. 107; 4 Asp. M. C. 482	516
Hore v. Whitmore, 2 Cowp. 784	635, 637, 641
Hornby, v. Lacy, 6 M. & S. 166; 18 R. R. 245	112
Horncastle v. Haworth, 1 Marsh. Ins. 681	1263
Horncastle v. Suart, 7 East, 400; 8 R. R. 649	266, 272, **274**, 276, 513, 1088
Horneyer v. Lushington, 15 East, 46; 3 Camp. 85; 13 R. R. 759	153, 448, **490**, 666, 732
Hoskins v. Pickersgill, 3 Dougl. 222	68, 219
Hough v. Head, 55 L. J. Q. B. 43; 53 L. T. 809; 34 W. R. 160; 5 Asp. M. C. 505	438
Houghton v. Gilbart, 7 C. & P. 701	70, 1274
Houlder v. Merchants' Mar. Ins. Co., 17 Q. B. D. 354; 55 L. J. Q. B. 420; 55 L. T. 244; 34 W. R. 673; 6 Asp. M. C. 12	458, 459
Houstman v. Thornton, Holt, N. P. 242; 17 R. R. 632	813, 814, 1048, 1190, 1214
Houston v. Bordenave, 6 Taunt. 451; 2 Marsh. 141; 16 R. R. 657	117, 118
Houston v. Robertson, 6 Taunt. 448; 2 Marsh. 138; 4 Camp. 342; Holt, 88; 16 R. R. 655	117, 118
Howard v. Refuge Friendly Society, 54 L. T. 644	1255
Hoyt v. Gilman, 8 Mass. 336	598

	SECT.
Hubbard v. Glover, 3 Camp. 313	548
Hubbard v. Hartford Fire Ins. Co., 33 Iowa, 325	797
Hubbard v. Jackson, 4 Taunt. 169; 13 R. R. 574	47, 48
Hucks v. Thornton, Holt, N. P. 30; 17 R. R. 594	437, 708, 723, 848
Hudson v. Guestier, 4 Cranch, 293	677
Hudson v. Harrison, 6 Moore, 288; 3 Br. & B. 97; 23 R. R. 575	**1160,** 1197, 1199, 1201
Hudson v. Marjoribanks, 7 Moore, 463; 1 Bing. 393	1019
Hughes v. Cornelius, Carth. 32; T. Raym. 473; 2 Shower, 232	678, 681
Hughes v. Tindall, 18 C. B. 98; 107 R. R. 225	52, 82
Hughes v. Union Ins. Co., 3 Wheat. 159	408
Hughes v. Wilson, 1 Stark. 180	1281
Hull v. Cooper, 14 East, 479; 13 R. R. 287	479
Hull Dock Co. v. Browne, 2 B. & Ad. 43; 36 R. R. 459	485
Hume v. Frenz, 150 Fed. R. 502	216, 1220
Humfrey v. Dale, 7 E. & B. 266; E. B. & E. 1004; 27 L. J. Q. B. 390; 5 Jur. (N. S.) 191; 6 W. R. 854; 110 R. R. 587	71, 72
Humphreys v. Union Ins. Co., 3 Mason, 429	1028, 1084
Hunt v. Royal Exch. Ass. Co., 5 M. & S. 47; 17 R. R. 264	206, **1148,** 1188, 1193
Hunter, The, 1 Dod. Adm. R. 480	666
Hunter v. Leathley, 8 L. J. (O. S.) K. B. 274; 9 L. J. (O. S.) Ex. 118; 10 B. & C. 858; 5 M. & P. 457; 7 Bing. 517; 1 C. & J. 423; 1 Tyr. 355; Ll. & Wels. 125, 244; 53 R. R. 179	134, 188, **404,** 452
Hunter v. Molineux, cited 6 East, 385	182
Hunter v. Northern Marine Ins. Co., 14 Ct. of Sess. Cas. (4th Ser.) 544; 13 App. Cas. 717	485, 495, 640
Hunter v. Parker, 10 L. J. Ex. 281; 7 M. & W. 322; 56 R. R. 723	202, 203, 1118, 1119
Hunter v. Potts, 4 Camp. 203; 16 R. R. 776	723, 777, 825
Hunter v. Prinsep, 1 Marsh. Ins. 323; 10 East, 378; 10 R. R. 328	228
Hunter v. Wright, 10 B. & C. 714; 8 L. J. (O. S.) K. B. 259	1267
Hunting v. Boulton, 1 Com. Cas. 120	473, 477, 508
Hurlbut v. Turnure, 81 Fed. R. 208	918
Hurrell v. Bullard, 3 F. & F. 445	150
Hurry v. Royal Exch. Ass. Co., 2 B. & P. 430; 3 B. & P. 308; 3 Esp. 289; 5 R. R. 639; 6 R. R. 804	447, 457, 458, 1014
Hurtin v. Phœnix Ins. Co., 1 Wash. C. C. R. 400	1104
Hurtin v. Union Ins. Co., 1 Wash. C. C. R. 530	1089
Hutchins v. Royal Exch. Ass. Corp., [1911] 2 K. B. 398; 80 L. J. K. B. 1169; 105 L. T. 6; 16 Com. Cas. 242; 12 Asp. M. C. 21; 27 Times L. R. 482	784, 885, 861a
Hutchinson v. Aberdeen Sea Ins. Co., 3 Ct. of Sess. Cas. (4th Ser.) 682	534
Hutchinson v. Bowker, 5 M. & W. 535; 9 L. J. Ex. 24; 52 R. R. 821	1274
Hutchinson v. Wright, 27 L. J. Ch. 834; 25 Beav. 444; 4 Jur. (N. S.) 749; 6 W. R. 475; 119 R. R. 482	82, 299
Huth v. Lamport, 16 Q. B. D. 442, 735; 55 L. J. Q. B. 239; 54 L. T. 663; 34 W. R. 386; 5 Asp. M. C. 593	1004
Hyams v. Stuart King, [1908] 2 K. B. 696	313a

SECT.

Hydarnes Steamship Co. v. Indemnity Mutual Mar. Ass. Co., [1895] 1
    Q. B. 500; 64 L. J. Q. B. 353; 14 R. 216; 72 L. T. 103; 7 Asp.
    M. C. 553 ....73, 516
Hyde v. Bruce, 3 Dougl. 213 638
Hyde v. Louisiana State Ins. Co., 2 Martin (N. S.), 410 1131
Hyderabad (Deccan) Co. v. Willoughby, [1899] 2 Q. B. 530; 68 L. J.
    Q. B. 862; 4 Com. Cas. 270 ....376, 414, 425, 446

I.

Ide v. Chalmers, 5 Com. Cas. 212 447
Idle v. Royal Exch. Ass. Co., 8 Taunt. 755; 3 Br. & B. 151, n. (*d*);
    3 Moore, 115; 21 R. R. 538 ....203, 1055, 1058, **1118**, 1119, 1122,
                                                1161, 1164, 1169, **1171**
Imina, The, 3 C. Rob. 167 764
Immanuel, The, 2 C. Rob. 186 ....98, 664, 771
Imperial Mar. Ins. Co. v. Fire Ins. Corp., 4 C. P. D. 166; 48 L. J.
    C. P. 424; 40 L. T. 166; 27 W. R. 680; 4 Asp. M. C. 71............ 188
Indian Chief, The, 3 C. Rob. 12............................90, 92, 93, 98, 100, 657
Industrie, The, Spinks' Prize Cases, 54 661
Inglis v. Stock, 9 Q. B. D. 708; 12 Q. B. D. 564; 10 App. Cas. 263; 53
    L. J. Q. B. 356; 54 L. J. Q. B. 582; 51 L. T. 449; 52 L. T. 821;
    33 W. R. 877; 5 Asp. M. C. 294, 422 ....185, 186, 188, 259a, **284**
Inglis v. Vaux, 3 Camp. 437; 14 R. R. 778............................409, 465, **496**
Ingram and Royle v. Services Maritimes du Tréport, [1913] 1 K. B.
    538; [1914] 1 K. B. 545; 82 L. J. K. B. 374; 83 L. J. K. B. 382;
    108 L. T. 304; 109 L. T. 733; 18 Com. Cas. 109; 19 Com. Cas. 105;
    12 Asp. M. C. 295, 387; 57 S. J. 375; 58 S. J. 172; 29 Times
    L. R. 274; 30 Times L. R. 79 717
Inman Steamship Co. v. Bischoff, 6 Q. B. D. 648; 7 App. Cas. 670;
    52 L. J. Q. B. 169; 47 L. T. 581; 31 W. R. 141; 5 Asp. M. C. 6.. 608,
                                                         785, 786, 788, 1089
Insurance Co. v. Folsom, 18 Wallace, 237 13
Insurance Co. v. Gossler, 96 U. S. 645 ....1137, 1217
Insurance Co. v. Stimson, 103 U. S. 25 299
Insurance Co. v. Transportation Co., 12 Wall. 194 819
International Navigation Co. v. Atlantic Mut. Ins. Co., 100 Fed. R.
    304; 108 Fed. R. 988 ....247, 340, 932, 1005, 1006, 1023
International Navigation Co. v. Sea Ins. Co., 124 Fed. R. 93; 129
    Fed. R. 13 ....1000, 1006
Ionides v. Harford, 29 L. J. Ex. 36; 121 R. R. 866 ......54, 180, 469, 1267
Ionides v. Pacific Fire & Mar. Ins. Co., L. R. 6 Q. B. 674; L. R. 7
    Q. B. 517; 41 L. J. Q. B. 190; 26 L. T. 738; 21 W. R. 22; 1
    Asp. M. C. 141, 330...34, 37, 182, **183**, 185, 188, 555, **568**, 575, 576
Ionides v. Pender, L. R. 9 Q. B. 531; 43 L. J. Q. B. 227; 30 L. T. 547;
    22 W. R. 884; 1 Asp. M. C. 432; 2 Asp. M. C. 266 ....20, 342, 343,
                                                          575, **589**, 626, 627

xlvi TABLE OF CASES.

SECT.

Ionides v. Universal Mar. Ins. Assn., 14 C. B. (N. S.) 259; 32 L. J.
 C. P. 170; 10 Jur. (N. S.) 18; 8 L. T. 705; 11 W. R. 858; 135
 R. R. 686 ....**790**, 819, **820**, 905
Iredale v. China Traders' Ins. Co. [1899] 2 Q. B. 356; [1900] 2 Q. B.
 515; 68 L. J. Q. B. 1021; 69 L. J. Q. B. 783; 81 L. T. 231; 83
 L. T. 299; 48 W. R. 48; 49 W. R. 107; 8 Asp. M. C. 580; 4 Com.
 Cas. 256; 5 Com. Cas. 337 ....929, 940
Ireland v. Livingstone, L. R. 2 Q. B. 99; L. R. 5 Q. B. 516; L. R. 5
 H. L. 395; 41 L. J. Q. B. 201; 27 L. T. 79; 15 W. R. 152 155
Irene, The, 5 C. Rob. 76 770
Ironmaster, The, Sw. 441 1135
Iroquois, The, 194 U. S. 240 430
Irrawaddy, The, 171 U. S. 187 918
Irving v. Manning, 1 C. B. 168; 2 C. B. 784; 6 C. B. 391; 1 H. L. Cas.
 287; 73 R. R. 69, 73 ....3, 340, 341, 348, 1053, 1123, **1133**
Irving v. Richardson, 9 L. J. (O. S.) K. B. 225; 2 B. & Ad. 193; 1 M.
 & Rob. 153; 36 R. R. 541 ....173, 251, 298, 349, 1274
Isaacs v. Royal Ins. Co., L. R. 5 Ex. 296; 39 L. J. Ex. 189; 22 L. T.
 681; 18 W. R. 982 441
Isberg v. Bowden, 22 L. J. Ex. 322; 8 Ex. 852; 1 C. L. R. 722 110

J.

Jackson v. Mumford, 8 Com. Cas. 61; 9 Com. Cas. 114; 52 W. R. 342;
 20 Times L. R. 172 .... 861a
Jackson v. Union Mar. Ins. Co., L. R. 8 C. P. 572; L. R. 10 C. P. 125;
 44 L. J. C. P. 27; 31 L. T. 789; 23 W. R. 169; 2 Asp. M. C.
 435 ....784, 785, 786, 787, 1089
Jackson, Sir John, Ltd. v. Owners of SS. Blanche. (See The
 Hopper No. 66.)
Jacob v. Gaviller, 7 Com. Cas. 116; 87 L. T. 26; 50 W. R. 428 783
James Nelson & Sons v. Nelson Line, Ltd., [1906] 2 K. B. 217; 75 L. J.
 K. B. 895; 95 L. T. 180; 54 W. R. 546; 11 Com. Cas. 228; 10 Asp.
 M. C. 265; 22 Times L. R. 630 ....1231, 1272
Jameson v. Swainstone, 2 Camp. 546, n.; 11 R. R. 794, n. 120
Jamieson & Newcastle SS. Freight Ins. Assn., In re, [1895] 2 Q. B. 90;
 64 L. J. Q. B. 560; 14 R. 444; 72 L. T. 648; 43 W. R. 530; 7 Asp.
 M. C. 593; 1 Com. Cas. 395 ....785, 788, 1089
Jan Frederick, The, 5 C. Rob. 128 ....659, 660
Jane, The, 2 Hag. Adm. R. 345 434
Janson v. Driefontein Consolidated Mines, [1900] 2 Q. B. 339; [1901]
 2 K. B. 419; [1902] A. C. 484; 71 L. J. K. B. 857; 87 L. T. 372;
 51 W. R. 142; 7 Com. Cas. 268...**86**, 89, 93, 99, 307, 753, 803, 833, 834
Jarman v. Coape, 13 East, 394; 2 Camp. 613; 12 R. R. 374 ....903, 905
Jarratt v. Ward, 1 Camp. 263; 10 R. R. 677 ....418, 423
Jason, The, 178 Fed. R. 414; 225 U. S. 32 918
Jefferyes v. Legendra, 3 Lev. 320; 1 Show. 320; 2 Salk. 443; 4 Mod.
 58; Carth. 216 654
Jell v. Pratt, 2 Stark. 67 125

TABLE OF CASES. xlvii

SECT.

Jenkins v. Power, 6 M. & S. 282; 18 R. R. 375 ....108, 109, 740
Job v. Langton, 6 E. & B. 779; 26 L. J. Q. B. 97; 3 Jur. (N. S.) 109;
    4 W. R. 641; 106 R. R. 797 ....911, 948, 952, **967**
Johnson v. Bryant, 1 Com. Cas. 363 436
Johnson v. Chapman, 35 L. J. C. P. 23; 19 C. B. (N. S.) 563; 15 L. T.
    70; 14 W. R. 264 ....60, **920**, 929, 930
Johnson v. Greaves, 2 Taunt. 344..96, 756, 758
Johnson v. Sheddon, 2 East, 581; 6 R. R. 516 ....1014, 1015
Johnson v. Ward, 6 Esp. 47 1279
Johnston v. Hogg, 10 Q. B. D. 432; 52 L. J. Q. B. 343; 48 L. T. 435;
    31 W. R. 768; 5 Asp. M. C. 51 905
Johnston v. Sutton, 1 Dougl. 254 749
Jolly v. Walker, 2 Park, Ins. (8th ed.) 630 420
Jones v. Neptune Mar. Ins. Co., L. R. 7 Q. B. 702; 41 L. J. Q. B.
    370; 27 L. T. 308; 1 Asp. M. C. 416 ....510, 514, **516**
Jones v. Nicholson, 10 Exch. 28; 23 L. J. Ex. 330; 2 C. L. R. 1236;
    102 R. R. 458 ....840, 849, 852
Jones v. Schmoll, cited 1 T. R. 130; 1 R. R. 196, n. 781
Jonge Klassina, The, 5 C. Rob. 297 ....97, 658
Jonge Margaretha, The, 1 C. Rob. 189 ....762, 763
Jonge Tobias, The, 1 C. Rob. 329 763
Jorden v. Money, 5 H. L. Cas. 185; 23 L. J. Ch. 865; 101 R. R. 116... 542
Joseph, The, 1 Gallison, 558 306
Journu v. Bourdieu, 1 Park, Ins. 245 ....68, 883
Joyce v. Kennard, L. R. 7 Q. B. 78; 41 L. J. Q. B. 17; 25 L. T. 932;
    20 W. R. 233; 1 Asp. M. C. 194 ....252, 309, **368**
Joyce v. Realm Mar. Ins. Co., L. R. 7 Q. B. 580; 41 L. J. Q. B. 356;
    27 L. T. 144; 1 Asp. M. C. 194 ....73, 328, 450
Joyce v. Swann, 17 C. B. (N. S.) 84; 142 R. R. 258 282
Joyce v. Williamson, 3 Dougl. 164 1137
Juffrow Maria Schrœder, The, 3 C. Rob. 147 ....668, 768
Juhel v. Church, 2 Johns. Cas. 333 321
Juhel v. Rhinelander, 2 Johns. Cas. 120, 487 613
Julia Blake, The, 107 U. S. 418 200
Jumel v. Mar. Ins. Co., 7 Johns. 423 ....1219, 1220

K.

Kacianoff v. China Traders' Ins. Co., Ltd., [1913] 3 K. B. 407; [1914]
    W. N. 245; 83 L. J. K. B. 58; 109 L. T. 365; 12 Asp. M. C. 395;
    18 Com. Cas. 290; 29 Times L. R. 642; 30 Times L. R. 546...784, 805,
                                                       807, 830, 1143
Kaines v. Knightly, Skinner, 54 42
Kaltenbach v. Mackenzie, 3 C. P. D. 467; 48 L. J. C. P. 9; 39 L. T.
    215; 26 W. R. 844; 4 Asp. M. C. 39......1045, 1055, 1058, 1059, **1061**,
               1062, 1092, 1164, 1182, 1191, 1192, 1194, 1214, 1274
Kane v. Columbian Ins. Co., 2 Johns. 264 ....394, 408
Karnak, The, 6 Moo. P. C. (N. S.) 136; L. R. 2 A. & E. 289; L. R. 2
    P. C. 505; 38 L. J. Adm. 57; 21 L. T. 159; 17 W. R. 1028...263, 264
Kearley v. Thompson, 24 Q. B. D. 742; 59 L. J. Q. B. 288; 63 L. T.
    150; 38 W. R. 604; 54 J. P. 804 1254

TABLE OF CASES.

	SECT.
Keighley, Maxted & Co. v. Durant, [1901] A. C. 240; 70 L. J. K. B. 662; 84 L. T. 777	140, 143
Keir v. Andrade, 6 Taunt. 498; 2 Marsh. 196; 16 R. R. 660	750
Keith v. Burrows, 1 C. P. D. 722; 2 C. P. D. 163; 2 App. Cas. 636; 46 L. J. C. P. 801; 37 L. T. 291; 25 W. R. 831; 3 Asp. M. C. 481.	1227
Keith v. Protection Marine Ins. Co. of Paris, 10 L. R. Ir. 51	311, 313
Kellner v. Le Mesurier, 4 East, 396; 1 Smith, 72; 7 R. R. 581	85, 86, 831, **1264**
Kelly v. Solari, 11 L. J. Ex. 10; 9 M. & W. 54; 6 Jur. 107; 60 R. R. 666	1244
Kemp v. Halliday, 6 B. & S. 723; L. R. 1 Q. B. 520; 34 L. J. Q. B. 233; 35 L. J. Q. B. 156; 12 Jur. (N. S.) 582; 14 L. T. 762; 14 W. R. 697; 141 R. R. 579	911, 965, 969, 1048, 1123, 1125, 1274
Kendrick v. Delafield, 2 Caines, 67	852
Kenny v. Clarkson, 1 Johns. 385	350
Kensington v. Inglis, 8 East, 273; 9 R. R. 438	47, 48, 88
Kent v. Bird, 2 Cowp. 583	316
Kent v. Manufacturers' Ins. Co., 18 Pick. R. 19	444
Kenyon v. Berthon, 1 Dougl. 12, n.	29, 629, 630, 640
Ker v. Osborne, 9 East, 378	1175
Kerr v. Union Mar. Ins. Co., 124 Fed. R. 835; 130 Fed. R. 415	39, 555, 561
Kettell v. Wiggin, 13 Mass. R. 68	427, 430
Kettlewell v. Refuge Ass. Co., [1907] 2 K. B. 242; [1908] 1 K. B. 545; 76 L. J. K. B. 711; 77 L. J. K. B. 421; 97 L. T. 106, 896; 23 Times L. R. 506	1256
Kewley v. Ryan, 2 H. Bl. 343; 3 R. R. 408	16, 185, **189**, 378, 380, 381, 388
Keyser v. Scott, 4 Taunt. 660; 13 R. R. 721	903
Khedive, The, 5 App. Cas. 876; 7 App. Cas. 795; 52 L. J. Adm. 1; 47 L. T. 198; 31 W. R. 249; 5 Asp. M. C. 360, 567	793
Kidston v. Empire Mar. Ins. Co., L. R. 1 C. P. 535; 2 C. P. 357; 36 L. J. C. P. 156; 12 Jur. (N. S.) 665; 16 L. T. 119, 286; 15 W. R. 769	22, 25, 207, 214, 215, 799a, 811, 869, 870, 871, 881, 885, 896, 1008, 1009, 1041, 1088, 1168
Kimball v. Ætna Ins. Co., 9 Allen (Mass.), 540	543
Kindersley v. Chase, 1 Marsh. Ins. 425	680, 682
King v. Glover, 2 B. & P. (N. R.) 206; 9 R. R. 638	240, 244, 245, 308
King v. Middletown Ins. Co., 1 Conn. 184	497
King v. Victoria Ins. Co., [1896] A. C. 250; 65 L. J. P. C. 38; 74 L. T. 206; 44 W. R. 592	1225, 1230
King v. Walker, 33 L. J. Ex. 167, 325; 2 H. & C. 384; 3 H. & C. 209; 11 Jur. (N. S.) 43; 13 W. R. 232; 133 R. R. 717, 726	110, 1189, 1284
Kingsford v. Marshall, 8 Bing. 458; 1 M. & Scott, 657; 1 L. J. C. P. 135; 34 R. R. 756	889, 890
Kingston v. Girard, 4 Dall. R. 274; Condy's Marshall, 189	408
Kingston v. Knibbs, 1 Camp. 508, n.; 10 R. R. 742, n.	59, 485, 610
Kingston v. M'Intosh, 1 Camp. 518	1284
Kingston v. Phelps, cited 7 T. R. 165	381
Kirby v. Smith, 1 B. & Ald. 672; 19 R. R. 412	560, 564, **595**
Kirchner v. Venus, 12 Moo. P. C. C. 361, 390; 5 Jur. (N. S.) 395; 7 W. R. 455; 124 R. R. 95	233

TABLE OF CASES. xlix

SECT.
Kish v. Taylor, [1910] 2 K. B. 309; [1911] 1 K. B. 625; [1912] A. C.
 604; 79 L. J. K. B. 1113; 80 L. J. K. B. 601; 81 L. J. K. B.
 1027; 102 L. T. 910; 103 L. T. 785; 106 L. T. 900; 15 Com. Cas.
 268; 16 Com. Cas. 59; 17 Com. Cas. 355; 54 S. J. 565; 56 S. J.
 518; 11 Asp. M. C. 544; 26 Times L. R. 504; 27 Times L. R. 174;
 28 Times L. R. 425 430
Klein v. Lindsay, [1910] Sess. Cas. 231; [1911] A. C. 194; 80 L. J.
 P. C. 161; 104 L. T. 261; 11 Asp. M. C. 563 .... 195, 918
Kleinwort v. Shepard, 1 E. & E. 447; 28 L. J. Q. B. 147; 5 Jur. (N. S.)
 863; 7 W. R. 227; 117 R. R. 275 .... 829, 836, 905
Knight v. Cambridge, 1 Str. 581; 2 Ld. Raym. 1540; 1 Mod. 230,
 cited 8 East, 135 .... 838, 841
Knight v. Cotesworth, 1 Cab. & E. 48 .... 186, 607
Knight v. Faith, 15 Q. B. 649; 19 L. J. Q. B. 509; 14 Jur. 1114; 81
 R. R. 725...203, 438, 819, 1032, 1032b, 1056, **1062**, 1063, 1121, 1122, 1184
Knight of St. Michael, The, [1898] P. 30; 67 L. J. P. 19; 78 L. T. 90;
 46 W. R. 396; 8 Asp. M. C. 360; 3 Com. Cas. 62......... 807, 828, 830, 860
Knill v. Hooper, 2 H. & N. 277; 26 L. J. Ex. 377; 5 W. R. 791; 115
 R. R. 531 710
Knox v. Wood, 1 Camp. 543; 10 R. R. 746 .... 240, 297
Koebel v. Saunders, 17 C. B. (N. S.) 71; 33 L. J. C. P. 310; 10 Jur.
 (N. S.) 920; 10 L. T. 695; 12 W. R. 1106; 142 R. R. 254......... 689
Koster v. Eason, 2 M. & S. 112; 14 R. R. 603 ....112, 113, 118
Koster v. Innes, Ry. & M. 333; 27 R. R. 755 ....814, 1281
Koster v. Reed, 6 B. & C. 19; 9 D. & R. 2; 30 R. R. 239 ......813, 814, 1048
Kulen Kemp v. Vigne, 1 T. R. 304; 1 R. R. 205 ....310, 320
Kung v. Methuen, 24 Times L. R. 145 232
Kynance SS. Co. v. Young, 16 Com. Cas. 123; 104 L. T. 397; 11 Asp.
 M. C. 596; 27 Times L. R. 306.................252b, 382a, **486a**, 495, 500

L.

Ladbroke v. Lee, 4 De G. & S. 106; 87 R. R. 306 299
Lady Durham, The, 3 Hag. Adm. 196 244
Laing v. Glover, 5 Taunt. 49 433
Laing v. Union Marine Ins. Co., 1 Com. Cas. 11 ....405, 605
Laird v. Robertson, 4 Bro. P. C. 488 ....29, 42, 43
Lambert v. Liddard, 5 Taunt. 480; 1 Marsh. R. 149; 15 R. R. 557... 396,
 402, **484**, 485
L'Amerique, 35 Fed. R. 835 924
Lamont, Nisbet & Co. v. Hamilton, [1907] Sess. Cas. 628; 44 Sc. L. R.
 490 106
Landauer v. Asser, [1905] 2 K. B. 184; 74 L. J. K. B. 659; 93 L. T.
 20; 53 W. R. 534; 10 Com. Cas. 265; 21 Times L. R. 429 181
Lane v. Nixon, L. R. 1 C. P. 412; 35 L. J. C. P. 243; 12 Jur. (N. S.)
 392; 14 W. R. 641 ....457, 689
Lang v. Anderdon, 5 D. & R. 393; 3 B. & C. 495; 1 Car. & P. 171;
 3 L. J. (O. S.) K. B. 62; 27 R. R. 412 ....647, 653
Langhorn v. Allnutt, 4 Taunt. 510; 12 R. R. 660.................405, 481, 1266
Langhorn v. Cologan, 4 Taunt. 330; 13 R. R. 613 ....42, 43, 1256

TABLE OF CASES.

	SECT.
Langhorn v. Hardy, 4 Taunt. 628; 13 R. R. 708	448
Lanyon v. Blanchard, 2 Camp. 597; 11 R. R. 808	132
Lapham v. Atlas Ins. Co., 24 Pick. R. 1	417, 498
Laroche v. Oswin, 12 East, 131; 11 R. R. 337	407, 408
Lateward v. Curling, 1 Park, Ins. (8th ed.) 288	876
Laurie v. West Hartlepool Thirds Indemnity Assn., 4 Com. Cas. 323	82, 180
Lavabre v. Wilson, 1 Dougl. 284	85, **401**, 425, **426**
Laveroni v. Drury, 8 Ex. 166; 22 L. J. Ex. 2; 16 Jur. 1024; 1 W. R. 55; 91 R. R. 415	777, 825
La Virginie, 5 C. Rob. 98	92
Law v. Hollingworth, 7 T. R. 160	702, **703**, 724, 745
Law Car and General Ins. Corpn., In re, (1911) W. N. 91, 101; 55 S. J. 407	104
Lawrence v. Aberdein, 5 B. & Ald. 107; 24 R. R. 299	227, **782**, 824, 1273
Lawrence v. Ocean Ins. Co., 11 Johns. 240	386
Lawrence v. Sydebotham, 6 East, 45; 2 Smith, 214; 8 R. R. 385	422, 423, 434
Lawther v. Black, 6 Com. Cas. 5, 196; 17 Times L. R. 8	239, 247
Leatham v. Terry, 3 B. & P. 479	1175
Leavenworth v. Delafield, 1 Caines, 578	1179
Lebeau v. General Steam Nav. Co., L. R. 8 C. P. 88; 42 L. J. C. P. 1; 27 L. T. 447; 21 W. R. 146; 1 Asp. M. C. 435	982
Lebon v. Straits Ins. Co., 10 Times L. R. 517	623
Le Cheminant v. Allnutt, 4 Taunt. 367; 13 R. R. 636	730
Le Cheminant v. Pearson, 4 Taunt. 367; 13 R. R. 636	10, 731, 869, 1032, **1032a**
Le Cras v. Hughes, 3 Dougl. 81	240, 301
Leduc v. Ward, 20 Q. B. D. 475; 57 L. J. Q. B. 379; 54 L. T. 214; 58 L. T. 908; 36 W. R. 537; 5 Asp. M. C. 571; 6 Asp. M. C. 290	57, 379, 401
Lee v. Beach, 1 Park, Ins. (8th ed.) 468	688
Lee v. Bullen, 27 L. J. Q. B. 161; 8 E. & B. 692, n.; 4 Jur. (N. S.) 557; 112 R. R. 733, n.	114, 118
Lee v. Gray, 7 Mass. R. 349	427
Lee v. Southern Ins. Co., L. R. 5 C. P. 397; 39 L. J. C. P. 218; 22 L. T. 443; 18 W. R. 863	874, 963
Lees v. Smith, 7 T. R. 338	80
Leevin v. Cormac, 4 Taunt. 483, n.; 13 R. R. 654	1264
Legge v. Byas, 7 Com. Cas. 16	125, 128
Leigh v. Adams, 25 L. T. (N. S.) 566; 1 Asp. M. C. 147	602, 607
Leigh v. Mather, 1 Esp. 412; 5 R. R. 740	464, **465**, 496, 497
Leitrim, The, [1902] P. 256; 71 L. J. P. 108; 87 L. T. 240; 51 W. R. 158; 9 Asp. M. C. 317; 8 Com. Cas. 6	907, 961
Le Louis, 2 Dod. 210	674
Le Lnneville v. Phillips, 2 B. & P. (N. R.) 97	85
Le Mesurier v. Vaughan, 6 East, 382; 2 Smith, 492; 8 R. R. 500	182
Lenox v. United Ins. Co., 3 Johns. Cas. 178	936
Leo SS. Co., Ltd. v. Corderoy, 1 Com. Cas. 300, 379	26
Leonis SS. Co., Ltd. v. Rank, Ltd., [1908] 1 K. B. 499; 77 L. J. K. B. 224; 13 Com. Cas. 136; 24 Times L. R. 128	270, 512
Letchford v. Oldham, 5 Q. B. D. 538; 49 L. J. Q. B. 458; 28 W. R. 789	890

TABLE OF CASES.

SECT.
Lever v. Fletcher, 1 Park, Ins. (8th ed.) 507; 1 Marsh. Ins. 45...612, 742, 809
Levi v. Allnutt, 15 East, 267 904
Levin v. Newenham, 4 Taunt. 722; 14 R. R. 648 903
Levy v. Barnard, 2 J. B. Moore 34; 8 Taunt. 149; 19 R. R. 484...... 134
Levy v. Merchants' Mar. Ins. Co., 5 Asp. M. C. 407; 1 Cab. & E. 474;
   52 L. T. 263; 1 Times L. R. 228 ....902, 1054
Levy v. Vaughan, 4 Taunt. 387; 13 R. R. 643 903
Lewen v. Swasso, Postlethwaite's Dict. Art. Assur. 147 ....839, 852
Lewis v. Rucker, 2 Burr. 1167............20, 318, 319, 339, 340, 342, 1011, 1014
Liddard v. Lopes, 10 East, 526; 10 R. R. 368 876
Lidgett v. Secretan, L. R. 5 C. P. 190; L. R. 6 C. P. 616; 39 L. J.
   C. P. 196; 40 L. J. C. P. 257; 24 L. T. 942; 19 W. R. 1088; 1
   Asp. M. C. 95......................342, 343, **489**, 819, 1024, 1032, **1032b**
Lilly v. Ewer, 1 Dougl. 72 654
Lindsay v. Janson, 28 L. J. Ex. 315; 4 H. & N. 699; 118 R. R. 698...59, 494
L'Invincible, 1 Wheat. 238 676
Lion Mutual Mar. Ins. Assn. v. Tucker, 12 Q. B. D. 176; 53 L. J. Q. B.
   185; 49 L. T. 764; 32 W. R. 546 ....2, 80
Lishman v. Northern Maritime Ins. Co., L. R. 8 C. P. 216; L. R. 10
   C. P. 179; 44 L. J. C. P. 185; 32 L. T. 170; 23 W. R. 733; 2
   Asp. M. C. 504 ....34, 37, 53, 82, 440, 568, 576
Littledale v. Dixon, 1 B. & P. (N. R.) 151; 8 R. R. 774......**594**, 626, 1274
Livermore v. Newburyport Mar. Ins. Co., 1 Mass. 281.................. 1197
Livesay v. Rider, cited 7 T. R. 269; 4 R. R. 439 1246
Livie v. Janson, 12 East, 648; 11 R. R. 513...784, **819**, 829, 867, 869, 875,
   905, 1032, **1032a**
Livingston v. Maryland Ins. Co., 6 Cranch, 274; 7 Cranch. 536......658, 666
Livingstone, The, 122 Fed. R. 278; 130 Fed. R. 746....................... 1230
Lloyd v. Fleming, L. R. 7 Q. B. 299; 41 L. J. Q. B. 93; 25 L. T. 824;
   20 W. R. 296; 1 Asp. M. C. 192 175
Lloyd v. Spence. (See Lloyd v. Fleming.)
Lloyd's v. Harper, 16 Ch. D. 290; 50 L. J. Ch. 140; 43 L. T. 481; 29
   W. R. 452 77
Locke v. North American Ins. Co., 13 Mass. 61 292
Lockyer v. Offley, 1 T. R. 252; 1 R. R. 194 ....438, 490, 838
Lohre v. Aitchison. (See Aitchison v. Lohre.)
London and Provincial Ins. Co. v. Chambers, 5 Com. Cas. 241 1272
London Ass. Co. v. Companhia de Moagens, 167 U. S. 149 ....886, 891
London Ass. Corp. v. Williams, 9 Times L. R. 96, 257..................... 1207
London Mar. Ins. Assn., In re, Smith's Case, L. R. 4 Ch. 611; 38
   L. J. Ch. 681; 21 L. T. 97; 17 W. R. 941 ....36, 39, 80, 82
London SS. Ins. Co. v. Grampian SS. Co., 24 Q. B. D. 32, 663; 59
   L. J. Q. B. 549; 62 L. T. 784; 38 W. R. 651; 6 Asp. M. C. 506...10, 793
Long v. Allen, 4 Dougl. 276 ....55, 60, 1250
Long v. Bolton, 2 B. & P. 209 599
Long v. Duff, 2 B. & P. 209 599
Loomis v. Shaw, 2 Johns. Cas. 36 ....287, 881
Lorraine v. Thomlinson, 2 Dougl. 585 ....437, 1251
Lothian v. Henderson, 3 B. & P. 499; 7 R. R. 829 ......630, 655, 680, 683

TABLE OF CASES.

SECT.

Lower Rhine Co. *v.* Sedgwick, [1898] 1 Q. B. 739; [1899] 1 Q. B. 179;
    67 L. J. Q. B. 330; 68 L. J. Q. B. 186; 78 L. T. 496; 80 L. T. 6;
    46 W. R. 380; 47 W. R. 261; 8 Asp. M. C. 380, 466.................. 328a
Lowry *v.* Bourdieu, 2 Dougl. 468 ....310, 313a, **316**, 1253, 1254
Lozano *v.* Janson, 2 E. & E. 160; 28 L. J. Q. B. 337; 5 Jur. (N. S.)
    1401; 7 W. R. 654; 119 R. R. 673...829, 1105, 1107, 1141, **1143**, 1285
Lubbock *v.* Potts, 7 East, 449 ....86, 87, 740, 1255
Lubbock *v.* Rowcroft, 5 Esp. 50; 8 R. R. 830 ....784, 804, **806**
Lucena *v.* Craufurd, 3 B. & P. 75; 2 B. & P. (N. R.) 269; 1 Taunt.
    325; 6 R. R. 623......3, 4, 140, 142, 171, 230, 241, 249, 254, 255, 255a,
                  256, 257, 258, 260, 266, 267, 287, 291, 297, 300,
                  302, 303, **304**, 306, 307, 311, 313, 1275
Luckett *v.* Wood, 26 Times L. R. 617 315
Luckie *v.* Bushby, 22 L. J. C. P. 220; **13** C. B. 864; 1 C. L. R. 685; 17
    Jur. 625; 1 W. R. 455; 93 R. R. 780 ....110, 1243
Luke *v.* Lyde, 2 Burr. 882; 1 W. Bl. 190.. 1177
Lund *v.* Thames and Mersey Mar. Ins. Co., 17 Times L. R. 566 716
Lunt *v.* Boston Mar. Ins. Co., 6 Fed. R. 562; 17 Fed. R. 411 543
Lynch *v.* Dunsford, 14 East, 494; 13 R. R. 295...186, 587, 590, 602, 607, 616
Lynch *v.* Hamilton, 3 Taunt. 37; 12 R. R. 591............186, **590**, 602, 607
Lysaght *v.* Coleman, [1895] 1 Q. B. 49; 64 L. J. Q. B. 175; 14 R.
    22; 71 L. T. 830; 7 Asp. M. C. 552 ....1018, 1019

M.

Maanss *v.* Henderson, 1 East, 334 132
Macardier *v.* Chesapeake Ins. Co., 8 Cranch, 39............................... 1117
Macbeth & Co., Ltd. *v.* Maritime Ins. Co., Ltd., [1908] A. C. 144;
    77 L. J. K. B. 498; 98 L. T. 594; 13 Com. Cas. 222; 24 Times
    L. R. 403 ....1124, 1125
Macfarlane *v.* Giaunocopulo, 28 L. J. Ex. 72; 3 H. & N. 860; 32 L. T.
    (O. S.) 133; 117 R. R. 1014 127
Mackenzie *v.* Coulson, L. R. 8 Eq. 368 41
Mackenzie *v.* Shedden, 2 Camp. 431; 11 R. R. 759 ....272, 513, 1088
Mackenzie *v.* Whitworth, L. R. 10 Ex. 142; 1 Ex. D. 36; 45 L. J.
    Ex. 233; 33 L. T. 655; 24 W. R. 287; 2 Asp. M. C. 490...241, 243, 251,
                                             252a, 257, 323
Mackie *v.* Pleasants, 2 Binn. 363 631
Mackintosh *v.* Marshall, 11 M. & W. 116; 12 L. J. Ex. 337; 63 R. R.
    531 ....556, 557, 593, **595**, 614, 615, 626, 1274
Maclean *v.* Fleming, L. R. 2 H. L. (Sc.) 128; 25 L. T. 317; 1 Asp.
    M. C. 160 1279
Mackrell *v.* Simond, 2 Chit. 660 1089
M'Andrew *v.* Bell, 1 Esp. 373 ....292, 593, 596, 1279
McAndrews *v.* Thatcher, 3 Wall. 370 ....911, 969
McAndrews *v.* Vaughan, 1 Park, Ins. (8th ed.) 252 1075
M'Call *v.* Houlder Bros., 2 Com. Cas. 129; 66 L. J. Q. B. 408; 76 L. T.
    469; 8 Asp. M. C. 252 ....924, 944, 948

TABLE OF CASES. liii

	SECT.
M'Carthy v. Abel, 5 East, 388; 1 Smith, 524; 7 R. R. 711	785, **1165**, 1175, 1176
M'Connell v. Hector, 3 B. & P. 113; 6 R. R. 724	85, 93, 657
M'Culloch v. Royal Exch. Ass. Co., 3 Camp. 406; 14 R. R. 765	1258
M'Dougle v. Royal Exch. Ass. Co., 4 Camp. 283; 4 M. & S. 503; 16 R. R. 532	888
M'Dowell v. Fraser, 1 Dougl. 260	529, 535, 550, 555, 557, 560, 1274
M'Iver v. Henderson, 4 M. & S. 576; 16 R. R. 550	1105, 1141
M'Kim v. Phœnix Ins. Co., 2 Wash. C. C. R. 89	360
M'Lanahan v. Universal Ins. Co., 1 Peters S. C. R. 170	160, 570, 577, 626
M'Masters v. Schoolbred, 1 Esp. 237; 5 R. R. 735	1110, 1219
M'Swiney v. Royal Exch. Ass. Co., 18 L. J. Q. B. 193; 19 L. J. Q. B. 222; 14 Q. B. 634; 14 Jur. 998; 80 R. R. 345	**238**, 288, 297, 805
Madison, The, Edw. Adm. Rep. 224	760
Maddison v. Alderson, 5 Ex. D. 293; 7 Q. B. D. 174; 8 App. Cas. 467; 52 L. J. Q. B. 737; 49 L. T. 303; 31 W. R. 820; 47 J. P. 821	542
Maggrath v. Church, 1 Caines, 196	986
Magnus v. Buttemer, 11 C. B. 876; 21 L. J. C. P. 119; 16 Jur. 480; 87 R. R. 795	816, 889
Main, The, [1894] P. 320; 63 L. J. Adm. 69; 6 R. 775; 70 L. T. 247; 7 Asp. M. C. 424	345, 1041
Maldonado v. British and Foreign Mar. Ins. Co., 182 Fed. R. 744	986, 1006
Mallet v. Bateman, L. R. 1 C. P. 163; 35 L. J. C. P. 40; 1 H. & R. 109; 12 Jur. (N. S.) 122; 13 L. T. 410; 14 W. R. 225	39
Mallough v. Barber, 4 Camp. 150	153
Man v. Shiffner, 2 East, 523	132, 133, 134
Manchester Liners v. British and Foreign Mar. Ins. Co., 7 Com. Cas. 26; 86 L. T. 148; 9 Asp. M. C. 266	233, 239, 279, 288, 785
Manfield v. Maitland, 4 B. & Ald. 582; 23 R. R. 402	232, 263, 264
Manilla, The, Edw. Adm. R. 1, 2	96
Manley v. United Marine & Fire Ins. Co., 9 Mass. 85	444
Mann v. Forrester, 4 Camp. 60; 15 R. R. 724	133, 134
Mannheim Ins. Co. v. Hollander, 111 Fed. R. 549	106
Manning v. Irving. (See Irving v. Manning.)	
Manning v. Newnham, 3 Dougl. 130; 2 Camp. 624, n.; 12 R. R. 761	1146, 1158
Mansell v. Hoade, 20 Times L. R. 150	832, 1142
Marean v. U. S. Ins. Co., 3 Wash. C. C. R. 256	1068, 1076
Margaret Mitchell, The, Swabey, 382; 4 Jur. (N. S.) 1193	202
Margetson v. Glynn. (See Glynn v. Margetson.)	
Margetts v. Ocean Corporation, [1901] 2 K. B. 792; 70 L. J. K. B. 762; 85 L. T. 94; 49 W. R. 669; 9 Asp. M. C. 217	795
Maria, The, 1 C. Rob. 340	667, 671, 673, 674, 763
Maria, The, 5 C. Rob. 365	660, 665
Marianna Flora, The, 11 Wheat. 42	671
Marine Ins. Co. v. China Transpacific SS. Co. (See Vancouver, The.)	
Marine Ins. Co. v. United Ins. Co., 9 Johns. 186	1179
Marine Mutual Ins. Ass. v. Young, 43 L. T. (N. S.) 441; 4 Asp. M. C. 357	26, 80

TABLE OF CASES.

SECT.

Maritime Ins. Co. v. Alianza Ins. Co., [1907] 2 K. B. 660; 77 L. J.
K. B. 69; 97 L. J. 606; 10 Asp. M. C. 579; 13 Com. Cas. 46; 23
Times L. R. 703 ....443, 485, **508**
Maritime Ins. Co. v. Stearns, [1901] 2 K. B. 912; 71 L. J. K. B. 86;
6 Com. Cas. 182 ....376, 380, 479, 480
Marriot v. Hampton, 7 T. R. 269; 2 Esp. 546; 4 R. R. 439 ....1244, 1246
Marryatt v. Wilson, 1 B. & P. 430; 8 T. R. 31; 53 R. R. 113............ 91
Marsden v. City and County Ass. Co., 1 H. & R. 53; L. R. 1 C. P. 232;
35 L. J. C. P. 60; 12 Jur. (N. S.) 76; 13 L. T. 465; 14 W. R. 106... 790
Marsden v. Reid, 3 East, 572; 7 R. R. 516............10, 34, 388, 394, 571, 572
Marsh v. Robinson, 4 Esp. 98; 2 Anstr. 479; 3 R. R. 617............258, 266
Marshall v. Delaware Ins. Co., 4 Cranch, 202 1138
Marshall v. Parker, 2 Camp. 69; 11 R. R. 665 ....342, 1281, 1283
Marshall v. Union Ins. Co., 2 Wash. C. C. R. 357 597
Marsham v. Dutrey, Select Cases, 58 928
Marten v. Nippon Sea Ins. Co., 3 Com. Cas. 164 ....328, 456, 460
Marten v. Steamship Owners' Underwriting Assn., 7 Com. Cas. 195;
71 L. J. K. B. 718; 87 L. T. 208; 50 W. R. 587; 9 Asp. M. C.
339 ....324, 327, 328, 1134
Martin v. Crokatt, 14 East, 465; 13 R. R. 281 1060
Martin v. Delaware Ins. Co., 2 Wash. C. C. R. 254 ....62, 391
Martin v. Fishing Ins. Co., 20 Pick. 389 444
Martin v. Salem Ins. Co., 2 Mass. 429 825
Martin v. Sitwell, 1 Shower, 156 1258
Marwick v. Rogers, 163 Mass. 50 908
Mary & Eva, The, 6 Fed. R. 628 922
Mary Thomas, The, [1894] P. 108; 63 L. J. Adm. 49; 6 R. 792; 71
L. T. 104; 7 Asp. M. C. 495...918, 976, 977, 996, **1001**, 1003, 1004, 1005
Mashona, The, 17 Cape of Good Hope Sup. Ct. Rep. 129, 135; Journal
of Comparative Legislation, August, 1900 ....764, 774
Mason v. Joseph, 1 Smith, 406 167
Mason v. Mar. Ins. Co., 110 Fed. R. 453...1178, 1179, 1187, 1208, 1215, 1232
Mason v. Sainsbury, 3 Dougl. 61 ....1226, 1227, 1231
Mason v. Skurray, 1 Marsh. Ins. 218, 219, 226; 1 Park, Ins. 245, 253... 55,
68, 883, 1075
Maspons y Hermano v. Mildred, Goyeneche & Co., 9 Q. B. D. 530; 8
App. Cas. 874; 53 L. J. Q. B. 33; 32 W. R. 135; 5 Asp. M. C.
182 131
Master v. Miller, 4 T. R. 320; 5 T. R. 367; 2 H. Bl. 141; 1 Anst. 225;
2 R. R. 399; 1 Smith, L. C. 40
Matheson v. Equitable Mar. Ins. Co., 118 Mass. 209 ....1032, 1032a
Matthews v. Gibbs, 30 L. J. Q. B. 55; 7 Jur. (N. S.) 186; 3 L. T. 551;
9 W. R. 200 ....207, 213, 1220
Matthie v. Potts, 3 B. & P. 23 457
Matvieff v. Crosfield, 8 Com. Cas. 120; 51 W. R. 365 ....65, 128
Mauran v. Insurance Co., 6 Wall. 1 829
Maury v. Shedden, 10 East, 540 803
Mavor v. Simeon, 3 Taunt. 497 ....24, 107
Mavro v. Ocean Marine Ins. Co., L. R. 9 C. P. 595; L. R. 10 C. P. 414;
44 L. J. C. P. 229; 32 L. T. 743; 23 W. R. 758; 2 Asp. M. C.
590 ....981, 992, 996, 997, **1001**

TABLE OF CASES. lv

	SECT.
Maxwell v. Robinson, 1 Johns. R. 333	496
May v. Christie, Holt, N. P. 67; 17 R. R. 608	1244
May v. Keystone Yellow Pine Co., 117 Fed. R. 287	929
Maydew v. Forrester, 5 Taunt. 615; 15 R. R. 597	152, 162
Maydhew v. Scott, 3 Camp. 205	908
Mayne v. Walter, 3 Dougl. 79	597, 612, 663, 684
Mayo v. India Mutual Ins. Co., 152 Mass. 172	1145
Mayo v. Maine Fire and Mar. Ins. Co., 12 Mass. 259	360
Mead v. Davison, 3 A. & E. 303; 4 N. & M. 701; 1 H. & W. 156; 4 L. J. K. B. 193; 42 R. R. 401	13, 35, 167
Medeiros v. Hill, 8 Bing. 231; 1 M. & Scott, 311; 5 Car. & P. 182; 1 L. J. C. P. 77; 34 R. R. 696	760, 770
Mellen v. National Ins. Co., 1 Hall, 452	234, 262
Mellish v. Allnutt, 2 M. & S. 106; 14 R. R. 599	153, 448, 450
Mellish v. Andrews, 2 M. & S. 27; 5 Taunt. 496; 15 East, 13; 16 East, 312; 13 R. R. 351	395, **403**, 1045, **1049**, 1092, 1138, 1182, 1184, 1191, **1194**, 1274
Mellish v. Bell, 15 East, 4; 13 R. R. 344	1275
Mellish v. Staniforth, 3 Taunt. 499	903
Mennett v. Bonham, 15 East, 477	803
Mentz, Decker & Co. v. Maritime Ins. Co., [1910] 1 K. B. 132; 79 L. J. K. B. 104; 101 L. T. 808; 15 Com. Cas. 17; 11 Asp. M. C. 339	376, 847, 858
Mercantile Mar. Ins. Co. v. Titherington, 5 B. & S. 765; 34 L. J. Q. B. 11; 11 Jur. (N. S.) 62; 11 L. T. (N. S.) 340; 13 W. R. 141; 136 R. R. 732	489, **495**
Mercantile SS. Co. v. Tyser, 7 Q. B. D. 73; 29 W. R. 790; 5 Asp. M. C. 6, n.	608, 785, 786, 788, 1089
Merchant Shipping Co. v. Armitage, L. R. 9 Q. B. 99; 43 L. J. Q. B. 24; 29 L. T. 809; 2 Asp. M. C. 185	789, 878
Merchants' Trading Co. v. Universal Mar. Ins. Co., cited L. R. 9 Q. B. 596; 2 Asp. M. C. 431, n.	775, 777, 812
Mercurius, The, 1 C. Rob. 80	668, 766, 767
Mercurius, The, 1 C. Rob. 288	763
Meretony v. Dunlope, cited 1 T. R. 260; 1 R. R. 194	438
Mersey Mutual Underwriting Assn. v. Poland, 15 Com. Cas. 205; 26 Times L. R. 386	70, 508
Metcalfe v. Britannia Ironworks Co., 1 Q. B. D. 613; 2 Q. B. D. 423; 46 L. J. Q. B. 443; 36 L. T. 451; 25 W. R. 720; 3 Asp. M. C. 407	212
Metcalfe v. Parry, 4 Camp. 123; 15 R. R. 734	399, **402**, 745, 801
Mexican Prince, The, 82 Fed. R. 484	720
Meyer v. Gregson, 3 Dougl. 402	1249, 1266
Meyer v. Ralli, 1 C. P. D. 358; 45 L. J. C. P. 741; 35 L. T. 838; 24 W. R. 963; 3 Asp. M. C. 324	22, 206, 799a, 801, **873**, 1145, 1158
Michael v. Gillespy, 2 C. B. (N. S.) 627; 26 L. J. C. P. 306; 3 Jur. (N. S.) 1219; 109 R. R. 809	53, 232, 438, 440, 521, 1172
Michael v. Tredwin, 17 C. B. 551; 25 L. J. C. P. 83; 4 W. R. 297; 104 R. R. 789	697
Middlewood v. Blakes, 7 T. R. 162; 4 R. R. 405	389, 606

lvi TABLE OF CASES.

SECT.

Midland Ins. Co. v. Smith, 6 Q. B. D. 561; 50 L. J. Q. B. 329; 45 L. T. 411; 29 W. R. 850; 45 J. P. 699 1231
Milburn v. Jamaica Fruit Importing Co. of London, [1900] 2 Q. B. 540; 69 L. J. Q. B. 860; 83 L. T. 321; 5 Com. Cas. 346......908, 918
Miller v. Law Accident Ins. Co., [1903] 1 K. B. 712; 72 L. J. K. B. 428; 88 L. T. 370; 51 W. R. 420; 8 Com. Cas. 161; 9 Asp. M. C. 386 ....804, **807**, 829, 832, 905
Miller v. Titherington, 30 L. J. Ex. 217; 31 L. J. Ex. 363; 6 H. & N. 278; 7 H. & N. 954; 7 Jur. (N. S.) 214; 8 Jur. (N. S.) 1039; 3 L. T. (N. S.) 893; 9 L. T. (N. S.) 231; 9 W. R. 437; 10 W. R. 356; 123 R. R. 503, 512 ....60, 920
Miller v. Woodfall, 8 E. & B. 493; 27 L. J. Q. B. 120; 4 Jur. (N. S.) 302; 112 R. R. 663 ....1178, 1208
Milles v. Fletcher, 1 Dougl. 231a..................1104, 1105, **1146**
Mills v. Roebuck, 1 Marsh. Ins. 154; 1 Park, Ins. (8th ed.) 460; 1 Phillips, s. 699 714
Milward v. Hibbert, 3 Q. B. 120; 11 L. J. Q. B. 137; 2 G. & D. 142; 6 Jur. 706; 61 R. R. 155 ....60, 225, 801, 920, 1273
Miner v. Tagert, 3 Binn. 204 161
Minett v. Anderson, 1 Peake, N. P. 277; 3 R. R. 692 490
Minett v. Forrester, 4 Taunt. 541; 13 R. R. 676 ....116, 117, 118
Minneapolis, St. P. & B. SS. Co. v. Manister Transit Co., 156 Fed. R. 424 909
Mirabita v. Imperial Ottoman Bank, 3 Ex. D. 164; 47 L. J. Ex. 418; 38 L. T. 597; 3 Asp. M. C. 591 282
Missouri Co., In re, 42 Ch. D. 321; 58 L. J. Ch. 721; 61 L. T. 306; 37 W. R. 696 744
Mitchel v. Ede, 11 A. & E. 888; 3 P. & D. 513; 9 L. J. Q. B. 187; 52 R. R. 525 282
Mitchell v. Edie, 1 T. R. 608; 1 R. R. 318 ....22, 799a, 1052, 1183, 1197
Moffatt v. Ward, 4 Dougl. 29, n. (a), 31, n. (b) 501
Moir v. Royal Exch. Ass. Co., 4 Camp. 84; 6 Taunt. 241; 1 Marsh. R. 570; 3 M. & S. 461; 16 R. R. 330 652
Monmouth County Fire Ins. Co. v. Hutchinson, 21 N. J. Eq. 107...... 1240
Montara, The 771
Montgomerie v. United Kingdom Mutual SS. Ass. Assn., [1891] 1 Q. B. 370; 60 L. J. Q. B. 429; 64 L. T. 323; 39 W. R. 351; 7 Asp. M. C. 19 83
Montgomery v. Egginton, 3 T. R. 362; 1 R. R. 718............266, 268, 511
Montgomery v. Indemnity Mutual Mar. Ins. Co., [1901] 1 K. B. 147; [1902] 1 K. B. 734; 70 L. J. K. B. 45; 71 L. J. K. B. 467; 84 L. T. 57; 86 L. T. 462; 49 W. R. 221; 50 W. R. 440; 9 Asp. M. C. 141; 6 Com. Cas. 19; 7 Com. Cas. 120......907, 929, 1001, 1005
Montoya v. London Ass. Co., 6 Ex. 451; 20 L. J. Ex. 254; 17 L. T. (O. S.) 82; 86 R. R. 364 ....**784**, 811, 822, 828
Montreal Light, &c. Co. v. Sedgwick, [1910] A. C. 598; 80 L. J. P. C. 11; 103 L. T. 234; 11 Asp. M. C. 437; 26 Times L. R. 657...1048, 1080
Moody v. Surridge, 2 Esp. 633; 1 Park, Ins. 245 ....68, 883
Moore v. Mourgue, Cowp. 480 156
Moore v. Taylor, 3 N. & M. 406; 1 A. & E. 25; 3 L. J. K. B. 132; 40 R. R. 242 ....465, **496**, 501

TABLE OF CASES. lvii

SECT.

Moores v. Louisville Underwriters, 14 Fed. R. 226 ....710, 714, 725
Moran v. Jones, 7 E. & B. 523; 26 L. J. Q. B. 187; 3 Jur. (N. S.) 663;
   5 W. R. 503; 110 R. R. 710..**967**, 987
Moran v. Uzielli, [1905] 2 K. B. 555; 74 L. J. K. B. 494; 10 Com. Cas.
   203; 21 Times L. R. 378 ....246, 247, 255a, 257, **257a**, 260, 279,
                                                                 286, 307, 310
Morck v. Abel, 3 B. & P. 35 ....87, 1255
Mordy v. Jones, 4 B. & C. 394; 6 D. & Ry. 479; 3 L. J. (O. S.) K. B.
   250; 28 R. R. 305 ....784, 785, **879**, 1172
Morgan v. Price, 19 L. J. Ex. 201; 4 Exch. 615; 80 R. R. 720 349
Morocco Land and Trading Co. v. Fry, 11 L. T. (N. S.) 618; 11 Jur.
   (N. S.) 76; 13 W. R. 310 35
Morris v. Cleasby, 1 M. & S. 575; 4 M. & S. 566; 14 R. R. 531; 16
   R. R. 544 112
Morris v. Robinson, 3 B. & C. 196; 5 D. & R. 35; 27 R. R. 322....206, 1120,
                                                                    1128, 1158
Morrison v. Universal Mar. Ins. Co., L. R. 8 Ex. 40, 197; 42 L. J. Ex.
   115; 21 W. R. 774; 25 L. T. 108; 27 L. T. 791; 1 Asp. M. C. 100,
   503..27, 35, 523, **524**, 525, 569, **601**, 614
Morse v. St. Paul Fire and Mar. Ins. Co., 122 Fed. R. 748 695
Mortimer v. Broadwood, 20 L. T. 398; 17 W. R. 653 313
Moses v. Macfarlane, 2 Burr. 1005; 1 W. Bl. 219 1246
Moses v. Pratt, 4 Camp. 297; 16 R. R. 794 1251
Moss v. Byrom, 6 T. R. 379; 3 R. R. 208 ....418, 843
Moss v. Smith, 9 C. B. 94; 19 L. J. C. P. 225; 14 Jur. 1003; 82 R. R.
   307 ....878, 879, 1046, 1091, 1152, 1158, **1173**
Motteux v. London Ass. Co., 1 Atk. 545, 548.........14, 41, 374, 413, 429, 474,
                                                                         475, 478, 481
Mount v. Harrison, 4 Bing. 338; 1 M. & P. 14; 6 L. J. (O. S.) C. P.
   6; 29 R. R. 580 ....202, 1119, 1129, 1161, 1164, **1171**
Mount v. Larkins, 8 Bing. 108; 1 M. & Scott, 165; 1 L. J. C. P. 20;
   1 Dowl. P. C. 262; 34 R. R. 631 ....412, 414, 479, 483, 618, 1274
Mouse's Case, 12 Coke, R. 63... 909
Moxon v. Atkins, 3 Camp. 200; 13 R. R. 789...............59, 70, 454, 610, 1274
Muir v. Fleming, 1 D. & R. N. P. 29; 25 R. R. 775 133
Muirhead v. Forth and North Sea Mutual Ins. Assn., [1894] A. C. 72;
   20 Ct. of Sess. Cas. (4th Ser.) 442; 6 R. 59 ....81, 341, 797
Muller v. Thompson, 2 Camp. 610; 12 R. R. 753 ....630, 756, 757
Mullett v. Shedden, 13 East, 304; 12 R. R. 347.........**1050**, 1138, 1191, 1194
Munro v. Vandam, 1 Park, Ins. (8th ed.) 469 ....714, 725
Munroe, The, [1893] P. 248; 1 R. 642; 70 L. T. 246; 7 Asp. M. C.
   407 ....795, 826
Munson v. Standard Mar. Ins. Co., 156 Fed. R. 44.......................... 872
Murdock v. Potts, 1 Marsh. Ins. 332; 2 Park, Ins. 634...............232, 518
Murphy v. Bell, 4 Bing. 567; 1 M. & P. 493; 6 L. J. (O. S.) C. P. 118;
   29 R. R. 630 ....9, 311, 312, 317, 318
Murray v. Alsop, 3 Johns. Cas. 47... 543
Murray v. Columbian Ins. Co., 11 Johns. R. 302.................293, 451, 454
Murray v. Hatch, 6 Mass. 465 1046
Murray v. United Ins. Co., 2 Johns. Cas. 168 658

lviii   TABLE OF CASES.

                                                              SECT.
Myers v. Perigal, 18 L. J. Ch. 185; 22 L. J. Ch. 431; 16 Sim. 533;
  2 De G. M. & G. 599; 13 Jur. 223; 17 Jur. 145; 1 W. R. 57;
  20 L. T. (O. S.) 229; 95 R. R. 245 ....99, 307
Myers v. Sarle, 30 L. J. Q. B. 9; 7 Jur. (N. S.) 97; 9 W. R. 96......... 72

                               N.

Nantes v. Thompson, 2 East, 385; 6 R. R. 458 311
Natusch v. Hendewerk, cited 7 Q. B. D. 460................................. 1248
National Protector Fire Ins. Co. v. Nivert, [1913] A. C. 507; W. C.
  & I. Rep. 363; 82 L. J. P. C. 95; 108 L. T. 390; 29 Times L. R.
  363 75
Navone v. Haddon, 9 C. B. 30; 19 L. J. C. P. 161; 82 R. R. 267...1055, **1073**,
                                                         1145, 1149, 1159
Naylor v. Palmer, 8 Ex. 739; 10 Ex. 382; 22 L. J. Ex. 329; 23 L. J.
  Ex. 323; 21 L. T. (O. S.) 168; 24 L. T. (O. S.) 83; 91 R. R. 731... 836
Naylor v. Taylor, 9 B. & C. 718; 4 M. & Ry. 526; Dans. & Ll. 240;
  Moo. & M. 205; 33 R. R. 305 ....760, 770, 808, 1096, 1100,
                                      1101, 1102, 1104, **1139**, 1274
Neal v. Erving, 1 Esp. 61; 5 R. R. 720 166
Neale v. Reid, 1 B. & C. 657; 3 D. & R. 158 296
Neale v. Rose, 3 Com. Cas. 236.. 468
Neilson v. Columbian Ins. Co., 3 Caines, 108; 1 Johns. 301......1068, 1077
Neilson v. Delacour, 2 Esp. 619 502
Nelson v. Empress Ass. Corp., [1905] 2 K. B. 281; 74 L. J. K. B. 699;
  93 L. T. 62; 53 W. R. 648; 10 Com. Cas. 237; 10 Asp. M. C. 68;
  21 Times L. R. 555 ....322, 323, 324
Nelson v. Nelson Line, Ltd. (See James Nelson & Sons v. Nelson
  Line, Ltd.)
Nelson v. Salvador, Moo. & M. 309; Dan. & Ll. 219; 31 R. R. 733...... 650
Neptune, The, 1 Hag. Adm. 227, 239 244
Neptunus, The, 1 C. Rob. 170; 3 C. Rob. 173 769
Neptunus, The, 2 C. Rob. 110 ....768, 770
Neptunus, The, 3 C. Rob. 108 ....762, 763
Nereide, The, 9 Cranch, 388 ....92, 671
Nesbitt v. Lushington, 4 T. R. 783; 2 R. R. 519......832, 836, 886, 910, 925
Neutralitet, The, 3 C. Rob. 295 763
Newby v. Reed, 1 W. Bl. 416 ....331, 349, 814, 1283
Newcastle Fire Ins. Co. v. Macmorran, 3 Dow. 255; 15 R. R. 67...... 632
Newfoundland (Government of) v. Newfoundland Ry. Co., 13 App.
  Cas. 199; 57 L. J. P. C. 35; 58 L. T. 285 110
Newman v. Cazalet, 2 Park, Ins. 900 ....**995**, 997
New Orleans SS. Co. v. London Provincial Mar. &c. Ins. Co., [1909]
  1 K. B. 943; 78 L. J. K. B. 473; 100 L. T. 595; 14 Com. Cas. 111;
  11 Asp. M. C. 225; 53 S. J. 286 1274
Newtown Creek Towing Co. v. Ætna Ins. Co., 163 N. Y. 114.........795, 826
New York Bowery Fire Ins. Co. v. N. Y. Fire Ins. Co., 17 Wend. 359... 323,
                                                         324, 589
New York and Cuba Mail SS. Co. v. Royal Exch. Assn., 154 Fed. R.
  315 ....233, 355, 358

TABLE OF CASES. lix

	SECT.
New York Firemen Ins. Co. *v.* Lawrence, 14 Johns. 46............380,	386
New York and P. R. SS. Co. *v.* Ætna Ins. Co., 204 Fed. R. 255	697
New York State Ins. Co. *v.* Protection Ins. Co., 1 Story, 458; 2 Phillips, s. 2145	326
New Zealand Shipping Co. *v.* Duke, [1914] 2 K. B. 682; 30 Times L. R. 385 235,	880
Nicholson *v.* Chapman, 2 H. Bl. 254; 3 R. R. 374	865
Nicholson *v.* Croft, 2 Burr. 1188...............	166
Nicholson *v.* Gooch, 5 E. & B. 999; 25 L. J. Q. B. 137; 2 Jur. (N. S.) 303; 103 R. R. 842	109
Nicholson *v.* Power, 20 L. T. (N. S.) 580.....................600, 614,	616
Nickels *v.* London and Provincial Mar. and Gen. Ins. Co., 6 Com. Cas. 15; 70 L. J. K. B. 29 ....784, 785, 790,	805
Nigel Gold Mining Co. *v.* Hoade, [1901] 2 K. B. 849; 70 L. J. K. B. 1006; 85 L. T. 482; 50 W. R. 108; 6 Com. Cas. 268...94, **95**, 97, 99,	660
Niobe, The, [1891] A. C. 401; 17 Ct. of Sess. Cas. (4th Ser.) 1016; 65 L. T. 502; 7 Asp. M. C. 89	795
Nixon *v.* Albion Marine Ins. Co., L. R. 2 Ex. 338; 36 L. J. Ex. 180; 16 L. T. 568; 15 W. R. 964	32
Nobel's Explosives Co. *v.* Rea, 2 Com. Cas. 293...................	1004
Noble *v.* Kennoway, 2 Dougl. 510 ....30, 57, 58, 63, 463,	1273
Nome Beach Co. *v.* Munich Ass. Co., 123 Fed. R. 820	726
Nonnen *v.* Kettlewell, 16 East, 176 ....451, 530,	559
Nord Deutscher Lloyd *v.* Ins. Co. of N. America, 110 Fed. R. 420......	1225
Norden SS. Co. *v.* Dempsey, 1 C. P. D. 654; 45 L. J. C. P. 764; 24 W. R. 984	59
North Atlantic SS. Co. *v.* Burr, 9 Com. Cas. 164; 20 Times L. R. 266... 1023, 1127,	1134
North Britain, The, [1894] P. 77; 63 L. J. Adm. 33; 6 R. 673; 70 L. T. 210; 42 W. R. 243; 7 Asp. M. C. 413	795
North British and Mercantile Ins. Co. *v.* London Liverpool and Globe Ins. Co., 5 Ch. D. 569; 46 L. J. Ch. 537; 36 L. T. 629...333, 1237,	1238
North Eastern 100A SS. Ins. Assn. *v.* Red "S" Steamship Co., 10 Com. Cas. 245; 12 Com. Cas. 26; 21 Times L. R. 665; 22 Times L. R. 692 ....80, 82,	1248
North of England Iron SS. Ins. Assn. *v.* Armstrong, L. R. 5 Q. B. 244; 39 L. J. Q. B. 81; 21 L. T. 822; 18 W. R. 520........**339**, 341, 351, 352,	**1228**
North of England Oil Cake Co. *v.* Archangel Maritime Ins. Co., L. R. 10 Q. B. 249; 44 L. J. Q. B. 121; 32 L. T. 561; 24 W. R. 162; 2 Asp. M. C. 571 ....175, 178, 181,	469
North Queensland Ins. Co. *v.* Rhenish Westphalian Ins. Co. (unreported)	41
North Star, The, 106 U. S. 17	793
North-Western Salt Co. *v.* Electrolytic Alkali Co., [1913] 3 K. B. 422; [1914] A. C. 461; 83 L. J. K. B. 530; 107 L. T. 439; 58 S. J. 338; 30 Times L. R. 313	315
Northcote *v.* Owners of The Henrich Björn. (*See* Henrich Björn.)	

TABLE OF CASES.

	SECT.
Northey v. Trevillion, 7 Com. Cas. 201	70
Norway, The, Br. & Lush. 377; 3 Moo. P. C. (N. S.) 246; 11 Jur. (N. S.) 892; 13 L. T. 50; 13 W. R. 1085	1004
Norwich and N. Y. Transport Co. v. Ins. Co. of N. America, 118 Fed. R. 307; 129 Fed. R. 1006; 194 U. S. 637	937
Notara v. Henderson, L. R. 5 Q. B. 346; 7 Q. B. 225; 41 L. J. Q. B. 158; 26 L. T. 442; 20 W. R. 442; 1 Asp. M. C. 278...207, 215, 428,	880
Nourse v. Liverpool Sailing Shipowners' Assn., [1896] 2 Q. B. 16; 65 L. J. Q. B. 507; 74 L. T. 543; 44 W. R. 500; 8 Asp. M. C. 144; 1 Com. Cas. 388	868
Nutt v. Bourdieu, 1 T. R. 323; 1 R. R. 211 ....838, 849, 850,	856

O.

Ocean, The, 3 C. Rob. 297	769
Ocean, The, 5 C. Rob. 90 ....90, 91,	94
Ocean Ins. Co. v. Carrington, 3 Conn. R. 357	898
Ocean Ins. Co. v. Francis, 2 Wend. 64	803
Ocean Iron SS. Assn. v. Leslie, 22 Q. B. D. 722, n.; 57 L. T. 722; 6 Asp. M. C. 226	83
Oceanic SS. Co. v. Faber, 11 Com. Cas. 179; 13 Com. Cas. 28; 95 L. T. 607; 97 L. T. 466; 22 Times L. R. 527; 23 Times L. R. 673; 10 Asp. M. C. 303, 515 55,	861a
Oddy v. Bovill, 2 East, 473; 6 R. R. 482	676
Ogden v. Columbian Ins. Co., 10 Johns. 273	361
Ogden v. Fire Ins. Co., 10 Johns. 177; 12 Johns. 25	1203
Ogg v. Shuter, 1 C. P. D. 47; 45 L. J. C. P. 44; 33 L. T. 492; 24 W. R. 100; 3 Asp. M. C. 77	282
Olinda Rodrigues, The, 67 Davis (174 U. S.) 510	767
Olive v. Smith, 5 Taunt. 56; 2 Rose, 122 131,	134
Oliver v. Cowley, 1 Park, Ins. (8th ed.) 470	689
Oliver v. Greene, 3 Mass. 133	261
Oliver v. Maryland Ins. Co., 7 Cranch, 493	432
Oliverson v. Brightman, 8 Q. B. 781; 1 Car. & K. 360; 15 L. J. Q. B. 274; 10 Jur. 875; 70 R. R. 642 ....467, 468,	502
Oliverson v. Loughman, 4 M. & S. 346; cited 2 B. & Ald. 322	700
O'Mealey v. Wilson, 1 Camp. 482; 10 R. R. 732............93,	94
Oom v. Bruce, 12 East, 225; 11 R. R. 367 ....87, 740,	1255
Oom v. Taylor, 3 Camp. 204	903
Oppenheim v. Fry, 3 B. & S. 873; 5 B. & S. 348; 33 L. J. Q. B. 267; 10 L. T. (N. S.) 539; 12 W. R. 831; 136 R. R. 568 ....25, 218,	910
O'Reilly v. Gonne, 4 Camp. 249; 16 R. R. 788 ....432, 435,	905
O'Reilly v. Royal Exch. Ass. Co., 4 Camp. 246; 16 R. R. 786......435,	905
Orient Co. v. Brekke, [1913] 1 K. B. 531; 82 L. J. K. B. 427; 108 L. T. 507; 18 Com. Cas. 101	148
Oriental SS. Co. v. Tyler, [1893] 2 Q. B. 518; 63 L. J. Q. B. 128; 4 R. 554; 69 L. T. 577; 42 W. R. 89; 7 Asp. M. C. 377	263
Orozembo, The, 6 C. Rob. 430	760
Orrok v. Commonwealth Ins. Co., 38 Mass. R. 456	1030

TABLE OF CASES.   lxi

SECT.
Osacar *v.* Louisiana Ins. Co., 5 Martin (N. S.) 386 457
O'Sullivan *v.* Thomas, [1895] 1 Q. B. 698; 64 L. J. Q. B. 398; 15 R. 253; 72 L. T. 285; 43 W. R. 269; 59 J. P. 134..................121, 1255
Oswell *v.* Vigne, 15 East, 70; 13 R. R. 375 ....666, 732
Otago Farmers' Co-operative Assn. of New Zealand *v.* Thompson, [1910] 2 K. B. 145; 79 L. J. K. B. 692; 102 L. T. 711; 15 Com. Cas. 28; 11 Asp. M. C. 403 ....10, 55, 70, 901
Ougier *v.* Jennings, 1 Camp. 505, n.; 10 R. R. 739...58, 64, 391, 463, 483, 610
Ovington *v.* Bell, 3 Camp. 237 120

P.

Pacific Mail Steamship Co. *v.* N. Y. Min. Co., 74 Fed. R. 564...918, 933, 936
Packet, The Ship, 3 Mason, 255 1284
Paddock *v.* Franklin Ins. Co., 11 Pick, 227 709
Padstow Ass. Assn., *In re,* 20 Ch. D. 137; 51 L. J. Ch. 344; 45 L. T. 744; 30 W. R. 326 ....79, 80
Page *v.* Rogers, 2 Marsh. Ins. 739 1280
Page *v.* Thompson, 1 Park, Ins. (8th ed.) 175 803
Palmer *v.* Blackburn, 1 L. J. (O. S.) C. P. 1; 1 Bing. 61; 7 Moore, 339; 25 R. R. 599 ....66, 365, 1041
Palmer *v.* Day, [1895] 2 Q. B. 618; 64 L. J. Q. B. 807; 15 R. 523; 44 W. R. 14; 2 Manson, 386 110
Palmer *v.* Fenning, 9 Bing. 460; 2 M. & Scott, 624 482
Palmer *v.* Marshall, 8 Bing. 79, 317; 1 M. & Scott, 161, 454; 1 L. J. C. P. 19; 34 R. R. 628 ....413, 474, 475, 482
Palmer *v.* Pratt, 3 L. J. (O. S.) C. P. 250; 9 Moore, 358; 2 Bing. 185; 27 R. R. 583 ....224, **248**, 252, 310
Palyart *v.* Leckie, 6 M. & S. 290; 18 R. R. 381.....................87, 740, 1254
Papayanni *v.* Grampian SS. Co., 1 Com. Cas. 448.......................909, 936
Parfitt *v.* Thompson, 13 M. & W. 392; 14 L. J. Ex. 73; 67 R. R. 649... 694, 725
Park *v.* Hammond, Holt, N. P. 80; 4 Camp. 344; 2 Marsh, 189; 6 Taunt. 495; 16 R. R. 658 153
Parke *v.* Hebson, cited 2 B. & B. 326; 23 R. R. 451 ...266, **268**, 270, 271, 511
Parker *v.* Beasley, 2 M. & S. 423; 15 R. R. 299 ....114, 118
Parker *v.* Carter, cited Cook's Bankrupt Laws, 547 (7th ed.) 131
Parker *v.* Potts, 3 Dow, 23; 15 R. R. 1.............................698, **714**, 725
Parker *v.* Smith, 16 East, 382; 14 R. R. 366 ....112, 117, 118
Parkin *v.* Dick, 2 Camp. 221; 11 East, 502; 11 R. R. 258 749
Parkin *v.* Tunno, 11 East, 22; 2 Camp. 59; 10 R. R. 422...504, **806**, 1282
Parkinson *v.* Collier, 1 Park, Ins. 47; 2 Park, Ins. 653; 1 Marsh. Ins. 255 .... 72, 463
Parmeter *v.* Cousins, 2 Camp. 235; 11 R. R. 702 ....475, **478**, 698
Parmeter *v.* Todhunter, 1 Camp. 541 ....1091, **1170**, 1189
Parr *v.* Anderson, 6 East, 202; 2 Smith, 316; 8 R. R. 461......68, 390, 420, 422, 1274

TABLE OF CASES.

	SECT.
Parry v. Aberdein, 4 Man. & Ry. 343; 9 B. & C. 411; 7 L. J. (O. S.) K. B. 260; Dan. & Ll. 228; 33 R. R. 221	1140
Parsons v. Mass. Fire and Mar. Ins. Co., 6 Mass. 197	460
Parsons v. Scott, 2 Taunt. 363; 11 R. R. 610	831, 1095, 1100, 1104
Patapsco Ins. Co. v. Coulter, 3 Peters, S. C. R. 222	237, 287, 828, 845
Patapsco Ins. Co. v. Southgate, 5 Peters, S. C. R. 604	1055, 1190
Paterson v. Harris, 30 L. J. Q. B. 354; 31 L. J. Q. B. 277; 1 B. & S. 336; 2 B. & S. 814; 7 Jur. (N. S.) 1276; 9 Jur. (N. S.) 173; 9 W. R. 743; 124 R. R. 585	**249**, 307, 825
Patrick v. Eames, 3 Camp. 441	269, 1282
Patrick v. Ludlow, 3 Johns. Cas. 10	433
Patterson v. Mills, 1 Dow (N. S.), 342; 3 Wils. & Shaw, 218	35
Patterson v. Ritchie, 4 M. & S. 393; 16 R. R. 498	1096, 1102
Paul v. Insurance Co. of North America, 15 Times L. R. 535	458
Pawson v. Barnevelt, 1 Dougl. 12, n. 4	529, 629
Pawson v. Watson, 2 Cowp. 785; 1 Dougl. 11, n	528, 529, 530, 535, **538**, 546, 555, 559, 571, 1256
Payne v. Hutchinson, 2 Taunt. 405, n.; 11 R. R. 620	69, 454, 485
Pearce v. Gardner, [1897] 1 Q. B. 688	529, 629
Pearson v. Commercial Union Ass. Co., 15 C. B. (N. S.) 304; L. R. 8 C. P. 548; 1 App. Cas. 498; 33 L. J. C. P. 85; 45 L. J. O. P. 761; 35 L. T. 455; 24 W. R. 951; 10 Jur. (N. S.) 517; 3 Asp. M. C. 275	57, 376, 414, **509**
Peat v. Jones, 8 Q. B. D. 147; 51 L. J. Q. B. 128; 30 W. R. 433	110
Peek v. Derry. (See Derry v. Peek.)	
Peele v. Merchants' Ins. Co., 3 Mason 27	1097, 1099, 1126, 1129, 1136, 1200, 1201, 1203
Peele v. Northcote, 7 Taunt. 478; 1 Moore, 178; 16 R. R. 655; 18 R. R. 549	112, 115, 118
Peisch v. Dixon, 1 Mason, 10	70
Pelican, The, Edw. Adm. R. App. D.	96
Pellas v. Neptune Marine Ins. Co., 5 C. P. D. 34; 49 L. J. C. P. 153; 42 L. T. 35; 28 W. R. 405; 4 Asp. M. C. 213	110, 175, 176
Pelly v. Royal Exch. Ass. Co., 1 Burr. 341	30, 57, 58, 457, 460, 507, 828, 1273
Penson v. Lee, 2 B. & P. 330; 5 R. R. 614	1268
Peppin v. Solomons, 5 T. R. 496	1281
Perkin v. Auguste Ins. Co., 2 Parsons, Ins. 34, n.	430
Peterhoff, The, 5 Wallace, 28	764, 769
Peters v. Milligan, 1 Park, Ins. 296	972
Peters v. Warren Ins. Co., 3 Sumn. 389; 14 Peters, S. C. R. 99	791, 821, 964, 993
Peterson v. The Chandos, 4 Fed. R. 645	430, 434
Phelps v. Auldjo, 2 Camp. 350; 11 R. R. 725	427
Phelps v. Hill, [1891] 1 Q. B. 605; 60 L. J. Q. B. 382; 64 L. T. 610; 7 Asp. M. C. 42	425, 428, 429
Phillips v. Barber, 5 B. & Ald. 161; 24 R. R. 317	817, 860
Phillips v. Headlam, 2 B. & Ad. 380; 9 L. J. (O. S.) K. B. 238; 36 R. R. 595	692, **702**, 704, 721, 724, 798
Phillips v. Irving, 7 Man. & G. 325; 8 Scott (N. R.), 3; 13 L. J. C. P. 145	414, 415, 416, 481, 1274

SECT.

Phillips v. Nairne, 4 C. B. 343; 16 L. J. C. P. 194; 11 Jur. 455; 72
R. R. 610 ....692, **694**, 725, **1130**
Philpot v. Swann, 11 C. B. (N. S.) 270; 30 L. J. C. P. 358; 7 Jur.
(N. S.) 1291; 5 L. T. 183 ....784, 785, 879, 1172
Phœnix, The, 5 C. Rob. 20, 167 ....97, 660
Phœnix Ass. Co. v. Spooner, [1905] 2 K. B. 753; 74 L. J. K. B. 792;
93 L. T. 306; 54 W. R. 313; 10 Com. Cas. 282; 21 Times L. R.
577 1240
Phœnix Ins. Co. v. Erie Transport Co., 117 U. S. 312..................... 1231
Phœnix Ins. Co. v. Moog, 78 Ala. 284 849
Phœnix Ins. Co. v. Pratt, 2 Binn. 308 666
Phœnix Life Ass. Co., *In re*. (*See* Burges v. Stocks.)
Phyn v. Royal Exch. Ass. Co., 7 T. R. 505; 4 R. R. 508..378, 425, 840, 846
Pickersgill v. London and Provincial Mar. and Gen. Ins. Co., [1912] 3
K. B. 614; 82 L. J. K. B. 130; 107 L. T. 305; 18 Com. Cas. 1; 12
Asp. M. C. 263; 57 S. J. 11; 28 Times L. R. 591 ....176, 535, 589
Pickup v. Thames and Mersey Mar. Ins. Co., 3 Q. B. D. 594; 47 L. J.
Q. B. 749; 39 L. T. 341; 26 W. R. 689; 4 Asp. M. C. 43............ 714,
725, 1277
Pieschell v. Allnutt, 4 Taunt. 792 750
Pink v. Fleming, 25 Q. B. D. 396; 59 L. J. Q. B. 559; 63 L. T. 413;
6 Asp. M. C. 554 ....778, 783, 790, 818, 824
Pipon v. Cope, 1 Camp. 434; 10 R. R. 720 ....840, 844, 848
Pirie v. Middle Dock Co., 44 L. T. 426; 4 Asp. M. C. 388...908, 936, 978, 982
Pirie v. Steele, 8 C. & P. 200; 2 M. & Rob. 49; 56 R. R. 840.............. 1027
Pitman v. Universal Mar. Ins. Co., 9 Q. B. D. 192; 51 L. J. Q. B.
561; 46 L. T. 863; 30 W. R. 906; 4 Asp. M. C. 544...1023, 1032, 1032b,
1034, 1038, 1092
Pittegrew v. Pringle, 3 B. & Ad. 514; 37 R. R. 493 ....473, 629, **647**
Pizarro, The, 2 Wheat. 227 666
Planché v. Fletcher, 1 Dougl. 251 ....85, 388, 610, 742, 809, 810
Plantamour v. Staples, 1 T. R. 611, n.; 3 Dougl. 1 ....192, 468
Plummer v. Wildman, 3 M. & S. 482; 16 R. R. 334 ....948, 958
Poingdestre v. Royal Exch. Ass. Co., Ry. & M. 378; 27 R. R. 759..1024, 1028
Pole v. Fitzgerald, Willes, 641; Amb. 145; 4 Bro. P. C. 439; 5 Bro.
P. C. 131 ....307, 1104
Polka, The, Spinks' Prize Cases, 57 677
Pollard v. Bell, 8 T. R. 434; 5 R. R. 404 ....662, 663, 683, 684
Polly, The, 2 C. Rob. 361 ....660, 665
Polurrian SS. Co. v. Young, 19 Com. Cas. 143; 109 L. T. 901; 30
Times L. R. 126...784, 835, 1099, **1108**
Pomeranian, The, [1895] P. 349; 65 L. J. Adm. 39 ....870, 873
Pond v. King, 1 Wils. 191 1104
Pontida, The, 9 P. D. 177; 53 L. J. Adm. 78; 51 L. T. 849; 33 W. R.
38; 5 Asp. M. C. 330 196
Popham v. St. Petersburgh Ins. Co., 10 Com. Cas. 31, 276...812, 869, 1161
Portland, The, 3 C. Rob. 41 ....93, 97, 658, 755
Postilion, The, Hay & Marriott, 245 ....93, 657
Potter v. Campbell, 16 W. R. 401 1198
Potter v. Marine Ins. Co., 2 Mason, 475 331
Potter v. Ocean Ins. Co., 3 Sumner, 27 1005

TABLE OF CASES.

SECT.

Potter v. Rankin. (*See* Rankin v. Potter.)
Potts v. Bell, 8 T. R. 548; 2 Esp. 612; 5 R. R. 452 ....93, 754
Powell v. Gudgeon, 5 M. & S. 431; 17 R. R. 385...784, 811, 821, 877, 926,
    978, 1115
Powell v. Hyde, 5 E. & B. 607; 25 L. J. Q. B. 65; 2 Jur. (N. S.) 87;
    4 W. R. 51; 103 R. R. 644 ....829, 905
Powell v. Kempton Park Racecourse Co., [1899] A. C. 143; 68 L. J.
    Q. B. 392; 80 L. T. 538; 47 W. R. 585; 63 J. P. 260; 15 Times
    L. R. 266 .... 313a
Power v. Butcher, 10 B. & C. 329; 5 Man. & Ry. 327; 8 L. J. (O. S.)
    K. B. 217; 34 R. R. 432 ....106, 107, 108, 123
Power v. Whitmore, 4 M. & S. 141; 16 R. R. 416 ....948, 961, 996
Powles v. Innes, 12 L. J. Ex. 163; 11 M. & W. 10; 63 R. R. 496...175, 176,
    178, 258

Pray v. Edie, 1 T. R. 313 169
President, The, 5 C. Rob. 277 ....90, 93, 95, 657
Preston v. Greenwood, 4 Dougl. 28....................................55, 501, 505
Price v. A 1 Ships' Small Damage Ins. Assn., 22 Q. B. D. 580; 58
    L. J. Q. B. 269; 61 L. T. 278; 37 W. R. 566; 6 Asp. M. C. 435... 885,
    893, 1003
Price v. Bell, 1 East, 663 ....663, 684, 728, **730**
Price v. Maritime Ins. Co., [1901] 2 K. B. 412; 70 L. J. K. B. 780; 85
    L. T. 101; 49 W. R. 645; 5 Com. Cas. 332; 9 Asp. M. C. 213... 246,
    289, 879, 1166
Price v. Noble, 4 Taunt. 123; 13 R. R. 566 ....909, 928
Prince v. Clark, 1 L. J. (O. S.) K. B. 69; 1 B. & C. 186; 2 D. & R.
    266; 25 R. R. 352 148
Princess Charlotte, The, Br. & L. 75 1278
Prinz Heinrich, The, 13 P. D. 31; 57 L. J. Adm. 17; 58 L. T. 593;
    36 W. R. 511; 6 Asp. M. C. 273 965
Priscilla, The, Lush. 1; 1 L. T. 272; 5 Jur. (N. S.) 1421.................. 198
Property Ins. Co. v. National Protector Ins. Co., 18 Com. Cas. 119;
    108 L. T. 104; 12 Asp. M. C. 287; 57 S. J. 284......324, 328, 608, 618
Proudfoot v. Montefiore, 8 B. & S. 510; L. R. 2 Q. B. 511; 36 L. J.
    Q. B. 225; 16 L. T. 585; 15 W. R. 920.........570, 577, 578, 579, 581,
    582, 583, 585, 586
Providence Washington Ins. Co. v. Adler, 65 Maryland, 162......778, 828
Provincial Ins. Co. of Canada v. Leduc, L. R. 6 P. C. 224; 43 L. J.
    P. C. 49; 31 L. T. 141; 22 W. R. 929; 2 Asp. M. C. 338......71, **639**,
    1200, 1201, 1273
Puller v. Glover, 12 East, 124 262
Puller v. Halliday, 12 East, 494; 11 R. R. 464 262
Puller v. Staniforth, 11 East, 232; 10 R. R. 486 ....262, 266
Pulsford v. Richards, 17 Beav. 87; 22 L. J. Ch. 559; 17 Jur. 865;
    1 W. R. 295; 99 R. R. 48 536
Purissima Conception, The, 6 C. Rob. 45 677
Pyman v. Marten, 22 Times L. R. 834; 24 Times L. R. 10; 13 Com.
    Cas. 64 ....175, 1267

TABLE OF CASES. lxv

Q.

SECT.
Quebec Marine Ins. Co. v. Commercial Bank of Canada, L. R. 3 P. C.
  234; 39 L. J. P. C. 53; 22 L. T. 559; 18 W. R. 769......49, 70, 429, 686,
  688, 690, 698, 699, 701, 718

R.

R. v. Arnaud, 16 L. J. Q. B. 50; 9 Q. B. 806 ....99, 307
Raine v. Bell, 9 East, 195; 9 R. R. 533............**407**, 410, 418, 430, 481
Raisby, The, 10 P. D. 114; 54 L. J. Adm. 65; 53 L. T. 56; 33 W. R.
  938; 5 Asp. M. C. 473 ....964, 965
Ralli v. Janson, 25 L. J. Q. B. 300; 6 E. & B. 422; 106 R. R. 650...
  359, 878, 1069, 1082, **1084**, 1086
Ralli v. Troop, 157 U. S. 386...................................909, 911, 933, 936
Ralli v. Universal Marine Ins. Co., 31 L. J. Ch. 207, 313; 4 De G. F.
  & J. 1; 2 J. & H. 159; 8 Jur. (N. S.) 495; 6 L. T. 34; 10 W. R.
  278; 135 R. R. 1 ....180, 181
Ralston v. Union Ins. Co., 4 Binn. 386 1064
Ramstrom v. Bell, 5 M. & S. 267 47
Randal v. Cochrane, 1 Ves. sen. 98...1209, 1214, 1226, 1231, 1234, 1235, 1236
Ranger, The, 6 C. Rob. 125 763
Ranken v. Reeve, 2 Park, Ins. 627 401
Rankin v. Potter, L. R. 3 C. P. 562; L. R. 4 C. P. 76; L. R. 5
  C. P. 354, 518; L. R. 6 H. L. 83; 42 L. J. C. P. 169; 29 L. T.
  142; 22 W. R. 1; 2 Asp. M. C. 65......267, 271, 272, **273**, 275, 297, **513**,
  1045, 1056, 1059, 1062, 1087, 1088, 1117, 1144, 1161, **1162**,
  1163, 1164, 1168, 1182, 1191, 1192, 1195, 1198, 1214
Rapid, The, Edwd. Adm. R. 228 760
Ratcliffe v. Shoolbred, 1 Park, Ins. (8th ed.) 413; 1 Marsh. Ins. 466 ... 564,
  575, 593
Rawlins v. Desborough, 2 M. & Rob. 328....................................... 1274
Rayner v. Godmond, 5 B. & Ald. 225; 24 R. R. 335....................... 890
Rayner v. Preston, 18 Ch. D. 1; 50 L. J. Ch. 472; 44 L. T. 787; 29
  W. R. 546; 45 J. P. 829 1
Rayner v. Ritson, 6 B. & S. 888; 35 L. J. Q. B. 59; 14 W. R. 81...... 1272
Read v. Anderson, 10 Q. B. D. 100; 13 Q. B. D. 779; 53 L. J. Q. B.
  532; 51 L. T. 55; 32 W. R. 950; 49 J. P. 4 ....313a, 315
Read v. Bonham, 3 Br. & B. 147; 6 Moore, 397; 23 R. R. 587......168, 202,
  1116, 1128, 1189, 1193, 1274
Reade v. Commercial Ins. Co., 3 Johns. R. 352................................ 432
Redman v. Loudon, 3 Camp. 503; 5 Taunt. 462; 1 Marsh. 136......379, 405
Redman v. Wilson, 14 M. & W. 476; 14 L. J. Ex. 333; 9 Jur. 714;
  69 R. R. 740 ....691, 692, **693**, 717, 784, **798**
Redmond v. Smith, 7 M. & G. 457; 2 D. & L. 280; 8 Scott (N. R.),
  250; 13 L. J. C. P. 159; 8 Jur. 711; 66 R. R. 734...............735, 747
Red Sea, The, [1895] P. 293; [1896] P. 20; 65 L. J. Adm. 9; 73 L. T.
  462; 44 W. R. 306; 8 Asp. M. C. 102...232, 264, 1177, 1205, **1206**, 1207
Reed v. Cole, 3 Burr. 1512 281
Reed v. Deere, 7 B. & C. 261; 2 Car. & P. 624; 31 R. R. 190............29, 51
Reid v. Allan, 4 Ex. 326; 19 L. J. Ex. 39; 13 Jur. 1082; 80 R. R. 577...26, 79

A.—VOL. I. e

lxvi TABLE OF CASES.

SECT.
Reid v. Darby, 10 East, 143; 10 R. R. 246.........203, 206, 1118, 1127, 1158
Reid v. Harvey, 4 Dow, 97; 16 R. R. 38 ....533, 599
Reid v. Macbeth, [1904] A. C. 223; 73 L. J. P. C. 57; 90 L. T. 422;
   20 Times L. R. 316 282
Reid v. Standard Mar. Ins. Co., 2 Times L. R. 807........................... 442
Reimer v. Ringrose, 6 Ex. 263; 20 L. J. Ex. 175; 86 R. R. 280...1145, 1151
Reischer v. Borwick, [1894] 2 Q. B. 548; 63 L. J. Q. B. 753; 9 R.
   558; 71 L. T. 238; 7 Asp. M. C. 493 ....783, 822
Reliance Mar. Ins. Co. v. Duder, [1913] 1 K. B. 265; 81 L. J. K. B.
   870; 106 L. T. 936; 12 Asp. M. C. 223; 17 Com. Cas. 24, 227;
   28 Times L. R. 469 ....172, **252b**, 328a, 475, 486, 486a
Reliance Mar. Ins. Co. v. N. Y. & C. Mail SS. Co., 77 Fed. R. 317...... 933,
                                                                    936, 969
Rendsborg, The, 4 C. Rob. 121 660
Renpor, The, 8 P. D. 115; 52 L. J. Adm. 49; 48 L. T. 887; 31 W. R.
   640; 5 Asp. M. C. 98 868
Republic of Bolivia v. Indemnity Mutual Mar. Ass. Co., [1909] 1 K. B.
   785; 78 L. J. K. B. 596; 100 L. T. 503; 11 Asp. M. C. 218; 14
   Com. Cas. 156, 166; 53 S. J. 266; 24 Times L. R. 724; 25 Times
   L. R. 254 ....588, 598, 607, 617, 836, 860, 905
Reyner v. Hall, 4 Taunt. 725; 14 R. R. 650 ....1243, 1244
Reyner v. Pearson, 4 Taunt. 662; 13 R. R. 723 903
Rhind v. Wilkinson, 2 Taunt. 237; 11 R. R. 551 258
Rhodes, In re, 36 Ch. D. 586; 56 L. J. Ch. 825; 57 L. T. 652........... 442
Rice v. New England Mar. Ins. Co., 4 Pick. 439 543
Rich v. Parker, 2 Esp. 615; 7 T. R. 705; 4 R. R. 552.........661, **662**, 727
Richardson v. Anderson, 1 Camp. 43, n.; 10 R. R. 628, n. 119, 168
Richardson v. Burrows, Lowndes Mar. Ins. (2nd ed.) 199............... 826
Richardson v. London Ass. Co., 4 Camp. 94................................... 466
Richardson v. Maine Ins. Co., 6 Mass. 102................................... 760
Richardson v. Nourse, 3 B. & Ald. 237; 22 R. R. 368...200, 927, 978, 982, 1031
Rickards v. Murdock, 8 L. J. (O. S.) K. B. 210; 10 B. & C. 527; 5
   Man. & Ry. 418; Dan. & Ll. 221; Ll. & Wels. 132; 34 R. R.
   511 ....152, 159, **595**, 626
Rickman v. Carstairs, 2 N. & M. 562; 5 B. & Ad. 651; 3 L. J. K. B.
   28; 39 R. R. 603 ....**346**, 347, 448, **449**, 455, 1021, 1259
Ridolpho v. Nunez, Selden Society Publications, Vol. 2, p. 52............ 11
Ridsdale v. Newnham, 4 Camp. 111; 3 M. & S. 546; 16 R. R. 327...647, 723
Ridsdale v. Shedden, 4 Camp. 107 ....29, 47, 647
Riley v. Delafield, 7 Johns. 522..234, 262
Ringende Jacob, The, 1 C. Rob. 89 763
Rising v. Burnett, 2 Marsh. Ins. 738 ....251, 1280
Rivaz v. Gerussi, 6 Q. B. D. 222; 50 L. J. Q. B. 176; 44 L. T. 79;
   4 Asp. M. C. 377 ....185, 526, 554, **589**, 1256
Roanoke, The, 59 Fed. R. 161 908
Robbins v. New York Ins. Co., 1 Hall, 363.................................... 233
Robert S. Besnard Co., Ltd. v. Murton, 14 Com. Cas. 267; 101 L. T.
   285; 53 S. J. 717; 11 Asp. M. C. 299 1165
Roberts v. Fonnereau, 1 Park, Ins. (8th ed.) 405............................ 536
Roberts v. Hardy, 3 M. & S. 533; 16 R. R. 347.............................. 93

TABLE OF CASES. lxvii

	SECT.
Roberts v. Ogilby, 9 Price, 269; 23 R. R. 761	121, 136
Robertson v. Carruthers, 2 Stark. 571; 20 R. R. 738	1055, 1119, 1122
Robertson v. Clarke, 2 L. J. (O. S.) C. P. 71; 1 Bing. 445; 8 Moore, 622; 25 R. R. 676	70, 202, 372, 486, 1055, 1119, 1274
Robertson v. Columbian Ins. Co., 8 Johns. 491	427
Robertson v. Ewer, 1 T. R. 127; 1 R. R. 164	219, 784, 835, 841, 876, 961
Robertson v. French, 4 East, 130; 4 Esp. 246; 7 R. R. 535	15, 18, 56, 73, 75, 153, 218, 443, 448, 1278
Robertson v. Hamilton, 14 East, 522; 13 R. R. 303	139, 259a, **294**
Robertson v. Marjoribanks, 2 Stark. N. P. 573; 20 R. R. 740	573, 627, 1164
Robertson v. Money, Ry. & M. 75; 27 R. R. 732	486
Robertson v. United Ins. Co., 2 Johns. Cas. 250	243
Robinows v. Ewing's Trustees, 3 Ct. of Sess. Cas. (4th series) 1134	999
Robinson Gold Mining Co. v. Alliance Ins. Co., [1901] 2 K. B. 919; [1902] 2 K. B. 489; [1904] A. C. 359; 70 L. J. K. B. 892; 71 L. J. K. B. 942; 73 L. J. K. B. 898; 85 L. T. 419; 86 L. T. 858; 91 L. T. 202; 50 W. R. 109; 51 W. R. 105; 53 W. R. 160; 6 Com. Cas. 244; 7 Com. Cas. 219; 9 Com. Cas. 301; 20 Times L. R. 645	99, 790, 829, 905
Robinson v. Gleadow, 2 Bing. (N. C.) 156; 2 Scott, 250; 1 Hodges, 245; 42 R. R. 568	136, 140, 141
Robinson v. Mar. Ins. Co. of New York, 2 Johns. 89	425, 435
Robinson v. Mollett, L. R. 7 H. L. 802; 44 L. J. C. P, 362; 33 L. T. 544.	128
Robinson v. Price, 2 Q. B. D. 91, 295; 46 L. J. Q. B. 551; 36 L. T. 354; 25 W. R. 469; 3 Asp. M. C. 407	916, 932
Robinson v. Tobin, 1 Stark. 336	15, 40, 42, 73
Robinson v. Touray, 3 Camp. 158; 1 M. & S. 217; 13 R. R. 781	41, 50, 187, 757
Robson v. Wilson, 1 Marsh. Ins. 301	108
Roddick v. Indemnity Mutual Mar. Ins. Co., [1895] 1 Q. B. 836; [1895] 2 Q. B. 380; 64 L. J. Q. B. 733; 14 R. 516; 72 L. T. 860; 44 W. R. 27; 8 Asp. M. C. 24	218, 219, 220, 246, 365, **637**, 797
Roderick v. Hovil, 3 Camp. 103	32
Rodocanachi v. Elliott, L. R. 8 C. P. 649; L. R. 9 C. P. 518; 43 L. J. C. P. 255; 31 L. T. 239; 2 Asp. M. C. 399	470, **807**, 832, 1138, 1143
Rodocanachi v. Milburn, 17 Q. B. D. 316; 18 Q. B. D. 67; 56 L. J. Q. B. 202; 56 L. T. 594; 35 W. R. 241; 6 Asp. M. C. 100	264
Roelandts v. Harrison, 9 Ex. 444; 2 C. L. R. 995; 23 L. J. Ex. 169; 22 L. T. (O. S.) 289; 96 R. R. 786	485
Rogers v. Ætna Ins. Co., 76 Fed. R. 569	721
Rogers v. British Shipowners' Mut. Prot. Assn., 1 Com. Cas. 414	81
Rogers v. Davis, 1 Marsh. Ins. 140; 2 Park, Ins. 601	331
Rogers v. Maylor, 1 Park. Ins. 267; 2 Marsh. Ins. 644	1242
Rohl v. Parr, 1 Esp. 445; 5 R. R. 741	777, 825, 898
Rolla, The, 6 C. Rob. 344	767
Rona, The, 51 L. T. 28; 5 Asp. M. C. 259	428
Roscow v. Corson, 8 Taunt. 684; 21 R. R. 507	847
Rose v. Bank of Australasia, [1894] A. C. 687; 63 L. J. Q. B. 504; 6 R. 121; 70 L. T. 422; 7 Asp. M. C. 445	215, 881, 960, 964, 969

lxviii   TABLE OF CASES.

SECT.

Rose v. Hart, 8 Taunt. 499; 2 Moore, 547; 2 Smith, L. C.; 20 R. R.
   533 ....110, 134
Rosetto v. Gurney, 11 C. B. 176; 20 L. J. C. P. 257; 15 Jur. 1177; 17
   L. T. (O. S.) 242; 87 R. R. 629...1106, 1145, **1151**, 1152, 1154, 1157,
                                                                    1158, 1159
Ross v. Hunter, 4 T. R. 33; 2 R. R. 319 ....424a, 847, 852
Ross v. Thwaites, 1 Park, Ins. (8th ed.) 23 ....224, 225, 801
Rossiter v. Miller, 3 App. Cas. 1124; 48 L. J. Ch. 10; 39 L. T. 173; 26
   W. R. 865 37
Rotch v. Edie, 6 T. R. 413; 3 R. R. 222.........95, 833, 834, 1104, 1108
Rothwell v. Cooke, 1 B. & P. 172 1250
Routh v. Thompson, 11 East, 428; 13 East, 274; 10 R. R. 539...140, 142,
                  171, 172, 173, 252a, 301, 302, **305**, 306, 1258, 1275
Routledge v. Burrell, 1 H. Bl. 255 629
Roux v. Salvador, 7 L. J. Ex. 328; 1 Bing. (N. C.) 536; 3 Bing.
   (N. C.) 266; 4 Scott, 1; 2 Hodges, 209; 43 R. R. 638...205, 206, 887,
          1044, 1045, 1052, 1054, 1055, 1059, 1063, 1065, 1066, **1070**,
          1076, 1142, 1144, 1149, 1184, 1191, 1192, 1197, 1214, 1246
Rowcroft v. Dunmore, cited 3 Taunt. 228; 12 R. R. 643 817
Rowland and Marwood's Steamship Co. v. Maritime Ins. Co., 6 Com.
   Cas. 160 1091
Royal Exch. Ass. Co. v. Tod, 8 Times L. R. 669 ....39, 70
Royal Exch. Ass. Corp. v. Sjorforsakrings Aktiebolaget Vega, [1901]
   2 K. B. 567; [1902] 2 K. B. 384; 70 L. J. K. B. 874; 71 L. J.
   K. B. 739; 85 L. T. 241; 87 L. T. 356; 50 W. R. 25, 694; 6 Com.
   Cas. 189; 7 Com. Cas. 205; 9 Asp. M. C. 329.........440, 708, 744
Royal Exch. Shipping Co. v. Dixon, 12 App. Cas. 11; 56 L. J. Q. B.
   266; 56 L. T. 206; 35 W. R. 461; 6 Asp. M. C. 92 920
Royal Mail Steam Packet Co. v. English Bank of Rio de Janeiro, 19
   Q. B. D. 362; 57 L. J. Q. B. 31; 36 W. R. 105...911, 924, **968**, 969, 970
Ruabon Steamship Co. v. London Assurance, [1897] 2 Q. B. 456;
   [1898] 1 Q. B. 722; [1900] A. C. 6; 66 L. J. Q. B. 841; 67 L. J.
   Q. B. 548; 69 L. J. Q. B. 86; 77 L. T. 402; 78 L. T. 402; 81
   L. T. 585; 46 W. R. 417; 48 W. R. 225; 8 Asp. M. C. 346, 369;
   9 Asp. M. C. 2; 2 Com. Cas. 295; 3 Com. Cas. 148; 5 Com. Cas.
   71 ....1037, 1038, 1039, 1040
Rucker v. Allnutt, 15 East, 278; 13 R. R. 465 ....403, 405
Rucker v. Ansley, 5 M. & S. 25; 17 R. R. 251 758
Rucker v. London Ass. Co., 2 B. & P. 432, n.; 3 Esp. 290; 5 R. R.
   639, n. 457
Ruckman v. Merchants' Louisville Ins. Co., 5 Duer, 342 1116
Ruger v. Firemen's Fund Ins. Co., 90 Fed. R. 310 ....611, 785
Ruggles v. General Interest Ins. Co., 4 Mass. 74; 12 Wheat. S. C. R.
   408 ....553, **583**, 602, 617, 623
Rumball v. Metropolitan Bank, 2 Q. B. D. 194; 46 L. J. Q. B. 346;
   36 L. T. 240; 25 W. R. 366 63
Rummens v. Hare, 1 Ex. D. 169; 46 L. J. Ex. 30; 34 L. T. 407; 24
   W. R. 385 134
Russell v. Bangley, 4 B. & Ald. 395 125
Russell v. Boehm, 2 Str. 1127 1279
Russell v. Dunskey, 6 Moore, 283 1224

TABLE OF CASES. lxix

SECT.
Russell v. Thornton, 4 H. & N. 788; 6 H. & N. 140; 29 L. J. Ex. 9; 30
L. J. Ex. 69; 6 Jur. (N. S.) 1080; 2 L. T. 574; 8 W. R. 615;
118 R. R. 762, 774 ....52, 54, 600, 619
Ruys v. Royal Exchange Ass. Corp., [1897] 2 Q. B. 135; 66 L. J. Q. B.
534; 77 L. T. 23; 8 Asp. M. C. 294; 2 Com. Cas. 201...764, 830, 1096,
1099, 1102, 1139, 1202, 1214

S.

Sadler v. Dixon (see Dixon v. Sadler), 8 M. & W. 895; 11 L. J. Ex.
435; 52 R. R. 784 ....702, 703
Saffery v. Mayer, [1901] 1 Q. B. 11... 315
Sage v. Middletown Ins. Co., 1 Conn. R. 239............................... 497
Saidler v. Church, 1 Caines, 303; 2 Caines, 286 1220
Sailing Ship "Blairmore" Co. v. Macredie, [1898] A. C. 593; 67 L. J.
P. C. 96; 24 R. 893; 79 L. T. 217; 8 Asp. M. C. 429; 3 Com.
Cas. 241 ....1047, 1048, 1091, 1096, 1097, 1099, 1123, **1126**, 1204
Sailing Ship "Dewa Gungadhur" Co. v. United Kingdom Mar. Mut.
Ins. Assn., 2 Times L. R. 366 84
Sailing Ship "Garston" Co. v. Hickie, 15 Q. B. D. 580; 18 Q. B. D.
17; 56 L. J. Q. B. 38; 53 L. T. 795; 55 L. T. 879; 35 W. R. 33;
5 Asp. M. C. 499; 6 Asp. M. C. 71..........................69, 454, 456, 485
St. Johns, The, 101 Fed. R. 469 ....339, 1092, 1184, 1227, 1230, 1240
St. Paul Fire, &c. Co. v. Morice, 11 Com. Cas. 153; 22 Times L. R. 449.. 783,
829, 832
St. Paul Fire, &c. Co. v. Pacific Cold Storage Co., 157 Fed. R. 627 869
St. Paul Fire & Mar. Ins. Co. v. Knickerbocker, 93 Fed. R. 931......... 637
Salisbury v. Townson, Miller, Ins. 418 ....62, 391
Sally, The, 3 C. Rob. 300, n. 659
Salomon v. Salomon & Co., [1897] A. C. 22; 66 L. J. Ch. 35; 75 L. T.
426; 45 W. R. 193; 4 Manson, 89 ....99, 307
Saloucci v. Johnson, 4 Dougl. 224; cited 8 East, 129 ....656, 842
Saloucci v. Woodmass, 2 Park, Ins. 727; 1 Marsh. Ins. 405 680
Saltus v. Ocean Ins. Co., 12 Johns. R. 107 ....881, 1172
Saltus v. Ocean Ins. Co., 14 Johns. 138 1068
Salvador v. Hopkins, 3 Burr. 1707 ....58, 391, 505, 610, 611
Samuel v. Royal Exch. Ass. Co., 8 B. & C. 119; 6 L. J. (O. S.) K. B.
315; 32 R. R. 352 ....414, **491**, 1064
Sanches v. Davenport, 6 Mass. R. 258 151
Sandeman v. Tyzack and Branfoot SS. Co., [1913] A. C. 680; 83 L. J.
P. C. 23; 109 L. T. 580; 57 S. J. 752; 29 Times L. R. 694 780
Sanderson v. McCallum, 4 J. B. Moore, 5 44
Sanderson v. Symonds, 1 Br. & B. 426; 4 J. B. Moore, 42; 21 R. R.
675 ....42, 44
San José Indiano, The, 2 Gall. 268 658
San Roman, The, L. R. 3 A. & E. 583; L. R. 5 P. C. 301; 41 L.J.
Adm. 72; 42 L. J. Adm. 46; 26 L. T. 948; 21 W. R. 393; 1 Asp.
M. C. 603 432
Santa Ana, The, 154 Fed. R. 800 ....923, 1004
Santissima Trinidad, The, 7 Wheat. 283 760
Sarah Ann, The, 2 Sumn. R. 206 ....204, 1117

TABLE OF CASES.

SECT.

Sarquy v. Hobson, 3 D. & R. 192; 2 B. & C. 7; 4 Bing. 131; 12 Moore, 474; 1 Y. & J. 347; 1 L. J. (O. S.) K. B. 222; 26 R. R. 251...784, 811, 821, 877, 927, 1115

Sassoon v. Western Ass. Co., [1912] A. C. 561; 81 L. J. P. C. 231; 106 L. T. 929; 12 Asp. M. C. 206; 17 Com. Cas. 274...777, 812, 825

Saunders v. Baring, 34 L. T. (N. S.) 419; 3 Asp. M. C. 133...1071, 1197, 1214

Saunders v. Drew, 3 B. & Ad. 445; 37 R. R. 460 264

Sawtell v. London, 5 Taunt. 359; 1 Marsh. R. 99 ....50, 576, **599**

Scadding v. Eyles, 9 Q. B. 858; 15 L. J. Q. B. 364 36

Scaife v. Tobin, 3 B. & Ad. 523; 1 L. J. K. B. 183; 37 R. R. 500... 1004

Scaramanga v. Stamp, 5 C. P. D. 295; 49 L. J. C. P. 674; 42 L. T. 840; 28 W. R. 691; 4 Asp. M. C. 295 434

Schibsby v. Westenholz, L. R. 6 Q. B. 155; 40 L. J. Q. B. 73; 24 L. T. 93; 19 W. R. 587 ....678, 682

Schieffelin v. New York Ins. Co., 9 Johns. 21 881

Schiller, The Cargo ex, 2 P. D. 145; 36 L. T. 714; 3 Asp. M. C. 439... 868

Schloss v. Heriot, 14 C. B. (N. S.) 59; 32 L. J. C. P. 211; 10 Jur. (N. S.) 76; 8 L. T. 246; 11 W. R. 596; 135 R. R. 602 918

Schloss v. Stevens, [1906] 2 K. B. 665; 75 L. J. K. B. 927; 96 L. T. 205; 10 Com. Cas. 224; 10 Asp. M. C. 331; 22 Times L. R. 774... 470, 860, 1272

Schmidt v. Royal Mail SS. Co., 45 L. J. Q. B. 646; 4 Asp. M. C. 217, n. 923, 936

Schooner Boston, The, 1 Sumn. 328 434

Schooner Jasper, In re, 3 Sumner, 308; cited 2 Phillips, Ins. s. 1345... 973

Schooner Reeside, The, 2 Sumn. 567 56

Schroder v. Thompson, 7 Taunt. 462; 1 Moore, 163; 18 R. R. 540 416

Schrœder v. Vaux, 15 East, 52; 13 R. R. 758, n. 758

Schulz v. Ohio Ins. Co., 1 Monroe's Kentucky R. 339 214

Schwartz v. Ins. Co. of North America, 3 Wash. C. C. R. 117 666

Scotland, The, 105 U. S. 24 793

Scott v. Avery, 22 L. J. Ex. 157; 25 L. J. Ex. 308; 8 Exch. 487; 5 H. L. Cas. 811; 2 Jur. (N. S.) 815; 4 W. R. 746; 91 R. R. 580; 101 R. R. 392 82

Scott v. Bourdillon, 2 B. & P. (N. R.) 213; 9 R. R. 644 ....68, 883

Scott v. Globe Marine Ins. Co., 1 Com. Cas. 370 ....173, 185, 1274

Scott v. Irving, 9 L. J. (O. S.) K. B. 89; 1 B. & Ad. 605; 35 R. R. 396 ....65, 125, 127, **128**

Scott v. Thompson, 1 B. & P. (N. R.) 181; 8 R. R. 780 ....427, 435, 848

Scottish Mar. Ins. Co. v. Turner, 4 H. L. Cas. 312; 1 Macq. H. L. 334; 17 Jur. 631; 1 W. R. 527...785, 1064, 1164, **1165**, 1176, 1188, 1190, 1205

Scottish National Ins. Co. v. Poole, 18 Com. Cas. 9; 107 L. T. 687; 12 Asp. M. C. 266; 57 S. J. 45; 29 Times L. R. 16 .... 328a

Scottish Shire Line, Ltd. v. London and Provincial Mar. Ins. Co., [1912] 3 K. B. 51; 81 L. J. K. B. 1066; 107 L. T. 46; 17 Com. Cas. 240; 12 Asp. M. C. 253; 56 S. J. 551......233, 269, 608, 626, 788, 1089, 1166

Scull v. Briddle, 2 Wash. C. C. R. 150 204

Seagrave v. Union Mar. Ins. Co., L. R. 1 C. P. 305; 35 L. J. C. P. 172; 1 H. & R. 302; 12 Jur. (N. S.) 358; 14 L. T. 479; 14 W. R. 690 ....282, 291

	SECT.
Sea Ins. Co. v. Blogg, [1898] 2 Q. B. 398; 67 L. J. Q. B. 757; 78 L. T. 785; 47 W. R. 71; 3 Com. Cas. 1218	651
Sea Ins. Co. v. Gavin, 4 Bligh (N. S.) 578; 2 Dow & C. 129; 33 R. R. 77	485
Sea Ins. Co. v. Hadden, 13 Q. B. D. 706; 53 L. J. Q. B. 252; 50 L. T. 657; 32 W. R. 841; 5 Asp. M. C. 230...1175, **1178**, 1205, 1208, 1211, 1227, **1232**	
Seaman v. Fonnereau, 2 Str. 1183	590, 602
Seaman v. Loring, 1 Mason, 127, 140	474, 475, 481
Searle v. Scovell, 4 Johns. Ch. C. 218	989, 1041
Seaton v. Burnand, [1900] A. C. 135; 69 L. J. K. B. 409; 82 L. T. 205; 5 Com. Cas. 198	329
Seller v. M'Vicar, 1 B. & P. (N. R.) 23; 8 R. R. 744	517
Seller v. Work, 1 Marsh. Ins. 305, 306	152, 162
Seton v. Low, 1 Johns. Cas. 1	613
Sewell v. Burdick, 10 Q. B. D. 363; 13 Q. B. D. 159; 10 App. Cas. 74; 54 L. J. Q. B. 156; 52 L. T. 445; 33 W. R. 461; 5 Asp. M. C. 376	292
Sewell v. Royal Exch. Ass. Co., 4 Taunt. 855	736
Seymour v. London and Prov. Mar. Ins. Co., 41 L. J. C. P. 193; 27 L. T. 417; 1 Asp. M. C. 423	670, 764
Sharp v. Gladstone, 7 East, 24; 3 Smith, 39; 8 R. R. 583...835, 876, 880, 1175, 1181, 1211	
Shaw v. Benson, 11 Q. B. D. 563; 52 L. J. Q. B. 575	79
Shawe v. Felton, 2 East, 109; 6 R. R. 394 ......339, 340, 341, 345, 356, **489**, 1064	
Shee v. Clarkson, 12 East, 507; 11 R. R. 473	116, 118
Shelbourne v. Law Investment Corp., [1898] 2 Q. B. 626; 67 L. J. Q. B. 944; 79 L. T. 278; 3 Com. Cas. 304	250
Shepeler v. Durant, 14 C. B. 582; 23 L. J. C. P. 140	89
Shepherd v. Chewter, 1 Camp. 274; 10 R. R. 681	1243
Shepherd v. Harrison, L. R. 4 Q. B. 196, 493; L. R. 5 H. L. 116; 40 L. J. Q. B. 148; 24 L. T. 857; 20 W. R. 1; 1 Asp. M. C. 66	282
Shepherd v. Henderson, 7 App. Cas. 49; 9 Ct. of Sess. Cas. (4th Ser.) 1	1096, 1106, 1188, 1200
Shepherd v. Kottgen, 2 C. P. D. 578, 585; 47 L. J. C. P. 67; 37 L. T. 618; 26 W. R. 120; 3 Asp. M. C. 544	929, 942
Shepherdess, The, 5 C. Rob. 264	770
Sheriff v. Potts, 5 Esp. 96	407, 1242
Shiffner v. Gordon, 12 East, 296	750
Shipton v. Thornton, 8 L. J. Q. B. 73; 9 A. & E. 314; 1 P. & D. 216; 48 R. R. 507	192, **207**, 211, 811, 1087, 1168
Shirley v. Wilkinson, 1 Dougl. 306, n.; 3 Dougl. 41	557, 575, 591
Shoe v. Craig, 189 Fed. R. 227; 194 Fed. R. 678; Lowndes, Gen. Av., 5th ed., pp. 756—759, Add.	963
Shoe v. Low Moor Iron Co., 49 Fed. R. 252	942
Shoolbred v. Nutt, 1 Park, Ins. 493; 1 Marsh. Ins. 474	555, 600, 619
Shore v. Bentall, 7 B. & C. 798, n.; 31 R. R. 302, n.	723, 798
Sibbald v. Hill, 2 Dow, 263; 14 R. R. 160	536, 554, 564, 574, 623
Siffken v. Allnutt, 1 M. & S. 39	245, 1255
Siffken v. Lee, 2 B. & P. (N. R.) 484; 9 R. R. 676	661

lxxii   TABLE OF CASES.

	SECT.
Silvia, The, 171 U. S. (64 Davis) 462	720
Simson v. Bazett, 2 M. & S. 94	803, 833
Simon, Israel & Co. v. Sedgwick, [1893] 1 Q. B. 303; 62 L. J. Q. B. 163; 4 R. 128; 67 L. T. 785; 41 W. R. 163; 7 Asp. M. C. 245...	376, 380, 387, 470
Simond v. Boydell, 1 Dougl. 268	1263, 1264
Simonds v. Hodgson, 7 L. J. (O. S.) C. P. 239; 1 L. J. K. B. 51; 3 B. & Ad. 50; 3 M. & P. 385; 6 Bing. 114; 37 R. R. 319	218, 242, 243, 289
Simonds v. White, 4 D. & R. 375; 2 B. & C. 805; 2 L. J. (O. S.) K. B. 159; 26 R. R. 560	981, 992, 993
Simpson v. Thomson, 3 App. Cas. 279; 4 Sc. Cas. (4th Ser.) 177; 38 L. T. 1; 3 Asp. M. C. 567	1226, 1227, 1231
Simpson SS. Co. v. Premier Underwriting Assn., 10 Com. Cas. 198; 92 L. T. 730; 53 W. R. 512; 10 Asp. M. C. 127; 21 Times L. R. 485	436, 639
Sims v. Willing, 8 Serg. & Rawle, 103	1004
Sir John Jackson, Ltd. v. Owners of SS. Blanche. (See Hopper No. 66.)	
Sisters, The, 3 C. Rob. 213; 4 C. Rob. 275; 5 C. Rob. 155	661
Sleigh v. Tyser, [1900] 2 Q. B. 333; 69 L. J. Q. B. 626; 82 L. T. 804; 5 Com. Cas. 271; 9 Asp. M. C. 97	686, 689, 712
Small v. Gibson, 16 Q. B. 128; 19 L. J. Q. B. 147; 20 L. J. Q. B. 152; 14 Jur. 368; 15 Jur. 325 (see Gibson v. Small)	630
Small v. United Kingdom Mar. Mut. Ins. Assn., [1897] 2 Q. B. 42, 311; 66 L. J. Q. B. 736; 76 L. T. 828; 46 W. R. 24; 8 Asp. M. C. 293; 2 Com. Cas. 133, 267	173, 840, 849, 852
Smith and Scaramanga v. Fenning, 3 Com. Cas. 75; 14 Times L. R. 222	239
Smith v. Chadwick, 20 Ch. D. 27; 9 App. Cas. 187; 53 L. J. Ch. 873; 50 L. T. 697; 32 W. R. 687; 48 J. P. 644	536, 555
Smith v. Cologan, 2 T. R. 188, n.	150
Smith v. Kay, 7 Cl. & F. 759; cited [1899] 2 Q. B. 646	536
Smith v. Lascelles, 2 T. R. 187; 1 R. R. 457	138, 146, 148, 298
Smith v. Price, 2 F. & F. 748	148
Smith v. Pyman, [1891] 1 Q. B. 742; 60 L. J. Q. B. 621; 64 L. T. 436; 39 W. R. 466; 7 Asp. M. C. 7	263
Smith v. Reynolds, 25 L. J. Ex. 337; 1 H. & N. 221; 4 W. R. 644; 108 R. R. 534	241, 313
Smith v. Robertson, 2 Dow, 474; 14 R. R. 174	1096, 1097, 1102, 1199, 1201
Smith v. Scott, 4 Taunt. 125; 13 R. R. 568	827a
Smith v. Surridge, 4 Esp. 25; 6 R. R. 837	415, 481, 698
Smith v. Wright, 1 Caines, 43	62
Snook v. Davidson, 2 Camp. 218; 11 R. R. 696	132
Soares v. Thornton, 7 Taunt. 627; 1 Moore, 373; 18 R. R. 615	844, 855, **857**
Soelberg v. Western Ass. Co. of Toronto, 119 Fed. R. 23	1200
Solly v. Whitmore, 5 B. & Ald. 45; 24 R. R. 274	405
Somes v. Sugrue, 4 C. & P. 274; 34 R. R. 797	203, 1114, 1116, 1117, 1120, 1128
Sousmith v. The J. P. Donaldson, 21 Fed. R. 671	938

	SECT.

South British Fire and Mar. Ins. Co. of New Zealand v. Da Costa, [1906] 1 K. B. 456; 75 L. J. K. B. 276; 94 L. T. 435; 54 W. R. 420; 11 Com. Cas. 81; 10 Asp. M. C. 227; 22 Times L. R. 305... 1085

South Staffordshire Tramways Co. v. Sickness, &c. Ass. Assn., [1891] 1 Q. B. 402; 60 L. J. Q. B. 47; 63 L. T. 807; 55 J. P. 168......... 441

Spafford v. Dodge, 14 Mass. 66 ....977, 986

Spalding v. Crocker, 2 Com. Cas. 189 ....41, 503

Sparkes v. Marshall, 5 L. J. C. P. 286; 2 Bing. (N. C.) 761; 3 Scott, 172; 2 Hodges, 44; 42 R. R. 725..............176, 180, 255a, 258, 282, 287

Sparrow v. Carruthers, 2 Str. 1236 458

Spence v. Union Mar. Ins. Co., L. R. 3 C. P. 427; 37 L. J. C. P. 169; 18 L. T. 632; 16 W. R. 1010................................. 780

Spencer v. Franco, Beawes, 316; cited 2 Burr. 1211................831, 1104

Spitta v. Woodman, 2 Taunt. 416; 16 East, 188, n.; 11 R. R. 628...... 153, 448, 450

Sprague v. Overton, 1 Sprague's Decisions, 462............................ 430

Spring v. South Carolina Ins. Co., 8 Wheat. 268............................ 134

Springbok, The, 5 Wallace, 1...................................... 764

Stackpole v. Simon, 2 Park, Ins. 933.............................. 571

Stadt Embden, The, 1 C. Rob. 26 763

Stainbank v. Fenning, 20 L. J. C. P. 226; 11 C. B. 51; 15 Jur. 1082; 87 R. R. 561 ....198, 199, 242, 243, 289

Stainbank v. Shepard, 22 L. J. Ex. 341; 13 C. B. 418; 1 C. L. R. 609; 17 Jur. 1032; 1 W. R. 505; 93 R. R. 599..............199, 242, 243, 289

Stamma v. Brown, 2 Str. 1173; cited 8 East, 135, 136; 9 R. R. 389... 838, 840, 841, 850

Standard Mar. Ins. Co. v. Nome Beach Co., 133 Fed. R. 636............ 799

Stanley v. Berners, 3 Hagg. Eccl. Rep. 374..................... 90

Stanton v. Richardson, L. R. 7 C. P. 421; 9 C. P. 390; 41 L. J. C. P. 180; 43 L. J. C. P. 230; 45 L. J. C. P. 78; 33 L. T. 193; 24 W. R. 324; 3 Asp. M. C. 23 ....710, 717

Stanwood v. Rich, State Ct. Mass: 1817........................... 720

Star of Hope, The, 9 Wall. 203..............................937, 938, 942, 961

Stead v. Salt, 3 L. J. (O. S.) C. P. 175; 3 Bing. 101; 10 Moore, 389; 28 R. R. 602 168

Stearns v. Village Main Reef Gold Mining Co., 10 Com. Cas. 88; 21 Times L. R. 236 ....1235, 1236

Steel v. Lacy, 3 Taunt. 285; 12 R. R. 658 ....543, 666, **729**, 732, 1243

Steel v. State Line SS. Co., 3 App. Cas. 72; 4 Sc. Cas. (4th Ser.) 657; 37 L. T. 333; 3 Asp. M. C. 516 ....710, 720

Steinback v. Rhinelander, 3 Johns. N. Y. Cas. 281...................... 171

Stephens v. Australasian Ins. Co., L. R. 8 C. P. 18; 42 L. J. C. P. 12; 27 L. T. 585; 21 W. R. 228; 1 Asp. M. C. 458............41, 188, 309

Stephens v. Broomfield, L. R. 2 P. C. 516........................290, 1137, 1217

Stert, The, 4 C. Rob. 65..767, 769

Stevens v. Beverley Ins. Co., 1 Phillips, Ins. s. 963...................... 498

Stevenson v. Snow, 3 Burr. 1237; 1 W. Bl. 318........................ 1249

Stewart v. Aberdein, 7 L. J. Ex. 292; 4 M. & W. 211; 1 H. & H. 284; 51 R. R. 536 ....65, 125, **128**, 1273

Stewart v. Bell, 5 B. & Ald. 238; 24 R. R. 342...................457, 579, 610

TABLE OF CASES.

SECT.

Stewart v. Dunlop, 4 Bro. P. C. 482... 579
Stewart v. Greenock Mar. Ins. Co., 2 H. L. Cas. 159; 1 Macq. H. L.
    328; 81 R. R. 91 ....1063, 1064, 1165, **1176**, 1203, 1205, 1206, 1213
Stewart v. Merchants' Mar. Ins. Co., 16 Q. B. D. 619; 55 L. J. Q. B.
    81; 53 L. T. 892; 34 W. R. 208; 5 Asp. M. C. 506.................75, 893
Stewart v. Morrison, Millar, Ins. 59 532
Stewart v. Steele, 11 L. J. C. P. 155; 5 Scott (N. R.), 927 ....1032, 1032a
Stewart v. West Indian and Pacific Steamship Co., L. R. 8 Q. B. 88,
    362; 42 L. J. Q. B. 191; 28 L. T. 742; 21 W. R. 953; 1 Asp.
    M. C. 528 ....936, 996
Stewart v. Wilson, 12 M. & W. 11; 13 L. J. Ex. 27; 7 Jur. 1020; 67
    R. R. 234 ....84, 719
Stirling v. Vaughan, 11 East, 619; 2 Camp. 225; 11 R. R. 276...140, 171,
    255, 255a, 301, 305, 306
Stitt v. Wardell, 2 Esp. 610.. 407
Stock v. Inglis. (See Inglis v. Stock.)
Stockdale v. Dunlop, 9 L. J. Ex. 83; 6 M. & W. 224; 4 Jur. 681; 55
    R. R. 592...257, 287, 288
Stocker v. Harris, 3 Mass. 415; 2 Phillips, s. 1203 361
Stocker v. Merrimack Fire and Mar. Ins. Co., 6 Mass. 220.............. 598
Stockton and Darl. Ry. Co. v. Barrett, 11 Cl. & F. 590; 8 Scott (N. R.),
    641; 7 Man. & G. 870; 65 R. R. 261 485
Stone v. Marine Ins. Co. of Gothenburg, 1 Ex. D. 81; 45 L. J. Ex. 361;
    34 L. T. 490; 24 W. R. 55; 3 Asp. M. C. 152...13, 54, 491, 493, **506**
Stoomvart Maatschappy Nederland v. P. and O. Steam Nav. Co. (See
    Khedive, The.)
Stott (Baltic) Steamers, Ltd. v. Marten, [1914] 1 K. B. 442; [1914]
    W. N. 345; 83 L. J. K. B. 406; 109 L. T. 899; 19 Com. Cas. 93;
    30 Times L. R. 85 .... 861a
Stowe v. Querner, L. R. 5 Ex. 155; 39 L. J. Ex. 60; 22 L. T. 29; 18
    W. R. 466 ....7, 1277
Strang v. Scott, 14 App. Cas. 601; 59 L. J. P. C. 1; 61 L. T. 597;
    38 W. R. 452; 6 Asp. M. C. 419 ....918, 920, 921, 1004
Strass v. Spillers and Bakers, [1911] 2 K. B. 759; 80 L. J. K. B. 1218;
    104 L. T. 284; 16 Com. Cas. 166; 11 Asp. M. C. 590 181
Strathdon, The, 94 Fed. R. 206; 101 Fed. R. 600 918
Street v. Royal Exchange Ass., 18 Com. Cas. 284; [1914] W. N. 197;
    109 L. T. 215; 12 Asp. M. C. 356; 30 Times L. R. 495 328
Stribley v. Imperial Mar. Ins. Co., 1 Q. B. D. 507; 45 L. J. Q. B. 396;
    34 L. T. 281; 24 W. R. 701; 3 Asp. M. C. 134.........**584**, 585, 590, **592**,
    594, 606, 627
Stringer v. English and Scottish Mar. Ins. Co., L. R. 4 Q. B. 676; 5
    Q. B. 599; 39 L. J. Q. B. 214; 10 B. & S. 770; 22 L. T. 802; 18
    W. R. 1201 ....23, 1050, **1057**, 1138, 1192, **1195**, 1218
Strong v. Harvey, 4 L. J. (O. S.) C. P. 57; 3 Bing. 304; 11 Moore,
    C. P. 72 80
Strong v. Natally, 1 B. & P. (N. R.) 16; 8 R. R. 741.................. 458
Strong v. New York Firemen's Ins. Co., 11 Johns. 315.................... 986
Suart v. Merchants' Mar. Ins. Co., 3 Com. Cas. 312; 14 Times L. R. 564.
    1213, 1218

TABLE OF CASES. lxxv

	SECT.
Success, The, 1 Dod. 131	661
Suckley v. Delafield, 2 Caines, 222	543
Suffell v. Bank of England, 9 Q. B. D. 555; 51 L. J. Q. B. 401; 17 L. T. 146; 30 W. R. 932; 46 J. P. 500	40
Sun Mutual Ins. Co. v. Ocean Ins. Co., 107 U. S. (17 Otto) 485	589, 609
Sunderland Mar. Ins. Co. v. Kearney, 16 Q. B. 925; 20 L. J. Q. B. 417; 15 Jur. 1006	1273
Sunderland Steamship Co. v. North of England Iron Steamship Ins. Assn., 11 Times L. R. 106; 14 R. 196	1091
Susa, The, 2 C. Rob. 251	658
Sutherland v. Pratt, 11 M. & W. 296; 12 M. & W. 16; 2 Dowl. (N. S.) 813; 12 L. J. Ex. 235; 13 L. J. Ex. 246; 7 Jur. 261; 63 R. R. 606; 67 R. R. 238	13, 259, 292
Suydam v. Marine Ins. Co., 2 Johns. R. 138; 1 Phillips, Ins. s. 1002	416, 417, 1190

Svendsen v. Wallace, 11 Q. B. D. 616; 13 Q. B. D. 69; 10 A. C. 404; 54 L. J. Q. B. 497; 46 L. T. 742; 52 L. T. 901; 30 W. R. 841; 34 W. R. 369; 4 Asp. M. C. 550; 5 Asp. M. C. 453...906, 907, 927, 944, 947, 948, 949, **950**, 951, 952, 953, 954, 955, 956, 957, 958, 959, 960, 961, 962, 964, 966, 967

Swan v. Maritime Ins. Co., [1907] 1 K. B. 116; 76 L. J. K. B. 160; 96 L. T. 839; 12 Com. Cas. 73; 10 Asp. M. C. 450; 23 Times L. R. 101 ....103, 110, 119, 175, 176, 177, 299, 1273

Sweeting v. Pearce, 29 L. J. C. P. 265; 30 L. J. C. P. 109; 7 C. B. (N. S.) 449; 9 C. B. (N. S.) 534; 7 Jur. (N. S.) 800; 5 L. T. 79; 9 W. R. 343; 121 R. R. 584 ......65, 124, 125, 126, **127**, 128, 1273

Syers v. Bridge, 2 Dougl. 527 ....14, 419, 422, 437

T.

Tabbs v. Bendelack, 4 Esp. 108; 3 B. & P. 207, n. 91, 93, 657
Tait v. Levi, 14 East, 481; 13 R. R. 289 ....721, 799, 1251
Tamvaco v. Lucas, 30 L. J. Q. B. 234; 31 L. J. Q. B. 296; 1 B. & S. 185; 3 B. & S. 89; 1 E. & E. 581; 6 L. T. 697; 10 W. R. 733; 5 Jur. (N. S.) 1258; 117 R. R. 355, 360 181
Tannenbaum v. Heath, [1908] 1 K. B. 1032; 77 L. J. K. B. 634; 99 L. T. 237; 13 Com. Cas. 264; 24 Times L. R. 450 1272
Tanner v. Bennett, Ry. & M. 182; 27 R. R. 743......**800**, 1057, 1115, 1284
Tappenden v. Randall, 2 B. & P. 467; 5 R. R. 662 1254
Tasker v. Cunningham, 1 Bligh, 87, 102; 20 R. R. 33 385
Tasker v. Scott, 1 Marsh. R. 556; 6 Taunt. 234; 16 R. R. 608...310, 313a, 315
Tatam v. Reeve, [1893] 1 Q. B. 44; 62 L. J. Q. B. 30; 5 R. 83; 67 L. T. 683; 41 W. R. 174; 57 J. P. 118 ....107, 315
Tate v. Hyslop, 15 Q. B. D. 368; 54 L. J. Q. B. 592; 53 L. T. 581; 5 Asp. M. C. 487 ....556, **608**, 1238
Tatham v. Burr, [1898] A. C. 382 ....10, 795
Tatham v. Hodgson, 6 T. R. 656 ....781, 824
Taylor, In re, Ex parte Norvell, [1910] 1 K. B. 562; 79 L. J. K. B. 610; 102 L. T. 84; 17 Manson, 145; 54 S. J. 271; 26 Times L. R. 270 ....110, 134

TABLE OF CASES.

SECT.

Taylor *v.* Bowers, 1 Q. B. D. 291; 46 L. J. Q. B. 39; 34 L. T. 938; 24 W. R. 499 1254
Taylor *v.* Curtis, 6 Taunt. 608; 2 Marsh. R. 309; Holt, N. P. 192; 4 Camp. 337; 16 R. R. 686 .... 777, 823, 935
Taylor *v.* Dewar, 5 B. & S. 58; 33 L. J. Q. B. 141; 10 Jur. (N. S.) 361; 10 L. T. 267; 12 W. R. 579; 136 R. R. 479 10
Taylor *v.* Dunbar, L. R. 4 C. P. 206; 38 L. J. C. P. 178; 17 W. R. 382 .... 778, 782, 824
Taylor *v.* Wilson, 15 East, 324; 13 R. R. 488 .... 232, 518
Teignmouth and General Mutual Shipping Assn., *In re*, L. R. 14 Eq. 148; 41 L. J. Ch. 679; 26 L. T. 684; 1 Asp. M. C. 325 .... 36, 82
Tenant *v.* Elliott, 1 B. & P. 3; 4 R. R. 755 .... 109, 121, 1255
Tennant *v.* Henderson, 1 Dow, 324 610
Teutonia, The, 8 Moo. P. C. (N. S.) 411; L. R. 3 A. & E. 394; L. R. 4 P. C. 171; 41 L. J. Adm. 57; 26 L. T. 48; 20 W. R. 421 ...... 432, 435
Thacker *v.* Hardy, 4 Q. B. D. 685; 48 L. J. Q. B. 289; 39 L. T. 595; 27 W. R. 158 .... 313a
Thames and Mersey Mar. Ins. Co. *v.* "Gunford" Ship. Co. (*See* "Gunford" Ship Co. *v.* Thames and Mersey Mar. Ins. Co.)
Thames and Mersey Mar. Ins. Co. *v.* Hamilton, Fraser & Co., 17 Q. B. D. 195; 12 App. Cas. 484; 56 L. J. Q. B. 626; 57 L. T. 695; 36 W. R. 337; 6 Asp. M. C. 200 .... 812, 823, 828, 860, **861**
Thames and Mersey Mar. Ins. Co. *v.* O'Connell, 86 Fed. R. 150 639
Thames and Mersey Mar. Ins. Co. *v.* Pitts, [1893] 1 Q. B. 476; 5 R. 168; 68 L. T. 524; 41 W. R. 346; 7 Asp. M. C. 302...... 233, 343, 361, 886, 887
Thames and Mersey Mar. Ins. Co. *v.* Van Laun, Shipping Gazette, 25th July, 1905 .... 376, **382a**, 405, 414, 832, 905
Thellusson *v.* Bewick, 1 Esp. 77 366
Thellusson *v.* Fergusson, 1 Dougl. 361 .... 378, 380, **381**, 645, 649
Thellusson *v.* Fletcher, 1 Dougl. 315; 1 Esp. 72........ 313, 1091, 1189, 1200
Thellusson *v.* Pigou, 1 Dougl. 366, n. 645
Thellusson *v.* Shedden, 2 B. & P. (N. R.) 228 1284
Thellusson *v.* Staples, 1 Dougl. 366, n. 645
Thin *v.* Richards, [1892] 2 Q. B. 141; 62 L. J. Q. B. 39; 66 L. T. 584; 40 W. R. 617; 7 Asp. M. C. 165 .... 705, 706
Thomas & Son Shipping Co., Ltd. *v.* London and Prov. Mar. Ins. Co., Ltd., 29 Times L. R. 736 .... 697, 799
Thomas *v.* Atherton, 10 Ch. D. 185; 48 L. J. Ch. 370; 40 L. T. 77 ... 168
Thomas *v.* Builders' Fire Ins. Co., 119 Mass. 121 797
Thomas *v.* Foyle, 5 Esp. 88 1278
Thomas *v.* Royal Exch. Ass. Co., 1 Price, 195 .... 430, 431
Thompson *v.* Adams, 23 Q. B. D. 361 37
Thompson *v.* Buchanan, 4 Bro. P. C. 482 575
Thompson *v.* Colvin, Ll. & Wels. 140 .... 1127, 1128, 1130
Thompson *v.* Gillespie, 5 E. & B. 209; 24 L. J. Q. B. 340; 1 Jur. (N. S.) 779; 3 W. R. 505; 103 R. R. 438 647
Thompson *v.* Hopper, 26 L. J. Q. B. 22; 27 L. J. Q. B. 441; 6 E. & B. 172, 937; E. B. & E. 1038; 5 W. R. 83; 6 W. R. 857; 106 R. R. 547, 872; 113 R. R. 986........ 377, 695, 697, 699, 727, 799, 801
Thompson *v.* Hunter, cited 2 M. & Rob. 51 1027

TABLE OF CASES. lxxvii

	SECT.
Thompson v. Redman, 12 L. J. Ex. 310; 11 M. & W. 487; 2 Dowl. (N. S.) 1028	110
Thompson v. Reynolds, 7 E. & B. 172; 26 L. J. Q. B. 93; 3 Jur. (N. S.) 464; 110 R. R. 543	10, 341
Thompson v. Rowcroft, 4 East, 34	1164, 1175, 1177
Thompson v. Royal Exch. Ass. Co., 16 East, 214	**1072**, 1137, **1149**
Thompson v. Taylor, 6 T. R. 478; 3 R. R. 233	266, 268, **272**, 513, 1088
Thompson v. Whitmore, 3 Taunt. 227; 12 R. R. 642	817
Thorne v. Deas, 4 Johns. 84	145
Thorneley v. Hebson, 2 B. & Ald. 513; 21 R. R. 381	1093, 1107
Thornton v. Lance, 4 Camp. 231	1285
Thornton v. Royal Exch. Ass. Co., 1 Peake, 25	726
Tidmarsh v. Washington Ins. Co., 4 Mason, 439	711
Tierney v. Etherington, 1 Burr. 348	461, 468
Tilley v. Bowman, [1910] 1 K. B. 745; 79 L. J. K. B. 547; 102 L. T. 318; 17 Manson, 97; 54 S. J. 342	134
Tobin v. Harford, 32 L. J. C. P. 134; 34 L. J. C. P. 37; 13 C. B. (N. S.) 791; 17 C. B. (N. S.) 528; 10 Jur. (N. S.) 859; 10 L. T. 817; 12 W. R. 1062; 134 R. R. 734; 142 R. R. 497	222, 345, **346**, 347, 455, 1021, 1041, 1259
Todd v. Reid, 4 B. & Ald. 210	125
Todd v. Ritchie, 1 Stark. 240; 18 R. R. 768	840
Tonge v. Watts, 2 Str. 1251	268
Toulmin v. Anderson, 1 Taunt. 227	848
Toulmin v. Inglis, 1 Camp. 421; 10 R. R. 715	424, 848
Touteng v. Hubbard, 3 B. & P. 291; 6 R. R. 791	803, 834
Townsend v. Crowdy, 8 C. B. (N. S.) 477; 29 L. J. C. P. 300; 7 Jur. (N. S.) 71; 2 L. T. 537; 125 R. R. 740	1244
Townson v. Guyon, 2 Park, Ins. (8th ed.) 620	390
Travelers' Ins. Co. v. McConkey, 127 U. S. 666	75
Trayes v. Worms, 34 L. J. C. P. 274; 19 C. B. (N. S.) 159, 177; 11 Jur. (N. S.) 639; 12 L. T. 547; 13 W. R. 898	233, 986
Treadwell v. Union Ins. Co., 6 Cowen, 270	700
Tregelles v. Sewell, 7 H. & N. 574; 126 R. R. 558	282
Trinder, Anderson & Co. v. Thames & Mersey Mar. Ins. Co., [1898] 2 Q. B. 114; 67 L. J. Q. B. 666; 78 L. T. 485; 46 W. R. 561; 8 Asp. M. C. 373; 3 Com. Cas. 123	424, 656, 692, 695, 697, 704, 724, 727, 798, **799**, 799a, 801, 827a, 828, 844, 1164, 1191
Trinity House Corp. v. Clark, 4 M. & S. 288	855
Trott v. Wood, 1 Gallison, 443	62
Trueman v. Loder, 11 A. & E. 589; 3 P. & D. 267; 9 L. J. Q. B. 165; 52 R. R. 451	56
Truscott v. Christie, 2 Br. & B. 320; 5 Moore, 33; 23 R. R. 446	266, 267, **268**, 270, 511
Tudor v. Macomber, 14 Pick. 34	981
Tuite v. Royal Exchange Ass. Co., 1 Park, Ins. (8th ed.) 224, 225; 1 Marsh. Ins. 232	365, 1010
Tunno v. Edwards, 12 East, 488; 11 R. R. 458	340, **1051**, 1138, 1184, 1214, 1227, 1245
Turnbull v. Janson, 36 L. T. 635; 3 Asp. M. C. 433	710

lxxviii   TABLE OF CASES.

Turnbull, Martin & Co. *v.* Hull Underwriters' Assn., [1900] 2 Q. B. 402; 69 L. J. Q. B. 588; 82 L. T. 818; 5 Com. Cas. 248; 9 Asp. M. C. 93 ....
Turnbull *v.* Woolfe, 7 L. T. (N. S.) 483; 9 Jur. (N. S.) 57; 11 W. R. 55 ....52, 81
Turner *v.* Trustees of Liverpool Docks, 20 L. J. Ex. 393; 6 Exch. 543; 17 L. T. (O. S.) 212; 86 R. R. 377 ....
Turpin *v.* Bilton, 12 L. J. C. P. 167; 5 M. & G. 455; 6 Scott (N. R.), 447; 7 Jur. 950 ....
Tutela, The, 6 C. Rob. 177 ....
Twee Frienden, The, cited 3 C. Rob. 29 ....
Twee Juffrowen, The, 4 C. Rob. 242 ....
Twemlow *v.* Oswin, 2 Camp. 85; 11 R. R. 670 ....814, 1
Tyler *v.* Horne, 1 Park, Ins. (8th ed.) 455 1
Tyrie *v.* Fletcher, 2 Cowp. 666 ....437, 1247, 1249, 1
Tyser *v.* Shipowners' Syndicate, [1896] 1 Q. B. 135; 65 L. J. Q. B. 238; 73 L. T. 605; 44 W. R. 207; 8 Asp. M. C. 81; 1 Com. Cas. 224 ....
Tyson *v.* Gurney, 3 T. R. 477 ....

U.

Udny *v.* Udny, L. R. 1 H. L. (Sc.) 441; 5 Ct. of Sess. Cas. (3rd ser.) 164 90
Uhde *v.* Walters, 3 Camp. 16; 13 R. R. 737 ....70, 372,
Underwood *v.* Robertson, 4 Camp. 138; 16 R. R. 760 1057,
Union Ins. Co. *v.* Smith, 124 U. S. 405 ....
Union Mar. Ins. Co. *v.* Borwick, [1895] 2 Q. B. 279; 64 L. J. Q. B. 679; 15 R. 546; 73 L. T. 156; 8 Asp. M. C. 71; 1 Com. Cas. 87... 795,
Union Mar. Ins. Co. *v.* Martin, 35 L. J. C. P. 181 330,
United Ins. Co. *v.* Lenox, 1 Johns. 377; 2 Johns. 443 ....
United Ins. Co. *v.* Robinson, 1 Johns. R. 592; 2 Caines, 279......1219,
United Kingdom Mutual SS. Ass. Assn. *v.* Boulton, 3 Com. Cas. 330..81,
United Kingdom Mutual SS. Ass. Assn. *v.* Nevill, 19 Q. B. D. 110; 22 Q. B. D. 719; 56 L. J. Q. B. 522; 35 W. R. 746; 6 Asp. M. C. 226, n. ....
United States *v.* Wilder, 3 Sumn. 308 ....
United States Shipping Co. *v.* Empress Ass. Corp., [1907] 1 K. B. 259; [1908] 1 K. B. 115; 76 L. J. K. B. 225; 77 L. J. K. B. 120; 12 Com. Cas. 142; 13 Com. Cas. 90; 23 Times L. R. 137; 24 Times L. R. 45 ....262, 363, 365,
Universo Ins. Co. of Milan *v.* Merchants' Marine Ins. Co., [1897] 1 Q. B. 205; [1897] 2 Q. B. 93; 66 L. J. Q. B. 564; 77 L. T. 748; 45 W. R. 625; 2 Com. Cas. 28, 180 ....24, 56,
Urquhart *v.* Bernard, 1 Taunt. 450; 10 R. R. 574 61,
Ursula Bright SS. Co. *v.* Arnsinck, 115 Fed. R. 242 ....
Usher *v.* Noble, 12 East, 639; 11 R. R. 505...340, 343, 365, 1010, 1013,
Usparicha *v.* Noble, 13 East, 332; 12 R. R. 360 88,
Uzielli *v.* Boston Mar. Ins. Co., 15 Q. B. D. 11; 54 L. J. Q. B. 142; 52 L. T. 787; 33 W. R. 293; 5 Asp. M. C. 405...**325**, 327, **886**, 902,

TABLE OF CASES. lxxix

V.

	SECT.
Vacher v. London Society of Compositors, [1912] 3 K. B. 547; [1913] A. C. 107; 81 L. J. K. B. 1014; 82 L. J. K. B. 232; 106 L. T. 778; 107 L. T. 722; 56 S. J. 442; 57 S. J. 75; 28 Times L. R. 366; 29 Times L. R. 73	1
Vallance v. Dewar, 1 Camp. 503; 10 R. R. 738...58, 62, 391, 463, 482, 483, 610	
Vallejo v. Wheeler, 1 Cowp. 124; Lofft, 645...838, 847, 848, 849, 855, **856**, 857	
Van Baggen v. Baines, 9 Ex. 523; 2 C. L. R. 543; 23 L. J. Ex. 213; 96 R. R. 821	485
Vancouver, The, 11 App. Cas. 573; 56 L. J. Q. B. 100; 55 L. T. 491; 35 W. R. 169; 6 Asp. M. C. 68 ....965, **1035**, 1036	
Vancouver Nat. Bank v. Law, &c. Ins. Co., 153 Fed. R. 440	257a
Vanderheuvel v. Church, 2 Johns. 127, 173, n.	543
Vandyck v. Hewitt, 1 East, 96; 5 R. R. 516 ....87, 740, 1255	
Vandyck v. Whitmore, 1 East, 475	758
Van Laun v. Thames and Mersey Mar. Ins. Co. (28th March; 9th Nov. 1903), unreported. (See Thames and Mersey Co. v. Van Laun.)	
Van Omeron v. Dowick, 2 Camp. 42; 11 R. R. 656 ....206, 1148	
Vardon v. Wilmot, 2 Park, Ins. 696, n.	654
Venus, The, 8 Cranch, 253 ....92, 93, 94	
Vezian v. Grant, 1 Marsh. Ins. 359; 2 Park, Ins. 670	641
Victoria, The, Edwards' Adm. R. 97	676
Victorin v. Cleeve, 2 Str. 1250	654
Vigilantia, The, 1 C. Rob. 1 ....93, 97, 658, 661, 755	
Vigilantia, The, 6 C. Rob. 122	769
Village Main Reef Co. v. Stearns, 5 Com. Cas. 246	1272
Vincentelli v. Rowlett, 16 Com. Cas. 310; 105 L. T. 411; 12 Asp. M. C. 34	156
Violett v. Allnutt, 3 Taunt. 419; 13 R. R. 676 ....402, 452	
Virginia Carolina Chemical Co. v. Norfolk, &c. SS. Co., 17 Com. Cas. 277; 107 L. T. 320; 12 Asp. M. C. 233; 56 S. J. 722; 28 Times L. R. 513	720
Vlierboom v. Chapman, 13 L. J. Ex. 384; 13 M. & W. 230; 8 Jur. 811; 67 R. R. 582 ....205, 206, 785	
Von Tungeln v. Dubois, 2 Camp. 151.............530, 543, 559	
Vortigern, The, [1899] P. 140; 68 L. J. P. 49; 80 L. T. 382; 47 W. R. 437; 8 Asp. M. C. 523 ....701, 705, **706**, 710	
Vreede Scholtys, The, 5 C. Rob. 5, n.	661
Vrow Anna Catharina, The, 5 C. Rob. 161 ....97, 660	
Vrow Barbara, The, 3 C. Rob. 158, n.	768
Vrow Elizabeth, The, 5 C. Rob. 2	661
Vrow Howina, The, Calvo, Droit International, 4th ed. Vol. 5, s. 2767	764
Vrow Judith, The, 1 C. Rob. 150	769
Vrow Margaretha, The, 1 C. Rob. 336	659

W.

Wadsworth v. Pacific Ins. Co., 4 Wend. 33 ....457, 1084	
Wait v. Baker, 17 L. J. Ex. 307; 2 Ex. 1; 76 R. R. 469	282
Wake v. Atty, 4 Taunt. 493; 13 R. R. 660 ....152, 577	

TABLE OF CASES.

Walden *v.* New York Firemen Ins. Co., 12 Johns. 128 194,
Walden *v.* Phœnix Ins. Co., 5 Johns. 310 ....
Waldron *v.* Coombe, 3 Taunt. 162; '12 R. R. 629 ....
Walford, de Baerdemaecher & Co. *v.* Galindez Bros., 2 Com. Cas. 137...
Walker *v.* Maitland, 5 B. & Ald. 171; 24 R. R. 320......692, 723, **798**,
Walker *v.* Protection Ins. Co., 29 Maine R. 317 ....
Walker *v.* United States Ins. Co., 11 Serg. & Rawle, 51 ....
Wallace *v.* Tellfair, 2 T. R. 188, n., cited 1 Esp. 75 145,
Waller *v.* Louisiana Ins. Co., 9 Martin, 276 ....
Wallerstein *v.* Columbian Ins. Co., 44 N. Y. 204 1068,
Waln *v.* Thompson, 9 Serg. & Rawle, 115 ....
Walpole *v.* Ewer, 2 Park, Ins. (8th ed.) 898 995,
Walthew *v.* Mavrojani, L. R. 5 Ex. 116; 39 L. J. Ex. 81; 22 L. T.
    310 ....911, 948, 952,
Wamsutta Mills *v.* Old Colony Steamboat Co., 137 Mass. 471 ....
Waples *v.* Eames, 2 Str. 1243 ....
Ward *v.* Beck, 32 L. J. C. P. 113; 13 C. B. (N. S.) 668; 9 Jur.
    (N. S.) 912; 134 R. R. 691 ....
Ward *v.* Weir, 4 Com. Cas. 222 279,
Ward *v.* Wood, 13 Mass. 539 ....
Warkworth, The, 9 P. D. 145; 53 L. J. Adm. 65; 51 L. T. 558; 33
    W. R. 112; 5 Asp. M. C. 326 ....
Warre *v.* Miller, 4 L. J. (O. S.) K. B. 8; 4 B. & C. 538; 7 D. & R. 1;
    1 Car. & P. 237; 28 R. R. 382......**268**, 269, 270, 275, **409**, 455,
                                                                                                     486
Warwick, The, 15 P. D. 189; 63 L. T. 561; 6 Asp. M. C. 545 ....
Warwick *v.* Scott, 4 Camp. 62 ....
Warwick *v.* Slade, 3 Camp. 127; 13 R. R. 772 34,
Washburn Manufacturing Co. *v.* Reliance Mar. Ins. Co., 179 U. S. 1...
                                                                                                    1117,
Waters *v.* Allen, 5 Hill, N. Y. 421 ....
Waters *v.* Merchants' Ins. Co., 11 Peters, S. C. R. 213 ....
Watson *v.* Clark, 1 Dow, 336; 14 R. R. 73 ....691, 698, 714,
Watson *v.* Ins. Co. of North America, 1 Binn. 47 ....
Watson *v.* King, 1 Stark. 121; 4 Camp. 272; 16 R. R. 790 ....
Watson *v.* Shankland, L. R. 2 H. L. (Sc.) 304; 29 L. T. 349; 10 Ct. of
    Sess. Cas. (3rd ser.) 142; 2 Asp. M. C. 115 ....
Watson *v.* Swann, 31 L. J. C. P. 210; 11 C. B. (N. S.) 756; 132
    R. R. 746 ....140, 143, 172
Watt *v.* Morris, 1 Dow, 32 ....
Watt *v.* Potter, 2 Mason, 77 ....
Watts *v.* Bacon ....
Waugh *v.* Morris, L. R. 8 Q. B. 202; 42 L. J. Q. B. 57; 28 L. T. 265;
    21 W. R. 438; 1 Asp. M. C. 573 ....
Wavertree Sailing Ship Co. *v.* Love, [1897] A. C. 373; 66 L. J. P. C.
    77; 76 L. T. 576; 16 N. S. W. L. R. 271 103
Way *v.* Modigliani, 2 T. R. 30; 1 R. R. 412..................371, 380, **384**
Webb *v.* Thompson, 1 B. & P. 5; 4 R. R. 757 ....
Webster *v.* De Tastet, 7 T. R. 157; 4 R. R. 402 ....161, 244

	SECT.
Webster v. Foster, 1 Esp. 407	593
Wedderburn v. Bell, 1 Camp. 1; 10 R. R. 615	686, 718, 719
Weir v. Aberdein, 2 B. & Ald. 320; 20 R. R. 450...49, 52, 429, **690**, 717, 1274	
Weir v. Girvin, [1900] 1 K. B. 45; 69 L. J. Q. B. 168; 81 L. T. 687; 48 W. R. 179; 9 Asp. M. C. 7; 5 Com. Cas. 40	264
Wellman v. Morse, 76 Fed. R. 573	1004
Wells v. Hopwood, 3 B. & Ad. 20; 37 R. R. 307	888, 889, 890
Wells v. Philadelphia Ins. Co., 9 Serg. & Rawle, 103	292
Wells v. Williams, 1 Salk. 45; 1 Ld. Raym. 282	88
Welvaart Van Pillaw, The, 2 C. Rob. 128	668
West of England Bank v. Batchelor, 51 L. J. Ch. 199; 46 L. T. 132; 30 W. R. 364	134
West of England Fire Ins. Co. v. Isaacs, [1896] 2 Q. B. 377; [1897] 1 Q. B. 226; 66 L. J. Q. B. 36; 75 L. T. 564	1240
West of England and South Wales District Bank v. Canton Ins. Co., 2 Ex. D. 472	1271, 1272
West India and Panama Telegraph Co. v. Home and Colonial Mar. Ins. Co., 6 Q. B. D. 51; 50 L. J. Q. B. 41; 43 L. T. 420; 29 W. R. 92; 4 Asp. M. C. 341	828, 861
West Rand Central Gold Mines Co. v. Rougemont, [1900] 2 Q. B. 346; 69 L. J. Q. B. 771; 83 L. T. 79; 48 W. R. 619; 5 Com. Cas. 296	428
Westbury v. Aberdein, 2 M. & W. 267; M. & H. 49; 6 L. J. Ex. 83; 1 Jur. 201; 46 R. R. 598	595, 626, 1274
Western Ass. Co. v. Southern Cotton Oil Co., 68 Fed. R. 924	694
Western Ass. Co. of Toronto v. Poole, [1903] 1 K. B. 376; 72 L. J. K. B. 195; 88 L. T. 362; 8 Com. Cas. 108; 9 Asp. M. C. 390...73, 324, 325, 327, 866, 872, 1091, 1191	
Western Transit Co. v. Brown, 152 Fed. R. 476	795
Westminster Fire Office v. Reliance Mar. Ins. Co., 19 Times L. R. 668	470
Weston v. Emes, 1 Taunt. 115	56
Westwood v. Bell, 4 Camp. 349; 16 R. R. 800	131, 132, 133
White, Ex parte, In re Nevill, L. R. 6 Ch. 403; 40 L. J. Bk. 73; 24 L. T. 45; 19 W. R. 488	115
White v. Republic Fire Ins. Co., 57 Maine, 91	869
Whitecross Wire Co. v. Savill, 8 Q. B. D. 653; 51 L. J. Q. B. 426; 46 L. T. 643; 30 W. R. 588; 4 Asp. M. C. 531	936
Whitehead v. Bance, 4 Bro. P. C. 446, n.	1104
Whitehead v. Vaughan, 6 East, 523, n.; 8 R. R. 524, n.	131, 134
Whitney v. American Ins. Co., 3 Cowen, 210; 5 Cowen, 712	360, 455
Whitney v. Haven, 13 Mass. 172	432
Whittingham v. Thornburgh, 2 Vernon, 206	574, 1256
Whitwell v. Harrison, 2 Ex. 127; 18 L. J. Ex. 465; 76 R. R. 526	492
Whitworth Bros. v. Shepherd, 12 Ct. of Sess. Cas. (4th ser.) 204	1188
Wiggin v. Amory, 13 Mass. 118	421, 427
Wiggin v. Boardman, 14 Mass. 12	421
Wilbraham v. Wartnaby, Ll. & Wels. 144	765
Wilcocks v. Union Ins. Co., 2 Binn. 574	674, 842
Wild Rose SS. Co. v. Jupe, 19 Times L. R. 289	1127
Wilkes v. People's Fire Ins. Co., 19 N. Y. 184	255
Wilkie v. Geddes, 3 Dow, 57; 15 R. R. 17	686, 718
Wilkinson v. Clay, 4 Camp. 171; 6 Taunt. 110; 10 R. R. 591	119

lxxxii   TABLE OF CASES.

                                                                      SECT.
Wilkinson v. Coverdale, 1 Esp. 75; 53 R. R. 256 ....145, 161
Wilkinson v. Hyde, 27 L. J. C. P. 116; 3 C. B. (N. S.) 30; 4 Jur.
  (N. S.) 482; 111 R. R. 529 ....224, 359, 1021, 1086
Wilkinson v. Lindo, 7 M. & W. 81; 10 L. J. Ex. 94; 56 R. R. 638...... 129
Willard v. Dorr, 3 Mason, 161 1220
Willes v. Glover, 1 B. & P. (N. R.) 14; 8 R. R. 739............557, **593**, 626
William, The, 5 C. Rob. 385 ....660, 668
William J. Quillan, The, 180 Fed. R. 681 918
Williams v. Armroyd, 7 Cranch, 423 67
Williams v. British Mutual Marine Ins. Co., 3 Times L. R. 314; 57
  L. T. 27; 6 Asp. M. C. 134 8
Williams v. Canton Ins. Office, [1901] A. C. 462; 70 L. J. K. B. 962;
  85 L. T. 317; 6 Com. Cas. 256 ....233, **789**, **879**
Williams v. London Ass. Co., 1 M. & S. 318; 14 R. R. 441 ....358, 980
Williams v. Marshall, 6 Taunt. 390; 7 Taunt. 468; 2 Marsh. 292; 1
  Moore, 168; 18 R. R. 542 63
Williams v. North China Ins. Co., 1 C. P. D. 757; 35 L. T. 884; 3
  Asp. M. C. 342.........................142, 171, 232, 233, 252b, 264, 345, 127
Williams v. Shee, 3 Camp. 469; 14 R. R. 811 ....405, 40
Williams v. Smith, 2 Caines, 20 121
Williamson v. Innes, cited 8 Bing. 81; 1 Moo. & R. 88; 34 R. R.
  629, n.; 42 R. R. 765 ....269, 27
Willis v. Baddeley, [1892] 2 Q. B. 324; 61 L. J. Q. B. 769; 67 L. T.
  206; 40 W. R. 577 127
Willis v. Cooke, 25 L. J. Q. B. 16; 5 E. & B. 641; 1 Jur. (N. S.)
  1164; 4 W. R. 54; 103 R. R. 659 ....235, 28
Willis v. Joyce, 16 Com. Cas. 190; 104 L. T. 576; 11 Asp. M. C. 601;
  55 S. J. 443; 27 Times L. R. 388 16
Willison v. Patteson, 7 Taunt. 439; 1 Moore, 133; 18 R. R. 525 9
Wills & Sons v. The World Marine Ins., Ltd., The Times, March 14th,
  1911 861
Wilson v. Bank of Victoria, L. R. 2 Q. B. 203; 36 L. J. Q. B. 89; 16
  L. T. 9; 15 W. R. 693 ....916, 932, 948, 96
Wilson v. Creighton, 3 Dougl. 132, cited 1 T. R. 113 11
Wilson v. Duckett, 3 Burr. 1361 ....574, 128
Wilson v. Forster, 1 Marsh. R. 425; 6 Taunt. 25; 16 R. R. 560... 108
                                                             1110, 1164, 12
Wilson v. Jones, L. R. 1 Ex. 193; L. R. 2 Ex. 139; 36 L. J. Ex. 78;
  15 L. T. 669; 15 W. R. 435...238, **249**, 259a, 260, 288, 307, 315, 714, 7
Wilson v. Marryatt, 8 T. R. 31; 1 B. & P. 430; 53 R. R. 104...92, 93, 9
                                                             657, 735, 746, 7
Wilson v. Martin, 25 L. J. Ex. 217; 11 Exch. 684; 105 R. R. 726...232, 23
                                                             248, 263, 2
Wilson v. Millar, 2 Stark. N. P. 1; 19 R. R. 670 ....206, 11
Wilson v. Nelson, 5 B. & S. 354; 33 L. J. Q. B. 220; 10 Jur. (N. S.)
  1044; 10 L. T. 523; 12 W. R. 795; 133 R. R. 579 ....20, 3
Wilson v. Rankin, L. R. 1 Q. B. 162; 34 L. J. Q. B. 62; 35 L. J.
  Q. B. 87; 13 L. T. 564; 14 W. R. 198 ....704, 745, 8
Wilson v. Royal Exch. Ass. Co., 2 Camp. 623; 12 R. R. 760..206, 245, **114**
Wilson v. Salamandra Ass. Co. of St. Petersburgh, 8 Com. Cas. 129;
  88 L. T. 96; 9 Asp. M. C. 370 ....77, 5

	SECT.
Wilson v. Smith, 3 Burr. 1550; 1 W. Bl. 507	885, 886
Wilton v. Reatson, 1 Park, Ins. (8th ed.) 16	169
Wimble v. Rosenberg, [1913] 2 K. B. 94; 3 K. B. 743; 81 L. J. K. B. 650; 82 L. J. K. B. 1251; 106 L. T. 298; 109 L. T. 294; 17 Com. Cas. 193; 18 Com. Cas. 302; 12 Asp. M. C. 182, 373; 56 S. J. 274; 57 S. J. 784; 29 Times L. R. 752	148
Winder v. Wise, Danson & Lloyd, 238	768, 770, 1274
Wingate v. Foster, 3 Q. B. D. 582; 47 L. J. Q. B. 525; 38 L. T. 737; 26 W. R. 650; 3 Asp. M. C. 598	431, 471
Winter v. Haldimand, 2 B. & Ad. 649; 9 L. J. (O. S.) K. B. 313; 36 R. R. 693	229, 232, 233, **248**, 264
Winthrop v. Union Ins. Co., 2 Wash. C. C. R. 7	427, 430
Wolcott v. Eagle Ins. Co., 4 Pick. 429	224, 226, 227
Wolff v. Horncastle, 1 B. & P. 316; 4 R. R. 808	138, 140, 169, 170, 171, 291, **293**, 1275
Wood v. Phœnix Co., 8 Fed. R. 27	922
Wood v. Worsley. (See Worsley v. Wood.)	
Woodrop-Sims, The, 2 Dod. 83	827
Woods v. Olsen, 99 Fed. R. 451	964
Woodside v. Globe Marine Ins. Co., [1896] 1 Q. B. 105; 65 L. J. Q. B. 117; 73 L. T. 626; 44 W. R. 187; 8 Asp. M. C. 118; 1 Com. Cas. 237	20, 339, 1033, **1092**, 1184
Woolf v. Claggett, 3 Esp. 257; 6 R. R. 830	430, 719
Woolmer v. Muilman, 1 W. Bl. 427; 3 Burr. 1419	657
Woolridge v. Boydell, 1 Dougl. 16	371, 380, 381
Wordsworth, The, 88 Fed. R. 313	913
Work v. Leathers, 97 U. S. (7 Otto) 379	714
Worsley v. Wood, 6 T. R. 710; 2 H. Bl. 574; 3 R. R. 323	629
Wright v. Barnard, 2 Esp. 700; 5 R. R. 767	726
Wright v. Marwood, 7 Q. B. D. 62; 50 L. J. Q. B. 643; 45 L. T. 297; 29 W. R. 673; 4 Asp. M. C. 451	908, **921**, 922
Wright v. Shiffner, 2 Camp. 247; 11 East, 515; 11 R. R. 263	646
Wright v. Welbie, 1 Chit. 49; 22 R. R. 792	756
Wyllie v. Povah, 12 Com. Cas. 317; 23 Times L. R. 687	238

X.

Xantho, The, 11 P. D. 170; 12 App. Cas. 503; 56 L. J. Adm. 116; 57 L. T. 701; 36 W. R. 353; 6 Asp. M. C. 207	775, 812, 823
Xenos v. Fox, L. R. 3 C. P. 630; L. R. 4 C. P. 665; 38 L. J. C. P. 351; 17 W. R. 893	10, 872
Xenos v. Wickham, 13 C. B. (N. S.) 381; 14 C. B. (N. S.) 435; L. R. 2 H. L. 296; 31 L. J. C. P. 364; 33 L. J. C. P. 13; 36 L. J. C. P. 313; 16 L. T. 800; 11 W. R. 1067; 16 W. R. 38; 135 R. R. 757	27, 35, 54, 107, 108, 119, 124, 163, 165, 168

Y.

Yangtze Ins. Assn. *v.* Indemnity Mut. Mar. Ass. Co., [1908] 1 K. B. 911; [1908] 2 K. B. 504; 77 L. J. K. B. 392, 995; 73 Com. Cas. 283; 24 Times L. R. 687 ....
Yates *v.* White, 4 Bing. (N. C.) 272; 5 Scott, 640; 7 L. J. C. P. 116; 44 R. R. 708 ....1226, 1227, 1
Yonge Pieter, The, 4 C. Rob. 79 ....
Young *v.* Bank of Bengal, 1 Moo. Ind. App. Cas. 87; 1 Moo. P. C. 50; 1 Deac. 622; 43 R. R. 8 ....
Young *v.* Kitchin, 3 Ex. D. 127; 47 L. J. Ex. 579; 26 W. R. 403......
Young *v.* Turing, 2 M. & G. 593; 2 Scott (N. R.) 752; 58 R. R. 477... 8
1123, 1128, 1
Yuill *v.* Scott-Robson, [1907] 1 K. B. 685; [1908] 1 K. B. 270; 76 L. J. K. B. 469; 77 L. J. K. B. 259; 96 L. T. 842; 98 L. T. 364; 12 Com. Cas. 196; 13 Com. Cas. 166; 10 Asp. M. C. 453; 23 Times L. R. 247; 24 Times L. R. 180 10,

Z.

Zacharie *v.* New Orleans Ins. Co., 5 Martin (N. S.), 637 ....
Zelden Rust, The, 6 C. Rob. 93 ....

MARINE INSURANCE.

PART I.

OF THE NATURE, FORMATION, AND SUBJECT-MATTER OF THE CONTRACT OF MARINE INSURANCE.

CHAPTER I.

THE CONTRACT OF MARINE INSURANCE GENERALLY.

	SECT.
Definition of Terms	1, 2
Nature of the Indemnity afforded by Marine Insurance	3—6

1. UNTIL the year 1907 the Law of Marine Insurance was derived mainly from the decisions of the Courts and the treatises of text-writers; but its leading principles are now contained in the Marine Insurance Act, 1906 (6 Edw. 7, c. 41), the full title of which is "An Act to codify the Law relating to Marine Insurance" (*a*). The Act came into force on the 1st of January, 1907 (*b*).

Codification of the Law of Marine Insurance.

The nature and scope of the contract of Marine Insurance are explained in the first three sections of the Act in the following terms:—

> Section 1. A contract of marine insurance is a contract whereby the insurer undertakes to indemnify the assured,

Marine insurance defined.

(*a*) The title of an Act of Parliament is now a part of the Act, and may be taken into consideration for the purpose of construing it. See May's Parliamentary Practice, 10th ed. 462, 473; Fielden *v.* Morley Corporation, [1899] 1 Ch. 1, 3; per Lord Haldane, L. C., and Lord Moulton in Vacher *v.* London Society of Compositors, [1913] A. C. 107, 113, 128. For the rules of construction applicable to a codifying statute, see per Lord Herschell, in Bank of England *v.* Vagliano, [1891] A. C. 107, 144.

(*b*) Mar. Ins. Act, 1906, s. 93.

Sect. 1.

Mixed sea and land risks.

in manner and to the extent thereby agreed, agai marine losses, that is to say, the losses incident marine adventure (*c*).

Section 2.—(1) A contract of marine insurance m by its express terms, or by usage of trade, be extend so as to protect the assured against losses on inla waters or on any land risk which may be incidental any sea voyage (*d*).

(2) Where a ship in course of building, or the laur of a ship, or any adventure analogous to a marine adve ture, is covered by a policy in the form of a marine poli the provisions of this Act, in so far as applicable, sh apply thereto (*e*); but, except as by this section provide nothing in this Act shall alter or affect any rule of l applicable to any contract of insurance other than contract of marine insurance as by this Act defined.

Marine adventure and maritime perils defined.

Section 3.—(1) Subject to the provisions of this A every lawful marine adventure may be the subject o contract of marine insurance (*f*).

(2) In particular there is a marine adventure wher
  (a) Any ship goods or other moveables are expo to maritime perils. Such property is in t Act referred to as "insurable property";
  (b) The earning or acquisition of any freig passage money, commission, profit, or ot pecuniary benefit, or the security for advances, loan, or disbursements, is end gered by the exposure of insurable prope to maritime perils;

(*c*) In the seventh edition of this work Marine Insurance was defined as "a contract whereby one party, for an agreed consideration, undertakes to indemnify the other against loss arising from certain perils or sea-risks, to which his ship, merchandise, or other interest in a maritime adventure, may be exposed during a certain voyage, or a certain period of time."

(*d*) See *post*, §§ 447, 457, 460, 470, 507.

(*e*) The stamping of a policy on ship under construction or repair, or on trial, is regulated by Revenue Act, 1903, s. 8.

(*f*) It is said that sect. 3 is tended to express the principle the insurance is effected in res of the pecuniary interest of assured in a marine adventure. Chalmers & Owen, Mar. Ins. 2nd ed. p. 6. For the distinc between the *subject-matter insu* and the *subject of a contrac Marine Insurance*, see *ibid.*, per Brett, L. J., in Rayne Preston (1881), 18 Ch. D. 1, 7. to the effect of illegality, see Part II. Chap. V.

(c) Any liability to a third party may be incurred by the owner of, or other person interested in or responsible for, insurable property, by reason of maritime perils.

"Maritime perils" means the perils consequent on, or incidental to, the navigation of the sea, that is to say, perils of the seas, fire, war perils, pirates, rovers, thieves, captures, seisures, restraints, and detainments of princes and peoples, jettisons, barratry, and any other perils, either of the like kind or which may be designated by the policy (*g*).

2. The party indemnified, called the *assured* in the Act, is sometimes also called the *insured*.

The property or thing insured itself is called in the Act the *subject-matter insured* (*h*). In this work it has hitherto been called the *subject of insurance*.

The title or interest which the assured has in the subject-matter insured is called his *insurable interest*.

The party undertaking to indemnify the assured against loss, called the *insurer* in the Act, is also generally called the *underwriter*.

The consideration for which he so undertakes to indemnify the assured is called the *premium* (*i*).

The instrument by which the contract of indemnity is effected is called in England the *policy*.

That which is insured against is, as appears in sect. 3 (2), loss arising from maritime perils or casualties.

These casualties are in technical language called, some-

(*g*) See *post*, Part III. Chap. II., "Losses by the Perils insured against."

(*h*) See s. 6 (1), *post*, § 254, and of. s. 3 (1), *supra*, in which a marine adventure is said to be the "subject of a contract of marine insurance."

(*i*) The word *premium* is used in the Act and in general language only to denote the stipulated sum of money which the assured usually pays to the underwriter. Lord Esher pointed out that the word might be used in a wider sense, to cover the consideration (whatever it may be) which moves from the assured to the insurer. In this sense the premium which a member of a mutual insurance association pays is his liability to contribute to the losses of other members. See Lion Insurance Association v. Tucker (1883), 12 Q. B. D. 176, 187. The term is not used in this sense in the Act. See s. 85 (2).

sect. 2. times, *the perils insured against* and sometimes the *risks covered by the policy,* expressions which mean one and the same thing, and are employed to signify those causes of loss against the effect of which the underwriter undertakes by his contract to indemnify the assured.

The interest of the assured is technically said to be *covered by the policy,* when the sum or aggregate of sums insured in the policy is sufficient to afford him full compensation for whatever loss that interest may sustain.

If the value of his interest exceeds the sum insured, the excess of interest is said to be "*uncovered by the policy,*" and the assured to be "*his own insurer in respect of the uninsured balance*" (k).

When the liability of the underwriter commences under the contract, the technical mode of expressing this is by saying that "*the policy attaches,*" or "*the risk begins to run,*" or "*the risk attaches*" (l) from that time.

ure of the mnity rded by ine rance.

3. The very essence of the contract of Marine Insurance is that it is a contract of INDEMNITY (m); its sole and exclusive object is to procure for the assured indemnity, in the strictest

(k) See Mar. Ins. Act, 1906, s. 81, *post,* § 1215.

(l) This is the term used in the Act. See ss. 43, 44, and Schedule I., rr. 1—4.

(m) This principle may, however, be violated by means of a valued policy, the valuation of the subject of insurance therein being in general conclusive against both parties. Therefore it has been said that "a policy of insurance is not a perfect contract of indemnity. It must be taken with this qualification, that the parties may agree beforehand in estimating the value of the subject assured, by way of liquidated damages, as, indeed, they may in any other contract to indemnify." Opinion of the Judges in Irving v. Manning (1847), 1 H. L. C. 287, 307; see also McArthur, Marine Ins. p. 68, where it is shown that in open policies on ship, in consequence of the recognized method of computing the value after a loss, the assured recovers more than his real loss when the freight is also insured. Under policies on freight, again, the assured may recover more than an indemnity, as in case of a loss he is entitled to be paid the gross freight, *i.e.,* without any deduction in respect of the expenses which would have been incurred after the loss to earn the freight. On the other hand, in respect of cargo generally, he recovers less than his loss under an open policy. See *post,* Part I. Chap. XIII. "Valuation."

CHAP. I.] MARINE INSURANCE GENERALLY. 5

sense of that word, for any losses he may sustain through the agency of those sea-risks against the effect of which the underwriter by the terms of his policy stands pledged to protect him. To prevent the assured from suffering loss by means of any of the perils insured against is the single aim of a contract of Marine Insurance, and its whole spirit would be violated if he could make the occurrence of any such casualties a means of gain, for this would be to give him an interest in procuring sea-losses, which would be opposed to every principle of commercial policy (*n*). Hence an interest in the subject-matter insured is of the very essence of the right to recover upon the contract (*o*). In the absence of such an interest the plaintiff is not damnified, although there may have been a total loss of the thing insured.

Sect. 3.

4. Indemnity, then, being the sole object of the contract of Marine Insurance, it becomes important to inquire into the nature and extent of the indemnity it professes to afford.

Nature and extent of the indemnity.

In France and some other foreign countries the contract used to be rigorously confined to an indemnity against such losses only as might be caused by the perils of the sea to some property of which the assured was actually in possession at the time of the loss; it was not allowed to extend to an indemnity against the loss of that gain or profit which the same perils prevented him from realising (*p*).

In France.

In this country, however, and in the United States, a more liberal policy has always prevailed, and the contract of Marine Insurance was always considered applicable to protect men, not only against such events as may occasion the deprivation of that which they may actually possess, but against those also which would intercept from them the

In this country and in the United States.

(*n*) Assecuratus non quærit lucrum sed agit ne in damno sit. Straccha de Assecurationibus, gl. 20, No. 4.

(*o*) Lucena *v.* Craufurd (1806), 2 B. & P. N. R. 269.

(*p*) By a law of the 12th August, 1885, Articles 334 and 347 of the French Code de Commerce were amended, and now insurances may be effected on profits. The prohibition of insurances on freight was at the same time removed. See the present Article 334 of the Code.

Sect. 4. advantage or profit which, but for such events, they would acquire in the ordinary and probable course of things (*q*).

Hence in this country, as we shall see more at large hereafter, the loss arising from the interception, by the perils insured against, of future freight and expected profit is quite as legitimate an object of that indemnity which Marine Insurance can afford as the damage actually inflicted by the same perils upon ships or merchandise.

Interest exposed to risk indispensable to every contract of marine insurance.

5. Not only, as we have already seen, must the assured have an interest in the subject-matter insured, but it is an indispensable requisite of every contract of Marine Insurance, properly so called, that the subject-matter insured should be exposed to the risk of loss from the perils insured against, upon the voyage or during the period over which the indemnity is by the terms of the contract made to extend (*r*). This is the most fundamental principle in the whole law of Marine Insurance. *Principale fundamentum assecurationis est risicum seu interesse assecuratorum; sine quo non potest subsistere assecuratio* (*s*).

The contract of Marine Insurance, in short, is nothing but a contract of indemnity against the risk of loss by sea perils, and the premium is nothing but the price paid for this indemnity; it is obvious, therefore, that if the assured is not really interested in something which he runs the risk of losing by the perils of the sea, there is no consideration for the sum he has paid: and as the foreign jurists express it, no matter on which the contract can work, for its very constituent element is the possibility of loss from marine casualties (*t*). With

---

(*q*) Per Lawrence, J., in Lucena *v.* Craufurd (1806), 2 B. & P. N. R. 301.

(*r*) 1 Emerigon, c. i. s. 1, p. 6; 1 Benecke, System des Assecuranz, c. i. p. 23.

(*s*) Casaregis, Disc. 4, No. 1, cited by Emerigon, *ubi supra*.

(*t*) Si non adest risicum assecuratio non valet, nam non adest materia in quâ forma potest fundari. Roccus, No. 88. En un mot, la perte ou le dommage considerés dans l'incertitude des évènemens sont la matière de ce contrat. 1 Emerigon, c. i. e. 1, p. 6.

CHAP. I.] MARINE INSURANCE GENERALLY. 7

the commencement of exposure to the risk of loss by the perils insured against the policy or risk is said to *attach;* and any loss that occurs earlier, let the cause be what it may, is uncovered. Therefore, if the subject-matter insured be totally lost before the policy has attached, the underwriter pays nothing; but he must return the premium received, because there has been a complete failure of consideration for what was otherwise a valid and binding contract.

Sect. 5.

6. Thus it appears that two things are mainly essential to every contract of Marine Insurance:—
  1. An interest in the subject-matter insured.
  2. Exposure of that interest to risk of loss or detriment by sea perils.

Distinction between contracts of marine insurance and wagers.

It is the necessity for these requisites which entirely distinguishes contracts of Marine Insurance, properly so called, from mere wagers upon the issue of maritime adventures.

Such maritime wagers, although framed externally as policies of sea-assurance, and therefore called wager policies, were, as we shall see more at large hereafter, prohibited in this country nearly two centuries ago by a solemn act of the legislature, and in most other maritime states are either expressly forbidden or practically disused: and this on the ground that it is plainly opposed to the true interests of a mercantile state to enable those who have no real stake in the safety of a maritime adventure to give themselves (by means of such a contract) a great interest in its loss or destruction.

CHAPTER II.

FORM AND CONTENTS OF SEA-POLICIES.

SECT.	SECT.
What Insurances must be made by a Policy ....7—8	Conditions implied in the Policy 30
Different kinds of Policies 9	The Stamping of Policies ...31—33
Form of Lloyd's Policy 10	The Slip ....34—39
Clauses and formal Requisites of the Policy ....11—28	Corrections and Alterations in the Policy ....40—51
Express Warranties and occasional Clauses 29	Forfeiture, Renewal and Rescission of the Policy ....52—54

What is a policy.

7. THE instrument in which the contract of sea-insurance is generally embodied is called a policy of insurance (*a*). In the Marine Insurance Act, 1906, it is called a marine policy (*b*).

What insurances must be made by a policy.

In the interest of the revenue various Stamp Acts have made the use of stamped policies compulsory (*c*). The Stamp Act, 1891, which repealed all the enactments then in force relating to the stamping of policies, provides that a contract for sea-insurance (other than such insurance as is referred to in the 55th section of the Merchant Shipping Act Amendment Act, 1862 (25 & 26 Vict. c. 63), for which the corresponding section 506 of the Merchant Shipping Act, 1894, must now be substituted (*d*)) shall not be valid unless it is expressed in a policy of sea-insurance (*e*).

A policy of insurance is defined in the Stamp Act as

(*a*) From the Italian *polizza d'asseourazione*.

(*b*) See Mar. Ins. Act, 1906, s. 22, *infra*, § 8.

(*o*) 35 Geo. 3, c. 63; 54 Geo. 3, c. 144; 30 Vict. o. 23.

(*d*) See *infra*, note (*j*).

(*e*) 54 & 55 Vict. c. 39, s. 93 (1), re-enacting in substance the provision of 30 Vict. c. 23, s. 7, as to the stamping of the policy: see *post*, §§ 31—33. As to admitting an alleged copy of a policy when the execution of a policy is itself in issue, see Stowe *v.* Querner, (1870), L. R. 5 Ex. 155.

CHAP. II.] FORM AND CONTENTS OF SEA-POLICIES. 9

including "every writing whereby any contract of insurance is made or agreed to be made, or is evidenced" (*f*).

Sect. 7.

For the purposes of the Stamp Act, the expression "policy of sea-insurance" (*g*) means "any insurance (including re-insurance) made upon any ship or vessel, or upon the machinery, tackle, or furniture of any ship or vessel, or upon any goods, merchandise, or property of any description whatever on board of any ship or vessel, or upon the freight of, or any other interest which may be lawfully insured in or relating to, any ship or vessel, and includes any insurance of goods, merchandise, or property for any transit which includes not only a sea-risk, but also any other risk incidental to the transit insured from the commencement of the transit to the ultimate destination covered by the insurance" (*h*).

Further, by the Stamp Act, "a contract for sea-insurance" includes any agreement whereby "any person, in consideration of any sum of money paid or to be paid for additional freight or otherwise, takes upon himself any risk attending goods, merchandise, or property of any description whatever, while on board of any ship or vessel, or engages to indemnify the owner of any such goods, merchandise, or property from any risk, loss, or damage" (*i*).

The insurances referred to in the 55th section of the Merchant Shipping Act Amendment Act, 1862, and the 506th section of the Merchant Shipping Act, 1894 (*j*), which therefore do not require a policy, are insurances by owners of ships against claims for (1) loss of life or personal injury caused to any persons carried in such ships, (2) damage or loss

---

(*f*) 54 & 55 Vict. c. 39, s. 91. Cf. 30 Vict. c. 23, s. 4; and see Home Mar. Ins. Co. *v.* Smith, [1898] 2 Q. B. 351.

(*g*) "Policy of sea insurance" seems in this definition to be used in the sense of "contract for sea insurance."

(*h*) 54 & 55 Vict. c. 39, s. 92 (1).
(*i*) *Ibid.* s. 92 (2).

(*j*) The former Act is repealed by the Merchant Shipping Act, 1894. S. 54, which is referred to in s. 55, is in substance re-enacted in s. 503 of the later Act. By s. 38 (1) of the Interpretation Act, 1889, the references to the sections of the repealed Act must be construed as references to the corresponding sections of the Merchant Shipping Act, 1894.

Sect. 7. caused to any goods, merchandise, or other things whatsoever on board such ships, (3) loss of life or personal injuries caused by the improper navigation of such ships to persons carried in other ships or boats, (4) loss or damage caused by the improper navigation of such ships to any goods, merchandise, or other things whatsoever on board other ships and boats.

Statutory requisites of a policy.
8. Subject to the provisions of sect. 11 of the Finance Act, 1901 (*k*), no policy of sea-insurance made for time may be made for any time exceeding twelve months (*l*).

A policy of sea-insurance is not valid unless it specifies the particular risk or adventure (*m*), the names of the subscribers or underwriters, and the sum or sums insured (*n*).

By a document called an "open cover" an underwriter agreed to re-insure an insurance company to the extent of the excess, over certain amounts mentioned in the document, of the risks to be undertaken by the company from time to time, on goods shipped by certain steamship lines. The limit of the excess on any one ship was specified. The Court of Appeal held that the document was a contract for sea-insurance within sect. 93 (1) of the Stamp Act, 1891, and that it did not specify the sum insured, and was therefore invalid as a policy (*o*).

Sect. 91 of the Marine Insurance Act, 1906, declares that nothing therein "shall affect the provisions of the Stamp Act, 1891, or any enactment for the time being in force relating to the revenue." The Marine Insurance Act, however, also contains provisions relating to the particulars which a policy must contain, which overlap those of the Stamp

---

(*k*) See *infra*, § 31.

(*l*) Stamp Act, 1891, s. 93 (2), (3). Similarly s. 25 (2) of the Mar. Ins. Act, 1906, declares that subject to these provisions "a time policy which is made for any time exceeding twelve months is invalid."

(*m*) See Edwards *v.* Aberayron Mutual Ship Ins. Society (1875), 1 Q. B. D. 563.

(*n*) Stamp Act, 1891, s. 93 (3). In re The Arthur Average Association (1875), L. R. 10 Ch. 542, on the similar provision in 30 Vict. c. 23, s. 7; Home Mar. Ins. Co. *v.* Smith, [1898] 2 Q. B. 351.

(*o*) *Ibid.*

Act hereinbefore mentioned (*p*). Sect. 22 of the Marine Insurance Act declares that "subject to the provisions of any statute, a contract of marine insurance is inadmissible in evidence unless it is embodied in a marine policy in accordance with this Act." By sect. 23 "a marine policy must specify (1) the name of the assured, or of some person who effects the insurance on his behalf; (2) the subject-matter insured and the risk insured against; (3) the voyage, or period of time, or both, as the case may be, covered by the insurance; (4) the sum or sums insured; (5) the name or names of the subscribers"; and sect. 24 (1) declares that "a marine policy must be signed by or on behalf of the insurer."

9. We will now advert briefly to the division frequently made of policies into interest and wager, valued and unvalued or open, named and floating, time and voyage policies.

An *interest policy* is one which shows by its form that the assured has a real, substantial interest in the thing insured: in other words, that the contract embodied by the policy is a contract of indemnity, and not a wager. All the common forms of policy are adapted to transactions of this nature; and every policy is taken to be an interest policy, unless the contrary is clearly expressed on the face of it (*q*).

A *wager policy* (sometimes called an *honour policy*) is one which contains words implying that the contract it embodies is not really an insurance, but a wager; *i.e.*, a pretended insurance, founded on a fictitious risk, where the assured has no interest in any thing insured, and can, therefore, sustain no loss by the happening of any of the casualties against which the supposed insurance professes to protect him (*r*).

A wager policy is generally known by having one or other

Sect. 8.

Classifications of policies.

Interest and wager policies.

Definition of a wager policy.

Form of a wager policy.

(*p*) § 7, *supra*.
(*q*) See Cousins *v.* Nantes (1811), 3 Taunt. 513.
(*r*) Though such a policy is termed a wager policy, it may in fact be made in order to protect an insurable interest. On the other hand a policy in form an interest policy may not be intended to protect a real interest, and may be void for want of insurable interest. See *post*, § 311.

Sect. 9. of the following clauses written on the face of it:—"interest or no interest"; or, "without further proof of interest than the policy"; or, "policy to be deemed sufficient proof of interest" (*s*); or, "without benefit of salvage to the insurer," or some analogous clause, showing that the assured means to give no proof of his having any interest whatever in the subject insured, except the mere production of the policy itself; and thereby bringing him directly within the scope of sect. 4 of the Marine Insurance Act, 1906, which prohibits all such policies, as gaming policies, except in one specified case (*t*).

Definition of a valued,

A *valued policy* is defined in sect. 27 (2) of the Marine Insurance Act, 1906, as "a policy which specifies the agreed value of the subject-matter insured."

and of an unvalued or open policy.

An *unvalued policy* is defined in sect. 28 as "a policy which does not specify the value of the subject-matter insured, but, subject to the limit of the sum insured, leaves the insurable value to be subsequently ascertained, in the manner" specified in the Act (*u*).

Hitherto the policy called an unvalued policy in the Act has usually been called an *open policy*. The reason why the former name has been adopted in the Act is that the term *open policy* is sometimes used in mercantile language to denote a floating policy (*x*) which has not been exhausted by declarations (*y*).

The chief practical difference between valued and unvalued policies in case of loss is that in the former the value is fixed

---

(*s*) Murphy *v.* Bell (1828), 4 Bing. 567. The clause which makes the policy itself proof of interest is commonly called the "p. p. i." clause.

(*t*) See *post*, § 313.

(*u*) The following were the definitions in the previous editions of this work:—A *valued policy* is one in which the agreed value of the subject insured, as between the assured and underwriter, for the purposes of the insurance, is expressed on the face of the policy. An *open policy* is one in which the value of the subject insured is not thus fixed or agreed in the policy, as between the assured and the underwriter, but is left to be estimated in case of loss.

(*x*) See *infra*.

(*y*) Chalmers & Owen, Mar. Ins. Act, 2nd ed. p. 45.

by the policy; in the latter it must be proved by the production of tradesman's bills, invoices, bills of shipping charges, surveyor's estimates, and other necessary vouchers.

Sect. 9.

As the value of ship and freight is more difficult to prove in this way than the value of goods, the former interests are generally insured in valued, the latter frequently in open policies.

Voyage and *time policies* are defined in sect. 25 (1) of the Marine Insurance Act, 1906, in the following terms:— "Where the contract is to insure the subject-matter at and from, or from one place to another or others, the policy is called a 'voyage policy,' and where the contract is to insure the subject-matter for a definite period of time the policy is called a 'time policy.'"

Voyage and time policies.

An instance of a voyage policy is where a ship is insured "at and from London to Buenos Ayres." The place at which the voyage is to begin is called the *terminus a quo*, and that at which it is to end is called the *terminus ad quem*.

An example of a time policy is an insurance on a ship "from the first day of January, 1914, to the 30th day of June, 1914, inclusive."

Sect. 25 of the Marine Insurance Act, 1906, declares that "a contract for both voyage and time may be included in the same policy." An insurance on a ship for a voyage to a named terminus and for thirty days after arrival is a contract of this kind.

Policies are also occasionally effected which, in form, partake of the nature both of time and voyage policies; as where a ship is insured "from London to Buenos Ayres for six months"; or, "from the first of January, 1914, to the 1st of July, in the same year, on the ship at and from London to Buenos Ayres"; or, "for twelve months from the date of sailing from Leith."

Policies which in form are both time and voyage policies.

These policies, however, as we shall see more at large hereafter, are effectively time policies, the risk commencing and expiring with the limits of time specified therein.

A *named policy* is one in which the adventure is limited

Named and

Sect. 9.
floating policies.

to a ship specifically named therein, as where goods by the ship *Emma* are insured from Hamburg to London.

A *floating policy* was defined in this work as one in which there is no limitation of the risk to a particular ship, as where goods " on ship or ships " are insured for the same voyage. In sect. 29 (1) of the Marine Insurance Act, 1906, it is more broadly defined as " a policy which describes the insurance in general terms, and leaves either the name of the ship or ships or other particulars to be defined by subsequent declaration."

Our common form of sea-policy.

10. The Forms of Policy employed in different mercantile communities are exceedingly various; the merchants and underwriters of our own country have adhered with persevering tenacity to the old and hardly intelligible form which was introduced at an early period into England (*z*); and although this has always been regarded by our Courts of Law as an absurd and incoherent instrument (*a*), yet length of time and a variety of decisions have now given it such a degree of certainty that it is likely now to be retained among the chief instruments of English commerce, especially as it is recognized in the Marine Insurance Act, 1906, as the standard form of policy, and is printed in the First Schedule, with a series of rules for its construction (*b*).

(*z*) It was adopted as a statutory form of policy in 35 Geo. 3, c. 63, and 30 Vict. c. 23, the schedules annexed to which contained this form. These Acts provided for the issue of printed forms of this policy in blank, duly stamped, by the Commissioners of Stamps and the Commissioners of Inland Revenue respectively. There is no such provision in the Stamp Act, 1891.

(*a*) Per Buller, J., 4 T. R. 210.

" It is wonderful that policies should be drawn with so much laxity ": Lawrence, J., in Marsden *v.* Reid (1803), 3 East, 579. " This policy of insurance is a very strange instrument, as we all know and feel ": per Mansfield, C. J., in Le Cheminant *v.* Pearson (1812), 4 Taunt. 380, &c.

(*b*) See Mar. Ins. Act, 1906, s. 30, sub-s. 1.

OF SEA-POLICIES.

The following is the form of this policy:—

S. G. (c).
£ ―――――
[Stamp.]

Sect. 10.

Common printed form of the policy in blank.

BE IT KNOWN THAT (1) [   ] as well in [   ] own name as for and in the name and names of all and every other person or persons, to whom the same doth, may or shall appertain, in part or in all, doth make assurance, and cause (2) [   ] and them and every of them to be insured, (3) lost or not lost, at and from (4) [   ] (5) upon any kind of goods and merchandises, and also upon the body, tackle, apparel, ordnance, munition, artillery, boat and other furniture, of and in the good ship or vessel, (6) called the [   ]; whereof is master, under God, for the present voyage (6) [   ], or whosoever else shall go for master in the said ship, or by whatsoever other name or names the same ship or the master thereof is or shall be named and called.

(1) & (2) Blanks for the name or names of the party for whom or by whom the policy is effected.

(3) Clause "lost or not lost."
(4) Blank for the description of the voyage insured.
(5) Clause specifying the subject insured.
(6) Blanks for the name of ship and master.

(7) BEGINNING the adventure upon the said goods and merchandises from the loading thereof aboard the said ship [   ]; upon the said ship, &c. [   ], and so shall continue and endure, during her abode there, on the said ship, &c.; and further, until the said ship, with all her ordnance, tackle, apparel, &c., and goods and merchandises whatsoever, shall be arrived at [   ]; upon the said ship, &c., until she hath moored at anchor twenty-four hours in good safety, and upon the goods and merchandises, until the same be there discharged and safely landed.

(7) Description of the commencement, continuance, and termination of the risk.

(8) AND it shall be lawful for the said ship, &c., in this voyage, to proceed and sail to and touch and stay at any ports or places whatsoever, [   ] without prejudice to this insurance.

(8) Liberty to touch and stay.

(9) THE said ship, &c., goods and merchandises, &c., for so much as concerns the assured, by agreement

(9) Valuation clause, and blank for inserting value.

(c) For the suggested meanings of these letters, see Gow, p. 30.

Sect. 10. between the assured and assurers in this policy, are and shall be valued at [

].

(10) TOUCHING the adventures and perils which we, the assurers, are contented to bear and do take upon us in this voyage, they are of the seas, men-of-war, fire, enemies, pirates, rovers, thieves, jettisons, letters of mart and counter-mart, surprisals, takings at sea, arrests, restraints, and detainments of all kings, princes and people, of what nation, condition, or quality soever, barratry of the master and mariners, and of all other perils, losses and misfortunes that have or shall come to the hurt, detriment, or damage of the said goods and merchandises, and ship, &c., or any part thereof. *(10) Clause enumerating the perils insured against.*

(11) AND in case of any loss or misfortune, it shall be lawful to the assured, their factors, servants and assigns, to sue, labour, and travel for, in and about the defence, safeguard, and recovery of the said goods and merchandises, and ship, &c., or any part thereof, without prejudice to this insurance; to the charges whereof we, the assurers, will contribute, each one according to the rate and quantity of his sum herein assured. *(11) Sue and labour clauses.*

(12) AND it is especially declared and agreed that no acts of the insurer or insured, in recovering, saving, or preserving the property insured, shall be considered as a waiver or acceptance of abandonment (*d*). *(12) Waiver clause.*

(13) AND it is agreed by us, the insurers, that this writing, or policy of assurance, shall be of as much force and effect as the surest writing or policy of assurance heretofore made in Lombard Street or in the Royal Exchange, or elsewhere in London. *(13) Clause as to the binding effect of the policy.*

(14) AND so we the assurers are contented and do promise and bind ourselves, each one for his own part, our heirs, executors and goods, to the assured, their executors, administrators, and assigns, for the true performance of the premises. *(14) Promise of the underwriters to indemnify.*

(15) CONFESSING ourselves paid the consideration due unto us for this assurance by the assured, at and after the rate of (16) [

]. *(15) Acknowledgment of receipt of premium.*
(16) Blank for inserting rate of premium.

(*d*) The waiver clause is not found in the policies set out in the former Stamp Acts.

(17) IN witness whereof we, the assurers, have subscribed our names and sums insured in London. *(17) Attestation clause.*

(18) N.B. Corn, fish, salt, fruit, flour, and seed are warranted free from average, unless general, or the ship be stranded; sugar, tobacco, hemp, flax, hides and skins are warranted free from average under 5*l.* per cent.; and all other goods, also the ship and freight, are warranted free from average under 3*l.* per cent., unless general, or the ship be stranded. *(18) Common memorandum.*

(19) [*(19) Blank space in which is to be inserted the subscription of each underwriter, the sum he insures, and the date of his subscription.*

£ (*sum in figures*) A. B. (*sum in words*)   day of
£ (*ditto*   ) C. D. (*ditto*   )   day of
£ (*ditto*   ) E. F. (*ditto*   )   day of

(*and so on, until the aggregate amount of the different sums subscribed by each underwriter equals the amount required to be insured*).

This form of policy is known as Lloyd's policy. It has been in use not only among the underwriters at Lloyd's, but also very generally among private underwriters throughout the United Kingdom, and has been in substance adopted by the companies. Strictly speaking, however, the term "Lloyd's policy" denotes a policy with the device of an anchor in the margin, encircled by the words: "For signature by the underwriting members of Lloyd's only." Any person who without the authority of the society, or without lawful excuse, imitates the stamp or mark used to denote a Lloyd's policy, or utters or uses a policy with such stamp or mark, is liable to a penalty under Lloyd's Act, 1871 (34 Vict. c. xxi). The peculiar value of such a policy lies in the fact that great care is exercised in the election of members of the society, and that each member is required on election to deposit securities of the value of at least 5,000*l.* to cover his engagements on marine and transport risks. *Lloyd's policy.*

"Anchor Policy."

In 1898, owing to a feeling that war risks should not be covered by any ordinary insurance, the policy in use at Lloyd's was by a resolution of the members modified by the insertion of the following clause between the clauses num-

Sect. 10. bered (13) and (14) above: "Warranted nevertheless free of capture, seizure and detention, and the consequences thereof, or of any attempt thereat, piracy excepted, and also from all consequences of hostilities or warlike operations, whether before or after declaration of war." At the beginning of 1899, however, this resolution was superseded by another resolution which declared that all policies at Lloyd's should contain this warranty against (or, to use a more correct expression, this exception of) war risks, unless the contrary be written or printed in the slip or the agreement previously signed or initialed by the underwriters (*e*). Since then, the Committee of Lloyd's have supplied policies either with or without this "free of capture" clause.

Additional clauses. Other clauses are usually inserted in policies so as to meet the circumstances of the adventure insured. In insurances on ships and freight the general practice now is to incorporate in voyage and time policies respectively a number of printed clauses, called the "Institute Voyage Clauses" and the "Institute Time Clauses." There are also Institute Clauses for port risks and builders' risks, and Institute Cargo Clauses (*f*). The Institute Clauses are revised from time to time. The most important of these clauses in policies on ships is the clause known as the *collision* or *running-down clause*, which was originally introduced in consequence of the decision in *De Vaux* v. *Salvador* (*g*), and has been expanded to meet the requirements of underwriters and assured (*h*).

(*e*) In Yuill *v.* Scott Robson, [1907] 1 K. B. 685, Channell, J., said that as between brokers and underwriters a policy "against all risks" would nevertheless contain this "free of capture" clause. See, further, as to insurances against all risks, § 156.

(*f*) For specimens, see App. B. For the effect of the incorporation of Institute clauses, "as far as they apply," see Otago Farmers' Co-operative Assn. *v.* Thompson, [1910] 2 K. B. 145.

(*g*) (1836), 4 A. & E. 420.

(*h*) For older forms of the collision clause, and their effect, see Thompson *v.* Reynolds (1857), 7 E. & B. 172; Taylor *v.* Dewar (1864), 5 B. & S. 58; Xenos *v.* Fox (1868), L. R. 3 C. P. 630.

The following is the collision clause in the Institute clauses for 1914 (*i*):—   Sect. 10.

> And it is further agreed that if the ship hereby insured shall come into collision with any other ship or vessel, and the assured shall in consequence thereof become liable to pay, and shall pay by way of damages to any other person or persons any sum or sums not exceeding in respect of any one such collision the value of the ship hereby insured, we, the assurers will pay the assured such proportion of three-fourths of such sum or sums so paid as our respective subscriptions hereto bear to the value of the ship hereby insured, and in cases in which the liability of the ship has been contested, or proceedings have been taken to limit liability, with the consent in writing of two-thirds of the subscribers to this policy *in amount*, we will also pay a like proportion of three-fourths of the costs which the assured shall thereby incur, or be compelled to pay; but when both vessels are to blame, then unless the liability of the owners of one or both of such vessels becomes limited by law, claims under this clause shall be settled on the principle of cross-liabilities as if the owners of each vessel had been compelled to pay to the owners of the other of such vessels such one-half or other proportion of the latter's damages as may have been properly allowed in ascertaining the balance or sum payable by or to the assured in consequence of such collision (*k*).
>
> Provided always that this clause shall in no case extend to any sum which the assured may become liable to pay, or shall pay for removal of obstructions under statutory powers (*l*), for injury to harbours, wharves, piers, stages, and similar structures, consequent on such collision; or in respect of the cargo or engagements of the insured vessel, or for loss of life or personal injury.

(*i*) This form of the clause is used with Lloyd's policies. For the slightly different form used with a company's policy, see Vol. II. App. B.

(*k*) The stipulation as to the cost of proceedings was inserted in consequence of Xenos *v.* Fox, *supra*.

The present rule as to cross-liabilities was introduced in consequence of the decision in London SS. Ins. Co. *v.* Grampian SS. Co. (1889), 24 Q. B. D. 663.

(*l*) As to removal of obstructions, see Tatham *v.* Burr, [1898] A. C. 382.

Sect. 10.
Club policies.

Lloyd's policy is not altogether adapted to insurances by mutual insurance associations (or clubs, as they are commonly called), whose policies are by no means identical in conditions or wording. The present tendency of the associations is, however, to use policies which as to many of their clauses are the same as Lloyd's policy. A specimen of a "club" policy will be found in the Appendix.

Of the usual clauses and formal requisites of the policy.

11. We will now consider in their order the common clauses which a Lloyd's policy usually comprises, and the main requisites which are essential to the validity of a policy as a contract under our law.

The name of the assured or his agent.

A policy without the names of the parties by or for whom it is effected is called a policy in blank, and is either prohibited by the laws, or rejected by the practice, of all mercantile states.

28 Geo. 3, c. 56.

In our own country the law used to require that no policy should be effected without first inserting therein "the name or names, or the usual style and firm of dealing," either—(1) Of one or more of the persons interested; or, (2) of the consignors or consignees of the property to be insured; or, (3) of the persons resident in Great Britain who received the order for and effected the policy; or, (4) of the persons who gave the order to the agent immediately employed to effect it (*m*).

Under the liberal construction put by the Courts of Law on this Act of Parliament, it was reduced to a mere prohibition against policies in blank; and the Marine Insurance Act, 1906, sect. 92 of which repealed it, simply provides in sect. 23 that "a marine policy must specify the name of the assured, or of some person who effects the insurance on his behalf."

In practice the name usually inserted in the policy is that of the insurance broker, who insures either in his own name

(*m*) 28 Geo. 3, c. 56.

and on his own account (*n*), or in his own name and on account of his principals (*o*).

In the first case the blanks marked numbers (1) and (2) in the printed form are filled up thus:—

"A. B. & Co. (style of the insurance broker's firm), as well in their own names, as for and in the name and names of all and every other persons to whom the same doth, may or shall appertain, in part or in all, do make assurance and cause themselves and them and every of them to be insured," &c.

In the second case the blanks are filled up thus:—

"A. B. & Co., as well in their own names, as for and in the name and names of all and every other persons to whom the same doth, may or shall appertain, in whole or in part, do make assurance and cause C. D. & Co. (name or firm of their employers, the parties interested), and them and every of them, to be insured," &c.

If the party interested effects the policy, without the intervention of a broker, he of course expresses himself to have so effected it in his own name and on his own account, as in the first form, merely substituting the name or style of the principal for that of the broker.

Such are the usual modes in which these blanks are filled up in English policies; in practice, some slight variation of form occasionally occurs; sometimes, for instance, it is stated on the face of the policy that the party effecting it does so " as agent for," or " at the request of " the principal; but these variations are immaterial.

The party who has thus effected the policy on account of a principal is called "the nominal assured"; the principal himself, for whom it is effected, is called "the party interested," or "the assured."

(*n*) When he insures in this way he is not bound to disclose the name of the real assured: Glasgow Ass. Corpn. *v.* Symondson (1911), 16 Com. Cas. 109.

(*o*) The practice of effecting the policy in the name of the agent is a very old one. See an allegation of custom in Ridolpho *v.* Nunez (1562), Selden Society Publications, vol. ii. p. 52.

Sect. 12.
Assignment clause.

12. "*For and in the names of all persons to whom the same doth, may, or shall appertain, in part or in all.*"

The insertion of this clause, which is invariably introduced into all our common printed forms of policy, is of great importance, as without it no one could take advantage of the policy except the party expressly named in it, or his principal (*p*); but by the aid of this clause, as we shall have occasion to see more at large hereafter, any party may avail himself of the policy who can prove that he was interested in the subject-matter of the insurance during the risk and at the time of loss, and is the person upon whose account the insurance was *bonâ fide* intended to be made (*q*). The clause also made it possible to assign the benefit of the policy, but for this purpose is now unnecessary, as sect. 50 (1) of the Marine Insurance Act, 1906, declares that "a marine policy is assignable unless it contains terms expressly prohibiting assignment," and "may be assigned either before or after loss." An assignee of the policy may by sect. 50 (2) sue in his own name (*r*).

"Lost or not lost" clause.

13. As policies are frequently effected on ships and goods believed to be in foreign ports, or at sea, it being then uncertain whether they may not actually have been lost before the policy was effected, these words, "lost or not lost," are inserted in every form of policy as a matter of course. Their effect is thus stated in Rule 1 of the Rules for the construction of the policy (*s*):—"Where the subject-matter is insured 'lost or not lost,' and the loss has occurred before the contract is concluded, the risk attaches unless, at such time, the assured was aware of the loss, and the insurer was not."

It has been decided that a policy containing this clause

(*p*) Browning *v.* Provincial Ins. Co. of Canada (1873), L. R. 5 P. C. 263.

(*q*) See *infra*, §§ 172, 173.

(*r*) 31 & 32 Vict. c. 86, s. 1 (repealed by the Marine Insurance Act) contained a similar provision. Neither Act requires notice of assignment such as is necessary under the Judicature Act. See *post*, § 176.

(*s*) Mar. Ins. Act, 1906, Sched. I.

CHAP. II.] OF SEA-POLICIES. 23

was good, where the subject of insurance was accepted for insurance, and the premium paid, before loss, although the policy was not executed until after a loss had happened, to the knowledge both of the assured and the underwriter (*t*).

Sect. 13.

If indeed the loss, at the time of effecting the policy, were known to the assured only, then, on the plainest general principles, the policy would be void; but no case has determined that an underwriter, who chooses to effect a policy with full knowledge that the loss has actually happened, may not be bound by it (*u*).

A policy, indeed, containing this clause, is, in the words of Parke, B., "clearly a contract of indemnity against all past as well as all future losses sustained by the assured, in respect of the interest insured" (*x*). Accordingly, where on a policy on goods "lost or not lost" the pleadings raised the question, whether it was any answer to an action on such policy that the plaintiff did not acquire an interest in the goods till after an average loss by sea damage, the Court held that it was not (*y*). Such a contract, they considered, "operated just in the same way as if, the plaintiff having purchased goods at sea, the defendant, for a premium, had agreed that if the goods, at the time of the purchase, had sustained any damage by the perils of the sea, he would make it good" (*z*).

A policy with this clause affords indemnity against past losses.

(*t*) Mead *v.* Davison (1835), 3 A. & E. 303; *S. C.* 4 Nev. & Man. 701. The report in Adolphus & Ellis represents the loss as an *average* one only; that in Nevile & Manning states that, before execution, an *average*, and subsequently a *total*, loss had occurred; the difference does not affect the principle of the decision.

(*u*) Per Lord Denman in 3 A. & E. 308; per Brett, L. J., Bradford *v.* Symondson (1881), 7 Q. B. D. 456, 463.

(*x*) Per Parke, B., delivering the judgment of the Court in Sutherland *v.* Pratt (1843), 11 M. & W. 311, 312.

(*y*) Sutherland *v.* Pratt (1843), 11 M. & W. 296.

(*z*) *Ibid.* p. 312. "This decision," says Judge Duer, "does not embrace the case of a total loss by an actual destruction of the whole or part of the goods that are the subject of the contract of sale. Where such a loss has occurred, the purchaser, in proportion to its extent, is exonerated from his contract, and it is by the seller, not by himself, that the loss must be sustained. As it is not a risk to

Sect. 13.

Effect is given to this decision in sect. 6 (1) of the Marine Insurance Act, 1906, which qualifies the statement that the assured must be interested in the subject-matter insured at the time of the loss, by the proviso that " where the subject-matter is insured 'lost or not lost,' the assured may recover although he may not have acquired his interest until after the loss, unless at the time of effecting the contract of insurance the assured was aware of the loss, and the insurer was not."

Another result of the clause, as stated in sect. 84 (3) (b) of the Marine Insurance Act, 1906, is that " when the subject-matter has been insured 'lost or not lost,' and has arrived in safety at the time when the contract is concluded, the premium is not returnable unless, at such time, the insurer knew of the safe arrival " (*a*).

Whether this clause is necessary.

The provisions of the Marine Insurance Act with regard to the effect of the words " lost or not lost " suggests that the words are necessary in order to make the insurance retrospective. There is, however, no statement in the Act that a policy without the clause is not retrospective. The opinion expressed in the seventh edition of this work, founded on that of the author, was that the clause does not appear to be in all cases strictly necessary, as there can be no reason why a

which he is subject he cannot cover it by an insurance": 2 Duer, 7. These remarks are completely borne out by the observations of Coleridge, J., in delivering the judgment of the Court of Exchequer Chamber in Hastie *v.* Couturier (1853), 9 Exch. 110: " If the goods had been totally lost before the contract of purchase was made, there would not be an insurable interest, as a person cannot buy a thing that is *totally lost*." It appears, nevertheless, to the present editors that although ordinary contracts of sale are conditional on the existence of the subject-matter intended to be sold, yet there is no reason why it should not be expressly provided that the risk of the thing having been already lost at the date of the contract should be borne by the purchaser. In such a case it is conceived that the contract of sale would be a valid one, and that the purchaser would have an insurable interest in the property, even although it had been totally lost prior to the insurance, and would be entitled to recover under a policy "lost or not lost."

(*a*) Bradford *v.* Symondson (1881), 7 Q. B. D. 456 (C. A.), a case of a re-insurance on a ship supposed to be overdue when the policy was effected.

previous loss of the subject-matter insured should prejudice an insurance subsequently effected, if at the time the assured was ignorant of the loss, or he and the underwriter were equally cognizant thereof (*b*). This view agrees with a decision of the Supreme Court of the United States. "It is sufficient," said the Court, "if it appear by the description of the risk and the subject-matter of the contract that the policy was intended to cover a previous loss" (*c*). Accordingly, it is submitted that a policy without the clause may be retrospective, at any rate where it appears clearly from the terms of the policy that this was the intention of the parties; for instance, if a ship were insured "from the 1st of January" by a time policy effected in February. The point does not seem, however, to have any practical importance in this country.

Sect. 13.

14. In the case of a voyage policy the underwriter cannot know the nature of the risk he is asked to insure, nor, consequently, the amount of premium he ought to require, unless he knows the nature of the voyage on which the ship is to sail, or the goods are to be conveyed. It is therefore one of the most essential requisites of a policy of insurance, that it should contain an accurate description of the voyage insured. By this is meant, not that it should describe the whole course of the voyage to be actually taken by the ship; the track which she is to pursue through the waters; the straits she is to pass; the islands which she is to leave on the one side or the other; the capes she is to double; the reefs and shoals she has to avoid:—all this is supposed to be so familiar to

Description of the voyage insured.

(*b*) See 1 Marshall, Ins. 338—340; 1 Phillips, Ins. s. 925; 3 Kent's Comm. 258, n. (*c*); 2 Parsons, Ins. 44; Lord Denman in Mead *v.* Davison, 3 A. & E. 303, 307; per Bramwell, B., Stone *v.* Marine Ins. Co. of Gothenburg (1876), 1 Ex. D. 81, 85; per Cockburn, C. J., in Gledstanes *v.* Royal Exchange Ass. Co. (1864), 34 L. J. Q. B. 30, 35; Story, J., Hammond *v.* Allen (1836), 2 Sumner's R. 397. See an interesting discussion of the "lost or not lost" clause, Gow, 33.

(*c*) Insurance Co. *v.* Folsom (1873), 18 Wallace, 237; *S. C.* Folsom *v.* Mercantile Mutual Ins. Co. (1871), 8 Blatchford, 170; 9 *ibid.* 201.

Sect. 14.

The voyage need only be described by its termini.

the underwriter from his acquaintance with the course of the trade and navigation which the insurance is designed to protect, that it is never expressly inserted in any policy. All that is necessary to be expressed in the policy is the place or period at which the voyage insured is to begin, and the place or period at which it is to end, and which are called in technical language the *terminus a quo* and the *terminus ad quem* of the voyage insured, or of the risk.

These termini must be expressed with great care and distinctness in the policy, and any failure herein will, as we shall see hereafter, have the effect of vitiating that instrument (*d*). We shall here only mention, by way of explaining the language of the instrument, the distinction between insuring with the words "at and from" a place, and simply insuring "from" it. An insurance expressed in the policy to be "from A. to B." only protects the subject insured from the moment of the ship's sailing from A. (*e*): an insurance "at and from" protects the subject insured during her stay at the *terminus a quo* and after she has sailed from it (*f*).

As it is especially desirable, in cases where a ship is expected to arrive at a certain port abroad, to protect her during her whole stay in such port from the moment of her arrival, the form of insurance "at and from" ought always to be adopted in insuring homeward voyages; indeed, in English policies, from the many advantages it presents, it is the form almost always employed in practice.

Time policies.

What precedes is applicable chiefly, if not entirely, to voyage policies; time policies, instead of the *termini* of the adventure, contain here the limits of the period over which the insurance is to extend.

Description of

15. It is a rule, founded on very plain principles, that

(*d*) Mar. Ins. Act, 1906, ss. 43, 44. See Molloy, book ii. c. 11, s. 14, as cited 1 Marshall, Ins. 328; Syers *v.* Bridge (1780), 2 Dougl. 527.

(*e*) Mar. Ins. Act, 1906, Sched. I., rule 2.

(*f*) Per Lord Hardwicke in Motteux *v.* London Ass. (1739), 1 Atkyns, 548. See Mar. Ins. Act, 1906, Sched. I., rule 3.

every contract of insurance ought distinctly to specify the subject intended to be insured, whether it be ship, goods, freight, profit, money advanced on bottomry and respondentia, disbursements, or other interest. Accordingly, sect. 26 (1) of the Marine Insurance Act, 1906, states that "the subject-matter insured must be designated in a marine policy with reasonable certainty."

Sect. 15. the subject-matter insured.

The clause in the common printed form of policy, in which the subject-matter of insurance is set forth, is as follows:— "Upon any kind of goods and merchandises, and also upon the body, tackle, apparel, ordnance, munition, artillery, boat, and other furniture of and in the good ship or vessel," &c.

The common printed clause is only applicable to an insurance on ships and merchandise.

This clause is, in terms, only applicable to the case in which the same party being interested in both ship and cargo wishes to insure both in one common policy: the reason of this is, that in the earlier ages of maritime commerce, when our present form of policy was framed, merchants employed their own ships to carry on their own trade. Now, however, the trade of the ship-owner has become a distinct business from that of the merchant, and this clause, as it stands in the common printed form of policy, is wholly inadequate, without alteration, to meet the exigencies of modern commerce. Instead, however, of providing different forms to meet the various cases of insurances on ship or cargo separately, on freight, on profits, and other interests now held capable of protection by insurance, the English underwriters adhere to the old form, and for the requisite particularity of description resort to the expedient of writing in the body, at the foot, or on the margin of the policy, a statement of the real nature of the subject-matter intended to be insured (as, e.g., "*on profits,*" "*on freight,*" "*on bottomry,*" "*on disbursements,*" "*on 100 bales of cotton, marked, &c.*"), leaving the printed clause entirely unaltered.

How this clause is rendered applicable to other subjects of insurance.

The written words thus inserted in the body, margin, or at the foot of the policy, apply indefinitely to the whole instrument, and control the sense of the general printed clause applicable to ship and goods, and narrow it in point of

Sect. 15. construction to the particular species of interest, whether "ship," "goods," "freight," "profit," &c., the name of which is so inserted (*g*). The policy, in fact, becomes a policy on that subject alone; and in suing thereon no notice need be taken of the formal printed clause as to ship and goods (*h*).

"The meaning of this marginal memorandum," says Lord Ellenborough, in a case where the written insertion was in the margin of the policy, "may be translated thus:—We mean to insure the subject so named 'freight,' for instance, arising and accruing during the limits of the voyage within described, from the carriage of goods on board the ship within mentioned, against the perils within enumerated, and upon the premium herein specified" (*i*).

Whether the mere indorsement on the back of the policy of such written description of the subject of insurance, without reference on the face of it to such indorsement, would have the effect of thus controlling the policy, may be doubted; unquestionably it would do so, if referred to in the body of the policy, or initialed by the underwriters (*k*).

Name of the ship.

16. As the nature of the risk depends very materially on the character of the ship employed, it is of great importance to the underwriter to know the name of the ship on which the insurance is to be effected, or on which the property insured is to be embarked. Hence, as a general rule, in all insurances, whether on ship or goods, the name of the ship ought to be accurately inserted in the policy.

Principle as to naming the ship.

Yet, if the underwriter really know what ship is intended, since the purpose of inserting the name is answered in fact, an error in the name of the ship will not vitiate the policy. *On ne doit pas pointiller sur le nom du navire, pourvu que*

(*g*) Per Lord Ellenborough, Robertson *v.* French (1803), 4 East, 130, 140; per Lord Penzance, Dudgeon *v.* Pembroke (1877), 2 App. Cas. 284, 293; Haughton *v.* Ewbank (1814), 4 Camp. 89.

(*h*) See Robinson *v.* Tobin (1816), 1 Stark, 336.
(*i*) Per Lord Ellenborough, Robertson *v.* French (1803), 4 East, 130, 141.
(*k*) See 1 Duer, 76.

l'erreur qui s'y est glissée n'empêche pas d'en reconnaître l'identité (*l*).

Hence, immediately following the blank left in our common policy for inserting the name of the ship or master come the words, "or by whatsoever other name or names the same ship or the master thereof is or shall be named and called."

As, moreover, circumstances may frequently arise, especially in case of shipments made from abroad, in which the merchant, though desirous of protecting his goods by an immediate insurance, may be utterly ignorant of the particular vessel by which they may be consigned to him, a relaxation of the rule requiring the insertion of the name of the ship in the policy is in such cases permitted; and the party insuring is allowed to effect the policy on his property "on board any ship or ships," on condition of declaring, as soon as he becomes aware of it, the name of the ship or ships on board which it has actually been loaded (*m*).

Insurance on ship or ships.

17. The name of the master, like that of the ship, ought, said Arnould, if known, to be truly inserted in the policy, and that for the same reason, viz., that the safety of the adventure is in some degree dependent on the character of the master.

Name of the master.

As, however, many occasions may arise in the course of the voyage which may make it necessary to change the master, and in cases of insurance on "ship or ships" at sea, or from a distant port, the name of the master for the time being may not be known, in our common form after the blank left for the name of the master these words follow: "or

---

(*l*) Emerigon, c. vi. s. 2, vol. i. p. 160, citing Casaregis, Disc. I. No. 159.

(*m*) The legality of the insurance on ship or ships, which is recognized in s. 29 of the Mar. Ins. Act, 1906, was declared, more than a century ago, to be too well established by usage and authority to admit of dispute: Kewley *v.* Ryan (1794), 2 H. Bl. 348. In France an insurance of this nature is called "assurance in quovis," and is expressly permitted by the Code de Commerce, art. 337. It is ably explained in 1 Emerigon, c. vi. s. 5, p. 173.

Sect. 17. whoever else shall go for master in the said ship " (*n*), and the words already cited, " or by whatsoever name or names the same ship or the master thereof is or shall be named or called." It is not usual, now, to insert the name of the master in the policy (*o*).

Duration of the risk;

18. In the ordinary form of policy the duration of the risk on ship and goods is described in the following clause, the blanks in which must be filled up according to the nature of the adventure which the party effecting the policy wishes to insure.

" Beginning the adventure upon the said goods and merchandises from the loading thereof on board the said ship [at A.   ] upon the said ship, &c. [at and from A.], and so shall continue and endure, during her abode there, on the said ship, &c.; and further until the said ship, with all her ordnance, tackle, apparel, &c., and goods and merchandises whatsoever, shall be arrived at [B.], upon the said ship, &c., until she hath moored at anchor twenty-four hours in good safety, and upon the goods and merchandises, until the same be there discharged and safely landed."

on goods;

The meaning of this clause, when stripped of its verbiage, is, that the risk upon the goods is to commence from their being loaded on board the ship wherever that may be; to continue upon them during the whole time they remain on board, and not to terminate until they have been discharged from the ship and safely landed at the port of delivery.

on ship.

The risk upon the ship is to commence at the port from which she sails on the voyage insured, wherever that may be, to continue during her stay there, and not to terminate until

---

(*n*) The French effect the same object by inserting the words " ou autre pour lui ": see 1 Emerigon, c. vii. s. 1, pp. 184—187.

(*o*) " It is conclusively established by the evidence that the name of the master is not inserted in the policy at all, but is always left blank ": Lord Salvesen in Gunford Ship Co. *v.* Thames & Mersey Mar. Ins. Co., [1910] Sess. Cas. 1072, 1084. See per Lord Alverstone, C. J., *S. C.*, [1911] A. C. at p. 533; see also McArthur, p. 79.

CHAP. II.] OF SEA-POLICIES. 31

after she has moored at anchor for twenty-four hours in good safety at her port of destination.

Sect. 18.

The effect of this clause, however, depends, of course, upon the mode in which the blanks are filled up (*p*). The multifarious exigencies of commerce in a country like our own, which lead our merchants and shipowners to engage in enterprises almost infinitely varied, require the same diversity in describing as is displayed in undertaking them; and policies are accordingly filled up in every variety of form, as we shall have occasion to see more at length when we come to consider the construction put from time to time by our Courts upon the loosely drawn and imperfectly expressed clauses by which our merchants have endeavoured to adapt the old policy to the widely extended commerce of modern times.

By sect. 93 (3) of the Stamp Act, 1891, a policy of sea insurance is not valid unless it specifies the particular risk or adventure (*q*).

19. The course of the ship's navigation is, as we have seen, never in terms expressed in any policy. It is an implied condition of every policy, as we shall see more at large hereafter, that the ship, in sailing between the termini of the voyage insured, shall pursue that course or track which long usage has established to be the safest and most direct mode of navigation, without deviating from it to touch at any ports or places whatsoever which lie between the extreme points of the voyage, unless express liberty for that purpose be inserted in the policy (*r*).

Liberty to touch and stay.

(*p*) See Robertson *v.* French (1803), 4 East, 130.

(*q*) See Edwards *v.* Aberayron Mutual Ship Ins. Society (1875), 1 Q. B. D. 563. Cf. Mar. Ins. Act, 1906, s. 23, which requires, *inter alia*, the risk insured against and the voyage, or period of time, covered by the policy to be specified, and see *ibid.* s. 22. "Risk or adventure" in the Stamp Act seems to have a wider meaning than "risk" in s. 22 of the Mar. Ins. Act. In the latter it obviously does not include the voyage or period covered by the policy, nor a description of the subject-matter insured, and apparently has reference only to the perils insured against.

(*r*) See Mar. Ins. Act, 1906, s. 46.

Sect. 19.

As very few voyages, however, occur, in which it is not desirable that the ship should have the power of touching at intermediate ports, the common printed form of policy invariably contains this clause: "*And it shall be lawful for the said ship, &c., in this voyage to proceed and sail to and touch and stay at any ports or places whatsoever* [   ] *without prejudice to this insurance.*" The blank which is left is for the purpose of specifying the particular ports and places at which it is intended this liberty shall be exercised; and the various modes in which this blank may be filled up, together with the numerous cases decided on the construction of this clause in the policy, will be referred to hereafter under the head of Deviation.

Valuation clause.

20. *The said ship, &c., goods and merchandises, &c., for so much as concerns the assured by agreement between the assured and assurers in this policy are and shall be valued at (s)* [   ].

This clause is in all the common printed forms of policy, though the blank it contains is not always filled up; if filled up, the policy is called a *valued policy*; if not filled up, an *open* or *unvalued policy (t)*.

When inserted, the value ought to be, but frequently is not, the real value of the ship or the prime cost of the goods at the time of effecting the policy, together with the amount of the shipping charges, premiums, and other expenses of the insurance (*u*).

As will appear from the language of the clause, this valuation is agreed to be final and conclusive " between the assured and assurers " on the particular policy; and consequently it

---

(*s*) The words " as under " were here written in, and the following blank was not filled up; lower down in the margin was written " 13,000*l.*," and opposite to this, but in the body of the policy, following the 3 per cent. memorandum clause, were written these words: "on freight, warranted free of capture, seizure," &c. This was held not to be a valued policy. Wilson *v.* Nelson (1864), 5 B. & S. 354; see also Asfar *v.* Blundell, [1895] 2 Q. B. 196, 201.

(*t*) Mar. Ins. Act, 1906, ss. 27, 28.

(*u*) Stevens on Average, Pt. ii. art. i.

cannot be set aside (*x*). But, as will appear hereafter, the contract is vitiated by an over-valuation which is fraudulent, or so excessive as to make the contract a mere wager (*y*), or which is material to be disclosed (*z*), yet has in fact been concealed (*a*).

Sect. 20.

It is not unfrequently the case that where the interest intended to be insured requires a more specific description than that contained in the general printed form, such description is inserted in this clause; as, *e.g.*, the said ship and goods, &c., " are and shall be valued [at one thousand pounds, being on twenty bales of cotton, marked $\frac{1}{x}$ to $\frac{20}{x}$, the said twenty bales valued at that sum] or [at one thousand pounds, being on the interest which I. S. has as owner in one-fourth share of the said ship, the said one-fourth share being valued at that sum]," or the words "valued at" are frequently struck out, and a description of the real subject of insurance then inserted without any valuation; as, *e.g.*, the said ship and goods, &c., for so much as concerns the assured and assurers in this policy are "freight," or "profits," or "money lent on bottomry."

Description of subject of insurance in valuation clause.

In this case it is obvious that the words "the said ship and goods," &c. are to be read as though they meant "the subject insured by this policy, as far as concerns the assured and underwriters, is taken to be 'freight,' 'profits,' 'bottomry,'" &c.

(*x*) Mar. Ins. Act, 1906, s. 27. See Barker *v.* Janson (1868), L. R. 3 C. P. 303; Woodside *v.* Globe Marine Ins. Co. (1895), 1 Com. Cas. 237.

(*y*) Per Lord Mansfield, Lewis *v.* Rucker (1761), 2 Burr. 1167, 1171; Haigh *v.* De la Cour (1812), 3 Camp. 319. See *post*, § 342.

(*z*) Ionides *v.* Pender (1874), L. R. 9 Q. B. 531; Thames & Mersey Mar. Ins. Co. *v.* "Gunford" Ship Co., [1911] A. C. 529. See also the questions left by Mathew, J., to the jury in Herring *v.* Janson (1895), 1 Com. Cas. 177.

(*a*) Arnould (2nd ed. p. 30) says that the valuation "cannot be set aside, except in cases of fraudulent or excessive over-valuation," and similar language is used in s. 27 (3) of the Mar. Ins. Act, 1906. It is not, however, strictly correct to say that the valuation can be set aside. In some Continental countries this can be done, and another valuation substituted; but according to English law the valuation cannot be altered, though in the cases mentioned in the text the policy can be entirely avoided. See *post*, Part I. Chap. XIII. § 341 *et seq.*

Sect. 20.   The words " valued at " are frequently struck out, and the sum insured is then inserted, thus, " 1,000*l*. on ship," or " on goods," &c.; and if the policy is intended to be a valued one, it proceeds, " 1,000*l*. on ship valued at 2,000*l*.," " 2,000*l*. on goods valued at 11,000*l*."

By statute the policy is not valid unless it specifies the sum or sums insured (*b*).

The perils insured against.   21. The next clause in the policy contains an enumeration of the perils against which the underwriters undertake to insure the property on which the policy is effected; or, in the language of the clause, which they " are contented to bear, and do take upon them " in the voyage insured.

As the underwriter is, on plain principles, considered not to be liable to indemnify the assured against loss arising from any perils not specified in the policy or embraced in the general clause, great care has been taken to make this form of words as comprehensive as possible; and the clause in its present state may fairly be regarded as affording a protection against almost every casualty which can possibly happen in the course of any voyage, and for which it is meant that the underwriter shall be answerable. The effect of it is frequently modified by exceptions inserted on the face of the policy, *e.g.*, "warranted free from capture or any attempts thereat, or the consequences thereof."

Sue and labour clauses.   22. " *And in case of any loss or misfortune, it shall be lawful to the Assured, their Factors, Servants, and Assigns, to sue, labour, and travel for, in, or about the Defence, Safeguard, and Recovery of the said Goods and Merchandises, and Ship, &c., or any part thereof, without prejudice to this insurance: To the charges whereof, we, the Assurers, will contribute, each one according to the Rate and Quality of his sum herein insured.*"

Reason of   This clause was introduced to obviate a notion which

---

(*b*) Stamp Act, 1891, s. 93 (3); cf. Mar. Ins. Act, 1906, s. 23 (4), and see *id.*, s. 22.

appears at one time to have prevailed, that if the assured, after a loss which threatened the total destruction of the property insured, were, either by himself or his agents, to take active measures for its recovery or restoration, he would thereby lose the right to abandon, which he might otherwise have exercised. The object of this clause, therefore, is to permit the assured in such cases to take every measure for the recovery of the property without waiving his right of abandonment, and also to bind the underwriters to contribute in proportion to the amount of their several subscriptions, to reimburse the assured for the expenses which he may thereby have incurred (c). The language of the clause is only permissive, but it has long since been settled that it is a clear duty of the assured so to labour for the recovery and restitution of the detained or damaged property (d).

Sect. 22.
introducing this clause.

The effect of it.

The clause does not entitle the assured to recover moneys spent in averting losses for which the underwriter would not have been liable if they had actually happened (e).

23. "*And it is especially declared and agreed that no acts of the Insurer or Insured in recovering, saving, or preserving the property insured shall be considered as a waiver or acceptance of abandonment.*"

Waiver clause.

The object of this clause is to insure that when the assured has given notice of abandonment and claimed for a constructive total loss, the legal position of neither party shall be prejudiced by any act done by him for the purpose of averting a loss. In one case the Court of Queen's Bench expressed the opinion that the clause is superfluous (f).

(c) Mitchell v. Edie (1787), 1 T. R. 608. See 2 Marshall, Ins. 625; and the elaborate discussion of this clause in the learned judgment of Willes, J., in Kidston v. Empire Ins. Co. (1866), L. R. 1 C. P. 535; in error (1867), L. R. 2 C. P. 357; see also Lord Blackburn's judgment in Aitchison v. Lohre (1879), 4 App. Cas. 755, 764.

(d) This is Arnould's language. See *post*, § 799a, and Mar. Ins. Act, 1906, s. 78 (4).
(e) Great Indian Peninsular Ry. v. Saunders (1861), 1 B. & S. 41; (1862), 2 *ibid*. 266; Booth v. Gair (1863), 33 L. J. C. P. 99; Meyer v. Ralli (1876), 1 C. P. D. 358.
(f) Stringer v. English, &c. Ins. Co. (1869), L. R. 4 Q. B. 676, 686.

Sect. 24.

Promise to insure and acknowledgment of receipt of premium.

24. "*And so we the insurers are contented and do promise and bind ourselves, each one for his own part, our heirs, executors, and goods, to the assured, their executors, administrators and assigns, for the true performance of the premises: confessing ourselves paid the consideration due unto us for this assurance by the assured,*" &c.

The policy, it will be observed, contains only a promise *by the underwriters,* without anything in the nature of a counter-promise on the part of the assured; the reason of this is, that the premium, or, as it is described in this clause of the policy, "the consideration due unto them for the assurance," is always supposed to have been paid to the underwriters at the time the policy is subscribed by them, and is accordingly acknowledged to have been so paid on the face of the instrument.

Premium never paid beforehand in practice.

In point of fact the premium is scarcely ever, in the actual course of London business, paid till long after the policy is effected; and is in most cases never paid in money at all, but passed in account between the insurance broker and the underwriter, between whom a running account is kept of premiums and losses, which is settled from time to time.

Acknowledgment of the receipt binds the underwriter.

Although this is the actual course of practice, yet the acknowledgment of the receipt of premium in the policy is so far binding on the underwriter, as to prevent him, in the absence of fraud, from seeking to recover his premium from the assured himself (*g*). Even when the policy contains a promise by the assured to pay the premium, the usage that the underwriter must look to the broker for payment has been held to apply (*h*).

The premium is commonly described in the policy as at so much "per cent.," meaning on the amount subscribed by the underwriter. 35 Geo. 3, c. 63, s. 11, required the premium

---

(*g*) Mar. Ins. Act, 1906, s. 54. See Dalzell *v.* Mair (1808), 1 Camp. 532; De Gaminde *v.* Pigou (1812), 4 Taunt. 246. Mavor *v.* Simeon (1810), 3 Taunt. 497, n.; and Foy *v.* Bell (1811), 3 Taunt. 493, are cases in which, under peculiar circumstances, fraud on the part of the assured was alleged.

(*h*) Universo Ins. Co. *v.* Merchants' Mar. Ins. Co., C. A. [1897] 2 Q. B. 93.

or consideration in the nature of the premium to be expressed in the policy. There was no express provision to that effect in 30 Vict. c. 23, nor is there in the Stamp Act, 1891, or the Marine Insurance Act, 1906.

Sect. 24.

25. This clause is introduced into all policies for the purpose of exempting the underwriters from liability for trivial losses, or for partial losses in respect of certain articles of a perishable nature. In Lloyd's policy it is expressed in the following uncouth form of words:—

The memorandum: its object.

Memorandum clause in use at Lloyd's.

N.B.—Corn, fish, salt, fruit, flour, and seed are warranted free from average, unless general, or the ship be stranded (A); sugar, tobacco, hemp, flax, hides, and skins are warranted free from average under five pounds per cent. (B); and all other goods, also the ship and freight, are warranted free from average under three pounds per cent., unless general, or the ship be stranded (C) (*i*).

In order to make this form of words at all intelligible, it must be carefully borne in mind that the word "AVERAGE," as employed in this clause, means damage to or partial loss of the subject of insurance (*k*), and that the expression "WARRANTED FREE FROM AVERAGE" means, "so insured as to exclude all liability for such damage or partial loss." Hence the whole meaning of the clause is as follows:—

On certain articles of a peculiarly perishable nature, enumerated in paragraph (A), the underwriter shall be answerable for a total loss only (*l*).

On certain other articles of a less perishable nature, but still very liable to be destroyed, enumerated in paragraph (B), he shall only be answerable when the amount of damage exceeds 5 per cent. of their value.

On ship, freight, and all other goods, he shall only be liable when the amount of damage exceeds 3 per cent.

(*i*) The words "sunk or burnt" are often added.
(*k*) See Kidston *v.* Empire Ins. Co. (1866), L. R. 1 C. P. 535;
Oppenheim *v.* Fry (1863), 3 B. & S. 873; Ex. Ch. (1864), 5 *ibid.* 348.
(*l*) Per Willes, J., Kidston *v.* Empire Ins. Co. (1886), L. R. 1 C. P. 535, 544.

Sect. 25.

But in all the three cases alike, the clause provides that the underwriter will be liable for any amount of damage or partial loss, however small, in case the ship be stranded; and it also provides, that he shall in every case be liable for every loss, however small, of the nature of general average (*m*).

The subscription, sum insured, and date.

26. The only parties who sign their names at the foot of the policies, in other words, underwrite them, are the insurers, who are hence called the underwriters or subscribers. By sect. 24 (1) of the Marine Insurance Act, 1906, "a marine policy must be signed (*n*) by or on behalf of the insurer (*o*), provided that in the case of a corporation the corporate seal may be sufficient (*p*), but nothing in this section shall be construed as requiring the subscription of a corporation to be under seal."

Mode of subscribing the policy.

In policies of insurance effected with private underwriters, the first underwriter to whom the policy is tendered subscribes the policy with his name, and the sum he intends to insure, which is generally written in words at length. The next underwriter to whom the policy is tendered then, in like manner, writes under the first subscription his name and the sum he means to insure; and the rest follow in order until the aggregate of the separate sums written opposite to the name of each underwriter, or, in technical

---

(*m*) The bad punctuation of the Memorandum in Lloyd's form (see above) makes it read as if the words "unless general, or the ship be stranded" have no application to the articles in the five per cent. class. Such a construction of the clause, the effect of which would be to make an utterly unreasonable distinction between the articles in paragraphs (B) and (C), has, however, never been adopted in practice. The Memorandum is differently punctuated in Sched. I. of the Mar. Ins. Act, 1906 (see Vol. II. App. A.); but a comma is required after "under three pounds per cent." to make it clear that the meaning of the clause is that stated in the text.

(*n*) An impression of the names from a rubber stamp is a sufficient signature: Cope *v.* Miller (1896), 1 Com. Cas. 296; see also Bennett *v.* Brumfield (1867), L. R. 3 C. P. 28.

(*o*) The effect of s. 22 is apparently that an unsigned policy cannot be given in evidence.

(*p*) In Marine Mutual Ins. Ass. *v.* Young (1880), 43 L. T. 441, the seal of the association, attested by the manager, was held to be sufficient.

CHAP. II.] OF SEA-POLICIES. 39

language, till the "aggregate of their several subscriptions" amounts to the sum which the party effecting the policy desires to protect by the insurance. But since the repeal (in 1825) of the 6 Geo. 1, c. 18 (which prohibited any partnership other than the two chartered companies from underwriting sea-policies), a subscription in the name of a partnership firm has been held sufficient (*q*).

By the Stamp Act, 1891, s. 93 (3), "a policy of insurance shall not be valid unless it specifies the names of the underwriters and the sum or sums insured" (*r*). In addition to this specification of the sums underwritten, a sum large enough to cover the aggregate amount insured is usually in practice expressed in figures on the margin of the policy, either just under or just over the stamp.

Sect. 26.

Policy must specify the sum insured.

Where the aggregate sum insured appears on the face of the policy, and the proportion which each underwriter bears is mentioned, "the sum or sums insured" are sufficiently described in the policy (*s*).

Sect. 24 (2) of the Marine Insurance Act, 1906, provides that "where a policy is subscribed by or on behalf of two insurers, each subscription, unless the contrary be expressed, constitutes a distinct contract with the assured" (*t*). Therefore each underwriter is, generally speaking, only liable, in case of total loss, to pay the assured to the extent of the sum he has thus written against his own name, *i.e.*, to the

Each subscription makes a distinct contract.

(*q*) Reid *v.* Allan (1849), 4 Exch. 326; Dowdall *v.* Allan (1849), 19 L. J. Q. B. 41, S. P. It is a fundamental rule of Lloyd's that no member shall in the City of London underwrite in the name of a partnership.

(*r*) See also Mar. Ins. Act, 1906, ss. 22, 23. A club policy signed "A. & B., per procuration of the several members of the A. A. Association," was held to be void because the names of the insurers were not specified: In re The Arthur Average Association (1875), L. R. 10 Ch. 542. Where the sum insured was left undetermined, because it could not be exactly fixed, the insurance was held to be void: Home Mar. Ins. Co. *v.* Smith, C. A. [1898] 2 Q. B. 351.

(*s*) Dowell *v.* Moon (1815), 4 Camp. 166; Tyser *v.* Shipowners' Syndicate, [1896] 1 Q. B. 135; 1 Com. Cas. 224.

(*t*) See Leo SS. Co., Ltd. *v.* Corderoy (1896), 1 Com. Cas. 300, 379.

Sect. 26. amount of his subscription; or, in case of partial loss, some proportion or aliquot part of that sum (*u*).

The date and subscription.
Formerly the date used not to be inserted in the body of the policy, but was affixed by each underwriter to that which forms the real contract between himself and the assured, viz., the subscription. Now, however, it is usual to insert a date in the policy, which is not necessarily that on which the underwriters actually subscribe it, and the underwriters do not usually add a date to their subscriptions (*x*). These are inserted at the foot of the policy, and generally in the blank space which is left in our common policies under the memorandum.

Supposing the sum which the party effecting the policy wishes to insure be 1,000*l*., of which A. B. is willing to take on himself 500*l*., C. D. 300*l*., and E. F. 200*l*., then the policy would be thus subscribed:—

500*l*. A. B. [*name at length*] Five hundred pounds.
300*l*. C. D. [*name at length*] Three hundred pounds.
200*l*. E. F. [*name at length*] Two hundred pounds.

Delivery of the policy.
27. After the policy has been executed in the form which is binding on the insurer, it must be delivered to make a valid contract. If the underwriter hands over the policy to his clerk, to be kept until called for, the presumption is that this amounts to a delivery (*y*). Little room for questions of this nature is left by the practice at Lloyd's, where it is usual for the broker to carry round the policy for the subscription of the underwriters who have initialed the slip. With com-

---

(*u*) See Tyser *v*. Shipowners' Syndicate, *supra*. If there be a partnership, the fact of there being separate subscriptions by the partners individually does not bar the assured from resorting to the partnership assets: Brett *v*. Beckwith (1856), 26 L. J. Ch. 130, *coram* M. R. A number of underwriters may have one representative insuring for all of them without being partners: per Mathew, J., Tyser *v*. Shipowners' Syndicate, *supra*.

(*x*) The Code de Commerce, Art. 332, requires the policy to be dated on the day and *hour* when executed, distinguishing whether before or after noon. The date in France is conclusive.

(*y*) Cope *v*. Miller (1896), 1 Com. Cas. 296.

CHAP. II.] OF SEA-POLICIES. 39

language, till the "aggregate of their several subscriptions" amounts to the sum which the party effecting the policy desires to protect by the insurance. But since the repeal (in 1825) of the 6 Geo. 1, c. 18 (which prohibited any partnership other than the two chartered companies from underwriting sea-policies), a subscription in the name of a partnership firm has been held sufficient (*q*).

<small>Sect. 26.</small>

By the Stamp Act, 1891, s. 93 (3), "a policy of insurance shall not be valid unless it specifies the names of the underwriters and the sum or sums insured" (*r*). In addition to this specification of the sums underwritten, a sum large enough to cover the aggregate amount insured is usually in practice expressed in figures on the margin of the policy, either just under or just over the stamp.

<small>Policy must specify the sum insured.</small>

Where the aggregate sum insured appears on the face of the policy, and the proportion which each underwriter bears is mentioned, "the sum or sums insured" are sufficiently described in the policy (*s*).

Sect. 24 (2) of the Marine Insurance Act, 1906, provides that "where a policy is subscribed by or on behalf of two insurers, each subscription, unless the contrary be expressed, constitutes a distinct contract with the assured" (*t*). Therefore each underwriter is, generally speaking, only liable, in case of total loss, to pay the assured to the extent of the sum he has thus written against his own name, *i.e.*, to the

<small>Each subscription makes a distinct contract.</small>

(*q*) Reid *v.* Allan (1849), 4 Exch. 326; Dowdall *v.* Allan (1849), 19 L. J. Q. B. 41, S. P. It is a fundamental rule of Lloyd's that no member shall in the City of London underwrite in the name of a partnership.

(*r*) See also Mar. Ins. Act, 1906, ss. 22, 23. A club policy signed "A. & B., per procuration of the several members of the A. A. Association," was held to be void because the names of the insurers were not specified: In re The Arthur Average Association (1875), L. R. 10 Ch. 542. Where the sum insured was left undetermined, because it could not be exactly fixed, the insurance was held to be void: Home Mar. Ins. Co. *v.* Smith, C. A. [1898] 2 Q. B. 351.

(*s*) Dowell *v.* Moon (1815), 4 Camp. 166; Tyser *v.* Shipowners' Syndicate, [1896] 1 Q. B. 135; 1 Com. Cas. 224.

(*t*) See Leo SS. Co., Ltd. *v.* Corderoy (1896), 1 Com. Cas. 300, 379.

Sect. 26.

The date and subscription.

amount of his subscription; or, in case of partial loss, some proportion or aliquot part of that sum (*u*).

Formerly the date used not to be inserted in the body of the policy, but was affixed by each underwriter to that which forms the real contract between himself and the assured, viz., the subscription. Now, however, it is usual to insert a date in the policy, which is not necessarily that on which the underwriters actually subscribe it, and the underwriters do not usually add a date to their subscriptions (*x*). These are inserted at the foot of the policy, and generally in the blank space which is left in our common policies under the memorandum.

Supposing the sum which the party effecting the policy wishes to insure be 1,000*l*., of which A. B. is willing to take on himself 500*l*., C. D. 300*l*., and E. F. 200*l*., then the policy would be thus subscribed:—

    500*l*.   A. B. [*name at length*] Five hundred pounds.
    300*l*.   C. D. [*name at length*] Three hundred pounds.
    200*l*.   E. F. [*name at length*] Two hundred pounds.

Delivery of the policy.

27. After the policy has been executed in the form which is binding on the insurer, it must be delivered to make a valid contract. If the underwriter hands over the policy to his clerk, to be kept until called for, the presumption is that this amounts to a delivery (*y*). Little room for questions of this nature is left by the practice at Lloyd's, where it is usual for the broker to carry round the policy for the subscription of the underwriters who have initialed the slip. With com-

---

(*u*) See Tyser *v.* Shipowners' Syndicate, *supra*. If there be a partnership, the fact of there being separate subscriptions by the partners individually does not bar the assured from resorting to the partnership assets: Brett *v.* Beckwith (1856), 26 L. J. Ch. 130, *coram* M. R. A number of underwriters may have one representative insuring for all of them without being partners: per Mathew, J., Tyser *v.* Shipowners' Syndicate, *supra*.

(*x*) The Code de Commerce, Art. 332, requires the policy to be dated on the day and *hour* when executed, distinguishing whether before or after noon. The date in France is conclusive.

(*y*) Cope *v.* Miller (1896), 1 Com. Cas. 296.

panies the practice is different, for the execution usually takes place in the absence of the assured and his broker. The presumption, therefore, is that when the instrument, completed and executed, passes into the hands of the company's servants, to be kept until called for by the assured, it is already a valid policy (z).

Sect. 27.

28. Every policy must be duly stamped, before it is signed or underwritten by any person, with the amount of duty required by the Stamp Act, 1891 (a). If not stamped in the first instance, it cannot, with two exceptions, be stamped afterwards (b), unless on payment of a penalty of 100l. (c); and a failure to comply with the provision of the Stamp Act in this respect not only renders the policy void, but entails a considerable penalty upon all those concerned in so effecting or subscribing it (d). But we reserve the effect of the Stamp Laws for consideration separately.

Stamping the policy.

We have seen that a contract of sea-insurance, other than such as is referred to in sect. 506 of the Merchant Shipping Act, 1894, is not valid unless expressed in a policy. In substance, a policy contains the following particulars (e):—
1. The name of some party either really or nominally insured. 2. A description of the voyage or risk insured. 3. Of the subject insured. 4. Of the perils insured against. 5. The name of the ship (except where the insurance is on ship or ships, or on cargo to be carried by

Recapitulation

(z) Xenos v. Wickham (1867), L. R. 2 H. L. 296; Ex. Ch. (1863), 33 L. J. C. P. 13; 14 C. B. N. S. 435; Cox v. Troy (1822), 5 B. & Ald. 474. For limited effect that may be given to delivery out of a policy, see Morrison v. Universal Marine Ins. Co. (1873), L. R. 8 Ex. 197.
(a) Stamp Act, 1891 (54 & 55 Vict. c. 39), ss. 1, 95 (1), and Sched. I.
(b) Ibid. s. 95 (1) (a), (b).
(c) Ibid. s. 95 (2).

(d) Ibid. s. 97.
(e) The statutory requisites under the Stamp Act, 1891, are—(1) the stamp; (2) the risk or adventure; (3) the names of the underwriters; (4) the sums insured. The Mar. Ins. Act, 1906, requires—(1) the name of the assured, or of some person who effects the insurance on his behalf; (2) the subject-matter and the risk; (3) the voyage or period of time covered; (4) the sums insured; (5) the names of the insurers; (6) their signature.

Sect. 28. ships unknown). 6. The premium or consideration for the risk. 7. The sums insured. 8. The subscription of the underwriter. It is, moreover, requisite that every policy should be, 9. Dated; and 10, Stamped, before execution (*f*).

Express warranties and other occasional clauses contained in policies.

29. The clauses hitherto considered are for the most part to be found in the common printed forms of policy. With the varying exigencies of commerce, however, and the fluctuating character of the political relations between mercantile states, occasions frequently arise which render the assured, on the one hand, desirous of extending the degree of indemnity which is afforded him by the common form of policy; and warn the underwriter, on the other, to limit the amount of responsibility he takes on himself, by declaring in writing on the face of the policy that he will only undertake to indemnify the assured against the usual risks upon certain specified conditions, which are inserted in writing on the face of the policy, and, in English Law, are called Express Warranties.

Form of express warranties, and mode of inserting them in policies.

The effect of these warranties will be fully discussed hereafter. With regard to their form they are generally expressed thus:—" Warranted to sail on or before the 1st day of June, 1914." " Warranted well, this 1st day of June, 1914." " Warranted to depart with convoy." " Warranted neutral ship and neutral property." " Warranted a Dane," &c.; or the word " warranted " is altogether omitted, and the words " to sail," or " to sail with convoy," &c. alone inserted. The clause of warranty is sometimes introduced into the policy immediately after that describing the voyage; but this is not necessary; all that is essential is, that it should be included in, or written upon, the policy, or contained in some document incorporated by reference into the policy (*g*): it need not appear in the body of it (*i.e.*, the written or printed

---

(*f*) See, however, Stamp Act, 1891, s. 95, *post*, § 32, for certain exceptions, and for the stamping of a policy after execution on payment of a penalty.

(*g*) Mar. Ins. Act, 1906, s. 35 (2).

part); it may be written either at the foot (*h*), or on the margin of the policy (*i*), and that either in the usual way or transversely (*k*); for, wherever or however written, so long as it be on the face of the policy, it will be a good warranty; for whatever is contained in the policy at the time of signing is a part of the contract, and is adopted by the signature (*l*). It is apprehended, however, that, unless initialed by the underwriters, or referred to in the body of the instrument (in either of which cases it would, no doubt, be operative (*m*)), a memorandum indorsed on the back of the policy would not be permitted to have any effect in varying or modifying its terms (*n*).

Sect. 29.

30. Besides the different express clauses and stipulations, both ordinary and extraordinary, already considered, every policy of insurance implicitly contains within itself certain terms and conditions, which, though not on the face of the instrument, are of the same binding authority as though they were, and combine with the express clauses to make up the whole of the contract between the assured and the underwriters.

Of the implied conditions and terms contained in every policy.

They are, in fact, the terms upon which the parties mutually understand their contract to be based; and are regarded as so much a matter of course, that it would be a needless ceremony to express them in form. If either of the parties fail to comply with any one of these conditions, he will in most cases be entirely precluded from taking any advantage of his contract.

1. Thus, it is an implied condition in every policy that the assured, at the time of procuring the policy, shall fairly

Representation and concealment.

(*h*) Blackhurst *v.* Cockell (1789), 3 T. R. 360.
(*i*) Bean *v.* Stupart (1778), 1 Dougl. 11.
(*k*) Kenyon *v.* Berthon (1778), 1 Dougl. 12, n.
(*l*) Cockran *v.* Retberg (1800), 3 Esp. 121; see also De Hahn *v.* Hartley (1786), 1 T. R. 343.

(*m*) See Laird *v.* Robertson (1791), 4 Br. P. Cases, 488; Ridsdale *v.* Shedden (1814), 4 Camp. 107; Reed *v.* Deere (1827), 7 B. & Cr. 261; and *post*, § 42.
(*n*) 1 Duer, 76. Phillips, however, vol. i. s. 68, appears to take a contrary view.

Sect. 30. and truly disclose to the underwriters every fact material to the risk which is exclusively within his own knowledge, and which is not embraced by some agreement in the policy: if this condition is not complied with, the policy may be avoided by the underwriter (*o*).

Implied warranty of seaworthiness.

2. Again, in voyage policies the assured is understood by the very act of procuring the insurance to warrant that the vessel is seaworthy and in every way fit for the voyage or service on which it is employed; accordingly this warranty, though it is never expressed, is uniformly implied as a part of the contract (*p*).

Usual course to be followed.

3. The actual navigation of the ship between the termini of the voyage is, as we have seen, never inserted in any policy; because every underwriter is presumed to be acquainted with the usual mode of conducting the voyage on which he has assured the risk; but, although never inserted, the usual course of the voyage is supposed to be incorporated in every policy, and as much forms part of its legal effect as though it were set out in terms on the face of the instrument (*q*).

Implied condition not to deviate.

4. It is always an implied condition of every policy, that the ship, in proceeding from one terminus to the other, shall pursue this usual course of the voyage, without any delay or deviation: this implied condition is generally termed a condition not to deviate; and any failure to comply with it exempts the underwriter from all liability from the moment of deviation (*r*).

All generally known mercantile usages are incorporated.

5. Not only the course of the voyage insured, but all generally established usages of trade and navigation, applicable to the subject of their contract, are always supposed to be known by the parties contracting for a mercantile indemnity; and therefore, though never expressly inserted

---

(*o*) *Post,* Part II. Chap. II. "Concealment."

(*p*) *Post,* Part II. Chap. IV. "Seaworthiness."

(*q*) Noble *v.* Kennoway (1780),

2 Dougl. 510; Pelly *v.* Royal Exch. Co. (1757), 1 Burr. 341.

(*r*) See *post,* Part I. Chap. XV. "Deviation."

CHAP. II.] OF SEA-POLICIES. 45

in any policy, are as binding on the parties as though they were. <small>Sect. 30.</small>

6. It must never be forgotten, therefore, that the whole contract between the assured and the underwriters is only partially expressed in the policy; and that the real contract between them is, that, supposing the underwriters to have been informed beforehand of the real nature of the risk, supposing also (except in time policies) the ship to have been seaworthy when the risk commenced, and never afterwards to have deviated from the usual course of the voyage insured, and the assured not to have precluded himself from recovery on the ground of illegality of the risk, then the underwriters engage to indemnify him, according to the terms of the policy as explained by usage, for any loss he may sustain as a direct consequence of the enumerated perils. <small>Real nature and effect of the contract.</small>

31. The stamping of policies in the United Kingdom is mainly regulated by the Stamp Act, 1891 (54 & 55 Vict. c. 39), by which all then-existing enactments dealing with the stamping of policies were repealed, as amended by the Finance Act, 1908 (8 Edw. 7, c. 16), s. 5. <small>The stamping of policies.</small>

All policies of sea insurance must be stamped according to the following scale (*s*):— <small>Scale of stamp duties.</small>

	Duty.
	£ *s. d.*
(1) Where the premium or consideration does not exceed the rate of 2*s*. 6*d*. per centum of the sum insured (*t*)	0 0 1

(*s*) See Stamp Act, 1891, s. 1 and Sched. I.; Finance Act, 1908, s. 5.

(*t*) By the Finance Act, 1912, s. 8, where such premium is subject to an increase upon the occurrence of a specified contingency, it is still to be treated as not exceeding the rate of 2*s*. 6*d*. per cent. of the sum insured. But if, owing to the occurrence of the contingency, the premium is increased so as to exceed this rate, the policy or a new policy to be thereupon issued must be stamped with the additional sum required to represent the additional duty, and may be so stamped without penalty within thirty days after the increased premium becomes ascertained.

FORM AND CONTENTS [PART I.

Sect. 31.

(2) In any other case—
 (a) For or upon any voyage—
  In respect of every full sum of 100*l*., and also any fractional part of 100*l*. thereby insured ....   Duty. £ s. d.   0 0 1
 (b) For time—
  In respect of every full sum (*u*) of 100*l*., and also any fractional part of 100*l*. thereby insured—
  Where the insurance shall be made for any time not exceeding six months ...   0 0 3
  Where the insurance shall be made for any time exceeding six months and not exceeding twelve months 0 0 6

By sect. 91, the expression "policy of insurance" for the purposes of the Act includes every writing whereby any contract of insurance is made or agreed to be made, or is evidenced. The meaning of the term "policy of sea insurance" for the purposes of the Act is defined in sect. 92 (*x*).

Sect. 93 (1) provides that a contract for sea insurance (other than such insurance as is referred to in sect. 55 of the Merchant Shipping Act Amendment Act, 1862, re-enacted in sect. 506 of the Merchant Shipping Act, 1894 (*y*)) shall not be valid unless it is expressed in a policy of sea insurance (*z*).

By sect. 93 (2), no policy of sea insurance made for time shall be made for any time exceeding twelve months.

Sect. 93 (3) declares that a policy of sea insurance shall not be valid unless it specifies the particular risk or adventure, the names of the subscribers or underwriters, and the

---

(*u*) A time policy embracing a number of ships with separate sums insured on each is properly stamped at the duty corresponding to the aggregate sum insured. Great Britain S.S. Premium Association *v.* White (1891), 19 Ct. of Sess. Cas. 4th Ser. 109; (1896) W. N. 91.

(*x*) See *ante*, § 7.

(*y*) *Ibid.*

(*z*) As to costs, where the insurer has successfully pleaded this provision of the Stamp Act, after leading the insured to believe that he would not rely on it, see Genforsikrings Aktieselskabet *v.* Da Costa, [1911] 1 K. B. 137.

CHAP. II.] OF SEA-POLICIES. 47

sum or sums insured (*a*), and is made for a period not exceeding twelve months.

Sect. 31.

By sect. 94, where any sea insurance is made for a voyage and also for time, or to extend to or cover any time beyond thirty days after the ship shall have arrived at her destination and been there moored at anchor, the policy is to be charged with duty as a policy for a voyage, and also with duty as a policy for time.

The prohibition of insurances for a time exceeding twelve months has been modified by sect. 11 of the Finance Act, 1901 (1 Edw. 7, c. 7), which provides that notwithstanding anything contained in the Stamp Act, 1891, a policy of sea insurance made for time may contain a continuation clause as defined in the section, and shall not be invalid on the ground only that by reason of the clause it may become available for a period exceeding twelve months (*b*). A policy with such a clause is chargeable with a stamp duty of sixpence in addition to the duty otherwise chargeable; and if the risk covered by the clause attaches, and a new policy is not issued covering the risk, the clause shall be deemed to be a separate contract of insurance, not covered by the stamp on the original policy, which must be stamped anew in respect of that contract. It may be so stamped without penalty at any time not exceeding thirty days after the risk has so attached.

Sect. 8 of the Revenue Act, 1903 (3 Edw. 7, c. 46), provides that a policy of insurance upon any ship, or its machinery or fittings, while under construction or repair, or on trial, need only be stamped as a policy for a voyage, and though made for a time exceeding twelve months, shall not be deemed to be a policy made for time.

32. The first Act relating to the stamping of sea-policies (35 Geo. 3, c. 63), declared that a policy should neither be given in evidence nor available in law or equity unless duly

Effect of omission to stamp the policy under the old law.

(*a*) See also Mar. Ins. Act, 1906, ss. 22—24, *ante*, §§ 8, 26.

(*b*) See *post*, § 440, for the definition of a continuation clause.

… FORM AND CONTENTS [PART I.

Sect. 32.

stamped, and it absolutely prohibited the stamping of a policy after it was underwritten (sect. 14). The effect of this provision was that a policy not properly stamped at the time when it was made was wholly null and void (*c*).

Stamping the policy after execution.

The rigour of the law has been considerably modified. Sect. 95 (1) of the Stamp Act, 1891, after declaring that a policy of sea insurance may not be stamped at any time after it is signed or underwritten by any person, makes the two following exceptions:—

(a) Any policy of mutual insurance having a stamp impressed thereon may, if required, be stamped with an additional stamp, provided that at the time when the additional stamp is required the policy has not been signed or underwritten to an amount exceeding the sum or sums which the duty impressed thereon extends to cover.

(b) Any policy made or executed out of, but being in any manner enforceable within, the United Kingdom may be stamped at any time within ten days after it has been first received in the United Kingdom on payment of the duty only.

Further, sect. 95 (2) allows a policy of sea insurance for the purpose of production in evidence to be stamped after the execution thereof, on payment of a penalty of 100*l*. (*d*). This is a provision of the greatest importance. The contract is good *ab initio*, and either party can enforce it by paying

(*c*) Roderick *v.* Hovil (1811), 3 Camp. 103. See the 2nd edition of this work, pp. 41—50, for the law as to the stamping of policies before 30 Vict. c. 23.

(*d*) This was first allowed in 1876, by 39 Vict. c. 6, s. 2 (repealed by the Act of 1891), which made sea-policies instruments within the Stamp Act, 1870 (33 & 34 Vict. c. 97), s. 16. Before this provision a special case stating that the parties agreed that a valid (*i.e.*, stamped) policy should be deemed to have been issued was ordered to be struck out as sanctioning an evasion of the stamp laws: Nixon *v.* Albion Marine Ins. Co. (1867), L. R. 2 Ex. 338. Where the question in issue was whether an unstamped document was a policy of insurance, an order was made in chambers that for the purposes of the trial the Court was to assume that all penalties (if any were necessary) had been paid: Home Marine Ins. Co. *v.* Smith, [1898] 2 Q. B. 351.

CHAP. II] OF SEA-POLICIES. 49

the penalty. Under the old law, as we have seen, there was no enforceable contract (e). Sect. 32.

33. Sect. 97 (1) of the Act imposes a penalty of 100*l*. on any person who becomes an insurer, or settles for a loss, or effects an insurance, or knowingly procures one to be effected, unless the insurance is expressed in a duly stamped policy of sea insurance, or who fraudulently or wilfully seeks to evade the duty payable on a policy. By sect. 97 (2), a broker, agent, or other person who negotiates a sea insurance contrary to the Act, or writes a policy upon material not duly stamped, is liable to a similar penalty, and has no legal claim to any charge for brokerage or commission, or for any money paid by him with reference to the insurance. Further, any money paid to him in respect of any such charge shall remain the property of his employer. Penalties for breaches of the Stamp Act.

Sect. 97 (3) imposes a similar penalty on anyone who makes or issues a document purporting to be a copy of a policy, unless there be a duly stamped policy in existence of which it is a copy.

The Stamp Duties Management Act, 1891 (54 & 55 Vict. c. 38, ss. 9—12), as amended by 61 & 62 Vict. c. 46, deals with the question of allowances for spoiled stamps. Spoiled stamps.

34. The most difficult questions raised by the Stamp Acts relate to the legal effect of the slip. The slip.

The broker, when requested to effect an insurance, prepares a brief memorandum of the leading particulars of the proposed risk, such as convey at a glance to those who are skilled in the business a sufficient notion of the intended policy to enable them to say whether, and at what premium, they will underwrite it. This memorandum, called the *slip*, is presented, if the insurance is effected at Lloyd's, successively to the underwriters there, who, if they think well of the risk and the premium at which it is offered, initial the slip,

(e) Arnould, 2nd ed. pp. 43, 44.

A.—VOL. I. 4

Sect. 34. each for the sum he thinks proper to underwrite, and so on until the whole amount is subscribed (*f*).

The legal effect of the slip was explained by Blackburn, J., in the year 1871, when the Act of 1867 (30 Vict. c. 23) was in force. "The slip," said the learned judge (*g*), "is in practice, and according to the understanding of those engaged in marine insurance, the complete and final contract between the parties, fixing the terms of the insurance and the premium, and neither party can, without the assent of the other, deviate from the terms thus agreed on without a breach of faith, for which he would suffer severely in his credit and future business.

"The Legislature, for the purpose of protecting the revenue, had by the very strongest enactments provided that no such instrument should be given in evidence for any purpose (*h*). But all those enactments are repealed by the 30 Vict. c. 23; and the law is now governed by the 7th and 9th sections of that Act. By sect. 7 no contract or agreement for sea insurance shall be valid unless expressed in a policy. And by sect. 9 no policy shall be pleaded or given in evidence in any Court unless duly stamped. As the slip is clearly a contract for marine insurance, and is equally clearly not a policy, it is, by virtue of these enactments, not

---

(*f*) Another document of similar import, sometimes also called a slip, is that which is known as a *cover note* or *covering note*. It is a memorandum containing similar particulars of the terms of an insurance signed on behalf of, and issued to the broker or assured by, a company on accepting the risk. See *post*, § 102, *n*.

(*g*) Ionides *v*. Pacific Fire and Marine Ins. Co. (1871), L. R. 6 Q. B. 674, 684, 685; affd. on appeal (1872), L. R. 7 Q. B. 517.

(*h*) So much so that Lord Ellenborough, C. J., refused to look at it as a means of showing the order in which the underwriters had taken the risk: Marsden *v*. Reid (1803), 3 East, 572, 573; see also Warwick *v*. Slade (1811), 3 Camp. 127. 35 Geo. 3, c. 63, s. 14, provided that no insurance whereon duty was payable, nor any contract or agreement for such insurance, should be given in evidence unless stamped. 30 Vict. c. 23, only says that no unstamped policy shall be given in evidence; yet there is a wide definition of the term "policy" in s. 4 of that Act. In Fisher *v*. Liverpool Marine Ins. Co. (1873), L. R. 8 Q. B. 469, 474, Lord Blackburn hinted at a doubt whether Lord Ellenborough was right in refusing to look at the slip.

CHAP. II.] OF SEA-POLICIES. 51

valid—that is, not enforceable at law or in equity; but it Sect. 34.
may be given in evidence wherever it is, though not valid,
material."

Nevertheless, when a stamped policy had been issued, the
Courts recognized the practice of underwriters to consider
the agreement complete when the slip was initialed, to the
extent of holding that any fact coming to the knowledge of
the assured between the time when the slip was initialed
and the execution of the policy, however material it might be,
need not be communicated to the underwriter, even though
the slip was initialed for the agent of the assured, subject to
confirmation by his principal; and since the Act of 1867 the
Courts have held that the slip could be looked at to show
when the bargain was made (i). Now sect. 21 of the Marine
Insurance Act, 1906, declares that for the purpose of showing
when the contract was concluded, reference may be made to
the slip or covering note or other customary memorandum
of the contract, although it be unstamped.

35. Arnould was of opinion that a memorandum embody- Arnould's
ing an agreement to execute a regular stamped policy, accom- view that the
panied by the payment of the premium, could be enforced in by the slip
a court of equity (k); but in support of this view he was only able in equity.
able to cite a dictum of Lord Denman's (l), and a Scotch
case in which the House of Lords recognized the validity of
a written agreement to execute a policy. The report, however, does not state whether the memorandum was stamped,
and it does not appear that any question arising out of
35 Geo. 3, c. 65, the Stamp Act then in force, was raised or
considered in the case (m).

A subsequent decision of the Court of Exchequer Chamber

(i) Cory v. Patton (1872), L. R.   (l) In Mead v. Davison (1835),
7 Q. B. 304; (1874), L. R. 9 Q. B.   3 A. & E. 303.
577; Lishman v. Northern Mari-   (m) Patterson v. Mills (1828), 1
time Ins. Co. (1873), L. R. 8 C. P.   Dow, N. S. 342. The case in the
216, 225; in the Exchequer Cham-   Court of Session is reported as
ber (1875), L. R. 10 C. P. 179.   Albion Life and Fire Ins. Co. v.
(k) 2nd ed. p. 52.   Mills, 3 Wils. & Shaw, 218.

Sect. 35.

Decision to the contrary.

shows that this opinion could not be supported under the former Stamp Acts.

The facts in that case (*n*) were that the London agent of the defendant company initialed a slip, and received from the brokers a copy of the slip, which he forwarded to his principals to have a policy prepared, and the amount of the premium and stamp duty was subsequently paid by the brokers to the defendants' agents. No policy was executed by the defendants, and an action was brought for damages. In the Court of Queen's Bench, Blackburn, J., held, not that the defendants were legally bound to execute a policy, but that by accepting the copy slip they agreed to use due diligence either to execute a stamped policy or to repudiate the transaction. But in this opinion he was not sustained, the other members of the Court and the Exchequer Chamber holding that the initialing of the slip and the forwarding of the copy slip were parts of one contract—a contract of insurance which could not, by reason of 30 Vict. c. 23, be enforced.

Thus it is clear that before 1876 the assured had no remedy upon an unstamped slip, because, even if the slip satisfied the other requirements of the Stamp Acts, it was unstamped and therefore invalid as a policy (*o*).

Cases in which assured recovered

36. Only under exceptional circumstances—for instance, where the claimant has been able to prove his case without actual production of a stamped policy—have actions been

---

(*n*) Fisher *v*. Liverpool Marine Ins. Co. (1873), L. R. 8 Q. B. 469; in the Exchequer Chamber (1874), L. R. 9 Q. B. 418. In Morrison *v*. Universal Marine Ins. Co. (1871), 25 L. T. 108, Kelly, C. B., had previously ruled that a custom whereby an underwriter is bound to issue a policy in accordance with the terms of the slip is bad. See also Morocco Land and Trading Co. *v*. Fry (1865), 11 L. T. N. S. 618; and the opinion of Willes, J., in Xenos *v*. Wickham (1867), L. R. 2 H. L. 296, 314.

(*o*) As we have just seen, it was held by Blackburn, J., not to be a policy under the Act of 1867; and if this be a correct interpretation of that Act, it could not have been stamped under the Act of 1876 as a policy. See per Mathew, J., in Home Mar. Ins. Co. *v*. Smith, [1898] 1 Q. B. 829, 835.

CHAP. II.] OF SEA-POLICIES. 53

successfully maintained when no stamped policy was in existence.

Sect. 36.
without a policy.

Thus, in one case the assured was held entitled to receive the amount of a loss from a mutual insurance association, as on an account stated, where only an unstamped policy had been issued, but a sufficient admission of liability appeared in the books of the association (*q*).

In another case a member of such an association was held by the Court of Appeal to be liable to pay calls (although the association issued no policies), on the ground that he had assented to the payment of the losses in respect of which the calls were made, and was therefore estopped from saying that the payments were improperly made (*r*).

37. The question now to be considered is, whether the provision of sect. 95 (2) of the Stamp Act, 1891 (re-enacting the similar provision of the Act of 1876), which enables policies of insurance to be stamped after execution on payment of a penalty, also enables a slip to be stamped so as to give it the force and effect of a policy.

Is the slip a policy under the Stamp Act, 1891?

By sect. 91 of the Stamp Act, 1891, the expression "policy of insurance" includes, for the purposes of the Act, every writing whereby any contract of insurance is made or agreed to be made, or is evidenced. Is a slip a writing of this kind? There can be no doubt that, according to the practice of those engaged in the business of marine insurance, the slip is the writing by which the contract is really made, although the subsequent issue of a formal policy is contemplated. But it is clear that the mere fact that the parties intend that an

---

(*q*) In re Teignmouth and General Mutual Shipping Association (1872), L. R. 14 Eq. 148. It may, however, be doubted whether an account stated in respect of a contract declared by statute to be invalid is binding. See Scadding *v.* Eyles (1846), 9 Q. B. 858; Cocking *v.* Ward (1845), 1 C. B. 858, per Tindal, C. J., p. 870; but see Barrow Mutual Ship Ins. Co. *v.* Ashburner (1885), 54 L. J. Q. B. 377, for the view taken by the Court of Appeal of the effect of the Stamp Act.

(*r*) Barrow Mutual Ship Insurance Co. *v.* Ashburner, *supra*. Cf. In re London Marine Ins. Association, Smith's Case (1869), L. R. 4 Ch. 611.

Sect. 37. agreement which they have arrived at shall be subsequently embodied in a more formal document does not prevent the earlier agreement from constituting a binding engagement (*s*). *Primâ facie,* therefore, it does seem that on general principles the slip is a policy of insurance within the very wide definition of the Act. The consequences, however, of the adoption of this view, to which it must be conceded that the wording of the Act of Parliament gives great support, are curious; for it seems to follow that every broker who procures the initialing of a slip, and every underwriter who initials it, breaks the law and makes himself liable to a penalty.

Against the view that the slip is itself a policy, the decisions in the cases to which we have already referred may fairly be urged (*t*). The question in these cases was whether, where a slip had been duly followed by a formal stamped policy, the former might be looked at for the purpose of explaining the latter. The Act of 1867 (*u*), which was in force when these cases were decided, provided (sect. 9) that no policy should be given in evidence unless duly stamped; and it defined a policy (sect. 4) as "any instrument whereby a contract or agreement for any sea insurance is made or entered into." In the earliest of these cases (*x*), as we have seen, the Court of Queen's Bench held that a slip is not a policy, and in all of the cases it was held that the slip could be given in evidence.

We have already quoted from the judgment of the Court of Queen's Bench, delivered by Blackburn, J., in the earliest of these cases (*y*). Strangely enough, the learned Judge agrees that the slip is a contract for marine insurance, but

---

(*s*) For the general principle see Rossiter *v.* Miller, (1878), 3 App. Cas. 1124, and cases there cited.

(*t*) Ionides *v.* Pacific Fire, &c. Co. (1871), L. R. 6 Q. B. 674; (1872), 7 Q. B. 517; Cory *v.* Patton (1872), L. R. 7 Q. B. 304; (1874), L. R. 9 Q. B. 577; Lishman *v.* Northern Mar. Ins. Co. (1873), L. R. 8 C. P. 216; (1875), L. R. 10 C. P. 179.

(*u*) 30 Vict. c. 23.

(*x*) Ionides *v.* Pacific Fire Ins. Co., *supra.*

(*y*) *Ante,* § 34.

does not notice the comprehensive definition of a policy in sect. 4 of the Act then in force, which we have just cited (z). Whether or not, had the Court duly considered this definition, they would have held, in view of their opinion that the slip was a contract of marine insurance, that the slip was nevertheless in no sense of the word a policy capable of being, and liable to be, stamped, may perhaps be open to question. And what view would now be taken in a Court of last instance as to the effect of the provisions of the Stamp Act now in force, it is equally impossible to say.

Sect. 37.

In 1898 the question arose whether a certain covering note initialed by the underwriters was a policy of insurance within the meaning of the Stamp Act, 1891, and could be stamped after execution. Mathew, J., held that it was a slip, and that a slip is not a policy of sea insurance, and therefore cannot be stamped (a). The chief ground on which the learned judge based his decision was that both the language of 30 Vict. c. 23, and the cases upon the Act show that a slip was not a policy within its meaning. The Court of Appeal, on the other hand, held that the covering note was a contract for sea insurance within the meaning of the Stamp Act, 1891; though they affirmed the decision of Mathew, J., on another ground, viz., that it was invalid as a policy because it did not specify the "sum or sums insured" (b).

Home Marine Insurance Co. v. Smith.

The Court were careful to limit their decision to the particular document, and to say nothing on the general question whether a slip can ever be stamped and sued upon. The decision of Mathew, J., on this point has, therefore, not been expressly overruled. It is, however, difficult to see how, in view of this decision of the Court of Appeal, it is now possible to contend that a cover note which specifies the

---

(z) *Supra.*
(a) Home Mar. Ins. Co. v. Smith, [1898] 1 Q. B. 829. Cf. Thompson v. Adams (1889), 23 Q. B. D. 361, where Mathew, J., held that, as the statute did not apply, a slip initialed by a Lloyd's underwriter was a valid contract of fire insurance.
(b) [1898] 2 Q. B. 351.

Sect. 37. sum insured, and in other respects conforms with the requirements of the Stamp Act, is not a valid policy (*c*). Further, it seems difficult to distinguish the covering note, either as regards its form or its object, from an ordinary slip. The result seems to follow that an ordinary slip is a policy, and that Mathew, J.'s, decision to the contrary has been impliedly overruled (*d*). The remarkable consequences, if this opinion be well founded, have already been pointed out. The language of sects. 21 and 89 of the Marine Insurance Act, 1906 (*e*), may be cited in support of the view that a slip is not a contract of insurance, but only a memorandum of such contract. This, however, does not seem to be a conclusive answer to the contention that the slip is a writing whereby a contract of insurance is evidenced, within the definition of sect. 91 of the Stamp Act, and it is a matter of regret that the Legislature did not take advantage of the opportunity given by the passing of the Marine Insurance Act to settle this question (*f*).

(*c*) In Empress Ass. Corp. *v.* Bowring (1906), 11 Com. Cas. 107, however, Kennedy, J., held that an open cover slip was not a policy of sea insurance.

(*d*) In a note to this passage the question was raised in the seventh edition whether, if a slip can be considered a policy of insurance, as it can be stamped on payment of a penalty, it can ever properly be admitted in evidence when unstamped: Stamp Act, 1891, s. 14 (1). In Ionides *v.* Pacific Fire Ins. Co. (1871), L. R. 6 Q. B. 674, the Court of Queen's Bench seem clearly to have considered that if they had held the slip to be a policy, they would have been obliged to reject it as evidence. The Court of Exchequer Chamber (L. R. 7 Q. B. 517) only said that the slip, though a nullity as a contract, could be put in evidence for a collateral purpose. Now s. 21 of the Mar. Ins. Act, 1906, provides that an unstamped slip, or covering note, or other customary memorandum may be referred to for the purpose of showing when the contract was made, and s. 89 declares generally that "where there is a duly stamped policy, reference may be made, as heretofore, to the slip or covering note, in any legal proceeding." In view of the practice of forty years, during which slips have constantly been used in evidence, their admissibility, whatever be the answer to the question under discussion, is thus established.

(*e*) See note (*d*), *supra*.

(*f*) In an article in the Law Quarterly Review for January, 1914, Mr. Arthur Cohen discusses the effect of the stamp laws, and expresses the view that a slip is not a policy, but an honorary and legally unenforceable agreement as to the terms of the policy which is

CHAP. II.] OF SEA-POLICIES. 57

38. We have already seen that a policy of insurance is not valid, by reason of sect. 93 (3) of the Stamp Act, 1891, unless it specifies the particular risk or adventure (*g*), the names of the subscribers or underwriters, and the sum or sums insured. Further, by sect. 23 of the Marine Insurance Act, 1906, it must specify the name of the assured, or of someone effecting the policy on his behalf, the subject-matter insured and the risk insured against (*h*), the voyage or period of time covered by the insurance, the sums insured, and the names of the insurers; and by sect. 24 it must be signed by or on behalf of the insurers. Assuming that a slip can be treated as a policy, it will not be available unless it contains these particulars. There are, no doubt, slips or cover notes for floating policies in which some of these particulars are not sufficiently described; but it is submitted that the ordinary slip for a voyage or time policy contains an adequate specification of the necessary particulars (*i*).

The ordinary perils insured against are not usually specified in the slip; but there is authority for saying that these perils are not required to be expressly stated in a policy, as being the risk or adventure insured, within the meaning of the Stamp Act (*k*), and their subsequent insertion in the policy is not in consequence of any express agreement between the parties. An expert can say with certainty, from

Sect. 38.
Does the slip contain the requisites of a valid policy?

subsequently to be delivered, and that it cannot therefore be stamped after execution. In arriving at this conclusion he is largely influenced by the fact that s. 97 of the Stamp Act, 1891 (see *ante*, § 33), would lead to results so manifestly unjust and absurd, if a slip were held to be a policy under s. 91, that such a construction must, if possible, be avoided.

(*g*) In Edwards *v.* Aberayron Mutual Ship Ins. Society (1875), 1 Q. B. D. 563, the Court of Queen's Bench seem to have held that "risk or adventure" includes the voyage or period of time covered by the insurance. There is no clear statement on the point whether the perils insured against are part of the "risk or adventure"; but art. 83 of the articles of association, which were held to form part of the policy, does indicate that certain perils were covered.

(*h*) As has already been pointed out, "risk" seems here to be used in a narrower sense than in the Stamp Act, and to denote the perils insured against.

(*i*) See Gow, 24.

(*k*) Edwards *v.* Aberayron, &c. Ins. Society, *supra*.

Sect. 38. a mere perusal of the slip, what these perils and all the terms and conditions of the insurance are intended to be (*l*). It may be suggested that when the slip is only initialed the names of the underwriters do not sufficiently appear; but this is probably an ambiguity which can be explained by parol evidence. There can be little doubt that the initials are a sufficient signature within sect. 24 of the Marine Insurance Act, 1906 (*m*).

Agreements to issue policies.

39. An express agreement to issue a policy sometimes forms part of a cover note issued by a company. As by sect. 91 of the Stamp Act, 1891, the term "policy of insurance" includes every writing whereby any contract of insurance is agreed to be made, it seems that an agreement to issue a policy, if in writing, would be a policy within that Act, and that it could not be enforced unless it contained the particulars required by the Act. Moreover, any agreement to execute a policy is itself a contract of sea insurance within the meaning of sect. 93 (1) of the Act (*n*), and therefore, if verbal, is invalid under the Act (*o*).

Apart from the provisions of the Stamp Act, there is no reason why specific performance of an agreement to issue a policy should not be ordered in a proper case (*p*).

(*l*) A specimen of a slip for a Lloyd's policy is given in Appendix B.

(*m*) See 1 Smith's L. C. 11th ed. 335.

(*n*) See Mallet *v.* Bateman (1865), L. R. 1 C. P. 163, that an agreement for guaranty is a guaranty within the meaning of the Statute of Frauds. See also In re London Mar. Ins. Association, Smith's Case (1869), L. R. 4 Ch. 611, per Selwyn, L. J., at p. 614, that a contract for a policy of insurance was within the terms of 35 Geo. 3, c. 63.

(*o*) Genforsikrings Aktieselskabet *v.* Da Costa, [1911] 1 K. B. 137.

(*p*) See Bhugwandass *v.* Netherlands India Ins. Co. (1888), 14 App. Cas. 83, a Rangoon case in which the Privy Council ordered specific performance of a contract to issue a policy in terms of an open cover note. Royal Exchange Ass. Co. *v.* Tod (1892), 8 Times L. R. 669, was an action before Romer, J., for specific performance of an agreement to issue a policy, in which the question at issue was what classes of voyages were covered by the slip. The claim was dismissed on the merits, and the point that an unstamped slip did not constitute an enforceable contract seems neither to have been taken by the defendant nor by the learned judge.

CHAP. II.] OF SEA-POLICIES. 59

In the United States, where the restrictions of the revenue law do not interfere, and the great bulk of sea insurance business is carried on by companies, it is very generally the case that a memorandum of the contract, or an agreement to insure, is made out and subscribed before executing the policy: in such case "the usual practice," says Phillips, is, "to enter the agreement on the books of the insurance company, subscribed by some officer authorized to bind the company. Such a memorandum is binding on the company to make out a policy if the premium is paid in due time " (*q*).

Sect. 39.
The practice in the United States.

Many questions have arisen, and very elaborate decisions taken place, in the United States as to what will amount to the consummation of an agreement to insure between parties in different places, communicating by letter or message (*r*).

40. The policy is the only legal evidence of the terms of the contract of marine insurance; and, as such, will be avoided, according to one of the best-known rules of the common law (*s*), as against any party, by any material alteration introduced into it, without his consent, after it has once been entered into by him (*t*).

Corrections and alterations in the policy at Common Law.

41. Whether, when there has been a mistake made in drawing up the policy, and its terms do not rightly express the true intention of the parties at the time they entered into

Can a policy be rectified?

(*q*) 1 Phillips, s. 13. "It has long since been established that such a binding slip is itself a contract of insurance, and that a direct action at law will lie upon it, as well as a suit in equity": per Holt, D. J., in Kerr *v.* Union Mar. Ins. Co. (1903), 124 Fed. R. 835, 837.

(*r*) 1 Phillips, s. 13 *et seq.* Phillips details at length the cases on this subject; see also 1 Duer, 66, 109 *et seq.*

(*s*) Master *v.* Miller (1797), 4 T. R. 320; 2 H. Bl. 140; 1 Smith's L. C. 11th ed. 767; Fairlie *v.* Christie (1817), 7 Taunt. 416;

Davidson *v.* Cooper (1843), 11 M. & W. 778, 802; in error (1844), 13 M. & W. 343; Suffell *v.* Bank of England (1882), 9 Q. B. D. 555— C. A. See the cases on policies, *post*, §§ 43, 44.

(*t*) There is a questionable ruling of Lord Ellenborough's, that (although the contract of each underwriter is separate) the policy is to be deemed to be still in *fieri*, still incomplete, until the whole amount of the insurance has been subscribed: Robinson *v.* Tobin (1816), 1 Stark. 336. The point decided in that case was one of pleading.

Sect. 41. the contract, there is power to rectify it, is a question on which there have been conflicting decisions. There can be no doubt that before the Stamp Act of 1795 the Courts of Equity did exercise such a power when, in the words of Story, J., the mistake was "made out by the clearest evidence, according to the understanding of both parties, and upon testimony entirely exact and satisfactory" (*u*).

Case in which a Court of Equity has exercised this power.

Thus, where the risk was described in the early part of a policy as a voyage "at and from Fort St. George," yet in that part of the policy which defines the duration of the risk, the words were "beginning the adventure from and immediately following the ship's departure from Fort St. George," and it was proved that the policy had been filled up from a label, signed by the agent of the assured and two of the directors of the company, in which the risk was described to be "at and from" Fort St. George, and it was not disputed by the underwriters that the label expressed the intention of both parties, Lord Hardwicke held that the policy should be considered one "at and from" (*x*).

Case in which the Court refused to exercise this power.

In another case, where rectification of a policy was sought, but the evidence appeared to be contradictory, Lord Hardwicke dismissed the bill, at the same time stating that while the Court of Chancery had jurisdiction to relieve in respect of a plain mistake in contracts, if reduced into writing contrary to the intention of the parties, it would only exert such power upon being satisfied by the strongest possible evidence that a mistake had really been made (*y*).

Mackenzie v. Coulson.

In 1869, in Mackenzie *v.* Coulson (*z*), a bill was filed by underwriters for the rectification of a policy, for the reason that the clause "warranted free of particular average" had by mistake been omitted, and they produced the slip in which the clause appeared. But James, V.-C., dismissed the bill

---

(*u*) Andrews *v.* Essex Fire and Marine Ins. Co. (1822), 3 Mason's Rep. 6.

(*x*) Motteux *v.* London Ass. Co. (1739), 1 Atkyns, 545. Phillips (vol. i. s. 117) remarks that the policy itself appears to have authorised such a construction, without rectification.

(*y*) Henkle *v.* Royal Exch. Ass. (1749), 1 Ves. Sen. 317.

(*z*) (1869), L. R. 8 Eq. 368.

CHAP. II.] OF SEA-POLICIES. 61

on the ground that there can be no rectification, unless there has been an actual concluded contract antecedent to the instrument which it is sought to rectify, and that the slip did not constitute a contract (*a*).

Sect. 41.

On the other hand, Barnes, J., in a subsequent case ordered the rectification of a policy which was not in accordance with the slip (*b*); and, in a later case, in which Mackenzie *v.* Coulson was cited, Mathew, J., held that he had power to order the rectification of a policy, though in the absence of clear evidence of a common mistake he refused to do so (*c*).

In another case, Bigham, J., rectified a policy by inserting a clause which was not in the cover note, but was contained in an earlier policy, with which the judge found that the policy in dispute was intended to be identical in terms; and the Court of Appeal decided the case on the construction of the clause which the learned judge had inserted (*d*).

Thus the weight of authority supports the view that, notwithstanding the provisions of the Stamp Act, a policy can be rectified, and, with the exception of James, V.-C., the

---

(*a*) The principle of this decision is approved by Sir Edward Fry; Specific Performance, s. 791. S. 21 of the Mar. Ins. Act, 1906, declares that "a contract of marine insurance is deemed to be concluded when the proposal of the assured is accepted by the insurer, whether the policy be then issued or not," and in the ordinary course of business the insurer signifies his acceptance by initialing the slip. But although the statement in s. 21 is general in its terms, it seems to be made with reference to the provisions of ss. 18 and 20.

(*b*) The Aikshaw (1893), 9 T. L. R. 605. The report does not show whether the point was taken that there was no power to rectify.

(*c*) Spalding *v.* Crocker (1897), 2 Com. Cas. 189. In Empress Ass. Corp. *v.* Bowring (1906), 11 Com. Cas. 107, Kennedy, J., although he refused to rectify the policies, obviously considered that he had power to rectify them after ascertaining the intention of the parties from the slip.

(*d*) North Queensland Ins. Co. *v.* Rhenish Westphalian Ins. Co., *coram* Bigham, J., 21st February, 1901, C. A., 21st March, 1902, unreported. No question was raised, either at the trial or on appeal, as to the power of the judge to rectify the policy. In Emanuel *v.* Weir (1914), 30 T. L. R. 518, Bailhache, J., rectified a policy, to make it agree with the usual form covered by the slip.

Sect. 41. judges have referred to the slip or cover note in order to ascertain the intention of the parties. As sect. 89 of the Marine Insurance Act declares that "where there is a duly stamped policy, reference may be made, as heretofore, to the slip or covering note, in any legal proceeding," it now seems impossible in an action for rectification to reject the evidence of the slip (*e*).

Correction of a mistake in declaring interest.

The contract of the underwriters is complete in fact and in form when they have signed the policy; but a declaration of interest to be afterwards made stands on a different footing to a contract; it is the mere exercise of a power conferred on the insured, and need not of necessity be in writing; if, therefore, a broker has committed a blunder in making this declaration, as where he has declared goods by the wrong ship, this blunder may be rectified by parol evidence, either with or without the assent of the underwriters (*f*).

Corrections by consent.

42. The parties themselves may, by consent, introduce any alterations into the policy, even after it is underwritten, whether by an erasure, an interlineation (*g*), or an addition in a blank space, which may be required by their mutual interests, and sanctioned by their mutual agreement (subject, however, to the provisions of the Stamp Act); and such alterations, if properly signed, and not infringing the provisions of the Stamp Act, form as valid a contract between the parties as the terms of the original policy.

Alterations must be in writing,

As, however, no contract can have the effect of varying or altering another, unless it be of as high a nature as the

(*e*) If, indeed, the view that the ordinary slip is a valid policy be correct, the ground of James, V.-C.'s, decision no longer exists, and the only question that can arise when it is sought to rectify a policy by such a slip is whether the slip can be given in evidence without being stamped. On that question s. 89 of the Mar. Ins. Act, 1906, seems decisive.

(*f*) Mar. Ins. Act, 1906, s. 29;

Robinson *v.* Touray (1811), 3 Camp. 158; *S. C.*, 1 M. & S. 217. See the usage stated in Stephens *v.* Australasian Ins. Co. (1872), L. R. 8 C. P. 18, and other cases which are noticed in Chap. IX. Part I., where such declarations are discussed.

(*g*) Striking a pen across words is a cancelling of the words: Fairlie *v.* Christie (1817), 7 Taunt. 416.

instrument upon which it so professes to operate, these alterations must be in writing, either in a separate instrument referring to the original policy, or by memorandum on the face or back of the policy; and, in either case, subscribed by or, as is most usual in practice, signed by the initials of the underwriters who are intended to be bound by them (*h*).

<small>Sect. 42.</small>

The only ground upon which a written alteration of this kind can be binding upon any of the parties to the original policy is his assent thereto signified by his signature; although, therefore, all the rest of the underwriters may have signed such an indorsement, yet if only one have not done so, he is not bound by the policy as altered (*i*).

<small>Initialed by the parties.</small>

The general rule, then, is, that any material alteration of the policy by the assured avoids the policy, except as to those underwriters who have consented to it in writing by signing their initials to the memorandum in which the alteration is specified, or to the interlineation, erasure, or addition by which it is effected (*k*).

<small>General rule.</small>

43. The question has generally been, What constitutes a material alteration? To use the language of Judge Duer, does it change the sense, or affect in any degree the substance, of the contract?

<small>What are material alterations.</small>

Where a ship was insured from Virginia to Rotterdam, with leave to call at a port in England, and the assured, after the policy was underwritten, by consent of some of the underwriters (indorsed on the policy), altered her destination from Rotterdam to Hull; this was held to avoid the policy as to all the underwriters, except those who had signed the indorsement (*l*).

<small>Alteration of destination.</small>

(*h*) Kaines *v.* Knightly (1682), Skinner, 54; Robinson *v.* Tobin (1816), 1 Stark. 336.

(*i*) Forshaw *v.* Chabert (1821), 3 Brod. & B. 158; see also 1 Duer, 78—81, 142 *et seq.*

(*k*) Laird *v.* Robertson (1791), 4 Brown's Parl. Cases, 488; Langhorn *v.* Cologan (1812), 4 Taunt.

330; Fairlie *v.* Christie (1817), 7 Taunt. 416; Campbell *v.* Christie (1817), 2 Stark. 64; Sanderson *v.* Symonds (1819), 1 Brod. & B. 426; Forshaw *v.* Chabert (1821), 3 Brod. & B. 158.

(*l*) Laird *v.* Robertson (1791), 4 Brown's Parl. Cases, 488.

Sect. 43.
The insertion of a subject of insurance.
Altering time of sailing.
Adding alternative *terminus ad quem*.

So the insertion of a specific subject of insurance in a policy which had been executed in blank (*m*); the alteration of the specified day in a warranty as to the time of sailing (*n*); the alteration of a policy "from Colmar to Portsmouth" into a policy "from Colmar to Portsmouth, or Weymouth" (*o*), were held to be material alterations which prevented the assured from recovering against those underwriters who had not subscribed the alteration, and this in the last-cited case although the underwriter, when first informed of the alteration, had said he would not take advantage of it.

Inserting liberty to call.

So, where a ship was insured from "Cuba to Liverpool, with liberty in that voyage to proceed to and touch and stay at and discharge and take in at any ports or places whatsoever, without prejudice":—after the subscription of the policy a leave "to call off Jamaica" was inserted in the body of it. The Court held, that, as Jamaica was out of the direct course of the voyage insured, this was a material alteration which avoided the policy as to an underwriter who had not signed it; although his not doing so appeared to have arisen solely from his being out of the way when the other underwriters initialed the alteration (*p*).

Immaterial alterations.

44. On the other hand, where the alteration is not material, it will not vitiate the policy; but in such case, if some of the underwriters have consented to the alteration, after the policy is executed, and others refuse, those who consent make the altered instrument their own; but those who do not, remain liable on their original contract (*q*).

The following alterations have been considered not to be material. A policy was originally filled up,." on the Three Sisters, at and from Cadiz and Seville to Liverpool": after the policy was underwritten the broker added the words

---

(*m*) Langhorn *v.* Cologan (1812), 4 Taunt. 330.

(*n*) Fairlie *v.* Christie (1817), 7 Taunt. 416; *S. C.* at N. P. (1816), Holt, 331.

(*o*) Campbell *v.* Christie (1817),

(*p*) Forshaw *v.* Chabert (1821), 3 Brod. & B. 158.

(*q*) Per Richardson, J., in Sanderson *v.* M'Callum (1819), 4 J. B. Moore, 5.

"Tres Hermanas" (Spanish for "the Three Sisters") and also the words "both or either" to the description of the voyage: Lord Ellenborough said that, "as the English name, the Three Sisters, did not amount to a warranty that the ship was an English ship, the policy was not avoided by merely inserting the equivalent Spanish name of 'Tres Hermanas.'" As to the words "both or either," his Lordship said, that "as the ship, as originally insured, had the option of going both to Seville and Cadiz or not, as it might suit the exigencies of the adventure, these words did not give any additional liberty, and therefore did not affect the legal operation of the instrument" (r).

<small>Sect. 44. "Tres Hermanas," inserted after "The Three Sisters," as the Spanish name of the ship.</small>

A ship was insured "from Liverpool to her port or ports of discharge and loading in Africa, during her stay there and back to Liverpool, with liberty to proceed and sail to and touch and stay at any ports or places wheresoever, to sell, barter, and exchange, and load, unload, or reload goods at any or all of the ports and places she may call at or proceed to." The broker, after the subscription of the policy, fearing that the words employed might not be sufficiently extensive to include a trading, added the words "and trade." He then presented it to the various underwriters for their consent to this alteration, which most of them signified by signing their initials to the underlined words: the defendant, however, refused to do so, alleging that he never underwrote trading policies to Africa. It was contended that, as the defendant had expressly refused to underwrite a trading policy to Africa, the alteration in question must be deemed material; but the Court were clearly of opinion that it was not so, because, independently of the words inserted, the plaintiff had, upon the true construction of the policy as it originally stood, liberty to trade on the coast of Africa (s).

<small>"To trade," inserted in a liberty "to sell, barter, and exchange."</small>

(r) Clapham v. Cologan (1813), 3 Camp. 382.
(s) Sanderson v. Symonds (1819), 1 Brod. & Bing. 426; Sanderson v. M'Callum (1819), 4 J. B. Moore, 5, S. P. See the remarks of Duer, vol. i. pp. 78—81, on the general principle involved in the cases, and

Sect. 45.
Material alterations on the face,

45. There seems no doubt that a material alteration, unassented to, will avoid the policy wherever made on the face thereof, *i.e.*, in the margin as much as in the body of the instrument: (in fact, in Fairlie *v.* Christie, cited above, the alteration was in the margin.) With regard to memoranda on the back of the policy, and not signed by any of the underwriters, as they could not generally be operative, Judge Duer (no doubt with reason) thinks they would not avoid the policy, even if embodying material alterations (*t*).

and on the back of the policy.

Alterations in relation to the Stamp Act.

46. The cases hitherto considered were decided upon the principles of the common law. We will now discuss the effect of the stamp laws upon the same subject.

S. 96 of 54 & 55 Vict. c. 39.

The Stamp Act, 1891, s. 96, in effect provides, that even where the underwriter has so consented to the alteration in the policy, the altered policy cannot be enforced without a fresh stamp (*u*) unless the alteration comply with all the requisites specified in the clause. The clause is as follows: "Nothing in this Act shall prohibit the making of any alteration which may lawfully be made in the terms and conditions of any policy of sea-insurance after the policy has been underwritten; provided that the alteration be made before notice of the determination of the risk originally insured, and that it do not prolong the time covered by the insurance thereby made beyond the period of six months in the case of a policy made for a less period than six months, or beyond the period of twelve months in the case of a policy made for a greater period than six months, and that the articles insured remain the property of the same person or persons, and that no

---

pp. 142—146 for illustrations, including some American authorities: see also 1 Phillips, s. 109 *et seq.*

(*t*) 1 Duer, 82; see also Henderson *v.* Stevenson (1875), L. R. 2 H. of L. (Sc.) 470. Duer also thinks that the addition of a new clause will not avoid the policy, if it has a new date affixed to it, subsequent to that of the policy, since the invalidity of the alteration, when not signed by the insurers, is then apparent on its face, and hence the possibility of fraud is excluded: 1 Duer, 82.

(*u*) See *ante*, § 32, as to stamping a policy after execution, on payment of a penalty.

additional or further sum be insured by reason or means of the alteration." Sect. 46.

This section (which ought to have a liberal construction (*x*)) does not legalize any alteration in policies, which would have been illegal at common law, without the assent of the underwriter; but even though the underwriter have assented to it, the policy if not re-stamped cannot be enforced, unless the alteration comply with all the requisites of this section. Effect of the provision in this section.

47. From the cases on the similarly worded section of 35 Geo. 3, c. 63 (s. 13), it appears that by the words "before notice of the determination of the risk originally insured" is meant that determination of the risk which is caused "by the loss, or safe arrival, of the thing insured, or by the final end and conclusion of the voyage" (*y*). Cases on the construction of the section.

Hence the determination of the risk by non-compliance with a warranty to sail before a given day is not within the meaning of this term. Thus, where a policy "on goods to be shipped on board ship or ships which should sail between the 1st of October, 1799, and the 1st of June, 1800," was altered by a memorandum extending the time of sailing until the 1st of August, 1800, after the original time for sailing had expired, but before the loss happened, Lord Ellenborough and the Court of King's Bench held that this was an alteration made before notice of the determination of the risk (*z*). Extending time of sailing.

Where a ship was insured "from Stockholm to Swinemunde," and while she was lying at Wisby for repairs, as it was doubtful whether the enemy might not be at Swinemunde, the underwriters consented to alter the policy by adding the words "Kœnigsberg or Memel" after the word "Swinemunde," the Court held that the alteration was Change of terminus.

(*x*) Per Lord Tenterden in Brockelbank *v.* Sugrue (1830), 1 B. & Ad. 88, on the similar provision of 35 Geo. 3, c. 63.

(*y*) Per Lord Ellenborough in Kensington *v.* Inglis (1807), 8 East, 291.

(*z*) Kensington *v.* Inglis (1807), 8 East, 273; see also Hubbard *v.* Jackson (1811), 4 Taunt. 169; Ridsdale *v.* Shedden (1814), 4 Camp. 107.

5 (2)

Sect. 47. made while there was only an intention to determine the risk originally insured, and before its actual determination (*a*). If, indeed, the change of terminus were such as to involve the entire substitution of a new adventure for that originally insured, the case would, no doubt, be different (*b*).

A release from a warranty to sail before a certain day which has the effect of changing a summer risk to a winter risk is not the substitution of a new adventure. It is, therefore, not a determination of the risk, but only a change in the conditions of the policy, which may be made without a fresh stamp (*c*).

Condition that the thing insured shall remain the property of the same person.

48. Another of the conditions on which an alteration may be made in the terms of the policy is that "the articles insured shall remain the property of the same person or persons."

"The words, the thing insured shall remain the property, &c., appear to us," says Lord Ellenborough, "properly to require and apply to one identical and continued subject-matter of insurance, ... and to be ill-suited to a case where the thing last insured is not only in fact, but in name and in kind (as a specific subject of insurance), essentially different from the thing first insured." (*d*).

"Ship and outfit" altered to "ship and goods."

Hence where a policy was effected "at and from London to the South Seas, during the ship's stay and fishing there, and at and from thence to Great Britain," "on ship and outfit"; and then, with the consent of the underwriters, after the subscription of the policy, but before notice of loss, was altered into a policy "on ship and goods"; it was held, that the policy after this alteration required a new stamp, because the outfit originally insured was a totally different

(*a*) Ramstrom *v.* Bell (1816), 5 M. & S. 267; see also Brockelbank *v.* Sugrue (1830), 1 B. & Ad. 81.

(*b*) See 1 Duer, 84; the argument for the defendant in Brockelbank *v.* Sugrue, *supra;* and Lord Tenterden's illustration in the same case of a change to a voyage requiring a different stamp.

(*c*) Hubbard *v.* Jackson (1811), 4 Taunt. 169.

(*d*) Per Lord Ellenborough in Hill *v.* Patten (1807), 8 East, 375.

CHAP. II.] OF SEA-POLICIES. 69

kind of thing, on a whaling voyage, from "goods" to which the altered policy was made to apply (e). Sect. 48.

It must, however, be borne in mind, that the above decision is confined to cases where, by the alteration, the kind or description of the original subject of insurance is wholly changed: it is not at all intended that the subject of insurance should, throughout the voyage, continue the same specific thing, but only the same denomination of thing. The subject of insurance need not continue the same specific thing, only the same denomination of thing.

Thus, where an insurance was effected "on goods, which should first sail on board any ship or ships sailing between the 1st of October, 1799, to the 1st of June, 1800, to the amount of 45,000l.," it was held, that an alteration extending the time of sailing from the 1st of June to the 1st of August did not require a new stamp; for it was a mere alteration in the terms and conditions of the policy, and not in the subject-matter of the insurance; for, *non constat*, that the goods shipped on board before the altered time of sailing were different goods from those intended to be shipped on board originally (f). So, where a policy was "on hemp, marked R.," it was held that a memorandum withdrawing the mark did not make a fresh stamp necessary (g).

49. We have already seen that an express warranty may be altered without a fresh stamp (h); it has also been decided that a memorandum by which the underwriter consents to waive the implied warranty that the ship was seaworthy at the time of sailing is not such an alteration of the policy as to require a fresh stamp, for such consent prevents the inference which would otherwise arise, that the unseaworthiness was a determination of the risk (i). Memorandum waiving implied warranty of seaworthiness.

50. Even where an alteration is not within the exemption created by sect. 96 of the Stamp Act, it will not require a Correction of a mistake.

(e) Hill v. Patten (1807), 8 East, 373.

(f) Kensington v. Inglis (1807), 8 East, 273.

(g) Hubbard v. Jackson (1811), 4 Taunt. 169.

(h) *Ante*, § 47.

(i) Weir v. Aberdein (1820), 2 B. & Ald. 320, as explained in Quebec Marine Ins. Co. v. Commercial Bank of Canada (1870), L. R. 3 P. C. 234.

Sect. 50. fresh stamp if it be merely the correction of a mistake. There is a wide difference, as regards the stamp, between cases in which the alteration is such a correction only, and those in which it is in fact intended to make a new instrument: the one is an alteration of the contract for the mere purpose of making it express in terms what both parties intended it should express at the time of making it; the other is an alteration for the purpose of giving it a different meaning and extent to that which both parties intended it to bear at the moment of its execution. It is for this reason that alterations of the first class require no fresh stamp, while those of the second do (*k*).

Thus, in a case where, the assured having no interest in the ship, but only in the cargo, the words "on ship," which had been inserted by pure mistake, were struck out, and the words "on goods as interest may appear" substituted in their room, it was held, that the memorandum empowering this alteration required no new stamp (*l*). This case is distinguished from that of Hill *v*. Patten on the ground that there the assured was owner of the ship, and, as such, interested in the outfit: and also, that there the intention really was to alter the nature of the subject-matter from what the parties had originally meant and understood it to be; whereas here the intention only was to correct an error, and the alteration had only the effect of putting the policy into the state in which it was originally intended to have been framed.

Effect of not re-stamping on the original instrument.
51. Where no rights or liabilities can be enforced under the altered instrument by reason of the stamp laws, the rights and liabilities which existed under the original instrument are nevertheless destroyed by the alteration (*m*).

(*k*) Cole *v*. Parkin (1810), 12 East, 471.

(*l*) Sawtell *v*. Loudon (1814), 5 Taunt. 359; see also Robinson *v*. Touray (1811), 3 Camp. 158; 1 M. & S. 217. In that case the policy was on goods by "ship or ships" to be thereafter declared, and the broker by mistake made declaration of a wrong ship. It was held that a memorandum rectifying this mistake required no fresh stamp.

(*m*) Per Bayley, J., in Reed *v*. Deere (1827), 7 B. & C. 264.

OF SEA-POLICIES.

After the Court, in Hill v. Patten, had decided that the alteration of "outfits" into "goods" was one which could not be made without a fresh stamp, and therefore that the plaintiff could not recover on the policy as altered, the plaintiff brought an action upon the policy in its original form; but the Court held he could not recover on that either (*n*). Lord Ellenborough said, "that the altered policy, though ineffectual as an instrument to sue on, was effectual to do away with the former agreement, which was thereby abandoned" (*o*); and Le Blanc, J., asks "how the Court can enforce an agreement, after the parties themselves, upon the very face of the same instrument, have declared that it is not their agreement, and have actually written another and a different agreement in the place of it" (*p*). It would seem to make no difference whether the memorandum embodying the alteration is written on the back or the face of the original policy (*q*), provided it be signed by the underwriter.

Sect. 51.

52. The assured, after acceptance of a valid policy, may forfeit all benefit under it; for instance, by breach or non-performance of one of the warranties expressed or implied in the instrument itself, or of a condition precedent under which the instrument was granted (*r*), or by such an alteration of the instrument as at common law or by virtue of the Stamp Acts renders it a nullity, or by such illegality affecting the assured adventure as makes it incapable of protection under the sanction of the law.

Forfeiture of policy.

We have seen that a forfeiture for breach of a warranty may be waived by a memorandum endorsed on the policy and signed by the underwriter (*s*). But when a policy was vitiated by concealment of a material fact on the part of the assured's agent, and afterwards the underwriter, upon learn-

Waiver of forfeiture.

(*n*) (1807), 1 Camp. 72; French v. Patten (1808), 9 East, 351.
(*o*) Ibid. 355.
(*p*) Ibid. 357.
(*q*) Reed v. Deere (1827), 7 B. & C. 261.

(*r*) Hughes v. Tindall (1856), 18 C. B. 98; Turnbull v. Woolfe (1863), 9 Jur. N. S. 57.

(*s*) Weir v. Aberdein, *ante*, § 49.

Sect. 52. ing what had happened, wrote to the plaintiff's agents in these words: "Understanding that the steamer B. has been on shore, I do not consider that my risk commences until the vessel has been surveyed and repaired"—this letter was held not to be a waiver of the breach of the warranty (*t*).

Continuing or renewing policy.

53. The question of continuing or renewing a policy has been considered in a couple of cases (*u*). Subject to the provisions of the Stamp Act being complied with, there is no reason why a time policy should not be expressed to continue or to be renewable for a further period of time, unless determined by notice (*x*).

Rescission of contract.

54. The rescission of the contract must be the act of both parties to it, the assured and the insurer. The insurance broker, acting for the former, has no implied authority, merely by virtue of his capacity as such agent, to demand or consent to the cancellation of the policy, even though it had been left in his hands (*y*). But the conduct of the principals in this matter may be so ambiguous that their intention may become a question of law for the Court upon the construction of their written communications, or a question of fact for a jury upon consideration of what was said and done between them (*z*).

A vessel insured against fire for twelve months, ending the 29th of July, arrived at Liverpool on the 12th of April, and the assured wrote a letter to the insurance broker, proposing

---

(*t*) Russell *v*. Thornton (1859), 4 H. & N. 788; 29 L. J. Ex. 9; in orror (1860), 6 H. & N. 140; 30 L. J. Ex. 69. It was also held that the letter could not create a fresh contract, being at the utmost a mere unaccepted proposal.

(*u*) See per Cockburn, C. J., in Michael *v*. Gillespy (1857), 2 C. B. N. S. 627; Lishman *v*. Northern Marit. Ins. Co. (1873), L. R. 8 C. P. 216; Charlesworth *v*. Faber (1900), 5 Com. Cas. 408.

(*x*) A policy cannot, of course, be prolonged, except by a continuation clause, so as to cover a period of more than one year. Stamp Act, 1891, ss. 93 (2), 96; Finance Act, 1901, s. 11. See Charlesworth *v*. Faber (1900), 5 Com. Cas. 408; *ante*, § 31; and *post*, § 440.

(*y*) Xenos *v*. Wickham (1866), L. R. 2 H. L. 296; in the Ex. Ch. (1865), 14 C. B. N. S. 435, 449, 463; see also Russell *v*. Thornton (1859), 4 H. & N. 788.

(*z*) Ionides *v*. Harford (1859), 29 L. J. Ex. 36.

a cancellation of the policy and return of premium, "say from the 12th of April." The other sent for the policy "to put forward returns for cancellation," and received it. On the 21st of April the broker cancelled it on the terms of returning premium from the 30th April to the 30th July, alleging a custom of insurance brokers not to reckon broken months. The ship was burnt on the 22nd April, and that same day the assured wrote a letter, withdrawing his proposal to cancel, as he had then received no answer; and whether, under these circumstances, there had been a cancellation, and on what terms, was the question. It was held that the broker, by sending for the policy on receipt of the proposal to cancel, must be taken to have acceded to the terms proposed, and to have cancelled on those terms. The plaintiff therefore lost the insurance, and recovered the difference on the return of premium for the period between the 12th and 30th April (a).

A policy on ship from Liverpool to Philadelphia and United Kingdom was altered by memorandum substituting Baltimore for Philadelphia, and was afterwards further altered by this memorandum: "In consideration of an additional premium, it is hereby agreed to allow the vessel to go to Antwerp." In this state of the policy, the ship arrived at Antwerp and was ordered to Leith, but was lost on her way thither. It was held that she was uninsured at the time of the loss, as the effect of the second memorandum was to terminate the risk at Antwerp (b).

Sect. 54.

(a) Baines v. Woodfall (1859), 6 C. B. N. S. 657; 28 L. J. C. P. 338.

(b) Stone v. Marine Ins. Co. Ocean, Ltd. of Gothenburg (1876), 1 Ex. D. 81.

CHAPTER III.

OF THE CONSTRUCTION OF SEA-POLICIES.

SECT.	SECT.
Evidence of Usage of Trade, &c. ...55—61	Explanation of Ambiguities in Contract ...67—72
	Written and Printed Clauses.73, 74
Usage must be notorious, &c..62—66	Inexplicable Ambiguities 75

The principles of construction applicable to sea-policies are the same as those applied to other mercantile contracts.

55. THE principles which govern the construction of sea-policies do not vary from those applicable to all other mercantile instruments.

The language of sea-policies is frequently indeterminate, ambiguous, or technical. When this is so, parol evidence, as in the case of other contracts, is admissible to explain it (*a*). The language of sea-policies is also frequently incomplete as an expression of the meaning of the parties, because it is employed, and is understood so to be, with reference to the usages of trade (*b*): in this latter class of cases (and they are very numerous) the meaning of the contract embodied in a sea-policy may, nay must, be explained by parol evidence of

(*a*) Thus where the description of the voyage insured was ambiguous, evidence that the rate of premium was the same, whether the wider or narrower meaning was given to the words, was admitted in Preston *v.* Greenwood (1784), 4 Dougl. 28. In Oceanic SS. Co. *v.* Faber (1907), 13 Com. Cas. 28, Buckley, L. J., took the smallness of the premium into consideration in determining the construction of the Inchmaree clause (see § 861a) in a policy on port risks. In Otago Farmers' Co-op. Ass. *v.* Thompson, [1910] 2 K. B. 145, the policy contained an ambiguously worded warranty; and Hamilton, J., seems to have doubted the admissibility of evidence (given without objection) that the rate of premium usually charged for such an insurance as, according to the contention of the assured, was effected by the policy was much higher than the premium actually charged.

(*b*) *I.e.*, as Judge Duer very correctly expresses it, "not of trade in the largest sense of the word, but of that export and import trade which is conducted by navigation." 1 Duer, 180.

CHAP. III.] CONSTRUCTION OF SEA-POLICIES. 75

those usages, a knowledge of which in such cases forms the only available key to the real intention of the parties (c).

Sect. 55.

In this class of cases, even where the language of the policy is on the face of it unambiguous, yet, as without reference to the usage, the mere terms employed would not be a complete expression of the mind and intention of the contracting parties, evidence of usage, if not repugnant to the express terms of the instrument, is always admitted to show what the true nature of the contract, as mutually understood by the parties, really was.

Evidence of usage.

In such cases, in the language of Lord Mansfield, "the question is, whether the usage has not explained the generality of the words. If it has, every man who contracts under a usage does it as if the point of usage were inserted in the contract in terms" (d).

(c) Mason v. Skurray (1780), 1 Marsh, 226; 1 Park, 253.

(d) The following is Arnould's note on this passage (see 2nd ed. of this work, p. 70):—"It is to these "cases (viz., where the terms of "the policy are employed with "reference to the usages of trade, "and incomplete as an expression "of the meaning of the parties "without such reference) that we "must apply the strong expressions "of Lord Mansfield and some other "judges as to the force of usage in "interpreting policies. Thus, in "Preston v. Greenwood (1784), 4 "Dougl. 28, Lord Mansfield says: "'Usage is always considered in "'policies of insurance, even where "'the words are plain'; and Buller, "J., in Long v. Allen, ibid. 276: "'In policies of insurance in par- "'ticular, a great latitude of con- "'struction as to usage has been "'admitted'; and again (which is "the strongest expression on the "subject to be found in the books): "'Usage not only explains but con- "'trols the policy.' Judge Duer

"considers Buller, J., strictly accu- "rate in the use of the word con- "trol, which, as he truly states, does "not necessarily imply to contra- "dict: 'The distinction made by "'the learned judge between ex- "'plaining and controlling really "'does exist. Where the words to "'be interpreted are indeterminate "'or ambiguous, the usage explains "'them; but when they convey a "'definite meaning that the Court "'would be bound to adopt, or their "'construction has been settled by "'law, the usage controls them; "'and in these cases it does set "'aside what, judging only from "'the terms of the policy or the "'rule of law, was the plain in- "'tention of the parties; but, in "'controlling, the usage does not "'contradict the words, it merely "'varies, by restraining or enlarg- "'ing, their application.' Duer, "vol. i. pp. 245, 246."

This note is retained by the present editors because of the high authority from which it emanates. It is, however, impossible not to feel

Sect. 55.
Provisions of Marine Insurance Act as to effect of usage.

The Marine Insurance Act, 1906, expressly recognizes the effect of usage upon the construction of the contract. By sect. 87:—

(1) Where any right, duty, or liability would arise under a contract of marine insurance by implication of law, it may be negatived or varied by express agreement, or by usage, if the usage be such as to bind both parties to the contract.

(2) The provisions of this section extend to any right, duty, or liability declared by this Act which may be lawfully modified by agreement.

Former notion as to construction of policies.

56. From the frequency, probably, of such cases as those just referred to in this branch of the law, a notion appears at one time to have prevailed (favoured unquestionably by certain reported expressions of the earlier judges) that sea-policies were not amenable to the rules of construction generally applicable to all other mercantile contracts, but were to be interpreted so as to carry out the assumed intentions of the parties, even though repugnant to the terms in which their intentions purported to be expressed on the face of the instrument itself.

Usage cannot vary express terms of policy.

This notion is now discarded as erroneous (*e*). Parol evidence, whether of usage or otherwise, can in no case be admitted to contradict or materially vary the plain and express terms of a sea-policy (*f*); it can only be admitted either to explain those terms where technical or ambiguous, or to modify and add to them where they are plainly employed with reference to some usage of trade, and without

---

the force of Phillips' criticisms (in s. 133) on Duer's explanation of the word "control." If the word means no more than to "interpret," or "explain," then clearly a usage which "controls" the policy does not necessarily contradict it; but understanding the word in the sense in which Judge Duer evidently understood it, it is difficult to see how a usage which "varies, by restraining or enlarging," the application of words does not *pro tanto* contradict them.

(*e*) Weston *v.* Emes (1808), 1 Taunt. 115.

(*f*) The case, however, of Universo Ins. Co. of Milan *v.* The Merchants' Mar. Ins. Co., [1897] 1 Q. B. 205; 2 Q. B. 93, is difficult to reconcile with this rule.

CHAP. III.] CONSTRUCTION OF SEA-POLICIES. 77

such reference would, accordingly, be incomplete as an Sect. 56.
expression of the mind of the parties contracting: in such
cases the Courts may resort to any means of interpreting the
policy so as to effectuate the real intention of the parties,
which may be supplied either by the rules of the common
law, the general usages of trade, or the particular circumstances of the case (*g*).

"The same rule of construction," said Lord Ellenborough, Rule as laid
"which applies to other instruments applies equally to this, Ellenborough
viz., that it is to be construed according to the sense and *v*. French.
meaning, as collected in the first place from the terms used in
it, which terms are to be understood in their plain, ordinary,
and popular sense, unless they have generally, in respect to
the subject-matter, as by the known usage of trade or the
like, acquired a peculiar sense, distinct from the popular
sense of the same words, or unless the context evidently
points out that they must in the particular instance, and in
order to effectuate the immediate intention of the parties, be
understood in some other special and peculiar sense" (*h*).

(*g*) See 1 Emerigon, c. i. s. 5, p. 17; and c. ii. pp. 55, 56; see the judgment of Lord Denman in Trueman *v.* Loder (1840), 11 A. & E. 589; and that of Story, J., in The Schooner Reeside, 2 Sumn. 567; and the remarks of Mathew, L. J., in Ellinger *v.* Mutual Life Ins. Co. of New York (1904), 10 Com. Cas. 22, 30; *S. C.*, [1905] 1 K. B. 31; see also the admirable remarks of Mr. Chancellor Kent (Com. iii. p. 260, n. (*f*)); and especially the two very able and elaborate chapters of Judge Duer (1 Duer, 158—311). "The meaning of the rule excluding parol evidence is, that such evidence shall never be received to show the intention of the parties to have been directly opposite to that which their language expresses, or substantially different from any meaning which the words they have used upon any construction will admit or convey; but there are cases in which the language of a policy, in entire consistency with the rules of law, may be interpreted in different senses, or with a modification which, though not express, is implied: in such cases parol evidence may be admitted to determine the construction that, following the intention, ought to be adopted. The admission of such evidence varies the construction of the contract, but does not contradict or vary the agreement embodied in the policy; on the contrary, it establishes its true meaning." 1 Duer, 176, 177.

The present editors, while retaining this note, conceive that their criticisms in note (*d*), *supra*, apply also, to some extent at least, here.

(*h*) Robertson *v.* French (1803), 4 East, 135. These words were cited

Sect. 56.

"A contract of insurance," said Erle, C. J., "is a commercial instrument, and is to be construed, like all others, so as to give effect to the intention of the parties, and that intention is to be gathered from the words of the instrument interpreted by the surrounding circumstances. If the words are clear, the proper effect is to be given to them; if the words are capable of more interpretations than one, the judge, with the aid of the jury and of the surrounding circumstances, is to put the true construction upon the contract" (*i*).

57. The following are some of the more prominent rules of construction that appear to have been acted upon by our Courts in the interpretation of sea-policies.

I. Every well-settled usage of trade is *primâ facie* part of the policy.

I. Every usage of a particular branch of maritime trade which is so well settled, or so generally known, that all persons engaged in that trade may fairly be taken as contracting with reference to it, is considered to form part of every sea-policy, designed to protect risks in such trade, unless the express terms of the policy decisively repel the inference (*k*). Nor need any evidence be given in such cases that the usage has been communicated to the underwriter; for, as Lord Mansfield says, "every underwriter is presumed to be acquainted with the usage of the particular trade he insures; and if he does not know it, he ought to inform himself" (*l*). The description of the voyage in the policy, he says, in another case, "is an express reference to the usual manner of making it, as much as if every circumstance were mentioned" on the face of the instrument. "What is usually done by such a ship, on such a cargo, in such a voyage, is understood to be

---

with approval by Bowen, L. J., in Hart *v.* Standard Mar. Ins. Co. (1889), 22 Q. B. D. 499.

(*i*) Carr *v.* Montefiore (Ex. Ch. 1864), 33 L. J. Q. B. at p. 258.

(*k*) See, where in case of a fire policy on a ship, an alleged usage was not permitted to extend the risks, Pearson *v.* Commercial Union Ass. Co. (1873), L. R. 8 C. P. 548; 1 A. C. 498. The usage in this case was merely collateral to, and not necessarily connected with, the adventure insured.

(*l*) Lord Mansfield in Noble *v.* Kennoway (1780), 2 Dougl. 513; and Lord Ellenborough in Da Costa *v.* Edmunds (1815), 4 Camp. 143.

CHAP. III.] CONSTRUCTION OF SEA-POLICIES. 79

referred to in every policy, and to make a part of it as much Sect. 57.
as if it was expressed" (*m*).

Evidence of usage in these and the like cases does not
vary the terms of the policy; but, as it is expressed by Lord
Lyndhurst, merely "introduces matter upon which the policy
is silent" (*n*).

It appears that an established usage, which is not expressly Parol
excluded by the terms of the written contract, cannot be agreement insufficient to
excluded by parol agreement (*o*); *a fortiori* it seems to exclude established
follow that a representation by an assured of an intention to usage.
vary from a usage, whether such representation amount to
an agreement or not, cannot be binding on the underwriter
if not made part of the written contract (*p*).

58. The following cases illustrate the application of these China trade.
principles:—It having been the universal custom for many
years in the China trade, for all European ships, while at
Canton, to store all their rigging and furniture in storehouses,
built for that purpose on sand banks in the Canton river,
called banksauls, it was held that every underwriter insuring
a risk in the Canton trade must be considered to have done
so with reference to this usage; that the storing of the
rigging in the banksaul must be deemed to have been quite
as much part of the risk insured as though it had been expressed so to be in the policy; and that the underwriter was,
therefore, as much liable for a loss by fire happening to the
rigging so stored as for any similar loss occurring in any
other part of the adventure (*q*).

(*m*) Lord Mansfield in Pelly *v.* Royal Exch. Ass. Co. (1757), 1 Burr. 341.

(*n*) Blackett *v.* Royal Exch. Ass. Co. (1832), 2 Cr. & Jer. 249.

(*o*) See Fawkes *v.* Lamb (1862), 31 L. J. Q. B. 98. Arnould (2nd ed. p. 577), Phillips (vol. i. s. 594), Parsons (vol. i. p. 432), and Duer (vol. ii. p. 608) state the contrary, but as Maclachlan observes, without any judicial authority in support of their view. See Maclachlan's remarks in the 6th ed. of this work, pp. 541, 542. In Burges *v.* Wickham (1863), 33 L. J. Q. B. at p. 23, Cockburn, C. J., did indeed express an opinion to the contrary, but Blackburn, J., at p. 28, strongly affirmed the view in our text.

(*p*) See Leduc *v.* Ward (1888), 20 Q. B. D. 475.

(*q*) Pelly *v.* Royal Exch. Ass. Co. (1757), 1 Burr. 341; Brough *v.*

Sect. 58
East India trade.

It was formerly the uniform and well-known practice of the East India Company to reserve in their charter-parties the liberty of employing the vessel in what is called the country trade, that is, on intermediate voyages from one port to another in India. All parties engaged in this trade were taken to be fully cognizant of this usage; accordingly, under policies on ships employed by the company, though nothing was said of an intermediate voyage in the policy, yet, because the voyage insured was known by the underwriter to be an East India voyage, the Courts held that he must be presumed to have contracted with reference to all the known usages of the East India trade; and therefore that the construction of the policy should be the same as if liberty had been expressly reserved, on the face of it, to make such intermediate voyage (*r*).

Newfoundland trade.

In the Newfoundland and Labrador trades, where the main object of the voyage is to take fish, it was a well-known and general usage that the cargoes insured on such voyages, being chiefly salt and provisions, were taken out as they were wanted, and not landed, like other cargoes, on arrival; under an insurance, therefore, on such a fishing voyage, on "goods" in the usual form, "until discharged and safely landed," it was held that the underwriter, who must be taken to have insured with full cognizance of this usage, could not exempt himself from liability for a loss upon the goods because such loss had not taken place until long after the time when, but for such custom of the trade, his liability under the mere terms of the policy would have been at an end (*s*).

It was also a well-understood and familiar usage of the

Whitmore (1791), 4 T. R. 206. So also in Dennis *v.* Home Ins. Co. (1905), 136 Fed. R. 481, the defendants were held to be liable for the loss of a ship's launch while being used between the ship and the shore.

(*r*) Salvador *v.* Hopkins (1765), 3 Burr. 1707; Gregory *v.* Christie (1784), 3 Dougl. 419; Farquharson *v.* Hunter (1785), 1 Park, 105.

(*s*) Noble *v.* Kennoway (1780), 2 Dougl. 510. The voyage in this case was to the coast of Labrador, but evidence was admitted to show the usage in such case to be the same as on fishing voyages to the coast of Newfoundland.

Newfoundland trade that the ships engaged in it, after their arrival at Newfoundland, were either engaged for some time in fishing (called banking), or made intermediate voyages from one American port to another before beginning to load a cargo on the homeward voyage. It was ruled, both by Lord Eldon and Lord Ellenborough, that underwriters who had insured homeward risks on ships engaged in this trade, under policies "at and from Newfoundland," were bound to know this usage; and were not entitled to contend that such intermediate voyages vitiated the policy, by varying the risks they had intended to insure, so as to discharge them from a loss happening upon the final voyage home (*t*).

"According to the general import of the words 'at and from,'" says Lord Ellenborough, in one of these cases, "the policy would attach on the ship's first mooring in a harbour on the coast, but it doubtless may be explained differently by usage, and, as between these parties, the policy must be taken to be the same as if it had been expressed to attach on the expiration of the banking or intermediate voyage" (*u*). This certainly seems an instance of usage being permitted to control the general import of a clause in the policy as fixed by legal construction (*x*).

59. The risk on ship and goods, generally speaking, only commences at the very port or place named in the policy as that whence the ship is to sail, or where the goods are to be loaded; but if a general and well-known usage of the particular trade can be shown, that the ship under certain circumstances is to sail from, or the goods are to be loaded at, not that very port or place, but some port near it, the underwriter

Usage governs the commencement and termination of the risk.

(*t*) Vallance *v.* Dewar (1808), 1 Camp. 503; Ongier *v.* Jennings, *ibid. in notis*, per Lord Eldon in 1801, when Chief Justice of the Common Pleas.
(*u*) 1 Camp. 508.
(*x*) So Arnould, 2nd ed. p. 74. But is it not in reality simply a case where, the policy being on its face ambiguous as to the time when the voyage which it was intended to cover should commence, evidence was admitted to remove such ambiguity, by showing that it was a voyage home after the intermediate fishing voyage, and no other, which the parties had in their minds? See Duer, vol. i. p. 203.

Sect. 59. will be bound by such usage, and not allowed to dispute his liability on the ground that the risk, under the precise terms of the policy, never commenced on the subject insured.

Oporto trade. Thus, where it was shown to be a well-known usage in the Oporto trade for ships to complete their loading for the homeward voyage outside the bar, whenever from the low state of water in the River Tagus they could not conveniently do so withinside the bar, Lord Ellenborough ruled, that an underwriter who had insured a ship "at and from Oporto to London" could not object that he was discharged from his liability because the ship, without his knowledge, had finished

Florida trade. her loading outside the bar (*y*). So, where it was proved to be customary in the Florida trade for ships to take in their homeward cargoes at Tigre Island in St. Mary's River, and then drop down to Amelia Island, a little lower down the river, for the purpose of paying dues and clearing; it was held that an underwriter who had insured goods "at and from the ship's loading port or ports in Amelia Island to London" was not entitled to object that the policy never attached because the goods had been loaded, not at Amelia Island, but at Tigre Island (*z*).

Archangel. It was formerly the well-known custom at Archangel, immediately on a ship's arrival, to seal down her hatches, send a custom-house officer on board till she was unloaded, and carry the goods to the government warehouses, where they remained till the duty was paid; a merchant who had insured his goods from London to Archangel "until they should be there discharged and safely landed" was held to have no right of action against the underwriter, for any loss that had occurred on the goods after they had been landed

---

(*y*) Kingston *v.* Knibbs (1808), 1 Camp. 507, *in notis*, a very strong case, as it appeared that in such policies liberty was often expressly given to load on either side the bar; so that the underwriter might not unfairly have contended that he was misled by the omission of this stipulation.

(*z*) Moxon *v.* Atkins (1812), 3 Camp. 200. In this case it should be remarked that, as there were no ports at all in Amelia Island, the policy could not be construed literally.

CHAP. III.] CONSTRUCTION OF SEA-POLICIES. 83

and lodged in a government warehouse in accordance with the custom; for, as Lord Ellenborough said, the goods were then landed, according to the usual course of trade, at the port of Archangel, which was all the underwriter undertook for (*a*). So, on proof of an ancient and well-known custom at the port of Leghorn, that certain goods for that port should be invariably landed at the Lazaretto, it was held, in the United States, that a merchant who had insured goods of this description "till they were safely landed at Leghorn" could not protect them by such policy after they were once landed at the Lazaretto, such being by the custom of the trade equivalent to a landing at Leghorn (*b*).

_{Sect. 59.}

_{Leghorn.}

Under a policy on a ship at Mauritius, and for thirty days after arrival, evidence was admitted of a usage to anchor at the Bell Buoy, outside the harbour of Port Louis, where vessels calling for orders, seeking freight, or receiving or discharging part—not the whole—of their cargo, waited, and that they were then considered to be at Mauritius, and a total loss at this place within the thirty days was held to be covered by the policy (*c*).

60. Such are some of the applications that have occurred in practice of the principle now under consideration; those that immediately follow illustrate the position, that, where the usage of the particular trade with reference to which the underwriter insures is opposed to any of those general usages of maritime trade with reference to which all policies are *primâ facie* supposed to be made, the former is to be taken as the true key to the construction of the policy in preference to the latter.

_{Particular usage prevails over general maritime usage.}

On an insurance on goods, the underwriter is in general

_{Goods carried}

(*a*) Brown *v.* Carstairs (1811), 3 Camp. 161.
(*b*) Gracie *v.* Maryland Ins. Co. (1814), 8 Cranch's Sup. Ct. Rep. 75.
(*c*) Lindsay *v.* Janson (1859), 28 L. J. Ex. 315; 4 H. & N. 699. As to determination of risk "to Jamaica," see Camden *v.* Cowley (1762), 1 W. Bl. 417. See the effect of usage at the Port of Liverpool on the law of demurrage, Norden SS. Co. *v.* Dempsey (1876), 1 C. P. D. 654.

CONSTRUCTION OF SEA-POLICIES. [PART I.

Sect. 60.
on deck by usage.

entitled to expect that they will be carried in the hold, and not on deck, which is regarded as an unusual and dangerous place for that purpose. Every policy, then, in the absence of any express stipulation to the contrary, is generally read as though it contained on the face of it an exemption in terms against all liability on goods so carried (*d*). But whenever it can be shown that, by a well-settled and generally-known usage of the particular trade on which the underwriter insures, goods of the specific description of those on which the policy is effected are customarily carried on deck, the more general usage gives way to the more particular one, and the underwriter is liable for any loss upon the goods so carried, without any necessity of proving notice (*e*).

Stopping at intersjacent port.

In the same way it is a general usage of maritime trade, incorporated as we have seen into all policies, that the ship, in the absence of any express permission on the face of the policy to do otherwise, shall pursue a direct course between the two termini of the voyage, without stopping at any intermediate places; if, however, it be the notorious and well-settled usage of any given trade to stop at certain interjacent ports, this usage of the particular trade would doubtless countervail the general maritime usage, and the stopping at such ports, although not authorized by any express clause in the policy, be deemed no deviation (*f*).

Return of premium.

Again, it is a settled rule, that where the risk and premium are both entire, if the policy have once attached, the whole premium is to be retained. Yet Lord Mansfield, in an action for return of premium, allowed evidence of a constant and

---

(*d*) See the judgment of Lord Lyndhurst in Blackett *v.* Royal Exch. Ass. Co. (1832), 2 Cr. & J. 249, 250. In Apollinaris Co. *v.* Nord Deutsche Ins. Co., [1904] 1 K. B. 252, Walton, J., doubted whether this rule has any application to a river voyage.

(*e*) Da Costa *v.* Edmunds (1814), 4 Camp. 142; Gould *v.* Oliver (1837), 4 Bing. N. C. 134; Milward *v.* Hibbert (1842), 3 Q. B. 120; Miller *v.* Titherington (1862), 6 H. & N. 278; 7 H. & N. 954; Johnson *v.* Chapman (1865), 35 L. J. C. P. 23; Apollinaris Co. *v.* Nord Deutsche Ins. Co., *supra*.

(*f*) 1 Marshall, 186; 1 Phillips, Ins. s. 133.

CHAP. III.] CONSTRUCTION OF SEA-POLICIES. 85

invariable usage in the trade between London and Jamaica, Sect. 60.
infringing this rule in particular cases (*g*).

61. Where the legal construction of a clause is not thus Liberty "to
clearly settled and fixed, but comparatively doubtful, evidence enlarged
of usage is *à fortiori* admitted to explain the sense in which by usage.
it is used in the particular policy. Thus, where a clause in
a policy gave a "liberty to touch" at certain islands, and the
ship not only touched but took in salt there, the Court of
Common Pleas, after adverting to the doubtful meaning of
a liberty to touch, as contradistinguished from a liberty to
"touch and stay," admitted evidence of a usage of trade for
ships on the voyage insured to call at the islands in question
to take in salt (*h*).

62. II. The usage, in order to be binding, must be either II. The usage
a general and notorious trade usage of the whole mercantile general and
world (of which the Court will take judicial notice), or a notorious in
particular proved usage of universal prevalence and notoriety branch of
in the trade upon which, and of the place in respect of trade.
which, the insurance is effected: the usage of a particular
place, or of a particular class of persons, cannot be binding
on non-residents, or on other persons, unless they are shown
to have been cognizant of it (*i*).

"To make an usage obligatory on the parties," says It must be
Story, J., "it should be so well settled that all persons well settled,
engaged in the trade must be considered as contracting with

(*g*) Long *v*. Allen (1785), 4 of usage being admitted to control
Dougl. 276; 2 Park, 797; 2 Marsh. the settled legal construction of a
660. Judge Duer is of opinion that clause in the policy. On examina-
where, as in these cases, evidence of tion of the case, however, it appa-
usage is adduced to vary the settled rently amounts to no more than an
construction of the policy or super- authority for permitting evidence
sede a rule of maritime law, it must, of usage to settle the construction
in order to be binding, be shown in the particular policy of a clause
to be invariable. 1 Duer, 265. in itself ambiguous.

(*h*) Urquhart *v*. Bernard (1809), (*i*) Per Lord Tenterden in Bart-
1 Taunt. 450. Judge Duer cites lett *v*. Pentland (1830), 10 B. &
this case as an instance of evidence Cr. 760.

Sect. 62.   reference to it" (*k*). Hence, where, in case of an insurance effected from Liverpool to Jamaica, the ship put into the Isle of Man; and it appeared that ships bound on this voyage sometimes put in there, but not usually; it was held, that this proof did not amount to such a well-known and settled usage of the trade between Liverpool and the West Indies as to prevent this from being a deviation (*l*).

general, if not uniform.   The usage need not, in the strict sense of the word, be uniform, that is, followed invariably and without exception at all times and by all persons in the trade to which it relates: it is enough that it should be general. Thus, in the case of intermediate voyages in the Newfoundland fishery trade, to which reference has already been made, the objection was taken before Lord Ellenborough that the suggested usage was not uniform, for whenever a ship engaged in the trade could procure a cargo on her arrival at Newfoundland, she would prefer returning direct to Europe to taking an intermediate voyage in America. As to this objection, his Lordship said, "although there should be exceptions to the usage, that would be immaterial. Things are presumed to go on in their ordinary course, and if an usage be general, though not uniform, the underwriters are bound to take notice of it" (*m*).

must be notorious.   "The usage must be notorious; *i.e.*, it must have existed under such circumstances, or for such a length of time, as to have become generally well known to all persons concerned in or about the branch of trade to which it relates, and so as to warrant a presumption that contracts are made with reference to it" (*n*).

(*k*) In Trott *v.* Wood (1813), 1 Gallison's Rep. 443, cited 1 Phillips, s. 138.

(*l*) 1 Marshall, Ins. 186; Salisbury *v.* Townson, Millar's Ins. 418; Martin *v.* Delaware Ins. Co. (1808), 2 Wash. C. C. 254; Condy's Marshall, 186, n.

(*m*) Vallance *v.* Dewar (1808),

1 Camp. 508; see also 1 Duer, 264, 265. Judge Duer is of opinion (p. 265) that when "the usage settles the construction of the policy, or supersedes a rule of law, its constancy of observance, to render it binding, must be invariable"; but *quære*.

(*n*) This test, with a slight diffe-

CHAP. III.] CONSTRUCTION OF SEA-POLICIES. 87

63. If the usage proved can satisfactorily be shown to have been general and notorious, as long as the course of trade in which it prevails has lasted, it makes no difference that such trade is itself of recent origin.

Sect. 63.
Usage may be binding although trade of recent origin.

Thus, when the trade to Labrador, which was first opened to English shipping after the Peace of Paris in 1763, had been carried on only three years, Lord Mansfield held, that a custom which had been invariably observed ever since its opening was binding on those who insured on Labrador risks, as though the trade itself had been of much longer continuance. In this case, Lord Mansfield considered that evidence of a usage which had prevailed in one trade was rightly admitted to prove that the same usage was binding on those engaged in another trade of the same kind, carried on in the same way (*o*).

64. It need hardly be said that such usage must be reasonable. When the case of intermediate voyages in the Newfoundland fishing trade came before Lord Eldon, he is reported to have said to the jury as to this point, "If the evidence leads to this, that the ship may make an intermediate voyage of several years, it is too dangerous for you to give it effect." "If you think this usage does exist, if you think it reasonable, and if you think this ship acted *bonâ fide* in taking the intermediate voyage, you will find for the plaintiff" (*p*). Lord Eldon could hardly have meant by this to leave the question of reasonableness to the jury

The usage must be reasonable.

---

rence in the phraseology, is adopted from the judgment of the Supreme Court of New York in Smith *v.* Wright (1803), 1 Caines, 43, cited 1 Duer, 267, n. (*a*).

(*o*) Noble *v.* Kennoway (1780), 2 Dougl. 510. Judge Duer remarks, and very properly, on this case, that as the observance of such a usage seems to have been almost a necessary result from the nature of the trade, the Court were probably satisfied with slighter proof of its existence than they would otherwise have required. 1 Duer, 255. As to when a usage of recent origin becomes binding in law, see the judgment, per Cockburn, C. J., in Goodwin *v.* Roberts (1875), L. R. 10 Ex. 337, 346; 1 App. Cas. 476; Rumball *v.* Metropolitan Bank (1877), 2 Q. B. D. 194.

(*p*) Ougier *v.* Jennings (1808), 1 Camp. 506, *in notis;* see 1 Duer, 269.

88   CONSTRUCTION OF SEA-POLICIES.   [PART I.

Sect. 64.

(a question which must always, it should seem, be for the Court): what he intended must have been to ask them whether they thought the evidence established the existence of such a usage as he had already pointed out as reasonable, or of one which, as he had already told them, was too dangerous to give effect to.

And not merely local or particular.

Although with regard to usages which are either common to all trades, or perfectly well known and settled in the particular course of trade to which the insurance relates, it is obviously a fair presumption that the parties to the policy, as mercantile men, are conversant with such usages, and have contracted with reference to them, with regard to usages which only prevail in a given place, or amongst a particular description of persons, the presumption is the other way; and in such cases, accordingly, it must be satisfactorily shown that the party sought to be affected by the usage had knowledge of it at the time of contracting. In the language of Lord Tenterden: "the usage of a particular place or a particular class of persons cannot be binding on non-residents or on other persons, unless they are shown to have been cognizant of it" (*q*).

Usage at Lloyd's.

65. Thus, even though clear proof may be given of a particular usage being established at Lloyd's, and even though the fact may be that the policy was effected by a broker at Lloyd's, in the common course of business, for a party resident in this country; yet, such party cannot be affected by the usage, unless it can be further shown, either that he was actually cognizant of it, or from his general modes of dealing, habits of life, or place of business, cannot be supposed to have been ignorant of it (*r*).

"Free of mortality."

A Liverpool house, through the agency of a London broker,

(*q*) Per Lord Tenterden in Bartlett *v.* Pentland (1830), 10 B. & Cr. 760.

(*r*) Gabay *v.* Lloyd (1825), 3 B. & Cr. 793; Bartlett *v.* Pentland (1830), 10 B. & Cr. 760; Scott *v.* Irving (1830), 1 B. & Ad. 605; Stewart *v.* Aberdein (1838), 4 M. & W. 211; Sweeting *v.* Pearce (1861), 9 C. B. N. S. 534; 30 L. J. C. P. 109; Matvieff *v.* Crosfield (1903), 8 Com. Cas. 120.

CHAP. III.] CONSTRUCTION OF SEA-POLICIES.

effected a policy, at Lloyd's, on horses "warranted free of jettison and mortality," from Liverpool to Jamaica. During a storm in the course of the voyage, three of the horses were kicked to death by the others—a loss which the Court held to be owing to perils of the sea, and not to "mortality," or death from natural causes, so that the warranty did not apply. The underwriters nevertheless refused to make good this loss, on the ground that, on policies containing this warranty, it was contrary to the usage of Lloyd's to pay in respect of any loss of live stock occurring in the course of the voyage, except where the ship was lost before arrival. The facts of the case were stated in the form of a special verdict, which set out the custom at Lloyd's, as proved at the trial, but did not contain any finding that the plaintiff was cognizant of such usage. The Court, under these circumstances, held that the plaintiff was not bound by the usage: it was not found to be a general usage of the whole trade in the city of London; and therefore, in order to render it binding on the plaintiff, it ought to have been distinctly found that he was cognizant of it (*s*).

Sect. 65.

66. By the general usage of the law mercantile, to which effect is given in sect. 53 (1) of the Marine Insurance Act, 1906, the insurance broker is considered as debtor to the underwriter for the premiums, while the underwriter is debtor to the assured for the loss (*t*): a custom, however, has long prevailed at Lloyd's, and is well known to all who transact business there, that the brokers settle with the underwriters according to the state of their accounts with them, in which accounts the broker is made the debtor to the underwriter for all premiums on any policies effected by him with such underwriter, no matter on whose account; and the underwriter, in the same way, is made debtor to the broker for all losses, as between the underwriter and the broker. Such

Settlement between broker and underwriter.

(*s*) Gabay *v.* Lloyd (1825), 3 B. & Cr. 793.

(*t*) Per Lord Tenterden in Bartlett *v.* Pentland (1830), 10 B. & Cr. 760.

Sect. 66. settlement on account is considered as payment according to the custom of Lloyd's; but whether the assured is bound by such a settlement, so as to oblige him to look to the broker only for what before the settlement was a debt due from the underwriter, depends upon his cognizance of the usage, as we shall see elsewhere (*u*).

Gross freight. So strong, however, has the binding force of a usage at Lloyd's been considered, with regard to all those in the habit of transacting business there, that in one case it was even admitted to prove a mode of adjustment inconsistent with the true principles of Marine Insurance as a contract of indemnity. Thus, where in an open policy on freight the assured contended that he was entitled, in case of a total loss, to recover the amount of the gross freight without any reduction; and to establish this right called witnesses of thirty or forty years' experience at Lloyd's, who stated that, though open policies on freight were rare, yet the uniform custom of settling losses upon them had been to pay the assured the amount of the gross freight, the Court admitted the evidence, although they allowed that the practice seemed inconsistent with the true principles of indemnity (*x*).

III. Patent or latent ambiguity of words.

67. III. Where the sense of the words and expressions used in a policy is either ambiguous or obscure on the face of the instrument, or is made so by proof of extrinsic circumstances, parol evidence is admissible to explain by usage their meaning in the given case.

Technical or local terms.

The words and phrases employed in policies may be obscure in themselves, as when they are entirely technical and local, so as to be quite unintelligible to the generality of persons, without explanation; in this case, the ambiguity as to their meaning arises upon merely reading them as they

(*u*) See *post*, § 124 *et seq.*
(*x*) Palmer *v.* Blackburn (1822), 1 Bing. 61. In this case Dallas, C. J., doubted, but Park, J., and Burroughs, J., the other two members of the Court then present, were clear that the evidence had been rightly admitted. The custom became, in consequence of this decision, a settled rule of law, which is recognized in s. 16 (2) of the Mar. Ins. Act, 1906.

CHAP. III.] CONSTRUCTION OF SEA-POLICIES. 91

stand in the instrument. So, again, although the words *Sect. 67.* employed may have an ordinary meaning intelligible to people not engaged in the business to which they relate; yet, *Terms used in a secondary* if they have also another meaning when employed by those *sense.* engaged in that business, and the circumstances of the case show that such secondary or less general sense must have been that in which they were used in the particular instrument whose meaning is to be ascertained, parol evidence must be equally resorted to in this, as in the former case, to explain the real meaning of the contract, by showing the sense in which the parties meant it to be understood (*y*).

68. Several instances of the application of this rule have *Instances.* arisen in the construction of the memorandum, by which the underwriters exempt themselves from liability on certain perishable articles; thus, evidence of usage has been admitted to show that the term "corn," as used in the memorandum, is meant to comprehend every sort of grain, and also beans and peas (*z*) and malt (*a*); but that it does not include rice (*b*); also that the term "salt" does not include saltpetre (*c*).

Upon the same principle, in the United States, where the memorandum contained the exception of roots, the evidence of mercantile men was admitted to show that the word as used in the memorandum was in practice confined in its application to perishable roots, such as beets and other garden roots; and, therefore, that sarsaparilla, being a dry hard root,

---

(*y*) Judge Duer, whose observations on this point are eminently valuable, states, as the general conclusion from the cases, "that the question whether a particular word in the policy has acquired by the usage of trade a technical meaning, distinct from its popular sense, is always to be determined by the inquiry whether such has been its use and practical interpretation in other mercantile instruments and contracts:" 1 Duer, 184.

(*z*) Mason *v.* Skurray (1780), 1 Park, Ins. 245.
(*a*) Moody *v.* Surridge (1798), *ibid.*
(*b*) Scott *v.* Bourdillon (1806), 2 B. & P. N. R. 213.
(*c*) By Wilson, J., in Journu *v.* Bourdieu (1787), 1 Park, 245. Cf. Hart *v.* Standard Co. (1889), 22 Q. B. D. 499, where it was held that in the absence of a usage limiting the meaning of the word, "iron" in the clause "warranted no iron" included steel.

Sect. 68. and not liable to decay, was not included in the memorandum (*d*). So, in a policy on furs, similar evidence was admitted, to prove that the word "skins" in the memorandum should not exempt the underwriter from liability to an average loss on bear skins; it being shown that such skins were chiefly valuable as furs (*e*).

In a case before Lord Mansfield, where the insurance was on ship, furniture, &c., in the usual words of the printed sea-policy, the ship was employed in the Greenland fishery, and the question was whether the words of the policy covered fishing tackle and stores. His Lordship said this would depend on the usage of trade, and admitted evidence of such usage accordingly (*f*).

"With or without letters of marque."

A vessel was insured "either with or without letters of marque," the intention of course being to have the liberty of using it, but to what extent, whether solely in acting on the defensive, or in giving chase, or in cruising generally, were questions not settled by the obvious and general import of the words; Lord Ellenborough said, "it may be material to ascertain in what manner parties to contracts containing this form of words have acted upon them in former instances, and whether they have obtained, as between the assured and assurers, any known and definite import." (*g*).

"Port."

69. The risk on ship and goods is often specified to begin and end from their arrival, sailing from, or loading at one port, until their arrival or safe discharge at another port; in these cases the meaning in which the word "port" is used in

(*d*) Coit *v.* Commercial Ins. Co. (1811), 7 Johnson's N. Y. Rep. 385. The words of the memorandum in this case were, "roots and all other articles of a perishable nature," so that the very language of the clause formed a clue to its construction.

(*e*) Astor *v.* Union Ins. Co. (1827), 7 Cowen's Rep. 202.

(*f*) Hoskins *v.* Pickersgill (1783), 2 Marsh. 735; 1 Park, 126.

(*g*) Parr *v.* Anderson (1805), 6 East, 207. Duer (vol. i. p. 187) observes that "this mode of interpreting a contract by a reference to the practice of other parties in similar cases is almost peculiar to a policy of insurance, nor is it easy to be reconciled with the ordinary rules of evidence," and follows with some excellent remarks in explanation.

CHAP. III.] CONSTRUCTION OF SEA-POLICIES. 93

the policy must be ascertained by admitting parol evidence to show what meaning and extent, in the general understanding of the mercantile world, is attached to the word "port" as applied to the place where, by the policy, the risk is made to begin or end (*h*); and, although the mercantile sense attached to the term may give the port in question a greater or a less extent than its legal or political limits, yet the mercantile sense, and not the legal import of the word, shall prevail. Thus, although Llanelly is, legally speaking, considered to be a part of the port of Carmarthen, and Bridport of the port of Lyme Regis, yet neither was considered to be so within the meaning of the words "port of Carmarthen" and "port of Lyme Regis," in a policy of insurance; those words meaning, in a mercantile sense, "the town and port of Lyme Regis," and "the town and port of Carmarthen" (*i*).

Sect. 69.

70. So, again, where words descriptive of seas or countries have acquired a sense among mercantile men differing from their common geographical import, parol evidence of the meaning put upon them by the mercantile world is admissible, to show the sense put on them by the parties to the policy.

Thus, under a policy "from Van Dieman's Land to a port or ports of loading in India and the Indian Islands," the Court held that, though, amongst geographers, Mauritius was deemed an African island, yet parol evidence was admissible to prove that, in commercial language, it was considered an Indian island (*k*). So, where an insurance was made "from London to any port in the Baltic," and

"Indian Islands."

"Baltic."

(*h*) Constable *v.* Noble (1810), 2 Taunt. 403; Payne *v.* Hutchinson (1810), *ibid.* 405, *in notis;* Cockey *v.* Atkinson (1819), 2 B. & Ald. 460; Brown *v.* Tayleur (1835), 4 A. & E. 241.

(*i*) Constable *v.* Noble (1810), 2 Taunt. 403; Payne *v.* Hutchinson (1810), *ibid.* 405, n. See per Brett, M. R., in Sailing Ship Garston Co. *v.* Hickie (1885), 15 Q. B. D. 580.

(*k*) Robertson *v.* Clarke (1824), 1 Bing. 445. See also Northey *v.* Trevillion (1902), 7 Com. Cas. 201, where with reference to an agency contract it was held that Rangoon is not in India.

94   CONSTRUCTION OF SEA-POLICIES.   [PART I.

Sect. 70.   the vessel sailed for Revel in the Gulf of Finland, which, among geographers, is considered a different sea to the Baltic, yet, upon evidence that it is comprehended in the Baltic in commercial language, the Court gave this extension to the term "Baltic" in the policy (*l*).

"The Pacific."   So, in a case of re-insurance "from the Pacific," where the evidence showed that the plaintiffs' policies with the defendants and other underwriters, containing these words, had always been limited to vessels sailing from ports on the West Coast of South America, it was held by Romer, J., that the words must be construed accordingly (*m*).

"No St. Lawrence."   But in the absence of any such usage or custom among mercantile men, with regard to the phraseology in the policy, the meaning must be ascertained by the ordinary rules of construction. Thus in a policy on ship in which the warranty was "No St. Lawrence" between certain dates, it was held that both the river and the gulf of that name were within the terms of the warranty (*n*).

"Cargo."   Where a question arose in an action on a policy as to the meaning of the word "cargo," Tindal, C. J., ruled that, being a term of mercantile import, its sense, as used in the policy, was a question for the jury, and could not be decided by the dictionary (*o*). So with regard to "freight," Story, J., on the ground that it was a word which, in common parlance, has several meanings, admitted parol evidence to be given of the circumstances under which the contract was made, in order to show its meaning in the particular case; as, for instance, to show whether it meant "goods on board ship," or "an interest in the earnings of the ship" (*p*).

"Port risk" policy.   In one case Hamilton, J., admitted evidence that the term

(*l*) Uhde *v.* Walters (1811), 3 Camp. 16; see also Moxon *v.* Atkins (1811), *ibid.* 200.
(*m*) Royal Exch. Ass. Co. *v.* Tod (1892), 8 Times L. R. 669.
(*n*) Birrell *v.* Dryer (1884), 9 App. Cas. 345; cf. also The Beacon Fire and Life Ass. Co. *v.* Gibb (1862), 1 Moore, P. C. N. S. 73; Quebec Marine Ins. Co. *v.* Commercial Bank of Canada (1870), L. R. 3 P. C. 234.
(*o*) Houghton *v.* Gilbart (1836), 7 C. & P. 701.
(*p*) Peisch *v.* Dixon (1815), 1 Mason, 10; 1 Duer, 168, 169.

CHAP. III.] CONSTRUCTION OF SEA-POLICIES. 95

"port risk" has a well-recognized meaning at Lloyd's, and Sect. 70.
that the risk under a "port risk" policy ceases when the
insured vessel leaves her anchorage (*q*).

In another case the same learned judge admitted the Warranty
evidence of underwriters as to the meaning of a warranty against "p. a. and loss."
against "particular average and loss" in policies on frozen
meat (*r*).

71. IV. A resort to parol evidence, however, whether of IV. Usage
usage or otherwise, is only permitted in order either to only admissible to
explain the policy where it is technical or ambiguous, or to explain what is doubtful,
fill out and add to it where it is silent: such evidence will not to
never be admitted to contradict, set aside or control its contradict what is plain.
express, plain and unambiguous terms.

No evidence can be admitted of a usage which is at direct
variance with the plain terms of the policy: it may be
admitted to explain technical terms or ambiguous clauses,
or "to introduce matter on which the policy is silent," but
not to show that the policy has a meaning in plain opposition to its language; "usage is only admissible to explain
what is doubtful, it is never admissible to contradict what is
plain" (*s*).

"Usage," says Lord Campbell, "may be relied upon to
show the sense in which an expression found in a written
contract is used in a particular trade; and a usage, consistent
with a written contract, may be introduced into it: as both
parties being aware of it, may be supposed to have intended
that it shall form part of their bargain. But to let in verbal
evidence of a usage for the purpose of contradicting and
nullifying an express written contract, would be contrary to
all principle, and has been forbidden as often as the attempt
has been made" (*t*).

(*q*) Mersey Mutual Underwriting Assn. *v.* Poland (1910), 15 Com. Cas. 205.
(*r*) Otago Farmers' Co-op. Ass. *v.* Thompson, [1910] 2 K. B. 145.
(*s*) Per Lord Lyndhurst in

Blackett *v.* Royal Exch. Ass. Co. (1832), 2 Cr. & J. 244. See Provincial Ins. Co. of Canada *v.* Leduc (1874), L. R. 6 P. C. 224.
(*t*) Hall *v.* Janson (1855), 4 E. & B. 504; 24 L. J. Q. B. 101; cf.

96 CONSTRUCTION OF SEA-POLICIES. [PART I.

Sect. 71.

"Where the terms," says Judge Duer, "in which the usage must be expressed, if introduced into the policy, would be directly and irreconcilably repugnant to an express clause or provision, the evidence must doubtless be rejected, otherwise the policy would be void for uncertainty. A usage may explain, modify and control (*u*), but cannot contradict a policy; by restriction or addition it may qualify the construction of particular words and clauses, but can never be permitted to nullify or expunge them" (*x*).

Parkinson *v.* Collier.

72. These principles, notwithstanding some apparent discrepancy in the expressions of the judges, have been uniformly acted upon in the construction of sea-policies. Thus, where the risk on goods was, by the policy, made to continue "till discharged and safely landed," Lord Kenyon would not admit evidence of usage to show that this expression, in the particular trade insured, meant "until the ship was moored twenty-four hours in safety"; because this was inconsistent with the plain meaning of the policy, which was too clearly expressed to require or allow of any such explanation (*y*).

Blackett *v.* Royal Exch. Ass. Co.

So where a policy was in the common form upon the ship, that is, "upon the body, tackel, apparel, ordnance, munition, boat, and other furniture of the ship called the 'Thames,'" Lord Lyndhurst would not admit evidence of a usage at Lloyd's, that boats slung on the ship's quarter (which was proved to be the invariable mode of carrying them on such voyages as that insured) were not protected by such policy (*z*). "The objection," said his Lordship, "to the parol evidence is, that it was not to explain any ambiguous words in the policy, any words which might admit of doubt, nor to intro-

---

also Humfrey *v.* Dale (1856), 7 E. & B. 266; E. B. & E. 1004; Brown *v.* Byrne (1854), 3 E. & B. 703.

(*u*) The word "control" was queried by Arnould (see 2nd ed. p. 88). The point is discussed

ante, § 55, note (*d*).

(*x*) 1 Duer, 270.

(*y*) Parkinson *v.* Collier (1797), 2 Park, 653; 1 Marshall, 255.

(*z*) Blackett *v.* Royal Exch. Ass. Co. (1832), 2 Cr. & J. 244.

CHAP. III.] CONSTRUCTION OF SEA-POLICIES. 97

duce matter on which the policy was silent, but was at direct variance with the terms of the policy and in plain opposition to the language it used; that whereas the policy purported to be upon the ship, furniture and apparel generally, the usage is to say, that it is not upon all the furniture and apparel, but upon part only, excluding the boat " (*a*). On the same ground, in a case where it appeared that oil had been lost by leakage, caused by the violent labouring of the ship in a cross sea, Lord Denman refused to admit evidence of a usage of Lloyd's, to the effect, that unless the cargo shifted, or the casks were damaged, underwriters were not liable for any extent of leakage, however caused, as a loss by perils of the seas (*b*). His Lordship told the jury to consider for themselves whether, in their opinion, the damage to the oil was in fact caused by perils of the seas. "It may be very convenient for the underwriters to have such a general rule, and for the commercial world to submit to it; but if they mean thereby to control the effect of a plain instrument, they should introduce its terms into the policy" (*c*).

Sect. 72.

Crofts *v.* Marshall.

In an action for contribution in general average against one of the underwriters on a policy "on money advanced on account of freight," containing the usual clause in the memorandum by which "freight, &c. is warranted free of average unless general or the ship be stranded," the plea set up a usage of merchants, &c., effecting and underwriting policies in London, not to pay general average contribution under such a policy. The Court held the plea bad on general demurrer, on the ground that it attempted to set up in bar to the action a usage in derogation and contradiction of the written contract which, by virtue of the clause in the memorandum, plainly and expressly rendered the underwriter on freight liable for general average without regard to the extent of the loss (*d*).

Hall *v.* Janson.

(*a*) Per Lord Lyndhurst, 2 Cr. & J. 249; criticised in Myers *v.* Sarl (1860), 30 L. J. Q. B. 9; cf. also Humfrey *v.* Dale, *ubi supra*.
(*b*) Crofts *v.* Marshall (1836), 7

C. & P. 597.
(*c*) Crofts *v.* Marshall (1836), 7 C. & P. 607.
(*d*) Hall *v.* Janson (1855), 4 E. & B. 500; 24 L. J. Q. B. 97. As

A.—VOL. I. 7

Sect. 73.
V. The written clauses have greater weight than the printed and formal parts of the policy.

73. V. The policy being a printed form with the blanks filled up in writing, it is a rule that "if there is any doubt about the sense or meaning of the whole, the words superadded in writing are entitled to have a greater effect attributed to them than the printed words; inasmuch as the written words are the immediate language and terms selected by the parties themselves for the expression of their meaning" (e).

Effect of inapplicable printed words left in the policy.

In a case where the Lloyd's form of policy was filled up as a time policy on ship, it was argued that various clauses which were clearly only intended to refer to a voyage policy, but which had, nevertheless, been in this case, as in other similar cases, left standing, therefore applied to the policy in question. The House of Lords, however, reversing the judgment in the Exchequer Chamber, decided otherwise. "It has been suggested," said Lord Penzance, "that by reason of the policy having been drawn up on a printed form, the printed terms of which are applicable to a voyage, and also to goods as well as to the ship, the policy is something less or something more than a time policy. But the practice of mercantile men of writing into their printed forms the terms by which they desire to describe and limit the risk intended to be insured against, without striking out the words which may be applicable to a larger or different contract, is too well known, and has been too constantly recognized in courts of law, to permit of any such conclusion" (f).

Hence it is, that in the familiar instance of words written to the liability of the underwriter by express contract on the face of the policy, the Court says: "The policy not only contains general words to indemnify the assured on account of loss, but it expressly declares that 'freight is warranted free of average, unless general, or the ship stranded.' Therefore the underwriters on freight expressly, absolutely, and universally undertake to pay general average, however large or however minute the amount may be."

(e) Per Lord Ellenborough in Robertson v. French (1803), 4 East, 130; per curiam, Gumm v. Tyrie (1864), 33 L. J. Q. B. 97; per Blackburn, J., in Joyce v. Realm Ins. Co. (1872), L. R. 7 Q. B. 583; per Lord Penzance in Dudgeon v. Pembroke (1877), 2 App. Cas. 293. See Hagan v. Scottish Ins. Co. (1901), 186 U. S. 423; 3 Kent's Comm. 260.

(f) Dudgeon v. Pembroke (1877), 2 App. Cas. 284; 1 Q. B. D. 96; L. R. 9 Q. B. 581.

in the margin, or at the foot of policies, such written words are considered as applying indefinitely to the whole of the policy, and as controlling the sense of those parts of the printed policy to which they apply.

Thus, where the word "ship," or "freight," or "goods," is written in the margin of the policy, the general terms of the policy, applicable to other subjects besides the particular one mentioned on the margin, are thereby considered as narrowed in point of construction by relation to the word so written (*g*).

Moreover, printed words of general application may be entirely rejected when they are inapplicable to the insurance intended by the parties (*h*). Thus the suing and labouring clause has been held to be inapplicable to an insurance against the liability of shipowners to the owners of cargo for negligence (*i*).

The subsequent portions of this work will furnish abundant instances of this rule of construction.

74. VI. It is also a rule, founded on the same principle, that greater strictness of construction should be applied to those clauses and stipulations, which the parties have themselves introduced, than to the words of the printed formula, which are adapted to all other cases of insurance on similar subjects, and not confined to the circumstances of the particular adventure (*k*).

Frequent illustrations of this rule will be afforded when we come to speak of clauses giving a liberty to touch and stay, express warranties and other written stipulations, by which the parties to the policy seek either to enlarge or to limit the protection afforded by the common printed form.

(*g*) 4 East, 140; and see Robinson *v.* Tobin (1816), 1 Stark. 336; see also Haughton *v.* Ewbank (1814), 4 Camp. 88.
(*h*) See Hydarnes SS. Co. *v.* Indemnity, &c. Ass. Co., [1905] 1 K. B. 500 (C. A.).
(*i*) Cunard SS. Co. *v.* Marten, [1902] 2 K. B. 624; [1903] 2 K. B. 511 (C. A.). See also Western Ass. Co. of Toronto *v.* Poole, [1903] 1 K. B. 376.
(*k*) 1 Emerigon, cii. s. 7, p. 55.

Sect. 75.
VII. As to inexplicable ambiguity.

75. VII. If conditions which are inserted for the protection of the underwriter be ambiguous, and the ambiguity is such as to be inexplicable by extrinsic evidence if admitted, the construction will lean towards the side of the assured rather than of the insurer (*l*), proper regard being, however, always paid to the business aspect of the case (*m*).

(*l*) Blackett *v.* Royal Exch. Ass. Co. (1832), 2 Cr. & J. 244. See also Birrell *v.* Dryer (1884), 9 App. Cas. 345. In a case on an accident policy, In re Etherington and Lancashire & Yorkshire Accident Ins. Co., [1909] 1 K. B. 591, 596, Vaughan Williams, L. J., began his judgment by laying down a broader rule, so far as the policies of companies are concerned. "I start with the consideration," he said, "that it has been established by the authorities that in dealing with the construction of policies, whether they be life, or fire, or marine policies, an ambiguous clause must be construed against, rather than in favour of the company." Farwell, L. J., said (p. 600): "I agree that the insurance company which prepares these documents is bound to make their meaning as clear as possible, and, if there is any ambiguity in the document, it does not lie in the mouth of the company, who may have been receiving premiums under it for years, to insist on that construction of an ambiguous clause which is in their favour." Lord Justice Vaughan Williams' rule is criticized by Mr. Arthur Cohen (Laws of England, vol. xvii. § 688), who considers it inconsistent with Birrell *v.* Dryer, *supra*, and points out that a marine policy, unlike fire and life policies, is framed in accordance with the slip prepared by the assured's broker (see *post*, § 102). In the later case of National Protector Fire Ins. Co. *v.* Nivert (1913), 108 L. T. 390, the Privy Council applied the rule stated in the text to the construction of a fire policy. In America there is authority for the wider doctrine, that the whole of the policy is deemed to be the writing of the insurers, and is therefore in all cases of ambiguity to be construed against them. Parsons dissents from this doctrine (see 1 Parsons, Ins. p. 67); but it has been affirmed in recent cases. See First Nat. Bank of Kansas City *v.* Hartford F. Ins. Co. (1877), 95 U. S. 678; Travelers' Ins. Co. *v.* McConkey (1887), 127 *ibid.* 666; American SS. Co. *v.* Indemnity Mutual Ins. Co. (1901), 108 Fed. R. 421; Hagan *v.* Scottish Ins. Co. (1901), 186 U. S. 423. A number of cases are collected in the 14th vol. of Campbell's Ruling Cases, notes to Robertson *v.* French.

(*m*) Stewart *v.* Merchants' Marine Ins. Co. (1885), 16 Q. B. D. at p. 626.

CHAPTER IV.

DIFFERENT CLASSES OF INSURERS ON SEA-POLICIES.

	SECT.
Who may be Insurers	76
Lloyd's Underwriters	77
Insurance Companies and Partnerships	78, 79
Mutual Insurance Associations or Clubs	80—84

76. EVERY person capable of making a contract may be an insurer, and may authorize any person capable of being an agent to underwrite policies in his name and on his behalf. The practice of insuring with individuals was the earliest in use anywhere, and long continued to be followed in this country.

<small>Who may be insurers.</small>

77. In the time of William III. and of Queen Anne, Lloyd's Coffee-house, at the corner of Abchurch Lane, in Lombard Street, was the celebrated resort of seafaring men, and those that did business with them. There, and subsequently in Pope's Head Alley, and ultimately on the west side of the old Royal Exchange, at this coffee-house congregated the underwriters of London. For some time they had no organization; but in the latter part of the eighteenth century they formed themselves into an association or society with a committee of management, which became famous under the name of Lloyd's, and was in 1871 incorporated by a special Act of Parliament into a society under the same title (a). In connection with this society

<small>Lloyd's underwriters.</small>

(a) Lloyd's Act, 1871, 34 Vict. c. xxi. The objects of the society were declared to be the carrying on of the business of marine insurance by the members, the protection of their interests, and the collection and diffusion of intelligence. As insurance business other than marine business has been largely carried on at Lloyd's, an amending Act was recently passed (Lloyd's Act, 1911, 1 & 2 Geo. 5, c. lxii.),

Sect. 77. they have developed a ramified system of agency radiating everywhere to the ports of the world, which is now become of imposing magnitude, essential to the business of marine insurance whether in the hands of individuals or of companies, and to the general interests of British commerce.

Lloyd's rooms.

Lloyd's underwriters now meet and carry on their business in spacious rooms over the Royal Exchange. In the underwriting rooms the underwriters sit at tables of the coffee-house type, while the brokers and other subscribers pass from one underwriter to another and submit their "slips." There are also (1) an apartment in which the latest telegrams are exhibited for the information of members, and (2) a large room called the reading room, where all this information is carefully tabulated in volumes ranged alphabetically from one end of the room to the other.

The corporate affairs of members, as distinguished from their underwriting business, are managed by a committee, elected by and from the members of Lloyd's and presided over by a chairman and deputy-chairman, the latter being the acting president.

Lloyd's agents.

The committee, on the recommendation of an agency committee, on which the insurance companies are also represented, appoint agents of the corporation (generally called Lloyd's agents) in all the principal ports of the world, whose business it is regularly to forward to Lloyd's accounts of all departures from and arrivals at their ports, as well as of losses and casualties; and also general information bearing upon shipping and insurance (*b*). This information, which is now of course largely transmitted by telegraph, is posted up, when received, in the apartment mentioned above. The information thus received during each day is forthwith published in the "Shipping and Mercantile Gazette," a newspaper in

Shipping Gazette and Lloyd's List.

which extended the objects of the society to the carrying on by the members of every kind of insurance business, including guarantee business.

(*b*) By Lloyd's Signal Act, 1888 (51 & 52 Vict. c. 29), s. 2, the society may compulsorily acquire land for the purpose of erecting signal stations.

CHAP. IV.]   INSURERS ON SEA-POLICIES.   103

which is incorporated what was formerly known as Lloyd's   Sect. 77.
List. The columns of this "Gazette" are numbered, and
the information is immediately indexed in the volumes
referred to above—the date and column number of the
"Gazette" being recorded against each entry (c). There is
also at Lloyd's a register of captains, giving the record of
every master during his whole career.

It should be noted that Lloyd's agents, who, as has just
been said, are appointed by the corporation, are not the
agents of the individual underwriters (d). Still, they perform very important functions, e.g., as surveyors of damaged
cargo, and in many ways render assistance. where vessels
put into a port of distress (e).

The development of the telegraph system, however, which
enables masters of ships in most cases to communicate
quickly with their owners, and through them to obtain
instructions from the underwriters, has relieved the agents
of much responsibility.

Lloyd's underwriters individually sign their names at the   Form of
foot of the policy, and write opposite thereto the sum insured   underwriting.
by each in figures and also in words, and sometimes (though
not usually) the date of so doing (f). Each thereby makes

(c) "The receipt of official news of capture, &c.," being a term in a policy, news of an embargo entered in Lloyd's "Lost Book" was held by a special jury at Guildhall, Erle, C. J., presiding, to be official news: Fowler v. English & Scottish Marine Ins. Co., Guildhall Sittings, post M. T. 1864.

(d) Wilson v. Salamandra Ins. Co. (1903), 8 Com. Cas. 129.

(e) S. 11 of Lloyd's Act, 1911 (1 & 2 Geo. 5, c. lxii.), authorizes the corporation to use its funds and employ agents for the taking charge of the interests of members and others in insurable property of every description.

(f) Rule 4 in the Sched. to the special Act (34 Vict. c. xxi.), incorporating the Society of Lloyd's, is as follows:—

"An underwriting member shall not, by himself or by any partner or other substitute, directly or indirectly underwrite in the city of London a policy of insurance as follows: (1) In the name of a partnership, or otherwise than in the name of one individual (being an underwriting member of the society) for each separate sum subscribed; or (2) for the account, benefit, or advantage of any company or association, unless they are subscribers to the society, nor unless every policy underwritten for their account, benefit, or advantage is

Sect. 77. a separate contract in the terms of the instrument with the assured of the particular amount set opposite to his name. The right of action in the assured is consequently against each separately, and not against all jointly (*g*).

With a view to maintaining the credit of the room, the committee of Lloyd's now require a deposit of securities, of the minimum value of 5,000*l*., to cover the engagements of each member in his capacity as an underwriter of marine and transport risks. Formerly the committee were satisfied with a written guaranty to cover these engagements, and now a guaranty is sometimes required in addition to the deposit. The corporation of Lloyd's being thus constituted trustees of the benefit of the guaranty on behalf of those who had sustained damage by the failure of the underwriting member in respect of his engagements in that capacity, were held entitled to put it in suit, although they had themselves suffered no loss (*h*).

The two Old Companies.

78. By virtue of an Act of 1719 (6 Geo. 1, c. 18), two companies, the Royal Exchange Assurance Corporation and the London Assurance Corporation, were incorporated, with the exclusive right of making sea insurances in their corporate capacity, and all others were restrained from granting insurances as companies or partnerships on a joint capital. A subsequent Act, 8 Geo. 1, c. 15, relieved them of any liability to double damages or costs at law, at that time an important privilege; and the 11 Geo. 1, c. 30, s. 43, gave them the right of pleading the general issue to all actions of debt and

underwritten in their ordinary place of business."

A Lloyd's underwriter sometimes carries on business on behalf of other underwriters called his "names," subscribing policies on their behalf. See In re Burnand, [1904] 2 K. B. 68 (C. A.), where it was held that under their agreements all the parties had a joint property in the books kept by the underwriting member.

(*g*) See *ante*, § 26.

(*h*) Lloyd's *v.* Harper (1880), 16 Ch. D. 290. By s. 10 of Lloyd's Act, 1911 (1 & 2 Geo. 5, c. lxii.), the society has power to make bye-laws enabling it to make good any deficiency arising from the insufficiency of any security furnished by a member.

CHAP. IV.] INSURERS ON SEA-POLICIES. 105

covenant on their policies (*i*). Their main privilege of Sect. 78.
exclusively granting marine policies as corporate bodies was
retained by them until the year 1824, when the 5 Geo. 4,
c. 114, repealed so much of the 6 Geo. 1, c. 18, as restrains
"any corporation or body politic, society or partnership, or
persons acting in any society or partnership," from underwriting sea-policies or lending money on bottomry.

79. The repeal of the monopoly formerly possessed by the Consequences
two old companies was succeeded by the rapid multiplication of the repeal
of public companies, some of them incorporated by special monopoly.
statutes, some by charter from the Crown, and others formed
upon the provisions of a partnership deed, for the purpose of
granting marine policies (*k*).

By the Joint Stock Companies Act, 1844 (7 & 8 Vict. Companies
c. 110), it was enacted that every company insuring ships Companies
and their cargoes against loss and damage must be regis- Act.
tered (*l*). This Act was repealed by the Companies Act,
1862, which provided that every insurance company completely registered under the Act of 1844 should register
itself under the Act of 1862 (*m*). By such registration
these companies obtained the advantages suitable to each
as provided by the Act of 1862 (*n*). By doing so, they

(*i*) The right to plead the general issue and give special matter in evidence was also given to the two companies when the insurance is on inland navigation by 41 Geo. 3, cc. lvii., lviii. respectively, but the latter Act was repealed by the London Assurance Act, 1891 (54 & 55 Vict. c. cxxvi.). This right of pleading the general issue was not affected by the 5 & 6 Vict. c. 97, s. 3 (Carr *v.* Royal Exch. Ass. (1861), 1 B. & S. 956; 31 L. J. Q. B. 93), and it is clearly not affected by the Public Authorities Protection Act, 1893, s. 2 (e). Whether, however, it survived the changes in pleading effected by the Rules under the Judicature Acts is a matter of some doubt. Maclachlan expressed the view that the privilege remains unchanged. (Arnould, 6th ed. vol. i. p. 151, n. (2).)

(*k*) See Hallett *v.* Dowdall (1852), 18 Q. B. 2, 17.

(*l*) The Act of 1844 extended to companies established in England, Wales, or Ireland, or if established in Scotland, having an office in the former country: s. 2.

(*m*) Companies Act, 1862, s. 209. For the purposes of that Act, a company that carried on the business of insurance in common with any other business was deemed to be an insurance company: s. 3.

(*n*) Companies Act, 1862, ss. 6, 180, 206. The corresponding pro-

Sect. 79. retained all property, and all rights, interests, and obligations in connection with property, their rights and liabilities in respect of debts, obligations, and contracts; and the peculiar modifications impressed on their constitution—and their rights and liabilities in connection therewith—by the statute, charter, or deed, under which they might have been formed (*o*). Moreover, any stipulation or condition in any policy affecting the liability of members, or of the funds of any company, remained in full force and effect, notwithstanding registration of the company under that Act (*p*). The repeal of the Act of 1862 by the Companies (Consolidation) Act, 1908, s. 286, does not affect the position of these companies (*q*).

Any company registered under the 7 & 8 Vict. c. 110, if not registered under the Companies Act, 1862, did not become illegal, but was subjected to the following consequences:—1. It was incapable of suing, yet not incapable of being sued, either at law or in equity; 2. No dividend was payable to any of its shareholders; and 3. Each director or manager incurred a penalty of 5*l.* a day during default in registering under the Act of 1862 (*r*). Policies issued under these circumstances appear to be valid notwithstanding, and they may be enforced against the company.

No partnership or company consisting of more than twenty persons, which has been formed on or after the 2nd of November, 1862, for the acquisition of gain by the company or its members, is legal unless registered under the Act of 1862 or the Act of 1908 (*s*), or formed in pursuance of some other Act, or of letters patent. The effect of this

visions of the Companies (Consolidation) Act, 1908, are in ss. 2, 249, 286.

(*o*) Companies Act, 1862, ss. 193, 194, 196, re-enacted in ss. 260, 261, 263 of the Companies (Consolidation) Act, 1908.

(*p*) Companies Act, 1862, s. 38 (6); Companies (Consolidation) Act, 1908, s. 123 (6).

(*q*) See Companies (Consolidation) Act, 1908, ss. 245, 246, 247.

(*r*) Companies Act, 1862, s. 210.

(*s*) *Ibid.* s. 4; Companies (Consolidation) Act, 1908, s. 1. See Shaw *v.* Benson (1883), 11 Q. B. D. 563; 52 L. J. Q. B. 575; In re Padstow Ass. Association (1882), 20 Ch. D. 137; 51 L. J. Ch. 344.

provision on policies made by such a partnership or company, if not registered, is a point which remains unsettled. The better opinion seems to be that an illegal association and its creditors who are cognizant of the illegality will not be assisted by the Courts; but that the association cannot avail itself of its illegality to defeat a claim made by a person who had contracted with it in ignorance of the illegality (*t*).

If the issue of marine policies be *ultra vires* of the company, the policies are invalid, and the premiums paid may be recovered back (*u*).

Since the 5 Geo. 4, c. 114, legalized insurance companies and partnerships, the mode of making them parties to a policy varies with the constitution of each. For this purpose, the several names of all the members of the partnership or company never were necessarily subscribed, notwithstanding the 36 Geo. 3, c. 63, s. 11 (*x*). In some cases, the matter is left as at common law, so that a valid policy is made by the subscription of the partnership firm, or the application of the seal of the body corporate (*y*). But the form of execution may be indefinitely varied by the statute, charter, deed, or articles of association under which the company is constituted (*z*).

<small>Sect. 79.

Consequences of issuing marine policies *ultra vires* of the company. Form of underwriting by companies.</small>

(*t*) See Buckley on Companies, 9th ed. pp. 4, 5, where the authorities are cited; see also Lindley on Partnership, 8th ed. p. 127.

(*u*) Re Phœnix Life Ass. Co., Burges *v.* Stocks (1862), 2 J. & H. 441. Accord. Hambro' *v.* Hull & London Fire Ass. Co. (1858), 3 H. & N. 789.

That the objects of a company incorporated under the Act of 1862 or of 1908, as stated in the memorandum of association, cannot be departed from, and consequently that a contract made by the directors in respect of a matter not included in such memorandum, or not fairly incidental to the company's objects as defined therein, is *ultra vires* of the directors, and not binding on the company, is now matter of clear law. See Ashbury Railway Carriage, &c. Co. *v.* Riche (1875), L. R. 7 H. L. 653; A.-G. *v.* Gt. Eastern Ry. Co. (1880), 5 App. Cas. 473.

(*x*) Repealed by the 30 & 31 Vict. c. 23. If partners do underwrite their several names for separate sums, the right of the assured against the partnership assets is not thereby invalidated. Brett *v.* Beckwith (1856), 26 L. J. Ch. 130, *coram* M. R.

(*y*) Mar. Ins. Act, 1906, s. 24 (1), *ante*, § 26.

(*z*) See the general principle laid down and applied in Reid *v.* Allan

Sect. 80.
Association of shipowners for mutual assurance.

80. The business of insurance is carried on, not only by individual underwriters and companies, for the purpose of earning profits, but also largely by associations of shipowners, who agree, each entering his ships for a certain amount, to divide among themselves one another's loss. These are called mutual insurance associations or clubs.

These clubs appear to have originated in the prohibition imposed by the Act of 1719 against insurance by chartered companies, and to have been designed to afford their members a more adequate protection than that furnished by private underwriters for a smaller rate of premium than they required (*a*). The Courts, however, in their endeavour to preserve to the two old companies the monopoly secured to them by the Act of 1719, as against every other public body formed for the purposes of marine insurance, decided that the members of such associations could only be individually, and not collectively, liable to such of their members as sustained a loss (*b*). Consequently, where, in case of the insolvency of any one of the members, all the others covenanted that they would be liable to make good his losses, Lord Kenyon held that such association was illegal, although, except in case of insolvency, each member only covenanted severally to pay for his separate share (*c*). The result of these decisions, of course, was that the objects which such associations had in view were only imperfectly obtained.

(1849), 4 Exch. 326; Dowdall *v.* Allan (1849), 19 L. J. Q. B. 41. In an unreported case where a rule for a new trial or to enter a verdict for the defendants was obtained on the ground, among others, that the declaration purported to be on a simple contract, whereas the policy was made by a company under seal, when cause came to be shown on that point, Blackburn, J., inquired whether the seal in that case had any other legal effect than merely to put the contract in the form proper to the company. The point was not further pressed by the defendants. Roper *v.* English and Scotch Marine Ins. Co., *coram* Q. B.

(*a*) See per Pollock, B., in Marine Mutual Ins. Assn. *v.* Young (1880), 4 Asp. M. C. 357.

(*b*) Harrison *v.* Millar (1796), 7 T. R. 340, n.; Lees *v.* Smith (1797), *ibid.* 338; and see Strong *v.* Harvey (1825), 3 Bing. 304.

(*c*) Lees *v.* Smith (1797), 7 T. R. 338. It was decided not to be necessary to specify on the face of the policy the respective sums for which the members severally insure. Dowell *v.* Moon (1815), 4 Camp. 166.

CHAP. IV.] INSURERS ON SEA-POLICIES. 109

The system of mutual insurance has, however, been entirely altered, in consequence of the abolition of the prohibition of insurance by corporations and partnerships, and as a result of the Companies Act, 1862. It has been established that a mutual insurance association is a company for the acquisition of gain by the company or its members within sect. 4 of that Act, and is therefore, when consisting of more than twenty members, an illegal association unless registered (*d*).

Sect. 80. Associations under the Companies Act, 1862.

The consequence is that the associations are now always registered under the Act, usually as unlimited companies, or companies limited by guarantee (*e*). In general, it is now the association itself which is the insurer, not as formerly the individual members, and the cause of action of the member, as assured, is against the association itself, not against the other members. The consideration which the member gives for his insurance is his liability to contribute in the manner provided by the rules of the association to the losses of other members (*f*) and to the expenses of management (*g*), and often also the payment, in addition, of an initial premium, or entrance fee (*h*).

(*d*) In re Arthur Average Association (1875), L. R. 10 Ch. 542; In re Padstow Total Loss Association (1882), 20 Ch. D. 137, in which case an order for the winding-up of an unregistered association of more than twenty members was discharged.

(*e*) See Lion Mutual Marine Ins. Association *v.* Tucker (1883), 12 Q. B. D. 176; In re Bangor & North Wales Mutual, &c. Association, Baird's Case, [1899] 2 Ch. 593; and Corfield *v.* Buchanan (1913), 29 Times L. R. 258, as to the effect of a limitation by guarantee in the event of the winding-up of an association.

(*f*) See the remarks of Brett, M. R., in Lion Ins. Association *v.* Tucker (1883), 12 Q. B. D. 176, 187, on the question of consideration, where the members of the association were themselves the insurers.

(*g*) There are now some clubs, whose policy-holders are divided into two classes—(1) those who pay a fixed premium only, (2) those who are liable to contribute by calls to the losses of other members. If the fixed premiums are insufficient to meet the aggregate losses of the former class, the deficiency is made good by contributions from the members in the latter class; if they exceed the amount of such losses, the surplus is appropriated

(*h*) See note (*h*), next page.

Sect. 80.
The Stamp Acts apply to mutual insurance.

At one time an opinion prevailed that a policy was not necessary for the validity of contracts of mutual insurance (*i*), but it has been established that the Stamp Acts apply to such insurances, for the validity of which, therefore, a policy containing the particulars required by the Stamp Act, 1891, is requisite (*k*).

In favour of these clubs an exception has been made to the general rule that policies may not be stamped after they have been underwritten (except on payment of a penalty). By sect. 95 of the Stamp Act, 1891, a policy of mutual insurance, originally sufficiently stamped, may, if required, be stamped with an additional stamp.

A club policy has been held to be properly signed within the meaning of the Stamp Act when sealed with the seal of the association, and attested by the manager (*l*); and sect. 24 (1) of the Marine Insurance Act, 1906, declares that the seal of a corporation may be a sufficient signature to a policy.

Mutual insurance is specifically dealt with in sect. 85 of the Marine Insurance Act, 1906, the terms of which are as follow:—

> (1) Where two or more persons mutually agree to insure each other against marine losses there is said to be a mutual insurance.
>
> (2) The provisions of this Act relating to the premium do not apply to mutual insurance, but a guarantee, or such other arrangement as may be agreed upon, may be substituted for the premium.
>
> (3) The provisions of this Act, in so far as they may be modified by the agreement of the parties, may in the

---

to the payment of the losses of the second class. See, *e.g.*, Corfield *v.* Buchanan (1913), 29 Times L. R. 258, *infra*, § 83.

(*h*) For a series of modern rules fixing the liabilities of members, see North-Eastern 100 A SS. Ins. Ass. *v.* Red " S " Steamship Co. (1906), 12 Com. Cas. 26.

(*i*) Bromley *v.* Williams (1863), 32 L. J. Ch. 716; see also Harvey *v.* Beckwith (1864), 2 H. & M. 429.

(*k*) In re London Marine Ins. Association, Smith's Case (1869), L. R. 4 Ch. 611; In re Arthur Average Association (1875), L. R. 10 Ch. 542.

(*l*) Marine Mutual Ins. Ass. *v.* Young (1880), 43 L. T. N. S. 441.

case of mutual insurance be modified by the terms of the policies issued by the association, or by the rules and regulations of the association.

Sect. 80.

(4) Subject to the exceptions mentioned in this section, the provisions of this Act apply to a mutual insurance.

Sub-sect. (1) does not correctly describe the existing system of mutual insurance; for, as we have seen, it is the associations, not the members, who are now the insurers.

81. The system of mutual insurance is now used by shipowners, not only for the ordinary insurance of ship and freight, but also to cover a number of risks and liabilities which are not protected by the ordinary policies. The insurances are made subject to the articles of association and the rules and regulations of the particular association (*m*), which are usually by express reference incorporated into the policies issued to the members (*n*). One class of mutual insurance associations insures the ships of the members against the same risks as are undertaken by Lloyd's underwriters under their ordinary policies. The policies are made subject to exceptions and special clauses similar in most respects to those contained in the time policies subscribed at Lloyd's. The exception of particular average is, however, not always the same as in the memorandum of Lloyd's policy. Sometimes the amount is not 3*l*. per cent. as in the latter, but 1*l*. per cent. or at a certain rate (*e.g.*, 3*s*.)

Risks and liabilities insured by the club.

Ordinary time insurances on ship.

(*m*) A knowledge of the rules by which a member of an association has agreed to be bound will be imputed to him. Turnbull *v.* Woolfe (1862), 7 L. T. N. S. 483.

(*n*) A policy incorporated the provisions of the articles of association, which were indorsed on the policy. One of these articles, which provided that the assured should keep one-fifth of the ship's value uninsured, was invalid for non-compliance with the formalities of the Companies Act. The House of Lords held that the condition was nevertheless binding as a contract. Muirhead *v.* Forth, &c. Mutual Ins. Association, [1894] A. C. 72. Where the policy contained no reference to the rules, it was held that the member who had by letter agreed to be bound by the rules could be sued for a contribution, and that the letter, though unstamped, could be given in evidence. In re Albert Average Association, Blyth's Case (1872), L. R. 13 Eq. 529.

Sect. 81. per gross registered ton. Sometimes the ship is warranted free from particular average under a specified sum, *e.g.*, under 500*l.*

Freight. Another class comprises mutual associations for the insurance of freight. Not only do the policies of these associations insure the members against a loss of freight in respect of which there is an insurable interest, but they commonly incorporate a rule which provides that in case of the total loss of a member's ship, the amount insured with the association shall be deemed to be his interest at risk. This provision seems to amount to an admission of interest, and to make a policy into which the rules are incorporated a wager policy (*o*).

"Thirds." Mutual associations have been established to indemnify the members against loss caused by the customary deduction of "thirds" and "sixths" from the cost of new materials or of repairs to their ships (*p*).

Small damage. Other associations insure their members against certain kinds of losses, not covered by the ordinary insurances, which are included under the head of "small damage." Among these losses are—(1) particular average losses on ship under 3*l.* per cent. or other small particular average losses which the underwriters except in the ordinary policies; (2) the cost of the wages and provisions of the crew while the ship is ashore, or disabled, or under average repairs; (3) damage

(*o*) See *post*, "Wager Policies," §§ 311, 312. In United Kingdom Mutual SS. Ass. Association *v.* Boulton (1898), 3 Com. Cas. 330, a rule of a freight club provided that "the interest insured shall be the amount entered in the association, which amount shall be paid in the event of the total loss of the steamship entered, whether the vessel be loaded, in ballast, or under time charter." Bigham, J., thought that the rule was framed to cover loss of freight consequent on the total loss of the ship, and not caused by perils of the sea. See also Coker *v.* Bolton, [1912] 3 K. B. 315. The plain meaning, however, of this and similar rules seems to be that the assured shall recover in the event of a total loss of ship, whether or not he has any freight at risk, and it is believed that this is the construction which in practice has been put upon these rules.

(*p*) See, as to these deductions, *post*, §§ 1024—1030.

CHAP. IV.] INSURERS ON SEA-POLICIES. 113

to the ship by striking the ground when such striking does Sect. 81.
not amount to stranding.

Other associations insure shipowners against loss caused Detention.
by the detention of their ships from various causes, such as
detention while stranded or sunk, or under repair, detention
by breakdown of machinery, in quarantine, through the
arrest of the ship, or when the ship is ice-bound in consequence of damage.

An important class of mutual insurance associations are Protection
those called protection and indemnity associations. Their and indemnity.
object is not only to indemnify their members against certain
liabilities, but also to assist them in certain kinds of litigation
in respect of their ships, *e.g.*, with charterers, cargo-owners,
seamen and public authorities. They usually undertake,
inter alia, to indemnify their members against liabilities—
(1) for life salvage, and for damages in respect of loss of
life and personal injury, including now compensation payable to members of the crew and their dependants under the
Workmen's Compensation Act, 1906; (2) for medical and
funeral expenses, &c. incurred in respect of the crews of their
ships (*q*); (3) for the loss of or damage to goods carried on
their ships (*r*); (4) for the one-fourth of the damages and
expenses consequent on collision, which is not covered by
the ordinary collision clause; (5) for damage to harbours,
piers, &c.; (6) for the expenses of raising wrecks; (7) for
quarantine expenses, and the expenses of disinfection in
consequence of outbreaks of disease on their ships. They

(*q*) See Rogers *v.* British Shipowners' Mutual Protection, &c. Association (1896), 1 Com. Cas. 414, in which it was held that the club was not liable under its rules for expenses incurred in obtaining substitutes for members of the crew disabled by illness.

(*r*) For the meaning of the term "improper navigation," where the shipowners were protected against damage to goods on board when caused by the improper navigation of their ship, see Good *v.* London SS. Owners' Mutual Protecting Association (1871), L. R. 6 C. P. 563; Carmichael *v.* Liverpool Sailing Ship Owners' Mutual Indemnity Association (1887), 19 Q. B. D. 242; Canada Shipping Co. *v.* British Shipowners' Mutual Protection Association (1889), 23 Q. B. D. 342. See also The Warkworth, C. A. (1884), 9 P. D. 145.

Sect. 81. also usually undertake to pay to the shipowner the cargo's proportion of general average (not including damage to the ship) when it is not recoverable from the cargo-owner or the ship's underwriter (*s*).

(*s*) It is not the practice of protection and indemnity associations to issue policies to their members. The contract between the association and the member is effected by a request, usually made on a printed form on the part of the shipowner addressed to the association, to enter the specified ship or ships for protection and indemnity for specified tonnages, and the acceptance of such request by the association. Whether or not this procedure is sufficient to make a valid contract depends on whether the contract is "a contract for sea insurance" within the meaning of s. 93 of the Stamp Act, 1891. It would, in fact, be impossible to comply with the provisions of s. 93 (3), which requires that a policy of sea insurance shall specify *inter alia* the sum or sums insured. (See also Mar. Ins. Act, ss. 22, 23 (4), 91 (1) (a).) This impossibility is due to the fact that the liability of the association is not restricted to any particular sum, and any such restriction would defeat the main object for which the association exists—*i.e.*, to protect its members against liabilities which are themselves indefinite.

A contract of this nature differs from an ordinary contract of marine insurance, inasmuch as it does not pretend to recoup a member for damage affecting any subject-matter of insurance. And it is not at all clear from the Stamp Act that an agreement of indemnity against a liability to a third person, although such liability may itself arise indirectly from a sea peril, is itself a contract for sea insurance requiring a policy. Of the liabilities ordinarily undertaken by such associations, that which it is most difficult to distinguish from a sea risk is the liability to pay the shipowner the cargo's proportion of general average in certain cases.

On the other hand, s. 93 (1) of the Stamp Act expressly exempts the insurances referred to in s. 55 of the Merchant Shipping Act Amendment Act, 1862, from the necessity of being expressed in a policy of sea insurance. These are insurances against liability for damages, in respect of which a shipowner was thereby entitled to limit his liability—*i.e.*, for loss of life and loss of or damage to goods on board his ship. This sub-section is unnecessary unless a policy of sea insurance would otherwise be requisite. Its existence is, therefore, some ground for the argument that, inasmuch as the associations undertake other risks of the same nature as those referred to in the 55th section of the Merchant Shipping Act Amendment Act, 1862, which, however, are not excepted by s. 93 (1) of the Stamp Act, 1891, a policy in respect thereof is necessary.

The question might also be raised whether an agreement between such an association and a member, if containing several provisions of which some taken by themselves do, but others do not, amount to sea insurance, is severable, so that the contract would be good so far as its terms were not required to be

CHAP. IV.] INSURERS ON SEA-POLICIES. 115

In consequence of the modern practice of inserting in the ordinary policies the clause excepting capture and seizure, associations have also been founded for mutual insurance against war risks.

Sect. 81. War risks.

82. The rules of the mutual insurance associations vary according to their objects, and to some extent according to the views of their directors and members; but there are certain provisions which are almost invariably to be found in the rules of all.

Rules of mutual insurance associations.

It is usually provided that a person desiring to insure a ship shall deliver to the association a proposal in writing, authorizing the directors, if they accept the proposal, to enter his name in the register of members, and the insurance in the register of insurances (*t*).

We have already seen that a contract for sea insurance must, with certain exceptions, to be valid, comply with the requirements of the Stamp Act. Where, however, a member of a mutual association, having vessels on its books as insured, paid calls and otherwise acted as if he were a member, he was held to be estopped, in an action for calls on losses, from denying his liability on the ground that the losses were paid without any stamped policies having been issued (*u*). Again, where a ship insured with an association was lost, and the

---

expressed in a policy, and bad only as to the remainder; or whether, on the other hand, the whole agreement is void. In many cases there would undoubtedly be much difficulty in severing the different provisions of such an agreement from each other. It may be arguable that where the agreement between the association and the member provides for an indemnity against a large number of liabilities, only one or two of which require to be insured against by a policy, the contract, taken as a whole, is not one which requires to be expressed in a policy of sea insurance.

(*t*) Where a rule provided that a person became a member only by signing the articles, the association was held to be estopped from asserting that a person was not a member who had not so signed, but who had paid contributions claimed by the association from him. Edwards *v.* Aberayron Mutual Ship Ins. Society (1875), 1 Q. B. D. 563.

(*u*) Barrow-in-Furness Mutual Ship Ins. Co. *v.* Ashburner (1885), 54 L. J. Q. B. 377. See, however, In re London Marine Ins. Association, Smith's Case (1869), L. R. 4 Ch. 611.

Sect. 82. books showed that the sum due to the member for the loss had been assessed by the committee and paid by the members, it was held that there was a sufficient admission of liability in the books to enable the assured to recover without producing a stamped policy (*x*).

The practice is to insure by time policies from noon of the 20th of February, Greenwich time, or from noon of the date entered in the register of insurances, until noon of the following 20th of February. There is usually a rule which provides that the insurances shall be renewed from year to year on the 20th of February, unless either the member or the association gives notice to terminate the insurance in the manner and at the time prescribed by the rules (*y*).

There is almost always a rule declaring that no policy issued by the association shall be assigned, mortgaged, or disposed of, so as to pass any part of the beneficial interest in the policy, without the consent of the association endorsed upon the policy (*z*). Another usual rule provides that the association shall not be bound to take notice of the interest of any person, other than the member insuring, in any ship or insurance, unless a memorandum of the name and interest of such person has been endorsed on the policy with the consent of the association.

Usually the rules provide that the insurance shall cease on the death, insolvency, or lunacy of the member, or if the member mortgages the ship (*a*), unless a sufficient guarantee

---

(*x*) In re Teignmouth and General Mutual Shipping Association (1872), L. R. 14 Eq. 148; 41 L. J. Ch. 679.

(*y*) This rule has been held not to make a club policy a continuing policy beyond the day on which it is expressed to terminate: Lishman *v.* Northern Maritime Ins. Co. (1873), L. R. 8 C. P. 216; in the Exch. Ch. (1875), L. R. 10 C. P. 179. See *post*, § 440.

(*z*) See Laurie *v.* West Hartlepool Thirds Indemnity Association (1899), 4 Com. Cas. 323.

(*a*) See Turnbull *v.* Woolfe (1862), 7 L. T. N. S. 483; Alexander *v.* Campbell (1872), 41 L. J. Ch. 478. A rule which provided that "no vessel which is mortgaged shall be insured unless the mortgagee gives a written guarantee, &c.," was held to apply only to a ship mortgaged at the time when the insurance was made, and not to render a guarantee necessary when a ship was mortgaged afterwards. Hutchinson *v.* Wright (1858), 25 Beav. 444; 27 L. J. Ch. 834. For the construction of this rule, see

for the payment of all contributions be given to the associa- Sect. 82.
tion (*b*). In general, also, the liability to contribute to future
losses ceases on the loss or sale of the ship.

In case of a dispute between a member and the association
with regard to a claim, the rules almost invariably make a
reference to arbitration a condition precedent to the right of
the member to bring an action (*c*).

83. The most characteristic feature of the system of Contributions.
mutual insurance, viz., that the losses are divided among the
members, has already been pointed out. Frequently an
entrance fee is paid when a ship is accepted for insurance,
and many associations require an initial premium to be paid
every year in respect of each ship insured. When a claim
for a loss has been allowed and there is no fund, such as the
initial premiums, out of which it can be paid, the necessary
sum is raised by a call on all the members. The contribu- How assessed.
tions are assessed on them either in proportion to the amounts
for which they are insured, or in proportion to the gross
registered tonnage of their ships, as the rules prescribe.
Sometimes in insurances on ships, contributions in respect of
total and general average losses are levied on the amounts
insured, while contributions for particular average losses are
assessed according to tonnage.

Where an association was by the terms of its policies under Claims for
liability only to the member, it was held that a part-owner contributions
of a ship other than the member could not bring an action by or against
on the policy for a loss (*d*). Similarly, it was held that an other than
members.

also North-Eastern 100 A SS. Ins. Ass. *v.* Red "S" Steamship Co. (1905—6), 10 Com. Cas. 245; 12 Com. Cas. 26. In that case the Court of Appeal held, affirming Channell, J., that the member, although unprotected in consequence of the rule, was liable under the rules of the association to pay contributions.

(*b*) See Hughes *v.* Tindall (1856), 18 C. B. 98.

(*c*) See Scott *v.* Avery (1855), 5 H. L. Cas. 811; 25 L. J. Ex. 308.

For the effect of a rule which provided that in certain events the decision of the directors should be final, see The Warwick (1890), 15 P. D. 189. An improper hearing by the directors does not preclude a member from bringing an action. *Ibid.*; Edwards *v.* Aberayron Mutual Ship Ins. Society (1876), 1 Q. B. D. 563.

(*d*) Montgomerie *v.* United Kingdom Mutual SS. Assurance Association, [1891] 1 Q. B. 370.

Sect. 83. association could not bring an action for contributions against a part-owner, as the undisclosed principal of the managing owner who had become a member of the association in respect of the ship, when the policy was expressed in a form which made the member only liable upon it (*e*). Where, however, the policy issued to the managing owners of a ship, who insured her in their own names, was an adaptation of Lloyd's policy, containing the clause "as well in his or their own names as for and in the name or names of all and every other person to whom the same doth, may, or shall appertain, &c.," it was held that the other owners could be sued for contributions, as being the persons insured by the policy (*f*).

The result of the cases is that, generally speaking, under the rules and policies of the associations, the owners of a ship, who authorize a person to effect an insurance with and to become a member of an association, are liable, as assured, to be sued for contributions. They ought, therefore, on general principles to be able themselves to enforce claims for losses; but the rules often provide that claims can only be enforced by the member. The question whether the owners who authorize the insurance are themselves members was raised but not decided in one of the cases. "It may be," said Lord Esher, "that the defendants" (the assured) "are members for the purpose of paying contributions, though not for the purpose of voting, and that they are not liable to contribute to the expenses of the association other than in respect of losses of other ships insured" (*g*). Subject to any special rules of the particular association, it is submitted that this is a correct view of their position.

(*e*) United Kingdom Mutual SS. Ass. Association *v.* Nevill, C. A. (1887), 19 Q. B. D. 110. See per Lord Esher, M. R., 22 Q. B. D. 719.

(*f*) Great Britain 100 A 1 SS. Ins. Association *v.* Wyllie, C. A. (1889), 22 Q. B. D. 710; following Ocean Iron SS. Association *v.* Leslie (1887), *ibid.* 722, n.; British Marine Mutual Ins. Co. *v.* Jenkins, [1900] 1 Q. B. 299. In the last-mentioned case Bigham, J., held that this liability was not inconsistent with the rule that "a member shall be uninsured in respect of any interest entered if he becomes bankrupt or insolvent," unless an approved guarantee be given.

(*g*) Great Britain 100 A 1 SS. Ins. Association *v.* Wylie (1889), 22 Q. B. D. at p. 717.

CHAP. IV.] INSURERS ON SEA-POLICIES. 119

The memorandum of a mutual insurance association enabled it to undertake re-insurance risks generally, and the policies of re-insurance issued by the association at fixed rates of premium declared that the assured should not be liable for further contributions, nor entitled to share in any profit, and that they waived any right of voting at the general meetings. One of the articles of association provided that every person effecting an insurance or re-insurance should be deemed to have become a member. The House of Lords held that, notwithstanding this article, this class of policy-holders were not members, and could not be made contributories in the winding-up, and also that the issue of the fixed-premium policies was not *ultra vires* (h).

Sect. 83.
Issue of policies to non-members.

84. Sometimes compliance with a rule which is incorporated in a policy is expressly made a condition precedent to the liability of the association (i). Whether a rule, not expressed to create a condition precedent, is a warranty, depends on its nature. Thus a rule providing that ships should not sail on certain voyages between certain dates was held to be a warranty. In the same case the Court said that a rule which provided that a vessel beaching before or after a specified time was not entitled to recover for any subsequent loss until surveyed and reported sufficient, was an exception as to the damage taking place between the beaching and the survey (k).

(h) Corfield v. Buchanan (1913), 29 Times L. R. 258.
(i) See Stewart v. Wilson (1843), 12 M. & W. 11. See Sailing Ship Dewa Gungadhur Co. v. United Kingdom Maritime Mutual Ins. Association (1886), 2 T. L. R. 366, for a decision on a rule providing that the insurance should cease if the member neglected to pay calls. In Williams v. British Mutual Marine Ins. Co. (1887), 3 T. L. R. 314, the Court of Appeal held that the member could set off against a call a loss, the amount of which had been adjusted, and that the association could therefore not forfeit the policy for non-payment of the call.

(k) Colledge v. Harty (1851), 6 Exch. 205; 20 L. J. Ex. 146. See also Harrison v. Douglas (1835), 3 A. & E. 396.

CHAPTER V.

OF THE ASSURED; WHO MAY BE INSURED.

	SECT.
Insurances on Enemy's Property	85—89
Who is for commercial purposes an Alien Enemy	90—100

<small>All persons may be insured except alien enemies.</small> 85. ALL persons, whether aliens or British subjects, may be insured, with the exception of alien enemies; that is, persons who, either by birth or domicil, belong to a state actually engaged in war with our own.

This restriction is an obvious consequence of that universally recognized principle in the law of nations, viz., that the object of a maritime war is the destruction of the enemy's commerce and navigation, in order to weaken and destroy the foundations of his naval power. As marine insurance has for its object the protection of commerce and navigation, it would obviously be inconsistent with the very purposes of a maritime war, to permit insurance on the shipping and trade of the enemy. "*Hostium enim pericula in se suscipere, quid est aliud quam eorum commercia maritima promovere ?*"(*a*).

<small>Lord Mansfield upheld insurances by alien enemies.</small> It was for a long time, however, an unsettled question in English law, whether the insurance of enemy's property was or was not illegal at common law. Lord Hardwicke, in the year 1749, said it had never been declared in our Courts to be unlawful (*b*); and Lord Mansfield supported the practice, not apparently upon any principles of law (*c*), but on fancied grounds of expediency; supposing that English underwriters would thereby gain more in premiums than they would lose

---

(*a*) Bynkershoek, Quæst. Jur. Publ., l. 1, c. 21.
(*b*) Henkle *v.* Royal Exch. Co. (1749), 1 Ves. Sen. 317, 320.

(*c*) Buller, J., said that he never could get him to give any opinion as to their legality: Bell *v.* Gilson (1798), 1 B. & P. 345, 354.

ALIEN ENEMIES. 121

by captures (*d*). Valin, however, followed by Pothier and Emerigon, declares that owing to the permission of this practice in England, one part of our nation restored to theirs, by the effect of insurances, what the other part took from them by the rights of war (*e*).

Sect. 85.

The English legislature by two temporary statutes, one in 1748 (*f*), and another in 1792 (*g*), prohibited the insurance of any ships or merchandise belonging to France during the wars then pending with the subjects of that nation.

Temporary prohibition by statute.

At length the Courts of Westminster Hall took the whole subject into consideration upon general principles, and established, by a long course of decisions, under Lord Kenyon, Lord Alvanley, and Lord Ellenborough, that such insurances were not only illegal and void, but repugnant to every principle of public policy (*h*).

Such insurances finally determined to be illegal.

"The question is," says Lord Alvanley, "whether it be competent to an English underwriter to indemnify persons who are engaged in war with his own sovereign, from the consequences of that war; and we are all of opinion that, on the principles of the English law, it is not competent to any subject to enter into a contract to do anything which may be detrimental to the interests of his own country; and that such contract is as much prohibited as if it had been expressly forbidden by Act of Parliament" (*i*).

86. The first two cases in which the question was formally

Cases which established this rule.

(*d*) Planché *v*. Fletcher (1779), 1 Dougl. 251; Gist *v*. Mason (1786), 1 T. R. 88; Lavabre *v*. Wilson (1779), 1 Dougl. 284.

(*e*) 2 Valin, tit. vi. Des Assurances, art. 3, p. 215 (he is speaking of the war terminated by the Peace of Paris, 1763); Pothier, Traité d'Assurance, No. 95; Emerigon, c. iv. s. 9, vol. i. p. 128. Boulay-Paty says that by French law such insurances are illegal; Comment. on Emerigon, vol. i. p. 131.

(*f*) 21 Geo. 2, c. 4.

(*g*) 33 Geo. 3, c. 27.

(*h*) Brandon *v*. Nesbitt (1794), 6 T. R. 23; Bristow *v*. Towers (1794), *ibid*. 35; Furtado *v*. Rogers (1802), 3 B. & P. 191; Kellner *v*. Le Mesurier (1803), 4 East, 396; Gamba *v*. Le Mesurier (1803), *ibid*. 407; Brandon *v*. Curling (1803), *ibid*. 410; M'Connell *v*. Hector (1802), 3 B. & P. 113; Le Luneville *v*. Phillips (1806), 2 B. & P. N. R. 97.

(*i*) In Furtado *v*. Rogers (1802), 3 B. & P. 198.

Sect. 86. decided (Brandon *v.* Nesbitt and Bristow *v.* Towers (*k*)) proceeded exclusively on the ground that such a contract could not be enforced in our Courts. They did not directly decide the question whether such insurances were absolutely illegal in their own nature. But in the case of Furtado *v.* Rogers, Lord Alvanley, then presiding in the Court of Common Pleas, laid it down decisively, that insurances effected on behalf of an alien enemy, though made previously to the commencement of hostilities, and therefore legal in their inception, could not cover a loss by British capture after war had broken out; and that no action could be brought upon them in our Courts even after the restoration of peace (*l*).

Decisions of Lord Ellenborough.

The language of Lord Ellenborough in condemning these insurances was even stronger than that of Lord Alvanley; he pronounced them to be not only illegal and void, but repugnant to every principle of public policy. Whether the loss in respect of which the assured sought to recover were a loss by British capture (*m*), or by capture by a co-belligerent (*n*); whether the insurance were effected before or after the breaking out of hostilities (*o*); or whether the action were brought during war or after the restoration of peace (*p*); Lord Ellenborough's decision was uniformly the same; and he declared, that every insurance on alien property by a British subject must be understood with this limitation, that it shall not extend to cover any loss happening during the existence of hostilities between the respective countries of the assured and the underwriters.

Semble, insurance on a British ship against British capture legal.

When, however, it was attempted to extend this principle still further, to an insurance on a British ship against British capture, the point was not decided, but the Court intimated a

---

(*k*) (1794), 6 T. R. 23, 25.

(*l*) Furtado *v.* Rogers (1802), 3 B. & P. 191.

(*m*) As in Kellner *v.* Le Mesurier (1803), 4 East, 396.

(*n*) As in Brandon *v.* Curling (1803), 4 East, 410.

(*o*) As in Furtado *v.* Rogers (1802), 3 B. & P. 191; or Brandon *v.* Curling (1803), 4 East, 410.

(*p*) As in Gamba *v.* Le Mesurier (1803), 4 East, 407.

CHAP. V.] ALIEN ENEMIES. 123

pretty clear opinion, that it would only be illegal in the case of a foreign ship (*q*). Sect. 86.

Thus it came to be established during the great French war, 1st, that an insurance effected by an alien enemy is an illegal contract, and therefore void *ab initio;* 2ndly, that an alien enemy cannot recover for a loss occurring during the existence of the war, even though the insurance was effected before its commencement. Neither of these propositions was disputed in the case of Janson *v.* Driefontein Consolidated Mines, which will now be considered, and both of them are confirmed by the judgments delivered therein. In that case an attempt was made to extend the rule that losses incurred by an alien enemy are not recoverable. On the 2nd of October, 1899, when the relations between the British Government and the South African Republic had become strained, a quantity of gold in transit to the United Kingdom, belonging to a company incorporated under the laws of the Republic, was seized by order of the Government of the Republic. War broke out on the 11th of October. In an action on a policy by which the gold had previously been insured against capture, the insurers contended that the company could not recover, as the gold had been seized by its own Government for the purposes of hostilities against this country; and in the Court of Appeal Vaughan Williams, L. J., held that, on grounds of public policy, a British subject cannot legally contract to indemnify the subject of a foreign state against a loss by the forcible seizure of his property by the foreign Government for the purpose of an imminent war with this country. The other members of the Court of Appeal held, however, that as at the time of the seizure the two countries were still at peace, the assured could recover for the loss (*r*), and the House of Lords unanimously affirmed their decision (*s*). "The authorities referred to in the

Summary of Rules established during great French war.

Attempt to extend rules.

Insurers liable for capture by foreign Government in time of peace, though war imminent.

(*q*) Lubbock *v.* Potts (1806), 7 East, 449.
(*r*) Driefontein Consolidated Mines *v.* Janson, [1901] 2 K. B. 419, affirming the decision of Mathew, J., [1900] 2 Q. B. 339.
(*s*) Janson *v.* Driefontein Consolidated Mines, [1902] A. C. 484.

Sect. 86. argument," said Lord Halsbury, L. C., "do not justify the proposition that expected wars render a contract illegal between citizens of the two nations between whom war is anticipated, and to lay down such a rule would be to establish an entirely new code, for which there is no authority in the law."

Return of premium.

87. If the contract of insurance be effected before the commencement of hostilities, it is legal in its inception; and if the risk have once attached on such policy, there can be no return of premium (*t*). If the policy be knowingly effected after hostilities have commenced, the assured has no right to a return of premium (*u*), unless before the commencement of the risk he has duly renounced the contract (*x*). If, however, an agent in this country innocently effects an insurance for one, who has become an alien enemy by the breaking out of hostilities before the policy was effected, the agent being unaware of that fact at the time he procured it, the premium thus paid under a mistake of fact may be recovered back from the underwriter (*y*).

An alien enemy who is licensed to trade may be insured.

88. An alien enemy having a licence or privilege to trade has the right of insuring his property as incident to the right of trading (*z*). Such a licence not only legalizes the commerce, and therefore the insurance by which it is sought to be protected (*a*), but also enables the alien enemy, so licensed, to sue upon the policy, not only in the name of the agent, but in his own (*b*). "Whatever commerce of this kind,"

The doctrine of public policy is elaborately discussed in the judgments.

(*t*) Furtado *v*. Rogers (1802), 3 B. & P. 191.

(*u*) Vandyck *v*. Hewitt (1800), 1 East, 96; Morck *v*. Abel (1802), 3 B. & P. 35; Lubbock *v*. Potts (1806), 7 East, 449.

(*x*) Palyart *v*. Leckie (1817), 6 M. & S. 290; and the cases cited *post*, Vol. II. "Return of Premium."

(*y*) Oom *v*. Bruce (1810), 12 East, 225; Hentig *v*. Staniforth (1816), 5 M. & S. 122.

(*z*) Wells *v*. Williams (1697), 1 Salk. 45; 1 Lord Raymond, 282, S. C.

(*a*) Kensington *v*. Inglis (1807), 8 East, 273; Conway *v*. Gray (1809), 10 East, 536.

(*b*) Usparicha *v*. Noble (1811), 13 East, 332.

says Lord Ellenborough (c), "the Crown has thought fit to permit, must be regarded by the Courts of Law as legal with all the consequences of its being legal; one of which consequences is a right to contract with other subjects of the country for the purpose of protecting such property by insurance."

Hence, where a licence to trade with the enemy was given to three persons, two of whom themselves became alien enemies before action brought; it was held, that the broker, who had effected the policy for all the three, might, nevertheless, recover upon it (d).

89. Where the party intended to be insured by the policy does not become an alien enemy, until after the loss and the cause of action have arisen, his right to sue on the policy is only suspended during the continuance of hostilities, and revives on the restoration of peace (e); and where the policy had been made out in the name of a British agent, and the underwriter had only pleaded the general issue, it was held that the agent could recover on it during the war (f). Hence, the defence of alien enemy in such cases is only a temporary bar to the plaintiff's right to sue (g). Where the war has broken out before the loss, the policy, as we have already seen, becomes wholly illegal and void (h).

The defence that the plaintiff is an alien enemy is not regarded in our Courts with indulgence (i). Thus, where

Sect. 88.

Right to sue suspended during war.

Defence that defendant an enemy not favoured.

(c) 13 East, 341.
(d) De Tastet v. Taylor (1812), 4 Taunt. 233.
(e) Flindt v. Waters (1812), 15 East, 260. See also Janson v. Driefontein Consolidated Mines, [1902] A. C. 454, at pp. 493, 499, 508.
(f) Flindt v. Waters, *supra*. See note (k), *infra*.
(g) In Harman v. Kingston (1811), 3 Camp. 152, Lord Ellenborough held that such a defence could only be taken advantage of by a plea in abatement, and was not maintainable under the general issue. As to the replication to such a plea, see Bolton v. Dobree (1808), 2 Camp. 163; and see Alcenius (or Alcinons) v. Nigren (1854), 4 E. & B. 217; 23 L. J. Q. B. 287; Shepeler v. Durant (1854), 14 C. B. 582; 23 L. J. C. P. 140.
(h) Gamba v. Le Mesurier (1803), 4 East, 407.
(i) Per Lord Kenyon, Casseres v. Bell (1799), 8 T. R. 166.

Sect. 89. a defendant had obtained time to plead, on the terms that he should plead issuably, and afterwards war was declared between this country and the state of which the plaintiff was a subject, the Court refused leave to the defendant to plead that the plaintiff was an enemy (*k*).

Who are alien enemies.

Domicil the leading test of national character.

90. An alien enemy, in the primary sense of the words, is the natural-born subject of a state actually engaged in war with our own; but for all commercial purposes the domicil of the party, without reference to his place of birth, is the leading test of national character. Every person domiciled in a state actually engaged in hostilities with our own is an alien enemy, whether he be a subject of that state or not (*l*).

(*k*) Shepeler *v.* Durant (1854), 14 C. B. 582; 23 L. J. C. P. 140. In Driefontein Consolidated Mines *v.* Janson, [1900] 2 Q. B. 339, a company incorporated under the law of the South African Republic brought an action on a policy of insurance during the war between the Republic and this country. The parties agreed that no dilatory plea should be set up on the ground that the plaintiffs were an alien enemy, and the action was tried while a state of war existed. In the Court of Appeal Vaughan Williams, L. J., expressed a doubt whether it was not against public policy for the Court to give effect to such an agreement: [1901] 2 K. B. at p. 432; and a similar doubt was expressed in the House of Lords by Lord Davey: [1902] A. C. at p. 499. Lord Lindley, on the other hand, approved of the course taken in this case, which he considered justified by the decision in Flindt *v.* Waters: *ibid.* at p. 509.

(*l*) The Indian Chief (1801), 3 C. Rob. 12, 18. For a general exposition of the law of domicil, see Lord Westbury's judgment in Udny *v.* Udny (1869), L. R. 1 H. L. Sc. 441, 457. Domicil, for commercial purposes in time of war, must, however, not be confounded with domicil in the technical sense which the word has now acquired. In that sense, as Professor Dicey points out, domicil denotes the place or country which the law deems to be a person's permanent home. Thus, an Englishman who goes to France and sets up in trade there with the intention of returning in ten years, does not acquire a French domicil. He retains his English domicil of origin. But if war broke out between England and France, and he continued to reside and trade in France, he would, under the maritime law of England, undoubtedly be treated as an enemy. In order, therefore, to distinguish between the legal domicil and that domicil or residence which determines the character of a person in time of war, the learned professor calls the former the civil and the latter the commercial domicil. Dicey, Conflict of Laws, 2nd ed. App. n. 7, p. 741. The term "domicil" is used in the latter sense by Arnould, as well as by Duer (Ins. vol. i. p. 495) and Marshall (Ins. vol. i. p. 390). Lord Stowell in his judgments uses

ALIEN ENEMIES.

That is properly the domicil of a person, where he has his true fixed home, and principal establishment; in which, when present, he has the intention of remaining (*animus manendi*), and from which he is never absent without the intention of returning (*animo revertendi*) directly he shall have accomplished the purpose for which he left it (*m*).

<small>Sect. 90.
Definition of domicil.</small>

The two great tests of domicil are: 1. The fact of residing in a place (*factum manendi*); 2. The intention of abiding there (*animus manendi*), either for a permanency or an indefinite period (*n*).

<small>Tests of domicil.</small>

Primâ facie the presumption arising from actual residence in a place, is that the party is there *animo manendi* (*o*). Directly, however, it appears that the residence was not coupled with any real *animus manendi*, the presumption arising from the mere fact of actual residence is rebutted. Hence, if a man has merely come into a foreign country for a definite period, or to accomplish a particular purpose intending to return to his own country directly such period has elapsed, or such purpose been accomplished, he will not be considered to have acquired a new domicil by a residence connected with such purpose, although his stay may exceed

<small>Presumption of domicil arises from residence. How rebutted.</small>

---

the words "domicil" and "residence" indifferently.

The rule that national character in time of war depends on commercial domicil is recognized in the Prize Law of the United States and of Japan; but the general rule in Continental states is that the national character of property is determined by the national character of the owner.

(*m*) This agrees almost verbatim with the definition given in the Civil Law, Code, lib. x. tit. 39, f. 7, as cited in Story's Conflict of Laws, c. iii. s. 42.

(*n*) Story's Conflict of Laws, c. iii. s. 44. Lord Stowell's opinion, as expressed in The Harmony (1800), 2 C. Rob. 324, 325, seems to be that an intention to remain for a definite period of time may be enough to confer a commercial domicil, if the period be a considerable one. This view has been adopted by Mr. Dicey (Conflict of Laws, 2nd ed. 743). See also 1 Duer, 498, 501.

(*o*) "The actual place where a man is, is *primâ facie* to a great many purposes his domicil": per Lord Thurlow in Bempdé v. Johnstone (1796), 3 Ves. 198; see also The Bernon (1798), 1 C. Rob. 102; The Diana (1803), 5 C. Rob. 60; The President (1804), *ibid.* 277; The Ocean (1804), *ibid.* 90; Bruce v. Bruce (before the House of Lords) (1790), 2 B. & P. 229, n.; Stanley v. Berners (1830), 3 Hagg. Eccl. Rep. 374.

128   OF THE ASSURED.   [PART I.

Sect. 90. the period originally contemplated, and extend over a considerable time (*p*). And the same principle applies to all cases of involuntary residence in a foreign country; for instance, if a man is detained on the breaking out of hostilities in an enemy's country, this forced residence will not impress him with the character of an alien enemy (*q*). In the latter class of cases there is no *animus manendi* at all, but merely a *compulsio manendi*: in the former there is no *animus manendi* in the sense requisite to gain a domicil.

Residence in belligerent country after accomplishment of special purpose.

91. It is principally in these cases, in which parties having originally left their own country for some special purposes of pleasure, or of business, continue to reside for a long time in a foreign country in the prosecution of such purposes, that the question of domicil becomes most difficult.

It may be considered as settled, that, if the party continues to reside in the foreign land for some time after he has accomplished the purpose for which he originally went there, such continued residence, especially if accompanied by trading, will be held to operate a change of domicil (*r*). Further, a party cannot remain an unlimited or indefinite time in a foreign country, even for the accomplishment of a special purpose, without assuming the national character of the country of his residence (*s*).

Purpose for which residence changed important in questions of domicil.

In the determination of the question, the purpose for which the party changed his place of residence has to be considered; if that purpose be one which, to the knowledge of the party, will necessarily oblige him to reside in the foreign country for a considerable or indefinite time, the

---

(*p*) The Harmony (1800), 2 C. Rob. 322. See, however, n. (*n*), *supra*, as to the view really expressed by Lord Stowell.

(*q*) Per Lord Ellenborough in Bromley *v.* Hesseltine (1807), 1 Camp. 77; The Ocean (1804), 5 C. Rob. 90.

(*r*) So held in a case decided in the United States, where a foreigner, having come to New York for the recovery of his health, continued there after he had recovered, and engaged more or less in trade: Elbers *v.* United Ins. Co. (1819), 16 Johns. New York Rep. 128.

(*s*) See the judgment of Lord Stowell in The Harmony (1800), 2 C. Rob. 322.

length of his stay, for that purpose, becomes an important element of consideration; and circumstances may easily be conceived in which a protracted stay in a foreign country, especially if accompanied by trading or any other evidence of a settled establishment, would be held to change the domicil, though the party may all along have been engaged in forwarding the special purpose of his visit, and may, throughout, have kept up the intention of returning, when he should have accomplished such purpose, to his native country (*t*). On the other hand, where there has not been originally any intention of making a protracted stay, but only of residing for a limited time, and a definite purpose; but the period of residence has been extended by direct constraint, such residence, however protracted, will not change the original domicil (*u*); and where a treaty allows aliens a definite period of time for the purpose of realising their property and leaving the territory, no presumption of an intention to reside will arise from their stay during that period (*x*).

Sect. 91.

92. It may therefore be laid down as a general rule that, in all questions with regard to domicil, the chief point to be considered is the *animus manendi*: if there be no intention of making a fixed and permanent abode in a foreign country, even a somewhat protracted residence there will not change the domicil; while, on the other hand, even the shortest residence, if with a design of a permanent settlement, stamps the party so residing with the national character (*y*).

The great test of domicil is the *animus manendi*.

(*t*) The Harmony (1800), 2 C. Rob. 322. It is in reference to this class of cases that Lord Stowell there says, "Be the occupation what it may, it cannot happen, but with few exceptions, that mere length of time shall not constitute domicil." See the case of Tabbs v. Bendelack (1801), 4 Esp. 108; The Ann Green (1812), 1 Gallison, Adm. Rep. 274; see also Marryatt v. Wilson, Ex. Ch. (1799), 1 B. & P. 430; *S. C.*, in the K. B. (1798), 8 T. R. 31; The Friendschaft (1818), 3 Wheaton, 14, 51.

(*u*) See The Ocean (1804), 5 C. Rob. 90.

(*x*) The Diana (1803), 5 C. Rob. 60.

(*y*) The Diana (1803), 5 C. Rob. 60; The Venus (1814), 8 Cranch, S. C. R. 253; 1 Kent, Com. 76.

Sect. 92.

What will be considered as evidence of an animus manendi.

To ascertain the real intention of the party himself, no circumstance can be regarded as unimportant which can in any way tend to throw light upon it, and the amount of evidence required to establish an *animus manendi* must, of course, vary with the circumstances of the particular case.

Thus, slighter evidence would be required to determine the domicil of a man returning to his own country, than of the same man going to reside in a foreign land. In the former case there is a natural presumption that the party is returning to re-assume his original character; in the other the natural presumption rather is, that he is not going to make his home in the foreign country, but intends to return thence to his own, when he shall have accomplished the objects of his journey. Hence a national character, acquired in a foreign country by residence, changes immediately the party has left such country *animo non revertendi;* and this is especially the case if he be returning to his native country, *sine animo revertendi.* In such case the native domicil revives while he is yet *in transitu,* for it very easily reverts, and is re-acquired the moment the foreign domicil is abandoned (*z*). But here, as in all other cases, the *animus manendi,* or, rather, the *animus non revertendi,* is the all-important test; and therefore a mere return to a man's native country, without any intention to abandon his foreign domicil, does not, as we have seen, work any change of domicil (*a*). Thus, where a British-born subject, who had been adopted, and acquired a domicil, as a citizen of the United States, returned for a few days to the British dominions, in the course of prosecuting a voyage from America to the East Indies, his native national character was held not to have reverted by this limited stay in his native country for a temporary purpose (*b*). So a British-

Leaving a foreign country animo non revertendi.

(*z*) Per Lord Westbury, Udny *v.* Udny, L. R. 1 H. L. Sc. 458; The Indian Chief (1801), 3 C. Rob. 12; La Virginie (1804), 5 C. Rob. 98; see 1 Kent, Com. 76; Story's Conflict of Laws, c. iii. s. 48.

(*a*) Wilson *v.* Marryatt (1798), 8

T. R. 31; The Friendschaft (1818), 3 Wheaton's Supreme Court R. 14, 51; The Ann Green (1812), 1 Gallison's R. 274; see also The Indian Chief (1801), 3 C. Rob. 12.

(*b*) Wilson *v.* Marryatt (1798), 8 T. R. 31.

born subject, having a mercantile establishment in Lisbon, was held, in the United States, not to have lost the Portuguese national character by returning to England for a special purpose (*c*).

Sect. 92.

93. The strongest proof of a domicil in a foreign country is a commercial establishment there; this fact alone is sufficient to impress a man with the national character as far as relates to all his property connected with such establishment, even though he may not be actually resident in the country (*d*): when coupled with the additional fact of residence, it amounts to the strongest conceivable case of domicil. "No position, in fact," says Chancellor Kent, "is more clear than this, that if a person goes into a foreign country and engages in a trade there, he is to be considered a merchant of that country, and a subject to all civil purposes, whether that country be hostile or neutral" (*e*). "Persons resident in a country and carrying on trade there, by which both they and the country are benefited, are to be considered the subjects of that country, at least, so far as to subject their property to capture by a country at war with that in which they live" (*f*). This rule applies to the consul of a neutral state in the enemy's country, when he carries on trade there (*g*).

Trading the strongest proof of *animus manendi*.

In the same way, if the natives of a belligerent state are resident and carrying on their business in a neutral country, they are, for all commercial purposes, regarded as subjects

---

(*c*) The Friendschaft (1818), 3 Wheaton's Supreme Court R. 14, 51; see also the case of the Ann Green (1812), 1 Gallison, already cited *supra;* see also The Nereide (1815), 9 Cranch's Supreme Court R. 388.

(*d*) The Vigilantia (1798), 1 C. Rob. 1; The Portland (1800), 3 C. Rob. 41: sustained in the United States in the Antonia Johanna (1816), 1 Wheaton, 159 ; The Friendschaft (1819), 4 Wheaton, 105. See per Lord Lindley in

Janson *v.* Driefontein Consolidated Mines, Ltd., [1902] A. C. at p. 505.

(*e*) 1 Kent, Com. 74.

(*f*) Per Lord Kenyon in Tabbs *v.* Bendelack (1801), 4 Esp. 108; see Wilson *v.* Marryatt (1798), 8 T. R. 31; The Indian Chief (1801), 3 C. Rob. 12; The Anna Catherina (1802), 4 C. Rob. 107; The President (1804), 5 C. Rob. 277.

(*g*) The Aina (1854), Spinks' Prize Cas. 8; The Baltica (1855), *ibid.* 264.

Sect. 93. of the neutral state, and enjoy all the privileges, and are subjected to all the inconveniences, of a neutral trade (*h*).

Every party, in short, who resides and trades in a country is regarded, in mercantile law, as a subject of that country, and must take the advantages and disadvantages, whatever they may be, of the country of his residence.

British subjects residing and trading in hostile country deemed to be enemies.

This general principle extends to the case of British subjects, residing either in hostile or neutral countries (*i*). The rigour of this principle, indeed, must not be extended to cases in which the residence in the hostile country is not accompanied with trading, and does not clearly appear to have been voluntary. Thus, where the partner of a mercantile house here sailed for America, with his wife and family, after war had, in fact, been declared between this country and the States, but before he knew of it, or had any reason to suspect it; and after his arrival in America he continued to reside there throughout the war, but without engaging in trade; and it did not clearly appear that his stay was not compulsory; Lord Ellenborough held, that he could not, by such residence, be considered to have acquired a hostile character (*k*).

Involuntary residence in a hostile country unaccompanied by trading not a proof of hostile character.

Subject domiciled when war breaks out in the enemy's country.
The Venus.

94. If the subject of one state has acquired a domicil in a hostile state, by residing and keeping up a commercial establishment there before the breaking out of hostilities, it has been decided in the United States that his property, shipped before knowledge of the war, but while his acquired domicil continued, would be liable to capture, on the ground

---

(*h*) The Postilion, Hay & Marriott, 245; Wilson *v.* Marryatt (1798), 8 T. R. 31; M'Connell *v.* Hector (1802), 3 B. & P. 113; The Danaŏus (in the House of Lords) (1802), cited 4 C. Rob. 255; Bell *v.* Reid (1813), 1 M. & S. 726; The Abo (1854), Spinks' Prize Cas. 42, 45. The cases in the United States on the same subject are referred to, 1 Kent, Com. 75, n. (*a*). The most important are The Venus (1814), 8 Cranch's Supreme Court R. 253; The Frances (1814), *ibid.* 363.

(*i*) Potts *v.* Bell (1800), 8 T. R. 548; M'Connell *v.* Hector (1802), 3 B. & P. 113; Roberts *v.* Hardy (1815), 3 M. & S. 533; Willison *v.* Patteson (1817), 7 Taunt. 439; O'Mealey *v.* Wilson (1808), 1 Camp. 482.

(*k*) Roberts *v.* Hardy (1815), 3 M. & S. 533, as explained in the case of Willison *v.* Patteson (1817), 7 Taunt. 439.

CHAP. V.]   ALIEN ENEMIES.   133

that his permanent residence had stamped him with the national character of the hostile country. This was the point decided in the celebrated case of The Venus (*l*). In that case some American merchants, who had gained a domicil by residing and carrying on trade in England, before hearing of the declaration of war by the United States against Great Britain in 1812, and while they had no particular expectation of it, nor any intention of ceasing to reside in this country, shipped cargoes to the United States, which were captured by American cruisers, after the declaration of hostilities: a majority of the judges of the Supreme Court decided (against the opinion, however, of Marshall, C. J.) that the property was liable to capture as belonging to those who, by trading and residing in an actually hostile country, were to be regarded, for all commercial purposes, as alien enemies. Marshall, C. J., dissented, on the ground that the parties should have had an opportunity given them, after they knew of the declaration of war, to show by their acts whether or not they intended to continue to make the hostile country the place of their permanent abode (*m*).

In one case Lord Ellenborough held that a British-born subject became an alien enemy by residing and trading in a hostile country, even though he had been adopted as the citizen of a neutral state, and was then residing and carrying on his business in the hostile country as the recognized agent of such neutral state (*n*).

Sect. 94.

95. Upon the same principle British subjects residing and carrying on trade in a neutral country are admitted, in

British subjects residing in a neutral country.

(*l*) The Venus (1814), 8 Cranch's Supreme Court R. 253; see 1 Kent, Com. 78; and the remarks of Phillips, vol. i. s. 159, and n. (*a*), who inclines to the opinion of Marshall, C. J., and refers to The Ocean (1804), 5 C. Rob. 90, as supporting his view of the case.

(*m*) There appears to be some leaning towards this opinion in the judgment of the Queen's Bench in Esposito *v.* Bowden (1855), 4 E. & B. 963; 24 L. J. Q. B. 210, 215; and it was approved by Mathew, J., in Nigel Gold Mining Co. *v.* Hoade, [1901] 2 K. B. 849, 853. See § 95, *infra*.

(*n*) O'Mealey *v.* Wilson (1808), 1 Camp. 482.

respect to their *bonâ fide* trade, to all the privileges of a neutral character (*o*). Thus, a British subject, adopted by and trading in the United States, was permitted to prosecute a voyage from America to the East Indies in a manner which would have been illegal in a British subject, but was permitted by treaty to the citizens of the United States (*p*).

He may also, like any other neutral, carry on trade with powers at war with his own country. Thus, in the case of The Danaöus, which came before the House of Lords in 1802, a British-born subject, resident and trading in Portugal, was allowed the benefit of the Portuguese neutral character, so far as to render his trade with Holland, then at war with England, not impeachable as an illegal trade (*q*). The same rule was afterwards applied to a natural-born British subject, domiciled in the United States; and it was held that he might lawfully trade to a country at war with England, but at peace with the United States (*r*).

Alien enemy migrating flagrante bello.

It has, however, been decided in the United States (and the decision seems thoroughly well founded), that an alien enemy is not permitted to acquire a neutral domicil for the purpose of protecting his trade if he emigrate into the neutral country from his own, *flagrante bello*. At all events, the circumstances attending such a course will be closely scrutinized, with a view of ascertaining his object (*s*).

Neutral leaving belligerent country on outbreak of war.

Though a neutral may have been resident and carrying on trade in a foreign country, up to the time of the breaking out of hostilities between that country and our own; yet if

(*o*) See The Emanuel (1799), 1 C. Rob. 302. Lord Stowell annexes to this rule the qualification that he must do nothing inconsistent with his allegiance: *Ibid*.

(*p*) Wilson *v*. Marryatt (1798), 8 T. R. 31.

(*q*) (1802); cited in 4 C. Rob. 255, n.

(*r*) Bell *v*. Reid (1813), 1 M. & S. 726.

(*s*) The Dos Hermanos (1817), 2 Wheaton's Supreme Court R. 76; cited 1 Kent, Com. 75; 1 Phillips, Ins. s. 166. There is an earlier decision of the New York Court of Errors (Dugnet *v*. Rhinelander (1802), 2 Johns. 476), that when a subject of a belligerent state migrated *flagrante bello* to the United States, then neutral, and became naturalized, such naturalization would support a warranty of neutral property in a policy of insurance.

he then, or shortly afterwards, breaks up his establishment in the enemy's country and comes to reside here, he will not be precluded from recovering in our Courts, during the war, on a policy effected before the commencement of hostilities, to protect his separate share as part owner in a ship and cargo, the other moiety of which was owned by the alien enemy, in conjunction with whom he had, before the declaration of hostilities, been carrying on his establishment in the foreign country (*t*).

Sect. 95.

96. Where the party interested is himself a neutral, and the policy is effected to cover goods consigned to him at a neutral port, such policy is not rendered void by the neutral's happening at the time to be resident in a place, which, though situated in the dominions of a neutral, is then occupied by the troops of the enemy (*u*).

National character of ports occupied by the enemy.

During the unexampled circumstances of Napoleon's wars, it frequently became important to decide upon the national

---

(*t*) Rotch *v*. Edie (1795), 6 T. R. 413. Such seems to be the true effect of the case. See a note of Lord Campbell's to his report of Bromley *v*. Hesseltine (1807), 1 Camp. 75. The rule may be stated generally that a neutral who resides or trades in a belligerent country will preserve his neutral character if he leave the country with his property *sine animo revertendi*. If on the outbreak of hostilities he promptly take steps to leave, he will not be considered an enemy, even when still in the belligerent state, provided that he carries on his preparations without delay. But a mere intention to leave, not accompanied by any overt act, is not sufficient: The President (1804), 5 C. Rob. 277, 280; The Baltica (1855), Spinks' Prize Cas. 264, 267; 1 Kent, Com. 78. In Nigel Gold Mining Co. *v*. Hoade, [1901] 2 K. B. 849, 853, the plaintiffs were a metal company which owned a mine in the Transvaal. A few days after war was declared by the South African Republic against this country some gold, the product of their mine, was seized therein by the agents of the Republic. The plaintiffs shut down their mine when war was declared, and there was nothing to show that they intended to continue their business or mining operations in the Transvaal during the war. Mathew, J., held that they could recover on a policy on the gold. "The sounder opinion," said the learned judge, "would seem to be that the subject of one country, surprised by a declaration of war in the country where he has a commercial domicil, ought to have time allowed him to free himself from his commercial engagements and effect a removal of his property."

(*u*) Bromley *v*. Hesseltine (1807), 1 Camp. 75.

Sect. 96. character of ports, which, though nominally neutral, were yet under military occupation by the troops of the French Emperor. As we shall have occasion to consider these cases elsewhere, it will be sufficient in this place to state the two principles upon which they were mainly decided. 1st. That a port belonging to a neutral state, though coerced, or even occupied, by the forces of a belligerent, does not, by virtue of such aggression, cease to be neutral and become hostile, provided it still retains its own institutions and its own civil government. 2nd. That the most potent evidence in time of general war, as to the hostile or non-hostile character of any port, is the declaration of our own government regarding it; if our own government, either directly or indirectly, recognizes any of the ports of a hostile state, or of its colonial possessions, as neutral, or non-hostile ports, that is binding on our Courts of Justice (*x*).

Property connected with trading establishment in hostile country.

97. Domicil, however, is not always the test of national character for commercial purposes. Thus, the act of trading or keeping on foot a mercantile establishment in the enemy's country, even without residence there, impresses a hostile character on all the property connected with such establishment (*y*).

This principle, however, only applies to property or transactions connected with the hostile firm. If a neutral have

---

(*x*) The Dart and The Happy Couple (1808), cited in The Manilla, Edwards' Adm. R. 1, 2; The Pelican (1809), Edwards' Adm. R. App. D.; Bromley *v.* Hesseltine (1807), 1 Camp. 75; Donaldson *v.* Thompson (1808), *ibid.* 429; Johnson *v.* Greaves (1810), 2 Taunt. 344; Atkinson *v.* Abbott (1809), 11 East, 135; Hagedorn *v.* Bell (1813), 1 M. & S. 450; see also Blackburn *v.* Thompson (1811), 3 Camp. 61. See *post*, §§ 757, 758.

(*y*) The Vigilantia (1798), 1 C. Rob. 1; The Portland (1800), 3 C. Rob. 41; The Dree Gebroeders (1802), 4 C. Rob. 232. A different rule prevails in the case of a resident in a hostile country who is interested in a neutral house of business. All his property, whatever be the nature of the trade in which it is engaged, is considered enemy's property. 1 Duer, Ins. 524. Similarly, the interest of a British merchant in the goods of a neutral firm has been held to be British property. The Franklin (1805), 6 C. Rob. 127, 132.

two houses of business, one in the neutral and the other in the belligerent country, his property connected with the neutral house will be protected from seizure, while his property connected with the hostile establishment will be liable to it (z). On the same principle, there may be a partnership between two persons, one residing in a neutral and the other in a belligerent country, and the trade of one of them with the enemy will be held lawful, and that of the other unlawful, and consequently the share of one partner in the joint traffic will be condemned, and that of the other restored (a).

Sect. 97.

It has been held that the possession of an estate in the enemy's dominions impresses on the owner a hostile character in respect of the produce of his estate, during its transportation to another country, although he reside in a neutral State (b). The reason is that the proprietor has incorporated himself with the permanent interests of the nation, as a holder of the soil (c).

Produce of enemy's soil.

In a case tried during the South African war, Mathew, J., declined to apply this rule where an insurance had been effected on gold, the product of a mine in the Transvaal, owned by a British company (d). The learned judge's opinion seems to have been that the rule would not be followed at the present time; but the *ratio decidendi* was that "the subject of one country, surprised by a declaration of war in a country where he has a commercial domicil, ought to have time allowed him to free himself from his commercial engagements and effect a removal of his property" (e).

(z) The Portland (1800), 3 C. Rob. 41.
(a) *Ibid.*; The Herman (1801), 4 C. Rob. 228; The Jonge Klassina (1804), 5 C. Rob. 297.
(b) The Phœnix (1803), 5 C. Rob. 20; The Vrow Anna Catharina (1804), 5 C. Rob. 161, 167. The Supreme Court of the United States assented to this rule in Bentzon v. Boyle (1815), 9 Cranch, 191.
(c) Per Lord Stowell, 5 C. Rob. at p. 167.

(d) Nigel Gold Mining Co. v. Hoade, [1901] 2 K. B. 849.
(e) It is, of course, impossible to say whether a somewhat harsh rule which there has been no opportunity to reconsider for a whole century would be abandoned in any future maritime war. The editors have throughout retained the statements in the text which are founded upon the decisions of the British Prize Courts.

138   OF THE ASSURED.   [PART I.

Sect. 98.
Neutral engaging in privileged colonial or coasting trade of the enemy.

98. A neutral, on the breaking out of hostilities, has the same rights of carrying on trade with either of the belligerents as he had before the war commenced, and therefore his property engaged in trade with the enemy is in general insurable in this country (*h*); but if instead of carrying on his trade on the ordinary footing of a foreign merchant in time of peace, he do so as a privileged trader of the enemy; or if the trade itself consist of a colonial carrying trade between the hostile mother country and any one of her foreign settlements to which neutral nations had not been admitted previous to the war, the neutral, in respect of such privileged or unusual trade, is regarded as an alien enemy, and cannot maintain an action here on a policy effected to protect it (*i*).

Consuls carrying on such trade.

The consul of a neutral nation in this country, if engaged in such privileged colonial or coasting trade of the enemy, loses his neutral character (*k*); and his consular residence does not protect his goods concerned in such trade from seizure and condemnation as enemy's property (*l*).

National character of a corporation.

99. The question what is the national character of a company incorporated under the law of an enemy has become one of great practical importance. A corporation is an entity, having an independent legal existence (*m*), and there is strong authority for the rule that it derives its national character from the State under whose laws it is incorporated, whatever be the nationality of its members. Thus it has been held that a ship owned by a British company can be registered as a British ship under the Merchant Shipping Act, although some of the shareholders are aliens, and aliens are not quali-

---

(*h*) See Bell *v.* Reid (1813), 1 M. & S. 726.

(*i*) See the judgments of Sir W. Scott in The Immanuel (1799), 2 C. Rob. 186; The Anna Catherina (1802), 4 C. Rob. 107; The Dree Gebroeders (1802), *ibid.* 232; and see Berens *v.* Rucker (1761), 1 W. Bl. 313; Brymer *v.* Atkins (1789),

1 H. Bl. 165, 191. See *post*, §§ 664, 665, 771.

(*k*) The Dree Gebroeders (1802), 4 C. Rob. 232.

(*l*) The Indian Chief (1800), 3 C. Rob. 22.

(*m*) See Myers *v.* Perigal, 2 De G. M. & G. 599; Salomon *v.* Salomon & Co., [1897] A. C. 22.

fied to own British ships, or shares in British ships (*n*). In Driefontein Consolidated Mines *v.* Janson (*o*), the plaintiffs were a Transvaal mining company, incorporated and registered according to the laws of the South African Republic, and carrying on in the territory of the latter the business of extracting gold from their mines. The company had a London office and committee of management, and its shareholders were nearly all resident outside the Transvaal, and not subjects of the Republic. The question was raised whether the company was an enemy during the war between the Republic and this country, and although, except for the purposes of the judgment of Vaughan Williams, L. J., it was unnecessary to determine this question, as it was held that the loss took place before the commencement of hostilities, there was a large consensus of judicial opinion that the company was a subject of the Republic, and, therefore, during the continuance of the war, an enemy (*p*). The judgment of Vaughan Williams, L. J., however, is necessarily founded on an actual decision that the company was a subject of the Republic (*q*). But where a company registered in Natal, whose only property was a gold mine in the Transvaal, had received a supplementary incorporation in the Transvaal (the object of which was to enable the company to sue and be sued there in its corporate name), Mathew, J., held that it was a British company and could therefore recover under a policy of insurance for a loss which occurred after the war had commenced (*r*).

Another question which may possibly arise, hereafter, is whether a company registered under the laws of one State can

(*n*) R. *v.* Arnaud (1846), 9 Q. B. 806; 16 L. J. Q. B. 50.
(*o*) [1900] 2 Q. B. 339; [1901] 2 K. B. 419, C. A.; [1902] A. C. 484.
(*p*) See per Mathew, J., [1900] 2 Q. B. at p. 346; per Romer, L. J., [1901] 2 K. B. at p. 437; per Lords Davey, Brampton and Lindley, [1902] A. C. at pp. 498, 501, 505.

The same view was expressed by Phillimore, J., in Robinson Gold Mining Co. *v.* Alliance Ins. Co., [1901] 2 K. B. 919, at p. 923. The only contrary expression of opinion is that of A. L. Smith, M. R., [1901] 2 K. B. at pp. 426, 427.
(*q*) See [1901] 2 K. B. at p. 430.
(*r*) Nigel Gold Mining Co. *v.* Hoade, [1901] 2 K. B. 849.

Sect. 99. have a commercial domicil in the territory of another State. The test of residence in the ordinary sense of the word is inapplicable to a corporation, which has not a physical existence, and it is submitted that the business of a company may be so entirely controlled and carried on in a country other than that in which it is registered, that the company will be deemed to have acquired a commercial domicil there (*s*).

Europeans residing and trading in Asiatic or African factories.

100. Europeans, residing and trading under the protection of factories or colonial establishments in Asia or Africa, have the national character of the European mother State to which the establishment belongs, and under whose protection they live and trade; and the reason of this is obvious: Europeans, so circumstanced, do not become the subjects of the Asiatic or African power in whose dominions such trading establishment is situated (*t*).

Such are some of the more important points in the jurisprudence of this country and the United States on the subject of national character, as affected by domicil or course of trade. It has not been deemed desirable further to encumber a work devoted to a special subject, by references to authorities which more properly range themselves under other heads of legal inquiry.

(*s*) See De Beers Consolidated Mines, Ltd. *v.* Howe, [1906] A. C. 455, in which the House of Lords decided that a foreign corporation may "reside" in this country within the meaning of the Income Tax Act, 1853. See also per Lord Lindley in Janson *v.* Driefontein Consolidated Mines, Ltd., [1902] A. C. at p. 505.

(*t*) The Indian Chief (1800), 3 C. Rob. 22; The Etrusco (1798), cited *ibid.* 11; The Twee Frienden (1784), cited *ibid.* 29.

CHAPTER VI.

COURSE OF BUSINESS IN SEA INSURANCE—RELATIONS BETWEEN ASSURED, BROKER, AND UNDERWRITER.

SECT.	SECT.
Actual Course of Business as between Assured, Broker and Underwriter ....101—105	Rights and Duties as between Assured and Broker......119—123
Legal Position ....106—109	Rights of Assured against Underwriter—What discharges the Underwriter ....124—129
Rights of Set-off, and application of Mutual Credit Clause in event of Bankruptcy..110—118	Broker's Lien on Policy...130—134

101. In this country almost all policies are effected by insurance brokers, whose business it is to act as middlemen between those merchants and shipowners who wish to insure their property, on the one hand, and the private underwriters or public insurance companies, on the other. The broker is the agent of the assured, not of the underwriter, and therefore he owes no duty in the transaction to the latter, on which an action for negligence can be founded (a). *Primâ facie,* the business of an insurance broker would seem to be limited to receiving instructions from his principal as to the nature of the risk, and the rate of premium at which he wishes to insure; communicating these facts to the underwriters; effecting the policy with them on the best possible terms for his employer; paying them the premium; and receiving from them whatever may be due in case of loss.

The usage, however, of our great commercial metropolis

<small>Employment of insurance brokers.</small>

(a) Empress Ass. Corp. *v.* C. T. Bowring & Co., Ltd. (1905), 11 Com. Cas. 107. See also Glasgow Ass. Corpn. *v.* Symondson (1911), 16 Com. Cas. 109. Sometimes, however, the broker may be the agent of both parties with regard to returns of premium. See *post,* § 116.

142   COURSE OF BUSINESS   [PART I.

Sect. 101. has introduced modes of transacting business between insurance brokers and underwriters in London, apparently intended to facilitate the transaction of insurance business on an extensive scale, by substituting, as far as possible, credits for payments, in all dealings between broker and underwriter; but one effect of the system has been to introduce a considerable degree of complexity into the relations subsisting between the assured, the broker, and the underwriter.

Provisions of the Act as to the course of business.

The provisions of the Marine Insurance Act, 1906, which concern these relations are contained in sects. 52, 53 and 54, and are as follow:—

When premium payable.

Sect. 52. Unless otherwise agreed, the duty of the assured or his agent to pay the premium, and the duty of the insurer to issue the policy to the assured or his agent, are concurrent conditions, and the insurer is not bound to issue the policy until payment or tender of the premium.

Policy effected through broker.

Sect. 53.—(1) Unless otherwise agreed, where a marine policy is effected on behalf of the assured by a broker, the broker is directly responsible to the insurer for the premium, and the insurer is directly responsible to the assured for the amount which may be payable in respect of losses, or in respect of returnable premium.

(2) Unless otherwise agreed, the broker has, as against the assured, a lien upon the policy for the amount of the premium and his charges in respect of effecting the policy; and, where he has dealt with the person who employs him as a principal, he has also a lien on the policy in respect of any balance on any insurance account which may be due to him from such person, unless when the debt was incurred he had reason to believe that such person was only an agent (*b*).

Effect of receipt on policy.

Sect. 54. Where a marine policy effected on behalf of the assured by a broker acknowledges the receipt of the premium, such acknowledgment is, in the absence of fraud, conclusive as between the insurer and the assured, but not as between the insurer and broker.

(*b*) An insurance is not a necessary for a ship, and therefore neither the broker nor the underwriter can proceed *in rem* under s. 6 of the Admiralty Court Act, 1840, against a foreign ship for premiums: The André Théodore (1904), 10 Asp. M. C. 94.

CHAP. VI.] IN SEA INSURANCE. 143

Further, as the course of business in marine insurance is to a large extent regulated by usage, sect. 87 of the Act (c) must be considered in connection with these provisions. For, as we have already seen in the chapter on the Construction of Sea-Policies, the usages of trade are often part of the contract. Indeed the rules contained in sect. 53 of the Act are themselves derived from mercantile usage (d).

102. The actual course of the business of marine insurance, as carried on in London and elsewhere in this country, is as follows:—A broker on receiving orders from his principal to effect an insurance prepares what is commonly known as a "slip." This is merely a slip of paper containing rough notes relating to the intended insurance. It is, however, sufficiently precise to enable anyone conversant with the business to draw up, without difficulty and without going beyond its four corners, the policy which it is proposed to effect. The broker then takes the slip round to the various underwriters to whom he may be disposed to offer the business; these may be private Lloyd's underwriters, or they may be underwriters on behalf of companies, or some of one class and some of another. Those underwriters who are willing to accept the risk, whether private or representing companies, signify their willingness by initialing the slip for the amounts for which they are willing to become insurers. When the broker has succeeded in getting the slip initialed for the full amount required, it is then his duty to procure the execution of policies in accordance therewith. So far as the initials on the slip are those of Lloyd's underwriters, a policy is prepared by the broker, and taken round by him to the different underwriters in succession for their signature. The insurance companies, however, always prepare their own policies, and in order to enable them to do so, the broker fills up a form which is also called a slip, and sends one to each company. This slip is an entirely distinct document from the slip which we have already explained, and is merely

Sect. 101.

Outline of course of business between assured, broker, and underwriter. The slip.

(c) See ante, § 55.   (d) Ante, § 66.

144 COURSE OF BUSINESS [PART I.

Sect. 102. a memorandum of the engagement which the particular company has already entered into by initialing the "slip" proper (*e*).

As soon as the policy is completed, the underwriters enter the risk in their books, and debit the broker with the premium.

Possession of policy.

103. The broker, having effected the policy, usually retains it in his possession (*f*). He may do so either as of right, in exercise of his lien for premiums, or as a matter of convenience; for insurance brokers are now very generally employed not merely to effect insurances, but to attend to all business relating thereto that may subsequently arise, which the possession of the policy enables them to do.

When a loss occurs in respect of which the assured desires to make a claim on the policy, he instructs the broker to do so, sending him the policy if it is not already in the broker's possession (*g*). The broker then ascertains (*h*) the percentage of the loss which ought to fall upon the policy—100 per cent. if it be a total loss, or a smaller percentage in case of an average loss—employing average adjusters if necessary, and endorses the ascertained percentage upon the policy, with the

---

(*e*) The term "slip" is used, in Liverpool at least, in yet a third sense, to denote the covering or insurance note, by way of provisional insurance, issued by a company in order to signify its acceptance of a risk, and its undertaking for the subsequent issue of a stamped policy. See Gow, App. CA. and CB.

(*f*) This is so more particularly as regards policies on ship. Those on goods are often handed over forthwith to the assured who then may pass them on to bankers or other parties, together with bills of lading, as security for advances or otherwise.

(*g*) In a recent case it was contended that an action cannot be maintained for a loss, unless the plaintiff has the policy in his possession; but Channell, J., did not agree with this contention, although he admitted that non-production of the policy may be a ground for suspecting that some one other than the person putting forward the claim has an interest in the policy: Swan *v.* Maritime Ins. Co., [1907] 1 K. B. 117.

(*h*) In a great majority of cases this work has been already done by an average adjuster employed by the assured. As to the position and functions of an average adjuster, see Wavertree Sailing Ship Co. *v.* Love, [1897] A. C. 373.

word "settled" prefixed. He then takes the policy, so endorsed, round to the several underwriters, who, unless they see reason for resisting the claim, sanction it with their initials and enter the amount to the broker's credit. This process is called "settling the claim." Any underwriter who is not satisfied as to the claim, or who proposes to resist it, simply refuses to attach his initials. Disputed claims are dealt with in the ordinary course of law. Of course, if the claim is one which it is known will be generally disputed, the process of ascertainment of the percentage, and the attempt to settle will be postponed until after the question of liability has been determined (*i*).

Sect. 103. "Settling the claim."

104. Sect. 52 of the Marine Insurance Act, as we have seen, provides that, unless otherwise agreed, the insurer is not bound to issue the policy until payment or tender of the premium (*k*). When, however, the insurance is made through a broker, the recognized course of business, as will appear presently, is such that the insurer may have no right to an immediate payment (*l*).

Payment of premium.

The custom of the marine insurance companies is that the premium of all policies issued during the month falls due upon the 8th of the following month. Premiums are subject to a deduction of 5 per cent. brokerage and 10 per cent. discount. The 5 per cent. brokerage is of course retained by the broker; the 10 per cent. discount is allowed by the broker to his principal (*m*). Where, as is sometimes done in

Accounts as between broker and underwriter.

(*i*) Such is the present practice. In order, however, to understand expressions which occur in some of the earlier cases, it should be noted that what is now called "settling the claim" used to be called "adjusting the policy." "Striking off the loss" was where the underwriter, on passing the loss to the credit of the broker, struck through his subscription to the policy with his pen. See 6th ed. p. 198, present ed. § 1241. These expressions and formalities are not now used.

(*k*) *Ante*, § 101.

(*l*) See Mar. Ins. Act, 1906, s. 87, *ante*, § 55.

(*m*) This custom, as a whole, was recognized by Scrutton, J., in Glasgow Ass. Corp. *v.* Symondson (1911), 16 Com. Cas. (see p. 114), and was proved in Green *v.* Tughan (1913), 30 Times L. R. 64, Pickford, J. In an earlier case, when the right of the principal to

Sect. 104. insuring with companies, the insurance is effected direct, without the intervention of a broker, the whole 15 per cent. is allowed by the company to the assured.

Losses and averages are paid by cheque in each case—the cheque being signed at the board meeting at which the claim is passed, and delivered to the broker on his calling for it. It is not the practice for brokers and the insurance companies to have cross accounts for premiums and for losses, and to settle balances. Separate cheques for each are written out and handed over (*n*).

In the case of Lloyd's underwriters, the premiums on insurances effected during the month likewise become due on the 8th of the following month. Claims fall due seven days after settlement. It is customary, however, to carry on current accounts, setting claims against premiums, and passing cheques for the balance due at the end of each quarter. When a total loss, or a heavy average loss occurs, the broker may, if he please, claim payment seven days after settlement; but he will in this case be expected to pay the underwriter all premiums due on the 8th of the current month. Lloyd's underwriters allow the same brokerage and discount as those allowed by the companies.

Accounts between broker and assured.

105. The broker usually keeps his account with the assured in a manner similar to that which governs his own relations with the companies. Thus, premiums for the month are due on the 8th of the succeeding month; and losses are payable as soon as the amounts are actually received from the under-

---

the discount seems not to have been so well established, the Court of Appeal allowed the agents to retain the 10 per. cent. discount which they had received for many years, during which the principal made no enquiry as to their remuneration: Baring *v.* Stanton (1876), 3 Ch. D. 502; see also Great Western Ins. Co. *v.* Cunliffe (1874), L. R. 9 Ch. 525.

(*n*) For a running contract of re-insurance, under which monthly losses were to be deducted from monthly premiums, and the balance paid to the brokers, and by them to trustees to secure the re-insurers against further losses, and for the position after the re-insuring company was ordered to be wound up, see In re Law Car and General Ins. Corp. (1911), W. N. 91, 101,

writer, or if the amount of a loss is not actually so received, but merely placed by the underwriter to the broker's credit in current account, then seven days after settlement of such loss. The broker deducts from the claim a commission of 1 per cent. and remits the balance to the assured.

<small>Sect. 105.</small>

This practice, however, merely illustrates what is usual. There is no recognized or binding custom as to these matters, and in fact special arrangements are often made. For example, if a large steamer is insured for twelve months, or if a floating policy is taken out on a series of cargoes, the premiums payable by the broker to the underwriter may amount to several thousands of pounds, which it may be inconvenient to the assured to provide all at once at the inception of the risk. In such a case special arrangements are sometimes made between the broker and the assured for the premiums to be paid by instalments. When this is done, the assured usually gives the broker written authority to cancel the policy in the event of any instalment not being duly paid. The broker is thus enabled to protect himself by cancelling the policy and receiving from the underwriter the monthly return of premium, which its terms provide for.

For greater security to their customers, insurance brokers frequently guarantee the solvency of the underwriters. This exposes them to greater hazard, and of course entitles them to a higher, or as usually it is, an additional, commission upon the business they perform. In such cases the brokers are said to act *del credere,* and the percentage which they are entitled to receive is called a commission *del credere.* This commission they are legally considered to be entitled to immediately upon entering into the contract, without waiting to see whether such guaranty do in the event subject them to loss (*o*). "The commission," said Lord Ellenborough in such a case, "was earned and to be paid to the party for entering into the contract of guaranty, and not in respect of the event, which was perfectly collateral" (*p*).

<small>Commissions del credere.</small>

(*o*) Caruthers *v.* Graham (1811), 14 East, 578.

(*p*) *Ibid.* As to the general law relating to the liability of *del*

Sect. 105. The above sketch is only intended to explain generally the course of business actually adopted in our commercial world. We do not say that in all points such practice tallies with the law. In what follows we propose to indicate the extent to which the practice is consistent with the law, either by being in original accord therewith, or by having become engrafted thereon by constant usage.

Broker alone liable to underwriter for premiums.

106. By virtue of a custom which had existed for more than a hundred years, it became established law that the assured could not be sued by the underwriter for premiums (*q*), nor could the latter set off unpaid premiums in an action brought by the assured on the policy for losses. Accordingly, sect. 53 (1) of the Marine Insurance Act, 1906, declares that "unless otherwise agreed, where a marine policy is effected on behalf of the assured by a broker, the broker is directly responsible to the insurer for the premium, and the insurer is directly responsible to the assured for the amount which may be payable in respect of losses, or in respect of returnable premium."

Legal relation of the parties and their broker.

The position is briefly but comprehensively described by Bayley, J., in these words: "According to the ordinary course of trade between the assured, the broker and the underwriter, the assured does not in the first instance pay the premium to the broker, nor does the latter pay it to the underwriter. But, as between the assured and the underwriter, the premiums are considered as paid. The under-

credere agents, the reader is referred to a masterly exposition of the subject by Judge Duer, who, as usual, collects and exhausts all the authorities. 2 Duer, 331—339, especially 337, *in notis*. Since the publication of Duer's work, it has been settled, in accordance with his view, that the *del credere* contract between the agent and his principal is not within the Statute of Frauds; Couturier *v.* Hastie (1852), 8 Exch. 40. See Harburg India Rubber Comb Co. *v.* Martin, [1902] 1 K. B. 778.

(*q*) In the United States it was held in Mannheim Ins. Co. *v.* Hollander (1901), 111 Fed. R. 549, that, no usage similar to the English one having been proved, the assured was liable to the underwriter for the premium on a policy effected by the broker.

CHAP. VI.] IN SEA INSURANCE. 149

writer, to whom, in most instances, the assured are unknown, looks to the broker for payment, and he to the assured. The latter pay the premiums to the broker only, who is a middleman between the assured and the underwriter. But he is not merely an agent: he is a principal to receive the money from the assured, and to pay it to the underwriters" (*r*). Sect. 106.

By sect. 54 of the Marine Insurance Act, 1906, "where a marine policy effected on behalf of the assured by a broker acknowledges the receipt of the premium, such acknowledgment is, in the absence of fraud, conclusive as between the insurer and the assured, but not as between the insurer and broker." Effect of acknowledgment in policy of payment of premium.

The earlier editions of this work appear to have confined the rule that, as regards premiums, the broker is the debtor of the underwriter to policies which, such as Lloyd's, contain an express acknowledgment by the underwriter of the receipt of premium from the assured. There is undoubtedly some judicial sanction for this view of the origin of the present state of the law. But a few years ago it was held that the rule under discussion was based, not upon the receipt clause, but upon a general custom, and that it applied accordingly to all policies of marine insurance, whether containing such receipt clause or not. The action was brought by an insurance company against the assured for premiums on a policy which, so far from containing the receipt clause, embraced an express promise by the assured to pay the premiums to the company, and for the latter it was argued that the custom, which admittedly obtained in the case of Lloyd's policies, to treat the broker and not the assured as liable for the premiums had no application to, and was in fact inconsistent with, the present policy. But Collins, J., after explaining the origin of the custom, rejected this contention. "It is a well- Origin of rule that broker alone liable for premiums.

Broker alone liable, even where policy contains express promise by assured to pay the insurer.

(*r*) In Power *v.* Butcher (1829), 10 B. & Cr. 340; see also per Parke, J., at p. 347. The course of dealing between the parties may be such that the liability of a third party to the broker for premiums is substituted for that of the assured, *e.g.*, the liability of the managing owner of a ship. See Lamont, Nisbet & Co. *v.* Hamilton, (1907) Sess. Cas. 628.

Sect. 106. recognised practice in marine insurance," said the learned judge, "for the broker to treat himself as responsible to the underwriter for the premiums; by a fiction he is deemed to have paid the underwriter, and to have borrowed from him the money with which he pays. If that is a correct explanation of the origin of the custom, it is as applicable to this form of policy as to a Lloyd's policy. No doubt there is here a contract to pay by the assured, but by custom the broker is treated as personally liable, the same fiction being applicable, namely, that the broker has paid the premium, and has so absolved the assured from his liability, having first borrowed the money from the underwriter to make the payment." This decision was confirmed by the Court of Appeal (*s*).

Assured at once liable to broker for premiums.

107. It further follows from what has been above stated that, as a general rule, the assured is liable to the broker for premiums as for money paid, whether they have been in fact paid over by the broker to the underwriter or not. This is because, in accordance with the system which we have just explained, the premiums are, as between the broker and the underwriter, considered as paid. The broker, being thus deemed to have paid the underwriter, can at once recover the amount from the assured as money paid to his use (*t*). Simi-

---

(*s*) Universo Ins. Co. of Milan *v.* Merchants' Marine Ins. Co., [1897] 2 Q. B. 93; see also Power *v.* Butcher, *ubi supra*, especially at p. 347, per Parke, J.; and Dalzell *v.* Mair (1808), 1 Camp. 533; De Gaminde *v.* Pigou (1812), 4 Taunt. 246. In Dalzell *v.* Mair, which was an action by the assured against the underwriter to recover back a premium where the risk had never attached, Lord Ellenborough said: "I should completely knock up the insurance business if I were to allow this acknowledgment [in the policy] to be impeached." In the last-mentioned case, which was an attempt by an underwriter, in an action by the assured, to set off premiums, Heath, J., said: "When the assured is admitted to have paid the premium, it is as between the assured and the underwriter actually paid." We have already suggested that the decision in Universo Ins. Co. *v.* Merchants' Mar. Ins. Co. is difficult to reconcile with established rules of construction (see *ante*, § 56), and the qualifying words, "unless otherwise agreed," in sect. 53 (1) of the Mar. Ins. Act, 1906, leave that decision still open to review by the House of Lords.

(*t*) Power *v.* Butcher (1829), 10 B. & Cr. 347. See also Airy *v.* Bland (1774), 2 Park, Ins. 811.

larly, in case the assured becomes entitled to claim a return Sect. 107.
of premiums, inasmuch as these are deemed to have been paid
by the broker to the underwriter on account of the assured,
they can at once be recovered from the underwriter by the
assured as money had and received "without any reference
as to whether or not the year during which the broker
generally has credit has run out, so as to make them payable
in cash by the broker to the underwriter" (*u*).

Of course, if there be fraud or collusion on the part of the
assured, or of the assured and broker jointly, in their dealings
with the underwriter, the acknowledgment in the policy will
not be held binding (*x*).

108. As we have seen, the general rule is, that the broker, **The broker is the debtor**
and not the assured, is the debtor of the underwriter for the **of the underwriter**
premiums. "By the course of dealing," says Parke, J., **for premiums.**
"the broker gives the underwriter credit for the premium
when the policy is effected, and he, as the agent of both the
assured and the underwriter, is considered as having paid the
premium to the underwriter, and the latter as having lent it
to the broker again, and so becoming his creditor" (*y*).

Generally speaking, however, it is only the broker imme- *I.e.* generally
diately concerned in effecting the policy to whom the under- immediately
writer can resort for premiums, on the plain principle that it effecting the
is to him alone he has given credit for them (*z*). policy.

In the case of policies which are gaming or wagering contracts within the Gaming Act, 1845 (see *post*, § 315), it seems that the Gaming Act, 1892, would bar the right of the broker to recover the premiums from the assured even though he was not aware of the true nature of the transaction: see Tatam *v.* Reeve, [1893] 1 Q. B. 44.

(*u*) Per Blackburn, J., in Xenos *v.* Wickham (1863), 33 L. J. C. P. 18; 14 C. B. N. S. 452; Dalzell *v.* Mair (1808), 1 Camp. 532.

(*x*) Foy *v.* Bell (1811), 3 Taunt. 491; Mavor *v.* Simeon (1810), *ibid.* 497.

(*y*) Per Parke, J., Power *v.* Butcher (1829), 10 B. & Cr. 347; and per Blackburn, J., Xenos *v.* Wickham (1863), 33 L. J. C. P. 13, 17; 14 C. B. N. S. 452.

(*z*) In a case of Robson *v.* Wilson (1797), cited 1 Marsh. Ins. 301, where the assured had employed broker A., who in his turn employed broker B., to effect a policy, the Court allowed the underwriter to recover against broker A. when

Sect. 108.
Broker, to action by underwriter, has the same grounds of defence as the assured.

Being thus substituted for the assured, the broker generally has the same grounds of defence against the claim for the premium as the assured would have had if he had effected the policy without the intervention of a broker (*a*).

Premiums for an illegal insurance.

109. Hence a broker is only legally liable to the underwriter for premiums due on legal insurances. Therefore, in the case of premiums for re-insurance, which was then known by all to be illegal, where no money had passed, and the assured had ordered the brokers not to pay the underwriters on the ground of illegality, Lord Ellenborough held that no action could be maintained by the assignees of the underwriters against the brokers for the recovery of the premiums as money paid to the use of the bankrupt. "The money," said his Lordship, "does not appear to have been actually paid into the defendants' (brokers') hands. In case of illegal transactions, it may always be stopped while it is *in transitu* to the party entitled to receive it. We cannot consider this as money paid for the use of the bankrupt; no money has, in fact, been paid, but only an account stated: if, indeed, this had been a legal transaction, the money might have been considered as paid, but we will not assist an illegal transaction in any respect, we leave the matter as we find it, and then the rule applies *melior est conditio possidentis*" (*b*).

If the premiums had actually been paid to the brokers by their employers, in such case it seems that the action would be maintainable (*c*); and where the insurance is void under

---

broker B. had become bankrupt; but this case is of doubtful authority.

(*a*) Per Lord Ellenborough, in Jenkins *v.* Power (1817), 6 M. & S. 282, 287.

(*b*) Edgar *v.* Fowler (1803), 3 East, 222; and see *ibid.* 224. So, where the language of the policy was large enough to comprise an illegal adventure, and the assured contemplated it, the underwriter was held not entitled to sue for the premium which had not been paid by the assured to the broker. Jenkins *v.* Power, *supra*.

(*c*) In Tenant *v.* Elliott (1797), 1 B. & P. 3, it was held in an action by the assured against the broker, that the defendant had no right to retain as against the plaintiff moneys paid to him by the underwriter as the amount of loss on an illegal insurance on the ground, as Judge Duer remarks, "that the person to whom moneys have been

the Gaming Act, 1845, as being a gaming or wagering transaction, the Gaming Act, 1892, does not seem to bar the right to recover (*d*).

Sect. 109.

If an underwriter have, by mistake, paid a loss to the broker to which the assured is not entitled, he may recover it back as money had and received to his use, if the broker have not in fact paid it over to his principal. Merely passing it in account with his principal is not equivalent to paying it over, and no answer to such an action; *secus*, retaining a portion of the money in payment of an adjusted balance due to him from his principal (*e*).

Losses paid to broker by mistake and not actually paid over by broker to his principal.

110. In considering the right of set-off, it is as well to remember that the contract of marine insurance is still a contract sounding in unliquidated damages, even after an adjustment of a loss under the policy (*f*), and notwithstanding it be a valued policy (*g*). It consequently follows that any claim for such a loss cannot give a right of set-off, in the strict sense in which that term was used in the old statutes of set-off. This point is, however, not of so much importance as it used to be, inasmuch as by modern practice a defendant can by counterclaiming usually secure most, if not all, the advantages which he formerly could only obtain in cases where he was entitled to set-off (*h*).

Right of set-off.

actually paid to the use of another has no right to inquire into the legality of the transaction out of which the payment arose." See 2 Duer, 366—371. See also per Lord Campbell, C. J., and Crompton, J., in Nicholson *v.* Good (1856), 5 E. & B. 999, 1015, 1017.

(*d*) See De Mattos *v.* Benjamin (1894), 63 L. J. Q. B. 248; and § 121, *infra*.

(*e*) Buller *v.* Harrison (1777), 2 Cowp. 565; *i.e.*, as Judge Duer observes, supposing the circumstances to be such that the broker had a right to revoke the credit he had given to the assured; 2 Duer,

269, n. (*a*); Holland *v.* Russell (1861), 1 B. & S. 424; 30 L. J. Q. B. 308; 4 B. & S. 14; 32 L. J. Q. B. 297.

(*f*) Castelli *v.* Boddington (1852), 1 E. & B. 66; 22 L. J. Q. B. 5; Luckie *v.* Bushby (1853), 13 C. B. 864; Thompson *v.* Redman (1843), 11 M. & W. 487; Pellas *v.* Neptune Marine Ins. Co. (1879), 5 C. P. D. 34. See, however, Swan *v.* Marit. Ins. Co., [1907] 1 K. B. 117, 123.

(*g*) King *v.* Walker (1863), 2 H. & C. 384; 3 *ibid*. 209; 33 L. J. Ex. 167, 325.

(*h*) Similarly, Young *v.* Kitchin (1878), 3 Ex. D. 127 (approved in

154 COURSE OF BUSINESS [PART I.

Sect. 110.
In bankruptcy.

It is nevertheless still important, in the event of the bankruptcy of one of the parties, say of the underwriter or of the broker, to consider the question of the right of set-off in the wider sense (*i*) in which the expression is used in the Bankruptcy Act, 1883. The right depends on whether there have been, in relation to the policy, mutual "credits, debts, or other dealings" between the parties within the meaning of sect. 38 of that Act, at the time of the receiving order (*j*).

Principle of the mutual credit clause.

"The principle of the mutual credit clause," says Tindal, C. J., after a luminous review of the whole course of legislation on the subject, "is this, that where persons have dealt with each other on mutual credit, and one of them becomes bankrupt, the account shall be settled between them, and the balance only payable on either side. From the earliest practice to the latest provision by statute, the object seems to have been that the account should be settled as between merchant and merchant, and whatever would be in ordinary practice a pecuniary item in such account, should be the subject of set-off" (*k*).

Primâ facie no mutuality as regards claims for premiums and losses.

111. We have seen that the ordinary relations between the three parties to the contract result in this, that the broker is the debtor of the underwriter for premiums, and the underwriter the debtor of the assured for losses. *Primâ facie*, therefore, there is no such mutuality between the claim of the underwriter against the broker for the premium

---

Government of Newfoundland *v.* Newfoundland Ry. Co. (1887), 13 App. Cas. 199), shows that in an action by the assignee of a debt a defendant with cross-claims is, as against the plaintiff, in as good a position whether his cross-claims are liquidated or unliquidated.

(*i*) See per Parke, B., in Forster *v.* Wilson (1843), 12 M. & W. 203; see also Isberg *v.* Bowden (1853), 22 L. J. Ex. 322.

(*j*) In re Daintrey, Ex parte Mant, [1900] 1 Q. B. 546, C. A.

(*k*) Gibson *v.* Bell (1835), 1 Bing. N. C. 743, 754; see also Rose *v.* Hart, 2 Smith's Leading Cases; Palmer *v.* Day, [1895] 2 Q. B. 618; In re Taylor, [1910] 1 K. B. 562. It is immaterial whether a debt is liquidated or not (Peat *v.* Jones (1881), 8 Q. B. D. 147); and even if the amount of a liability be not ascertainable until after the date of the receiving order, it may nevertheless be the subject of set-off: In re Daintrey, Ex parte Mant, *supra*.

CHAP. VI.]   IN SEA INSURANCE.   155

(as a claim of principal against principal) and the claim of **Sect. 111.**
the broker against the underwriter for losses and returns (a
claim of agent against principal) as to entitle the broker
(whether in cases of solvency or bankruptcy) to set off the
latter claim against the former (*l*). Hence, in many of the
cases, we shall observe the endeavour has been to show that
this *primâ facie* objection did not apply, but that the broker,
from his course of dealing, either generally or in the particular transaction, must be taken as standing in the place
of the assured, and entitled, as principal, to claim losses and
returns from the underwriter.

One of the earliest reported cases in which the effect of
this clause (*m*) on claims arising out of policies of assurance,
as between the assignees of the bankrupt underwriter and
the broker, came before the Courts, was Wilson *v.* Creighton, Wilson *v.*
decided in 1782. It was an action by the assignees of a Creighton.
bankrupt underwriter against an insurance agent for premiums passed in account in the usual way. The defendant
claimed to set off losses and returns of premium due to him
from the bankrupt on the same risks. He had not acted *del
credere*, but simply as agent in this country for various foreign
correspondents, effecting the policies on goods consigned by
him to his principals abroad, to all of whom, except one, he
was, at the time of action brought, in advance, more or less,
on the insurance account between them. The Court (Lord
Mansfield, Willes, Ashurst and Buller, JJ.) unanimously
held that the losses and returns of premium were not the
subject of set-off under the mutual credit clause, because
there was no mutuality—the debts were in different rights
and due to different parties (*n*).

The next case in which the question arose was the often- Grove *v.*
                                                           Dubois.

(*l*) It is, however, a common practice for the broker, on receiving credit for a claim from the underwriter, to pay the assured
forthwith. The reasoning in the text would not apply to such a
case.

(*m*) Or the corresponding clause in the Act then in force. On the
point of "mutuality" the old de-
cisions are still of effect.

(*n*) Wilson *v.* Creighton (1782), cited in 1 T. R. 113, and reported
in 3 Dougl. 132.

Sect. 111. cited one of Grove v. Dubois, 1786, also an action by the assignees of a bankrupt underwriter for premiums. The defendant had effected the policies in his own name with the bankrupt for foreign correspondents, unknown to the bankrupt, under a commission *del credere*, being debited in his underwriter's accounts for premiums, and always retained the policies in his own hands. Under these circumstances the Court of King's Bench held, that the defendant had a right, under the mutual credit clause, to the set-off he claimed (*o*).

Remarks on Grove v. Dubois.

112. In this case three points must be particularly noticed:— 1st, the insurance agent had effected the policies in his own name, on account of whom it might concern, so that his employers were unknown to the underwriter; 2nd, he always retained the policies in his own hands; 3rd, he acted for his employers on a commission *del credere*. The ground of the decision, therefore, might well have been that the insurance agent appeared, from all these circumstances, to have been the only party of whom the underwriters knew anything in the transaction; in fact, as Lord Ellenborough says, in Cumming v. Forrester, "that the dealing was with him as principal" (*p*), and therefore that it might be inferred that, as he gave them credit for premiums, so they gave him credit for losses.

Lord Mansfield on the effect of a commission *del credere*.

Lord Mansfield, however, certainly put the decision of the Court entirely on the last of the above-mentioned circumstances. "The whole turns," says his Lordship, "on the nature of a commission *del credere*. Then what is it? It is an absolute engagement to the principal from the broker that makes him liable in the first instance"(*q*).

(*o*) Grove v. Dubois (1786), 1 T. R. 112.
(*p*) In Cumming v. Forrester (1813), 1 M. & S. 498. Again, in Parker v. Smith (1812), 16 East, 386, Lord Ellenborough speaks of Grove v. Dubois as having been determined on the special ground that the dealings with the broker in respect of his commission *del credere* were considered as virtually had with the assured themselves.
(*q*) 1 T. R. 115.

CHAP. VI.] IN SEA INSURANCE. 157

Lórd Ellenborough and Sir Vicary Gibbs, especially the latter, frequently professed their inability to understand the ground of the decision as thus stated by Lord Mansfield (*r*); they refused, however, to disturb the case, which, as it had been long acted upon, might have been attended with inconvenience; but, on the other hand, they carefully avoided applying it by analogy to other cases, as will sufficiently appear by the following decisions:—

Sect. 112.
Opinions of Lord Ellenborough and Sir V. Gibbs.

113. The assignees of a bankrupt underwriter sued defendants, insurance brokers, for premiums due from them before the bankruptcy on the balance of their underwriting account with the bankrupt, upon nineteen policies of insurance which they had effected with the bankrupt. The defendants acted under a *del credere* commission for their employers; but this fact was not known to the bankrupt. The defendants claimed to be allowed to set off, as mutual credits, unadjusted losses due from the bankrupt, before his bankruptcy, on the account current between them, and for which they, the defendants, had given credit in account with their respective principals. It appeared that five out of the nineteen policies were effected by defendants in their own name and on their own account: as to these, the Court allowed the claim of set-off on the authority of Grove *v*. Dubois: four out of the nineteen policies were in the name, but not on the account, of the defendants; as to these also the Court held that the right of set-off might be claimed, because upon these policies the defendants could sue in their own names and on their own

Koster *v.* Eason, as to right of *del credere* broker to set off losses in an action by the assignees of a bankrupt underwriter for premiums.

(*r*) Lord Ellenborough says: "I cannot conceive how a contract between A. and B. can vary the rights between B. and a third person, who is a stranger to it, and empower B. to set up a claim upon him derived from that contract": 1 M. & S. 498. See also in Koster *v.* Eason (1813), 2 M. & S. 117; and Morris *v.* Cleasby (1816), 4 M. & S. 566; Hornby *v.* Lacy (1817), 6 M. & S. 166. Gibbs, C. J., declared that he had often endeavoured, but in vain, to discover the principle on which Grove and Dubois was founded. See Baker *v.* Langhorn (1816), 2 Marshall's R. at p. 216, *S. C.*, 6 Taunt. 519; see also Peele *v.* Northcote (1817), 7 Taunt. 478. The American jurists treat the case of Grove *v.* Dubois as clearly overruled on this point by the subsequent authorities. See 2 Duer, 375, who collects them all,

Sect. 113. account, provided they had a lien on the policies, or had paid the losses over to their employers; and the bankrupt, by subscribing to a policy so effected, had consented that they should stand as principals, and be considered as giving him credit on the policy at their own risk and on their own account. The remaining ten out of the nineteen policies were neither in the name nor on the account of the defendants, and as to these the Court held, on the ground of want of mutuality of credit, that the claim of set-off could not be allowed; because upon these policies the defendants, even though they had a lien, or had paid over losses, could never sue in their own names, but only in the names of their principals, nor had the bankrupt consented that as to these policies they should ever stand as principals, so as to be considered as giving him credit on their own risk and on their own account: the guaranty of the bankrupt's solvency, given by defendants to their employers under the commission *del credere*, being a transaction to which the bankrupt was not privy, could not affect the rights of the parties (*s*). With regard to these ten policies also, the Court considered that the right of the defendants to set off losses was precluded by the fact that they had not actually paid over such losses to their principals, but only allowed them in account (*t*).

Parker *v.* Beasley, as to right of broker who has a lien on a policy to set off losses in an action for premiums by the trustee of a bankrupt underwriter.

114. An agent who has a lien upon a policy which he has effected in his own name, though not on his own account, may set off losses, as mutual credits, in an action brought against him by the trustee of a bankrupt underwriter for premiums due before the bankruptcy, even though he has not a *del credere* commission; *e.g.*, the consignees of a cargo, having a lien thereon in respect of bills drawn on them on account of such cargo (*u*). "Here," said Lord Ellenborough, "if the parties had not had a lien, their names would have stood on the policy as mere naked names, not coupled with an interest;

(*s*) Koster *v.* Eason (1813), 2 M. & S. 112.
(*t*) *Ibid.* 119.

(*u*) Parker *v.* Beasley (1814), 2 M. & S. 423.

but they may have an interest not only by a *del credere* commission, but also by a lien" (*x*).

Accordingly, in a similar action against a broker who had effected a policy in his own name at the request of a principal, who was indebted to him at the time in a greater sum than that which the broker claimed to set off in the action, the Court of Common Pleas held, on the authority of the case just cited, that, as the broker himself might have sued on the policy, and had a lien on it for more than the amount of his set-off, he might be allowed to reduce the claim of the assignees by availing himself of such defence, though he did not act under a *del credere* commission (*y*).

In 1858 the principle underlying these decisions was again brought into question in the case of Lee *v*. Bullen. That was an action for premiums by assignees of a bankrupt underwriter against brokers, who pleaded a set-off for return of premiums and for losses. The policies had been effected by the defendants in their own names, "$\frac{\text{and}}{\text{or}}$ as agents," they had given the assured a *del credere* guaranty, and continued to hold the policies. Lord Campbell, C. J., said: "Both on principle and according to decided cases, I am quite clear that the facts raised a good defence. There was mutual credit between the parties; the underwriter trusts the brokers for the premiums, and they on the policy trust him that he will fulfil his engagement. The policy being effected in the names of the defendants, and they guaranteeing the solvency of the underwriter, the defendants are not merely nominal contractors, but had a real interest in the contract. This, therefore, is a case of mutual credit, both on principle and the cases decided. Koster *v*. Eason and Parker *v*. Beasley are especially in point as to the construction to be put on the mutual credit clauses as between an underwriter and the person thus effecting the policy" (*z*).

(*x*) *Ibid*. 427.
(*y*) Davies *v*. Wilkinson (1828), 4 Bing. 573.
(*z*) Lee *v*. Bullen (1858), 27 L. J. Q. B. 161; 8 E. & B. 692, n,

Sect. 115.
Baker v. Langhorn.

115. Where, however, brokers, not having a *del credere* commission, effected the policy in their own names, but expressly on the face of the policy "as agents," Gibbs, C. J., held, that although they had always retained the policy in their own hands, they could not set off losses in an action by the assignees for premiums (*a*). "If," said the Chief Justice, "I underwrite for A. B. in his own name without proof that he is acting for another, I must take him to be the principal; but if he be acting expressly as agent, I know that he is not the principal, and that any contract I may enter into with him is not a contract of insurance" (*b*). The result was the

Peele v. Northcote.

same in a case where a broker effected a policy, not in his own name or account, but in the name and on the account of his principals, under a commission *del credere* (*c*), and it was proved that the policy had throughout remained in the hands of the assured. The underwriter having become bankrupt, his assignees sued the broker for premiums due before the bankruptcy: the broker claimed to set off losses which had not only accrued before the bankruptcy, but which had actually been paid over by the broker to his employers before that event.

Sir Vicary Gibbs, however, disallowed his claim on the grounds,—

1. That the policy was not effected in the name of the broker at all.

2. That it was not left in his hands.

3. That the mere fact of its having been effected *del credere* could not alter the relations of the broker and the underwriter, nor let in the claim to set off; for the guarantee of the underwriter's solvency interested no one but the assured, who paid the broker accordingly his commission *del credere* (*d*).

(*a*) Baker v. Langhorn (1816), 2 Marshall's R. 215; 6 Taunt. 519, S. C.; 4 Camp. 396.
(*b*) 2 Marshall's R. 216.
(*c*) A declaration was written on the policy that it was agreed that the broker should guarantee the underwriters thereon.
(*d*) Peele v. Northcote (1817), 7 Taunt. 478. See, too, Ex parte White (1871), L. R. 6 Ch. at p. 403, per Mellish, L. J.

116. The cases hitherto considered have turned upon the right of the broker to deduct losses from premiums; those which follow relate to the broker's right to make a similar deduction in respect of returns of premium, and depend upon different principles.

Sect. 116.
Right of broker to make deductions in respect of returns of premium.

The amount of premium ultimately payable to the underwriter may very frequently depend on contingencies which cannot for some time be ascertained; as, for instance, where goods coming from abroad are insured at a premium of ten guineas per cent., to be reduced to five if the ship sail with convoy, and to be further reduced in case of short interest; the amount of premium, in fact, payable cannot in such case be ascertained until it be known whether the ship, in fact, sailed with convoy or not, and whether the interest really falls below the amount insured (*e*).

Principles on which it rests.

Accordingly, the general custom as between insurance brokers and underwriters was (*f*), that if on the settlement of their mutual account there were any returns of premium then pending, the balance of the account, instead of being paid over, became the first item of account for the ensuing year and the pending returns of premium, as they successively became due, were carried to the debit of the underwriter in such subsequent account, and the adjusted balance was not paid over to the underwriter until all returns of premium were actually ascertained and deducted (*g*).

Usage as to the allowance in account for returns of premium.

Until the sum to be deducted for returns of premium is ascertained—that is, in other words, until the events

Legal position.

(*e*) A more modern illustration would be the case of a steamer insured for twelve months with broad liberties of trading, say, at eight guineas per cent., with a return of one guinea per cent. should she be engaged solely in Eastern voyages.

(*f*) This custom is now quite extinct. Returns of premium are now dealt with as losses or averages. The underwriter is credited with the agreed initial premium, and if a return is afterwards found to be due, it is adjusted on the policy and credited to the broker, just as a loss would be adjusted or credited. It has nevertheless been thought necessary to retain in the text the passages and decisions relating to the old practice, for the sake of the principles which they illustrate.

(*g*) See Goldschmidt *v.* Lyon (1812), 4 Taunt. 534.

Sect. 116. are determined upon which the amount of premium, actually payable to the underwriter, depends—the broker is the mutual agent of the assured and the underwriters, for the one to pay and for the other to receive (*h*).

Either party may, indeed, determine this agency when he pleases: the assured by taking the policy out of the hands of the broker who has effected it (*i*), paying him, of course, what he owes him at the time, and placing it in the hands of another broker to get it adjusted (*k*); and the underwriter by at once calling on the broker for the full premium, leaving nothing in reserve in the broker's hands to answer any returns of premium that the underwriter, at a subsequent time, may be bound to pay the assured (*l*).

If, however, the underwriter do not determine the broker's agency before the event arises on which the return of premium depends, the broker still continues his agent for the deduction of such return from the full amount of premium; and, consequently, when the underwriter brings his action against the broker for such full amount of premium, the broker is entitled in his defence to set off the amount of returns which, as his agent, he was authorized to deduct.

The single question, then, as to the broker's right to set off returns in an action for premiums was considered, under the old practice, to resolve itself into this: Was or was not his agency determined before the right to returns of premium accrued?

Hence, where the underwriter himself sued the broker for premiums, the Court held, that the broker, although not acting under a *del credere* commission, might deduct, by way of set-off, sums due for returns of premium, though it did not appear that the broker had either received the premiums from his principals or credited them with returns of pre-

(*h*) Per Lord Ellenborough in Shee *v.* Clarkson (1810), 12 East, 510.

(*i*) See Mar. Ins. Act, 1906, s. 53 (1), *ante*, § 101, that the underwriter is directly responsible to the assured for losses.

(*k*) Per Mansfield, C. J., in Minett *v.* Forrester (1811), 4 Taunt. 543.

(*l*) *Ibid.* 544.

mium; and although the return of premium claimed to be deducted had never been adjusted as between the broker and the underwriter (*m*). Sect. 116.

117. As, however, the authority thus given by the underwriter ceases *ipso facto* by his bankruptcy or his death, the broker cannot avail himself of this defence when the action is brought by the trustee of a bankrupt or the executors of a deceased underwriter, unless, indeed, the sums payable by way of returns of premium have been actually adjusted in account between the broker and the underwriter before the bankruptcy or the death. Death or bankruptcy of underwriter terminates broker's agency.

Thus, where the assignees of a bankrupt underwriter brought their action against a broker for premiums due on two policies of insurance, in respect of which he claimed to deduct, by way of set-off, certain sums for returns of premium, and it appeared that the events which entitled the broker to make this deduction had occurred and become known to him—on the one policy before the bankruptcy; on the other policy not till after that event; but that no adjustment had been made on either policy: the Court held, that, as the agency of the broker had been determined by the bankruptcy of the underwriter, he was not entitled to this set-off either on the one policy or on the other (*n*). Upon the same principles the Court of King's Bench subsequently decided in a similar action the three following points:— Minett *v.* Forrester.

1. That no such returns of premium can be set off against a claim by the assignees (or now the trustee) of a bankrupt underwriter for premiums, even though forming part of an adjusted account, where the events entitling to such returns were not known to have happened until after the adjustment. Parker *v.* Smith.

2. That no such set-off can be allowed where the events entitling to the return happened before the bankruptcy, but

(*m*) Shee *v.* Clarkson (1810), 12 East, 507.

(*n*) Minett *v.* Forrester (1811), 4 Taunt. 541; Goldschmidt *v.* Lyon (1812), 4 Taunt. 534.

Sect. 117. the amount of return claimed was never adjusted with the bankrupt.

3. That such set-off cannot be allowed in any case where the events entitling to the return are not known till after the bankruptcy (*o*).

Houston v. Robertson.

The Court of Common Pleas extended the same principles to actions brought by the executors of a deceased underwriter, and decided that no set-off could be allowed in respect of returns of premium, the events entitling to which were not known till after the underwriter's death (*p*). In a subsequent case they also explicitly decided that all these rules applied exactly in the same way, whether the broker acted under a *del credere* commission or not (*q*). And the same principles have recently been held to apply to a case where a broker was sued by the underwriter's trustee for sums which, subsequently to the bankruptcy, he had received on the underwriter's account for certain salvages on losses which, prior to his bankruptcy, the underwriter had paid. It was held by Collins, J., that he was not entitled to deduct from the amount so received by him payments to the assured for losses which he had made in pursuance of his *del credere* obligation (*r*).

Whether the broker be acting del credere or not makes no difference: Houston v. Bordenave.

Such, then, are the principal decisions that have taken place on the right of the broker to set off losses and returns of premium in actions brought against him by the underwriter for his premiums—decisions complicated from the variety of circumstances involved in them, and from the difficulty of reconciling the relations arising out of the actual course of dealing between the broker and the underwriter with those which flow from the general principle that the underwriter is debtor, not to the broker, but to the assured.

(*o*) Parker *v.* Smith (1812), 16 East, 382.

(*p*) Houston *v.* Robertson (1816), 6 Taunt. 448.

(*q*) Houston *v.* Bordenave (1816), 6 Taunt. 451.

(*r*) Elgood *v.* Harris, [1896] 2 Q. B. 491.

CHAP. VI.] IN SEA INSURANCE. 165

118. The cases above discussed seem to support the following positions (*s*):—

1. In respect of setting off losses—

a. Where bankruptcy has intervened, and the action is brought on behalf of the creditors of the bankrupt underwriter, the broker who has effected the policy in his own name and on his own account, or in his own name, but on the account of his principals (provided in this last case he has also a lien on the policy to the extent of his set-off), may set off losses allowed to him on account by the underwriter before his bankruptcy, though unadjusted, because losses so allowed in account are mutual credits within the meaning of those words in the Statutes of Bankruptcy (*t*).

b. But where he effects the policy both in the name and on account of his principals; or where, when effected in his own name, but on their account, he has no lien on it; or where he effects it in his own name, but expressly on the face of the policy as agent, he has no such right of set-off, even though he acts under a *del credere* commission (*u*).

Sect. 118.
Summary of the positions established by the cases in respect, 1st, to setting off losses; 2nd, to setting off returns of premium.

(*s*) The summary which here follows is taken from the 2nd edition of this work, pp. 139, 140. It is conceived, however, that the modern tendency is rather to treat these and similar questions as questions of fact, each to be determined according to circumstances, the question in each case being, Did the broker contemplate having an interest in the policy, or was he acting merely as agent for the assured? In the former case he will be entitled to set off; in the latter he will not. The fact of the broker's receiving a *del credere* commission, the fact of the policy being expressed to be in his name, and of his retaining the policy in his own hands, are none of them conclusive, though each of them important pieces of evidence in his favour. Apart from other circumstances which might lead to a contrary conclusion, a modern tribunal would probably, upon proof of the several facts and circumstances detailed in the text, arrive at the several positions indicated—rather, however, as questions of fact than of law.

(*t*) Grove *v.* Dubois (1786), 1 T. R. 112; Koster *v.* Eason (1813), 2 M. & S. 112; Parker *v.* Beasley, *ibid.* 423; Davies *v.* Wilkinson (1828), 4 Bing. 573; Lee *v.* Bullen (1858), 27 L. J. Q. B. 161; 8 E. & B. 692, n.

(*u*) Koster *v.* Eason (1813), 2 M. & S. 112; Baker *v.* Langhorn (1816), 6 Taunt. 519; Peele *v.* Northcote (1817), 7 Taunt. 478.

Sect. 118.

c. For a *del credere* commission, being a contract wholly between the broker and the assured, cannot affect the mutual rights and liabilities of the broker and the underwriter; and therefore does not, *per se*, and without other requisites, entitle the broker to his right of set-off (*x*).

2. As to returns of premium (*y*)—

a. The broker, being the agent of the underwriter for deducting returns of premium in the account between them, may, in an action by the underwriter himself for premiums, set off sums due for returns of premium (*z*).

b. But the death or bankruptcy of the underwriter operates as a revocation of this agency, and the broker, therefore, cannot, in an action by the trustee in bankruptcy, or by the executors, set off unadjusted returns of premium, whether the events entitling to those returns were known before or after the death or bankruptcy (*a*).

Effect of leaving policy in the hands of the broker.

119. In the usual course of business, the assured leaves the policy in the hands of the broker until the settlement of claims. By doing so the assured probably holds the broker out as having authority, or in other words gives him ostensible authority, to act as his agent in all matters arising on the policy—to claim and receive returns of premium, to settle losses, and to receive the amount of them in cash, or, if the assured is cognizant of the usage at Lloyd's, to pass them in account—probably to do all that is incidentally necessary for carrying out the contract contained in the policy thus left in his hands (*b*). If, however, the insurer pays a loss to an

---

(*x*) Peele *v.* Northcote (1817), 7 Taunt. 478; Houston *v.* Bordenave (1816), 6 Taunt. 451; Elgood *v.* Harris, [1896] 2 Q. B. 491.

(*y*) As has been already pointed out, the alteration in the course of business, by which returns of premium are now regarded and treated as losses on the policy, has rendered obsolete the distinction which was properly drawn by Arnould.

(*z*) Shee *v.* Clarkson (1810), 12 East, 507.

(*a*) Minett *v.* Forrester (1812), 4 Taunt. 541; Goldschmidt *v.* Lyon (1812), *ibid*. 534; Parker *v.* Smith (1812), 16 East, 382; Houston *v.* Robertson (1816), 6 Taunt. 448; Houston *v.* Bordenave (1816), 6 Taunt. 451.

(*b*) See the cautiously expressed opinion of Blackburn, J., in Xenos

agent of the assured without the production of the policy, he no doubt does so at his peril, and will be liable to pay it a second time if the agent had not in fact authority to receive the money (c).

Sect. 119.

Whenever the assured leaves the policy in the hands of the insurance broker for the purpose just explained, the broker is, in law, presumed to promise, in consideration of his commission, that he will use all reasonable diligence to procure from the underwriter a speedy settlement of the claim, and, without delay, collect and pay over to the assured the sums due. If he fail to do so, an action for damages at the suit of the assured will lie against him in respect of such failure (d).

Duty of broker thus entrusted with the policy.

The broker, therefore, after thus allowing the loss in account, and so depriving the assured, when cognizant of the usage, of all legal remedy against the underwriter, will be liable to the assured for the amount, as money had and received to his use; and this although no proof be given that he has actually received any money from the underwriter, for in such action he will be estopped from saying that he has not such money in his hands for the plaintiff's use (e).

May be sued for money received.

120. The assured, however, may be found, by his subsequent course of dealing, to have waived his right to resort to the broker. The following is a case of the kind:—The brokers, after a loss had occurred, allowed the underwriter's name to be struck off the policy, and he gave them credit in his books for the amount. They did not, however, take credit for it on their side of the account; and, on the underwriter's bankruptcy, which took place soon after, gave notice thereof to the assured, telling him he must prove for his loss under the commission. Six months after this the assured settled an

Unless assured has waived his right.

v. Wickham (1863), 14 C. B. N. S. 452; 33 L. J. C. P. 13, 21; Richardson v. Anderson (1807), 1 Camp. 43, n.; Goodson v. Brooke (1815), 4 Camp. 163; per Lord Esher, M. R., Hine v. Steamship Ins. Syndicate (1895), 72 L. T. 79, 81; see *infra*, §§ 124—129.

(c) See Swan v. Marit. Ins. Co., [1907] 1 K. B. 117.
(d) Bousfield v. Cresswell (1810), 2 Camp. 545.
(e) Andrew v. Robinson (1812), 3 Camp. 199; Wilkinson v. Clay (1814), 4 Camp. 171; *S. C.* in banc, 6 Taunt. 110.

Sect. 120. account with the brokers, including the very policy in question, without making any complaint of the erasure of the underwriter's name, or any claim in respect of the loss. Lord Ellenborough ruled, that, under these circumstances, the assured must be considered to have waived his right against the broker, and to have elected to seek his remedy under the bankrupt's commission (*f*).

Broker who has paid a loss, or allowed it in account, cannot recover it back.

If an insurance broker, in case of a loss, pays the assured the full amount of the money subscribed, he cannot afterwards recover back any part of it on the ground that, before the loss happened, one of the underwriters became insolvent, and that he, the broker, was not aware of that fact when he paid the money (*g*). The same rule applies where the broker, instead of paying the loss over to his principal in money, has allowed it to him on account, especially if a considerable period has been suffered to elapse between such allowance and the claim to recover back the money (*h*).

When can broker set up defence of illegality.

121. An agent, to whom monies have actually been paid to the use of the principal, has no right to inquire into the legality of the transactions out of which the payment arose. Hence, where a loss has actually been paid over by the underwriter to the broker, the latter cannot, to an action for money had and received by the assured, set up the illegality of the insurance (*i*). But where the money is not paid, but only allowed in account, as the course of dealing is not suffered to

---

(*f*) Ovington *v.* Bell (1812), 3 Camp. 237.

(*g*) Edgar *v.* Bumstead (1808), 1 Camp. 411.

(*h*) Jameson *v.* Swainstone (1810), 2 Camp. 546, *in notis*. In this case two years had elapsed between the allowance of the loss in account and the attempt to recover it back by action. Mansfield, C. J., held, that after such a lapse of time the brokers, as between themselves and their principal, must be held to have received actual payment from the underwriters.

(*i*) Tenant *v.* Elliott (1797), 1 B. & P. 3; Farmer *v.* Russell, *ibid.* 298. As regards policies which are gaming and wagering contracts within the Gaming Act, 1845 (see *infra*, § 315), the position does not appear to be affected by the Gaming Act, 1892. See De Mattos *v.* Benjamin (1894), 63 L. J. Q. B. 248; Burge *v.* Ashley, [1900] 1 Q. B. 744, approving O'Sullivan *v.* Thomas, [1895] 1 Q. B. 698.

operate in illegal transactions, the money may always be stopped by the principal whilst in transitu to the person for whom it is intended; *e.g.*, premiums on illegal insurances may be stopped by the assured whilst in the hands of the broker (*k*).

Sect. **121.**

An agent cannot dispute the title of his principal; nor shall he, after accounting with his principal, and receiving money for him in that capacity, afterwards say that he did not so receive it, but for the benefit of some other person.

Broker cannot dispute the title of his employer.

An action was brought for money had and received, to recover from a policy broker the amount of a loss he had received from the underwriters on a policy effected on ship on behalf of the plaintiff, a part-owner and ship's husband. The other part-owners had never given the plaintiff any directions to insure for them, and the defendant, in effecting the policy, looked to the plaintiff alone as his employer. A loss having occurred, the defendant collected the amount thereof from the underwriters, but did not pay it over to the plaintiff, in consequence of having received notice not to do so from the other part-owners. On this evidence, a verdict having passed for the plaintiff, the Court refused to set it aside, on the plain ground that the plaintiff alone employed the defendant, and that the defendant, as his agent, having since received the money from the underwriters, must be held to have received it for his use (*l*).

Roberts *v.* Ogilby.

Flowerden and Davidson were partners: Flowerden having mortgaged a ship which belonged to him in his separate right, Hamond, the defendant, paid off the debt, 900*l.*, and got his own name substituted for that of the former mortgagee as registered owner. Some time subsequently defendant effected an insurance for 2,800*l.* on the ship and freight, as agent for and by the direction of Flowerden and Davidson, and charged the partnership with the premiums. The ship having been lost, the underwriters paid the whole amount insured to defendant, as agent for Flowerden and Davidson, who refused

Dixon *v.* Hamond.

(*k*) Edgar *v.* Fowler (1803), 3 East, 222.

(*l*) Roberts *v.* Ogilby (1821), 9 Price, 269.

Sect. 121. to pay over the difference between the 900*l.* and the 2,800*l.* to the assignees of Davidson, the surviving partner, on the ground that, 1st, the defendant, being the sole registered owner of the ship, was not liable at all; 2nd, if he was, as the ship never belonged to the partnership, he was only liable to the executors of Flowerden, and not to the assignees of the surviving partner. The Court overruled both objections on the single ground, that as the defendant had received the money as the agent for the partnership, he could not, when claimed of him, be permitted to say that he had received it for the benefit of Flowerden alone (*m*).

Bell *v.* Jutting.

122. The case of Bell *v.* Jutting has been frequently cited (*n*) in support of the proposition that brokers will, generally speaking, be safe in paying over a loss to the party for whom they have effected a policy as for a principal, and whom alone they knew as such, even after notice—unless, indeed, satisfactory proof can be given that he only effected the policy as agent. The facts were that the defendants, as brokers, by directions of Brown, the charterer of the "Lady Hood," effected an insurance for 2,000*l.* on her freight. A total loss having ensued, the defendants collected the 2,000*l.*, and although they received notice, whilst part of the money was still in their hands, that the plaintiffs, as owners of the vessel, claimed the benefit of the insurance, they nevertheless paid the balance over to Brown. The plaintiffs failed in an action to recover this sum, not, however, on the ground that the defendants were justified in paying the money to an agent, but because the Court held, on the facts, that Brown had effected the policy on his own account, and had never intended to act as the plaintiffs' agent at all. The case, therefore, decides nothing with respect to the duties or liabilities of the broker towards an agent and his undisclosed principal (*o*).

(*m*) Dixon *v.* Hamond (1819), 2 B. & Ald. 310.
(*n*) 2nd ed. of this work, p. 145; 6th ed. p. 209.

(*o*) Bell *v.* Jutting (1817), 1 J. B. Moore, 155. The true effect of this case is pointed out by Duer, vol. ii. pp. 176, 361—363.

123. We have already seen that the rule is that the assured is liable to the broker for premiums as for money paid, whether they have been paid over by the broker to the underwriter or not (*p*).

Sect. 123.

Where a policy by deed, instead of acknowledging receipt of the premium, contained a covenant from the brokers to pay it, and was expressed to be effected in consideration of that covenant, the Court held, that the premiums not paid by the broker before his bankruptcy to the underwriters could be recovered by his assignees from the assured, not, indeed, as money paid, but as "money due for premiums for policies caused and procured to be underwritten by the bankrupt" (*q*).

If a broker engages to effect an insurance with such names as should be to the satisfaction of the assured, it is no defence for the assured, after lying by till the voyage is completed, to set up against an action for premiums that the names of the underwriters had never been submitted to him for approval (*r*).

Assured cannot object to policy after voyage ended.

124. We now proceed to discuss the right of the assured to maintain an action on the policy for a loss.

We have already detailed the course of practice as to the settlement of claims in case of loss. Such a mode of settlement is binding by the usage of business upon the broker and the underwriter as between themselves. But whether it be of any binding effect upon the assured is a question of fact as to his assent to this kind of settlement.

Whether the usage of Lloyd's binds the assured.

We have seen that it is a usual thing for the assured to leave the policy in the hands of the broker. The effect is, probably, that he has ostensible authority to settle the loss and to receive the money (*s*). But it is of no effect

(*p*) See *ante*, § 107.
(*q*) Power *v*. Butcher (1829), 10 B. & Cr. 329.
(*r*) Dixon *v*. Hovill (1828), 4 Bing. 665.
(*s*) *Ante*, § 119. See per Blackburn, J., in Xenos *v*. Wickham (1863), 33 L. J. C. P. 13, 21; 14 C. B. N. S. 452. There is no clear judicial decision on the point. It arose in Sweeting *v*. Pearce, *infra*, §§ 126, 127, but in the event did

Sect. 124. whatever to bind the assured by the peculiar usages of Lloyd's (t).

What discharges the underwriter as to the assured.

125. Thus, if the underwriter pays the loss in money (u) to the broker who has been allowed to retain possession of the policy, and *à fortiori* to a broker to whom the policy has been expressly sent for the purpose of settling for the loss, the underwriter is thereby discharged at common law from any claim by the assured for the same loss (x). So he is, if the assured can be shown to have actually assented to the usage at Lloyd's in settling the claim, by allowing the amount to be credited by the underwriter to the broker in account (y); or if, from all the circumstances of the case, he must reasonably be presumed to have acquiesced in it (z).

The question involved in this is not appreciated in all its importance until the bankruptcy of the broker threatens one of the two other parties to the insurance with serious loss. Very strict views of the broker's authority, under any circumstances whatever, were at one time entertained by the judges,

---

not need to be decided. In the Court of Common Pleas, Cockburn, C. J., expressed the opinion that when the assured leaves the policy with the broker he is estopped from saying that the latter has no authority to receive payment for a loss (see 29 L. J. C. P. at p. 270); and Byles, J., agreed with this opinion (*ibid.* p. 272); but the judges in the Court of Exchequer Chamber carefully refrained from giving any opinion. Phillips (vol. i. s. 1882), Duer (vol. i. Lect. XI. ss. 8, 42), and apparently Arnould (§ 129, *infra*) agree with the view of Cockburn, C. J., and Byles and Blackburn, JJ. (*ubi supra*), which is also to some extent supported by the decisions that a broker who retains possession of the policy owes a duty to the assured to collect losses from the underwriters with diligence.

See *post*, §§ 163, 164. It is apprehended that the legal position is the same whether the assured voluntarily leaves the policy in the hands of the broker, or the latter retains it in the exercise of his lien.

(t) As to this, see *post*, §§ 126—128.

(u) As to payment by bill, see Hine v. Steamship Ins. Syndicate (1895), 72 L. T. 79.

(x) Scott v. Irving (1830), 1 B. & Ad. 605; see also Legge v. Byas (1901), 7 Com. Cas. 16, per Walton, J.

(y) See Bartlett v. Pentland (1830), 10 B. & Cr. 760. This usage does not extend to dealings between the brokers and insurance companies: Hine v. Steamship Ins. Syndicate, *supra*.

(z) Andrew v. Robinson (1812), 3 Camp. 199.

much to the prejudice of the underwriter (a). The leaning Sect. 125.
of the Courts, however, speedily altered. The right of the
assured in such cases to recover from the underwriter is now
a pure question of evidence, and depends solely upon the
point whether the assured, upon a view of all the facts,
must not be taken to have been cognizant of the usage, and
an assenting party, therefore, to its observance (b). For the
usage of Lloyd's as to settling losses in account, being "the
usage of a particular place, or of a particular set of persons,
cannot be binding on other persons, unless those other
persons are acquainted with that usage and adopt it" (c).

126. The law applicable to this question is strikingly Common law
expounded by Bramwell, B., in the following passage, and Lloyd's
in delivering his opinion in the case of Sweeting v. usage contrasted.
Pearce (d):—

"This is a question," says the learned judge, "of the
broker's authority. The legal presumption of authority
given to a person who is to receive satisfaction for another
for a money demand is, that he is to receive it by payment
of money only. It is also a rule of good sense. The custom
[*i.e.*, of Lloyd's] set up is, that the persons who are by legal
presumption to receive in money, and in money only, are
not to receive in money. The custom is therefore in contradiction to the authority given to the agents by their principal.
It is a custom not to do the thing which the law implies they
are to do. That shows it to be unreasonable" [*i.e.*, if it
were to be supposed to be binding on a person ignorant of
it and consequently not assenting to it].

(a) See the case before Lord
Ellenborough of Jell v. Pratt
(1817), 2 Stark. N. P. 67; and the
cases before Lord Tenterden of
Todd v. Reid (1821), 4 B. & Ald.
210; and Russell v. Bangley (1821),
ibid. 395.

(b) Bartlett v. Pentland (1830),
10 B. & Cr. 760; Scott v. Irving
(1830), 1 B. & Ad. 605; Stewart v.
Aberdein (1838), 4 M. & W. 211;
Sweeting v. Pearce (1861), 9 C. B.
N. S. 534; 30 L. J. C. P. 109.

(c) Per Lord Tenterden in Bartlett v. Pentland (1830), 10 B. &
Cr. 770.

(d) Sweeting v. Pearce (1861)
(in error), 9 C. B. N. S. 534, 540;
30 L. J. C. P. 109, 112.

Sect. 126.

"There is a great distinction between it and the cases which have been relied upon. If I set a man generally to do a thing, a custom may well apply to regulate the mode of doing it. So, with regard to usages of the Stock Exchange which have been referred to. If I tell a broker to purchase such and such stock, I impliedly say to him, deal upon terms upon which you can deal, that is, according to the usage. If the tenor of my authority is to exclude the operation of any custom, I give him no authority to act according to the custom; but if the authority I give is consistent with the custom, then the custom may come into play. Thus, in the case before us, the plaintiff [who was ignorant of the usage at Lloyd's and consequently non-assenting to it] says to the broker 'receive payment in money'; that means receive it in money and not otherwise.

"Mr. Arnould, in his work on Marine Insurance, 2nd edit. p. 81, says:—'It might have been considered not a very violent presumption that all parties resident in this country employing brokers to effect policies for them in the common course of business should be considered to have done so with reference to the usages established at Lloyd's.' I beg leave to say that I think it would have been an unreasonable presumption. I can well understand, if a man who knows of this usage of Lloyd's gives his policy to the broker, with directions to do the needful, a jury might well find that he authorizes the broker to do the needful according to the custom. Probably Mr. Arnould meant no more than that. But it would be a question for the jury in each case whether the presumption that the authority [was] to receive payment in money was rebutted by the principal's knowledge of the custom. This custom, in truth, goes not to say how the presumed authority to receive payment in cash is to be exercised, but that it should not be exercised at all."

Sweeting v. Pearce.

127. The case in which these observations were made was singularly suitable to bring out the antagonism between

Lloyd's usage and the general law of the country. The London brokers had become bankrupt after debiting the underwriter with the loss as against a large sum due to him from them on account of premiums. This was in accordance with the usage, which the jury found to be generally known amongst merchants and shipowners effecting insurances, and would have been a bar to the action of the assured against the underwriter, if the usage were binding on the plaintiff. It was admitted, however, by the defendant, in accordance with the plaintiff's evidence, that, the policy being in the hands of the brokers for safe custody only, the ship's papers were delivered to them after the loss for no other purpose than to obtain an adjustment. The plaintiff was ignorant of Lloyd's usage, and had not intended his brokers should ever receive the money in payment for the loss. Under these circumstances it was determined in the Court below, and affirmed by the Exchequer Chamber, that the general law, and not the usage at Lloyd's, governed the case and entitled the plaintiff, notwithstanding the settlement with the broker, to recover against the underwriter (e).

Sect. 127.

In Bartlett v. Pentland (f), the plaintiffs, corn merchants in Plymouth, had a policy effected for them by a London broker with the St. Patrick's Insurance Company at their office in Lombard Street, London; a total loss having taken place, a pen was struck through the company's subscription to the policy, and the loss passed in account, as between broker and underwriter, in the usual way, the company being at that time indebted to the broker on the general account between them. The plaintiffs, although in the habit for thirty years of procuring insurances, were yet unacquainted with the usage at Lloyd's, and were misled by a false request of the broker to draw on him instead of the underwriter (g) three months' bills, which he accepted but

Bartlett v. Pentland.

(e) Sweeting v. Pearce (1861), 7 C. B. N. S. 449; 29 L. J. C. P. 265; (in error), 9 C. B. N. S. 534; 30 L. J. C. P. 109.

(f) Bartlett v. Pentland (1830),
10 B. & Cr. 760.

(g) The practice of drawing bills, whether on brokers or underwriters, for the settlement of claims is now obsolete.

Sect. 127. never paid, having failed before they became due. Previous to his bankruptcy, the insurance company, which had all along been indebted to him on the general account between them (including many transactions besides the policy in question), settled such general account with him by paying in money the balance due to him for losses, including the loss in question, after deducting the amount of the premiums due to them from the broker. The question in the case was, whether such settlement with the broker was binding on the assured, as being in law a payment to them.

When payment not a discharge.

The Court were clearly of opinion that there was nothing in the case before them to raise any presumption against the plaintiffs, that they had given an implied authority to the broker to settle according to Lloyd's usage; and consequently that the money paid to the broker, being not a specific payment on account of a specific loss, but merely a general payment on a general account, was not to be deemed in law payment as against the assured (*h*).

When *laches* is a discharge.

They further held that, notwithstanding the plaintiffs had been induced to give credit to the broker, and had not applied to the company until after the broker's failure, when the company had already settled their general account with him, yet, as the company had not been damnified by the laches of the plaintiffs, they could not be discharged by it (*i*).

Scott *v.* Irving.

128. In the next case of the same kind, the plaintiff, a merchant in Glasgow, had employed a London broker to procure an insurance for him at Lloyd's. A total loss having occurred on the policy, the plaintiff wrote to the broker, enclosing a bill drawn on the broker, payable ten days after sight, and stating that he did not know at what date it was proper to draw for the balance, this being the first total loss he had ever had in London. The Court upon these facts

---

(*h*) Per Bayley, J., Bartlett *v.* Pentland (1830), 10 B. & Cr. 773; and see Scott *v.* Irving (1830), 1 B. & Ad. 605; and Macfarlane *v.* Giaunocopulo, *infra.*

(*i*) Per Lord Tenterden, C. J., 10 B. & Cr. 770; accord. *per curiam*, Macfarlane *v.* Giaunocopulo (1858), 3 H. & N. 860; 28 L. J. Ex. 72.

held that the plaintiff was not cognizant of the usage of Lloyd's so as to be precluded from suing the underwriter even two years after the broker's insolvency; but that to the extent of a payment made in cash by the underwriter to the broker within the month on account of this loss the underwriter was discharged as against the assured, since the payment made was in strict accordance with his general authority to the broker (*k*).

Sect. 128.

In the next case the plaintiffs were merchants at Liverpool, who, for a long course of years, had employed the same firm of London brokers to effect their insurance business in London, which was of a very extensive character. The London brokers kept both a general and also an insurance account with the plaintiffs, in the latter of which they debited them with all premiums, and credited them with all losses allowed in account by the different underwriters; and the balance, after deducting the premiums, was then carried into the general account with the plaintiffs. Some evidence was given that Lloyd's usage was well known in Liverpool. A loss on a policy effected with the defendant, who was an underwriter at Lloyd's, was settled and passed in account as between the brokers and the defendant in the usual way, and the defendant's name was struck off the policy. An adjustment of this and other losses having been obtained by the brokers, they advised the plaintiffs (to whom they were then considerably indebted on the general account) of the fact; and the plaintiffs then drew upon them for the amount (*l*). Shortly after this the London brokers, who were still greatly indebted to the plaintiffs, became bankrupt, and the plaintiffs thereupon immediately sued the defendant for the loss already mentioned as passed in account with the brokers. But the Court held that, under the circumstances, the plaintiffs' claim could not be supported, on the ground stated by Lord Abinger, "that there was sufficient evidence in the case of the knowledge of the plaintiffs of the custom,

Stewart *v.* Aberdein.

(*k*) Scott *v.* Irving (1830), 1 B. & Ad. 605.

(*l*) This practice is now obsolete. See *ante*, § 127, note (*g*).

Sect. 128.

and of their authorizing the brokers to settle with the underwriters, desiring them to credit the plaintiffs with the loss, and to permit them to draw on the brokers for the amount (*m*).

Opinion of Lord Abinger upon the general question.

Upon the general question, the Court were of opinion, "that where an insurance broker, or other mercantile agent, has been employed to receive money for another, in the general course of his business, and where the known general course of business is for the agent to keep a running account with the principal, and to credit him with sums which he (the agent or broker) may have received by credits in account with the debtors (the underwriters, &c.), with whom he also keeps running accounts, and not with monies actually received, it must be understood, that where an account has been *bonâ fide* discharged and settled according to that known usage, the original debtor (*i.e.*, the underwriter) is discharged; and the agent (*i.e.*, the insurance broker) becomes the debtor, according to the meaning and intention, and with the authority of the principal" (*n*).

Recent cases.

Unsuccessful attempts were made in two recent cases to bind the assured by a settlement in account between the broker and underwriter (*o*). In Matvieff *v.* Crosfield it was contended that Sweeting *v.* Pearce has been overruled by Robinson *v.* Mollett (*p*), a case in which the House of Lords affirmed (though without applying) the rule that "if a person employs a broker to transact for him upon a market with the usages of which the principal is unacquainted, he gives authority to the broker to make contracts upon the

---

(*m*) Stewart *v.* Aberdein (1838), 4 M. & W. 211.

(*n*) Per Lord Abinger, delivering the judgment of the Court in Stewart *v.* Aberdein (1838), 4 M. & W. 228. Duer is in many respects very dissatisfied with the report of this case (see remarks on it, 2 Duer, 260, 261); but although some of the reported expressions of Lord Abinger at N. P. and in Banc may be difficult to defend, yet the case, as Duer himself admits, is unexceptionable if only used as an authority for the position, that where the assured is fairly shown to be cognizant of the usage, he is bound by it.

(*o*) Legge *v.* Byas (1901), 7 Com. Cas. 16; Matvieff *v.* Crosfield (1903), 8 Com. Cas. 120.

(*p*) (1875), L. R. 7 H. L. 802.

footing of such usages, provided they are such as regulate the mode of performing the contract, and do not change their intrinsic character" (*q*). The judgments in Sweeting *v.* Pearce, however, expressly negative the application of this rule in the case of a Lloyd's usage which conflicts with the duty of an agent to receive payment in money; and Kennedy, J., held that Sweeting *v.* Pearce was not affected by Robinson *v.* Mollett.

Sect. 128.

129. The following propositions seem to embrace the law on this subject:—

Summary of the law on this point.

1. Unless the assured by evidence reasonably sufficient can be shown to be cognizant of this usage of settling claims in account and to have assented to it, he is not bound by it; but may recover against the underwriter, although the claim has, as between broker and underwriter, been settled, and passed in account.

2. Payment in cash by the underwriter to the broker of the balance of a general account is not payment as against the assured, if ignorant of Lloyd's usage. But a specific money payment by the underwriter to the broker in respect of the specific loss claimed by the assured in the action, and within the time appointed for cash payments, is, as against the assured, payment *pro tanto*.

3. If upon the facts of the case it is to be inferred that the assured was cognizant of this usage and assenting to it, he is bound by it, and cannot recover against the underwriter claims settled and passed in account as between underwriter and broker.

But the assured may lose his right to recover against the underwriter by suing in the name of the broker, since every defence which is good against the actual plaintiff is open to the defendant. Consequently, a settlement by passing the claim in account with the broker is a bar to the action when

(*q*) Per Lord Chelmsford, L. R. 7 H. L. at p. 836.

12 (2)

Sect. 129. it is brought in the broker's name (*r*). But the assured has the right of action in his own name.

The broker's lien on the policy.

130. The policy, when effected, becomes in law the property of the assured, who may maintain trover for it, subject to any lien which the broker may have for premiums and commission, or for the general balance of his insurance account. In practice the policy, after being effected, is sometimes handed over by the broker to the assured, and afterwards remitted by the assured to him for the settlement of claims on the occurrence of a loss; or the broker himself, as is very generally the case, keeps it throughout in his own possession.

If the broker represents to the assured that he has effected a policy according to their orders, they may maintain an action of trover against him although such policy has never in fact been effected at all; and in such action the plaintiff shall prove his loss, as in an action against the underwriter, and the defendant shall not be permitted to say that no such policy exists (*s*).

Particular lien.

As regards the broker's lien for the premium and commission due in respect of a particular policy which he has himself effected, the law is thus stated by Phillips (*t*):—"The agent who effects a policy for his principal and advances the premium or becomes responsible for it, and retains the policy in his hands, has a lien upon it for his commission and the premium until the same are paid to him or he is supplied with funds for the payment, whether his immediate employer is the assured himself or an intermediate agent, and in the latter case whether the intermediate agency was known or not known to the sub-agent claiming the lien." And this is

---

(*r*) Gibson *v.* Winter (1833), 5 B. & Ad. 96. This is so wherever the action is brought in the name of one in trust for another (see the observations of Parke, B., in Wilkinson *v.* Lindo (1840), 7 M. & W. 87). So, the Judicature Act, 1873, s. 25, sub-s. 6.

(*s*) Harding *v.* Carter, before Lord Mansfield (1781), Park, Ins. 5; 1 Marshall, 309.

(*t*) 2 Phillips, s. 1909, quoted with approval in Fisher *v.* Smith (1878), 4 App. Cas. at p. 12.

IN SEA INSURANCE.

so, even where the assured has paid the intermediary, in a case where the latter has not paid the broker (*u*).   Sect. 130.

131. His lien, however, for the balance of his general account depends on circumstances. Where he has been employed immediately by the assured himself, he has a lien on the policy, not only for the premium and commission due on the particular transaction, but for the amount of the general balance of his insurance account (*x*).   General lien.

But where he is employed not immediately by the assured himself but by some intermediate agent, and he knows that to be the case, he has no lien on the policy in respect of his general balance against such his immediate employer. Where, however, he is ignorant that the policy is not really effected for the party by whom he is immediately employed, he may refuse to give it up to the assured until he is paid the amount of the general balance of his insurance account against his immediate employer. "The only question," says Gibbs, C. J., "is whether he knew or had reason to believe that the person by whom he was employed was merely an agent" (*y*).

The broker may, however, be precluded by his conduct from enforcing a general lien, though he was not aware when he made the assurance that his employer was only an agent. Thus, where a firm of brokers who had effected policies on the instructions of an intermediate party, were requested

---

(*u*) Fisher *v.* Smith, *ubi supra*.

(*x*) Whitehead *v.* Vaughan, and Parker *v.* Carter, cited in Cook's Bankrupt Laws, 547, 7th ed.; see also Olive *v.* Smith (1813), 5 Taunt. 56, where Gibbs, J., says: "I came to London in 1775. I was pretty early conversant with some business of that sort, and never remember any doubt to have existed in the profession whether a policy broker had a lien for his general balance on the insurance accounts."

(*y*) See the general rule as laid down by Gibbs, C. J., in Westwood *v.* Bell (1814), 4 Camp. 352, 353; and cf. Maspons *v.* Mildred (1882), 9 Q. B. D. 530, affd. (1883), 8 App. Cas. 874; and Cahill *v.* Dawson (1857), 3 C. B. N. S. 106; 26 L. J. C. P. 253. Duer, vol. ii. pp. 353—371, reviews all the cases and agrees with the rule as stated above. It is, however, forcibly contended by Phillips, vol. ii. s. 1916, that the sub-agent, even if ignorant of the true position of his immediate employer, cannot maintain a general lien. The rule, however, seems to be now well established.

Sect. 131. by the latter to hold the policies to the order of the plaintiffs, and wrote to them to say they would do so subject to their lien for unpaid premium, Scrutton, J., held that the brokers were estopped from asserting against the plaintiffs a general lien for the premiums of other insurances effected for the intermediaries (z).

132. It is not necessary, in order to deprive the broker of his general lien against his immediate employer, to show that he had express notice that the party so employing him was only an agent: it is enough if he was reasonably bound to infer this from the circumstances proved (a). The party, however, who seeks to deprive the broker of his lien, on the ground of his knowledge of agency, must make out the affirmative, for, in the absence of reasonable proof to the contrary, it will be presumed that the broker believed his immediate employer to be the principal (b).

Cahill v. Dawson. D., at Liverpool, received orders from his principal abroad to effect an insurance on a cargo of fruit, but thinking to effect it more economically in London, wrote to L. there, who employed N. to procure the policy. A loss was afterwards paid on it to N., who retained the whole for his general balance against L., and D. was sued by his principal for negligence. It was held that, assuming D. to have been guilty of negligence in insuring at London instead of at Liverpool, the plaintiff's right to recover substantial damages from D. depended on whether L. had or had not shown to N. his letter of instructions, as, if he had, N. would not be entitled to retain the money for his general balance of account (c).

Maanss v. Henderson. An English merchant effected a policy for a neutral foreigner in his own name, but informed the broker at the

---

(z) Fairfield Shipbuilding Co. v. Gardner, Mountain & Co. (1911), 104 L. T. 288.

(a) Maanss v. Henderson (1801), 1 East, 334.

(b) Per Gibbs, C. J., in Westwood v. Bell (1814), 4 Camp. 353.

(c) Cahill v. Dawson (1857), 3 C. B. N. S. 106; 26 L. J. C. P. 253; Man v. Shiffner (1802), 2 East, 523.

CHAP. VI.] IN SEA INSURANCE. 183

time that the property was neutral, and the policy was effected Sect. 132.
with a warranty of neutrality. This was held a sufficient
indication to the broker, at a time when this country was at
war, that the English merchant was acting as agent, and not
on his own account, so as to deprive the broker of any lien
except for the premiums due on the particular policy (*d*).

Trover for a policy: The plaintiffs, it appeared, had told Snook *v.*
Carter, an insurance broker, to effect several policies for them; Davidson.
instead of effecting them himself he employed the defendants,
who were also insurance brokers, to do so, telling them at the
time that they were for correspondents in the country: it also
appeared from the policies themselves that they were in fact
for the plaintiffs, as they were all filled up in their names:
the defendants claimed to retain for the general balance of
their insurance account with Carter; but Lord Ellenborough
held that they could not do so, and the plaintiffs had a verdict
on paying the amount due for premium and commissions on
the policy for which the action was brought (*e*).

Action to recover a loss received by the defendant from the Lanyon *v.*
underwriters, on a policy effected by him as broker: The Blanchard.
plaintiff, then abroad, had instructed one Crowgy to effect an
insurance here, on goods which he, the plaintiff, had shipped
and consigned to Crowgy for sale, together with the bill of
lading unindorsed. Crowgy employed the defendant, as his
broker, to effect the policy, representing to him at the time
that he (Crowgy) had authority to indorse the bill of lading,
which he accordingly did, to a person named by the defen-

(*d*) Maanss *v.* Henderson (1801), 1 East, 334.

(*e*) Snook *v.* Davidson (1809), 2 Camp. 218. Lord Ellenborough puts the case on the want of privity between Carter and the defendants, and says: "A sub-agent, employed as the defendants were, cannot acquire the broker's general lien." It is clear, from the observations of Gibbs, C. J., in Westwood *v.* Bell, that the real ground of decision was the same as in Maanss *v.* Henderson, viz., that defendants must have known Carter to be only an agent. See 2 Duer, pp. 354, 355. Phillips, however, vol. ii. s. 1916, declines to accept this view of the case, which he cites as an authority for the position that a sub-agent, whether ignorant or not of the true position of his immediate employer, can have no general lien.

Sect. 132. dant. Under these circumstances, the defendant claimed to retain for the general balance on his insurance account with Crowgy. Lord Ellenborough, however, ruled that he could not do so, and the plaintiff had a verdict, subject only to a deduction for the premium and other charges on the particular policy (*f*).

Westwood *v.* Bell.

133. Where, on the other hand, in an action of trover for a policy, it appeared that the plaintiff (through several intermediate agencies) had employed one Clarkson to effect the policy, and Clarkson, instead of doing so himself, had instructed the defendants, who were regular insurance brokers, to effect it, as for him, representing himself and leading the defendants to believe that he was principal in the transaction, and the defendants accordingly effected the policy in their own names, "as agents," and debited Clarkson with the premiums; it was held that, under these circumstances, the defendants, as against the plaintiff, had a right of lien on the policy so effected for the amount of their general balance of their insurance account with Clarkson (*g*). In such a case the broker may still satisfy his lien, notwithstanding that before receiving the money he have notice that his immediate employer is only an agent. But if after

Mann *v.* Forrester.

(*f*) Lanyon *v.* Blanchard (1811), 2 Camp. 597. Per Gibbs, C. J.: "In Lanyon *v.* Blanchard, the defendant must be taken to have had notice that the person who employed him was not the principal. The representation made by Crowgy that he had authority to indorse the bill of lading was abundantly sufficient to show that he was only an agent": in Westwood *v.* Bell (1815), 4 Camp. 353. As Duer ably puts it: "The unindorsed bill of lading was conclusive to show that the ownership of the goods was still vested in the plaintiff, the shipper, and that it could only be divested by an indorsement made by him, or by his authorized agent. It was this authority that Crowgy represented himself as possessing, and the representation was, in its very terms, an admission of agency": 2 Duer, p. 357. Note that the truth or falsehood of the representation was not the material point, but whether or not the representation, as believed and acted upon by the defendant, necessarily and in its very terms conveyed to his mind the notion that Crowgy, in procuring the insurance to be effected, was acting as agent, and not as principal.

(*g*) Westwood *v.* Bell (1815), 4 Camp. 349.

such notice he pay over the surplus to his immediate Sect. 133.
employer, the principal will nevertheless be entitled to
recover the amount from him in an action for money had
and received (*h*).

A mercantile agent in this country of a merchant abroad
has a lien on the policy that he is authorized to effect, for
the general balance due to him, or becoming due on his
accounts with his principal, while the policy remains in his
hands (*i*). If he has procured the policy to be effected
through an insurance broker, this lien of his attaches on the
policy while in the possession of the broker, for the possession
of the broker in such case is regarded as that of his employer.
The assignee, therefore, of such policy, who becomes so by
the indorsement to him of the bill of lading, takes it subject
to the correspondent's lien: if the amount of such lien
exceeds that of the loss, the assignee of the policy, as against
the broker, can recover nothing (*k*).

If a policy be left in the hands of an agent merely as a No general
depositary and for safe custody, he acquires no general lien lien on policy
thereon, although he may have advanced money to the safe custody.
assured without any other security than the policy (*l*).

134. It must be clearly understood that the general lien of General lien
an insurance broker is only for the balance of his insurance is only for the
account: it does not comprehend transactions between the insurance
broker and his employer on a distinct account having no demands, not
relation to insurance. In cases, indeed, where bankruptcy of lien, may
has intervened, demands which cannot be made the subject be items of
of lien may frequently be embraced as items of mutual Olive *v.*
credit, so as to enable the broker to avail himself of a sub- Smith.
stantial benefit although no lien attaches (*m*).

Such appears to have been the principle of decision in the
case of Olive *v.* Smith: in the subsequent case of Rose *v.*

(*h*) Mann *v.* Forrester (1814), 4 Camp. 60.
(*i*) Godin *v.* London Ass. Co. (1758), 1 Burr. 493.
(*k*) Man *v.* Shiffner (1802), 2 East, 523.
(*l*) Muir *v.* Fleming (1822), 1 Dowl. & Ryl. N. P. C. 29. This was a case on a life policy, which had been left with defendant, he paying the premiums as they became due. So 2 Phillips, s. 1909.
(*m*) Olive *v.* Smith (1813), 5 Taunt. 56.

Sect. 134.   Hart the doctrine of mutual credit was limited to cases where the credits given must in their nature terminate in debts; but Gibbs, C. J., as the organ of the Court, was careful to state expressly that the principle so laid down would support Olive *v.* Smith, on the ground that in that case "the bankrupts were indebted to the defendants, and, being so indebted, delivered policies of insurance to them to collect losses under them, which, when so collected, would make the defendants their debtors for the amount" (*n*).

When lien of broker is lost,

The lien of an insurance agent, as of every other agent, depends at common law on the continuance of possession: when he voluntarily delivers up the policy to his principal, or to his order, his lien is extinguished; so it is if he parts with the policy wrongfully, as by pledging it as his own; but not so where it is taken from him by force, or fraud, or parted with by mistake (*o*).

and revives.

As a general rule, the lien of the broker revives where the policy comes again into his possession (*p*); but there are excepted cases. If, for instance, when the policy comes again into the broker's hands he knows, or has reasonable grounds to believe, that his immediate employer was a mere agent (he having been ignorant of the fact when he before held the policy), it seems that his general lien for the balance of his insurance account with his immediate employer will not revive with the re-possession of the policy, as against the claims of the party really assured (*q*). So, if during the time

---

(*n*) Rose *v.* Hart (1818), 8 Taunt. 499; 2 Smith's L. C.; and see, as to Olive *v.* Smith, the observations of Lord Brougham in Young *v.* Bank of Bengal (1836), 1 Moore's Ind. App. Cas. 87; and of Maule, J., in Dixon *v.* Stanfield (1850), 10 C. B. 413. It must be remembered that the words of the statute at present in force (s. 38 of the Bankruptcy Act, 1883) are wider than they were under the statute in force when many of the older cases were decided. Modern decisions have extended the applicability of the "mutual credits" clause: see, for example, In re Daintrey, [1900] 1 Q. B. 546; In re Taylor, [1910] 1 K. B. 562; Tilley *v.* Bowman, [1910] 1 K. B. 745.

(*o*) 2 Duer, 289. The learned jurist, as usual, supports these positions by incontestable authorities.

(*p*) Whitehead *v.* Vaughan, Cook's Bankrupt Laws, 547, 7th ed.; Levy *v.* Barnard (1818), 8 Taunt. 149; 2 J. B. Moore, 34.

(*q*) Levy *v.* Barnard (1818), 8 Taunt. 149; *S. C.*, 2 J. B. Moore,

...e policy has been out of the broker's possession, it has been assigned over by his employer in good faith and for a valuble consideration to a third party, the broker's general lien ...n the insurance account with his employer would not, it has ...en held in the United States, revive as against the claim of ...ch assignee (*r*).

Sect. 134.

If an insurance broker, having a lien on a policy, be sum...oned as a witness to produce it under a *subpœna duces tecum*, ... an action by his employer against the underwriter, he is ...mpellable to produce the policy; but the Court will, if the ...aintiff in such action obtain a verdict, prevent the money ...om being paid over to him until the broker's lien is ...tisfied (*s*).

Broker under a *sub. duc. tec.* must produce policy, but his lien will be satisfied.

... This was probably the point ...cided in this case; but it is ...tter, with Judge Duer, to speak ...ubtfully on the matter: 2 Duer, ...0, 359, 360.

(*r*) Spring *v.* S. Carolina Ins. ...). (1823), 8 Wheat. 268, cited 2 ...uer, 290.

(*s*) Hunter *v.* Leathley (1830), ... B. & Cr. 858; *S. C.*, at N. P., ...oyd & Welsby, 125. It appears, ... the Nisi Prius report, that the ...oker, after objection made, pro...ced the policy " on an assurance ...om Lord Tenterden that if the ...aintiffs recovered a verdict, the ...urt would prevent the money ...m being paid over to them till ... witness's lien was discharged ": ...oyd & Welsby, 125. This ex...ins the meaning of what Lord ...nterden is reported to have said ...banc: " We do not by this deci...n " (*i.e.*, that the broker was ...pellable to produce the policy) ...eprive the party of his lien; he ...l has the policy in his posses...n, and has the same right of lien ... before." His lordship obviously ...ans that the Court would take ...e that the broker's lien should ... satisfied out of the fruits of

the judgment, if it passed for the plaintiffs; if it did not, he would, of course, be in the same position as before. See 2 Duer, 294, 297.

In Fairfield Shipbuilding Co. *v.* Gardner, Mountain & Co. (1911), 104 L. T. 288, Scrutton, J., expressed a doubt whether a lien on a policy gives a lien on the proceeds collected under it, though the plaintiffs had declined to take this point. There may be a possessory lien on a document, which is merely a right to hold it until a claim is satisfied, giving no right to obtain payment of any debt of which the document is evidence: see Rummens *v.* Hare (1876), 1 Ex. D. 169; West of England Bank *v.* Batchelor (1882), 51 L. J. Ch. 199. When, however, a broker, being in possession of a policy, is authorized to collect losses or returns of premiums, his right to retain the sum for which he has a lien out of moneys received by him under the policy has been expressly recognized in Mann *v.* Forrester, *ante*, § 133, and impliedly in Cahill *v.* Dawson, *ante*, § 132. See also Man *v.* Shiffner (1802), 2 East, 523, at p. 530, *ante*, § 133.

CHAPTER VII.

INSURANCE AGENTS GENERALLY—THEIR RIGHTS, DUTIES AND LIABILITIES.

	SECT.		SECT.
Agents of the Assured	135	Agents of the Assured—*contd.*	
Their authority, express	135	Their Duties and Liabilities	145—162
implied	136—139	Their Duties when Policy left	163—165
Ratification	140—143	Agents of the Insurer	166
Revocation of authority	144	Their authority	166—168

Insurance agents acting for the assured.

135. IN the last chapter we considered the actual course of sea insurance business as carried on in London and elsewhere in Great Britain, and the relative rights, duties and liabilities of insurance agents and their principals as affected thereby. In the present chapter an endeavour will be made to discuss the relations of insurance agents to their employers, first, as governed by the general principles of the law of agency; and, secondly, as affected by the general course of business in sea insurance, in so far as that has grown to be a custom.

Insurance agents may be employed either for the assured to effect, or for the underwriters to subscribe, policies. We will for the present confine our attention to insurance agents acting on behalf of the assured, and consider, in the first place, the nature of the authority under which they act. Insurance agents may procure policies to be effected either, first, in consequence of orders expressly given them by their employers; or, secondly, by virtue of an implied authority arising out of the relation in which they stand to the persons for whom, or the property on which, they procure the insurance to be effected; or, thirdly, insurance made by them without the prior authority, may be ratified by the subsequent adoption, of the assured. — Sect. 135.

First, with regard to persons procuring sea insurances to be effected at the express request, instance or direction of the assured. In these cases no difficulty can arise as to the authority to insure: every person who is specially requested or directed so to do by the party interested may effect a policy to protect the interests of his employer; if, indeed, he himself puts the policy in suit or founds any legal claim upon it, he must, of course, be prepared, in the first instance, to prove the express authority, as given, whether verbally or in writing. The questions that have arisen in these cases of express authority turn mainly on the point: Under what circumstances does the express order to insure impose on the agent the positive duty of causing the insurance to be effected? And this will be more properly considered when we are discussing the duties and liabilities of insurance agents. — Their express authority.

136. As to the implied authority to insure arising out of the relation of the agent to the parties for whom, or the property on which, the insurance is effected, the following are some of the principal points that have been decided. — Their implied authority.

A partner may, without express authority from the other members of the firm, procure an insurance to be effected for him and them on partnership property; and if, by his directions, such an insurance is effected " on account of the firm," all the members of such firm are liable to the broker, by whom the policy was so effected, for premiums and commissions (a). — A partner has an implied authority to bind his co-partners by insurance;

But the same rule does not apply to part owners, who cannot bind the other part owners by any policy originally — but a part owner, as such, has not.

(a) Hooper v. Lusby (1814), 4 Camp. 66. The vessels in this case, however, were not partnership property, though the defendants carried on business in partnership. It should seem that, in order to constitute a joint liability, general partnership is not necessary; it will be sufficient if the defendants were special partners in the particular adventure intended to be protected by the insurance. See the *dicta* of the judges in Robinson v. Gleadow (1835), 2 Bing. N. C. 156.

Sect. 136. effected without their authority, and not subsequently adopted by their ratification. The reason of this difference is thus stated by Lord Ellenborough: "Each separate share in the ship is the distinct property of each individual part owner, whose business it is to protect it by insurance; so that the insurance of another cannot be binding on such proprietors without some evidence importing an authority by them" (b).

Not even where the part owner is ship's husband.

This is so even where the part owner, who has given orders for the insurance, is ship's husband, or managing owner, appointed by deed in the usual form to act discretionally for all the other owners. Nothing will make his insurance binding on the others, except either a particular direction from them to insure, or satisfactory proof that the other part owners approved and ratified the insurance after it came to their knowledge as a step taken for the general benefit (c). Consequently, without such express direction, or subsequent ratification, the brokers who effect the policy under his directions can only look to him for premiums, and are liable to him alone for the amount received by them for the underwriters on account of losses (d).

Aliter, where the part owners are jointly interested in the adventure insured.

Where, indeed, all the part owners are jointly interested in the particular adventure insured, and the insurance is made by one of them, who is managing owner, for their joint account and benefit, they having full opportunity of learning what has been done, and never objecting to it, this is sufficient to warrant a jury in inferring a joint authority to insure, and will render all the part owners liable to the broker, or his assignees, for premiums, notwithstanding the broker may have debited the managing owner only, and divided with him the profits of commission on effecting the insurance (e).

(b) Per Lord Ellenborough in Bell v. Humphries (1818), 2 Stark. 345. See French v. Backhouse (1771), 5 Burr. 2727.

(c) French v. Backhouse (1771), 5 Burr. 2727; Robinson v. Gleadow (1835), 2 Bing. N. C. 156.

(d) Roberts v. Ogilby (1821), 9 Price, 269.

(e) Robinson v. Gleadow (1835), 2 Bing. N. C. 156. Several of the judges put this decision on the ground, that though the defendants were not general partners, yet they

137. Has a consignor or commission agent, to whom funds are remitted to purchase and ship goods for his employer, an implied authority, as such, in the absence of express orders, to insure such goods on behalf of his principal? No doubt such insurances are not unfrequently made in reliance on their being subsequently adopted by the principal. In the absence of any established course of dealing, prior authority or subsequent adoption, would such insurances be upheld, so as to give the agent who has effected them a right to charge the premium to his principal, or to demand a loss from the underwriter? As a general rule, and in accordance with ordinary mercantile practice, it seems that the answer to this question must be in the negative. Where orders are given to consign, and no orders given to insure, the practical inference generally would be, either that the principal meant to effect the insurance himself, or intended to remain uninsured. Exceptions to the general rule may, of course, be created by circumstances. An established course of dealing between the principal and agent, or the usage of a particular port or trade (*f*), may be reasonably held to confer an implied authority in the consignor to effect an insurance on behalf of his principal (*g*).

Sect. 137.
Implied authority of consignor to insure.

138. The same question may be put with regard to the implied authority of the consignee, as such, to insure. The answer to this question depends on the sense in which the word consignee is used. A consignee who has made advances has, it is clear, not only the right to effect an insurance on

Implied authority of consignee to insure.

---

were special partners in the adventure in which the ships insured were engaged.

(*f*) Duer adds (vol. ii. p. 103): "An authority to insure may probably arise by implication in all cases where, from special or unforeseen circumstances, the agent is justified in believing that the property, unless insured by himself, will be unprotected, and that his principal, if on the spot, would himself direct the insurance." Arnould (2nd ed. p. 167) adopted this on the high authority of Judge Duer; but it may be doubted whether authority could be implied from such a state of things, however reasonable it would be in the agent to insure, relying on the ratification of his principal.

(*g*) 2 Duer, 101—104.

Sect. 138. his own behalf, and to recover thereon to the extent of those advances, but he has also an implied authority to insure on behalf of his consignor (*h*). But a more naked consignee—one, that is, who has no personal interest in the property consigned to him, but is the mere transmittee of the bill of lading, with directions to sell or otherwise dispose of the goods to which it relates—has no implied authority (in the absence of any established course of dealing) to effect insurances on behalf of his consignor, at all events while the goods are in course of transit, and before they have reached his hands (*i*).

Implied authority of general agents of foreign merchants to insure.

Has the general agent of a foreign merchant an implied authority to insure on his behalf? Here, again, the answer to the question must depend on the extent of trust and authority embraced by the term general agency. Where the general agency consists in this, that a merchant in one country consigns all his goods intended for sale in another country to a particular merchant there resident, and effects through him all his purchases, this alone, without some evidence of a special course of dealing in regard to insurances, would not show that either correspondent had implied authority to insure on behalf of the other. But where the trust reposed is more extensive, as, for instance, where a foreign merchant employs a general agent to procure consignments, and make advances and shipments on his account, leaving the whole conduct and management of the business entirely in the agent's uncontrolled and unassisted discretion, no doubt an authority to insure on the foreign merchant's behalf would be implied as a necessary means of conducting the business of such an agency (*k*).

(*h*) Wolff *v.* Horncastle (1798), 1 B. & P. 316; Carruthers *v.* Shedden (1815), 6 Taunt. 14; Smith *v.* Lascelles (1788), 2 T. R. 188; Craufurd *v.* Hunter (1798), 8 T. R. 23.

(*i*) 2 Duer, 104—111; see 2 Phillips, s. 1858.

(*k*) 2 Duer, 111—113. Judge Duer says: "Such agents as those last mentioned are to be found in all our principal cities; and their universal practice is either to insure themselves the shipments made to their principals, or to take an assignment of the policies that, for the security of their principals, they require to be effected": p. 113.

139. An implied authority to insure may arise from the peculiar situation of the property with which the agent effecting the insurance is entrusted. Thus, although the master, as such, has not in general an implied authority to effect insurance either on ship, freight, or cargo (*l*), yet there seems little doubt that cases may arise which would confer that authority on him. Where the ship is lost, but the cargo, or part of it, saved, under such circumstances as to make it impossible either to sell it at the place of disaster or to forward it to the port of destination, the master, if he had the chance of so doing, would be justified, as agent for all parties concerned, in sending it on to some other port for sale. In such a case, if there were no means of speedy communication with the owners, the law that confers the agency would seem also to confer upon the agent authority to insure (*m*). It has been intimated by a learned judge in the United States, that in a similar case a like authority would be implied in the supercargo (*n*). A merchant who has ordered goods from a foreign correspondent may refuse to receive them, if in excess of or not according to order; in such case, if he elect to re-ship them, he has, in the opinion of Lord Hardwicke, an implied authority to insure them on behalf of the consignor (*o*). Generally speaking, as we have seen, a mere order to consign or forward goods will not carry with it an implied authority to insure on behalf of the party giving the order. In a case, however, where an agent was empowered by the owners of a ship and cargo, captured as prize, to prosecute their claims in the foreign

Sect. 139.
Implied authority to insure, arising from the peculiar situation of the property; as of master and supercargo in case of wreck, &c., or prize agents and the like.

(*l*) Craufurd *v.* Hunter (1798), T. R. 23.
(*m*) 2 Duer, 101.
(*n*) Per Jones, J., in De Forest *v.* Fulton Ins. Co. (1828), 1 Hall, 4, cited in 2 Phillips, s. 1856.
(*o*) Cornwall *v.* Wilson (1750), Ves. sen. 214. A buyer who rejects the goods owes no duty to the seller to return them (Sale of Goods Act, 1893, s. 36); and it may be doubted whether, in general, he is entitled, without instructions, to send them back at the seller's expense. See as to his duty, Couston *v.* Chapman (1872), L. R. 2 H. L. Sc. 250; Grimoldby *v.* Wells (1875), L. R. 10 C. P. 391. Mr. Arthur Cohen questions Lord Hardwicke's dictum: Laws of England, vol. xvii. § 699, note (*b*).

Sect. 139. prize court, to make such compromise as he might deem advisable, and, in case of restitution, "to forward the ship to London:" it having been objected that these circumstances raised no implied authority in the agent to direct an insurance on the property after restitution, Lord Ellenborough held that the order to forward the ship to London was an authority to insure her (*p*).

Ratification equivalent to a prior authority.

140. The cases hitherto considered have been those in which a prior authority to insure has either been expressly given, or has been implied from the relation of the parties effecting the policy, either to those for whose benefit the insurance is intended, or to the property designed to be protected. It is not, however, essential to prove any prior authority, either expressed or implied. By sect. 86 of the Marine Insurance Act, 1906, "where a contract of marine insurance is in good faith effected by one person on behalf of another, the person on whose behalf it is effected may ratify the contract even after he is aware of the loss" (*q*). Such subsequent ratification is equivalent to a prior authority (*omnis ratihabitio retrotrahitur et mandato æquiparatur*) (*r*).

(*p*) Robertson *v.* Hamilton (1811), 14 East, 522. See the case stated and commented on, 2 Duer, 101, 102.

(*q*) The leading authorities are: Wolff *v.* Horncastle (1798), 1 B. & P. 316; Lucena *v.* Craufurd (1806), 2 B. & P. N. R. 269; Stirling *v.* Vaughan (1809), 11 East, 623; Routh *v.* Thompson (1811), 13 East, 274; Hagedorn *v.* Oliverson (1814), 2 M. & S. 485; Robinson *v.* Gleadow (1835), 2 Bing. N. C. 156; Watson *v.* Swann (1862), 11 C. B. N. S. 756; 31 L. J. C. P. 210; Boston Fruit Co. *v.* British & Foreign Mar. Ins. Co., [1906] A. C. 336.

(*r*) In Keighley, Maxted & Co. *v.* Durant, [1901] A. C. 240, the House of Lords held that the doctrine of ratification has no application where the person who made the contract did not profess at the time of making it to be acting on behalf of any principal. In Boston Fruit Co. *v.* British & Foreign Mar. Ins. Co., [1906] A. C. at p. 343, Lord Atkinson doubted whether since this decision the doctrine can survive that an insurance, if ratified, protects those whom the person dealing with the underwriter intended to be insured, when such intention was not communicated to the underwriter. As, however, the ordinary English policy professes in terms to be effected on behalf of other persons interested in the subject-matter insured, the editors submit that the decision in Keighley, Maxted & Co. *v.* Durant

Thus, although one part owner has no original implied authority from the rest to insure on their account, yet, if he does so, and they subsequently adopt the insurance, they are bound by it (*s*). So, although the captors of a prize have no original implied authority to insure, yet, if they do insure, for whom it may concern, and the Crown, in whom the legal interest vests, subsequently adopts the insurance, it is thereby rendered valid (*t*). Whether the clerk of a foreign consignee has, as such, a prior implied authority to direct an insurance to be effected by English correspondents of his master on a consignment made by them on account, and to the orders, of his employer, may be doubtful; but subsequent adoption by the foreign principal of the insurance so effected will amply warrant a jury in finding that such insurance was made with his authority (*u*).

<small>Sect. 140.</small>

141. With regard to the nature of the evidence required to establish the fact of ratification, positive proof of an express ratification is not needful. The adoption of the policy may be inferred from the conduct of him for whose benefit it was originally intended. If he means to reject it, he should express his dissent as soon as he is informed of the fact; if he fail in so doing, his adoption of the contract will, generally speaking, be inferred from his silence (*x*). At all events, this will be so in cases where those who have effected the insurance, instead of being mere strangers or volunteers,

<small>Ratification of insurance may be implied from conduct.</small>

---

does not affect the right of the intended principal to ratify the contract. See *post*, §§ 172, 173.

(*s*) French *v.* Backhouse (1771), 5 Burr. 2727; Robinson *v.* Gleadow (1835), 2 Bing. N. C. 156.

(*t*) Routh *v.* Thompson (1811), 13 East, 274. So of the Dutch Prize Commissioners, Lucena *v.* Cranfurd (1806), 2 B. & P. N. R. 269.

(*u*) Barlow *v.* Leckie (1819), 4 J. B. Moore, 8.

(*x*) So Phillips (vol. i. s. 390).

In view of the now-established doctrine in this country, that a principal may ratify even after knowledge of a loss (Mar. Ins. Act, 1906, s. 86, *ante*, § 140), this would probably be held to be law here; otherwise a party interested would be able to lie by for an indefinite time, and eventually elect to take the benefit of the insurance in case of a loss, or to repudiate liability for premiums in case of safe arrival.

Sect. 141. stand in such relations of business or correspondence as would give them, not indeed an implied authority to insure, but a reasonable ground for anticipating that the policy, when made, would be adopted by him for whom it was designed (*y*).

Evidence of ratification.

Thus, in the case of part owners: where no proof could be adduced of an express authority to insure, but evidence was given that the part owner insuring had "told all his co-partners that he had insured, and that they did not object to it" (*z*); or where it appeared that the part owner insuring had entered the premium in his books, which were open to the inspection of the other owners, and that they had actually inspected an extract made from these books relating to the insurance transaction without objecting to it; juries were held to be justified in finding that the part owner insuring had done so with the authority of his co-owners (*a*).

Conditional ratification.

142. A ratification, conditional in its terms, has been held in the United States to be equivalent to a prior authority as soon as the contingency on which it was to depend has happened. The general agent, at New York, of a merchant resident at Carthagena, having effected an insurance for him without instructions, gave him notice of what he had done. The Carthagena merchant wrote in answer, that, if other insurances which he had ordered should not have been made, and if the ship should not have arrived safe, he wished the policy to stand, otherwise to be cancelled. When this answer was received in New York the other insurance referred to had not been made, and the ship (which was then out of

---

(*y*) This distinction is suggested by Judge Duer, vol. ii. pp. 151—154. See also note (*v*) to sect. x. pp. 178—182, in which he discusses the question "whether the mere omission of the principal to reply to a letter of advice from a self-constituted agent is to be regarded as evidence of an adoption of the agent's act." The learned jurist takes the negative view.

(*z*) French *v.* Backhouse (1771), 5 Burr. 2727. The action here was by the ship's husband against his co-part-owners to recover back premiums on a policy effected by him on the owners' behalf.

(*a*) Robinson *v.* Gleadow (1835), 2 Bing. N. C. 156. The action was by the assignees of the broker against all the part owners for premiums.

time) had not arrived; in fact, was totally lost. An action having been brought in the Superior Court of New York on the policy, Oakley, J., before whom the case was tried, held the ratification sufficient, and a judgment was recovered for the loss (*b*).

The adoption, as we have seen, may be made not only after a loss has taken place, but even after it has become known to the principal (*c*); and in one case the only evidence of adoption was a letter written by the principal two years after the making of the insurance, and nearly as long after he had become aware of the loss, expressing a hope that the party who had effected the policy had procured a final settlement from the underwriters (*d*). Accordingly, the Court of Appeal, when asked to review these cases in order to limit more narrowly the time for valid ratification, recognized the rule as one that had been long established, and no doubt found convenient in the case of marine insurance, and therefore refused to disturb it (*e*).

That, however, which is relied upon as a ratification must be done, said, or written by the principal after he is cognizant of the insurance. A general order to insure, given by the principal before knowledge of the particular insurance, though not received by the party insuring till after the policy was effected, cannot, it seems, be construed into an adoption of such policy (*f*).

Sect. 142.

When the adoption must be made.

(*b*) Bridge *v.* Niagara Ins. Co. (1828), 1 Hall, 247, cited 2 Phillips on Ins. s. 1868. In point of fact, a conditional order ceases to be so, and becomes positive, when, before receipt by the party who is to execute it, its conditions have been fulfilled.

(*c*) Mar. Ins. Act, 1906, s. 86, *ante*, § 140. Lucena *v.* Craufurd; Routh *v.* Thompson; Barlow *v.* Leckie, *ubi supra*, are all cases in which the principal ratified the insurance with knowledge of the loss. This rule is peculiar to marine insurances: Grover *v.* Mathews, [1910] 2 K. B. 401.

(*d*) Hagedorn *v.* Oliverson (1814), 2 M. & S. 485.

(*e*) Williams *v.* North China Ins. Co. (1876), 1 C. P. D. 757. In view of this decision, it is probably the law now, as stated by Phillips, vol. i. s. 390, that ratification, and consequent liability for premiums, is presumed in the absence of express repudiation within a reasonable time after notice. See *ante*, § 141, note (*x*).

(*f*) Bell *v.* Janson (1813), 1 M. & S. 201.

Sect. 143.
Ratification of an insurance effected by a voluntary agent.

143. It is, however, necessary, in order to justify an adoption or ratification of such a contract, that the "voluntary agent"—or, in other words, the party who has without authority effected the contract—should have intended to be acting on behalf of the person claiming to adopt or ratify it. He must also have intended to look to such person for the reimbursement of his necessary expenses in the transaction (*g*). "It is clear," said Erle, C. J., "that no one can use on a contract but the person who made it, or the person who ratified what purported (*h*) to be a contract made by his agent. . . . A very wide extension has been given to this principle . . . in respect of a policy of assurance, and persons who could not be named at the time, if intended to come within it, and so capable of being ascertained, have been allowed to be entitled to the benefit of the same: but they must have been such as were contemplated at the time when the policy was made" (*i*).

In Byas *v.* Miller, an insurance broker at Lloyd's was instructed by principals at Liverpool to reinsure goods for a voyage at a certain premium. He was unable to execute the order at the rate mentioned, but obtained from the defendant, an underwriter, a slip at a higher premium, and

---

(*g*) See 2 Duer, 135. The whole subject of voluntary agency and ratification is learnedly discussed in pp. 132—155.

(*h*) As to the meaning of this word, the Lords Justices in Durant *v.* Roberts, [1900] 1 Q. B. 629, took different views. The dissenting opinion of A. L. Smith, L. J., was approved by the House of Lords, Keighley, Maxted & Co. *v.* Durant, [1901] A. C. 240. The fact that a person who effects a policy in his own name is an insurance broker may, it is suggested, be enough to show that he professes to be acting for a principal.

(*i*) In Watson *v.* Swann (1862), 11 C. B. N. S. 756; 31 L. J. C. P. 210, Willes, J., considered that the intended principal must be a person who is capable of being ascertained at the time the contract is made. Mathew, J., seems to have been of the same opinion. "It is imperatively necessary," he said in Byas *v.* Miller (1897), 3 Com. Cas. 39, "that the insurance should be intended to be effected by the agent on behalf of some person capable of identification, and responsible to the broker for the premiums that the broker undertakes to pay to the underwriter." See further on this point, *post*, §§ 171—173, and see also Keighley, Maxted & Co. *v.* Durant, *ubi supra.*

CHAP. VII.] THEIR RIGHTS, DUTIES AND LIABILITIES. 199

sent to the Liverpool firm a cover-note stating that he had Sect. 143.
reinsured provisionally for their account at the higher rate:
this insurance, however, the Liverpool firm refused to accept.
The broker shortly afterwards issued to the plaintiffs a fresh
cover-note in respect of an interest which they had in the
same goods, the defendant's name being inserted therein as
underwriter; and within two or three weeks the goods were
totally lost. A few days later a policy in the ordinary form
was tendered to, and signed by, the defendant in accordance
with the slip. The defendant never knew the names of the
original principals of the broker, nor did he ever know, until
after the loss, that the broker had appropriated the slip to
clients for whom he was not acting at the time when the slip
was signed. It was held, in accordance with the principles
above stated, that there was no contract between the plaintiffs
and the defendant (*k*).

144. With regard to the revocation of an express authority *When an*
to insure given to an agent, the time within which it may be *express*
made depends, of course, upon this: whether the agent, acting *insure may*
in pursuance of the authority, has conclusively bound himself *be revoked.*
or third parties before receiving notice of the revocation. If
he have not, the revocation will be operative; if he have, it
will be ineffectual. In this country no contract for sea
insurance is valid unless it be expressed in a policy containing
the particulars required by the Stamp Act, 1891 (*l*). Hence,
the authority given to an insurance agent may be revoked,
notwithstanding the initialing of the slip by the underwriters, at any time before the formal policy is subscribed;

(*k*) Byas *v.* Miller, *ubi supra*. Act, 1906, *ante*, § 140, may be con-
The facts and the decision in strued as implying that the volun-
Watson *v.* Swann were very similar. tary agent must have an honest
In Byas *v.* Miller, Mathew, J., belief that the intended principal
seems to have considered that a expects, or would, if aware of the
purely speculative insurance cannot facts, expect that he will effect the
be ratified. Such a limitation of insurance.
the rule is not unreasonable, and it (*l*) See also Mar. Ins. Act, ss. 22
is possible that the words "in good —24.
faith" in s. 86 of the Mar. Ins.

Sect. 144. and if a broker, having procured a slip to be written on terms within the scope of his original authority, afterwards receive an intimation from his principals that they will not consent to such terms, and, notwithstanding such notice, effect a policy on those terms, and pay the premiums to the underwriters, he cannot recover against his employers for the premiums so paid (*m*), nor for his commission (*n*).

Duties and liabilities of agents for the assured.
Agents paid and unpaid, skilled and unskilled.

145. The liability of insurance agents to their employers for negligence is determined by the general principles of the law of agency (*o*). All such agents, whether paid or unpaid, skilled or unskilled, are bound to exercise due care in the performance of the duties which they have undertaken. A greater degree of care, however, is required from a paid than from an unpaid, from a skilled than from an unskilled, agent. In other words, conduct which amounts to actionable negligence in a paid or in a skilled agent may not amount to such in one who is unpaid or unskilled. In view of recent authorities, this seems to be a better way of stating the law than to say that the one is liable for ordinary, but the other only liable for gross negligence (*p*).

Application of these principles.

The great majority of persons employed in the business of sea insurances are both paid and skilled agents, or, at all

---

(*m*) Warwick *v.* Slade (1811), 3 Camp. 127. We have, however, elsewhere advanced the view that the slip may itself be a valid policy: if this view be correct, the revocation by the principals would be too late. See *ante*, §§ 37, 38.

(*n*) So Arnould, 2nd ed. p. 174. But no question of commission appears to have been raised in Warwick *v.* Slade, and the editors suggest that under the circumstances the principals might have been liable to pay, if not commission, at least damages for preventing the broker from earning it. The editors are, however, informed that it is not the practice to claim brokerage when the insurance is cancelled before the policy has been issued. Whether such practice amounts to a binding usage, they are unable to say.

(*o*) See Coggs *v.* Bernard and notes, in Smith's Leading Cases; Story on Agency, 149, 150. A broker who effects a contract of insurance with an underwriter is not his agent, and owes no duty of care or skill to him: Empress Ass. Corporation *v.* Bowring (1906), 11 Com. Cas. 107; Glasgow Ass. Corpn. *v.* Symondson (1911), 16 Com. Cas. 109.

(*p*) Cf. 2nd ed. of this work, pp. 174, 175

CHAP. VII.] THEIR RIGHTS, DUTIES AND LIABILITIES. 201

events, either the one or the other. Generally speaking, therefore, the question of their liability for negligence turns on the point, whether they exerted such an amount of reasonable skill in effecting the policy as is ordinarily possessed and exercised by persons of common capacity, engaged in the same business or employment. From a policy broker, whose main occupation it is to manage sea insurance transactions, a higher degree of skill may fairly be claimed than from a merchant or commission agent, who may be expected, indeed, to possess a general knowledge of maritime and mercantile affairs, but no special knowledge of the business of sea insurance.

Sect. 145.

Notwithstanding doubts which at one time prevailed, it may now be considered as settled law, that a person who voluntarily and without consideration undertakes to effect insurances for another is liable for negligence in doing so, if he takes any steps towards performance of his undertaking (*q*). But if the person who voluntarily promises, without any kind of consideration, to procure an insurance never takes any steps whatever towards the performance of his promise, he is not liable to an action for the non-feasance (*r*).

Liability of a party voluntarily undertaking to procure an insurance for another.

146. Generally speaking, a person to whom an order to insure has been transmitted is under no obligation to accept the trust; but there are certain cases in which an express order to insure, not only may, but must be complied with.

Three cases in which agents requested to procure insurance must do so.

1. Where a merchant abroad has effects in the hands of his

(*q*) Wallace *v.* Tellfair (1788), 2 T. R. 188, n., before Buller, J., at N. P., cited in Wilkinson *v.* Coverdale (1793), 1 Esp. 75. In the latter case Lord Kenyon held, that where the seller of a house had voluntarily undertaken to get a fire policy renewed for the plaintiff, and had in fact renewed it, but without procuring a proper indorsement, whereby plaintiff was deprived of the benefit of the insurance, this was actionable negligence.

(*r*) Thorne *v.* Deas (1809), 4 Johns. N. Y. R. 84—a decision of Chief Justice (afterwards Chancellor) Kent. Duer approves of this decision as a correct exposition of the law, though he remarks forcibly on the hardship which may thus be inflicted on the party who trusts to the promise of the volunteer. 2 Duer, 128—130; see the Carpenters' Case, Year Books, xi. H. iv. p. 33, ed. 1679.

Sect. 146. agent or correspondent here, he has a right to expect that the agent will comply with an order to insure; because he is entitled to call his money out of the other's hands when, and in what manner, he pleases.

2. Where the merchant abroad has no effects in the hands of his correspondent here, but the course of dealing between them has been such that the one has been used to send orders for insurance, and the other to execute them, the former has a right to expect that his orders for insurance will still be obeyed, unless the latter give him notice to discontinue that course of dealing.

3. Where the merchant abroad sends bills of lading to his correspondent here, with an order to insure as the implied condition on which he is to accept the bills of lading, and the correspondent accepts the bills of lading, he must obey the order; for it is one entire transaction, and the acceptance of the bills of lading amounts to an implied agreement to perform the condition (*s*).

The rules thus stated are believed to be as universal in their observance as they are unquestionably well founded in justice and equity.

Where the obligation to insure arises from a previous course of dealing, and the agent has no funds in hand.

147. Where the obligation to insure arises from a previous course of dealing, and the agent has no funds in hand, Duer suggests that he would be excused from compliance if, when he receives the order, he has just grounds for believing that his correspondent is insolvent (*t*). This may be so; but in practice it will be the safer course for the agent to obey the order, unless his information of his correspondent's insolvency be of such a nature as leave him no ground for doubt.

Where the insurances are out of the usual course.

Duer also thinks that "the obligation to insure that arises from a previous course of dealing can only apply to insurances similar to those that the agent had been in the habit of effecting. If the past assurances had all been effected in a time of peace, at a low rate of premium, and requiring in

(*s*) Per Buller, J., in Smith *v.* Lascelles (1788), 2 T. R. 189, 190.
(*t*) 2 Duer, 124.

each case only a moderate advance, they would give the principal no right to expect that an order to insure in a time of war, not accompanied by a remittance of the necessary funds, would be obeyed" (*u*). It may be a question, however, how far this would be so held in this country, where an immediate advance in respect of the premium is hardly ever required in practice at the time of effecting the policy.

There can be no doubt as to another position of the very learned American jurist, "that where the necessary funds for procuring the insurance are remitted to a commission merchant or insurance broker, he is under an equal obligation to apply them to the purpose directed as where the funds are in his hands when the order is received" (*x*). {*Where funds are remitted.*}

It also seems free from doubt that the duty of insuring may be imposed on an agent, even in the absence of express directions to insure, by the usage of the particular trade to which his agency and the insurance relate (*y*).

148. If an agent is employed by a foreign correspondent to procure an insurance under circumstances which, according to the rules laid down by Buller, J., in Smith *v.* Lascelles, give the correspondent a right to expect such orders will be complied with, a total failure to comply with such orders, without notice, will subject such agent to an action for all the loss which his correspondent may have sustained from the non-insurance (*z*). It is his duty to give prompt notice of his refusal to act upon such orders, in order that his employer may not be deprived of the opportunity of effecting the insurance elsewhere. If, in consequence of his failure to give such notice, no insurance be made, the agent will be answerable to his employer for the loss arising from his neglect (*a*). {*Agent instructed to insure will be liable for neglect to do so.*} {*Unless he give prompt notice of dissent.*}

(*u*) 2 Duer, 125.
(*x*) *Ibid.*
(*y*) *Ibid.* 127, 128.
(*z*) Smith *v.* Lascelles (1788), 2 T. R. 187; Smith *v.* Price, *coram* Erle, C. J. (1862), 2 F. & F. 748. See 2 Duer, 120.
(*a*) *Ibid.* Observations of Ashurst, J., 2 T. R. 188. See the general principle in Prince *v.* Clark (1823), 1 B. & Cr. 186. On an analogous principle, unless otherwise agreed, where goods are sent by the seller to the buyer by a route involving sea transit, under circumstances in which it is usual

Sect. 148.   Hence, where a merchant in this country received from a merchant abroad, with whom he had no previous connection, a bill of lading, with a request to insure the goods, and the merchant, not wishing to take to the consignment, but without giving any notice to the consignor that he rejected it, handed over the bill of lading and the order to insure to a creditor of the consignor, who effected the insurance and received the goods, and afterwards became insolvent with the proceeds in his hands; it was held, that the merchant, who had his election either to accept or reject the bill of lading, was yet bound, if he accepted it, to comply with the terms of the consignment, and was liable for the consequences of not having done so (*b*). So also, in the event of any difficulties in procuring the insurance on the terms prescribed by the principal, it is the duty of the parties employed to give notice of such difficulties to their employer within a reasonable time.

Or of difficulties.

Callander *v.* Oelrichs.

149. The plaintiff, a merchant in this country, had instructed the defendants, who were his commission agents and correspondents in America, to effect an insurance for him, on certain prescribed terms (viz., that the insurers should be liable for every average loss above 10*l*. per cent.), upon a cargo of wheat shipped by him from London to Baltimore, and consigned to the defendants, to be sold and disposed of on commission. The defendants attempted in vain to procure an insurance on the terms prescribed, but gave no notice to

to insure, the seller must give such notice to the buyer as may enable him to insure them, and if he fails to do so, they will be at his risk during the voyage: Sale of Goods Act, 1893, s. 32 (3). As to the position of the parties, with regard to insurance, under a "c.i.f." contract, see Orient Co. *v.* Brekke, [1913] 1 K. B. 531, and cases there cited; for the position under a "f.o.b." contract, see Wimble *v.* Rosenberg, [1913] 3 K. B. 743.

(*b*) Corlett *v.* Gordon (1813), 3 Camp. 472. The action, however, was in trover and conversion, for allowing the creditor to obtain possession of the goods. It does not necessarily follow from this case that if the defendants had done nothing they would have been liable. The case might be different where there have been previous dealings between the parties. See the cases above cited.

the plaintiff of their failure to do so, and instead thereof effected an insurance on the usual terms (by which the insurers on wheat are exempted from all liability for average, unless general, or the ship stranded). The Court of Common Pleas held, that the giving of such notice was part of the common law duty of the defendants, to be implied from their retainer as commission agents with express orders to insure, and that the plaintiff, therefore, was entitled to recover in an action brought against them for the breach of such duty (*c*). In this case the damage alleged was, that by reason of the defendants' failure in giving notice, the plaintiff had been prevented from effecting an insurance on the wheat on the terms proposed, and thereby precluded from recovering for an average loss. As Judge Duer remarks, no proof appears to have been given that an insurance could have been effected on the terms proposed; as, however, by agreeing to refer the amount of damages, it was conceded that some *damnum* had been incurred (and none could have been incurred if no insurance could have been effected as ordered), it must be taken to have been admitted that the protection which the plaintiff wished might, with due diligence and a proper exercise of discretion, have been procured (*d*).

Sect. 149.

150. A foreign principal has a right to expect the same amount of ordinary care, skill and diligence in procuring an insurance that the principal himself, as a man of common prudence and knowledge of business, might reasonably have been expected to exercise, had he been upon the spot and himself engaged in endeavouring to effect it. Hence, where the foreign correspondent of a mercantile firm in this country directed them, as his agents, to procure an insurance for him, without prescribing any limit of premium, and they limited the broker to so low a rate of premium that it was impossible to effect an insurance on such terms, they were held liable to their foreign employer for the loss arising from the failure to

A correspondent for a foreign house must show the skill and diligence of a prudent man of business.

(*c*) Callander *v.* Oelrichs (1838), 5 Bing. N. C. 58; 6 Scott, 761.
(*d*) 2 Duer, 222—225.

Sect. 150. insure (*e*). On the same principle, where a policy had been effected, but the agents neglected to ascertain the solvency of the underwriters, and to communicate the names of the brokers, by whom it was effected in their own names, so that, when a loss on the property occurred, the assured were unable to obtain payment of the whole insurance money, the agent was held liable for the deficiency caused by the insolvency of the brokers and of one of the underwriters (*f*).

If, however, the agent does all that the foreign principal, on the spot and acting with due care, skill and diligence as a man of business, could reasonably be expected to do, he will not be liable for the consequences of a failure to procure insurance. Thus, where the correspondents in London of a foreign merchant, being directed by him to procure an insurance, and, having failed to do so at Lloyd's because the ship was not in Lloyd's register, ultimately caused it to be effected with a Newcastle company through the medium of the shipowners, who afterwards refused to deliver up the policy, or pay over a loss they had received on it from the underwriters, it was intimated to the jury by Buller, J., before whom the case was tried, that this afforded no ground of action against the agents for negligence in effecting the policy (*g*). "If," said the learned Judge, "the defendants had made a blunder in effecting the insurance, which would have avoided the policy, that would have been negligence; but the policy is a good one, and it was only owing to the knavery and insolvency of the shipowners that the plaintiffs have lost the benefit of it" (*g*).

How far must agent go in quest of insurance?

At the present day, Buller, J., would hardly be justified in the doubt, which he expressed in this case, whether the defendants, who lived in London, were bound to seek insurance elsewhere than at Lloyd's, as, for instance, at the public

---

(*e*) Wallace *v.* Tellfair (1788), 2 T. R. 188, *in notis*.

(*f*) Hurrell *v.* Bullard, *coram* Cockburn, C. J. (1863), 3 F. & F. 445.

(*g*) Smith *v.* Cologan (1788), at N. P., 2 T. R. 188, *in notis*. The verdict was given partly, if not principally, on the ground that the foreign correspondents had adopted the agents' acts.

metropolitan insurance offices. They would perhaps, however, not be bound to extend their endeavours beyond the limits of the metropolis. In the case of correspondents resident in provincial towns the obligation might be different.

Sect. 150.

151. In the United States the extent of the obligation to procure insurance has been well illustrated in the following case:—The correspondents in Boston of shippers at Surinam received orders to effect insurance on a valuable cargo on their account. When this order was received the ship was out of time, and the insurance was declined, on that ground, by the insurers at Boston, to whom the agents applied on the very day they received the letter. They subsequently tried in vain to effect the insurance at Salem, Newburyport, Portsmouth and Providence, the principal commercial places within sixty miles. They then wrote to New York for the same purpose, fixing a limit (but a very high one) to the rate of premium; part of the amount was eventually insured there at high premiums (the highest being $33\frac{1}{2}$ per cent.); the rest could not be done at the limit. An action having been subsequently brought against them for not having insured the whole amount, a verdict was found for the defendants under the direction of the presiding Judge, on the ground that in their prompt endeavours to procure insurance at Boston and the other neighbouring ports, they had extended their efforts at least as far as their duty required, and that, having done so, they were not liable for having failed in procuring a full insurance at New York, though such failure might possibly have been ascribed to their having set a limit on the premium (*h*).

152. In none of these cases does the law require an extraordinary degree of skill on the part of the agent, but only such a reasonable and ordinary proportion of it as persons of

A reasonable and average degree of skill is all that is required.

(*h*) Sanches *v.* Davenport (1810), 6 Mass. R. 258; cited 2 Duer, 242 —244; 2 Phillips, s. 1890. It might, however, now be considered reasonable to take steps which a hundred years ago would not have been required.

Sect. 152. average capacity in his situation and profession might fairly be expected to exert. In inquiries, therefore, as to his liability in case of loss, the question is, whether the act or omission complained of is inconsistent with that reasonable and proper degree of care, skill and judgment which persons of common prudence or ordinary ability might be expected to show in the situation and profession of the defendant (*i*).

Duty of broker to communicate the time of the ship's sailing.

Every policy broker of average capacity must know that all communications respecting the time of the ship's sailing are material to be submitted to the underwriter. Hence, where a policy broker, who was supplied by his principal with the requisite information as to the time of sailing, omitted, through inadvertence, to forward it to a second broker, who at the wish of the principal was employed to effect the policy, it was held that the first broker was liable to his principal for the failure of insurance arising out of this neglect; for although he personally was to receive no remuneration, he had yet undertaken to employ the other (*k*).

Effect of withholding information, the materiality of which is a doubtful point.

Where, however, the materiality of the information is of a more doubtful description, and has been made the subject of nicely-balanced legal decisions, or may fairly be a matter of divided opinion amongst persons conversant with the trade, it may very reasonably be urged that a policy broker, though acting in the ordinary way as a paid agent, may be ignorant of the point without such a degree of negligence as to make him responsible for the failure of a policy he was directed to effect, owing to the withholding by him of such information (*l*).

(*i*) Per Tindal, C. J., in Chapman *v.* Walton (1833), 10 Bing. 63.

(*k*) Seller *v.* Work (1801), 1 Marshall on Ins. 306. See Duer's remarks on this case, vol. ii. pp. 202, 203; see also Maydew *v.* Forrester (1814), 5 Taunt. 615, as to the point that, whenever the information concealed is unquestionably material, the broker will be liable; see also, as to what constitutes negligence, Wake *v.* Atty (1812), 4 Taunt. 493.

(*l*) See the observations of Lord Denman in Campbell *v.* Rickards (1833), 5 B. & Ad. 844, 845; see also Rickards *v.* Murdock (1830), 10 B. & Cr. 527.

153. Every policy broker is bound to know all the ordinary and formal details necessary to be complied with in order to make a sea-policy a legally valid instrument.

Sect. 153.

Hence, a policy broker employed to effect a policy on a ship, having negotiated an insurance with the Newcastle Commercial Insurance Company on the terms directed, was held liable for not procuring a stamped policy, in consequence of which neglect the shipowner was unable to recover from the company in respect of a loss that subsequently took place (*m*).

Duty of broker to procure the delivery of a stamped policy.

Every policy broker, or other insurance agent, is bound, without any express directions, to insert in the policy all the ordinary risks and customary clauses, which are usual and proper in respect of the contemplated voyage. Thus, as it was shown to be the invariable practice in all voyages from Teneriffe to London to insert a clause giving liberty "to touch and stay at all or any of the Canary Islands," it was held that a London policy broker was guilty of actionable negligence in omitting this clause, and thereby causing the failure of the insurance (*n*).

Duty of broker to insert all usual and ordinary clauses.

It has been repeatedly and notoriously decided, that a policy on goods, "beginning the adventure from the loading thereof on board," without any addition, only attaches on goods loaded at the port which is the terminus *a quo* of the voyage insured (*o*). So completely is this settled law, that all insurance brokers are bound to know and act on it. Hence, a London policy broker, being directed to effect a policy for a voyage "from Gibraltar to Dublin" upon goods which, by his instructions, clearly appeared to have been

Commencement of risk on goods must be properly described.

(*m*) Turpin *v.* Bilton (1843), 5 M. & G. 455. By s. 97 of the Stamp Act, 1891, a broker writing any policy of sea insurance upon material not duly stamped, or otherwise offending against the true intent of the Act, forfeits all claim for brokerage and expenses, and is also liable to penalties.

(*n*) Mallough *v.* Barber (1814), 4 Camp. 150.

(*o*) Robertson *v.* French (1803), 4 East, 130; Spitta *v.* Woodman (1810), 2 Taunt. 416; Horneyer *v.* Lushington (1812), 15 East, 46; Mellish *v.* Allnutt (1813), 2 M. & S. 106.

Sect. 153. loaded on board at Malaga, was held liable for negligence in having effected the policy on such goods in the common printed form, "at and from Gibraltar to Dublin, beginning the adventure upon the said goods and merchandise from the loading thereof aboard the said ship" (*p*).

Broker not liable where mistake due to uncertainty of law or practice.

154. The rule which we have been discussing regards what is ordinary, usual, and settled; when we leave the common beaten track it ceases to be applicable. As Judge Duer well expresses it, "The mistake of the agent, where the practice is unsettled, or the law uncertain, affords no evidence of that want of reasonable skill and ordinary diligence for which alone he is responsible" (*q*).

Unless the directions of his principal are clear and precise.

If the directions given be clear, precise and intelligible, the failure of the insurance agent to comply therewith is actionable, where it has caused damage to the principal, although the directions may embrace a partially illegal insurance. Thus, where clear directions were given by the plaintiffs (foreign merchants) to the defendants, (their London mercantile agents) to insure goods and also the premium, and the defendants insured the goods but not the premium; it was held that they were liable to the plaintiffs in damages for not complying with this order to insure, and that they could not avail themselves of the defence that the order also directed them to insure against British capture, for although on that ground they might have renounced the order altogether, yet, having adopted it, they were bound to execute it as far as by law they might *secundum formam jubentis* (*r*).

All prior verbal communications are superseded by subsequent written instructions.

155. An agent who has faithfully followed express written instructions to insure will not be liable for having omitted to insert a provision in the policy which, according to the verbal

(*p*) Park *v.* Hammond (1814), Holt, N. P. 80; *S. C.*, 4 Camp. 344; 2 Marshall's R. 189; 6 Taunt. 495. This last report, as Duer points out, commits the absurd mistake of stating the risk under the policy to have been on the goods "from the loading thereof on board at Gibraltar": 2 Duer, 209, n. (*b*).

(*q*) 2 Duer, 214.

(*r*) Glaser *v.* Cowie (1813), 1 M. & S. 52.

communications of his principal, he might fairly have inferred to be necessary for the complete protection of the insured property. Thus, where the captain of a ship told a policy broker, in the course of conversation, that the ship was to carry simulated papers, but afterwards sent him written instructions for effecting a policy on the ship, in which nothing whatever was said as to inserting a liberty to carry them, the broker was held not to be liable in an action for negligence in not inserting the clause, though the ship was subsequently condemned for carrying such papers (*s*).

Sect. 155.

In case the orders of the principal are so ambiguous as to be susceptible of two distinct meanings, and the agent *bonâ fide* adopts one of them and acts upon it, it is not competent to the principal to complain of the act as unauthorized, because he meant the order to be read in the other sense, of which it is equally capable (*t*).

Where instructions are ambiguous.

156. An agent acting under a general order to insure is not bound to do more than effect an insurance in the form in general use at the place to which the order refers (*u*). If the principal wishes to have the insurance effected in a particular mode, or with a particular class of insurers, he should give specific instructions to that effect.

An agent acting under a general order to insure need only effect a policy in the general form.

In the case, indeed, of a foreign principal, who is not proved to have, and cannot reasonably be presumed to have, a know-

---

(*s*) Fomin *v.* Oswell (1813), 3 Camp. 357. "The captain," Lord Ellenborough remarked, "notwithstanding his prior conversation, might have resolved not to carry any such papers, or if he still meant to carry them, might not have wished that a leave for that purpose should have been inserted in the policy."

(*t*) Ireland *v.* Livingstone (1871), L. R. 5 H. L. 395.

(*u*) Cf. Yuill *v.* Scott-Robson, [1907] 1 K. B. 685; [1908] 1 K. B. 270, C. A., in which a seller of cattle who had contracted to insure them "against all risks" was held not to have satisfied the contract by procuring a Lloyd's policy in the usual form, containing the "free of capture" clause.

Where a sale contract contained a clause: "Insurance to be effected by (the sellers) all risks," Hamilton, J., held that they had satisfied the contract by effecting an insurance covering the entire quantum of damage, although it did not cover a loss of cargo improperly shipped on deck in breach of the contract of carriage: Vincentelli *v.* Rowlett (1911), 16 Com. Cas. 310.

Sect. 156. ledge of the different usages of the various offices or classes of insurers at the place to which the order refers, it might *à priori* have been fairly deemed part of the agent's duty, even though acting only under a general order to insure, to take care and select that office, or that class of insurers, with whom he might have secured the most complete protection of the property to be insured, on the most advantageous terms. If directed, for instance, under a general order, to insure a certain description of goods, which at some of the insurance offices of the place to which the order referred might be completely protected, and at others not, the premium in both cases being the same, and the solvency of the insurers equal, the agent of a foreign principal would seem not to exercise that amount of reasonable skill to be fairly required of him by insuring with the office which, for the same amount of premium, afforded the less complete amount of protection.

Moore *v.* Mourgue.

The following case, however, is to the contrary:—The plaintiff (a merchant of Alicant) brought his action against the defendant (his agent in London) for not insuring the plaintiff's goods agreeably to his directions. The goods were a cargo of fruit: the plaintiff had given the defendant no particular directions how or with whom to insure, but only a general order "to insure the cargo." The defendant effected the policy with the London Insurance Office, who only insured fruit "free from particular average"—an exception not to be found in the policies of Lloyd's, or the Royal Exchange, who, however, insured fruit at the same premium as the London. An average loss having happened on the fruit, the plaintiff was precluded from recovering anything, owing to the exception. For the plaintiff it was contended, that though the order to insure was general, yet the defendant was bound to execute it in such a manner as would effectually answer the end proposed; that the very nature of the commodity showed it was liable to an average loss, a danger against which the defendant ought accordingly to have guarded; that, as there were two offices in London (Lloyd's and the Royal Exchange) where this exception was never put in, it was gross negligence in the defendant not to have insured with them. Lord Mansfield left it generally to the jury, that if they thought there was gross negligence, or that the defendant had acted *malâ fide,* they should find for the plaintiff, otherwise for the defendant; the jury found for the defendant, on the ground that they thought he had acted *bonâ fide* and to the best of his judgment, and this verdict the Court in Banc refused to disturb. "The plaintiff," said Lord Mansfield, "if he pleased, might have given orders to the defendant not to insure at the London Insurance Office, but at some other office where this exception would not have been insisted on. But he gives no directions at all. Therefore he left it to the discretion of his correspondent, who, if he meant no fraud, was at liberty to elect between the underwriters" (*x*). Unless we suppose that proof was given (of which no trace appears in the report) that the plaintiff, a foreign merchant, was cognizant of the different usages of the London Insurance Offices, this decision certainly seems unsatisfactory: the question is not only whether the agent acted *bonâ fide* in insuring as he did, but whether he exercised that reasonable amount of skill and diligence which could fairly be required of him: upon this point there is great weight in the following observations of Judge Duer: "A general order to insure implies a direction to make the insurance on the best terms that the agent, in the exercise of reasonable diligence, will be able to obtain, and binds the agent, at least, to that degree of diligence that a person of ordinary prudence is accustomed to employ in his own affairs. Certainly no person of ordinary prudence, about to determine on an insurance, would fail to ascertain the usual terms of the respective companies, or sets of underwriters, to whom he might apply; nor would fail, if the credit of the underwriters was equally solid, to effect his insurance at that office, whose terms, at an equal premium, secured to him the largest indemnity. Hence, an agent who, in acting for another, should omit to make the same

Sect. 156.

Remarks on Moore *v.* Mourgue.

(*x*) Moore *v.* Mourgue (1776), Cowp. 480.

Sect. 156. inquiries, and pursue the same course, would be chargeable with such a want of reasonable and ordinary diligence as would render him justly liable for a resulting loss " (*y*).

Comber *v.* Anderson.

157. In the following case the plaintiff was a British merchant, and although the decision seems partly to have proceeded on the fact that he must be taken to have acquiesced in the policy, yet Lord Ellenborough undoubtedly ruled that he must also be presumed cognizant of the tenor of the policies adopted by the different classes of insurers in London. The defendants, London insurance brokers, having received from the plaintiff, a merchant in Liverpool, general orders to insure a cargo of wheat on his account, but no specific instructions as to how or with whom to insure, effected a policy with the Royal Exchange Assurance Company, who at that time left out of their memorandum the exception which makes them liable for an average loss on wheat in case of stranding. The ship having been stranded, and the wheat having sustained an average loss, the plaintiff, owing to the peculiar form of the policy, was precluded from recovering anything under it. He lay by for some time after the loss had happened, without complaining of the form of the policy, and then brought his action against the defendants for not having effected such a policy as would have secured to him an indemnity for average loss in case of stranding. Lord Ellenborough, as to this part of the case, said: the plaintiff must be taken to have been cognizant of the existence of the chartered companies and the tenor of their policies. If he wished that the policy on this cargo should not be effected on the terms of the Royal Exchange Assurance Company, he ought to have given special directions to the defendants for this purpose; and, at any rate, having been so late in reproaching them with what they had done, he had acquiesced in and adopted the policy which they had actually effected (*z*).

(*y*) 2 Duer on Ins. 231; and see also pp. 229—232.

(*z*) Comber *v.* Anderson and another (1808), 1 Camp. 523.

158. A question of some importance in relation to the subject of a broker's duty in a particular case has been agitated, but not yet authoritatively determined. It is whether other persons engaged in the same business as the defendant may be examined as experts, and asked what an insurance broker of reasonable skill would, in their judgment, have done under the circumstances.

Primâ facie it should seem that, in order to know what amount of negligence will make an agent liable, the Court must know what amount of skill may fairly be expected of him; and this, in cases where the agent is engaged in a particular course of business, can best, it should seem, be ascertained by inquiring from persons engaged in that business, whether such due amount of skill was, in their opinion, exercised on the particular occasion in question.

In the only two cases, however, which have been decided on the express point, the Court of King's Bench and Common Pleas were at variance.

Sect. 158. Doubt as to the admissibility of the evidence of experts to prove what a broker of reasonable skill would have done under the circumstances.

159. The former was a case where the plaintiff, a merchant in Sydney, had shipped a consignment of seal skins to England on board the ship "Cumberland." By the ship "Australia," which sailed from the same place a month later, he wrote to the defendants, his correspondents in London, informing them of the time when the "Cumberland" had sailed, and desiring them, if that ship should not have arrived in England when they received the letter, to wait thirty days, and then to effect an insurance on the consignment. The defendants received this letter by the "Australia," and after having waited thirty-six days, effected an insurance, telling the underwriters when the "Cumberland" had sailed, and also when the letter directing the insurance had been written, but not informing them when that letter had been received, nor that it contained directions for not insuring for thirty days after its reception. The "Cumberland" having been lost, and the plaintiff having failed to recover anything on his policy against the underwriters, on the ground of this concealment,

Campbell v. Rickards.

Sect. 159. now brought this action against the defendants for the loss which he had sustained by their negligence in not taking care that the policy was properly effected. At the trial, several brokers and underwriters were called for the plaintiff, and the letter of instructions, which the plaintiff sent to the defendants by the "Australia," being put into their hands, they were asked, "whether it was material to have communicated the fact that that letter had arrived in this country thirty days before effecting the insurance?" The jury having found for the plaintiff, a new trial was obtained, on the ground that this evidence was improperly admitted (*a*). Lord Denman pronounced the evidence inadmissible, on the ground that the opinion of the underwriters and brokers had been asked, not as to a matter of prevalent practice in their trade, but on a matter of legal obligation, which was itself the very point on which the jury were called upon to pronounce a verdict; viz., whether the fact concealed was or was not material, and ought to have been communicated (*b*).

Chapman *v.* Walton.

160. In the other case, the plaintiff, a London merchant, employed the defendant to effect a policy on his goods for a voyage "at and from London to St. Thomas's, with leave to call at Madeira or Teneriffe": the defendant effected the policy accordingly. Shortly afterwards the plaintiff received the following letter from his supercargo, who was then at Funchal in Madeira: "I have now nearly completed, and expect to sail to-morrow or next day at farthest for the Canaries, from whence, as I have taken more wines here than I at first contemplated, it is my intention, for your government, to visit one or more of the West India Islands,

(*a*) Campbell *v.* Rickards (1833), 5 B. & Ad. 840. The same evidence had been admitted by Lord Tenterden at Nisi Prius, in the action brought by these same agents for the plaintiff against the underwriters; and in Banco he seemed strongly of opinion that it had been admitted rightly, saying, "I know not how the materiality of any matter is to be ascertained but by the evidence of persons conversant with the subject-matter of the inquiry." See Rickards *v.* Murdock (1830), 10 B. & Cr. 541.

(*b*) 5 B. & Ad. 846. See, however, Mar. Ins. Act, 1906, s. 20 (7).

say Barbadoes, St. Kitt's, and St. Thomas; in one or other of which, I am told, I cannot fail of getting a market for the wines, and such part of the cargo as I do not dispose of in the Canaries. I have not sold a single package of linens, but could have disposed of a much larger quantity of cottons. With respect to the linens I have no fear, as in Canary any reasonable quantity is desirable." The plaintiff took this letter to the defendant, telling him, "that the voyage was altered, and that he left him the letter to do the needful with." The defendant, upon this, altered the policy, by adding to it a liberty for the ship " to proceed to St. Kitt's and Barbadoes for all purposes," but did not also add any liberty to proceed to or touch at the Canary Islands.

The ship was lost at the Grand Canary Island; and in an action against the underwriter on the altered policy the plaintiff failed, on the ground that the place where the ship was lost was not included within the limits of the voyage therein described. Upon this the plaintiff brought an action against the defendant for the want of proper care and skill in the execution of his duty as a policy broker, by not having procured the proper alterations to be made in the policy according to the instructions he had received.

At the trial several policy brokers were called for the defendant; and the altered policy, together with the bills of lading and invoices, and the supercargo's letter, being placed in their hands, they were asked what alterations of the policy a skilful insurance broker ought in their judgment to have procured, having these documents in his possession, and being instructed to do the needful. The witnesses having replied, that they thought a policy broker could have done ample justice to such instructions by effecting the alterations as made, the jury found for the defendant; and on motion to set aside their verdict, on the ground of the improper reception of this evidence, the Court refused to do so, and held the evidence admissible (c).

(c) Chapman *v.* Walton (1833), 10 Bing. 57.

Sect. 160.   Tindal, C. J., said: "This action is brought for the want of reasonable and proper care, skill and judgment shown by the defendant under certain circumstances, in the exercise of his employment as a policy broker. The point, therefore, to be determined is, not whether the defendant arrived at a correct conclusion upon reading the letter, but whether upon the occasion in question he did or did not exercise a reasonable and proper care, skill and judgment. This is a question of fact, the decision of which appears to rest on this further inquiry, viz., whether other persons exercising the same profession or calling, and being men of experience and skill therein, would or would not have come to the same conclusion as the defendant. For the defendant did not contract that he would bring to the performance of his duty, on this occasion, an extraordinary degree of skill, but only a reasonable and ordinary proportion of it; and it appears to us that it is not only an unobjectionable mode, but the most satisfactory mode of determining this question, to show by evidence whether a majority of skilful and experienced brokers would have come to the same conclusion with the defendant" (d).

Although this question, as far as authority is concerned, must still be regarded as doubtful in English law, yet it must be confessed that the opinion of Tindal, C. J., for the reasons he has so forcibly urged, appears most consistent with sound principle; it seems also to have been adopted as the preferable rule on the other side the Atlantic (e).

(d) Chapman v. Walton (1833), 10 Bing. 63. This admirable judgment deserves a very careful and attentive perusal throughout.

(e) 1 Smith's Leading Cases, notes to Carter v. Boehm. As to the American decisions, see M'Lanahan v. Univ. Ins. Co. (1828), 1 Peter's Supreme Court R. 188; 3 Kent, 285, n. (b). Duer, vol. ii. pp. 780—788, gives a very learned review of the whole question. Cf. also, 2 Phillips, s. 2112. A similar question is discussed, and these and other cases referred to, in the chapter on "Concealment," where the point is whether expert evidence is admissible to show what facts are material, and, as such, necessary to be communicated. See *post*, § 626.

161. In order to fix the liability of an insurance agent, it [is] not sufficient to show that the insurance directed has failed through his default; it must also be proved that his principal has been damnified by the failure. Hence, if an agent fails to procure an insurance directed by his principal, which, if made as directed, would not be binding on the insurer, the agent is not liable in damages on the plain ground that his principal has not been damnified (*f*). If the neglect complained of be the non-communication of a material fact, the insurance agent may defend himself on the ground that, had the fact been communicated, it would have been impossible to procure an insurance at the premium limited in the instructions (*g*); but unless the policy, if made as directed, would have been wholly void or voidable, this defence, arising out of the absence of *damnum* to the principal, cannot be set up, as in the case of an agent directed to insure against British capture,—a direction which, if complied with, would only have avoided the policy *pro tanto* (*h*).

Sect. 161. The agent is not liable where principal is not damnified.

An insurance agent in this form of action may avail himself of any defence that would be open to the underwriters; as breach of warranty (*i*), unseaworthiness (*k*), deviations (*l*), and the like: the only exception to this rule is, that the agent cannot, of course, take advantage of any defence founded on his own act or default.

Insurance agent may avail himself of any defence open to the underwriters.

The insuring agent's liability in such actions is, as a general rule, co-extensive with that of the underwriters if sued on the policy; thus he is entitled, in such action, to deduct from the damages the premium, and any other items which

Extent of liability.

(*f*) Webster *v.* De Tastet (1797), T. R. 157. The assurance directed to be made in this case was on slaves, the privilege of transporting which was given to the mate of a slave ship in lieu of wages. This being an illegal subject of insurance; the policy, if made as directed, would have been void.

(*g*) Anonymous case before Chambre, J. (1808), cited in Paley's Principal and Agent, 20.

(*h*) Glaser *v.* Cowie (1813), 1 M. & S. 52.

(*i*) Alsop *v.* Coit (1815), 12 Mass. R. 40, cited 2 Duer, 325; 2 Phillips, s. 1904.

(*k*) Miner *v.* Tagert (1810), 3 Binn. 204, cited Duer and Phillips, *loc. cit.*

(*l*) Delaney *v.* Stoddart (1785), 1 T. R. 22.

Sect. 161. might have been deducted by the underwriter, such as (under the old practice) the one-half per cent. on the amount of loss (*m*).

It may sometimes be greater.

162. It may happen that the agent, in an action for negligence, is liable beyond the amount for which the underwriters would have been liable on the policy.

This may be for the costs of a previous action on the policy when brought at his desire or with his concurrence; and so it seemingly may be when the action on the policy, though brought without his concurrence, is defeated by some misconduct of his in effecting the insurance not disclosed to his principal until action brought (*n*). Not so, however, where the principal knows of the invalidity of the insurance and the misconduct of the agent, before suing, unless the suit be at the agent's request. Thus, where the principal sued the underwriters, although he knew that they had refused to pay on the ground that the agent had concealed a material fact, Lord Eldon would not suffer him to charge the agent with the costs, as the action was not necessary to entitle the principal to recover, and did not appear to have been brought at the desire or with the concurrence of the agent (*o*).

Insurance brokers were sued for negligence in not having communicated certain material letters to the underwriters, whereby the plaintiff, their principal, had failed in two actions on the policies, and incurred costs to a large amount in addition to very heavy losses. It appeared that the plaintiff had since offered the defendants permission to try on his behalf as many other actions as they liked on the policies, and that, on this offer being declined, he at once, without further communication with the defendants, paid back to certain of the underwriters the losses which they had

(*m*) Harding *v.* Carter (1781), 1 Marshall, 309; Delaney *v.* Stoddart (1785), 1 T. R. 22; Wilkinson *v.* Coverdale (1793), 1 Esp. 75; Glaser *v.* Cowie (1813), 1 M. & S. 52.

(*n*) 2 Duer, 330. This may sometimes be the case where the underwriters' ground of defence is concealment or misrepresentation by the agent.

(*o*) Seller *v.* Work, 1 Marshall, Ins. 305, 306; Duer, *ubi supra*.

aid over to him without suit. It was held that the plaintiff **Sect. 162.**
had a right so to do without waiting to resist an action at
the suit of these underwriters, and that, having done so, he
had a right to recover from the defendants the amount of the
losses, so paid over, in addition to his other losses and costs
of action (*p*).

Judge Duer raises the question, whether, in cases of con- *Agent is entitled to the fruits of abandonment.*
structive total loss, it is necessary, in order to charge the
agent, in an action for negligence, with the whole amount
that would have been due under the policy, to vest the
remains of the property in the agent by abandonment: he
concludes that it is, on grounds in every way reasonable,
being the principal is entitled in law against the defaulting
agent to the extent and in form as if he were the underwriter
on a valid policy, such as ought to have been effected (*q*).

163. So much for the duties of the insurance agent as to *Duties of insurance agent entrusted with the policy.*
effecting an insurance. If, after the insurance is effected, the
agent, as is generally the case, keeps the policy in his own
hands, another class of duties is imposed upon him, his negligence or unskilfulness in the discharge of which may also
render him personally liable to the assured.

Generally speaking, the agent so entrusted with the policy
after its execution is the substitute for the assured in all the
relations of the latter with the underwriters, and has cast
upon him the duty of enforcing the rights and protecting the
interests of his principal in all matters arising out of the
contract of insurance (*r*). Thus, according as circumstances
may arise, it may be his duty to demand a return of the
premium; to prepare and submit the proof of a loss, settle
and adjust the amount, and at the proper time collect and

(*p*) Maydew *v.* Forrester (1814), Taunt. 615.
(*q*) 2 Duer, 326, 327.
(*r*) 2 Duer, 245. "Perhaps," says Blackburn, J., "it may be put as high as to say that he is clothed with authority to do all that is incidentally necessary for carrying out the contract in the policy thus left in his hands. I do not wish to be understood as giving a decided opinion that he has so much authority, but there are at least grounds for so contending." Xenos *v.* Wickham (1863), 33 L. J. C. P. at p. 21.

Sect. 163. receive the various sums from the underwriters, and pay them over to his principals; where an abandonment is requisite, he must take care to give notice thereof in due time and in proper form. In this country these duties are generally discharged by professed insurance brokers, who, as we have already seen, are the parties usually employed in actually effecting the insurance. They will, however, equally be expected of any mercantile commission agent, who chooses to place himself in the same responsible relations to his principal.

Neglect of broker, having policy in his hands, to collect and pay over losses with due promptness. Bousfield v. Cresswell.

164. One of the most important of these subsequent duties of the insurance agent is to collect, receive, and promptly pay over losses to his principal. In an action against an insurance broker for not having duly called on certain underwriters to settle the loss and pay the sums insured, there was no other evidence offered of such obligation, except that the policy remained in his hands after the loss. Lord Ellenborough: "If an insurance broker keeps the policy in his hands he shall be presumed to promise that he will collect the sum due from the underwriters on a loss happening, in consideration of the commission he receives for effecting the insurance. Here the broker, if he chose to part with his lien, might have handed over the policy to the assured, as soon as it was effected, and his responsibility would then have been at an end; but as he retained it he was bound to use all reasonable diligence to bring the underwriters to a settlement of the loss according to the usage of trade in this respect" (*s*).

Duty to give notice of abandonment.

165. The insurance agent is no doubt bound, as to giving notice of abandonment, by any express instructions received from his principal, and to carry them out with such reasonable skill as may fairly be expected of him. Where, however, he is left to his own discretion in the matter, the question whether he is liable in an action for not having given due or timely notice of abandonment, must depend upon the circum-

---

(*s*) Bousfield *v*. Cresswell (1810), 2 Camp. 545. The usage of trade referred to by his Lordship is, that losses ought to be collected from the underwriters a month after the adjustment, and paid over forthwith to the assured.

stances of the case. In the case of principals living at too great a distance to be consulted on the matter, the agent having the policy in his hands would no doubt be held bound to act in their behalf by giving due notice of abandonment, where the circumstances are such as to require it. In such cases, if the agent have done all that his principal, as a prudent, careful and skilful man of business, if on the spot, could reasonably be expected to do, he will be free from liability; but if he have failed in this, he will be liable for the consequences of his negligence. In the case of principals living sufficiently near to be consulted, the agent, in a point of such difficult discretion as a question of abandonment frequently is, would always do wisely to refer to his employers for instructions. The only case in which the agent's liability for neglect to give due notice of abandonment has come in question in our Courts is the following:—Action by assured against insurance brokers for negligence in not giving due notice of abandonment to the underwriters, so as to have enabled the plaintiff to recover for a total loss. The plaintiff, a merchant of Liverpool, had insured through the defendants, insurance brokers in London, a cargo of wheat from Waterford to Liverpool. On going down the Waterford river on the 28th January, 1807, the ship struck and filled. The greater part of plaintiff's wheat was got out, but damaged 95 per cent. on its value. On the 2nd February the plaintiff wrote to the defendants a letter, which they received on the 4th, directing them, if any steps could be taken for his interest with the underwriters, "to do the needful," adding, "I should wish to abandon, if it be admitted of." The defendants, by return of post, wrote back to say, "that it would be imprudent to say anything to the underwriters without learning further particulars." The plaintiff did not write again till the 9th, when he neither complained of the abandonment not being made, nor directed the defendants to abandon. On the 18th of the same month they sent in a notice of abandonment, which was held to be too late (*t*).

Sect. 165.

Comber *v.* Anderson.

(*t*) In Anderson *v.* Royal Exchange Ass. Co. (1805), 7 East, 38.

Sect. 165. It was contended for the plaintiff, that the defendants, after receiving the letter of the 2nd of February, ought to have given immediate notice of abandonment.

Lord Ellenborough, however, held, that no negligence could be imputed to the defendants for not abandoning before the 18th. The letter of the 2nd left it to the defendants' discretion to act as they should think most expedient; and, if the plaintiff was dissatisfied with their conduct, he ought at once to have said so. Instead of that he lay by till the 9th, and did not even then complain or give them any fresh orders. Had he positively required them to abandon, they would have been answerable for not complying with his request as soon as possible; but he had referred them to their own judgment, and it seemed as if he himself at the time had thought that they acted judiciously (u).

The above case has been cited at greater length than usual, as it appears to afford a good illustration of the principles that in this matter regulate the insurance agent's liability: he will not, in cases of difficulty, as questions of abandonment generally are, be held liable for not having exerted the best possible judgment that could, under the circumstances, have been found; it is enough if he acted with reasonable skill and discretion, and as his principal would probably have done had he himself taken the management of the business.

Broker has no authority to cancel a policy.

A broker has, in the absence of the express authority of his principal, no authority to cancel a policy, whether it be left in his hands or not (x).

Agents of the insurer.

166. Agents may be appointed for the purpose not only of effecting sea-policies for the assured, but also of subscribing them for the underwriters (y). In this latter case they are

---

(u) Comber v. Anderson (1808), 1 Camp. 525.

(x) Xenos v. Wickham (in error) (1863), 14 C. B. N. S. 452; 33 L. J. C. P. 13; (1867) L. R. 2 H. L. 296.

(y) In Nicholson v. Croft (1761), 2 Burr. 1188, it was held that proof of subscription by an authorized agent will satisfy an allegation of signature by the principal. See also Cope v. Miller (1896), 1 Com. Cas. 296, and Mar. Ins. Act, 1906, s. 24, *ante*, § 26.

CHAP. VII.] THEIR RIGHTS, DUTIES AND LIABILITIES.

generally authorized to act by power of attorney; but it is not requisite that such power should be produced at the trial, if satisfactory evidence can be given of the agent's authority without its production.

Sect. 166.

As to what shall be satisfactory evidence in the absence of the written authority, is a point on which there has been some little fluctuation in the decisions. Thus, where a broker called by the plaintiff proved that the defendant's name had been subscribed by one Hutchins, who was in the constant habit of subscribing policies in the defendant's name, and had done several for the witness and for others to his knowledge, Lord Kenyon ruled that this was sufficient evidence to charge the defendant, without the production of the written authority under which he acted (*z*); but Lord Ellenborough, in a later case, held precisely similar evidence insufficient (*a*), unless it was also proved that the defendant had ratified such subscription, as, *e.g.*, by paying losses upon policies so subscribed (*b*).

Evidence of authority.

A memorandum indorsed on a policy for change of voyage was signed by the agent of an insurance company. It was proved that the agent had signed similar memorandums on many other policies, and that his habit was to do so, and advise the company of it. This was held by Lord Tenterden to be sufficient proof of the agent's authority to sign such memorandums; and that the other policies on which the memorandums had been signed need not be produced (*c*).

After an agent's authority to underwrite policies has expired, the principal may, nevertheless, under a rule of the general law of agency, be estopped from denying the continuation of the authority as against parties who had previously effected insurances with the agent, if the principal has not given them notice of the termination of the authority (*d*).

(*z*) Neal *v*. Erving (1793), 1 Esp. 61.

(*a*) Courteen *v*. Touse (1807), 1 Camp. 43, n.; and rightly, see 2 Duer, 341, n. (*a*).

(*b*) Haughton *v*. Ewbank (1814), 4 Camp. 88.

(*c*) Brockelbank *v*. Sugrue (1831), 5 C. & P. 21.

(*d*) Willis *v*. Joyce (1911), 16 Com. Cas. 190.

A.—VOL. I.

Sect. 167.

What is a sufficient execution of a power to sign policies.

167. Where a power was given to fifteen persons, "jointly or separately, to sign policies on such ships as they or any of them should think proper," after four of the original fifteen had died, a policy was executed, in the name of the principal, by four of the survivors, and this was held to be a sufficient pursuance of the authority (*e*).

Where the power of attorney was to execute policies on which the risk should commence from the day on which the ship was accepted by the association, the Court held that the agent had sufficiently complied with this power by executing a retrospective policy (with the clause "lost or not lost"), to commence on the day the ship had been accepted, although, at the time of so executing it, the agent and the assured were both aware that two average losses had, in the meantime, happened on the ship (*f*).

In virtue of a power "to underwrite any policy of insurance not exceeding 100*l*., and to subscribe the same in his (the underwriter's) name, and to settle and adjust losses," the broker signed a slip for a policy within the terms of the power, and the Court were of opinion that the signature of the broker's clerk to the policy, made in pursuance of the slip, was a good execution of this power, this being a mere ministerial act. There was, however, in the same case, a ratification of this signature by the underwriter (*g*).

Limited authority.

168. The ostensible authority of an agent to underwrite policies may be controlled by local usage. A broker at Liverpool, who had a written authority to underwrite for not more than 100*l*. by any one slip, underwrote a policy for 150*l*. The Court held that the principal was not bound by the subscription, inasmuch as in the place where it was made by the broker, it was common knowledge that such agents had only a limited authority (*h*).

(*e*) Guthrie *v.* Armstrong (1822), 1 Dowl. & Ryl. 248.
(*f*) Mead *v.* Davison (1835), 3 Ad. & E. 303. Cf. Mason *v.* Joseph, *infra*.
(*g*) Mason *v.* Joseph, 1 Smith. 406.
(*h*) Baines *v.* Ewing (1866), L. R. 1 Exch. 320.

CHAP. VII.] THEIR RIGHTS, DUTIES AND LIABILITIES. 227

An agent, whose original authority to subscribe a policy has been proved, has an implied authority to perform any subsequent act on behalf of his principal that the relation between the latter and the assured may render necessary.

Sect. 168.

Thus: the authority to sign or subscribe a policy for the underwriter involves that of signing the adjustment of a loss (*i*). And an agent proved to have been in the habit of subscribing policies and settling losses, was held, by Gibbs, C. J., to have an implied authority to submit a dispute, concerning a loss, to arbitration (*k*).

The authority to sign involves that of settling claims, and of submitting to arbitration.

These were cases of implied authority, arising out of the proved relationship subsisting between the underwriter and the agent. Where, however, the agent of the underwriters derives his authority from express instructions, which profess to define and regulate the duties of his agency, he cannot, as agent, bind his principal by any act which exceeds the limits of such instructions, much less by one that violates or contravenes them, unless the principal have held him out to the public as being invested with a general authority.

Thus: Lloyd's agents have no other authority than what they derive from the printed instructions under which they act. By these instructions it is expressly declared that no Lloyd's agent is to make up or sign any adjustment of loss as the representative of the underwriters. Where, therefore, such an agent, in a foreign port, signed a certificate that certain sugars were damaged over 5 per cent., the Court held that he had exceeded his authority, and that the certificate so given was not binding on the underwriters (*l*). By the same in-

Authority of Lloyd's agents.

(*i*) Richardson *v.* Anderson (1805), 1 Camp. 43, n.; and per Blackburn, J., Xenos *v.* Wickham (1863), 33 L. J. C. P. 13—19.

(*k*) Goodson *v.* Brooke (1814), 4 Camp. 163. *Sed quære*. The report no doubt bears out the text, but it is a report *ex relatione* of another, and it seems contrary to Stead *v.* Salt (1825), 3 Bing. 101;

Adams *v.* Bankart (1835), 1 C. M. & R. 681; confirmed by Hatton *v.* Royle (1858), 3 H. & N. 500; 27 L. J. Ex. 486, that even a partner has no implied authority to submit a partnership dispute to arbitration. Cf. also Thomas *v.* Atherton (1878), 10 Ch. D. 185.

(*l*) Drake *v.* Marryatt (1823), 1 B. & Cr. 473.

Sect. 168. structions no Lloyd's agent "is to accept an abandonment as the representative of the underwriters"; and although such acceptance of an abandonment by a Lloyd's agent seemed in one case to have been regarded as binding in the Common Pleas (*m*), Lord Tenterden remarked that, in the case referred to, the instructions to Lloyd's agents could not have been before the Court (*n*).

(*m*) Read *v.* Bonham (1821), 3 Brod. & B. 147. See the *dicta* of Burroughs, J., as there reported at p. 155.

(*n*) Lord Tenterden in Drake *v.* Marryatt (1823), 1 B. & Cr. 478. See further as to the position of Lloyd's agents, § 77, *supra*.

CHAPTER VIII.

DESCRIPTION OF THE ASSURED IN THE POLICY—
ASSIGNMENT OF THE POLICY.

SECT.	SECT.
Policies in Blank 169	Who may avail themselves of
Construction of 28 Geo. 3, c. 56. 170	an Insurance 172, 173
Ratification of Insurance 171	Assignment of Policy ......174—181

169. WE have already, in briefly noticing the main requisites of the policy, stated how the blanks in the common printed forms are generally filled up with the names either of the assured himself or of the insurance agent by whose instrumentality the policy is effected. We will now proceed to give, more at large, the history and present state of the law as it relates to the filling up of these blanks in the printed forms. *Description of the assured in the policy.*

A practice appears to have sprung up in this country in the middle of the eighteenth century of effecting policies in blank; *i.e.*, without inserting the names either of the party for whom or by whom they were effected (*a*). In consequence of complaints on the part of the underwriters, an Act was passed in the year 1784 (*b*), directing that the name of the person interested, or of his agent, should in all cases be inserted in the policy. *Practice of effecting policies in blank.*

The provisions of this Act appear to have been founded on a misconception of the real nature of that grievance of which the underwriters complained. What the underwriters really wanted was merely to know the name of someone concerned in effecting the policy, no matter whether principal or agent, *25 Geo. 3, c. 44.*

(*a*) Pray *v.* Edie (1786), 1 T. R. 313; see also the judgment of Buller, J., in Wolff *v.* Horncastle (1798), 1 B. & P. 316, 321.
(*b*) 25 Geo. 3, c. 44.

Sect. 169. to whom they could look as a responsible debtor. What the Legislature appears to have aimed at was, as far as possible, to compel a disclosure of the name of the person really interested as principal.

The Courts interpreted the Act strictly. Very soon after it was passed an underwriter took advantage of it to evade his contract on the ground that the agent's name was not inserted, *eo nomine*, as agent (*c*); and another policy was held void under the same law, because the names of all the parties interested were not inserted therein (*d*).

28 Geo. 3, c. 56.

170. This was evidently going too far. Another statute, therefore, was passed in the year 1787 (*e*), which provided that no policy should be effected without first inserting therein "the name or names, or the usual style and firm of dealing," either—1st, of one or more of the persons interested; or, 2nd, of the consignor or consignee of the property to be insured; or, 3rd, of the person resident in Great Britain who received the order for and effected the policy (*f*); or, 4th, of the person who gave the order to the agent immediately employed to effect it.

Marine Insurance Act, s. 23 (1).

The Courts of Law gave this Act the most liberal construction the words would bear (*g*), so that in practice it was reduced to a mere prohibition of policies in blank. Accordingly when it was repealed by the Marine Insurance Act, 1906, the simpler provision of sect. 23 (1) was substituted, which declares that "a marine policy must specify the name of the assured or of some person who effects the insurance on his behalf" (*h*).

(*c*) Pray *v.* Edie (1786), 1 T. R. 313.

(*d*) Wilton *v.* Reatson (1787), 1 Park, 16; Cox *v.* Parry (1786), 1 T. R. 464.

(*e*) 28 Geo. 3, c. 56.

(*f*) It was held in Bell *v.* Gilson (1798), 1 B. & P. 345, that an insurance broker was such a person; and in De Vignier *v.* Swanson, *ibid.* 346, n., that the person need not be described in the policy as an agent.

(*g*) See Wolff *v.* Horncastle (1798), 1 B. & P. 316.

(*h*) In Wolff *v.* Horncastle *supra*, it was held that an agent who employed the broker by whom the policy was effected was a person who received the order for and effected the policy, within the meaning of 28 Geo. 3, c. 56.

171. Sect. 86 of the Marine Insurance Act, 1906, provides that "where a contract of marine insurance is in good faith effected by one person on behalf of another, the person on whose behalf it is effected may ratify the contract even after he is aware of a loss" (*i*). As an instance of ratification the following case may be cited:—A policy was effected in London, through the medium of a broker, by the orders of Hagedorn, in the usual form, "as well in his own name as for and in the name and names of all whom it might concern." This policy was effected by Hagedorn for Schrœder, a foreign merchant, who had given him no previous authority for that purpose, and who did not do any act to adopt the policy till nearly two years after it was effected; and then, long after a loss had occurred, he wrote to Hagedorn "hoping that he had settled the loss with the underwriters on the policy in question." Such adoption was held by Lord Ellenborough and the rest of the Court to be equivalent to a previous authority to insure (*k*).

Of course, as no act of one man can be ratified by another, unless that other is cognizant of what has previously been done, so the party for whom the insurance is intended to be made cannot, by any after authority to insure, be considered to adopt the previous insurance, unless at the time of giving such authority he knew as a fact that the prior insurance had been made. This, indeed, is so plain on principle, that it requires no authority to enforce it; and it is all that was really decided in the earlier case of Bell *v.* Janson, in which Lord Ellenborough had thrown doubt upon the application

---

(*i*) See as to ratification, Lucena *v.* Craufurd (1808), 1 Taunt. 325; *S. C.*, in the House of Lords (1806), 2 B. & P. N. R. 269; Stirling *v.* Vaughan (1809), 11 East, 623; Routh *v.* Thompson (1811), 13 East, 274; Hagedorn *v.* Oliverson (1814), 2 M. & S. 485; Barlow *v.* Leckie (1819), 4 J. B. Moore, 8; and the cases cited *ante*, §§ 140—143. The law is the same in the United States; see per Kent, J., in Steinback *v.* Rhinelander (1803), 3 John. New York Cases, 281; 1 Phillips on Ins. s. 388; 3 Kent, Com. 256.

(*k*) Hagedorn *v.* Oliverson (1814), 2 M. & S. 485. So, also, Williams *v.* North China Ins. Co., C. A. (1875), 1 C. P. D. 757.

Sect. 171. of the principle of ratification to the Act of 28 Geo. 3 (*l*). One of the points determined in Wolff *v.* Horncastle (*m*) was this: that the subsequent adoption of the policy by the party for whom it was intended to be made constituted the party making it a "person who received the order for and effected the policy" within the meaning of 28 Geo. 3, c. 56. It therefore seems clear that where a policy has been made, without any previous instruction or authority, by the broker, its adoption or ratification by his principal, after the fact of its having been so effected has been made known, is equivalent to a previous authority to effect it, and constitutes the party by whom the policy has been made a "person who effects the insurance" on behalf of his principal, within the meaning of sect. 23 (1) of the Marine Insurance Act, 1906 (*n*).

Who may avail themselves of an insurance.

172. We have seen that the parties really interested in the subject of the insurance are in our common forms of policy not generally described by name at all, but are comprehended under the clause by which the insurance is expressed to be made by the person effecting it, "as well in his own name as for and in the name and names of all and every other person and persons to whom the same (*i.e.*, the thing insured) doth, may, or shall appertain in part or in all."

Questions have been raised as to the parties who may avail themselves of these very broad and comprehensive terms. In the first place it is clear they must be persons who may lawfully be insured. In the next place they must be persons who, at some time or other during the risk, have an insurable interest in the property, either as the persons originally insured or as their assignees. Beyond this, it must be shown that the person effecting the insurance either intended it for their benefit, or at all events, did not intend it exclusively for the benefit of others having a conflicting or inconsistent

---

(*l*) Bell *v.* Janson (1813), 1 M. & S. 201.
(*m*) (1798), 1 B. & P. 316.

(*n*) For a curious illustration of the general principle, see Barlow *v.* Leckie (1819), 4 J. B. Moore, 8.

interest, but meant it to apply generally, so as to cover the interests of those who should ultimately appear concerned (*o*); if this be shown, a subsequent adoption of the policy by the parties so intended to be insured, or so appearing ultimately concerned in interest, will be held equivalent to a previous order, and entitle them, under the words of the general clause, to avail themselves of the benefit of the insurance (*p*).

Sect. 172.

It is possible that sect. 26 (3) of the Marine Insurance Act, which declares that "where the policy designates the subject-matter insured in general terms, it shall be construed to apply to the interest intended by the assured to be covered," was intended to affirm the rule that a policy covers the interest of any person whose interest it was intended to protect, though the context suggests that the sub-section was perhaps intended to declare a different principle, and that "interest" is equivalent to "subject-matter" (*q*).

173. The intention, at the time, of the party who directs the insurance to be effected is the great point to be ascer-

The intention of the party directing the

(*o*) "I agree that a policy may be made for the benefit of all such persons (*i.e.*, all persons to whom the subject-matter does, may, or shall appertain in part or in all). But where it has been established that in fact the person claiming the benefit was not such a person as those who effected the policy had in contemplation, Courts have disallowed his claim though he might be within the description" (per Lord Loreburn, L. C., in Boston Fruit Co. *v.* British and Foreign Mar. Ins. Co., [1906] A. C. 336, at p. 339).

(*p*) In this passage the text of the second edition is reproduced. It implies that the person who procures the insurance need not, at the time when he insures, have a definite person in his mind as his intended principal; and Routh *v.* Thompson (1811), 13 East, 274, is a clear authority for the statement. See also Duer, vol. ii., p. 36, cited by Vaughan Williams, L. J., in Boston Fruit Co. *v.* British and Foreign Mar. Ins. Co., [1905] 1 K. B. at p. 647, and § 143, *ante*. The view of Mathew, J., as expressed in Byas *v.* Miller (1897), 3 Com. Cas. at p. 42, seems to be that a voluntary agent must intend to benefit a particular person, and this seems also to be the view of Willes, J., according to his judgment in Watson *v.* Swann (1862), 11 C. B. N. S. 756. For the rule laid down by the U. S. Supreme Court where the policy was expressed to be "on account of whom it may concern," see Hooper *v.* Robinson (1878), 98 U. S. 528.

(*q*) See per Kennedy, L. J., in Reliance Mar. Ins. Co. *v.* Duder, [1913] 1 K. B. at p. 275, and *post*, § 252b.

Sect. 173.
insurance to be effected is the test.

tained in determining whose interests the policy can be applied to protect; and this point is to be determined, as a question of fact, upon a consideration of all the circumstances (r).

Where the intention of the party directing the insurance is to embrace the interests of any person whatever who may ultimately appear to be concerned, there can be no doubt that any person coming within that category, who subsequently chooses to adopt the policy, may obtain the benefit of it.

Routh v. Thompson.

Thus, where a prize agent abroad, who at the time did not know to whose benefit the prize would ultimately accrue, wrote directions to this country for the insurance to be made for the benefit of those concerned, and it ultimately turned out that the Crown had an insurable interest, and had adopted the insurance by an Order in Council, it was held that the nominal plaintiffs might recover in an action on the policy in which the interest was averred in the Crown alone (s). In a former action on the same policy, it having been stated as a fact, in the special case on which the argument proceeded, that the policy had been in reality effected on account of the captors, the plaintiffs failed, because the Court were of opinion that the captors had no insurable interest, and they considered themselves precluded, by the statement in the special case, from applying the benefit of the policy to any other parties than those for whom alone it was found to have been effected (t).

Irving v. Richardson.

So where a party had insured 3,700*l.* on a ship in which he was interested only as mortgagee, and only to the extent of 900*l.*, Lord Tenterden left it to the jury to say, on the evidence, whether they thought he intended by the insurance

(r) Grant v. Hill (1812), 4 Taunt. 380; Irving v. Richardson (1831), 2 B. & Ad. 193; Hill v. Scott (1895), 1 Com. Cas. 140, 200; Scott v. Globe Mar. Ins. Co. (1896), 1 Com. Cas. 370; Boston Fruit Co. v. British and Foreign Mar. Ins. Co., [1906] A. C. 336. The intention of the broker or other person who, upon instructions, effects the insurance is immaterial: *S. C.*, [1905] 1 K. B. 637, 648, per Mathew, J.; Small v. United Kingdom Mar. Mutual Ins. Assn., [1897] 2 Q. B. 42, 45.

(s) Routh v. Thompson (1811), 13 East, 274. See note (p), *supra*.

(t) Routh v. Thompson (1809), 11 East, 428.

to cover his own interest only, as mortgagee, or that also of the mortgagor. The jury having found that he meant only to insure his own interest, the Court would not permit the policy to be extended, by virtue of the general clause, so as to cover the interest of the mortgagor (*u*). In another case, where an insurance agent, being unable to effect such a policy as the plaintiff required, indorsed the risk on his own general policy, it was held that the plaintiff could not recover under it, as it had not been effected on his behalf, nor was it a contract purporting to be made for, and afterwards ratified by, him; the plaintiff was no party to the contract, and consequently could not put it in suit (*x*).

Sect. 173.

Watson *v.* Swann.

Where a ship was demised by a charter-party which provided that the shipowners should pay for the insurance, but which was held on the construction of the whole instrument not to impose upon them a duty to insure for the benefit of the charterers, and there was no evidence outside of the charter-party that the shipowners intended, in effecting an insurance, to cover the interest of the charterers, the House of Lords held that the latter could not sue upon the policy (*y*).

The true rule, then, would appear to be, that any party to whom an interest in the property insured "doth, may, or shall appertain," at any time during the pendency of the risk, nay, under the general words, by subsequent adoption, take advantage of the policy to protect such interest, if it appears from extrinsic evidence that the person directing the policy to be effected intended at the time to protect this particular interest, or at any rate to protect the interests generally of the parties who should ultimately appear to be concerned (*z*).

(*u*) Irving *v.* Richardson (1831), B. & Ad. 193.

(*x*) Watson *v.* Swann (1862), 11 C. B. N. S. 756; 31 L. J. C. P. 210; followed in Byas *v.* Miller (1897), 3 Com. Cas. 39.

(*y*) Boston Fruit Co. *v.* British and Foreign Mar. Ins. Co., *infra*.

(*z*) See *ante*, § 172. This, of course, has no application to the question of assignment of a policy, as to which, see the following sections.

Sect. 173. The onus of proving that the plaintiff's interest was intended to be insured under these general words is on him (*a*).

A contract of insurance is not an incident of the thing insured.

174. Sect. 15 of the Marine Insurance Act, 1906, provides that—

> Where the assured assigns or otherwise parts with his interest in the subject-matter insured, he does not thereby transfer to the assignee his rights under the contract of insurance, unless there be an express or implied agreement with the assignee to that effect.
>
> But the provisions of this section do not affect a transmission of interest by operation of law (*b*).

A sea-policy, in its ordinary form, is not an incident of the property insured, so as to follow its transmission from hand to hand during the continuance of the risks; in other words, the purchaser of the property insured does not, by the simple fact of such purchase without more, entitle himself also to the protection of the policy. In order to enable a purchaser of the insured property to derive the substantial benefit of the insurance, there must have been an assignment to him of the policy by the party originally insured, or, at all events, an agreement or understanding to assign it, or to hold it for the benefit of the purchaser (*c*).

When and how policy is assignable.

175. The assignment of marine policies is dealt with in sects. 50 and 51 of the Marine Insurance Act, 1906, in the following terms:—

> Section **50.**—(1) A marine policy is assignable unless

(*a*) Boston Fruit Co. *v.* British and Foreign Mar. Ins. Co., [1905] 1 K. B. 637, per Vaughan Williams, L. J., at p. 646; [1906] A. C. 336.

(*b*) This qualification was, no doubt, inserted *ex abundanti cautela*. Except possibly in the case of death or bankruptcy it is difficult to suggest any transmission of interest by operation of law to which it is applicable: see, however, Chalmers & Owen, Mar. Ins. Act, 2nd ed. p. 23, where it is suggested that subrogation comes under the same category.

(*c*) See Mar. Ins. Act, 1906, s. 51, *infra*. The remedy was entirely at law, and not in equity. De Ghetoff *v.* London Ass. Co. (1730), 4 Brown's Parl. Cas. 436, Tomlin's ed.

it contains terms expressly prohibiting assignment (d). **Sect. 175.**
It may be assigned either before or after loss.

(2) Where a marine policy has been assigned so as to pass the beneficial interest in such policy, the assignee of the policy is entitled to sue thereon in his own name; and the defendant is entitled to make any defence arising out of the contract which he would have been entitled to make if the action had been brought in the name of the person by or on behalf of whom the policy was effected.

(3) A marine policy may be assigned by indorsement thereon or in other customary manner.

Section **51.** Where the assured has parted with or lost his interest in the subject-matter insured, and has not, before or at the time of so doing, expressly or impliedly agreed to assign the policy (e), any subsequent assignment of the policy is inoperative: *Assured who has no interest cannot assign.*

Provided that nothing in this section affects the assignment of a policy after loss.

A valid assignment before loss supposes the co-existence of three things at the time of assignment:—(1) An insurable interest in the subject-matter of the policy in the assignor; (2) the continuance of the risk insured in the policy; (3) the assignment of an insurable interest in the subject-matter of the policy to the assignee, and its exposure to the perils during the continuance of the risk. *Conditions of valid assignment before loss.*

A cargo of linseed was insured from Constantinople to a port of call and discharge in the United Kingdom to be named, including all risk of craft or lighters to and from the brig, each lighter to be considered as if separately insured. Whilst it was on the voyage the cargo was sold in London to the plaintiffs on the following terms:—To be delivered at destined port in sound merchantable condition, and paid for in fourteen days from being ready for delivery by cash, less

---

(d) For a clause providing that policy should "become cancelled" if the vessel insured were sold or transferred to new management, see Pyman v. Marten (1906), Times L. R. 834.

(e) An agreement to "keep the policy alive," or to "hold it" for the benefit of the assignee of the interest insured (see Powles v. Innes (1843), 11 M. & W. 10; *ante*, § 174; *infra*, § 178), implies, it is submitted, an agreement to assign it.

Sect. 175. 2½ per cent. discount, or on seller's option on handing shipping documents, less 5 per cent. The vessel to go to any safe floating port in the United Kingdom. A safe floating port was named. The ship had arrived there in February, and the cargo was being landed in public lighters employed by the plaintiffs, when one of the lighters with her cargo on board was sunk, and would have been a loss within the meaning of the risk in the policy. The policy was assigned to the plaintiffs in the following June, and the assignment indorsed on it in the following October. The plaintiffs sued on it in their own names, but did not recover, because at the time of the assignment the assignor had no interest to assign, the same having ceased by delivery of the goods into the plaintiffs' lighter, and there was no agreement to assign the policy to them, which might otherwise have kept it alive for their benefit when they had become capable of taking an assignment (*f*).

Assignment after loss.

After a total loss, the property insured ceases to be covered by the policy; but there remains a right in the assured to recover damages from the insurer in respect of his loss. Although, technically, a claim for a loss under a policy is for unliquidated damages (*g*), the proposition that a right to unliquidated damages cannot be assigned has no application to policies of marine insurance, and the effect of an assignment after loss is to transfer this chose in action to the assignee (*h*).

Assignee may sue in his own name, or that of another.

176. When there had been an assignment of the policy, or an agreement to assign it or keep it alive for the benefit of the transferee of the thing insured, the transferee could not at common law sue in his own name on the policy, but an action could be brought by the party, by whom or on whose behalf the insurance was originally effected, as trustee for the

---

(*f*) North of England Oil Cake Co. *v.* Archangel Maritime Ins. Co. (1875), L. R. 10 Q. B. 249.

(*g*) See Pellas *v.* Neptune Marine Ins. Co., *infra*; Baker *v.* Adam (1910), 15 Com. Cas. 227.

(*h*) Lloyd *v.* Fleming (1872), L. R. 7 Q. B. 299, 303; Swan *v.* Maritime Ins. Co., [1907] 1 K. B. 116, 123.

transferee (*i*). In such cases, it was no objection to the right Sect. 176. of the nominal plaintiff to recover, as trustee, on the policy, that the property had not been transferred, nor the policy assigned by him, until after the loss was known to all parties (*k*).

By 31 & 32 Vict. c. 86, s. 1, however, whenever a policy on ship, goods or freight had been assigned "so as to pass the beneficial interest in such policy to any person entitled to the property thereby insured," the assignee might sue on the policy in his own name. This provision was repealed by sect. 92 of the Marine Insurance Act, 1906, and re-enacted in sect. 50 (2) (*l*), with the omission of the words "to any person entitled to the property thereby insured." It is apprehended that the omission of these words makes no difference. The principle that the contract is one of indemnity implies that the beneficial interest in the policy cannot while it remains in force be severed from the interest insured. In other words, a person cannot retain the interest insured by the policy and assign the right to recover whenever a loss takes place to another person (*m*). The Court of Appeal held that sect. 1 of 31 & 32 Vict. c. 86 was merely intended to amend procedure, and not alter the rights of the parties (*n*), and the same construction is applicable to sect. 50 (2) of the Marine Insurance Act.

(*i*) Gibson *v.* Winter (1833), 5 B. & Ad. 96; Sparkes *v.* Marshall (1836), 2 Bing. N. C. 761; Powles *v.* Innes (1843), 11 M. & W. 10. The assignor could sue for a loss as trustee, even though he became bankrupt: Castelli *v.* Boddington (1852), 1 E. & B. 66, 879.

(*k*) In Sparkes *v.* Marshall, *supra*, it was generally believed in December, 1831, that a missing ship was lost. The policy was transferred in April, 1832.

(*l*) *Ante*, § 175.

(*m*) The assured can, however, after a partial loss assign the amount recoverable in respect thereof to another person: Swan *v.* Maritime Ins. Co., [1907] 1 K. B. 116.

(*n*) Pellas *v.* Neptune Marine Ins. Co. (1879), 5 C. P. D. 34, C. A. Therefore the Court of Appeal held in that case that the insurers could not, in an action by the assignee of a policy, set off a debt incurred with them by the assured, as a set-off could not be pleaded to a claim for unliquidated damages, either under the statutes of set-off or in equity. In De Mattos *v.* Saunders (1872),

Sect. 176. There is no reason why the assignee should not, as formerly, sue in the name of the assignor, or of the brokers named in it as effecting the policy; but in this case he sues subject to all rights of defence that may be set up against the nominal plaintiff (*o*). And so now, when he sues in his own name, he does so subject to those same rights, they being expressly preserved to the defendant by the provision in sect. 50 (2) of the Marine Insurance Act, 1906, that "the defendant is entitled to make any defence arising out of the contract which he would have been entitled to make if the action had been brought in the name of the person by or on behalf of whom the policy was effected" (*p*). Thus the underwriter can set up, against an innocent assignee of a policy, the concealment of a material fact on the part of the person by or on behalf of whom the policy was effected (*q*). He cannot, however, set off against an assignee any claims that he may have against the assignor under other policies, as such claims do not arise out of the contract sued upon (*r*).

Mode and form of assignment.

177. "A marine policy may be assigned by indorsement thereon or in other customary manner" (*s*). The Act of

L. R. 7 C. P. 570, it was held that the underwriters could not, as against an assured who was suing on behalf of third persons, set off under the mutual credit clause of 12 & 13 Vict. c. 106, a debt due to them from the assured.

(*o*) Gibson *v.* Winter (1833), 5 B. & Ad. 96; 2 Smith's L. C. 11th ed. p. 417. If inequitable defences, such as a release by the nominal plaintiff after assignment, be set up, the plaintiff may set out the true facts by way of reply: De Pothonier *v.* De Mattos (1858), E. B. & E. 461; and the Courts have interfered upon motion to protect the rights of the parties. See Gibson *v.* Winter, *supra*, and the cases therein cited in the judgment.

(*p*) The Judicature Act, 1873 (36 & 37 Vict. c. 66), s. 25, sub-s. 6, making choses in action assignable with a complete transfer of remedies to the assignee, does it with this reservation—"Subject to all equities which would have been entitled to priority over the right of the assignee." Notice of the assignment is required by this Act, which is not necessary under the Mar. Ins. Act, s. 50 (2).

(*q*) Pickersgill *v.* London and Provincial Gen. Ins. Co., [1912] 3 K. B. 614.

(*r*) Baker *v.* Adam (1910), 15 Com. Cas. 227.

(*s*) Mar. Ins. Act, s. 50 (3). The learned author of this work stated that assignment of the policy might be made by delivery merely

CHAP. VIII.] ASSIGNMENT OF THE POLICY. 241

31 & 32 Vict. gave a form of assignment, though it did not require that form to be followed, nor make indorsement imperative (*t*); but no form of indorsement is given in the Marine Insurance Act, 1906.

Sect. 177.

When the assignment is made by indorsement, this may be put upon the back of the instrument, either at the time of the transfer of the property insured, or at any other time between the making of the policy and the bringing of the action (*u*).

Time of indorsement.

178. An absolute sale or transfer by the party originally insured of all his interest in the insured property before the loss, incapacitates him, or the party who has effected the insurance for him, from recovering on the policy on his own account; nor can he, or the party who has so effected the policy, sue thereon as trustee for the purchaser unless there have been either an assignment of the policy, or something which the Courts will consider as equivalent thereto, or as evidence of an agreement or understanding between the vendor and vendee that the policy should be kept alive for the benefit of the latter (*x*).

Rights of parties after assignment of the insurable interest.

of the policy with intention to assign it (see 2nd ed. p. 211). The editors were, however, informed before the seventh edition of this work was published, that the modern practice is to indorse the assignment on the policy; and the case of Baker *v.* Adam (1910), 15 Com. Cas. 227, confirms their belief that mere delivery of the policy is not now a customary mode of assignment. It is possible, however, that the policy may be handed over without indorsement with the other shipping documents, as security for an advance: see De Mattos *v.* Saunders, *supra*, and the dictum of Channell, J., in Swan *v.* Maritime Ins. Co. (1906), 12 Com. Cas. [3, 79.

(*t*) The form given by the Act was as follows:—

I, A. B., of, &c., do hereby assign unto C. D., &c., his executors, administrators and assigns, the within policy of assurance on the ship, freight and the goods therein carried [or on the ship, or freight, or goods, as the case may be]. In witness whereof, &c.

(*u*) Of course, an assignment subsequent to the transfer of the property would be inoperative, if there had not been an agreement, express or implied, to assign the policy: Mar. Ins. Act, s. 51, *ante*, § 175.

(*x*) Hibbert *v.* Carter (1787), 1 T. R. 745; Delaney *v.* Stoddart (1785), *ibid.* 22; Powles *v.* Innes

A.—VOL. I. 16

Sect. 178.
Powles v. Innes.

Thus, where a part owner of a ship, after insurance and before loss, had by bill of sale absolutely transferred his share to a third party who was an entire stranger to the insurance, it was held that the plaintiffs, who had effected the policy under the vendor's directions, could neither recover as his agents under a count averring interest in him—for he had no interest left at the time of loss—nor as trustees for the purchaser of his share, because there were no facts stated in the case to warrant the inference that the policy had been handed over with the bill of sale, or that there had been an order on the broker to hand it over, or any understanding that the policy should be kept alive for the purchaser's benefit (*y*).

Right of assured in whom some interest remains.

179. Nothing short of an absolute transfer, however, of the insured property, will preclude the party originally insured from recovering on the policy, either for his own benefit or, even where there has been no assignment of the policy, and nothing that amounts to it, for the benefit of the transferee(*z*); a mere pledge of the bill of lading, as a collateral security, does not divest the assured of all his insurable interest.

Hibbert v. Carter.

Thus, where Kerr, having consigned a cargo of produce to this country, and directed an insurance to be made thereon by the plaintiffs, his correspondents in London, subsequently, but before the policy was actually effected, assigned the bill of lading over to Dellprat, the Court of King's Bench, proceeding upon the ground that an indorsement of the bill of lading passed the whole property, at first held that the plaintiffs could not recover on the policy;—not as agents for Kerr, because he had absolutely divested himself of all interest before the policy was effected, nor as trustees for Dellprat, because there had been no transfer to him of the policy and no agreement to transfer it. Subsequently, however, on affidavits that Kerr had no intention to pass the

(1843), 11 M. & W. 10; North of England Oil Cake Co. *v.* Archangel Maritime Ins. Co. (1875), L. R. 10 Q. B. 249, stated *ante*, § 175.

(*y*) Powles *v.* Innes (1843), 11 M. & W. 10.

(*z*) Hibbert *v.* Carter (1787), 1 T. R. 745; Alston *v.* Campbell (1779), 4 Brown's P. C. 476, Tomlin's ed.

whole property by indorsement of the bill of lading, but only to bind it to the extent of the net proceeds, as a security for Dellprat's debt, which debt had since been paid on Kerr's behalf, a new trial was granted, and on the second trial, the facts appearing as set forth in the affidavits, the plaintiffs had a verdict for the whole amount of the loss (*a*).

Sect. 179.

180. An assignee of a policy can only avail himself of the insurance to the extent to which the assignor has agreed to assign his rights to him.

Right of assignee limited by the assignment.

A ship was chartered with grain from Galatz to Emden for orders, to discharge in a port of the United Kingdom, and the cargo-owners effected an insurance on the grain from Galatz to Emden and thence to the United Kingdom. The cargo was sold while on the voyage to Emden, the price "including freight and insurance to Emden," and the bill of lading and policy were delivered to the buyer. A loss having occurred between Emden and the port of discharge in the United Kingdom, the Court of Exchequer held that the buyer was only entitled to the insurance as far as Emden, and consequently that he could not recover against the underwriter for the loss (*b*).

Unless the policy (as is usually the case in insurances by mutual associations (*c*)) imposes such a condition, the consent of the underwriter is never necessary to the validity of an assignment of it (*d*).

Consent of insurer unnecessary.

(*a*) Hibbert *v*. Carter, *supra*.

(*b*) Ionides *v*. Harford (1859), 29 L. J. Ex. 36; see also Ralli *v*. Universal Marine Ins. Co. (1862), 31 L. J. Ch. 313, *post*, § 181.

(*c*) See, *e.g.*, Laurie *v*. West Hartlepool Thirds Indemnity Association (1899), 4 Com. Cas. 322.

(*d*) In Sparkes *v*. Marshall (1836), 2 Bing. N. C. 761, it was found as a fact that the defendants did not assent to the transfer of the property, or to the assignment of the policy. This practice of merchants with regard to marine policies accounts for the absence from the 31 & 32 Vict. c. 86, and the Mar. Ins. Act, of any such provision as is to be found in the Judicature Act, 1873, requiring notice to be given of the assignment of the chose in action. See 2 Duer, 62, 68, for clauses in American policies restricting the right of assignment.

Sect. 181.
Agreements to transfer insurances to buyer of property.

181. Where a policy is assigned to the purchaser of the insured property, it is usual to indorse on it a memorandum to the effect that "the interest in this policy is transferred" to the purchaser. When a floating cargo (*i.e.*, a cargo at sea) is sold in London, it is generally on what are called "The London Floating Conditions," which comprise the delivery to the purchaser for his benefit of the policies which have been effected on the cargo (*e*), the understanding being that it is insured to the full value. If it be objected by the buyer that the vendor has committed a breach of his contract in handing over policies apparently short of the full value of the cargo, the question whether the policies are sufficient as regards amount is one of fact, and if the sum by which they fall short is small, the jury are entitled to find that the contract has been fulfilled (*f*). In another case a cargo of wheat, still afloat, was sold at a depreciated price, and the vendor indorsed over the policy for so much only as would cover the depreciated price, being part merely of the sum insured in a valued policy. The underwriters having paid the full amount of the insurance into Court, it was held that the buyer was entitled to the full sum, the wheat having been sold as insured, so that the full benefit of the insurance passed by the contract to the buyer (*g*). Again, where a contract for the sale of goods contained a clause "insurance for 5 per cent. over net invoice amount to be effected by sellers for account of buyers," and the sellers obtained an insurance for a larger amount, and handed the cover-note to

---

(*e*) See North of England Oil Cake Co. *v.* Archangel Ins. Co. (1875), L. R. 10 Q. B. 249, 254.

(*f*) Tamvaco *v.* Lucas (1861), 1 B. & S. 185; 30 L. J. Q. B. 234; in error (1862), 3 B. & S. 89; 31 L. J. Q. B. 296.

(*g*) Ralli *v.* Universal Mar. Ins. Co. (1862), 31 L. J. Ch. 313; 2 John. & H. 159. The vendor claimed that by indorsing over the policy for only part of the amount insured, he had expressly reserved to himself, as against the buyer, an interest in the balance. If, however, the underwriters had not paid the full amount insured into Court and the Court had decided against the buyer's claim to the balance, it is difficult to understand upon what principle the vendor could have based his claim thereto. Cf. Harland *v.* Burstall (1901), 6 Com. Cas. 113.

CHAP. VIII.] ASSIGNMENT OF THE POLICY. 245

the buyers, it was held that the buyers were entitled to retain Sect. 181.
the whole of the insurance money, which the underwriters
were prepared to pay to them, and were not trustees for the
sellers for the amount by which it exceeded the invoice price
plus 5 per cent. (*h*). On the other hand, where a contract
for the sale of a cargo of wheat contained a clause "seller
to give policies of insurance . . . . for 2 per cent. over
the invoice amount, and any amount over this to be for
seller's account," and the sellers had effected policies sufficient to fulfil the contract, which were handed over to the
buyers, and two additional honour policies on "increased
profits," it was held that the sub-purchasers (to whom after
a loss the sellers caused the honour policies to be sent to have
the amount payable thereon adjusted) were not entitled as
against the sellers to retain the sum collected by them on the
honour policies. The contract of sale had been satisfied by
handing over policies for the specified amount, and could not
be construed as meaning that the sellers were bound to hand
over other policies which they had effected (*i*).

It is an implied condition in a contract which provides
that the seller shall hand over policies of insurance that the
policies handed over are valid (*k*).

(*h*) Landauer *v.* Asser, [1905] 2 K. B. 184.
(*i*) Strass *v.* Spillers & Bakers (1911), 16 Com. Cas. 166.
(*k*) Cantiere Meccanico Brindi-sino *v.* Constant (1912), 17 Com. Cas. 192; *S. C.*, in C. A., *id.* 346.

CHAPTER IX.

OF THE SHIP.

SECT.	SECT.
Naming Ship in Policy 182	Declarations under Floating Policies 187
Insurance on Goods by Ship or Ships 183	Appropriation of Losses 189
	Changing Ship when named ... 190 may discharge Underwriters.
Floating Policies 186	190—192

Reason why the ship must be named in the policy.

182. We have already seen (*a*) that the name of the ship in which the voyage is to be performed must be accurately specified in every policy, on the ground that the underwriter has a right to be informed of everything material to the risk; the nature of which would obviously be very different upon ships of different degrees of seaworthiness.

It has also appeared that, although the name must generally be inserted with accuracy, yet, as it is only required to be so inserted for the purpose of identifying the ship, an error in the name will be unimportant, if it can be clearly shown that the underwriters were not misled by it, but that they really intended to insure a risk to be carried on in the very ship on which the loss occurred, the principle being that *nil facit error nominis cum de corpore constat* (*b*). Accordingly, in our common policies, after the names of the ship and master, come the words, "or by whatsoever other name or names the same ship or the master thereof, is or shall be named or called."

Degree of accuracy required.

The following cases show the degree of accuracy practically required on this subject:—An insurance was effected on ship as on a ship called the "Leopard"; it appeared that the name

---

(*a*) *Ante*, § 16.

(*b*) See 1 Emerigon, 160: "Error nominis alicujus navis non attenditur, quando ex aliis circumstanciis constat de navis identitate."

CHAP. IX.] OF THE SHIP. 247

of the ship was in fact the "Leonard," and that she had never been called the "Leopard"; it being proved, however, that the ship lost was the same that the underwriters intended to insure, the Court held, that by virtue of the above clause in the policy, the variance in the name had no effect on the validity of the insurance (c). So, where an American ship called the "President" was described in the policy as "the good ship called 'The American ship President'"; but it clearly appeared that the error had arisen from the blunder of the broker's clerk, and that the ship lost was really that on which the underwriters meant to insure, the error of name was held immaterial (d). And the decision of the Court was the same in another case, where a ship really called by the Spanish name of "Las Tras Hermanas," was described in the policy by an English translation of the name, as "The Three Sisters" (e).

Sect. 182.

183. The importance of accuracy in cases where the underwriter may be misled by a mistake in the name of the ship is well illustrated by a case in which an insurance was effected on goods on board the "Socrates." During the negotiation reference was made by the insurer to Veritas, at the time lying on his desk, and when it was found that Veritas contained the "Socrates, Albertson," a new Norwegian ship, and the "Socrate, Jean Card," an old French ship, he asked whether it was the Norwegian ship that was proposed, and he was told by the broker's clerk that he thought it was (f). The goods were in fact loaded on

Mistake as to age of ship.

(c) Hunter v. Molineux, before Lee, C. J. (1744), cited in 6 East, 385. It appears, from the judgment in Ionides v. Pacific Ins. Co. (1871), L. R. 6 Q. B. at p. 683, that, apart from the clause, "or by whatsoever name, &c.," the decision would have been the same.

(d) Le Mesurier v. Vaughan (1805), 6 East, 382.

(e) Clapham v. Cologan (1813), 3 Camp. 382.

(f) The Court considered this expression tantamount to an assertion that the ship was the Norwegian; but added that even if it were a representation as to an expectation or belief, there were no reasonable grounds for the belief. The rule applicable to such a representation, as declared by sect. 20 (5) of the Marine Insurance Act, 1906, is that it is true if made in good faith; but the Court refrained from

Sect. 183.

the French ship the "Socrate, Jean Card," and were lo during the voyage; it was held that the underwriter was n liable on the policy for this loss, on the ground of a mi representation as to the age of the ship in which they we carried (*g*).

Mistake in name of ship immaterial when goods insured by floating policy.

On the other hand, when goods are insured "by ship ships," the underwriter engages, as will presently appear, insure them by any ship on which they are loaded. Co sequently in such an insurance a mistake made subsequent in the name of the ship is immaterial. Thus in the las mentioned case the insurer had also initialed a slip f 5,000*l.* on hides by ship or ships; and afterwards, at t request of the broker, he initialed a slip for 2,445*l.* on hid by the "Socrates," this second slip being expressly made order to be substituted for the slip "by ship or ship already mentioned. The jury found that the parties, entering into the contracts, both meant to insure the goo by the vessel on which they were actually shipped, whatev her name might be, and the assured recovered on the poli issued in respect of this insurance (*h*).

Importance of correct name with reference to maritime news.

One reason why accuracy in specifying the name of t ship may be required is that news calculated to make t underwriter cautious about undertaking the risk may ha come to hand; he may have heard of storms, of losses, a of facts affecting particular ships; and consequently it necessary that he should be able to identify the propo: ship in order to apply this information (*i*).

"Ship" in English policies applies to all builds of vessels.

184. Emerigon (*k*) has employed himself in pointing the varieties of build and size specifically designated technical words, as (in our language) by *ship, bark, b*

stating whether they thought that a want of good faith must be imputed to the clerk. See as to representations of matters of belief, *post*, §§ 545, 546.

(*g*) Ionides *v.* Pacific Fire and Mar. Ins. Co. (1871), L. R. 6 Q. B. 674.

(*h*) Ionides *v.* Pacific, &c. Co. (1872), L. R. 7 Q. B. 517, Ch.

(*i*) See Bates *v.* Hewitt (18 L. R. 2 Q. B. 595.

(*k*) 1 Emerigon, c. vi. s. pp. 163, 164.

schooner, sloop, and the like; and he has truly said that if the underwriter is fraudulently misled by the designation adopted for the vessel to suppose that he is insuring goods on board a *ship,* when the vessel intended is in size and rig a *sloop,* the policy would be void. But as the generic designation *ship* is used, probably invariably, in English policies for vessels of every build, it is difficult to see how, apart from fraud, any question of misrepresentation by the mere use of the generic term can arise.

<small>Sect. 184.</small>

185. It is now necessary to describe the system of insuring by floating policies, *i.e.,* policies in which the name of the ship is not specified. It is dealt with in sect. 29 of the Marine Insurance Act, 1906, in the following terms:—

<small>Floating policies by "ship or ships."</small>

> (1) A floating policy is a policy which describes the insurance in general terms, and leaves the name of the ship or ships and other particulars to be defined by subsequent declaration.
>
> (2) The subsequent declaration or declarations may be made by indorsement on the policy, or in other customary manner.
>
> (3) Unless the policy otherwise provides, the declarations must be made in the order of dispatch or shipment. They must, in the case of goods, comprise all consignments within the terms of the policy, and the value of the goods or other property must be honestly stated, but an omission or erroneous declaration may be rectified even after loss or arrival, provided the omission or declaration was made in good faith.
>
> (4) Unless the policy otherwise provides, where a declaration of value is not made until after notice of loss or arrival, the policy must be treated as an unvalued policy as regards the subject-matter of that declaration (*l*).

Insurances by floating policies are usually made to cover goods; for cases frequently occur in the extended operations of commerce in which it is utterly impossible, or would be highly injurious, to compel the insertion in the policy of the

<small>Object and effect of insurance on goods "on board ship or ships."</small>

(*l*) See *post,* § 360.

Sect. 185. name of the ship in which the goods intended to be insured will be carried.

"Floating Policies."

A merchant who has ordered goods from abroad may be anxious to effect an immediate insurance on them, while he is ignorant of the particular ship by which they may be sent. In time of war, when merchant vessels are obliged to take such opportunities of sailing as the varying fortunes of the hostile parties chance to afford, this uncertainty is, of course, considerably increased. By the laws and practice of all maritime states, it is allowable under such circumstances to effect a policy on goods "on board ship or ships" (*m*).

"The contract of an underwriter who subscribes a policy on goods by ship or ships to be declared is," said Blackburn, J., "that he will insure any goods of the description specified which may be shipped on any vessel answering the description, if any there be, in the policy, on the voyage specified in the policy, to which the assured elects to apply the policy. The object of the declaration is to earmark and identify the particular adventure to which the assured elects to apply the policy. The assent of the assurer is not required to this, for he has no option to reject any vessel which the assured may select, nor is it necessary that the declaration should do more than identify the adventure, and so prevent the possible dishonesty of a party insured, who might intend to apply the policy to particular goods, so that they should be at the risk of the assurers, and he should come on them if there was a loss; and then, when those goods had arrived safely, to pretend that he intended to apply the policy to another set of goods still subject to risks" (*n*).

(*m*) In England the legality of this practice was declared, as far back as 1794, to be too well established to be disputed. Kewley *v.* Ryan (1794), 2 H. Bl. 348. In France it has been ably explained by Emerigon, c. vi. s. 5, "Assurance in quovis," vol. i. p. 173; see also Ordonn. tit. vi. art. 4; Code de Comm. art. 337; 3 Boulay-Paty, Droit Mar. 410—416. So in the United States, see 3 Kent, Com. 257, 258; 1 Phillips, s. 438.

(*n*) Ionides *v.* Pacific Ins. Co. (1871), L. R. 6 Q. B. 674, at p. 682, cited with approval in Davies *v.* National Fire Co. of N. Z., [1891] A. C. 491. See also per Lord Blackburn in Inglis *v.* Stock (1885), 10 App. Cas. 263, 269. For an instance

A floating policy cannot, however, be applied to an interest which it was not intended to cover. A shipowner, who ordinarily carried goods on terms excluding liability for negligence, was in the habit of effecting floating policies for the purpose of protecting goods which he was requested to insure on behalf of the shippers; and the policies were not intended to insure his personal interest as carrier of the goods. It was held that he could not declare on one of these policies for a loss of goods for which he was responsible, because in this instance he was carrying them under the ordinary liability of a common carrier (*o*).

Sect. 185. Floating policies cannot be applied to interests not intended to be protected.

186. This mode of insuring, however, being an exception to the general rule, which requires the name of the ship in every case to be stated in the policy at the time of its subscription, can only be allowed in those cases in which the party effecting the insurance is *bonâ fide* and in fact ignorant of the name of the ship or ships by which the goods insured have been consigned.

This mode of insuring amounts to a representation of ignorance of the ship's name.

It amounts, indeed, to a representation of such ignorance; and therefore, if a party who has adopted this mode of insurance knew, at the time of effecting the policy, the name of any one of the ship or ships on board of which the goods insured were really loaded, the withholding such name would vitiate the policy (*p*).

Floating policies are very largely used by merchants at the present day, not only to protect particular consignments of goods actually ordered, but in order to cover all such

Use of floating policies.

---

such "possible dishonesty," see Ivaz *v.* Gerussi (1880), 6 Q. B. D. 222. Lord Blackburn's opinion that the assured may elect whether he will or will not disclaim a particular shipment is inconsistent with sect. 29 (3) of the Mar. Ins. Act, *supra*.
(*o*) Scott *v.* Globe Mar. Ins. Co. (1896), 1 Com. Cas. 370. See now Mar. Ins. Act, 1906, s. 26 (3), discussed *infra*, § 252b.

(*p*) Lynch *v.* Hamilton (1810), 3 Taunt. 37; confirmed in error in Lynch *v.* Dunsford (1811), 14 East, 494, *infra*, § 607. It should be noted, however, that in this instance there was a report to the effect that the ship in question had suffered a mishap. Her name, therefore, was a material fact of which the underwriters were entitled to be informed. See per Lawrence, J., 3 Taunt. at p. 38.

Sect. 186. property as the merchant expects to have at risk, to a certain specified amount, within stated limits of space and of time. Thus, a firm of merchants in London with a branch house in a foreign country will, at the beginning of their business year, take out a policy (*q*) upon all goods to be shipped on their account up to an aggregate value of, say, 100,000*l.* within the ensuing twelve months for carriage between termini more or less specifically designated. The policy will then attach automatically on all shipments comprised within its terms up to the amount insured; "declarations" being meanwhile made upon the policy by indorsing thereon the names of the vessels and the particulars of the cargoes to which it applies. When the amount insured is exhausted by such declarations, the policy is said to be "fully declared" or "written off" (*r*). By virtue of the words "to be hereafter declared and valued," the assured is enabled to make the policy a valued one as regards any particular consignment by declaring and valuing before a loss; otherwise the amount of interest must be proved at the trial as in the case of an open policy (*s*). A firm of merchants will often have a succession of such floating policies, each one being expressed "to follow policy for £——, No. ——," the meaning of which is that, "there being consecutive policies, any loss declared is to be borne first by the earlier policies, and that it is not till after the earlier policy is exhausted that the underwriters on the policy which follows are to bear the balance of the loss, if any" (*t*).

The point for which the case was cited by Arnould is expressly declared by Mansfield, C. J., to be left undecided. See 3 Taunt. at p. 45; see also Knight *v.* Cotesworth (1883), 1 Cab. & Ell. 48.

(*q*) A similar result is often effected in practice by "open covers." These are unstamped agreements to insure, and are commonly considered, whether rightly or wrongly, as binding in honour only. The insurance is not regarded as legally binding until the goods are "put on stamp," *i.e.*, until the underwriter, in pursuance of his undertaking, issues a policy covering the particular consignment. See Gow, 229.

(*r*) McArthur, 3.

(*s*) See Mar. Ins. Act, 1906, s. 29 (4), *supra*. The valuation must be communicated to the underwriters before loss: Harman *v.* Kingston (1811), 3 Camp. 150.

(*t*) Per Lord Blackburn in Inglis

then the policy contains a stipulation to this effect, it Sect. 186.
seems clear that, while the earlier policies are unexhausted,
no shipments of goods are within the terms of the later
policy; for they are excluded by the stipulation. Therefore
the provision of sect. 29 (3) of the Marine Insurance Act,
1906, that all consignments of goods within the terms of a
floating policy must be declared, does not, under these circumstances, apply to the later policy.

187. With regard to the subsequent declaration by the assured of the name of the ship or ships when known to him, the practice generally is for the broker, on ascertaining the fact, to indorse the declaration of the name or names as a memorandum on the policy. It is not, however, necessary that this declaration should be in writing, nor will an error in the declaration either as to the name of the ship or as to her particulars be fatal to the contract (*u*).
Name should be subsequently declared.

Thus: a policy was effected for a voyage "at and from Archangel to Great Britain," "on goods to be thereafter valued and declared by ship or ships." The broker, having received wrong information as to the ships on which the goods were to be loaded at Archangel, wrote the following declaration on the policy and got it signed by the underwriters:—
A mistake in such declaration may be corrected.

"The interest attached to this policy is hereby declared to be shipped on board the 'Tweende Venner' and the 'Neptunus.'" Shortly afterwards the broker, discovering that the goods had, in fact, been shipped, not on board the "Tweende Venner" and the "Neptunus," but on board the "America," inserted a fresh memorandum in the policy, by which the interest was declared to be on board the latter ship. This the underwriter would not sign, and afterwards refused to pay a loss on the goods, on the ground that the policy had never attached on any goods shipped by the "America." But Lord Ellenborough held, that, as the declaration of interest need not have been in

Stock (1885), 10 App. Cas. at 269.
(*u*) Mar. Ins. Act, 1906, s. 29, sub-ss. (2) and (3), *ante*, § 185.

Sect. 187. writing at all, the first declaration did not form any part of the contract, and that the mistake, being a mere blunder in the names of the ships first declared, might be corrected without any fresh stamp, and that the policy attached upon the goods shipped on board the "America," in the same manner as if the first declaration had never been made (*x*).

Where port of loading unknown.

188. As the merchant may be ignorant of the name of the exact port at which the goods may be loaded on board, an insurance on goods "on board ship or ships" will attach on goods loaded at any port within the limits of the voyage insured (*y*); though of course it would not cover a consignment sent from a different part of the world from that mentioned in the policy, or from any place, in short, not comprised within the limits of the risk, upon a fair construction of the terms of the policy (*z*).

Declaration before loss is not a condition precedent to plaintiff's recovery.

As a general rule, the name of the ship ought to be declared before notice of the loss. As, however, cases may occur in which this would not be possible, as where the assured does not ascertain the name of the ship till he hears of her loss, it is in no case a condition precedent to the plaintiff's right to recover on the policy (*a*). It was a recognized usage, now incorporated in sect. 29 of the Marine Insurance Act, 1906, that such a declaration may, and indeed must, be made, and if necessary rectified, even after the loss is known (*b*).

(*x*) Robinson *v.* Touray (1811), 3 Camp. 158; 1 M. & S. 217.

(*y*) Hunter *v.* Leathley (1830), 10 B. & C. 858. The policy in this case contained a very extensive licence to touch, stay and trade.

(*z*) 2 Valin, tit. vi. art. 4, p. 46; 3 Boulay-Paty, Droit Mar. 410; and his Comment. on Emerigon, vol. i. p. 175.

(*a*) Craufurd *v.* Hunter (1798), 8 T. R. 16; Harman *v.* Kingston (1811), 3 Camp. 150.

(*b*) Gledstanes *v.* Royal Exch. Ass. Co. (1864), 34 L. J. Q. B. 30; Ionides *v.* Pacific Fire and Mar. Ins. Co. (1871), L. R. 6 Q. B. 674; 7 Q. B. 517; and per Brett, J., Stephens *v.* Australasian Ins. Co. (1872), L. R. 8 C. P. 18, 23.

The usage on which s. 29 (3) of the Mar. Ins. Act, 1906, is based was stated in the last-mentioned case in these words:—" According to the usage of the insurance business, when a policy is effected on goods by ship or ships to be thereafter declared, the policy attaches

FLOATING POLICIES.

Sect. 188.
Gledstanes *v.* Royal Exch. Ass. Co.

The plaintiffs were the agents in London of the Hong Kong Insurance Company, and had for some time kept that company re-insured with the Royal Exchange Assurance Company for all sums in excess of 5,000*l.* upon goods by any one ship under a Hong Kong policy. The manner was to effect a policy of re-insurance for 7,000*l.* or 10,000*l.* on goods by ship or ships, to be afterwards declared as particulars came to hand by the Calcutta mail. On the 15th of February, 1860, the Calcutta agent of the Hong Kong company wrote to the plaintiffs notifying an excess in the cargo of the "Red Gauntlet." On the 16th of March the "Red Gauntlet" was posted at Lloyd's as having been burned and scuttled, with partial salvage of her cargo. On the 17th of March the plaintiffs appropriated the residue of the sum insured by the policy then current to other shipments underwritten by the Hong Kong company; and on the 19th they effected a new policy for 10,000*l.* on goods by ship or ships, lost or not lost, which new policy was expressly declared "to succeed" the

to the goods as soon as and in the order in which they are shipped; and directly the assured knows of the shipment of the goods, he is bound to declare them to the underwriter on the policy, and to declare them in the order in which they are shipped. He is not entitled to declare some of the risks, and remain his own insurer as to the others. In case, by oversight or otherwise, the goods are declared on the policy in an order different from that in which they were shipped, the assured is bound to rectify the declarations, and make them correspond with the order of shipment. The underwriter would require to see the bills of lading, and could insist on the declarations being made to follow the sequence of the bills of lading. Declarations are often thus rectified, and sometimes even after loss."

The usage, as here stated, was held in the case of the Imperial Mar. Ins. Co. *v.* Fire Ins. Corp., Ltd. (1879), 4 C. P. D. 166, to be binding on a fire insurance company which had re-insured a marine insurance company against fire risks.

In a later case, Inglis *v.* Stock (1885), 10 App. Cas. 263, 269, Lord Blackburn said that if the assured had several adventures, all within the description in the policy, the assured might select at his pleasure which was to be protected by the policy, subject to the qualification that if there was nothing to show that the first adventure which came in safe was selected not to be under the policy, it must be taken to have been covered, though not declared. This differs to some extent from the rule in the Mar. Ins. Act, 1906, s. 29 (3).

Sect. 188. last current policy. On the 21st the plaintiffs received from Calcutta the letter of the 15th February, and then for the first time learned that their Company had taken risks on the cargo of the "Red Gauntlet" in excess of 5,000*l*., whereupon they immediately desired the defendants to apply the new policy to the "Red Gauntlet." This was refused by the defendant company; but the Court held, to the contrary, that the plaintiffs were entitled to have the policy of the 19th of March so applied (*c*). It is always expected, and it may be made an express condition, that the assured shall declare his interest at the earliest possible opportunity (*d*).

How loss was formerly applied where there were two or more policies effected on goods on board "ship or ships."

189. A very nice question has sometimes arisen as to the application of the loss when there are two or more policies of this loose description on different parcels of goods. In this country it was established by the following decisions, that the assured, in case of loss, had a right to apply either policy to a loss on board any ship he pleased that came within the terms of such policy.

Honchman *v.* Offley.

A merchant in India caused two insurances to be effected by his agent in London, one for 6,000*l*: on goods "on board any ship or ships which should sail from Bengal to London between the 1st of November, 1779, and the 1st of July, 1780"; the other on goods "on board any ship or ships which should sail on the same voyage between 1st February and 31st December, 1780." He loaded goods to the amount of 4,889*l*. on board the "General Barker," and to the amount of 4,500*l*. on board the "Ganges," and entered a declaration before Sir Elijah Impey, then Chief Justice in Bengal, that he had shipped on board the "General Barker" 4,889*l*. of the risk intended to be covered by the 6,000*l*. policy (*e*). Both ships sailed within the time mentioned in both policies. The "Ganges" arrived safe, but the "General Barker" was lost. The plaintiff claimed a total

---

(*c*) Gledstanes *v.* Royal Exch. Ass. Co. (1864), 34 L. J. Q. B. 30.
(*d*) See Weskett, 520; 1 Phillips, s. 438.

(*e*) Lord Mansfield overruled an objection taken at the trial to the admissibility of this declaration in evidence, and allowed it to be read.

loss under the 6,000*l.* policy, which, under these circumstances, he contended he had a right to apply to the "General Barker." Lord Mansfield at the trial, and the Court in Banc, held that he had a right so to apply it, and he recovered accordingly 4,889*l.*, the value of the goods shipped on board the "General Barker" (*f*).

Sect. 189.

Freeland and Rigby, a mercantile house at St. Vincent, directed the plaintiffs, their Liverpool correspondents, to get 1,260*l.* insured on cotton on board the "Elizabeth" from Granada to London; and 1,300*l.* on other cotton, which they intended to send by some other ship that would sail by the first convoy. The plaintiffs accordingly got 1,260*l.* insured in London on goods on board the "Elizabeth," and also 1,300*l.* on goods "on board ship or ships," viz., 700*l.* in Liverpool and 600*l.* in London. The 700*l.* policy, on which the action was brought, was "at and from Granada to Liverpool, on any kind of goods as interest should appear in ship or ships on account of Freeland and Rigby, warranted to sail on or before the 1st of August, 1793," without any exception of the goods on board the "Elizabeth." The "Elizabeth" arrived safe in Liverpool: the "Heart of Oak," on board of which the second cargo ultimately turned out to have been shipped, was totally lost on the voyage. Both ships had sailed before the 1st of August, the time warranted for sailing in the 700*l.* policy (*g*). The plaintiffs' claim for a total loss under this policy was resisted, mainly (*h*) on the ground "that, as a ship, answering the description in the 700*l.* policy and having on board property of Freeland and Rigby to the full amount therein insured, had arrived, this policy, being on ship or ships, might and ought to be applied to that ship, and was satisfied." The Court, however, held, that the assured had clearly a right to apply such an insurance to whatever ship they thought proper, within the

Kewley *v.* Ryan.

(*f*) Henchman *v.* Offley (1782), H. Bl. 345, n.

(*g*) Marshall omits this circumstance, 1 Ins. 168.

(*h*) The other ground was the illegality of insurances on ship or ships, as to which, however, the Court entertained no doubt.

Sect. 189. terms of it; and were therefore, under the circumstances, entitled to recover the whole sum therein insured (*i*).

The rule that the assured may select the policy on which he will declare a particular shipment has no application where it is stipulated that one floating policy shall follow another (*k*). Moreover, as sect. 29 (3) of the Marine Insurance Act, 1906 (*l*), provides that the declarations under a floating policy must comprise all consignments within its terms, the rule seems to be no longer law (*m*); for when the assured has effected two or more floating policies not stated to be successive, it seems to follow from sect. 29 (3) that he must declare his shipments on all the policies on which it is possible to declare them. He cannot, of course, recover more in all than the value of the goods, and a difficulty arises, therefore, in determining when the policies become exhausted: must the whole value of each shipment be deducted for this purpose from the total sum insured by each policy, or must this value be divided rateably among the different policies?

Of changing the ship.

190. It is an implied condition of the policy, that the ship named therein should not, after the commencement of the risk, be changed without necessity or the consent of the underwriters; for such unnecessary or unsanctioned change of the ship produces an alteration of the risk, and therefore exempts them from liability (*n*).

(*i*) Kewley *v.* Ryan (1794), 2 H. Bl. 343; 1 Marshall, Ins. 168.
(*k*) See *ante*, § 186.
(*l*) *Ante*, § 185.
(*m*) Sir M. Chalmers and Mr. Owen are of opinion that the rule, for which Henchman *v.* Offley and Kewley *v.* Ryan are clear authorities, had ceased to be law before the Act was passed; but the only reason given for this statement is that floating policies are now commonly effected "to follow and succeed." See Chalmers and Owen, Mar. Ins. Act, p. 44. No usage has been established, by virtue of which the rule can be treated as having ceased to apply to policies not expressed to be consecutive.

(*n*) Upon this subject, generally, consult Emerigon (c. xii. s. 16, vol. i. pp. 419—425), who discusses it with his usual masterly display of research and reasoning; see also Pothier, d'Assurance, Nos. 68, 69, 70, 71.

CHAP. IX.]   CHANGE OF SHIP.   259

If the policy be upon ship, it is clear that the liability of the underwriters will be at an end directly the specific subject of insurance has been wholly lost, as by foundering at sea; or wholly destroyed as a ship, either by shipwreck or irreparable damage.

<small>Sect. 190.
In insurances on ship.</small>

191. It is only, therefore, in policies upon other subjects of insurance, as, for instance, goods, freight, profits, &c., that any question as to the effect of changing the ship can possibly arise. With regard to these it may be laid down, that if either before the commencement of the voyage or during the course of it, the ship named in the policy be changed without necessity, or without the consent of the underwriters, they will be discharged from their liability (o). This rule holds good even though the substituted ship may be of larger dimensions or greater strength than that originally named in the policy, or though both ships perish on the voyage (p); for, by the fact that a given ship is named in the instrument, the underwriter has a right to say that he had some peculiar reasons for insuring a risk on that very ship which would not apply to any other.

<small>In policies on goods, &c., an unnecessary change of ship will discharge the underwriters.</small>

Thus, if the underwriter has agreed to insure three several parcels of goods, each of the value of 1,000*l.*, one on board the "St. Joseph," another on board the "Triton," and a third on board the "Syren," making together 3,000*l.*, but the merchant afterwards loads these parcels all on board the "St. Joseph," the underwriter will only be liable upon the policy effected on goods on board the "St. Joseph," and that only to the extent of 1,000*l.*; and as to the remaining 2,000*l.* he will be discharged, although all the three ships may have perished in the course of the voyage (q).

(o) 1 Emerigon, c. xii. s. 16, p. 419. See *post*, § 468.

(p) Emerigon, *ibid.* 420; Pothier, d'Assurance, No. 68, p. 111, par Estrangin.

(q) Code de Commerce, art. 361: 4 Boulay-Paty, Droit Mar. 132.

Sect. 192.

192. By sect. 59 of the Marine Insurance Act, 1906—

Where, by a peril insured against (r), the voyage is interrupted at an intermediate port or place, under such circumstances as, apart from any special stipulation in the contract of affreightment (s), to justify the master in landing and re-shipping the goods or other moveables, or in transhipping them, and sending them on to their destination, the liability of the insurer continues, notwithstanding the landing or transhipment (t).

Transhipment by consent, or under necessity.

The general rule, as stated previously in this work, is that if the underwriters consent to the change of ship, or if in the course of the voyage the ship becomes so disabled (u) as to be incapable, by any means at the master's disposal, of being repaired at all, so as to take on the cargo, the master, as agent for all concerned, may procure another ship in which to forward the cargo to its port of destination; and in such case the change of ship does not discharge the underwriters, on goods, freight, or profits, from their liability for loss on the subjects insured, which may occur subsequently to such change of ship. Many cases will occur in the later part of this work, under the head of Constructive Total Loss of Goods and Freight, which will serve to illustrate this position: we shall also have occasion, in considering the duties of the master, to discuss those cases of necessity which give

---

(r) If these words imply that where the transhipment is made necessary by a peril not insured against, the liability of the insurer does not continue, they seem, so far as the insurance is concerned, to impose a restriction upon the right to recover, for which, before the Act, there was no authority. For instance, if goods insured only against war risks or fire are necessarily transhipped in consequence of the ship being disabled by perils of the sea, does the insurance come to an end?

(s) Wide powers of transhipment are sometimes given by the contract, especially by bills of lading for goods carried on a general ship. The transhipment must, however, be justifiable independently of the express terms of the contract of carriage, if the insurer's liability is to continue.

(t) See *post*, § 468.

(u) See note (r), *supra*, as to the position when the ship is disabled by a peril not insured against.

him the right, if they do not impose upon him the duty, of forwarding the goods in another ship. This position was first established in this country by the case of Plantamour v. Staples (x), and has ever since been recognized (y). It is apprehended that, even where goods are insured "on board ship or ships," there is no general right to tranship. As soon as the shipment has taken place, the effect is the same as if the ship selected had been expressly named in the policy (z).

Sect. 192.

(x) (1781), 1 T. R. 611, n.; S. C., 3 Dougl. 1.

(y) See the rule further discussed infra, § 207 et seq.; and cf. Shipton v. Thornton (1838), 9 A. & E. 314.

(z) See infra, § 468.

CHAPTER X.

OF THE MASTER.

SECT.	SECT.
Naming and Changing the Master 194	His Power to Sell the whole Cargo......... 205, 206
His Power to Borrow............ 195	to Tranship 207
to Hypothecate or Sell Cargo...196—200	Is it his Duty to Tranship? ... 208—212
to Sell Ship ...201—204	Effect of Transhipment ...213—215
	Master's Duties in Cases of Abandonment 216

Of the master.

193. It is not intended, in this place, to enter at any length into those general duties and obligations of the master, in regard to the conduct of the ship, which more properly form part of a professed treatise on shipping; nothing more is proposed than to notice such points only, in respect to the master, as have a bearing more or less direct on the subject of sea insurance; and to this end we will consider—(1) The naming of the master in the policy, and subsequently changing him; (2) His power, in a port of distress, of hypothecating the cargo, or selling part of it, in order to repair the ship; (3) His power, in certain cases, to sell the ship or the whole cargo; (4) His power, in case the first ship is disabled, of sending on the cargo in another; and (5) The relation in which he stands to the assured and to the underwriter in case of abandonment.

Of naming the master in the policy, and of subsequently changing him.

194. After the blank left in our common printed forms of policy for the name of the master come the following words: "or whosoever else shall go for master in the said ship, or by whatsoever other name or names the said ship, or the master thereof, is or shall be named or called."

CHAP. X.]   NAMING AND CHANGING THE MASTER.   263

From this clause it is abundantly evident, that it is no **Sect. 194.**
implied condition in our English policies either that the
master should be correctly named, or that the same master
should continue on board throughout the voyage (*a*).

The law is the same in France (*b*). Emerigon, however, **What change**
limits the generality of the words "or whosoever else shall **of master**
go for master" to this extent, that they shall not apply to a **policy.**
master who is of any other nation, especially in time of war,
so as to increase the risk of the underwriters, by substituting
a belligerent as master instead of a neutral (*c*).

Thus there seems no doubt that another master may be
substituted to command the ship, instead of him who is
named in the policy, without the consent of the underwriters, and before the commencement of the voyage; provided always that the change be made in perfect good faith,
and the substitute be competent (*d*). If the substitution can
be shown to have been effected for any fraudulent purpose,
it will, of course, vitiate the policy (*e*).

If in the course of the voyage, from death, disability, or
other necessary cause, the master originally named in the
policy be rendered incapable of acting, or if he abandon his
command, the substitution of another captain in such case of
necessity will, of course, make no difference to the policy (*f*).
Even in such case the command ought not in time of war to
be delegated to an enemy; nor, except in case of absolute

(*a*) The blank for the name of the master is now seldom filled up: *ante*, § 17.

(*b*) 1 Emerigon, c. vii. ss. 1, 2, 3, pp. 184—190.

(*c*) Ibid. p. 187; Boulay-Paty, in his Comment. *ibid*. p. 188, agrees with Emerigon in this construction of the clause. Arnould added: "This limitation seems very reasonable, and, should the case ever arise, would no doubt be ratified in our Courts." The Editors submit, however, that the shipowner is under no obligation to appoint a master of his own nation when, as under English law, an alien is not disqualified from acting as master.

(*d*) See Walden *v.* N. Y. Firemen's Ins. Co. (1815), 12 Johnson's R. 128; 3 Kent's Comm. 257.

(*e*) Boulay-Paty on Emerigon, c. vii. s. 2, p. 189. *Secus*, however, where the owners were not themselves parties to the fraud. See Dudgeon *v.* Pembroke (1874), L. R. 9 Q. B. 581.

(*f*) Emerigon, c. vii. s. 3, pp. 189, 190.

Sect. 194. necessity, if the ship be British, ought the appointment to be conferred on any one that does not possess a British certificate of qualification for master on such a voyage (*g*).

Master's powers of borrowing under necessity.

195. The duty of the master, in case of damage to the ship, is to do all that can be done towards bringing the adventure to a successful termination, to repair the ship (if there be a reasonable prospect of doing so at an expense not ruinous), and to bring home the cargo, and earn the freight if possible (*h*). To accomplish this object of repairing his vessel, the master is authorized to bind his owner, by causing the repairs to be done on his credit, in which case the tradesman may sue the owner; or by borrowing money on his credit where that is necessary, in which case the lender has his remedy against the owner; or by selling a portion of the cargo, which is in effect borrowing from the shipper through the medium of a sale, and in this case the shipper may sue the shipowner; or the master may hypothecate part or the whole of the cargo, which gives a right to the proprietor of it to recover a compensation from the owner of the vessel. All these are merely modes of raising money by the agent of the shipowner for his account and for his use, to enable him to do his duty by repairing the ship, and in all the shipowner must repay the lender. The agency to borrow by these various modes, and so to bind his employer to the lender, is cast upon the master by the necessity of the case (*i*). He may also hypothecate the ship or the freight, or both, which gives the lender a right of arrest by Admiralty process. There is this one condition, however, imposed by the law on these various powers as an indispensable pre-requisite to their exercise, that the master is bound to communicate with the owner of the subject to be so dealt with, whenever such communication is

(*g*) Merchant Shipping Act, 1894, s. 92; cf. Emerigon, c. vii. s. 3, pp. 189, 190.

(*h*) Opinion of the judges in Benson *v.* Chapman (1849), 2 H. L. Cas. 720. See also Hansen *v.* Dunn (1906), 11 Com. Cas. 100.

(*i*) Judgment of Court of Exchequer in Duncan *v.* Benson (1847), 1 Exch. 555; affirmed in Benson *v.* Duncan (1849), 3 Exch. 655.

196. It is not proposed to consider here the authority of the *Power to hypothecate or sell cargo.* master to bind his owner by borrowing money to repair, or by causing repairs to be done on his credit (*k*), but merely to notice a few points connected with his power to hypothecate and sell the cargo, or part of it. With regard to his right to hypothecate, it is now clear law, that in cases of justifying necessity, or—to use the language of Lord Stowell, in the celebrated case of The Gratitudine—" of instant, unforeseen, and unprovided necessity," the master having no other means whatever of procuring funds, may hypothecate not the ship only, but the cargo also, in order to raise money for the repairs of the ship (*l*). In such cases the master, who, in the ordinary course of things, is a stranger to the cargo, except for the purposes of safe custody and conveyance, has forced upon him the character of agent and supercargo, not by the immediate act and appointment of the owner, but by the general policy of the law (*m*).

The extent of this agency, thus created by necessity, is only to bind the owner of the cargo, or (in cases of hypothecation) the cargo itself, to the lender of the money: it does not bind the owner of the cargo as against the owner of the ship (*n*).

(*j*) See Carver on Carriage by Sea, s. 316, and cases there cited; to which may be added Australian Steam Nav. Co. *v.* Morse (1872), L. R. 4 P. C. 222; The Gipsy (1864), 33 L. J. Ad. 195; Maclachlan's Shipping, 5th ed. 59, 164. Such communication is not required, when it is not necessary under the law of the flag: The Gaetano and Maria (1882), 7 P. D. 137, C. A. When the master does not know who the owner of the cargo is, he will satisfy his obligation by communicating with the shipper of the cargo, or his agent: Klein *v.* Lindsay, [1910] S. C. 231.

(*k*) The authorities are collected in Maude & Pollock on Shipping, 4th ed. p. 564; and see Carver, s. 310.

(*l*) The Gratitudine (1801), 3 C. Rob. 240. See The Pontida (1884), 9 P. D. 177.

(*m*) The Gratitudine, *supra.*

(*n*) "The case of The Gratitudine dealt only with the authority of the master in respect of binding the cargo to the lender of the money, it determined nothing as to the relative rights of the owners of the ship, and of the cargo, *inter*

Sect. 197.

Benson v. Duncan.

197. An attempt was made in one case to carry the doctrine of Lord Stowell beyond this limit, and to contend that the act of the master, in necessarily and justifiably hypothecating the cargo, bound the owner thereof so as to preclude him from recovering against the owner of the ship for loss incurred in consequence of the hypothecation. The facts were shortly these: The master of the "Lord Cochrane," a ship damaged by perils of the seas, hypothecated at a foreign port (Pernambuco), by one bottomry bond, for necessary repairs, the ship, freight, and cargo, amongst which were the plaintiff's goods. The ship and freight realized less than the sum borrowed, and the plaintiff, being obliged to contribute towards the difference, and also to pay his proportion of the costs of a suit instituted in the Court of Admiralty by the obligee of the bond, brought his action against the defendant, as owner of the ship, on an implied promise to indemnify. The Court of Exchequer were unanimously of opinion that the plaintiff might maintain such action, on the simple principle, that as between him and the defendant (the shipowner), his cargo had been pledged to secure the defendant's debt, and therefore, as the plaintiff had been compelled to pay the debt through the medium of the pledge, he must be reimbursed by the defendant (*o*). The point was decided the same way by the Court of Exchequer Chamber on a bill of exceptions (*p*). Patteson, J., who delivered the judgment

se;" per Patteson, J., delivering the judgment of the Exchequer Chamber in Benson *v.* Duncan (1849), 3 Exch. 655. The passage in the text is taken from the 2nd ed. p. 229, but Arnould was probably wrong in suggesting that the master could involve the cargo-owner in any personal liability for the money borrowed for repairs of the ship.

(*o*) Duncan *v.* Benson (1847), 1 Exch. 537; *S. C.*, 17 L. J. Exch. 238.

(*p*) The bill of exceptions was tendered to the ruling of the learned judge who tried the cause on the second count; the second count was on the bill of lading for the non-delivery of the plaintiff's goods by the defendant, the shipowner, and the bill of exceptions raised two substantial questions, viz., whether, as against the owners of the ship, the master, under the circumstances, had authority (1) to order the repairs; (2) to execute the bottomry bond. The Court of Exchequer Chamber held in the affirmative on both.

that Court, thus stated the law as to the authority of the master and the liability of the shipowner:—

"In ordering the repairs of the ship, the master acts exclusively as the agent of the owner of the ship, and no other person but the owner of the ship and his agent can have any authority to order the repairs. The owner of the cargo cannot insist on such repairs being made, for the shipowner is absolved from his contract to carry if prevented by perils of the sea, and he is bound by it if prevented by inherent defects in the ship. Being, then, the agent of the shipowner in ordering the repairs, how can he be the agent of any one else in borrowing money to pay for them? If, in order to borrow that money, he is obliged to hypothecate not only the ship but the cargo, he, in effect, borrows money on the cargo for the benefit of the shipowner, just as much as he would have done had he sold a part of the cargo to raise the necessary funds, in which case it is not doubted that the shipowner must have indemnified the owner of the cargo" (*q*).

Sect. 197.

Master agent of shipowner.

198. The exercise of this power of hypothecation must be very strictly watched, and rigorously confined to cases of necessity. The master must, in the first instance, endeavour to raise the money upon the credit of his owners: it is only when he cannot otherwise obtain the money, that he will be justified in hypothecating (*r*). The ship and freight must always be resorted to in the first instance, even though the bond be upon the cargo alone (*s*), and even where there is an earlier bond on ship alone, and subsequent bonds include cargo, the latter will be enforced against the ship alone, even though the result may be to exhaust the proceeds of the ship and leave nothing to satisfy the earlier bond (*t*). The right to hypothecate is not absolutely confined to cases arising in a

Power to hypothecate strictly confined to cases of necessity.

(*q*) Benson *v.* Duncan (1849), 3 Exch. 665, 666; *S. C.*, 18 L. J. Exch. 172, 173.

(*r*) Per Jervis, C. J., in Stainbank *v.* Fenning (1851), 11 C. B.

(*s*) The Constancia (1845), 2 W. Rob. 404.

(*t*) *Ibid.*; The Priscilla (1859), Lush. 1; 1 L. T. 272; Carver on Carriage, s. 318.

Sect. 198. country other than that of the owner's residence. The master may, in cases that otherwise justify such a step, hypothecate, even although the ship is in a port of the country where his owners reside, provided he have no means of communicating with them, and there is no other mode of escaping from the pressure of the necessity (*u*).

Power to hypothecate, not to mortgage or pawn.

199. This power of the master is apparently confined solely to hypothecation, strictly and properly so called, as distinct either from a mortgage, which transfers the property, or a pledge or pawn at common law, which gives a lien on the chattel, and is void without actual possession. Hypothecation gives a maritime lien, which exists independently of possession, and which can be enforced against the subject of it, through the medium of legal process on the termination of the voyage: it is also essential to the validity of hypothecation, that the sea risk should be incurred by the lender, and that the privilege or claim should take effect only in the event of the ship's safe arrival (*x*).

Hence, where the master, besides drawing bills on his owners, also executed an instrument which purported to be an hypothecation of ship, cargo, and freight, whereby the merchant forbore to take maritime interest, and the master took on himself and his owner the risk of the voyage, making the money payable at all events, it was held that this was beyond the scope of his authority as agent, and did not, therefore, bind his owner to the merchant who had advanced the money (*y*).

But as instruments of hypothecation are the creatures of necessity and distress, and usually contain the language of commercial men and not of lawyers, they receive a liberal

(*u*) Maude & Pollock on Shipping, 4th ed. p. 565; Abbott, 14th ed. p. 163, and cases there cited.

(*x*) See the judgment of Jervis, C. J., in Stainbank *v.* Fenning (1851), 11 C. B. 88; and of Parke, B., in Stainbank *v.* Shopard (1853), 13 C. B. 441; see also Broomfield *v.* Southern Ins. Co. (1870), L. R. 5 Ex. 192.

(*y*) Stainbank *v.* Fenning (1851), 11 C. B. 51; Stainbank *v.* Shepard (1853) (in the Exch. Chamber), 13 C. B. 418; Carver on Carriage, s. 812.

instruction. It is not, therefore, necessary that the risk **Sect. 199.**
should be mentioned in express terms; it is sufficient, if it can
be fairly and reasonably inferred from the whole document,
that it was the intention of the parties to make the repayment
of the money dependent on this contingency (z).

200. The sale of a portion of the cargo by the master, for **Power to sell portion of** he repairs of the ship in a port of distress, stands on the **cargo in port** footing of a forced loan from the owner of the goods through **of distress for repairs.** the medium of a sale, and is only to be resorted to in cases
of necessity (a).

It can only be exercised in a port of distress, for the sole
purpose of enabling the ship (or a substituted ship as it should
seem) to proceed with the cargo, or the residue of it, on the
voyage chartered or insured: hence, if the master unduly puts
an end to the voyage insured, it has been held in the United
States, and apparently on very good grounds, that the master
is not justified in selling any part of the cargo for repairs for
a new voyage (b).

The owner of the goods, if the ship afterwards arrives at **Amount which the** her destination, is entitled to recover against the shipowner **owner of the goods sold is** in respect of the goods so sold: and he may claim, at his **entitled to** option, either the price for which the goods actually sold at **recover.** the port of distress (c), or, the amount for which they would
have sold at the port of discharge (d).

But the owner of goods sold for repairs at a port of distress,
is only entitled to recover the amount which they would have
realized at the port of discharge, in case of the ship's arrival

---

(z) The above passage was adopted literally by Arnould from Maude & Pollock on Shipping. See 4 ed. p. 571; see also The Great Pacific (1868), L. R. 2 A. & E. 4; The Haabet, [1899] P. 295.
(a) See the judgment of the Court of Exchequer in Duncan v. Benson (1847), 1 Exch. 555.
(b) Watt v. Potter (1820), 2 Mason's R. 77; 3 Kent, Com. 173;
and see The Julia Blake (1882), 107 U. S. 418.
(c) Campbell v. Thompson (1816), 1 Stark. 490; Richardson v. Nourse (1819), 3 B. & Ald. 237; cf. Hopper v. Burness (1876), 1 C. P. D. 137.
(d) Alers v. Tobin (1802), Abbott on Shipping, 14th ed. p. 551; Hallett v. Wigram (1850), 9 C. B. 580; S. C., 19 L. J. C. P. 281.

Sect. 200. there (*e*); whether, if the ship be lost, or fails to arrive at her port of destination after the repairs, to procure which the goods were sold, the owner of the goods can recover against the shipowner the price for which they actually sold at the port of distress, seems an open question in our Courts (*f*).

Right of sale for repairs can only extend to part of cargo.

As this power of selling the goods of the shipper for the repairs of the ship is conferred for the sake of ultimately procuring the arrival of some part of the cargo in the repaired ship, it is obvious that it can only extend to the sale of part of the cargo and not of the entirety; for it cannot be presumed to be for the interest of the shipper that the whole should be sold, in order to enable the ship to proceed empty to her port of destination (*g*).

But the whole cargo may be hypothecated.

On the other hand, the master may well hypothecate the entirety of the cargo, for the hypothecation of the whole may be for the benefit of the whole, because it may enable the whole to be brought to a proper market, where it may realize far more than the amount raised on hypothecation and the expenses of the loan (*h*). It will be sufficient here to have pointed out thus generally the extent and limits of this power, reserving any particular instances of its exercise for a more detailed examination in subsequent parts of this work (*i*).

(*e*) Atkinson *v.* Stephens (1852), 7 Exch. 567; *S. C.*, 21 L. J. Exch. 329.

(*f*) See the judgment of the Court in Atkinson *v.* Stephens. Lord Tenterden inclines to the opinion of Emerigon as the more reasonable, viz., that the money is only payable in case of the ship's arrival, on the ground that the merchant is thus not placed in a worse condition than if his goods had not been sold, but had remained on board. See Abbott on Shipping, 5th ed. p. 246; 14th ed. p. 551. It seems, nevertheless, to be always competent for the merchant to consider himself as having lent to the shipowner the money which the sale of his goods actually fetched, and to recover this amount, at least, in any event. See Hopper *v.* Burness (1876), 1 C. P. D. 137; cf. also Maclachlan on Shipping, pp. 491—494.

(*g*) Freeman *v.* East India Co. (1822), 5 B. & Ald. 617: *per curiam*, Duncan *v.* Benson (1847), 1 Exch. 537.

(*h*) The Gratitudine (1801), 3 C. Rob. 240; and see Duncan *v.* Benson (1847), 1 Exch. 537; Benson *v.* Duncan (1849), 3 Exch. 655. The Supreme Court of the United States affirmed the same principles in The Julia Blake (1882), 107 U. S. 418.

(*i*) See chapters on "Total Loss" and "Abandonment."

201. The point of the preceding inquiry was, the extent of the power vested in the master to hypothecate the ship and cargo, or to sell part of the cargo for the purpose of repairing the ship and enabling her to prosecute her voyage. The cases now to be considered are those in in which, where the further prosecution of the enterprise has become hopeless—where the ship cannot be repaired or the cargo forwarded—a still further extension is given to the powers of the master, and he is held justified, from the paramount necessity of the case, in selling the ship or the whole of the cargo, or both.

Sect. 201. Power of the master to sell ship, or the whole cargo.

It is obvious that nothing but a case of absolute and supreme necessity, such as sweeps all ordinary rules before it, can justify the master in such sale. He is employed, as servant of the owners, to navigate the ship, and, as agent for both the shipowner and the merchant, to carry the goods to their port of destination; his disposal by sale of that which he is thus entrusted solely to navigate or convey, would in ordinary cases be the mere unauthorized act of a servant manifestly exceeding his commission. Extreme emergencies, however, may arise in which the master, being at a distance from his home port, and without any opportunity of consulting either the shipowner or the merchant, has no alternative left him, acting with perfect good faith as a prudent and skilful man, and for the best interests of all concerned, but to sell the property entrusted to his charge. What those circumstances of emergency are that will justify him in thus acting, we shall have frequent occasion to consider in treating the question of constructive total loss on ship and goods; we, therefore, confine ourselves here to a brief statement of the nature of this power, and the limitations on its exercise (*k*).

(*k*) The statement which follows is retained in substance from the 2nd ed. pp. 235—237. In the chapters on "Absolute and Constructive Total Loss," the editors have ventured to discuss certain points in connection with this subject which appeared to them to be controversial; for instance, what constitutes such a necessity as will justify the master in selling.

Sect. 202.
Nature of this power as vested in the master by the necessity of the case.

202. The nature of the power has been thus expressed b Parke, B.: "The master has, by virtue of his employmen not merely those powers that are necessary for the navigatio of the ship, and the conduct of the adventure to a sai termination, but also a power when such termination become hopeless, and no prospect remains of bringing the vesse home, to do the best for all concerned, and therefore t dispose of her for their benefit" (*l*).

Limitations on this power, as it relates to sale of ship.

Thus, if the ship is driven ashore and wrecked to pieces or broken up so as no longer to retain the character of ship at all, the master will clearly be justified in selling th remains of the wreck (*m*).

It is not, however, necessary that the ship should be thu absolutely destroyed in order to justify a sale by the master

If by the perils of the sea she be reduced to such a con dition that, although her timbers still hold together, yet th master, after the utmost endeavours, is compelled to renounc all hope of repairing her so as to bring her home, either from the physical impossibility of extricating her from the peril a all with the utmost exertion of force he can command, or from his inability to find the necessary funds for the purpose, in such cases, if the danger is imminent, and delay likely t prove destructive, the master will be justified in selling th ship as she lies, although at the time of sale she may stil retain the character of a ship (*n*).

Thus, to take the case put by Lord Stowell, in The Fann; and Elmira, of a ship cast away in a foreign country where there is no correspondent of the owners, and no mone; to be had on hypothecation to put her in repair, and all thi at such a distance from the home port that the ship may ro before the master can hear from his owners, our Courts i such a case have held a sale by the master to be justifiable (*o*)

(*l*) Hunter *v.* Parker (1840), 7 M. & W. 342.

(*m*) Cambridge *v.* Anderton (1824), 2 B. & Cr. 691.

(*n*) Robertson *v.* Clarke (1824), 1 Bing. 445; Mount *v.* Harrison (1827), 4 Bing. 388; Hunter t Parker (1840), 7 M. & W. 342.

(*o*) Fanny and Elmira (1809) Edw. Ad. R. 117; see also Read t Bonham (1821), 3 Brod. & B. 147 The Margaret Mitchell (1858)

CHAP. X.] HIS POWERS. 273

203. The exercise, however, of this power is most jealously watched by the English Courts, and rigorously confined to cases of extreme necessity: such a necessity, that is, as leaves the master no alternative as a prudent and skilful man, acting *bonâ fide* for the best interests of all concerned, and with the best and soundest judgment that can be formed under the circumstances, except to sell the ship as she lies (*p*).

Sect. 203.
Sale of ship only justified by extreme necessity.

If he come to this conclusion hastily, either without sufficient examination into the actual state of the ship (*q*), or without having previously made every exertion in his power, with the means then at his disposal, to extricate her from the peril, or to raise funds for her repair (*r*), he will not be justified in selling, even though the danger at the time appear exceedingly imminent (*s*).

A mere difficulty in procuring the necessary funds for the purpose of the repairs (*t*), or the necessary materials (*u*), although it may be very considerable, and such as to impose great sacrifice of time and money, will not justify the master in selling instead of repairing; unless the difficulty is insurmountable by any means within the master's disposal at the time and on the spot, he is bound to repair.

If, indeed, it is clearly manifest, as a matter not of probable conjecture, but of absolute moral certainty, that, although the ship is not, in the literal sense, irreparable, yet the cost of

---

wab. Ad. 382; The Glasgow 1856), Swab. Ad. 145; The Bonita 1861), Lush. 252.

(*p*) Alcock *v.* Royal Exch. Co. 1849), 13 Q. B. 292; Knight *v.* aith (1850), 15 Q. B. 649. See arnworth *v.* Hyde (1865), 34 . J. C. P. 207.

(*q*) Hayman *v.* Moulton (1803), Esp. 65; Reid *v.* Darby (1808),) East, 143; Doyle *v.* Dallas 831), 1 Mood. & Rob. 48.

(*r*) Gardner *v.* Salvador (1831), Mood. & Rob. 118; The Fanny id Elmira (1809), Edw. Ad. R. 7.

(*s*) Idle *v.* Royal Exch. Co. (1821), 3 Brod. & B. 151, in which the Court of King's Bench reversed the judgment of the Common Pleas, which had been given in favour of the right to sell. *S. C.*, 8 Taunt. 755; Australian Steam Nav. Co. *v.* Morse (1872), L. R. 4 P. C. 222; Cobequid Marine Ins. Co. *v.* Barteaux (1875), L. R. 6 P. C. 319; see, however, Hunter *v.* Parker (1840), 7 M. & W. 342.

(*t*) Somes *v.* Sugrue (1830), 4 C. & P. 274.

(*u*) Furneaux *v.* Bradley (1780), 1 Park on Ins. 365.

A.—VOL. I. 18

Sect. 203. repairing her, so as to keep the sea, will exceed her value when repaired, the master, as agent for the owners, will be justified in selling her (*x*). The excess, however, of the cost of repairs above her value must be no mere measuring cast, no subject of probable conjecture, it must be so far certain that no prudent owner, if on the spot and uninsured, would hesitate for a moment, in the exercise of a sound discretion, to sell the ship as she lay, rather than attempt to repair her (*y*); neither will it be sufficient to justify the master in selling under such circumstances, that he acted *bonâ fide*, and for the best interests of all concerned: the sale will not be justified unless the master in selling acted upon the best and soundest judgment that could be formed under the existing circumstances (*z*).

In the United States.
204. In the United States, the limitations upon the exercise of this power do not seem to be very certainly defined: in some cases a more extensive liberty than that allowed by the English rule has been avowedly conceded; and the position advanced, that the master may sell in all cases where he has good reason to believe that the owner would elect to abandon, *i.e.*, in all cases of constructive total loss (*a*). On the other hand, the stricter doctrine of the English law has been asserted and maintained in decisions of the Courts of Massachusetts (*b*), which derive additional sanction from the opinion of Chancellor Kent, who declares "the strict rule to be the one best supported by reason and authority" (*c*).

(*x*) Cambridge *v.* Anderton (1824), 4 Dowl. & Ryl. 203; 1 C. & P. 213; Ryan & Mood. 60; 2 B. & Cr. 691. The editors have, however, ventured elsewhere to express the view that Cambridge *v.* Anderton is at best a doubtful authority in support of the position laid down in the text. See *post*, § 1054.

(*y*) Somes *v.* Sugrue (1830), 4 C. & P. 274; Doyle *v.* Dallas (1831), 1 Mood. & Rob. 48.

(*z*) Doyle *v.* Dallas (1831), 1 Mood. & Rob. 48.

(*a*) American Ins. Co. *v.* Center (1829), 4 Wendell's (Supreme Courts) R. 45.

(*b*) Gordon *v.* The Massachusetts Fire & Mar. Ins. Co. (1824), 2 Pickering's R. 249; Hall *v.* The Franklin Ins. Co. (1830), 9 Pickering, 466.

(*c*) 3 Kent, Com. 173, 174, n.; 2 Parsons on Insurance, 145.

CHAP. X.]   HIS POWERS.   275

In France, the Ordonnance de la Marine, following in this Sect. 204.
respect the maritime laws of the middle ages (*d*), absolutely In France.
prohibited the master from selling the ship in any case, except
by the special direction of the owners (*e*): but this prohibition was relaxed in the Code de Commerce, and the sale
of the ship by the master is permitted in the sole case of
"innavigability legally certified" *(innavigabilité légalement
constatée)*, that is, as Boulay-Paty explains it, upon the
report of experienced navigators appointed to act as surveyors by the local authorities, and followed by a formal
condemnation in the local tribunals (*f*).

The French jurists confine the "innavigability," spoken
of in the Code, to the single case in which the ship cannot
be repaired so as to continue its voyage or keep the sea (*g*).
Boulay-Paty considered this prohibition to sell as a very
important safeguard of the interests of shipowners against
the frauds of masters (*h*). It is remarkable, that among the
representations addressed to the French legislature, in order
to induce them to relax the ancient rule, one of the cases
stated as showing its hardship, is that in which the power of
sale is denied, where the cost of repairing the ship will exceed
its value when repaired: no notice, however, is taken of this
case, either by Boulay-Paty or Pardessus, in interpreting the
legal meaning of the word "innavigability" as used in the
237th article of the Code; from which it is fair to conclude
that, in the opinion of these eminent jurists, the case supposed
would not warrant the master in selling.

In one case in the United States, the power of the master

(*d*) The Jugements d'Oleron, art. 1; the Laws of Wisbuy, art. 13, and those of the Hanse Towns, art. 57, expressly prohibit the master from selling the ship in any case. 2 Boulay-Paty, Droit Mar. 85.

(*e*) Ord. de la Marine, liv. ii. tit. 1, du Capitaine, art. 19.

(*f*) 2 Boulay-Paty, 86; Code de Com. art. 237. See, however,

Lyon-Caen & Renault, vol. v. s. 137, as to a sale in a place where the legal formalities cannot be observed.

(*g*) 2 Boulay-Paty, Droit Mar. 88; see also 3 Pardessus, Droit Com. No. 606. Cf. Lyon-Caen & Renault, vol. v. s. 135.

(*h*) 2 Boulay-Paty, 89.

Sect. 204. to sell was limited to stranding on a foreign coast (*i*); but it has since been decided there, by Story, J., that in a case of overwhelmingly urgent necessity, the master has a right to sell the vessel as well on a home as on a foreign shore, and whether the owner's residence be near or at a distance (*j*).

Power of master to sell the whole cargo.

205. The power to sell the whole cargo.

This depends on exactly the same principles as the power to sell the ship, and, like it, can only be exercised in cases of extreme necessity.

In the admirable language of Lord Stowell, "though the master, in the ordinary state of things, is a stranger to the cargo, except for the purposes of custody and conveyance; yet in cases of instant and unforeseen and unprovided necessity his character of supercargo or agent is forced on him by the general policy of the law, unless the law can be supposed to mean that valuable property in his hands is to be left without protection or care. Suppose the case of a ship driven into port with a perishable cargo; or suppose the vessel unable to proceed, or to stand in need of repairs, what must be done? The master, in such case, must exercise his judgment, whether it would be better to tranship the cargo, if he has the means, or to sell it: he is not bound to tranship, he may not have the means of transhipment, but even if he has, he may act for the best in deciding to sell. If he has not the means of transhipment, he is under an obligation to sell the cargo, unless it can be said that he is under an obligation to let it perish" (*k*).

Where the ship is disabled, and the cargo, being sea-damaged and of a perishable nature, is in danger of being destroyed by the rapid progress of putrefaction if not sold, it is the master's right, if not his duty, immediately to sell it (*l*); and the duty, it seems, would be equally imperative,

(*i*) Scull *v.* Briddle (1808), 2 Wash. Circ. Court R. 150.

(*j*) The brig Sarah Ann (1835), 2 Sumner's R. 206, cited 3 Kent, Com. 174, n. (*d*).

(*k*) Per Lord Stowell in The Gratitudine (1801), 3 C. Rob. 240.

(*l*) Vlierboom *v.* Chapman (1844), 13 M. & W. 230.

CHAP. X.] POWER TO SELL CARGO. 277

or, at all events, the right equally clear, in such case, even Sect. 205.
where the ship is not permanently disabled, but capable,
after repair, of taking on the cargo (*m*). But a sale even of
perishable goods is not justifiable, unless it be practically
impossible to obtain the instructions of their owner before
they perish (*n*).

206. The power of sale, however, where the ship is not Power to sell strictly
disabled, or where there exist means of transhipment, must limited.
be strictly confined to cases in which the cargo is of a perishable nature, and has suffered so much sea-damage as renders
it physically impossible, that, if sent on, it can arrive in
specie at its port of destination (*o*).

Where the original ship is disabled, but there exist means
of transhipment, and the cargo is not of a perishable nature,
and not sea-damaged, the master will not be justified in selling, but is bound, or, at all events, entitled to tranship (*p*).

Where the original ship is disabled, and there exist no
means of transhipment, or hope of any,—as where the ship is
cast away on some desolate and unfrequented coast, or if the
cost of saving and transhipping and sending home the cargo
would be more than its worth when landed at its port of
destination—the master might possibly be held empowered
to sell the cargo if he had the opportunity, even though it
were neither sea-damaged nor of a perishable nature (*q*).
But if not otherwise justifiable, a sale will not be justified
by a decree of a Vice-Admiralty Court ordering it (*r*).

(*m*) Roux *v.* Salvador (1836), 3 Bing. N. C. 266; Australian Steam Nav. Co. *v.* Morse (1872), L. R. 4 P. C. 222.

(*n*) Acatos *v.* Burns (1878), 3 Ex. D. 282, C. A.; Carver, s. 297.

(*o*) Hunt *v.* Royal Exch. Ass. Co. (1816), 5 M. & S. 55; Roux *v.* Salvador (1836), 3 Bing. N. C. 266; Wilson *v.* Royal Exch. Co. (1811), 2 Camp. 623; Meyer *v.* Ralli (1876), 1 C. P. D. 358.

(*p*) Anderson *v.* Wallis (1813), 2 M. & S. 240; Wilson *v.* Millar (1816), 2 Stark. N. P. 1; Morris *v.* Robinson (1824), 3 B. & Cr. 196; Freeman *v.* East India Co. (1822), 5 B. & Ald. 617.

(*q*) Per Bayley, J., in Hunt *v.* Royal Exch. Ass. Co. (1816), 5 M. & S. 56, 57; Farnworth *v.* Hyde (1865), 34 L. J. C. P. 207.

(*r*) Van Omeron *v.* Dowick (1809), 2 Camp. 43; Reid *v.* Darby (1808), 10 East, 143; Morris *v.* Robinson (1824), 3 B. & Cr. 196.

Sect. 206. "In our opinion," say James and Cotton, L. JJ., "purchasers of cargo from a master cannot justify the sale, unless it is established that the master used all reasonable efforts to have the goods conveyed to their destination as merchantable articles, or could not do so without an expenditure clearly exceeding their value after their arrival at their destination." In this case, the insurers of cargo filed a bill against the purchasers of cargo to have the purchase set aside and the purchasers treated as salvors only. The plaintiffs were successful (*s*).

The master is not the agent of the shipper for purpose of creating pro ratâ freight.

The justifiable sale by the master of a perishable cargo at a port of distress transfers the property, and binds the shipper, on the ground that the character of agent for the shipper is necessarily devolved on the master by the emergency; but the master cannot in such case be considered as the agent of the shipper for the purpose of receiving the damaged goods at the port of distress, dispensing with their further carriage, and thereby entitling the shipowner to *pro ratâ* freight. The presumption that he is agent for the shipper in such cases in selling the goods is incompatible with the presumption that he is also agent for the shipper in dispensing with their further carriage, "for the agency of the master from necessity, arises from his total inability to carry the goods to the place of destination, which dispensed with the performance of that primary duty altogether; and the right to freight *pro ratâ* arises from the presumed waiver on the part of the shipper of the performance of a duty which the master (on behalf of the shipowner) was ready to execute" (*t*).

Power of the master, in case the first ship is disabled, to send on the cargo in another.

207. The subject of which we now come to treat has been in some degree anticipated in our discussion of the continuing liability of the underwriter, notwithstanding the shifting of the goods, in cases of necessity, into a ship different to that named in the policy.

(*s*) Atlantic Mutual Ins. Co. *v.* Huth (1880), 16 Ch. D. 474, 481.
(*t*) Per Parke, B., Vlierboom *v.* Chapman (1844), 13 M. & W. 230;
Hopper *v.* Burness (1876), 1 C. P. D. 137. See also Acatos *v.* Burns (1878), 3 Ex. D. 282, 288, C. A.

CHAP. X.] POWER TO TRANSHIP. 279

In the first place, it is now clearly established in English Sect. 207.
law, in conformity with the uniform tenor of the Continental
and American authorities, that in cases where the original
ship is disabled by the perils of the seas the master is
empowered to procure another ship in which to forward the
goods to their place of destination, and on their arrival by
such substituted ship, the owner is entitled to receive from
the merchant the whole amount of freight which he might
have claimed, had they arrived on board the original ship (u).

This position was first directly established in English law Shipton v. Thornton.
by the case of Shipton v. Thornton (x); in that case the
"James Scott," a general ship of which the plaintiff was
owner and master, had taken on board at Singapore certain
goods, of which the defendant was owner, under bills of
lading according to which they were to be delivered to him
in London. The "James Scott" sailed from Singapore with
the goods on board, but having suffered much injury from
tempest was obliged to put into Batavia to refit, where she
was found to be so disabled that it became necessary to
tranship the goods, and they were accordingly forwarded
by two other vessels, the "Mountaineer" and "Sesostris,"
by which they were duly delivered to the defendant at
London.

The freight payable for the transport of these goods from
Batavia to London, in the "Mountaineer" and "Sesostris,"
was less than it would have been had it been sent on thence in
the "James Scott." The defendant paid the freight actually
due for their carriage by the "Mountaineer" and "Sesostris,"
but refused to pay the higher rate of freight that would have
been due had they been sent on in the "James Scott" (y):

(u) Shipton v. Thornton (1838), 9 A. & E. 314; Matthews v. Gibbs (1860), 30 L. J. Q. B. 55; Blasco v. Fletcher (1863), 32 L. J. C. P. 284; The Hamburg (1864), 33 L. J. Ad. 116; 2 Moore, P. C. N. S. 289; De Cuadra v. Swann (1864), 16 C. B. N. S. 772; Kidston v. Empire Ins. Co. (1866), L. R. 1 C. P. 535; Notara v. Henderson (1870—2), L. R. 5 Q. B. 346; 7 Q. B. 225; Hansen v. Dunn (1906), 11 Com. Cas. 100.

(x) 9 A. & E. 314.

(y) The freight due for their transport by the "James Scott," from Singapore to Batavia, was also paid.

Sect. 207. the plaintiff brought this action for the difference, and the Court of Queen's Bench, after a very elaborate discussion of the whole question and a copious reference to foreign authorities, held that he was entitled to recover what he claimed, on the ground that, where transhipment is necessary, the master is at all events empowered, if not bound, to send on the cargo in a substituted ship for the purpose of earning freight (*z*).

Master's duty to his owners to tranship?

208. In the case just cited, inasmuch as the freight by the substituted was lower than that by the original ship, it was obviously to the interest of the shipowners that the master should effect the transhipment and so earn the whole freight. It was therefore clearly a duty which the master owed to his employers, the shipowners, to take this course.

When the freight by the substituted ship is higher.

Where, however, the transhipment and conveyance by a substituted ship can only be effected at a higher than the original amount of freight, it may not be for the interest of the shipowner to tranship. In such a case, therefore, it is difficult to see how, merely as between the master and shipowner, there can be any duty on the master to take measures which will not be for his employers' benefit.

Does he owe a duty to cargo owners to tranship?

209. But there are other considerations to which weight must be given. It may be the law that the master, though owing no duty to his employers, may nevertheless under certain circumstances owe a duty to the owners of the cargo, and that in their interest he may be bound to tranship, although at a higher rate of freight than they had agreed to pay to the owners of the original vessel.

It never has been formally decided in this country whether, under any circumstances, he is bound to do so.

" By the Rhodian law (*a*), it is left discretionary, as it is by the laws of Oleron (*b*), and would appear to be so left by the ordinance of Wisby, did not a subsequent article, copied also

---

(*z*) Shipton *v.* Thornton (1838), 9 A. & E. 314.

(*a*) Chap. 42, 1 Pardess. 256.
(*b*) Art. 4, 1 Pardess. 325.

nto the Hanse Ordinance (*c*), bear testimony of a contrary disposition, thereby agreeing with the maritime law of Amsterdam (*d*). According to the interpretation put by Vinnius upon the Roman law, the master is thereby under no obligation to procure another ship when that by which he contracted to carry the goods is disabled (*e*). But the Antwerp (*f*) and Rotterdam (*g*) Ordinances, as translated by Magens, employed the strongest terms of obligation. The French law is so framed as to leave the intention thereof in doubt (*h*), and the most distinguished jurists of that country divided in opinion, Valin (*i*) and Pothier (*j*) holding that he is no further bound to procure another vessel than by losing his freight if he omit to do so, while Emerigon (*k*), followed by Pardessus (*l*), and Boulay-Paty (*m*), maintained that, by the express language of the law and the nature of the trusts reposed in the master, it is his duty to hire another vessel, if it be possible, for the cargo, and that he is answerable in damages if he neglect it" (*n*).

{Sect. 209.}

210. Chancellor Kent (*o*), stating the law of America, says: "In this country we have followed the doctrine of Emerigon and the spirit of the English cases, and hold it to be the duty of the master, from his character of agent of the owner of the cargo, which is cast upon him from the necessity of the case, to act in the port of necessity for the best interest of all concerned; and he has powers and discretion adequate to the trust, and requisite for the safe delivery of the cargo at the port of destination. If there be another vessel in the same or in a contiguous port, which can be had, the duty is clear

{Statement by Chancellor Kent of the law as to this point in the United States.}

(*o*) Ord. Wisby, art. 18, 1 Pardess. 472; Hans. Ord. (1614), t. iii. art. 17, 2 Pardess. 536.

(*d*) Art. 17, 1 Pardess. 413.

(*e*) Vinnius in Peckium, 285, 295.

(*f*) Art. 3, 2 Magens, 14.

(*g*) Art. 148, 2 Magens, 105.

(*h*) Co. Com. art. 296, 391; Ord. 1681, liv. 3, t. iii. art. 11, 4 Pardess. 362.

(*i*) 1 Valin, 651.

(*j*) Charte-partie, No. 68.

(*k*) 1 Emerig. 422, 423, 427.

(*l*) 3 Pardess. Droit Com. No. 715, and No. 644.

(*m*) 3 Boulay-Paty, Droit Mar. 400—405.

(*n*) The above paragraph is abbreviated from Maclachlan on Shipping, 5th ed. pp. 479, 480.

(*o*) 3 Kent, Com. 212.

Sect. 210. and imperative upon the master to hire it; but still the master is to exercise a sound discretion adapted to the case."

The same learned jurist adds: "He may tranship the cargo, if he has the means, or let it remain. He may bind it for repairs to the ship. He may sell part, or hypothecate the whole. If he hires another vessel for the completion of the voyage, he may charge the cargo with the increased freight, arising from the hire of the new ship. . . . The master may refuse to hire another vessel, and insist on repairing his own; and whether the freighter be bound to wait for the time to repair, or becomes entitled to his goods without any charge of freight, will depend upon circumstances. What would be a reasonable time for the merchant to wait for the repairs cannot be defined, and must be governed by the facts applicable to the place and time, and to the nature and condition of the cargo. A cargo of a perishable nature may be so deteriorated as not to endure the delay for repairs, or may be too unfit and worthless to be carried on. The master is not bound to go to a distance to procure another vessel, and encounter serious impediments in the way of putting the cargo on board another vessel. His duty is only imperative when another vessel can be had in the same or in a contiguous port, or at one within a reasonable distance, and there be no great difficulties in the way of a safe reshipment of the cargo."

English authorities as to duty of master to tranship.

211. As to the English authorities, Lord Tenterden appears to have thought that where the cargo is perishable, and the master has no opportunity of consulting the merchant, he ought either to tranship or sell, according as the one or the other course will be more beneficial to the merchant, and sums up the case a little later on by saying, "in general, he is to do that which a wise and prudent man will think most conducive to the benefit of all concerned" (*p*). And such was the view of Lord Denman and the Court of Queen's Bench, expressed in the case of Shipton *v.* Thornton (*q*), as follows:

(*p*) Abbott on Shipping, 5th ed. pp. 240, 243; 14th ed. pp. 528, 530.
(*q*) (1838); 9 A. & E. 314.

For it must never be forgotten that the master acts in a double capacity, as agent of the owner as to the ship and freight, and agent of the merchant as to the goods; these interests may sometimes conflict with each other; and from that circumstance may have arisen the difficulty of defining the master's duty under all circumstances in any but very general terms. The case now put supposes an inability to complete the contract on its original terms in another bottom, and, therefore, the owner's *right* to tranship will be at an end; but still, all circumstances considered, it may be greatly for the benefit of the freighter that the goods should be forwarded to their destination, even at an increased rate of freight; and, if so, it will be the duty of the master, as his agent, to do so. *In such a case* the freighter will be bound by the act of his agent, and, of course, be liable for the increased freight. The rule will be the same whether the transhipment be made by the shipowner or the master; and, in applying it, circumstances make it necessary on the one hand to repose a large discretion in the master or owner, while the same circumstances require that the exercise of that large discretion should be very narrowly watched."

Sect. 211.

212. There are, however, undoubtedly dicta to be found in our reports to a different effect from those already quoted. For example, in Metcalfe *v.* The Britannia Ironworks Co. (*r*), Cockburn, C. J., appears to have said: " If the master desires to earn the entire freight, he must cause the ship to be repaired, or send on the cargo in another vessel. But if he chooses to forego the freight, he is not bound to do either." But this can hardly be regarded as a deliberate expression of opinion by that learned judge, as it is clear that three years afterwards (*s*) he regarded the point at present under discussion as being still an open question.

On the whole, it is submitted that the weight of authority in England, as in America, is in favour of the position that

Result of authorities.

(*r*) (1876), 1 Q. B. D. 613.
(*s*) In Atwood *v.* Sellar (1879), 4 Q. B. D. at p. 359.

Sect. 212. under certain circumstances, the master may owe a duty [to] the owners of the cargo, even where he owes none to his o[wn] employers, to tranship. For instance, where the cargo [is] perishable, where there is an emergency, and it is impossib[le] to obtain instructions, it is his duty to remember the doub[le] capacity in which he acts, and to take such measures for t[he] protection of the cargo as the exercise of a sound discreti[on] may dictate (*t*). If, after the exercise of such a discretio[n] under such circumstances, he forms the opinion that the rig[ht] thing to do is to tranship, and that this course can be adopt[ed] without prejudicing the interests of his owners, it is his du[ty] to do so. And in such a case he will have power to bind t[he] cargo-owners to pay any freight, which he may on the[ir] behalf have properly agreed to pay.

Whose agent is the master when he tranships?

213. The question whether the master, if he tranship, [is] acting as the agent of his owners or of the freighters w[as] discussed in Matthews *v.* Gibbs (*u*), and appears to be a ques[-] tion of fact in each case. It is a natural presumption, if th[e] freight of the substituted ship be lower than the freight o[f] the original ship, that in hiring her he is agent for his owner[s], and that he is agent for the freighters if he *bonâ fide* send o[n] the goods at an increased freight. Where the transhipme[nt] is effected on the shipowner's behalf, the latter remains und[er] the same liabilities with respect to the completion of t[he] voyage as were imposed upon him by his original contract [of] carriage (*x*).

Is underwriter on goods liable for increased freight?

214. Where the cargo is forwarded in the freighter[s'] interest at an increased freight, is such increased charge t[o] be made good by the underwriters on the goods? This [is] a question which was not dealt with by Lord Denman i[n] Shipton *v.* Thornton.

In France the law upon this point is, that such excess [of]

(*t*) See Hansen *v.* Dunn (1906), 11 Com. Cas. 100, as to the duty of the master, where the cargo is perishable and he can communicate with its owners.
(*u*) (1860), 30 L. J. Q. B. 55.
(*x*) The Bernina (1886), 12 P. [D.] 36.

...ight by the substituted ship, together with all expenses unloading, warehousing, and reloading the goods, shall made good by the insurer up to the amount of his sub- ...iption (*y*).

In the United States it has been decided that the under- ...iter on goods is not liable for the loss occasioned by such ...tra freight, because he only guarantees the safe arrival in ...ecie of the goods (*z*); to which Phillips adds, that such loss ...ems to be not a proximate, but only an indirect consequence ...the perils insured against (*a*).

Arnould was of opinion (*b*) that on these grounds the under- ...iter would in this country be exempt from liability in ...spect of this claim; which, moreover, seemed to him to fall ...early within the principle established by the case of Baillie ... Moudigliani (*c*), that the underwriter on goods can never ...affected by any loss occasioned by the payment of freight. ...is not clear, however, that this case has any relation to the ...yment of extra freight, which, we may remark, may have ...be taken into consideration in determining whether there is constructive total loss of goods (*d*). When, in consequence ...a peril insured against, the voyage cannot be accomplished ...the original ship, it seems that the excess of the expense which the owner of the goods is put in bringing them ...their destination over the freight which he would have ...d to pay in the ordinary course is a loss directly due to ...ch peril. The practice of underwriters has been to pay ...ch excess as particular charges (*e*), and as one of the objects ...an insurance on goods is to guarantee that the goods shall ...ach their destination, it is submitted that this practice is

---

(*y*) 1 Emerigon, c. xii. s. 16, 426; Code de Commerce, art. 392, 3; and see a very able statement ...the French law as to this point ...2 Boulay-Paty, Droit Mar. ...viii. s. 8, Du Fret en Cas de ...doub, et d'Innavigabilité du ...vire, pp. 398—416.

(*z*) Schulz *v.* Ohio Ins. Co., 1 ...nroe's Kentucky R. 339; 3 ...nt's Com. 212, n. (*a*).

(*a*) 2 Phillips, s. 1462.

(*b*) 2nd ed. p. 246.

(*c*) (1785), 2 Marshall, Ins. 736; 1 Park, Ins. 116.

(*d*) Farnworth *v.* Hyde (Ex. Ch.) (1866), L. R. 2 C. P. 204.

(*e*) See Booth *v.* Gair (1863), 15 C. B. N. S. 291; 33 L. J. C. P. 99; and the remarks of Willes, J., in Kidston *v.* Empire Ins. Co. (1866), L. R. 1 C. P. 548—550.

Sect. 214. correct in principle (*f*). It is certainly not inconsistent with the provisions of the Marine Insurance Act, 1906 (*g*).

Duty of master to check progress of damage,

215. In this country it has been held, in respect of perishable cargo sustaining such damage as may, if not checked, go on increasing, that the master, being in an intermediate port, is not entitled to proceed on his voyage with such damaged cargo on board, the progress of the damage being unchecked, and that if he do so he or his owners are liable for the further loss that ensues in consequence (*h*). If in such a case, instead of proceeding on his voyage with the damaged cargo, he incurs expense in checking the progress of the damage, he is entitled to be recouped by the owner of the goods, who has a

and liability of underwriters for expense of doing so.

right of action over against his underwriter, under the sue and labour clause of the policy, notwithstanding the damage actually sustained does not reach the memorandum percentage, provided it appear that but for such expenditure the damage would have increased until it had become a loss for which the insurer was answerable (*i*). In short, if it appear that a loss which would have fallen on the insurer has been prevented or mitigated by the expenditure of money, the insurer is liable for the expense. Accordingly, where the vessel, in consequence of the perils insured against, was properly abandoned at an intermediate port, and the goods were transhipped and carried on to their destination at a heavy cost for incidental charges and for freight, the underwriter on freight was held liable for the whole of this expense, because thereby a total loss of the original freight was prevented (*k*).

(*f*) When the policy is against total loss only, the owner of goods cannot, however, recover the excess of freight, except where a total loss has been prevented by the expenditure: Booth *v.* Gair, *supra;* Great Indian Peninsular Rail. Co. *v.* Saunders (1862), 2 B. & S. 266; 31 L. J. Q. B. 206.

(*g*) See the definition in s. 64 (2), *post*, § 869, of particular charges, which are recoverable under the suing and labouring clause: s. 78, *post*, § 870.

(*h*) Notara *v.* Henderson (1870—2), L. R. 5 Q. B. 346; 7 Q. B. 225.

(*i*) Per Willes, J., in Kidston *v.* Empire Marine Ins. Co. (1866), L. R. 1 C. P. 535.

(*k*) Kidston *v.* Empire Marine Ins. Co. (1866), L. R. 1 C. P. 535; 2 C. P. 357; cf. Rose *v.* The Bank of Australasia, [1894] A. C. 687.

216. By a clause invariably inserted in our common forms of policy, "the assured, his factors, servants, and assigns," are allowed, or, as the law construes it, are bound, "in case of any loss or misfortune," to make every exertion in their power "for the defence, safeguard and recovery" of the property which is the subject of the insurance. In almost all cases of "loss or misfortune," the duty of acting for the benefit of all concerned, under the emergency, is thrown upon the master. If the casualty should prove to be of such a nature as to justify the assured in giving notice of abandonment, a question may, and frequently does, arise as to whose agent the master is in taking the steps which in his judgment are necessary under the circumstances. This is not the place for entering at any length into the discussion of the question, which will be more fully noticed when we come to treat on the subject of abandonment; it will be sufficient here to state the principle upon which it depends, which is, that as the effect of a notice of abandonment, if accepted, or made on good grounds, is to entitle the underwriter to take over the interest of the assured in whatever remains of the subject-matter insured as from the moment of the loss (*l*), the master will be considered, if the ownership of the abandoned property has thus vested in the underwriter, as the agent of the latter in all acts done by him from that time, within the scope of the authority given to him by the policy "to sue, labour, and travel," for "the defence, safeguard, and recovery of the subject insured" (*m*).

If no effective notice of abandonment is given, the master, in all that he does within the scope of his duty, is the agent of the assured (*n*); and it is his duty, as such, to take such measures as may be reasonable for the purpose of averting or minimizing a loss (*o*).

Sect. 216.
Of the powers and duties of the master in cases of abandonment.

(*l*) Mar. Ins. Act, 1906, s. 63, *post*, § 1205.
(*m*) See *post*, §§ 1218, 1220; Phillips, vol. ii. s. 1584. See also Gilchrist *v.* Chicago Ins. Co.
(1899), 104 Fed. R. 566; Hume *v.* Frenz (1907), 150 Fed. R. 502.
(*n*) Fleming *v.* Smith (1848), 1 H. L. Cas. 513.
(*o*) Mar. Ins. Act, 1906, s. 78 (4).

CHAPTER XI.

THE SUBJECTS OF MARINE INSURANCE.

	SECT.		SECT.
Introduction	217	Seamen's and Master's Wages and Effects	244, 245
Ship	218—221	Disbursements	246, 247
Goods	222—228	Miscellaneous	248
Freight	229—234	Shares in Companies	249
Passage Money	235	Shipowner's Liability for Damages	250
Profits and Commission	236—241	Description of Nature and Extent of Risk usually unnecessary	251, 252
Bottomry and Respondentia	242, 243		

What may and may not be insured.

217. GENERALLY speaking, everything which is exposed to risk by the perils of the seas may be made the subject of a contract of marine insurance, unless its insurance is prohibited by law—including in this term the general law maritime, and the rules of international law so far as they form part of the law of the land. "Subject to the provisions of this Act," it is declared in sect. 3 (1) of the Marine Insurance Act, 1906, " every lawful marine adventure may be the subject of a contract of marine insurance" (a).

In this chapter we will consider what may be insured, and what is covered by the description in the policy of the usual subjects of insurance, leaving to another part of the work the consideration of those things the insurance of which is unlawful, owing to the prohibited nature of the traffic, or voyage, for or on which they are insured. The reason for this arrangement is that, as the prohibition of insurance in these latter cases generally arises not from anything in the nature of the things themselves considered as subjects of insurance,

---

(a) For the meaning of "marine adventure," see s. 3 (2) of the Act, *ante*, § 1.

but solely from the illegality of the risk on which they are embarked, it seems more natural to treat of them, under the general head of the illegality of the risk, in that division of the work devoted to the discussion of the causes that avoid the insurance.

Sect. 217.

Ships and goods have always, and universally, been regarded as the proper and main subjects of insurance, and in dealing with them it will only be necessary to consider what is covered by a policy on "ship" or "goods" respectively.

218. In our common printed forms the policy, after stating that it is effected "upon any kind of goods and merchandises," proceeds thus—"and also upon the body, tackle, apparel, ordnance, munition, artillery, boat, and other furniture, of and in the good ship or vessel called the," &c.

What is covered by a policy on ship.

When the insurance is intended to be confined to the ship alone, this is generally effected by inserting, either at the foot or margin of the policy, the words "on ship"; or by stating in the valuation clause that, as between the assured and underwriters on the particular policy, the subject of insurance is agreed to be the ship, or as many sixty-fourth shares thereof as the assured owns. The effect of either mode of specifying the subject of insurance is to obliterate, as it were, such other words of the general form as are inapplicable to the specified subject (*b*). It is hardly necessary to remark that a policy in this form on ship alone, even when effected by one who is owner both of the ship and cargo, cannot extend to protect the latter (*c*).

Not any part of the cargo.

(*b*) See Robertson *v.* French (1803), 4 East, 130, 140, 141; Haughton *v.* Ewbank (1814), 4 Camp. 89; and the other cases cited *ante*, § 73, which lay down the general principle which subordinates the printed portions of the policy to the effect of those in manuscript. Thus, the interest of a mortgagee, if misdescribed as bottomry, would remain uncovered by the policy, although there are printed words in the policy which would cover a mortgage notwithstanding the misdescription in manuscript. See Simonds *v.* Hodgson (1829), 6 Bing. 114; and *S. C.* (in error), per Lord Tenterden (1832), 3 B. & Ad. 50.

(*c*) 1 Marshall, Ins. 328; per Smith, L. J., Field SS. Co. *v.* Burr, [1899] 1 Q. B. 585.

Sect. 218.
Policies on hull and machinery.

Sometimes a policy is made upon the hull and machiner[y] of a steamship, and in valued policies on steamships it is common practice to have separate valuations of hull an[d] machinery. It is unnecessary to mention the machinery i[n] the policy, for the term *ship* in a policy upon a steamshi[p] covers the machinery as well as the hull (*d*). The object [of] the separate valuation is to provide that for certain purpose[s] in particular as regards average, the hull and the machiner[y] are to be considered separately insured (*e*).

Sched. I. Rule 15 of Marine Insurance Act.

219. Rule 15 in Schedule I. of the Marine Insurance Ac[t] 1906, declares that in the ordinary English policy "the ter[m] 'ship' includes the hull, materials and outfit, stores ar[d] provisions for the officers and crew, and, in the case of vesse[ls] engaged in a special trade, the ordinary fittings requisi[te] for the trade, and also, in the case of a steamship, t[he] machinery, boilers, and coals and engine stores, if owne[d] by the assured" (*f*).

The clause "and also upon the body, tackle, &c.," in th[e] policy made it unnecessary before the Act to decide wheth[er]

Provisions are comprised as part of the ship, under the word "furniture."

fittings or stores were covered by the word "ship." Thus [it] was held that the provisions put on board the ship, when s[he] sails, for the use of the crew on the voyage, are comprehend[ed] under the word "furniture," and protected by an insuran[ce] on the "body, tackle, apparel, ordnance, furniture," &c. [of] the ship in the common printed form (*g*). The contra[ry] position had been erroneously inferred from the case [of] Robertson *v*. Ewer, which decided no such point, but mere[ly] established that the underwriter on ship could not be lial[ble] for the consumption of such provisions while the ship w[as] detained by an embargo (*h*).

(*d*) Mar. Ins. Act, 1906, Sched. I. r. 15, *infra*. See per Kennedy, J., in Roddick *v*. Indemnity Mutual Marine Ins. Co., [1895] 1 Q. B. 842.

(*e*) See Oppenheim . *v*. Fry (1863), 3 B. & S. 873; in the Ex. Ch. (1864), 5 *id*. 348; 33 L. J. Q. B. 267.

(*f*) Cf. s. 16 of the Act, p[ost] § 365, by which the insurable va[lue] of a ship includes also money [ad]vanced for seamen's wages. [See] s. 30 (2).

(*g*) Brough *v*. Whitmore (17[9]) 4 T. R. 206.

(*h*) Robertson *v*. Ewer (1786) T. R. 127; and see per Buller,

CHAP. XI.] INSURANCE ON SHIP. 291

It was admitted, in Brough v. Whitmore, that all the ship's stores and tackle were also included in the insurance on ship in the common form (*i*).

The word "outfit" is sometimes used to denote the necessary stores and provisions put on board the ship for the use of the crew on the voyage; and, in this sense, outfit is included in a general insurance on ship. It is in this sense that Lord Ellenborough uses the word when he says that hull and outfit are both protected by an insurance on ship (*k*).

In whaling voyages, however, the word "outfit" has a peculiar sense, and means the fishing stores of the ships so employed; *i.e.*, the harpoons, lances, spears, and whale lines, for the purpose of catching whales and seals on the voyage, and the casks, cisterns, boilers, &c. for preparing and containing the oil and blubber: in a word, all the instruments and apparatus necessary for taking the fish, and preparing and bringing home their animal produce (*l*). It is established, in accordance with the general custom of whaling voyages, that outfits in this sense are not protected by a general insurance in the common form on the "body, tackle, apparel, &c. of the ship" (*m*); and the practice in

Sect. 219.
Stores and tackle also included in insurance on ship.
And outfit in the sense of stores and provisions.

Not so the fishing stores for whaling voyages.

Mode of insuring

---

4 T. R. 210. Maclachlan said that if provisions for the crew are laid in double, for reasons of economy or necessity, the policy on the ship will only cover the provisions for the voyage insured; the provisions in excess being cargo. Rule 15, *supra*, may be construed in accordance with this opinion. He also said that provisions intended for the use of passengers, although incidental to the earning of passage money, are not covered by an insurance on ship, but should be insured *eo nomine*. Arnould, 6th ed. p. 48; and see McArthur, Ins. 58. This view is confirmed by Rule 15.

(*i*) 4 T. R. 206. The doubts expressed by Lord Esher, M. R., and Smith, L. J., in Roddick *v.* In-

demnity Mutual Marine Ins. Co., [1895] 2 Q. B. 380, whether the word "ship" alone covers provisions or stores, are removed by Rule 15.

(*k*) Hill *v.* Patten (1807), 8 East, 373, 375; Forbes *v.* Aspinall (1811), 13 East, 323, 325.

(*l*) 8 East, 375; Gale *v.* Laurie (1826), 5 B. & Cr. 156.

(*m*) Hoskina *v.* Pickersgill (1783), 3 Dougl. 222; 1 Marshall, Ins. 241; 1 Park, Ins. 126. Admitted in the case of The Dundee by Lord Stowell (1823), 1 Hagg. Ad. R. 109, 123 (see 1 Marshall, Ins. 241); and by Lord Tenterden in Gale *v.* Laurie (1826), 5 B. & Cr. 156, 164. See Hill *v.* Patten (1807), 8 East, 373, 375. It is possible that some of these stores are "fittings" requisite

Sect. 219.
whaling risks in the United States.
the United States, accordingly, is stated by Phillips to to describe the different interests insured in a fishi voyage as "ship, outfit, and cargo" (*n*).

Fittings and damage.
According to Mr. McArthur, temporary dunnage, ball or fittings are in practice not treated as covered by a gene policy on ship, but the rule is different when they are permanent use on a ship regularly employed in a particu trade (*o*). It is probable that the words "vessels engag in a special trade" in Rule 15 will, at any rate to sor extent, be construed in accordance with this practice, so th fittings required specially for a single voyage will not covered by the common policy.

The word "furniture," in a time policy on a ship employ in the grain trade, has been held to cover separation clot and dunnage mats required for the proper carriage of gra cargoes, although in the particular voyage, not being in us they were temporarily stowed away in the fore-peak (*p*).

Bunker coals and engine stores.
220. The bunker coals and engine stores of a steamsh necessary for the voyage are covered by an insurance for voyage in the common form (*q*). When the insurance for time, it seems that proper effect will be given to t words of the policy and to Rule 15 by allowing the policy cover a reasonable quantity of coals and stores, regard bei had to the service on which the ship is engaged, and avera adjusters usually allow such a quantity.

Roddick v. Indemnity Mutual Mar. Ins. Co.
In Roddick *v.* Indemnity Mutual Marine Insurance C the question arose whether a time policy on the "hull a machinery" of a steamship covered her bunker coals a stores. Evidence was given that in a voyage policy insurance on hull covers, according to the practice of unde writers, the coals and stores necessary for the voyage describ for the special trade in which the vessels are engaged, within the meaning of Rule 15, *supra*.

(*n*) 1 Phillips, Ins. ss. 496, 497.
(*o*) McArthur, Mar. Ins. 58.
(*p*) Hogarth *v.* Walker, [1899] 2 Q. B. 401; 68 L. J. Q. B. 888;

affirmed by the Court of App [1900] 2 Q. B. 283; 69 L. J. Q. 634.

(*q*) Mar. Ins. Act, 1906, Sched r. 15, *supra*. See Lowndes, I 2nd ed. s. 65; McArthur, 57; G 46.

CHAP. XI.] INSURANCE ON SHIP. 293

in the policy. Kennedy, J., however, held that, in a time Sect. 220.
policy at any rate, they were not covered by the term
"hull" (*r*), and this judgment was affirmed in the Court of
Appeal (*s*). Further, the learned judge thought that, even in
a voyage policy, this extended meaning of the word "hull"
could not be adopted, and both Lord Esher and Smith, L. J.,
seem to have been of the same opinion (*t*). It may be remarked, however, that policies simply on hull and machinery
are not common. There are often words in the policy which
show that the intention was to insure such stores, &c. as
would be covered by a policy in the ordinary form.

221. The "boat" is included by name as part of the ship The boat.
in the common policies of insurance (*u*); hence, in a policy on
ship in the common form upon the "body, tackle, apparel,
munition, ordnance, boat, and other furniture" of the ship,
Lord Lyndhurst would not admit evidence of a usage to show
that underwriters never paid for boats outside the ship slung
upon the quarters, on the ground that, though "usage may
be admissible to explain what is doubtful, it is never
admissible to contradict what is plain" (*x*).

In this case it had been proved on the part of the plaintiffs
that such slinging of the boat on the quarters was proper and
necessary in voyages of the description insured against: if it
could be shown that the boat was carried in any way which,
while exposing it to extraordinary risk, was not proper and
necessary on the voyage insured, it might fairly be considered
that, as in the case of goods carried on deck, the underwriter
would not be liable unless informed by the policy of the nature
of the risk. Thus, in a case decided in the United States it
seems to have been assumed that, if it could be clearly shown
that carrying boats slung at the stern davits, besides being a
dangerous, was also an unusual mode of carrying them on

(*r*) [1895] 1 Q. B. 836.
(*s*) [1895] 2 Q. B. 380.
(*t*) [1895] 1 Q. B. 842; 2 Q. B. 384, 386.
(*u*) See Dennis *v.* Home Ins. Co. (1905), 136 Fed. R. 481, where it was held that a launch was covered by the policy while being used in the ordinary way between the vessel and the shore.
(*x*) Blackett *v.* Royal Exch. Ass. Co. (1832), 2 Cr. & J. 244, 250.

Sect. 221.   the voyage insured, the underwriter, under the common for[m] of policy, could not be liable for their loss (*y*).

What is covered by a general insurance on "goods" or "merchandise."

222. According to Rule 17 in Schedule I. of the Mari[ne] Insurance Act, 1906, "the term 'goods' means goods in t[he] nature of merchandise, and does not include personal effec[ts] or provisions and stores for use on board." This definiti[on] is, however, qualified by the statement that "in the absen[ce] of any usage to the contrary, deck cargo and living anima[ls] must be insured specifically, and not under the gener[al] denomination of goods." Thus, it is unnecessary, in mo[st] cases, for the merchant who wishes to insure his merchandi[se] against sea risks to do more than give a general descriptio[n] of it as "goods" or "merchandise." Under such a polic[y,] in case of loss, the merchant would, in general, recover f[or] any goods of his which ultimately proved to be on board [at] the time of the loss (*z*).

Successive cargoes shipped in the course of the same voyage.

Hence it is laid down by the French jurists, and apparentl[y] on sound principles, that if, under such a general form o[f] insurance, the ship, in the course of the voyage insured, an[d] under liberty given her for that purpose in the policy, touche[s] at an intermediate port, and there lands the goods which we[re] on board at the commencement of the risk, and takes on boa[rd] others on account of the assured, such substituted goods a[re] comprehended under the general words of the policy, an[d] their value is recoverable in case of loss (*a*).

So, in this country, although after a policy has been on[ce] effected on a particular subject of insurance, it cannot, [in] consequence of the stamp laws, be so changed in its terms [as] to be made to attach on a totally different subject, "Yet [it] is not to be inferred from hence," says Lord Ellenboroug[h,] "that shifting or successive cargoes on board the same shi[p] in the course of the same continued adventure, as in th[e]

(*y*) Hall *v.* Ocean Ins. Co. (1839), 21 Pick. 472; cited 1 Phillips, s. 465.

(*z*) Pour que telle assurance soit valable, il suffit que l'aliment du risque existe lors du sinistre. Emerigon, c. x. s. 1, p. 296.

(*a*) Emerigon, *ibid.*; see also Boulay - Paty, Droit Com. M[ar.] tit. x. s. 6, p. 384.

African and other trades, out and home, may not properly be the subject of insurance under the word 'goods'; for in some of these cases the successive cargoes—*i.e.* (1) of English goods; (2) African articles of traffic; and, lastly, West India produce—are, according to the course of such trading adventures, one continued subject-matter of insurance under the one name of 'goods'" (*b*). Sect. 222.

223. The law of France is, that goods subject to deterioration or leakage must be specifically described in the policy (except where the assured is ignorant of the nature of the cargo at the time of effecting the insurance); otherwise no loss is recoverable upon such goods under the general description. The same rule is extended to perishable articles and to contraband of war, by the laws of other foreign states (*c*). Goods subject to leakage, perishable articles, and contraband are insurable under a general policy in this country.

No such rule exists in this country. As to articles liable to leakage or deterioration, the underwriters, by the common memorandum, expressly exempt themselves either from all liability for particular average losses, or from liability for such losses not amounting to a certain percentage. As to contraband of war, although the underwriter might avoid the insurance, unless he were told of the nature of the intended risk, yet it has never been decided that the contraband character of the cargo must be specified in the policy.

224. Considerable doubt appears at one time to have been entertained whether money, bullion or jewels could be insured under the general denomination of "goods, wares and merchandise." This doubt, in all probability, arose from mistaken theories of the balance of trade, which led to the notion that all exportation of such commodities, as articles of trade, Bullion, coin and jewels put on board for the purposes of commerce.

(*b*) Hill *v.* Patten (1807), 8 East, 373, 377; see also Tobin *v.* Harford (1863), 32 L. J. C. P. 134; in error (1864), 13 C. B. N. S. 791; 34 L. J. C. P. 37.

(*c*) Ord. de la Marine, 1. iii. t. 6, art. 31; Code de Commerce, art. 355; 1 Emerigon, c. x. s. 2, pp. 302 —307. See the Commercial Codes of Belgium, art. 208; Holland, art. 596; Spain, art. 745; Chile, art. 1215. The earlier ordinances are collected in the learned work of Magens, n. (*a*) to s. 14, vol. i. p. 9; and in Nolte's edition of Benecke, vol. i. pt. ii. tit. iii. c. ii. pp. 549 —552.

Sect. 224. was detrimental to the common weal. There is now, howeve no doubt that, when put on board as merchandise, they ma be insured, in this country, under the general description of goods and merchandise (though in actual practice they a generally insured under a specific description); it being a the same time understood that the underwriter is not liab for the risk of a clandestine exportation (*d*). The laws of some Continental states require these commodities to l specifically designated in the policy (*e*).

Bank notes and bills of exchange. Bank notes and bills of exchange should, it seems, l specifically described (*f*). A policy "on goods" means onl such goods as are merchantable (*merces*), *i.e.*, cargo put c board for the purposes of commerce (*g*). Hence it is tha clothes and other personal effects are not covered by general policy on goods and merchandise, nor the ship provisions (*h*), even though the ship carries nothing bu passengers (*i*).

(*d*) For an instance, see the case of Da Costa *v.* Firth (1766), 4 Burr. 1966. "Goods, wares and merchandise" will cover dollars, if entered at the custom-house: per Dampier, J. (1815), in Manning's Dig. Index to N. P. Rep. 164, n. 5, 2nd ed.; see also 1 Magens, art. 15, p. 10. Phillips points out (vol. i. s. 432) that there is no reason for this exception of clandestine trade which is made by the text-writers, saying that the fact that the trade is prohibited appears to involve the question of concealment, or the legality of the contract, rather than that of the sufficiency of the description.

(*e*) Dutch Code, art. 596; Spanish Code, art. 745.

(*f*) Per Dampier, J., Manning's Index, 165; Palmer *v.* Pratt (1824), 2 Bing. 185.

(*g*) So stated by underwriters in Ross *v.* Thwaites, before Lord Mansfield (1776), 1 Park, 23, 24; and so defined by Best, C. J., in Brown *v.* Stapyleton (1827), 4 Bing 121. "Wares or cargo for sale, per Lord Ellenborough in Hill Patten (1807), 8 East, 375. See however, Wilkinson *v.* Hyde, *infr*.

(*h*) Mar. Ins. Act, 1906, Sched. r. 17, *ante*, § 222; Ross *v.* Thwait (1776), 1 Park, 23. It is submitte however, that the personal effec of persons on board are covered, shipped as cargo. See 1 Parsor Ins. 521. It was not disputed Wilkinson *v.* Hyde (1858), 3 C. N. S. 30; 27 L. J. C. P. 116, th a policy on goods covered an en grant's outfit. In Duff *v.* Ma kenzie (1857), 3 C. B. N. S. 16; L. J. C. P. 313, the master insur his clothes, charts, instruments, & as master's effects, and this see the proper way to describe the Provisions are covered by t common policy on ship. Steve on Average, 60; *ante*, § 219.

(*i*) Brown *v.* Stapyleton (182; 4 Bing. 119, 122.

"In merchandise," says Park, J., "is included all property of great value, unless attached to the persons of the passengers" (k). Thus jewels, ornaments, cash, &c. not designed for trade, but carried about, or belonging to the persons of those on board, do not (as the better opinion seems to be) fall within the general description of goods and merchandise; and in case of loss would not, it seems, be recoverable under a policy on goods in the general form (l).

Sect. 224. Money and jewels attached to the person.

225. The reason why goods carried on deck are not usually covered by a general insurance in the common form on goods and merchandise is that they are exposed to a greater hazard than goods carried in the ordinary way (m); if, indeed, they are carried on deck by virtue of a general custom of the particular trade on which the insurance is effected, the underwriter is presumed to be acquainted with such usage without having notice of it, and therefore may fairly be supposed to undertake the risk of their being so carried on deck. As, however, the custom only applies to certain descriptions of goods in any trade (n), it may be doubtful whether, even in this case, the goods ought not to be specifically described in the policy, in order that the underwriter may be apprised that he is to run the extra risk. In the only case in which the point directly arose, the insurance was declared by the policy to be "on forty carboys of vitriol" (o). The observa-

Goods on deck are not covered by a general policy "on goods," unless there is a usage.

(k) Brown v. Stapyleton (1827), 4 Bing. 122; and see S. P., as to provender of live stock, Wolcott v. Eagle Ins. Co. (1827), 4 Pick. 429.

(l) Mar. Ins. Act, 1906, Sched. I. r. 17, *ante*, § 222. See 1 Park, Ins. 30; 1 Marshall, Ins. 327; 1 Emerigon, c. xii. s. 42; and c. x. s. 11.

(m) Ross v. Thwaites (1776), 1 Park, 23; and Backhouse v. Ripley (1802), *ibid.* 24. Deck goods are sometimes covered by the "in and over" clause.

(n) In Apollinaris Co. v. Nord Deutsche Ins. Co., [1904] 1 K. B. 252, a general custom to carry deck cargo on Rhine voyages was established, and the insurer was held to be liable for such cargo.

(o) Da Costa v. Edmunds (1815), 4 Camp. 142. So in the instance given by Phillips, in which an insurance on "outfits and catchings" was held to cover "blubber" remaining on deck, to be "tried" according to the usage of the whale fishery. Here, as Phillips remarks, "there is an uniform usage to carry on deck, and also an indication by the description of the subject and the voyage, that the part of the

Sect. 225.
Observations of Lord Lyndhurst.

tions of Lord Lyndhurst on this point are well deserving [of] attention. "Goods carried on deck," he says, "are not [in] the part of the ship where goods are usually carried; the[y] are in more than usual peril, and an usage that they are n[ot] covered by an ordinary policy on goods, but that they requi[re] a distinct explanation to the underwriter, of the part of th[e] ship in which they are to be carried, or (where that wi[ll] imply the same information) of the nature of the goods, not at variance with any part of the policy, is essential to th[e] information which the underwriter ought to receive, to enab[le] him to estimate the risk and calculate the premiums, and is [a] portion of that fairness which ought to be rigidly observe[d] upon all these contracts " (*p*).

The general conclusion arrived at by Phillips is, that, [if] by the description of the voyage, or the character of th[e] article specified in the policy, the underwriter may be pre[]sumed to be apprised of a usage to carry it on deck, th[e] policy will attach to it so carried (*q*). This appears ver[y] fairly to represent, if not the actual doctrine of the authoritie[s,] at all events the result of established principles.

The language of Rule 17 in Schedule I. of the Marin[e] Insurance Act, 1906 (*r*), does not altogether agree with th[e] foregoing statement, which is reproduced from the secon[d] edition of this work. The rule implies that deck cargo mus[t] be insured specifically, unless the usage be not merely to carr[y]

---

subject in the form of 'blubber' is to be on deck": 1 Phillips, s. 460. In the two cases of Gould *v.* Oliver (1837), 4 Bing. N. C. 134, and Milward *v.* Hibbert (1842), 3 Q. B. 120, the point decided was, that goods carried on deck by the usage of trade are entitled, if jettisoned, to contribution in general average; but there is nothing in either case upon the point how far such goods are insurable under the general description.

(*p*) Per Lord Lyndhurst, C. B.,

in Blackett *v.* Royal Exch. Ass. Co. (1832), 2 Cr. & J. 250.

(*q*) 1 Phillips, s. 460 *ad finem*. Phillips considers that when a article is sometimes carried on dec[k] and sometimes in the hold, there [is] no usage to carry on deck of whi[ch] the underwriter is bound to tal[e] notice. Da Costa *v.* Edmun[ds] (1815), 4 Camp. 142, however, [in] which it appeared that vitriol w[as] carried either on deck or below, [is] not consistent with this opinion.

(*r*) *Ante*, § 222.

the cargo on deck, but to insure it when so carried under the general denomination.

_{Sect. 225.}

In a recent case it was doubted whether the rule that deck cargo is not in general covered by an insurance on "goods" has any application to inland voyages by river or canal (*rr*); and inasmuch as the reason for the rule, viz., the increased hazard when goods are carried on deck, does not exist, the doubt seems to be well founded.

226. In whaling voyages the only cargo, properly so called, on board the ship, from first to last, is in general the homeward-bound cargo, consisting of the immediate produce and result of the fishing adventure; such proceeds, therefore (*i.e.*, the oil, whalebone, &c. taken in the fishery), may be covered under the general designation of "goods and merchandise" (*s*).

_{The produce of the whale fishery in whaling ships is covered by "goods" or "merchandise."}

Outfit in such voyages principally consists of the apparatus and instruments necessary for taking fish, seals, &c., and the disposing of them when taken in such a manner as to bring home the oil, whalebone and other animal produce of the adventure. Outfit, therefore, in such a voyage cannot be considered as "goods" in any proper sense of that word; *i.e.*, as Lord Ellenborough defines it, "as part of the wares or cargo for sale laden on board the ship"; accordingly it cannot be recovered under a general policy on goods (*t*).

_{Not so the outfit.}

227. It has been held in the United States that a general insurance on "cargo" will not cover provender taken on board for live stock, which constituted a great part of the cargo (*u*); nor will it cover the live stock itself (*x*).

_{Nor live stock or provender.}

With regard to live stock, the rule has been the same in this country; such interest being always, in fact, described

_{Live stock must be specifically described.}

(*rr*) Apollinaris Co. *v.* Nord Dentsche Ins. Co., [1904] 1 K. B. 252.

(*s*) Hill *v.* Patten (1807), 8 East, 374. So held also in the United States, in a case where the insurance was "on the cargo of a ship for a whaling voyage." Wolcott *v.* Eagle Ins. Co. (1827), 4 Pick. 429.

(*t*) Hill *v.* Patten (1807), 8 East, 373.

(*u*) Wolcott *v.* Eagle Ins. Co. (1827), 4 Pick. 429, cited 1 Phillips, Ins. s. 452; and see Brown *v.* Stapyleton (1827), 4 Bing. 119.

(*x*) Wolcott *v.* Eagle Ins. Co., *supra*, cited 1 Phillips, s. 453.

Sect. 227. specifically. Thus, where a general policy on goods w[as] intended to cover live stock, the insurance was declared, [at] the foot of the policy, "to be on thirty mules, ten asses, a[nd] thirty oxen," &c. (*y*); and in another case, where a poli[cy] was effected "on goods, as per annexed statement, valued [at] 2,800*l*.," the horses, a loss on which was claimed under t[he] policy, were specifically valued in the statement (*z*). As [we] have seen, the Marine Insurance Act, 1906, declares th[at] living animals must, in the absence of any usage to t[he] contrary, be insured specifically (*a*).

General practice, when the cargo consists of few commodities, to specify.

228. Although the interests and commodities alrea[dy] mentioned comprise the greater number of those which m[ust] be specifically designated in the policy, yet in practice, whe[n]ever the cargo consists of few commodities, or where [the] goods are valued by the hogshead, pipe, bale, &c., it is alm[ost] invariable to specify the commodities by name and numb[er]. This is generally done by writing at the foot or on the marg[in] of the policy "on woollen goods," "on piece goods," " one hundred tierces of coffee," "on twenty hogsheads [of] sugar," adding also the mark of each bale, cask, &c. (*b*); it may be done by altering the valuation clause so as to m[eet] the views of the parties.

When goods are specified the description must be accurate.

"Hats" not covered by "piece goods."

It must be carefully borne in mind that, whenever goods are specified in the policy, if no property of [the] assured be on board which fairly answers the descript[ion] given, the policy will not attach (*c*). Thus, if an insura[nce] be made on goods described in the policy as "piece good[s]," and by the invoice it appears that the goods really ship[ped] were "hats," the underwriter will not be liable for any [loss].

(*y*) Lawrence *v*. Aberdein (1821), 5 B. & Ald. 107.

(*z*) Gabay *v*. Lloyd (1825), 3 B. & Cr. 793.

(*a*) Sched. I. r. 17, *ante*, § 222.

(*b*) De Symonds *v*. Shedden (1800), 2 B. & P. 153. In Brown *v*. Fleming (1902), 7 Com. Cas. 245, Bigham, J., held that a policy on "228 cases whisky" covered the labels on the bottles and the st[raw] in which the bottles were pac[ked].

(*c*) A clause providing that [the] assured should be held covere[d on] a premium to be arranged in [case] of any incorrect definition of [the] interest insured, was held to [pro]tect him only where there wa[s no] intentional misdescription: H[ood] *v*. Wilson (1914), 30 T. L. R.

CHAP. XI.] INSURANCE ON GOODS. 301

on the hats (*d*): so an insurance on tortoiseshell will not cover a loss on indigo, &c. (*e*).

Sect. 228.

If an insurance purports to be effected on several ingredients, described *nominatim* in the policy, which enter into the composition of a manufactured article, such policy will not cover a loss on the manufactured article itself, which is a new product, and has a distinct appropriate name: thus, though oil and barilla both enter into the composition of soap, yet an insurance on oil and barilla will not cover a loss on soap (*f*). An insurance, however, effected on the raw material of a simple fabric, or utensil, into the composition of which no other ingredient enters to any extent, will, according to Emerigon, cover a loss on such fabric or utensil: thus, an insurance on "gold" or "silver" will, according to this doctrine, cover the loss of a gold cup or silver spoons (*g*).

Nor a manufactured article by the separate ingredients of it.

229. The next subject demanding our attention is freight. The word freight in insurance law has a more extensive signification than in the general law of shipping, and is used comprehensively to denote "the benefit derived by the shipowner from the employment of his ship" (*h*).

Freight. Meaning of the word in insurance law.

Freight, strictly speaking, as between the shipowner and the freighter, is the price to be paid by the latter to the former for the carriage of goods in the ship, and is only payable on the arrival of the goods at their port of destination; but in policies of insurance it also denotes that which is less properly

---

(*d*) Hunter *v.* Prinsep (1806), per Sir J. Mansfield, 1 Marshall, Ins. 323.

(*e*) 1 Emerigon, c. x. s. 1, p. 294.

(*f*) 1 Emerigon, c. x. s. 3, p. 306.

(*g*) *Ibid., ubi supra*. Maclachlan suspected "that this is a solitary instance of a peculiar *usus loquendi* as to the precious metals, and that it will not bear to be extended." Arnould, 6th ed. p. 30. There are few things, except metals, which can be restored to their original form; but Emerigon's distinction, which is derived from the Roman law of accession, is intelligible, and, if the principle be sound, is there any good reason for limiting it to the precious metals? Where a policy contained a warranty against more than a certain quantity of "iron cargo," the Court of Appeal held that the warranty applied to a cargo of steel blooms. Hart *v.* Standard Marine Ins. Co. (1889), 22 Q. B. D. 499.

(*h*) Per Lord Tenterden in Flint *v.* Flemyng (1830), 1 B. & Ad. 48.

Sect. 229. called freight, viz., the price agreed to be paid by the charterer to the shipowner for the hire of his ship, or a part of it, under a charter-party or other contract of affreightment (*i*), and also the benefit which the shipowner expects to derive from the carriage of his own goods in his own ship in the shape of their increased value to him at the port of delivery (*k*). As Lord Tenterden observes: "If the term freight, as used in policies of insurance, imports the benefit derived from the employment of the ship, it is the same thing to the shipowner whether he receives that benefit of the use of his ship (1st) by a money payment from one person who charters the whole ship; or (2nd) from various persons who put specific quantities of goods on board; or (3rd) from persons who pay him the value of his own goods at the port of delivery, increased by their carriage in his own ship " (*l*).

Definition of freight in Mar. Ins. Act.
Rule 16 in Schedule I. of the Marine Insurance Act, 1906 states that in the ordinary policy "the term 'freight' includes the profit derivable by a shipowner from the employment of his ship to carry his own goods or moveables (*m*), as well as freight payable by a third party, but does not include passage money" (*n*). Both freight in the strict sense of the word and the price paid for the hire of a ship under a charter party are no doubt covered by the words "freight payable by a third party."

Expected freight is a lawful subject of insurance in this country.
230. In whichever of these three senses the word is used it has long been a clearly established principle in this country that expected freight is a lawful subject of marine insurance "It would, indeed, be extraordinary," says Chambers, J., in *Lucena v. Craufurd*, "if freight could not be made the

(*i*) Per Lord Tenterden in *Winter v. Haldimand* (1831), 2 B. & Ad. 649; per Lord Ellenborough in *Forbes v. Aspinall* (1811), 13 East, 323, 325.

(*k*) *Flint v. Flemyng* (1830), 1 B. & Ad. 45; *Devaux v. J'Anson* (1839), 5 Bing. N. C. 519.

(*l*) 1 B. & Ad. 48.

(*m*) "Moveables" means any moveable tangible property, other than the ship, and includes money, valuable securities, and other documents: Mar. Ins. Act, 1906, s. 90.

(*n*) The definition of freight in the interpretation clause, s. 90, is literally the same.

subject of protection by an instrument which had its origin in commerce, and was introduced for the very purpose of giving security to mercantile transactions; it is a solid substantial interest ascertained by contract, and arising out of labour and capital employed for the purposes of commerce" (*o*).

Sect. 230.

As we shall see more at large hereafter, the party who insures freight must have an inchoate right to it, in order to entitle him so to insure; *i.e.*, he must be in such a position with regard to the expected freight that in the ordinary course nothing would prevent him from ultimately having a perfect right to it but the intervention of the perils insured against, or other maritime perils incident to the voyage (*p*).

The party insuring must have an inchoate right to the freight.

If, by the perils of the sea, the shipowner is prevented from realizing that which, but for the intervention of those perils, he would have earned, it is but fair and reasonable that he should have the means of protecting himself, by a policy of marine insurance, against the loss he is thus exposed to. For this reason, in this country, in America, and now in most of the Continental states, the shipowner is allowed to effect an insurance on that freight which he expects to earn, and which he may be prevented from earning by maritime perils.

231. The French legislature, proceeding rather on scholastic refinements than mercantile considerations, used to prohibit all insurance of expected or future freight (*q*), on the ground that expected freight is a mere contingency in which there is no present existing interest; that it is but a gain which the assured may miss making, not a property which he can risk losing. By a law of the 12th August, 1885, however, the law of France as to the insurance of expected gains has been completely altered, and the net freight (*le fret net*) is now insurable (*r*).

French law.

(*o*) 3 B. & P. 102.

(*p*) The question when this inchoate right begins belongs to the subject of insurable interest, and is fully discussed under that head, *post*, § 265 *et seq.*

(*q*) "Fret à faire," Ord. de la Marine, tit. vi. art. 15. "Fret des marchandises existant à bord," former art. 347 of the Code de Commerce.

(*r*) See Code de Commerce, art. 334.

Sect. 232.
Advances on freight.

232. Sect. 12 of the Marine Insurance Act, 1906, decl[ares] that "in the case of advance freight, the person advanc[ing] the freight has an insurable interest, in so far as such frei[ght] is not repayable in case of loss." Therefore sums paid [by] the charterer or his agent as an advance of part of the frei[ght] are insurable by him in this country. The question [that] usually arises as regards payments by the charterer is whet[her] the sum paid is an advance of freight (in which case it can[not] be recovered back if the goods are lost on the voyage [by] excepted perils), or merely a loan which the shipowner m[ust] repay though no freight be subsequently earned; and [the] question usually depends, as we shall see hereafter, on [the] particular terms of the charter-party (*s*).

Contingency freight.

The owner of goods who, if they arrive sea-damaged, [will] still have to pay full freight for their carriage will, by rea[son] of the damage, lose in whole or in part the benefit wh[ich] he would otherwise derive from the enhancement of [the] value of goods by their carriage to their destination. So[me]times cargo-owners protect themselves against such loss b[y a] policy on "contingency freight," *i.e.*, the freight payable [on] the delivery of the goods (*t*); but the insurance in such c[ase] is not really one on freight. It is substantially one on [the] interest in the goods akin to an insurance on profits.

(*s*) See next chapter, §§ 263, 264, and the discussion in Allison *v.* Bristol Mar. Ins. Co. (1875, 1876), 1 App. Cas. 209; De Silvale *v.* Kendall (1815), 4 M. & S. 37; Manfield *v.* Maitland (1821), 4 B. & Ald. 582; Winter *v.* Haldimand (1831), 2 B. & Ad. 649; Wilson *v.* Martin (1856), 11 Ex. 684; Hicks *v.* Shield (1857), 7 E. & B. 633; 26 L. J. Q. B. 205; Williams *v.* North China Ins. Co. (1876), 1 C. P. D. 757; The Red Sea, [1896] P. 20, C. A.; Maclachlan, Merchant Shipping, pp. 575—577.

(*t*) The policy usually contains a clause stating that "the freight insured under this policy b[eing] payable at port of destination, [the] amount shall be treated as an a[ddi]tional valuation of cargo, and [the] insurance is to cover only partic[ular] average on such additional v[alue] over and above the amount cl[aim]able in the usual way on the g[oods] themselves." When no freigh[t is] payable in the event of the los[s of] the goods or ship, the assured [has] obviously no insurable interes[t in] the "contingency freight" so [far] as total loss is concerned: see K[elly] *v.* Methuen (1907), 24 Times L[. R.] 145, C. A.

It was laid down by Lord Kenyon, at Nisi Prius, that freight could not be insured for part of the intended voyage (*u*); but this position, for which no ground of principle ever existed, was subsequently overruled by Lord Ellenborough and the Court of King's Bench, and it is now quite clear that freight, like any other subject, may be insured either for part or for the whole of the voyage or of the time over which it is likely to extend (*x*). A portion only of the freight at risk on a particular voyage may also be insured (*y*).

<small>Sect. 232.
Freight may be insured for part of the voyage or time.</small>

233. Freight must be insured *eo nomine* in the policy, which is generally adapted to an insurance on this interest by inserting the words "on freight" at the foot or in the margin of the instrument (*z*).

<small>Freight must be insured *nominatim*.</small>

Such a policy would cover not only freight in its strictest acceptation, but also the chartered hire of the vessel (whether a gross sum for the whole voyage, or a fixed sum per month payable as long as the voyage lasts) (*a*), and the benefit derived by the shipowner from carrying his own goods in his own vessel (*b*).

<small>What is covered by the word "freight."</small>

(*u*) Murdock *v.* Potts (1795). See 1 Marshall, Ins. 332; 2 Park, Ins. 634.

(*x*) Taylor *v.* Wilson (1812), 15 East, 324; Hall *v.* Brown (1814), 2 Dow, 367; Michael *v.* Gillespy (1857), 2 C. B. N. S. 627; 26 L. J. C. P. 306.

(*y*) Griffiths *v.* Bramley-Moore, C. A. (1878), 4 Q. B. D. 70.

(*z*) Frequently the insurance is expressed to be on "freight chartered $\frac{\text{and}}{\text{or}}$ as if chartered, on board or not on board." See as to the meaning of this clause, per Lord Esher, M. R., in The Bedouin, [1894] P. 1, 12; the judgments in Williams *v.* Canton Ins. Office, [1901] A. C. 462; per Hamilton, J., in Scottish Shire Line, Ld. *v.* London & Provincial, &c. Ins. Co.,

[1912] 3 K. B. 51, 62. The words "as if chartered" do not cover expected freight not yet contracted for: *ibid.* p. 63. See also, as to the meaning of "on board or not on board," New York & Cuba Mail SS. Co. *v.* Royal Exch. Assn. (1907), 154 Fed. Rep. 315.

(*a*) Etches *v.* Aldan (1827), 1 Man. & R. 157; S. P., Clark *v.* Ocean Ins. Co. (1835), 16 Pick. 289. For an insurance of such monthly hire specifically as "chartered or hiremoneys," see Manchester Liners *v.* British & Foreign Mar. Ins. Co. (1901), 7 Com. Cas. 26.

(*b*) Mar. Ins. Act, 1906, Sched. I. r. 16, *ante*, § 229. See Flint *v.* Flemyng (1830), 1 B. & Ad. 45, 48; Devaux *v.* J'Anson (1839), 5 Bing. N. C. 519.

Sect. 233.
Advance freight.

The charterer may insure advance freight—*i.e.*, mo[ney] advanced by him to the shipowner under their agreement [as] part payment of the freight—specifically, *e.g.*, as "advan[ce] on account of freight," or "advances against freight" ( ) It used to be thought that advances against freight at [the] time of loading could not be insured by the charterer sim[ply] as "freight"; the reason being that several eminent jud[ges] have said that such a payment is not freight (which is not earned until the goods are delivered), but money paid [for] taking the goods on board and undertaking to carry them ( ). Arnould, however, thought that the charterer could ins[ure] advance freight *eo nomine* as freight, though it might [be] safer to insure it specifically; and his opinion is suppor[ted] by high judicial authority (*e*). Rule 16 in Schedule I. [to] the Marine Insurance Act, 1906 (*f*), does not profess to [be] exhaustive, and therefore it does not prevent the insura[nce] of advance freight simply as "freight."

In a case before the Privy Council, where a charterer [had] insured an advance of freight by a policy on disburseme[nts] it was not questioned that the subject of the insurance [was] properly described, and the assured recovered for a loss ( ). It is not, however, the practice in this country to ins[ure] advance freight as disbursements. The owner of goods [who] has made an advance of freight sometimes insures the go[ods] and the advance by the same policy, the amount of [the] insurance on the advance freight being expressly stated ( ).

(*c*) Wilson *v.* Martin (1856), 11 Ex. 684; 25 L. J. Ex. 217; Williams *v.* North China Ins. Co. (1876), 1 C. P. D. 757, 761.

(*d*) See Blakey *v.* Dixon (1800), 2 B. & P. 321; Winter *v.* Haldimand (1831), 2 B. & Ad. 649, 653, 658; Etches *v.* Aldan (1827), 1 Man. & R. 157; Kirchner *v.* Venus (1859), 12 Moore, P. C. C. 361, 390; per Blackburn, J., Allison *v.* Bristol Mar. Ins. Co. (1876), 1 App. Cas. 229.

(*e*) See Arnould, 2nd ed. p. 272; Allison *v.* Bristol Mar. Ins. Co. (1876), 1 App. Cas. 209; per [Lord] Chelmsford, p. 223; Lord Hat[her]ley, p. 239; Lord O'Hagan, p. [ ] *per our.* Hall *v.* Janson (185[7]) E. & B. 509; per Byles, J., Tr[ ] *v.* Worms (1865), 19 C. B. N[.S.] 177; and see Robbins *v.* New [York] Ins. Co. (1828), 1 Hall, 363.

(*f*) *Ante*, § 229.

(*g*) Currie *v.* Bombay N[ative] Ins. Co. (1869), L. R. 3 P. C[.]

(*h*) See, however, Thames [&] Mersey Mar. Ins. Co. *v.* [ ] [1893] 1 Q. B. 476.

234. It has been doubted in the United States whether a charterer who hires a vessel for a voyage at a certain rate per month, payable on completion of the voyage, can insure, under a general policy on freight, the freight payable to him for carrying the goods of other persons (*i*); and also whether such a policy will cover the interest of a party who has sold his vessel, reserving to himself a right to receive the freight for the voyage insured (*k*). The ground of this doubt is the same in both cases, viz., that the assured has not the same stake in the safety of the ship as though he were owner; and that the underwriters, when asked to insure freight generally, may presume that they are dealing with the owner of the ship. The objection, however, is not well founded; for the charterer or former owner must be regarded as owner *pro hâc vice*, having as much interest in the ship's arriving so as to earn freight as the owners would have if insured to the full value of the freight to be earned (*l*).

Sect. 234. The charterer who carries goods on freight, or the owner who sells his ship, reserving the freight, may insure by a policy on freight.

235. In some respects similar to freight, in others very different, is our next subject of insurance—passage money (*m*). It differs from freight in point of practice, if not of principle, by a very important usage that requires it to be paid before sailing. Yet "no liability is by the common law thrown upon the owner or master of a ship, if the ship be lost, to forward passengers to their place of destination. Nor usually is there any obligation to do this imposed by the actual contract between the parties" (*n*).

Passage money. At common law no liability when ship lost to forward passengers.

(*i*) Riley *v.* Delafield (1811), 7 Johns. 522; cited 1 Phillips, s. 480.

(*k*) Mellen *v.* National Ins. Co. (1829), 1 Hall, 452; cited 1 Phillips, ss. 337, 480.

(*l*) See 1 Phillips, ss. 339, 480. For insurances by a charterer of his expected profit on subletting the ship, see *post*, § 239.

(*m*) See, generally, Maclachlan on Shipping, c. vii. *Passengers.* The insurability of passage money is recognized in s. 3 (2) (b) of the Mar. Ins. Act, 1906, *ante*, § 1.

(*n*) Per Lord Campbell, C. J., in Gibson *v.* Bradford (1855), 4 E. & B. 586, 589; 24 L. J. Q. B. 159, 160; Gillan *v.* Simpkin (1815), 4 Camp. 241. If, however, the ship be lost before the voyage commences, the passenger is entitled at common law to recover the passage money, as for a total failure of consideration: per Gibbs, C. J., Gillan *v.* Simpkin (1815), 4 Camp. 241.

Sect. 235.   A passenger who has paid his passage money under these conditions has an insurable interest analogous to that of the merchant upon freight paid in advance.

Statutory liabilities.   The law has been materially altered by statute; and it is now in many cases the duty of the owner, charterer, or master of a ship to have the passenger carried to his destination even when the vessel is lost (*o*). The Merchant Shipping Act, 1894, expressly provides that no insurance in respect of any steerage passage or of any steerage passage or compensation money which any person is by the Act made liable to provide or pay, or in respect of any other risk under Part III. of the Act, shall be invalid on account of the nature of the risk or interest insured (*p*).

Under a policy against all costs, charges and liabilities to which the owner or charterer might be subjected under sections 46, 47, 48, 49, 50 and 51 of the repealed Passengers Act, 15 & 16 Vict. c. 44, the owner recovered against the underwriter for money expended in forwarding the passengers to their ultimate port from New Providence, off which place the vessel in the course of her voyage had been totally lost (*q*). A year after, under another policy "on passage money of emigrants, to pay a loss *pro rata* subject to (the same clauses almost as in the foregoing case) and against these risks only," the owner sought to recover the money spent in provisions for the emigrants during six weeks' stay at Fayal whilst the ship was being repaired after sea damage, and failed in his suit simply because his obligation to maintain the passengers during the detention was imposed by a section not included in the policy (*r*).

Passage money is not covered by a policy on "freight," unless the context of the particular policy necessitates a

---

(*o*) Merchant Shipping Act, 1894, ss. 331—335. The Act repealed the Passenger Acts then in force.

(*p*) Merchant Shipping Act, 1894, s. 335.

(*q*) Gibson *v.* Bradford (1855), 4 E. & B. 586; 24 L. J. Q. B. 159.

See New Zealand Shipping Co. *v.* Duke (1914), 30 Times L. R. 385, for a modern form of policy covering disbursements on account of passengers.

(*r*) Willis *v.* Cooke (1855), 5 E. & B. 641; 25 L. J. Q. B. 16.

CHAP. XI.]   PROFITS.   309

different construction (*s*). A ship was partly laden with goods, and also carried a number of coolies whose passage money was only payable on arrival. The shipowner took out a policy on freight, the risk to attach "from the loading of the said goods or merchandise on board the said ship." It was contended, but not established, that by the custom of the particular trade freight included passage money. In this state of facts, and on the construction of the policy, the Court of Common Pleas held that the freight of the merchandise only was insured (*t*).

Sect. 235.

236. Insurances on expected profits are lawful in this country (*u*) and in the United States, and are in general expressly allowed by the commercial codes of the Continental States (*x*). From the same train of reasoning which led them to prohibit all insurances on freight, the jurists and lawgivers of France forbade all insurances on expected profits (*y*); but the law of the 12th August, 1885, introduced a more liberal rule, and profits are now insurable in France (*z*).

Insurance on profits.

The grounds upon which profits are insurable are expressed with admirable force and clearness in the following passage from Lawrence, J.'s, judgment in the case of Barclay *v.* Cousins. "As insurance is a contract of indemnity, it cannot be said to be extended beyond what the design of such species of contract will embrace, if it be applied to protect men from those losses and disadvantages which but for the perils insured against the assured would not suffer; and in every maritime adventure the adventurer is liable to be deprived, not only of the things immediately subjected to the

Principle upon which they are insurable, as expressed by Lawrence, J.

(*s*) Mar. Ins. Act, 1906, s. 30, Sched. I. Introduction and r. 16, *ante*, § 229.

(*t*) Dencon *v.* Home & Colonial Ins. Co. (1872), L. R. 7 C. P. 341; 41 L. J. C. P. 162.

(*u*) See Mar. Ins. Act, 1906, s. 3 (2) (b), *ante*, § 1.

(*x*) See the Codes of Holland, art. 593; Spain, arts. 743, 748; Germany, art. 779; Russia, art.

545; Scandinavia, art. 230; Belgium, art. 191.

(*y*) See 1 Emerigon, c. viii. s. 9, pp. 236—239, and the former art. 347 of the Code de Com.

(*z*) Code de Com. art. 334. In Spain and Denmark, also, profits were formerly uninsurable, but in those countries also the law has been altered. See the Spanish and Scandinavian Codes, *ubi supra*.

Sect. 236. perils insured against, but also of the advantages to be derived from the arrival of those things at their destined port. If they do not arrive, his loss is not merely that of his goods, but of the benefits which he might obtain were his money employed in an undertaking not subject to the perils. If it be allowable for the merchant to protect capital, subject to the risk of maritime commerce, by insuring it, why may he not protect those advantages he is in danger of losing by their being exposed to the same risks? It is surely not an improper encouragement of trade to provide that merchants, in case of adverse fortune, should not only not lose the principal adventure, but that the principal should not, in consequence of such bad fortune, be totally unproductive; and that men of small fortune should be encouraged to engage in commerce by their having the means of preserving their capitals entire" (a).

Such are the principles upon which insurances on expected profits are allowed in this country.

Profits may be insured either in valued or open policies. The assured must give evidence that some profit would have been made.

237. Profits may be insured equally by valued and by open policies (b); but, whether insured by one or the other, it has been held in this country (as we shall see more at large when treating of insurable interest) that the assured cannot recover unless he prove that but for the intervention of the perils insured against some profit would in fact have been realized by the sale of his goods on arrival (c).

The ordinary policy does not cover loss of profits on goods not shipped.

238. He must also, said Arnould, prove that the goods from the sale of which the profits were expected to arise were at one time or other actually exposed to the perils of the sea (d). It was so held in one case, where the policy

(a) Per Lawrence, J., delivering the judgment of the Court in Barclay v. Cousins (1802), 2 East, 544.
(b) Eyre v. Glover (1812), 3 Camp. 276; 16 East, 218.
(c) Hodgson v. Glover (1805), 6 East, 316; Eyre v. Glover, *supra*. The law is different in the United States. See Patapsco Ins. Co. v. Coulter (1830), 3 Peters' Supreme Court R. 222; 1 Phillips, Ins. s. 318. It is there a conclusive presumption that some profit would have accrued had the goods arrived, and upon this the valuation in the policy attaches. 1 Parsons, Ins. 194, 195.
(d) 2nd ed. p. 255; 6th ed. p. 38.

CHAP. XI.] INSURANCE ON PROFITS. 311

was in the ordinary form, with the term "beginning the adventure from the loading of the goods" (e); but the Court admitted in that case, and in the later case of Halhead v. Young (f), that where a loss of profit will be caused by the happening of some event before the goods are shipped, the assured may protect himself against such loss by a properly framed policy.

Sect. 238.

The facts in McSwiney v. Royal Exchange Assurance Co. were as follows. McSwiney, who had bought 6,000 bags of rice to arrive from Madras by the ship "E. B." before the end of May, effected an insurance at and from Madras to London on profit on rice loaden or to be loaden on the "E. B." When 1,200 bags were on board, the other 4,800 bags being ready to be shipped, the "E. B." was disabled by perils of the sea and prevented from performing the voyage, and the rice on board was spoiled. McSwiney's purchase thus became inoperative. The policy was in the ordinary form, and the adventure was to begin from and after the loading on board. The Exchequer Chamber held that the policy only attached to the rice which was on board, and also that the losses insured against were only losses by perils of the seas directly affecting the goods and consequently the profits on the goods. Therefore, even if the rice on shore had been covered by the policy, the loss of profit on such rice was not caused by a peril of the seas within the meaning of the policy (g). The Court, however, said: "We have no doubt that the plaintiff might have recovered, in the events which have happened, a total loss if he had been insured by a policy properly adapted to the case, and so drawn as to cover his special interest from the time that the rice was appropriated by the vendors and ready to be shipped at Madras, and also to assure him against losses of the expected profits, not merely by the loss of all the rice by perils of the

McSwiney v. Royal Ex. Ass. Co.

Opinion of Court that profits are insurable before goods shipped.

(e) McSwiney v. Royal Exchange Ass. Co. (1849), 14 Q. B. 634; S. C., in error (1850), ibid. 646.

(f) (1856), 6 E. & B. 312; 25 L. J. Q. B. 290.

(g) McSwiney v. Royal Exchange Assurance (1849), 14 Q. B. 634, 646.

Sect. 238.

seas, but by the loss of any part of it, or the loss of the ship, or delay of the voyage beyond the month of May; in any of which contingencies this special interest in profits would have been entirely defeated" (*h*).

Halhead v. Young.

H. contracted to buy a cargo of timber at Quebec, and chartered a ship then on her way to New York to proceed thence to Quebec and take the cargo to Liverpool. He effected a policy "on profit on cargo" for a voyage from New York to Quebec and thence to Liverpool, beginning the adventure from the loading of the goods. The ship was lost between New York and Quebec; in consequence of which the cargo which was ready at Quebec could not be shipped during the shipping season, and the plaintiff lost his profit. The Court of Queen's Bench held that the policy had not attached; but they were of opinion that where the profits of a purchaser of goods depend on the contingency of a particular ship carrying them on a particular voyage a policy might be framed to indemnify him for a loss of profits caused by the ship being lost before she reaches the port of loading (*i*).

Profits on cargo are sometimes insured by a policy with a clause "to pay on non-arrival of the cargo at its destination," to which sometimes the words "in such ship" (*i.e.*, the ship in which they are intended to be carried) are added (*j*).

Profits on charter.

239. A charterer who enters into a sub-charter or contracts to carry goods in the ship may insure his expected profit,

---

(*h*) 14 Q. B. 660. Cf. Wilson *v.* Jones (1867), L. R. 2 Ex. 139.

(*i*) Halhead *v.* Young (1856), 6 E. & B. 312; 25 L. J. Q. B. 290. In this case an attempt was made by parol evidence to set up a different risk from that which was expressed in the policy, but it failed.

(*j*) In Wyllie *v.* Povah (1907), 12 Com. Cas. 317, the clause without the words "in such ship" was adopted. The ship became a total wreck in the course of the voyage; but the goods were carried to their destination in another ship, and tendered to the assured, the purchasers, who refused to accept them as they seem to have been entitled to do under the contract of sale. Pickford, J., held that they could not recover.

CHAP. XI.] PROFITS AND COMMISSIONS. 313

which is properly described as "profit on charter" (k), or **Sect. 239.**
"difference of freight" (l).

Whether a shipowner can insure the profit which he **Profits from use of ship.**
expects to make by the use of his ship is a question which
has not been determined (m). In a recent case the plaintiff
contended that the benefit to be derived from the use of a
ship is insurable, although there be no actual contract for
freight, and Walton, J., agreed that a shipowner has an
interest in the use of his vessel, and may insure against loss
through his being deprived of such use by perils of the sea,
or other causes (n).

240. A party may also insure the sums which he is to **Commissions.**
receive by way of commission on the sale of merchandise;
and if the merchandise from the sale of which such commissions were to arise was only prevented from arriving at
the place of sale by the perils insured against, the assured
may recover to the extent of his loss (o).

It was held in 1809 that the goods from the sale of which
the commissions are to arise must also have been on board at
the time of the loss (p). There is, however, a close analogy
between profits and commissions; and it is submitted, on the
authority of the later cases relating to the insurance of profits,
that on a properly framed policy the assured may recover

(k) See Asfar v. Blundell, [1895] 2 Q. B. 196; C. A., [1896] 1 Q. B. 123, for the nature of such an insurance.

(l) See Smith v. Fenning (1898), 3 Com. Cas. 75. The contract was "to pay a total loss in the event of the steamer being unable to fulfil her charter, through inability to load by November 20," and Kennedy, J., held that the assured could not recover where a part-cargo had been loaded before that date.

(m) It is clear that he cannot insure such profit as "freight" unless he has entered into a binding contract for freight: see *post*, § 269.

(n) Manchester Liners v. British and Foreign Mar. Ins. Co. (1901), 7 Com. Cas. 26, 33. See also per Mathew, J., in Lawther v. Black (1900), 6 Com. Cas. 5, 8, and *post*, § 288.

(o) Mar. Ins. Act, 1906, s. 3 (2) (b), *ante*, § 1; Flint v. Le Mesurier (1796), before Lord Kenyon, 2 Park, Ins. 563; Barclay v. Cousins (1802), 2 East, 544; King v. Glover (1806), 2 B. & P. N. R. 206.

(p) Knox v. Wood (1809), 2 Park, Ins. 564; *S. C.*, 1 Camp. 543.

314 SUBJECTS OF MARINE INSURANCE. [PART I.

Sect. 240. although the goods were not on board at the time of the loss, provided that he had an insurable interest.

The commission or brokerage which a ship's husband or shipbroker expects to earn under a binding contract can, no doubt, be insured if the earning thereof is liable to be prevented by maritime perils affecting the ship (*q*).

Profits and commissions must be specifically named.

241. Profits and commissions to arise from the sale of goods are really an interest in the goods themselves, and in one sense an insurance on them is an insurance on goods (*r*). It is, however, well established that such profits or commissions are not covered by a policy on *goods* or *merchandise;* they must be specifically named (*s*). This rule is absolute in England (*t*). In the United States it appears to have been held that "a right to a certain percentage, proportion, or share of a cargo as commissions or profits is covered by a policy on 'property'" (*u*).

Lloyd's form of policy is adapted, as usual, by insertion of the words *profits* or *commissions* in the margin; or in the valuation clause, adopting or adapting the language of the clause according as the subject of the policy is valued or not (*x*).

Bottomry and respondentia loans.

242. Loans on bottomry and respondentia, though themselves a species of insurance, may yet be the subjects of

(*q*) See Buchanan *v.* Faber (1899), 4 Com. Cas. 223; and per Lord Mansfield as to prize agents in Le Cras *v.* Hughes (1782), 2 Park, Ins. 569.

(*r*) See Smith *v.* Reynolds (1856), 1 H. & N. 221; 25 L. J. Ex. 337; Allkins *v.* Jupe (1877), 2 C. P. D. 375; Berridge *v.* Man On Ins. Co. (1887), 18 Q. B. D. 346.

(*s*) So resolved by all the judges in Lucena *v.* Craufurd (in Dom. Proc.) (1806), 2 B. & P. N. R. 315; Anderson *v.* Morrice (1875), L. R. 10 C. P. 609, 622, 624. For the reason see Mackenzie *v.* Whitworth (1875), 1 Ex. D. 36, 43. See, however, Buchanan *v.* Faber (1899), 4 Com. Cas. 223; *post,* "Disbursements," § 246.

(*t*) In a valued policy the owner of the goods may, of course, include his expected profit in the valuation. See Lowndes, Mar. Ins. s. 25.

(*u*) Holbrook *v.* Brown (1807), 2 Mass. R. 280; cited 1 Phillips, s. 462. It has been stated to be the custom in Philadelphia to insure profits under the general denomination of goods. 1 Phillips, s. 462.

(*x*) See Eyre *v.* Glover (1812), 16 East, 218.

insurance, inasmuch as they are an interest exposed to risk from the perils of the sea (y).

Sect. 242.

Sect. 10 of the Marine Insurance Act, 1906, declares that "the lender of money on bottomry or respondentia has an insurable interest in respect of the loan." The lender alone can insure the sum advanced: the nature of the contract shows this. The condition of the bond is that if the ship perishes the borrower is to pay him nothing; if it arrives safely he pays the capital and the maritime interest. The lender therefore, risks his capital and interest, and may consequently insure them (z). Where the loan is made repayable in any event, the lender cannot insure it as a bottomry loan (a).

Who can insure them.

The borrower clearly cannot insure the sum advanced, for the risk of its loss does not fall upon him, and as in case of loss of the ship he would have nothing to pay the lender, were he to receive the whole sum insured from the underwriters he would have a direct interest in the destruction of the vessel (b).

In France, though the capital lent on bottomry was insurable, the maritime interest which the lender on bottomry is to receive on the prosperous termination of the voyage used not to be, on the ground, as Pothier expresses it, that such interest is a gain, which the lender will miss making if the ship perishes, and not a loss by the perils of the sea (c). Now, however, the maritime interest (*le profit maritime*) is insurable in France as well as the sum lent (d).

The law in France.

In this country, and also in the United States, a more liberal practice has always prevailed, and both bottomry and

In this country and the United States.

(y) 1 Emerigon, c. viii. s. 11, pp. 241, 243; Pothier, Traité d'Assurance, Nos. 30, 31; Glover *v.* Black (1763), 3 Burr. 1394; 1 W. Bl. 405.
(z) 1 Emerigon, c. viii. s. 11, p. 243; 1 Nolte's Benecke, 295, 296.
(a) Stainbank *v.* Fenning (1851), 11 C. B. 51; 20 L. J. C. P. 226; Stainbank *v.* Shepard (1853), 13 C. B. 418; 22 L. J. Ex. 341; and see Simonds *v.* Hodgson (1829), 6 Bing. 114; *S. C.*, in error (1832), 3 B. & Ad. 50.
(b) Pothier, Traité d'Assurance, Nos. 31, 32.
(c) *Ibid.* No. 32, p. 40, edit. par Estrangin.
(d) Code de Com. art. 334.

Sect. 242. respondentia interest have always been lawful subjects of insurance.

Respondentia and bottomry loans must be specifically insured.

243. It has always been said that respondentia and bottomry loans must be specifically described in the policy; they cannot be insured under the general denomination of goods and merchandise. Lord Mansfield put this on the ground "that by the custom of merchants respondentia is insured under a special denomination" (*e*); but Kent, J., has also suggested, as a reason for the rule, "that the risk is peculiar, as there is neither average nor salvage; and a capture does not mean a temporary taking only, but one that occasions a total loss" (*f*). It is doubtful whether the latter ground can now be considered sufficient; but, notwithstanding sect. 26 (2) of the Marine Insurance Act, 1906, on the ground of usage it will apparently still be necessary, by reason of sect. 26 (4), to insure bottomry and respondentia loans specifically (*g*).

Unless there be a usage to the contrary.

Yet if it can be shown to be the usage of any particular course of trade to insure these interests under the general words, they may be recovered under a policy containing such words only. Thus, on the ground of such a custom of the East India trade, an East India captain was permitted to recover, at respondentia interest, money he had laid out for the use of the ship, under the general words "goods, specie, and effects on board" (*h*).

The specific description should be true.

Of course, if the instrument of hypothecation be not in law what it is described in the policy to be, the policy is invalid. The Court of Common Pleas, therefore, upon the construction of such an instrument, being of opinion that it was not a bottomry bond, because it made the lender's claim under it depend, not on the arrival of the ship, but on the arrival of

---

(*e*) Glover *v.* Black (1763), 2 Burr. 1394; 1 W. Bl. 399, 405, 422; see also Simonds *v.* Hodgson (1832), 3 B. & Ad. 50. Glover *v.* Black was commented on in Mackenzie *v.* Whitworth (1875), L. R. 10 Exch. 142; C. A., 1 Ex. D. 36.

(*f*) Robertson *v.* United Ins. Co. (1801), 2 Johnson's Cases, 250; cited 1 Phillips, Ins. s. 427.

(*g*) See *post*, §§ 251, 252.

(*h*) Gregory *v.* Christie (1784), 3 Dougl. 419; 1 Marshall, Ins. 326.

the master, held that the lender could not recover under a policy "on bottomry" (*i*). The Court of King's Bench, in error, admitted that, had the Court of Common Pleas been correct in their construction of the instrument, the policy as framed would not have covered the interest of the lenders (*k*).

Sect. 243.

The master of a ship borrowed money in a foreign port for necessary repairs and disbursements, to secure which he drew bills on his owner, and executed what purported to be an hypothecation of ship, cargo, and freight. By this instrument the lender forbore all interest beyond the amount necessary to insure the ship and cover the advances; and the master took upon himself and his owner the risk of the voyage, making the money payable at all events, and subjecting the ship to seizure and sale in the event of the bills being refused acceptance or dishonoured. The Court held, that as this was not such an hypothecation as would be enforced by the Court of Admiralty, the merchant had no insurable interest in the ship (*l*). The interest was described in this policy as "1,500*l*. advances for repairs and disbursements, the whole valued at 1,675*l*., including premiums of insurance." *Semble* that this was not a good description whether the insurance was to be taken as on the ship in respect of the advance, or on the debt (*m*).

Stainbank *v.* Fenning.

244. Seamen have been debarred by the laws of most, if not of all, maritime states from insuring their wages, the reason being the belief that such an insurance might tempt them in time of danger not to exert themselves to the utmost for the preservation of the ship. By the law of England it was an implied condition of the seaman's contract with the shipowner that his wages were dependent on the earning of freight by the ship. This rule was generally expressed by

Seamen's wages formerly not insurable. The maritime law of England.

(*i*) Simonds *v.* Hodgson (1829), 6 Bing. 114.
(*k*) See remarks of Lord Tenterden in delivering the judgment of the Court in Simonds *v.* Hodgson (1832), 3 B. & Ad. 57.

(*l*) Stainbank *v.* Fenning (1851), 11 C. B. 51; 20 L. J. C. P. 226; Stainbank *v.* Shepard (1853), 13 C. B. 418; 22 L. J. Ex. 341; cf. The Haabet, [1899] P. 295.
(*m*) 11 C. B. 74, 78.

Sect. 244. saying that freight is the mother of wages. Therefore, when a ship was lost in the course of a voyage, the seaman was usually a loser to the extent of the wages already earned by him, and also (except when he obtained another ship) in respect of the wages which he would have earned during the remainder of the voyage. Yet, on grounds of policy, as has just been said, the insurance of his wages, or of any commodities which he was to receive at the end of the voyage in lieu of wages, was not permitted (*n*).

The Merchant Shipping Acts. The law relating to the earning of wages was altered by the Merchant Shipping Act, 1854. Wages are no longer dependent on freight being earned, and seamen are now entitled, in the event of the ship being lost, to be paid their wages until the time of the loss (*o*). Thus the loss of the ship cannot now be the immediate cause of a loss of wages already earned. Such loss of wages can only be directly due to the inability of the shipowner to pay his debt to the seaman; but indirectly it may be caused by the loss of the ship, as the seaman's lien on the ship for his wages may become valueless (*p*). But the loss of the ship may still involve a loss of the wages which the seamen would have earned during the remainder of the voyage, or of the period of time for which they were engaged.

Wages are now insurable. In a previous edition of this work (*q*), Maclachlan raised the question whether, as a result of the alteration in the law made by the Merchant Shipping Act, 1854, seamen's wages became insurable. It is, however, unnecessary to repeat his

---

(*n*) Webster *v.* De Tastet (1797), 7 T. R. 157; King *v.* Glover (1806), 2 B. & P. N. R. 206, 209, 210; The Neptune (1824), 1 Hagg. Ad. 227, 232, 239; The Lady Durham (1835), 3 Hagg. Ad. 196, 201; 1 Emerigon, c. viii. s. 10, p. 235, where all the learning of the foreign jurists on this point is collected. So in the United States, Galloway *v.* Morris (1802), 3 Yeates, R. 445.

(*o*) 17 & 18 Vict. c. 104, ss. 183,
184; repealed by the Merchant Shipping Act, 1894, and therein re-enacted by ss. 156, 157.

(*p*) The seaman retains his lien on the wreck (The Neptune (1824), 1 Hagg. Ad. 239); but he has no claim for his wages out of the owner's insurance on the lost vessel. The Lady Durham (1835), 3 Hagg. Ad. 196.

(*q*) 6th ed. p. 44.

arguments, which the present editors did not think convincing; for when the Marine Insurance Act, 1906, was passed there was a consensus of opinion that seamen should be allowed to insure their wages, and sect. 11 declares that "the master or any member of the crew of a ship has an insurable interest in respect of his wages" (*r*). {Sect. 244.}

Even when they were debarred from insuring their wages, seamen were allowed to insure any goods which they might have purchased with their wages and shipped on board (*s*). So it has been held in the United States that a mariner, who has the privilege of carrying a certain quantity of goods, may insure them (*t*). {Goods purchased by seamen with their wages.} {Goods they are privileged to carry (United States).}

245. All that has been said of the crew's wages applied to all officers of lower rank than the master, *e.g.*, the mate (*u*). The master, however, was regarded as a person of too much trust and character to be rendered indifferent to the fate of the adventure merely by having secured his own interest in it. He was, therefore, allowed to insure his wages, or his commissions, or any interest he might have in the vessel as part owner (*x*); and his right to insure his wages is, as we have seen, affirmed in sect. 11 of the Marine Insurance Act, 1906 (*y*). {The master's wages and commissions insurable.}

The master may insure his personal effects; they must, however, be specifically mentioned, and are not protected by a policy on goods (*z*). There is no decision as to the in- {Master's effects.} {Seamen's effects.}

(*r*) In France seamen's wages have been insurable since the Law of 1885 (Code de Com. art. 334), and they are also insurable in Belgium (Code, art. 191).

(*s*) 1 Emerigon, c. viii. s. 10, 240; 1 Park, 11.

(*t*) Galloway *v.* Morris (1802), 3 Yeates, R. 445.

(*u*) Webster *v.* De Tastet (1797), 7 T. R. 157.

(*x*) King *v.* Glover (1806), 2 B. & P. N. R. 206; Hawkins *v.* Twizell (1856), 5 E. & B. 883; 25 L. J. Q. B. 160. Wilson *v.* Royal Exchange Ass. Co. (1811), 2 Camp. 626, decided that a policy effected by the lender on money advanced to the captain payable out of freight was void; see also Siffken *v.* Allnutt (1813), 1 M. & S. 39.

(*y*) *Supra*, § 244.

(*z*) Mar. Ins. Act, 1906, Sched. I. r. 17, *ante*, §§ 222, 224. See Duff *v.* Mackenzie (1857), 3 C. B. N. S. 16; 26 L. J. C. P. 313; Anstey *v.* Ocean Mar. Ins. Co. (1913), 19 Com. Cas. 8.

Sect. 245. surability of seamen's effects; but it is impossible to suppose that the prohibition against insuring wages, which the Legislature has removed, would now apply to personal effects, especially as it was conceded that seamen might insure merchandise on board belonging to them (*a*).

Disbursements.

246. In recent times "disbursements" have become a common, and important, subject-matter of insurance. Inasmuch, however, as the policies are usually "honour" or "p. p. i." policies, and for an agreed valuation, they have given rise to comparatively little litigation, and there is consequently a dearth of legal decision as to what items of loss are properly recoverable thereunder. In its ordinary sense, a disbursement means an expenditure of money. In this sense it may be said that all expenditures the benefit of which will be lost, or the object of which will be frustrated, by marine perils would be properly covered by a "disbursement" policy, and these alone (*b*). But inasmuch as money expended

Ordinary meaning of "disbursements."

(*a*) After seamen's wages, Arnould in the 2nd edition (vol. i. p. 259) dealt with slaves as a subject of insurance. He mentioned that the practice of insuring slaves as articles of traffic was prohibited in this country in 1806 by 47 Geo. 3, c. 36, s. 5. They must therefore, he said, be more properly classed with those subjects the insurance of which is prohibited by the positive laws of our own country than with those which in their own nature are not insurable. Although the practice required to be suppressed by a positive prohibition, and when he wrote was still permitted in other states, " it will yet be allowable in writing, as an Englishman to Englishmen," he said, " to consider the statute which exterminated the practice as a mere affirmation of the law of nature, and to declare that a man, whatever be his race or colour, cannot, from the nature of things, be made the subject of insurance as an article of merchandise."

(*b*) Where a charterer who had made an advance of freight for the ship's purposes protected himself by a policy on disbursements, it was not disputed that the subject was properly described, and the assured recovered. Currie *v.* Bombay Native Ins. Co. (1869), L. R. 3 P. C. 72. It is not, however, usual to insure advance freight as disbursements. For an instance of an insurance on disbursements made to cover an expenditure on coal, engine-room stores, provisions and port charges, see Roddick *v.* Indemnity Mutual Marine Ins. Co., [1895] 1 Q. B. 836; 2 Q. B. 380. The editors have been informed that in some trades when a ship has sustained damage and been repaired, it is usual for the assured to effect a policy on "disbursements" against total loss only, in respect of the repairs, for the benefit of his underwriter, who invariably pays the premium.

cannot be itself at risk, this statement is probably subject to the qualification that a disbursement, to be insurable, must be represented by some interest in the tangible property at risk, *i.e.*, in the ship or the property on board (*c*). Yet it was stated by Bigham, J., that the term is used at Lloyd's in a sense which in some respects is undoubtedly wider, and in other respects is probably narrower, than the meaning now suggested. The learned Judge said that it was a "compendious term commonly used to describe any interest which is outside the ordinary and well-known interests of 'hull,' 'machinery,' 'cargo,' and 'freight,'" and that it would cover the commission and brokerage which the managing owners and insurance brokers of a ship expected to earn in the future (*d*). Expected commission and brokerage, however, can clearly in no sense be said to be expenditures; therefore, if the learned Judge be correct, disbursements must in this case be used in a wider sense than the ordinary meaning of the word. On the other hand, the learned Judge intimated that the term does not include all expenditures, but only such as are not covered ordinarily by insurances on hull, machinery, cargo, and freight. In this respect the meaning

Sect. 246.

Meaning of term according to Bigham, J.

(*c*) See Moran *v.* Uzielli, [1905] 2 K. B. 555. In that case the plaintiffs, who were agents for a foreign ship, the owners of which were indebted to them for advances for her necessary disbursements, effected a policy "on disbursements" for a voyage of the ship to this country. It was admitted that the plaintiffs' interest, if insurable, was sufficiently described, and Walton, J., held that as the plaintiffs had a right to enforce their claim for advances by an action *in rem* and the arrest of the ship, they had an insurable interest and could recover to the extent of the advances. On the other hand, where the managing owner of a British ship, who had no lien on her, insured the amount of the company's indebtedness to him by policies or disbursements, Lord Shaw said that any payments made under these insurances would not be payments made to indemnify him for loss, but would be of the nature of presents: Thames & Mersey Mar. Ins. Co. *v.* "Gunford" Ship Co., [1911] A. C. 529, 542. In Price *v.* Maritime Ins. Co., [1901] 2 K. B. 412, the plaintiffs who had advanced money to the master of the ship on the security of the ship and freight, effected a policy "on advances in the ship or vessel C."

(*d*) Buchanan *v.* Faber (1899), 4 Com. Cas. 223.

322   SUBJECTS OF MARINE INSURANCE.   [PART I.

Sect. 246. of the word is limited by the learned Judge to something less than its ordinary meaning.

Object of disbursement policies.

247. As a matter of fact, however, policies on disbursements are largely used in practice to insure that the shipowner may recover additional sums in respect of his adventure beyond the amount covered by his insurances on ship and freight; and irrespective of any particular items of expenditure or obligation (e). Such insurances are probably always made against total loss only. Thus the object of the assured is in reality to increase the insurance on the ship without increasing the valuation in the policies (f). The question has been raised—What is the real subject-matter of insurance in a disbursement policy? The answer to this inquiry is attended with some difficulty, especially when it is sought to give a special or customary meaning to the word. It can only be proved that a word has an extraordinary or technical meaning in a particular trade or business by calling experts engaged in such trade or business to give evidence that such peculiar meaning has become well recognized and established by general usage. But inasmuch as nearly all disbursement policies are valued, and contain the "p. p. i." clause, whereby the underwriter agrees that he will not contend that the assured has no interest in the thing insured (in effect that he will pay the amount at which the disbursements are valued without any inquiry as to the nature of the claim), it is difficult to see that there can be scope for sufficient controversy on the subject in business

Difficulty in establishing a technical meaning of "disbursements."

(e) See Thames & Mersey Mar. Ins. Co. v. "Gunford" Ship Co., [1911] A. C. 529; Gow, 232. In the case of steamships, according to Mr. Gow, the policies are usually on time, and, as he points out, a time policy on disbursements can scarcely be intended to insure any real interest in disbursements.

(f) The club insurances on freight are partly of a similar nature. It is commonly provided that in the event of the loss of the ship the amount insured shall be deemed the shipowner's interest at risk, and that he shall be paid such amount whether the ship be laden, in ballast, or under a time charter. Such an insurance seems to be a wager policy: see *ante*, § 81, note.

circles to establish a technical meaning which our Courts would recognize.

Sect. 247.

Usually policies on disbursements are expressed to be free of average or against total loss only. In the case of Lawther *v.* Black (*g*), the question, what is covered by a policy on disbursements "warranted free from all average," was considered by Mathew, J. The assured maintained that he intended by such a policy on a voyage to South America to insure the profits which he expected to realize from the homeward voyage of the ship. The underwriter maintained that a policy on disbursements, warranted free from all average, is, by custom, an extra insurance on the ship against total loss only, and he called witnesses to prove the alleged custom. As regards the contention of the assured, the learned Judge said that it would be a straining of language to say that the policy covered the expectation of profit to be earned on the homeward voyage, though he was not prepared to say that such an interest could not be protected by a properly worded policy. He also declined to find that the meaning which the underwriter said the term disbursements had acquired by custom had been proved by the evidence. He then proceeded to consider a list of disbursements which the assured had produced, covering stores, port dues, dry dock and painting expenses, ropemaker's accounts, and the cost of insurance. A part of this expenditure, as the learned Judge pointed out, was represented either by stores or by the enhanced value of the ship. The ship had not been lost, and there was no clear evidence as to what had become of the stores and outfit. He therefore held that there had not been a total loss of the items mentioned in the list of disbursements, and that the assured could not recover.

Policy on disbursements against total loss only. Lawther v. Black.

The decision is thus, to some extent, an authority for the proposition that a policy on disbursements by a shipowner covers all expenditures of money incurred in equipping the

Shipowner's policy on disbursements.

(*g*) (1900), 6 Com. Cas. 5; affirmed on appeal, *ibid.* 196.

Sect. 247. ship, or for other purposes of the voyage. On this point it agrees with the view expressed in a later case by Walton, J. In the case of an ordinary shipowner's policy, said the learned Judge, "the disbursements represent expenditure by the shipowner either on his ship, or for the purpose of earning his freight, and such policies are in the nature of insurances of the shipowner, either upon his ship or upon his freight" (*h*). If this be the proper construction of a policy on disbursements, there are some peculiarities of the insurance which deserve notice. An expenditure on repairs or permanent fittings is represented by some part of the value of the ship at the beginning of the voyage; an expenditure on stores may be represented by stores on board at the time of the loss, which are covered in a policy on the body, tackle, &c. of the ship in the common form, but perhaps not in a policy on hull and machinery only (*i*). Other items, again—such as payments in respect of port charges—will be ultimately defrayed out of freight; and therefore, if there be some freight at risk which is covered by insurance, these items are also indirectly covered by the policies on freight. The result is, that there may often be in fact, though not in form, a double insurance—*i.e.*, where the ship and freight are already fully covered by the ordinary policies on ship and freight (*k*). This was said to be the result in the case

---

(*h*) Moran *v.* Uzielli, [1905] 2 K. B. 555, 558.

(*i*) See *ante*, § 220.

(*k*) A difficult question which arises on these disbursement policies against total loss only is as to the meaning of the term "total loss." The question does not admit of a satisfactory answer, because it is at present quite uncertain what is covered by the term "disbursements." Underwriters maintain that by total loss is meant "total loss of the ship," and the loss under a policy on disbursements is frequently expressed to be payable only in case of the actual or constructive total loss of ship. *Primâ facie*, total loss must mean total loss of the thing insured. If the thing insured be not the ship as a whole, but that part of the value of the ship to its owner which represents the expenditure, this construction seems to be inadmissible, unless it be proved that the words "total loss" in a policy on disbursements have acquired a well-known technical meaning which limits the right of the assured to recover to cases where the ship itself has been lost. If the intention of the parties (assuming that it can be carried out by a policy on

of The Gunford (*l*), where the vessel was insured on a valuation on ship, largely in excess of the amount which could have been recovered on an open policy, and the freight was insured on a valuation exceeding its gross amount. The owners had in addition effected a valued honour policy on disbursements for 4,600*l*., and they produced a list of the payments on account of which they sought to justify this insurance. "So far as these payments consisted of current working expenses necessary to earn freight," said Lord Robson, "they were covered by the insurance on the gross freight, and so far as they consisted of repairs, outfit, and insurance premium on hull, they would ordinarily be included in the policy on ship and materials. This policy was therefore an over-insurance by double insurance. The plaintiffs could not legally avail themselves of it to enforce recovery of any sum in excess of the indemnity allowed by law" (*m*).

Sect. 247.

disbursements) is to effect an extra insurance on the ship, "total loss" may well mean total loss of the ship. In Lawther *v.* Black, as we have seen, the underwriter brought forward evidence of a custom under which a disbursement policy, when against total loss only, is understood to be on the ship; but Mathew, J., did not find it necessary to decide whether the evidence established the alleged custom. Sometimes, as in Moran *v.* Uzielli, *supra*, the policy is expressed to be on disbursements against the risk of total loss of ship only. For a clause providing that a total loss paid by underwriters on hull and machinery should constitute a total loss under a policy on disbursements, see Andersen *v.* Marten, [1907] 2 K. B. 248. The question, what is covered by a disbursement policy against total loss only, arose in the United States, in International Nav. Co. *v.* Atlantic Mut. Ins. Co. (1900), 100 Fed. R. 304. Brown, D. J., after hearing evidence on this question, held that such a disbursement policy was not "another insurance upon the premises aforesaid" within the meaning of a policy on the ship against partial, as well as total, loss: affirmed on appeal (1901), 108 Fed. R. 988. Cf. Brown *v.* Merchants' Mar. Ins. Co. (1907), 152 Fed. R. 411, in which the Circuit Court of Appeals held that the underwriters of a policy against total loss only on "disbursement $\frac{\text{and}}{\text{or}}$ increased value," who had paid for a total loss, were entitled to share with the insurers on ship in a fund recovered in a collision suit.

(*l*) Thames & Mersey Mar. Ins. Co. *v.* "Gunford" Ship Co., [1911] A. C. 529.

(*m*) [1911] A. C. at p. 549. See also Lord Alverstone's judgment, *ibid.* pp. 535, 536. Lord Shaw condemned disbursement policies which are duplications of insurances on freight as "a gamble, discountenanced by sound principle and not enforceable by law": *ibid.* p. 545.

Sect. 248.
Miscellaneous subjects of insurance.

248. There is sometimes a difficulty in accurately describing the subject of the insurance, and yet substantial accuracy, is requisite in every case where a specific description is necessary.

A policy on "bills of exchange" will not cover instruments not legally bills.

The case of Palmer *v.* Pratt is an extreme illustration of the degree of accuracy at one time required in this respect. The policy was effected "upon any kind of goods and merchandise," &c. in the common printed form, for a voyage from London to Calcutta, and the insurance, by a memorandum on the face of the policy, was declared to be "on two bills of exchange": as, however, it appeared that the supposed bills were drawn on a contingency, being made payable at thirty days after the ship's arrival at Calcutta, the Court held that such instruments, being mere waste paper, were improperly described as bills of exchange, and that therefore, on this ground, their value, in case of loss, could not be recovered under such a policy (*n*).

As Phillips well remarks, "this construction was very strict on the assured," and, as a precedent, would probably not now be followed. Lord Campbell, in delivering judgment in the case of Hall *v.* Janson, appears to lay down a far more sensible rule. "Great latitude," he says, "is allowed in describing the interest on a policy of insurance, provided that the nature of it is intelligibly disclosed" (*o*).

A policy "on specie and returns" will not cover an advance by charterer.

The ship "Leonidas" was chartered for a voyage from Buenos Ayres to Canton and back, at a gross sum payable, not as freight properly so-called, but as the price of the hire of the ship for the voyage. Part of this sum was paid, as stipulated by the charter-party, by the charterer's agents at Canton, to cover the port charges and incidental expenses of the ship there. The charterers, who had shipped on board the vessel at Buenos Ayres a large sum of dollars to be invested in produce at Canton, being desirous of securing their interest in the adventure, caused a policy to be effected, in

---

(*n*) Palmer *v.* Pratt (1824), 2 Bing. 185. A strong decision, for the underwriter was fully informed of the real facts as to the drawing and payment of the bills.

(*o*) Hall *v.* Janson (1855), 4 E. & B. 500, 509; 24 L. J. Q. B. 97, 101.

CHAP. XI.] MISCELLANEOUS SUBJECTS. 327

the common form, for the proposed voyage, "on specie, &c. Sect. 248.
shipped on board the 'Leonidas' in the River Plate, and on
the same or the returns thereof, as interest might appear, in
any description of merchandise," &c. The Court of King's
Bench held, that under a policy so framed the assured could
not recover, in addition to what is usually recoverable as the
value of goods in an open policy, the sum paid at Canton,
under the charter-party, for the port charges, &c. (*p*). Lord
Tenterden, however, in the course of the argument, intimated
that, although such sum could not be recovered under a mere
policy on merchandise, yet it might have been insured as
money paid for shipment of goods to be transported to Buenos
Ayres (*q*); and in delivering the judgment of the Court he
said: "We have no doubt that these payments might have
been made the subject of a special and distinct insurance" (*r*).

A policy "on money advanced on account of freight" will cover advances for necessary repairs abroad,

In a case where the policy described the insurance to be
"on money advanced on account of freight," the shipowner
was allowed to recover in respect of advances made for
necessary expenses incurred by the master at a foreign port
for repairs, and loading and unloading cargo, on the terms
that the loan should be deducted from the freight or repaid
if the freight were not ultimately earned. Lord Campbell,
delivering the judgment of the Court, said: "There seems
no reason why the money advanced may not be insured as
freight, as well as the money to grow due on the charter,
which is undoubtedly insurable as freight, although not properly freight, and rather the price of the hire of the ship.
Nor do we see how we can be called upon to infer that the expression 'money advanced on account of freight' necessarily
indicates that the insurance is effected by the shipper, and
that the freight paid in advance is at his risk, not at the risk
of the shipowner" (*s*). A similar policy will cover bills
drawn abroad against freight by captains and accepted by

and bills drawn abroad against freight.

(*p*) Winter *v.* Haldimand (1831), 2 B. & Ad. 649.
(*q*) Ibid. 654.
(*r*) Ibid. 658. There can be little doubt, as we have seen, that the advance might have been insured as freight. *Ante,* § 233.
(*s*) Hall *v.* Janson (1855), 4 E. & B. 500; 24 L. J. Q. B. 97.

Sect. 248. agents here. The agents in this country of foreign principals having accepted bills drawn abroad by the captain of a ship, taken up by their principals for a general cargo, against freight, it was held that they had an insurable interest in respect thereof, and that such interest was well described in the policy as "an advance on account of freight" (*t*).

Share in company uninsurable.

249. A shareholder in the Atlantic Telegraph Company, before any attempt had been made to lay the cable between the Irish and American coasts, effected a policy to secure himself against loss when the attempt was made; and in the valuation clause (the policy being in the form usual at Lloyd's) occurred the only specification of the subject of insurance in these words: "The said ship, &c. goods and merchandise, &c. .... are, and shall be, valued as on one 1,000*l*. share in the Atlantic Telegraph Company, said share valued at 1,100*l*." Stopping here, the policy would have been construed as being on a subject—a share in a company—incapable of exposure to, and consequently not covered by a policy against, maritime risks. But this other sentence followed: "In case of loss, the part saved to be sold or appraised for the benefit of the underwriters." The Court, regarding the whole in the light of these latter words, held that it was a policy on the cable, and that the assured under the circumstances was entitled to recover for an average loss if above 3 per cent. (*u*).

As shares in an incorporated company cannot be exposed to maritime perils, it seems to follow that they cannot be the subject of maritime insurance (*x*); and as the shareholder in such a company has no property in the estate or chattels of the company, such a chattel as the Atlantic Cable, though exposed to maritime perils, cannot for him be the subject of a valid policy (*y*). But it has been held that

---

(*t*) Wilson *v*. Martin (1856), 11 Exch. 684; 25 L. J. Ex. 217.

(*u*) Paterson *v*. Harris (1861), 1 B. & S. 336; 30 L. J. Q. B. 354. There was no plea on the record to the insurable interest of the claimant.

(*x*) See *par cur*. Paterson *v*. Harris (1861), 1 B. & S. 354, 355; 30 L. J. Q. B. 361.

(*y*) See *post*, § 307.

his right to a share of the profits of such a company gives him an insurable interest in an adventure such as that of laying the Atlantic Cable, which interest, by the use of suitable language, may be covered by a policy of insurance (z).

Sect. 249.

In Wilson v. Jones (a), a shareholder in the Atlantic Telegraph Company, before the cable had been laid, effected a policy to cover his interest in the concern, describing the subject of insurance in a cloud of ambiguous words, as follows:—" The said ship, &c., goods and merchandises, &c., for so much as concerns the assured by agreement between the assured and assurers, on this policy, are and shall be valued at 200*l*. on the Atlantic Cable, value say on twenty shares, valued at 10*l*. per share." Then on the margin, over against the statement of perils insured against, were written these words: " It is hereby understood and agreed that this policy, in addition to all perils and casualties herein specified, shall cover every risk and contingency attending the conveyance and successful laying of the cable." Having regard to these latter words, both the Court of Exchequer and the Court of Exchequer Chamber held that the subject intended to be insured was the plaintiff's interest in the adventure, and that this might be the subject of a valid policy of marine insurance (b).

A ship is now frequently the property, not of individuals (each holding severally one or more of the sixty-four shares into which the property is legally divided), but of a limited company. From what has just been said, it appears that a shareholder in the company cannot insure his shares in it against maritime risks. Moreover he cannot, apparently, effect a valid insurance on the ship itself, for want of an

Share in company owning ship.

(z) Cf. Mar. Ins. Act, 1906, s. 3, which declares (sub-s. 1) that every lawful marine adventure may be the subject of a contract of marine insurance, and (sub-s. 2 (b)) that there is a marine adventure where the earning of any pecuniary benefit is endangered by the exposure of insurable property to maritime perils.

(a) (1866), L. R. 1 Exch. 193; in error (1867), L. R. 2 Exch. 139.

(b) Reference was made by Blackburn, J., to the language of Lawrence, J., in Barclay v. Cousins (1802), 2 East, 544; and in Lucena v. Craufurd (1806), 2 B. & P. N. R. 301.

Sect. 249. insurable interest (*c*). Yet the company may be a "single-ship company," whose only asset is the ship; she may not be insured or may be inadequately insured by the company, and her loss may therefore either render the shares valueless or greatly depreciate their value. The decision in Wilson *v.* Jones suggests that by a properly worded policy a shareholder can protect himself against loss due to the depreciation of his shares consequent on maritime perils affecting the ship.

Shipowner's liability for loss of life, injury and damage.

250. A shipowner may become liable to pay large sums in consequence of loss of life, injury to person, or damage to property caused by the improper navigation of his vessel. Sect. 506 of the Merchant Shipping Act, 1894, expressly recognizes the validity of insurances by shipowners against their liability to pay damages for such loss of life, injury or damage, in the cases enumerated in sect. 503 of the Act (*d*), and sect. 3 (2) (c) (*e*) of the Marine Insurance Act, 1906, recognizes in general terms the right of a person interested in insurable property to protect himself against his liabilities in respect thereof.

In policies on " ship " it is now usual for the shipowner to insure himself in part or in whole by the collision clause against the liability to pay damages in consequence of a collision between his ship and any other vessel, and against the costs of litigation arising out of such a collision (*f*).

The shipowner's liability to pay damages, so far as it is not covered by policies in the ordinary form, is usually insured with mutual associations, called Protection and Indemnity Associations; and there are some other risks and liabilities, not within the scope of the ordinary insurances, which are also undertaken by such associations (*g*).

(*c*) *Post,* § 307.
(*d*) *Ante,* § 7.
(*e*) *Ante,* § 1.
(*f*) *Ante,* § 10. Sometimes the collision clause also covers liability for damage caused by the ship insured to buoys, moorings, piers, bridges, &c. See, *e.g.,* Shelbourne *v.* Law Investment and Insurance Corporation (1898), 3 Com. Cas. 304.
(*g*) The Workmen's Compensa-

CHAP. XI.] SPECIFICATION OF INTEREST. 331

251. With regard to the designation of the subject-matter of the insurance in the policy, sect. 26 of the Marine Insurance Act, 1906, lays down the following rules:—

Sect. 251.
Designation of subject-matter in policy.

(1) The subject-matter insured must be designated in a marine policy with reasonable certainty.

(2) The nature and extent of the interest of the assured in the subject-matter insured need not be specified in the policy.

(3) Where the policy designates the subject-matter insured in general terms, it shall be construed to apply to the interest intended by the assured to be covered.

(4) In the application of this section regard shall be had to any usage regulating the designation of the subject-matter insured.

The manner in which the various subject-matters of insurance are described has already been sufficiently indicated.

That the nature of the interest of the assured need not be specified is well established (*h*). Thus, where a policy expressed to be "5,000*l*. on cotton" was a re-insurance, but it was not so expressed on the face of it, nor was any notice of this fact given to the underwriter, the Court of Appeal held that the interest of the assured did not need to be described. "The assured here had a direct interest in the safe arrival of the cotton, not in any way a collateral interest in something else after the cotton arrived. It was, though not a property in the cotton, an interest in the cotton created and evidenced by a binding legal contract between them and the owners of that cotton; and if the mode in which they acquired that interest had been stated in the policy, it would have in no way altered the effect of the defendant's contract, which would still have remained a contract to

The nature of the interest of the assured need not generally be described.

---

tion Act, 1906, has imposed upon shipowners large liabilities for injuries sustained by seamen in their employment; but they are seldom insured by policies effected against the ordinary marine risks. The protecting and indemnity associations undertake to indemnify their members against claims for compensation under the Act, which it is beyond the scope of this work to discuss.

(*h*) See per Lord Tenterden in Crowley *v.* Cohen (1832), 3 B. & Ad. 478, 485.

Sect. 251.

The extent of the interest need not be specified.

Interest in ship and freight.

indemnify against all damage sustained by the cotton in consequence of any of the perils insured against" (*i*).

So, also, it is a well-established rule that a party interested only to a certain extent in property, which he owns in common with others, may effect insurance generally without specifying his interest, and will recover for such interest as he has (*k*). Thus, a mortgagee may recover under a policy on ship to the extent of his mortgage (*l*); or one of several part-owners of a ship may insure the freight generally without specifying what share he has in the ship, and he may declare generally and recover for such interest as he has (*m*).

Cases on rule that interest need not be specified.

252. The above positions have received abundant illustration in the jurisprudence of this country and the United States (*n*). Thus, with regard to the nature of the interest, Lord Mansfield, in the case of Glover *v*. Black, after deciding, solely on the ground of the usage of merchants, that the interest of the lender on bottomry and respondentia must be specifically described in the policy, adds: "But we by no means say that, under an insurance on goods at large, a man may not be permitted to give in evidence a mortgage or other special lien" (*o*). "I admit," says Park, J., "that a party who has only a special interest in goods may recover, in respect of that interest, on a general insurance" (*p*).

One of the first cases, in direct illustration of this point, is that of Carruthers *v*. Shedden, in which it appeared that a general insurance " on coffee " had been effected by a London broker, " by order and for account of N. D. & Co.," a London mercantile firm, who were interested as part-owners with others in seven-tenths of the coffee, but who had also an

---

(*i*) Mackenzie *v*. Whitworth (1875), 1 Ex. D. 36, 44; below, L. R. 10 Ex. 142.

(*k*) The principle is laid down, 1 Emerigon, c. x. s. 1, p. 299.

(*l*) Irving *v*. Richardson (1831), 1 Mood. & Rob. 153; 2 B. & Ad. 193.

(*m*) Rising *v*. Burnett (1798), 2 Marshall, Ins. 738.

(*n*) See 1 Phillips, §§ 421 *et seq.*, for the cases in the United States.

(*o*) Glover *v*. Black (1763), 1 W. Bl. 423; see also 3 Burr. 1401. As to bottomry and respondentia, see *ante*, § 243.

(*p*) Palmer *v*. Pratt (1824), 2 Bing. 192.

insurable interest in the whole of it as consignees of the Sect. 252.
cargo, and as having a lien on the whole for advances. The
Court held that, under the general form of policy, N. D. &
Co. might protect any or all of these different species of
interest; that the nature of the several interests need not be
expressed in the policy; and that the assured were not bound
to elect on which they would proceed (*q*).

Upon the same principle, a general policy "on goods" (*r*)
has been held sufficient to cover the interest of carriers on
goods entrusted to their care, so as to protect them against
loss arising from damage done to such property by the perils
insured against, whereby they were obliged to make compensation to the owners, and were, besides, put to other
expenses (*s*). It was objected that such a policy could not
cover such an interest, since it merely purported to protect
goods against the usual risks to which the owners of goods
are liable; whereas the loss alleged was one arising out of
a risk to which carriers are liable. But the Court, although
Lord Tenterden admitted that it might have been better if
the policy had expressly shown that the object was to indemnify the plaintiffs as carriers, were yet unanimously of opinion
that it was sufficient in its present form, on the ground that

---

(*q*) Carruthers *v*. Sheddon (1815), 6 Taunt. 14; *S. C.*, 1 Marshall, R. 416.

(*r*) The policy, which was intended to cover the interest of plaintiffs, as barge-owners, in the property carried to and fro for hire in their barges for a year, was a common printed form of policy on ship and goods, filled up and altered in a very clumsy manner so as to adapt it to the object in view. By it the plaintiffs were insured for twelve months "by canal navigation boats, containing goods, at work between London, Wolverhampton and Birmingham, &c., backwards and forwards, and in any rotation, upon goods, and on the body and tackle, &c., on thirty boats, as per margin." In the valuation clause it was declared that the subject of insurance was agreed between the parties to be "twelve thousand pounds on goods as interest shall appear hereafter."

(*s*) Crowley *v*. Cohen (1832), 3 B. & Ad. 478; *S. P.*, Joyce *v*. Kennard (1871), L. R. 7 Q. B. 78. Cf. Cunard SS. Co. *v*. Marten, [1902] 2 K. B. 624; [1903] 2 K. B. 511, in which Bigham, J., and the Court of Appeal held that an insurance by shipowners "against liability of any kind to owners of cargo up to 20,000*l*." was not an insurance on the cargo, but a contract to indemnify them in full to the amount of 20,000*l*. in respect of their liability as carriers.

Sect. 252. it is only necessary to state accurately the subject-matter, not the interest which the assured has in it (*t*).

The rule in the United States is to the same effect.

The decisions upon this subject in the United States go to the full extent of the English law; and the doctrine seems to be established there, that a mortgagee may insure the subject of the mortgage, either generally or under a direct description, without specifying his interest to be that of a mortgagee (*u*).

The nature of the interest need not be described though it affects the risk.

252a. There is some authority for saying that where the peculiar nature of the interest increases or alters the character of the risk, the nature of the interest should be specified in the policy (*x*); and the rule that bottomry and respondentia loans must be specifically described has, as we have seen, been explained on the ground that the risk is peculiar (*y*).

In view of the unqualified statement in sect. 26 (2) (*z*), that the interest of the assured need not be specified, the principle that the peculiar nature of the interest may require to be stated in the policy cannot now be accepted as law. Nevertheless, it is apprehended that where the risk is of an exceptional kind, the insurer may be entitled to avoid the insurance, if the nature of the risk has not been disclosed to him (*a*).

(*t*) In Joyce v. Kennard, *supra*, the fact that the insurance was of a carrier's interest was specifically stated in the policy.

(*u*) See the cases collected, 1 Phillips, Ins. ss. 419 *et seq.*

(*x*) See per Blackburn, J., in Mackenzie v. Whitworth (1875), 1 Ex. D. 36, 42. See also per Lord Ellenborough in Routh v. Thompson (1809), 11 East, 428, 433.

(*y*) See *ante*, § 243. When the Marine Insurance Bill left the House of Lords, sub-sect. 2 of sect. 26 contained a proviso that when an insurance is effected by a lender on bottomry or respondentia, the nature of his interest must be specified. The sub-section was amended in the House of Commons by omitting the proviso, and adding the words "but when the interest is of such a kind as to affect the character of the risk it must be stated; and in particular a loan on bottomry or respondentia is not effectually insured by a policy on ship or goods, unless the nature of the interest is stated." The amendment was not accepted by the House of Lords, but the proviso was not restored.

(*z*) *Ante*, § 251.

(*a*) See *post*, Part II., Chap. II., "Concealment."

CHAP. XI.] SPECIFICATION OF INTEREST. 335

On the ground of usage it will apparently still be necessary, by reason of sect. 26 (4), to insure bottomry and respondentia loans specifically (*b*).

Sect. 252a.
Except by usage, as in policies on bottomry and respondentia loans.

252b. There is a difficulty in construing sect. 26 (3) of the Marine Insurance Act, 1906, which says that "where the policy designates the subject-matter insured in general terms, it must be construed to apply to the interest intended by the assured to be covered." The difficulty is to give a precise meaning to the word "interest" in this vague proposition. It may be suggested that "interest" is in this sub-section equivalent to "subject-matter." To construe "interest" as simply denoting "subject-matter" is, however, to give a forced meaning to the word, and involves a proposition which could not formerly have been maintained. For instance, where the assured simply insured "freight," and did not earn the freight which he intended to insure, but completed the voyage and earned freight under another contract of affreightment, it was held that the policy applied to the freight which had been earned, although he had not intended to insure it (*c*). The sub-section is founded on a passage in the opinion of Brett, J., in Allison *v*. Bristol Marine Insurance Co. (*d*), and when read in the light of that passage may be construed to bear the following meaning:—Where the policy designates the subject-matter insured in general terms, it must be construed to apply to the subject-matter described in the policy, so far as the assured has an interest therein which he intended to cover. For such a proposition there is no doubt authority (*e*), but

Policy applies to interest intended by assured to be covered.
Mar. Ins. Act, s. 26 (3).

(*b*) See Glover *v*. Black (1763), 3 Burr. 1394; 1 Wm. Bl. 399, *ante*, § 243.

(*c*) See Everth *v*. Smith, *post*, § 1166.

(*d*) (1875), 1 App. Cas. 209, at p. 216. See Chalmers & Owen, Mar. Ins. Act, 2nd ed. p. 40. "Wherever the subject-matter of a policy is described in it in general terms," said Brett, J., "it is to be taken to cover the interest which is within its terms, which the assured has at risk, unless the contrary appears to have been the intention of the assured from other parts of the policy, or other proof."

(*e*) See Feise *v*. Aguilar (1811), 3 Taunt. 506; Forbes *v*. Aspinall (1811), 13 East, 323; Allison *v*.

Sect. 252b. it could not before the Act have been accepted without qualification. Thus, it has been held that a valued policy on freight must be construed as referring to the freight of a full cargo, although the assured intended (but without communicating his intention to the insurers) only to insure the freight of a smaller shipment of goods (*f*). The question may arise whether, by reason of the wide language of the sub-section, the assured will in future be entitled in a similar case to recover the full amount of his valuation (*g*).

In order that this may not be so, it might be necessary to hold that the words "it must be, construed to apply to the interest intended by the assured to be covered" do not necessarily mean that the policy is to apply exclusively to such interest, and therefore do not oust the rule that a valuation of freight refers to a full cargo unless the contrary intention is communicated to the insurer.

Another interpretation, based on the context, was recently suggested by Kennedy, L. J. (*h*), viz., that the principal object of the sub-section is to prevent an assured, who has only a limited interest in the subject-matter which is designated by the policy in general terms, from being prejudiced by such generality of designation, provided that the designation is not inappropriate (*i*). The learned Lord Justice added that, having regard to the words "interest intended by the assured to be covered," those who introduced the sub-section into the Act may also have had in view the one class of cases in which the "intention" of one of the parties to the contract—*i.e.*, the assured—is under the very terms of

Bristol Mar. Ins. Co. (1875), 1 App. Cas. 209; Williams *v.* North China Ins. Co. (1876), 1 C. P. D. 757.

(*f*) Denoon *v.* Home & Colonial Ass. Co. (1872), L. R. 7 C. P. 341.

(*g*) See per Kennedy, L. J., in Reliance Mar. Ins. Co. *v.* Duder, [1913] 1 K. B. 265, 275.

(*h*) The purpose of the section, as appears by the marginal note, said the Lord Justice, is to deal with "designation of subject-matter": *ibid.*

(*i*) *Ibid.* See also Chalmers & Owen, Mar. Ins. Act, 2nd ed. p. 42, where it is stated that the sub-section was intended to protect the assured against technical objections to the description of the interest insured.

the contract matter of inquiry in regard to rights under the contract, viz., the class in which (the insurance having been effected in the common form by insurance brokers "for and in the name and names of all and every other person or persons, &c.") the persons for whose benefit the policy is available have to be ascertained (*j*).

However this may be, a majority in the Court of Appeal have expressed the view that the sub-section does not mean that an insurer is entitled to exclude the assured from the benefit of the insurance of any of the risks which are within the terms expressed in the written policy, by showing that at the time when the insurance was effected, the assured "intended" in his own mind to cover only some of them.

In the case which elicited this opinion, a ship was insured by two policies for a voyage from New South Wales "to port or ports . . . . on the West Coast of South America," and by a later policy, subscribed by the same underwriters for a voyage "at and from Valparaiso and/or port or ports . . . . on the West Coast of South America" to Europe, the "risk to commence from expiration of previous policy." The underwriters effected a policy of re-insurance in which the voyage was described exactly as in the later policy, viz., "at and from Valparaiso and/or port or ports . . . . on the West Coast of South America" to Europe. The ship was chartered to carry a cargo from New South Wales to the West Coast, to be discharged at Valparaiso or at a safe port as ordered. She discharged a portion at Valparaiso, and then, by arrangement with the charterers, proceeded with the rest of the cargo on board towards Tocopilla, another West Coast port, where she was to complete her discharge and load a cargo under another charter-party for a European port. She was lost on the way to Tocopilla, and it was held that the shipowners were entitled to recover for the

---

(*j*) See *ante*, § 172. An objection to this interpretation is that the sub-section states a general rule, not a rule for the construction of a particular clause in the policy, the appropriate place for which would have been the First Schedule of the Act.

Sect. 252b. loss on the policies for the voyage from New South Wales (*k*). The underwriters then sued on the policy of re-insurance, and were met by the defence that they only intended to re-insure their risk under the policy from the West Coast to Europe, and could not recover by reason of sect. 26 (3) of the Act. Bray, J., held on the evidence that the defendants had not proved that the intention of the plaintiffs was only to re-insure their liability under the later policy, and that, as the loss had occurred on the voyage described in the policy of re-insurance, the plaintiffs were entitled to recover (*l*). His decision was affirmed on the same grounds by the Court of Appeal (*m*). It was therefore unnecessary for the Court to decide the point of law, with regard to which the meaning of sect. 26 (3) was material; but as this point had been fully discussed, Kennedy, L. J., gave his reasons for thinking that the defendants' contention was unsound, and Cozens-Hardy, M. R., concurred in his judgment. The learned Lord Justice referred to the fundamental rule that where a contract has a plain natural meaning, it is not permissible to alter its effect according to the intention of one of the two contracting parties, or to adduce evidence in order to show such intention; and, as we have already said, his view was that the sub-section does not enable the underwriter to assert that the assured did not intend to cover a risk which is within the terms of the policy.

(*k*) Kynance SS. Co. *v.* Young (1911), 16 Com. Cas. 123. This action was on another but similar policy for the voyage from New South Wales to the West Coast. The point was taken by the underwriters that at the time when the policy was effected the shipowners only contemplated a discharge at one port, and that the general words in the policy describing the voyage must be limited by their intention at such time (p. 130).

Scrutton, J., held that the assured did not mean to shut himself out from varying the charter-party in its mode of performance. See his remarks (p. 131) as to the suggested limitation of general words in the policy by the intention of the parties.

(*l*) Reliance Marine Ins. Co. *v.* Duder (1911), 17 Com. Cas. 24.

(*m*) *Ibid.* p. 227; [1913] 1 K. B. 265 (Buckley, L. J., doubting).

CHAPTER XII.

OF THE INTEREST THAT GIVES A TITLE TO INSURE;
i.e., INSURABLE INTEREST.

SECT.	SECT.
Insurable Interest generally... 253—260	Insurable Interest of Mortgagors and Mortgagees ... 298, 299
Insurable Interest of Shipowner and Charterer in Ship. 261	Of Trustees 300
Insurable Interest of Shipowner and Charterer in Freight ....262—279	Of Captors and Prize Agents 301—306
	Of Shareholders 307
Shipowner's Insurable Interest in Liabilities 280	Of Masters and Mariners ... 308
	Of Carriers 309
Insurable Interest of Vendors and Vendees ....281—286	Miscellaneous Cases of Insurable Interest 310
In Profits 287, 288	Wager Policies ....311—321
Of Lenders and Borrowers on Bottomry and Respondentia 289, 290	Re-insurance ....322—328
	Insuring the Underwriter's Solvency 329
Of Consignees, Factors and Agents ....291—297	Double and Over Insurance ... 330—335

253. THE definition of the contract of marine insurance in sect. 1 of the Marine Insurance Act, 1906, viz., a contract whereby the insurer undertakes to indemnify the assured against marine losses (*a*), embodies the principle that it is a contract of indemnity. It is obvious that a contract which purports to provide an indemnity for the assured against loss becomes, when perverted to the purposes of one who has no interest in the subject insured in respect of which he can suffer loss, nothing better than a bet or wager upon the event of the voyage or adventure described in the policy. Such policies, with no interest to justify the assured in making them, came into frequent use in the reign of Charles the Second, and in the time of Queen Anne our Courts of

Of insurable interest generally.

(*a*) See *ante*, § 1.

Sect. 253. Justice unfortunately pronounced them to be valid and legal. An Act of Parliament (19 Geo. 2, c. 37) afterwards declared them illegal in respect of British ships and their cargoes, and thus reduced the policy once more to a contract of indemnity; and now by sect. 4 of the Marine Insurance Act, 1906, a contract of marine insurance is void where the assured has no insurable interest, and enters into the contract without any expectation of acquiring one (*b*).

Description of insurable interest.

254. It is very difficult to give any definition of an insurable interest, and the Marine Insurance Act, 1906, does not purport to do so exhaustively. Sect. 5 deals with it in the following terms:—

(1) Subject to the provisions of this Act, every person has an insurable interest who is interested in a marine adventure (*c*).

(2) In particular a person is interested in a marine adventure where he stands in any legal or equitable relation to the adventure or to any insurable property at risk therein, in consequence of which he may benefit by the safety or due arrival of insurable property, or may be prejudiced by its loss, or by damage thereto, or by the detention thereof, or may incur liability in respect thereof.

Therefore, in order to have an insurable interest, it is not necessary to have an absolute vested ownership or property in that which is insured: it is sufficient to have a right in the thing insured, or to have a right or be under a liability arising out of some contract relating to the thing insured, of such a nature that the party insuring may have benefit from its preservation, or prejudice from its destruction (*d*).

(*b*) See *post*, § 314. By sect. 92 of the Act, the statute of 19 Geo. 2 is repealed.

(*c*) For the meaning of "marine adventure," see s. 3 of the Act, *ante*, § 1.

(*d*) See the *dicta* of Lawrence, J., in Lucena *v*. Craufurd (1806),
2 B. & P. N. R. 302; and of Lord Eldon, *ibid*. 321; Crowley *v*. Cohen (1832), 3 B. & Ad. 478. For a possible exception in the case of captors to the rule that an insurable interest depends on some right relating to the thing insured, see *post*, §§ 301—303.

GENERAL PRINCIPLES.

An insurable interest is thus described by a Judge of the highest legal reputation:—"A man," says Lawrence, J., "is interested in a thing to whom advantage may arise or prejudice happen from the circumstances which may attend it; and whom it importeth that its condition as to safety or other quality should continue. Interest does not necessarily imply a right to the whole or part of the thing, nor necessarily and exclusively that which may be the subject of privation, but the having some relation to, or concern in, the subject of the insurance; which relation or concern, by the happening of the perils insured against, may be so affected as to produce a damage, detriment or prejudice to the person insuring. And where a man is so circumstanced with respect to matters exposed to certain risks and dangers as to have a moral certainty of advantage or benefit but for those risks and dangers, he may be said to be interested in the safety of the thing. To be interested in the preservation of a thing is to be so circumstanced with respect to it as to have benefit from its existence, prejudice from its destruction. The property of the thing and the interest derivable from it may be very different. Of the first the price is generally the measure; but by interest in a thing, every benefit and advantage arising out of or depending on such thing may be considered as being comprehended" (e).

Sect. 254.
Lawrence, J., in Lucena v. Craufurd.

255. The plainest instance of an insurable interest is the ownership of a chattel. The variety of ways in which this ownership may be modified suggests, again, the various questions, some of them of considerable nicety, by which the

Ownership of a thing may be indefinitely modified.

(e) Lucena v. Craufurd (1806), 2 B. & P. N. R. 269, 302; see also the same learned Judge's decision in Barclay v. Cousins (1802), 2 East, 544; also 1 Marshall, Ins. 101, 102; 1 Phillips, Ins. ss. 172 et seq.; 3 Kent, Com. 276, 277. It may be remarked that some of these observations of Lawrence, J., are more applicable to insurances on tangible objects than to insurances on such subjects as disbursements or commissions. It may also be remarked that the statement, that benefit from the existence of a thing, or prejudice from its destruction, gives an insurable interest, can probably only be accepted with the limitation that there must be some legal relation between the assured and the thing insured. See *post,* §§ 257, 257a.

Sect. 255 inquiry as to the insurable interest of the assured may be perplexed. The chattel owned may be held in trust; or may be subjected to incumbrances, such as mortgages and liens; or to rights in other persons, as by deed of demise or contract of charter-party; or it may be sold under a reservation of rights or liabilities in the vendor; or may be possessed so conditionally (*f*) as to be liable to defeasance at the will of another; or to seizure for a forfeiture incurred before the voyage described in the policy (*g*). In all these instances an insurable interest undoubtedly exists, and independent insurable interests may co-exist, in several persons at the same time; but whether under certain circumstances an insurable interest does exist in a particular person may be a somewhat difficult question.

Defeasible or contingent interest is insurable.
Mar. Ins. Act, s. 7.

255a. Sect. 7 of the Marine Insurance Act, 1906, declares that—

(1) A defeasible interest is insurable, as also is a contingent interest.

(2) In particular where the buyer of goods has insured them, he has an insurable interest, notwithstanding that he might, at his election, have rejected the goods, or have treated them as at the seller's risk, by reason of the latter's delay in making delivery or otherwise (*h*).

Sub-sect. (2) is an example of an interest defeasible by the act of the assured (*i*). Another instance of a defeasible interest is the right of captors to their prize under the Prize Acts, which was held to be an insurable interest before condemnation, though defeasible before that event by the release

---

(*f*) Per Lord Ellenborough, Stirling *v.* Vaughan (1809), 11 East, 619, 629.

(*g*) Wilkes *v.* People's Fire Ins. Co. (1859), 19 N. Y. 184; 1 Phillips, s. 195; per Lord Eldon, Lucena *v.* Craufurd (1806), 2 B. & P. N. R. 319, 320.

(*h*) See Sparkes *v.* Marshall (1836), 2 Bing. N. C. 761, and the remarks of Lord Chelmsford and Lord Hatherley on this case in Anderson *v.* Morice (1876), 1 App. Cas. 713, 727, 735; Colonial Ins. Co. of New Zealand *v.* Adelaide Mar. Ins. Co. (1886), 12 App. Cas. 128, 140.

(*i*) See Chalmers & Owen, Mar. Ins. Act, 2nd ed. p. 16.

CHAP. XII.] GENERAL PRINCIPLES. 343

of the Crown, or by sentence of restoration (k). It is difficult Sect. 255a.
to say precisely what is covered by the term "contingent
interest." The expression occurs in the opinion of seven
judges in Lucena v. Craufurd, and they seem, from a preceding remark, to have considered the interest of a captor
a contingent one (l). It may be suggested that a liability
gives rise to a contingent interest (m), and that such expec-
tancies and inchoate rights as are insurable (n) may also be
regarded as contingent interests.

256. A vested interest in possession is not necessary to give Vested
the right of insuring. An expectancy, coupled with a present possession not
existing title to that out of which the expectancy arises, is an necessary.
insurable interest. Inchoate rights founded on titles subsisting at the time of loss are insurable interests: thus
freight, payable either on the arrival of the goods or under
a charter-party, is insurable by the shipowner, provided
his title to the freight has accrued, so that only the intervention of the maritime perils will in the ordinary course
prevent him from earning it. Thus, again, profits expected
to arise out of the sale or disposal of the goods on their
arrival are insurable by the owner of the goods, provided
that but for the perils of the voyage a profit will be made
on them. Again, commissions the earning of which will
be prevented only by the perils of the voyage are insurable,
though there is generally a total absence of ownership
of the chattel from which the commissions are derivable.

(k) See Lucena v. Craufurd (1806), 2 B. & P. N. R. at p. 295; Stirling v. Vaughan (1809), 11 East, 619, 628. The insurable interest which Walton, J., held in Moran v. Uzielli, [1905] 2 K. B. 555, to result from the right to bring an action *in rem* against a ship, is defeasible by the sale of the ship; see The Henrich Björn (1886), 11 App. Cas. 270.

(l) See Lucena v. Craufurd, *ubi sup.*

(m) See Chalmers & Owen, Mar. Ins. Act, 2nd ed. p. 16, where it is said that re-insurance is a good example of a contingent interest. It seems, however, unnecessary, in view of s. 5 (2) of the Mar. Ins. Act (*ante*, § 254), to consider whether the interest arising from a liability is a contingent one, and re-insurance is specifically dealt with in s. 9 of the Act (*post*, § 322).

(n) See *infra*, § 256.

Sect. 256. In fact, every kind of interest that may subsist in, and be dependent upon, things exposed to the dangers to which mercantile adventures are subjected may be protected by a policy of insurance effected on account and for the benefit of those who are so far interested in the things thus exposed to sea risks as to have a benefit from their preservation, or damage from their destruction (*o*).

The expectation of an expectation is not an insurable interest.

257. But although a vested interest in possession is not necessary to entitle a party to insure on his own account, yet where the interest insured is the expectancy of benefit to arise out of the safe arrival of some subject of insurance, a title to such subject must be subsisting in the assured at the time of loss to enable him to recover (*p*). The expectation of benefit to arise from some subject in which the party insuring is not actually interested, but only expects to be interested, is the mere expectation of an expectation, and is not an insurable interest. Such would be the expectation of commissions to arise out of the sale and disposal of a homeward cargo not contracted for at the time of the ship's loss (*q*). So also the expectation of profit to arise out of the sale of goods which have neither vested nor will vest on arrival in the party insuring, under any legal contract, is not an insurable interest (*r*).

Expectation of profit on goods.

Insurable interest arising from a liability.

A liability in case of the loss of a thing gives an insurable interest in the thing to the person on whom the liability rests (*s*). Thus, the liability of carriers or of insurers to compensate or indemnify in respect of losses affecting pro-

---

(*o*) See the opinions of the Judges generally, and of Lawrence, J., in particular, on the fifth question submitted to them by the House of Lords in Lucena *v.* Craufurd (1806), 2 B. & P. N. R. 289—310.

(*p*) This is the original text; but it would be more correct to say "yet where the interest insured is the expectancy of benefit to arise out of the safe arrival of some insurable property, some legal right in relation to such property must be subsisting," &c. For a possible exception to this principle, see *post*, §§ 301—303. See also Moran *v.* Uzielli, [1905] 2 K. B. 555, and the remarks on that case, *infra*, § 257a.

(*q*) See Buchanan *v.* Faber (1899), 4 Com. Cas. 223.

(*r*) Stockdale *v.* Dunlop (1840), 6 M. & W. 224.

(*s*) Mar. Ins. Act, 1906, s. 3 (2) (c), *ante*, § 1; s. 5 (2), *ante*, § 254.

perty carried or insured by them is an interest in the property which is insurable (*t*).

_{Sect. 257.}

257a. The decision of Walton, J., in a recent case (*u*), does not agree with the statement that when the interest insured is the expectancy of benefit to arise out of the safe arrival of some subject of insurance, the assured, in order to recover, must have a title to such subject at the time of loss, or some legal right in relation thereto. In that case the agents in the United Kingdom of a foreign ship effected an insurance for a voyage of the ship from Vancouver to any ports in the United Kingdom "on disbursements." At the date of the policy the owners of the ship were largely indebted to them for advances in respect of the ship's disbursements; and the learned judge held that the agents, having an existing right to enforce their claim for advances in respect of necessaries supplied to the ship by an action *in rem*, and in such an action to arrest the ship (*x*), had an insurable interest in the ship to the extent of such advances. It is clear that if the assured had gained a lien on the ship they would, to the extent thereof, have had an insurable interest. It is, however, submitted that the circumstance that a person will, if he takes legal proceedings, obtain a lien on insurable property does not give an insurable interest. If it did, the result would seem to be that every judgment creditor would have an insurable interest in all the property of his debtor which was capable of being taken in execution. The decision of the learned judge does not obtain any support from the definition of an insurable interest in sect. 5 of the Marine Insurance Act, 1906 (*y*); for it can hardly be maintained

_{Does the right to arrest insurable property give an interest?}

(*t*) Crowley *v.* Cohen (1832), 3 B. & Ad. 478; Mackenzie *v.* Whitworth (1875), 1 Ex. D. 36. So the liability of captors to pay costs and charges if they had taken possession improperly, and also their liability to render back property which should turn out to be neutral: per Lord Eldon in Lucena *v.* Craufurd (1806), 2 B. & P. N. R. 323.

(*u*) Moran *v.* Uzielli, [1905] 2 K. B. 555.

(*x*) This "existing right" would cease if the ship were sold to a *bonâ fide* purchaser: see The Henrich Björn (1886), 11 App. Cas. 270.

(*y*) *Ante*, § 254.

Sect. 257a. that a person who, if he begins an action *in rem*, will have a right to arrest insurable property, stands thereby in any "legal or equitable relation" to the property. It is true that the definition in sect. 5 does not profess to be exhaustive; but the proposition that the possibility of obtaining a lien upon property is a right which gives an insurable interest, seems to the editors unduly to extend the legal conception of an insurable interest (*z*).

When the interest must attach.

258. With regard to the time when the interest must attach, sect. 6 of the Marine Insurance Act, 1906, lays down the following rules:—

(1) The assured must be interested in the subject-matter insured at the time of the loss though he need not be interested when the insurance is effected:

Provided that where the subject-matter is insured "lost or not lost," the assured may recover although he may not have acquired his interest until after the loss, unless at the time of effecting the contract of insurance the assured was aware of the loss and the insurer was not.

(2) Where the assured has no interest at the time of the loss, he cannot acquire interest by any act or election after he is aware of the loss (*a*).

The interest must be subsisting at the time of loss.

Formerly the rule was laid down to be that the assured, besides being interested at the time of the loss, must also be interested at the time of effecting the policy (*b*); but it is

(*z*) The learned judge adopts the view that the definition of insurable interest has been continually expanding: [1905] 2 K. B. 563, citing Chalmers & Owen, Mar. Ins. Dig. 2nd ed. p. 11. In the United States it has been decided that advances for repairs of a ship give no insurable interest, unless when secured by a lien: see *post*, § 310. It has also been held there that a general creditor has no insurable interest in the property of his debtor: Vancouver Nat. Bank *v.* Law, &c. Ins. Co. (1907), 153 Fed. R. 440.

(*a*) Anderson *v.* Morice (1875—6), L. R. 10 C. P. 609, 620, 623; 1 App. Cas. 713, 726, 733, 749. In this case the assured bought a cargo of rice under a contract by which the property did not pass until the whole cargo was shipped. The ship was lost with part of the cargo on board, and it was held that the assured, who afterwards paid for the lost cargo, could not recover from the underwriters: see *post*, § 283.

(*b*) Lucena *v.* Craufurd (1806), 2 B. & P. N. R. 295; see also Marsh *v.* Robinson (1804), 4 Esp. 98.

now established that an insurable interest subsisting at the time of loss is sufficient (c); indeed, it is every day's practice to effect insurances in which the allegation of interest at the time of effecting the policy could not be made with any degree of truth, as, for instance, where goods are insured on a return voyage long before they are bought (d).

It must, however, be alleged, and, if traversed, be proved in all cases, that the party on whose account and for whose benefit the policy was made was interested in the subject of insurance at the time of loss. Where, therefore, interest being averred in three part owners of a ship, it appeared that one of them had, before the loss, parted with his share to one of the other part owners, it was held that there was no right of action in the three jointly (e). If, however, the party in whom interest is averred has parted with his interest after the loss, the underwriter cannot, on that ground, resist his claim on the policy (f).

Sect. 258.

259. As the proviso to sect. 6 (1) of the Marine Insurance Act, 1906, shows, the rule that the party insuring must be interested at the time of loss does not apply to a policy containing the "lost or not lost" clause, so as to preclude a party who has become interested in goods after the commencement of the risk from recovering for an average loss on such goods which occurred before his interest commenced, when the loss in question falls on him (g). If, however, the assured effects an insurance with knowledge of a loss and without disclosing

Loss of goods before interest acquired may be recoverable.

(c) Arnould stated that the interest must also be subsisting "during the risk," but the editors submitted in the seventh edition that the words "during the risk" were superfluous; for, to enable the assured to recover, the loss must have been during the risk—*i.e.*, within the limits of place or time prescribed in the policy; and it is surely immaterial whether the interest came into existence at the moment of the loss or at some time before. Their view is confirmed by the language of sect. 6 (1).

(d) Rhind v. Wilkinson (1810), 2 Taunt. 237.

(e) Powles v. Innes (1843), 11 M. & W. 10.

(f) Sparkes v. Marshall (1836), 2 Bing. N. C. 776.

(g) Sutherland v. Pratt (1843), 11 M. & W. 296.

Sect. 259. his information to the underwriter, the latter, if at that time ignorant of the loss, can avoid the policy (*h*).

A partial interest may be insured.

259a. Sect. 8 of the Marine Insurance Act, 1906, declares that—"A partial interest of any nature is insurable."

The term "partial interest" may be construed as meaning an undivided or "hotchpot" interest in the subject-matter insured (*i*), *e.g.*, the interest of a part owner (whether joint tenant or tenant in common) of insurable property (*k*), or the interest of one of a body of adventurers in their common adventure (*l*). It may also be construed more widely so as to cover other interests which do not extend to the full value of the subject-matter insured, *e.g.*, the interest of a party having a mortgage or lien on insurable property, in respect of the amount of his lien (*m*).

The power to abandon, a suggested test of insurable interest.

260. The power to abandon has been suggested as a test of an insurable interest; but it is not a certain criterion, as there are insurable interests in things which from their nature are incapable of abandonment, as profits, disbursements, bottomry, and respondentia (*n*). If, however, the nature of the subject admits of abandonment, an incapacity to abandon certainly shows a want of insurable interest in the subject of insurance at the time of the loss; for an abandonment is nothing else than a divesting out of the assured of all the interest he had in the thing insured at the moment of the loss, on condition of his being paid by the underwriters the whole amount of the insurance (*o*).

(*h*) See *post*, §§ 575, 609.

(*i*) See Robertson *v.* Hamilton (1811), 14 East, 522; Inglis *v.* Stock (1885), 10 App. Cas. 263, 274, *post*, § 284.

(*k*) Thus, the registered owner of one or more sixty-fourth shares in a ship, who is a tenant in common of the ship with the owners of the other shares, can protect his interest by a separate insurance.

(*l*) Wilson *v.* Jones (1867), L. R. 2 Ex. 139.

(*m*) See *post*, §§ 292, 298.

(*n*) See the opinions of the Judges generally, and of Lawrence, J., in particular, on the fifth question submitted to them by the House of Lords in Lucena *v.* Craufurd (1806), 2 B. & P. N. R. 289 —310; see also the opinion of Lord Eldon, *ibid*. 315—327.

(*o*) See the observations of Lawrence, J., in Lucena *v.* Cranfurd (1806), 2 B. & P. N. R. 312; and Conway *v.* Gray (1809), 10 East,

CHAP. XII.] OF SHIPOWNER AND CHARTERER. 349

An interest, in order to be insurable against particular perils, must be such as to be immediately, and not only by way of consequence, affected by those perils. Thus, if profits, by evidence of the state of the market, would have been secured but for the loss of the goods on the voyage, commissions but for the same calamity, freight but for the disabling of the ship by the perils of the sea, they are insurable. A person, however, who advances money in this country to a British shipowner for the repair of his ship acquires thereby no insurable interest, unless the money be secured by some such legal interest in the vessel as a mortgage, or bottomry lien, and yet the loss of the ship may by way of consequence involve the loss of the money (*p*).

Sect. 260.
Interest must be directly liable to the perils insured against.

261. The owner has in all cases an insurable interest in the ship. Even where he lets her out under a contract of affreightment to a charterer who covenants, in case of loss, to pay him her full value, he has a right to insure to the full amount; for he is not bound to trust exclusively to the credit of the charterer (*q*). The charterer also has, in such case, an insurable interest in the ship to the full extent of his liability. Thus, in the United States, where the owner of one-half of a schooner hired the other half, with a covenant that, in case of her being lost within the terms of the charter-party, he would pay the other part owner the value of his moiety, he was held to have an insurable interest to the full value of the ship (*r*).

Insurable interest of shipowner and charterer in ship.

262. Generally speaking, the shipowner alone has an insurable interest in freight, whether by that word be meant

Shipowner's interest in freight.

536, where the want of power to abandon, and the absence of insurable interest in goods, are apparently treated as resting on the same ground.

(*p*) For a further illustration of the principle under consideration, see Wilson *v.* Jones (1866), L. R. 1 Ex. 193; in the Ex. Ch. (1867),

L. R. 2 Ex. 139; *post*, § 307. As regards advances to the owner of a foreign ship, see Moran *v.* Uzielli, [1905] 2 K. B. 555, *ante*, § 257a.

(*q*) Hobbs *v.* Hannam (1811), 3 Camp. 93.

(*r*) Oliver *v.* Greene (1807), 3 Mass. R. 133; cited 1 Phillips, s. 325.

Sect. 262.

Charterer's interest in freight.

freight properly so called, or the chartered hire of his ship (*s*).

In some cases, however, the charterer may have an insurable interest in freight. Where he relets the ship, or puts her up as a general ship for the transport of other people's goods on freight, there seems no doubt that, as he stands, *pro hâc vice*, in the position of a shipowner, he has an insurable interest in the freight (*t*) he so expects to earn (*u*). Moreover, as the shipowner has an insurable interest in the benefit which he expects to derive, or the profit he expects to make, by carrying his own goods in his own ship, and may protect this interest by an insurance on freight (*x*), there is no reason why the charterer, when he stands in the same position, may not do the same (*y*).

(*s*) As to insurances by cargo-owners on "contingency freight," see *ante*, § 232.

(*t*) The American case of Mellen *v.* National Ins. Co. (1829), 1 Hall, 452, cited 1 Phillips, Ins. ss. 337, 480, decided that a charterer could not insure his interest under the description of freight; but it appears wrongly decided. See the observations of Phillips, vol. i. s. 480. In United States Shipping Co. *v.* Empress Ass. Co., [1907] 1 K. B. 259, it was not disputed that the charterer could insure his interest as freight.

(*u*) Arnould added (2nd ed. vol. i. p. 311): "At all events, for the surplus by which such freight exceeds the sum he has engaged to pay the shipowner as charter-money." This qualification agrees with Phillips' opinion, if it means that where by the operation of the same peril the charterer loses the freight which he would otherwise receive, and is discharged from his liability to pay freight to the shipowner, he is, on the principle of indemnity, only entitled to recover such surplus. See 1 Phillips, s. 337; see also 1 Parsons, 175. In U. S. Shipping Co. *v.* Empress Ass. Co., *supra*, Channell, J., held, however, that a charterer was entitled on a policy on freight to recover the gross freight which he would have received under a sub-charter, without deducting the hire which he would have had to pay to the shipowner. The decision was affirmed on a question of fact, [1908] 1 K. B. 115. See also Mar. Ins. Act, 1906, s. 16 (2), *infra*, § 365, where it is stated in general terms that in insurance on freight the insurable value is the gross amount of the freight at the risk of the assured.

(*x*) Flint *v.* Flemyng (1830), 1 B. & Ad. 45; Devaux *v.* J'Anson (1839), 5 Bing. N. C. 519. See Mar. Ins. Act, 1906, Sched. I. rule 16, *ante*, § 229.

(*y*) The contrary was held in the American case of Mellen *v.* National Ins. Co. (1829), above cited; but the case of Flint *v.* Flemyng was not adverted to.

CHAP. XII.] OF SHIPOWNER AND CHARTERER. 351

A charterer who wishes only to insure the surplus of the freight which he expects to receive over the freight which he will have to pay, can do so by a policy on "profits on charter," or "difference of freight" (*z*). {Sect. 262.}

The vendor of a ship who reserves his right to the freight being earned at the time is in a similar situation to a charterer who takes goods on freight, and ought, therefore, to have an insurable interest in such freight (*a*). {Owner who sells his ship, reserving right to the freight.}

A charterer who agrees to pay dead freight, in case the ship be prevented by political or other circumstances from discharging her outward, or shipping her return, cargo, has an insurable interest to the same extent, and may protect himself by a policy properly framed to cover his liability under the terms of the charter-party (*b*). The risk insured against in this case was the contingent determination of the adventure by the foreign government at the port of discharge, and it was insured for the charterer; the shipowner might also have insured his interest in the freight under a common policy against ordinary sea risks (*c*). {Charterer's interest in dead freight.}

263. Sect. 12 of the Marine Insurance Act, 1906, declares that— {Advance freight.}

> "In the case of advance freight, the person advancing the freight has an insurable interest, in so far as such freight is not repayable in case of loss."

A charterer who advances money under the terms of the charter-party in part payment of the freight has, therefore, an insurable interest in the money so advanced; for as such money cannot, in case of the loss of the ship or cargo, be recovered back, the loss of the ship or cargo involves the loss of the benefit which the charterer expected to derive from the {Charterer's interest in advances on freight.}

(*z*) See *ante*, § 239.

(*a*) The contrary has been decided in the United States (Riley *v*. Delafield (1811), 7 Johns R. 522); but this decision, as Phillips has ably pointed out, does not rest on satisfactory grounds. See 1 Phillips, Ins. s. 480.

(*b*) Puller *v*. Staniforth (1809), 11 East, 232; see also Puller *v*. Glover (1810), 12 East, 124; Puller *v*. Halliday (1810), 12 East, 494.

(*c*) See the observations in 1 Phillips, Ins. s. 336.

Sect. 263. payment (*d*). But in order to give him such an insurable interest it must appear, by fair and reasonable inference from the words in the charter-party, that the money advanced is an advance in part payment of the freight.

When, as is usually the case, the advance is made under a stipulation in the charter-party, the question whether the advance is a mere loan to the shipowner to be repaid in any event, and therefore not insurable by the charterer, or whether it is an advance in part payment of freight, which the charterer therefore can insure, depends on the construction of the charter-party alone. An advance which is not stipulated for in a charter-party will be treated as made on account of freight if it clearly appears, from the transaction between the parties, that this was their intention (*e*).

As soon as the advance freight becomes due, the charterer's insurable interest therein commences; for even though a loss should take place before any payment has been made, the charterer is liable to pay the advance freight (*f*).

When an advance is part payment of freight.

264. No rule can be laid down to determine generally when an advance is a part payment of freight. When the question is one of the construction of the charter-party, such construction should not depend "on strict grammatical form, or on the apparent meaning of any one phrase in (the charter-party) taken by itself, but on the apparent expressed meaning, as to practical results, of the whole. It should be construed by considering the terms of it, and the decisions in former cases of terms similar, though perhaps not identical" (*g*).

(*d*) Anonymous case, 2 Shower, 283; De Silvale *v.* Kendall (1815), 4 M. & S. 37; per Bayley, J., in Manfield *v.* Maitland (1821), 4 B. & Ald. 582, 585; and the discussion in Allison *v.* Bristol Mar. Ins. Co. (1876), 1 App. Cas. 209.

(*e*) Per Brett, J., Allison *v.* Bristol Marine Ins. Co. (1876), 1 App. Cas. 209, 217; Wilson *v.* Martin (1856), 11 Exch. 684; 25 L. J. Ex. 217; The Karnak (1869),

L. R. 2 P. C. 505, 514.

(*f*) See per Lord Esher in Smith *v.* Pyman, [1891] 1 Q. B. 742, 744; Oriental SS. Co. *v.* Tyler, [1893] 2 Q. B. 518 (C. A.).

(*g*) Per Brett, J., *ubi supra*. On the question, when an advance is held to be on account of freight, see, in addition to the cases cited *supra*, Hicks *v.* Shield (1857), 7 E. & B. 633; 26 L. J. Q. B. 205; Williams *v.* North China Ins. Co.

CHAP. XII.] ADVANCE FREIGHT. 353

The following cases are instructive examples of the grounds on which the question was decided in the particular instances. The covenant as to payment of freight in a charter-party on a ship bound from Liverpool to Maranham and back, was in the following terms:—" Such freight to be paid as follows, viz., 120*l*. British sterling for freight of the outward cargo to Maranham, and as much cash as may be found necessary for the ship's disbursements at Maranham, to be advanced by the charterer or his agents to the master when required, free from interest or commission, &c., and the residue of such freight to be paid on the delivery of the cargo in Liverpool," &c.: Lord Ellenborough and the Court of King's Bench held, that under the special terms of this charter-party the money advanced must be held to have been advanced specifically on account of freight, and therefore, upon the loss of the ship before any freight earned, could not be recovered back by the charterer from the owner as money had and received (*h*). "In this case," as Lord Tenterden remarks, "the instrument was studiously framed so as to make the freighter lose the money advanced by him unless the owner reaped the benefit by the ship's coming home safe" (*i*).

Sect. 264.
Cases on the point.
De Silvale v. Kendall.

Where, however, the charter-party did not on the face of it clearly and distinctly import that the sum advanced was a payment on account of freight, but merely contained the words, "The captain to be supplied with cash for the ship's use," the Court held, that the charterer had no insurable interest in bills of exchange drawn on him by the master in respect of cash so supplied, it not appearing by the charter-party to be advanced as a part payment of freight (*k*). But

Manfield v. Maitland.

(1876), 1 C. P. D. 757; Byrne *v.* Schiller (1870, 1871), L. R. 6 Ex. 20, 319; 40 L. J. Ex. 177; Watson *v.* Shankland (1873), L. R. 2 H. L. (Sc.) 304; The Red Sea, C. A., [1896] P. 20; Weir *v.* Girvin, [1900] 1 K. B. 45; Carver, ss. 564 —566.

(*h*) De Silvale *v.* Kendall (1815), 4 M. & S. 87. Lord Ellenborough

and Dampier, J., lay some stress upon the words "free from interest and commission," as showing that the money advanced was not intended to be a loan.

(*i*) Per Abbott, C. J., in 4 B. & Ald. 585.

(*k*) Manfield *v.* Maitland (1821), 4 B. & Ald. 582; see also Saunders *v.* Drew (1832), 3 B. & Ad. 445.

A.—VOL. I. 23

Sect. 264.

Wilson v. Martin.

where the freighters of a general ship paid her disbursements abroad, and by the request of the owners took the captain's bill, drawn against freight, on the consignees of the cargo in this country, in discharge of such disbursements, it was held, that as the freighters had agreed to advance on credit of the freight, which was distinctly pledged by the captain's bill, they had an insurable interest in freight, and might recover on a policy describing their interest as "an advance on account of freight" (*l*).

Winter v. Haldimand.

By a charter-party the freighters were to pay, for the use of the ship "for the voyage, 10,000 dollars in manner following:—viz., in China, all the sums that might be necessary for the payment of port charges and other incidental expenses (the latter not to exceed 2,000 dollars), and the balance at thirty days after the ship's return to the port at Buenos Ayres": and Lord Tenterden admitted that the freighters had an insurable interest in payments made under this stipulation by their agents at Canton in respect of port charges and incidental expenses, and that they might insure such payments as "money paid for shipment of goods to be transported to Buenos Ayres" (*m*).

Effect of term "subject to insurance."

A stipulation in the charter-party that an advance is "subject to insurance," or subject to a deduction on account of insurance, is sufficient to show that it is a payment on account of freight, and not a mere loan (*n*). The term "subject to insurance" does not imply any liability on the part of the shipowner to insure on behalf of the charterer, but only that a sum equal to the premium is to be allowed to the latter, who can insure if he chooses (*o*).

(*l*) Wilson *v.* Martin (1856), 11 Exch. 684; *S. C.*, 25 L. J. Exch. 217.

(*m*) Winter *v.* Haldimand (1831), 2 B. & Ad. 649. The dicta of Lord Tenterden above referred to are in pp. 653, 658 of the report. See, however, *ante*, § 233.

(*n*) Hicks *v.* Shield (1857), 7 E. & B. 633; 26 L. J. Q. B. 205; accord. The Karnak (1869), L. R. 2 P. C. 505, 514; Allison *v.* Bristol Marine Ins. Co. (1876), 1 App. Cas. 209, 222, 229, 234.

(*o*) Watson *v.* Shankland (1873), L. R. 2 H. L. (Sc.) 304; per Manisty, J., Rodoconachi *v.* Milburn (1886), 17 Q. B. D. 316, 321.

CHAP. XII.] IN FREIGHT. 355

265. We will now consider when the insurable interest of the shipowner (or of the charterer who is in the position of a shipowner) in the freight begins. The question whether the assured on freight has at the time of the loss an insurable interest in the freight is one which is often treated in the cases and text-books in a way which causes a difficulty in distinguishing it from the question of the duration of the risk under a policy on freight. Yet these questions are different ones. Whether there be an insurable interest is a matter independent of the policy. In the absence of an insurable interest, the assured cannot maintain an action, however the policy be worded. If, on the other hand, he had an insurable interest, the question arises whether the loss occurred within the limits of place or time fixed by the policy. Arnould confined himself in this chapter to a statement of general principles, and afterwards discussed at length the question of insurable interest in freight in connection with that of the duration of the risk. In the previous edition it was thought advisable to deal fully with the question of insurable interest in its proper place, especially as in the opinion of the editors the author's statement of the law on the subject was not altogether supported by the authorities, and the same course is adopted in the present edition.

Sect. 265. Insurable interest in freight usually confounded with duration of risk.

266. Arnould, in the second edition of this work (*p*), stated the law as to insurable interest in freight in the following terms:—" In order to give an insurable interest on freight, there must be, 1. A title, either legal or equitable, in the party insuring, subsisting at the time of loss, in the subject out of the ownership of which the right to freight accrues, *i.e.*, the ship. 2. There must be, at the time of loss, an inchoate right to the freight; in other words, the position of things must be this, that but for the intervention of the loss freight would have been realized by the party insuring.

Arnould's doctrine as to insurable interest in freight.

" First, then, the party effecting an insurance on freight must have a title in the ship, either legal or equitable, sub-

(*p*) Vol. i. pp. 287—289.

Sect. 266. sisting at the time of loss; 'for the right to freight results from the right of ownership, and if the assured have no title to the ship they have no interest in the freight' (*q*).

" Secondly, at the time of the loss there must be an inchoate right to the freight in the party insuring; in other words, he must be so situated with respect to it as that he would certainly have earned freight but for the intervention of the loss. The principle here is, that where nothing intervenes between the subject insured and the possession of it but the perils insured against, the person so situated may insure the safety of such subject of insurance, for he has an interest to avert the perils insured against (*r*). We shall have occasion elsewhere to investigate more at large the numerous decisions that show when an inchoate right to freight may be considered to have vested in the party effecting an insurance on that interest.

" It will be sufficient here to state the principles established by these decisions, and draw those conclusions from them that have a more particular application to the subject of insurable interest.

" The word freight, in policies of insurance, means, as we have already had occasion to observe, either, 1. Freight properly so called, *i.e.*, the sum paid to the shipowner for the transport of goods in his ship; or, 2nd, The price agreed to be paid by charter-party for the hire of the ship, which is, strictly speaking, rather to be called charter-money than freight.

" The shipowner's right to freight in the former case does not accrue—in other words, he has no inchoate right to freight —and therefore no insurable interest thereon, unless the goods or a part of them are actually loaded on board the ship before the loss; ' or are so situated with respect to the ship as to create a well-grounded expectation of freight being realized ' (*s*).

(*q*) Camden *v.* Anderson (1794), 5 T. R. 709; and see *S. C.* (1796), 6 T. R. 723; (1798), 1 B. & P. 272; see also Marsh *v.* Robinson (1802), 4 Esp. 98.

(*r*) Lucena *v.* Craufurd (in error) (1802), 3 B. & P. 95.

(*s*) Dictum of Eyre, C. J., in Curling *v.* Long (1797), 1 B. & P. 636.

"The true proposition, in fact, as far as regards freight properly so called, is this: that, in order to give the shipowner an insurable interest in such freight, he must prove that but for the intervention of the perils insured against some freight would have been earned, either by showing that some of the goods for the transport of which it was to be paid were actually put on board, or that there was some contract for putting them on board, that the ship was ready to receive the goods, and the goods ready to be shipped under such contract, before the loss (*t*).

Sect. 266.

"On the other hand, where the freight intended to be insured is the price of the hire of the ship under a charter-party, the cases show that the inchoate right to such freight vests in the shipowner directly the ship has broken ground on the voyage described in the charter-party; from that moment nothing can intercept the earning of freight under the terms of the charter-party, except the breaking-up of the voyage by the perils insured against; and, consequently, from that moment the shipowner has an insurable interest in the freight, which but for the intervention of such perils he has thus put himself in a position to earn (*u*).

"The shipowner has an insurable interest in the profit he expects to make by carrying his own goods in his own ship, and this interest he may protect by a general policy on freight (*x*).

"The charterer, as we shall see more at large hereafter, has an insurable interest in protecting himself against the liability of having to pay dead freight, under the covenants of a charter-party, to the full amount of the sum he has covenanted so to pay" (*y*).

(*t*) Montgomery *v*. Eggington (1789), 3 T. R. 362; Truscott *v*. Christie (1820), 2 Brod. & B. 320; Parke *v*. Hebson (*circa* 1820), *ibid*. 326; Forbes *v*. Aspinall (1811), 13 East, 331; Flint *v*. Flemyng (1830), 1 B. & Ad. 45; Devaux *v*. J'Anson (1839), 5 Bing. N. C. 519.

(*u*) Thompson *v*. Taylor (1795),
6 T. R. 478; Horncastle *v*. Suart (1806), 7 East, 400; Atty *v*. Lindo (1805), 1 B. & P. N. R. 236; Davidson *v*. Willasey (1813), 1 M. & S. 313.

(*x*) Flint *v*. Flemyng (1830), 1 B. & Ad. 45; Devaux *v*. J'Anson (1839), 5 Bing. N. C. 519.

(*y*) Puller *v*. Staniforth (1809), 11 East, 232.

358 INSURABLE INTEREST [PART I.

Sect. 267.
Misleading expressions in relation to insurable interest in freight.

267. We propose to consider in detail the cases cited by Arnould (*z*) on the question when the insurable interest commences. Before doing so, however, we think it advisable to draw attention to certain expressions which have been generally used both by Judges and text-writers, but which in their literal sense bear a meaning which it is safe to say they could not be intended to convey. We refer to such expressions as that the assured must prove that he "would certainly have earned freight but for the intervention of the loss," or that "but for the perils insured against some freight would have been earned," or that "nothing could intercept the earning of the freight under the terms of the charter-party except the breaking-up of the voyage by the perils insured against" (*a*). There need not be a *certainty* that but for the loss freight would have been earned. All that can be required is, that in the ordinary course of things, each party performing his contract, some freight would have been earned (*b*). Thus, if a ship be lost while sailing under the terms of a charter-party to her port of loading, the shipowner has, as will presently appear, an insurable interest in the freight to be earned under the contract; and he can, therefore, recover the consequent loss of freight under a properly worded policy, although if the loss had not taken place he might still have lost the freight through the subsequent

Not necessary that earning of freight would have been certain but for loss.

(*z*) 2nd ed. vol. i. pp. 522—532.
(*a*) *Supra.*
(*b*) Thus, Lawrence, J., says that an insurance may be to protect men against the loss by uncertain events of the advantage or profit which but for such events they would acquire *according to the ordinary and probable course of things.* Lucena *v.* Craufurd (1806), 2 B. & P. N. R. 269, 301. So also, in Davidson *v.* Willasey (1813), 1 M. & S. 313, 317, Le Blanc, J., speaks of "a contract for freight, under which, except for the wrongful act of the party with whom he has contracted, he (the assured) would be in a condition to earn his freight if the voyage were not stopped by a peril insured against." See also per Richardson, J., in Truscott *v.* Christie (1820), 2 Brod. & B. 320, 532. In Rankin *v.* Potter (1873), L. R. 6 H. L. 83, where the claim was for a total loss of freight by perils of the sea, it appeared that the charterer became insolvent after the ship was damaged, but before she was abandoned, and had actually failed to supply a cargo: the House of Lords held, that this did not prevent the assured from recovering. See L. R. 6 H. L. 154, 160, 167.

insolvency of the charterer, and the latter's inability to provide a cargo or pay dead freight (c). Again, the use of the words "perils insured against" in the expressions cited above is obviously incorrect. A more accurate term would be "perils insured against or other perils incident to the voyage." Thus, if the insurance were against capture only, it could not be said that nothing but a capture could intercept the earning of the freight. Yet a loss by capture would none the less be recoverable under the policy.

268. The insurable interest in freight properly so called (*i.e.*, the price to be paid to the shipowner by the owner of goods on their arrival for their carriage in the ship) will first be considered.

In the earliest reported case, it was decided by Lee, C. J., that the assured could not recover for the freight of goods ready to be shipped, but not yet loaded on board, at the time of the loss (d); but a more liberal rule was established by the later cases.

The first case which extended the rule laid down by Lee, C. J., was Montgomery *v.* Eggington, which established that, where part of the goods were actually on board at the time of the loss, and all were ready to be shipped, the policy attached on the whole freight. The insurance was on freight valued at 1,500*l.*: when only 500*l.* worth of freight was on board, the ship was driven from her moorings and lost, but goods to the amount of the rest of the freight were ready to be shipped, and were lying on the quay for that purpose, at the time of the loss. The jury, under the direction of Lord Kenyon, found a verdict for the whole sum, which the Court of King's Bench, on motion for a new trial, refused to disturb (e).

(c) Rankin *v.* Potter (1873), L. R. 6 H. L. 83.
(d) Tonge *v.* Watts (1746), 2 Str. 1251.
(e) Montgomery *v.* Eggington (1789), 3 T. R. 362. Lord Kenyon, in Thompson *v.* Taylor (1795), 6 T. R. 482, thus distinguishes this case from that of Tonge *v.* Watts: "In the case in Strange, the inception of the contract would have been the taking of the goods on

Sect. 268.
Parke v. Hebson.

The same principle was applied in other cases. Thus, an insurance was effected on the freight of a general ship, which was to complete her lading at a number of different ports, and to be paid freight for the same according to the terms usual in the colonial trade. The ship, after having taken on board part only of her return cargo, was lost at Jamaica, while passing from port to port in that island in order to complete it. It appeared, however, that, although only part of the cargo was shipped at the time of the loss, yet contracts had previously been made for the whole of the residue: upon this evidence plaintiff was allowed to recover for the whole freight (*f*).

Truscott v. Christie.

A shipowner insured freight and passage money for a homeward voyage "at and from Madras and all ports and places in the East Indies to the United Kingdom." He had agreed with the government of Madras to carry goods for them on board his ship at certain freight, and also to fit her up with an extra deck, and make other alterations for the purpose of accommodating 200 invalids, whom the company engaged to send home in his ship at a fixed rate of passage money. He had commenced making the alterations, had received on board the greater part of the cargo, and had shipped water for 100 invalids, when, before the alterations were completed, or any of the invalids embarked, the ship was driven from her moorings and totally disabled. The Court held that he was entitled to recover the whole freight for all the goods that were to be shipped under the contract, and passage money for as many invalids as his ship would have carried, on the ground that he had a contract for both the freight and the passage money, and that he had begun to execute his part of the contract, the completion of which

board; but as the loss happened before the goods were put on board, there was no inception of the contract, and the plaintiff was nonsuited: but in the case of Montgomery *v.* Eggington there was an inception of the contract, because part of the goods had been put on board."

(*f*) Parke *v.* Hebson (*circa* 1820), cited 2 Brod. & B. 326.

would have entitled him to his money, and had been prevented by perils of the sea (*g*).

Sect. 268.

In these cases some portion of the goods from the carriage of which freight was to arise had been actually shipped on board at the time of the loss; in later cases the assured recovered for the freight for the whole cargo though no part had been shipped, but the whole had been purchased or contracted for at the time of the loss. Thus, where freight was insured for a homeward voyage "at and from the Island of Granada to London," and the ship was lost while she was proceeding from one port of Granada to another, before she had discharged all her outward cargo, and before any of the homeward cargo had been actually shipped on board, but it appeared that a full homeward cargo had been contracted for at the time of the loss, it was not disputed that the risk had attached on the whole freight for the homeward voyage (*h*). So, where freight was insured on a homeward voyage "at and from Madras to London," and the day after the ship had finished discharging her outward cargo at Madras she was totally lost by the perils of the sea, and no part of the homeward cargo was then shipped, but the captain had purchased for the ship a quantity of red wood to be laden on board, and a mercantile house at Madras had also engaged to ship a quantity of saltpetre, the Court held, that the plaintiff was entitled to his full freight for the red wood and saltpetre (*i*).

Cases in which the assured recovered though no goods had been shipped.
Warre v. Miller.

Flint v. Flemyng.

An insurance was effected on freight "from Calcutta or any port or place on the Coromandel Coast to Bourbon;" the ship, on arrival at Coringa, on the Coromandel Coast, was taken into dry dock for repairs: during which the supercargo purchased, on behalf of the owners, a return cargo to Bourbon, which was warehoused at a place seven miles from Coringa, and was there lying ready to be conveyed on board the ship on the day when she was reported ready for sea. On that day she was still in the dock, but on being floated

Devaux v J'Anson.

(*g*) Truscott *v.* Christie (1820), 2 Brod. & B. 320.
(*h*) Warre *v.* Miller (1825), 4 B. & Cr. 538.
(*i*) Flint *v.* Flemyng (1830), 1 B. & Ad. 45. See *post*, § 269.

Sect. 268. into the river would have been ready to receive her cargo; but in attempting to leave the dock she was so much damaged that she was obliged to be broken up and sold. Under these circumstances, the Court of Common Pleas held, that as the whole of the return cargo was purchased and ready to be put on board at the time of the ship's loss, and as that loss was occasioned by a peril within the policy, the plaintiffs were entitled to recover the full freight on the whole of the return cargo (*k*).

It must be observed that in this case the intended cargo was the property of the shipowners. There could not, therefore, be any contract for its shipment or for the payment of freight for its carriage. Under such circumstances, all that the Court deemed it necessary to determine with regard to the cargo was, that it must have become the property of the parties insured (*l*) by a contract made with a view to its being sent on board, and must actually be in a state of readiness, reference being had to the nature and description of the voyage insured, to be put on board when the ship arrived at the place of loading (*m*).

The form of the contract of affreightment is immaterial,

269. As to the contract under which the cargo is to be shipped on board, all that is required is, that it should be valid and binding at law; its form is not material (*n*).

provided there is a binding contract.

It is, however, essential, where the plaintiff seeks to recover the whole freight for a cargo only part of which, or none of which, has been actually loaded on board, that he should prove the existence of some actual binding contract for shipping such cargo.

Patrick v. Eames.

Thus, under a policy on freight, the ship had sailed from Sierra Leone with the intention of taking in a complete cargo of orchella weed from the Cape de Verd Islands, and was lost

---

(*k*) Devaux *v.* J'Anson (1839), 5 Bing. N. C. 519.

(*l*) " Freighters " must be substituted for " parties insured," to make this statement applicable where the shipowner is not the cargo-owner.

(*m*) Devaux *v.* J'Anson (1839), 5 Bing. N. C. 539.

(*n*) Per Lord Ellenborough in Patrick *v.* Eames (1813), 3 Camp. 441.

when only 150 bags had been shipped on board, and it did not appear that any more orchella weed was then ready to be loaded (*o*), or that any binding contract, whether verbal or otherwise, had been made for supplying it; Lord Ellenborough held, that the plaintiff was only entitled to the freight on the 150 bags actually shipped (*p*). So in the case of Flint *v*. Flemyng, in addition to the red wood which the captain had purchased, and the saltpetre which the mercantile house had formally contracted to put on board, it was proved that a partner in that house had also engaged verbally to ship on board ninety tons of light goods. With regard to these ninety tons, the Court ordered a new trial, because the question was not distinctly submitted to the jury, whether there was any binding contract for shipping those goods (*q*).

Two other cases were cited by Arnould to establish the proposition that the assured cannot recover for a loss of freight unless the ship was at the time of the loss ready to receive the cargo and the cargo ready to be shipped. One was Forbes *v*. Aspinall, in which the facts were as follow.

A policy was effected on freight valued at 6,500*l*., for a homeward voyage "at and from any port or ports in Hayti to Liverpool, or the ship's port of discharge in the United Kingdom." There was no charter-party; and the ship, which was a general or seeking ship, sailed from Liverpool to Hayti with a cargo intended for barter. At Jacmel, in

---

(*o*) It was proved that persons were actually engaged in the different islands in picking and preparing it. See the report.

(*p*) Patrick *v*. Eames (1813), 3 Camp. 441.

(*q*) Flint *v*. Flemyng (1830), 1 B. & Ad. 45. The principle of these cases was applied by Hamilton, J., in Scottish Shire Line, Ld. *v*. London & Provincial Mar. Ins. Co., [1912] 3 K. B. 51. This was an insurance on freight "chartered or as if chartered," and the plaintiffs contended that under the words "as if chartered" they were entitled to recover for a loss of the freight of cargo which the ship was expected to load, but for which there was not a binding contract. "I cannot find," said the learned judge (p. 65), "that the words 'freight, or chartered freight, or freight as if chartered' have ever been applied to the expectation, however well founded, that a ship's agent will procure a cargo for her, where there is no actual binding engagement to that effect."

Sect. 269. Hayti, she bartered away part of her outward cargo, and took in exchange fifty-five bales of cotton as part of her homeward lading. She was proceeding from Jacmel to Aux Cayes, another port in Hayti, to barter away the rest of her outward cargo and complete her lading home, when, with the great bulk of her outward cargo still on board, she was totally lost by the perils of the sea. It did not appear that any goods were ready, or had been contracted for, at Aux Cayes, to be loaded on board the ship at the time of the loss; and the Court held, that the plaintiffs could only recover for a part of the agreed value of the freight in the same proportion as the fifty-five bales bore to a full cargo (*r*). Lord Ellenborough—after distinguishing the case from those in which the freight was secured under a charter-party, and in which, consequently, the risk on the whole freight commenced by the inception of the voyage—went on to show in what the case before the Court differed from Montgomery *v.* Eggington and the other decisions by which that case was supported and confirmed. "There," said his Lordship, "a full cargo was ready to be laden, and the ship in a state ready to receive it; and nothing but the perils insured against did or (as it appears) could prevent its being received; here it was uncertain whether any additional cargo could have been ever procured, and the outward cargo must also have been discharged before the homeward cargo could have been completed. So that the ship was not ever in a condition to receive her homeward cargo, even if the cargo had been ready, which it never was, to have been put on board."

Lord Ellenborough's judgment.

Arnould, after citing this passage, states (*s*) that the grounds upon which this decision proceeds are:—

1. That, as in this case there was no entire contract for freight under a charter-party for the whole voyage out and home, the right to the whole freight did not accrue by the

(*r*) Forbes *v.* Aspinall (1811), 13 East, 323. Forbes *v.* Cowie (1808), 1 Camp. 520, was the same case, only on an open instead of on a valued policy, and the result was the same.

(*s*) 2nd ed. vol. i. p. 531.

inception of the outward voyage. 2. That none of the cargo in respect of which freight was claimed was ever ready for the ship. 3. That, even had it been so, the ship at the time of the loss was not in a state of readiness to receive the cargo (*t*).

Sect. 269.

The real ground of the decision seems, however, to be that, except as to the fifty-five bales on board, there was no contract at the time of the loss under which the shipowner could claim freight. "In a case, therefore, circumstanced as this is," Lord Ellenborough said in conclusion, "where the valuation was with reference to freight upon a *complete* cargo; where a complete cargo, or anything like a complete cargo, never was in fact obtained, and for all that appears never might have been obtained; where there was no contract by any person to load a complete cargo or pay dead freight, but the ship was a mere seeking ship; we cannot feel ourselves warranted in saying that there has been a total loss by any peril insured against of that which the insurance was intended to cover" (*u*).

The following were the facts in the remaining case. A policy was effected on freight for a homeward voyage "at and from Algoa Bay to London." There was a charter-party. The ship, after she had arrived at Algoa Bay, and had unloaded there all the outward cargo destined for that place that she safely could, was just about commencing to load on board her homeward cargo, which was there lying ready for her, when she was lost by a hurricane. The report of Lord Lyndhurst's ruling merely states that he told the jury that if the ship was in a condition to begin to take in her homeward cargo, the plaintiff was entitled to recover; if not, then the verdict ought to be for the defendants; and the jury found for the plaintiff (*x*).

Williamson *v.* Innes.

(*t*) See, as to the ship, per Tindal, C. J., in Devaux *v.* J'Anson (1839), 5 Bing. N. C. 538.

(*u*) 13 East, 331.

(*x*) Williamson *v.* Innes (1831), cited in 8 Bing. 81; see also Warre *v.* Miller (1825), 4 B. & Cr. 538.

Sect. 270.
Result of the cases on insurable interest in freight proper.

270. The question must now be considered, whether these cases establish the proposition that the assured on freight, in order to show an insurable interest, must prove that "the ship was ready to receive the goods, and the goods ready to be shipped under the contract" (*y*).

Must the ship be ready to receive the cargo?

First, must the ship be ready to receive the goods? In Parke *v.* Hebson (*z*), the ship, having taken on board part of her cargo, was lost while proceeding to another port to load other goods which had been contracted for. She was certainly not ready to receive those goods, yet the shipowner recovered the freight on them. In Truscott *v.* Christie (*a*), the ship at the time of the loss was being altered to make her able to accommodate 200 invalids. The alterations were not completed, and the point was taken that at the time of the loss the ship was not ready to receive the invalids. The Court, however, held that the assured could recover on a policy on the passage money, to which obviously the same principles must apply as to a policy on freight. The ground of the decision was, that there was a contract for the passage money, and that something was done under the contract. In Warre *v.* Miller (*b*), the ship had not unloaded all her outward cargo; but as it was not disputed at the trial that the risk had attached, the Court would not allow the point to be taken that the ship was not ready, and therefore the case cannot be relied on as an authority. In Devaux *v.* J'Anson (*c*), again, the loss took place while the ship was still in the dry dock in which she had been repaired. It is true that Tindal, C. J., did say that the ship was ready to receive her cargo; but it is difficult to reconcile this statement with the fact that she was not yet at the actual place where she was to take the cargo on board (*d*).

(*y*) *Ante*, § 266.
(*z*) Cited 2 Brod. & B. 326.
(*a*) (1820), 2 Brod. & B. 320.
(*b*) (1825), 4 B. & Cr. 538.
(*c*) (1839), 5 Bing. N. C. 519.
(*d*) It may, however, be argued that the term "ready" is used in a somewhat different sense, which does not require that the vessel should be at the precise spot where the loading will commence: see Leonis SS. Co., Ltd. *v.* Rank, Ltd., [1908] 1 K. B. 499.

IN FREIGHT.

Sect. 270

Against these decisions there are only a passage in Lord Ellenborough's judgment in Forbes *v.* Aspinall (*e*) (the true *ratio decidendi* of which case seems to have been that there was no contract for the return cargo) and the reported ruling of Lord Lyndhurst in Williamson *v.* Innes (*f*). As to the latter, it may be remarked, it was only a *nisi prius* ruling. The freight was chartered freight, and the ruling, as reported, is opposed to the cases on chartered freight, such as Barber *v.* Fleming (*g*) and Foley *v.* United Fire and Marine Insurance Co. (*h*), as well as to the cases already considered (*i*).

271. Again, must the cargo be ready to be shipped before the insurable interest commences, or is it enough that there is a binding contract for freight? It was unnecessary to decide this point in Forbes *v.* Aspinall (*k*), as the cargo was not contracted for. In Parke *v.* Hebson (*l*) and Flint *v.* Flemyng (*m*), only the question whether there was a contract seems to have been considered. In Devaux *v.* J'Anson (*n*), the point whether the cargo was ready to be shipped was discussed; but that was the case of a shipowner insuring the freight of his own goods, to which, as has already been suggested and as will be shown hereafter, different considerations apply (*o*). The case is therefore not a true authority to prove that where the shipowner does not carry his own goods the cargo must be actually ready. All that the cases really establish on the point is that there must, at the time of the loss, be a valid contract under which goods are to be loaded, and on principle this seems all that should be neces-

Must the cargo be ready to be shipped?

(*e*) (1818), 13 East, 323, 331. See the remarks of Tindal, C. J., in Devaux *v.* J'Anson (1839), 5 Bing. N. C. 519, 538, as to the hearing upon the case of the fact that the ship was not ready to load.

(*f*) (1831), cited 8 Bing. 81.

(*g*) (1869), L. R. 5 Q. B. 59. See *post*, § 275.

(*h*) (1870), L. R. 5 C. P. 155, 160, 164. See *post*, § 273.

(*i*) Mr. Arthur Cohen agrees with the editors' opinion that those cases are opposed to the view that the ship must be ready to receive the cargo: see Halsbury's Laws of England, vol. xvii. § 775. See *infra*, § 511, n. (*z*).

(*k*) (1811), 13 East, 323.

(*l*) Cited 2 Brod. & B. 326.

(*m*) (1830), 1 B. & Ad. 45.

(*n*) (1839), 5 Bing. N. C. 519.

(*o*) *Post*, § 277.

Sect. 271. sary (*p*). The shipowner is entitled to assume that the goods contracted for will be ready at the proper time (*q*).

It is submitted that these cases do not establish the rule that the insurable interest in freight proper only begins when the ship is ready to receive the goods, and the goods are ready to be shipped. They show that there is at any rate an insurable interest when the assured, having a valid contract for freight, has taken steps towards the earning of the freight. The view that under the circumstances there is an insurable interest is supported by the decision of the Court of Queen's Bench in Barber *v.* Fleming (*r*). That was a case of chartered freight, but the decision is of general application, as it did not depend on the question whether there had been an inception of the charter-party contract. Whether it may not be possible to state the rule even more broadly will be considered presently (*s*).

Insurable interest in chartered freight.

272. We have now to consider insurable interest in chartered freight, *i.e.*, in a fixed sum stipulated to be paid to the shipowner by the terms of a charter-party for the use of his ship, or part of it, on an entire voyage therein described.

Under such a contract the ship may earn freight though no goods may ever be put on board, and the question whether, at the time of loss, she had taken any goods on board for the voyage insured, or whether any were contracted to be shipped, does not arise.

Result of the cases.

A series of cases shows that there is an inchoate right to such freight, and therefore an insurable interest from the inception of the voyage described in the charter-party (*t*).

(*p*) See 1 Parsons, pp. 169, 178.
(*q*) See Rankin *v.* Potter (1873), L. R. 6 H. L. 83; and *ante*, § 267.
(*r*) (1869), L. R. 5 Q. B. 59. See particularly the judgment of Blackburn, J., pp. 71, 73.
(*s*) See *post*, § 279.
(*t*) Thompson *v.* Taylor (1795), 6 T. R. 478; Horncastle *v.* Suart (1806), 7 East, 400; Atty *v.* Lindo (1805), 1 B. & P. N. R. 236; Mackenzie *v.* Shedden (1810), 2 Camp. 431; Davidson *v.* Willasey (1813), 1 M. & S. 312; Ellis *v.* Lafone (1853), 8 Exch. 546; 22 L. J. Ex. 124; Foley *v.* United Fire and Marine Ins. Co. of Sydney (Ex. Ch.) (1870), L. R. 5 C. P. 155; Rankin *v.* Potter (1873), L. R. 6 H. L. 83.

On this principle, when by the terms of the charter-party **Sect. 272.**
the ship is to proceed from A. to B., and at B. load a cargo
for C., there has been held to be an insurable interest in the
freight of this cargo, as soon as the ship breaks ground at A.
to proceed to B.

In the first of these series of cases the facts were as follow: Thompson v.
A shipowner who insured half the freight of his ship on a Taylor.
voyage "at and from London to Teneriffe, and at and from
thence to the Bay of Honduras," had chartered the ship to
sail from London to Teneriffe, where she was to take wine
on board and carry it out to the West Indies; freight for the
whole voyage to be paid at the rate of 35s. per pipe. The
ship sailed from London on her voyage under the charter-
party; and before her arrival at Teneriffe, and, of course,
before any of the wine was taken on board, she was captured
by the French. The Court held that the insurable interest
and the risk upon the freight had commenced directly the
ship sailed from London on her voyage by which the freight
was to be earned. Lord Kenyon said: "As the plaintiff had
begun to perform his part of the contract, as he had done
something under it which, if matured, would have entitled
him to his freight, I think he may recover under this policy,
which was an insurance on that freight" (*u*).

273. A previous voyage may be incorporated into the Previous
charter-party, so that there is an inception of the voyage voyage incorporated
described in the charter-party during the performance of the by the
prior voyage. charter-party.

By charter-party it was agreed that the "Sir William Rankin v.
Eyre," then on a voyage from the Clyde to New Zealand, Potter.
should proceed to New Zealand with a cargo for owners'
benefit, and thence to Calcutta, and there load a cargo for
Liverpool for the freighter. The owners of the ship effected
a policy on homeward chartered freight from Calcutta to
Liverpool, at and from the Clyde to Otago, New Zealand,

(*u*) Thompson *v*. Taylor (1795), 6 T. R. 478; *S. P.*, Atty *v*. Lindo
(1805), 1 B. & P. N. R. 236.

Sect. 273. and for thirty days in port there after arrival. At New Zealand the vessel grounded, and received such damage by sea perils as to become a constructive total loss, and in the result she was not repaired, and the homeward freight was not earned. It was not disputed that there was an insurable interest in such freight, and the House of Lords decided that the plaintiff was entitled to recover under the policy (*x*).

Foley v. United Fire and Marine Ins. Co.

A vessel when about to sail with cargo from Calcutta to Mauritius was chartered to carry a cargo of rice from Akyab to the United Kingdom. The charter-party stipulated that she should "with all convenient speed sail on her present voyage to Mauritius, and having discharged her cargo there," should proceed to Akyab and there load the rice. She arrived at Mauritius in good safety, and when about two-fifths of her cargo were discharged, she was wrecked with the residue on board. Upon a policy on chartered freight "at and from Mauritius to rice ports," the Exchequer Chamber held that the shipowner could recover. "It is the express condition in the charter-party," said Kelly, C. B., "that the voyage shall commence at Calcutta, and the inchoate right to freight attached when the voyage from Calcutta commenced." There being thus an insurable interest, it followed that the risk under the policy began upon the arrival of the ship at Mauritius (*y*).

Contract may be entire though there be separate payments of freight.

274. When a ship is chartered for a double voyage, as from A. to B., and from B. to C., or back to A., the contract is none the less an entire one because separate sums are to be paid as freight for the different parts of the voyage (*z*). Therefore the shipowner's interest in the whole freight commences at the inception of the first part of the voyage.

Horncastle v. Suart.

A shipowner effected an insurance on the freight of his

(*x*) Rankin *v.* Potter (1873), L. R. 6 H. L. 83.

(*y*) Foley *v.* United Fire and Marine Ins. Co. of Sydney (Ex. Ch.) (1870), L. R. 5 C. P. 155.

(*z*) Horncastle *v.* Suart (1806), 7 East, 400; Davidson *v.* Willasey (1813), 1 M. & S. 312. See also Ellis *v.* Lafone (1853), 8 Exch. 546; 22 L. J. Ex. 124.

ship for a voyage at and from Dominica to London. He had previously chartered the ship for a voyage from London to the Island of Dominica and back to London, on the terms of being paid half the net freight of the outward voyage, if it exceeded 1,000*l.*, but if not, then he should be paid 500*l.*; and, as to the homeward freight, the charterers covenanted to load a full cargo at the current freight, or, if the cargo should not be full, to pay dead freight for the deficiency. The ship was captured at Dominica before she had unloaded all her outward cargo. A full cargo of produce had been procured by the charterer's agents at Dominica, and was ready to be loaded on board the ship there. The Court held that as the voyage had commenced under which the freight was to be earned according to the terms of the charter-party, which made it one entire contract, the assured was entitled to recover for the homeward freight (*a*).

Sect. 274.

Upon the same principle, where an insurance was effected on the homeward freight of a West Indian ship, chartered for a voyage out and home, on the terms of taking in a full cargo of produce for the homeward voyage, and the ship, after arriving at her out-port of discharge in the West Indies, was lost there, when she had taken on board only half her homeward cargo; the Court held that as there had been, at the time of loss, an inception of the entire voyage out and home, the risk had attached on the homeward freight, and the whole was recoverable (*b*).

Davidson *v.* Willasey.

A shipowner insured the outward freight of a West Indian ship "at and from London to Jamaica, with liberty to touch at Madeira, and discharge and take on board goods there." Under her charter-party, the ship was to sail from London, with a cargo, which she was to dispose of at Madeira, and there receive from the charterers' agents wine to be taken on to Jamaica. The freight or hire for the whole voyage was 135*l.*, to be paid at Madeira, on delivery of the London

Atty *v.* Lindo.

(*a*) Horncastle *v.* Suart (1806), 7 East, 400.
(*b*) Davidson *v.* Willasey (1813), 1 M. & S. 312.

cargo, in wine to be taken on board, and carried on, with the rest, to Jamaica, free of freight, under the denomination of freight wine. The ship at Madeira had taken in part of her Jamaica cargo, but not the freight wine, when she was blown out to sea and captured by the French.

The assured recovered the whole amount insured, on the ground that as soon as the ship broke ground from London on the voyage, an inchoate right to the whole freight attached, which was defeated only by the intervention of a peril insured against (c).

Ellis v. Lafone.

The principle is illustrated by the following case. A ship, then at Monte Video, was chartered to proceed to the Falkland Islands, to sail thence to Santa Cruz and there load part of her cargo, and then to proceed to Monte Video and complete her cargo, and with it to proceed to Havre. Freight was to be paid at the rate of 250*l*. a month, the first payment of 250*l*. to be made when the ship sailed from the Falkland Islands (d). The charterer accordingly paid this sum of 250*l*. The ship took her cargo on board at Santa Cruz and Monte Video, and was afterwards lost on the voyage to Havre. The charterer had effected a policy on advance freight from Monte Video to Havre, on which he claimed this sum of 250*l*. It was contended that this was a separate sum paid for the voyage to the Falkland Islands; but the Exchequer Chamber held, that it was part of an entire sum payable for the whole voyage insured, and therefore remained at risk until the ship arrived at Havre (e).

Insurable interest before commencement of charter-party voyage.

275. In the cases that have been considered there had been an inception of the voyage described in terms in the charter-party. The next case to be mentioned shows that there may be an insurable interest in freight, although the ship is not yet on the voyage so described.

(c) Atty v. Lindo (1805), 1 B. & P. N. R. 236.

(d) This was not the original charter-party, but it is a sufficiently correct statement, for the purpose of the text, of the contract as altered by agreement between the parties.

(e) Ellis v. Lafone (1853), 8 Exch. 546; 22 L. J. Ex. 124.

A ship, stated to be lying at Bombay, was chartered for a voyage from Howland's Island to the United Kingdom with a cargo of guano. A policy was effected "on freight chartered or otherwise" at and from Bombay to Howland's Island, while there and thence to the United Kingdom. The ship sailed in ballast from Bombay to Howland's Island, and was lost on the voyage thither. The charter-party had been entered into on the 7th of August, and the ship was required to be at Howland's Island on or before the 1st June of the following year; but it was not stipulated that she should sail direct or by any particular route. On this ground the underwriter contended that nothing had been done under the charter-party to make the freight an inchoate interest. The Court of Queen's Bench, however, held, that as the ship had sailed from Bombay to Howland's Island in order to earn the freight under the charter from there to the United Kingdom, the interest in the chartered freight had commenced, and that the plaintiff could recover under the policy for its loss (*f*).

Sect. 275.
Barber *v.* Fleming.

Cockburn, C. J., treated the voyage from Bombay to Howland's Island as part of the whole voyage necessary to earn the freight.

"From the moment," he says, "that a vessel is chartered to go from port A. to port B., and at port B. to take a cargo and bring it home to England, or to take it to any port, which I will call port C., for freight, the shipowner having got such a contract, has an interest unquestionably in earning the freight secured to him by the charter; and having such an interest it is manifest that that interest is insurable; and he loses the freight and benefit of his charter just as much by the ship being disabled on her voyage to the port at which the cargo is to be loaded, and from which it is to be brought, as he would lose it by the disaster arising from the perils insured against between the port of loading and the port of discharge. It is therefore an appreciable

(*f*) Barber *v.* Fleming (1867), L. R. 5 Q. B. 59.

Sect. 275. tangible interest, and I entertain no doubt that it can be insured" (g).

Blackburn, J., said: "There is a policy of insurance made upon a voyage 'from Bombay to Howland's Island and from thence to England.' That is the description of the voyage. The nature of the thing insured is 'freight chartered or otherwise.' So that upon the face of the policy there is a bargain between the assured and the underwriters by which, if during that voyage, by one of the perils insured against, freight is lost, the underwriters should pay. We have, therefore, to see whether there was freight lost during the voyage, which involves the question whether this chartered freight had come into existence at the time the accident happened which caused the alleged loss; whether at that time the interest had commenced. When there is an insurance upon freight, so long as the matter remains merely contingent, so long as the shipowners have only a good hope of getting freight, no freight is in existence; and if the ship is lost there would be no loss of freight, inasmuch as the freight had never come into existence, and all that the shipowners have lost is the hope of earning the freight. But on the other hand, the law seems perfectly settled by a variety of cases, as I find it laid down by Mr. Phillips, in his book on Insurance, at s. 328, where he says: 'In regard to the commencement of this interest (on freight), it is a general rule that it commences, not only by the vessel sailing with the cargo on board, but also when the owner or hirer, having goods ready to ship, or a contract with another person for freight, has commenced the voyage, or incurred expenses and taken steps towards earning the freight.' I think that is the accurate rule. When a shipowner has got a contract with another person under which he will earn freight, and has taken steps and incurred expense upon the voyage towards earning it, then his interest ceases to be a contingent thing, but becomes an inchoate interest, and is an interest which, if

---

(g) Barber v. Fleming (1867), L. R. 5 Q. B. 67.

afterwards destroyed by one of the perils insured against, is lost, and ought to be paid for by the underwriters."

Sect. 275.

In answer to the argument that the interest had not commenced because the charter-party did not require the ship to sail at once or direct to Howland's Island, the learned judge said: "The spirit and reason of the rule are, that the interest commenced, not because the man acted under compulsion of the contract, but because he has acted so far under the contract as to show it is no longer speculative, but he had actually begun to do something which makes the inchoate interest attach, and makes it a real thing; and it seems to me that as soon as the ship, although not bound to go direct from Bombay to (Howland's Island), had begun to sail there, the interest had sufficiently attached" (h).

Cockburn, C. J., and Blackburn, J., both referred to the following passage in Phillips on Insurance, s. 335: "A vessel being chartered from A. to B., the interest in the freight commences under the charter-party on the vessel's sailing for A., either in ballast or with a small quantity only of goods for B." Phillips does not consider the case of a ship sailing for A. with a full cargo; and in Barber *v.* Fleming it was not necessary to decide whether, if the ship had been carrying a cargo to Howland's Island, there would have been an insurable interest in the freight from Howland's Island to the United Kingdom. It is submitted that this would have made no difference, for there is authority for saying that an act done for the purpose of one voyage may also be an act of preparation for the next voyage (*i*). In such a case, however, it would have been advisable to insure the freight from Howland's Island specifically (*k*). Under an insurance on freight simply, it might have been argued that only the freight of the cargo carried from Bombay to Howland's

---

(*h*) L. R. 5 Q. B. p. 73.
(*i*) Warre *v.* Miller (1825), 4 B. & Cr. 538; Foley *v.* United Fire and Marine Ins. Co. of Sydney (1870), L. R. 5 C. P. 155, 160, 164.

(*k*) In Rankin *v.* Potter (1873), L. R. 6 H. L. 83, the ship carried a cargo on the outward voyage, and the insurance was on "homeward chartered freight."

Sect. 275. Island was recoverable in case of a loss on that part of the insured voyage (*l*).

Insurable interest when ship let on time charter.

276. When a ship is let on a time charter, the usual stipulation is that she shall be placed at the disposal of the charterer at a given port. Barber *v.* Fleming (*m*) shows that under such a charter-party the shipowner has an insurable interest in the chartered hire or freight when he sends the ship to such port for the purpose of placing her at the charterer's disposal. The charter-party generally provides for monthly payments of the freight at a given rate. The contract, is, however, usually an entire one, and, therefore, when the insurable interest has begun, there can be no doubt that it extends to the freight for the whole agreed period, or such part of it as still remains at risk (*n*). The general practice is to insure this chartered hire or freight by a time policy on freight with a "diminishing clause," *i.e.*, a clause by which the amount insured is reduced monthly as each payment becomes due (*o*).

Insurable interest in freight of shipowner's own goods.

277. When the shipowner wishes to insure as freight the benefit to be derived from the carriage of his own goods, the case is obviously very different from that of an insurance on the goods of others. There is no contract, and therefore no cargo-owner's obligation to provide a cargo, or shipowner's to load one. As the shipowner cannot call upon someone else to supply cargo he would be insuring a mere expectation, unless he has goods of his own which he is in a position to ship. The cases show that to give him an insurable interest he must have goods definitely intended for shipment, which are so far ready that he will be able to ship them in the ordinary course when the ship reaches her loading place (*p*).

(*l*) See *post*, § 358.
(*m*) (1869), L. R. 5 Q. B. 59; *ante*, § 275.
(*n*) See Horncastle *v.* Suart (1806), 7 East, 400; Ellis *v.* Lafone (1853), 8 Exch. 546; 22 L. J. Ex. 124; *ante*, § 274.

(*o*) See Gow, p. 233.
(*p*) Flint *v.* Flemyng (1830), 1 B. & Ad. 45; Devaux *v.* J'Anson (1839), 5 Bing. N. C. 519. The facts of the latter case are set out *ante*, § 268.

In Devaux v. J'Anson (q), the ship was not actually ready to take the goods on board, as the casualty which caused the loss of freight, for which the assured recovered, occurred while she was preparing to leave a dry dock (r). In answer, however, to the objection that the ship was not ready, the Court held that she was "quite ready to go to sea and to receive the cargo on board, that nothing remained to prevent her sailing, but the getting her out of dock" (s). The Court did not, however, actually determine that readiness of the ship was essential.

Rule 3 (d) in the first schedule of the Marine Insurance Act, 1906 (t) provides that when the freight of goods belonging to the shipowner is insured by the ordinary English policy "at and from" a particular place, the risk attaches as soon as the cargo is in readiness and the ship is ready to receive the cargo. This rule supports the view that the insurable interest does not begin until the ship is ready to take the goods on board, but the editors submit that it is not necessarily conclusive on the question of insurable interest (u).

278. In conclusion, it is submitted that the following propositions are supported by the authorities:— *Result of the authorities.*

(1.) In respect of freight in the strict sense of the word, the shipowner has an insurable interest when, having a valid contract for the carriage of goods, he takes steps towards the earning of the freight.

(2.) In respect of chartered freight, he has an insurable interest when there is an inception of the voyage described in the charter-party, or when he does something for the purpose of performing his contract, as by sending the ship to the port of loading to ship the cargo.

(q) *Supra.*
(r) See, however, *ante*, § 270, note (d).
(s) In Flint v. Flemyng, *supra*, the ship had finished discharging her outward cargo the day before the loss. Whether she was in other respects ready to receive her homeward cargo does not appear.
(t) See *infra*, § 279a.
(u) See their remarks, *ibid.*

Sect. 279.
Is there an insurable interest in freight as soon as the contract is made? Tendency of the decisions.

279. The further question may be raised, whether an insurable interest in freight may not commence at an earlier period. The series of cases on the subject began in 1746 with Tonge *v.* Watts, in which the Court held that the insurable interest did not begin until the goods were actually loaded. The cases on freight proper show how the Courts, wherever there was an actual contract for freight, invariably relaxed the rule laid down in Tonge *v.* Watts sufficiently to enable the assured to recover. As regards charter-party freight, the principle first applied in 1795, in Thompson *v.* Taylor, that there is an insurable interest in the whole freight as soon as the chartered voyage has begun, enabled the Courts to decide every case before Barber *v.* Fleming in favour of the assured. In Barber *v.* Fleming, where the voyage described in the charter-party had not begun, the Court went beyond this principle and declared that the shipowner had an insurable interest when the ship was on her way to her loading port for the purpose of fulfilling her charter (*x*).

It may be urged that when a shipowner has made a contract under which he will in the ordinary course earn freight, he ought at once to be entitled to protect himself against a loss of that freight by the maritime risks to which his ship is exposed (*y*). If, for instance, a shipowner has entered into a very lucrative charter-party, by which his ship

---

(*x*) In Ward *v.* Weir (1899), 4 Com. Cas. 222, Mathew, J., said: "There is abundant authority that during the pendency of the outward voyage the homeward freight may be insured."

(*y*) Cockburn, C. J., meant, perhaps, to state as broad a principle as this when he said, in Barber *v.* Fleming: "From the moment that a vessel is chartered to go from port A. to port B., and at port B. to take a cargo and bring home that cargo to England, or to take it to any port, which I will call port C., for freight, the shipowner, having got such a contract, has an interest unquestionably in earning the freight secured to him by the charter; and having such an interest, it is manifest that that interest is insurable": L. R. 5 Q. B. at p. 67. The context, however, makes it doubtful whether the learned Chief Justice did not intend his remarks to refer only to a ship already at A. or on the way from A. to B. This passage from the judgment of Cockburn, C. J., was quoted with approval by Martin, B., in Foley *v.* United Fire, &c. Ins. Co. (1870), L. R. 5 C. P. 163.

is let for six months, there being only a stipulation that she shall be placed at the charterer's disposal on or before a given day, the shipowner, however, being left free to employ her as he thinks fit in the meanwhile, he may be prevented from earning freight under this charter-party by the loss of or damage to his ship in the course of an interim voyage. If he has effected a policy so worded as to cover a loss of this freight by the perils of the interim voyage, ought he not to be able to recover under the policy?

Sect. 279.

Against this contention there is, no doubt, the weighty argument that freight is not altogether a profit, but is only earned by the expenditure of money, and that to allow a shipowner to recover for a loss of freight, when he has, perhaps, incurred no expense for the purpose of earning it, is to depart from the principle that insurance is a contract of indemnity (*z*). Blackburn, J., in Barber *v*. Fleming, and Phillips, whom he quotes with approval, make the insurable interest in freight commence when expense is incurred to earn the freight (*a*). Yet the principle of indemnity was long ago departed from in insurances on freight, when the right of the assured to recover in all cases the gross freight was recognized, and it is now clearly possible to recover for a loss of freight when little or no expense has been incurred by the assured. Thus, if a ship on an outward voyage from A. to B. be chartered to complete that voyage, and then take a homeward cargo from B. to A., the homeward freight can at once be insured and recovered if the ship be lost the next day (*b*).

Principle of indemnity relaxed in insurances on freight.

As we have already pointed out, all the cases on insurable interest, in which there has been an actual contract for freight, have been decided in favour of the assured. The

---

(*z*) This argument could not be used in the case of a policy on profits of charter.

(*a*) See Barber *v*. Fleming (1869), L. R. 5 Q. B. 59, 71; 1 Phillips, s. 328.

(*b*) It may, however, be said that the expenses of the outward voyage are in every case incurred partly or in whole for the homeward voyage. See per Cockburn, C. J., in Barber *v*. Fleming (1869), L. R. 5 Q. B. 67.

Sect. 279. legal conception of insurable interest has been continuously expanding (c), and possibly the Courts may on some future occasion continue this process of expansion, and hold that the existence of a contract for freight in itself gives an insurable interest in the freight. But the existing authorities do not support this extension of the rule.

If, however, it should be considered that the wide principle cannot be supported, there are strong grounds for thinking that the profits which a shipowner expects to make on a contract of affreightment may be insurable as soon as the contract has been made (d).

<small>The Marine Insurance Act and insurable interest in freight.</small>

279a. It is now necessary to consider the bearing of the Marine Insurance Act, 1906, upon the subject of this discussion. In Rule 3 of the rules for the construction of the policy in Schedule I., which must be applied unless the context otherwise requires, the following rules are laid down with reference to the attachment of the risk on freight:—

> (c) Where chartered freight is insured "at and from" a particular place, and the ship is at that place in good safety when the contract is concluded, the risk attaches immediately. If she be not there when the contract is concluded, the risk attaches as soon as she arrives there in good safety.
>
> (d) Where freight, other than chartered freight, is payable without special conditions and is insured "at and from" a particular place, the risk attaches *pro ratâ* as the goods or merchandise are shipped; provided that if there be cargo in readiness which belongs to the shipowner, or which some other person has contracted with him to ship, the risk attaches as soon as the ship is ready to receive such cargo.

There is nothing in rule 3 (c) which conflicts with the principles relating to the commencement of the insurable

---

(c) See per Walton, J., in Moran v. Uzielli, [1905] 2 K. B. 563.

(d) In Manchester Liners v. British and Foreign Mar. Ins. Co. (1901), 7 Com. Cas. 26, 33, Walton, J., expressed the view that a shipowner has an insurable interest in the use of his ship, independent of any particular contract of affreightment; but was seemingly of opinion that such interest is not insurable as freight. See, further, *infra*, § 288.

interest in chartered freight which the editors have deduced Sect. 279a.
from the decisions. As regards the insurable interest in
freight, other than chartered freight, however, rule 3 (d)
must not be overlooked. The question whether the assured
had at the time of the loss an insurable interest, and the
question whether the risk has attached under the policy, have
usually been treated together (*e*). If, as was Arnould's view,
the *ratio decidendi* of the cases was that the risk under a
policy "at and from" the place of loading attached when
the ship was at such place as soon as there was an insurable
interest in the freight, it may be argued that rule 3 (d) is
based on the view that, as regards freight proper and the
freight of the shipowner's goods, the insurable interest does
not begin until the cargo is in readiness, and the ship is
ready to receive it, and that the rule disregards the decisions
which, in the opinion of the editors, extended the principle
laid down by Arnould. Inasmuch, however, as the Act
nowhere lays down any rule in relation to the commencement
of the insurable interest in freight, it is submitted that
rule 3 (d) does not affect these decisions so far as they determine the question of insurable interest. If this be correct,
and the insurable interest do commence before the ship and
cargo are ready, it will be possible, notwithstanding
rule 3 (d), to recover under a properly worded policy for any
loss of freight which has occurred after the commencement
of such interest.

280. A shipowner who has entered into recognizances in Shipowner's
the Admiralty Court to pay the salvors of ship and cargo insurable
has a lien on, and therefore an insurable interest in, the interest in
cargo for the average contribution due to him from its average
owners (*f*). He may also protect himself by insurance In liabilities
against charges imposed by the Merchant Shipping Act in under
Passenger
Acts, &c.

(*e*) See, for instance, Arnould, It was held that the interest was
2nd ed. pp. 287—289, 522 *et seq.*, sufficiently described as "average
and the remarks, *ante*, § 265. expenses." Cf. Dodwell *v.* Munich
(*f*) Briggs *v.* Merchant Traders' Ass. Co. (1903), 123 Fed. R. 841;
Association (1849), 13 Q. B. 167. affd. (1904), 128 Fed. R. 835.

Sect. 280. respect of the carriage of passengers (*g*). He has, besides, an insurable interest in respect of liabilities consequent on the casualties enumerated in Part VIII. of the Merchant Shipping Act, 1894 (*h*), and of other liabilities resulting from casualties happening in the course of the navigation of his ship.

Insurable interest of vendor and vendee.

281. A party seeking to recover on a policy must, as we have already seen, have been interested in the subject of insurance at the time of loss (*i*). If, therefore, the insurable interest depends upon a sale, the vendee must have acquired a complete title to the thing insured before the loss, or it must be at his risk under the contract of sale, otherwise he can recover nothing on his policy; and, on the same grounds, the vendor, if he have not absolutely parted with all his interest before the loss, may still recover in respect of such interest as remains in him at that time.

Vendor retaining interest in chattel.

Thus, where the owner of a ship had sold her to a purchaser, under an agreement that he would pay the purchaser 500*l*. if a loss happened within three months, the Court held that to this extent he still had an interest in the safety of the ship, and therefore might recover against the members of a mutual insurance society, to which he belonged, for such amount of contribution as, by the rules of the society, he was entitled to receive (*k*).

Insurable interest in goods usually depends on property.

282. When the buyer and seller of goods do not live in the same place, it is generally necessary, in order to determine who has an insurable interest during the transit, to ascertain when the property passes to the buyer. This question belongs to the law relating to the sale of goods, and only a

---

(*g*) Merchant Shipping Act, 1894, ss. 328—335. See Gibson *v.* Bradford (1855), 4 E. & B. 586; Willis *v.* Cooke (1855), 5 E. & B. 641.

(*h*) Merchant Shipping Act, 1894, s. 506.

(*i*) See *ante*, §§ 254, 258. The statement in the text is subject to the proviso in sect. 6 (1) of the Mar. Ins. Act, 1906.

(*k*) Reed *v.* Cole (1764), 3 Burr. 1512.

CHAP. XII.] OF VENDOR AND VENDEE. 383

few leading principles will be stated here, in the terms of the Sale of Goods Act, 1893 (*l*).

Sect. 282.

Rules in Sale of Goods Act as to transfer of property.

Where there is a contract for the sale of specific or ascertained goods, the property in them is transferred to the buyer at such time as the parties intend it to be transferred (*m*). Where the contract is unconditional and the goods are specific goods in a deliverable state, the property passes when the contract is made (*n*).

Where there is a contract for the sale of unascertained or future goods by description, and goods of that description and in a deliverable state are unconditionally appropriated to the contract, either by the seller with the assent express or implied of the buyer, or by the buyer with the assent of the seller, the property passes to the buyer (*o*). Such unconditional appropriation takes place when, in pursuance of the contract, the seller delivers the goods to the buyer or to a carrier or other bailee for the purpose of transmission to the buyer, and does not reserve the right of disposal (*p*).

If the seller of goods by the terms of the contract or appropriation reserves the right of disposal of the goods until certain conditions are fulfilled, then, notwithstanding the delivery of the goods to the buyer or to a carrier or other bailee for transmission, the property does not pass to the buyer until the condition is fulfilled (*q*). When goods shipped are by the bill of lading deliverable to the order of

---

(*l*) See generally the Sale of Goods Act, 1893 (56 & 57 Vict. c. 71), ss. 18—26, as to the transfer of property in goods and as to the title to goods; also Benjamin on Sale, bk. ii. co. 2—6, pp. 313—401, 5th ed.

(*m*) Sale of Goods Act, s. 17. See Anderson *v.* Morice (1876), 1 App. Cas. 713; Reid *v.* Macbeth, [1904] A. C. 223.

(*n*) Sale of Goods Act, s. 18, r. 1.

(*o*) Sale of Goods Act, s. 18, r. 5 (1); see Sparkes *v.* Marshall (1836), 2 Bing. N. C. 761.

(*p*) *Ibid.* r. 5 (2). See Fragano *v.* Long (1825), 4 B. & Cr. 219; Mitchel *v.* Ede (1840), 11 A. & E. 888; 9 L. J. Q. B. 187; Tregellas *v.* Sewell (1862), 7 H. & N. 574; Joyce *v.* Swann (1864), 17 C. B. N. S. 84; Castle *v.* Playford (Ex. Ch.) (1872), L. R. 7 Ex. 98; Mirabita *v.* Imperial Ottoman Bank (C. A.) (1878), 3 Ex. D. 164; Colonial Ins. Co. of New Zealand *v.* Adelaide Marine Ins. Co. (1886), 12 App. Cas. 128.

(*q*) Sale of Goods Act, s. 19 (2). See Mitchel *v.* Ede (1840), 11 A. & E. 888; 9 L. J. Q. B. 187, and the cases in the next note.

Sect. 282. the seller or his agent, the seller is *primâ facie* deemed to reserve the right of disposal (*r*).

Where the seller of goods draws on the buyer for the price and transmits the bill of exchange and bill of lading together to him, to secure acceptance or payment of the bill of exchange, the buyer is bound to return the bill of lading if he does not honour the bill of exchange; and if he wrongfully retains the bill of lading the property in the goods does not pass to him (*s*).

Cases on insurable interest in goods.
Anderson *v.* Morice.

283. The following cases illustrate the application of these rules to questions of insurable interest:—

A. entered into a contract for the purchase of a cargo of Rangoon rice. The bought note, as far as is material, was in these terms: "Bought .... the cargo of .... rice, per 'Sunbeam' .... Payment by sellers' draft on purchaser at six months' sight, with documents attached." A. insured the cargo "at and from Rangoon." The "Sunbeam" was loading the agreed cargo of rice in the Irrawaddy River, off Rangoon, and had received on board the larger portion thereof, when she was lost with the rice then on board. In the Common Pleas it was held that, when the rice was appro-

---

(*r*) *Ibid.* s. 19 (2). See Wait *v.* Baker (1848), 2 Ex. 1; 17 L. J. Ex. 307; Ogg *v.* Shuter (C. A.) (1875), 1 C. P. D. 47. In Joyce *v.* Swann (1864), 17 C. B. N. S. 84, the *primâ facie* inference was negatived by the jury, and their finding that the seller had taken the bills of lading in his own name only as agent for the buyer was upheld. See Seagrave *v.* Union Marine Ins. Co. (1866), L. R. 1 C. P. 305, another action on a policy in respect of the same loss, in which the evidence was somewhat different. The *primâ facie* inference is not negatived by the mere fact that the ship belongs to or is chartered by the buyer. Turner *v.* Trustees of Liverpool Docks (Ex. Ch.) (1851), 6 Ex. 543; 20 L. J. Ex. 393; Gabarron *v.* Kreeft (1875), L. R. 10 Ex. 274, 280, 285. When the property has already passed by an unconditional appropriation, the fact that the bills of lading afterwards make the goods deliverable to the order of the seller does not destroy the effect of the appropriation. Sparkes *v.* Marshall (1836), 2 Bing. N. C. 761; and see Coxe *v.* Harden (1803), 4 East, 211.

(*s*) Sale of Goods Act, s. 19 (3); Shepherd *v.* Harrison (1871), L. R. 5 H. L. 116. The buyer may, however, by transfer of the bill of lading give a good title to an innocent transferee. S. 25 (2); see Cahn *v.* Pockett's Bristol Channel Co. (C. A.), [1899] 1 Q. B. 643.

priated to the contract by putting it on board, an insurable interest therein passed to the buyer, the plaintiff. In the Exchequer Chamber it was held that the contract, being for the cargo of rice per the "Sunbeam," and the time for making out the shipping documents (which were to be attached to the sellers' draft) not having arrived at the time of the loss, no interest had passed to the buyer, or would pass until the complete cargo was loaded on board. In the House of Lords the law lords were equally divided, and therefore the judgment of the Exchequer Chamber was affirmed, and A. did not recover on the policy (*t*).

M. & G. agreed to purchase a cargo of wheat, free on board at Timaru, at 4*s.* 7*d.* per sack. They chartered a steamer, which began to load at Timaru, and before the loading was completed the ship and cargo were there lost. The Privy Council held that delivery from time to time to the master of the ship vested the property in the wheat as it was delivered in the buyers, and consequently that the latter had an insurable interest in the cargo on board at the time of the loss. They distinguished Anderson *v.* Morice (*u*) on the ground that there the vendors sold a particular cargo on a ship chartered by them. "The cargo to be purchased in that case was an entire thing . . . . and would not be in existence until the whole cargo should be put on board." "The master of the 'Sunbeam' received it on their account, and not on account of the purchasers. The purchasers' right was to depend on the shipping documents, which were to be under the direction of the sellers. In the present case . . . the contractors were delivering it (the wheat) to the purchasers in pursuance of their contract to put it free on board, the master of the vessel which had been chartered by them being their agent to receive it on their account" (*x*).

Sect. 283.

Colonial Ins. Co. of New Zealand *v.* Adelaide Marine Ins. Co.

(*t*) Anderson *v.* Morice (1874), L. R. 10 C. P. 58; in the Ex. Ch. (1875), *ibid.* 609; (1876), 1 App. Cas. 713.

(*u*) *Supra.*
(*x*) Colonial Ins. Co. of New Zealand *v.* Adelaide Marine Ins. Co. (1886), 12 App. Cas. 128.

386 INSURABLE INTEREST [PART I.

Sect. 284.

In general goods are at risk of owner.

284. Unless otherwise agreed, goods are at the seller's risk until the property is transferred to the buyer, and from the time of such transfer they are at the buyer's risk, whether delivery has been made or not (*y*). Therefore, in general, if under a contract of sale the property in sea-borne goods does not vest in the buyer until arrival, he has no insurable interest

In contract of sale the parties may agree otherwise.

in them during the transit. If, however, by the contract, the goods are to be at his risk during the voyage, he has an insurable interest in them during the same (*z*).

Similarly, the parties may agree that the property in goods shall vest in the buyer at the time of shipment; but that the goods shall be at the seller's risk during the transit, or that the price shall not be paid unless they arrive safely. Obviously the seller has an insurable interest in this case (*a*).

Inglis v. Stock.

D. & Co. sold to the plaintiff, Stock, 200 tons of sugar, f. o. b. at Hamburg; payment to be by cash in London in exchange for bills of lading. D. & Co. had already sold to B. 200 tons of the same quality of sugar on the same terms, and the plaintiff ultimately became the purchaser from B. of this parcel also, with no other change of terms except a slight increase of price. The plaintiff engaged room for both parcels of sugar on board a steamer trading from Hamburg to Bristol, and D. & Co. by their agent at Hamburg shipped sugar for both contracts in bags, without allocating the bags to the respective contracts. They intended, according to their usual practice, of which the plaintiff had knowledge, to make such appropriation on the arrival of the sugar in England. The sugar was totally lost on the voyage to England, and D. & Co., in England, after hearing of the loss, allocated the various bags to the two contracts. The plaintiff declared for both parcels under a floating policy, and in an action on the policy the underwriters contended that he had

---

(*y*) Sale of Goods Act, 1893, s. 20.
(*z*) Inglis *v.* Stock (1885), 10 App. Cas. 263; 53 L. J. Q. B. 356; see also Castle *v.* Playford (1872), L. R. 7 Ex. 98.

(*a*) Per Blackburn, J., Calcutta and Burmah Steam Navigation Co. *v.* De Mattos (1863), 32 L. J. Q. B. 322, 328.

CHAP. XII.] OF VENDOR AND VENDEE. 387

no insurable interest. In the Court of Appeal, Brett, M. R., held that, as no appropriation of a specific portion of the goods had been made at the time of the loss, the property had not passed; but that, under such a course of dealing as existed between the parties, when part of a cargo in bulk had been sold "free on board," the goods were at the risk of the buyer, and therefore the plaintiff had an insurable interest. Baggallay, L. J., thought this correct; but he and Lindley, L. J., decided the case on the ground that, apart from the effect of the "f. o. b." condition, the goods were at the buyer's risk (b).

Sect. 284.

The House of Lords affirmed the judgment of the Court of Appeal, also on the ground that the goods when shipped were at the buyer's risk (c). Lord Selborne's decision seems to be based on the "f. o. b." condition; while Lord Blackburn said that whether the sugar arrived or not the plaintiff was bound by his contract to pay for it on presentation of the bills of lading. In answer to the argument that there was no insurable interest because there had been no allocation of bags to the two contracts, Lord Blackburn said he could see no reason why an undivided interest in a parcel of goods might not be described as an interest in goods just as much as if it were an interest in every portion of the goods (d). Sect. 8 of the Marine Insurance Act, 1906, which declares that "partial interest of any nature is insurable," seems to affirm Lord Blackburn's view on this point (e).

285. An arrangement by which the buyer undertakes the risk before the property in the goods passes to him may be implied from the acts of the parties, when not inconsistent with the express terms of their agreement (f); but these

Agreement to take risk may be implied from acts of parties.

(b) Stock v. Inglis (1884), 12 Q. B. D. 564; 53 L. J. Q. B. 356.

(c) Inglis v. Stock (1885), 10 App. Cas. 263.

(d) Ibid.

(e) See ante, § 259a.

(f) Anderson v. Morice (1876), 1 App. Cas. 713; 46 L. J. C. P. 11; per Lord Hatherley, 1 App. Cas. 729; Lord O'Hagan, ibid. 743; Lord Selborne, ibid. 746.

Sect. 285. acts, said Lord Chelmsford, must manifest the intention of the parties without ambiguity (*g*). In Anderson *v.* Morice (*h*), the sellers having sent a telegram advising the buyers as to insuring, and the latter having effected an insurance "at and from Rangoon," it was contended that thereby the intention of the buyer to take the risk as soon as any rice was shipped was established. Lord O'Hagan and Lord Selborne thought that such an intention was proved, while Lord Chelmsford and Lord Hatherley were of a contrary opinion.

It is submitted, adopting the construction of the contract which prevailed (viz., that what was sold was a complete cargo, and therefore the property did not vest until the whole cargo was on board), that the decision of Lord Chelmsford and Lord Hatherley is sound. While the ship remained at Rangoon, after the loading was complete, the cargo would have been at the buyer's risk. Therefore the fact that, after being warned, he insured the cargo "at Rangoon" does not necessarily show that the parties had intended the risk to be his during the time of loading. And the principle laid down by Lord Chelmsford that where the acts, and not the express contract of the parties, are relied on to prove that goods are not at the owner's risk, the acts must be free from ambiguity, is essentially a reasonable one, though in this case it may have led to a hard result.

Effect of stoppage *in transitu.*

286. When an unpaid seller of goods exercises the right of stoppage *in transitu*, his act does not amount to a rescission of the contract, so as to deprive the buyer of the property which he has acquired in the goods; but it gives the seller a lien on the goods for the price (*i*). It follows that the exercise of the right of stoppage *in transitu* does not put an end to the insurable interest of the buyer; for he remains the owner of the goods subject to the lien, and is in the same position as a

---

(*g*) Anderson *v.* Morice (1876), 1 App. Cas. 713, at p. 723.
(*h*) *Supra.* See the facts stated, *ante,* § 283.

(*i*) Sale of Goods Act, 1893, ss. 44, 48. For the duration of the transit, see *ibid.* s. 45.

mortgagor who has an insurable interest to the full value of the property (k). **Sect. 286.**

The seller who has exercised the right of stoppage *in transitu* has obviously an insurable interest, to the extent at least of his lien.

Parsons is of opinion that an unpaid seller of goods has an insurable interest in them until they reach the buyer, on the ground that he has a lien until this takes place (l). It seems clear, however, that an unpaid seller who has parted both with the possession of the goods and the property in them, has in general no insurable interest until he exercises his right of stoppage. He has no right to stop the goods unless the buyer is insolvent, and not even then if the buyer has sold them and transferred the bill of lading or other document of title (m). It would be contrary to the principles on which an insurable interest depends if a seller who had parted with the property and possession could insure the goods and, if they were lost and the buyer afterwards became insolvent, recover their value, since at the time of the loss he had no right to take possession. Even if the buyer became insolvent and the goods were afterwards lost, the vendor not having exercised the right of stoppage, the latter, it is submitted, could not recover on an insurance; he had not gained a lien, and the loss made it impossible for him ever to acquire one (n).

287. An insurable interest in profits, it has been said, is constituted by "an expectancy coupled with a present existing title" (o). If the term "a present existing title" implies that the property in the goods from which profits are expected to arise must at the time of the loss be in the assured, the use **Insurable interest in profits.**

(k) *Post*, § 299. Arnould seems to have limited his right or that of his assignees to recover, to losses occurring before the right of stoppage was exercised (2nd ed. vol. i. p. 310). The principle stated in the text seems to the editors, however, to be clear.

(l) 1 Parsons, Ins. 232.

(m) Sale of Goods Act, 1893, s. 47.

(n) See, however, Moran *v.* Uzielli, [1905] 2 K. B. 555, *ante*, § 257a.

(o) 2nd ed. of this work, p. 290.

Sect. 287. of this term is not accurate (*p*). It is in general, however, true that the existence of an insurable interest depends on ownership in this sense, that unless the assured is or has been the owner of the goods, he must have entered into a binding contract for the purchase of them (*q*).

A vague possibility of realizing profits, which may or may not be made, will not suffice (*r*). In this country the right to recover on the policy is dependent on proof that profits would have been made if the goods had arrived. In the earliest cases, indeed, such as Grant *v.* Parkinson, and Barclay *v.* Cousins, the Court was satisfied with evidence of a general probability of the profitable issue of the adventure founded on the course and character of the trade in which it was made (*s*); but in subsequent cases the Courts adopted a stricter rule.

Thus in Hodgson *v.* Glover, where the policy was on "profits" upon an adventure from Liverpool to the African coast, the outward cargo to be bartered for slaves, and the slaves to be carried on in the ship to the West Indies for sale, the Court nonsuited the plaintiff, because he did not show that, if no loss had intervened and the slaves had all got to a market, any profit would have been produced (*t*).

Accordingly, in the next case of a similar kind which came before the Court, and in which the profit insured was upon sale of a homeward cargo of flax shipped at Riga for Hull, care was taken to allege in the declaration, and to prove at

---

(*p*) See Mar. Ins. Act, 1906, s. 5 (2), *ante*, § 254.

(*q*) See Stockdale *v.* Dunlop (1840), 6 M. & W. 224; and the remarks on this case, 1 Parsons, Ins. 193.

(*r*) Sparkes *v.* Marshall (1836), 2 Bing. N. C. 761.

(*s*) Grant *v.* Parkinson (1781), 3 Dougl. 16 (see also Lucena *v.* Craufurd (1802), 3 B. & P. 85, where a report of the case is given from Mr. Dunning's brief and a MS. note; 1 Marshall, Ins. 95; 2 Park, Ins. 561); Barclay *v.* Cousins (1802), 2 East, 544. See the observations of Lawrence, J., *ibid.*, p. 550.

(*t*) Hodgson *v.* Glover (1805), 6 East, 316. In this case Lawrence, J., differing from what he had said in Barclay *v.* Cousins, where the adventure was exactly similar, agreed with the rest of the Court, and said: "The case is defective in not showing that if there had been no shipwreck there would have been some profit."

the trial, that the flax, had it arrived sound, would have realized a profit to the amount insured (*u*). This case accordingly gives the rule which should be observed in pleading and in preparing the evidence.

Sect. 287.

In America the rule is different, and several cases there decided establish the doctrine, which has been adopted by the Supreme Court of the United States, that it is a conclusive presumption arising on proof of ownership of the goods shipped that they would have realized a profit in the foreign market (*x*). Thus, where three-eighths of the goods were lost, the Court held it to be a loss of that proportion of the profits, without inquiring whether there would have been any profits had the goods arrived (*y*).

In the United States.

288. It has been said that the assured must have not only an expectancy of profit, but, coupled therewith, a present existing title to the subject-matter out of which the profits are expected to arise (*z*). "The doctrine," says Mr. Justice (afterwards Chancellor) Kent, "that runs through all the cases, is, that the assured must have an interest in the subject-matter from which the profits are to proceed, in order to prevent the policy from being considered a wager" (*a*).

Insurable interest in profits, when the goods are not the property of the assured.

There can, however, be no doubt that an insurable interest in profits on goods may exist, although the goods are not, at the time of the loss, the property of the assured (*b*). Thus, where a purchaser of goods "to arrive" sold them before shipment on the same terms, but at a higher price, the Exchequer Chamber had no doubt that he had an insurable interest in his profit; yet the property in the goods would at

---

(*u*) Eyre *v.* Glover (1812), 16 East, 218.

(*x*) Patapsco Ins. Co. *v.* Coulter (1830), 3 Peters' Sup. Court R. 222; 1 Phillips, Ins. s. 318; 1 Parsons, Ins. 195.

(*y*) Loomis *v.* Shaw (1800), 2 Johns. Cas. 36.

(*z*) "I admit," says Parke, B., "that profits may be insured, but that is on the ground that they form an additional part of the value of the goods in which the plaintiff has already an interest": see Stockdale *v.* Dunlop (1840), 6 M. & W. 224, 232.

(*a*) Per Kent, J., in Abbott *v.* Sebor (1802), 3 John. Cas. (N. Y.) 39.

(*b*) See Mar. Ins. Act, 1906, s. 5 (2); *ante*, § 254.

Sect. 288. no time be in him (c). *A fortiori*, the assured in profits has an insurable interest, when there is a contract under which the goods will, on arrival, become his property (d). We have seen, however, that unless the goods, out of which such profit is to arise, were actually shipped on board at time of loss, he cannot protect such interest under a policy in the common form with the clause "beginning the adventure in the said goods from the loading thereof on board" (e).

Insurable interest of shipowner in use of his ship.

Whether a shipowner has an insurable interest in the profit which he expects to make by the use of his ship on a voyage or during a period for which he has not entered into a contract for freight is a question which has not been determined. There is some authority for the view that he has an insurable interest in the use of his ship (f); but if this view be correct, it is apprehended that he could only recover in an exceptional case, in which there is definite proof that the profit would have been realized if perils of the sea had not intervened; *e.g.*, where the vessel is lost on her way to a port, where the shipowner intends to put her "on the berth" to load a general cargo, and there is evidence that a remunerative cargo would in the ordinary course have been obtained.

Insurable interest of lender on bottomry and respondentia.

289. Sect. 10 of the Marine Insurance Act, 1906, declares that—"The lender of money on bottomry or respondentia has an insurable interest in respect of the loan."

By the contract of bottomry, if the ship be lost, the lender loses all his money; but if the ship arrive in safety, then he

(c) McSwiney v. Royal Exchange Ass. Co. (1850), 14 Q. B. 646, 659; see also 1 Parsons, Ins. 191—194.

(d) It is, in fact, in cases of this kind that insurances on profits are usually effected. A buyer of goods to whom the property has already passed, and who wishes to insure his profits, usually takes out a valued policy on goods, and includes the profits in his valuation.

(e) McSwiney v. Royal Exchange Ass. Co. (1849), 14 Q. B. 634; in error (1850), *ibid.* 646; *S. C.*, 18 L. J. Q. B. 193; *S. P.*, Halhead v. Young (1856), 6 E. & B. 312; 25 L. J. Q. B. 290; *ante*, § 238, where the facts of these cases are set out; see also per Willes, J., in Wilson v. Jones (1867), L. R. 2 Ex. 139, 146.

(f) Per Walton, J., Manchester Liners v. British and Foreign Marine Ins. Co. (1907), 7 Com. Cas. 26, 33; *ante*, § 239.

CHAP. XII.] OF BORROWER ON BOTTOMRY. 393

Sect. 289.

receives back his principal, and also the premium or maritime interest agreed upon. The lender on bottomry has a lien on the ship, and an insurable interest in her safety, and accordingly money lent on bottomry may, when so described, be the subject of marine insurance (*g*).

The insurable interest of the lender in these cases will depend upon the validity of the bottomry bond. In order to give an insurable interest the money secured by the instrument of hypothecation must, upon a fair construction of its terms, be made to depend on the arrival of the ship (*h*). Where the words of the instrument were, "I bind myself, my ship and tackle, &c., to pay the sum borrowed . . . after my arrival at the port of London"; . . . "and I do hereby make liable the said vessel, her freight and cargo, whether she do or do not arrive at the above-mentioned port of London": it was contended that, as the master had thus bound himself personally, the payment of the sum borrowed never depended on the arrival of the ship; and, consequently, that the lender had no such interest in the risk of the voyage as to entitle him to insure the money lent. The Court of King's Bench, however, reversing the judgment of the Court of Common Pleas, held that the words "my arrival" must be taken to mean, not the personal arrival of the master, but his arrival in the ship; and the clause "whether she do or do not arrive in the port of London," to mean not "whether she be lost or not," but "whether she arrives in the port of London or some other port"; they were of opinion, therefore, that the loss of the ship involved the loss of the money lent, and therefore that the lender might insure his interest by a policy on "bottomry" (*i*).

Simonds v. Hodgson.

The master of a ship which had put into a foreign port of distress to refit, borrowed money of a merchant there for

Stainbank v. Fenning.

(*g*) *Ante*, §§ 242, 243.

(*h*) In The Haabet, [1899] P. 295, Bucknill, J., held that an instrument was a valid bottomry bond, although the loan became payable if the vessel put into a port of refuge.

(*i*) Simonds v. Hodgson (1829), 6 Bing. 114; in error (1832), 3 B. & Ad. 50; cf. Price v. Maritime Ins. Co., [1901] 2 K. B. 412, C. A.

Sect. 289. necessary repairs, to secure which he drew bills on his owner, and executed what purported to be an hypothecation of ship, cargo and freight. But this instrument made the money payable at all events, and it was, therefore, held that the lender had no insurable interest (*k*).

Insurable interest of lender on respondentia.

Respondentia is a loan upon the goods, to be repaid to the lender, together with the marine interest, if the goods arrive; not to be paid if they are lost; the insurable interest, therefore, of the lender on respondentia, stands on the same ground with that of the lender on bottomry, viz., that he has a direct interest in the arrival of the goods.

Insurable interest of borrower on bottomry and respondentia.

290. "The borrower on bottomry and respondentia," said Arnould, "has no insurable interest in the property pledged, except in as far as the value of such property exceeds the amount for which it is pledged. If pledged to its full value, it is obvious that the borrower can have no insurable interest in its safety; for in such case, if the property arrives, it goes to satisfy the debt; if lost by the risks within the hypothecation, the borrower is discharged" (*l*).

Mr. Arthur Cohen, in discussing this passage, has, however, pointed out that the soundness of the principle stated therein may be questioned (*m*). This follows from the fact that if the bottomry bond be in the ordinary form, the money lent on bottomry is due in every case except that of an absolute total loss (*n*). If the shipowner is himself the borrower, and has made himself personally liable on the bond in case of the ship's arrival, it follows that in the case of any damage or loss not amounting to such a loss, he may, in the

---

(*k*) Stainbank *v.* Fenning (1851), 11 C. B. 51; Stainbank *v.* Shepard (1853), 13 C. B. 418. The description of the subject of insurance in the policy ran thus: "The said ship, goods and merchandizes, &c., for so much as concerns the assured by agreement between the assured and assurers in that policy, are and shall be 1,500*l.* advances for repairs and disbursements; the whole valued at 1,675*l.*, including premiums of insurance."

(*l*) 2nd ed. vol. i. p. 299.

(*m*) Law Quarterly Review, April, 1895, vol. ii. p. 120.

(*n*) Stephens *v.* Broomfield (1869), L. R. 2 P. C. 516; Broomfield *v.* Southern Ins. Co. (1870), L. R. 5 Ex. 192.

result, suffer to the extent of the damage which his ship has sustained; and on this ground he ought to have an insurable interest in his ship in respect of such damage. When, as is the usual case, the master is the borrower, and has made himself personally liable to pay the amount due under the bond, the shipowner may, if the ship arrives damaged, have to indemnify the master against any claim that may be made against him. In this case also the shipowner may be a loser to the extent of the damage which his ship has suffered, and ought to be able to protect himself against loss in consequence of such damage.

Sect. 290.

It may also be argued that, apart from any question of the shipowner's personal liability on the bond, or his liability to indemnify the master, the shipowner has an insurable interest on the following ground in respect of damage which the ship may sustain on the voyage: he has the right to redeem his ship by discharging the bond, and should therefore be entitled to protect himself against the loss which he will suffer in the exercise of this right if the ship should suffer damage.

291. "There are different sorts of consignees: some have a power to sell, manage, and dispose of the property, subject only to the rights of the consignor; others have a mere naked right to take possession" (*o*); others, again, it may be added, though not entrusted to sell, are yet interested in the property, as having a lien or claim upon it for their advances. It is obvious that the rights of these different kinds of consignees to effect an insurance must vary with the various relations in which they stand to the property and to the consignor.

Insurable interest of consignees, factors or agents.

Different kinds of consignees.

With regard to consignees who have a mere naked right to take possession, without being either entrusted to sell it on commission, or having a lien upon it for their advances, Lord Eldon says, "I will not say that they may not insure if they state the interest to be in their principal"; and they may do so, under sect. 23 (1) of the Marine Insurance Act, 1906, in their own names on account of the consignors,

Naked consignees.

(*o*) Per Lord Eldon, Lucena *v.* Craufurd (1806); 2 B. & P. N. R. 324.

Sect. 291. who will be bound by the policy so effected if they have already authorized it, or, if they subsequently adopt it, after notice (*p*).

But such mere naked consignees have no insurable interest so as to enable them to effect the policy in their own names, and on their own account, and to recover upon it, averring the interest to be in themselves. They have no legal property in the subject-matter of the insurance; they are not beneficially interested in it; and they can therefore only effect the insurance on account of those who are so interested and so entitled; and must aver the interest to be in those on whose account the insurance was made (*q*).

<small>Consignees having a lien or charge.</small>

292. Sect. 14 (2) of the Marine Insurance Act, 1906, declares that "a mortgagee, consignee, or other person having an interest in the subject-matter insured may insure on behalf and for the benefit of other persons interested as well as for his own benefit."

Thus, consignees who have a lien or claim on the property in respect of advances, or commission agents to whom it is entrusted for the purposes of sale, or indorsees of the bill of lading to whom a general balance is due, can effect an insurance on their own account and recover, averring the interest to be in themselves, to the amount of their lien, claim, or balance (*r*). They can also, by the same insurance, protect both their own interest and the interests of other parties in the property (*s*).

<small>What they can recover on an averment of interest in themselves.</small>

It is not settled whether an equitable mortgagee, or a consignee of goods to whom the legal property in goods has not passed, but who is beneficially interested in the whole of

---

(*p*) Wolff *v.* Herncastle (1798), 1 B. & P. 316.

(*q*) See the admirable remarks of Lawrence, J., in his celebrated judgment in Lucena *v.* Craufurd (1806), 2 B. & P. N. R. 307; per Willes, J., in Seagrave *v.* Union Marine Ins. Co. (1866), L. R. 1 C. P. 307, 319, 320; and see a very able note of Judge Duer, 2 Ins. n. 2 to s. 10, pp. 160—174.

(*r*) Ebsworth *v.* Alliance Marine Ins. Co. (1873), L. R. 8 C. P. 596; Godin *v.* London Ass. Co. (1758), 1 Burr. 489; 1 W. Bl. 103.

(*s*) See per Bowen, L. J., Castellain *v.* Preston (1883), 11 Q. B. D. 380, 398.

them, can recover the full value on such an averment, or whether he must also aver the interest of the other parties. On this point the Court of Common Pleas were equally divided in the latest case, in which the question was fully discussed and all the authorities considered (*t*).

Sect. 292.

The effect of the assignment of a bill of lading depends on the intention of the parties (*u*).

Indorsee of bill of lading.

Primâ facie, the indorsement and delivery of a bill of lading vests the whole property and interest in the goods in the indorsee (*x*), and gives him, from the moment of indorsement, an insurable interest in them to the full extent of their value. If, however, it be established that the assignment of the bill of lading is only intended to have a limited effect, as, *e.g.*, to be a pledge of the goods, the whole property does not pass (*y*), and the assignor still has an insurable interest in the goods. Thus where the purpose of the transfer of a bill of lading was to bind the net proceeds of the consignment in the hands of the consignor's agents, the consignor, notwithstanding such transfer, recovered for their loss (*z*).

It has been held in the United States, that where one takes a bill of lading to secure advances of money on a shipment of goods, and makes out the invoice in his own name, the shipper of the goods has still an insurable interest in them to their full value (*a*).

From the principle that a creditor who has a lien on the subject of insurance has an insurance to the extent of his lien, it follows that any creditor to whom goods are consigned as a collateral security has an insurable interest in them to the amount of his debt (*b*).

(*t*) Ebsworth *v.* Alliance Marine Ins. Co., *supra*.

(*u*) Sewell *v.* Burdick (1884), 10 App. Cas. 74.

(*x*) M'Andrew *v.* Bell (1795), 1 Esp. 373; Hibbert *v.* Carter (1787), 1 T. R. 745.

(*y*) Sewell *v.* Burdick (1884), 10 App. Cas. 74.

(*z*) Hibbert *v.* Carter (1787), 1 T. R. 745.

(*a*) Locke *v.* North American Ins. Co. (1816), 13 Mass. R. 61; 1 Phillips, s. 286.

(*b*) Wells *v.* Philadelphia Ins. Co. (1822), 9 Serg. & Rawle, 103; 1 Phillips, s. 292.

Sect. 292.
Pledgee of consignee.

So where the bill of lading is pledged by the consignees of the goods as a security for advances to them, the pledgee has an insurable interest in the goods; and may sue in his own name on a policy effected by the consignees, under his instructions, in their own names "for account of whom it may concern," and deposited with him as an additional security (*c*).

Cases on insurable interest of consignee, commission agent, or indorsee of bill of lading.

293. That a consignee of goods who is entrusted as a commission agent to sell them, or who has accepted bills on them, or has a general balance against the consignor, has an insurable interest in such goods, at all events to the extent of his claim, is a position which has received frequent illustration in our jurisprudence.

Wolff *v.* Horncastle

Thus, where the general agents of the consignor, on the refusal of the consignees to accept the goods, retained the bills of lading in their own hands, and accepted bills on account of the consignment to the amount of 300*l.*, they were held to have an insurable interest to the amount of their acceptances, on the ground, as stated by Buller, J., that "a debt which arises in consequence of the article insured, and which would have given a lien upon it, does give an insurable interest" (*d*).

Hill *v.* Secretan.

The house of De la Torre, in Spain, consigned a cargo of wool, with the bill of lading indorsed, to Du Bois & Son in London, directing them to hold part of it for Hill & Co. of Exeter. Hill & Co. had given no orders for the wool, but De la Torre & Co. were indebted to them in the sum of 500*l.* The Court held that, under these circumstances, Hill & Co. had clearly an insurable interest in that part of the wool which was held by Du Bois & Son as trustees for their benefit, and might recover under a count averring the interest to be in themselves (*e*).

Where, however, the consignor directed the consignees to hold, not the goods, but the proceeds of the goods, to the use

(*c*) Sutherland *v.* Pratt (1843), 1 B. & P. 316, 323.
12 M. & W. 16.
(*d*) Wolff *v.* Horncastle (1798), (*e*) Hill *v.* Secretan (1798), 1 B. & P. 315.

of his creditor, this was held, in the United States, not to give such creditor an insurable interest in the goods (*f*). Sect. 293.

294. Two British ships, the "Ross" and the "Atlantic," having, with their cargoes, been captured by the Spaniards, the plaintiffs (who were owners of the "Ross"), the owners of the "Atlantic," and the proprietors of the cargoes gave a joint authority to one Cowan to endeavour to obtain restitution. Cowan, by giving up part of the cargoes to the captors, obtained restitution of the rest, together with the two ships, in a mass, for the benefit of all concerned. He drew bills on the plaintiffs for his general expenses, 'which the plaintiffs accepted and paid; and he also, together with the rest of the property, consigned to them the "Atlantic" (of which they were not owners), in order, as he expressed it, to simplify the concern. Lord Ellenborough and the rest of the Court were of opinion that they had a clear insurable interest in the "Atlantic;" they were the original owners of one of the captured ships, and after the whole of the captured property had been redeemed *en masse* at their expense they became interested in the whole. They were also the consignees of the ship in question from Cowan; and having as such consignees accepted and paid bills for the expenses of restoring this ship, conjointly with the rest of the property, they had on this ground likewise a clear insurable interest. The Court accordingly held that the plaintiffs could recover the whole amount of the insurance; in trust, however, as to the surplus over their advances for those interested with themselves in the whole (*g*). Robertson *v.* Hamilton.

295. As a general principle, then, there can be no doubt that consignees of the goods being in advance to the consignors, or under acceptances for them, may insure, in General principle as to consignees.

(*f*) Murray *v.* Columbian Ins. Co. (1814), 11 Johnson's R. 302. This was apparently on the assumption that the creditor could not under the circumstances have claimed possession of the goods.

Phillips (vol. i. s. 291) says that the creditor has an insurable interest, and cites Hill *v.* Secretan, *supra*.

(*g*) Robertson *v.* Hamilton (1811), 14 East, 522.

Sect. 295. their own name (*h*), to the full value of the goods, and apply the proceeds of the policies to their own benefit to the extent of their claims in respect of such advances or acceptances, holding the residue in trust for the consignors if they intended when effecting the policies to cover the interest of the latter (*i*).

Consignee claiming under policy effected to protect the interest of the consignor.

It has been held, however, that such a consignee is so far identified in interest and right with his consignor as not to be able to apply with effect to his own interest, which is derived out of that of the consignor, an insurance which was effected in order to cover the interest of the latter, but which, owing to the intervention of some principle of law, cannot be available for such purpose.

Conway v. Gray.

Thus, Townsend, an American merchant, had consigned to Conway & Co., of Liverpool, a cargo of American produce for sale, and assigned to them the bill of lading. Conway & Co. effected an insurance on the cargo, in their own names, "as interest might appear," and debited Townsend with the premiums; they were then, and down to the time of loss, in advance to Townsend on account of the cargo, and had a general balance against him to a greater amount than the sum insured. The goods were detained in the United States under an American embargo; whereupon Conway & Co. gave notice of abandonment, and in an action on the policy averred the interest in the first count of the declaration to be in themselves. Lord Ellenborough and the Court of King's Bench, while admitting that a consignee so circumstanced might insure on his own account, held that, as the American consignor could not insure against acts done by the government of his own country, so the British consignees were as much incapacitated from applying the policy to their interest as though it had been made on their account (*k*).

(*h*) Arnould added "and on their own account." See on this point *ante*, § 292.

(*i*) See, in addition to the cases already cited, Carruthers v. Sheddon (1815), 6 Taunt. 14. The same position is established in the United States. De Forest v. The Fulton Ins. Co. (1828), 1 Hall's R. 84; cited 1 Phillips, Ins. s. 311.

(*k*) Conway v. Gray (1809), 10 East, 536. As regards the right of

296. The general agents of a purchaser of goods, who, by his directions and at his cost, have effected an insurance on the goods in order to cover bills drawn on them by him in favour of the seller, need only apply the proceeds of such policy to the payment of such drafts as far as the state of their accounts with the purchaser may enable them to do so without loss to themselves, and are entitled to hold the residue to their own benefit (*l*). "It has never been decided," says Bayley, J., "that a person not bound to insure, but who elects to insure in order to cover payments if the goods do not arrive, may not apply the proceeds of the policy to his own use. The premium for the insurance comes out of the general means of the party effecting it, and diminishes the fund applicable to the claims of the general creditors. As between them and the seller of the particular goods, they certainly would be entitled to the money secured by the policy" (*m*).

Sect. 296. General agents of a purchaser entitled to benefit of insurance.

297. A consignee has an insurable interest in the commission which he expects to earn on goods consigned to him, but must specifically describe his interest (*n*). The mere expectation, however, that goods will be consigned to a person of course gives him no insurable interest in the commission which he hopes to earn (*o*).

Insurable interest of consignee in his commission.

It seems to have been decided by Lord Ellenborough that there is no insurable interest in commissions unless the goods on which they are to be earned are already on board the ship. A merchant effected an insurance at and from Bristol to Jamaica and back to Dublin, on commission to arise upon the

Knox v. Wood.

---

the consignor to recover, the case has been overruled by the Exchequer Chamber in Aubert *v.* Gray (1862), 3 B. & S. 163, 169; 32 L. J. Q. B. 50. The decision is, however, not affected as regards the principle for which the case is cited in the text.

(*l*) Neale *v.* Reid (1823), 1 B. & Cr. 657.

(*m*) *Ibid.* 662.

(*n*) Per Lord Kenyon, Flint *v.* Le Mesurier (1796), 2 Park, Ins. 563; Lucena *v.* Craufurd (1806), 2 B. & P. N. R. 315.

(*o*) Knox *v.* Wood (1808), 1 Camp. 543. See per Bigham, J., Buchanan *v.* Faber (1899), 4 Com. Cas. 223.

402   INSURABLE INTEREST   [PART I.

Sect. 297. sale in Dublin of produce expected to be shipped at Jamaica
for the homeward voyage, under an agreement between himself and a Jamaica house. He chartered a ship to load the
produce. She was, however, captured on her outward
voyage; but being released she proceeded to Jamaica, and
found that her cargo had been forwarded by another ship.
Meanwhile she had also lost the season, and had to return
home in ballast. In an action to recover the loss of commission, it was held that the plaintiff had no insurable
interest in such commission; and Lord Ellenborough said:
"It strikes me that this was a mere expectation. The
expectation is frustrated by the capture, and the interest was
never on board; this is an insurance of the expectation of an
expectation." The defendant accordingly had a verdict;
and on motion for a new trial the Court were clearly of
opinion that the plaintiff had not an insurable interest when
the loss happened. Lord Ellenborough on that occasion
said: "This case carries us into the land of dreams; and, if
supported, would introduce the practice of insuring a 20,000*l.*
prize in the lottery without purchasing a ticket" (*p*).

If the case was decided on the ground that the plaintiff
had no contract for the consignment to him of a cargo by this
ship, its authority cannot be questioned (*q*). If, however,
as the report in Campbell implies, there was a binding contract under which the plaintiff was entitled to have the vessel
loaded, it would seem on principle that the plaintiff had an
insurable interest in the commission which but for the perils
of the voyage he would in the ordinary course of things
have earned (*r*). He would have been entitled to assume

(*p*) Knox *v.* Wood (1808), 1 Camp. 543; 2 Park, Ins. 564.
(*q*) The report in Park bears out this view.
(*r*) See per Mathew, J., in Ward *v.* Weir (1899), 4 Com. Cas. 216, 222. Phillips questions the decision in Knox *v.* Wood, 1 Phillips, s. 311. Other points might, however, be raised on this insurance. One (if, as is probable, the policy was in common form) is that the risk only attached on the loading of the goods. This depends on a further question, viz., whether commissions can, like profits, be deemed to be part of the value of the goods so as to make the clause as to the goods applicable. Another is, that the loss was due merely to a re-

that the cargo would be loaded if the ship arrived at Jamaica (*s*). *Sect.* 297.

A shipbroker to whom by agreement a ship is addressed, so that if she arrives at the port where he carries on his business he will earn brokerage, has an insurable interest in his brokerage during the voyage of the ship to the port (*t*). A mere hope or expectation, however, on the part of the broker that the owner of a ship will continue to employ him gives him no insurable interest in the brokerage, which he hopes to earn on the arrival of the ship (*u*). *Insurable interest of shipbrokers.*

298. The rule with regard to the insurable interest of mortgagor and mortgagee is thus stated in sect. 14 (1) of the Marine Insurance Act, 1906:— *Insurable interest of mortgagor and mortgagee.*

> Where the subject-matter insured is mortgaged, the mortgagor has an insurable interest in the full value thereof, and the mortgagee has an insurable interest in respect of any sum due or to become due under the mortgage.

From the general principle, that any creditor having a claim on property pledged to him for advances has an insurable interest to the extent of his claim, it follows that a mortgagee of ship or goods has a distinct insurable interest in the mortgaged property, and may recover in an action upon a policy effected for his benefit, averring the interest to be in himself, to the full amount of the mortgage debt. At the same time the equitable title that still remains in the mortgagor is in him an insurable interest which he may protect by a separate insurance.

Thus, a factor resident in this country, to whom goods and freight have been mortgaged by his foreign principal for

---

tardation of the voyage, and that the policy ought, therefore, to have been specially framed to cover such a risk. See M'Swiney *v.* Royal Exchange Ass. Co. (1850), Ex. Ch. 14 Q. B. 646. The case was, however, clearly not decided on either of these grounds.

(*s*) Rankin *v.* Potter (1873), L. R. 6 H. L. 83.

(*t*) Watts *v.* Bacon, *coram* Mathew, J., 18th Jan. 1900.

(*u*) Per Bigham, J., Buchanan *v.* Faber (1899), 4 Com. Cas. 223.

Sect. 298. advances, may, upon consignment to himself of the goods, with the bill of lading indorsed, insure the legal interest in the property on his own account, and the equitable interest remaining in his principal on account of the latter (x).

Amount which mortgagee can recover.

Although the ownership of the mortgagee is distinguished in the register from the absolute ownership (y), the mortgagee of a ship may protect his interest therein by a general policy on the ship in the common form: and he may insure to the full value of the ship, but can only recover to the extent of his mortgage debt, unless in effecting the policy he intended to cover, not his own interest only, but that of the mortgagor also (z).

The amount recoverable under an open policy effected by a mortgagee depends upon his intention in effecting the policy. Sect. 14 (2) of the Marine Insurance Act, 1906 (a), declares that a mortgagee "may insure on behalf and for the benefit of other persons interested as well as for his own benefit." If he intended it to cover the whole interest, both legal and equitable, he may recover the whole amount of the insurance, under trust as to the surplus, to hold it for the mortgagor; if he intended it only to cover his own interest as mortgagee, and the insurance is for more than the mortgage debt, he can recover to the extent only of his charge (b). If, under such circumstances, he have recovered the whole sum in an action on the policy, and retains the surplus, it may be recovered back from him by the underwriters (c).

The mortgagor's interest.

299. The mortgagor has an insurable interest in the mortgaged property to its full value, because in case of loss he would not only be deprived of the thing insured, but still remain liable for the mortgage debt: hence the mortgagor of

---

(x) Smith v. Lascelles (1788), 2 T. R. 187.

(y) See now the Merchant Shipping Act, 1894, s. 34.

(z) Irving v. Richardson (1831), 2 B. & Ad. 193; *S. C.* at N. P., 1 Mood. & R. 153.

(a) *Ante*, § 292.

(b) So in Carruthers v. Sheddon (1815), 6 Taunt. 17, Gibbs, C. J., told the jury to consider what amount of interest the policy was in fact intended to cover by those who caused it to be effected.

(c) Irving v. Richardson (1831), 2 B. & Ad. 193.

the ship has been held to have an insurable interest, though the ship be mortgaged to her full value (*d*).   Sect. 299.

When the mortgagor has covenanted to insure the mortgaged property on account of the mortgagees, he is, of course, a trustee for them of the proceeds of the policy (*e*). The owner, by a duly registered deed to which he and two trustees were the only parties, assigned six ships to the trustees for securing sums of money expressed to be lent by them, but which in fact were lent by the plaintiffs, and covenanted to insure each vessel in the sum of 1,500*l.* at the least, and, on request, to assign the policies to the trustees. He did insure in his own name through a broker who knew of the mortgage, but to whom he misrepresented the object of the insurance. Upon the loss of one of the ships and the bankruptcy of the owner, the plaintiffs obtained a decree in equity declaring their right to the proceeds of the policies, and setting aside the broker's general lien and the claim of the bankrupt's assignees under the reputed ownership section of the statute (*f*).   *Mortgagor insuring as trustee for mortgagee.*

The indorser of a bill of lading who did not intend to pass his whole property in the goods by the assignment, but only to give a charge on their net proceeds, stands in the same position as a mortgagor, and retains an insurable interest to their full value, since he continues to be as directly concerned in the safety of the goods as he was before assigning the bill of lading (*g*). A consignee of goods who has a lien   *When the indorser of a bill of lading is in the position of a mortgagor.*

(*d*) See Alston *v.* Campbell (1779), 4 Brown's Parl. Cas. 476; Hutchinson *v.* Wright (1858), 25 Beav. 444; 27 L. J. Ch. 834; Higginson *v.* Dall (1816), 13 Mass. R. 96; cited 1 Phillips, Ins. s. 286. The circumstance that in form the registered deed of mortgage is an absolute transfer of the ship does not affect the mortgagor's insurable interest. Hutchinson *v.* Wright, *supra;* and see Ward *v.* Beck (1863), 32 L. J. C. P. 113. In Ins. Co. *v.* Stimson (1880), 103 U. S. 25, the question of the insurable interest of mortgagor and mortgagee was considered.

(*e*) See as to the right of the mortgagor or the assignees of his interest to sue on the policy, when he has handed it over to the mortgagee, Swan *v.* Maritime Ins. Co., [1907] 1 K. B. 116; 12 Com. Cas. 73.

(*f*) Ladbroke *v.* Lee (1850), 4 De G. & S. 106.

(*g*) Hibbert *v.* Carter (1787), 1 T. R. 745. See *ante*, § 292.

Sect. 299. on them for a debt is in the position of a mortgagee. The question of the insurable interest of consignees has already been considered (*h*).

Insurable interest of a trustee.

300. There is no doubt that a trustee, having the legal interest in the thing insured, may insure, in respect of such interest, to the full value of the goods (*i*).

Insurable interest of captors, prize agents, &c.

301. The insurable interest of captors, prize agents, &c. in captured property has been the subject of very elaborate and refined discussion in the English Courts.

Le Cras v. Hughes, or the Omoa case.

The first case in which the question arose was that of Le Cras *v.* Hughes, before Lord Mansfield, generally known in insurance law as the Omoa case. A detachment of the sea and land forces of Great Britain jointly captured the fort of Omoa and two Spanish ships then lying under its protection. One of these ships, together with her cargo, was insured on account of the officers and crews of the British ships "at and from Omoa to London," and was lost on her homeward voyage. An action being brought on the policy, averring the interest to be in the officers and crews of the ships, two questions were made—1. Whether the sea officers had an insurable interest under the then Prize Act (19 Geo. 3, c. 67); 2. Whether possession of the ship would entitle them to insure upon the bare contingency of a future grant from the Crown.

The consideration of the second question became unnecessary, except speculatively, for Lord Mansfield was clearly of opinion that the officers and crew had an insurable interest under the Prize Act. The objection on this point being that the capture was not a sole capture by the sea forces, but a capture by the land and sea forces jointly, Lord Mansfield said: "The Act gives to the officers, seamen, marines and soldiers on board every ship of war the sole property in all ships and goods which they shall take during war, after

---

(*h*) *Ante*, §§ 291 *et seq.*
(*i*) Per Lord Eldon, in Lucena *v.* Craufurd (1806), 2 B. & P. N. R.

324. See also per Brett, J., in Ebsworth *v.* Alliance Marine Ins. Co. (1873), L. R. 8 C. P. 596, 638.

condemnation. It does not require that the seamen only shall take; where soldiers assist, their right may be doubtful, but that does not lessen the right of the navy" (*k*).

"As to the second ground," Lord Mansfield proceeded to say, "the Crown always makes the grant, and there is no instance to the contrary. Here the possession is in the assured, and a certain expectation of receiving the property captured from the Crown, which gives him an interest in its arrival" (*l*).

302. The position thus advanced by Lord Mansfield, "that possession, coupled with the expectation of future benefit, founded on the contingency of a future grant from the Crown, but warranted by universal practice, amounts to an insurable interest," has been considerably shaken by the observations of succeeding and scarcely less eminent judges. "If the Omoa case," says Lord Eldon, in Lucena *v.* Craufurd, "was decided upon the expectation of a grant from the Crown, I never can give my assent to that doctrine. That expectation, though founded on the highest probability, was not interest, and it was equally not interest whatever might have been the chances in favour of the expectation. That which was wholly in the Crown, and which it was in the power of his Majesty to give or withhold, could not belong to the captors so as to create any right in them" (*m*). Lord Ellenborough, in Routh *v.* Thompson (*n*), and Tindal, C. J., in Devaux *v.* Steele (*o*), both seem to consider that, after these observations of Lord Eldon's, the doctrine of Lord Mansfield, if it can still be treated as a binding authority, must be considered

Sect. 301.

Query, whether captors have an insurable interest on the ground of an expectation.

(*k*) Le Cras *v.* Hughes (1782), 1 Marshall, Ins. 105; 2 Park, Ins. 568; 3 Dougl. 81. See the judgment of Lord Ellenborough in Routh *v.* Thompson (1809), 11 East, 433, 434. That captors of a prize in case of joint capture had an insurable interest in such prize under the 45 Geo. 3, c. 72, was held in Stirling *v.* Vaughan (1809), 11 East, 619.

(*l*) Le Cras *v.* Hughes (1782), 1 Marsh. Ins. 105; 2 Park, Ins. 568; 3 Dougl. 81.

(*m*) Lucena *v.* Craufurd (1806), 2 B. & P. N. R. 323.

(*n*) 11 East, 434.

(*o*) 6 Bing. N. C. 358, 370, 371.

INSURABLE INTEREST [PART I.

Sect. 302. incapable of being extended, and as confined to cases falling strictly within the same circumstances (*p*).

Result of the authorities.

303. If the law, therefore, on this subject be that possession, coupled with the expectation of a future grant from the Crown, gives an insurable interest, it is so only in cases where a long and uniform course of practice can be shown for the Crown always to make such grant and no instance can be given to the contrary (*q*).

Lord Eldon, however, pointed out other grounds on which the right of the captors to insure might have been put. "The captors," said his Lordship, "not only had the possession, but a possession coupled with the liability to pay costs and charges, if they had taken possession improperly, and also a liability to render back property which should turn out to be neutral" (*r*). It was upon this very ground that Lord Kenyon had previously put the insurable interest of captors in the case of Boehm *v.* Bell (*s*).

Lucena *v.* Craufurd.

304. The next case to be considered is the famous one of the Dutch Commissioners, which, for more than eight years, was litigated in the English Courts of law, and in the House of Lords gave rise to one of the most elaborate and ingenious legal discussions ever raised upon a point of maritime law (*t*).

(*p*) Sect. 5 of the Mar. Ins. Act, 1906 (*ante*, § 254), in which there is a definition of insurable interest (which, however, does not profess to be exhaustive) does not affect this question. The section contained an additional sub-section which declared that "a prospect or possibility of loss or gain, which is not founded on any right or liability in, or in respect of, the subject-matter insured, is not insurable"; but it was struck out in Committee.

(*q*) See Devaux *v.* Steele (1840), 6 Bing. N. C. 358.

(*r*) 2 B. & P. N. R. 323.

(*s*) Boehm *v.* Bell (1799), 8 T. R. 154. See the judgment of Lord Kenyon, *ibid.* 161.

(*t*) The case first came before the Court of King's Bench under the name of Craufurd *v.* Hunter in 1798, 8 T. R. 13. It came before the Exchequer Chamber as Lucena *v.* Craufurd, in 1802, 3 B. & P. 75; before the House of Lords, under the same name, in 1806, 2 B. & P. N. R. 269. It then came before Lord Ellenborough at the Sittings after Michaelmas Term, 1806, on the *venire de novo*, and was ulti-

CHAP. XII.] OF THE DUTCH COMMISSIONERS. 409

The facts were as follow:—Holland having been in 1794 Sect. 304. overrun and occupied by the armies of the French Republic, with whom we were then at war, and it being probable that her reduction to French subjection might be permanent, our Government, by an Order in Council of February, 1795, directed that all Dutch ships bound to and from the ports of Holland should be seized for the purpose of being brought into this country and there provisionally detained. With a view to provide for the custody of such ships, an Act was passed empowering his Majesty in Council to appoint commissioners for the care, management, sale, or other disposal, according to his Majesty's instructions, of all Dutch ships or cargoes "which had been, and might be thereafter, detained in or brought into the ports of the United Kingdom"; and on the 15th June, 1795, a commission issued under this Act to Craufurd and others, appointing them to act as commissioners for the purposes specified in the Act. Before this commission was issued, a man-of-war, in company with some East India Company's ships, acting under the order in Council of February, 1795, had captured a fleet of Dutch merchantmen and carried them into St. Helena for the purpose of being brought into this country. Accordingly, in July, four of these ships, the "Hooghley," the "Dordrecht," the "Surcheance," and the "Zeelelye," sailed from St. Helena with their Dutch cargoes on board for this country; and on the 22nd of August (*u*) Craufurd and his co-commissioners, having received notice to that effect, caused an insurance to be effected on these ships and their cargoes on their own account, under the name and style of "The Honourable Commissioners for the Sale of Dutch Property." All the four ships thus insured, together with their cargoes, were totally lost before arriving in this country; one of them, however, the "Zeelelye," was not so lost till after the 15th of September. This date is important, because on that day a proclamation of reprisals—in other words, an open declara-

mately disposed of by the House of Lords on the 29th June, 1808, as   Lucena *v.* Craufurd, 1 Taunt. 325. (*u*) 1 Taunt. 329.

Sect. 304. tion of war—was made by his Majesty against the ships, goods, and subjects of the United Provinces.

On the loss of the ships becoming known, Craufurd and his co-commissioners brought an action upon the policy, averring the interest, in the first count of the declaration, to be in themselves "as such commissioners"; in the second count, to be in the Crown.

Question in the case. The main question in the cause was, whether the plaintiffs, under the circumstances, had an insurable interest, under the commission, in the ships and cargoes insured before their arrival in this country. It would be impossible to report at length, and useless to attempt to abridge, the able and ingenious disquisitions to which this question gave rise; the reader is referred to the reports at large, especially to the judgment of Chambre, J., in the Exchequer Chamber (*x*), of the same learned Judge (*y*), of Lawrence, J. (*z*), and of Lord Eldon (*a*), in the House of Lords.

Judgment of the Court of King's Bench. In the Court of King's Bench, Lord Kenyon and the rest of the Court held that the plaintiffs had an insurable interest sufficient to sustain the first count of the declaration, either as trustees for the Crown or for the parties who should ultimately be entitled, as consignees, or as prize agents; and judgment accordingly was given for the plaintiffs for the whole sum.

Judgment of the majority in the Exchequer Chamber. In the Exchequer Chamber this judgment was affirmed by a majority of the Judges, including Heath, J., and Lord Alvanley, Chambre, J., delivering a very forcible opinion the other way.

The grounds on which the majority founded their judgment were substantially the same as those which had prevailed with the Court of King's Bench; and rested on the principle "that an inchoate interest, though imperfect till a given contingency shall take place, is nevertheless insurable" (*b*).

Chambre, J., on the other hand, rested entirely on the fact

(*x*) 3 B. & P. 99—105.
(*y*) 2 B. & P. N. R. 298—300.
(*z*) *Ibid.* 300—307.
(*a*) *Ibid.* 315—326.
(*b*) 3 B. & P. 98.

CHAP. XII.] OF THE DUTCH COMMISSIONERS. 411

that, under the terms of the Act and the commission, the powers of the commissioners were strictly limited to the case of Dutch ships actually brought into the ports of the United Kingdom and provisionally detained there; that, as the ships had never been brought into this country at all, they had never become the objects of the plaintiffs' authority or powers under the commission, and consequently that the plaintiffs had no such relation, concern, or interest therein as to entitle them to insure.

<small>Sect. 304.</small>

Before the House of Lords, eight of the Judges were of opinion, upon the same grounds as before, that the plaintiffs had an insurable interest sufficient to sustain the first count; "they had a contingent interest, and, supposing the intentions of the Crown to remain unaltered, nothing stood between them and the vesting of that contingent interest but the perils insured against" (c).

<small>Opinion of the majority of the Judges in the House of Lords.</small>

Chambre, J., adhered to his former opinion, which was supported by Lawrence, J., by the great authority of Lord Eldon, by Lord Erskine, and, as is inferred rather from the known course of his subsequent decisions than from anything that fell from him at the time, by Lord Ellenborough (d). To these learned persons the plaintiffs' claim of interest seemed to have "no other foundation than a mere naked expectation of acquiring a trust, or charge, respecting the property, without a scintilla of present right, either absolute or contingent" (e). By the letter of the commission and the statute, they remarked, the plaintiffs' care was confined to ships which had been detained, or might be brought into the ports of this kingdom; so that, until arrival here, no Dutch property was clothed with those circumstances which designated it to be the object of their commission, and made it their duty to interfere in its preservation (f). Under these circumstances, they professed themselves unable to conceive

<small>Opinions of Chambre and Lawrence, JJ., and judgment of the House of Lords.</small>

(c) 2 B. & P. N. R. 289—298.
(d) Chambre, J., 2 B. & P. N. R. 298—300; Lawrence, J., 300—307; Lord Eldon, 315—326; Lord Ellenborough, 397; Lord Erskine, 328.
(e) Per Chambre, J., 2 B. & P. N. R. 299.
(f) Per Lawrence, J., ibid. 305.

Sect. 304. an interest dependent on a thing, with which thing the persons supposed to be interested had nothing to do (*g*); and Lord Eldon, in particular, declared he could "not point out what is an interest unless it be a right in the property, or a right derivable out of some contract about the property, which in either case may be lost upon some contingency affecting the possession or enjoyment of the party" (*h*). Notwithstanding this clear declaration of opinion, the House of Lords did not directly reverse the decision of the majority of the Judges, but, upon the advice of Lord Eldon, sent the case down for a new trial under a *venire de novo* on the following collateral ground.

Venire de novo.

The declaration of hostilities against the United Provinces took place on the 15th of September, and the "Zeelelye," one of the ships insured, was not lost till the 20th of September. Damages, nevertheless, had been assessed at a total sum in respect of all the ships, including the "Zeelelye." As, however, the House of Lords were clearly of opinion that whatever insurable interest (if any) the plaintiffs, as commissioners, might ever have had, had at all events been taken out of them by this declaration of hostilities, which vested the ownership of all captured property in the Crown *jure belli*, it followed that the plaintiffs had no interest in the "Zeelelye" at the time of her loss, and the finding of the jury, inasmuch as it gave general damages partly made up of the loss on the "Zeelelye," was erroneous.

Final result of the case.

The cause, accordingly, came on for trial before Lord Ellenborough on the *venire de novo*, when a verdict was found for the plaintiffs upon the second count of the declaration, which averred the interest to be in the king (*i*).

Cases since Lucena *v.* Craufurd.

305. Although, however, the House of Lords in this case avoided a decision diametrically opposed to the opinion of a

---

(*g*) 2 B. & P. N. R. 306.
(*h*) Per Lord Eldon, *ibid.* 321.
(*i*) 2 B. & P. N. R. 329. A bill of exceptions was taken to his Lordship's judgment, which was,

however, affirmed by the House of Lords without calling upon counsel in reply on 29th June, 1808. Lucena *v.* Craufurd, 1 Taunt. 325.

majority of the Judges, yet the subsequent course of our jurisprudence sufficiently shows the influence of this discussion to have been adverse to all claims of interest founded on mere contingent grants from the Crown (*k*).

Sect. 305.

Thus: in pursuance of an Order in Council, of September, 1807, by which all Danish ships were directed to "be detained and brought into port," a Danish ship was seized by a British privateer and carried into Lisbon. Thence, after repairs and the sale of her original cargo, she was despatched by the captors with another cargo to London on the 3rd of November, the very day on which a formal declaration of hostilities had been made by Great Britain against Denmark. Subsequently an insurance was effected on account of the captors, and, the ship and cargo being totally lost, an action was brought on the policy. Interest was averred in the captors, which it was contended that they had on two grounds:—(1) Because they had a possession, coupled with a well-grounded expectation of a grant from the Crown; (2) Because such possession rendered them liable, either to the Crown or to the foreign owner, for the safe custody of the ship, and therefore gave them an interest in her safety.

Routh *v.* Thompson.

As to the first, it was answered, that the ship was taken, not as a prize of war after a declaration of hostilities, but merely under an Order in Council "to detain and bring into port"; that, even if the ship had arrived in safety, the captors would have had nothing "but the chance of a grant": the Court accordingly held that they had no insurable interest on the short ground, "that a man has no right to an indemnity because he has lost the chance of receiving a gift."

A mere chance not an insurable interest.

As to the second ground, which, it will be recollected, was the foundation of Lord Kenyon's decision in Boehm *v.* Bell, and approved of by Lord Eldon in Lucena *v.* Craufurd, it was held by Lord Ellenborough to be inapplicable; because

(*k*) What was determined by this celebrated case, and the application of the rule so determined, was canvassed anew in the case of Ebsworth *v.* Alliance Marine Ins. Co. (1873), L. R. 8 C. P. 596; but the discussion, as the Court was equally divided, ended without result.

Sect. 305. a formal declaration of hostilities had intervened before the loss, which at once vested the right of ownership in the Crown, put an end to all claim on the part of the foreign owners, and freed the captors, as agents for the Crown, from all liability for acts done within the scope of their authority, which it did not appear that they had in any degree exceeded (*l*). As, however, there was no fraud in the captors in effecting the policy, nor anything illegal in the voyage or insurance, the assured were held entitled to recover back the premiums (*m*).

Secus, of a vested right. Stirling *v.* Vaughan.

In the case just cited, the captors had no claim to prize under any Prize Acts, for the ship was taken before the declaration of hostilities. Where they had such claim, they were held to have an insurable interest in ships taken as prize before condemnation, *e.g.*, under the Prize Act (45 Geo. 3, c. 72), s. 3, which vested the property in the captors after condemnation, subject to the right of the Crown to release the prize before condemnation, and to the effect of a sentence of restoration by a Court of Admiralty (*n*).

Policy effected by prize agent may be adopted by the Crown.

306. Whether the insurance and the loss took place before or after open declaration of war or order for reprisals; whether the parties insuring effected the policy under the orders and expressly on account of the captors, or otherwise; the Crown has in all cases an insurable interest in ships lawfully detained and captured under any Order in Council: and if such insurance was made for the benefit of all whom it might concern, the Crown, by a subsequent ratification, may adopt the insurance (*o*).

Express ratification not necessary.

It would seem by what fell from the Court in the case of Stirling *v.* Vaughan, and upon the principle that the law will

---

(*l*) Routh *v.* Thompson (1809), 11 East, 428.
(*m*) *Ibid.*
(*n*) Stirling *v.* Vaughan (1809), 11 East, 619. The Naval Prize Act now in force, 27 & 28 Vict. c. 25, declares (s. 55) that nothing in the Act shall give the captors any right in prize ships or goods, and that they shall continue to take only such interest (if any) as may be granted them by the Crown.
(*o*) Lucena *v.* Craufurd (1808), 1 Taunt. 325; Routh *v.* Thompson (1811), 13 East, 274, 284, 285. See *ante*, § 140.

presume, if nothing appears to the contrary, that every person accepts what is for his benefit, that captors, in every case of legal capture, have an implied authority to insure on behalf of the Crown, and may therefore, in all such cases, recover on a count averring the interest to be in the Crown, without any express subsequent ratification by it (*p*).

Sect. 306.

The law in the United States as to this subject seems to be, that an insurable interest in prizes can be acquired only by an actual grant from the government (*q*).

Law in the United States.

307. Ships are now frequently owned, not by individual shareholders, but by limited liability companies, whose whole property often consists of a single ship. The question whether a shareholder in an incorporated company has an insurable interest in the property owned by the company is therefore not without practical importance. The shareholder in a ship-owning company, to apply the much quoted test of Lawrence, J., is undoubtedly interested in the preservation of the ship, inasmuch as he has "benefit from its existence, prejudice from its destruction." Yet there is no case, except that of a captor, which is considered an exceptional one (*r*), where the validity of an insurance of a chattel has been recognized, unless the assured had some legal or equitable title to or charge upon the actual thing insured, or was under some contractual liability to indemnify another person in case of its loss or of damage to it.

Insurable interest of shareholders.

It has been decided that the property of an incorporated company is not the property of its shareholders; for the company is not a mere collection of individuals, but itself a legal personage (*s*). On this ground it has been held, that

Their relation to the property of the company.

(*p*) Stirling *v.* Vaughan (1809), 11 East, 623.

(*q*) See the observations of Story, J., in The Joseph (1813), 1 Gallison, 558; 1 Phillips, ss. 320 *et seq.*

(*r*) The judgment of Walton, J., in Moran *v.* Uzielli, [1905] 2 K. B. 555, seems to create another exception. See as to this case, *ante*, § 257a.

(*s*) R. *v.* Arnaud (1846), 9 Q. B. 806; 16 L. J. Q. B. 50; Myers *v.* Perigal (1852), 2 De G. M. & G. 599; 22 L. J. Ch. 431. See also Salomon *v.* Salomon & Co., [1897] A. C. 22; Janson *v.* Driefontein Consolidated Mines, Ltd., [1902] A. C. 484; Harburg India Rubber Comb Co. *v.* Martin, [1902] 1 K. B. 778.

Sect. 307. although an alien is not qualified to own a British ship, either wholly or in part, yet a British company is not disqualified from being the registered owner of a British ship by the fact that one of its shareholders is an alien (*t*).

The consequence seems to be that the insurable interest in a ship or other property belonging to a company is only in the company itself, not in the individual shareholders; and this was the view expressed by the Exchequer Chamber in Wilson *v.* Jones, in which the policy was effected to protect the interest of a shareholder in the Atlantic Cable Company (*u*).

The insurable interest of shareholder in the company's adventure.

In that case, however, the Court held that a shareholder in the Atlantic Telegraph Company had an insurable interest in the benefit which he expected to derive from the success of the adventure of laying the cable. His interest in that adventure, which in the policy was valued at the nominal value of his shares, was held to be protected by the ingeniously worded policy, which has elsewhere been set out (*x*).

Shares in company not exposed to maritime risks.

It has been said that shares in a company cannot be insured against maritime risks on the technical ground that being of an incorporeal nature, they cannot be exposed to those risks, nor are they directly liable to be lost in consequence of them (*y*).

Undoubtedly, however, shares in a company owning a ship are liable to be depreciated, or to become valueless, in consequence of casualties affecting the ship, and it may well be argued that a shareholder is as much interested in the safety of the ship as the shareholders in the Atlantic Telegraph

---

(*t*) R. *v.* Arnaud, *supra*.

(*u*) (1867), L. R. 2 Ex. 139; see per Willes, J., p. 144. The *dictum* of Smith, M. R., in Driefontein Consolidated Gold Mines, Ltd. *v.* Janson, [1901] 2 K. B. 419, 427, that the beneficial ownership in the property of the plaintiff company belonged to the shareholders is inconsistent with the authorities cited in note (*s*), *supra*. In Paterson *v.* Harris (1861), 1 B. & S. 336; 30 L. J. Q. B. 354, a shareholder recovered for a loss of part of the Atlantic cable; but there was no plea traversing his interest in the cable, and the question now discussed was not raised.

(*x*) *Ante*, § 249.

(*y*) Paterson *v.* Harris (1861), 1 B. & S. 354, 355; 30 L. J. Q. B. 361.

Company were in the laying of the cable. The opinion has already been expressed that a shareholder can protect himself against such depreciation by a properly worded policy (z).

Sect. 307.

308. We have seen (a) that the master has an insurable interest in his wages, and may effect a policy on these and on any commissions he is properly entitled to (b).

Master's wages and commission.

It seems that in the United States, the Courts, regarding him in the relation of a confidential agent, have held that if he buys on his own account ship or cargo, when sold in case of misfortune abroad, he has no insurable interest therein, unless the purchase be ratified by those whom it may concern (c).

Master buying ship or cargo.

Sect. 11 of the Marine Insurance Act, 1906, enables seamen and officers under the master to insure their wages, and this enactment will no doubt apply to any profits which they are to receive in lieu of wages (d).

Seamen's wages.

In the United States a seaman is allowed to insure any goods put on board by him as merchandise, notwithstanding the freight of these be a perquisite and so form a part of his wages (e).

Seamen's merchandise, by American law.

309. A shipowner or other carrier has an insurable interest in the goods which he carries in respect of his liability for loss or damage that may happen to them during transit (f).

Insurable interest of carriers.

(z) *Ante*, § 249. In Pole v. Fitzgerald (1752), Willes, 641, Willes, C. J., held that there cannot be an insurance on a voyage, on the ground that it was impossible to estimate the loss of a voyage; but he was speaking of a loss of hypothetical profits of a voyage, which might never have been earned. See the remarks of Lawrence, J., on this case, 2 B. & P. N. R. p. 301.

(a) Mar. Ins. Act, 1906, s. 11; *ante*, § 245.

(b) King v. Glover (1806), 2 B. & P. N. R. 206; and see Hawkins v. Twizell (1856), 5 E. & B. 883; 25 L. J. Q. B. 160.

(c) Copeland v. Mercantile Ins. Co. (1828), 6 Pick. 198; Barker v. Marine Ins. Co. (1821), 2 Mason, 369.

(d) See *ante*, § 244.

(e) Galloway v. Morris (1802), 3 Yeates, 445.

(f) Mar. Ins. Act, 1906, s. 3 (2) (c); *ante*, § 1. See Crowley v. Cohen (1832), 3 B. & Ad. 478; Joyce v. Kennard (1871), L. R. 7 Q. B. 78; Stephens v. Australasian Ins. Co. (1872), L. R. 8 C. P. 18; Hill v. Scott (C. A.), [1895] 2 Q. B. 713; Munich Ass. Co. v. Dodwell (1904), 128 Fed. R. 410.

A.—VOL. I.

418   INSURABLE INTEREST.   [PART I.

Sect. 309.
Of owner of property who is indemnified against loss.

At the same time the insurable interest of the owner of the goods is not affected by the existence of this liability. The general rule is thus stated in sect. 14 (3) of the Marine Insurance Act, 1906:—

> The owner of insurable property has an insurable interest in respect of the full value thereof, notwithstanding that some third person may have agreed, or be liable, to indemnify him in case of loss (*g*).

Miscellaneous cases of insurable interest.

310. There are other cases of insurable interest which cannot be ranged under any of the foregoing heads.

A party interested in cargo alone has no insurable interest in the ship; for the goods may arrive safe though the ship be lost, and *vice versâ*. Hence, where the owners of the cargo effected a policy on goods, with a memorandum declaring the insurance to be "on money expended for reclaiming ship and cargo"; "the loss to be paid in case the ship does not arrive" at the port of destination; it was held that the assured had no insurable interest in the subject insured, against the event sought to be provided for by this policy (*h*).

The owner of the cargo has no insurable interest in the ship.

Bills of exchange.

A bill of exchange drawn by the captain abroad to cover ship's disbursements gives the holder no lien on the ship by British law (*i*). It follows that he has no insurable interest in the ship; and the opinion to the contrary expressed by Gibbs, C. J., in Tasker *v.* Scott (*k*) seems to be an *obiter dictum* unnecessary to the case before him. The question

---

(*g*) See Hobbs *v.* Hannam (1811), 3 Camp. 93, a case of an insurance by a shipowner, to whom the charterer had undertaken to pay the value of the ship if lost during the voyage. The doctrine of subrogation will, of course, prevent the assured from recovering in all more than the value of his property: see *post*, Part III., Chap. IX., "Subrogation."

(*h*) Kulen Kemp *v.* Vigne (1786), 1 T. R. 304. The expenditure, it may be noticed, was ordered by the Admiralty Court to be a charge on the cargo.

(*i*) It seems to be otherwise by French law. Castrique *v.* Imrie (1861), 8 C. B. N. S. 405; (1870), L. R. 4 H. of L. 414. This law was in that case applied by a French Court to a British ship, no doubt erroneously; but as the judgment was *in rem*, it was held binding on the Courts of this country. The remedy, if any, was by appeal to the Cour de Cassation in France.

(*k*) Tasker *v.* Scott (1815), 1 Marsh. R. 556; *S. C.*, 6 Taunt. 234.

really at issue was whether the holder of the bill could recover *Sect. 310.* the premium from the master of the ship on the ground that the latter had authorized him to insure.

Instead of borrowing at respondentia, captains engaged in the East India Company's trade had, since the year 1810, practised the following mode of raising money to pay for their outward investments. Bills were drawn for the required amount upon the captain's agents in India, payable in so many days after the ship's arrival outwards; these bills, drawn in two sets, were indorsed to the person in this country who had made the required advances. One set was left with him; the other set, together with the goods, consigned to the captain's agents, was taken out in the ship, and the indorsee of the bills then effected insurance on them for his own benefit: the understanding was, that if the ship arrived safe the bills were to be paid; if she did not arrive they were not to be paid. After the practice had prevailed some time a case came before the Court of Common Pleas in which the indorsees of bills so drawn and insured sued the underwriter, describing them as "bills of exchange," and averring the total loss of ship, goods, and the set of bills on board of her: Best, C. J., held that upon such policy the assured could recover nothing; the instruments, being drawn on a contingency, were not bills, but so much waste paper; the plaintiffs had lost nothing by them, because they could have recovered nothing by them; they had, therefore, no insurable interest, because they had nothing at risk (*l*).

It has been decided in the United States that advances for repairs of ship give no insurable interest in the ship, unless when secured by a lien by law or contract (*m*). *Money advanced for repairs.*

(*l*) Palmer *v.* Pratt (1824), 2 Bing. 185. "I quite concur with Mr. Phillips," said Arnould, "that this is, both in itself and in reference to the grounds of the judgment, a very unsatisfactory decision." See 1 Phillips, s. 203, n.; see also Lowry *v.* Bourdieu (1780), 2 Dougl. 468.

(*m*) Buchanan *v.* Ocean Ins. Co. (1826), 6 Cowen, 318; 1 Phillips, s. 202. See, however, Moran *v.* Uzielli, [1905] 2 K. B. 555, *ante*, § 257a.

Sect. 310.
Interest of insurer.

An insurer has, for the purpose of re-insurance, an insurable interest in the thing insured. In view of the importance in modern times of the question of re-insurance, the subject will presently be dealt with as a whole at some length (*n*).

Wager policies.

311. The term *Wager Policy* relates to the form of the instrument as well as to the nature of the contract.

Definition of a wager policy.

A wager (or honour) policy may be defined to be one in which the parties, by express terms, disclaim, on the face of it, the intention of making a contract of indemnity.

Form of wager policies.

Such a policy is generally known by having one or other of the following clauses written on the face of it:—" Interest or no interest," or " Without further proof of interest than the policy," or " This policy to be deemed sufficient proof of interest," or any other terms which purport either to entitle the assured to recover against the underwriters a stipulated sum of money, whether he has any interest in the ship or cargo or not; or to bind the underwriter not to require any proof of the assured's interest other than the policy itself (*o*). As, moreover, in these cases there is nothing actually at risk which can be sea-damaged or abandoned, such policies frequently also contain the clause, "Free of all average, and without benefit of salvage."

Wager policies were at one time deemed legal.

It has been made a subject of very learned inquiry whether such policies were legal at common law. It will at present be sufficient to give what is now firmly established as the true result of the authorities, viz.:—

1. That by the law of England, as it stood at the time of passing the Act of 19 Geo. 2, c. 37, a wager policy properly so called, *i.e.*, one in which the parties, by express terms, such as the words " interest or no interest," or " without proof of interest," disclaimed making a contract of indemnity, was

---

(*n*) *Post*, §§ 322—328.
(*o*) See the judgment of Best, C. J., in Murphy *v.* Bell (1828), 4 Bing. 569—572. A clause of this kind is usually called a "p.p.i." (policy proof of interest) clause, and the policy containing it is also known as a "p.p.i." policy.

CHAP. XII.] WAGER POLICIES. 421

then (contrary to older determinations) deemed a valid contract of insurance (*p*). Sect. 311.

2. That a policy, containing no such clause disclaiming or dispensing with the proof of interest, but effected in the common form, was, at common law, as it still is, considered to be a contract of indemnity only, upon which the assured could never recover without averment and proof of interest (*q*). A policy in the common form was always a policy upon interest.

312. About the year 1746 wager policies became so prevalent that the Legislature, wisely considering it to be against the policy of this country, as a great maritime state, to permit parties who had no interest in the safety of British ships and cargoes, by means of these policies, to give themselves a direct interest in their loss, interfered by the 19th Geo. 2, c. 37, to suppress the practice. 19 Geo. 2, c. 37.

That Act prohibited the making of insurances on British ships and their cargoes "interest or no interest," or "without further proof of interest than the policy," or "without benefit of salvage to the insurer," or by way of gaming or wagering (*r*). Such insurances, as the preamble recites, had been

---

(*p*) This point was established by Assieviedo *v.* Cambridge (1710), 10 Mod. 77; Depaba *v.* Ludlow (1721), 1 Comyns, 360; Dean *v.* Dicker (1746), 2 Str. 1250. They were also recognized as legal by Lord Mansfield, and were held legal at common law in Ireland in Keith *v.* Protection Ins. Co. of Paris (1882), 10 L. R. Ir. 51.

(*q*) For this latter position, see the observations of Lord Eldon in Lucena *v.* Craufurd (1806), 2 B. & P. N. R. 321, dissenting from the *dictum* of Lord Kenyon in Craufurd *v.* Hunter (1798), 8 T. R. 23, in which that learned judge had said "that a person at common law might have insured without interest." The position, as stated in the text, was laid down as law by Chambre, J., in Lucena *v.* Craufurd (1802), 3 B. & P. 101, and was finally established by the judgment of the Exchequer Chamber in Cousin *v.* Nantes (1811), 3 Taunt. 513, in which the *dictum* of Lord Kenyon and the case of Nantes *v.* Thompson (1802), 2 East, 385, founded upon it, were decisively overruled.

(*r*) The following is the text of this provision:—"Be it enacted that no assurance or assurances shall be made by any person or persons, bodies corporate or politic, on any ship or ships belonging to his Majesty or any of his subjects, or on any goods, merchandises or effects laden or to be laden on board of any such ship or ships, interest or no interest, or without further proof of interest than the policy, or by way of gaming or wagering,

Sect. 312. found to be productive of many pernicious practices; such as the "fraudulent loss, destruction or capture of great numbers of ships, with their cargoes"; the "encouragement of the exportation of wool, and the carrying on of many prohibited and clandestine trades, which, by means of such insurances, have been concealed"; the introduction of "a mischievous kind of gaming, under pretence of insuring against the risk on shipping and fair trade."

"Thus," as Best, C. J., observes, "gaming was by no means the sole evil which the Legislature, by this Act, proposed to remedy; but its object also, and perhaps chiefly, was to prevent policies in this form from being 'used to protect persons who were carrying on an illegal traffic, or made the means of profiting by the wilful destruction and capture of ships'" (*s*).

Mar. Ins. Act, 1906, s. 4.

313. This Act has been repealed by sect. 92 of the Marine Insurance Act, 1906, sect. 4 of which deals with wager policies and insurances in general made by way of gaming and wagering in the following terms:—

(1) Every contract of marine insurance by way of gaming or wagering is void.

(2) A contract of marine insurance is deemed to be a gaming or wagering contract—

(a) Where the assured has not an insurable interest as defined by this Act (*t*), and the contract is entered into with no expectation of acquiring such an interest; or

(b) Where the policy is made "interest or no interest," or "without further proof of interest than the policy itself," or "without benefit of salvage to the insurer," or subject to any other like term:

Provided that, where there is no possibility of salvage, a policy may be effected without benefit of salvage to the insurer (*u*).

or without benefit of salvage to the assurer; and that every such assurance shall be null and void to all intents and purposes."

(*s*) Per Best, C. J., in Murphy *v.* Bell (1828), 4 Bing. 569, 570.

(*t*) See *ante*, § 254.

(*u*) This proviso gives effect to the opinion of nine of the judges in Lucena *v.* Craufurd (1806), 2

WAGER POLICIES.

An important change has been effected by this section. 19 Geo. 2, c. 37, in terms only prohibited wager policies on British ships and their cargoes (*x*), and was held not to extend to foreign vessels (*y*). There is no such limitation in the Marine Insurance Act, under which every insurance by way of gaming and wagering within the meaning of sect. 4 is void.

Sect. 313. Changes which it effects. Insurances on foreign ship.

Another change effected by the Marine Insurance Act, 1906, is that wager policies are now void in Ireland. The Irish Court had previously held that 19 Geo. 2, c. 37, was not extended to Ireland by the Irish Act, 21 & 22 Geo. 3, c. 48, and consequently that wager policies, being legal at common law, were valid (*z*).

Wager policies now void in Ireland.

313a. Wager policies, as we have seen, were expressly prohibited by 19 Geo. 2, c. 37, and under that Act were considered illegal (*a*).

B. & P. N. R. at p. 310. There seems to be no possibility of salvage in insurances on profits or commissions.

(*x*) It was held to apply to other subjects of insurance as well as "ship" and "goods." In a certain sense a marine insurance must in general be either on the ship or on the goods on board of her; for being against maritime perils, it must be against loss caused by some event which physically affects some tangible property at risk. Accordingly, for the purposes of the Act, an insurance was deemed to be on the thing physically at risk, the loss of which involved the loss of the subject-matter insured. Thus policies on "profits," "commissions," and "cash advances" were held to be within the Act. See Smith *v.* Reynolds (1856), 1 H. & N. 221; 25 L. J. Ex. 337; De Mattos *v.* North (1868), L. R. 3 Ex. 185; Allkins *v.* Jupe (1877), 2 C. P. D. 375; Mortimer *v.* Broadwood (1869), 17 W. R. 653; Berridge *v.* Man On Ins. Co. (1887), 18 Q. B. D. 346. In fact it was no doubt correct to say that the Act made every marine policy relating to a British ship void, which on the face of it was a wager policy.

(*y*) Thellusson *v.* Fletcher (1780), 1 Dougl. 315.

(*z*) Keith *v.* Protection Marine Ins. Co. of Paris (1882), 10 L. R. Ir. 51.

(*a*) Allkins *v.* Jupe (1877), 2 C. P. D. 375; Gedge *v.* Royal Exchange Ass. Corpn., [1900] 2 Q. B. 214. See also Lowry *v.* Bourdieu (1780), 2 Dougl. 468; Andree *v.* Fletcher (1789), 3 T. R. 266. In Tasker *v.* Scott (1815), 6 Taunt. 234, Gibbs, C. J., held, on the contrary, that a person who authorized another to effect a wager policy was liable to repay him the premium, on the ground that 19 Geo. 2, c. 37, made the insurance not illegal, but only unavailable.

Sect. 313a.

Wager policies not illegal under Mar. Ins. Act, 1906.

Sect. 4 (1) of the Marine Insurance Act, 1906, however, merely declares that they are void. As wager policies were not illegal at common law, the result seems to be the same as has been held to follow, as regards wagering contracts, from the similar provision of the Gaming Act, 1845, s. 18, *i.e.*, though void, they are not illegal under the Act of 1906 (*b*). A later statute, however, the Marine Insurance (Gambling Policies) Act, 1909 (9 Edw. 7, c. 12)(*c*), prohibits certain insurances, which in the Act are termed "contracts by way of gambling on loss by maritime perils," by making them criminal.

When prohibited by Mar. Ins. Act, 1909.

It is now an offence to effect a contract of marine insurance without having any *bonâ fide* interest, direct or indirect, either in the safe arrival of the ship in relation to which the contract is made or in the safety or preservation of the subject-matter insured, or a *bonâ fide* expectation of acquiring such an interest. The offender is liable, on summary conviction, to imprisonment for not more than six months, with or without hard labour, or to a fine not exceeding 100*l.*, and also to forfeit to the Crown any money he may receive under the contract (*d*). It is also an offence under this Act, entailing the same penalties, for any person in the employment of the owner (*e*) of a ship, not being a part-owner, to effect a contract of marine insurance in relation to the ship, "interest or no interest," or "without further proof of interest than the policy itself," or "without benefit of salvage to the insurer," or subject to any other like term (*f*). Further, any broker or other person through

---

(*b*) For the effect of the Gaming Act, 1845, see Fitch *v.* Jones (1855), 5 E. & B. 238; per Lush, J., Haigh *v.* Sheffield Town Council (1874), L. R. 10 Q. B. 102, 109; Beeston *v.* Beeston (1875), 1 Ex. D. 13; per Hawkins, J., Read *v.* Anderson (1882), 10 Q. B. D. 100, 104; per Bowen, L. J., Bridger *v.* Savage (1885), 15 Q. B. D. 363, 367; Powell *v.* Kempton Park Racecourse Co., [1899] A. C. 143, 170; Hyams *v.* Stuart King, [1908] 2 K. B. 696, 707, 727.

(*c*) For the text of this Act, see Vol. II. Appendix A.

(*d*) Mar. Ins. Act, 1909, s. 1, sub-s. 1 (a).

(*e*) "Owner" includes "charterer": Mar. Ins. Act, 1909, s. 1 (8).

(*f*) Mar. Ins. Act, 1909, s. 1, sub-s. 1 (b).

whom, and any insurer with whom, an insurance is effected is also guilty of an offence, punishable in like manner, if he acted with knowledge that the insurance was one prohibited by this Act (*g*). Proceedings under the Act cannot be instituted without the consent in England or Ireland of the Attorney-General, or in Scotland of the Lord Advocate; nor can they be instituted against any person (except one in the employment of the shipowner who has effected an honour policy), until an opportunity has been afforded him of showing that the contract was not one prohibited by the Act, and any information given by him for that purpose is not admissible in evidence against him (*h*).

Thus the Act of 1909 prohibits, without any qualification, insurances in relation to a ship effected by means of honour policies by persons in the employment of the owners, other than part-owners. Even if the assured had an insurable interest, that fact would afford no defence to a charge under sect. 1, sub-s. (b). On the other hand, it seems that an insurance effected by a person who has a genuine interest, direct or indirect, in the subject-matter insured cannot be within sub-s. 1 (a), even though the insurance be made on a valuation so excessive as to render the contract one by way of gaming or wagering within the meaning of the Marine Insurance Act, 1906, s. 4, or of the Gaming Act, 1845, s. 18 (*i*). But when proceedings have been taken under sect. 1, sub-s. 1 (a) of the Act of 1909 against any person who has effected a policy with a " p.p.i." or like clause, the onus of proving that he has not committed an offence of effecting a contract by way of gambling is thrown on him (*k*). One effect of the Act is, no doubt, that a broker who has committed an offence by knowingly making a contract prohibited by the Act cannot claim any remuneration or any indemnity from his principal for payments made by him in respect of the transaction (*l*).

Sect. 313a.

(*g*) *Id.* s. 1 (2).
(*h*) *Id.* s. 1 (4).
(*i*) See *infra*, §§ 314, 319.
(*k*) Mar. Ins. Act, 1909, s. 1 (5).
(*l*) See Thacker *v.* Hardy (1878), 4 Q. B. D. 685, 687.

Sect. 314.
Effect of no expectation of interest.

314. Sect. 4 (2) (a) of the Marine Insurance Act, 1906, declares, as we have seen, that a contract of marine insurance is deemed to be a gaming or wagering contract, where the assured has not an insurable interest, and the contract is entered into with no expectation of acquiring one. The words " where the assured has not an insurable interest" apparently relate to the time when the contract is made. By sect. 6 (1) of the Act it is not necessary that the assured should have an insurable interest at this time (*m*). Therefore if he effects the insurance, believing that he will acquire such an interest, and acquires it before the loss, he can recover. But it seems to follow from sect. 4 that if he insures at a time when he has no insurable interest and does not expect to acquire one, he cannot even recover when at the time of the loss he has an insurable interest, though the policy contains no express terms which show that it was intended to be a gaming or wagering contract. Under the Act of Geo. II. it was held that all policies must be taken to be on interest, unless something was stated showing the contrary, and were not valid, whether on foreign or British ships, unless the assured had an interest; and that it was not possible to recover by action upon them without averment of interest, and proof thereof when that averment was traversed (*n*).

Are wager policies void under the Gaming Act, 1845?

315. Whether a policy expressly admitting interest is void under the Gaming Act, 1845 (8 & 9 Vict. c. 109), s. 18, which provides that all contracts or agreements by way of gaming or wagering shall be null and void, is a question which no underwriter has raised. Arnould seemed to think that the policy is void under this Act (*o*). In support of this view it may be argued that the form itself of the policy shows that it was not intended to be a contract of indemnity. Yet the stipulation that proof of interest is dispensed with is not inconsistent with there being an insurable interest in the assured; and as a matter of fact it is well known that these

---

(*m*) See *ante*, § 258.
(*n*) Cousins *v.* Nantes (1811), 3

Taunt. 513.
(*o*) 2nd ed. vol. i. p. 333, n.

policies are constantly effected on behalf of persons who have an interest in the subject of the insurance, sometimes, perhaps, on account of some difficulty in proving interest (p).

It is submitted that a policy in which interest is admitted is not void under the Gaming Act, 1845 (and therefore that the Gaming Act, 1892, has no application to it), if in fact the assured has or expects to acquire such an interest as shows that he did not intend to make a wager (q). If such a policy

---

(p) See per Kennedy, J., in Gedge v. Royal Exchange Ass. Corporation, [1900] 2 Q. B. 214, 223. The fact that there may be a real insurable interest is, no doubt, the reason why Bigham, J., after consulting Mathew, J., announced that he would, with the consent of the parties, hear a case in which the policy contained a "p.p.i." clause, as if the policy did not contain the clause. Buchanan v. Faber (1899), 4 Com. Cas. 227, n. In a later case, where there was no agreement that the clause should be deemed to be deleted, and the assured was relying on the fact that the Act of George II. was not pleaded to enable him to recover without having any insurable interest, Kennedy, J., held that he was bound to take notice of the illegality and the fact that the insurance was a mere wager. Gedge v. Royal Exchange Ass. Corporation, supra. Wager policies are no longer prohibited in terms, as they were by 19 Geo. 2, c. 37; they are only declared to be void (see infra, note (q)). Yet, even though it be not pleaded that a "p.p.i." policy is void under sect. 4 of the Mar. Ins. Act, 1906, or under the Gaming Act, 1845, it seems, according to the decision of the Divisional Court in Luckett v. Wood (1908), 26 Times L. R. 617, to be the duty of the Court, in an action on the policy, to take notice of the fact that the contract is not enforceable. See also North-Western Salt Co. v. Electrolytic Alkali Co., [1913] 3 K. B. 422 (C. A.).

(q) "The Act," said Willes, J., "has no application to a contract upon a matter in which the parties have an interest." Wilson v. Jones (1867), L. R. 2 Ex. 139. Cf. however, Lord Shaw's *dictum* in Thames & Mersey Mar. Ins. Co. v. "Gunford" Ship Co., [1911] A. C. at p. 543. It may be pointed out that under the Gaming Act, 1892, any promise, express or implied, to repay any sum of money paid in respect of a contract made void by 8 & 9 Vict. c. 109, or to pay any money by way of commission, reward, or otherwise in respect of such contract or of any services in relation thereto, is null and void. See Tatam v. Reeve, [1893] 1 Q. B. 44; 62 L. J. Q. B. 30; De Mattos v. Benjamin (1894), 63 L. J. Q. B. 248; Saffery v. Mayer, [1901] 1 Q. B. 11. In Tasker v. Scott (1815), 6 Taunt. 234, Gibbs, C. J., held that a person who authorized another to effect a wager policy was liable to repay him the premium, on the ground that 19 Geo. 2, c. 37, made the insurance, not illegal, but only unavailable. In Allkins v. Jupe (1877), 2 C. P. D. 375, the Court

Sect. 315. has hitherto not been within the Gaming Acts, it is apprehended that it is not brought within those Acts by sect. 4 (2) of the Marine Insurance Act, 1906, which declares that every policy containing a "p.p.i." clause is deemed to be a gaming or wagering contract. The definition of such a contract for the purposes of the Marine Insurance Act, 1906, cannot, it is submitted, enlarge the meaning of the term "contracts by way of gaming or wagering" in the Gaming Act, 1845 (*r*).

Dictum that wager policies vitiate other insurances.

315a. The "Gunford" case, in which insurances on a vessel were held to be avoided by the concealment of a large over-insurance by means of "p.p.i." policies on disbursements, elicited a remarkable *dictum* of Lord Shaw of Dunfermline's that such policies, apart from the effect of their non-disclosure, vitiate all other insurances effected by the same assured on the same adventure (*s*). "It is necessary," said his Lordship, "to examine fundamentally the position of an owner who has made legitimate insurances upon ship, cargo, or freight, and also made separate gambling insurances. My Lords, it appears to me that, whenever owners enter into gambling transactions of this kind, these transactions themselves are not only invalid, but they infect and invalidate the entire insurances which the same assured have made upon vessel, freight, or cargo. The reason of that is this: the voyage is one, and the ship, its earnings, its cargo, its crew, all are involved in that one and single hazard which has been undertaken and which is by the gambling transaction improperly weighted towards loss—a loss which, falling upon

---

of Common Pleas held that wager policies were rendered illegal by 19 Geo. 2, c. 37. Sect. 4 of the Mar. Ins. Act, 1906, however, only declares that wager policies are void. Read *v.* Anderson (1884), 13 Q. B. D. 779 (C. A.), is therefore an authority in support of the liability of the assured to repay the premium, if the Gaming Acts be not applicable, unless the agent in effecting a wager policy was guilty of an offence under the Marine Ins. Act, 1909 (see *ante*, § 313a).

(*r*) Mr. Arthur Cohen comes to the same conclusion on this point: see Halsbury's Laws of England, vol. xvii. § 746.

(*s*) Thames & Mersey Mar. Ins. Co. *v.* "Gunford" Ship Co., [1911] A. C. 529, 543. This question was not raised by the appellants' case; they relied entirely on the concealment.

the ship, would not rest there, but spread to unsalved cargo and to freight, not to speak of the peril to human life which would be thus encountered. The line of plain duty for all parties to the contract is that the ship shall be preserved; but when a gamble has been made by one of the parties for gain upon the event of loss of ship, although the subject of the particular gamble be not the ship itself, the interest of that party is that the ship shall be destroyed. This hazard against the life of the vessel humbly appears to me to taint every policy entered upon by the same gambling adventurer, and no such policy thus depending upon the same hazard is enforceable. The rule governing this is simple and familiar, namely, that the law will not enforce a transaction which is thus tainted by conflict between duty and self-interest. The rarity and difficulty, my Lords, of a right adjustment of the wavering balance swayed by self-interest have been memorably phrased. But the law does not attempt the task; the penalty against such a conflict between interest and duty is the invalidation of the bargain. I remark, however, that the foregoing observations are not directed to the case of insurance upon ships in which third parties have acquired, in ignorance of the other and over-insurances and in good faith and for valuable consideration, separate interests. The rights of such parties would require to be separately and fully considered."

The editors are not aware that there is any direct authority, except this *dictum*, for the general proposition that an insurance otherwise valid will be vitiated by the gambling nature of an independent insurance effected by the same assured.

316. We will now consider some of the cases on the question what policies are or are not within the prohibition contained in the first section of 19 Geo. 2, c. 37, and the fourth section of the Marine Insurance Act, 1906.

Sect. 315a.

Cases on 19 Geo. 2, c. 37.

Where the surgeon of an East Indiaman agreed to pay 20*l*. to a passenger in the same ship at the next port she should reach, provided that if she did not save her passage to China, the passenger should pay him 1,000*l*. within one month after

Kent *v.* Bird.

430   INSURABLE INTEREST.   [PART I.

Sect. 316. her arrival in the river Thames, without reference to any property; this agreement was held void, as being a contract by way of gaming or wagering within the first section of the stat. 19 Geo. 2, c. 37, though the surgeon had some goods on board which were liable to suffer by the loss of the season (*t*).

Lowry v. Bourdieu. Lowry, having advanced to Lawson, the captain of an East India ship, 26,000*l*. on the security of a common money bond, effected a policy for the amount, which appeared on the face of it to be "on Captain Lawson's bond for 26,000*l*."—"in case of loss no other proof of interest to be required than the bond, warranted free of average, and without benefit of salvage to the insurer,"—Lord Mansfield, Ashurst, J., and Buller, J., held that this was void, as a gaming policy under the statute. "The plaintiffs," observed his Lordship, "say, 'We mean to game, but we give our reason for it: Captain Lawson owes us a sum of money, and we want to be secure in case he should not be in a situation to pay us.' It was a hedge; but they had no interest: for if the ship had been lost, and the underwriters had paid, still the plaintiffs would have been entitled to recover the amount of the bond from Lawson" (*u*).

Rule. 317. Any policy which by express terms dispensed with all proof of interest was held to be within the Act of 19 Geo. 2, c. 37, and void, though the clause by which the proof of interest was dispensed with was not in terms identical with those specified in the first section, even when it was manifest that the insurance was not a gaming one (*x*).

(*t*) Kent *v.* Bird (1777), 2 Cowp. 583. The 20*l*. which the surgeon had paid by way of premium was returned. See also Gedge *v.* Royal Exchange Ass. Co., [1900] 2 Q. B. 214.

(*u*) Lowry *v.* Bourdieu (1780), 2 Dougl. 468. Willes, J., only thought it an unavailable, not an illegal, insurance; the rest of the Court, however, holding it illegal, the premium was not returned.

(*x*) Murphy *v.* Bell (1828), 4 Bing. 567; Berridge *v.* Man On Ins. Co. (C. A.) (1887), 18 Q. B. D. 346. In the latter case the clause was "Full interest admitted." In Grant *v.* Parkinson (1782), 2 Park, 561, the terms of an insurance on profits were: "In case of loss it

CHAP. XII.] WAGER POLICIES. 431

Hence, where a policy of insurance stipulated "that the goods insured were and should be valued at five tierces coffee, valued at 27*l*. per tierce, say 135*l*., that policy to be deemed sufficient proof of interest," the Court of Common Pleas held that the policy was void, for the object of the statute was to prevent insurances in which the policy was to be proof, not of the amount, but of the existence of interest (*y*).

<small>Sect. 317.
Murphy *v.* Bell.</small>

Sect. 4 (2) of the Marine Insurance Act, 1906, expressly includes in the definition of gaming and wagering contracts policies subject to any term like those previously specified.

<small>"Any other like term."</small>

It has been held that a stipulation in one of the Institute Time Clauses that, in the event of a total loss of ship, the freight insurance should be paid "in full" was not equivalent to a stipulation that it should be paid "without benefit of salvage" (*z*).

<small>Insurance to be paid "in full."</small>

318. It was thought at one time that all valued policies were within 19 Geo. 2, c. 37, on the ground that frauds by the wilful loss or destruction of ships and cargoes might be accomplished by means of policies in which a higher value is put on the articles insured than they were worth; but the distinction between wager and valued policies is very clear. If the policy dispenses with all proof of the existence of interest, it is a wager policy, and void; but where the policy contains on the face of it no such dispensation, but only saves the plaintiff the trouble of showing the amount of his interest, leaving him still to prove some interest, it is a valued policy and good (*a*).

<small>Valued policies not within the Act:</small>

319. If, indeed, there appears to be an enormous disproportion between the real value of the articles insured and that inserted in the policy as their agreed value between the

<small>unless valuation enormously exaggerated.</small>

---

is agreed that the profits shall be valued at 1,000*l*., without any other voucher than the policy." The Court held that the last words were mere surplusage, referring to the valuation, not the interest, and that the policy was valid.

(*y*) Murphy *v.* Bell, *supra*.
(*z*) Coker *v.* Bolton, [1912] 3 K. B. 315, Hamilton, J.
(*a*) Lewis *v.* Rucker (1761), 2 Burr. 1171; Murphy *v.* Bell (1828), 4 Bing. 572.

Sect. 319. parties—for instance, if, in the words of Lord Mansfield, "it should come out in proof that a man had insured 2,000*l*., and had interest on board to the value of a cable only"—such policy, it was said, would have been within 19 Geo. 2, c. 37, and on that ground void, though the underwriter was aware of the extent of the over-valuation (*b*). Such a case is not covered by the definition of a gaming and wagering contract in sect. 4 (2) of the Marine Insurance Act, 1906 (*c*). It is, however, submitted that sect. 4 (2) is not exhaustive, and has, therefore, not the effect of preventing such a policy from being void under sect. 4 (1) (*d*). Of course, if the underwriter was kept ignorant of the excessive valuation he might avoid the policy on the ground of such concealment (*e*).

Exceptions made by 19 Geo. 2, c. 37, abolished by the Mar. Ins. Act.

320. From the prohibition of all wager policies on British ships and goods, 19 Geo. 2, c. 37, made an exception in the case of insurances on privateers and on effects from places in the possession of the Crowns of Spain and Portugal. As we have seen, the Marine Insurance Act, 1906, which repeals the whole Act of 19 Geo. 2, declares all wager policies, without exception, to be void.

Incidents of a wager policy.

It has been held that there can be no abandonment under a wagering policy (*f*); also that a recapture, after the ship has been in an enemy's port, will not avail the underwriter (*g*).

(*b*) Lewis *v.* Rucker, *quâ supra.* "In the absence of proof," said Willes, J., "that the value fixed by the contract is so exaggerated as to be a mere cloak for gambling, in representing more than any possible interest which the assured could have in the ship and outfit, or that the exaggeration was fraudulent with a view to cheat the underwriter, the latter is bound in case of total loss to pay the agreed sum." (Memorandum printed as App. LVII. to vol. ii. of the Report of the Unseaworthy Ships Commission of 1874; cited by Mathew, J., in Herring *v.* Janson (1895), 1 Com. Cas. 177.)

(*c*) *Ante*, § 313.

(*d*) This submission is not inconsistent with the language of s. 27 (3) of the Mar. Ins. Act, 1906, *post*, § 338; and the *dicta* of Lord Shaw and Lord Robson in Thames & Mersey Mar. Ins. Co. *v.* "Gunford" Ship Co., [1911] A. C. at pp. 542, 548, were probably not intended to apply to the case under discussion.

(*e*) *Post*, § 604.

(*f*) Kulen Kemp *v.* Vigne (1786), 1 T. R. 304.

(*g*) Dean *v.* Dicker (1746), 2 Str. 1250.

321. It is not only in our own country that insurances by way of wager are held illegal; in most countries their illegality is equally established by general mercantile usage or positive enactment.

Sect. 321. Wagering policies are illegal in most foreign countries.

In France, though not prohibited in express terms, they were held unlawful as opposed to the spirit of the Ordonnance de la Marine (*h*) and the text of the Code Civil (*i*). When the provisions of the Code de Commerce were under the consideration of the French legislature, an attempt was made to procure the protection of the law for this species of contract, but it was immediately checked by the indignant exclamation of the Imperial orator, that "it was not for a great nation like France to legalize the immorality of gambling contracts (*des paris*)" (*k*).

In France.

In the greater number of the United States of America these policies, though not prohibited by positive statute, have invariably been considered illegal (*l*). In New York, however, they were held legal (*m*), but are now prohibited by the revised statutes of that State (*n*).

In the United States.

322. After an insurance has been made, the underwriter may, by the law and practice of all countries (*o*), have the

Re-insurance.

(*h*) L. 3, t. 6, art. 22, 23; 2 Valin, Comment. sur l'Ordonnance de la marine, vol. ii. p. 73, ed. 1766; pp. 286—290, ed. Becane, A.D. 1829.

(*i*) Code Civil, art. 1965, 1966, which declares all wagers illegal. The Code de Commerce, says Boulay-Paty, cannot be more indulgent on this point than the Code Civil, Droit Mar. tom. iii. tit. x. p. 238. They seem now to be impliedly prohibited by art. 334 of the Code de Commerce as altered in 1885. The article formerly began: "L'assurance peut avoir pour objet" (the various subjects of insurance); now it runs: "Toute personne intéressée peut faire assurer," &c.

(*k*) See Estrangin, note to

Pothier, Traité d'Assurance, p. 14; Boulay-Paty, *quâ supra*, note by M. Becane to his edition of Valin, tom. ii. p. 285.

(*l*) 1 Phillips, Ins. ss. 5, 7, 211; 3 Kent, Com. 277, n. (*d*). According to American law "p.p.i." policies are not necessarily treated as wagering policies; they are deemed to be policies on interest, if the parties so intended: Brown *v.* Merchants' Mar. Ins. Co. (1907), 152 Fed. R. 411. See also 1 Phillips, s. 7.

(*m*) Juhel *v.* Church (1801), 2 Johnson's Cases, 333.

(*n*) N. Y. Rev. St. Pt. I. c. xx. tit. viii. ss. 8, 9, 10, cited in Kent's Com., *ubi supra*.

(*o*) Re-insurances are expressly

Sect. 322. whole amount at risk (or, as in France, the whole minus the premium) re-insured to him by some other underwriter. The object of this is to enable him to indemnify himself against the consequences of his own act, whenever he finds he has undertaken a risk on imprudent terms or bound himself to a greater amount than he may be able to discharge (*p*). If he gives a less premium for the re-insurance than he receives on the original policy, he gains the difference; he gains nothing if he gives the same premium, and suffers a loss if he gives more, as may sometimes happen, to cover a dangerous risk.

Formerly illegal in this country.

This means of protection for insurers was formerly illegal by the law of this country. About the middle of the eighteenth century this practice of re-insurance, having in this country come to be employed as a mode of speculating in the rise and fall of premiums, and being likely to be used as a cover for wager policies, was declared by the 4th section of the 19 Geo. 2, c. 37, unlawful, unless the insurer were insolvent, bankrupt, or dead. This was repealed and re-insurances made lawful by the 27 & 28 Vict. c. 56, s. 1 (*q*). Now by sect. 9 of the Marine Insurance Act, 1906—

Now permitted.

Mar. Ins. Act, 1906, s. 9.

(1) The insurer under a contract of marine insurance has an insurable interest in his risk, and may re-insure in respect of it.

(2) Unless the policy otherwise provides, the original assured has no right or interest in respect of such re-insurance.

323. There have been several decisions in our Courts within the last few years upon policies which happened, in

sanctioned by most of the Continental Commercial Codes. See that of France, art. 342; Spain, art. 749; Italy, art. 426; Germany, art. 779; Holland, art. 271; Scandinavia, art. 230. They are permitted in the United States, 3 Kent, Com. 278. See also 1 Emerigon, c. viii. ss. 14, 15, 16, pp. 252—261; 3 Boulay-Paty, Droit Mar. 429— 446; 1 Benecke, 281—289.

(*p*) A policy of re-insurance is, however, not a mere contract of indemnity. See Nelson *v.* Empress Assurance Corporation (1905), 10 Com. Cas. 237 (C. A.), *infra*, § 323.

(*q*) This statute was repealed by 30 & 31 Vict. c. 23, the schedule to which again repealed 19 Geo. 2, c. 37, s. 4.

fact, to be policies of re-insurance. This is a circumstance which is interesting as illustrating the large extent to which policies of this nature are now used. The decisions themselves, however, do not turn as a rule upon questions peculiar to re-insurance, and will be found to be noticed in their proper places so far as they illustrate any points of marine insurance law in general. The law relating to contracts of re-insurance is, generally speaking and apart from special circumstances, the same as that which governs the original contract.

Sect. 323.

The thing which the re-assured insures is the thing originally insured. In this thing he has an insurable interest to the extent of the liability which he may incur under and by reason of his original contract of insurance (*r*). As it is, apart from usage, never necessary in a contract of insurance to describe the interest of the assured, but is sufficient to specify simply what is the thing insured, it follows that a contract of re-insurance need only show that the thing intended to be covered is ship, freight, goods, or whatever it may be; it is not as a matter of law necessary that it should appear on the face of it to be a contract of re-insurance (*s*). In English policies, however, it is now an almost universal practice to insert in re-insurance policies a clause (the effect of which will be discussed hereafter) by which this particular circumstance is specially called to the underwriter's attention (*t*). And though, generally speaking, it seems unneces-

The re-insurance contract.

(*r*) "A policy of re-insurance is a policy on an interest in the subject-matter of the insurance, that interest being different from that protected by the original policy and acquired by the fact that the assured is the underwriter under the original policy": per Mathew, L. J., in Nelson v. Empress Assurance Corporation (1905), 10 Com. Cas. 237, 240.

(*s*) Mar. Ins. Act, 1906, s. 26, *ante*, §§ 251, 252; Mackenzie v. Whitworth (1875), L. R. 10 Ex. 142; 1 Ex. D. 36 (C. A.). By the 19 Geo. 2, c. 37, the policy was required to express that it was a re-insurance, and this remained the law till 1867.

(*t*) In Mackenzie v. Whitworth, *ubi supra*, a Liverpool jury refused to find for an underwriter upon the issue that the fact that the contract is one of re-insurance must be disclosed. A Commons' amendment to sect. 18 of the Marine Insurance Bill declared that "the fact that a policy is effected by way of re-

Sect. 323. sary to disclose the fact that the risk is one of re-insurance, there might in a particular case be circumstances attending the original contract which would affect the mind of a re-insurer. If, for instance, the original assured were known to the original insurer to be a person who on previous occasions had attempted to defraud his underwriters, it might be incumbent on the original insurer to disclose to a re-insurer the character of the original assured, and therefore also the fact that the risk is one of re-insurance (*u*).

Definition of re-insurance.

324. Re-insurance is defined to be a contract by which, in consideration of a certain premium, the original insurer throws upon another the risk for which he has made himself responsible to the original assured, to whom, however, he alone remains liable on the original insurance (*x*).

Totally distinct from the original insurance.

Sect. 9 (2) of the Marine Insurance Act, 1906, states that "unless the policy otherwise provides, the original assured has no right or interest in respect of such insurance." Thus, in general, the contract of re-insurance is totally distinct from and unconnected with the original insurance (*y*); the original assured has no kind of claim against the re-insurer, or against any moneys paid by the re-insurer to the re-assured (*z*). The re-assured remains solely liable on the original insurance and alone has any claim against the re-insurer (*a*).

Hence, supposing the original insurer to have become bankrupt and the assured to have been paid a small dividend out of his estate, the re-insurer is still liable to pay the whole

insurance is material," but it was not agreed to by the House of Lords.

(*u*) Cf. New York Bowery Fire Ins. Co. *v.* N. Y. Fire Ins. Co. (1837), 17 Wend. 359.

(*x*) 1 Emerigon, c. viii. s. 14, p. 252; 3 Boulay-Paty, Droit Mar. 329.

(*y*) See Nelson *v.* Empress Assurance Corporation (1905), 10 Com. Cas. 237, in which the Court of Appeal held that the original insurer cannot bring the re-insurers in as third parties to an action on the original policy.

(*z*) Herckenrath *v.* The American Mut. Ins. Co. (1848), 3 Barb. Ch. N. Y. 63; 1 Parsons, 301.

(*a*) Le premier contrat subsiste tel qu'il a été conçu, sans novation ni altération. La réassurance est absolument étrangère à l'assuré primitif, avec le quel le réassureur ne contracte aucune sorte d'obligation: 1 Emerigon, c. viii. s. 14, p. 252.

amount of the re-insurance to the trustee of the original insurer and not merely the dividend (*b*).

The re-assured, in order to recover against the re-insurers, must prove the loss in the same manner as the original assured must have proved it against them (*c*). The re-insurers are entitled to raise all defences which were open to the re-assured against the original assured (*d*), and they are also entitled in the action to have from the re-assured all the information and assistance which the latter were entitled to have from the original assured (*e*). If the original insurance was in fact void, this affords a good defence to the re-insurers, although there may have been no irregularity in connection with the contract of re-insurance, and although the re-assured may not have availed themselves of the defect in the original policy and may actually have paid thereon (*f*); for the re-assured, not being themselves really liable, had no insurable interest. Whether or not the same reasoning would be applied to a case where the original insurance was not void, but voidable merely, and

_{Sect. 324.}

_{Defences open to re-insurers.}

(*b*) Herckenrath *v.* The American Mut. Ins. Co., *ubi supra;* 2 Phillips, s. 1752; 1 Parsons, 300; Emerigon, 253. In In re Eddystone Marine Insurance Co., [1892] 2 Ch. 423, where the policy of re-insurance contained the words "to pay as may be paid thereon," the re-assured, who had paid nothing to the original assured, were nevertheless held entitled to recover the whole sum from their re-insurers. So, in the United States, Allemannia Ins. Co. *v.* Firemen's Ins. Co. (1907), 209 U. S. 326. In British Dominions Gen. Ins. Co. *v.* Duder, [1914] W. N. 311, Bailhache, J., held that re-insurers, who had refused to agree to a compromise with the original assured, were not entitled to the benefit of it, but must pay in full.

(*c*) Chippendale *v.* Holt (1895), 65 L. J. Q. B. 104; 1 Com. Cas. 197; 1 Parsons, 301.

(*d*) See Marten *v.* Steamship Owners' Underwriting Association (1902), 7 Com. Cas. 195, in which Bigham, J., held that in an action for a constructive total loss the re-insurers could set up a clause in the original policy providing that the insured value of the ship should be taken to be her repaired value.

(*e*) Thus the re-insurers are entitled to an affidavit of ship's papers, though they be not in the custody of the plaintiffs: China Traders Ins. Co. *v.* Royal Exchange Ass. Co., [1898] 2 Q. B. 187 (C. A.).

(*f*) The position is apparently the same even when the policy contains the clause "to pay as may be paid thereon": Chippendale *v.* Holt, *ubi supra*. See per Bigham, J., Western Assurance Co. of Toronto *v.* Poole, [1903] 1 K. B. 376, 386.

Sect. 324. where the original insurer has elected to waive the irregularity and has affirmed the contract after becoming aware of it, is a different question. It might be considered, under such circumstances, that no such election to affirm the contract should be allowed to prejudice the re-insurer, unless he also has agreed thereto, or should preclude him from contending that the original insurer need not, but for such election, have come under any liability on his contract.

It may even happen that a re-insurer has additional defences which were not open to the re-assured; for example, the original insurance may have been regularly effected, but the re-insurance may be voidable for concealment (*g*) or misrepresentation, or on any other grounds.

325. Likewise it appears that there may be cases in which the liability of a re-insurer may, even as regards amount, and even where the policies are in the same terms, be either greater or less than that of the re-assured (*h*). This result seems to be brought about by the operation of the suing and labouring clause.

Effect of suing and labouring clause in re-insurance contracts.

For example, let us suppose A., a shipowner, to abandon his vessel to B., his underwriter, who has in turn re-insured with C. B. spends 1,000*l.* in fruitless endeavours to save the vessel, which is worth 10,000*l.* B. only pays A. 10,000*l.*, the value of the vessel, but by virtue of the suing and labouring clause recovers 1,000*l.* beyond that sum from C. It is surprising, however, to note that if C. have re-insured with D., the latter is not necessarily liable for the whole of the 11,000*l.* which C. has paid B., even although all the policies contain the suing and labouring clause, and although C.'s re-insurance with D. was for the same amount as B.'s re-insurance with C. For in order to entitle C. to recover

---

(*g*) See Property Ins. Co. *v.* National Protector Ins. Co. (1913), 18 Com. Cas. 119. A possible example is New York Bowery Fire Ins. Co. *v.* N. Y. Fire Ins. Co. (1837), 17 Wend. 359.

(*h*) Phillips, vol. ii. s. 1751, citing Herckenrath *v.* American Mut. Ins. Co., 3 Barbour's Ch. R. 63, probably goes too far in stating that a re-insurer is never liable beyond the amount for which the insurer is legally liable.

the additional 1,000*l.* from D., the former would have to show that he or his agents had sued or laboured for the safety of the vessel. But inasmuch as the expense was incurred not by C. but by B., it seems to follow that C., although he has properly paid 11,000*l.* to B., nevertheless can only recover 10,000*l.* from D. This somewhat anomalous result seems to follow from the decision of the Court of Appeal in Uzielli *v.* The Boston Marine Insurance Co. (*i*). The facts of that case may be shortly summarized as follow. The "Rosa Middleton" was insured at Lloyd's for 1,500*l.* The Lloyd's underwriters re-insured with the plaintiffs, who in their turn re-insured with the defendants for the sum of 1,000*l.* The vessel became a constructive total loss, which the Lloyd's underwriters compromised by a payment of 88 per cent. They had, however, spent sums amounting to 24 per cent. in getting the ship off, and were entitled to recover the total, or 112 per cent., by virtue of the suing and labouring clause, from the plaintiffs. For this 112 per cent. the plaintiffs then brought their action against the defendants, claiming accordingly the sum of 1,120*l.*, and relying on the suing and labouring clause, and also on the clause by which the defendants undertook to pay as might be paid on the policy entered into between the plaintiffs and the Lloyd's underwriters. Mathew, J., gave judgment for the plaintiffs for the whole sum claimed, but the Court of Appeal held that the suing and labouring clause did not apply, and that the other special clause extended the liability of the defendants to 1,000*l.*, the sum for which they had insured, but not beyond (*k*).

Sect. 325.

Uzielli *v.* Boston Marine Insurance Co.

326. A question has been raised amongst foreign jurists as to whether, in an open policy of re-insurance, the re-assured is entitled to recover the whole amount of the original

Amount recoverable on open policy of re-insurance.

(*i*) (1884), 15 Q. B. D. 11. See Bigham, J.'s remarks on this case in Western Assurance Co. of Toronto *v.* Poole, [1903] 1 K. B. 376.

(*k*) The special clause is here noticed incidentally only; it is proposed to discuss it in more detail subsequently.

Sect. 326. insurance without deducting therefrom the premiums of the original insurance or the premium of the premium. Emerigon (*l*) supported the practice, which was stated by Arnould (*m*) to prevail in every other foreign country except France, whereby the whole amount was recoverable. But Pothier (*n*), Valin (*o*), Estrangin (*p*), and Boulay-Paty (*q*) were all opposed to Emerigon on the point upon the ground that, the premium of the original insurance having been already paid to the underwriter, he runs no risk upon it and therefore cannot insure it.

Re-insurer not entitled to notice of abandonment.

In cases of constructive total loss the re-assured need not give notice of abandonment to the re-insurer (*r*).

Expense of resisting original claim.

It has been held in the United States that the amount of loss recoverable on a policy of re-insurance will include the expense of resisting the claim of the original assured, provided the original insurer was justified in contesting the claim (*s*).

The re-insurance clause, "to pay as may be paid thereon."

327. It now remains to consider the effect of a clause which is found almost universally in policies of re-insurance. The clause is to the following effect:—" Being a re-insurance, subject to the same clauses and conditions as the original policy, and to pay as may be paid thereon" (*t*).

It has been decided that this clause does not preclude the re-insurer from insisting upon proper proof that a loss strictly within the terms of the original policy has taken place. Where, therefore, the plaintiffs, who were the original insurers, had accepted a notice of abandonment, and actually

---

(*l*) Vol. i. c. viii. s. 14, sub-s. 4, pp. 253—256.

(*m*) 2nd ed. p. 341.

(*n*) D'Assurance, No. 36.

(*o*) Comment. vol. ii. p. 279.

(*p*) Comment. on Pothier, No. 36, p. 46.

(*q*) 3 Droit Mar. tit. x. s. 10, p. 429 *et seq.*

(*r*) Mar. Ins. Act, 1906, s. 62 (9). See *post*, § 1191.

(*s*) Hastie *v.* De Peyster (1805), 3 Caines, 190; N. Y. State Ins. Co. *v.* Protection Ins. Co. (1841), 1 Story, 458; 2 Phillips, s. 2145.

(*t*) Commonly known as one of the "rubber clauses," from being usually stamped on the margin of the policy with a rubber stamp. The original policy or policies to which the re-insurance is intended to apply are sometimes specified.

in good faith paid their assured for a constructive total loss, it was held that these facts alone did not entitle them to recover from their re-insurers, without proof that a constructive total loss had in fact occurred (*u*). Conversely, it has been held that where the liability of the original insurer is once established, it is not necessary that he should prove actual payment. The trustee, therefore, of an insolvent underwriter, though he may have paid nothing, or only a small dividend, on the original policy, may nevertheless, notwithstanding the clause, recover from the re-insurers to the full extent of the liability which they have undertaken (*x*).

<small>Sect. 327.</small>

This clause does not enable the original underwriter to recover from his re-insurer to an extent beyond the subscription of the latter. Thus, as we have already seen, in Uzielli *v.* The Boston Marine Insurance Co. (*y*), an underwriter had paid a loss amounting in all to 112*l.* per cent., of which amount 88 per cent. was payable in respect of the constructive total loss of the vessel, and the remaining 24 per cent. for suing and labouring charges. He had re-insured for 1,000*l.* only, but sought to recover 112*l.* per cent. or 1,120*l.*, on his policy of re-insurance. It was held, first, for reasons which we have already explained, that the re-insurer was not liable under the suing and labouring clause; and secondly, that the special clause which we are now considering could not render him liable beyond the amount which he had agreed to re-insure. He was accordingly held liable for 1,000*l.* and no more.

<small>Re-insurer not liable, beyond his subscription, for suing and labouring expenses.</small>

The precise effect of the clause under consideration has not been judicially determined. In one case, Bigham, J., expressed his view as to the effect of a policy of re-insurance on ship containing this clause in the following terms:—" The re-insurer, when called upon to perform his promise, is entitled to require the re-assured first to show that a loss of the

---

(*u*) Chippendale *v.* Holt (1895), 65 L. J. Q. B. 104; 1 Com. Cas. 197. See also Marten *v.* Steamship Owners' Underwriting Association (1902), 7 Com. Cas. 195.
(*x*) See *ante*, § 324.
(*y*) (1884), 15 Q. B. D. 11.

Sect. 327. kind re-insured has in fact happened; and, secondly, that the re-assured has taken all proper and business-like steps to have the amount of it fairly and carefully ascertained. That is all. He must then pay. There is nothing in his contract either express or implied which entitles him to have the ship or to deal with it in any way: though he is, no doubt, entitled to require that the original underwriter should realise it in such a way as to reduce the loss as much as may be reasonably possible. Nor is he entitled to rip up the settlement between the shipowner and the original underwriter, except upon the ground that it is dishonest, or has been arrived at carelessly. So long as liability exists, the mere fact of some honest mistake having occurred in fixing the exact amount of it will afford no excuse for not paying. He has promised 'to pay as may be paid thereon.' Such is, in my opinion, the meaning and effect of these re-insurance policies" (z). If this view be correct, the result is anomalous. The re-insurer is entitled, notwithstanding his promise "to pay as may be paid thereon," to say that the original insurer was not liable to pay anything. Yet he may not say that as regards part of the claim the original insurer was under no liability to pay.

Where original policy and re-insurance policy contain different clauses.

328. Difficult questions have arisen where the policy of re-insurance, while expressed to be subject to the clauses and conditions of the original policy, has been found to contain clauses which are inconsistent with them. Of course, if the re-insurance policy contains a special clause by which it is obviously intended to limit the risks covered by the original policy—as, for example, where the re-insurance is expressed to be against total loss only, or against fire risks only—the risks will be limited accordingly (a). But sometimes the

(z) Western Assurance Co. of Toronto v. Poole, [1903] 1 K. B. 376, 386.

(a) See Chippendale v. Holt and Marten v. Steamship Owners' Underwriting Association, *ante*, § 327. Where the clause, after stating that the re-insurance was against total or constructive total loss only, ended with the words "but to follow hull underwriters in event of a compromised or arranged loss being settled," and a claim against these underwriters

RE-INSURANCE.

intention of the parties has not been so obvious. In Joyce *v.* Realm Marine Insurance Co. (*b*), the original insurance was on cargo, for voyages both outward and homeward between Liverpool and West African ports, and it was declared that outward cargoes should be considered as homeward interest twenty-four hours after the vessel's arrival at her first port of discharge. The re-insurance policy was upon cargo, at and from West African ports to the vessel's ports of discharge in the United Kingdom, "to commence from the loading of the goods at as above." Goods shipped at Liverpool were lost more than twenty-four hours after the ship's arrival at her first port of discharge in West Africa. The re-insurers contended that their risk had not attached, inasmuch as the goods had not been loaded on the coast of Africa. The Court of Queen's Bench, however, held that the clause in the original policy prevailed, and that the re-insurers were therefore liable.

Joyce v. Realm Insurance Co.

In 1888 Day, J., appears to have held that where a twelve months' policy expired on 1st June, 1883, subject, however, to a "continuation clause," which provided that if at the expiration of the twelve months the ship should be at any place other than her home port of discharge in Europe, the risk should be prolonged until her arrival at such port, the clause under discussion did not extend the liability of re-insurers so as to render them responsible for a loss which took place after the expiration of the twelve months, and was only covered by the continuation clause. He considered that time was of the essence of a contract of this description, and that the clause only incorporated such conditions as were applicable to an insurance ending on the 1st June, 1883 (*c*).

Franco-Hungarian Insurance Co. v. Merchants' Marine Insurance Co.

---

for a constructive total loss or in the alternative for a partial loss had been compromised for a considerable sum, Bray, J., held that the re-insurers were liable: Street *v.* Royal Exchange Ass. (1913), 18 Com. Cas. 284; and his decision was affirmed by the Court of Appeal, [1914] W. N. 197.

(*b*) (1872), L. R. 7 Q. B. 580.

(*c*) Franco-Hungarian Ins. Co. *v.* Merchants' Mar. Ins. Co. (1888), Shipping Gazette Weekly Summary, 15th June, 1888. The statement of the case is taken from McArthur, p. 336. The validity of

Sect. 328.
Charlesworth v. Faber.

In Charlesworth v. Faber (d) the same question was litigated, and Bigham, J., held that the "continuation clause," being a usual one, was incorporated in the policy of re-insurance. The learned judge distinguished the previous case on the ground that no evidence appeared to have been given before Day, J., to show that the clause was in common use; but such evidence would apparently have been irrelevant, according to the *ratio decidendi* of the case, and the two judgments cannot thus be reconciled.

Marten v. Nippon Sea Insurance Co.

Charlesworth v. Faber is, however, in agreement with the earlier decision of Bigham, J., in Marten v. The Nippon Sea Insurance Co. (e). The original policy, which was on goods at and from Liverpool to Guayaquil until there discharged and safely landed, contained in the margin what is called the "warehouse to warehouse" clause, whereby all risks whatsoever are included until the goods are safely delivered to the consignee. The re-insurance policy contained the usual clause by which the risk is made to determine on the discharge and safe landing of the goods, also the common re-insurance clause. It was held that the "warehouse to warehouse" clause, being such a common clause that the re-insurers ought to have known that it was in the original policy, was incorporated into the policy of re-insurance.

Property Insurance Co. v. National Protector Insurance Co.

The judgment of Scrutton, J., in a recent case seems to be founded on the view that the "rubber" clause has the effect of incorporating unusual as well as usual conditions in the original policy, but that if the original policy contains unusual clauses, the existence of which has not been disclosed to the re-insurer, he may avoid the re-insurance on the ground of concealment. This view accords best with the wording of the clause. In the case in question the clause ran:— "subject without notice to the same clause and conditions, &c." The original insurance in this case gave liberty to navigate the Canadian lakes, and the learned judge held that

a "continuation clause" has been established by legislation: see *post*, § 440.

(d) (1900), 5 Com. Cas. 408.
(e) (1898), 3 Com. Cas. 164.

the clause giving this liberty was so unusual that ordinarily **Sect. 328.**
it ought to be disclosed; but he also held that the effect of the
words "without notice" was that the re-insurers waived information as to unusual conditions in the original policy, and
were liable for a loss which occurred while the insured vessel
was in the lakes (*f*).

328a. The "rubber" re-insurance clause often contains a **To which of several**
blank space intended to be filled up by words identifying the **insurances the**
very policies which it is intended to re-insure. Where this **re-insurance policy applies.**
space is filled up, it seems clear that the re-assured will only **Lower Rhine**
be protected against liabilities incurred under those particular **Co. v. Sedgwick.**
policies. Where the space is not filled up, the presumption
will be that the re-insurance is only against risks actually
existing at the date of the re-insurance policy, and not
against other liabilities which the original insurer may subsequently undertake in relation to the same subject-matter.
At any rate, if subsequent policies are to be covered, they
must not differ in their terms from those of the original
policies (*g*).

In a recent case the re-insurance was expressed to be **Reliance Mar. Ins. Co. v.**
"subject to the same terms, clauses and conditions as the **Duder.**
original policy or policies." The original assured had effected
two insurances on ship for a voyage from Australia to the
West Coast of South America, and a third insurance, with
the same underwriters, at and from ports on the West Coast
to Europe, "risk to commence from expiration of previous
policy." The re-insurance policy was for a voyage at and
from the West Coast to Europe, the termini being described
exactly as in the third policy. A loss took place on the West
Coast, for which the shipowners were paid under the two

(*f*) Property Ins. Co. *v.* National Protector Ins. Co. (1913), 18 Com. Cas. 119. The "original insurance" in this statement of this case was itself a re-insurance.

(*g*) The Lower Rhine Co. *v.* Sedgwick, [1898] 1 Q. B. 739;

[1899] 1 Q. B. 179. The facts of the case are somewhat complicated, but the decision supports the above conclusions. See, as to the grounds of the decision, per Kennedy, L. J., in Reliance Mar. Ins. Co. *v.* Duder, [1913] 1 K. B. 265, 277.

Sect. 328a. earlier policies; but it also occurred within the limits of space and time covered by the words of the re-insurance policy. In answer to a claim on this policy, the re-insurers set up the defence that the original insurers had only intended to re-insure their risk under the third policy, and that they could not recover by reason of sect. 26 (3) of the Marine Insurance Act, 1906. The Court of Appeal, however, while holding that an intention only to cover this risk had not been proved, also said that as the loss was within the terms of the policy of re-insurance, evidence was not admissible of an intention, not communicated to the re-insurer, to re-insure only the risk under one of the original policies (*h*).

Of insuring the solvency of the underwriter.

329. Besides re-insurances, properly so called, *i.e.*, insurances effected by one underwriter with another to secure himself, the assured may also, if he pleases, insure the solvency of the underwriter with whom he has effected the policy. As, however, this practice tends greatly to lessen the profits of the voyage by multiplying the charges of it, it will not frequently be resorted to in any country and appears never to have been in use in our own, though it is neither prohibited by statute nor illegal at common law (*i*).

Double insurance.

330. Double insurance takes place when the assured makes two or more insurances on the same subject, the same risk and the same interest (*j*). It is therefore a totally different

(*h*) Reliance Marine Ins. Co. *v.* Duder, [1913] 1 K. B. 265, Cozens-Hardy, M. R., and Kennedy, L. J. (Buckley, L. J., *dubitante*). See, further, as to this case, *ante*, § 252b. A similar view was expressed by Bray, J., in Scottish National Ins. Co. *v.* Poole (1912), 18 Com. Cas. 9, viz., that the policy of re-insurance applied to any original policy which the original insurers had subscribed at the time when the re-insurer executed the policy, and which corresponded with the terms of the slip that he had initialed.

(*i*) Park on Ins. vol. ii. p. 599, seems to have thought that it would be void as a wager policy under the statute; but Arnould (2nd ed. p. 343) agreed with Benecke that it would be difficult to discover any satisfactory ground for this opinion. Policies guaranteeing the solvency of third parties other than underwriters are sometimes effected at Lloyds: see Seaton *v.* Burnand, [1900] A. C. 135; Hambro *v.* Burnand, [1904] 2 K. B. 10.

(*j*) See Union Mar. Ins. Co. *v.* Martin (1866), 35 L. J. C. P. 181, thing from a re-insurance, which, as we have seen, is effected by the underwriter to secure himself from having to pay a loss.

Double insurances are not prohibited by the law maritime unless made fraudulently: in fact, a moment's consideration will show that they are in many cases of necessary use.

A merchant, who expects consignments from abroad, may be ignorant of their exact value; he may, in the first instance, have effected an insurance on them only to an amount which subsequent information may lead him to think inadequate to cover their full value, and on that ground he may be desirous of effecting a further insurance; or he may have insured as much as he is able in one place, and being desirous of further security may then proceed to effect additional insurances elsewhere. If it turns out that the whole amount insured is greater than the whole value of the interest at risk, this is called an over-insurance.

The legal position when there has been a double insurance resulting in over-insurance is now regulated by sects. 32 and 80 of the Marine Insurance Act, 1906. Sect. 32 is as follows:—

> (1) Where two or more policies are effected by or on behalf of the assured on the same adventure and interest or any part thereof, and the sums insured exceed the indemnity allowed by this Act (k), the assured is said to be over-insured by double insurance.
>
> (2) Where the assured is over-insured by double insurance—
>
>> (a) The assured, unless the policy otherwise provides, may claim payment from the insurers in such order as he may think fit, provided that he is not entitled to receive any sum in excess of the indemnity allowed by this Act;

for a case in which the question arose whether there was a double insurance, or whether the second of two overlapping policies effected with the same insurer was in substitution for the earlier one. As to the "same subject," see the remarks, *infra*, § 331, on disbursement policies.

(k) For the insurable value on which the measure of indemnity (*infra*, § 338) depends, see Mar. Ins. Act, 1906, ss. 16, 27, *infra*, Part I., Chap. XIII,

Sect. 330.

(b) Where the policy under which the assured claims is a valued policy, the assured must give credit as against the valuation for any sum received by him under any other policy without regard to the actual value of the subject-matter insured (*l*);

(c) Where the policy under which the assured claims is an unvalued policy he must give credit, as against the full insurable value, for any sum received by him under any other policy;

(d) Where the assured receives any sum in excess of the indemnity allowed by this Act, he is deemed to hold such sum in trust for the insurers, according to their right of contribution among themselves.

By sect. 80:—

(1) Where the assured is over-insured by double insurance, each insurer is bound, as between himself and the other insurers, to contribute rateably to the loss in proportion to the amount for which he is liable under his contract (*m*).

(2) If any insurer pays more than his proportion of the loss, he is entitled to maintain an action for contribution against the other insurers, and is entitled to the like remedies as a surety who has paid more than his proportion of the debt (*n*).

According to sect. 32, to constitute an over-insurance by double insurance the policies must be on the same adventure and the same interest of the assured. It is possible, in fact, that an insurance on disbursements, though nominally on a different subject-matter from ship or freight, is intended to cover expenditures which are made to earn the freight, and therefore covered by the insurance on the gross freight, or which are made for items ordinarily included in the insurance on ship. In such a case it seems that the policy on

---

(*l*) See *infra*, §§ 349—352, for the effect of different valuations.

(*m*) See the remarks of Hamilton, J., on this provision in American Surety Co. *v.* Wrightson (1910), 16 Com. Cas. 37, 54.

(*n*) See *infra*, § 354, for the adjustment of the contributions when the policies contain different valuations.

disbursements is on the same interest of the assured as that covered by one or the other of the policies on ship or freight, and that there may be an over-insurance by double insurance within the meaning of sect. 32. There are *dicta* in the "Gunford" case to this effect (*o*). When, however, as was done in this case, and is almost invariably done, the insurance on disbursements is made by a "p.p.i." policy, it is submitted that the disbursement policy cannot be taken into account in order to determine, for the purposes of sect. 32, whether there has been an over-insurance. It is implied in sect. 80, which provides for contribution between the different sets of insurers, that the policies are valid policies.

_{Sect. 330.}

331. The rule that now prevails in this country may therefore be summarized as follows: In case of over-insurance the different sets of policies are considered as making but one insurance, and are good to the extent of the value of the effects put in risk; the assured can recover on the different policies no more than their value, but he may sue the underwriters on any of the policies, and recover from those he so sues to the full extent of his loss, supposing it to be covered by the policy on which he elects to sue, leaving the underwriters on that policy to recover a rateable sum by way of contribution from the underwriters on the other policy (*p*). Hence where a merchant, the value of whose whole interest was 2,200*l*., first effected a policy on this interest at Liverpool for 1,700*l*., and then (without fraud) another policy on the same interest (*q*) at London for 2,200*l*., he was allowed to recover the whole amount on the London policy, and the London underwriters were allowed to recover a rateable

_{Rule of contribution in case of over-insurance.}

_{Davis *v.* Gildart.}

(*o*) See Thames & Mersey Mar. Ins. Co. *v.* "Gunford" Ship Co., [1911] A. C. 529, per Lord Alverstone, C. J. (p. 536), and Lord Robson (p. 549).

(*p*) Newby *v.* Reid (1763), 1 W. Bl. 416; Rogers *v.* Davis, and Davis *v.* Gildart (1776), cited 1 Marshall, Ins. 140, 141; 2 Park, Ins. 601. As regards the amount of the contribution, difficulties may arise when some of the policies cover other subject-matters in addition to those covered by a different set: see American Surety Co. *v.* Wrightson (1910), 16 Com. Cas. 37.

(*q*) But for a different risk, see Rogers *v.* Davis, *quâ supra*.

Sect. 331. amount by way of contribution from the Liverpool underwriters (*r*).

Rule in France and the United States. The rule of contribution in cases of over-insurance by double insurance was established by Lord Mansfield (*s*). It is not the rule which formerly prevailed in this country, which now prevails in France, and which in the United States is generally rendered binding on the parties to the second policy by an express clause relating to prior insurance.

That rule is, in the words of the Code de Commerce, "that where there exist several contracts (N.B., not necessarily 'policies') (*t*) of insurance effected without fraud on the same subject, if the first contract insures the total value of the subject at risk, it alone shall be enforced." The insurers who have signed the subsequent contracts are freed from liability, and only receive $\frac{1}{2}$ per cent. on the sum insured.

If the whole value of the subject insured is not covered by the first contract, those insurers who have signed the subsequent contracts shall be responsible for the surplus in the order of the date of their respective signatures (*u*).

Formerly the rule in this country. So in this country it was once pleaded, and "proved by all the exchange," to be the custom of merchants "that where a policy is subscribed by a number of underwriters, and the goods are not equal in value to the sums subscribed (taken together), the underwriters in case of loss shall be liable in the order in which they subscribe, and the remaining underwriters shall be exonerated from all liability and return the premium, deducting $\frac{1}{2}$ per cent." (*v*).

The American clause. The common law rule in the United States is that laid down by Lord Mansfield; but the law as it anciently prevailed in England, and is now established in France, is

---

(*r*) Davis *v.* Gildart, *quà supra*.
(*s*) In Newby *v.* Reid, *supra*.
(*t*) Each subscription to the policy forms a new contract if it bears a separate date.
(*u*) Code de Commerce, art. 359.
(*v*) The African Co. *v.* Bull (1690), 1 Show. 132; see also Malynes, Lex Mercatoria, 112. But the rule in France was never applied to several subscriptions to one policy, unless they bore different dates; and this probably is the true meaning of the English rule.

CHAP. XII.] DOUBLE INSURANCE. 451

deemed by the American merchants so preferable, in point of simplicity and convenience, that clauses are very generally introduced into their policies to prevent the rule of contribution, and to make the insurers responsible according to the order of date of their subscriptions.

The following clause has been used in the second policy for this purpose:—"It is further agreed, that if the assured shall have made any other assurance upon the premises prior in date to this policy, the assurers shall be answerable only for so much as the amount of such prior insurance may be deficient."

The following is a form adapted to the first policy:— "In case of any subsequent assurance, the insurer shall, nevertheless, be answerable for the full extent of the sum subscribed by him without right to claim contribution from subsequent assurers" (x).

In France and in the United States (in cases where this rule has been adopted), it has been decided that, even where the second policy is dated on the same day as the first, inquiry may be made as to which of the two was actually first effected in point of time, and that which was so will alone bear the loss (y).

In France and the United States policies prior in time bear the loss.

This rule, however, does not in France extend to different subscriptions of uniform date to the same policy; for if they all bear one date they make but one contract, and the whole body of the underwriters, in case the sum insured in such policy exceeds the value at risk, contribute rateably to the loss and return a rateable share of premium for the excess (z).

332. Sect. 84 (3) (f) of the Marine Insurance Act, 1906, declares that, subject to the other provisions of the section relating to the return of premium, "where the assured has

Rule as to return of premium in case of over-insurance.

(x) 3 Kent, Com. 281.
(y) 4 Boulay-Paty, Droit Mar. 122, 123; Brown *v.* Hartford Ins. Co. (1808), 3 Day's R. 58; cited 1 Parsons, 287; Potter *v.* Marine Ins. Co. (1822), 2 Mason's R. 475; cited 3 Kent, Com. 281.
(z) 4 Boulay-Paty, Droit Mar. 116, 117.

Sect. 332. over-insured by double insurance, a proportionate part of the several premiums is returnable" (a).

This rule is, however, subject to a limitation expressed in the following proviso:—

> Provided that, if the policies are effected at different times, and any earlier policy has at any time borne the entire risk, or if a claim has been paid on the policy in respect of the full sum insured thereby, no premium is returnable in respect of that policy, and when the double insurance is effected knowingly by the assured no premium is returnable.

The reason why, where two sets of policies of different date are effected on the same property, the underwriters on the later set in point of date are alone called on for a rateable return of premium, if these policies were effected after the risk had attached on the earlier set, is that as the underwriters on the first set of policies were at one time liable to the whole extent of the sum therein insured, so they are fairly entitled to retain the whole premium (b).

The provision that there is no return of premium if the full sum insured has been paid on the policy seems to have made a change in the law. The insurer has a claim for contribution under sect. 80, and the only reason that can be suggested for the provision is that if he be compelled to pay in full, he does run the risk of not recovering the contributions of other underwriters in case of their becoming insolvent (c). The provision that there is to be no return of premium when the double insurance has been effected knowingly also effects a change of law, which seems to have been made with the object of discouraging double insurance (d).

Insurances of different interests in the same subject.

333. Although in cases of double insurance, properly so called, *i.e.*, where the same person insures the same interest by several policies on the same risk, he cannot recover more

(a) See 2 Marshall, Ins. 649.
(b) Fisk *v.* Masterman (1841), 8 M. & W. 165.
(c) See *post*, § 1262, where the effect of this provision is further discussed.
(d) See Chalmers & Owen, Mar. Ins. Act, 2nd ed. 136.

CHAP. XII.] CO-EXISTING INSURABLE INTERESTS. 453

than an indemnity—*i.e.*, more than the real or declared value Sect. 333.
of the thing insured, under all the policies put together—yet
it is different where two or more persons insure the same
thing against the same risks on distinct interests.

In such case each of the parties, having such distinct
interests in the thing insured, may effect insurance in respect
thereof to the full value of the thing insured, and each in
case of loss may recover to the full extent of his interest.

This, as Lord Mansfield remarks, "is by no means within
the idea of a double insurance, which is where the same man
is to receive two sums instead of one, or the same sum twice
over for the same loss by reason of his having made two
insurances upon the same goods or the same ship;" whereas
the case now referred to is the insurance by two different
persons of two different interests each to the whole value.

The doctrine of subrogation must, however, apply in cases Effect of
where more than the value of the thing insured is recovered doctrine of subrogation.
from the underwriters, so that in the result the whole sum
retained by the assured will be no more than such value.
The principle is well illustrated by the following passage
from the judgment of Cotton, L. J., in an action arising out
of a fire insurance:—

"The rule is perfectly established in the case of a marine
policy," said the learned Lord Justice, "that contribution
only applies where it is an insurance by the same person
having the same rights, and does not apply where different
persons insure in respect of different rights. The reason of
that is obvious enough. Where different persons insure the
same property in respect of their different rights, they may
be divided into two classes. It may be that the interest of
the two between them makes up the whole property, as in the
case of a tenant for life and remainderman. Then if each
insures, although they may use words apparently insuring
the whole property, yet they would recover from their respective insurance companies the value of their own interests, and
of course those values added together would make up the
value of the whole property. Therefore it would not be a

Sect. 333. case either of subrogation or contribution, because the loss would be divided between the two companies in proportion to the interests which the respective persons assured had in the property. But then there may be cases where, although two different persons insure in respect of different rights, each of them can recover the whole, as in the case of a mortgagor and mortgagee. But wherever this is the case it will necessarily follow that one of these two has a remedy over against the other, because the same property cannot in value belong at the same time to two different persons. Each of them may have an interest which entitles him to insure for the full value, because in certain events, for instance, if the other person becomes insolvent, it may be he would lose the full value of the property, and therefore would have in law an insurable interest; but yet it must be that if each recover the full value of the property from their respective offices with whom they insure, one office must have a remedy against the other" (e).

Godin *v*. London Ass. Co.

334. The following case was quoted by Arnould as a good illustration of the principle:—

Meybohm, of St. Petersburg, was in debt for advances both to Amyand, of London, and to Tamesz, of Moscow. Under these circumstances, Meybohm wrote to Amyand, who was then in expectation of a consignment from him, to the effect that he should send him goods, as per invoice, and directing him to insure. Amyand, accordingly, who had already insured to a certain extent on the expected consignment, effected a further insurance, thus making the aggregate sum insured by him more than sufficient to cover the full value of the consignment, but less than the amount of the balance then due to him from Meybohm in account. Meybohm shipped the goods as per invoice, but instead of indorsing the bill of lading to Amyand he indorsed it to Tamesz, to whom at that time he was also indebted to a greater amount than the value of the goods shipped.

(e) North British, &c. Ins. Co. *v*. London, Liverpool & Globe Ins. Co. (1877), 5 Ch. D. 583.

CHAP. XII.] INSURABLE INTERESTS.

Sect. 334.

Tamesz subsequently procured a policy to be effected with the London Assurance Company, by Godin & Co., to the full value of the goods, the brokers informing the company of the prior insurance by a prior consignee and that both parties wished to be safe. The ship and goods having been lost, the Court (the judgment of which was delivered by Lord Mansfield) held that Tamesz could recover the full amount of his insurance (*f*).

Remarks on this case.

That Tamesz, indeed, as indorsee of the bill of lading and in advance to Meybohm to a greater amount than the sum insured in the policy, had a clear insurable interest to the full extent of his claim, and therefore might recover the whole sum insured, is a position that can hardly be disputed. Whether Amyand could also recover on the policies effected by him was a point not before the Court, and therefore not decided. Lord Mansfield intimated a pretty clear opinion that he could, on the ground that, as a factor to whom a balance was due, he had under the circumstances an insurable interest distinct from the interest of Meybohm. At all events, his Lordship was clear that, assuming Amyand to have insured as agent only, he had a lien on the policies to the extent of his general balance.

Arnould thought that Lord Mansfield was right in both points, notwithstanding the doubts of Marshall as to the former position (*g*); but that it is, perhaps, safer on the whole to consider the case as a mere illustration of the undoubted principle, "that where each of two parties, having distinct interests in the subject to its full value, insures upon it to its full value, independently of the other, it is not a case of double insurance" (*h*).

Maclachlan maintained, however, that Amyand would not

(*f*) Godin *v.* London Ass. Co. (1758), 1 Burr. 489; 1 W. Bl. 103; 2 Park, Ins. 603 *et seq.*; 1 Marshall, Ins. 143.

(*g*) 1 Marshall, Ins. 145. Judge Duer, vol. ii. p. 163, n., cites Godin *v.* London Ass. Co., with other cases, as an authority for the position that the insurable interest of a factor or consignee is limited to his advances constituting a lien on the property.

(*h*) Phillips, vol. i. p. 209, 3rd ed.

Sect. 334. have been able to recover on his policy. "Amyand," he said, "*primâ facie* at the moment of the shipment had an insurable interest, and he was justified, therefore, in insuring on his own account. But Meybohm held in his hand the power of diverting the goods from Amyand, and exercised this power by indorsing the bill of lading to Tamesz for a debt greater than the value of the goods. That was the annihilation of any insurable interest held by Amyand, without the intervention of any of the perils insured against, and made his policy thenceforward of no effect" (*i*). The conclusion that at the time of the loss Amyand had ceased to have an insurable interest seems sound, and Lord Mansfield's opinion to the contrary is, of course, only an *obiter dictum* (*k*).

Discovery of over-insurance.

335. To enable the defendant to discover whether there was in any case a double or over-insurance, 19 Geo. 2, c. 37, s. 6, entitled him to call upon the plaintiff to declare in writing within fifteen days what sum he had insured on the whole, and how much he had borrowed on bottomry and respondentia for the voyage in question, or any part of it. This provision was not often put into use, perhaps because in most cases the underwriter was able to obtain the information he required by the order for discovery of ship's papers (*l*); and it has not been re-enacted by the Marine Insurance Act, 1906, which has repealed the whole of 19 Geo. 2, c. 37.

(*i*) Arnould, 6th ed. vol. i. p. 120.
(*k*) Phillips (1 Ins. s. 311) seems to agree with Lord Mansfield's opinion.
(*l*) See as to this order, *post*, vol. ii. § 1271.

CHAPTER XIII.

VALUATION OF INSURABLE INTERESTS.

	SECT.		SECT.
Theoretical Principle of Valuation	336, 337	Valued Policies—*contd.* On Freight	358
Practical Principle	338	On Goods	359—361
Valued Policies—		Open Policies— Estimation of Interest and Adjustment	362—364
Effect of Valuation	339—355	On Ship, Freight, Goods,	
On Ship	356, 357	&c.	365—368a

336. THE next point to be considered is the mode of estimating the insurable value of the interest at risk, with a view to procuring indemnity for the assured in case of loss.

Insurance being a contract of indemnity, it should seem that the true principle upon which the interest protected by a policy of insurance ought to be valued, is that which in case of loss will give the assured, as nearly as possible, a complete indemnity against the consequences of such loss. {Theoretical principle of valuation for the purposes of insurance.}

The object, therefore, of such valuation ought in theory to be to place the assured, in case of loss, in exactly the same situation as he would have been in if no loss had taken place.

To apply this principle to the case of ship, goods, and freight. {Applied to insurance on ship and freight.}

337. The ship, in view of modern commerce, is regarded by the shipowner, generally speaking, not so much as an instrument for carrying on his own traffic, as in itself a source of emolument, either by being used as a general ship for the purpose of carrying goods for freight, or by being let out on hire at a stipulated sum under contracts of affreightment. Out of such freight or hire the shipowner has to pay the seamen's wages, to furnish provisions, to {Wear and tear of the ship,}

458 VALUATION OF INSURABLE INTERESTS. [PART I.

Sect. 337.
and other deductions from the freight.

defray the expenses of the voyage, and to make good that diminution in the value of the ship and her apparel which necessarily takes place more or less in the course of every voyage, and which is familiarly called the wear and tear of the ship. What remains of the freight, after deducting these charges and outgoings, is the net profit of the voyage which the shipowner makes by the employment of his capital fixed in the ship.

Now, on the principle of valuation just adverted to, it is plain that the ship, for the purposes of insurance, ought to be estimated at her value after deducting the wear and tear of the voyage, for that is what the ship would have been worth to her owner on arrival but for the loss against which the insurance is intended to indemnify him.

In the same way with regard to freight, the true mode of estimating its value for the purposes of insurance on the above principle would be to take it at that sum, and no more, which the shipowner might calculate on receiving on the safe arrival of the ship—*i.e.*, the net freight, deducting seamen's wages and the other expenses of earning it—because, in case the ship is lost, that is all the shipowner loses (*a*).

As applied to insurances on goods.

So again with regard to goods, in order to put the merchant in the same situation as though no loss on his goods had taken place—in other words, to procure him a complete indemnity—it is clear that the value of the goods should be estimated, for the purpose of insurance, at the price which they would actually have produced had they arrived undamaged at their port of destination.

338. Such, unquestionably, as was very ably and unanswerably pointed out by Benecke, is the only mode of

---

(*a*) This is Arnould's text; but it would be more accurate to say that on principle the amount recoverable for a loss of freight ought to be the gross freight, less the expenses which would have been incurred after the time of the loss to earn the freight, but which, by reason of the loss, have been saved. For instance, in the case of a steamship, the expenses already incurred for coaling at an intermediate port ought not to be deducted. But as regards expenditures on stores, &c. included in the value of the ship, see *infra*, § 338, note (*c*).

CHAP. XIII.] VALUATION OF INSURABLE INTERESTS.

estimating the value of the interest at risk by which complete and absolute indemnity can in all cases be procured for the assured (*b*). Yet this, be the reason what it may, is not the principle of valuation which has been generally adopted in the practice of this or any other country. Parties engaged in the business of marine insurance are deemed to have contracted for an indemnity of a more limited description; and the object sought to be attained by the ordinary open policies on ship and goods, both in this and other countries, is to put the assured not in such a position as he would have been in if no loss had been incurred, but in the same situation he was in at the commencement of the risk.

_{Sect. 338.}

_{Practical principle of valuations not to put the assured in the same situation as if no loss had occurred, but to replace him in the same situation as he was in at the outset of the adventure.}

It is upon this basis that the insurable value of the interest at risk is invariably calculated in all open policies effected in this country. The worth of the thing insured to its owner at the outset of the risk covered with the expenses of the insurance is, in all open policies, its estimated value for the purposes of insurance.

As the ship in the course of every voyage is more or less diminished in value by wear and tear before the loss takes place; and as the goods would in most instances, but for the loss, have realized a higher sum at their port of destination than at their port of loading; it is very obvious that by this mode of insurance the assured on ship and on freight, in case of loss, will in all probability receive more than an indemnity, and the assured on goods less (*c*).

_{The assured on ship and freight generally receives more, and the assured on goods less, than an indemnity.}

(*b*) Principles of Indemnity, cc. i. ii. pp. 1—70, to which the reader is referred for a full exposition of the application of this principle to practice. See also McArthur, 2nd ed. p. 68, n. (*h*), where the advantages of valuing the various interests at the beginning and at the end of the voyage respectively are contrasted.

(*c*) McArthur (p. 68) points out an additional reason to account for the fact that the shipowner benefits by a loss, the fact being, as he states, that an owner who insures his ship and freight to the full extent which the law allows (as to which see § 365, *post*) is in reality effecting a double insurance on certain of the component parts of his insurable interest. "The expenditure in outfit, stores, provisions, and advances on account of crew's wages, which the law includes in the value of the ship, is also included in the gross freight, so that it is doubly insured." In principle, such expenditure should either be

Sect. 338.
Difference between valued and open or unvalued policies.

Policies for the purposes of this chapter may be divided into two classes, valued and open or unvalued, as policies of the latter class are called in the Marine Insurance Act, 1906 (*d*).

The difference between these two classes of policies, as regards their form and effect, is indicated in sects. 27 and 28 of the Marine Insurance Act, 1906, the terms of which are the following:—

Mar. Ins. Act, 1906, s. 27.

Section 27.—(1) A policy may be either valued or unvalued.

(2) A valued policy is a policy which specifies the agreed value of the subject-matter insured.

(3) Subject to the provisions of this Act (*e*), and in the absence of fraud, the value fixed by the policy is, as between the insurer and the assured, conclusive of the insurable value of the subject intended to be insured, whether the loss be total or partial.

(4) Unless the policy otherwise provides, the value fixed by the policy is not conclusive for the purpose of determining whether there has been a constructive total loss.

Sect. 28.

Section 28. An unvalued policy is a policy which does not specify the value of the subject-matter insured, but, subject to the limit of the sum insured, leaves the insurable value to be subsequently ascertained, in the manner herein-before specified.

We shall discuss these policies in their order, but first it is advisable to set out certain other provisions of the Marine Insurance Act, 1906, which are material to the discussion. They are contained in sects. 67 and 68 of the Act.

Measure of indemnity.

By sect. 67—

(1) The sum which the assured can recover in respect of a loss on a policy by which he is insured, in the case of an unvalued policy, to the full extent of the insurable value, or, in the case of a valued policy to the full extent

---

excluded in estimating the value of the ship, or it should be deducted from the gross amount of the freight.

(*d*) For the reason, see *ante*, § 9.

(*e*) *I.e.*, sect. 4, which avoids policies made by way of gaming and wagering, and sect. 18, which provides that the assured must disclose all material circumstances. See *infra*, § 342.

CHAP. XIII.] MEASURE OF INDEMNITY. 461

of the value fixed by the policy, is called the measure of indemnity (*f*). Sect. 338.

(2) Where there is a loss recoverable under the policy, the insurer, or each insurer if there be more than one, is liable for such proportion of the measure of indemnity as the amount of his subscription bears to the value fixed by the policy in the case of a valued policy, or to the insurable value in the case of an unvalued policy.

By sect. 68— Indemnity for total loss.

Subject to the provisions of this Act and to any express provision in the policy, where there is a total loss of the subject-matter insured,—

(1) If the policy be a valued policy, the measure of indemnity is the sum fixed by the policy:

(2) If the policy be an unvalued policy, the measure of indemnity is the insurable value of the subject-matter insured.

339. The statutory form, and usually every other form, of policy in this country contains the following clause:— Valued policies.

"The said ship, &c., goods and merchandises, &c., for so much as concerns the assured, by agreement between the assured and assurers in this policy, are and shall be valued at ——" (*g*).

The difference between an open and valued policy in form is solely this: that in a valued policy this blank is filled up with the sum at which the parties agree to fix the amount of the insurable interest; in an open policy it is left in blank.

The difference in effect between a valued and an open policy is that under an open policy, in case of loss, the assured must prove the actual value of the subject of insurance; under a valued policy he need not do so, the valuation in the policy being conclusive between the parties (*h*). Effect of valuation.

(*f*) "Measure of indemnity" is a new conventional expression introduced by this section.

(*g*) In a policy on freight the two words "as under" were added to this clause, and lower down in the margin was written "1,300*l*. on freight"—held, that this was not a valued policy: Wilson *v.* Nelson (1864), 5 B. & S. 354; 33 L. J. Q. B. 220; and see also Asfar *v.* Blundell, [1895] 2 Q. B. 196.

(*h*) Mar. Ins. Act, 1906, ss. 27, 28, *supra*, § 338; Barker *v.* Janson

Sect. 339. Thus, in Barker *v.* Janson (*i*), a vessel that had been worth 8,000*l.* was so much injured at sea that she was not worth repairing; this, however, being unknown at home, she was insured while in that condition by a time policy for 6,000*l.*, valued at 8,000*l.*, and after it attached she was totally destroyed by perils insured against. In this case the valuation was held binding and the policy valid. And in a more recent case (*k*), the vessel was driven on shore and was so badly damaged as to amount to a constructive total loss. Whilst in that condition she was completely destroyed by fire. It was held, first that her owners could recover as for a loss by fire, and secondly that, the policy being a valued policy, they could recover the full amount at which she was valued.

The rule that the valuation is conclusive between the parties applies equally in favour of the underwriter. For instance, in North of England Insurance Association *v.* Armstrong (*l*), a policy had been effected on the "Hetton" for 6,000*l.*, the vessel being valued at 6,000*l.* The "Hetton" was sunk by the "Uhlenhorst," whereupon the plaintiffs, who were the underwriters on the "Hetton," paid the defendants, the owners of the "Hetton," the sum of 6,000*l.* for this loss. The defendants then, under instructions from the plaintiffs took proceedings in the Court of Admiralty, and recovered 5,000*l.* from the owners of the "Uhlenhorst," this sum being apparently the limit of the liability of the latter. The whole of this sum was claimed by the plaintiffs as salvage. The defendants contended that the real value of the "Hetton" at the time of her loss was 9,000*l.*, and therefore they were entitled to participate in the said sum of 5,000*l.*; and it was urged on their behalf that, if the plaintiffs' contention were correct, it would follow, had the

(1868), L. R. 3 C. P. 303; North of England Ins. Assoc. *v.* Armstrong (1870), L. R. 5 Q. B. 244; Thames & Mersey Mar. Ins. Co. *v.* "Gunford" Ship Co., [1911] A. C. 529; Lewis *v.* Rucker (1761), 2 Burr. 1167; Shawe *v.* Felton (1801), 2 East, 109.

(*i*) L. R. 3 C. P. 303.

(*k*) Woodside *v.* Globe Marine Ins. Co., [1896] 1 Q. B. 105.

(*l*) (1870), L. R. 5 Q. B. 244.

owners of the "Uhlenhorst" been compelled to pay the full value of 9,000*l.*, that the underwriters would have been entitled to the whole, though they had only paid 6,000*l.* The Court regarded this anomaly (*m*) as one arising necessarily out of the peculiar nature of valued policies, and held that the underwriters were entitled to the whole sum (*n*).

Sect. 339.

The same principle was also applied in the underwriter's favour, in a later case where a vessel was undervalued in a policy and became liable to contribute to general average and salvage expenses. The SS. "Balmoral" was valued in the policy at 33,000*l.*, but her real value for the purpose of contribution was ascertained to be 40,000*l.*, and on this latter figure contribution was accordingly paid by her owners. It was held by the House of Lords, in an action by the owners against the underwriters to recover the whole amount of such contribution, that the valuation in the policy was binding and that the owners were only entitled to recover $\frac{33}{40}$ths of the ship's contribution (*o*).

340. As is expressly stated in sect. 27 (3) of the Marine Insurance Act, 1906 (*p*), the rule whereby the valuation in the contract is conclusive between the parties is the same, whether the loss be total or only partial (*q*). There was an opinion at one time entertained by writers of eminence that though conclusive in cases of total loss, yet it was not so in cases of average loss, but that in such cases the policy was to be opened. By this was meant that the agreed valuation was

Valuation applies in cases of partial, as well as total, loss.

(*m*) This point is further discussed in the chapter on "Subrogation," *post*, Vol. II. § 1230.

(*n*) The correctness of this decision was doubted by Lord Blackburn in Burnand *v.* Rodocanachi (1882), 7 App. Cas. 333, at p. 342; and it is perhaps not consistent with the reasoning of Lord Selborne at p. 335. The decision that the valuation is conclusive as between the parties is, however, confirmed by the language of sects. 67 and 68 of the Mar. Ins. Act, 1906, *ante*, § 338. See also Bruce *v.* Jones, *infra*, § 351; The St. Johns (1900), 101 Fed. R. 469.

(*o*) The SS. Balmoral Co. *v.* Marten, [1902] A. C. 511. See *post*, Vol. II. § 1006.

(*p*) *Ante*, § 338.

(*q*) See Mar. Ins. Act, 1906, ss. 70, 71, *post*, Vol. II. Pt. III. Chap. V., for its application to partial losses of freight and goods.

Sect. 340.

to be set aside as the standard and the basis of the underwriter's liability and the actual amount of interest at risk proved, just as in the case of an open policy.

Erroneous doctrine as to "opening the policy."

For instance, supposing a particular average loss to take place on a valued policy on goods, *insured to the full amount of their valuation,* and the damage ascertained to amount to one-fourth; according to the doctrine in question, it would be necessary for the assured, instead of at once calling upon the underwriters for a fourth part of the amount insured, to prove the insurable value of the goods, *i.e.,* their prime cost, together with the premiums of insurance, &c., just as though the policy were an open one, and the underwriters would, in case the agreed valuation proved to be greater than such insurable value, only be liable to pay a fourth of the latter.

This doctrine, wholly repugnant to the true construction of the valuation clause (*r*), appears to have arisen out of a *dictum* of Lord Mansfield, in the case of Erasmus *v.* Banks, where that great Judge is reported to have said, "an average loss opens the policy" (*s*). The phrase is unhappy, and suggestive of error, in consequence of the meaning attached

True meaning of opening the policy.

to the words "open the policy." It is quite clear, however, that the meaning of the expression is simply that, in case of an average loss the parties must necessarily go out of the policy to ascertain the extent of the damage done to the goods.

Of course, in the case of the goods being partially damaged, the policy alone can never show what the underwriter ought to pay; for the amount due from him is the same percentage on the sum he has agreed to insure, as the damage which the goods have suffered is upon their value: in other words, the proportion of the whole sum insured which the underwriter has to pay in case of loss, must depend upon the proportion in which the goods are damaged: as the one sum cannot be ascertained without fixing the other, and as the damage the goods have sustained can never

---

(*r*) Irving *v.* Manning (1848), 1 H. L. Cas. 287; 6 C. B. 391; 1 C. B. 168; 2 C. B. 784. Phillips (vol. ii. s. 1203) discusses the point.

(*s*) Cited in Shawe *v.* Felton (1801), 2 East, 113.

be made out except by calculations wholly extrinsic to the policy, every policy, whether open or valued, must in this sense be opened in every case of average loss (*t*).

Sect. 340.

Opening the policy, then, in this sense, means nothing more than resorting to extrinsic evidence, in order to ascertain the amount of damage sustained by the subject insured, so as to fix one element in calculating the amount of indemnification to which the assured is entitled; it is, in fact, merely ascertaining the percentage of damage sustained by the thing insured.

It has in fact long been established that a valuation has precisely the same effect in cases of particular average as it has in cases of total loss, viz., to relieve the assured from proving the prime cost, or insurable value (*u*).

There is moreover another sense in which the use of the phrase "opening the policy" has been used by a learned American judge. In cases of particular average on ship, the usual measure of the underwriter's liability is the repair bill, assuming always that its amount does not exceed the amount of the insurance (*x*). In particular average on goods, the amount of such liability is ascertained, in effect, by taking the proportion of loss to the sound value and then taking the same proportion of the amount for which the goods are insured (*y*). Judge Addison Brown points out that the result of these rules of adjustment is that "the policy value has no bearing upon the settlement of the amount to be paid by each underwriter, but only upon the amount of insurance that may be lawfully taken out; since each policy, up to the valuation, will pay the same amount, whether the valuation is high or low. Over-valuation in the policy, indeed, authorizes over-insurance to the same extent, if not fraudulent; because the insurer is estopped from asserting any

---

(*t*) See Mar. Ins. Act, 1906, s. 71 (3).

(*u*) See Lord Mansfield's observations in Lewis *v.* Rucker (1761), 2 Burr. 1167. See, too, Forbes *v.* Aspinall (1811), 13 East, 326;

Usher *v.* Noble (1810), 12 East, 639; Tunno *v.* Edwards (1810), 12 East, 488; Goldsmid *v.* Gillies (1813), 4 Taunt. 804.

(*x*) Mar. Ins. Act, 1906, s. 69 (1).
(*y*) Mar. Ins. Act, 1906, s. 71 (3).

466 VALUATION OF INSURABLE INTERESTS. [PART I.

Sect. 340. excess in the valuation. The owner, if insured above the actual value of his goods, will thereby realize from the insurer more than his actual loss. But the mode of settlement on each policy is precisely the same as upon an open policy; that is, to pay the same proportion of the insurance that the loss bears to the sound value; and if any one policy does not insure more than the actual value, which rarely happens, it will pay the same amount that it would pay if the policy were open. Hence the maxim as to goods, that 'a partial loss opens the policy,' which to the above extent is correct "(z).

The value in the policy is always conclusive.

341. In cases of total loss, the value in the policy has always been held as the conclusive standard of indemnity (a). Nor is it any exception to this rule, save in appearance, that where a ship, insured in a valued policy, was sold under an Admiralty decree in a collision suit for less than the amount in the policy, the assured did not recover more than she sold for, on this obviously just ground, that the contract in the running-down clause was to bear what the assured should be liable to pay, and should pay (b).

It is also established, that the valuation is binding generally, and not merely in cases where the question is as to the amount of payment to be made by underwriters in case of a loss. Thus where a vessel was valued at 3,750*l*., and the policy provided that the assured should keep one-fifth uninsured, it was held that there was a breach of this

---

(z) Per Brown, D. J., in Internat. Nav. Co. *v*. Atlantic Mut. Ins. Co. (1900), 100 F. 304. The following note at the end of his judgment explains how the valuation is a factor which is eliminated in the course of the calculation:—
"If *v* represents the policy value of goods, *s* the sound value at port of discharge, *d* the difference or loss as ascertained by sale, and *p* the amount insured by any particular policy, then each underwriter by the above rule must pay $\frac{d}{s} \times v \times \frac{p}{v} = \frac{dp}{s}$. This shows that the amount payable on any valued policy is independent of *v*, the policy value."

(a) Shawe *v*. Felton (1801), 2 East, 109; Irving *v*. Manning (1847), 1 H. L. Cas. 287; 6 C. B. 391; *S. C.*, 1 C. B. 168; 2 C. B. 784. See Mar. Ins. Act, 1906, s. 68 (1), *ante*, § 338.

(b) Thompson *v*. Reynolds (1857), 26 L. J. Q. B. 93; 7 E. & B. 172.

CHAP. XIII.] VALUED POLICIES. 467

stipulation as soon as there was an insurance for an amount exceeding four-fifths of 3,750*l*., although the shipowner was prepared to prove that the vessel was really worth 5,000*l*. (*c*).

Sect. 341.

There is, by English law, no exception to the rule under discussion. As long as the contract of insurance remains unimpeached, the valuation in the policy can under no circumstances be opened; or, to use the words of Cockburn, C. J. (*d*). "Where the value is stated in the policy in a manner to be conclusive between the two parties, the insurer and the insured, as regards the value, then in respect of all rights and obligations which arise upon the policy of insurance, the parties are estopped" from disputing the value stated.

Certain foreign codes differ from our law on this point. Thus in Germany (*e*) an excessive valuation may be reduced at the instance of the underwriter; and by the Dutch (*f*), Belgian (*g*), Italian (*h*), and Spanish (*i*) commercial codes, amongst others, an over-valuation may under certain circumstances be rectified.

342. In our own country language has undoubtedly been used not only by text writers (*k*), but also by judges (*l*) of

Effect of overvaluation in certain cases.

(*c*) Muirhead *v.* Forth and North Sea, &c. Assoc., [1894] A. C. 72; and see other cases there referred to.
(*d*) In North of England Ins. Assoc. *v.* Armstrong (1870), L. R. 5 Q. B. at p. 248.
(*e*) Commercial Code, s. 797.
(*f*) S. 274.
(*g*) S. 212.
(*h*) S. 612.
(*i*) S. 752.
(*k*) *E.g.*, Arnould, 2nd ed. pp. 361, 362; and in America, Phillips, ss. 1182, 1183; but see *contra*, 1 Parsons on Mar. Ins. p. 261.
(*l*) *E.g.*, Lord Ellenborough, as reported by Stevens on Average, 183, 5th ed.: "The valuation can only be opened where it is very exorbitant, or some proof of fraud can be established"; and again in Marshall *v.* Parker (1809), 2 Camp. 69: "Without evidence of fraud, I cannot disturb the valuation." So, too, per Bovill, C. J., in Barker *v.* Janson (1868), L. R. 3 C. P. 303: "An exorbitant valuation may be evidence of fraud; but when the transaction is *bonâ fide*, the valuation agreed upon is binding." So, also, per Willes, J., in Lidgett *v.* Secretan (1871), L. R. 6 C. P. 616, 629. "In the absence of fraud or wagering, it seems to me that the value is to be taken to be the conventional sum to be paid in the event of the loss"; and per Lord Robson in Thames & Mersey Mar. Ins. Co. *v.* "Gunford" Ship Co., [1911] A. C. at p. 548.

Sect. 342.

The valuation will not be set aside, but the policy itself may be avoided.

eminence, implying that an agreed valuation may in certain cases be set aside, and another apparently substituted; and the language of sect. 27 (3) of the Marine Insurance Act, 1906, also suggests that this may be so (*m*). It is clear, however, that by the law of this country no attack can be successfully made upon the valuation which will not also avoid the policy *in toto* (*n*). In such cases the object of attack is in reality not the valuation, but the policy itself, on the ground of irregularities relating to the valuation. It appears that there are three cases in which irregularities in the valuation may have the effect of avoiding the policy: (1) Where the subject of insurance has been fraudulently over-valued, with the object of cheating the underwriter (*o*); (2) Where circumstances show that the object was not to effect a *bonâ fide* insurance, but to gamble; (3) Where, apart from fraud in the assured, there is such an over-valuation of the interest of the assured in the adventure as alters the nature of the risk, making it, for example, one of a speculative, and not of an ordinary business nature, and it is found that this was a material fact which ought to have been, but was not, disclosed to the insurer.

Fraudulent over-valuation.

Thus in Haigh *v.* De la Cour (*p*) a fraudulent over-valuation of goods, made with intent to cheat the underwriters, was held to vitiate the policy. The actual value on board was only 1,400*l.*; the valuation in the policy was 5,000*l.*; the invoices were proved to be fictitious and the bills of lading to have been interpolated, after they were signed, by the captain; the ship was run away with, and carried to the West Indies (having been insured for Pernambuco), and the goods there disposed of by a person whom the assured had

---

(*m*) See sect. 27 (3), *ante*, § 338. The sub-section admits, however, of the construction that except in certain cases, for which see § 342, *infra*, the parties are precluded from giving evidence that the insured value is not the true one.

(*n*) See also the American authorities, cited 1 Parsons, 261, 262.

(*o*) "Had this over-valuation been tainted by fraud, the contract of insurance could not have been enforced": per Lord Shaw in Thames & Mersey Mar. Ins. Co. *v.* "Gunford" Ship Co., [1911] A. C. at p. 542.

(*p*) (1812), 3 Camp. 319.

put on board as a supercargo. A very high valuation is, however, not necessarily fraudulent (*q*).

<small>Sect. 342.</small>

Similarly, an over-valuation made in order to cover a gambling transaction will avoid the whole contract. This matter has already been dealt with in the chapter on wager policies (*r*). Here it will be sufficient to quote Lord Mansfield, who, after agreeing that upon valued policies "the merchant need only prove some interest to take it out of the stat. 19 Geo. 2, because the adverse party has admitted the value," adds: "If indeed it should come out in proof that a man had insured 2,000*l.*, and had interest on board to the value of a cable only, there never has been, and, I believe, never will be, a determination that by such an evasion the Act of Parliament may be defeated" (*s*). It is to be observed that in cases of this nature the policy will be just as much avoided even if both parties to the contract were throughout fully cognizant of all the facts. The ground of avoidance is not any unfair conduct of the one party towards the other, but the policy of the enactments directed against wagering or gaming transactions.

<small>Over-valuation by way of gaming.</small>

Thirdly, an over-valuation may under certain circumstances entitle the underwriter to avail himself of the doctrine of concealment (*t*), so as to avoid the policy. A good example of this is afforded by the case of Ionides *v.* Pender (*u*), where goods had been valued at an amount greatly exceeding any sum which they could possibly have realized. There were suspicious circumstances in the case, but the jury were unable to agree as to whether the assured's intentions were fraudulent. Evidence, however, from Lloyd's was produced to the effect that it was material for underwriters to know the extent of an over-valuation so excessive, as such speculative risks were either declined altogether, or only undertaken at high premiums. The jury found that the over-valuation was a material fact which had not been disclosed to the under-

<small>Over-valuation not disclosed, and such as to alter the nature of the risk.</small>

(*q*) See *infra*, § 343.
(*r*) See *ante*, § 319.
(*s*) Lewis *v.* Rucker (1761), 2 Burr. 1171.

(*t*) See Part II., Chap. II., "Concealment."
(*u*) (1874), L. R. 9 Q. B. 531.

470 VALUATION OF INSURABLE INTERESTS. [PART I.

Sect. 342. writers, and the Court of Queen's Bench affirmed a verdict which had been entered accordingly for the defendants (*x*).

It is obvious that in all these cases the question is not one of opening the valuation, but as to the validity of the policy.

Excessive valuation of ship.

343. No positive rules can be laid down as to what constitutes such an excess in valuation as will necessitate disclosure, or taint the transaction with fraud. A valuation which considerably exceeds the selling value of a ship is not necessarily fraudulent or so excessive as to need to be disclosed. In the case of the "Gunford" (*y*), though the selling value of the ship was about £9,000 and the valuation in the policies £18,500, the appellants did not allege fraud, or rely on the non-disclosure of the difference between the valuation and the selling value. It is impossible to say what view the House of Lords would, if the question had been raised, have taken of this exceedingly high valuation. But Lord Shaw, who referred to the valuation, said: "Where there is heavy overvaluation fraud is, *a priori*, not very far to seek. But fraud is not here pleaded; and upon the general question it ought to be remembered that to the insurer (*sic*) using a ship as part of the going concern of a business a statement of value going much beyond the amount to be realized if the concern was stopped and the asset put upon the market is intelligible and legitimate." And Lord Robson also expressed the view that there may be legitimate business reasons for a discrepancy between the selling value and the insured value (*z*). Moreover it must be remembered that underwriters are usually in a position to form a fairly accurate estimate of the real value of the ship, and that there are often reasons why they prefer a high valuation so long as they do not consider it a temptation to the assured (*a*).

(*x*) See also Herring *v.* Janson (1895), 1 Com. Cas. 177, where Mathew, J., quoted from a valuable memorandum of Willes, J., on this subject; and *infra*, § 589.

(*y*) Thames & Mersey Mar. Ins. Co. *v.* "Gunford" Ship Co., [1911] A. C. 529, *supra*, § 342.

(*z*) [1911] A. C. pp. 542, 548. See also per Willes, J., in Lidgett *v.* Secretan (1870), L. R. 6 C. P. p. 627.

(*a*) The higher the valuation, the greater is the immunity of the insurer from small claims, under the warranty against average under 3

In Ionides *v.* Pender it was stated, in evidence by under- *Sect. 343.*
writers (*b*), that an addition of 25 or even 30 per cent. to the *Excessive*
invoice value of the goods would not, but that any addition *valuation of goods.*
beyond this would, make the risk speculative. Yet each case
must depend on its own circumstances, and in each case the
question must be determined as one of fact. As Mr. Gow (*c*)
pertinently observes: "Cases have occurred in the history of
commerce in which the insurance of four times the amount
of invoice would be quite justifiable; for instance, that of
shipments of silver to Japan, made for the purpose of obtaining in exchange gold at the Japanese ratio of 4 to 1, when
the prevailing ratio in the rest of the world was about $15\frac{1}{2}$ to 1.
Similarly, in such insurances as those of contraband cargoes,
or cargoes destined to run a blockade, one can imagine a very
high valuation put on goods whose value would be enormously
enhanced by their mere arrival at their intended destination."

Apart from special circumstances, however, Lord Ellen- *Valuation of goods*
borough suggested that in fixing the valuation, "the assured, *may includ*)
if he wish to keep fairly within the principle of insurances, *expected profits.*
which is merely to obtain indemnity, will, in the case of
goods, never go beyond the first cost, adding thereto only the
premium and commission, and, if he see fit, the probable
profit; and, in the case of freight, he will not go beyond the
amount of what the ship would earn, with the premiums and
commissions thereupon" (*d*).

With regard to the case of goods, his Lordship, after adverting to the rule that, in open policies on goods, nothing more
can be recovered than the invoice price plus the premiums,
&c., and remarking that, as goods are generally sent to a
profitable market, this rule, in case of loss, operates favour-
ably for the underwriter, adds, "the assured may obviate

---

per cent. (see *post,* Vol. II. §§ 882, 892, 900); and the greater, also, is the difficulty of establishing a con- structive total loss by reason of the cost of repairs exceeding the re- paired value, if the policy contains the usual clause stipulating that the insured value shall be taken as the repaired value (see *post,* Vol. II. §§ 1091, 1132, 1133).

(*b*) L. R. 9 Q. B. at p. 535.
(*c*) Marine Insurance, p. 69.
(*d*) Forbes *v.* Aspinall (1811), 13 East, 327.

Sect. 343.

this inconvenience by making the policy a valued one, or by stipulating that, in case of loss, the loss shall be estimated according to the value of like goods at the port of delivery"(e): thus distinctly admitting that the assured may value his goods in the policy so as greatly to exceed the invoice price, and to cover the expected profit. And, indeed, as Stevens remarks, this is the real advantage that valued policies on goods hold out to the merchant (f).

Mode proposed by Benecke.

344. Benecke, agreeably to the principles already pointed out in the last section, shows how, by means of a valued policy, the merchant may cover, not only the profits he expects to make on his goods at the port of delivery, but also, in case of their arriving there in bulk, but sea-damaged, may protect himself against the loss to which he would otherwise be exposed, from having to pay full duty, freight, and landing charges (g). Thus, supposing the sum required to be insured on the goods themselves (*i.e.*, so as to cover their prime cost, premiums of insurance and commission) to be 2,000*l*.; freight payable on their arrival, 200*l*.; expected profit, 400*l*.; duty and landing charges at the port of delivery, 100*l*., the full duty and freight being payable on damaged goods arriving in bulk); then 2,700*l*. would be the sum required to be insured altogether. The plan recommended by Benecke is, to value at 2,700*l*., and add this clause:—" Of these 2,700*l*., 2,000*l*. are on the goods, 200*l*. on freight, 400*l*. on expected profit, 100*l*. on duty and landing charges " (h).

This clause, though unobjectionable, appears unnecessary in English policies, where, according to the liberal practice

(e) Usher *v.* Noble (1810), 12 East, 639.

(f) Stevens on Average, 179.

(g) Sometimes the owner of goods protects himself against the loss due to his having to pay the full freight by a policy against particular average on "contingency freight." See *ante*, § 232.

(h) Benecke, Pr. of Indem. pp. 24, 29. In Thames and Mersey Co. *v.* Pitts, [1893] 1 Q. B. 476, the merchant valued his cargo at a certain figure, and declared that a certain portion of such valuation was "for advance on freight." It was held that the policy was to be treated as one policy on valued goods, and not as a policy by which goods and advanced freight were separately insured.

CHAP. XIII.] VALUED POLICIES. 473

that prevails in the business of insurance, it seems very unlikely that any attempt would be made to set aside a valuation which was *bonâ fide* only intended to procure for the assured a complete indemnity in case of loss.

Sect. 344.

345. The value fixed by the policy is conclusive of the insurable value "of the subject intended to be insured" (*i*). It does not preclude the inquiry whether in fact the assured had an insurable interest in the whole of the subject of valuation, or whether the whole interest valued was ever at risk.

The valuation in the policy does not preclude the inquiry, whether or not the whole of the interest to which such valuation refers, has, in fact, been at risk.

Moreover, sect. 75 (2) of the Marine Insurance Act, 1906, expressly declares that—

> Nothing in the provisions of this Act relating to the measure of indemnity shall affect the rules relating to double insurance, or prohibit the insurer from disproving interest wholly or in part, or from showing that at the time of the loss the whole or any part of the subject-matter insured was not at risk under the policy.

For instance, if something has formed a constituent in the estimate of value in which the assured had no insurable interest (*e.g.*, if freight, paid in advance, were included in the valuation expressed in a policy on freight effected for the shipowner), it is clear that the underwriter, to the extent of this element of the value, would not be liable; and whether it was so or not may be investigated without infringing the valuation in the policy (*k*). Still more is it competent to the underwriter to show that the assured had no interest at all (*l*). The parties are only bound by the valuation as far as it goes; and if only part of the interest to which the valuation in the policy refers has ever been at risk on board, the assured, in case of loss, can only recover upon a proportionate amount of the valuation. For instance, if goods, the

---

(*i*) Mar. Ins. Act, s. 27 (3), *ante*, § 338.
(*k*) Williams *v.* North China Ins. Co. (1876), 1 C. P. D. 757; The Main, [1894] P. 320.

(*l*) Shawe *v.* Felton (1801), 2 East, 109; Burnand *v.* Rodocanachi (1882), 7 A. C. 333, per Lord Selborne.

Sect. 345. prime cost of which, including premiums and commissions, is 4,500*l*., are valued in the policy at 5,000*l*., and it should turn out that of these goods only two-thirds, or 3,000*l*. worth, were ever really shipped on board, the assured, in case of loss, would only recover the same proportion of 5,000*l*., the sum valued, that 3,000*l*. is of 4,500*l*., *i.e.*, two-thirds, or 3,333*l*. 6*s*. 8*d*. (*m*).

"The valuation," says Lord Ellenborough, "in case of goods, looks to all the goods intended to be loaded; and, in case of freight, it looks to the freight upon all the goods the ship is intended to carry on the voyage insured: and if, by the perils insured against in a valued policy on goods, part only of the goods intended to be covered be lost, the valuation must be opened, and the assured can only recover in respect of that part; and so if, by the perils insured against, the freight of part only of the goods to be carried be lost, the assured can only recover, in respect of that loss, according to the proportion which that part bears to the whole sum at which the entire freight was estimated in the valuation" (*n*).

Rule illustrated by case of a policy on freight; Forbes *v*. Aspinall.

346. Accordingly, in the case from which these remarks are taken, insurance having been made on freight "at and from Hayti to Liverpool," valued at 6,500*l*., and it appearing that the vessel was lost off the coast of Hayti, when the freight of only fifty-five bales of cotton was at risk, which formed but a small part of the cargo intended to be shipped on board her, and on which the freight was valued, the Court would not allow the assured to recover the whole amount of the valuation, but only such a proportion of it as the fifty-five bales bore to the full cargo intended to be loaded, and on which the freight was estimated (*o*).

By policy on goods; Rickman *v*. Carstairs.

Again, in the case of a policy on homeward cargo, it appeared that at the time of the loss, which was total, a considerable proportion of the homeward cargo was not on board, and that which was shipped was not equal to the value

(*m*) Phillips, s. 1196.
(*n*) In Forbes *v*. Aspinall (1811), 13 East, 327. See the judgment of

Blackburn, J., in Tobin *v*. Harford (1864), 34 L. J. C. P. 40.
(*o*) Forbes *v*. Aspinall, at p. 323.

CHAP. XIII.] VALUED POLICIES. 475

in the policy. At the same time enough of the outward Sect. 346.
cargo still remained on board to make up the amount named
in the valuation. As this, however, was not covered by the
policy, the Court, adopting the principle that the underwriter
is only bound by the valuation when the whole of the intended cargo is on board, held that the assured was entitled
to recover, not the whole amount of the insurance, but only
such proportion of it as the value of the homeward cargo, the
freight of which was at risk at the time of loss, bore to a full
homeward cargo (p).

Under a time policy on ship valued at 2,000l., and on cargo Tobin v.
valued at 8,000l., containing all the clauses proper to the Harford.
barter trade on the coast of Africa, outward cargo to be considered homeward interest twenty-four hours after arrival at
first port or place of trade, the ship reached Kinsembo with
a cargo on board worth 6,226l., of which part was there discharged to the value of 3,952l., and then without loading
other cargo, after being more than twenty-four hours at
Kinsembo, sailed for Congo with the residue, and was lost
on the way. The assured claimed 8,000l. in respect of the
"cargo," interpreting that word in the policy as signifying
any goods on board at the time of the loss. The Court, however, held that the valuation in the policy was of a substantially full cargo, and that the plaintiff could only recover, as
for an average loss, an aliquot part of that sum, corresponding to the proportion which the goods on board bore to a full
cargo, and that if this proportion could not be found, the
underwriters would be liable as upon an open policy underwritten for 8,000l.(q).

Similarly under a policy "upon chartered freight, valued Denoon v.
at 7,000l., at and from Sydney to Calcutta and London," the Colonial
remainder of the voyage was abandoned at Calcutta on account Ass. Co.
of the bankruptcy of the charterers, and the vessel took 360
coolies and part cargo of rice for Mauritius. Thereupon

(p) Rickman v. Carstairs (1833), L. J. C. P. 134; in error, 34 L. J.
5 B. & Ad. 651. C. P. 37; 13 C. B. N. S. 791; 17
(q) Tobin v. Harford (1864), 32 C. B. N. S. 528.

Sect. 346. the voyage described in the policy was altered by indorsement, and it was further indorsed as follows:—" The within interest is now declared to be on freight valued at 2,000*l*." The subscription of 1,000*l*. by the defendants remained unaltered. When near Mauritius the vessel was wrecked; there was a total loss of the rice and of the freight of it; the greater part of the coolies were saved, and their passage-money, but some were lost, and with them their passage-money. The question was what under this policy in these circumstances the assured was entitled to recover.

The Court, after holding that the word "freight" did not, as was contended by the defendants, include the passage-money, held further that inasmuch as there was not a full cargo on board or any estimation in the policy of what the freight of a full cargo would have been, the policy must be dealt with as an open policy, and, consequently, that the assured was entitled to recover in the proportion of 1,000*l*. to 2,000*l*., or one-half of the whole freight on board, not exceeding 1,000*l*., that is, one-half of 1,412*l*., being in fact 706*l*. (*r*).

In the United States.

These principles have received abundant illustration in the Courts of the United States. Thus, where seventy-four mules were insured, valued at 11,000 dollars, and only thirty-five mules were actually shipped, the assured, in case of loss, was only allowed to recover thirty-five 74th parts of 11,000 dollars (*s*).

Practical difficulties in applying this rule.

347. As to the rule thus well established, there is yet in many cases a difficulty about its practical application, arising out of the question, "what is a cargo, sufficient to entitle the jury to say, that that has been shipped to which the valuation in the policy refers?" (*t*).

(*r*) Denoon *v.* Home and Colonial Ass. Co. (1872), L. R. 7 C. P. 341. See further, as to this case, *ante*, § 252b.

(*s*) Brook *v.* Louisiana Ins. Co. (1826), 4 Martin, N. S. 640, 681;

2 Phillips, s. 1196; and other cases there cited.

(*t*) Per Parke, J., in 5 B. & Ad. 660; and see the judgment, per Blackburn J., in Tobin *v.* Harford (1864), 34 L. J. C. P. 37.

A difficulty was also at one time felt as to the principle upon which the amount of loss should be adjusted, but the following satisfactory solution of it, suggested in the argument in Rickman v. Carstairs, has since been accepted and sanctioned with the approval of the Court of Common Pleas and of Exchequer Chamber (*u*). The passage is this:— " Even supposing the policy to be opened, the valuation will not be altogether inoperative; for it will prevent any dispute as to the value of the whole contemplated cargo. Thus, if a valued policy on sugar be opened, on the ground of only four-fifths of the intended cargo having been shipped and lost, the underwriter will pay, not a value to be now put on the lost sugar, but four-fifths of the sum underwritten " (*x*).

Sect. 347. In case of average loss.

Where, however, it is impossible to ascertain the proportion which the cargo actually shipped bears to that intended to be shipped, it does seem to follow from the cases already cited that the valuation will be inoperative.

348. As we have seen (*y*), sect. 27 (4) of the Marine Insurance Act, 1906, declares that " unless the policy otherwise provides (*z*), the value fixed by the policy is not conclusive for the purpose of determining whether there has been a constructive total loss." The question, in order to ascertain whether a wrecked or stranded ship is so damaged as to entitle the assured to recover as for a total loss, upon giving due notice of abandonment, is not, will the cost of repairs exceed the value in the policy? but, will the cost of repairs exceed the ship's value when repaired? (*a*). " When this test has been applied, and the nature of the loss thus determined, the quantum of compensation is then to be fixed. In an open policy the compensation must then be ascertained by evidence. In a valued policy the agreed total value is conclusive; each party has conclusively admitted that this fixed

Valuation of ship is immaterial in questions of constructive total loss.

(*u*) Tobin *v.* Harford (1864), 32 L. J. C. P. 134, 136; 13 C. B. N. S. 791; in error, 34 L. J. C. P. 37.
(*x*) 5 B. & Ad. 662.
(*y*) *Ante*, § 338.
(*z*) The "Institute" Clauses pro-

vide that " the insured value shall be taken as the repaired value in ascertaining whether the vessel is a constructive total loss."
(*a*) See *post*, § 1124.

Sect. 348. sum shall be that which the assured is entitled to recover in case of a total loss" (*b*).

Effect of the valuation where there is a double insurance.

349. As we have already seen, sect. 32 (2) of the Marine Insurance Act, 1906, in which the results of double insurance are set out, provides that:—

(a) The assured, unless the policy otherwise provides, may claim payment from the insurers in such order as he may think fit (*c*), provided that he is not entitled to receive any sum in excess of the indemnity allowed by this Act;

(b) Where the policy under which the assured claims is a valued policy, the assured must give credit as against the valuation for any sum received by him under any other policy without regard to the actual value of the subject-matter insured.

Where the valuation is the same in both policies, there is little difficulty. The assured cannot recover in the whole more than the valuation, although the subject insured be proved to be really worth more (*d*). For instance, if he have insured his vessel in one policy for 3,000*l*., and in another for 4,000*l*., and the valuation in each be 6,000*l*., he cannot recover in the aggregate more than 6,000*l*., even though he prove the vessel to be really worth 7,000*l*. or more (*e*). He may, however, proceed first on whichever of the two policies he pleases, and then recover on the other policy the deficiency up to the 6,000*l*., leaving the underwriters on the two to adjust between themselves all questions of contribution. In the instance we have given, it appears that he would have a good claim for a return of premium in respect of the 1,000*l*. insured in excess of what he is entitled to recover.

(*b*) Opinion of the Judges in the House of Lords in Irving *v*. Manning (1847), 6 C. B. 422, supporting the previous decisions of Cambridge *v*. Anderton (1824), 2 B. & Cr. 691; Allen *v*. Sugrue (1828), 8 B. & Cr. 561; Young *v*. Turing (1841), 2 M. & G. 593; Manning *v*. Irving (1850), 1 C. B. 168. See Mar. Ins. Act, 1906, ss. 67, 68, *ante*, § 338.

(*c*) Newby *v*. Reed (1763), 1 W. Bl. 416.

(*d*) Mar. Ins. Act, 1906, ss. 67, 68, *ante*, § 338.

(*e*) Irving *v*. Richardson (1831), 1 Mood. & R. 153; 2 B. & Ad. 193; Morgan *v*. Price (1850), 4 Exch. 615.

CHAP. XIII.] VALUED POLICIES.

350. As, however, the valuation is only conclusive between the parties to the same policy, difficulties arose in cases where the assured had protected his interest in the subject of insurance by two or more valued policies containing different valuations.

Effect of several insurances on the same subject-matter, where the policies contain different valuations.

The first reported case of this kind is Bousfield *v.* Barnes (*f*). A vessel was valued in one policy at 8,000*l*., and insured for 6,000*l*.; in another policy she was valued at 6,000*l*. and insured for 600*l*. A total loss took place, and the underwriters on the first policy paid 6,000*l*., being the whole sum insured. The owners then brought an action on the second policy, and proved the real value of the vessel to have exceeded 8,000*l*. Lord Ellenborough, in answer to a claim by the underwriters to treat the 6,000*l*. already received under the first policy as salvage, held that the real value being over 8,000*l*., the plaintiff had therefore an interest to which he might still apply the policy on which the action was brought (*g*).

351. A similar point arose in Bruce *v.* Jones (*h*), the decision in which case virtually over-ruled that in Bousfield *v.* Barnes. A shipowner had effected four policies on the same ship: the first was for 725*l*. on a valuation of 3,000*l*.; the second was for 500*l*. on a valuation of 3,000*l*.; the third was for 3,450*l*. on a valuation of 5,000*l*.; and the fourth was for 2,400*l*. on a valuation of 3,200*l*. A total loss took place, and the assured received 3,126*l*. under the first three policies. He then sued on the fourth, and the question was how much was recoverable thereon. Willes, J., directed the jury that insurance was a contract of indemnity, and that for the purposes of the action 3,200*l*. must be taken to be the real value of the ship,—that the sum received on the other policies, whatever were the valuations therein, must therefore be deducted from such value, and that the plaintiff was

Bruce v. Jones.

(*f*) (1815), 4 Camp. 228.
(*g*) In America the case of Kenny *v.* Clarkson, 1 Johns. 385, is to the same effect. Other cases are cited in 1 Parsons, p. 264, where the point is discussed.
(*h*) (1863), 1 H. & C. 769; 32 L. J. Ex. 132.

480　VALUATION OF INSURABLE INTERESTS.　[PART I.

Sect. 351.　only entitled to recover the difference. The jury having accordingly found a verdict for 74*l*., the plaintiff obtained a rule calling on the defendant to show cause why there should not be a new trial on the ground of misdirection as to the measure of damages. Amongst other contentions put forward on behalf of the plaintiffs, it was urged that the payments made under the other policies must be taken into consideration, if at all, not as payments of so much cash, but merely as payments in respect of proportionate parts of the total loss sustained; so that, for instance, a sum of 500*l*. which had been paid by the underwriters on the first policy, the valuation wherein was 3,000*l*., should be regarded not as a payment of 500*l*. cash, but as a payment of one-sixth of a total loss, leaving five-sixths to which the other insurances might be applied (*i*). It was further pointed out that the contention of the underwriters would lead to this surprising anomaly,—that the whole sum recoverable would be less or greater, according as recovery were had in the first instance under policies of the greater or lesser valuation.

Anomalous result.

The Court (*k*), admitting this anomaly, decided nevertheless that the underwriters were entitled to treat the whole sum received by the assured under the other three policies as salvage, and that the total sum recoverable was the difference between such sum and the agreed value, namely, 74*l*. (*l*).

352. A rule which makes the aggregate sum recoverable on all the policies depend on the order in which recovery thereon is had may be considered unsatisfactory (*m*), and it is clear that an assured might be placed in a very awkward position, if the underwriter on the policy containing the greater valuation were to admit a claim and the underwriter on the policy with the smaller valuation were to contest his liability. Nevertheless, the effect of sect. 32 (2), (a) and (b),

---

(*i*) See 1 H. & C. at p. 773.
(*k*) Pollock, C. B., Martin & Channell, BB.
(*l*) See also North of England Ins. Association *v.* Armstrong (1870), L. R. 5 Q. B. 244, *ante*, § 339.
(*m*) See per Cockburn, C. J., in North of England Ins. Association *v.* Armstrong, *supra*.

CHAP. XIII.] VALUED POLICIES. 481

of the Marine Insurance Act, 1906, seems to be that the rule laid down in Bruce v. Jones is definitely established.

Sect. 352.

353. It is in accordance with the decision in Bruce v. Jones (n) that in all ordinary cases average adjusters in this country allow an assured to recover to the extent of the highest valuation, provided always that such amount be fully subscribed for in the aggregate. It is recognized, however, that the right of an assured to recover to this extent might be prejudiced, if he were to be so ill-advised or unfortunate as to have previously received payment upon a policy containing a higher valuation.

Practice of average adjusters.

354. The question how the total sum recovered by the assured should finally be apportioned as between the different underwriters, where there are several policies with different valuations, is not solved by the provisions of the Marine Insurance Act, 1906, which relate to the question of contribution (o). Nor is there any direct authority or established practice on this point. The difficulty may be well put by a simple illustration. Let us suppose that a ship is insured in two policies, A. and B. In policy A. she is valued at 8,000l., and is insured for 6,000l.; in policy B. she is valued at 7,000l. and insured for 4,000l. A total loss takes place, and the assured, having recourse in the first instance to policy B., recovers under the two policies 8,000l. in all. How is the liability under the two policies adjusted as between the respective sets of underwriters? The editors are informed that the average adjuster will probably state the case in the following form (p):—

Adjustment of contribution between underwriters on policies differently valued.

A. If 8,000l. pays 8,000l., 6,000l. insured would pay £6,000
B. If 7,000l. pays 7,000l., 4,000l. insured would pay 4,000

Total £10,000

(n) (1863), 1 H. & C. 769; 32 L. J. Ex. 132.
(o) Sects. 32 (2) (d), 80, *ante*, § 330. See American Surety Co.
v. Wrightson (1910), 16 Com. Cas. 37, 54.
(p) It is apparent that in cases of total loss this formula has very

A.—VOL. I. 31

Sect. 354. But inasmuch as the total sum to be made up is not 10,000*l*. but only 8,000*l*. (*q*), the amount payable by each set of underwriters must be proportionately reduced, so that eventually

$$\text{A. pays } \tfrac{6000}{10000} \text{ of } 8,000l. = £4,800$$
$$\text{B. pays } \tfrac{4000}{10000} \text{ of } 8,000l. = 3,200$$
$$\overline{£8,000}$$

And similarly, to take a case where the loss has been partial only, let us suppose that, upon the same policies, a loss takes place in respect of which the shipowner is entitled to be recouped to the extent of 4,000*l*. Then,

A. If 8,000*l*. pays 4,000*l*., 6,000*l*. insured would pay £3,000
B. If 7,000*l*. pays 4,000*l*., 4,000*l*. insured would pay 2,286

Total £5,286

Therefore, as before,

A. pays $\tfrac{3000}{5286}$ of 4,000*l*., or £2,270
B. pays $\tfrac{2286}{5286}$ of 4,000*l*., or 1,730

£4,000

In ordinary cases of partial loss, the method above indicated seems to be free from objection. In cases of total loss (*r*), however, as has been already observed, it involves the anomaly that an important part of the contract contained in B. policy, namely, the agreed valuation, is entirely ignored, and that the underwriters on that policy are made to contribute towards a sum in excess of any figure with which they have little utility. The result is based solely on a comparison of the amounts respectively subscribed, without any regard to the valuation in B. policy.

(*q*) There would also be a claim for return of premium on 2,000*l*. over-insured.

(*r*) The following objection applies also to cases of partial loss so great as to exceed the agreed valuation in any of the contributory policies.

CHAP. XIII.] VALUED POLICIES. 483

in any way agreed to be concerned. To such cases a somewhat different method of adjustment, which certainly seems to be free from these objections, is stated by Judge Carver (*s*) to be more properly applied. The sum of 1,000*l*. by which the valuation in A. exceeds that in B. is made to fall on A. alone, and only the balance of 7,000*l*. is treated as the subject of adjustment as between A. and B. This balance of 7,000*l*. is then apportioned between A. and B. according to their subscriptions, that of A. being of course reduced by the 1,000*l*. which he is deemed to have already contributed. In the result it will be found that

A. pays 1,000*l*. plus $\frac{5}{9}$ of 7,000*l*. = £4,889
B. pays $\frac{4}{9}$ of 7,000*l*. . . .= 3,111
————
£8,000

Sect. 354.
Alternative method.

Of the two methods suggested, the editors are disposed to prefer that of Judge Carver, who formulates (*t*) the position in the following terms:—

(1.) "In case of partial loss (*u*), the contribution is to be in proportion to the liabilities under the several policies in respect of that loss.

(2.) "In case of total loss, so much of the amount paid under any policy, as is ascribable to the part of the valuation therein which is covered by other policies, is to be contributed to by those policies in proportion to their liabilities in respect thereof."

355. The valuation is stated in sect. 27 (3) of the Marine Insurance Act, 1906 (*x*) to be conclusive of the insurable

The valuation in the policy is only a

(*s*) See pp. 130—133 of the Report of the Eighteenth Conference of the International Law Association held at Buffalo, U.S.A., in 1899 (Clowes & Sons, Ltd. 1900). Lowndes on Mar. Ins. 2nd ed. s. 38, appears to support the same view.

(*t*) Marine insurance proposals in Report of Buffalo Conference at p. 178, as amended for the Rouen Conference, 1900.

(*u*) The partial loss, however, ought not to exceed the valuation in any of the contributory policies; if it does, the adjustment should be regulated by the rule which follows.

(*x*) *Ante*, § 338. See also sect. 26 (3) of the Act, *ante*, § 252b,

Sect. 355.
valuation of the interest of the assured in the subject of insurance.

value of the "subject intended to be insured." It must therefore be understood that the valuation in the policy is not necessarily the whole estimated value of the subject of insurance, but only of the interest the assured has in such subject.

Hence, where insurance was made on goods "valued at 19,000*l.*," of which the assured owned four-ninths, it was contended that the valuation was intended for the entire property; and, accordingly, that the interest of the assured was to be taken as four-ninths of that sum; but the Court said, "We must take it that the value insured is the value of the assured's interest" (*y*).

Valued policies on ship, and on ship and freight.

356. From the difficulty of proving the insurable value of the ship in case of loss, almost all policies on ship are valued. The value is generally calculated in this country by estimating the ship's worth to her owner at the outset of the risk, including stores, outfit, and money advanced for seamen's wages, taking care to cover the whole with premiums and commissions (*z*).

However much the ship may be damaged by wear and tear, and consumption of her stores and provisions at the time of loss, even though the loss takes place at the very termination of a long voyage, yet the valuation so calculated determines the amount recoverable in case of loss (*a*).

---

which provides that the policy "shall be construed to apply to the interest intended by the assured to be covered."

(*y*) Feise *v.* Aguilar (1811), 3 Taunt. 506. See New York and Cuba Mail SS. Co. *v.* Royal Exch. Ass. (1907), 154 Fed. R. 315, in which the Circuit Court of Appeals held that the valuation in a time policy on freight was not intended to cover prepaid freight, but only the freight at the risk of the assured at the time of the loss.

(*z*) Stevens on Average, 190. So long as the ship is comparatively new, the owner, in estimating her worth, has regard principally to what she cost him, making allowance for her earnings; as she gets older the tendency is to consider her more and more as a freight-earning machine, and her worth as the present value of her future freights plus her breaking-up price. See Lowndes on Marine Insurance, 2nd ed. p. 13; Gow, p. 74. As to the valuation of a ship as "part of the going concern of a business," see *ante*, § 343.

(*a*) Shawe *v.* Felton (1801), 2 East, 109.

CHAP. XIII.] VALUED POLICIES. 485

As, moreover, it is frequently the practice in this country to value the freight also by a separate policy at its gross amount, without any deduction of the expenses of earning it, it is very clear that upon this principle, in case of loss, the shipowner receives far more than an indemnity.

Sect. 356.
Shipowner, in case of total loss, often receives more than an indemnity.

357. For example, suppose a ship chartered for a four months' voyage to be worth to her owner, in the port of loading, including rigging, &c., 2,000*l.*; provisions, 80*l.* more; petty expenses at port of loading, 18*l.* additional; seamen's wages, paid in advance to the extent of one-half, 75*l.*; making altogether, 2,173*l.*; add a premium on this sum at 3 per cent. and premium on premium, viz., 67*l.* 4*s.*, and the sum which the assured would be entitled to receive on the policy on ship in case of a total loss is 2,240*l.* 4*s.*

Examples.

So much for the policy on ship; but now as to the freight. Suppose the gross freight for the whole voyage, without deducting the expenses of earning it, to be 650*l.*; premium at 3 per cent., &c., 20*l.* 2*s.*, making together 670*l.* 2*s.*, which is the amount recoverable for freight, calculated according to the principle observed in this country in respect of open policies. Therefore the amount recoverable in respect of ship and freight under the two policies is 2,910*l.* 6*s.*

In order to show how much this exceeds an indemnity, let us see what the shipowner would net in case the ship arrived and full freight was earned. Taking the wear and tear of the ship for the four months' voyage at the moderate sum of 100*l.*, the ship would be worth to her owner on arrival (2,000*l.* -100*l.*) 1,900*l.*

Then as to freight, taking the expenses at the port of destination to be 25*l.*, and the seamen's wages for the last two months to be 75*l.*, these two items payable out of the gross freight of 650*l.* would reduce the net amount of freight to 550*l.* The sum, therefore, that the shipowner would net by the ship's safe arrival earning freight would be, for the ship, 1,900*l.*; for the freight, 550*l.*; making the total net value of the ship and freight to the owner on safe arrival, 2,450*l.*

Sect. 357. But in case of total loss he would receive 2,910*l.* 6*s.*, *i.e.*, he would be a gainer by the total loss of his ship to the extent of 460*l.* 6*s.* (*b*)—"a great inducement indeed to many," as Bénecke exclaims, "to convert a partial into a total loss!" (*c*).

Valued policies on freight.

358. Notwithstanding the theoretical difficulties attendant on the practice of insuring ship and freight separately (*d*), freight is still regularly insured in separate policies, and valued therein at a sum sufficient to cover its estimated gross amount.

In the United States.

But freight, as well as other subjects, may be valued even above its gross amount; and in one case in the United States the Court are reported to have said, "The parties agree that the freight shall be valued at a sum which eventually proves to be three times the value of the carriage of the goods, but we do not perceive that the estimate was made unfairly"; and it was adjudged that the underwriters should pay a loss according to the valuation (*e*).

Where the voyage is made up of distinct stages, and there is but one valuation.

The following question has arisen, and been a good deal discussed in the Courts of the United States:—

Suppose a policy to be on time, or on a voyage having intermediate stages, at each of which freight is earned and becomes due, independently of the circumstance of the vessel's arriving at subsequent stages; suppose, also, that the freight of the whole voyage, or for the whole time, is valued in gross—is this valuation to be applied to the aggregate amount of all the freights, or to the amount of each severally?

(*b*) A seaman's wages, in case of wreck or loss of ship, are now payable for the full time of service prior thereto, unless barred by proof that he has not exerted himself to the utmost to save ship, &c.; the Merchant Shipping Act, 1894, ss. 157, 158, re-enacting similar provisions in the Merchant Shipping Act of 1854. The difference, therefore, would not now be quite so great as stated in the text.

(*c*) Principles of Indem. c. ii. "As to Insurances on Ships," from which the whole of the above calculations are taken.

(*d*) As to which, see Bénecke, Pr. of Indem. c. ii. pp. 57—60; c. iv. pp. 133—136; and Dallas, C. J., in Case *v.* Davidson (1816), 2 Brod. & B. 387.

(*e*) Coolidge *v.* Gloucester Marine Ins. Co. (1819), 15 Mass. R. 341; cited 2 Phillips, s. 1267.

Phillips, after a learned examination of the authorities, states the result to be "in favour of such valuation being applied to the freight successively pending on the separate passages, and not to the aggregate freight for all the passages" (*f*). He concludes that the doctrine applicable to the subject is that "a valuation of freight in a time policy, or one for successive passages, is presumed to be of that successively pending;" but this presumption, he thinks, may be rebutted by showing that the valuation is applicable to the aggregate amount of the successive freights.

Sect. 358.

If there is any provision in the charter-party suspending the earning of freight till the completion of the homeward passage (as was frequently the case with ships chartered for the voyage out and home in the East India Company's trade), and the freight for the whole voyage be valued at a gross sum, it seems that the whole sum valued may be recovered whether the loss take place on the passage out or home (*g*).

Freight is now frequently insured in valued time policies, which are intended by both parties to be of constant effect during the whole period covered, quite independently of the ship's engagements. Thus, in the case of Club Insurances on freight, it is a common rule that, "in the event of the total loss of a ship, the freight of which is insured in this Association, the amount insured shall be deemed the owner's interest at risk, and he shall be paid such amount whether the vessel be loaded, in ballast or under time charter" (*h*). The effect of such an insurance is obviously to entitle the shipowner to receive a fixed sum in the event of a total loss, not necessarily of any freight at all, but of his ship; and this

Modern use of valued time policies on freight.

(*f*) 2 Phillips on Ins. s. 1208. See New York and Cuba Mail SS. Co. *v.* Royal Exch. Ass. (1907), 154 Fed. R. 315, *ante*, § 355, note (*y*).

(*g*) Williams *v.* London Ass. Co. (1813), 1 M. & S. 318.

(*h*) Similarly, one of the Institute Time Clauses, 1914, for insurances on freight provides that "in the event of the total loss, whether absolute or constructive, of the steamer the amount underwritten by this policy shall be paid in full, whether the steamer be fully or only partly loaded or in ballast, chartered or unchartered." See Appendix B.

Sect. 358. is no doubt the intention of the parties also. The rule appears clearly to make a policy framed in accordance therewith a contract of insurance by way of gaming and wagering, void therefore under sect. 4 of the Marine Insurance Act, 1906. Be this as it may, the object of the members of the Association is not to gamble with one another, but in this indirect way to increase the amount receivable in case of total loss of hull, which in their actual policies on hull they may have found it convenient to under-assess.

Valued policies on goods.

359. Valued policies on goods are stated by Stevens to have originated in insurances on colonial produce, of which, as no invoice could be had (no purchase having been made), a valuation was necessarily adopted such as would indemnify the planter in case of loss. The practice, being found very convenient on account of its enabling the merchant to include in the valuation a fair mercantile profit on his goods, which he could not do by an open policy, was extended to classes of goods to which the original reasons for its adoption would not apply.

Specific valuations.

When the cargo consists of different kinds of colonial produce, as sugars, coffees, tobacco, &c., it is more usual, because more convenient for the purpose of adjustment in case of loss, to value each species of produce separately; as "on sugars valued at 500*l*., on coffee valued at 600*l*.," or "on 100 hogsheads of sugar valued at," &c. Sometimes the valuation is at so much per hogshead, tierce, barrel, bale, hundredweight, &c. This is followed in most instances with appropriate clauses, " to pay average on each species, as if separate interests, separately insured," or " to pay average on each 10, 15, 20 hogsheads, &c., succeeding numbers, as if separately insured" (*i*). We shall see hereafter that the purpose of these specific insurances is in case of a partial loss to enable the assured to recover notwithstanding the memorandum clauses, and that the single word "effects" (*k*), or "goods" (*l*),

---

(*i*) Stevens on Average, 186, 224, 225; Benecke, Pr. of Indem. 158, 159.

(*k*) Duff *v.* Mackenzie (1857), 3 C. B. N. S. 16; 26 L. J. C. P. 313.

(*l*) Wilkinson *v.* Hyde (1857),

CHAP. XIII.] VALUATION IN FLOATING POLICIES. 489

describing the subjects of insurance, does not prevent the policy being construed distributively, when such word is descriptive of various kinds of goods or articles (*m*). It is quite otherwise if such word be descriptive of a homogeneous cargo only, such as linseed (*n*) or rice (*o*), notwithstanding it is packed in separate bags or packages; and the effect of such a policy is not altered by indorsement afterwards of a declaration of the ship, and of the packages and their separate value (*p*).

Sect. 359.

When goods are valued at so much per lb., this must be understood of the lb. of the place where the policy is made (*q*).

360. When the assured expects goods from abroad, but does not know the kind or the amount, he generally procures a floating policy to be effected "on goods to be hereafter declared and valued."

Goods "to be hereafter declared and valued."

Such declaration before loss is not a condition precedent to the right of the assured to recover; yet "unless the policy otherwise provides, where a declaration of value is not made until after notice of loss or arrival, the policy must be treated as an unvalued policy as regards the subject-matter of that declaration" (*r*).

Under a policy in this form, a clerk of the assured wrote out and signed a declaration of interest and value on a separate piece of paper, which he wafered to the policy, but it did not appear that this had been shown to the underwriter before the loss was known, and Lord Ellenborough held there was no declaration, and consequently that it was an open policy (*s*).

Valuation must be made and communicated to underwriter before loss.

3 C. B. N. S. 30; 27 L. J. C. P. 116.

(*m*) Cator *v.* Great Western Ins. Co. of New York (1873), L. R. 8 C. P. 552.

(*n*) Ralli *v.* Janson (1856), 6 E. & B. 422; 25 L. J. Q. B. 300.

(*o*) Entwistle *v.* Ellis (1857), 2 H. & N. 549; 27 L. J. Ex. 105.

(*p*) Ibid.

(*q*) Stevens on Average, 186; 2 Phillips, s. 1199.

(*r*) Mar. Ins. Act, 1906, s. 29 (4), ante, § 185. See Craufurd *v.* Hunter (1798), 8 T. R. 13, 15, n.; Gledstanes *v.* Royal Exchange Ass. Co. (1864), 34 L. J. Q. B. 30.

(*s*) Harman *v.* Kingston (1811), 3 Camp. 150. See per Mellor, J.: "It may be important that both parties should know as to value, but the risk is quite a different question;" Cockburn, C. J.: "There must be an agreement as to valua-

Sect. 360.

As we have seen elsewhere, a mistake made in declaring may be corrected without the assent of the underwriters, if made in good faith (*t*).

Applied to the proceeds or returns of the outward cargo.

Questions have arisen in the United States whether a valuation in a policy on goods for the voyage out and home applies to the proceeds or returns purchased by the sale of the outward cargo. This is a question of intention, and consequently to be determined upon a construction of the instrument in view of the circumstances of the case. "In the absence of any collateral considerations," says Phillips, "I conclude the preferable doctrine to be, that a valuation of the outward cargo in a policy for the round voyage is to be presumed to be a valuation of its whole proceeds for the return voyage or for subsequent passages" (*u*).

Premium.

Generally speaking, a valuation at a round sum is taken to include the premium, and this whether the valuation be on the subject in gross, or by the weight, measure, or piece, except where the contrary appears from the language of the policy, or from the scale of the valuation (*x*).

A stipulation as to rate of exchange does not make a valued policy.

361. Where goods are expected from abroad, and no value is put upon them in the policy, but it is only stipulated that the coin of the foreign port of loading at which they are invoiced shall be reduced into our own money, at so many shillings the dollar, livre, rupee, &c., it seems that this ought not to be taken as a valued, but as an open policy; for it contains no fixed valuation of the goods, but only an ascertainment of the value in our money of the foreign currency in which their invoice value is expressed. Accordingly it has

---

tion;" Gledstanes *v.* Royal Exchange Ass. Co. (1864), 34 L. J. Q. B. 30, 34.

(*t*) Mar. Ins. Act, 1906, s. 29 (3), *ante*, §§ 185, 187.

(*u*) See McKim *v.* Phœnix Ins. Co. (1807), 2 Wash. Circ. Court R. 89; Haven *v.* Gray (1815), 12 Mass. R. 71; Whitney *v.* American Ins. Co. (1824), 3 Cowen, 210; 5 Cowen, 712; 2 Phillips, ss. 1197, 1198; 1 Parsons, 270.

(*x*) This is the received doctrine in the United States; 2 Phillips, s. 1201. The learned author cites Mayo *v.* Maine Fire and Marine Ins. Co. (1815), 12 Mass. R. 259, where the Court concluded, from the scale of valuation merely, that the premium was not intended by the assured to be included.

been held in America, that the invoice value, thus calculated, must have the premium added to it, in order to ascertain the insurable value, just as in an open policy (*y*).

Sect. 361.

By sect. 72 of the Marine Insurance Act, 1906—

(1) Where different species of property are insured under a single valuation, the valuation must be apportioned over the different species in proportion to their respective insurable values, as in the case of an unvalued policy. The insured value of any part of a species is such proportion of the total insured value of the same as the insurable value of the part bears to the insurable value of the whole, ascertained in both cases as provided by this Act (*z*).

Apportionment of valuation where different kinds of property covered.

(2) Where a valuation has to be apportioned, and particulars of the prime cost of each separate species, quality, or description of goods cannot be ascertained, the division of the valuation may be made over the net arrived sound values of the different species, qualities, or descriptions of goods (*a*).

Thus, in the case of damage to goods, the insurable value of the different kinds of goods having been ascertained, the valuation is applied to each kind in the same proportion; and the percentage of damage sustained by any one kind of goods must then be applied to their portion of the value, in order to ascertain the amount due thereon from the underwriter.

If only part of the interest at risk is valued, it is easy to

---

(*y*) Ogden *v.* Columbian Ins. Co. (1813), 10 Johnson's R. 273, cited 2 Phillips, s. 1201. Benecke thought otherwise, but the rule in the text seems preferable. Pr. of Indem. 159.

(*z*) See s. 16, *post*, § 365.

(*a*) The provisions of this section are based on a rule of the Association of Average Adjusters. In one case in the United States the judges were equally divided in opinion whether a valuation in the lump on ship, cargo and freight in one policy, without specifying how much on each, was not void for uncertainty. Stocker *v.* Harris (1807), 3 Mass. R. 415; 2 Phillips, s. 1203. Arnould was of opinion that the valuation may be set aside, if it be impossible to ascertain, by the invoice or otherwise, in what way the valuation was intended to be apportioned on different parts of the cargo: 2nd ed. Vol. I. p. 376. It is, however, unlikely that a case will occur which cannot be settled by applying the alternative rule in sub-sect. (2).

492 VALUATION OF INSURABLE INTERESTS. [PART I.

Sect. 361.

Rule of adjustment where different subjects of insurance are separately valued in one policy, and only one subject is put at risk.

ascertain what amount that is not valued is covered, by deducting the amount of the valuation from the sum insured.

If several articles be insured at one sum, with a distinct valuation on each, as supposing ship and cargo insured for 5,500*l*., calculating the ship at 1,500*l*., and no part of the cargo to be taken on board, so that the risk on that never attaches; then, if the ship be lost, the assured shall recover such proportion of the sum insured as 1,500*l*., the value put upon the ship, bears to 5,500*l*., the value put upon the whole (*b*). The mere fact, however, that goods are valued at a certain sum, of which a certain portion is expressed to be in respect of advanced freight, does not necessarily prevent the whole valuation from being applied to the goods alone (*c*).

Of open policies.

362. In an unvalued or open policy the value of the interest at risk is not fixed in the policy, but is estimated by a certain standard, and in case of loss is made out by proof.

Estimation of interest.

As will presently appear, the amount of insurable interest in all open policies is the sum which measures its worth to the assured at the commencement of the risk, *plus* the charges of the insurance (*d*). The indemnity contemplated by this mode of estimation puts the assured as nearly as possible in the same position as he was in at the outset of the adventure, and before effecting the insurance, without paying any regard to the profit he may have missed making, or to the wear and tear which his property has or would have sustained.

Premium and premium thereon should be included.

It is clear that, upon this principle of indemnity, the charges of insurance should include the premium paid upon it, and also the premium upon the premiums down to the total extinction of the risk; otherwise the sum received by the assured in case of loss, as an indemnity, will not really put him in the same position he was in before effecting the insurance.

(*b*) Amery *v.* Rodgers (1794), 1 Esp. 208.
(*c*) Thames and Mersey Co. *v.* Pitts, [1893] 1 Q. B. 476.

(*d*) Sect. 13 of the Mar. Ins. Act, 1906, declares that "the assured has an insurable interest in the charges of any insurance which he may effect."

CHAP. XIII.] OPEN POLICIES. 493

For example, suppose goods, the invoice price of which, **Sect. 362.** together with shipping charges, amounts to 1,000*l.*, to be insured at 5 per cent.; it is plain that the merchant, by insuring 1,050*l.* is not fully covered; for the premium for insuring 1,050*l.* at 5 per cent. will be 52*l.* 10*s.*, and the whole sum at risk would thus be 1,052*l.* 10*s.*, while all that could be recovered, in case of a total loss upon the above supposition, would be 1,050*l.*; it is plain, therefore, that the assured, who wishes to be completely protected from loss, must go further, and insure the premium of the premiums, down to the extinction of the risk.

363. The simplest practical rule for ascertaining the sum **Practical rule** necessary for this purpose is as follows:—the premium being contained in the sum which the underwriter pays, the assured for his indemnification can clearly only receive that sum deducting the premium; hence, every 100*l.* meant to be insured must be so insured minus the premium. As this residue is to 100*l.*, so is the amount of interest intended to be insured to the sum required to be insured in order fully to protect it. Thus, suppose the amount of interest intended to be insured (no matter whether in ship, freight or goods, for the rule now under consideration extends to all alike) to be 1,000*l.* and the premium to be 5*l.* 5*s.* per cent.

Then, according to the rule, from the sum of £100 0 0
Deduct premium 5 5 0
Leaves £94 15 0

Then, as 94*l.* 15*s.* is to 100*l.*, so will 1,000*l.* be to the sum required to be insured, in order completely to cover the interest at risk, or about 1,055*l.* (*e*).

But besides the premium and premiums of premium, it is requisite also to cover the expenses of the policy; *i.e.*, the stamp duty and the broker's commission, if effected by a

(*e*) Stevens on Average, 193; Benecke, Pr. of Indem. 119, 120.

Sect. 363. broker (f). We have therefore, as before, on 100*l*., premium 5*l*. 5*s*., stamp duty, say 6*d*. (in case of a policy for twelve months), and the broker's commission ½ per cent.; *i.e.*, 5*l*. 15*s*. 6*d*. is to be deducted from the 100*l*., and the proportion is, as 94*l*. 4*s*. 6*d*. : 100*l*. :: 1,0000*l*. to the sum required to be insured, that is 1,062*l*.

Whatever be the subject-matter insured, whether ship, freight, goods, or profits, as the premium and the premium upon premium are always thus included in estimating the amount of the insurable interest, it follows, that in case of a stipulation for a return of premium on a certain contingency, the whole premium is, nevertheless, to be added in estimating the amount of the interest; since the assured may in the result be liable to pay the whole premium, or, which comes to the same thing, he may not be entitled to a return of any part of it (g).

Adjustment on open policies in cases of total and partial loss.

364. In case of total loss, the assured under an open policy is entitled to recover to the full extent of the value thus calculated, supposing the sum insured to amount to so much (h). In cases of partial loss the percentage of damage done to the subject insured having been first ascertained, the assured is entitled to recover the same percentage of the insurable value calculated as above; it being, of course, in every case understood that the underwriter is only proportionably liable upon the particular sum he has himself agreed to insure (i).

Thus, if an underwriter has insured 200*l*. on an open policy on goods, the estimated insurable value of which is 1,000*l*., and the ascertained amount of sea-damage 10*l*. per cent. on what they would have fetched at the port of delivery had

---

(f) The modern practice, however, is to include broker's commission in the premium: see per Channell, J., in United States Shipping Co. *v.* Empress Ass. Co., [1907] 1 K. B. 259, 262.

(g) 2 Phillips on Ins. s. 1221.

(h) Mar. Ins. Act, 1906, ss. 67, 68, *ante*, § 338.

(i) This is the rule in cases of particular average on goods: Mar. Ins. Act, 1906, s. 67. In case of ship there is no calculation of percentage of damage: the underwriter pays his proper proportion of the repair bill: Mar. Ins. Act, 1906, s. 69.

they arrived there sound, the underwriter pays as his share of the indemnification 10*l.* per cent. on the sum he has insured, *i.e.*, 20*l.*; in the same way, in case of total loss, he would have paid 200*l.* If the aggregate of the sums insured equals the whole amount of insurable value, the assured receives 10*l.* per cent. on 1,000*l.*, *i.e.*, 100*l.*; if it is less than this, he is his own insurer for the part uncovered by the policy (*k*), if more, it is an over-insurance.

<small>Sect. 364.</small>

The mode of proving the amount of insurable interest under an open policy in case of loss is;—for the goods, by the production of the invoice, bill of lading, policy, &c.;— for the ship, by the production of reports and estimates of surveyors, bills of sale, &c.;—for the freight, by the production of the manifest, bill of lading, charter-party, &c.

<small>Proof of interest at risk.</small>

365. The rules which are followed in estimating the value of the subject-matter insured for the purposes of an open policy are thus set out in sect. 16 of the Marine Insurance Act, 1906:—

<small>Measure of insurable value in an open policy—</small>

> Subject to any express provision or valuation in the policy, the insurable value of the subject-matter insured must be ascertained as follows:—
>
> (1) In insurance on ship, the insurable value is the value, at the commencement of the risk (*l*), of the ship, including her outfit, provisions and stores for the officers and crew, money advanced for seamen's wages, and other disbursements (if any) incurred to make the ship fit for the voyage or adventure contemplated by the policy, plus the charges of insurance upon the whole (*m*).

<small>on ship;</small>

(*k*) Mar. Ins. Act, 1906, s. 81, *post*, § 1215.

(*l*) The words "at the commencement of the risk" are unfortunate. In a policy "at and from" a particular port, the risk may well commence before her outfit, provisions, or stores are put on board (see *post*, § 475), and before the necessary disbursements are made.

(*m*) The items hereby expressly included were not, in the opinion of certain learned judges of the Court of Appeal, included, prior to the Act, in an insurance simply on "ship." See Roddick *v.* Indemnity Mutual Ins. Co., [1895] 2 Q. B. 380. It was probably only by reason of the general words "tackle, apparel, ordnance, munition, artillery, boat and other furniture," which

VALUATION OF INSURABLE INTERESTS. [PART I.

Sect. 365.

The insurable value, in the case of a steamship, includes also the machinery, boilers, and coals and engine stores if owned by the assured (*n*), and, in the case of a ship engaged in a special trade, the ordinary fittings requisite for that trade (*o*):

on freight;

(2) In insurance on freight, whether paid in advance or otherwise, the insurable value is the gross amount of the freight at the risk of the assured (*p*), plus the charges of insurance (*q*).

form part of the ordinary English policy, that such items were covered. There is a discrepancy between this provision and rule 15 of the 1st schedule to the Act, in which money advanced for seamen's wages is not included in the items covered by the term "ship" in the ordinary policy. On this point there is no judicial authority before the Act, but in Stevens on Average, p. 190, it is stated that such advances are included, and Stevens' statement was adopted by Arnould (2nd ed. Vol. I. p. 381; 7th ed. § 365) and by McArthur (Ins. p. 67). See generally *ante*, §§ 218—221, for what is covered by a policy on "ship."

(*n*) Ordinarily the coals and engine stores are provided by the shipowner, whether the vessel be under charter or not. Sometimes, however, the ship is let to a charterer, on the terms that the latter is to supply the coals and stores on his own account, and in this case they are not covered by an insurance effected to protect the shipowner's interest. It is not easy to see why the words "if owned by the assured," assuming them to be necessary here, were not also inserted after the words "provisions and stores for the officers" in the preceding paragraph of the subsection.

(*o*) These words possibly alter the law as to whaling, and other similar voyages. See *ante*, § 219.

(*p*) When during the voyage or time for which the insurance was effected there are successive shipments of goods, the question will arise whether or not the whole amount of the insurance must be applied to the freight at the risk of the assured at the time of the loss. If, for instance, a shipowner having at the commencement of the insured voyage only 500*l*. freight at risk, takes on board at an intermediate port additional cargo, the freight of which is the same in amount, will he, in the event of the whole cargo being lost, recover 1,000*l*. on his freight policy, or only 500*l*., the amount at risk at the commencement of the voyage? The result, it is apprehended, will in each case depend on the intention of the assured when he effected the insurance, and the wording of the policy. See Mar. Ins. Act, 1906, s. 26 (3), *ante*, § 251 *et seq.*; and see also *ante*, §§ 245, 246, 258, and *post*, §§ 367, 519.

(*q*) See per Lord Ellenborough, Forbes *v.* Aspinall (1811), 13 East, 326; Palmer *v.* Blackburn (1822), 1 Bing. 61; United States Shipping Co. *v.* Empress Assurance Corporation, [1907] 1 K. B. 259; [1908] 1 K. B. 115 (see § 262, note (*u*), *ante*); Stevens on Average, 192. The same rule appears most gene-

(3) In insurance on goods or merchandise, the insurable value is the prime cost of the property insured, plus the expenses of and incidental to shipping and the charges of insurance upon the whole (*r*).   *Sect.* 365. on goods;

(4) In insurance on any other subject-matter, the insurable value is the amount at the risk of the assured when the policy attaches, plus the charges of insurance (*s*).   or other subjects of insurance.

The prime cost of goods is generally evidenced by the invoice price, but is not conclusively fixed by it (*t*). In the United States it has been laid down on several occasions, that the market price of the goods at the commencement of the risk, is the true basis of calculation, and that the prime cost or invoice price furnishes no satisfactory rule of indemnity in any case where it exceeds, or is less than, this market value. "Suppose," says Washington, J., "the property to be destroyed within an hour after the risk has commenced, what is it the owner loses? Precisely as much as it is worth, or would have commanded in the market at the time and place of shipment. If the property cost him less than it was worth when shipped he

The invoice, and not the market price of the goods at the port of shipment.

rally to obtain in the United States, though in some of the States the insurable value of freight is taken to be two-thirds of its gross amount. See 2 Phillips, s. 1238. It is obvious that the rule by which gross freight is payable in case of a loss may in many cases give the assured much more than a mere indemnity. In United States Shipping Co. *v.* Empress Ass. Corporation, *supra,* Channell, J., held that in a charterers' policy on freight the commission for obtaining the charter could not be included in the valuation.

(*r*) See Usher *v.* Noble (1810), 12 East, 646; Tuite *v.* Royal Exchange Co. (1747), 1 Park, 224, 225; 1 Marshall, 232; Stevens on Average, 178 *et seq.;* Benecke, Pr.

of Indem. 12—14; 2 Phillips, s. 1232.

(*s*) The application of this rule to a policy on profits may have a curious result when the amount to be earned depends on fluctuating market prices. Thus, if goods could only have been sold at a loss at the time of shipment, but would have realized a profit if sold at the time of the loss or of their expected arrival, can the assured recover nothing on an open policy on profits? Moreover, the rule also seems inapplicable to a policy on commissions, when the amount thereof will depend on the sale of the goods during the voyage or upon arrival.

(*t*) 2 Phillips, s. 1229.

498 VALUATION OF INSURABLE INTERESTS. [PART I.

Sect. 365. loses (in case of total loss) as well the first cost as the increased value for which he is entitled to claim indemnity from the insurer" (*u*). In theory this is unquestionably true, but as a practical rule, the prime cost, as evidenced by the invoice price, is by far the most convenient standard.

Invoice price in foreign money.

366. When the invoice price of goods shipped from a foreign port, where there is no current rate of exchange, is expressed in the currency of the foreign country to which such port belongs, the true mode of ascertaining the insurable value is to estimate what would be the worth of the foreign money in which the invoice value is expressed, supposing that it had been shipped in specie, instead of the goods, to the port of destination: *i.e.*, the invoice value of the goods is to be ascertained by calculating what the foreign coin in which it is expressed would be worth to the consignee of the goods, after paying the premium of its insurance, the freight and other expenses of its transportation (*x*).

On the other hand, if there is a current rate of exchange at the foreign port of loading, the most equitable measure of the insurable value of the goods appears to be the rate of the exchange at the commencement of the risk (*y*).

Thellusson v. Bewick.

In one case, however, in this country, Lord Kenyon acted upon a different rule; a policy was effected in September, 1791, on sugar shipped from a French port: at the time of effecting the policy, the exchange in England on the French crown of 3 livres was 24*d*.; at the time of settling the loss, in January, 1792, it had fallen to $7\frac{3}{4}d$. Lord Kenyon held that as in case the exchange had risen the assured would have had the benefit of the rise, so in case of a fall they must submit to the loss; and he decided that the insurable value of the sugars must be estimated and the loss paid upon

---

(*u*) See 2 Phillips, s. 1229, citing Carron *v.* Marine Ins. Co. (1811), 2 Wash. C. C. R. 468. In one case the invoice value was taken, though higher than the actual cost to the assured. See *ibid.*; Coffin *v.* New-buryport Marine Ins. Co. (1812), 9 Mass. R. 436.

(*x*) See Magens on Ins. vol. i. p. 41, s. 40; Benecke, Pr. of Indem. 119.

(*y*) 2 Phillips, s. 1231.

the rate of exchange at the time of the adjustment, *i.e.*, at 7¾*d.* the French crown (*z*). {Sect. 366.}

If the goods are purchased by barter in a foreign port, with which there is no mode of estimating the rate of exchange, the French Code provides that the amount of interest shall be the cost and charges of the goods given in barter (*a*), by which word "charges" is meant the expenses of transporting and shipping them (*b*). {Goods purchased by barter.}

When goods are entitled to a drawback on exportation, a question has been raised whether in estimating the insurable value of such goods under an open policy the amount of this drawback is to be deducted. The Courts of the United States have held that it is not, on the ground that, though it may enter into the estimate of the value of the goods for exportation, it is no part of their actual market price at the port of departure (*c*); and these decisions seem conformable to sound principle (*d*). {Drawback.}

367. Where the provisions of the policy show that it is intended to cover any interest that the assured may have at risk within the limits of the time or the voyage for which the policy is effected, the amount of insurable interest fluctuates at different periods of the risk, and the loss must be apportioned between the parties in the proportion which the sum insured bears to the amount of insurable interest on board at the time of loss. {Of policies to cover fluctuating interest.}

For example, the plaintiffs, barge-masters, having several boats constantly engaged in carrying goods for hire by canal between London and Birmingham, for the purpose of pro- {Crowley *v.* Cohen.}

(*z*) Thellusson *v.* Bewick (1793), 1 Esp. 77. The rate of exchange at the commencement of the risk appears a preferable standard. In France the rule is to value the goods at the rate of exchange current at the time of subscribing the policy. Code de Commerce, art. 338.

(*a*) Code de Commerce, 339.
(*b*) Benecke, Pr. of Indem. 119.
(*c*) See these cases collected, 2 Phillips, s. 1235.
(*d*) Weskett says that when goods are entitled to a bounty on exportation the bounty is to be deducted, but the other seems the better rule. See Weskett's Digest, art. "Fish," No. 1.

Sect. 367. tecting their interest as carriers, caused themselves to be insured for twelve months, "by canal navigation boats, containing goods, at work between London, Wolverhampton, Birmingham, &c., backwards and forwards, and in any rotation, upon goods, and upon the body, tackle, &c., on thirty boats, as per margin of the policy," &c. The policy proceeded—"The said ship, &c., goods and merchandises, &c., for so much as concerns the assured, are and shall be (here the printed words 'valued at' were struck out) 12,000*l*., on goods, as interest may appear hereafter, to pay average on each package or description, as if separately insured, &c., the claim on this policy warranted not to exceed 100*l*. per cent." At the bottom of the policy was written "3,000*l*. only to be covered by the policy in any one boat on any one trip."

The facts were that within the time limited in the policy one of the thirty boats mentioned in the margin of the policy had sunk in the canal, with 1,700*l*. worth of goods on board of her, which was the loss in respect of which the action was brought; and that at the time of the loss every one of the thirty boats named in the margin had carried goods to the amount of 12,000*l*. and upwards, so that about 360,000*l*. worth of goods had been carried to and fro by the boats named in the policy between the commencement of the risk and the loss in question.

Under these circumstances the underwriters contended:—

1. That as soon as goods to the amount of 12,000*l*. had been carried by all the boats, or, at all events, by each boat, the policy was exhausted.

2. That, supposing the policy not to be so limited, still the underwriters were liable only for that proportion of the loss which 12,000*l*., the sum insured, bore to the whole amount of the goods carried by all the boats during the year for which the policy was effected (say 360,000*l*); for that must be taken as the whole insurable interest of the assured.

The Court, however, as to the first point, held that it was plainly inconsistent with the object of the policy and the real nature of the transaction, which was "in effect equivalent to a fresh insurance taking place at the time when each boat started, and governing all that were then afloat,—only that instead of a renewed insurance the object was attained by a continuing policy." As to the mode of calculating the indemnity, the Court held that the whole value of the goods afloat at the time of the loss must be taken, and the plaintiffs recover such a proportion of the loss as 12,000*l.* might bear to the value of all the property on board all the boats at the time of the accident, supposing that value to exceed 12,000*l.*; if not, then the plaintiffs would be entitled to the whole amount lost (*e*).

The true measure, therefore, of the insurable interest in such a policy is the amount at risk at the time of the loss (*f*).

368. In another case, the policy being differently framed, and indeed not properly a marine policy at all, there was a different result. The policy, an ordinary Lloyd's policy, was "lost or not lost at and from all or any of the wharves, banks, quays and places of arrival and departure in the river Thames, and any merchant or steam vessel of any description therein, comprising the whole extent of the said river, from Wandsworth downwards to the Victoria Docks, including all or any intermediate docks and wharves, and *vice versâ* until on board any merchant or steam vessel, barge or boat, or otherwise landed at any wharf, &c. The risk to commence on the 25th September, 1869, and to terminate on the 24th September, 1870, including both days, upon any kind of goods and merchandise in craft of every description, &c. The ship, and goods, and merchandise, &c., by agreement, &c., are and shall be valued at   on all goods and produce as interest may appear." The sum stated in the

Sect. 367.

Joyce *v.* Kennard.

(*e*) Crowley *v.* Cohen (1832), 3 B. & Ad. 478. The same principle was laid down by Story, J., in a similar case in the United States. See Columbian Ins. Co. *v.* Catlett (1827), 12 Wheaton, 383; 2 Phillips, s. 1228.

(*f*) Where the master of a ship had insured his effects by a time policy, Pickford, J., held that the policy covered all his effects at the time of the loss, including the clothes and watch which he was at that time wearing on shore: Anstey *v.* Ocean Mar. Ins. Co. (1913), 19 Com. Cas. 8.

Sect. 368. margin was 2,000*l*. At the bottom of the policy was written as follows:—" To cover and include all losses, damages, and accidents, amounting to 20*l*. and upwards, in each craft, to goods carried by Messrs. Joyce, as lightermen, or delivered to them to be waterborne, either in their own or other craft, and from (*sic*) which losses, damages, and accidents, Messrs. Joyce may be liable or responsible to the owners thereof, or others entrusted. It is agreed that the amount of each underwriter's liability shall not exceed the amount of his subscription." The defendants underwrote this policy for 100*l*.

During the continuance of the risk in this policy, a loss, damage, or accident, within the meaning of it, had occurred to goods loaded on board one of the assured's craft, called the "Lord Cardigan," to the amount of 1,100*l*., for which the assured were liable to the owners thereof and which they had paid. The total value of the goods at the time on board the "Lord Cardigan" was 2,906*l*., and the total value of the goods on board that and the other barges at the same time was 20,000*l* and upwards.

The Court said this was not an ordinary marine policy, but a policy of a mixed nature, by which the defendant indemnified the plaintiffs against any liability to the extent of the sum underwritten, which they might incur, as carriers, to the owners of the goods entrusted to them. It was, therefore, held, on the language of the policy, that the defendant was liable for the full amount underwritten by him (*g*).

Cunard SS. Co. v. Marten. In another case (*h*) the plaintiffs, having agreed to carry a cargo of mules under a contract without a negligence clause, effected an insurance with the defendant against "liability of any kind to owners of mules up to 20,000*l*., owing to the omission of the negligence clause in contract." The insurance was made by the ordinary form of Lloyd's policy, and

---

(*g*) Joyce *v.* Kennard (1871), L. R. 7 Q. B. 78. See also Ursula Bright SS. Co. *v.* Arnsinck (1902), 115 Fed. R. 242.

(*h*) Cunard SS. Co. *v.* Marten, [1902] 2 K. B. 624; [1903] 2 K. B. 511.

Walton, J., and the Court of Appeal held that it was not a policy on the mules, but a contract of indemnity under which the plaintiffs were entitled to recover in full any loss, up to 20,000*l.*, which they might incur.

<small>Sect. 368.</small>

368a. Sect. 74 of the Marine Insurance Act, 1906, declares that—

<small>Measure of indemnity in insurances against liabilities.</small>

> Where the assured has effected an insurance in express terms against any liability to a third party, the measure of indemnity, subject to any express provision in the policy, is the amount paid or payable by him to such third party in respect of such liability.

The preceding section affords some examples of insurances against liabilities. Other express insurances against liabilities are contained in the suing and labouring clause and the running-down clause, which will be discussed hereafter (*i*).

A general provision of the Act which has some bearing on the valuation of insurable interests is contained in sect. 75, as follows:—

<small>General provisions as to measure of indemnity.</small>

> (1) Where there has been a loss in respect of any subject-matter not expressly provided for in the foregoing provisions of this Act, the measure of indemnity shall be ascertained, as nearly as may be, in accordance with those provisions, in so far as applicable to the particular case.
>
> (2) Nothing in the provisions of this Act relating to the measure of indemnity shall affect the rules relating to double insurance, or prohibit the insurer from disproving interest wholly or in part, or from showing that at the time of the loss the whole or any part of the subject-matter insured was not at risk under the policy.

(*i*) See Vol. II. §§ 792 *et seq.*, §§ 864 *et seq.*

CHAPTER XIV.

THE VOYAGE INSURED.

SECT.
The Voyage insured distinguished from the Voyage of the Ship ... 369
Deviation and Change of Voyage 370, 371
Description of the Voyage insured ....372—375

Of the voyage insured, and the voyage of the ship. Difference between time and voyage policies.

369. USUALLY the risk undertaken by the underwriter is defined by certain limits of time or certain points of locality specified in the policy as the limits or termini of the risk (*a*). When the risk is limited by time, the policy is called a time policy; when by local termini, it is called a voyage policy (*b*).

Termini of a voyage policy.

In voyage policies, of which we are now treating, the *terminus a quo*, or place at which the risk commences, is usually, in the common policies on ship, the port of departure; in the common policies on goods, the port of loading, which frequently, but not necessarily, is the same place. The *terminus ad quem*, or point at which the risk ends, is the port of the ship's destination, or the port or ports of the cargo's discharge.

The voyage insured.

That which is limited or described in the policy, by these termini, is the voyage insured (*viaggium*); a technical term, which must be carefully distinguished from the actual voyage of the ship (*iter navis*) (*c*). The distinction is important.

The voyage insured (*viaggium*) is a transit at sea from the *terminus a quo* to the *terminus ad quem* in a prescribed course

---

(*a*) 2 Emerigon, c. xiii. p. 39;
2 Benecke, System des Assecuranz, c. viii. p. 203, ed. 1807.
(*b*) Mar. Ins. Act, 1906, s. 25 (1),

ante, § 9.
(*c*) Casaregis, Disc. 67, No. 31, as cited 2 Emerigon, c. xiii. s. 5, p. 60.

of navigation (*iter viaggii*), which is never set out in any policy, but virtually forms part of all policies, and is as binding on the parties thereto as though it were minutely detailed.

_{Sect. 369.}

The voyage of the ship (*iter navis*) is the course of navigation on and in which the ship actually sails.

_{The voyage of the ship.}

If the ship, in fact, sails in the prescribed course from the *terminus a quo* to the *terminus ad quem*, the voyage of the ship and the voyage described in the policy are identical.

370. If the ship, without entirely abandoning the prosecution of the voyage described in the policy (*viaggium*), yet voluntarily, and without justifying cause, departs from the prescribed course of that voyage (*iter viaggii*), this is a deviation, and the underwriter is liable for no loss occurring after the point (frequently called the dividing point) at which the ship first quits the prescribed course (*d*).

_{Deviation.}

If the ship either originally sail on a different voyage from that described in the policy, or if, after sailing, she entirely abandons all intention of prosecuting the voyage described in the policy, this is an abandonment or change of voyage, which avoids the policy from the moment the intention of so abandoning it is definitely formed (*e*); for it is an elementary principle in this branch of insurance law that the underwriter cannot be liable for a loss which does not take place in the course of prosecuting the very voyage described in the policy (*f*).

_{Abandonment, or change of voyage.}

(*d*) Mar. Ins. Act, 1906, s. 46, *post*, § 376.

(*e*) Mar. Ins. Act, 1906, ss. 43, 44, 45, *post*, § 380. The learned author of this work used the terms "change" and "abandonment" of voyage indifferently, as applicable in either case. In the Mar. Ins. Act "change of voyage" denotes only an abandonment thereof after the risk has attached; see sect. 45 (1).

No special term is used to describe the abandonment of the voyage before the risk has attached. In the earlier Marine Insurance Bills the term "abandonment" was used where the risk had never attached, and "change of voyage" in the same sense as in the Act.

(*f*) Roccus, No. 18, cited 2 Emerigon, c. xiii. p. 39.

Sect. 371.
Illustrations of the distinctions between— the voyage insured and the voyage of the ship.

371. The following simple illustrations may serve to place these distinctions in a clearer point of view:—

1. As to the voyage insured, and the voyage of the ship.

Suppose the ship to sail under a charter-party on a voyage from London to Sydney and back; a merchant who expects goods to be sent by her on her homeward voyage from Sydney to London, effects a policy on them on board the ship for a voyage "at and from Sydney to London": in this case, the voyage of the ship is the round voyage from London to Sydney, out and home: the voyage insured, or rather (for this is the more accurate mode of expression) the voyage on which the subject is insured, is only the home voyage from Sydney to London.

Between a deviation and change of voyage.

2. As to deviation and abandonment or change of voyage.

A ship insured on a voyage from London to Cadiz, sails from London with the intention of proceeding, not to Cadiz, but to Jamaica, or after sailing some distance with an intention of proceeding to Cadiz, changes that intention, and resolves to proceed to Jamaica.

In either case, as the voyage insured ceases to exist directly the purpose of prosecuting it is finally abandoned, any loss which may accrue afterwards does not take place in the course of prosecuting the voyage described in the policy; that is, not under those conditions on which the underwriter agreed to be responsible: the assured, therefore, ceased to be protected by the policy from that time (*g*). Even though, in the case supposed, the loss may take place while the ship is still sailing on the common course which leads indifferently either to the original *terminus ad quem* (Cadiz), or the substituted port of destination (Jamaica), yet the underwriter is equally freed from liability, for the voyage insured is broken up, not by altering its course, but by altering its termini (*h*).

(*g*) 3 Boulay-Paty, Droit Mar. tit. x. s. 9, p. 415.

(*h*) Si avant le départ, la destination était changée, le voyage sera rompu et l'assurance sera nulle, *etiamsi intra limites itineris destinati navis se contineat*. Casaregis, Disc. 67, No. 24; 2 Emerigon, c. iii. s. 11, p. 82; confirmed by Wooldridge *v.* Boydell (1778), 1 Dougl. 16; Way *v.* Modigliani (1787), 2 T. R. 30.

Again, supposing the ship to have been insured (say from London to Jamaica), and the prescribed or customary course of such voyage to be to sail to the south of St. Domingo, instead of which the ship, without any clause in the policy permitting her so to do, or without any necessity, or justifying excuse, sails to the north of that island: this is a deviation. Here the course actually taken by the ship (*iter navis*) differs from the prescribed course of the voyage insured (*iter viaggii*); the risk run is different from that which the underwriter agreed to take upon himself; and he is, therefore, liable for no loss that takes place after the ship has passed the dividing point at which the track to Jamaica by the south of St. Domingo branches off from that by the north (*i*).

Sect. 371.

372. The voyage insured must be accurately described in a voyage policy; that is, the local limits of the risk, the *terminus a quo*, or port where the voyage is to commence, and the *terminus ad quem*, or port where it is to conclude, must be each of them specified in the policy, which will be vitiated by any material failure in this respect (*k*). Thus, if the *terminus ad quem* or port of ultimate destination be left in blank, even though this were done for the purpose of deceiving the enemy, and private instructions were given to the captain as to the port for which the ship was really destined, the policy is nevertheless void (*l*).

Description of the voyage insured in the policy.

Where there is any doubt as to the precise mercantile limits of any place named in the policy, as one of the termini

How the limits of the termini must be ascertained.

(*i*) The whole subject of deviation and abandonment of voyage will be considered more at length in the next chapter; meanwhile the attention of the student may be directed to the thirteenth chapter of Emerigon's great work, an admirably arranged magazine of legal learning and accurate thought. Boulay-Paty, in his Cours de Droit Mar. vol. iii. tit. x. s. 9, has done little more than copy his distinguished predecessor.

(*k*) A terminus may, however, be described in general terms, as "at and from her port of loading" within a specified area, or "to any port in the Baltic," as in Uhde *v.* Walters (1811), 3 Camp. 16.

(*l*) Stamp Act, 1891, s. 93; Molloy, book ii. c. 7, s. 14, cited 1 Marshall on Ins. 328.

Sect. 372. of the voyage, such doubt, as we have already seen, must be cleared up by the evidence of mercantile men (*m*).

Thus, such evidence has been admitted to prove that the Gulf of Finland is, in the mercantile world, considered to be within the Baltic (*n*), and that Mauritius, although regarded by geographers as belonging to Africa, yet, in the common acceptation of mercantile men, is to be considered one of the East Indian Islands (*o*).

The proper course of the ship need not be described.

373. This description of the voyage insured by its termini is all that is necessary in the policy; it is not requisite, and in practice is never attempted to describe the track which the ship ought to take, for this, being fixed by general mercantile usage, is considered to be familiar to all mercantile men, and is as binding upon the parties to the policy as though it were inserted therein. The termini of the voyage insured must, however, be so clearly specified in the policy, that by means thereof, aided by a knowledge of the course of navigation prescribed by mercantile usage, both parties may know clearly when the subject of insurance will be within the protection of the policy.

Leave to touch at any place between the termini must be specially given.

Moreover, if it be desired that the ship should have the power of putting into any intermediate ports or places, the permission to do so must be clearly expressed in the policy by a clause in which the ports where, and the purposes for which, it is desired that the ship should have this power, must be accurately set forth. Of these clauses and their construction we shall treat at large elsewhere, and will here notice merely the more ordinary modes of describing the termini of the voyage insured.

Distinction between insuring

374. As appears from the common printed form of policy, the voyage insured is in this country generally made to

---

(*m*) *Ante,* Chap. III., on the construction of the policy.
(*n*) Uhde *v.* Walters (1811), 3 Camp. 16.

(*o*) Robertson *v.* Clarke (1824), 1 Bing. 445. See note at the end of the report, p. 451, *ibid.*

commence, not simply "from," but "at and from" the *terminus a quo*. The reason for this is, that, under an insurance simply from the *terminus a quo*, the voyage insured, and consequently the risk, does not commence until the ship actually sails on her voyage from that port; whereas, under the mode of insurance commonly adopted by virtue of the word "at" the ship is protected during the whole time that she is in the harbour of the *terminus a quo* preparing for the voyage insured (*p*).

<small>Sect. 374.
"from" and "at and from" the *terminus a quo*.</small>

375. Ships are very frequently insured in one policy and at one fixed premium for the round voyage out and home. In such cases the form generally adopted is to insure "at and from" the home port of loading "to" the out port of discharge, "and at and from" such out port (naming it), or "and at and from thence," back again to the home port or any other port of discharge which the parties may agree to name.

<small>Insurances for a round voyage.</small>

When the ship is thus insured for a voyage out and home, although she makes two separate passages (*itinera*), *i.e.*, from the home to the out port and then back again, yet the voyage insured (*viaggium*) is one and indivisible, and the underwriter is responsible for any loss that may happen in the whole course of its duration. The voyage insured is one, though the passages made by the ship are several.

<small>The voyage insured one and entire.</small>

This principle, which is incontestably established in the law of marine insurance, is thus expressed by Casaregis: *Falsum est omnino in casu nostro quod itus et reditus considerari debent pro diversis viagiis, sed pro unicâ tantum navigatione vel viaggio. Quia viaggium vel navigatio, cum sit nomen juris ac universale, potest complecti plura itinera* (*q*).

However complicated the voyage of the ship may be

(*p*) Motteux *v.* London Ass. Co. (1739), 1 Atkyns, 545; Forbes *v.* Wilson (1800), 1 Marshall, Ins. 148; 1 Park, 472.

(*q*) Disc. 67, No. 28, cited 2 Emerigon, c. xiii. s. 3, p. 52. For an illustration of this in our own jurisprudence, see Bermon *v.* Woodbridge (1781), 2 Dougl. 781.

Sect. 375. rendered by liberty given to touch and stay at intermediate ports, or by being broken up into a variety of successive stages, yet the voyage insured, if comprised between two specified termini and insured for one entire premium, is one and indivisible (*r*). Thus, where a ship was insured "at and from" Honfleur to the Coast of Angola, during her stay and trade there, at and from thence to her port or ports of discharge in St. Domingo, and at and from St. Domingo back again to Honfleur, at a premium of 11 per cent., Lord Mansfield and the Court of King's Bench determined, on great consideration, that as the premium here was entire and indivisible, so it was one voyage and one entire risk (*s*).

(*r*) 2 Emerigon, c. xiii. s. 3, p. 52.
(*s*) Bormon *v.* Woodbridge (1781), 2 Dougl. 781.

CHAPTER XV.

DEVIATION AND CHANGE OF RISK (a).

SECT.		SECT.
The general Doctrine of Deviation ....376—379	Deviation—*contd*. In relation to License Clauses	398—411
Change of Voyage ....380—389	By Delay ....412—417	
Deviation—	By Cruising ....418—424	
Without License Clauses .... 390—397	Causes which justify a Deviation ....424a—435	

376. IN almost all voyages, as we have already seen, experience and usage have prescribed a certain course of navigation, as the safest, directest, and most expeditious mode of proceeding from one of the termini to the other. The course thus prescribed is the lawful course of the voyage insured: and, being a matter of general mercantile notoriety, is presumed to have been contemplated by the parties to the policy at the time of entering into their contract, and is, therefore, considered as much to form part of the policy, as though it were in express terms set forth therein. *Of the general doctrine of deviation.*

In every contract of insurance by a voyage policy, the meaning of the parties is, in law, taken to be that the assured shall enjoy the protection of the policy, only as long as he strictly pursues this regular course of the voyage insured, and carries it on to its termination with all safe, convenient, and practicable expedition (b). It is only upon this condition, *An implied condition of the policy that there shall be no deviation.*

(a) The subject of this chapter affects voyage policies only. In a case on a fire policy on a ship while in a dock, it was suggested by Blackburn, J., that a departure from the prescribed locality would only suspend the risk until the ship returned to the locality—not terminate it, as in the case of a voyage policy. Pearson *v.* Commercial Union Ass. Co., in the Ex. Ch. (1873), L. R. 8 C. P. 548, 549; *S. C.*, in the House of Lords (1876), 1 App. Cas. 498.

(b) 3 Kent, Com. 312.

Sect. 376. never expressed, but universally implied, that the underwriter agrees to indemnify the assured; any failure, therefore, to comply with it, alters the nature of the risk which the underwriter has assumed, and frees him from liability for subsequent loss (*c*). This tacit understanding not to depart from the lawful course of the voyage insured is technically called an implied condition not to deviate (*d*).

Implied condition that there shall be no delay.

This implied condition extends as well to the time in which the voyage insured ought to be completed, as to the track or course of navigation by which it ought to be pursued. The understanding implied in the contract between the parties is not only that the ship, in sailing between the termini of the voyage insured, shall follow the course which custom has prescribed; but also that she shall commence and complete the voyage with that reasonable expedition which the underwriter has a right to expect (*e*).

Mar. Ins. Act, s. 42. Delay in attachment of risk.

The law on this subject is thus stated in sects. 42, 46, 47 and 48 of the Marine Insurance Act, 1906:—

Sect. 42.—(1) Where the subject-matter is insured by a voyage policy "at and from" or "from" a particular place, it is not necessary that the ship should be at that place when the contract is concluded, but there is an implied condition that the adventure shall be commenced within a reasonable time, and that if the adventure be not so commenced the insurer may avoid the contract.

(2) The implied condition may be negatived by showing that the delay was caused by circumstances known to the insurer before the contract was concluded, or by showing that he waived the condition (*f*).

(*c*) 2 Emerigon, c. xiii. s. 16, p. 98. For the effect of a deviation on a fire policy on a ship, see n. (*a*), *ante*.

(*d*) Cf. 2 Emerigon, c. xiii. s. 15, p. 94; 2 Benecke, System des Assecuranz, c. viii. s. 2, p. 234; 3 Kent, Com. 312. The language of Emerigon is marked with all his usual terseness and perspicuity. "Le navire change de route lorsqu', au lieu de suivre la voie usitée, il en prend une différente, sans perdre toutefois de vue l'endroit de sa destination"; *loc. cit.* Phillips defines deviation in more comprehensive terms, as "the enhancing or varying from the risks insured against." 1 Phillips, s. 977.

(*e*) 3 Kent, Com. 315.

(*f*) As to delay in the commencement of the risk, see *post*, §§ 479, 483.

Sect. 46.—(1) Where a ship, without lawful excuse, deviates from the voyage contemplated by the policy, the insurer is discharged from liability as from the time of deviation, and it is immaterial that the ship may have regained her route before any loss occurs.

Sect. 376.

Sect. 46. Deviation.

(2) There is a deviation from the voyage contemplated by the policy—

(a) Where the course of the voyage is specifically designated by the policy, and that course is departed from; or

(b) Where the course of the voyage is not specifically designated by the policy, but the usual and customary course is departed from.

(3) The intention to deviate is immaterial; there must be a deviation in fact to discharge the insurer from his liability under the contract.

Sect. 47.—(1) Where several ports of discharge are specified by the policy, the ship may proceed to all or any of them, but in the absence of any usage or sufficient cause to the contrary, she must proceed to them, or such of them as she goes to, in the order designated by the policy. If she does not there is a deviation (*g*).

Sect. 47. Order of ports of discharge.

(2) Where the policy is to "ports of discharge," within a given area, which are not named, the ship must, in the absence of any usage or sufficient cause to the contrary, proceed to them, or such of them as she goes to, in their geographical order. If she does not there is a deviation (*h*).

Sect. 48. In the case of a voyage policy, the adventure must be prosecuted throughout its course with reasonable despatch, and, if without lawful excuse it is not so prosecuted, the insurer is discharged from liability as from the time when the delay became unreasonable (*i*).

Sect. 48. Delay in voyage.

(*g*) See *post*, §§ 394, 395.
(*h*) See *post*, § 393.
(*i*) Hitherto the word "deviation" has in legal language been used to include delay. See Hartley *v.* Buggin (1781), 2 Park, Ins. 652; 3 Dougl. 39; and Company of African Merchants *v.* British and Foreign Mar. Ins. Co. (1873), L. R. 8 Ex. 154, where it was held that delay was covered by a plea of deviation. See also Hyderabad (Deccan) Co. *v.* Willoughby, *infra*. As the word "deviation" in its proper sense implies the idea of space or locality, it is an unhappy use of the term to make it cover delay, which refers to time; and there is no need for the fiction that an unjustifiable delay amounts to

514 DEVIATION AND CHANGE OF RISK. [PART I.

Sect. 376.
Deviation clause.

A clause by which the underwriter agrees to hold the assured covered in case of deviation, or of change of voyage, at an extra premium, is now commonly inserted in policies (*k*), and is one of the Institute Clauses (*l*). Such a clause, though it provides that notice must be given of a deviation, can be invoked after a loss (*m*); and where the clause stipulated that due notice should be given on receipt of advice of a deviation, and the assured, knowing that his ship had been lost, only gave notice many months later, Hamilton, J., thought that as nothing could have been done on receipt of the notice, it was given sufficiently early (*n*). Even when the clause does not expressly require notice to be given, it has been held by the House of Lords that it is an implied term of the contract that notice shall be given within a reasonable time after the assured has been advised of the deviation (*o*).

Sect. 31 (2) of the Marine Insurance Act, 1906, provides that—

> Where an insurance is effected on the terms that an additional premium is to be arranged in a given event, and that event happens but no arrangement is made, then a reasonable additional premium is payable.

The additional premium ought to be such as it would have

---

a deviation. In the Mar. Ins. Act, 1906, deviation is not defined as including delay.

(*k*) See Hyderabad (Deccan) Co. *v.* Willoughby, [1899] 2 Q. B. 530; Simon, Israel & Co. *v.* Sedgwick, [1893] 1 Q. B. 303, *post*, § 380, n. (*d*), § 387; Maritime Ins. Co. *v.* Stearns, [1901] 2 K. B. 912. It is apprehended, notwithstanding that in the Mar. Ins. Act of 1906 the term "deviation" does not cover delay, that the term ought in the deviation clause still to be construed, as in Hyderabad (Deccan) Co. *v.* Willoughby, to cover delay, in accordance with its well-established legal meaning. See note (*i*), *supra*.

(*l*) See Institute Voyage Clauses, Appendix B.

(*m*) Greenock SS. Co. *v.* Maritime Ins. Co., [1903] 1 K. B. 367, 374; Mentz, Decker & Co. *v.* Maritime Ins. Co., [1910] 1 K. B. 132; 15 Com. Cas. 17.

(*n*) Mentz, Decker & Co. *v.* Maritime Ins. Co., *supra*. *Sed quære*: see Thames & Mersey Mar. Ins. Co. *v.* Van Laun, *infra*.

(*o*) Thames & Mersey Mar. Ins. Co. *v.* Van Laun. Unreported; but the judgment of Lord Halsbury, L. C., is given in full in the Shipping Gazette, 25th July, 1905. The House of Lords held that a notice given fourteen days after receipt of information was not given within a reasonable time.

been reasonable to charge at the time of the deviation or change of voyage, if the parties had then been aware of it (*p*).

_{Sect. 376.}

377. It is not necessary to prove that the risk has been enhanced by the delay, or deviation. The underwriter only undertakes to indemnify the assured upon the implied condition, that the risk shall remain precisely the same, as it appears to be on the face of the policy, as interpreted by usage. Directly, by the act of the assured or his agents, this risk is in any degree varied, even though it be not increased, the underwriter's liability ceases by the breach of the condition on which alone he engaged to be liable: it is on this ground that every voluntary and unnecessitated departure from the prescribed course of the voyage, by which the risk is varied, has been held to be a deviation, whether the risk be thereby increased or not (*q*).

_{Not necessary that risk should be increased.}

On the same principle it was held not to be necessary, in order to discharge the underwriter, that the subsequent loss should be shown to be in any, even the remotest, degree connected with the prior deviation; the ship after the deviation may have returned in perfect safety to the direct course of the voyage, without having sustained the slightest injury in consequence of her departure from it; and yet on the ground that the risk incurred was thereby varied from the risk insured, the underwriter was held to be discharged from his liability for any loss subsequent to the deviation (*r*).

_{The loss need not be connected with the deviation.}

378. Deviation does not, however, like unseaworthiness, discharge the underwriter from liability on the policy, *ab initio;* he still remains liable for all loss incurred prior to the deviation. The reason is, that the implied condition of sea-

_{Deviation does not avoid the policy *ab initio*.}

(*p*) See Greenock SS. Co. *v.* Maritime Ins. Co., [1903] 1 K. B. at p. 375; Mentz, Decker & Co. *v.* Maritime Ins. Co., [1910] 1 K. B. at p. 135.

(*q*) Hartley *v.* Buggin (1781), 3 Dougl. 39, Lord Mansfield's judgment.

(*r*) Elliot *v.* Wilson (1776), 4 Br. Pr. Cas. 470; Davis *v.* Garrett (1830), 6 Bing. 716. See the principle expounded by Lord Campbell, C. J., in Thompson *v.* Hopper (1856), 6 E. & B. 948; 26 L. J. Q. B. 22.

516 DEVIATION AND CHANGE OF RISK. [PART I.

Sect. 378. worthiness relates to the state of the ship at the commencement of the risk, and is a condition precedent to the underwriter's liability on the policy; the implied condition not to deviate relates to the conduct of the ship in the course of the voyage, and cannot by relation be carried back, so as to exempt the underwriter from liabilities incurred prior to its being broken (*s*).

Intention to deviate does not discharge the underwriter.

There must, as we have already seen, be an actual deviation, in order to discharge the underwriter; a mere intention to deviate, never executed, is not sufficient (*t*).

The deviation must be voluntary.

Moreover, the departure from the usual course of the voyage must be voluntary, in order to make it a deviation (*u*); but it will be considered voluntary if it take place through the gross ignorance of the captain (*x*).

Notice to underwriter of intended deviation.

379. As the description of the voyage by its termini implies the condition that the regular course of the voyage will be pursued, it seems to follow that notice to the underwriter of an intention to depart from the usual course (no liberty to do so being given by the policy) will not prevent the underwriter from maintaining that such departure is a deviation from the voyage insured (*y*).

No implied waiver of a prior deviation.

It has even been held that if the underwriters insure a ship for a voyage, after she has sailed on it, and after notice that

(*s*) See Green *v.* Young (1702), 2 Salk. 444; Hare *v.* Travis (1827), 7 B. & Cr. 14.

(*t*) Mar. Ins. Act, 1906, s. 46 (3), *supra*, § 376; Kewley *v.* Ryan (1794), 2 H. Bl. 343; Thellusson *v.* Fergusson (1780), 1 Dougl. 361.

(*u*) Mar. Ins. Act, 1906, s. 49 (1) (b), *infra*, §§ 424a, 425.

(*x*) Phyn *v.* Royal Exch. Ass. Co. (1798), 7 T. R. 505.

(*y*) It has been held in the Court of Appeal that under a bill of lading contract it is a deviation to proceed to a port out of the regular course of the voyage, though notice of an intention to do so was given to the shipper of goods at the time when the bill of lading was given. Leduc *v.* Ward (1888), 20 Q. B. D. 475. Phillips considers that the underwriter ought not to be allowed to set up the defence of deviation, on the ground that it would be a palpable fraud on his part to subscribe and receive the premium, intending at the same time to avoid payment of a loss by alleging a deviation represented to be intended. 1 Phillips, s. 1041.

she has already deviated from its course, they will be dis- *Sect. 379.*
charged by the deviation from any subsequent loss (*z*).

380. The definition of what constitutes deviation requires *Distinction between a deviation and abandonment of voyage.* that it should be distinguished from what is called abandonment or change of voyage. The great distinction between a deviation and a change or abandonment of voyage is, that in the former the original voyage, as described in the policy, is not given up or lost sight of, while in the latter it is.

"A deviation," says Chancellor Kent, "is not a change of the voyage, but of the proper and usual course of performing it. The voyage insured is never lost sight of in cases of deviation, actual or intended. If, however, the original place of destination be abandoned, in order to get to another port of discharge, the voyage itself becomes changed, because one of the termini of the voyage is changed. The identity of the voyage is gone, and a new and distinct voyage is substituted" (*a*).

The results of the abandonment of the insured voyage are *Provisions of Mar. Ins. Act as to abandonment of voyage.* thus stated in sects. 43, 44 and 45 of the Marine Insurance Act, 1906:—

> Sect. 43. Where the place of departure is specified by *Alteration of port of departure.* the policy, and the ship instead of sailing from that place sails from any other place, the risk does not attach.

(*z*) Redman *v.* Loudon (1814), 3 Camp. 503; *S. C.*, 5 Taunt. 462; 1 Marshall, R. 136. The contrary has been ruled in the United States. Coles *v.* Marine Ins. Co. (1812), 3 Wash. C. C. R. 159. Phillips supports the American decision. See 1 Phillips, e. 1041. Maclachlan agrees with the English decision, but seems to suggest that the policy might be rectified. Arnould, 6th ed. vol. i. p. 452. As to rectification, see *ante*, § 41.

(*a*) In New York Firem. Ins. Co. *v.* Lawrence (1816), 14 Johnson's R. 46, and 3 Kent, Com. 317. The editors submitted, in the seventh edition of this work, that even though the intention of ultimately proceeding to the *terminus ad quem* of the voyage be not given up, the departure from the usual course may be so great that the voyage is really different from that described in the policy. This seems to be the view of Parsons (Ins. vol. ii. p. 41), of Phillips (vol. i. s. 992), and of Buller, J., in Way *v.* Modigliani (1787), 2 T. R. 30, 32, and perhaps of Arnould himself. See *post*, § 382, note (*n*). Sect. 45 of the Mar. Ins. Act, 1906, however, seems to make the change of destination the only test of a change of voyage.

Sect. 380.
Sailing for different destination.

Sect. 44. Where the destination is specified in the policy, and the ship, instead of sailing for that destination, sails for any other destination, the risk does not attach (b).

Change of voyage.

Sect. 45.—(1) Where, after the commencement of the risk, the destination of the ship is voluntarily changed from the destination contemplated by the policy, there is said to be a change of voyage.

(2) Unless the policy otherwise provides, where there is a change of voyage, the insurer is discharged from liability as from the time of change, that is to say, as from the time when the determination to change it is manifested; and it is immaterial that the ship may not in fact have left the course of voyage contemplated by the policy when the loss occurs.

Definition of a change of voyage.

As we have already pointed out (c), the expressions "change" and "abandonment" of voyage have commonly been used indifferently when, either before or after the commencement of the risk, the assured abandons all thought of proceeding to the port of destination originally prescribed by the policy. In the Marine Insurance Act, 1906, however, the term "change of voyage" is only used to denote an abandonment of the voyage after the risk has attached, and it is now, therefore, advisable to use it in this restricted sense. For this restricted use there was some authority before the Act (d).

(b) It is submitted that in the case of a policy "at and from" a place, sect. 44 must be read together with sect. 45, i.e., if the voyage was abandoned after the time when, according to ordinary principles, the risk has commenced "at" the *terminus a quo*, the case is one of change of voyage. Consequently the underwriter is liable for any loss which may have occurred "at" the *terminus a quo* before the voyage was changed, and the assured is not entitled to a return of premium, as he would be if the case were governed by sect. 44.

(c) *Ante,* § 370, note (e).

(d) See Simon, Israel & Co. v. Sedgwick (C. A.), [1893] 1 Q. B. 303, in which case a clause holding the assured covered at an extra premium in case of "change of voyage," was held to be inoperative where the ship sailed for a *terminus ad quem* other than that mentioned in the policy. So also, in Maritime Ins. Co. v. Stearns, [1901] 2 K. B. 912, Mathew, J., held that "change of voyage" in the deviation clause did not cover delay in the attachment of the risk.

There is, however, no necessity to limit the use of the term "abandonment of the voyage," which may with propriety be employed, whether the voyage was given up before the risk could attach or after its attachment.

The effect of an abandonment of the voyage is to discharge the underwriter from all liability on the policy from the moment the purpose of so abandoning the voyage is definitely formed. Hence, if the purpose be fixed before the commencement of the risk, the policy is void *ab initio*, and the risk never attaches; if it be not formed till after the risk attaches, the underwriter is discharged from all liability for losses which may accrue subsequently to its having been formed, although such loss may take place while the ship is still on the track common both to the voyage insured and to that which is substituted for it (*e*).

An intention to deviate, on the other hand, may be defined to be a purpose to depart from the true course of the voyage without giving up the design of ultimately proceeding to the *terminus ad quem;* however decisively such an intention may be formed, yet the underwriter remains liable for all loss incurred prior to its being actually carried into effect; *i.e.*, as long as the vessel is on the direct course of the voyage insured, and before she has reached the dividing point (*f*).

381. The following case well illustrates the difference between an abandonment of the voyage and an intention to

Sect. 380.

Effect of change or abandonment of voyage.

Definition of an intention to deviate.

Cases illustrating difference

(*e*) See 2 Emerigon, c. xiii. ss. 11 and 14, pp. 82, 92. Both the sections here referred to must be consulted in order to discover that the French law is identical with ours on the present subject. In the former of these sections the learned author discusses what he calls "*le voyage rompu avant le départ;*" in the second "*le voyage changé.*" See also 2 Benecke, System des Assecuranz, 314—325. In the United States the Court of Errors, in a case of N. Y. Firemen's Ins. Co. *v.* Lawrence (1816), 14 Johns.

46, reversing the decision below, held that the voyage was changed from the moment the master had determined upon a new destination, although he had not entered upon the altered route when his ship was captured. 1 Phillips, s. 966, where the author offers reasons against the decision.

(*f*) See Woolridge *v.* Boydell (1778), 1 Dougl. 16 (*a*); Thellusson *v.* Fergusson (1780), 1 Dougl. 361; Kewley *v.* Ryan (1794), 2 H. Bl. 343.

DEVIATION AND CHANGE OF RISK. [PART I.

Sect. 381.
Distinction between abandonment of voyage and intention to deviate.
Woolridge v. Boydell.

deviate:—A ship, insured "from Maryland to Cadiz," cleared out for Falmouth, in this country, gave bonds to land her cargo in Great Britain, and sailed with the intention of making Falmouth her port of destination: she was captured while on the common course both to Falmouth and Cadiz. It was contended that this was a mere case of intended deviation. The Court, however, said that it was a change of voyage; that on which the vessel sailed was different from the voyage insured, and they accordingly held the underwriter not to be liable for the loss, though it had taken place before the ship passed the dividing point (*g*). Lord Mansfield thus distinguished the case from that of an intended deviation:—" In all cases of that sort the *terminus a quo* and *ad quem* are certain and the same; but in the present case the *terminus ad quem* has been altered, for there was no intention of going into Cadiz at all."

Cases of intended deviation.

On the other hand, the principle that, if the *terminus ad quem* be not abandoned, a mere intention to deviate, not carried into effect, still leaves the underwriter liable for all loss that takes place before the ship has passed the dividing point, is illustrated by the following cases (*h*):—

Thellusson v. Fergusson.

The master of a vessel insured "from Guadaloupe to Havre" had, in pursuance of his instructions, formed the intention of sailing first to Brest, as the safest way, in time of war, of getting to Havre, which latter place still continued the port of the ship's ultimate destination; this was held to be a mere intention to deviate, leaving the underwriter liable for the loss of the ship before she had reached the dividing point at which the course to Brest diverges from that to Havre (*i*).

(*g*) Woolridge *v.* Boydell (1778), 1 Dougl. 16 (*a*).

(*h*) Foster *v.* Wilmer (1746), 2 Str. 1249; Carter *v.* Royal Exch. Ass. Co., cited *ibid.*; Thellusson *v.* Fergusson (1780), 1 Dougl. 361; Kewley *v.* Ryan (1794), 2 H. Bl. 343; Heselton *v.* Allnutt (1813), 1 M. & S. 46; Harc *v.* Travis (1827),

7 B. & Cr. 15.

(*i*) Thellusson *v.* Fergusson (1780), 1 Dougl. 361. If the master acted *bonâ fide* and reasonably for the purpose of avoiding capture, the insurance would have remained in force even after the ship left the direct course to Havre. See *post*, § 432.

CHAP. XV.]   CHANGE OF VOYAGE.   521

So, where a vessel insured from "Granada to Liverpool" took out clearances for Cork, at which place the master was instructed and intended to put in, though bound ultimately for Liverpool, and the ship was lost before reaching the dividing point, the Court held that the voyage continued the same; the design of putting into Cork being only an intention to deviate, which could not discharge the underwriter from the loss (*k*). {Sect. 381. *Kewley v. Ryan.*}

Goods were insured from Liverpool to London, but the master had taken in goods for Southampton, and did put in there. The Court held this a deviation which discharged the underwriters from subsequent loss, but not from loss occurring before the ship diverged from the course of her voyage to London in order to go into Southampton (*l*). {*Hare v. Travis.*}

Where a ship sailed with an intention to deviate by putting into an intermediate port, but before she turned off for that purpose was overtaken by a storm and driven into that very port, this was held no deviation, and of no effect on the underwriter's liability (*m*). {A ship driven by stress of weather into a port to which she intended to deviate.}

382. It is sometimes a matter of very nice discrimination to draw the line between an intention to deviate and an abandonment of the voyage; the test in all cases is whether the *terminus ad quem*, specified in the policy, remains the ultimate place of intended destination; if it does, then the design, though formed before sailing, of putting into any other port, or taking an intermediate voyage, in the way to such ultimate place of destination, does not amount to an abandonment of the voyage (*n*). {Test of distinction between intention to deviate and to abandon the voyage.}

In one case, where the voyage insured was "from Heligo- {*Heselton v. Allnutt.*}

(*k*) Kewley *v.* Ryan (1794), 2 H. Bl. 343.

(*l*) Hare *v.* Travis (1827), 7 B. & Cr. 14.

(*m*) Kingston *v.* Phelps (*circa* 1795), cited 7 T. R. 165; so held also in the United States, Hobart *v.* Norton (1829), 8 Pick. Mass. R. 159.

(*n*) Arnould's words were "does not necessarily amount to a change of voyage"; and the word "necessarily" suggests that he did not think the test mentioned in the text under all circumstances conclusive. See, however, the editors' note, *ante*, § 380.

Sect. 382. land to Memel," it appeared that the ship sailed with a preponderating purpose to proceed to Memel, but with orders to go into Gottenburg to learn whether it would be safer to proceed to Memel or to Anhalt; and the ship was afterwards captured in sailing from Heligoland to Gottenburg, while on the direct course both to Anhalt and to Memel. Lord Ellenborough held that there was only an intention to deviate to Gottenburg, and that the contingent purpose of going to Anhalt was not a change of voyage, and consequently that the underwriters were not discharged (*o*). His Lordship considered that, as the original port of destination had not been definitively abandoned, there had, in this case, been "a good inception of the voyage under a fluctuating purpose."

Thames & Mersey Mar. Ins. Co. *v.* Van Laun.

382a. In a case decided shortly before the Marine Insurance Act came into force, the House of Lords seem to have gone beyond the previous authorities in expressing the view that the insured voyage had been abandoned (*p*). The respondents had contracted to deliver a cargo of Australian cattle at a port in Northern China for the use of the German Government, though not by direct agreement with the Government, there being two intermediate contractors. The cattle under the contract were to be shipped in October; but the respondents only shipped them in November. In the bills of lading, Taku was made the port of delivery, and the master was given power, if Taku was unsafe by reason of ice, to land the cattle at any other safe port. The respondents effected two policies of insurance with the appellants on the cattle against mortality during transit. One policy was expressed to be from Australia "to the vessel's port or ports of discharge in China," and gave leave for the ship "to proceed and sail to and touch and stay at any ports or places whatsoever in

(*o*) Heselton *v.* Allnutt (1813), 1 M. & S. 46.

(*p*) Thames & Mersey Mar. Ins. Co. *v.* Van Laun (24th July, 1905). Unreported, but the judgment of Lord Halsbury, L. C., is set out verbatim in the Shipping Gazette, 25th July, 1905. The editors' summary of the very complicated facts of the case is based on the policies and a verbatim transcript of Kennedy, J.'s, judgment at the trial.

the course of her said voyage for all necessary purposes." The other policy was for a voyage from Australia "to China Ports"; it contained a similar license clause and an additional clause which gave liberty " to proceed to and call at any ports or places on this side and beyond the port of destination backwards and forwards for all purposes." On the 16th December, 1900, the vessel arrived at Wei-hai-Wei, where the master heard that Taku was blocked by ice. He was ordered by the assured to wait for further instructions. The German Government had previously intimated that in consequence of the delay in shipment they would not accept the cattle, and fruitless negotiations followed between all the parties concerned. At the same time the assured were also making inquiries as to the possibility of disposing of the cargo by sale afloat at Wei-hai-Wei or at Vladivostok. On the 25th December the master, being in want of water, went to Chefoo. Legal proceedings having been taken in Germany, the Court on the 2nd January, 1901, authorized the sale of the cattle without prejudice to the rights of the parties, and on the 3rd the assured telegraphed to the master to proceed to Shanghai. The ship arrived at Woosung on the 6th, and was kept there by the agents of the assured until the 16th, when by the agents' order she was taken up to Shanghai and at once commenced to land the cattle. During all this time there was great mortality among the cattle, and on the 26th, owing to an outbreak of rinderpest, the authorities ordered their discharge to be stopped, and the cattle remaining on board to be thrown into the sea. The action having been brought to recover for the loss of the cattle, Kennedy, J., held that there was a deviation, by reason of the delay at Wei-hai-Wei while the assured were trying to find a way out of the financial complications in which they were involved and were discussing the feasibility of selling the cargo afloat or sending the cargo to Vladivostok or elsewhere. He considered, however, that there was no proof of such a formal or definite intention not to send the cargo to a Chinese port of destination as would amount to an abandonment of the insured voyage. On the

Sect. 382a.

Sect. 382a. ground of delay and other grounds the learned judge gave judgment for the defendants (*q*). This decision was reversed by the Court of Appeal (*r*), but was restored by the House of Lords. Lord Halsbury, L. C., said that there was a clear deviation, and that he would be prepared to find as a fact that the voyage was abandoned, and that the real object of keeping the master waiting for orders was to see whether the cattle could not be disposed of to greater advantage than by attempting to deliver them in pursuance of bills of lading. Lord Macnaghten and Lord James concurred in this judgment, and expressly stated that in their opinion the voyage had been abandoned. Lord Robertson also concurred in the Lord Chancellor's judgment. Lord Davey agreed with Kennedy, J., that there had been a deviation, and inclined, though less strongly than the other Law Lords, to the view that the detention of the ship at Wei-hai-Wei amounted to an abandonment of the voyage. "It is often a nice question on the facts," he said, "whether an interruption of the voyage amounts to a deviation only or is a change of voyage. The usual test is whether the ultimate *terminus ad quem* remains the same. In the present case it may be doubted whether the detention of the ship at Wei-hai-Wei and Chefoo, not for any purpose connected with or for the purposes of the voyage insured, but for the reason and under the circumstances disclosed by the evidence, did not amount to an abandonment of that voyage. It may be that Shanghai was a port to which the master might have taken the ship when he found that the port of Taku was ice-bound, but he went there and was, in fact, ordered to go there for a purpose different from that contemplated in the original voyage."

The Lords appear to have been of opinion, though without deciding the case on this ground, that as regards a policy on cargo, the abandonment of the intention to deliver the cargo under the bill of lading contract amounts to a change of

(*q*) There is an epitome of his judgment in the Shipping Gazette, 2nd April, 1903.

(*r*) See Shipping Gazette, 10th Nov., 1903.

Sect. 382a.

voyage, although the assured has not given up the intention of landing the goods at a port which is covered by the description of the *terminus ad quem* in the policy. For this proposition the Marine Insurance Act, 1906, does not afford any support. Section 45 of the Act, the only section which deals with the point, says that there is a change of voyage where after the commencement of the risk the destination of the ship is voluntarily changed from the destination contemplated by the policy—not the destination contemplated by the contract between the cargo-owner and the shipowner (*s*).

A forced intermediate voyage has no effect.

383. The forced interposition of an intermediate voyage will not discharge the underwriters if there be no abandonment of the original adventure, but the ship be lost while prosecuting it (*t*).

Driscol *v.* Passmore.

A ship was insured on a round voyage "from Lisbon to Madeira, from Madeira to Saffi on the coast of Africa, in ballast, and thence back to Lisbon with a cargo of wheat," and an insurance on the freight of the wheat "from Saffi to Lisbon" was effected on a representation that the ship, which was then at Madeira, was about to pursue her voyage to Saffi immediately. Instead, however, of doing this, the captain was forced by his crew, alarmed by reports of Moorish cruisers, to take the ship back from Madeira to Lisbon. On his arrival at Lisbon the charterers insisted on his taking the ship direct from that port to Saffi in ballast, which he accordingly did, loaded a cargo of wheat at Saffi, and was captured while sailing on his homeward passage from Saffi to Lisbon. In an action on the freight policy, the Court were clearly of opinion that there had been no abandonment of the original adventure; and, moreover, that as, when taken, she

(*s*) In Kynance SS. Co. *v.* Young (1911), 16 Com. Cas. 123, Scrutton, J., refused to restrict the duration of the voyage described in the policy by reference to the charter-party. The ship was insured for a voyage to a port or ports of discharge in South America, while the charter-party only provided for a discharge at one port. The shipowner and the charterer afterwards agreed to have the cargo discharged at two ports, and the learned judge held that a loss on the voyage from the first to the second port was covered.

(*t*) See Mar. Ins. Act, 1906, s. 49 (1) (b), *post*, § 424a.

Sect. 383. was sailing from Saffi for Lisbon, the voyage actually insured in the freight policy, the underwriters were not discharged (*u*).

In general an intermediate voyage discharges the underwriter.

384. If, however, the ship, without justifying cause, after accomplishing part of her voyage insured, sails on a distinct intermediate voyage, not allowed by the usage of trade, and neither subordinate to nor connected with the voyage contemplated as the principal object of the contract, she will be considered as having, for the time at least, given up all intention of proceeding to her primary destination, and the underwriter will be discharged from all loss that may take place after she has engaged on such intermediate voyage, although the captain may still intend ultimately to proceed to the original *terminus ad quem* (*v*).

Way v. Modigliani.

How strictly this rule is enforced appears from the following case:—A ship, insured "at and from the 20th October, 1783, from any ports in Newfoundland to Falmouth or her port or ports of discharge in England," sailed on the 1st of October from her port in Newfoundland to fish on the Banks, where she continued fishing till the 7th, on which day she sailed from the Banks to England. On the 20th of October she was sailing on a course common both to a voyage from the Banks to England and from Newfoundland to England, and on this course she continued until and at the time of the loss for which the action was brought.

Buller, J., held, that as the voyage insured was from Newfoundland to England direct, and that on which the ship sailed was from Newfoundland to the Banks, and then to England, the ship had never sailed on the voyage insured, and the policy had never attached (*x*). Ashhurst, J., held,

---

(*u*) Driscol *v.* Passmore (1798), 1 B. & P. 200.

(*v*) Bottomley *v.* Bovill (1826), 5 B. & Cr. 210; see also Hamilton *v.* Sheddon (1837), 3 M. & W. 49.

(*x*) Way *v.* Modigliani (1787), 2 T. R. 30; see *ante*, § 380, note (*a*). Phillips and Benecke doubt the decision on the same ground, viz.,

that the *terminus a quo* of the risk was the 20th of October, before which day the vessel was "on the specified voyage": but was she so? She was on the same *iter*, but not on the same *viaggium*. See Benecke, System des Assecuranz, vol. ii. p. 331; and 1 Phillips, s. 992.

that either the ship sailed on a different voyage, or there had been a deviation. The grounds on which the remaining judge, Grose, J., decided do not appear clearly in the report.

Sect. 384.

385. Whether, in point of fact, the intention to abandon the original destination of the voyage had been definitively adopted at the time of the loss is sometimes a nice question of evidence, and the fact of sailing does not necessarily enter into the determination of it (*y*). The conduct of the assured while the ship is still in port may be such as, in case of a policy "at and from," will alter his relations with the underwriter entirely.

Evidence of intention to abandon voyage.

"When a person," says Lord Eldon, "is insured 'at and from' a port, the probable continuance of the ship in that port is in the contemplation of the parties to the contract. If the owners, or persons having authority from them, change their intention, and the ship is delayed in that port for the purpose of altering the voyage and taking in a different cargo, the underwriters run a different risk, if such change of intention is not to affect the contract" (*z*).

The case alluded to was this:—A British ship, being expected to arrive in Cadiz with a cargo of fish, her owners sent instructions to their agents there to ballast the ship, after she had discharged her cargo, with salt, and procure freight for her, if possible, to Clyde. When the ship arrived, the French army had got possession of the saltpans round Cadiz, so that no salt could be procured. The agents thereupon wrote to the owners that they had resolved, with the concurrence of the captain, to despatch the ship to Liverpool to load with salt for Newfoundland. The owners accordingly insured the ship "at and from Cadiz to her port or ports of discharge in St. George's Channel, including Clyde." Much time having been spent in discharging the fish at Cadiz the

Tasker v. Cunningham.

(*y*) For a good illustration of this, see Hall *v.* Brown (1814), 2 Dow, 367, a case which stands too much on its own particular circumstances to be of any value except as an illustration.

(*z*) 1 Bligh, 100.

528 DEVIATION AND CHANGE OF RISK. [PART I.

Sect. 385. agents, thinking that the ship would arrive too late at Newfoundland if sent first to Liverpool for salt, resolved, after consulting with the master, to load the ship with what salt they could procure at Cadiz, and despatch her direct for Newfoundland. They again wrote to the owners of this proposed alteration. About a week after the date of this last letter, the ship, while still in the bay of Cadiz, and before she had entirely discharged the fish, or taken any steps towards commencing the direct voyage from Cadiz to Newfoundland, was taken by the French and burnt where she lay.

Upon this state of facts, the Scotch Court three times decided that the ship, when so destroyed, was still under the protection of the policy; but the House of Lords finally reversed their decision on the ground that a fixed determination had been formed to abandon the voyage insured before the loss took place (*a*).

What is evidence of a definite intention to change the voyage.

Lord Eldon, in the course of his judgment, said: "It appears throughout the correspondence that the captain and the agents had taken upon themselves to direct and alter the destination of the ship with the acquiescence, at least, of the owners.—"Undoubtedly a mere meditated change does not affect a policy; but circumstances are to be taken as evidence of a determination; and what better evidence can we have than that those who were authorized had determined to change the voyage? In my opinion the voyage was abandoned, and I have the highest authority in Westminster Hall to confirm that opinion" (*b*).

Rule in the United States as to effect of change of voyage.

386. In the United States it was decided by the Supreme Court of New York, and in the Court of Errors, against the opinion of Chancellor Kent, that the assured may recover for any loss which may happen before the determination to change the voyage is manifested by some act whereby the risk insured against is affected and changed; and that consequently, though all intention of proceeding to the *terminus*

(*a*) Tasker *v.* Cunningham (1819), 1 Bligh, 87.
(*b*) *Ibid.* 99, 102.

CHAP. XV.] CHANGE OF VOYAGE. 529

ad quem may have been entirely abandoned at the time of loss, yet, if the vessel be lost before she reach the dividing point, this must be regarded as having only the same effect as an intention to deviate, and will not discharge the underwriter from antecedent loss (*c*).

Sect. 386.

This decision appears entirely irreconcilable with the principle which has been either admitted or acted on in all the English cases, and is affirmed in the Marine Insurance Act, 1906, viz., that the identity of the voyage depends on its termini, and that directly the intention has been deliberately formed of abandoning the *terminus ad quem* of the original voyage, the vessel is sailing on a new voyage, and is out of the protection of the policy (*d*).

But the English rule seems better founded on principle.

On the other hand, it is clearly implied in the provisions of the Act that the underwriter will be liable for all loss incurred prior to the formation of a definitive purpose of abandoning the original voyage, and that it is only where the purpose of changing the voyage has been fixed before the commencement of the risk that it can avoid the policy *ab initio* (*e*).

Abandonment is not retrospective in effect.

387. Where a marine policy on goods covered a land transit following a sea voyage, the Court of Appeal has held that to determine whether the policy ever attached, the *terminus ad quem* of the sea voyage only must be taken into consideration. Therefore, where the insurance was on goods from the Mersey to any port in Spain this side of Gibraltar, and thence by inland conveyance to any place in the interior, and the goods destined for Madrid were shipped to a port on the east side of Gibraltar, they held that the risk had never attached (*f*).

Change of voyage where both sea and land transit.

(*c*) Lawrence *v*. Ocean Ins. Co. (1814), 11 Johns. 240; N. Y. Firemen's Ins. Co. *v*. Lawrence (1816), 14 Johns. 46; cited 1 Phillips, Ins. s. 966, where the learned writer, who erroneously states that Chancellor Kent's judgment was concurred in by the rest of the Court, dissents from it.

(*d*) See 3 Kent, Com. 317, where the English rule is approved.

(*e*) See, upon this point, the remarks of M. Estrangin, in his learned notes on Pothier, in his Appendix, p. 471.

(*f*) Simon, Israel & Co. *v*. Sedgwick (C. A.), [1893] 1 Q. B. 303.

A.—VOL. I. 34

Sect. 387. The policy contained a clause, now very common, to the effect that deviation or change of voyage was to be held covered at a premium to be arranged; but the Court held that this stipulation did not apply, as the ship had never sailed on the voyage insured, and the policy, therefore, had never attached (*g*).

What is not change of voyage.

388. The mere fact of taking in goods, and clearing out for a different port to that named in the policy, as the *terminus ad quem*, does not *per se* amount to a change of voyage; for this may have been done with the design of putting into such port in the way to the original terminus, and of ultimately carrying out the original adventure. In this case it would be a mere intention to deviate, and not a change of voyage; and the assured would still be liable for all loss incurred before passing the dividing point (*h*). So, *à fortiori*, it is no change of voyage for a ship insured to two or more named ports of discharge to take in goods and clear out for only one of them (*i*).

Shortening the voyage.

With regard to shortening the voyage, it appears that a ship insured to several successive ports may terminate the voyage at one of the nearer ports without vitiating the policy (*k*); but it is otherwise if, being insured to a single port, she sail with a fixed purpose not to go beyond a nearer port not contemplated in the policy. Thus, Emerigon, after stating it as a general principle that a mere shortening of the voyage will not avoid the policy, adds, "provided that, at the outset, the voyage insured was not abandoned (*rompu*) by a change of destination" (*l*).

(*g*) Simon, Israel & Co. *v.* Sedgwick (C. A.), [1893] 1 Q. B. 303.

(*h*) 2 Emerigon, c. xiii. s. 14, p. 92; Henkle *v.* Royal Exch. Ass. Co. (1749), 1 Ves. Sr. 317; Planché *v.* Fletcher (1779), 1 Dougl. 251; Kewley *v.* Ryan (1794), 2 H. Bl. 343.

(*i*) Marsden *v.* Reid (1803), 3 East, 572.

(*k*) Mar. Ins. Act, 1906, s. 47, *ante*, § 376.

(*l*) See 2 Emerigon, c. xiii. s. 11, Voyage entièrement rompu avant le départ. See also the very lucid commentary of M. Estrangin on Pothier, Appendix, c. v. s. 3, p. 471.

389. The case of Middlewood *v.* Blakes, though it more properly belongs to the doctrine of concealment, may, in consequence of the discussion to which it has given rise, be conveniently mentioned here. In that case it appeared that usage in respect of the voyage insured (from London to Jamaica) left the captain, on arriving at a certain point, the choice of one of three tracks (one to the north, and two to the south of St. Domingo), all equally leading to the *terminus ad quem*. In the particular case the captain, by orders from his owners (not communicated to the underwriter), took the northernmost track in order to touch at Cape Nicola Mole, a port in that track, but out of the direct course from London to Jamaica; but while still pursuing a direct course to Jamaica, and before having turned off to make Cape Nicola Mole, the ship was lost by capture. On these facts, Lord Kenyon told the jury that in his opinion the underwriter was discharged, "because at the time the ship was captured she was bound to a different place to that to which she was insured" (as she had not abandoned Jamaica as the ultimate *terminus ad quem*, this seems hardly correct), "and with a view to which the captain, under compulsion of his orders, had taken this particular track, and was not left at liberty to exercise his judgment at the dividing point for the benefit of all concerned, as the underwriters had a right to insist on." The jury found for the underwriter, being, as they stated, unanimously of opinion "that the concealment of the intention to go to St. Domingo vitiated the policy." Lord Kenyon, Ashhurst, J., and Grose, J., supported the verdict on the ground of concealment; they thought the circumstance, "that the discretion of the captain had been taken away," ought to have been communicated. Lawrence, J., thought this ground not tenable. Had the ship been lost before reaching the dividing point of the three tracks, he should have held the underwriters bound, on the ground that there would then have been only an intention to deviate; as she was lost after passing that point, he thought them discharged, and on the following ground:—"When the ship

Sect. 389. came to the dividing point she was subjected to a risk, for which the underwriters did not make themselves responsible, for at that moment they were entitled to have the benefit of the captain's judgment, whether he would go to the north or to the south" (*m*).

Cases of deviation irrespective of the clauses giving a liberty to touch and stay.

390. In proceeding to examine more in detail the various decided cases by which the doctrine of deviation has been illustrated in English jurisprudence, we will confine our attention, in the first instance, to those instances of deviation which consist in a local divergence from the direct course of the voyage, and do not specially turn on the construction of the clauses giving a liberty " to touch, stay, or trade."

In the absence of any usage the ship must sail direct.

In the absence of any usage or stipulation to the contrary, the contract is invariably understood to be that the ship should proceed from one terminus of the voyage insured to the other, in a direct course, with all due expedition, and without touching at any interjacent port, or pursuing any intermediate adventure. Anything that she does to the contrary of this without such justification as shall be considered hereafter, or without leave expressly given in the policy, however trifling in extent or duration, is a fatal deviation, although the ship afterwards return to her proper course without having sustained the slightest damage in consequence of having thus departed from it (*n*).

(*m*) Middlewood *v.* Blakes (1797), 7 T. R. 162. For an elaborate discussion of this case, see 2 Duer on Ins. pp. 491—498. Judge Duer considers that the case cannot be put as one of deviation. He says that the majority in the Court of King's Bench placed their decision upon the true ground; but also considers that the case may be put on the ground of change of risk; for " where the master is bound to deviate, the voyage on which he sails is different in its very inception from that which the policy describes and is meant to cover "

(p. 497). "I confess," says Arnould, " it appears better, on the whole, to rest the decision where the majority of the Court put it, on the ground of concealment." 2nd ed. vol. i. p. 408, n. Applying the provisions of sect. 46 of the Mar. Ins. Act, 1906, to the facts of the case, there does not seem to have been a deviation at the time of the loss, but only a possible intention to deviate.

(*n*) See Fox *v.* Black (1767), 2 Park, 620; Townson *v.* Guyon (temp. Lord Mansfield), *ibid.*; Clason *v.* Simmonds (1741), cited 6 T. R. 533; Parr *v.* Anderson

391. Where, however, by the usage of trade it is customary in the course of the voyage insured to stop at interjacent ports, though out of the direct course, it is no deviation to stop there, though leave for that purpose be not expressly reserved; for, upon the principles already developed, such stopping is considered to be a regular part of the voyage insured, and to have been contemplated by the parties to the policy. It takes place in the words of the Marine Insurance Act, 1906, s. 46 (2) (b) (*o*), in the "usual and customary course" of the voyage. But for this purpose the usage must be precise, clear, and established. Thus, when all ships sailing through the Sound had to stop at Elsinore to pay the Sound dues, this was no deviation, though no liberty so to stop was reserved in the policy (*p*).

Sect. 391.
Effect of usage.

But a stoppage at the Isle of Man by a ship insured from Liverpool to the West Indies was held not to be justified by proof that ships insured on that voyage had occasionally, but not customarily, stopped there before (*q*). So in the United States, two instances of stopping at an intermediate port, not named in the policy, by other ships engaged in the same trade was held inadequate to prove a usage or justify a departure from the direct course (*r*).

On the same principle, in the East India and Newfoundland trades it was repeatedly held to be no deviation to engage in intermediate voyages, although no liberty was given in the policy so to do (*s*). In fact, where the termini only of the

(1805), 6 East, 202; 3 Kent, Com. 312. Phillips says (vol. i. s. 989) that the law does not regard such inconsiderable circumstances as "a delay of an hour, or a deviation of a mile." There is much to be said in favour of his rule, but his statement is not borne out by the authorities. Even if the rule "*De minimis,*" &c. can be applied in questions of deviation, it must be remembered that a deviation which may be of no importance in the case of a steamer may greatly affect the voyage of a sailing ship. See *post,* § 560.

(*o*) *Ante,* § 376.

(*p*) Cormack *v.* Gladstone (1809), 11 East, 347.

(*q*) Salisbury *v.* Townson, Millar, Ins. 418.

(*r*) Martin *v.* Delaware Ins. Co. (1808), 2 Wash. R. 254; Condy's Marshall, 186, n.

(*s*) As to the East Indian trade, see Salvador *v.* Hopkins (1765), 3 Burr. 1707; Gregory *v.* Christie (1784), 3 Dougl. 419; 1 Park, 104;

Sect. 391. voyage insured are indicated by the policy, and the parties to the contract have done nothing else towards indicating its course, the sole guide in determining what that course should be is mercantile usage; and nothing can be considered a deviation which only follows that course which usage has sanctioned.

Where the policy expressly excludes or is inconsistent with the usage.

392. Where, however, the policy itself, besides indicating the termini of the voyage, specifically designates the course which the ship shall take in sailing between them, such directions must be followed with the most scrupulous and literal exactness, and the slightest failure to comply with them will amount to a fatal deviation (*t*).

Hence, where liberty is given in the policy to touch at any one specified intermediate port, it will be a deviation to put into any other than that named in the policy, though calling at such port may be sanctioned by usage apart from the policy, and though neither the risk nor premium would have been increased had such port been substituted for that named in the clause. *Expressio unius est exclusio alterius.*

Elliott v. Wilson.

It seems to have been usual for vessels sailing from Carron for Hull, in going down the Frith of Forth, to touch at different places for the purpose of taking in and delivering goods, particularly at Burrowstowness, Leith and Morrison's Haven. A merchant desirous of insuring goods on a voyage from Carron to Hull directed his broker to effect an insurance with liberty in the policy "to call as usual" (which would have enabled the ship to touch at all or any of the three places above mentioned); instead of this the broker, contrary to the directions of the merchant, and without his knowledge, insured them from "Carron to Hull, with liberty to call at Leith." The premium was the same as though the general liberty to call as usual had been inserted in the policy.

The ship on her voyage passed by Leith, but put into

---

1 Marshall, Ins. 273; Farquharson v. Hunter (1785), 1 Park, 105; 1 Marshall, Ins. 274. As to the Newfoundland trade, see Vallance v. Dewar (1808), 1 Camp. 503; Ougier v. Jennings (1800), *ibid.* 505, n.

(*t*) Mar. Ins. Act, 1906, s. 46 (2) (a), *ante,* § 376.

Morrison's Haven, and afterwards, without damage, got safe again into the direct course of the voyage from Carron to Hull, and had been proceeding on such course for about a day, when she was overtaken by a storm and wrecked, with a total loss of the cargo.

Sect. 392.

The Scotch Courts, upon this state of facts, decreed that the underwriters should pay the loss, but the House of Lords reversed their judgment, on the ground that putting into Morrison's Haven, under a policy which contained no liberty so to do, but, on the contrary, gave express permission to put into another named port, was a deviation, discharging the underwriters from all further liability (*u*).

393. As is stated in sect. 47 (2) of the Marine Insurance Act, 1906—

When the ship must take ports in their geographical order.

> Where the policy is to "ports of discharge," within a given area, which are not named, the ship must, in the absence of any usage or sufficient cause to the contrary (*x*), proceed to them, or such of them as she goes to, in their geographical order. If she does not there is a deviation.

Thus where a ship, insured on a voyage "from London to her ports of discharge within the Straits (of Gibraltar) as high as Messina," sailed on her voyage, with a freight for Marseilles, but with instructions to go also to Genoa, Leghorn and Naples, and on arriving off Marseilles, her first port of discharge in geographical order, was prevented by contrary winds from putting in there, and therefore proceeded first to Genoa and then to Leghorn, from which latter place she was making her way back to Marseilles, when she was captured; a special jury found this sailing back to

Clason v. Simmonds.

(*u*) Elliot *v.* Wilson (1776), 4 Brown's P. Cases, 470.

(*x*) The decisions do not help to explain the effect of the words "sufficient cause to the contrary." A reference is probably intended to sect. 49 (1) of the Act, *post*, § 424a, in which the causes which excuse a deviation are set out; but then one would expect the same term to be used as in sect. 46 (1), *ante*, § 376, viz., "lawful excuse." Moreover, an express reference does not seem necessary in order to make the provisions of sect. 49 (1) applicable.

Sect. 393. Marseilles to be a deviation, which determined the policy from the moment of her leaving Leghorn (*y*).

When the policy determines the order of the ports.

394. Again, as is declared in sect. 47 (1) of the Marine Insurance Act, 1906—

Where several ports of discharge are specified by the policy, the ship may proceed to all or any of them, but in the absence of any usage or sufficient cause to the contrary (*z*) she must proceed to them, or such of them as she goes to, in the order designated by the policy. If she does not, there is a deviation.

Beatson v. Haworth.

Thus: A ship, insured on a voyage "at and from Fisherow to Gottenburg, and back to Leith and Cockenzie," was on her homeward passage, with goods on board both for Leith and Cockenzie (*a*). Cockenzie lies nearer to Gottenburg than Leith, and is about a mile and a half out of the direct course between the two; there appeared to be no settled course of trade as to the order of calling at the two places on such a voyage as this. The ship put first into Cockenzie, and in coming out was stranded and lost. Upon these facts the Court held that, as the termini of the intended voyage were in terms described in the policy, and as there was no regular and settled course known to all traders different from that so described, the ship was guilty of a deviation by putting first into Cockenzie, and the underwriter was discharged from his liability (*b*).

(*y*) Clason *v.* Simmonds (1741), 6 T. R. 533, *in notis*. The ship had also put in at Falmouth to load tin, which was also contended to be a deviation, and so held by the Chief Justice; in fact, it appears very doubtful on what precise ground the case was decided. See 1 Phillips on Ins. s. 1010. Sir Vicary Gibbs puts it on the ground that the assured had fixed upon Genoa for his port of discharge by passing Marseilles and proceeding to Genoa; and that, having done so, the ship was not warranted in returning to a port she had once passed, but was bound to take the remaining ports in the order of their succession. Andrews *v.* Mellish (in error) (1814), 5 Taunt. 502.

(*z*) See note (*x*), *supra*, § 393.

(*a*) See Lord Ellenborough's remarks on this case in Marsden *v.* Reid (1803), 3 East, 577.

(*b*) Beatson *v.* Haworth (1796), 6 T. R. 531; see also Marsden *v.* Reid (1803), 3 East, 571, 577. Phillips suggests (vol. i. s. 1012)

CHAP. XV.] ORDER OF THE PORTS. 537

It is not, however, necessary that a ship thus insured to several successive named ports of discharge, should sail to all the ports so named. She may omit any or only sail to one; the only limitation is, that if she visits more than one, she must take them in their due order. Thus, where a ship was insured "from Liverpool to Palermo, Messina and Naples," Lord Ellenborough held the true construction of the insurance to be that the assured might drop any of the places named, but that if he went to more than one he must take them in the order named in the policy (*c*). Sect. 394.
A ship insured to several ports need not visit them all.

Generally speaking, therefore, where there are several ports of discharge, the ship must take them either in the order in which they are named in the policy, or, if not named, then in the geographical order of their distance from the port of departure. If, however, long and uniform usage have established a different order, the geographical order may be disregarded and the other observed. It has been even intimated that the order fixed by usage overrules that specified in the policy (*d*). "This," said Arnould, "appears more doubtful," and sect. 47 (1) of the Marine Insurance Act, 1906, does not make it clear whether it is obligatory or only permissive to observe the order established by usage. Summary and rule.

395. In all cases the ports must be visited in the direct course of the voyage insured; and, generally speaking, it will be a deviation, after having once touched at one of such ports, to revisit it or to sail backwards and forwards from To revisit is to deviate, unless justified by the policy.

---

that in such a case, considering the relative position of the ports to each other and to the port of departure, the order in which they are visited should be regarded as indifferent. He considers it absurd that, even where there is no usage, it should in all cases be necessary to follow either the geographical order or the order in the policy. So far as English law is concerned, the controversy is, however, ended by the Mar. Ins. Act, 1906.

(*c*) Marsden *v*. Reid (1803), 3 East, 572. Same rule in the United States. See Kane *v*. Columbian Ins. Co. (1807), 2 Johnson, R. 264; and see other cases illustrating the same point, cited 1 Phillips, Ins. s. 1010.

(*d*) Beatson *v*. Haworth (1796), 6 T. R. 531, and Gairdner *v*. Senhouse (1810), 3 Taunt. 16, are cited by Arnould, but no judicial opinion on the point can be extracted from them.

Sect. 395. one to the other, unless express liberty for that purpose be inserted in the policy (*e*), or unless it appear from the terms of the policy that the purposes of the voyage as described necessarily involve such a liberty (*f*).

Thus, in the United States a ship insured on a West India voyage to any one of the islands, "and a market," was held to be justified in seeking a market at the different islands, without regard to their geographical order, and even in touching at the same port once and again, if done with the *bonâ fide* intention of finding a market (*g*).

Policy from a named terminus, and "other port or ports" not named.

396. Where a ship is insured "at and from" some one named port of departure, and "other port or ports," to a fixed terminus, it depends entirely on the language of the clause and the true construction of the policy, whether it be a deviation for the ship to depart from the direct course between the first-named port of departure and the *terminus ad quem* for a purpose connected with the main object of the voyage insured.

Bragg v. Anderson.

Thus, a ship insured on a homeward voyage "at and from Martinique and all or any of the other West India Islands to London," sailed to take in her cargo at St. Domingo, a place very wide of the direct course of a voyage from Martinique to London; this was yet held to be no deviation: "For in order to make it so," said Sir J. Mansfield, "you must read the insurance to be, not at and from Martinique and all or any other of the West India Islands, but 'at and from Martinique and such of the West India Islands as lie between Martinique and London'" (*h*).

Lambert v. Liddard.

So it was held no deviation for a ship insured "at and from Pernambuco or any other port or ports in the Brazils, to London," after touching at Pernambuco, and finding no cargo there, to sail to St. Salvador, another port in the

---

(*e*) Gairdner *v.* Senhouse, *supra*.
(*f*) Mellish *v.* Andrews (1813), 2 M. & S. 27; *S. C.* (1814), 5 Taunt. 496, in error.

(*g*) Deblois *v.* Ocean Ins. Co. (1835), 16 Pick. R. 303. See 1 Phillips, Ins. s. 1014.
(*h*) Bragg *v.* Anderson (1812), 4 Taunt. 229.

Brazils, in order to obtain one, although St. Salvador lies 500 miles to the south of Pernambuco, and therefore in a direction opposite to the course from Pernambuco to London. Gibbs, C. J., said that if the insurance had been at and from Pernambuco or any other port in the Brazils, there might have been something in the objection, as it might then have been contended that, by electing Pernambuco as the port of loading, the assured could not go to another without a deviation; but that the alternative being, any other port or ports, there must have been an intention of sending her to more than one (*i*).

Sect. 396.

A ship was insured "at and from Liverpool to ports and places in China and Manilla, all or any, during the ship's stay there for any purposes, and from thence to her port or ports of calling and discharge in the United Kingdom." The ship sailed from Liverpool for the coast of China, discharged part of her outward cargo at the Chinese port of Tonghoo, and proceeded to Manilla, where she discharged the residue. At Manilla, finding freights low, the captain took on board only a tenth part of a cargo and sailed back for Tonghoo with the intention of there completing his homeward cargo and sailing thence direct for England, but on this passage the ship was lost. Tonghoo is quite out of the direct course from Manilla to England. The Court of Exchequer, however, held this to be no deviation, for the words "from thence" in the policy meant not "from Manilla" only, but applied to "ports or places in China and Manilla, all or any" (*k*).

Ashley *v.* Pratt.

397. It may become a question, under a policy to or from "port A. and a port or ports in B.," of considerable nicety, whether a particular place be a port within the meaning of the policy, so as to excuse what would otherwise be a deviation. The cases show that usage may justify the application of this term to an anchorage in an open roadstead, though

Port and ports— meaning of.

(*i*) Lambert *v.* Liddard (1814), 5 Taunt. 480; 1 Marshall, R. 149.
(*k*) Ashley *v.* Pratt (1847), 16 M. & W. 471; affirmed in error, 1 Exch. 257; S. C., 17 L. J. Exch. 135.

Sect. 397. it may be an inconvenient place for loading or discharging cargo (*l*).

Harrower *v.* Hutchinson.

In one case where the alleged port was a roadstead or bay formed by headlands, and open to the east and north-east, without any other artificial formation than a jetty or pier attached to a slaughter-house, and vessels loading there were obliged to lie off in the roadstead a quarter of a mile from the jetty, and to load by means of craft,—this place although frequented only by coasters trading to Buenos Ayres, and not at all by vessels loading for Europe, and although it was unknown to underwriters as a place of loading, was nevertheless held by a majority in the Exchequer Chamber to be a port within the meaning of the policy (*m*).

As in this last case the vessel was obliged to sail back to Buenos Ayres to complete her cargo and obtain her clearances, it was argued that such sailing back was evidently not contemplated by a policy "from a port or ports of loading to a port or ports of call and discharge in the United Kingdom," and consequently was a deviation; but the Court of Queen's Bench held that the language of the policy permitted the ship to go from port to port and back to the same port until she had completed her cargo (*n*).

Everything, in these cases, depends upon the meaning of the parties, as ascertainable, first from the terms of the policy, and, if these leave the matter still doubtful, then upon extrinsic evidence.

Brown *v.* Tayleur.

Thus, where a ship was insured "at and from her port of loading in North America to Liverpool," it was held a deviation for the ship, after having taken in part of her loading at a place situated in one creek of a bay, to go afterwards to another place, lying eight miles off, on another creek of the

(*l*) See *post*, § 485.

(*m*) Harrower *v.* Hutchinson (1870), L. R. 5 Q. B. 584; affirming on this point the decision of the Court of Queen's Bench (1869), L. R. 4 Q. B. 523.

(*n*) In the Exchequer Chamber, Cleasby, B., held that the policy did not cover a voyage back to Buenos Ayres. The other Judges gave no decision on this point, the Court holding unanimously that the policy was void for concealment.

same bay, to take in the rest; for the terms of the policy clearly showed that the underwriter did not mean to run the risk of loading the ship at two such distant places, and there was no evidence to show that the two places were considered by the mercantile world as forming parts of the same port (*o*). If, indeed, the ship were at a particular quay on a river, as at Liverpool, and merely removed to another quay, a mile or two off, that would not be a deviation, for there the ship would be all the time at one port or place; but it is a deviation if she removes to a different town or different place of habitation, which might itself be a port of loading (*p*).

<small>Sect. 397.</small>

398. We next come to cases of deviation decided on the construction of those special clauses in the policy, by which liberty is given to the ship "to call," or "to touch," or "to touch and stay," or "to touch, stay and trade," either at certain specified ports, or "at all ports whatsoever, for all purposes whatsoever," &c.

<small>Deviation in relation to the clauses giving a liberty to touch and stay.</small>

These cases are generally divisible into two classes.

<small>Classes under which the cases range themselves.</small>

1st. Those in which the question is, whether the ship was justified, under the policy, in originally putting into the port at all; and this question mainly turns upon the two following points, viz.:—(a) Was the port one which, on the true construction of the policy, was within the course of the voyage as contemplated by the parties? (b) If so, was the purpose for which it was visited connected with, and in furtherance of, the main scope and object of the adventure?

2ndly. Supposing the ship to have been thus justified in originally visiting the port, as nothing which she does during the period of her lawful stay there, though foreign to the purposes of the adventure, and not specifically permitted by the policy, will be held to discharge the underwriter, unless it substantially varies the risk; the only question is, whether the trading, &c. at such port has, in fact, varied the risk originally assumed by the underwriter?

(*o*) Brown *v.* Tayleur (1835), 4 A. & E. 241.

(*p*) Per Patteson, J., Brown *v.* Tayleur (1835), 4 A. & E. 249.

542   DEVIATION AND CHANGE OF RISK.   [PART I.

Sect. 399.

Formerly the exact words of the clauses were chiefly considered.

399. Formerly, it appears to have been supposed that a great deal turned on the exact words of the clauses, without reference to the real scope and purpose of the adventure, as discoverable from the whole language of the policy. Thus, a liberty "to touch" was supposed to have a different meaning from a liberty "to touch and stay"; and a ship, insured under a policy containing only the former clause, was considered to have no power thereby conferred on her of trading in the port at which she had touched, though such trading was obviously contemplated as part of the adventure (*q*).

Present rule.

The Courts, however, conformably to the good sense of the matter, now hold that the liberty conferred by these words must depend upon the real object which the parties had in view when they inserted the clause in the policy.

Urquhart v. Bernard.

Thus, in the case of a ship insured "at and from Madeira to Santos, with liberty to touch at the Cape de Verd Islands," where it appeared from communications made to the underwriters, before effecting the policy, that the parties intended the ship to take in salt at one of the Cape de Verd Islands, she was held entitled to do so under the mere liberty to touch there (*r*).

Metcalfe v. Parry.

So, where a ship was insured from "Antigua to England," with an extensive "liberty to touch" at all or any of the West Indian Islands, Gibbs, C. J., held that as the main object of the voyage plainly appeared to be that the ship should go about from island to island seeking freight, the bare liberty "to touch" included a liberty to stay and take goods, and therefore that the ship's remaining two months at one of the islands waiting for a cargo was no deviation (*s*).

In short, wherever it appears to have been clearly contemplated by the parties, or necessary to the purposes of the voyage insured, that the ship should trade where she has liberty merely to touch, her doing so will not be deemed a deviation.

(*q*) Urquhart *v.* Bernard (1809), 1 Taunt. 450, 455, where Sir J. Mansfield said he could not find the distinction anywhere defined.

(*r*) Urquhart *v.* Bernard (1809), 1 Taunt. 450.

(*s*) Metcalfe *v.* Parry (1814), 4 Camp. 123.

CHAP. XV.] LICENSE CLAUSES. 543

400. We now revert to our classification of the cases illustrative of these principles of interpretation, and first take those in which the question is whether the ship was originally guilty of a deviation in visiting or staying at any given port.

<small>Sect. 400.
What ports may be visited, and for what purposes.</small>

Whatever may be the language of the clause, or however extensive its terms, it cannot convey a liberty of touching at any port out of that which, on the true construction of the policy, appears to have been the understood course of the voyage, nor of putting into any port within the limits of the voyage for purposes unconnected with the real objects of the adventure (*t*):

<small>Present rule.</small>

The true points of inquiry, then, are—1st. Was the port at which the ship touched a port in the course of the voyage as understood by the parties? 2nd. Was the purpose for which she so touched there *bonâ fide* connected with the main object of the adventure?

401. In the Marine Insurance Act, 1906, Schedule I., the first point is dealt with in Rule 6 of the Rules for the construction of a policy in the ordinary form in these terms—

<small>In general only ports in the direct course may be visited.</small>

> In the absence of any further license or usage, the liberty to touch and stay "at any port or place whatsoever" does not authorise the ship to depart from the course of her voyage from the port of departure to the port of destination.

Unless, therefore, upon the true construction of the policy, it appears manifest that the parties had a different meaning, it may be taken as a general rule that a liberty to touch and stay, though conceived in very extensive terms, can only confer a power of visiting such ports as lie in the usual and direct course between the termini of the voyage insured (*u*).

(*t*) This is but another instance under the general rule which restrains the effect of general terms to things *ejusdem generis,* or otherwise to matters of a tenor consistent with the context.

(*u*) In cases on charter-parties it has been held that a deviation clause, however wide its terms, must be construed with reference to the main object of the contract. See Margetson *v.* Glynn, [1893] A. C. 356; and Leduc *v.* Ward (C. A.) (1888), 20 Q. B. D. 475.

Sect. 401. This inference is insurmountably strong if there be anything in the language of the policy expressly favouring such an interpretation.

Lavabre v. Wilson.

Thus, a ship was insured on an East Indian voyage, "out and home," "with liberty to touch in the outward or homeward-bound voyage at the Isles of France and Bourbon, and at all or any other place or places what or wheresoever"; and with a stipulation "that it should be lawful for the said ship in this voyage to touch and stay at any ports or places whatsoever, as well on this side as on the other side of the Cape of Good Hope, without being deemed a deviation." Lord Mansfield, in the course of argument, intimated a clear opinion that the general words were, by the expressions "in the outward and homeward-bound voyage," and "in this voyage," qualified and restrained so as to mean "all places whatsoever in the usual course of the voyage to and from the places mentioned in the policy" (x).

Hogg v. Horner.

Upon the same principle, where a ship was insured "at and from Lisbon to a port in England, with liberty to call at any one port in Portugal for any purpose whatever," Lord Kenyon was of opinion that the liberty given by this policy must be confined to ports to the northward of Lisbon, and in the direct course of a voyage thence to England; and he held accordingly that the ship was guilty of deviation in sailing to Faro, a port to the southward of Lisbon, although she sailed there to complete her cargo—a purpose connected with the voyage insured (y).

Ranken v. Reeve.

So, where a ship was insured "at and from Africa to the Canaries, Madeira and Lisbon, with liberty to touch, stay and trade at all ports," &c. "in the voyage," it was held that,

---

(x) Lavabre v. Wilson (1779), 1 Dougl. 284.

(y) Hogg v. Horner (1797), 2 Park, 626 ; 1 Marshall, 184 ; Arnould (2nd ed. vol. i. p. 420) calls this "certainly a strong decision," but it is in accordance with the tenor of modern decisions. In the case of Ashley v. Pratt (1847), 16 M. & W. 471; 1 Exch. 257, which he appears to consider as of a contrary effect, it must be remembered that the words of the policy were peculiarly wide, and were construed as giving peculiarly wide powers of deviation.

CHAP. XV.] LICENSE CLAUSES. 545

after having once moored at anchor for twenty-four hours in **Sect. 401.**
a port in Africa, so as to give an inception to the risk, she
could not then proceed to the southward, but only northward,
towards Europe, the object being only to protect deviations
in the direct course of the voyage insured (*z*).

So, where a ship was insured "at and from London to *Gairdner v.*
Trinidad and the Spanish main," with liberty "to call at all *Senhouse.*
or any of the West Indian Islands and Settlements," Sir J.
Mansfield expressed a clear and undoubted opinion that this
liberty of calling must be confined to places taken in the
direct and customary course between the termini of the voyage
insured, and therefore could not be held to protect the ship,
after having once sailed southward as far as Demerara, in then
sailing up northward to Martinique and St. Thomas's, unless,
indeed, very satisfactory evidence were given that such was
a customary course on such voyages as those insured in this
policy (*a*).

402. Where, however, upon the true construction of the *The purposes*
whole policy, it plainly appears that the parties could not *of the voyage*
have intended to give this limited effect to these clauses, they *a wider*
will be held to confer a power of visiting any ports within *construction*
the scope of the policy, although they may lie wide of the *of the clause*
usual and direct course between the termini of the voyage,
and even, under very special circumstances, in a diametrically
opposite direction; provided that they be visited for some
purpose connected with the prosecution of the adventure contemplated by the policy.

Thus, where a trading ship was insured on a homeward *Bragg v.*
voyage "at and from Martinique, and all or any other of the *Anderson.*
West Indian Islands, to London," with liberty "in that
voyage to touch and stay at any ports or places whatever," it
was held to be no deviation under this policy for the ship,
after sailing from Martinique, to put in for a cargo at one of
the West Indian Isles (St. Domingo), which lay very wide of

(*z*) Ranken *v.* Reeve (1814), 2   (*a*) Gairdner *v.* Senhouse (1810),
Park, 627.   3 Taunt. 16.

A.—VOL. I.   35

Sect. 402. the direct course of the voyage from Martinique to London. Mansfield, C. J., said, "There is no getting over these words; instead of 'all' you must substitute the words 'some of the West Indian Islands, such as lie between Martinique and London.' That would make quite a new agreement" (*b*).

Metcalfe v. Parry.

So, where a ship was insured "at and from Antigua to England, with liberty to touch at all or any of the West Indian Islands, Jamaica included"; and the ship, in order to complete her homeward cargo, put into St. Kitts, which lies wide of the direct course of the voyage from Antigua to England; it was contended that this was a deviation; but Gibbs, C. J., ruled decisively that it was not, for, by including Jamaica, which lies at least 500 miles wide of the direct course of the voyage from Antigua to England, it plainly appeared to be the meaning of the parties that the islands might be touched at without regard to their lying on or off such direct course, and that the ship was to go about, if necessary, from island to island, for the purpose of seeking freight (*c*).

Baltic risks in the time of Napoleon's Continental system.

403. Many instances occurred, during the pressure of Napoleon's Continental system, of a liberal interpretation of such clauses in those adventures generally called "Baltic risks": not because the Courts in such cases were guided by any peculiar principles of interpretation, but because the troubled and shifting nature of our relations with the different ports in the Baltic, under the political circumstances of the time, was such as to render the voyages then insured for those seas more vague in their objects and less definite in their limits.

Rucker v. Allnutt.

Goods were insured "at and from London to any port or

(*b*) Bragg *v.* Anderson (1812), 4 Taunt. 229; see also Lambert *v.* Liddard (1814), 5 Taunt. 480. In the case of Violett *v.* Allnutt (1811), 3 Taunt. 419, the ship put into Penzance, where she had express liberty given her "to touch for any purpose whatever," in order to complete her cargo, and was afterwards lost there while waiting for a wind: the Court were clear this was no deviation.

(*c*) Metcalfe *v.* Parry (1814), 4 Camp. 123. This decision was not questioned. See also Barclay *v.* Stirling (1816), 5 M. & S. 6.

CHAP. XV.] LICENSE CLAUSES. 547

ports in the Baltic, backwards and forwards, &c., with leave to touch and stay at any ports or places for all purposes whatever"; and, by another clause, "particularly with leave to wait for information off any ports or places." The ship went into the port of Carlshamn to wait for information; while there an embargo was laid on her, and the goods were seized and confiscated. At the trial Lord Ellenborough intimated an opinion that the words reserving liberty to wait off any port for information abridged the liberty of "touching and staying for all purposes," and the jury accordingly found for the underwriters. On motion for a new trial Lord Ellenborough altered his view of the case, and, with the concurrence of the Court, directed a new trial, principally on the ground that obtaining information as to the political state of the Baltic ports was a necessary purpose intimately connected with the prosecution of such a voyage as that which was insured, in which no fixed ports of discharge were named, and the ship could not venture to proceed to any without first learning whether they were friendly or hostile (*d*).

Sect. 403.

So, where a ship was insured "at and from London to the ship's discharging port or ports in the Baltic," with liberty, "to touch at any port or ports for orders or any other purpose," it was held no deviation for the ship, before she had fixed upon her port of discharge, to call for orders twice at the same port (*e*). In this case, as Lord Ellenborough remarked, "the adventure is stated to be a voyage all over the Baltic, the object of the adventure was that the assured should call as often as necessity required, and there is nothing in the nature of the thing which makes calling again at the same port absurd or contrary to what may be presumed to have

Mellish *v.* Andrews.

(*d*) Rucker *v.* Allnutt (1812), 15 East, 278.

(*e*) Mellish *v.* Andrews (1813), 2 M. & S. 27. On the former trial of the same case Lord Ellenborough thought this was a deviation, especially as the policy did not contain the words "backwards and forwards" (see Mellish *v.* Andrews (1812), 16 East, 312); but in his judgment in 2 M. & S. he states that the non-introduction of these words could make no difference under the circumstances.

35 (2)

Sect. 403. been the intention of the parties" (*f*). When this case came before the Court of Error, the judgment of Lord Ellenborough was affirmed; but Sir Vicary Gibbs, who delivered the judgment in error, laid great stress on the point that no port of discharge had been fixed on when the ship put in a second time for orders; had this been otherwise, he thought she would then have been obliged to take the ports in their order of succession; as it was, he was of opinion that, under the terms of the policy, "the assured had a right to go backwards and forwards from port to port for orders as to his port of discharge until his port of discharge was fixed" (*g*).

Other case of extensive liberty to touch.
Arnett *v.* Innes.

404. The two following decisions proceed upon, and perhaps in some degree extend, the same principle:—

A convict ship was insured on a voyage "at and from London to New South Wales, and at and from thence to the ship's loading port or ports in the East Indies, Persia, China, or elsewhere, forwards and backwards, and backwards and forwards, as well on this side as on the other side of the Cape of Good Hope, until her safe arrival at her final port of discharge in Great Britain," with leave for the ship "in the voyage insured to proceed and sail, to touch and stay, at any ports or places whatsoever and wheresoever, and for any purpose whatsoever, without being deemed a deviation." The ship, after arriving at New South Wales and discharging her convicts there, sailed in ballast to Batavia, where she took in a cargo of iron for Sourabaya, sailed to that port, discharged her iron there and took in a cargo of rice for the Mauritius; at the Mauritius she unloaded part of the rice, intending to load there a cargo of cotton for England, but, being on survey found unseaworthy, was broken up there and sold.

The jury found at the trial that the ship had not touched at too many places, nor stayed there an unreasonable time, but had pursued the usual course on a voyage of this description. The defendant, however, contended that the having

---

(*f*) 2 M. & S. 34.

(*g*) Andrews *v.* Mellish (in error), (1814), 5 Taunt. 496.

touched at these different ports for the purpose not only of loading, but also of discharging goods, was under the terms of this policy a deviation, but the Court held it was not so (*h*). Park, J.: "The terms contained in the policy cannot be more general and extensive. The vessel might sail and touch at any ports or places whatsoever, for any purposes whatsoever. Is not trading a purpose? If an underwriter enters into a covenant of this kind it is his own fault."

Sect. 404.

The next case shows that, if consistent with and in furtherance of the general purposes of the voyage, the ship, under such a liberty, will be justified in calling and taking goods on board at a port which lies even directly out of the usual course from the *terminus a quo* to the *terminus ad quem*.

Hunter *v.* Leathley.

A merchant here, having reason to expect a shipment of goods on his account from some of the ports of the Indian Archipelago, without, however, knowing of what nature they were, at what port to be loaded, or by what ship to be sent, effected a policy on goods generally on board of some one out of four different ships named in the policy (with leave to declare his interest more particularly, as it might thereafter appear), upon a voyage "at and from Singapore, Penang, Malacca, and Batavia, all or any, to the ship's port or ports of discharge in Great Britain or Holland," &c., "with leave to touch, stay, and trade at all or any ports or places whatsoever and wheresoever in the East Indies, Persia (*i*), or elsewhere, and also with permission to touch and stay at any ports or places in any direction and for any purpose necessary or otherwise, particularly Singapore, Penang, Malacca, Batavia, the Cape of Good Hope and St. Helena, and to take on board, discharge, reload and exchange goods and passengers, without being deemed a deviation."

Under this policy the ship took in part of her cargo at Batavia, and then proceeded to Sourabaya (another port in

(*h*) Armett *v.* Innes (1820), 4 J. B. Moore, 150.

(*i*) It was expressly found by the special case that the nearest port or place in Persia was more than 1,000 miles out of the direct course of a voyage from either Singapore, or Penang, or Malacca, or Batavia, to Europe.

Sect. 404. Java, lying 400 miles to the eastward of Batavia, and directly out of the course from Batavia, or any other of the four ports mentioned in the policy, to Europe), where she took on board the remainder of her cargo and returned with it to Batavia, whence she sailed for Europe and was afterwards lost by the perils of the seas.

The Court of King's Bench held that this putting into Sourabaya for the purpose of completing her cargo was no deviation; and the Court of Exchequer Chamber confirmed their judgment (*k*).

Lord Tenterden remarked that, from the circumstances of the case and the terms of the policy, the object of the assured plainly appeared to be to protect himself against loss, whatever kind of goods might be sent him, at whatever port they might be loaded, and by whatever ship they might be sent; that the underwriter accordingly, by subscribing such a policy, must be understood to have intended to afford a protection equally extensive, if the language of the policy would admit of such a construction (*l*). In the opinion of the two Courts, the very extensive powers given by the policy, the order in which the four places named stood in the policy (*m*), and the mention of Persia, more than a thousand miles out of the direct course of the voyage, showed that a voyage in the direct geographical course was not intended.

The purpose of the visit must be within the scope of the voyage.

405. Even though the port visited may be within the terms of the policy, yet the question still remains, whether the purpose for which it was visited was within the scope of the adventure contemplated by the policy; otherwise the visit will be a deviation.

However extensive may be the language of the clauses, "the permission to stay 'for any purpose whatever,' must be

---

(*k*) Hunter *v.* Leathley (1830), 10 B. & C. 858; *S. C.*, confirmed in error (1831), 7 Bing. 517; *S. C.*, at N. P., Ll. & Wels. 244.

(*l*) See 10 B. & C. 871.

(*m*) The geographical order is—(1) Penang; (2) Malacca; (3) Singapore; (4) Batavia. The order in the policy is—(1) Singapore; (2) Penang; (3) Malacca; (4) Batavia.

for some purpose within the scope of the adventure" (*n*). "The liberty in the policy must always be construed with reference to the main scope of the voyage insured" (*o*).

Thus, where goods were insured "at and from London to Berbice, with liberty to touch and stay at any ports and places whatsoever and wheresoever, and for all purposes whatsoever, particularly to land, load and exchange goods, without being deemed a deviation," Lord Ellenborough held that, notwithstanding the extensive terms in which this liberty was conceived, the ship, which had sailed with convoy, was guilty of a deviation by putting in to Madeira for the purpose of unloading goods and taking on board wines (which did not form part of the subject of the insurance), and there delaying for that purpose till after the convoy had proceeded on the voyage (*p*).

A ship was insured "at and from Para to New York," during her stay there, and at and from thence to Para, "with leave to call at all or any of the Windward and Leeward Islands on her passage to New York, with leave to discharge, exchange and take on board the whole or any part of any cargo and cargoes at any ports or places she might call at or proceed to, particularly at all or any of the Windward and Leeward Islands, without being deemed any deviation and without prejudice to this insurance." Under this extensive liberty, the ship, after sailing from Para, on her passage to New York, put into St. Thomas's and St. Bartholomew's, two of the Leeward Islands, not for any purpose connected with the voyage insured, but in order to obtain information for the shipowner whether the state of the market in those islands was such as to make it worth his while to send goods

---

(*n*) Per Gibbs, J., in Langhorne *v.* Allnutt (1812), 4 Taunt. 510, 519; see also Rucker *v.* Allnutt (1812), 15 East, 278; Thames & Mersey Mar. Ins. Co. *v.* Van Laun, *ante*, § 382a.

(*o*) Per Lord Ellenborough in Williams *v.* Shee (1813), 3 Camp.

469.

(*p*) Williams *v.* Shee (1813), 3 Camp. 469; see also Redman *v.* Loudon (1813), *ibid.* 503, which was a policy on the same ship for the same voyage, without the clause, and in which it was admitted there had been a deviation.

Sect. 405. out there in another vessel of his, on a separate adventure, from New York. The Court held that, although these islands were undoubtedly within the language of the policy, yet putting into them for a purpose wholly unconnected with the voyage insured, and which had reference to some new adventure, subsequently to be undertaken in another vessel, was a deviation (*q*).

Solly *v.* Whitmore.

A ship was insured on an outward voyage, "at and from Hull to her port or ports of loading in the Baltic or Gulf of Finland, with liberty in the said voyage to touch and stay at any ports or places whatever, for all purposes, particularly at Elsinore, without being deemed a deviation." The ship's intended port of loading was Pillau; before sailing, however, she had taken goods on board for Elsinore and Dantzic, and on her voyage she stopped at both these places, in order to deliver those goods, and was afterwards lost before reaching Pillau: the Court held, under this policy, that the stopping to deliver goods, being a purpose wholly foreign to the main object of the voyage insured, was a deviation. "If," said Abbott, C. J., "the ship had gone into Elsinore or Dantzic, to see if she could get a cargo, that would have been a purpose connected with the voyage, and consequently would not have been a deviation. But the vessel, in fact, went into those ports for the purpose of delivering goods, which was wholly unconnected with the object of the voyage insured" (*r*).

Laing *v.* Union Mar. Ins. Co.

A ship was insured from Haiphong, in Tonquin, to any ports or places in any order in Japan, "with leave to call at any ports or places in or out of the customary route in any order for all purposes." She went from Haiphong to Hongay, where she loaded a cargo of coals for Hongkong, and was lost between Hongay and Hongkong. Mathew, J., held that the loss was not covered by the policy. There was no direct trade, he said, between Tonquin and Japan, and the

---

(*q*) Hammond *v.* Reid (1820), 4 B. & Ald. 72.

(*r*) Solly *v.* Whitmore (1821), 5 B. & Ald. 45. It is somewhat difficult to reconcile this case with Armett *v.* Innes, *ante*, § 404.

underwriter was entitled to assume that the ship would go in ballast straight to Japan, calling at "ports or places" for purposes incidental to a voyage from Tonquin to Japan (*s*).

Sect. 405.

A ship was insured "at and from Liverpool to the west and (or) south-west coast of Africa, during her stay and trade therein, and back to a port of call or (and) discharge in the United Kingdom." The vessel, after she had completed her loading for the return voyage, stayed a month on the African coast for the purpose of earning salvage; she was damaged while in that employment, and was afterwards totally lost on the voyage home. It was held that salvage, in the absence of usage, could not be construed to be a purpose within the licence contained in the policy, and consequently that the risk had been substantially varied by what had been done (*t*).

Company of African Merchants *v.* Brit. & For. Mar. Ins. Co.

406. In like manner, although the words of the clause are of the most extensive nature, the ship will not be protected by such a policy if, at the time of loss, she be on an intermediate voyage, not subordinate to or connected with the voyage or voyages contemplated by the parties as the principal objects of the contract (*u*) (unless sanctioned by a well-established usage).

An intermediate voyage not connected with that insured is not covered.

A ship was insured "at and from London to New South Wales, and at and from thence to all ports or places in the East Indies and South America," with liberty "to proceed and sail, to touch and stay at any ports whatsoever, &c., for all purposes whatsoever, particularly to trade and sail backwards and forwards and forwards and backwards." Under this policy the ship sailed from London with convicts for New South Wales, and soon after arriving there the captain received orders from his employers to proceed from New South Wales to the East Indies. Before this, however, he had entered into engagements for a voyage to New Zealand

Bottomley *v.* Bovill.

(*s*) Laing *v.* Union Marine Ins. Co. (1895), 1 Com. Cas. 11.
(*t*) Company of African Merchants *v.* Brit. & For. Mar. Ins. Co. (1873), L. R. 8 Exch. 154.

Whether and how far purposes of salvage will justify deviation is considered *post*, § 434.
(*u*) Bottomley *v.* Bovill (1826), 5 B. & Cr. 210.

Sect. 406. and back again to New South Wales, and accordingly sailed on this voyage, intending to return to New South Wales, and then to sail, as directed by his employers, for the East Indies. On his way back, however, from New Zealand, his ship was lost, and the underwriters resisted payment, on one ground, amongst others, that as New Zealand lay entirely out of the course of the voyage from New South Wales to the East Indies, the sailing thither was a deviation, even under the extensive terms of this policy, and the Court, on the principle already stated, held that it was so (*x*).

Hamilton v. Sheddon.

Upon the same principle, where an insurance was effected on goods on board a ship which, as appeared upon the face of the policy, was meant to act as a tender to other ships employed in the palm oil trade on the African coast, the Court held that it was a deviation for a ship so insured to sail away from the Benin river (where she had been for some time acting as a tender) to Cameroons with the cargo of one of the oil ships which had gone ashore at the bar of the Benin river, although the policy contained the most extensive liberty to touch and stay (*y*), because instead of her subsidiary duties as tender she had assumed the responsibilities of a principal voyage (*z*).

Trading no deviation if it has not caused delay.

407. We now come to the consideration of those cases which establish the position that if the ship under the terms of the policy was justified in originally visiting the port, any trading during her lawful stay, although foreign to the main

---

(*x*) Bottomley *v.* Bovill (1826), 5 B. & Cr. 210.

(*y*) The policy was "at and from Liverpool to any port or place of loading and trade on the African coast and islands during her stay and trade there, and at and from thence to her port or ports of discharge in the United Kingdom, with leave to call at all ports and places, backwards and forwards and, forwards and backwards, in any order, for any purpose, without being deemed a deviation; and with liberty also for the said ship in the said voyage to proceed and sail to and touch and stay at any ports or places whatsoever, and to load, unload, reload, sell, barter, and exchange goods and property, &c., particularly with liberty to tranship," and with a memorandum "that the said vessel might be employed and used as a tender to any other ship or vessel in the same employ."

(*z*) Hamilton *v.* Sheddon (1837), 3 M. & W. 49.

purposes of the adventure, is not a deviation unless it causes additional delay or otherwise substantially varies the risk.

Sect. 407.

Formerly this was otherwise. Thus, where a ship, under a general liberty "to touch and stay," was forced by stormy weather into a port of distress, and obliged to remain there three weeks, during which she broke bulk and discharged a quantity of coals, Lord Kenyon held this to be a deviation, though no additional delay was caused thereby (*a*). So where a ship was insured from Gibraltar to Guernsey, "with liberty to touch and discharge goods at Lisbon"; and the ship, while waiting at Lisbon for a convoy, not only discharged part of her loading there, but took in fresh goods for Gibraltar, Lord Ellenborough held that, under this policy, the taking in goods at Lisbon was a deviation, although no additional delay was caused thereby (*b*). These cases, however, are now overruled by the following authorities, which have established the more liberal rule stated above.

Formerly the rule was different.

Cases in the present rule.

Ship and freight were insured "from the ship's loading port or ports on the coast of Spain to London, with liberty to touch and stay at any port or place whatever without being deemed a deviation." The ship was obliged to put into Gibraltar for provisions, and while there the captain also took on board some chests of dollars on freight. The putting into Gibraltar was justifiable, and no additional delay was caused by taking the dollars on board. The Court, therefore, held that there had been no deviation (*c*). Lord Ellenborough also said that the increased temptation to attack caused by taking treasure on board was not such an alteration of the risk as to discharge the underwriter.

Raine *v.* Bell.

So, where a ship was insured "from Stockholm to New York," it was held no deviation for the owner of live stock on board to take in provender for their use, while the ship,

Cormack *v.* Gladstone.

(*a*) Stitt *v.* Wardell (1798), 2 Esp. 610.
(*b*) Sheriff *v.* Potts (1803), 5 Esp. 96. This case may be supposed to have proceeded partly on the principle that *expressio unius est exclusio alterius;* but even then it is overruled by Laroche *v.* Oswin (1810), 12 East, 131.
(*c*) Raine *v.* Bell (1808), 9 East, 195.

Sect. 407. as was then customary, was waiting at Elsinore for the purpose of taking convoy and paying Sound dues; the whole of such provender having been loaded on board before the Sound dues could be paid, so that no additional delay was thereby occasioned (*d*).

It makes no difference whether the policy is on ship or freight, or on goods.

408. In the case of Raine *v*. Bell, where the policy was on ship and freight, Lord Ellenborough expressly reserved his opinion as to the effect of a change in the state of the cargo upon a policy "on goods." The following case resolves this doubt, and shows that it makes no difference whether the policy be on goods or any other subject of insurance.

Laroche v. Oswin.

Goods were insured "at and from Gottenburg to a port or ports in the Baltic with liberty, in case of non-admittance, to unload at Carlshamn." After the ship had sailed from Gottenburg with convoy, and while she was lying in Malmoe Roads under orders of the commodore to prepare for sailing, a boat came alongside with some boxes of indigo, which formed no part of the original intended cargo, but were all got on board without any delay to the ship. The Court held this was no deviation (*e*), "for the risk insured was neither enhanced nor varied; but something was done in the course of the voyage which made no difference in either, and therefore was no discharge of the underwriter's liability" (*f*).

Cases in the United States.

The principle of interpretation thus established in English law has received abundant confirmation in the jurisprudence of the United States. Thus, where a ship, under liberty to touch and stay, sold part of her cargo while detained in port by an embargo (*g*), or while waiting for necessary repairs (*h*), or for fear of capture (*i*), such trading was held

---

(*d*) Cormack *v*. Gladstone (1809), 11 East, 347.

(*e*) Laroche *v*. Oswin (1810), 12 East, 131.

(*f*) Per Lord Ellenborough, 12 East, 133.

(*g*) Kingston *v*. Girard (1808),

4 Dall. R. 274; Condy's Marshall, 189; 1 Phillips, s. 999.

(*h*) Kane *v*. Columbian Ins. Co. (1807), 2 Johns. R. 264; 1 Phillips, s. 999.

(*i*) Hughes *v*. Union Ins. Co. (1818), 3 Wheaton, R. 159; 1 Phillips, s. 999.

not to amount to a deviation, because proved to have caused no delay and no variation of the risk.

Sect. 408.

409. In all such cases, however, if additional delay is caused by the trading, it will terminate the risk (*k*). Any act of trading not contemplated by the parties to the policy, and unconnected with the main object of the adventure, is justifiable only on condition that it be completed during the period of her lawful stay, at an allowed port, for a justifiable purpose (*l*).

Additional delay caused by such trading terminates the risk.

But, if no additional delay or variation of the risk is caused, the mere fact of putting into a port or place with a twofold purpose, partly connected and partly unconnected with the adventure contemplated by the policy, will not amount to a deviation or terminate the risk. Thus, where a vessel, sailing outwards from London to Grenada, was insured on freight homewards "at and from Grenada to London," and on arriving at the island (where there is but one custom-house) proceeded to deliver her outward cargo in different bays there, and was lost in entering one of these bays for the twofold purpose of delivering the remainder of her outward, and taking in a homeward, cargo, it was held that this was no deviation, but that the underwriters were liable for the loss of the homeward freight (*m*).

Aliter, if no additional delay. Warre *v.* Millar.

(*k*) "It will amount to a deviation" were Arnould's words. See, however, note (*i*) to sect. 48 of the Mar. Ins. Act, 1906, *ante*, § 376.

(*l*) Williams *v.* Shee (1813), 3 Camp. 469. See Company of African Merchants *v.* British and Foreign Mar. Ins. Co. (1873), L. R. 8 Ex. 154. Inglis *v.* Vaux (1813), 3 Camp. 437, was cited by Arnould as an authority for the rule that "even where the delay is partly for a purpose connected with the main objects of the voyage insured, if it be partly for another which is entirely foreign to it, such delay will be regarded as a deviation." Arnould, as his statement of the case shows, only meant that if the master of the ship stayed longer in Antigua than was reasonably necessary to dispose of the outward cargo, so that the real object of his prolonged stay was to procure a homeward cargo, the risk on the outward voyage came to an end. If Lord Ellenborough meant to decide that a stay in port, necessary for the purposes of the insured voyage, puts an end to the risk because the master also utilizes it for the purposes of the succeeding voyage, his decision is entirely opposed to the weight of authority.

(*m*) Warre *v.* Millar (1825), 4 B. & Cr. 538; *S. C.*, at N. P. (1824),

Sect. 410.

Distinction between Hammond v. Reid and Raine v. Bell.

410. The line of distinction between the class of cases of which Hammond v. Reid (n) is the leading authority and those which are governed by Raine v. Bell (o), though not at first sight obvious, is, in reality, sufficiently clear. In Hammond v. Reid, and cases of that class, the ship would not have touched at the port at all except for some purpose totally unconnected with the main object of the voyage insured; and the execution of that purpose was itself the sole cause of the delay. In Raine v. Bell, and the cases decided on its authority, the ship had originally put in, and was actually staying at, the port for some purpose connected with the voyage; and, during her justifiable and necessary stay there, some act was done, which, though in itself unconnected with the adventure, and not originally contemplated by the parties to the policy, was held not to be a deviation, because there was no material variation of the risk, and no delay which would not otherwise have occurred. For instance, in Hammond v. Reid, the ship would never have touched at St. Bartholomew's at all, except for the purpose,—wholly alien to the object of the voyage insured,—of procuring information for the guidance of another adventure. In Raine v. Bell, the ship, when the dollars were put on board, was actually staying at Gibraltar for provisions, without which the voyage insured could not have been prosecuted, and no extra delay or risk was incurred by taking the dollars on board.

Summary of the rules established by the cases.

411. The principles of law, therefore, applicable to the interpretation of these clauses, appear to be,—

1. That the extent of the powers they confer on the ship is to be judged of, not so much by verbal criticism on the terms employed (such as "to call," "to touch," or "to touch

---

1 C. & P. 237. In this case it was held that the delivery of the outward cargo was a necessary preparation for the homeward voyage, and therefore what was done for that purpose was no deviation. It is clear that the discharge of the outward cargo had occupied time.

(n) *Ante*, § 405.
(o) *Ante*, § 407.

and stay"), as by reference to the true scope and nature of the adventure contemplated by the policy.

Sect. 411.

2. That, however extensive the language of these clauses may be, they can never confer a power of visiting ports out of that which, upon a fair construction of the whole policy, appears to have been the course of the voyage insured as contemplated by the parties; nor can they justify the ship in visiting any port, even though within the local limits of the voyage insured, for any purpose unconnected with the main object of the adventure.

3. If the ship visits an allowed port for an allowed purpose, no trading, breaking bulk, landing, or loading cargo, however alien to the main object of the adventure, will make the visit a deviation if the trading, &c. be completed during the period of the ship's lawful stay in such port without additional delay or substantial variation of the risk.

4. If, however, such trading give rise to delay that would not otherwise have been incurred, it will, on that ground, discharge the underwriter from liability as from the time when the delay began (*p*).

412. Sect. 48 of the Marine Insurance Act, 1906, declares that—

Change of risk by delay.

> In the case of a voyage policy, the adventure insured must be prosecuted throughout its course with reasonable despatch, and, if without lawful excuse (*q*) it is not so prosecuted, the insurer is discharged from liability as from the time when the delay became unreasonable.

As the sole ground upon which a deviation discharges the underwriter is that it varies the risk, and as it is evident that the risk may be as much varied by a delay in commencing or prosecuting the voyage as by a local divergence from its prescribed course, the rule was established that every such delay, if unreasonable or unexcused, will discharge the underwriter.

(*p*) See Mar. Ins. Act, 1906, s. 48, *infra*.

(*q*) See sect. 49, *post*, § 424a.

560　DEVIATION AND CHANGE OF RISK.　[PART I.

Sect. 412.　　412. In the words of Tindal, C. J., "The voyage in the commencement or prosecution of which any unreasonable delay takes place, becomes a voyage at a different period of the year, at a more advanced age of the ship, and, in short, a different voyage than if it had been prosecuted with reasonable and ordinary diligence; the risk is altered from that which was intended by all parties when the policy was effected" (r).

Delay in commencing the voyage.　　413. To begin with the commencement of the voyage, it is clear that, under an insurance "at and from," any unreasonable delay that takes place between the time when the policy attaches on the ship "at" the port, and the time when she sails on her voyage, will discharge the underwriter (s). As long, indeed, as she is *bonâ fide* preparing for her voyage, as by repairs, &c., the delay will be held excused, and the underwriter liable; but if all thoughts of the voyage be laid aside, and the ship still kept lying in port, the underwriter is discharged (t). So, although the voyage be not abandoned, yet any waste of time or unnecessary delay in port, not excused by justifying cause, nor in any degree connected with the purposes of the voyage insured, is held to vary the risk; as where a yacht lying in Bristol harbour was insured on a voyage "at and from Bristol to London," and did not sail for five months after the policy was effected (u).

Delay in the course of the voyage.　　414. That an unreasonable delay in performing the voyage insured is equivalent to a deviation (x), was expressly ruled by Lord Mansfield, in the case of Hartley v. Buggin, in which, the ground of defence being the detention of the ship as a floating slave depôt on the African coast, his Lordship said,

---

(r) Per Tindal, C. J., in Mount v. Larkins (1831), 8 Bing. 122.

(s) The consequence is the same when the delay takes place before the risk has commenced; see Mar. Ins. Act, 1906, s. 42, *ante*, § 376; but delay, when it prevents the policy attaching, properly belongs to the subject of the chapter on duration of the risk, and is considered there. See *post*, §§ 479, 483.

(t) Per Lord Hardwicke in Motteux v. London Ass. Co. (1739), 1 Atkyns, 545; Chitty v. Selwyn (1742), 2 Atkyns, 359.

(u) Palmer v. Marshall (1831—1832), 8 Bing. 79, 317.

(x) See note (i), *ante*, § 376.

"The single point before the Court is, whether there has not been what is equivalent to a deviation—whether the risk has not been varied, no matter whether the risk has or has not been thereby increased" (*y*). So, where a vessel engaged in the African palm oil trade, with liberty to act as a tender to other ships in the same employ, was kept thirteen months in the Benin river, this was found by the jury to be an unreasonable delay, and the Court refused to disturb their verdict (*z*).

Sect. 414.

A delay at the termination of the voyage insured is, if unexcused and unreasonable, as fatal as though it had occurred in any of its intermediate stages. Thus, where a ship insured "at and from Sierra Leone to London" was delayed in the Thames, off Deptford dockyard, from the 18th to the 27th of February, before she was admitted into the dock to unload her cargo, it was not disputed that this delay, if unexcused or unnecessary, would amount to a deviation at that, as at any other, stage of the voyage (*a*).

Delay at the termination of the voyage.

When the master of a ship remained in port for several weeks for the purpose of building a house for himself, and waiting the issue of two sealing voyages on which he had despatched another vessel, this was found, on special verdict, to be an unreasonable and unjustifiable delay (*b*).

In short, whenever the delay exceeds a reasonable time, or is incurred for purposes unconnected with the true object of the voyage insured, it will determine the insurance (*c*).

As every special clause contained in the policy must be strictly construed, it follows that, if express permission be

Limit of express leave.

(*y*) Hartley *v.* Buggin (1781), 2 Park, 652. See, in illustration of the same principle, Phillips *v.* Irving (1844), 7 M. & Gr. 325; see also Pearson *v.* Commercial Union Ass. Co., in the Ex. Ch. (1873), L. R. 8 C. P. 548; in the House of Lords (1876), 1 App. Cas. 498 —a case on a fire policy which (although the result might have been different in a voyage policy) is an authority for the principle that a delay on a voyage for a collateral purpose is unjustifiable. The facts of the case are set out *post*, § 509.

(*z*) Hamilton *v.* Sheddon (1837), 3 M. & W. 49; see also Hyderabad (Deccan) Co. *v.* Willoughby, [1899] 2 Q. B. 530.

(*a*) Samuel *v.* Royal Exch. Ass. Co. (1828), 8 B. & Cr. 119.

(*b*) Mount *v.* Larkins (1831), 8 Bing. 108.

(*c*) See Thames & Mersey Mar. Ins. Co. *v.* Van Laun, *ante*, § 382a.

Sect. 414. given in the policy to delay for a given time specified in the policy, that delay cannot lawfully be prolonged. Thus, where liberty was given in the policy "to wait two months at Monte Video if needful," a longer delay than two months was held to discharge the underwriters (*d*).

Necessary delay for purpose of voyage justifiable.

415. It is only, however, an unreasonable or unexcused delay, *i.e.*, a wilful and unnecessary waste of time, that will put an end to the insurance; if justified by necessity, or incurred *bonâ fide* with a view to the purposes of the voyage insured, the underwriter will not be discharged by the delay, although its absolute duration may be very considerable. "To discharge the policy," says Lord Ellenborough, "there must be a clear imputation of waste of time; mere length of time elapsing between the sailing of the vessel and the underwriting of the policy is not of itself sufficient, for it is capable of explanation"(*e*). "What delay will constitute a deviation," says Story, J., "depends on the nature of the voyage and the usage of trade. That delay which is necessary to accomplish the objects of the voyage, according to the course of the trade, if incurred *bonâ fide*, cannot be admitted to avoid the insurance"(*f*). So, Tindal, C. J., lays it down that the "detention for a reasonable time, for the purposes of the adventure, must be allowed; and whether the delay be reasonable or not must be determined, not by any positive or arbitrary rule, but by the state of things existing at the time at the port where the ship happens to be" (*g*).

Smith v. Surridge.

A ship insured on the 15th of May "at and from Pillau to London," and then lying at Pillau, was obliged to be thoroughly repaired there before she could sail on the voyage insured; these repairs were not completed till the end of June, when the water in the harbour had become so low that she could not get over the bar, and she did not actually sail

(*d*) Doyle *v.* Powell (1832), 4 B. & Ad. 267.
(*e*) Grant *v.* King (1802), 4 Esp. 175.
(*f*) In Columbian Ins. Co. *v.* Catlett (1827), 12 Wheaton, R. 383; 1 Phillips, Ins. s. 1002.
(*g*) In Phillips *v.* Irving (1844), 7 M. & Gr. 328.

till November. Lord Kenyon held that this was not such a delay as to discharge the underwriter (*h*).

Sect. 415.

A policy was effected in August, 1789, on an American ship "at and from Brest to London," against British capture, while she was lying in Brest Harbour, then blockaded by the British. The ship did not sail till March, 1790. It was contended that this delay of nearly seven months discharged the underwriters; but proof having been given that the voyage had never been abandoned, and that the time had been consumed in *bonâ fide* attempting to procure an American crew from England (there being no possibility of doing so in France), a special jury, under the direction of Lord Ellenborough, found for the plaintiff. Lord Ellenborough told the jury that while the vessel was in a fair state of preparation for the voyage it was covered by the policy; but if the voyage was abandoned for a length of time, the underwriters would be discharged. "The question whether there was an abandonment of the original adventure is to be decided," said his Lordship, "from a fair review of all existing circumstances at the time when the voyage might reasonably be presumed to commence. Here the extreme difficulty of obtaining men is to be taken into consideration" (*i*).

Grant *v.* King.

416. The main point in all these cases is whether the delay was *bonâ fide* incurred with a view to promote and carry out the main objects of the voyage insured. If it was, there is no ground for saying that the voyage was not prosecuted with reasonable despatch.

When is the delay justifiable?

Thus, where a vessel, chartered for the timber trade between this country and the United States, was insured on a voyage "from London to her loading port in Virginia and back to London," it was held that her waiting fifteen months at Norfolk, her loading port, until an embargo was taken

Schroder *v.* Thompson.

(*h*) Smith *v.* Surridge (1801), 4 Esp. 25. The detention after the end of June was, of course, unavoidable; the previous delay was a necessary one.

(*i*) Grant *v.* King (1802), 4 Esp. 175.

Sect. 416. off, and long enough afterwards to take on board a cargo of lumber there, did not discharge the underwriter, although the ship might have sailed home in ballast immediately the embargo was laid on (*k*).

Bain *v.* Case. So, where the captain of a ship, insured on a trading voyage to all or any ports in the North or South Pacific Ocean, delayed one hundred and nine days at one of the ports in those seas in the hope of getting permission to land her outward cargo, for which purpose he was during that time negotiating with the government, a special jury, under the direction of Lord Tenterden, found that the delay under the circumstances was not unreasonable (*l*).

Phillips *v.* Irving. So, where a seeking ship, insured on a trading voyage "at and from London to Bombay and thence to China and back to the United Kingdom," stayed at Bombay for more than six months after she was ready to take in cargo there for the purpose of procuring a remunerative freight, such delay was held to be justifiable, since it was for a purpose strictly connected with the main object of the adventure (*m*).

The law is the same in the United States. 417. In the jurisprudence of the United States the same principle has been illustrated by several decisions, which appear to have proceeded on a very sound application of general rules (*n*). Thus, if a vessel enters a port to dispose of her cargo, it has been decided by Story, J., that the master may stay there a reasonable time for that purpose, though he meets with no success. In the case alluded to, insurance was made on a cargo of flour "from Alexandria to St. Thomas, and two other West Indian ports, and back to the United States"; and the ship on arriving at St. Thomas remained there seventy-two days, during which time the master

---

(*k*) Schroder *v.* Thompson (1817), 7 Taunt. 462.

(*l*) Bain *v.* Case (1829), 3 C. & P. 496; see also Suydam *v.* Mar. Ins. Co. (1807), 2 Johnson, R. 138; 1 Phillips, Ins. s. 1002.

(*m*) Phillips *v.* Irving (1844), 7 M. & Gr. 325.

(*n*) See 1 Phillips, Ins. s. 1002, and especially Suydam *v.* Mar. Ins. Co. (1807), 2 Johnson, R. 138; Lapham *v.* Atlas Ins. Co. (1833), 24 Pickering, R. 1.

endeavoured, but with only partial success, to dispose of his outward cargo at the price limited by his instructions: the Court held this delay no deviation, although it was proved that the captain might at once have sold his flour at half a dollar per barrel less than the limited price (*o*).

Sect. 417.

In answer to the argument that the delay to procure the limited price was unreasonable, Story, J., in delivering the judgment of the Court, says: "In almost every voyage of this nature, where different ports are to be visited for the purposes of trade, and to seek markets, it is almost universal to prescribe limits to the price of sales. It cannot be that the master, if entitled to go to a single port only, is bound to sell, at whatever sacrifice, as soon as he arrives at that port, and within that period at which he may unload and reload a return cargo. He must, from the very nature of the case, have a discretion on this subject. He is not bound to sell the whole cargo at once, whatever may be the sacrifice, and thus frustrate the projected adventure. He must exercise on this, as in all other cases, a sound discretion for the interests of all concerned. To be sure, if the owner should limit the price to an extravagant sum, or the master should delay, after all reasonable expectations of a change of market were extinguished, such circumstances might probably be left to a jury to infer a delay amounting to a deviation" (*p*).

Remarks of Story, J.

418. On the principle that every unexcused departure from the usual mode of conducting the voyage by which the risk can be varied amounts to a deviation, Lord Kenyon once held that the mere fact of carrying letters of marque without the cognizance or consent of the underwriters on

Deviation by cruising (q). Carrying letters of marque without leave not a deviation.

(*o*) Columbian Ins. Co. *v.* Catlett (1827), 12 Wheaton, R. 383; 1 Phillips, s. 1002.

(*p*) *Ibid.* See also Ellery *v.* New England Ins. Co. (1829), 8 Pickering, R. 14; 1 Phillips, s. 1002.

(*q*) Since the United States and Spain—the two most important maritime Powers who have not formally adhered to the Declaration of Paris—decided in their late war not to issue letters of marque, the cases on deviation by cruising have little practical importance. The editors only retain them in an abbreviated form because they illustrate principles of general importance.

Sect. 418. a ship insured on a trading voyage was a fatal deviation; for although she had never made use of such letters, nor ever diverged from the usual track of the voyage, they varied the risk which the underwriter had assumed by giving the assured a temptation to deviate (*r*).

The law, however, as thus laid down must now be considered to be overruled. Lord Kenyon himself, on a subsequent occasion, admitted that the case was decided on principles which were new, and which went to the very verge of the law (*s*), and he refused to extend them to a case where the letters of marque were taken on board without any intention of cruising, but solely for the purpose of more easily procuring a crew (*t*). Later judges have demurred entirely, not only to the law as laid down by Lord Kenyon, but to the principles on which he grounds it. Lawrence, J., says: "If an intention to deviate not carried into effect will not avoid a policy, still less can a temptation to deviate" (*u*). And Lord Ellenborough declared the general opinion in his time to be that a "mere irritation of this sort shall not operate as a deviation" (*x*).

Cruising by a trading ship is a deviation.

419. If a ship on a mere mercantile adventure carries letters of marque with the consent of the underwriters, but without express liberty in the policy so to do, there has been some doubt as to the extent to which she would be justified in departing from the direct course of the voyage insured.

The true principle, said Arnould, appears to be, that no departure from the usual course of the voyage caused by repelling hostile force, or even attacking an enemy's ship, will be held a deviation, provided it can fairly be attributed to motives of self-defence (*y*). If, however, such a vessel,

---

(*r*) Dennison *v.* Modigliani (1794), 5 T. R. 580.

(*s*) See 6 T. R. 382.

(*t*) Moss *v.* Byrom (1795), 6 T. R. 379.

(*u*) In Raine *v.* Bell (1808), 9 East, 201.

(*x*) Jarratt *v.* Ward (1808), 1 Camp. 266.

(*y*) The Mar. Ins. Act, 1906, s. 49 (1) (d), *post*, § 424a, provides that a deviation is excused, when reasonably necessary for the safety of the ship or subject-matter insured. Probably, therefore, it is now more correct to say that there

CHAP. XV.] DEVIATION BY CRUISING. 567

from a desire of profit, cruises, *i.e.*, lies by, or departs from the direct course of the voyage, in hopes of meeting with prizes, that is a deviation (*z*).

Sect. 419.

420. It is, however, admitted that if an enemy comes in the way she may engage in her own defence, and prosecute the engagement to capture, even though in so doing she may be obliged to depart from the direct course of the voyage (*a*). It appears equally clear that if an enemy comes across her course she may attack and take him from other motives than those of self-defence, if the so doing does not involve any departure from the direct course of the voyage (*b*).

Chasing an enemy in self-defence.

The really doubtful point is, whether a ship so circumstanced has a right to alter her course for the purpose of chasing a strange sail. Lord Mansfield held that the ship has a right to give chase (*c*); but in a subsequent case Lord Ellenborough was strongly inclined to think that if the departure from the course was for the purposes of hostile capture it was a deviation; but if it were *bonâ fide* for the purposes of defence, as by making a show of confidence to deter the enemy from attack, or with a view to obtain some advantage in the conflict, or the like, in that case it was no deviation (*d*).

421. The subject has occupied the attention of the Courts of the United States (*e*), and the law has been laid down by Story, J., in the following terms:—"Whether a vessel be commissioned or not, she has a right to repel any attempt of

Law on this point in the United States.

---

is a deviation when a merchant ship, not having leave to carry letters of marque, departs from her course to attack an enemy, but that the deviation may be excusable.

(*z*) Cock *v.* Townson (*temp.* Lord Camden), 2 Park, 630. As to what constitutes cruising, see Syers *v.* Bridge (1780), 2 Dougl. 527.

(*a*) Jolly *v.* Walker (1781), 2 Park, 630; Parr *v.* Anderson (1805), 6 East, 202.

(*b*) Jolly *v.* Walker (1781), 2 Park, 630.

(*c*) *Ibid.*

(*d*) Parr *v.* Anderson (1805), 6 East, 202.

(*e*) See the cases of Wiggin *v.* Amory (1816), 13 Mass. R. 127; Wiggin *v.* Boardman (1817), 14 Mass. R. 12; Haven *v.* Holland (1820), 2 Mason, R. 230; cited 1 Phillips, ss. 1029, 1030.

Sect. 421. an enemy, and to protect and defend herself by all reasonable precautions against a meditated hostile attack. If a vessel, supposed to be an enemy cruiser, be in sight, and apparently intend to attack a merchant vessel, the master of the latter is bound to exert his best skill and judgment as to the time and mode of his defence; and if he act honestly and fairly, he will be justified, whatever may be the event. He is not bound to endeavour to make his escape in the first instance; and on failure of this, to meet the enemy. He may lay-to or chase the enemy, if he deem that the most effectual way to secure his object. The only question in cases of this nature is whether what is done is fairly attributable to motives of self-defence or to motives of another nature—such as a desire to profit: if the latter, then it is a deviation" (*f*). The learned Judge further held that delay for the purpose of manning a prize justifiably captured by a merchant ship carrying letters of marque, but without express liberty so to do, was no deviation; for the right to make the capture at all drew after it the right to make the capture effectual, and it would be most mischievous to the interests of trade to discourage men from making a gallant defence, from the knowledge that in no event could they reap a reward for their victory (*g*).

Chancellor Kent, in his Commentaries, speaks of this case as having confided to the captain a pretty enlarged discretion as to the best mode of defence, and one carried to the very verge of the law (*h*); but the decision seems conformable to the spirit of the maritime law, if not to the very letter of the earlier authorities.

Construction of clauses giving a liberty "to cruise," &c.

422. The cases hitherto considered have been principally those in which the policy has contained no clauses empowering the ship " to cruise," " to carry letters of marque," &c.

The general rule of construction with regard to all such permissions is that they should be construed strictly, so as

(*f*) See 1 Phillips, s. 1030. Mason, R. 230.
(*g*) Haven *v.* Holland (1820), 2 (*h*) 3 Kent, Com. 316.

not to extend their force beyond the plain meaning of the words in relation to the subject-matter and the intention of the parties, as collected from the whole of the document (*i*). Thus, where a ship was insured " with a liberty to cruise six weeks," this was held to mean six weeks successively from the commencement of the cruise, and not for six weeks at different periods (*k*).

Sect. 422.

Again, where a ship, insured on a slaving voyage, " with or without letters of marque," saw a sail which she did not know to be an enemy, about a quarter of a point on her lee-bow, and she altered her course accordingly, and gave chase for about a quarter of an hour, when she abandoned it, and returned into the direct course of the voyage insured, Lord Ellenborough, at the trial, and afterwards in banc, was strongly inclined to think that under the clause in question this was a deviation (*l*).

Construction of the clause "with or without letters of marque." Under such clause may a trading ship alter her course to chase a strange sail?

423. When such clauses contain an express permission to do certain specified things, the principle *expressio unius est exclusio alterius* applies, and the permission cannot be extended to objects not mentioned in the policy.

Exclusive effect of a positive permission.

Thus, where a ship was insured on a slaving and trading adventure, " with or without letters of marque, with leave to chase, capture, and man prizes," Lord Ellenborough held that this permission did not authorize the captain, after having taken a prize, to shorten sail and lie to in order to keep company with the prize while convoying her to port, although the port to which he was so convoying her was within the limits of the voyage insured (*m*). In a similar case, however, in the United States, it has been held, apparently on good grounds, that the mere act of convoying a prize to port under

To man, not to convoy.

(*i*) Per Lord Ellenborough in Lawrence *v.* Sydebotham (1805), 6 East, 51.

(*k*) Syers *v.* Bridge (1780), 2 Dougl. 527.

(*l*) Parr *v.* Anderson (1805), 6 East, 202. See further as to this case, 2 Park, 632; and see 1 Phillips, ss. 1029, 1030; 3 Kent, Com. 315.

(*m*) Lawrence *v.* Sydebotham (1805), 6 East, 45.

570　　　DEVIATION AND CHANGE OF RISK.　　[PART I.

Sect. 423.

To "capture, man, and see into port" is not to delay in port.

Cruising restricted in locality.

such liberty, is not a deviation unless it involves delay or departure from the direct course of the voyage (*n*).

It has been held that leave to "capture, man, and see into port any enemy's ships,". did not authorize the ship to remain in port while a prize was receiving necessary repairs there, but at most to see the prize moored safely, and give the necessary orders for its final destination (*o*).

So, where a ship, insured for the Southern whale fishery, with liberty "to chase, capture, and man prizes, &c., and also to cruise thirty-one days, either together or separate, anywhere and in any latitude on the outward bound passage, on this side of Cape Horn," lay to for nine days, for the purpose of capturing a prize, off a port within the limits of her fishing ground, but on the other side of Cape Horn, the Court held: 1st. That such lying to was not within the liberty to chase, capture, or man, but was a cruising; 2nd. That, as such, it came within the clause giving liberty to cruise for thirty-one days on this side Cape Horn, and, therefore, that having taken place on the other side of Cape Horn, it was a deviation (*p*).

Rule as to acts which change the risk.

424. "From the above cases it has sufficiently appeared," said Arnould (*q*), "that the real ground of the underwriter's discharge is change of risk; any change of risk accordingly, though not arising from any of the causes hitherto considered, will be a good defence to the action, if the underwriter can show it to have arisen from the fault or with the knowledge of the assured, but not otherwise. Thus, where it appeared that three Spanish prisoners of war, who had been taken on board on parole, without the knowledge of the underwriters, had, together with the crew, mutinously run the ship ashore, and the insured on the goods brought an action for loss by barratry, Lord Ellenborough held that, though the taking these men on board might slightly have

---

(*n*) Ward *v.* Wood (1816), 13 Mass. R. 539; 1 Phillips, s. 1030.

(*o*) Jarratt *v.* Ward (1808), 1 Camp. 263.

(*p*) Hibbert *v.* Halliday (1810), 2 Taunt. 428.

(*q*) 2nd ed. p. 450; 6th ed. p. 498.

CHAP. XV.] CAUSES WHICH JUSTIFY DEVIATION. 571

increased the risk, yet, as there was no culpable intention in taking them on board, in the first instance, nor any gross negligence in watching them afterwards, the underwriters could not defend themselves on the ground that the risk had been thereby varied" (r). Sect. 424.

424a. Sects. 46 (1) and 48 of the Marine Insurance Act, 1906, declare, as we have seen (s), that a deviation or delay "without lawful excuse" discharges the underwriter from liability for subsequent losses. The causes which amount to a lawful excuse are summarized in sect. 49 of the Act, which is as follows:— Causes that justify a deviation or delay.

(1) Deviation or delay in prosecuting the voyage contemplated by the policy is excused—
(a) Where authorised by any special term in the policy; or
(b) Where caused by circumstances beyond the control of the master and his employer; or
(c) Where reasonably necessary in order to comply with an express or implied warranty (t); or

---

(r) Toulmin v. Inglis (1808), 1 Camp. 421. See 1 Phillips, s. 982, as to this case; and *post*, Part III. Chap. I., "Loss by Barratry." As regards deviation, it seems clear that the fault or knowledge of the assured has no bearing on the question. If the proper course of the voyage has in fact been departed from, the underwriter is discharged (subject to the exceptions in sect. 49 of the Mar. Ins. Act, 1906, *infra*, § 424a). It is submitted that if any act be done by the master which makes the risk a different one from that taken by the underwriter, the latter ought likewise to be discharged whether or not the assured was privy to the act. There cannot, however, be many acts (not amounting to barratry) except deviation or delay, which change the risk in the sense in which this term ought surely to be understood, viz., making the voyage a different one from that insured. It cannot be said that every voluntary act which increases the danger of loss makes the voyage a different one from that insured, and the general principle is that the underwriter is liable for a loss by a peril insured against, even though brought about by the act of the assured himself, unless such act amounts to wilful misconduct. Mar. Ins. Act, 1906, s. 55, *post*, § 775; see Trinder v. Thames and Mersey Mar. Ins. Co., [1898] 2 Q. B. 114 (C. A.).

(s) See *ante*, § 376.

(t) This is generalized from the decision in Bouillon v. Lupton (1863), 33 L. J. C. P. 37, where it was held that a delay at the end of the river stage of a voyage to fit the ship out for the sea portion of the voyage was justifiable: Chalmers & Owen, Mar. Ins. Act,

Sect. 424a.

(d) Where reasonably necessary for the safety of the ship or subject-matter insured (*u*); or

(e) For the purpose of saving human life, or aiding a ship in distress where human life may be in danger (*x*); or

(f) Where reasonably necessary for the purpose of obtaining medical or surgical aid for any person on board the ship; or

(g) Where caused by the barratrous conduct of the master or crew, if barratry be one of the perils insured against (*y*).

(2) When the cause excusing the deviation or delay ceases to operate, the ship must resume her course, and prosecute her voyage, with reasonable despatch (*z*).

Deviation or delay authorised by the policy.

We have already seen that where the policy gives liberty to call at an intermediate port for the purpose of trading, a delay for such purpose is authorised by the license clause. The "deviation clause," which usually provides that the subject-matter insured shall be held covered in case of deviation on payment of an additional premium (see *ante*, § 376), is also a special term within the meaning of sub-sect. (1) (a).

An involuntary deviation or delay is excusable.

425. Sect. 49 (1) (b) gives effect to the principle that it is only a voluntary departure from the course of the voyage which discharges the underwriter from all subsequent loss (*a*).

2nd ed. p. 71. The general rule stated in this sub-section is not laid down in that case.

(*u*) See *post*, § 428.

(*x*) It is now, under sect. 6 of the Maritime Conventions Act, 1911, the duty of the master or person in charge of a ship (so far as he can do so without serious danger to his own vessel and the persons on board of her) to render assistance to every person who is found at sea in danger of being lost. If he fails to do so, he is guilty of a misdemeanour.

(*y*) Ross *v.* Hunter (1790), 4 T. R. 33. Barratry of the crew may also be an excuse within sub-sect. (1) (b).

(*z*) See *post*, § 431.

(*a*) Arnould's statement was that it is only a voluntary and unexcused departure from the course of the voyage which amounts to a deviation. The provisions of sects. 46 and 49 of the Act have necessitated a change of language. The Act seems to regard even an involuntary departure from the proper course as a deviation, though excusable by reason of sect. 49 (1) (b).

CHAP. XV.] CAUSES WHICH JUSTIFY DEVIATION. 573

If produced, however, by the ignorance of the captain, however gross, it will not be the less considered a voluntary act (*b*). Hence, where a ship, insured on a voyage "at and from London to Jamaica," with directions to proceed direct to the latter place, was driven out of her course, by strong currents and other circumstances, to a point between the Grand Canary and Teneriffe, from which point the direct course to Jamaica was south-west, but the captain ignorantly bore up for Santa Cruz, which lies thirty miles to the north-west; this was held to be a deviation (*c*). {Sect. 425. A deviation is not excused by the ignorance of the captain.}

The general rule, to which effect is given in sect. 49, sub-sect. (1), (b) and (d), of the Marine Insurance Act, 1906, is that a departure from the course of the voyage, if necessitated either by moral or physical force, or reasonably necessary for the safety of the ship or of the subject-matter insured, will never discharge the underwriter. *Si iter mutaverit magister ex aliquâ justâ et necessariâ causâ, puta ex causâ refectionis navis, vel ad evitandam maris tempestatem, vel ne inciderit in hostibus, in istis casibus, mutato itinere, tenetur assecurator* (*d*). "There is not, probably, any exception to be met with," says Chancellor Kent, "to the application of the general rule, that if the vessel departs from the usual course of the voyage from necessity, and departs no further than that necessity requires, the voyage will still be protected by the policy" (*e*). {Deviation caused by moral or physical force, or necessary for the safety of the property at risk.}

The delay, or departure indeed, must be strictly commensurate with the necessity that justifies it; there must be no waste of time, nor any needless divergence from the course of the voyage (*f*). {Must be strictly commensurate with the necessity.}

(*b*) The reason given by Arnould (2nd ed. p. 451) is that it was the fault of the assured not to have appointed a competent captain. This reason seems to the editors both unnecessary and unsatisfactory.

(*c*) Phyn *v.* Royal Exch. Ass. Co. (1798), 7 T. R. 505.

(*d*) Roccus, not. 52, 53, cited 2 Emerigon, c. xiii. s. 15, p. 94; see also 2 Benecke, System des Assecuranz, c. viii. s. 2.

(*e*) In Robinson *v.* Marine Ins. Co. (1806), 2 Johnson, R. 89.

(*f*) Mar. Ins. Act, 1906, s. 49 (2), *supra*, § 424a. See Lavabre *v.* Wilson (1779), 1 Dougl. 284; Hyderabad (Deccan) Co. *v.* Willoughby, [1899] 2 Q. B. 530; see also Phelps *v.* Hill, [1891] 1 Q. B. 605.

Sect. 426.

Lavabre v. Wilson.

426. The following well-known case illustrates this principle:—The "Carnatic," a French East Indiaman, was insured "at and from Port L'Orient to Pondicherry, Madras, and China, and at and from thence back to the ship's port or ports of discharge in France." On her arrival at Pondicherry she was found to be so much damaged that it became necessary for her to go to Bengal for repairs, that being the only place where she could be properly repaired. The usual time in which the direct voyage from Pondicherry to Bengal is performed is about six or seven days; but the "Carnatic," by touching and trading at different intermediate ports, consumed six weeks in going to Bengal, and about two months in returning thence to Pondicherry. Lord Mansfield said that, even if necessity were admitted to have been the sole motive for substituting the voyage to Bengal in the place of that to China, still it was incumbent on the assured to have pursued that voyage of necessity directly in the shortest and most expeditious manner, and that the delay in going from Pondicherry to Bengal, and the repeated stoppages by touching at different places, and trading there, were deviations which discharged the underwriter (*g*).

Difficulty in determining when deviation is justifiable or excusable.

427. Though there is no doubt as to the principle of law, there is sometimes a difficulty in ascertaining—(1) what degree of force or constraint will amount to such an unavoidable necessity as, on that ground, to justify a departure from the course of the voyage; (2) what circumstances, short of such unavoidable necessity, will excuse the ship in departing from, or delaying, the usual course of the voyage.

What is unavoidable necessity?

1. With regard to what amounts to an unavoidable necessity, the following cases have been decided in this country:—

Violence of mutinous crew.

Where the crew of a letter of marque mutinously insisted on the captain's returning home with a prize he had taken, instead of proceeding on the voyage, and, on his remonstrating, forced him to submit; this compulsory return was

---

(*g*) Lavabre *v.* Wilson (1779), 1 Dougl. 284.

CHAP. XV.] CAUSES WHICH JUSTIFY DEVIATION. 575

held not to be such a deviation as to discharge the underwriters (*h*). So where a crew, dreading the attacks of pirates if they pursued their voyage, all left the ship and refused to return to her unless the captain would promise immediately to sail back to the home port: his returning thither in pursuance of such promise was held no deviation (*i*).

Sect. 427.

Where a neutral ship was carried out of her course by a British cruiser, and detained in a port far out of the limits of the policy for about six weeks, this was held to be no deviation, having been caused by overruling necessity (*k*).

Carried out of course by a ship of war.

On the other hand, where the master of a merchant ship, while he lay at a port in Iceland taking in his loading, was ordered by the captain of a king's ship to go out to sea and examine a strange sail in the offing bearing enemy's colours, which he did, without any remonstrance on his part, or any threat of force on the other, his so doing was held to amount to a deviation (*l*).

Mere orders by a ship of war are not a justifying necessity.

On the whole, therefore, it appears that when a deviation is sought to be justified on the ground of unavoidable necessity, it must be shown that a degree of force was exercised towards the captain, which either physically he could not resist, or morally, as a good subject, he ought not to resist (*m*).

Result.

The principle illustrated in these cases has been followed and maintained in the decisions of the Courts of the United States (*n*).

428. Where departure from the course has not been caused by force or constraint, moral or physical, it was laid down by Arnould as a general rule, that it cannot be excused unless the

Causes short of actual force or constraint which justify deviation.

(*h*) Elton *v.* Brogden (1747), 2 Strange, 1264.
(*i*) Driscol *v.* Bovil (1798), 1 B. & P. 313.
(*k*) Scott *v.* Thompson (1805), 1 B. & P. N. R. 181.
(*l*) Phelps *v.* Auldjo (1809), 2 Camp. 350.
(*m*) Per Lord Ellenborough, 2 Camp. 351.
(*n*) See Winthrop *v.* Union Ins. Co. (1807), 2 Wash. C. C. R. 7; Lee *v.* Gray (1811), 7 Mass. R. 349; Wiggin *v.* Amory (1816), 13 Mass. R. 123; Kettell *v.* Wiggin (1816), 13 Mass. R. 68; Robertson *v.* Columbian Ins. Co. (1811), 8 Johnson, 491.

576 DEVIATION AND CHANGE OF RISK. [PART I.

Sect. 428.

state of circumstances be such as to leave the master no alternative, as a reasonable and prudent man, exercising a sound judgment, and acting for the best interest of all concerned, but to depart from, or delay, the usual course of the voyage (*o*). An exception to this principle is that a deviation is allowed for the purpose of saving human life, or obtaining medical or surgical aid.

Deviation solely for the preservation of the cargo.

Sub-sect. (1) (d) of sect. 49 of the Marine Insurance Act, 1906, declares, as we have seen, that a deviation or delay is excused when reasonably necessary for the safety of the ship or subject-matter insured. Therefore it seems clear that a deviation or delay for the safety of the ship is always permissible, and that no underwriter, whether on ship or cargo, or any other subject-matter, can claim to be discharged by reason thereof. If, however, a deviation be made solely for the safety of the cargo, or a part thereof, this sub-section does not excuse it, so far as policies on the ship or on other parts of the cargo are concerned. Yet as between the shipowner and the owners of cargo there are possible cases in which it may be not only justifiable, but even the master's duty, taking into consideration the question of the whole adventure, to put into a near port or to incur some delay in port for the preservation of the cargo, or even of some part thereof (*p*).

Is sect. 49 of the Mar. Ins Act, 1906, exhaustive?

If sect. 49 is intended to be an exhaustive summary of the causes which justify a deviation or delay, the policies on the ship or on any portion of the cargo which was not in danger will be vitiated by the fulfilment of this duty. It is possible, however, that sect. 49 ought not to be construed as exhaustive (*q*), and that as regards all the policies on the

---

(*o*) See Phelps *v.* Hill (C. A.), [1891] 1 Q. B. 605; and Bouillon *v.* Lupton (1863), 33 L. J. C. P. 37. In the latter case it was held to be reasonable for a river steamer, about to perform a sea voyage, to wait for other ships in order to sail in company with them. See also West Rand Central Gold Mines Co. *v.* Rougemont, [1900] 2 Q. B. 346.

(*p*) See Carver, ss. 289—291; the judgment of Hannen, J., in The Rona (1884), 51 L. T. 28; Notara *v.* Henderson (1870), L. R. 7 Q. B. 225, 233, 237 (Ex. Ch.); but see per Cockburn, C. J., *S. C.* (1872), L. R. 5 Q. B. at p. 354.

(*q*) Mr. Arthur Cohen says (Halsbury's Laws of England, vol. xvii. § 784): "It seems somewhat

CHAP. XV.] CAUSES WHICH JUSTIFY DEVIATION. 577

adventure there is a "lawful excuse" for the deviation or delay within the meaning of sects. 46 and 48 of the Act.   Sect. 428.

We will now consider the chief cases in which a deviation is considered reasonably necessary for the safety of the property at risk. They may be thus enumerated:—(1) Making a port to refit; (2) or to recruit the crew when generally disabled by sickness, &c.; (3) stress of weather; (4) endeavouring to avoid capture; (5) or to join convoy.

429. *Making a port to refit.* (1) Making a port to refit.

The going into a port out of the usual course for necessary repairs, and staying there till such repairs can be completed, is justifiable, provided it plainly appear that such repairs under the circumstances, and at such port, were reasonably necessary, and that the delay was not longer than was requisite for repairs to enable the ship to proceed on her voyage (*r*). The same principle applies when it is necessary to ballast or lighten the ship. Thus, in one case, where a captain, finding he had too little ballast to steady his ship, at the importunity of the crew, and to save his and their lives, put into a port, out of the course of the voyage, where he took in 500 rolls of tobacco as ballast (*s*); and, in another case, where an overladen ship, shortly after sailing, put back into a port out of the course of her voyage, to unload part of her cargo—this was held no deviation (*t*).

In the United States it has been held that if the ship does not find in the first port she enters what is indispensable to

---

doubtful whether this section of the Act was intended to enumerate all the causes which will excuse deviation or delay."

(*r*) Motteux *v.* London Ass. Co. (1739), 1 Atkyns, 545.

(*s*) Guibert *v.* Readshaw (1781), 2 Park, 637.

(*t*) Weir *v.* Aberdein (1819), 2 B. & Ald. 320. These are both cases of unseaworthiness at sailing; but this objection seems not to have been taken in Guibert *v.* Readshaw, and in Weir *v.* Aberdein it was prevented by express license, indorsed on the policy by the underwriters, for the ship to go into Ramsgate and discharge part of her cargo. See as to the latter case, the judgment of the Privy Council pronounced by Lord Penzance in Quebec Maritime Ins. Co. *v.* Commercial Bank of Canada (1870), L. R. 3 P. C. 234, 244; and *post*, § 690.

Sect. 429.	refit her, she may seek it, if necessary, in a second port out of the course of the voyage (*u*).
The port need not always be the nearest.	Though, generally speaking, the ship must put into the nearest port where necessary repairs can be done, there may be considerations such as danger, time, expense or accommodation, which make a more distant port preferable. If the master, in the reasonable exercise of his judgment, proceed to the more distant port, the policy will still remain in force (*v*).
(2) To procure fresh hands or stores.	430. *To recruit disabled crew, or procure stores or fresh hands.*

There can be little doubt that if a ship, which was originally sufficiently manned and equipped for the voyage, were, in the course of it, to lose so great a proportion of her officers or crew by sickness or other cause, that it became impossible to continue the voyage without procuring more, and no more could be procured except by making a port out of the direct course of the voyage, the putting into such port for such purpose would be allowable. The deviation would be reasonably necessary for the safety of the ship and those on board of her.

Thus, in one Nisi Prius case, Lord Eldon admitted, "That, if by the visitation of God so many of the crew, who were otherwise sufficient, became so afflicted with sickness as to be incapable of managing the ship, such an illness of the crew was a necessity which might justify a deviation" (*x*).

So, it has been held in the United States, and apparently on good grounds, that the death of all the superior officers of an East India ship justified the crew in putting into the Isle of France, though out of the course of the voyage (*y*).

Secus, if the ship was   It was, however, laid down by Arnould (*z*) that going out

---

(*u*) Hall *v.* Franklin lns. Co. (1830), 9 Pickering, R. 466; 1 Phillips, Ins. s. 1020.

(*v*) Phelps *v.* Hill (C. A.), [1891] 1 Q. B. 605—a charter-party case, the decision in which is, however, applicable to contracts of insurance. See per Lindley, L. J., p. 612.

(*x*) In Woolf *v.* Claggett (1800), 3 Esp. 257.

(*y*) Winthrop *v.* Union Ins. Co. (1807), 2 Wash. R. 7.

(*z*) 2nd ed. p. 455.

CHAP. XV.] CAUSES WHICH JUSTIFY DEVIATION. 579

of the course for such purposes can only be justified when the ship was adequately manned, equipped and stored in the first instance: if the ship when she sailed was deficient in any of the elements of seaworthiness, the going into port to supply such deficiency, however necessary it may be, will, he said, be deemed a deviation (*a*).

Sect. 430.
originally
inadequately
fitted out.

For this statement there is some authority. Thus, where a ship put into a port out of her course in order to procure medicines and medical assistance, with which she ought to have been adequately provided when she sailed, this was held to amount to a deviation (*b*).

Upon the same principle it seems to have been held in the United States that the fact of a ship, insufficiently provisioned at the outset for the voyage, going off the course to procure provisions will, as a general rule, discharge the underwriter

Deviation to procure provisions.

(*a*) The chief authority for this proposition is Woolf *v.* Claggett, *infra*, the *ratio decidendi* of which was that the assured must show that the necessity for going into port arose without any default of the master or himself. The editors pointed out in previous editions that it is at any rate arguable that the deviation under such circumstances would not avoid the policy unless the deficiency was due to the wilful default of the assured himself. If the ship, reduced through the negligence of the assured or his servants to a state of disablement, were in consequence lost by perils insured against, the underwriter would be liable: Mar. Ins. Act, 1906, *s.* 55. It is therefore not apparent that a deviation, necessitated by the danger of such a loss, should avoid the policy. Of course, if there has been a breach of the warranty of seaworthiness, the insurer is entitled to avoid the policy on that ground. In Kish *v.* Taylor, [1912] A. C. 604, the House of Lords held, with regard to a contract of affreightment, that a deviation, necessary to save the ship and the lives of those on board, but caused by the master having taken her to sea in an unseaworthy state, was justifiable, though the right to recover damages for his previous wrongful act was preserved.

(*b*) Woolf *v.* Claggett (1800), 3 Esp. 257. Forshaw *v.* Chabert (1821), 3 Brod. & B. 158; 6 J. B. Moore, 369, which Arnould also cited, is a questionable authority. The ship, which ought to have sailed with a full complement of men engaged for the whole voyage, sailed with two of the number who were only engaged for part of the voyage, and put into a port out of the limits of the policy, in order to supply this deficiency. The ground of the decision was not really that there had been a deviation, but that the ship was unseaworthy at the start. The jury had found that to touch at Jamaica for fresh hands was justifiable, and the Court expressed neither approval of nor dissent from this finding.

Sect. 430. on the ground of deviation (*o*); though it would certainly be otherwise, were such lack of provisions due to unavoidable (and unusual) delay through causes over which the assured had no control (*d*).

It will be noticed that sub-sect. (1) (d) of sect. 49 of the Marine Insurance Act, 1906, states without qualification that a deviation reasonably necessary for the safety of the ship is excusable. It is therefore doubtful, whatever the law may previously have been, whether the insurer can now, in a case within the sub-section, rely on the fact that the necessity for the deviation was due to default (other, at any rate, than the wilful misconduct of the assured) in providing medicines or other stores.

Or medical aid.

The question whether a deviation to obtain medical aid for persons on board is justifiable when the navigation of the ship is not made unsafe by disablement has not arisen in this country, though it has been held in the United States that when there is an immediate need of medical aid for the preservation of human life, a deviation to obtain such aid is justifiable (*e*). Sub-sect. (1) (f) of sect. 49 of the Marine Insurance Act, 1906, as we have seen, lays down the rule that a deviation is allowable when it is "reasonably necessary for the purpose of obtaining medical or surgical aid for any person on board the ship."

(3) Stress of weather.

431. *Stress of weather*.

The deviation is excused if a ship be driven out of her course by stress of weather; or if the captain puts into a port out of his course, or delays his sailing, to take refuge from a tempest, or to wait for a wind, if in so acting the

---

(*o*) See the American case of Kettell *v.* Wiggin (1816), 13 Mass. R. 68, cited 1 Phillips, Ins. s. 1026.

(*d*) See Raine *v.* Bell (1808), 9 East, 195; Thomas *v.* Royal Exch. Ass. Co. (1814), 1 Price, 195.

(*e*) Perkin *v.* Auguste Ins. Co. (1855), 2 Parsons, Ins. p. 34, n.; Peterson *v.* The Chandos (1880), 4 Fed. R. 645; see also Sprague *v.* Overton (1859), 1 Sprague's Decisions, 462. The Supreme Court has held that it may even be the duty of the master to an injured seaman, for the breach of which damages are recoverable against the ship, to put into the nearest port where medical assistance can be obtained: The Iroquois (1903), 194 U. S. 240.

CHAP. XV.] CAUSES WHICH JUSTIFY DEVIATION. 581

captain did what a prudent man, in the exercise of sound Sect. 431.
judgment, would have done under the circumstances, with a
view to the safety of the ship or of the subject-matter
insured (*f*).

Sect. 49 (2) of the Marine Insurance Act, 1906, provides A ship driven
that " when the cause excusing the deviation or delay ceases course must
to operate, the ship must resume her course, and prosecute her prosecute her
voyage, with reasonable dispatch." The words " the ship the point
must resume her course" suggest that she must return to the has been
actual track from which she turned aside. Yet the deviation driven.
may have taken her to a place from which the usual or best
course to her destination is a different one. It is submitted
that the course ought to be determined with reference to the
actual situation of the ship, and this view agrees with the
decisions before the Act, according to which a ship driven
from her course is not obliged to sail back to the point
whence the storm first drove her; but she may make the
best of her way to her port of destination from the point
whither she has been driven.

Thus a ship, insured "from London to St. Kitts," was Harrington *v.*
separated from her convoy by a storm and afterwards cap- Halkeld.
tured while still out of her course, but taking the best course
for St. Kitts or the convoy; Lord Mansfield held this was no
deviation (*g*). So where a ship, insured from St. Kitts to Delaney *v.*
London, was driven by a storm out of St. Kitts and obliged Stoddart.
to run to St. Eustatia, and, after many unsuccessful efforts
to get back to St. Kitts, finally gave up the attempt and
completed her lading at St. Eustatia, whence she sailed for
London; Lord Mansfield held this no deviation, and said:
" If a storm drive a ship into any port out of the course of

(*f*) Mar. Ins. Act, 1906, s. 49 (1) tion to Belfast, undertaken to save
(b) and (d), *ante*, § 424a. Where the salved vessel from sinking, was
pumps, intended to be used in sal- not recoverable. Wingate *v.* Foster
vage operations, were insured from (1878), 3 Q. B. D. 582. See, how-
Ardrossan to a wreck, while being ever, as to this case, *post*, § 471.
used there and back to Ardrossan,
the Court of Appeal held that a (*g*) Harrington *v.* Halkeld (1778),
loss of the pumps during a devia- 2 Park, 639.

Sect. 431. her voyage, and, being there, she do the best she can to return " (*quære, proceed*) "to her port of destination, she is not obliged to return back to the port whence she is driven " (*h*).

Waiting until port open.

It has been suggested by Lord Ellenborough in this country (*i*), and decided in the United States (*k*), that if a ship find her port of destination blocked up by ice, or otherwise rendered inaccessible, she may make the nearest practicable port with a view of staying there till her own is open, without its being deemed a deviation. The rule in sect. 49 (2) of the Marine Insurance Act, 1906, is consistent with a stay in such port as long as the cause of the deviation is in operation.

Where a captain, delayed by adverse winds and dangerous weather, puts into a roadstead for safety, it has been held no deviation to send ashore for provisions if requisite (*l*).

(4) Endeavour to avoid capture.

432. *Endeavour to avoid capture.*

The endeavour to avoid the imminent peril of capture, either by lying to in the port of loading, or putting into a port out of the course of the voyage, or by departing from the track of the voyage insured, has always been held to justify a deviation, provided the danger was real and immediate, and the apprehension founded on reasonable evidence (*m*).

So a ship, insured "against capture in her port of loading," may hurry out of such port in order to avoid the imminent peril of capture, though only half loaded and totally unprepared for her voyage; and her afterwards putting into a port

---

(*h*) Delaney v. Stoddart (1785), 1 T. R. 22.

(*i*) Blankenhagen v. London Ass. Co. (1808), 1 Camp. 453.

(*k*) Graham v. Commercial Ins. Co. (1814), 11 Johnson, R. 352, cited 1 Phillips, s. 1023.

(*l*) Thomas v. Royal Exch. Ass. Co. (1814), 1 Price, 195.

(*m*) Driscol v. Bovil (1798), 1 B. & P. 313; Driscol v. Passmore (1798), *ibid*. 200; Blankenhagen v. London Ass. Co. (1808), 1 Camp. 453; O'Reilly v. Gonne (1815), 4 Camp. 249; see also The San Roman (1873), L. R. 5 P. C. 301. In The Teutonia (1872), L. R. 4 P. C. 171, an action on a charter-party, the Privy Council held that a master of a German ship bound for Dunkirk, having been told war had broken out between France and Germany, was justified in putting back to the Downs to make inquiries.

CHAP. XV.] CAUSES WHICH JUSTIFY DEVIATION. 583

out of the course of her voyage in order to repair damage Sect. 432.
occasioned by such hasty escape will not discharge the
insurer (*n*).

In the United States several cases have been decided upon
this principle, and in all the main point of inquiry seems to
have been whether the danger was so real and immediate as
to justify the deviation (*o*).

433. *Endeavour to join convoy.*

(5) Endeavour to join convoy.

It is justifiable, whether the ship be warranted to sail
with convoy or not (*p*), to depart from the direct course of
the voyage in order to seek convoy either at the usual place
of rendezvous or elsewhere; the only question in such cases is
whether the circumstances show to the satisfaction of the jury
that the captain, in so departing from the direct course of the
voyage, acted fairly and *bonâ fide* according to the best of his
judgment and with no other view or motive but to meet with
convoy, and thereby be enabled to reach the terminus of the
voyage by the safest way (*q*).

It has been held justifiable for a ship, warranted or not to
sail with convoy, if she has once sailed therewith and is afterwards driven back to port, to sail the second time without
convoy (*r*).

If it clearly appears that, in the common course of the
voyage insured, the ship might have obtained convoy at a
nearer port, her being limited by her instructions to call for
it at a more distant port may discharge the underwriter as
varying the risk (*s*).

(*n*) O'Reilly *v.* Gonne (1815), 4 Camp. 249.

(*o*) Oliver *v.* Maryland Ins. Co. (1813), 7 Cranch's S. C. R. 493; Whitney *v.* Haven (1816), 13 Mass. R. 172; Reade *v.* Com. Ins. Co. (1808), 3 Johnson, R. 352.

(*p*) D'Aguilar *v.* Tobin (1816), Holt, N. P. 185. So held also in the United States, Patrick *v.* Ludlow (1802), 3 Johnson's Cases, 10; 1 Phillips, Ins. s. 1023.

(*q*) Bond *v.* Gonzales (1704), 2 Salk. 445; Gordon *v.* Morley (1747), 2 Str. 1265; Campbell *v.* Bordieu (1747), *ibid.*; Bond *v.* Nutt (1777), 2 Cowp. 601; Enderby *v.* Fletcher (1780), 2 Park, 646; D'Aguilar *v.* Tobin (1816), Holt, N. P. 185; S. C., 2 Marshall, R. 265.

(*r*) Laing *v.* Glover (1813), 5 Taunt. 49.

(*s*) Heselton *v.* Allnutt (1813), 1 M. & S. 46.

Sect. 434.

(6) Succouring the distressed and saving property.

434. A doubt, dishonouring to the jurisprudence of Christian communities, appears for some time to have prevailed both in this country and the United States, whether a departure from the direct course of the voyage, for the purpose of saving the lives of men threatened with an imminent danger of shipwreck or foundering, was or was not a deviation which would discharge the underwriters; it was, however, before the Marine Insurance Act, 1906, was passed, considered clear law, both on this and the other side the Atlantic, that a deviation of this kind, sanctioned alike by the true interests of commerce and the clearest precepts of humanity, can in no instance be held to discharge the underwriters (*t*); and the Act declares that a deviation is justifiable for the purpose of saving human life, or aiding a ship in distress where human life may be in danger (*u*).

This liberty, however, does not extend to the case of a deviation solely for the purpose of saving property (*x*).

In an action by a goods owner against the shipowner, whose vessel and her cargo, including the plaintiff's goods, were lost whilst the ship was performing a salvage service for another vessel and her cargo, but not such a service as was reasonably necessary to save the lives of those on board, the Court of Appeal held the deviation to be unjustifiable (*y*). The Court regarded the case as one of the first impression in our Courts. Upon the American authorities they formulated

---

(*t*) See the *dictum* of Lawrence, J., in Lawrence *v.* Sydebotham (1805), 6 East, 54, and the judgments of Lord Stowell in The Beaver (1801), 3 C. Rob. 292, and The Jane (1831), 2 Hagg. Ad. R. 345. In the United States, see the cases collected in Phillips, Ins. s. 1027; 3 Kent, Com. 313. See especially the judgment of Story, J., in The Schooner Boston (1833), 1 Sumner, R. 328; see also Peterson *v.* The Chandos (1880), 4 Fed. R. 645.

(*u*) Sect. 49 (1) (e), *ante*, § 424a. See also Maritime Conventions Act, 1911, s. 6, *ibid.* u. (*x*), and the provisions of the Merchant Shipping (Convention) Act, 1914, as to the duty to render assistance on receiving a wireless distress call, and (in the case of passenger ships) to be provided with a wireless telegraphy installation.

(*x*) Scaramanga *v.* Stamp (1880) (C. A.), 5 C. P. D. 295. See, for the cases in the United States which establish this rule, 1 Phillips, Ins. s. 1028.

(*y*) Scaramanga *v.* Stamp (1880), 5 C. P. D. 295.

CHAP. XV.] CAUSES WHICH JUSTIFY DEVIATION. 585

the following propositions, as containing the existing law of Sect. 434.
the United States on the question, and expressed their cordial
concurrence with the law as thus laid down:—

"Deviation for the purpose of saving life is protected, and involves neither forfeiture of insurance nor liability to the goods owner in respect of loss which would otherwise be within the exception of perils of the seas. And, as a necessary consequence of the foregoing, deviation for the purpose of communicating with a ship in distress is allowable, inasmuch as the state of the vessel in distress may involve danger to life. On the other hand, deviation for the sole purpose of saving property is not thus privileged, but entails all the usual consequences of deviation.

"If, therefore, the lives on board a disabled ship can be saved without saving the ship, as by taking them off, deviation for the purpose of saving the ship will carry with it all the consequences of an unauthorized deviation.

"But where the preservation of life can only be effected through the concurrent saving of property, and the *bonâ fide* purpose of saving life forms part of the motive which leads to the deviation, the privilege will not be lost by reason of the purpose of saving property having formed a second motive for deviating" (*z*).

435. It has been clearly established that where the Irresistible force of a peril not insured against.
departure from the course of the voyage is necessitated by the
immediate and irresistible operation of a peril not insured
against, it will not discharge the underwriter, whether the
peril be one not included among the ordinary risks or expressly excluded by the specific terms of the policy. It is no
doubt excusable as being "caused by circumstances beyond
the control of the master and his employer" (*a*).

Thus, where a neutral ship, insured expressly "against sea risks and fire only," was carried out of her course and detained six weeks by a British cruiser, it was held that this

---

(*z*) See per Sprague, J., in Crocker *v.* Jackson, Sprague, R. 141.

(*a*) Mar. Ins. Act, 1906, s. 49 (1) (b), *ante*, § 424a.

Sect. 435. deviation had no effect on the obligation of the insurer, though capture and seizure were perils not insured against (*b*).

Avoiding peril not insured against.

It appears, however, to have been held at Nisi Prius that a departure from the course in order to avoid, or in consequence of endeavouring to avoid, a peril not insured against is a deviation, though it would not have been so had it taken place in order to avoid a peril insured against. In the case alluded to, the policy was on goods "at and from La Guayra," with the clause "warranted free of capture and seizure, and the consequences thereof, in the port of La Guayra." To avoid seizure the ship ran to sea before she was properly loaded, and was in consequence obliged to put into a port out of the course of the voyage insured and was there lost. Gibbs, C. J., told the jury that, upon these facts, the ship had been guilty of a deviation which discharged the underwriters, because it was the consequence of endeavouring to avoid a risk for which the underwriters had stipulated by the policy not to be liable (*c*). And this was the sole ground of his decision, for in a policy on the freight of the same ship, in which there was no such exception of capture and seizure in port, the Chief Justice held upon precisely the same state of facts that the ship was guilty of no deviation (*d*).

O'Reilly v. Royal Exchange Co.

Both Arnould and Phillips thought it doubtful whether the decision could be sustained as an authority (*e*), and the reasons which the latter gave for this opinion have great weight. As he points out, it cannot but be known to the parties to a policy against one or some only of the ordinary sea perils, that the vessel is to be subject to the other perils usually included in policies, and the fair inference is that they do not contemplate the forfeiture of the insurance by a reasonable departure from the course to avoid one of these risks (*f*).

(*b*) Scott *v.* Thompson (1805), 1 B. & P. N. R. 181. See also per Kent, C. J., in Robinson *v.* Marine Ins. Co. (1806), 2 Johnson, 89, cited 1 Phillips, s. 1025; 3 Kent, Com. 316.

(*c*) O'Reilly *v.* Royal Exch. Ass. Co. (1815), 4 Camp. 246.

(*d*) O'Reilly *v.* Gonne (1815), 4 Camp. 249.

(*e*) See Arnould, vol. i. 2nd ed. 461; 1 Phillips, s. 1025.

(*f*) For an analogous principle, see The Teutonia (1872), L. R. 4 P. C. 171, 180, where, the master having justifiably deviated for the

Sect. 49 (1) (d) of the Marine Insurance Act, 1906 (g), which states that a deviation is excused when reasonably necessary for the safety of the ship or subject-matter insured, seems not to contemplate any distinction between a deviation to escape a peril insured against and one to escape a peril for which the insurer would not be liable. It is submitted that such a distinction is not sound, and that, since the Act at any rate, it cannot be supported.

safety of the ship, Mellish, L. J., said: "It cannot be contended that the master is deprived of the right of taking reasonable and prudent steps for the preservation of his ship because, from the accident of the cargo not belonging to his own nation, the cargo is not exposed to the same danger as the ship."

(g) *Ante*, § 424a.

CHAPTER XVI.

NATURE AND DURATION OF THE RISK IN TIME POLICIES.

	SECT.
Nature of the Risk in Time Policies	436
Duration of the Risk	437—442
Mixed Policies	443—445

A time policy is one in which the risk is limited by time alone.

436. THE inconvenience or impossibility, when a ship was employed in such adventures as cruising, coasting or fishing voyages, of designating the risk by local termini led to the practice of limiting the risk to a certain fixed term or period of time specified in the policy (*a*). "Where the contract is to insure the subject-matter for a definite period of time, the policy is called a 'time policy'" (*b*). The use of time policies is now very extensive. In fact, they are now used much more than voyage policies for the insurance of steamships, and very largely for that of freight and disbursements. They are not in general suitable for the insurance of goods, which the assured usually wishes to protect during transit from one place to another (*c*). There is one kind of insurance of goods, viz., by floating policies, which, in a sense, is an insurance on time when it covers shipments of goods, made within a certain period of time fixed by the policy, as declared by the assured; but these floating policies are in reality insurances of goods for a series of voyages (*d*).

(*a*) 2 Emerigon, c. xiii. s. 1, p. 41; 2 Benecke, System des Assecuranz, o. viii. s. 3, p. 442.

(*b*) Mar. Ins. Act, 1906, s. 25 (1).

(*c*) See Gow, 228—238, for an account of the practice of insuring by time policies.

(*d*) Where a policy covered shipments of goods "from the loading thereof ... shipments held covered to December 31," "in as many voyages as may be required until 31/12/94," goods shipped on the 31st December, 1894, were held covered, though the ship only sailed on the 1st January, 1895. Johnson *v.* Bryant (1896), 1 Com. Cas. 363.

CHAP. XVI.] THE RISK IN TIME POLICIES.

In time policies the risk insured is entirely independent of the voyage of the ship (*iter navis*) (*e*), and the policy covers any voyage whatever which the ship may make, and any loss or damage sustained within the space of time limited in the policy (*f*). It is now, however, very common for the policy to except certain geographical limits, either entirely or for certain seasons of the year, as, *e.g.*, "Warranted no St. Lawrence between the 1st of October and the 1st of April." In that case a loss within the excepted limits of time and space is, of course, not covered by the policy (*g*).

Sect. 436.

There is no implied warranty of seaworthiness in time policies (*h*).

437. The two extremes of the time are the termini of the risk, and the adventure begins and ends with the term wherever the ship may then happen to be, and whether the object of the voyage be then accomplished or not (*i*). The risk necessarily ceases when the time limited in the policy comes to an end (*j*). From the instant that the policy attaches, the insurer's right to the full premium is complete, as is the right of the assured to a full indemnification in case of loss (*k*). Thenceforth there is no suspension of the risk

Duration of the risk.

(*e*) Ist von der Reise des Schiff's völlig unabhängig. 2 Benecke, System des Ass. c. 8, s. 3, 446.

(*f*) 3 Kent, Com. 307, n.

(*g*) See Birrell *v.* Dryer (1884), 9 App. Cas. 345. Where there was a warranty "not to proceed east of Singapore," Bigham, J., held that the assured could recover for a loss on a voyage to a port east of Singapore, at a time when the ship had not yet got as far as Singapore: Simpson SS. Co. *v.* Premier Underwriting Assn. (1905), 10 Com. Cas. 198.

(*h*) Dudgeon *v.* Pembroke (1877), 2 App. Cas. 284; *post*, Part II. Chap. IV.

(*i*) Casaregis, Disc. lxvii. No. 31, cited 2 Emerigon, o. xiii. s. 1, p. 42.

Lapso tempore extincta est materia obligationis et consequenter obligatio, quia post tempus, jam alia est materia, alia res. Dumoulin, tom. iii. p. 283, cited 4 Boulay-Paty, Droit Mar. 170.

(*j*) Il suffit que le risque ait commencé pour qu'il finisse au tems préscrit. 2 Emerigon, c. xiii. s. 1, p. 41.

(*k*) Tyrie *v.* Fletcher (1777), 2 Cowp. 666; Lorraine *v.* Thomlinson (1781), 2 Dougl. 585. A clause is usually inserted in time policies (see Institute Clauses, *post*, App. B.) providing for a return of an agreed part of the premium when the ship has been laid up for thirty consecutive days.

Sect. 437.

Time policy may be retrospective.

whether the ship be at sea or in port; it continues to run until the expiration of the period insured (*l*).

A time policy, like a voyage policy, may be effected retrospectively if it contain the clause "lost or not lost"; as where a policy was effected in August, 1807, "to commence from 1st August, 1806," on a ship engaged in the Southern whale fishery, which had sailed on her voyage in 1805 (*m*).

Loss caused within the limits of the time, but damage not ascertained till afterwards.

438. On general principles, it is clear that the underwriters on a time policy ought to be liable for any loss which happens within the limits of the time (*n*). It is supposed, however, to have been laid down in Meretony *v.* Dunlope, that where damage is caused within the limits of the time, but the extent of it not ascertained till afterwards, the underwriter is not liable. The case, as shortly stated by Willes, J., was that of an insurance for six months on a ship, which received her death-wound three days before, but was kept afloat by pumping till three days after, the expiration of the time: the verdict for the underwriters was confirmed by the Court (*o*). In Knight *v.* Faith (*p*), however, which subsequently raised the same point for decision, Lord Campbell, in giving the judgment of the Court, intimated considerable doubt whether the doctrine supposed to be established by Meretony *v.* Dunlope was ever laid down by Lord Mansfield,

Supposed doctrine of Meretony v. Dunlope overruled by Knight v. Faith.

(*l*) 2 Emerigon, c. xiii. s. 1, p. 41. See, to the same effect, Syers *v.* Bridge (1780), 2 Dougl. 527. A usual clause in time policies (see Institute Time Clauses, App. B.) makes the risk attach "in port and at sea, in docks and graving docks, and on ways, gridirons and pontoons at all times, in all places, and on all occasions, services and trades whatsoever and wheresoever, &c."

(*m*) Hucks *v.* Thornton (1815), Holt, N. P. 30. Could it possibly be argued that such an insurance, even without the clause, "lost or not lost," was not intended to be retrospective?

(*n*) A loss of freight in consequence of a casualty happening during the time limited by the policy is recoverable, although the voyage could not have been completed, and therefore the freight would not have been earned within such time. Michael *v.* Gillespy (1857), 2 C. B. N. S. 627; 26 L. J. C. P. 306.

(*o*) Meretony *v.* Dunlope (1783), stated by Willes, J., in giving judgment in Lockyer *v.* Offley (1786), 1 T. R. 260.

(*p*) Knight *v.* Faith (1850), 15 Q. B. 649.

and stated what the Court deemed to be the correct doctrine thus:—" If a ship, insured for time, during the time received damage from the perils of the seas, though the amount thereof be not ascertained till the expiration of that time, and she is kept afloat till then, upon the assured taking proper steps, there does not appear any good reason why they may not, according to the facts, proceed against the underwriters either for a total or for a partial loss " (*q*).

Sect. 438.

In the following case, although the casualty which caused a loss of freight took place before the policy expired, the loss was held to have occurred afterwards. The policy was expressed to be "from the 15th April to the 14th October, both inclusive, on chartered freight," to pay only loss of hire which might arise under the "forty-eight hours' clause" in a charter-party "for accidents occurring between the 15th April and the 15th October." The ship met with an accident in June, but was only docked for repairs in November, and the repairs were not completed until the 30th December, and in the meanwhile the payment of hire ceased. The Court of Appeal held, affirming the Divisional Court, that the underwriter was not liable, because freight had been paid for the whole period covered by the policy, and consequently there was no loss of freight within that period (*r*).

439. England appears to be the only commercial state in which any restriction is placed on the duration of time policies. The foreign codes, in general, expressly allow insurances on time without any limitation as to their extent (*s*); and the law is the same in the United States of America (*t*).

Time policies limited in England to a year; not so restricted elsewhere.

In England the law, as declared in the Stamp Act, 1891, was "that no policy of sea insurance made for time shall be made for any time exceeding twelve months," and a

---

(*q*) Knight *v.* Faith (1850), 15 Q. B. 667.
(*r*) Hough *v.* Head (1885), 55 L. J. Q. B. 43.

(*s*) See, *e.g.*, the Code of Holland, art. 256; German Code, art. 830; Code de Commerce, arts. 332, 363.
(*t*) 1 Phillips, Ins. s. 949, n.

Sect. 439. policy made for a longer period was expressly declared to be invalid (*u*).

Continuation clause.

440. In the English time policies it has been usual to provide by a clause attached to the policy, called the continuation clause, that if at the end of the period of the insurance the ship is at sea the insurance may be extended until her arrival at some port. The form of the clause in the Institute Time Clauses for policies on ship is now as follows:—"Should the vessel at the expiration of this policy be at sea, or in distress, or at a port of refuge or of call, she shall, provided previous notice be given to the underwriters, be held covered at a *pro ratâ* monthly premium to her port of destination."

Another form of continuation clause, which has sometimes been inserted in policies, does not make the prolongation of the risk conditional on notice being given, but provides simply that if the ship be at sea at the expiration of the policy the insurance shall continue until the ship arrives at some port (*x*).

For some time there was considerable doubt whether or not a continuation clause in a policy for twelve months had the effect of vitiating the whole insurance, on the ground that it made the policy one for a period exceeding twelve months within the meaning of the Stamp Act, 1891, s. 93 (*y*).

In two cases (*z*) it was held that the assured could not recover under this clause for a loss which took place after the expiration of the twelve months. The assured were thus relying on a contract of insurance alleged by themselves to be one for more than twelve months (*a*). Such a contract is

---

(*u*) Stamp Act, 1891, s. 93 (2), (3).

(*x*) See, *e.g.*, the continuation clause in Charlesworth *v.* Faber (1900), 5 Com. Cas. 408.

(*y*) See Gow, 237.

(*z*) Charlesworth *v.* Faber (1900), 5 Com. Cas. 408; Royal Exchange Ass. Corporation *v.* Sjoforsakrings Aktie-bolaget Vega, [1901] 2 K. B. 567; [1902] 2 K. B. 384, C. A.

(*a*) They also contended in the later case that the policy contained two separate contracts, one an insurance for twelve months, the other made by the continuation clause an insurance either for a voyage or for a further period. It

CHAP. XVI.] THE RISK IN TIME POLICIES. 593

plainly void. In the later case Bigham, J., expressed the opinion that the contract was severable, so that the illegal part could be rejected, and if the loss had taken place within the twelve months the assured could have recovered (*a*). The decision of the Court of Appeal was, however, based on the ground that the contract was indivisible and the policy therefore altogether void. "It is one time policy throughout," said Mathew, L. J., "for the period of twelve months and the additional time contemplated by this very extensive continuation clause" (*aa*). This decision agrees with the view expressed in the seventh edition of this work, viz., that any term prolonging an insurance for a year makes the policy one for a period exceeding twelve months.

Sect. 440.

Sect. 11 of the Finance Act, 1901 (1 Edw. 7, c. 7), has, however, provided that a policy of sea insurance shall not be invalid on the ground that by reason of a continuation clause it may become available for a period exceeding twelve months; and a continuation clause is defined as an agreement, the effect of which is that in the event of the ship being at sea, or the voyage otherwise not completed, on the expiration of the policy, the subject-matter of the insurance shall be held covered until the arrival of the ship, or for a reasonable time thereafter not exceeding thirty days (*b*).

Sect. 25 (2) of the Marine Insurance Act, 1906, declares that "subject to the provisions of sect. 11 of the Finance Act, 1901, a time policy which is made for any time exceeding twelve months is invalid" (*c*).

The question of continuing policies arose some time ago in connection with a club policy, of which a rule, declaring that the association should renew the policy unless they received

was, however, held that even if the clause could be regarded as a separate policy, it was invalid under sect. 93 (3) of the Stamp Act, because if for a voyage it did not sufficiently specify the termini, if for time it did not determine the period.
(*a*) [1901] 2 K. B. at p. 573.

(*aa*) [1902] 2 K. B. at p. 395.
(*b*) As to the stamping of a time policy with a continuation clause, see *ante*, § 31.
(*c*) A policy on a ship under construction or repair, though made for a time exceeding twelve months, is not deemed to be a time policy: Revenue Act, 1903, s. 8, *ante*, § 31.

A.—VOL. I. 38

594 NATURE AND DURATION OF [PART I.

Sect. 440. ten days' notice to the contrary, was expressly made a term. It was not necessary to decide whether the insurance (originally for thirty-eight days only) was thereby prolonged; but Cockburn, C. J., expressed the opinion that the policy was a continuing one (*d*). In a later case the question arose whether a club policy for twelve months was a continuing one by reason of a similar rule, and it was held that, according to the terms of the rule and the words of 30 & 31 Vict. c. 23, the policy was not a continuing one (*e*).

Duration of an insurance "from" a day.

441. When the insurance is expressed to be from one particular day to another, *e.g.*, "from the 14th day of February, 1914, until the 14th day of August, 1914," it has been held in the case of a fire policy that the risk does not in general commence to run until the former day has expired, and that it will cover losses happening on the latter day (*f*). The decision seems applicable to marine policies; but it appears that there is no hard-and-fast rule to this effect, and that in any particular case it would be open to one of the parties to prove that a different computation of time was intended.

(*d*) Michael *v.* Gillespy (1857), 2 C. B. N. S. 627; 26 L. J. C. P. 306.

(*e*) Lishman *v.* Northern Marit. Ins. Co. (1873), L. R. 8 C. P. 216; in the Exch. Ch. (1875), L. R. 10 C. P. 179. The assured, it must be noticed, was not suing on or asserting the validity of the policy. The question was whether he was insured by it, after the expiration of twelve months, within the terms of a warranty in another policy not to be insured beyond a certain amount. The rules of the mutual insurance associations commonly provide for the continuation of the insurance and the issue of a fresh policy from year to year, in default of notice by either party to terminate the insurance. The club policies are usually expressed to be made subject to the rules and regulations of the associations. If the rule prolonging the insurance be thereby incorporated in the policy, the latter is invalid, as being made for more than twelve months. But the correct view, it is submitted, is that the policy only incorporates those rules which are applicable to the risk for the year and not the antecedent agreement to issue a fresh policy at the expiration of the risk. This view agrees with the decision in Lishman *v.* Northern Maritime Ins. Co., *supra*.

(*f*) Isaacs *v.* Royal Ins. Co. (1870), L. R. 5 Ex. 296. Accord. South Staffordshire Tramways Co. *v.* Sickness and Accident Ass. Assn., [1891] 1 Q. B. 402, a case upon an accident insurance.

CHAP. XVI.] THE RISK IN TIME POLICIES. 595

Usually, however, in English policies the risk is declared to run from a particular hour of a particular day, *e.g.*, "from noon of the 20th day of February." It is evident that the time of the same place ought to determine the beginning and end of the risk, otherwise the ship, by sailing eastward or westward, might shorten or lengthen the duration of the risk. In the United States it has been decided that the time which determines the duration of the risk is that of the place where the contract was executed, unless it be shown that a different computation of time was contemplated (*g*). The same rule would no doubt be followed in the English Courts, if the question should arise here. It is, however, usually stipulated in the English policies that Greenwich mean time is the time which governs the risk. In view of the fact that in practice Greenwich mean time is everywhere used in England, even without this stipulation it would no doubt be held that this time was applicable to a policy made in this country (*h*).

Sect. 441. Time of what place determines the duration of the risk.

442. Sect. 58 of the Marine Insurance Act, 1906, declares that "where the ship concerned in the adventure is missing, and after the lapse of a reasonable time no news of her has been received, an actual total loss may be presumed." Still, the burden of proving that a loss took place within the time covered by the policy is on the assured, and there is no presumption in the case of a missing ship that the loss took place at a particular time (*i*). The assured must, therefore, in order to recover, produce some evidence on which a jury will be justified in finding that the loss took place while the

Proof of time of loss in case of missing ship.

(*g*) Walker *v.* Protection Ins. Co. (1849), 29 Maine R. 317; 1 Phillips, s. 949.

(*h*) By the Statutes (Definition of Time) Act, 1880, any expression of time in a statute, deed, or legal instrument shall, unless it be otherwise specifically stated, be held, in the case of Great Britain, to be Greenwich mean time, and in the case of Ireland, Dublin mean time.

(*i*) Brown *v.* Neilson (1804), 1 Caines, 525, cited 1 Parsons, 311, and followed by Field, J., in Reid *v.* Standard Marine Ins. Co. (1886), 2 Times L. R. 807. The rules of the mutual insurance associations, however, often provide that a missing ship shall be deemed to have been lost on the day when she was last heard of.

Sect. 442. policy was in force. Evidence that the ship must have encountered a violent storm which happened at a particular time may be sufficient (*k*). Again, if in the ordinary course the ship ought to have arrived at her destination before the expiration of the policy, a loss within the time limit may be inferred (*l*).

Mixed policies.

443. The policies hitherto considered have been purely time policies, in form as well as in effect; *i.e.*, the limits of the risk have been defined in the policy, solely by points of time, without any designation of local termini at all: policies, however, have sometimes, though not very frequently, been made, in which not only the time is specified for which the risk is limited, but the voyage also is described by its local termini (*m*). As, for instance, "at and from London to Cadiz for six months," or "from the 1st of January, 1914, to the 1st of June, 1914, at and from Bristol to Marseilles," &c., or "from the 1st of January, 1914, at and from Liverpool to New York."

Construction and effect of mixed policies.

These policies are neither time nor voyage policies, but partake of the nature of both, and, for the sake of convenience, may be called mixed policies. They are time policies in this, that the underwriter is not liable for any loss unless it occur within the limits of the time specified in the policy; and they are so far voyage policies, that the underwriter is not liable for any loss unless the ship originally sailed on the voyage described in the policy, and at the time of the loss be sailing on the prescribed course between the termini of such voyage (*n*), or if insured "at and from" a

(*k*) See a case before James, V.-C., cited by North, J., in In re Rhodes (1887), 36 Ch. D. 591.

(*l*) Brown *v*. Neilson, *supra*.

(*m*) Way *v*. Modigliani (1787), 2 T. R. 30; Robertson *v*. French (1803), 4 East, 130. See also Maritime Ins. Co. *v*. Alianza Ins. Co., [1907] 2 K. B. 661.

(*n*) Salvage pumps were insured "from the 30th of December, 1882, to the 12th of January, 1883, . . . whilst engaged in salvage operations at the wreck of the C.," "including all risk while being conveyed from B. to and/or on board the wreck." Cave, J., held that "at the wreck" meant at the locality of the wreck, and that the policy did not cover a loss of the pumps on board the wreck within the prescribed period, while it was

CHAP. XVI.] THE RISK IN TIME POLICIES. 597

place, be there at the time of the loss for the purposes of the voyage insured.

<small>Sect. 443.</small>

Thus, as we have already seen, where a Newfoundland ship was insured "at and from the 20th of October, from any ports in Newfoundland to Falmouth, or her port or ports of discharge in England"; it was held that, although under this policy the ship need not have been in any port in Newfoundland on the 20th of October, yet, in order to make the policy attach at all, the ship must have originally sailed on the voyage insured, and that as in this case she had not done so, the assured could not recover, though the loss took place after the 20th of October, and when the ship had got into the course of the voyage described in the policy (*o*).

<small>Way *v.* Modigliani.</small>

444. The point conceded in this case, viz., that in such a policy it is not necessary that the ship should be in the port named as the *terminus a quo* in the policy, at the time when the insurance is limited to commence, has been illustrated in the United States.

<small>The ship need not be at the *terminus a quo* on the day from which the policy takes effect.</small>

Thus, where a brig was insured "from Calais, in Maine, on the 16th day of July, to, at, and from all ports to which she may proceed in the coasting trade for six months"; and the brig was not at Calais on the 16th July, but had been there subsequently within the six months; the Court held that the policy had attached on the 16th July, "for it was the clear intent of the parties to insure on time, without regard to the place where the vessel might then be, but only with regard to the employment in which she was engaged, viz., the coasting trade" (*p*).

<small>American cases on this point.</small>

being towed to the nearest port of safety. Difiori *v.* Adams (1884), 53 L. J. Q. B. 437.

(*o*) Way *v.* Modigliani (1787), 2 T. R. 30. The ship had left Newfoundland on the 1st of October. If she had sailed after the 20th on the voyage insured, she would no doubt also have been protected by the policy when she broke ground, the mention of the date not being a warranty (it is apprehended) that she shall sail on or before that date, but only fixing the date before which the risk cannot attach. There may, however, be an implied condition in a policy like this, that the voyage shall at any rate commence within a reasonable time after the specified date. Cf. Mar. Ins. Act, 1906, s. 42 (2).

(*p*) Martin *v.* Fishing Ins. Co. (1838), 20 Pick. R. 389, cited 1 Phillips, Ins. s. 928.

Sect. 444. So where insurance was effected on a ship for a voyage "at and from Boston to Charlestown," the policy only to take effect so far as the ship was not covered by previous insurances; and it appeared that the ship, fully covered by a prior policy on time, had sailed from Boston before such prior policy had expired, the second policy was held to attach while the ship was at sea on the voyage, immediately upon the expiration of the first (*q*).

Where it is evident from the whole language of the instrument that, although the risk is expressly made to commence from a specified local terminus, yet the policy is substantially a time policy, it has been held in the United States that it will attach and operate as such, though the vessel may never within the term have been at the local *terminus a quo* named in the policy as the place where the risk is to commence. A policy was effected on ship "to, at, and from one or more ports in the globe, for one year, commencing the risk at Barbadoes the 7th of December, 1810, to continue till the vessel shall be arrived and moored at anchor twenty-four hours in safety within the year aforesaid." The vessel was not at Barbadoes, as supposed by the policy, having left on the 6th; but the Court said her being so was immaterial, and that the risk would end with the year without any regard to her being in any port, either at that time or before; the beginning, duration, and end of the risk being well enough described without any regard to the place where it was to commence, or to the vessel's being safe in port (*r*).

Difference in effect between these mixed policies and voyage policies.
Upon the whole it may be laid down that, supposing a policy in this mixed form once to have attached, the only difference in point of effect between it and an ordinary voyage policy will be that the risk upon the adventure will continue, not until the arrival of the ship or the landing of the goods, but until the completion of the time specified, whenever and wherever that may be, totally irrespective of the completion

(*q*) Kent *v.* Manufacturers' Ins. Co. (1836), 18 Pick. R. 19; 1 Phillips, Ins. s. 928.

(*r*) Manley *v.* United Marine and Fire Ins. Co. (1812), 9 Mass. R. 85, cited 1 Phillips, s. 928.

CHAP. XVI.] THE RISK IN TIME POLICIES.

or non-completion of the voyage. These policies, in fact, afford no more protection than, and not so much liberty as, time policies, and are, probably for that reason, comparatively of rare occurrence (s). {Sect. 444.}

445. Sect. 25 (1) of the Marine Insurance Act, 1906, declares that "a contract for both voyage and time may be included in the same policy"; and by the Stamp Act, 1891, s. 94, "where any sea insurance is made for a voyage, and also for time, or to extend to or cover any time beyond thirty days after the ship shall have arrived at her destination and been there moored at anchor, the policy is to be charged with duty as a policy for a voyage, and also with duty as a policy for time." {Policies for voyage and time.}

(s) Benecke, System des Assecuranz, c. viii. introductory section, p. 203.

CHAPTER XVII.

DURATION OF THE RISK IN VOYAGE POLICIES.

	SECT.
Duration Clause	446
Commencement of Risk on Goods	447—455
Continuance and End of Risk on Goods	456—471
Commencement of Risk on Ship	472—486
Continuance and End of Risk on Ship	487—509
Commencement of Risk on Freight	510—519
End of Risk on Freight	520, 521

Clause fixing the duration of the risk.

446. THE clause describing the voyage by its termini is distinct in our English policies from that which defines the commencement, continuance, and end of the risk. This latter clause, upon the construction of which the nature of the contract between the parties so materially depends, is in Lloyd's policies in the following form:—

"Beginning the adventure upon the said goods and merchandises from the loading thereof on board the said ship upon the said ship, &c. , and shall so continue and endure, during her abode there, upon the said ship, &c., and further, until the said ship, with all her ordnance, tackle, apparel, &c., and goods and merchandises whatsoever, shall be arrived at , upon the said ship, &c., until she hath moored at anchor twenty-four hours in good safety, and upon the goods and merchandises till the same be there discharged and safely landed" (a).

(a) By express stipulation the risk on goods is sometimes made to attach during a land transit preceding the marine voyage. See, e.g., Hyderabad Deccan Co. v. **Willoughby**, [1899] 2 Q. B. 530.

CHAP. XVII.] DURATION OF THE RISK ON GOODS. 601

As there are many decisions on the construction of this clause, and as the duration of the risk varies upon the different subjects of insurance, it will conduce to clearness if we discuss separately the duration of the risk: (1) on goods; (2) on ship; (3) on freight. It must, however, be noticed that in general, whatever be the subject-matter insured, there is an implied condition in a voyage policy that the adventure shall be commenced within a reasonable time, and that if the adventure be not so commenced, the insurer may avoid the policy (*b*).

Sect. 446.

447. "Beginning the adventure upon the said goods and merchandises from the loading thereof on board the said ship."

Commencement of the risk on goods.

Rule 4 of the Rules for the Construction of a Policy in this form, in the First Schedule of the Marine Insurance Act, 1906, provides that—

> Where goods or other moveables are insured "from the loading thereof," the risk does not attach until such goods or moveables are actually on board, and the insurer is not liable for them while in transit from the shore to the ship (*c*).

In this respect our practice differs from that of almost all continental states, which either decree by their laws or stipulate in their policies that the risk of the underwriters on goods shall commence directly the goods leave the shore in order to be loaded on board the ship (*d*).

(*b*) Mar. Ins. Act, 1906, s. 42 (1), *post*, § 480.

(*c*) The form of policy in the Schedule is for an insurance "at and from" a named port. If the insurance were expressed to be merely "from" the port of loading, it is apprehended that the risk would not commence until the ship started on the insured voyage, even though the printed clause as above were not deleted. See Mar. Ins. Act, 1906, Sched. I. rule 2, *post*, § 473.

(*d*) Thus the German Commercial Code (art. 824) provides that the risk on goods shall begin immediately from the time the goods leave the shore. By the Russian Commercial Code (art. 567) and the Egyptian Maritime Code (art. 184) the beginning of the risk is the same, unless the policy itself provides otherwise. By the Belgian Maritime Code (art. 195), when the duration of the risk is not settled by the policy, it runs as to goods from the moment they

602   DURATION OF THE RISK ON GOODS.   [PART I.

Sect. 447.
The commencement of the risk may be varied by a special clause.

Of course goods, even in this country, may be protected while thus in transit from quay to ship by any express clause in the policy duly framed for the purpose. Thus, where a policy on goods at and from St. Petersburg to London contained this clause: "Beginning the adventure on the said goods from and immediately following the loading thereof on board boats at St. Petersburg"; it was not disputed that the risk on the goods commenced directly they were put on board boats at St. Petersburg to be loaded (in the usual course of trade there) on board the ship at Cronstadt (*e*).

Commencement of the risk under the ordinary clause.

448. "From the loading thereof on board the said ship at."

Upon the construction of these words it has been decisively established that a policy on goods for a voyage "at and from" a specified terminus in which the risk is expressed to begin "from the loading thereof on board the ship," in the common form, will only attach upon goods loaded on board at the very

are loaded in the ship, or in lighters to convey them there. The Commercial Codes of Holland (art. 627) and of Spain (arts. 733, 761) go even further, and declare that the risk on goods shall commence from the time they are brought down to the quay or wharf in order to be loaded on board. The French Code de Commerce (arts. 328, 341) makes the risk attach from the loading of the goods on board the ship or the lighters that are to convey them thither. For the former laws of continental countries, see 3 Boulay-Paty, Droit Mar. tit. x. s. 9, pp. 418—420; 2 Emerigon, c. xiii. s. 2, p. 48; and 2 Benecke, System des Assecuranz, c. viii. s. 1, p. 205; Nolte's ed. vol. i. pp. 641—646.

(*e*) Hurry *v.* Royal Exch. Ass. Co. (1801), 2 B. & P. 430; see per Heath, J., *ibid.* 435. A clause such as "including risk of craft to and from the vessel" is commonly inserted in English policies. In some companies' policies a clause providing that "the insurance shall commence from the time when the goods shall be laden on board the said ship, or vessel, craft, or boat, as above" has taken the place of the ordinary clause relating to the commencement of the risk. See McArthur, p. 90. It has been usual for some time to insert in Lloyd's policies a clause, called the "warehouse to warehouse" clause, which covers "all and every risk in craft to and/or from the vessel or vessels, and all risks, including fire, from the warehouse of the consignor by any conveyances by land or by water, and until safely delivered into the warehouses of the consignees and/or their agents." See Ide *v.* Chalmers (1900), 5 Com. Cas. 212. Somewhat differently worded "warehouse to warehouse" and "craft" clauses are included in the Institute Cargo Clauses. See *post*, Vol. II. App. B.

place named as the *terminus a quo* of the voyage (*f*); and this even though it should plainly appear, from extrinsic evidence, that the underwriters knew that the goods had in fact been loaded on board prior to the ship's arrival at the place specified in the policy as the *terminus a quo* of the voyage, and that the assured effected the insurance with the intention of protecting the goods so loaded elsewhere (*g*). Most of these cases arose during the great wars of the French Revolution, when, in consequence of Napoleon's Berlin and Milan decrees, goods really shipped in this country were constantly insured as though shipped at some Baltic port.

Sect. 448.

Thus, to take one case as an illustration of many: a cargo insured "at and from Gottenburg to the ship's port or ports of discharge in the Baltic," with the usual clause, "beginning the adventure on the said goods from the loading thereof on board the said ship," had been loaded at London, carried to Gottenburg, where it was not taken out nor reloaded, and after leaving Gottenburg was totally lost by capture. Although the policy on which the action was brought was proved by parol evidence to be in continuation of another policy, from London to Gottenburg, effected with the same underwriter, as he well knew, the Court felt themselves bound by the express words of the policy, and held that, as the goods had been loaded on board, not at Gottenburg, the *terminus a quo* of the voyage insured, but at a previous port, the policy

Spitta *v.* Woodman.

(*f*) Robertson *v.* French (1803), 4 East, 130; Spitta *v.* Woodman (1810), 2 Taunt. 416; Horneyer *v.* Lushington (1812), 15 East, 46; Langhorn *v.* Hardy (1812), 4 Taunt. 628; Mellish *v.* Allnutt (1813), 2 M. & S. 106; Rickman *v.* Carstairs (1833), 5 B. & Ad. 651.

(*g*) Per Bayley, J., in Gladstone *v.* Clay (1813), 1 M. & S. 423; per Lord Denman in Rickman *v.* Carstairs, *supra;* and see the facts of Robertson *v.* French (1803), 4 East, 130; Spitta *v.* Woodman (1810), 2 Taunt. 416; Langhorn *v.* Hardy (1812), 4 Taunt. 628, in all which it plainly appeared that the underwriters knew the goods had been previously loaded. The principle of these decisions has been adversely criticised by Erle, C. J., in Carr *v.* Montefiore (1864), 5 B. & S. 408, 428; 33 L. J. Q. B. 256, 259; and by Mr. Arthur Cohen, who thinks that they will not in future be followed: Halsbury's Laws of England, vol. xvii. § 760. Alternatively, the Court might now entertain a claim for rectification of the policy.

Sect. 448. never attached at all, and that the assured could recover nothing (*h*).

In this case the risk was made to begin on the goods "from the loading thereof on board the ship" in blank, *i.e.*, without saying where: of course, if the risk is from their being "loaded on board the ship at" the *terminus a quo* or other named place, the reason for a strict construction of the policy is still more cogent (*i*).

Rickman *v.* Carstairs.

449. The strict rule of construction was not relaxed in the later case of Rickman *v.* Carstairs, which was an action on a policy on ship and goods for a homeward voyage "at and from the coast of Africa" to the ship's port of discharge in the United Kingdom, beginning the adventure on the goods from the loading thereof aboard the said ship twenty-four hours after her arrival on the coast of Africa." It was held by Lord Denman and the Court of King's Bench, that, in the absence of anything upon the face of the instrument to show the contrary, this policy did not attach on part of the outward cargo, which, although still remaining on board the ship on the coast of Africa more than twenty-four hours after her arrival there and at the time of loss, had been loaded on board at her port of departure in this country (*k*).

Lord Denman, in delivering the judgment of the Court in that case, said: "It appears very likely that the assured intended by this policy to insure both the outward and homeward cargo. Unfortunately, however, they have used words which will not, we think, effectuate that intention. The question in this and other cases of the construction of written

---

(*h*) Spitta *v.* Woodman (1810), 2 Taunt. 416; *S. C.*, 16 East, 188, n. See also Mellish *v.* Allnutt (1813), 2 M. & S. 106, where the risk was also made to begin "from the loading on board ship," without more.

(*i*) See, accordingly, Robertson *v.* French (1803), 4 East, 130;

Horneyer *v.* Lushington (1812), 15 East, 46; Langhorn *v.* Hardy (1812), 4 Taunt. 628; in all which the risk was made to commence from the loading on board at a named place.

(*k*) Rickman *v.* Carstairs (1833), 5 B. & Ad. 651.

instruments is, not what was the intention of the parties, but what is the meaning of the words they have used" (*l*).

Sect. 449.

450. The application of this rule to some of these cases was the subject of severe animadversion in Carr *v.* Montefiore. "In the several Gottenburg cases it seems to me," says Erle, C. J. (*m*), "that a construction was put on the policies so as to defeat the intention of the parties." Cockburn, C. J., in the same case below (*n*), expresses a hope that it might be brought under the consideration of the highest Court of Appeal. And Lord Ellenborough, C. J., himself an assisting party in the establishment of this construction, says of it: "A very strict and certainly a construction not to be favoured, and still less to be extended, was adopted in Spitta *v.* Woodman. But if there be anything to indicate that a prior loading was contemplated by the parties, it will release the case from that construction" (*o*).

The Courts take every opportunity afforded by the parties of modifying the strict rule.

Accordingly, where the words used on the face of the written instrument show, consistently with sound principles of interpretation, that the parties intended by the policy to protect goods loaded on board the ship elsewhere than at the *terminus a quo* of the voyage insured, the Court will relax the rigour of this rule.

Bell v. Hobson.

Thus, where a policy on American produce for a voyage at and from Gottenburg to any ports in the Baltic, "beginning

---

(*l*) 5 B. & Ad. 662. In Carr *v.* Montefiore (1864), 5 B. & S. 428; 33 L. J. Q. B. 256, Erle, C. J., formulated the following rule of construction: "If the words of the instrument are clear in themselves, the instrument must be construed accordingly; but if they are susceptible of more meanings than one, then the Judge must inform himself by the aid of the jury and the surrounding circumstances which bear on the contract"; and he was of opinion that the provision as to beginning the adventure from the loading at the *terminus a quo* is mere description, not a warranty that the cargo shall be loaded there. This is also Phillips' view. 1 Phillips, s. 939.

(*m*) (1864), 33 L. J. Q. B. 256, 259; 5 B. & S. 408, 429.

(*n*) 33 L. J. Q. B. 57, 63. The observation is not reported in Best & Smith.

(*o*) Bell *v.* Hobson (1812), 16 East, 240, 248. In the following year, however, Lord Ellenborough followed Spitta *v.* Woodman in Mellish *v.* Allnutt (1813), 2 M. & S. 106.

Sect. 450. the adventure on the goods from the loading thereof on board the ship," was on the face of it declared to be "in continuation of five other policies," and these were on the same cargo for a voyage from Norfolk in Virginia to Gottenburg: Lord Ellenborough held that, as it thus clearly appeared on the face of the policy that the parties to it must have known that the goods had been loaded on board before arriving at Gottenburg, the policy had attached (*p*).

Joyce v. Realm Insurance Co.
So a policy of re-insurance was in such terms as would have brought it within the rule in Spitta *v.* Woodman; but it was expressly made "subject to all clauses and conditions of the original policy," and as the original policy, being upon goods embarked in the barter trade on a voyage to Africa and back, stipulated that outward cargo should be considered homeward interest twenty-four hours after the ship's arrival at her first port of discharge, it was held that the policy of re-insurance was qualified by the terms of the original policy and had attached on the goods, although not loaded on the coast of Africa, but at Liverpool (*q*).

Effect of the words "wheresoever loaded." *Gladstone v. Clay.*
Lord Ellenborough had, in Bell *v.* Hobson, suggested the introduction of the words "wheresoever loaded" as a way of adapting the policy to the purposes of the parties. Accordingly a policy on a cargo for a homeward voyage "at and from Pernambuco to Maranham, and at and from thence to Liverpool"—"beginning the adventure on the said goods from the loading thereof on board the said ship wheresoever"—was held, by virtue of the word "wheresoever," to protect a portion of the outward cargo loaded at Liverpool and still on board at the time of the loss, while the ship was on her way from Pernambuco to Maranham, not having found a market at Pernambuco (*r*).

Constructive loading.
451. Moreover, if the goods, though originally loaded on board elsewhere, are afterwards, either wholly or in part, first

(*p*) Bell *v.* Hobson (1812), 16 East, 240; *S. C.*, at N. P. 3 Camp. 272.
(*q*) Joyce *v.* Realm Ins. Co. (1872), L. R. 7 Q. B. 580; 41 L. J. Q. B. 356.
(*r*) Gladstone *v.* Clay (1813), 1 M. & S. 418.

landed and then reloaded, at the port specified in the policy as the *terminus a quo* of the voyage, this is a sufficient "loading on board the ship" at that port to make the policy attach under the clause.

Sect. 451.

Thus, under a policy on ship and goods "at and from Landscrona to Wolgast," beginning the risk on the goods "from the loading on board the ship," the goods, though previously loaded on board at Gottenburg, were partly taken out of the hold on the ship's arrival at Landscrona and landed on the quay there, so as to enable the custom-house officers to ascertain the quality of the whole cargo and adjust the duties on it, after which they were reloaded on board. Lord Ellenborough held that this unloading and reloading distinguished the case from that of Spitta *v.* Woodman, and was sufficient to make the policy attach on the goods at and from Landscrona (*s*). Accordingly, under a similar policy on goods "from a port or ports in the River Plate," where the cargo on the forepeak down to the keelson was taken out and landed at Monte Video for the purpose of repairing the ship and then reloaded, it was held that this satisfied the clause "from the loading thereof on board," although it was a cargo of guano that had been originally shipped at Liones Island in Patagonia. Cockburn, C. J., however, said he relied more upon the additional fact that at Monte Video, after the repairs, both ship and cargo had changed hands by sale and a new destination was given to the adventure by the purchasers (*t*).

Nonnen *v.* Kettlewell.

Carr *v.* Montefiore.

In the United States, where the construction put upon this clause is as strict as in our own Courts, it has been held that merely unstowing the goods from the hold on the ship's arrival at the *terminus a quo* of the voyage insured, in order

Constructive loading in the United States.

(*s*) Nonnen *v.* Kettlewell (1812), 16 East, 176. In this case it was objected that the cargo had not been so far unloaded as to ascertain what amount of sea damage it had sustained on the voyage from its prior port of loading; but Lord Ellenborough held that as the goods were "warranted free of average," the objection at all events in this case would not apply.

(*t*) Carr *v.* Montefiore (1863), 5 B. & S. 408; 33 L. J. Q. B. 57; affirmed (in error) (1864), 5 B. & S. 425; 33 L. J. Q. B. 256.

608 DURATION OF THE RISK ON GOODS. [PART I.

Sect. 451. to make room for other goods there taken in, and then re-stowing them, is not equivalent to a loading on board at such terminus so as to make the policy attach on those goods (*u*). Phillips thinks that if the goods in this case had been landed on the wharf and then taken on board again, this would have been a loading within the terms of the policy.

The strict rule not applicable where there is a liberty to touch and stay.

452. This strict rule of construction, which has been applied in the case of goods loaded before the ship has reached the *terminus a quo*, does not prevail where, the voyage being a trading or bartering voyage, the policy contains a liberty " to touch, stay, trade, &c.," or any other clause of that kind; for in such cases it is obvious, on the face of the policy itself, that it must have been contemplated by the parties that other goods would be put on board in the course of the voyage than those loaded at the port of departure, and that they intended to protect such goods by the policy. Wherever, therefore, it can fairly be deduced from the whole construction of the policy that the parties contemplated loading, unloading, bartering or trading with goods at any intermediate ports in the course of the voyage insured, the policy attaches not only on goods loaded on board at the port of departure, but also on those loaded on board at any of the ports where the ship is empowered to touch and trade under the terms of the policy, or where, upon a true construction of the whole instrument, it must be presumed that such a loading was contemplated (*x*).

Violett v. Allnutt.

Barclay v. Stirling.

Thus, where a ship has liberty by such a policy to touch at a specified port, the policy attaches on goods loaded on board at that port in order to complete the cargo (*y*). So a freight policy, with liberty for the ship "to call, exchange, or take on board goods at any ports or places she may call at," was

(*u*) Murray *v.* Columbian Ins. Co. (1814), 11 Johnson, 302, cited 1 Phillips, Ins. s. 939.

(*x*) Violett *v.* Allnutt (1811), 3 Taunt. 419; Grant *v.* Delacour (1806), cited 1 Taunt. 466; Grant *v.* Paxton (1809), *ibid*. 463; Barclay *v.* Stirling (1816), 5 M. & S. 6; Hunter *v.* Leathley (1830), 10 B. & Cr. 858; affirmed (in error) (1831), 7 Bing. 517.

(*y*) Violett *v.* Allnutt (1811), 3 Taunt. 419.

held to cover the freight on fresh goods loaded on board the ship at a port of distress in order to replace part of the original cargo, which had been washed out of her as she lay ashore (z). So in the case of Hunter v. Leathley, the policy attached on goods shipped on board to complete the cargo at a port lying diametrically out of the course from the original port of loading to the ultimate ports of discharge, and not named in the policy, though embraced within its very extensive terms. Lord Tenterden intimated that in policies on trading voyages all places mentioned in the policy after the words "with liberty to touch, &c." may be considered as loading ports—*i.e.*, as ports, goods loaded at which will be protected by the policy (a).

Sect. 452.

Hunter v. Leathley.

453. The two following cases afford a good illustration of the mode in which the Courts apply policies containing such extensive liberties of touching and staying to the protection of goods laden on board in the course of the voyage.

An East India captain, being desirous of protecting his interest in the adventure for the voyage out and home, effected a policy "on goods as interest shall appear" "at and from London to all ports or places on this or the other side of the Cape of Good Hope forwards and backwards at sea, at all times, on all services, and all ports and places, until the ship's arrival back again to her last station of discharge at Blackwall or Deptford," "beginning the adventure on the said goods from the loading thereof on board the said ship at London."

Grant v. Delacour.

The Court held that, though these last words literally applied only to goods laden in London for the outward voyage, yet as these voyages were for the purposes of trading and barter, the policy attached upon any goods which the captain might acquire by trading with his outfit in the course

---

(z) Barclay v. Stirling (1816), 5 M. & S. 6.

(a) Hunter v. Leathley (1830), 10 B. & Cr. 858; in error (1831), 7 Bing. 517.

Sect. 453.

Grant v. Paxton.

of the voyage described in the policy, wherever they might be loaded on board (b).

The same captain, to protect his interest in the same adventure for the homeward voyage, effected an insurance on goods "at and from China to all or any other ports or places whatsoever and wheresoever in the East Indies, Persia, or elsewhere beyond the Cape of Good Hope, in port and at sea, in all places, at all times, and in all services, until the ship's safe arrival at London"—"beginning the adventure upon the said goods from the loading thereof on board at China," "with liberty for the ship in that voyage to proceed and sail to and touch and stay at any ports or places whatsoever, for any purposes whatsoever, without being deemed a deviation." With a cargo of tea originally loaded on board at China for the homeward voyage, the ship was afterwards obliged to put into Bombay to repair; the tea cargo was sent on to England in another vessel, and the captain, having repaired his ship, loaded a cargo of cottons at Bombay, and sent her therewith to Canton, on which voyage she was lost.

The Court held that this policy, unlike the former, had never attached on the goods so loaded at Bombay for the voyage to Canton; the insurance, they said, in this case was on nothing but the goods laden on board at China for the homeward voyage thence to London (c). The Court remarked that there was nothing on the face of this policy nor in the circumstances of the case to alter "the plain, fair, grammatical sense" of the words "beginning the risk on the goods from the loading thereof on board in China"; there was no custom of trade authorizing the company to send back the ship from Bombay to Canton, so as to keep her still within the protection of a policy effected on a homeward voyage from Canton to London; there was no intention of unloading the goods, for "it never was in the contemplation of the underwriters, or of any man, that a ship once laden

(b) Grant v. Delacour (1806), cited 1 Taunt. 466. See per Mansfield, C. J., *ibid.* 474.

(c) Grant v. Paxton (1809), 1 Taunt. 463.

CHAP. XVII.] DURATION OF THE RISK ON GOODS. 611

with tea, a very valuable cargo, would be unloaded and employed in some other trade."

Sect. 453.

454. The strict rule of construction which confines the policy to goods loaded at the *terminus a quo*, is not satisfied by their being loaded at a place within the legal limits merely of the port; unless it appears that the word used to describe the *terminus a quo* is understood in this extended sense by mercantile men (*d*).

Limits of the port for the purposes of this rule.

Thus, under a policy on goods "at and from Lyme to London," it appeared that the goods were loaded on board at Bridport, a town nine miles from Lyme town, but a member of the port of Lyme; the Court held, in the absence of any mercantile usage to show that goods insured from Lyme might be loaded at Bridport, that this policy never attached on these goods (*e*).

Constable v. Noble.

In this case it appeared that there was no separate custom-house at Bridport; *à fortiori* where goods insured "at and from Carmarthen to London" were in fact loaded on board at Llanelly, which, though legally speaking a member of the port of Carmarthen, yet has a separate custom-house at which vessels are cleared out independent of that at Carmarthen, the Court held that this policy had never attached on the goods loaded at Llanelly (*f*).

Payne v. Hutchinson.

If, on the contrary, there is a mercantile usage to ship goods under such policies, not at the place specified in the policy, but at some place adjoining thereto, the policy will attach on goods shipped in compliance with the usage. Thus where a policy was effected on goods "at and from the ship's loading port or ports in Amelia Island," and the ship never

Effect of usage.

Moxon v. Atkins.

(*d*) See *infra*, § 485, as to the meaning of "port" or "port of loading" in a policy. See also Sailing Ship Garston Co. v. Hickie (1885), 15 Q. B. D. 580, for a discussion by Lord Esher of the tests for determining the business meaning of the word "port" in a charter-party.

(*e*) Constable v. Noble (1810), 2 Taunt. 403.

(*f*) Payne v. Hutchinson (1808), 2 Taunt. 405, n. The law as to this point is the same in the United States. See Murray v. Columbian Ins. Co. (1809), 4 Johns. R. 443, cited 1 Phillips, s. 931.

Sect. 454. touched at Amelia Island at all, but took in her cargo at Tigre Island, which is a little higher up the river St. Mary's—but this was the usual manner in which ships took in their cargo in that trade—Lord Ellenborough held that the policy attached on the goods so loaded (*g*).

A policy on goods "at and from" for a homeward voyage, only protects the homeward cargo.

455. A policy on goods "at and from" a foreign port for the homeward voyage, only protects the homeward-bound cargo, and only runs from the time when such cargo is wholly or partially loaded on board there. If there be a policy on outward cargo "until discharged and safely landed" in the same port, both policies may operate concurrently, the outward policy to protect what remains on board of the outward cargo, and the homeward policy to protect what has been already loaded of the homeward cargo (*h*).

Policy at and from an island.

If the place be an island or other place having several ports, as Jamaica, and there be two several policies, one on the outward cargo, say "from London to Jamaica," and the other on the homeward cargo "at and from Jamaica to London," and the ship, after discharging part of her outward and shipping part of her homeward cargo at one port in Jamaica, be lost while proceeding to another port in that island in order to dispose of the residue of her outward and complete the loading of her homeward voyage, having thus part of both cargoes on board at the time of loss; in such case the true result of the authorities appears to be that the outward policy continues to protect what remains on board of the outward cargo, and the homeward policy attaches on what has been already taken on board of the homeward cargo (*i*).

(*g*) Moxon *v.* Atkins (1812), 3 Camp. 200.

(*h*) See 2 Emerigon, c. xiii. s. 20; 3 Boulay-Paty, Droit Mar. 421—428; and 3 Kent, Com. 309. The effect of the clause often inserted in African voyages, that outward cargo is considered homeward risk twenty-four hours after arrival at the first port of discharge, may be that the outward cargo is protected at the same time by different sets of policies—*i.e.*, those on the outward and homeward voyages.

(*i*) 2 Emerigon, c. xiii. s. 20, pp. 114, 115; 3 Boulay-Paty, Droit Mar. 422; Camden *v.* Cowley (1763), 1 W. Bl. 417; Forbes *v.* Aspinall (1811), 13 East, 323; Warre *v.* Miller (1825), 4 B. & Cr. 538; Rickman *v.* Carstairs (1833), 5 B. & Ad. 651; 3 Kent, Com. 309.

CHAP. XVII.] DURATION OF THE RISK ON GOODS. 613

In policies on the African barter traffic, after the usual clause giving extensive liberty to load, reload, exchange, sell, or barter, &c., there is usually a clause that outward cargo is to be considered homeward interest twenty-four hours after arrival at first port or place of trade, so that the new and the old cargo on board are protected during the barter transactions on the coast (*k*).

Sect. 455.
Barter policies.

Under such a policy on ship and goods for twelve months, an attempt was made to extend the barter clause so as to render the underwriter liable for loss by fire of cargo landed but not yet bartered, and of the produce received in exchange for part of it although not yet shipped; it was held, however, that the policy did not protect either kind of goods while on land (*l*).

It has been decided in the United States that a policy on goods outward and upon their proceeds home will apply to a homeward cargo procured by money or credit of the consignees at the port of discharge, though the outward goods, for want of a market, have not been in fact sold so as to realize any proceeds (*m*). A policy in this form will not, however, protect for the homeward voyage the same goods that were carried out but not landed at the outward port (*n*).

In the United States, policy on goods outward and on their proceeds home.

456. The common clause in our English policies makes the risk on goods continue during the voyage to the port of discharge, "until the same be there discharged and safely landed" (*o*).

Continuance and end of the risk on goods.

(*k*) See Tobin *v*. Harford (1863), 13 C. B. N. S. 791; 32 L. J. C. P. 134; in error (1864), 34 L. J. C. P. 37, for such a clause.

(*l*) Harrison *v*. Ellis (1857), 7 E. & B. 465; 26 L. J. Q. B. 239.

(*m*) Haven *v*. Gray (1815), 12 Mass. R. 71; Whitney *v*. The American Ins. Co. (1824), 3 Cowen, 210; 3 Kent, Com. 310.

(*n*) Ibid.

(*o*) In Marten *v*. Nippon, &c. Ins. Co. (1898), 3 Com. Cas. 164, the clause was "until safely delivered to consignees," and Bigham, J., held that placing the goods in the Customs warehouse was a safe delivery within the meaning of the clause. A "warehouse to warehouse" clause, which extends the risk until the goods are safely warehoused at their destination, is now usually inserted in the policy. See *ante*, § 447, note (*e*), and the Institute Cargo Clauses, *post*, Vol. II. App. B.

Sect. 456.
Meaning of "safely landed."

Rule 5 of the Rules for the Construction of the Policy in the First Schedule of the Marine Insurance Act, 1906, declares that—

> Where the risk on goods or other moveables continues until they are "safely landed," they must be landed in the customary manner and within a reasonable time after arrival at the port of discharge, and if they are not so landed the risk ceases.

By "safely landed" is meant safely delivered on shore, at the ordinary wharves and quays or customary landing-places within the limits of the port of discharge (*p*). These limits are to be ascertained in case of doubt by the evidence of mercantile usage (*q*).

Policy covers goods landed in lighters according to usage.

457. It is frequently necessary to employ smaller craft, such as lighters, shallops, &c., to carry the goods from the ship to the shore. Whenever it is established that such a usage exists by the general course of trade, the underwriters are liable for any loss or damage that may happen to the goods in the course of their being so carried; for they are being landed in the customary manner (*r*).

(*p*) See, as to this, Gatliffe *v.* Bourne (1838), 4 Bing. N. C. 314; Bourne *v.* Gatliffe (in error) (1841), 3 M. & Gr. 643; *S. C.*, before the House of Lords (1841), 7 M. & Gr. 850. The question in this case was what amounts to a delivery of goods under a charter-party to the consignee. The editors submit that the goods may be "landed" within the meaning of the policy, although the consignee may be entitled to say that there was not a good delivery to him because the landing-place was not a customary one.

(*q*) See per Lord Esher in Sailing Ship Garston Co. *v.* Hickie (1885), 15 Q. B. D. 580, for the meaning of the word "port" in a charter-party. See also *infra*, § 485.

(*r*) Whether the goods are protected while being discharged in a reasonable, though not the customary, manner was a moot point before the Mar. Ins. Act, 1906. Phillips (vol. i. s. 970) considered that goods are only protected in lighters when that is the usual mode of discharge. Parsons (vol. ii. p. 61) thought that the same rule should apply to any mode of conveyance by water made necessary by the circumstances of the case. Thus, if the usual mode of discharge is from the ship on to a quay, but in consequence of the crowded state of the quays the goods are taken ashore in lighters, they would, according to Parsons' rule, be protected. The rule in the Act agrees with Phillips' opinion.

CHAP. XVII.] DURATION OF THE RISK ON GOODS.

Sect. 457.

"The insurer," says Lord Mansfield, "in estimating the price at which he is willing to indemnify the trader against all risks, must have under his consideration the nature of the voyage to be performed, and the usual course and manner of doing it. He took the risk upon the supposition that what was usual and necessary would be done, and therefore when goods are insured 'till discharged and safely landed' the insurance, without express words, extends to the boat, the usual manner of landing goods out of a ship upon the shore" (s).

In the port of London public lighters being employed, in the general course of trade, to unload ships, goods on such lighters, while being conveyed from the ship to the wharf, are under the protection of the policy (t).

So, where formerly, in the contraband trade in the Spanish main, it was usual for ships to stand into shore as near as they could, and then run the cargo ashore in launches, it was held that goods insured for this traffic were protected while in such launches (u). So, where the general usage with regard to all goods destined for a certain shallow bay in Jamaica was to put the ship into the nearest practicable port, and thence send the goods ashore in shallops; Lord Tenterden held, that the goods while being so sent on were protected by the policy (v).

Goods for St. Petersburg, on board vessels of any burden, are unloaded at Cronstadt, about twenty miles from the capital, and thence sent on, up the Neva, in lighters. Before the cutting of the canal of the Helder to Amsterdam, vessels of large burden sometimes unloaded at the Texel, and

---

(s) 1 Burr. 348; see also Lane v. Nixon (1866), L. R. 1 C. P. 412; per Byles, J., ibid. 420. In France this general principle is confined to the taking of goods from the ship to the shore, and does not, as a general rule, extend to their transport from the ship up rivers to the port of discharge. 2 Emerigon, c. xiii. s. 2, p. 49;

3 Boulay-Paty, Droit Mar. 419.
(t) Rucker v. London Ass. Co. (1784), 2 B. & P. 432, in notis; Hurry v. Royal Exch. Ass. Co. (1801), ibid. 430.
(u) Matthie v. Potts (1802), 3 B. & P. 23.
(v) Stewart v. Bell (1821), 5 B. & Ald. 238.

Sect. 457. formerly the largest class of vessels were obliged to lighten between Cuxhaven and Hamburg. In such cases, as the river navigation is a foreseen and customary part of the voyage, and the risk thereof calculated in the rate of premium, the goods would be protected in the river craft under our common form of policies (*w*).

In France. In France, it seems that their policies, though not considered as a general rule to protect goods when sent on from the ship up a river to the port, will yet do so whenever there is a usage to unload goods at the seaboard, and thus send them on, as from Paimbœuf to Nantes, though the distance between the two places is ten French leagues (*x*).

In the United States. So, in the United States, on its being proved that hides were generally sent ashore at New York from the ship in boats, the Supreme Court of the United States held, that the risk continued on them while they were being so sent (*y*).

Where the assured receives the goods into his own care.
Sparrow v. Carruthers.

458. It has been held that in all such cases the assured may terminate the risk before the time when it would expire in the usual course under the policy, by receiving the goods out of the ship into his own care. Thus, although, as we have seen, goods while in a course of being carried in lighters from the ship to the shore are, generally speaking, protected in the port of London, yet a merchant of that port was held to have put an end to this protection by himself sending for them and bringing them ashore in his own lighter (*z*). Again, where

---

(*w*) See 2 Benecke, System des Assecuranz, 213.

(*x*) 2 Emerigon, 49; 3 Boulay-Paty, Droit Mar. 419, 420; 1 Nolte's Benecke, 654.

(*y*) Wadsworth *v.* Pacific Ins. Co. (1829), 4 Wendall's R. 33. Arnould stated that in Osacar *v.* Louisiana Ins. Co. (1827), 5 Martin, N. S. 386, cited 1 Phillips, s. 970, the principle was carried to the extent of protecting goods destined for a Mexican port, while being carried up from the river bar to the town, partly in boats and partly overland on mules, that being shown to be the general mode of conveying them to their place of destination (2nd ed. vol. i. p. 484). This is, however, erroneous. The decision was that the goods were protected while being conveyed ashore in launches; and the Court said that, as the insurance was a marine one, there was no responsibility for land risks.

(*z*) Sparrow *v.* Carruthers (1746), 2 Str. 1236. "The only strong ground upon which it (*i.e.*, this case) can be supported," said

CHAP. XVII.] DURATION OF THE RISK ON GOODS. 617

goods were brought in a public lighter in the port of London to the merchant's wharf, where, owing to the roughness of the weather, they could not then be unloaded; and thereupon the merchant dismissed the lighterman, and told him to leave his lighter all night moored to the wharf, where he himself would look after it, and in the course of the night the lighter with the goods on board sank: the Court held that the merchant, by thus taking the goods into his own care and possession, had discharged the underwriter from all liability (a).

Sect. 458.
Strong v. Natally.

The Court of Appeal said in one case: "It is perfectly true that by taking delivery short of the shore the consignee determines the risk insured. But this is not because in such a case the risk is terminated by an actual landing, but because the consignee waives the landing, and himself terminates the risk by taking delivery short of the land" (b). There is, however, nothing in the wording of the instrument to justify the rule that the policy does not protect the goods when the assured has taken possession of them. The risk is expressed to be, not until the owner of the goods takes delivery, but until the goods are safely landed (c).

In another case (d) there was a policy on goods from Baltimore to Ipswich, "including all risks of craft to and from the vessel." The evidence was that steamers bound to Ipswich usually proceeded up the Orwell to Butterman's Pool, where they discharged their cargoes into lighters;

Paul v. Ins. Co. of North America.

Chambre, J., in Hurry v. Royal Exchange Assurance, "is that the owner of the goods completely accepted them and discharged the shipowner" (2 B. & P. 436). The discharge of the shipowner cannot, however, be the test of the end of the risk; for, although the liability of the shipowner ceased when he delivered the goods to a public lighterman, it was held in that case that the risk was not thereby terminated. Whatever the correct rule may be, as Marshall remarks, if there were a custom for merchants in any port to use their own lighters in landing goods, they would, no doubt, be protected by the policy. See also 2 Benecke, System des Assecuranz, c. viii. s. 1, p. 213.

(a) Strong v. Natally (1804), 1 B. & P. N. R. 16.

(b) Houlder v. Merchants Marine Ins. Co. (1886), 17 Q. B. D. 354, 356. It was not necessary to decide this point. See post, § 459.

(c) Mr. Arthur Cohen agrees with this view: Halsbury's Laws of England, vol. xvii. § 764.

(d) Paul v. Insurance Co. of North America (1899), 15 Times L. R. 535.

Sect. 458. but by an arrangement made in this case, which was said not to be an unusual one, the owners of the goods insured took delivery of them into their own lighters, and some of the goods were lost alongside after they had been put into one of these lighters. Mathew, J., held that the assured could recover. He characterized the decisions in Sparrow v. Carruthers and Strong v. Natally as extraordinary, and said: "'Including risk of craft' covers carriage in a hired lighter; why not also in lighters belonging to the assured?" The only ground on which this judgment can be reconciled with that of the Court of Common Pleas in Strong v. Natally is that the clause "including risk of craft from the vessel" authorizes any reasonable use of lighters to discharge the goods, and thereby, even when the lighters belong to the assured, prevents the application of the principle of Strong v. Natally; but this is not a satisfactory reason for distinguishing the cases. For the reason already given, the editors consider Strong v. Natally a questionable decision. They further submit that, even if that case be supported, if the ship, owing to perils of the sea, had to abandon the voyage at an intermediate port, and the owner of goods, obliged to take possession of them there, carried them in his own ship to the *terminus ad quem,* the underwriter would not be discharged. This acceptance of the goods is not the same as a voluntary acceptance at the port of discharge.

Risk of craft till landed.

459. Where the policy expressly provided for "all risk of craft until the goods are discharged and safely landed," and the goods had been put into lighters at the port of destination named in the policy, not, however, for the purpose of being landed, but of being transhipped into export vessels bound for a foreign port, a loss of part of the goods was held not to be within the risk described in the policy. The goods were not in lighters for the purpose of being landed, but for the purpose of being transhipped, a purpose that could not be expressed by the term "landed" (*e*).

(*e*) Houlder v. Merchants Marine Ins. Co. (1886), 17 Q. B. D. 354. The rule is different when goods are, in the customary way, placed

CHAP. XVII.] DURATION OF THE RISK ON GOODS. 619

460. Whenever the goods can be considered as landed, according to the usual course of business at their port of destination, the risk ends, though they may never have been delivered into the hands of the consignees (*f*).

Sect. 460. When the goods are considered to have been "landed."

Thus at Reval, the port of discharge, the cargo was (according to the uniform course of business in that port) unloaded into government lighters by the revenue officers, and lodged in government warehouses, where it was afterwards confiscated, without ever coming into the hands of the consignees: Lord Ellenborough held, that the risk ceased on its so being landed, for that the policy protected it against the perils of the sea only, and not of the shore (*g*).

The general rule, in fact, is clear, that the underwriter in a sea policy insures only against sea risks; the risk on goods, therefore, ends directly they are put on terra firma, unless they are placed there only for a temporary purpose, subsidiary to the main purpose of the voyage, or under such circumstances as to be protected by the usage of the trade (*h*), or unless there be a special agreement to prolong the risk (*i*).

General rule.

The following American case, which seems to have been well decided, affords a good illustration of this rule. An insurance had been effected on "specie and merchandise out and merchandise home, at and from Boston to ports in the islands of Sumatra and Java, for the purpose of disposing of the outward and procuring a return cargo, &c., with liberty to touch at the usual places and trade thereat." The captain had landed, at a port in Sumatra, a chest of opium, part of the outward cargo, to be exchanged for a certain quantity of

in lighters at an intermediate port for transhipment, there being liberty to tranship.

(*f*) Gatliffe *v.* Bourne (1838), 4 Bing. N. C. 314; *S. C.*, before the House of Lords (1841), 7 M. & Gr. 850.

(*g*) Brown *v.* Carstairs (1811), 3 Camp. 161; see also Marten *v.* Nippon, &c. Ins. Co. (1898), 3 Com. Cas. 164.

(*h*) Harrison *v.* Ellis (1857), 7 E. & B. 465; 25 L. J. Q. B. 239; contrasted with Pelly *v.* Royal Exch. Ass. Co. (1757), 1 Burr. 341; Brough *v.* Whitmore (1791), 4 T. R. 206; see also Australian Agricultural Co. *v.* Saunders (1875), L. R. 10 C. P. 668.

(*i*) See *post*, § 470.

620 DURATION OF THE RISK ON GOODS. [PART I.

Sect. 460. pepper and dollars, but, not being able to come to terms, had taken up the chest and stowed it in the launch for the purpose of being carried back to the ship, when the natives made a rush on the crew, overpowered them, and carried off the opium: the Court in the United States held that, under these circumstances, the opium was protected by the policy. Sedgwick, J., in giving the judgment of the Court, said: "The goods were as much protected by the policy in the boats, while employed as auxiliary to the voyage, as they were on board the ship" (k).

Damage in unloading.
461. As by our law the risk on the goods continues until they are safely landed at the wharves or usual landing places of the port of discharge, any damage caused to the goods in the course of unloading them from the ship into the lighters, or from the lighters on to the wharf, would fall on the underwriters, always supposing, that is, that such damage be not imputable to the wilful default of the assured. Accordingly, where a policy, otherwise in the common form, gave a special power of shipping and reshipping the goods, Lee, C. J., held that the policy would extend to cover a loss happening in the unloading and reshipping from one ship to another (l).

In a more recent case, though the words were "risk of transhipment, or landing and reshipment," such as would cover a loss by fire during a continuous process of transhipment, or while the goods were being landed or reshipped, it was held that in the absence of custom they would not cover a loss by fire while the goods, after being landed, were stored in a warehouse and waiting to be shipped (m).

Time within which the goods must be landed.
462. In our common policies no fixed period of time is specified during which the risk on the goods is limited to continue after the ship's arrival; i.e., there is no specified time within which their landing must be completed, and

---

(k) Parsons v. Massachusetts Fire and Marine Ins. Co. (1810), 6 Mass. R. 197; 1 Phillips, s. 970.
(l) Tierney v. Etherington (1743),
1 Burr. 348.
(m) Australian Agricultural Co. v. Saunders (1875), L. R. 10 C. P. 668.

CHAP. XVII.] DURATION OF THE RISK ON GOODS. 621

beyond which they will be out of the protection of the policy. Sect. 462.
The rule, as we have seen, is that they must be landed "within a reasonable time after arrival at the port of discharge, and if they are not so landed the risk ceases" (*n*).

The law of France in this respect agrees with our own (*o*). Foreign law

By some of the foreign codes, on the other hand, it is provided that the risk upon the goods, unless they are previously landed, shall continue only for a certain limited number of days after the ship's arrival at the port of discharge (*p*).

The reasons given for preferring a fixed number of days are—1st, to avoid all litigation as to what shall be deemed reasonable time (as to which see presently); 2ndly, to compel a speedy clearance of the cargo. Benecke, however, after examining the different provisions of foreign states on this subject, concluded that the rule adopted in England and France is, upon the whole, preferable; and this opinion seems well founded (*q*).

It is, of course, competent to parties effecting insurances in this country to adopt special clauses, varying the duration of the risk as fixed by the common clauses. Duration of risk may be varied by a special clause.

463. The extent of a reasonable time for the unloading depends entirely on the nature and usages of the trade, the main object of the adventure, and the circumstances of the port of discharge at the time. What is a reasonable time for discharging cargo.

(*n*) Mar. Ins. Act, 1906, Sched. I. rule 5, *ante*, § 456.
(*o*) The Code de Commerce (arts. 328, 341) provides that the risk on goods shall continue "jusqu'au jour où elles sont délivrées à terre." The Belgian Code (art. 195) and the Spanish Code (art. 761) are similar. Except in the case of unjustifiable delay on the part of the assured or consignee, the risk endures by the German Code also (arts. 824, 821 (4)) until the goods are landed. By the Russian Code (art. 557) the risk ends when the goods are landed, or the time fixed for discharging has expired.
(*p*) By the Commercial Code of Holland (art. 627) the risk ends fifteen days after the ship's arrival. In case of delay through the fault of the consignee, the Italian Code (arts. 601, 611) makes the risk end one month after arrival. For the older laws, see 2 Magens, and 2 Benecke, System des Assecuranz, v. viii. s. 1, p. 209.
(*q*) 2 Benecke, System des Assecuranz, p. 223; Nolte agrees with him, vol. i. pp. 657—660.

Sect. 463.
In the barter trade.

Thus, under a policy for the African barter trade in gum, continuing the risk on the cargo "till discharged and safely landed," the ship was captured about a month after her arrival on the African coast, at which time, as no gums had been brought down to the coast by the natives, no part of her outward cargo had been landed for the purposes of barter: Lord Kenyon held, that as, under the circumstances, no unnecessary delay appeared to have taken place, the risk on the outward cargo was a continuing risk at the time of the loss (*r*).

In the Newfoundland trade.

In the Newfoundland and Labrador trade, as carried on early in the nineteenth century, the great object of the adventure being to catch fish, the outward cargo generally consisted in great part of salt and provisions for victualling the crew and curing the fish caught. This part of the cargo was naturally consumed as wanted, and never landed at all; even such part of it as consisted of merchandise was frequently not landed until the fishing, which was the main business of the adventure, left the crew at liberty to discharge it. In the case, therefore, of outward cargoes insured on board ships engaged in this trade by policies in the common form, continuing the risk on the goods "till discharged or safely landed," it was held that such outward cargoes were protected by the policy, though in one instance they were still on board for thirty, and in another for fifty, days after the ship's arrival off the coast (*s*).

As a general principle, the risk continues until the goods are landed at the ultimate port of discharge.

464. When goods are insured in the common form, the risk upon them continues until they are safely landed at the particular port which is either named in the policy as their ultimate port of discharge, or contemplated as such by the parties (*t*).

(*r*) Parkinson *v.* Collier (1797), 2 Park, Ins. 653; 1 Marshall, Ins. 255. It is obvious that in such a case as this a fixed rule of time would have operated unjustly.

(*s*) Noble *v.* Kennoway (1780), 2 Dougl. 510; see also Vallance *v.*
Dewar (1808), 1 Camp. 503; Ougier *v.* Jennings (1800), *ibid.* 505, n.

(*t*) Lord Mansfield in Barrass *v.* London Ass. Co. (1782), 1 Marshall, Ins. 266; Leigh *v.* Mather (1795), 1 Esp. 412.

CHAP. XVII.] DURATION OF THE RISK ON GOODS. 623

Even when the place named in the policy as the *terminus ad quem* of the voyage is one of the West Indian Islands, or other place containing several ports, an outward policy effected on the goods will, generally speaking, enure to protect them until the whole of the outward cargo, or, at all events, until the great bulk of it, has been safely landed at that port in the island which was, in fact, contemplated by the parties as the ultimate port of discharge (*u*).

Sect. 464.

465. Where, indeed, the great bulk of the outward cargo, under such a policy, has been unloaded and sold at any given port, either in that island or elsewhere within the limits of the voyage, and that which remains on board, being trifling in quantity, is taken on, either as ballast or because it could not be sold at the port where the rest was disposed of, in such cases the risk on the outward cargo will be held to have terminated at the port where the bulk of it was sold; and the liability of the underwriters on the outward policy will not be held to continue merely because at the time of the loss an insignificant portion of the outward cargo may still be on board.

Where the great bulk of the cargo has been discharged.

This principle, which is equitable and well adapted to the real intentions of the parties, has long been established in the law of France (*x*); and has received abundant confirmation in the jurisprudence of this country (*y*).

Thus, where an insurance was made on ship and goods "at and from Georgia to Jamaica," and the ship arrived at Montego Bay, which was the port to which the cargo was originally destined, where she remained a month, and during

Leigh *v.* Mather.

(*u*) Barrass *v.* London Ass. Co. (1782), 1 Marshall, 266.

(*x*) Emerigon, c. xiii. s. 20; 3 Boulay-Paty, Droit Mar. 421—429.

(*y*) Leigh *v.* Mather (1795), 1 Marshall, Ins. 266; 1 Park, 74. As to the ship, Inglis *v.* Vaux (1813), 3 Camp. 437; Moore *v.* Taylor (1834), 1 A. & E. 25. The editors submit that under a policy on a trading voyage the fact that only a small quantity of goods remains on board, because it has not been sold, will not determine the policy, except it be so trifling that the maxim "De minimis," &c., applies. Of course, if goods are kept as ballast only, they cease to be cargo and to be protected by the policy.

Sect. 465. that period sold and delivered the greatest part of her cargo, and would have disposed of the whole but for a verbal agreement with a party who chartered the vessel for a voyage from Montego Bay to St. Anne's, for a cargo, and thence to London, by which agreement part of the outward cargo, which was lumber, was to be carried in ballast to St. Anne's: Lord Kenyon held, that under these circumstances the risk on the outward cargo came to an end when the bulk of it was landed at Montego Bay, and did not continue on that part of it which was carried on as ballast to St. Anne's (*z*).

The subject will receive further illustration when we come to consider the duration of risk on the ship.

Goods insured "till arrived at the last place of discharge in the outward voyage."

466. In the following case a question was made as to the continuance of the risk on goods insured "until arrived at the last place of discharge in the outward voyage."

The goods in question were the investment of an East India captain, and the voyage for which they were insured was described in the policy to be "at and from London to Madeira, the Cape of Good Hope, and all or any of the ports or places in the East Indies, China, Persia, or elsewhere, on this or the other side the Cape," "until arrived at the last place of discharge on the outward voyage, with leave to exchange the goods in the course of the voyage." The ship arrived at Calcutta, and there discharged the whole of the cargo she carried out for the East India Company; after which she was ordered by the company on an intermediate voyage to Madras, and took on board a cargo to be conveyed thither. The captain had also landed the whole of his investment (the goods insured by this policy) at Calcutta, and had disposed of a considerable part of it; but, being unable to find purchasers for the residue, he resolved to carry it on to a new market, and, with this view, re-loaded it on board the ship for Madras. The ship was lost on the

(*z*) Leigh *v.* Mather (1795), as reported 1 Marshall, Ins. 266; 1 Park, Ins. 74. The case, as reported in 1 Esp. 412, is not consistent with the principles above laid down, nor, it is submitted, with law.

intermediate voyage from Calcutta to Madras. Lord Ellenborough held that the risk had ended at Calcutta; for, as all the company's outward cargo had been discharged there, that port was the "last place of discharge on the outward voyage," upon the true construction of the policy (a).

Sect. 466.

"If," said Lord Ellenborough, "the company's officers wish for the protection which is here sought (*i.e.*, until the goods are finally disposed of in some market in the East Indies), they must not limit the risk to the duration of the outward voyage, but extend it to the arrival of the goods to a market at their final port of discharge." No doubt an insurance in such form would effectually protect the goods until the whole were actually disposed of in some foreign market (b).

Goods insured "to a market."

467. When the risk on the goods is made by the policy to continue "until they shall be arrived at their final port of destination," it will frequently become a question of fact, depending upon the intentions of the parties, what "the final port of destination" really was.

Goods insured to their "final port of destination."

During the suspension of friendly relations between this country and China, in the year 1841, the "Penang" arrived in Macao Roads, with a cargo insured from Liverpool for various ports in China by a policy, containing the most extensive liberties, in the China Seas, to tranship cargo on board any other vessel, to visit any ports, and to remain there till it should be deemed expedient to proceed to her port or ports of discharge, continuing the risk "until the goods should be arrived at their final port of destination."

Oliverson v. Brightman.

The consignees at Macao, finding that it would be dangerous to send the goods up the river to Canton, and also that it would be necessary, owing to sea damage sustained in the voyage, to tranship them, hired the "James Laing" as a temporary receiving ship, and sent her with the "Penang"

(a) Richardson v. London Ass. Co. (1814), 4 Camp. 94.

(b) See the cases as to the continuance of risk on ship, *post*, §§ 496, 501.

Sect. 467. to Hong Kong—the safest anchorage in those seas—in order there to receive the cargo from the "Penang" for the purpose, 1st, of examining it; 2nd, of keeping it on board in a place of safety till it could be sent on to Canton, or some other market in China, where it could be sold; there being then no market whatever at Hong Kong. During the transhipment in Hong Kong Roads, the "James Laing," and all the goods that had, up to that time, been transhipped into her, were sunk in a typhoon and lost. In an action for this loss the Court were clearly of opinion that Hong Kong was not the final port of destination within the contemplation of the parties, and further, that the principle established by Brown v. Vigne (c)—that if a vessel, instead of proceeding to her originally destined port, chooses to wait at another until the termination of war, the voyage is thereby determined—was inapplicable to the circumstances of this case; for the fact in Brown v. Vigne was that there was actual war with Spain, which rendered it illegal to send on the goods to their original port of destination; whereas here, there having been no formal declaration of war against China, it would not have been illegal, but only dangerous and inexpedient, to send the goods on to Canton, or any other market in China. Accordingly, the risk on the goods lost in the "James Laing" was held to be a continuing risk at the time of the loss, and the plaintiff therefore recovered (d).

Effect of transhipment.

468. The general rule is, that if goods be transferred in the course of the voyage to another ship the risk is at an end, the English policy being worded to cover a voyage in one ship only. There are, however, two cases in which it was held—before the Marine Insurance Act, 1906—that the risk is not determined by a transhipment. One is where the

---

(c) (1810), 12 East, 283.

(d) Oliverson v. Brightman (1846), 8 Q. B. 781; 15 L. J. Q. B. 274. In this case the policy contained an express liberty "to tranship." In another case on the same adventure, where the policy contained no such liberty, the Court, on proof of the above facts, directed a nonsuit. Bold v. Rotherham (1846), 8 Q. B. 781; 15 L. J. Q. B. 279.

policy contains an express licence to tranship (*e*); the other is where it is impossible to carry the goods to their destination in the original vessel. Thus, if in the course of the voyage the original ship becomes disabled, and the goods are by the master sent on in another vessel, it was held that the risk on the goods continues until they are safely landed out of the substituted ship at the original port of destination (*f*), provided that a clear case of necessity is made out (*g*).

Sect. 468.

With reference to transhipment from necessity, sect. 59 of the Marine Insurance Act, 1906, contains the following provision:—

> Where, by a peril insured against, the voyage is interrupted at an intermediate port or place, under such circumstances as, apart from any special stipulation in the contract of affreightment (*h*), to justify the master in landing and reshipping the goods or other moveables, or in transhipping them, and sending them on to their destination, the liability of the insurer continues, notwithstanding the landing or transhipment (*i*).

When the policy gives leave to tranship, the insurer is liable for a loss happening in the course of a transhipment or landing and reshipment effected in the manner usual in the

(*e*) Where goods shipped on board a P. & O. steamer were insured to any ports in Australia " in P. & O. and Orient steamers, with all liberties and exceptions as per bill of lading," and by the bill of lading the goods were to be transhipped at Sydney into local steamers for delivery at Brisbane, Bigham, J., held that they were covered after transhipment into a local steamer which did not belong to the P. & O. Company, whose steamers do not run to Brisbane. Neale *v.* Rose (1898), 3 Com. Cas. 236.

(*f*) Plantamour *v.* Staples (1781), 1 T. R. 611, n.; 1 Marshall, Ins. 164. In that case a policy was effected on ship and goods for a trading voyage out and home. The ship was wrecked on the outward voyage, but some of the goods were saved and sent to their destination. It was held that the policy covered goods bought with the proceeds of the sale and sent home in another ship.

(*g*) Bold *v.* Rotherham (1846), 8 Q. B. 797; De Cuadra *v.* Swan (1864), 16 C. B. N. S. 772.

(*h*) See note (*s*), *ante*, § 192.

(*i*) *Quære* whether the effect of this provision has been to impose a restriction, as between the assured and insurer, upon the right of transhipment in case of necessity, which did not previously exist: see *ante*, § 192, note (*r*).

Sect. 468. port (*k*). Although the question has not arisen here, there is no doubt that if the transhipment or landing and reshipment do not put an end to the risk, the insurer is similarly liable (*l*).

Tierney v. Etherington.

In Tierney *v.* Etherington goods were insured on board a Dutch ship "from Malaga to Gibraltar, and at and from thence to England and Holland, both or either," continuing the risk "till the ship and goods be arrived at England or Holland, and there safely landed." There was a special clause in the policy, by which it was agreed that on the arrival of the ship at Gibraltar the goods might be unloaded and reshipped in one or more British ship or ships for England and Holland, &c. When the ship arrived at Gibraltar there was no British ship there, and the goods were unloaded and put into a store-ship (which it was proved was always considered as a warehouse), in order to be kept there till some British ship should arrive. Two days after the goods were put into this store-ship they were lost in a storm.

For the underwriters it was objected that the risk on the goods was at an end upon their being loaded into this store-ship, which was to be considered as a warehouse on land; but Lee, C. J., held that the construction should be according to the course of trade in Gibraltar; and that, as it appeared to be the usual method of unloading and reshipping in that place, that, when there is no British ship there, the goods should be kept in store-ships until one arrives, the risk upon the goods so loaded according to such custom should be held to continue, and the underwriters to be liable (*m*).

Pre-determination of the risk by sale of the goods.

469. Inasmuch as an assured must be interested in the subject-matter insured at the time of the loss (*n*), the under-

(*k*) Tierney *v.* Etherington (1743), cited 1 Burr. 348; Oliverson *v.* Brightman (1846), 8 Q. B. 781; 15 L. J. Q. B. 274; Australian Agricultural Co. *v.* Saunders (1875), L. R. 10 C. P. 668, 676, 678.

(*l*) The Supreme Court of Massachusetts said in one case that if it be necessary on account of the loss of the ship to carry the cargo overland for the purpose of transhipment, the underwriter is liable during the land transit. Bryant *v.* Commonwealth Ins. Co. (1833), 13 Pickering, 543, 555.

(*m*) Tierney *v.* Etherington (1743), cited 1 Burr. 348, 349.

(*n*) See § 258, *ante*.

writer's liability on the policy may be terminated before the end of the voyage, if the assured part with his interest without transferring the right to the protection of the policy. Thus, where a cargo of wheat insured from Galatz to Emden and (or) United Kingdom was sold by the assured, "including insurance to Emden," it was held that the purchaser could not recover for a loss between Emden and the port of discharge in the United Kingdom (*o*).

Sect. 469.

470. By express contract the protection of a marine policy may be prolonged after landing and during the subsequent transport of the goods overland (*p*). Thus, in a policy the voyage was described: "At and from Japan and (or) Shanghai to Marseilles and (or) Leghorn, and (or) London *viâ* Marseilles and (or) Southampton, and whilst remaining there for transit, with leave to call, &c., in the good ship or vessel called 'The ——' steamers or steamer, per overland, or *viâ* Suez Canal," &c. In the margin was this memorandum: "It is hereby agreed that the silks insured by this policy shall be shipped by Peninsular and Oriental Company, Messageries Impériales steamers, and (or) the steamers of the Mercantile Trading Company of Liverpool only."

Prolongation of the risk during land transit;

The goods were shipped and paid for to London by the Messageries Impériales steamers, whose customary route, followed in this instance, was from Shanghai to Marseilles, and thence overland, through France, *viâ* Paris, where they arrived on the 13th September, 1870; and while they were still there the German armies approached on the 19th September and surrounded the city, preventing the goods after that event from being forwarded to London. It was held that, the goods being still covered by the policy, there was a total loss within the meaning of the peril described

(*o*) Ionides *v.* Harford (1859), 29 L. J. Ex. 36; see also North of England Oilcake Co. *v.* Archangel Maritime Ins. Co. (1875), L. R. 10 Q. B. 249. As to the assignment of the policy to a purchaser, see *ante*, § 174 *et seq.*

(*p*) See, *e.g.*, Rodocanachi *v.* Elliott (1873), L. R. 8 C. P. 649. For other forms of policy prolonging the risk to cover a land transit, see Simon, Israel & Co. *v.* Sedgwick, [1893] 1 Q. B. 303; Schloss *v.* Stevens, [1906] 2 K. B. 665.

Sect. 470.

therein as "the arrests, restraints, and detainments of all kings, princes, and people" (*q*).

until goods warehoused.

It is now usual by means of a "warehouse to warehouse" clause to prolong the risk after the goods have been landed, until they have been warehoused at their destination (*r*).

Policy on pumps for a salvage adventure.

471. A somewhat peculiar case arose out of a policy specially worded to protect certain pumps used in salvage operations.

A salvage company intending to raise the steamer "Alexandra," ashore near Drogheda, effected a policy on four steam pumps, &c., valued at 2,000*l*., on the "Sea Mew" salvage steamer, "at and from Ardrossan to the 'Alexandra' steamer ashore in the neighbourhood of Drogheda, and whilst there engaged at the wreck, and until again returned to Ardrossan; the risk beginning from the loading on board the 'Sea Mew' upon the said ship and (or) wreck, &c." The pumps arrived safely at the wreck, were used on board of it, and were successful in raising it. The wreck, with the pumps still on board, then started for Ardrossan in tow of several tugs, the "Sea Mew" also acting in that capacity; but the weather became so foul that they necessarily put about for Belfast, and before that port could be reached the wreck went down with the pumps on board. The Court of Appeal held that the words of the policy did not cover the voyage to Belfast, that being a voyage undertaken for the safety of the wreck, and not intended to be insured (*s*).

(*q*) Rodocanachi *v.* Elliott, *supra*.

(*r*) See *ante*, § 447, n. (*e*). A policy on goods "to wharf or export vessel at port of discharge," was expressly stated to cover the goods while "temporarily placed upon the quay . . . and until delivered to the export vessel or at any wharf or warehouse within the limits of the port." They were placed in sheds on the quay while the consignee, who had not made up his mind as to their ultimate destination, was trying to find a purchaser, and were there damaged by fire; and it was held that they were covered: Westminster Fire Office *v.* Reliance Mar. Ins. Co. (1903), 19 Times L. R. 668. For the construction of a policy on goods "until safely delivered into warehouse or other place for which the goods have been entered, or in which it is intended they shall be lodged," see Deutsch-Australische Dampfschiffsgesellschaft *v.* Sturge (1913), 30 Times L. R. 137.

(*s*) Wingate *v.* Foster (1878), 3

CHAP. XVII.] DURATION OF THE RISK ON SHIP. 631

Cotton, L. J., and Thesiger, L. J., thought that it was not Sect. 471.
in the contemplation of the parties that the pumps should be
kept on the wreck after she was raised and while she was
being taken to a port of refuge. Brett, L. J., was of opinion
that the pumps would have been protected even on the wreck
if she had been returning to Ardrossan. It is submitted,
however, that the correctness of the decision may depend on
whether the policy was intended to cover the pumps on the
wreck after she was raised. If not, it is clear that the risk
was varied when the pumps were afterwards allowed to
remain on board of her, instead of being reloaded on the
" Sea Mew "; and the policy then came to an end. On the
other hand, if the policy covered the pumps on board the
wreck until their return to Ardrossan, although no doubt the
voyage to Belfast instead of to Ardrossan was not within the
scope of the policy, the deviation to Belfast might be
justifiable if it was properly made for the safety of the
" Alexandra." It was under such circumstances a deviation
for the safety, both of the vessel on which the assured was
entitled to have the pumps carried, and of the property on
board of her.

472. We come now to consider the duration of the risk on Duration of risk on the
ship, and first its commencement. In most of the Con- ship.
tinental states the period of the commencement of the risk
on the ship is fixed by their codes: subject, of course, to be
varied by the express stipulations of the parties. Thus, in Commencement of risk
France, unless otherwise stipulated by the policy, the risk on abroad.
ship commences from the day of the ship's sailing (*t*).

In this country the period at which the risk on the ship In this country.
commences depends on the terms of the policy, and the nature
of the voyage intended to be insured.

473. Rule 2 of the Rules for the Construction of the Policy

Q. B. D. 582. For another case of   (*t*) Code de Commerce, arts. 328,
a policy on pumps for a salvage   341.
adventure, see *ante*, § 443, note (*n*).

DURATION OF THE RISK ON SHIP. [PART I.

Sect. 473.
Insurance "from" a port.

in the first Schedule of the Marine Insurance Act, 1906, states that—

> Where the subject-matter is insured "from" a particular place, the risk does not attach until the ship starts on the voyage insured.

Thus, if the ship be insured simply "from" a port, or if the adventure on the ship be made by the policy "to begin on the ship from A. B.," the risk does not commence until the ship sails on her voyage "from" such port; *i.e.*, until she quits her moorings and breaks ground, being in a state of perfect equipment and readiness for her voyage (*u*).

"At and from" a port.

474. With regard to insurances on ship "at and from," the law was stated as follows in the second edition of this work:—

> "If the ship be insured 'at and from' a home port, *i.e.*, if the *terminus a quo* be a port in this country in which the ship is then lying, the risk commences on the ship immediately upon the execution of the policy, and continues during the whole time the ship remains in the home port in a course of preparation for her voyage.
>
> "If the ship be insured, and the adventure made to commence upon her 'at and from' some foreign port at which the ship is expected to arrive, with the view of protecting her for her homeward voyage, it is now settled in this country that, in order to make the risk under the homeward policy attach on the ship, she must have once been at the outward port in good physical safety" (*x*).

(*u*) Pittegrew *v.* Pringle (1832), 3 B. & Ad. 514; Hunting *v.* Boulton (1895), 1 Com. Cas. 120, in which the insurance was "from date of sailing from Leith;" 1 Marshall, Ins. 260. The law is the same in the United States. 3 Kent, Com. 307, n. (*a*). See what constitutes a sailing within the meaning of warranties to sail at a particular time, *post*, § 643 *et seq.*

(*x*) 2nd ed. p. 496; 6th ed. p. 404. The authorities cited are Motteux *v.* London Ass. Co. (1739), 1 Atkyns, 548; Palmer *v.* Marshall (1831), 8 Bing. 79. The same rule is stated by Story, J., in Seaman *v.* Loring (1816), 1 Mason, R. 127, 140. Chancellor Kent says that the risk "includes all the time the ship is in port, after the policy is subscribed, if the ship be at home," 3

CHAP. XVII.] DURATION OF THE RISK ON SHIP. 633

The language of this passage, and that used by many judges and text-writers, suggests that this question of the commencement of the risk is a different one according as the voyage is from a home or a foreign port (*y*). Yet there is no distinction in principle, as regards the attachment of the risk, between voyages beginning at home and those beginning at foreign ports; and no such distinction is made, as will presently appear, in the Rules for the Construction of the Policy in the Marine Insurance Act, 1906.

Sect. 474.

475. When the insurance is "at and from" there are three possible cases—(1) The ship may then be lying at the *terminus a quo*, (2) she may not have arrived there, (3) she may already have sailed.

Rules in Mar. Ins. Act for attachment of risk on ship.

In relation to the first and second cases, the Marine Insurance Act, 1906, lays down the following rule (*z*):—

(a) Where a ship is insured "at and from" a particular place, and she is at that place in good safety when the contract is concluded, the risk attaches immediately.

(b) If she be not at that place when the contract is concluded the risk attaches as soon as she arrives there in good safety, and, unless the policy otherwise provides, it is immaterial that she is covered by another policy for a specified time after arrival.

With regard to a ship lying at the *terminus a quo* when the policy is effected, it thus appears that the mere presence of the ship in port will not under all circumstances cause the policy to attach. She must be there "in good safety," and therefore the policy will not attach unless the ship is in a reasonable state of fitness for the harbour risk (*a*). And it is

Policy "at and from" a port effected when the ship is lying there.

Com. 307. See, as to this, Chitty *v.* Selwyn (1742), 2 Atk. 359, and *ante*, "Deviation."

(*y*) There is no suggestion of such a distinction in Phillips' treatise, unless it can be inferred from the statement (vol. i. s. 934) that under a policy "at and from" a foreign port the risk is held not to commence until the ship is there in good safety. The distinction is,

however, recognized by Chancellor Kent (3 Com. 307), and by Story, J., in Seaman *v.* Loring (1816), 1 Mason, R. 127, 140.

(*z*) Sched. I. rule 3.

(*a*) Forbes *v.* Wilson (1800), 1 Park, 472; see also Annen *v.* Woodman (1810), 3 Taunt. 299; Parmeter *v.* Cousins (1809), 2 Camp. 235. See further, as to good safety, *infra*, § 478.

Sect. 475. further submitted that the policy will not attach if the ship be not in the port for the purposes of the insured voyage (*b*). Thus, if the insured voyage be "at and from" A. to B. and at the time when the contract is made the ship be taking cargo on board for a voyage from A. to C., it seems clear that the risk will not attach even "at" A. So also, if a ship has been laid up for some time, it may be that the policy will not attach until preparations for the voyage are begun. This has been decided in the United States with regard to a ship lying in a foreign port (*c*).

Before the Marine Insurance Act, 1906, it had not been necessary to decide that a policy on a ship "at and from" a place where she was then lying did not attach retrospectively. There is no doubt authority for the view that the risk only attaches as from the time when the contract is made; and Rule 3 (*d*) in the First Schedule to the Act, which provides that the risk attaches immediately, certainly seems to be founded on this view. For the condition in the rule that the ship must at the time when the contract is concluded be in good safety at the *terminus a quo* cannot be reconciled with a right to recover for previous losses; for if the ship had already been totally lost during her stay "at" the *terminus a quo* it would be impossible to satisfy this condition. Rule 1 of the Rules for the Construction of the Policy declares, however, that "when the subject-matter is insured 'lost or not lost,' and the loss has occurred before the contract is

---

(*b*) See *infra*, note (*f*).

(*c*) Seaman *v.* Loring (1816), 1 Mason, R. 127, 140, cited 1 Phillips, s. 935. In Palmer *v.* Marshall, *supra*, the policy was on a yacht, then lying ready for sea. When vessels are laid up it is usual to insure them by "port" or "harbour" policies at a low premium. See *infra*, § 508.

(*d*) In Palmer *v.* Marshall (1831), 8 Bing. 79, the Judge had directed the jury that the policy only attached when the ship (a yacht lying at Bristol ready for sea, but apparently without reference to any particular voyage) commenced her voyage. This was held to be a wrong direction. There was a sufficient delay after the insurance was made to avoid the policy, and on a second trial the plaintiff was non-suited on this ground (8 Bing. 317). It was unnecessary to consider whether under ordinary circumstances the policy could have been retrospective; but Tindal, C. J., certainly said that the risk on the policy could only commence from its date.

CHAP. XVII.] DURATION OF THE RISK ON SHIP. 635

concluded, the risk attaches, unless at such time the assured **Sect. 475.**
was aware of the loss, and the insurer was not." The terms
mentioned in the Schedule are not to be construed as having
the scope and meaning assigned to them therein when the
context of the policy otherwise requires (*e*). It is therefore submitted that the rule which gives effect to the "lost
or not lost" clause ought to prevail, and that in a policy
"lost or not lost," "at and from" a port where the ship is
lying at the time when the policy is effected, the risk generally attaches as from the earliest time when the ship was
in the port in good safety for the purposes of the voyage
insured (*f*).

476. The same principle, it is submitted, applies when a Policy "at
and from"
a port from
which the
ship has
already
sailed.
ship is insured "at and from" a port from which she has
already sailed. This case is not dealt with in the Marine
Insurance Act, 1906; but if the rule applicable to it were that
an insurance "at and from" does not attach before the making
of the contract, such a policy on a vessel that had already
sailed would only amount to an insurance "from" the port.

477. The principle in virtue of which it is maintained that Construction
of words "at
and from"
with
reference to
circumstances.
a policy "at and from," with the "lost or not lost" clause,
attaches retrospectively during the whole stay of the ship at
the port for the purposes of the voyage is probably to be
regarded rather as a rule of construction than as a
principle of universal application. Ordinarily, that is to say,
the words ought so to be construed; but there may be special
circumstances in which the ambiguity of the word "at" (*g*)

(*e*) Mar. Ins. Act, 1906, s. 30 (2).
(*f*) See Phillips, s. 932. The rule, that in homeward policies the risk attaches from the arrival at the foreign port, is laid down in general terms by Lord Hardwicke in Motteux *v.* London Ass. Co. (1739), 1 Atkyns, 545, 548. It is not necessary for the attachment of the risk that the cargo of the previous voyage shall have been discharged. See Camden *v.* Cowley,

and Reliance Mar. Ins. Co. *v.* Duder, *infra*, § 485. For, as has been held with reference to insurances on freight, the discharge of the outward cargo is an act done for the purposes of the homeward voyage: Warre *v.* Miller (1825), 4 B. & Cr. 538. See also Foley *v.* United, &c. Ins. Co. (1870), L. R. 5 C. P. 160, 164.

(*g*) In Haughton *v.* Empire Mar. Ins. Co. (1866), L. R. 1 Exch. at

Sect. 477. may justify the admission of parol evidence to show that the real contract between the parties was different. If, for instance, the ship had, prior to the policy, sustained considerable damage, and a premium be agreed upon amounting to less than the sum to which both parties knew such damage amounted, it would be clear that such damage was not intended to be covered. It seems, then, that, in accordance with the opinion of Mathew, J., in a somewhat similar case (*h*), evidence would be admissible to show, consistently with the language of the policy, what the risk was. The effect of such evidence, in the instance we have given, would, no doubt, be that the words we are discussing would receive an interpretation not in conformity with the general principle, but limited in accordance with the intentions of the parties in the particular case.

Policy "at and from" a port where the ship has not yet arrived.

478. As we have seen, if the ship insured "at and from" a port be not yet arrived when the policy is effected, the risk attaches as soon as she arrives there in good safety (*i*).

Thus, under a policy on ship "at and from" Havana to Greenock, the ship arrived off Havana and the master engaged a tug and pilot for the purpose of taking her to a clear anchorage. She was towed into the harbour, past the place where she ultimately discharged her cargo, to a point at the head of the harbour called the Regla Shoal. There she grounded, and received damage from the anchor of

p. 210, Channell, B., seems to have considered that *primâ facie* the word "at" would cover the whole of the ship's stay at the port, but that this presumption might be controlled by extrinsic evidence.

(*h*) Hunting *v.* Boulton (1895), 1 Com. Cas. 120.

(*i*) Mar. Ins. Act, 1906, Sched. I. r. 3 (b), *ante*, § 475. See per Lord Hardwicke, Motteux *v.* London Ass. Co. (1739), 1 Atk. 545, 548; 1 Phillips, ss. 927, 932. Of course, if at the time of the ship's arrival there be no intention to send her on the insured voyage, the risk does not attach, by reason of the abandonment of the voyage. *Ante*, § 380. It is also submitted that the policy does not attach if the ship arrives for the purpose of an intermediate voyage. Thus if a ship be insured "at and from" A. to B., being then on her way to A., and the intention be then to send her first on a voyage from A. to C. and back to A., and then on the voyage from A. to B., the risk will only attach, if at all, on the second arrival of the ship at A.

another ship. "In my opinion," says Channell, B., delivering judgment in the case, "she was at that time at Havana, and consequently the risk under the policy had attached. The damage occurred at Havana, geographically speaking, and there is nothing which to my mind shows that the parties, at the time this policy was underwritten, contemplated any other meaning of the word 'at.' All the limitation which the law appears ever to have imposed as to the time of the commencement of the risk in such a case is, that the ship should arrive at the port at which she is insured in a state of sufficient repair or seaworthiness to be enabled to be there in safety " (k).

Sect. 478.

Good safety.

What constitutes good safety is well illustrated by the case of Parmeter v. Cousins. The policy was on ship "at and from St. Michael's, or all or any of the western islands, to England"; and it appeared that the ship, which had encountered very bad weather on the whole of the outward voyage, cast anchor off St. Michael's in such a leaky condition as to be unfit to take in a cargo, and was only kept afloat by pumping, and that, after lying in the roadstead there at anchor for upwards of twenty-four hours (during the whole of which time she was in great danger from the storm that still continued), she was blown out to sea and wrecked: Lord Ellenborough held that under these circumstances the risk had never commenced on the ship under the homeward policy, for the ship had never been at St. Michael's in good safety (l).

All that is required in such case is good physical safety; not that the ship should have been free during her stay at the *terminus a quo* from political danger.

Physical, not political, safety is necessary.

Thus, where a ship was insured "at and from Riga to her ports of discharge in the United Kingdom," and immediately upon her arrival at Riga her papers were seized by government and the ship and cargo sequestrated and condemned before the outward cargo had been discharged: Lord

Bell v. Bell.

(k) Haughton v. Empire Marine Ins. Co. (1866), L. R. 1 Ex. 206.

(l) Parmeter v. Cousins (1809), 2 Camp. 235.

638   DURATION OF THE RISK ON SHIP.   [PART I.

Sect. 478. Ellenborough held that, as the ship had been once "at" Riga in good physical safety, the risk under the homeward policy had attached on the ship (*m*).

What physical safety is required.

All that is required, in fact, is that the ship while at the *terminus a quo* of the voyage should "be in such a condition as to enable her to lie there in reasonable security till she is properly repaired and equipped for her voyage" (*n*).

Thus, where a ship, though leaky, was able to lie for a month loading in a river, it was held that the policy had attached (*o*). Of course the vessel must subsequently be made seaworthy for the marine risk.

The words "at and from" do not imply that the ship is at the place.

479. It follows from what has already been said that the words "at and from" do not imply a warranty or a representation that the ship is at the time of effecting the policy in the port in question; but it has been decided that the ship must be there within such a time afterwards that the risk shall not be materially varied; and that any delay between the making of the policy and the commencement of the risk, *whether such delay be voluntary or involuntary*, which has the effect of materially varying the risk, will prevent the policy from attaching (*p*).

The facts of the case on which this latter point was decided were these. The policy, "at and from Montreal," was effected on the 13th of July. No question was put by the underwriter as to where the ship then was, and no

---

(*m*) Bell *v.* Bell (1810), 2 Camp. 475.

(*n*) The stipulation as to "good safety" does not seem to mean anything more than that in this form of policy, as in all voyage policies, it is a condition precedent to the attachment of the risk that the vessel shall be seaworthy. This appears to have been the view of Channell, B., in Haughton *v.* Empire Mar. Ins. Co. (1866), L. R. 1 Exch. 210, and is consistent with that of Lord Ellenborough in Parmeter *v.* Cousins (1809), 2 Camp. 237. In Bell *v.* Bell (1810), 2 Camp. 475, Lord Ellenborough required "physical safety from the perils insured against."

(*o*) Annen *v.* Woodman (1810), 3 Taunt. 299; see also per Lord Kenyon in Forbes *v.* Wilson (1800), 1 Marshall, 148; 1 Park, 472.

(*p*) Hull *v.* Cooper (1811), 14 East, 479; De Wolf *v.* Archangel Marit. Bank & Ins. Co. (1874), L. R. 9 Q. B. 451; Maritime Ins. Co. *v.* Stearns, [1901] 2 K. B. 912.

information was offered by the assured; but in fact she was then at sea, on a voyage intended to end at Montreal. She did not arrive at Montreal till the 30th of August. Evidence was given on the trial that the delay of arrival at Montreal had materially varied the risk and the rate of premium. Evidence was offered, but not received, to show that the delay was not voluntary, but was due entirely to sea perils upon the voyage to Montreal. It was held that this evidence was properly rejected, as upon the facts of this case the only question for the jury was whether the delay had materially varied the risk (*q*).

Sect. 479.

The above decision is the earliest in our books as to the effect of involuntary delay preceding the time fixed for such a policy attaching. The question had come before the Court of Common Pleas in respect of voluntary delay, and was then decided adversely to the assured (*r*). Tindal, C. J., in delivering the judgment of the Court, seemed to intimate that his decision would have been the other way in case the underwriter had been prepared to expect delay by notice, or, what is equivalent to notice, by the existence of a usage (*s*). But Blackburn, J., in the later decision already cited, expressly reserved his opinion as to the effect of either notice or usage on the question (*t*).

480. On this subject sect. 42 of the Marine Insurance Act, 1906, lays down the following rules:—

The adventure must commence within a reasonable time.

(1) Where the subject-matter is insured by a voyage policy "at and from" or "from" a particular place, it is not necessary that the ship should be at that place when the contract is concluded, but there is an implied condition that the adventure shall be commenced within a reasonable time (*u*), and that if the adventure be not so commenced the insurer may avoid the contract (*x*).

(*q*) De Wolf *v.* Archangel Marit. Bank & Ins. Co., *supra*.
(*r*) Mount *v.* Larkins (1831), 8 Bing. 108.
(*s*) *Ibid.* 121.
(*t*) De Wolf *v.* Archangel, &c.

Co., *supra*. See *post*, § 483.
(*u*) By sect. 88 of the Act the question what is a reasonable time is one of fact.
(*x*) See Maritime Ins. Co. *v.* Stearns, *supra*.

Sect. 480.

(2) The implied condition may be negatived by showing that the delay was caused by circumstances known to the insurer before the contract was concluded, or by showing that he waived the condition.

The implied condition, as stated in this section, is that the adventure shall be commenced within a reasonable time; and it is arguable that such a condition is not the same as one that there shall not be a delay which materially varies the risk. In relation to contracts of affreightment it has been established by the House of Lords that an obligation to discharge a ship in a reasonable time must be construed with reference to the circumstances existing at the time of performance, so that the shipowner is not responsible for a delay arising from causes beyond his control, provided that he has not acted negligently or unreasonably (*y*). If the principle of this decision governs the construction of the words "reasonable time" in sect. 42, De Wolf *v.* Archangel Maritime is no longer law, in so far as it decides that an involuntary delay prevents the policy from attaching (*z*). Yet the condition that the adventure shall be commenced within a reasonable time is not the same as an obligation, a failure to discharge which will render the person on whom it is imposed liable to an action for breach of contract. The assured is under no obligation whatever to bring his ship to the *terminus a quo* and to prosecute the voyage insured. Therefore it is not clear that the rule laid down by the House of Lords with reference to the fulfilment of an obligation must be applied to the determination of the question what is a reasonable time within the meaning of sect. 42 of the Marine Insurance Act, 1906. The language of the section does not preclude a construction by which the question of reasonable time must be determined with reference to

---

(*y*) Hick *v.* Raymond, [1893] A. C. 22; Carlton SS. Co., Ltd. *v.* Castle Mail Packets Co., Ltd., [1898] A. C. 486. In the former case Lord Watson stated the rule as being one of general application and not confined to contracts for the carriage of goods: [1893] A. C. at p. 32.

(*z*) Mr. Arthur Cohen inclines to this view: Halsbury's Laws of England, vol. xvii. § 770.

the risk contemplated at the time of the insurance, and it is submitted that this construction, which gives effect to the rule laid down in De Wolf *v.* Archangel Maritime Bank, is the correct one.

Sect. 480.

481. Where the policy has once attached, length of time occupied in necessary repairs, though considerable, does not take the ship out of the protection of the policy, supposing those repairs to be made with an ultimate view of sending the ship on the voyage insured (*a*); nor does any other reasonable delay, if justified by necessity, or *bonâ fide* incurred for the purposes of the voyage (*b*)—as to take in simulated papers (*c*), or a particular description of crew (*d*); or provisions where rendered necessary by unavoidable delay (*e*).

What delay is excusable.

The principle, in short, established by the cases is, that where the risk "at and from" has once attached, "a detention for a reasonable time for the purposes of the adventure insured must be allowed, and whether the time is reasonable must be determined, not by any positive or arbitrary rule, but by the state of things existing in the port where the vessel happens to be" (*f*).

482. On the other hand, it has been said that a policy effected on a ship "at and from" a port implies that the voyage insured shall be very shortly commenced, or, at all events, be in the near contemplation of the parties (*g*). And the ship will not be under the protection of the policy if she lie at the port for a long time before sailing or preparing

What delay inexcusable.

(*a*) Mar. Ins. Act, 1906, s. 49 (c), *ante*, § 424a. Motteux *v.* London Ass. Co. (1739), 1 Atkyns, 545, 548.

(*b*) Smith *v.* Surridge (1801), 4 Esp. 25; Grant *v.* King (1802), 4 Esp. 175.

(*c*) Langhorn *v.* Allnutt (1812), 4 Taunt. 510.

(*d*) Grant *v.* King (1805), 4 Esp. 174.

(*e*) Raine *v.* Bell (1808), 9 East, 195.

(*f*) Per Tindal, C. J., in Phillips *v.* Irving (1844), 7 M. & Gr. 328. See, to the same effect, the remarks of Story, J., in Seaman *v.* Loring (1816), 1 Mason, R. 127, cited 1 Phillips, s. 935.

(*g*) Per Tindal, C. J., in Palmer *v.* Marshall (1832), 8 Bing. 317, 318; see also per Park, J., in Palmer *v.* Fenning (1833), 9 Bing. 462.

Sect. 482. for the voyage insured, and there be no reasonable excuse for delay (*h*).

Thus, for instance, if all thought of the voyage insured be laid aside, and the ship lie in the port for years, the risk would be held either never to have attached, or, at all events, to have come to an end directly the determination to abandon the voyage was finally fixed (*i*).

Exception by usage.

The general rule as to the attachment of the policies is subject to be modified by the usages of particular trades. Thus, in the Newfoundland trade, owing to the well-known practice of making fishing expeditions or intermediate trading voyages after the ship's first arrival off the coast of Newfoundland, the risk under policies for the homeward voyage though expressed to be "at and from" any port or ports in Newfoundland, was held not to attach upon the ships on their first arrival out, but only from their beginning to prepare for the homeward voyage (*k*).

Delay of which the underwriter has been informed.

483. If a communication has been made to the underwriter from which he ought to infer that there will be a delay in the attachment of the risk, it has been a matter of doubt whether he is discharged by such a delay? In De Wolf *v.* Archangel Maritime Bank and Insurance Co. (*l*) the Court indicated that there were two possible views: (1) that there is in every case the implied understanding that the risk is to commence within such a time that it will not be varied unless the policy contains some express condition on the subject; (2) that a communication, though not embodied in the policy, will qualify or rebut the implied understanding (*m*).

The latter view was supported by the Newfoundland voyage cases already referred to, in which even when the delay consequent on the customary fishing expedition or intermediate

---

(*h*) Palmer *v.* Marshall (1832), 8 Bing. 317.

(*i*) See the observations of Lord Hardwicke in Chitty *v.* Selwyn (1742), 2 Atkyns, 359.

(*k*) Vallance *v.* Dewar (1808),
1 Camp. 503, and the other cases there collected.

(*l*) *Ante*, § 479.

(*m*) See L. R. 9 Q. B. 456, 457; 1 Phillips, ss. 602, 690.

voyages changed a voyage back to Europe from a summer to a winter voyage, it was held that the policy on the homeward voyage remained good. Further, it was held that the assured was not bound to disclose the fact that the ship might be engaged in fishing, or sent on the intermediate voyage (after which, only, the policy by usage attached), because the underwriter was presumed to know the usage of the trade (*n*). Thus the *ratio decidendi* of these cases, as Chief Justice Tindal said in a later case, was that the usage of the trade was equivalent to notice (*o*).

In support of this view it was also argued that there is no express stipulation in the ordinary policy with regard to the time when the risk attaches. Therefore the time must be that which is contemplated by the parties. When no information is given to the underwriter, he is entitled to assume that the ship, if not yet arrived, will be at the *terminus a quo* within such time as is reasonable under ordinary circumstances. If facts relating to the previous voyage of the ship be communicated to him, he ought to keep these facts in mind in estimating the probable date when the voyage insured will commence. He is in a position to estimate the risk, he can fix the premium accordingly, and may, as is sometimes done, stipulate for a varying rate of premium, according to the time when the voyage begins.

The point has been settled by sect. 42 (2) of the Marine Insurance Act, 1906, which, as we have seen, provides that the implied condition that the adventure shall be commenced within a reasonable time may be negatived by showing that the delay was caused by circumstances known to the insurer before the contract was concluded.

Sect. 483.

484. It has sometimes been made a question when a ship begins to prepare for her homeward voyage. The following case illustrates the nature of the evidence with which the

What is a beginning to prepare for the homeward voyage.

(*n*) Vallance *v.* Dewar (1808), 1 Camp. 503; Ougier *v.* Jennings (1800), *ibid.* 505, n.

(*o*) Mount *v.* Larkins (1831), 8 Bing. 108, 122.

41 (2)

Sect. 484.
Lambert v. Liddard.

Courts will be satisfied on this point:—A ship engaged on a cruising voyage on the Southern Atlantic was insured for a trading voyage home by a policy effected on ship and freight "at and from Pernambuco or any other port or ports in the Brazils to London," "beginning the adventure on the goods from the loading thereof on board" the ship, "and upon the ship on the determination of her cruise, and preparing for her voyage to London," &c.

The cruise being ended, the captain went to Pernambuco, and, when off that place, sent in one of his officers to see if a cargo could be procured there; but as there was none, he sailed southward to St. Salvador for the same purpose, and was lost at sea between the two places. The Court held that his going to Pernambuco for a cargo, and sending in an officer there to inquire after one, was such "a preparing for his voyage to London" within the words of the policy, as to make the homeward risk attach from that moment and protect the ship at the time of loss (*p*).

What is included in "port."
Named port.

485. We have already seen that, when the terminus "at and from" which the voyage is made to commence is a named port, the name is, generally speaking, taken to include, not different places classed together in legal style, or for the purposes of revenue, as one port, but some one place, which in the more limited and popular sense is considered the port; in other words, the harbour-town (*q*). If the

"Port or ports."

policy be "at and from a port or ports" or "place or places" in the alternative, it must be supposed that the insurer meant to incur the greater risk of letting the ship sail to several

---

(*p*) *Lambert v. Liddard* (1814), 1 Marshall, R. 149; *S. C.*, 5 Taunt. 480. See also *ante*, § 475, note (*f*).

(*q*) *Constable v. Noble* (1810), 2 Taunt. 403; *Payne v. Hutchinson* (1808), *ibid.* 405, n.; *Brown v. Tayleur* (1835), 4 A. & E. 241; *ante*, § 454. See also, as to the meaning of the word "port," *Hull Dock Co. v. Browne* (1831), 2 B. & Ad. 43; *Stockton and Darlington Rail. Co. v. Barrett* (1844), 7 M. & Gr. 870, in Dom. Proc.; *Roelandts v. Harrison* (1854), 9 Ex. 444; *Van Baggen v. Baines* (1854), 9 Ex. 523; *SS. Garston Co. v. Hickie* (1885), 15 Q. B. D. 580; *Hunter v. Northern Marine Ins. Co.* (1888), 13 App. Cas. 717, 722, 726, 733; *Goodbody v. Balfour* (1899), 5 Com. Cas. 59 (C. A.).

CHAP. XVII.] DURATION OF THE RISK ON SHIP. 645

places in order to take in her cargo (*r*). But where a ship was insured "at and from her port of lading," the Court held that the expression "port of lading" pointed to one single place, and did not allow of the ship loading at two distinct places (though both lying within seven miles of one another in the same bay), in either of which there might have been a lading (*s*).

Sect. 485.
"Port of loading."

It is not at all necessary to the definition of the term "port," as used in policies, that it should be an artificial harbour shut in with regular moles or piers. If it be a natural basin protected by a headland, or even an open roadstead, provided it be the usual and sole place of loading and unloading, it will be sufficient, especially if there be provided the usual machinery and appendages of a harbour (*t*). Thus, in one case, the Court of King's Bench held that the expression "to any port or ports whatsoever," in a time policy, ought to be construed the same as "place or places," and would protect the ship while anchored in an open roadstead, that being the usual place for loading and unloading goods at the place where the loss occurred (*u*).

"Port" does not necessarily imply an artificial harbour.

A ship, insured "at and from Leith to Shetland, and from thence to Barcelona, and at and from thence and two other ports in Spain, to a port in Great Britain," was lost while loading at Saloe. The roadstead there was the usual station for vessels of her burden. Saloe town lay at the bottom of a natural basin, protected by a headland, and without any artificial harbour. It was frequented as a port, usually designated as such, and so recognized both by the Spanish Government and in this country, which

Sea Insurance Company *v.* Gavin.

(*r*) Brown *v.* Tayleur (1835), 4 Ad. & E. 241; see also Lambert *v.* Liddard, *supra*, § 484.

(*s*) Brown *v.* Tayleur (1835), 4 Ad. & E. 241. There may, however, be a usage by which a loading begun in a place designated in the policy may be finished elsewhere. Kingston *v.* Knibbs (1808), 1 Camp. 508, n.

(*t*) See SS. Garston Co. *v.* Hickie (1885), 15 Q. B. D. 580; and the judgments in Hunter *v.* Northern Marine Ins. Co. (1888), 13 App. Cas. 717.

(*u*) Cockey *v.* Atkinson (1819), 2 B. & Ald. 460; *S. P.*, in the United States, Delonguemere *v.* Fireman's Ins. Co. (1813), 10 Johnson, R. 126, cited 1 Phillips, Ins. s. 929.

Sect. 485. had a vice-consul there. It had a Custom House and harbour-master; port dues were levied there, and at the time of the loss conveniences were erected on the shore for the purpose of loading goods and of protecting smaller vessels from wind and weather. On this evidence the House of Lords, affirming the judgment of the Scotch Court of Session, decided that it was a port within the meaning of the policy (*x*).

Policy "at and from" an island or district containing several ports.

486. Where the policy is "at and from" an island or other district containing several ports, the risk on ship commences as soon as the ship has arrived in good safety at the first port at which she touches at the island or district for the purpose of discharging her outward cargo. Hence, where a ship, insured for her outward voyage from London to Jamaica, "until moored twenty-four hours in good safety," and by an homeward policy "at and from Jamaica to London," was lost in coasting the island after she had stayed some days at one port there, but before she had delivered all her outward cargo; a special jury found, and Lord Mansfield supported their finding, that this loss on the ship was at the risk of the underwriters on the homeward policy (*y*).

Ever since this case it has been clear insurance law that a ship insured for a homeward voyage "at and from" any of

(*x*) Sea Insurance Co. *v.* Gavin (1830), 4 Bligh, N. S. 578; 2 Dow & Clark, 129. Several additional cases as to the meaning of the word "port" will be found in §§ 903, 905, *post*, Vol. II. As to the meaning of the words "place or places" following the words "port or ports," see Maritime Ins. Co. *v.* Alianza Ins. Co., [1907] 2 K. B. 660, *infra*, § 508.

(*y*) Camden *v.* Cowley (1763), 1 W. Bl. 417, 418. See also Reliance Mar. Ins. Co. *v.* Duder, [1913] 1 K. B. 265 (C. A.); 17 Com. Cas. 24, 227. Arnould stated (2nd ed. p. 503) that the risk commences in such a case when the ship has been moored in good safety for twenty-four hours at the first port of discharge—*i.e.*, when the policy on the outward voyage expires. It was, however, established by Haughton *v.* Empire Marine Ins. Co. (1866), L. R. 1 Ex. 206, that the expiration of the outward policy is not the test of the commencement of the risk under the homeward policy, and it is so expressly declared in the Mar. Ins. Act, 1906, Sched. I., rule 3 (b), *ante*, § 475.

the West India Islands is protected by the word "at" in Sect. 486. going from port to port of the island (z).

In these cases, the general word by which the *terminus a quo* of the homeward voyage is described comprehends all ports and places in the island or country named; the construction would be different if the *terminus a quo* were otherwise described in the policy: thus if the policy were on the ship "at and from the ship's port of loading" in Jamaica, that would restrict the commencement of the risk to one particular port in the island (a).

When the insurance is from or to a district or island, evidence of usage is admissible to show what meaning is attached to the description of the terminus in the policy, as, *e.g.*, that the Baltic includes the Gulf of Finland (b), or that "East Indian Island" includes Mauritius (c).

486a. The attachment of the risk may of course be deferred by a stipulation that it is to commence on the happening of a particular event, such as the expiration of a previous policy. A ship was insured for a voyage from Australia "to port or ports, place or places of call and for discharge .... on the West Coast of South America," and by a later policy subscribed by the same underwriter for a voyage "at and from Valparaiso and/or port or ports .... on the West Coast of South America" to European ports, with the additional stipulation "risk to commence from expiration of previous policy." The vessel discharged part of her Australian cargo at Valparaiso, and was lost while proceeding from Valparaiso to Tocopilla, where she was to have discharged the remainder of her Australian cargo and taken on board a cargo for Europe. It was held by Scrutton,

Risk to commence on expiration of previous policy.

(z) Cruickshank v. Janson (1810), 2 Taunt. 301; Warre v. Miller (1825), 4 B. & Cr. 538.

(a) Per Patteson, J., in Brown v. Tayleur (1835), 4 A. & E. 248.

(b) Uhde v. Walters (1811), 3 Camp. 16.

(c) Robertson v. Money (1824), Ry. & M. 75. In a previous case the Court had held the evidence insufficient to establish this construction. Robertson v. Clarke (1824), 1 Bing. 445.

648   DURATION OF THE RISK ON SHIP.   [PART I.

Sect. 486a. J., that the liability of the underwriter was under the earlier policy (*d*), though, as is shown by a later decision, the vessel was also at the time of the loss on the voyage described in the second policy (*e*).

Continuance and termination of risk on ship.
Foreign law.

487. The risk on the ship is in all our common voyage policies expressed to continue "until the ship hath moored at anchor twenty-four hours in good safety."

In France the risk is declared by the Code de Commerce to end, unless determined by the contract, when the ship is anchored or moored at her destination (*f*).

According to the codes of some countries the risk on the ship continues either until the ship has entirely discharged her cargo, or for a certain specified number of days after her arrival (*g*).

Alteration proposed by Magens.

Magens, observing that it is impossible in most cases to discharge the cargo in twenty-four hours, recommended the insertion of a clause by which the risk shall be made to continue for twenty-one working days after the ship's commencing to unload (*h*); and a clause prolonging the risk for a given number of days after arrival (usually thirty) is now commonly inserted in voyage policies (*i*). In the absence of a clause of this kind the underwriters are not responsible for any loss that has happened after the ship has once been "moored twenty-four hours in good safety."

What is a "mooring in good safety."

488. The question on the ordinary English policy has generally been what constitutes a mooring in good safety.

The result of the cases appears to be that a ship cannot

(*d*) Kynance SS. Co. *v.* Young (1911), 16 Com. Cas. 123.

(*e*) Reliance Mar. Ins. Co. *v.* Duder, [1913] 1 K. B. 265 (C. A.).

(*f*) Code de Commerce, arts. 328, 341. The law is similar in Spain (Code, arts. 733, 761), and in Portugal (Code, art. 602). The Russian Code (art. 558) makes the risk end when the ship reaches her destination.

(*g*) See the Code of Holland (art. 625), of Belgium (art. 195), and of Germany (art. 823). For the former ordinances of Continental states, see Magens, vol. ii. *passim;* Benecke, System des Assecuranz, c. viii. s. 1, pp. 234—238; Nolte, vol. i. pp. 668—671, ed. 1851.

(*h*) 1 Magens, p. 47.

(*i*) See *infra*, § 495.

CHAP. XVII.]   DURATION OF THE RISK ON SHIP.   649

be considered to have been moored for twenty-four hours in good safety, unless she have been moored for that space of time in the harbour of her port of discharge: (1) in such a state of physical safety that she can keep afloat while her cargo is being unloaded; (2) in such a state of political safety that she shall not have been subjected during that time to any embargo, seizure, or capture on the part of the government of the port or of strangers; (3) under such circumstances as to have had an opportunity of unloading and discharging (*k*).

Sect. 488.

489. The ship must have been for the twenty-four hours moored in a state of physical safety.

1. Physical safety.

A ship arrived at Demerara, her port of destination, a perfect wreck, having received her death-wound at sea, and was with the utmost difficulty kept afloat by lashing her to a hulk, till all the people on board were landed, a few days after which, in an attempt to move her, she sank in the harbour; Lord Kenyon held that the risk under the policy still continued on the ship when she so sank, "for though she arrived at Demerara she was never moored twenty-four hours, nor a moment, in safety" (*l*).

Shawe *v.* Felton.

A ship was insured "at and from London to Calcutta, and for thirty days after arrival"; the words "until she have moored at anchor twenty-four hours in good safety" still remaining part of the policy. While on her voyage she struck on a reef, and thereby suffered such damage that her pumps required to be kept constantly going, and her steering gear was materially injured. In this condition, on the 28th of October, she came to anchor in the harbour of Calcutta, at a place in the river where vessels commonly discharge their cargo, and there she safely completed the discharge of her

Lidgett *v.* Secretan.

(*k*) A better expression would be, "under such circumstances as to have been free to unload and discharge." What is meant is not that there must have been nothing to prevent the immediate discharge of the ship, but that there shall have been no legal obstacle to the discharge, such as one arising from the quarantine regulations of the port. See *post*, § 491.

(*l*) Shawe *v.* Felton (1801), 2 East, 110.

Sect. 489. cargo on the 8th of November, a fire engine being used to pump the water out of her, until she lightened sufficiently to lessen the leak and to place the water under control of the ship's pumps. The ship while in this position was exposed to the perils common to all vessels so anchored, viz., the strong currents and the bore in the Hooghly, aggravated in her case, if she had broken adrift, by the bad condition of her steering gear. She was then placed in a dry dock for repairs, and while there, and after the lapse of twenty-four hours, and more than thirty days in addition, she was destroyed by fire.

It was unnecessary, in the events which had happened, to determine in this case whether under this policy the thirty days were to be reckoned from the arrival of the vessel at Calcutta, or from her having moored at anchor twenty-four hours in good safety (*m*). Bovill, C. J., delivering the judgment, said: "Assuming, then, that the thirty days are to be reckoned from the time of the ship being moored for twenty-four hours in good safety, the question arises, What is the meaning of those words in such a policy? We are of opinion that the meaning is not, as has been contended, that the moorings are safe, but that the words refer to the ship being in safety. The words cannot mean that the vessel is to arrive without any damage or injury whatever from the effects of the voyage; otherwise, the loss of a mast or even a spar, a sail, or rope, though the vessel was perfectly fit to keep not only the river but the sea, would, contrary to all the ordinary meaning of language, prevent her from being considered as in safety. So, on the other hand, the words would not, in our opinion, be satisfied by the vessel arriving and being moored in a sinking state, or as a mere wreck, or by a mere temporary mooring. We think, also, that the mere liability to damage, whether partial or total, during the twenty-four hours, by the occurrence of some or all of the perils insured against, cannot prevent the running of the twenty-four

---

(*m*) See, as to this point, Mercantile Marine Ins. Co. *v.* Titherington (1864), 5 B. & S. 765; 34 L. J. Q. B. 11, *post*, § 495.

hours, because the extension of the period of risk for twenty-four hours, after having moored in good safety, clearly implies that, notwithstanding the safety intended, the ship is liable to partial or total loss by the occurrence of a peril insured against.

". . . . In the present case the vessel, though considerably damaged and leaky, and with one compartment full of water, existed as a ship at the time of her arrival, and she was able to keep afloat, and did keep afloat as a ship more than twenty-four hours after being moored, by exerting the means within the power of the captain. She arrived and moored at the ordinary place for unloading, and was so moored as a ship in the possession or control of her owners for more than twenty-four hours; and she remained as a ship, and in possession of her owners, for more than thirty days after the lapse of the twenty-four hours before described, and until the time of the fire by which she was totally lost." It was therefore held, that the total loss which had occurred was not within the period of risk covered by the outward policy, and that only the average loss was recoverable under it (*n*).

490. The ship must have been for the twenty-four hours in a state of political safety.

2. Political safety.

Minett *v.* Anderson.

An English ship insured from Bilbao to Rouen was, the day after arrival at Rouen, laid under an embargo then existing there against all English ships, and her captain and crew treated as prisoners of war; Lord Kenyon held that the risk on the ship still continued, for she could not be said, under the circumstances, to have been twenty-four hours, or even a minute, moored in safety, having been, immediately she entered the port, to all intents and purposes captured by the French (*o*).

So, where immediately on the ship's arrival at Riga (which was her port of discharge under the policy), her hatches were

Horneyer *v.* Lushington.

(*n*) Lidgett *v.* Secretan (1870), L. R. 5 C. P. 190, 198, 199, 200. See this case considered with reference to another policy on a different point (L. R. 6 C. P. 616), *post*, vol. ii. § 1223.

(*o*) Minett *v.* Anderson (1794), Peake, N. P. R. 277.

Sect. 490. sealed down and her papers sent to St. Petersburg to be examined, on which examination the ship and cargo were seized and afterwards condemned; it was held, that as there had been an incipient seizure immediately on the ship's arrival which ended in condemnation, this was not a mooring twenty-four hours in good safety (*p*).

In the first of these cases a constructive, and in the second an actual, seizure had taken place immediately on the ship's arrival. Our Courts, however, have refused to regard a seizure as having a relation back to the moment of arrival, merely on the ground of the ship's liability to seizure from that moment onward.

Lockyer *v.* Offley.

A ship insured "from Hamburg to London," had rendered herself liable to forfeiture under our revenue laws for smuggling committed during the voyage; she arrived in the port of London on the 1st of September, and was not seized by the revenue officers for the said smuggling till the 27th, having been all that time safe at her moorings in the river Thames. The Court held that the risk in this case was at an end twenty-four hours after the ship's arrival (*q*).

3. Liberty to unload and discharge.

491. The ship must have been so moored as to have had an opportunity of unloading and discharging. Otherwise, whatever time may have elapsed since her arrival, the risk will be deemed to be still continuing.

Waples *v.* Eames.

A ship was moored on the 8th July at a wharf in London, but, that same day, was ordered back into quarantine for a fortnight; she did not go into quarantine till the 30th July, having all the time remained at her moorings; she was burnt on the 23rd August, before she could get permission to leave the quarantine ground.

The Court held that, though so long at her moorings before she ultimately went into quarantine, she had not been there in good safety, which must imply an opportunity of loading and discharging (*r*).

(*p*) Horneyer *v.* Lushington (1812), 15 East, 46.
(*q*) Lockyer *v.* Offley (1786), 1 T. R. 252.
(*r*) Waples *v.* Eames (1746), 2 Str. 1243.

CHAP. XVII.] DURATION OF THE RISK ON SHIP. 653

A ship insured from Sierra Leone to London was ordered into the King's Dock at Deptford, and on the 18th February arrived off the dock gates; not being able then to enter, the captain lashed her to a king's ship outside the gates. Owing to the quantity of ice that had drifted down the river, no attempt could be made to get her in until the 27th of February. On that day, while she was being warped towards the dock, the rope broke and she went ashore and was totally lost. The Court of King's Bench held, that as the captain was ordered to take the ship into the King's Dock, that was her place of discharge, and consequently, as she had never been there, she had not been moored twenty-four hours in good safety, and so the risk continued (s).

<small>Sect. 491.</small>
<small>Samuel v. Royal Exchange Assurance Co.</small>

If, however, the ship be moored in such a place and under such circumstances that she has only to wait till her turn of unloading comes without again unmooring, this is held a mooring in good safety.

A ship insured to London arrived at the wharf where it was intended she should unload, but was laid on the outside of the tier of shipping, there being no room to lay her inside, and remained so moored and lashed to other vessels for seven days, when she was forced adrift by the ice and lost: Lord Kenyon held that she had been moored twenty-four hours in good safety (t).

<small>Angerstein v. Bell.</small>

492. In Samuel v. Royal Exchange Assurance Company, the circumstances showed that the ship had not arrived at her true port of discharge. Where, however, she has once arrived at a port for the purpose of discharging, that will be deemed to be her true port of discharge, although a different port may have been agreed upon in her charter-party.

<small>Ship must have arrived at true port of discharge.</small>

Thus a ship insured from Liverpool to Quebec and back to

<small>Whitwell v. Harrison.</small>

(s) Samuel v. Royal Exch. Co. (1828), 8 B. & Cr. 119. See Stone v. Mar. Ins. Co. of Gothenburg (1876), 1 Ex. D. 81. See also Zacharie v. New Orleans Ins. Co. (1827), 5 Martin, Louisiana R. N. S. 637; and Dickey v. United Ins. Co. (1814), 11 Johns. 358; cited 1 Phillips, s. 968.

(t) Angerstein v. Bell (1795), 1 Park, 54; 1 Marshall, Ins. 263.

Sect. 492. her discharging port in the United Kingdom, and until she had moored at anchor twenty-four hours in good safety, was by her charter-party to take her cargo from Quebec " to Wallasey Pool, on the River Mersey, or as near thereto as she could safely get." She arrived in the Mersey on the 4th September, and was towed up the next morning abreast of Wallasey Pool, where, as she could not enter the port by reason of her great draft of water, the captain anchored, and reported the vessel at Liverpool. He engaged lumpers to unload and discharged the crew. After the deck cargo and a considerable portion of the other cargo had been discharged, the ship, on 14th September, fell over and sustained injury. The captain had always intended to take the vessel into Wallasey Pool with as much of the cargo as she could safely carry. The Court of Exchequer, nevertheless, held that the ship had been moored twenty-four hours in safety, and consequently that the underwriters were not liable (u).

Duration of risk without ordinary clause.

493. If the twenty-four hours' clause were struck out of the policy, the risk on the ship would still continue until her safe arrival at her port of destination, but would cease immediately on her being at her moorings (x).

Termination of risk where there is no cargo to discharge.

494. Where the ship is not proceeding to the *terminus ad quem* to discharge cargo, but for other purposes, the question where the risk ends may be one of fact, depending on usage with reference to the voyage. Thus, where a ship insured to the Mauritius and for thirty days after arrival, anchored at the entrance of the harbour, seeking freight, at a place where

---

(u) Whitwell v. Harrison (1848), 2 Ex. 127; 18 L. J. Ex. 465; approved in the United States in Bramhall v. Sun Ins. Co. (1870), 104 Mass. 510.

(x) Anonymous case (1685), Skinner's R. 243; see also the American case of Dickey v. United Ins. Co. (1814), 11 Johnson's Cases, 358, cited 1 Phillips, Ins. s. 968.

"I quite agree with the statement in Arnould, that where there is no clause as to mooring in good safety for any given time, if a vessel got to port, and was at moorings waiting her turn to unload, she would have finished her voyage": per Bramwell, B., in Stone v. Marine Ins. Co., Ocean, Ltd. of Gothenburg (1876), 1 Ex. D. 81, 85.

CHAP. XVII.] DURATION OF THE RISK ON SHIP. 655

vessels usually anchored for that purpose, the jury found that the ship had arrived at the place where the voyage ended, and the Court of Exchequer upheld the verdict (*y*).

Sect. 494.

495. The risk is frequently prolonged by express stipulation in the policy beyond the usual period of twenty-four hours.

Express prolongation of risk beyond the twenty-four hours.

Thus, a ship was insured, by a clause in writing, to any port in the Pacific Ocean, and during thirty days' stay in her last port of discharge. The printed twenty-four hours' clause remained in the policy. The ship arrived at her last port at 7 p.m. on the 25th of May, and was lost at 3.45 a.m. on the 24th of June. The underwriters contended (1) that in computing the thirty days the whole of the 25th of May should be reckoned; (2) that the printed twenty-four hours' clause was superseded by the written thirty days' clause. According to their argument, the 23rd of June was the last day of the risk. Crompton, J., however, said: "We must construe the policy so as to make all the parts of it available, and I cannot see why we should not read it as meaning that the thirty days should run from the expiration of twenty-four hours after the ship had moored at anchor." Cockburn, C. J., concurred, and there was judgment for the assured (*z*).

(*y*) Lindsay *v.* Janson (1859), 4 H. & N. 699; 28 L. J. Ex. 315.

(*z*) Mercantile Marine Ins. Co. *v.* Titherington (1864), 5 B. & S. 735; 34 L. J. Q. B. 11. Such a policy is a time policy engrafted on a voyage policy. Gambles *v.* Ocean Marine Ins. Co. of Bombay (1876), 1 Ex. D. 141; 45 L. J. Ex. 366. Where a ship was insured "while in port thirty days after arrival," Lord Trayner held that the risk ended when the ship left the public dock and was laid up for repairs in a private graving dock in Greenock Harbour, on the ground that she was no longer under the protection nor in the jurisdiction of the port authorities. It became unnecessary on appeal to consider this decision, but Lord Shand expressed a strong opinion that it could not be supported. Hunter *v.* Northern Mar. Ins. Co. (1887), 14 Ct. of Sess. Cas. 4th Ser. 544. In Union Mar. Ins. Co. *v.* Martin (1866), 35 L. J. C. P. 181, the Court of Common Pleas held, on the facts, that an insurance to A., and for thirty days after arrival, was terminated by a new insurance with the same underwriters " at and from A." Cf. Kynance SS. Co. *v.* Young (1911), 16 Com. Cas. 123, where the second policy contained a clause, "risk to commence from expiration of previous policy," and Scrutton, J., held that the earlier policy remained in force.

Sect. 495. In a recent case a ship was insured for a voyage to Algoa Bay "and for thirty days in port after arrival," the printed words "twenty-four hours" in the clause "until she hath there moored at anchor twenty-four hours in good safety" being struck out. The ship was moored in good safety at 11.30 a.m. on the 2nd of August; and the Court of Appeal held, affirming the judgment of Bigham, J., that the words "thirty days" meant thirty consecutive periods of twenty-four hours, beginning at 11.30 a.m. on that day, so that the assured could not recover for a loss which took place at 4.30 p.m. on the 1st of September (*a*).

End of risk when ship insured to an island.

496. When the ship is insured to an island or other district generally, comprising several ports, questions have been raised as to the duration of the outward risk on the ship so insured. This mode of insurance used to be exceedingly common in the West Indian trade. Circumstances which can only be ascertained on arrival may make it expedient for the ship to touch at more or fewer ports, or to visit them in any order which may seem most suitable on the spot.

The outward risk on ships so insured.

It was decided in the time of Lord Mansfield, and has ever since been a clear point in insurance law, that the risk on the outward voyage upon a ship insured to an island terminates immediately after the ship has moored for twenty-four hours in safety at the first port in the island at which she discharges the great bulk of her cargo, and that afterwards, if lost in coasting round the island, it is the underwriters on the homeward policy who are alone liable (*b*).

Nor does it make any difference to the liability of the underwriters under the outward policy on the ship that a small part of the outward cargo is still on board at the time of loss. Thus in Leigh *v.* Mather, as the ship had moored and unloaded the great bulk of her outward cargo at Montego Bay, in the island of Jamaica, the outward risk on the ship

---

(*a*) Cornfoot *v.* Royal Exchange Ass. Corporation, [1903] 2 K. B. 363; [1904] 1 K. B. 40.

(*b*) Camden *v.* Cowley (1763), 1 W. Bl. 417, 418; Barrass *v.* London Ass. Co. (1782), 1 Park, Ins. 74; 1 Marshall, Ins. 266; Cruickshank *v.* Janson (1810), 2 Taunt. 301.

CHAP. XVII.] DURATION OF THE RISK ON SHIP. 657

was thereby held to be at an end, although a small part was Sect. 496.
sent round as ballast to the port of St. Ann's in the same
island (c).

A ship insured "to Martinique and all or any of the Inglis v.
Windward and Leeward Islands, with liberty to touch at Vaux.
any ports or places whatsoever, to take on board and land
goods, stores," &c., arrived at Martinique, where the captain
disposed of all his outward cargo, except a small quantity
of lime and bricks, with which he sailed for, and arrived at,
Antigua, and there remained for about five weeks, partly, as
he said, to dispose of the remnant of the outward cargo, and
partly to procure a homeward cargo: at the end of this time
she went down in a hurricane, with the lime and bricks still
on board. Lord Ellenborough held the underwriters on the
outward policy not liable for this loss, the risk on the ship
having come to an end, at all events directly the disposal of
the outward cargo at Antigua ceased to be the sole object of
the captain's stay there (d).

A ship was insured for a trading voyage from the West Moore v.
Indies to this country and back, in the following terms: "At Taylor.
and from St. Vincent's, Barbadoes, and all or any other of
the West India Islands (Jamaica and St. Domingo excepted),
to her port or ports of discharge and loading in the United
Kingdom, during her stay there, and thence back again to
Barbadoes and all or any other West India Islands (Jamaica
and St. Domingo excepted), until the ship shall be arrived
at her final port as aforesaid, with liberty to the ship in this
voyage to proceed to and touch and stay at any port or places
whatsoever, and to load and unload goods at all places she
may call at." Having sailed to Liverpool, she took on board
for the return voyage, amongst other things, a quantity of
coals and bricks which in weight formed about one-third of
the whole cargo, but in value not above one-eighteenth. She
arrived at Barbadoes, where she disposed of all the cargo

(c) Leigh v. Mather (1795), 1 Camp. 437.
Marshall, Ins. 266; 1 Esp. 412; (d) Inglis v. Vaux (1813), 3
see also Inglis v. Vaux (1813), 3 Camp. 437.

Sect. 496. loaded on board her at Liverpool, except the coals and bricks; with these on board, and also with some empty sugar casks loaded on board her at Barbadoes, she was ordered to proceed to Berbice for the purpose of bringing back a cargo, when, just before sailing, she was lost by a hurricane off Barbadoes.

There was some doubt on the evidence whether the coals and bricks were on board as ballast, or whether they formed part of the outward cargo, and were intended to be disposed of at Berbice. Lord Denman directed the jury to find for the defendant (*i.e.*, that the risk on the ship was at an end at the time of loss) if they thought that the cargo had been substantially discharged at Barbadoes: the jury thought that it had, and found accordingly for the defendant. The Court held this direction right, and though they seemed to think that the jury had drawn an incorrect conclusion from the facts, refused to disturb the verdict (*e*).

Insurance to an island and a market.

It has been held in the United States that under a policy on ship to any named West India Island, as Barbadoes, " and a market," the ship will be protected in going *bonâ fide* from island to island till her cargo is disposed of (*f*).

Effect of unloading a small part of the cargo.

497. The discharge of a small part of the cargo at an intermediate port does not put an end to the risk. In Leigh *v.* Mather, Lord Kenyon stated (and the special jury seem to have been of the same opinion) that if a ship, insured from A. to B., be obliged to put into an intermediate port of distress, and there dispose of part of her cargo, the risk on the ship does not thereby terminate, but continues until her arrival at some port at which it was originally contemplated that she should discharge her cargo in whole or in part (*g*).

This appears to be a very just rule, and is illustrated and confirmed in the jurisprudence of the United States.

Thus, where a ship was insured from the United States

(*e*) Moore *v.* Taylor (1834), 1 A. & E. 25.

(*f*) Maxwell *v.* Robinson (1806), 1 Johnson, R. 333, cited 1 Phillips, Ins. s. 960. So, Deblois *v.* Ocean Ins. Co. (1835), 16 Pick. (Mass.) 303.

(*g*) Leigh *v.* Mather (1795), 1 Esp. 412.

to Europe, and back "to her port of discharge in the United States," it was held that the landing of 150 boxes of lemons at New York, a port into which the ship had put to wait for orders, the lemons being in a perishing state and likely to be spoiled, did not make New York the port of discharge under this policy, so as to terminate there the risk on the ship (*h*). Where a ship, under the same form of policy, having put into New York for orders, and being directed to proceed up the Connecticut River to Middletown, necessarily landed about 3,000 bushels of salt into lighters at New York to be carried up to Middletown, and then herself proceeded thither with the residue of her cargo, the same Court held that, notwithstanding this necessary discharge of part of the cargo there, New York was only the port of arrival, and not the port of discharge, and therefore that the risk continued to Middletown (*i*).

Sect. 497.

498. From these cases it is evidently not the fact of unloading at any port into which the ship runs in the course of the voyage which puts an end to the risk on the ship, when insured either generally to an island or country, or to her port or ports of discharge. It is not until she has moored twenty-four hours in good safety at a port at which she was intended to unload, and at which the master actually breaks bulk for the purpose of unloading either the whole or the greater part of her cargo, that the risk on the ship will be held to terminate.

Result.

If, indeed, the port into which she puts be one to which she was originally destined, then, if she be lost after having moored there twenty-four hours in good safety, the risk on the ship will no doubt be at an end, even although she has not actually broken bulk, but be only preparing to unload her cargo at the time of the loss.

On the other hand, if the ship enter a port with only a contingent purpose to unload there, if circumstances should

---

(*h*) Sage *v*. Middletown Ins. Co. (1814), 1 Connecticut R. 239; 1 Phillips, Ins. s. 962.

(*i*) King *v*. Middletown Ins. Co. (1814), 1 Connecticut R. 184; 1 Phillips, Ins. s. 962.

Sect. 498. render it expedient, it has been decided in the United States that such port shall not be deemed her port of discharge, so as to terminate the risk on the ship, by her mooring there for twenty-four hours in good safety. Thus, a vessel insured "to her port of discharge in the United States," put into Savannah, where the master intended to discharge his cargo if the market was favourable; but not finding it so, he resolved to proceed to Boston, and, accordingly, after doing repairs at Savannah, but without breaking bulk there, he sailed for Boston and was lost. The Court in Massachusetts held, apparently on very sound principles, that the risk on the ship, under the circumstances, continued to Boston (*k*). But where the insurance was to "Bilbao or a port of discharge," and the ship had put into Bilbao and discharged part of her cargo and then sailed to Lisbon: it was held in the United States that the outward risk ended at Bilbao (*l*).

Law of France as to end of risk in the West India trade.

499. The general rule in France as to the duration of the outward and commencement of the homeward risk on a ship insured for the West India trade seems to be substantially the same as our own, viz., that the risk on the ship under the outward policy continues till her arrival at the port of substantial discharge, and cannot be extended beyond that, merely because an inconsiderable portion of the outward cargo may still be on board after she has sailed from that port, or at the time of loss (*m*).

As it seems to be repugnant to French law that the outward and homeward policies on ship should be concurrent, Emerigon proceeds to consider what rules there are for ascertaining when the loss on the ship is at the risk of the outward and when at that of the homeward insurers (*n*). No such

---

(*k*) Lapham *v*. Atlas Ins. Co. (1833), 24 Pick. Mass. R. 1. See 1 Phillips, Ins. s. 962; 3 Kent, Com. p. 309; see also Coolidge *v*. Gray (1812), 8 Mass. R. 527, cited 1 Phillips, Ins. s. 962.

(*l*) Stevens *v*. Beverley Ins. Co. (1820), cited 1 Phillips, s. 963. "The plain meaning of the expression," said the Chief Justice, "is to Bilbao or some other port of discharge."

(*m*) 2 Emerigon, c. xiii. s. 18, p. 108.

(*n*) See 2 Emerigon, c. xiii. s. 20; see also 3 Boulay-Paty, Droit Mar. tit. x. s. 9, tom. iii. pp. 423—426.

CHAP. XVII.] DURATION OF THE RISK ON SHIP. 661

principle exists in the law of England; so that if the outward **Sect. 499.**
policy be "until moored twenty-four hours in good safety,"
and the homeward policy be "at and from" the same port,
both policies may well be concurrent during the twenty-four
hours (*o*).

500. Questions have arisen as to the duration of the risk **Insurance to "port of**
on the ship when she is insured "to her port of discharge," **discharge."**
or "to her port or ports of discharge," or to a named place
"and her port of discharge," or "to her final port of discharge or destination."

In one of the earlier English cases it was said that the
ship's port of discharge means that at which it was originally
intended that the goods should be delivered (*p*); and it has
been held in the United States, apparently on good grounds,
that the risk on the ship under an insurance "to her port of
discharge" (in the singular) terminates twenty-four hours
after she has moored in safety at the port, where, in pursuance of the original intentions of the parties to the policy,
she first breaks bulk for the purpose of discharging her
cargo (*q*).

Where the insurance is to her "port or ports of discharge," **"Port or**
in the alternative, the duration of the risk is not confined to **ports of discharge."**
the first port at which she breaks bulk, and discharges
cargo (*r*). According to Arnould's view, the risk would be
extended until twenty-four hours after her arrival at that

(*o*) See Mar. Ins. Act, 1906, Sched. I., rule 3 (b), *ante*, § 475; Haughton *v.* Empire Marine Ins. Co. (1866), L. R. 1 Ex. 206, 210, 211.

(*p*) Clason *v.* Simmonds (1741), cited 6 T. R. 533. See, however, Kynance SS. Co. *v.* Young, *infra*, note (*r*).

(*q*) Coolidge *v.* Gray (1812), 8 Mass. R. 527; 1 Phillips, s. 962.

(*r*) See Kynance SS. Co. *v.* Young (1911), 16 Com. Cas. 123. In that case the charter-party provided for a discharge at one port, but the shipowner and charterer afterwards agreed that the cargo should be discharged at two ports; and Scrutton, J., held that a loss while the ship was on her way from the first to the second port was covered by a policy to "port or ports of discharge."

Sect. 500. port, where, in fact, she substantially discharged her cargo, *i.e.*, the great bulk of it (*s*).

Final port of discharge.

501. This is unquestionably the rule when the ship is insured "to her final port of discharge," as the following cases sufficiently prove:—

Moffatt *v.* Ward.

A ship, insured "till her safe arrival at her last port of discharge in the East Indies or China," unloaded all her cargo at Madras, and was afterwards lost on her way to Bengal: the Court held that the risk on the ship was at an end at the time of the loss, for by the true interpretation of the policy, the last port of discharge was not that where the ship might have been originally destined to discharge any part of her cargo, but that where she actually did discharge the whole of it (*t*).

In this case the whole cargo had been discharged at Madras: in that which follows only a part of the cargo was unloaded there, and the residue, which was intended for an ulterior port, was still on board at the time of the loss.

Preston *v.* Greenwood.

A ship insured "from London to Madras and Bengal, or the ship's last port of discharge of her Europe cargo beyond the Cape of Good Hope," was, as the underwriters knew at the time of subscribing the policy, destined for China: on arriving at Madras she unloaded a considerable part of her cargo there, but still had on board all that part of it which had been originally destined for China, when she perished by a hurricane in Madras roads. Lord Mansfield held that the risk, under these circumstances, continued till the ship's arrival at China (*u*).

Substituted port where it is illegal to enter "last port of discharge."

502. If a ship insured to port or ports "until arrived at her last port of discharge" elects to put into some other port because it would be illegal by the laws of war to continue her voyage to the port of original destination, and disposes of a

---

(*s*) 2nd ed. p. 516; and see *ante*, § 498.

(*t*) Moffatt *v.* Ward (1784), 4 Dougl. 29, n. (*a*), 31, n. (*b*).

(*u*) Preston *v.* Greenwood (1784), 4 Dougl. 28, 33; see also Moore *v.* Taylor (1834), 1 A. & E. 25.

CHAP. XVII.]   DURATION OF THE RISK ON SHIP.   663

considerable part of her cargo in the substituted port, the risk   Sect. 502.
on the ship ends after she has moored there twenty-four hours,
even though the captain may not at the time of loss have
entirely abandoned the intention of ultimately proceeding to
the place of his original destination.

A ship was insured "at and from London to any port or   Brown v.
ports in the river Plate, until her arrival at her last port   Vigne.
of discharge in the river Plate." There are three ports
in the river Plate, which are reached in the following
order by a ship arriving from England:—1. Maldonado;
2. Monte Video; 3. Buenos Ayres. The captain, on sailing
from England, had intended to proceed to Buenos Ayres, but
on his arrival in the river Plate, learning that Buenos Ayres
was in the hands of the Spaniards, then at war with this
country, he sailed past Maldonado, and put into Monte Video,
which was then occupied by the English. His intention was
to land and sell his whole cargo there, and finish the voyage
at that place if he found the markets favourable; finding the
sale, however, duller than he expected, he had not given up
all thoughts of proceeding on to Buenos Ayres for a market
with that portion of the cargo which he could not sell at
Monte Video, when his ship was fouled in Monte Video
harbour and received the damage, to recover which the underwriter was now sued under this policy. The Court held that
the plaintiff could not recover, the risk on the ship having
come to an end after her being safely moored for twenty-four
hours in Monte Video (*x*).

In the course of the argument Bayley, J., intimated that
the words "last port of discharge" must mean "the last
practicable friendly port of discharge"; just as in an insurance on a ship "from Liverpool to any of the Windward
or Leeward Isles," Lord Kenyon had previously held that
the meaning of such policy must be to any of such isles as
were friendly; for that a hostile port could not be in the
contemplation of the parties at the time the policy was
effected (*y*).

(*x*) Brown *v.* Vigne (1810), 12   (*y*) Neilson *v.* Delacour (1798),
East, 283.   2 Esp. 619.

Sect. 502.

It will be observed that in this case the port originally contemplated as the final port of discharge was in a state of open hostility at the time the vessel reached the river Plate, so that it would have been absolutely illegal for her to have proceeded to such port: this is very different from the case of a mere temporary obstruction, or one in which, though there might be danger, yet there would be no illegality in proceeding to the final port; and this constitutes the point of distinction between this case and that of Oliverson *v.* Brightman (*z*).

Insurance to "final port."

503. A policy on ship to ports in a country or district may, of course, be so worded that the risk does not end at the last port of discharge.

Crocker *v.* Sturge.

A ship was insured from Australia "to any port or ports, place or places on the West Coast of South America .... while there and thence" to the United Kingdom. The underwriters re-insured the earlier portion of their risk by a policy "to any port or ports, place or places in any order on the West Coast of South America and for thirty days after arrival in final port, however employed." The ship, after discharging her cargo at a port on the West Coast, was lost on her way to a loading port on the West Coast. Mathew, J., held that the words "port or ports" and "final port" were not limited to ports of discharge, and that the risk still endured at the time of the loss (*a*).

"To any port or ports, however employed." Crocker *v.* General Insurance Co.

In another policy of re-insurance on the same risk, the clause was "to any port or ports, place or places, in any order on the West Coast of South America, and for thirty days in port after arrival however employed or until sailing on next voyage, whichever may first occur." The Court of Appeal held, affirming the decision of Mathew, J., that the loss was also covered by this policy. They considered that the words "however employed" applied to the words "to any port or ports," as well as to the words "for thirty days in port after

---

(*z*) Oliverson *v.* Brightman (1846), 8 Q. B. 781; *ante*, § 467.
(*a*) Crocker *v.* Sturge, [1897] 1 Q. B. 330; 66 L. J. Q. B. 514; Spalding *v.* Crocker (1897), 2 Com. Cas. 189.

arrival," and therefore that "port or ports" included loading ports for the next voyage as well as ports of discharge (*b*). Sect. 503.

504. If a ship entirely abandons the voyage insured, and finally gives up all hopes of proceeding to the port of her original destination, the risk on the ship is at an end immediately that determination is definitely formed. If, on the other hand, the ship, yielding to the irresistible force of present circumstances, merely puts back or lies by for a time with the intention of ultimately proceeding to the original terminus, she is deemed still to be on the voyage insured, and the risk continues till she arrives at the final terminus. In order, however, that this should be so, the obstruction must be only temporary in its nature; and the ultimate point of destination must continue the same. Final abandonment of intention to proceed to port of original destination.

A ship insured to a port in the Baltic, finding it blocked up with ice, took shelter for the winter in a place as near to it as she could safely go, and waited till the spring, when, on the first thaw, she sailed for it again; the risk on the ship was held to continue till her arrival there (*c*).

But where a ship insured from London to Revel, hearing of an embargo at Revel, sailed back from the Baltic, by orders of a British man-of-war, to Copenhagen Roads, and then, entirely abandoning her voyage, accompanied the fleet to England; Lord Ellenborough nonsuited the plaintiff on the ground that the risk had terminated under this policy, at all events, directly the ship had sailed back to England from Copenhagen Roads (*d*). Blackenhagen *v.* London Assurance Co.

His Lordship, however, remarked, that had the ship been coming home as the best means of getting finally to Revel, and had there been a possibility of her accomplishing that object when the loss happened, she might still have been considered in the course of the voyage insured; but that all

---

(*b*) Crocker *v.* General Ins. Co. of Trieste (1897), 2 Com. Cas. 233; in the C. A., 3 Com. Cas. 22.

(*c*) See Blackenhagen *v.* London Ass. Co. (1808), 1 Camp. 454, 455;

and Brown *v.* Vigne (1810), 12 East, 286.

(*d*) Blackenhagen *v.* London Ass. Co. (1808), 1 Camp. 454.

Sect. 504.

Parkin v. Tunno.

thought of completing her original voyage seemed to have been abandoned when she sailed home from Copenhagen with the fleet (e).

In such cases, in fact, the risk may be held to continue on the ship during the whole period in which she can be fairly considered as taking measures with a view to ultimately arriving at the port of destination; but she will not be protected if, when turned away or forced to desist from proceeding to her original port, from its being in the hands of the enemy, she forthwith prosecutes a new voyage to the nearest friendly port, even though it be a voyage of necessity (f).

Duration prolonged by usage.

505. The duration of the risk may be prolonged by usage, to illustrate which principle reference may still be made to the cases on the trade of the East India Company's ships. By the usual course of that trade, the ships on arriving out were liable to be employed, at the discretion of the different presidential governments, in intermediate voyages, or in what was called the country trade, the charter-parties giving permission to prolong the ship's stay for a year or more. The policies were generally adapted to this usage and were uniformly held to cover all intermediate voyages in the Indian seas, unless restricted by special clauses (g). So great, indeed, was the influence of usage in the construction of these policies that a policy on a company's ship containing a liberty to touch and stay, but not to trade, would yet protect the ship while engaged on one and even a second country voyage for trading purposes (h).

Preston v. Greenwood.

It was at one time a rule in the East India trade that a voyage to China was not to be held included in a policy on a company's ship, unless China were expressly named in the

---

(e) Blackenhagen v. London Ass. Co. (1808), 1 Camp. 455.

(f) Parkin v. Tunno (1809), 11 East, 22. The law of the United States seems to be different: see post, § 808.

(g) Salvador v. Hopkins (1765), 3 Burr. 1707; Gregory v. Christie (1784), 3 Dougl. 419; 1 Park, 104; 1 Marshall, Ins. 273.

(h) Farquharson v. Hunter (1785), 1 Park, 105; 1 Marshall, Ins. 274; Gregory v. Christie, quâ supra.

instrument; where, however, it clearly appeared that the ship's destination for China was publicly known at the India House, and that the premium was the same as it would have been on a China voyage—although the insurance in terms was only "from London to Madras and Bengal, or the ship's last port of discharge of her Europe cargo beyond the Cape of Good Hope"—Lord Mansfield held, that although the word China was not introduced into the policy, yet, as the words in themselves certainly extended to China, the risk under the circumstances must be considered as continuing on the ship till her arrival in China, for the underwriters must clearly be considered to have contemplated the ship's proceeding thither when they subscribed the policy (*i*).

Sect. 505.

506. If a new *terminus ad quem* be substituted for the original one by a memorandum indorsed on the policy, the risk will terminate there.

In the case of a ship reinsured "from Liverpool to Philadelphia and back to the United Kingdom," it was found that a large part of her homeward cargo had been sold by the charterer to persons in Antwerp, and the underwriters, at request of the assured, indorsed the policy thus: "In consideration of an additional premium of 7s. 6d. per cent., it is hereby agreed to allow the vessel to go to Antwerp." The vessel, without calling at the United Kingdom, had arrived in the outer dock of Antwerp when the captain was ordered by telegraph to Leith. He sailed for Leith as soon as he could, and on his way thither his ship was totally lost by perils of the seas. It was held that the memorandum construed with the policy might mean to Antwerp by way of the United Kingdom, but whether this or not, that Antwerp was certainly to be taken to be the final port of her destination, and consequently that the ship was not protected by the policy at the time of her loss (*k*).

Substitution of a new *terminus ad quem* by agreement.

Stone *v.* Mar. Ins. Co., Ocean Limited of Gothenburg.

(*i*) Preston *v.* Greenwood (1784), 4 Dougl. 28. See, however, *ante*, § 57. Buller, J., had on a former trial directed the jury to find for the defendants.

(*k*) Stone *v.* Marine Ins. Co., Ocean Ltd. of Gothenburg (1876), 1 Ex. D. 81.

Sect. 507.

Usage to cover ship's furniture on shore.

507. Generally speaking, the underwriter on a sea policy only insures against sea risks, and consequently is not responsible for any loss that may take place on shore. Usage, however, in this, as in all other cases, is the great regulator of the rights of parties under policies of insurance; and sect. 2 (1) of the Marine Insurance Act, 1906, declares that a contract of marine insurance may, by usage of trade, be extended so as to protect the assured against losses on any land risk which may be incidental to any sea voyage. Thus, if it can be shown that ship's furniture or stores are regularly landed at certain parts of a voyage by the usage of trade, they are as much within the protection of a policy on ship while thus put on shore as when on board the ship herself (*l*).

Insurance "at" a place only.

508. An insurance on a ship "at" a port or place in relation to a voyage is not common. In a recent case, however, the question whether the risk had attached arose on a policy of re-insurance expressed to be "at and from July 1, 1904, until August 31, 1904, ... whilst at port or ports, place or places in New Caledonia," the original insurance being for a voyage from New Zealand to Nehone, New Caledonia, and while there and thence to Grangemouth. A loss occurred while the ship was proceeding through Gazelle Passage on the coast of New Caledonia, on her way to Nehone. Walton, J., held that the assured could not recover (*m*).

"Port" or "harbour" policies.

Ships are frequently insured at low premiums against harbour risks by policies called "port" or "harbour" policies.

A ship was insured by such a policy for a week "while at Leith." Evidence was given to prove that it was the custom at Lloyd's to treat "port" policies as ceasing to attach when the vessel unmoors with the intention of proceeding on her voyage. Accordingly, Mathew, J., held that the words

---

(*l*) Pelly *v.* Royal Exch. Ass. Co. (1757), 1 Burr. 341; Brough *v.* Whitmore (1791), 4 T. R. 206.

(*m*) Maritime Ins. Co. *v.* Alianza Ins. Co., [1907] 2 K. B. 660.

"while at Leith" were equivalent to "while lying at the port of Leith," and that the risk terminated when the ship unmoored. The learned judge also intimated that a different construction might be put on the words if it could be shown that the underwriter intended to cover a larger risk (*n*).

In a later case Hamilton, J., held, after admitting evidence as to the meaning of "port risk," that in the absence of express words to the contrary, "the risk under a port risk policy ceases when the ship, being fitted and equipped for sea, and possessed of her clearances, crew, and, if necessary her cargo, commences to navigate upon her voyage, and no longer remains moored in the port in the course of preparing for the voyage" (*o*).

509. The question of the duration of the risk in a fire policy on a ship arose in a case in which the facts were as follow:—The policy was for a certain time on a steamship lying in the Victoria Docks, London, with liberty to go into a dry dock. In order to enable the ship to enter the dry dock, it was necessary to remove part of her paddle wheels. When she left the dry dock she was moored in the river for ten days, for the purpose of having her paddle wheels replaced before returning to the Victoria Docks, and before this operation was completed she was burnt in the river. The paddle wheels could have been replaced in the Victoria Docks, but it was cheaper to do this in the river, and there was evidence that in similar cases it was usual to replace them outside the docks. In the docks there were appliances for extinguishing fire, and precautions were taken against fire, which were wanting in the river. The House of Lords held, affirming the decisions of the Court of Common Pleas and of the Exchequer Chamber, that the assured could not recover. The Lords and the judges were almost unanimous in considering

---

(*n*) Hunting *v.* Boulton (1895), 1 Com. Cas. 120. A policy on a vessel in harbour "while securely moored" was held by Lord Ellenborough to allow of her being moved in the harbour. Anon. *v.* Westmore (1808), 6 Esp. 109.

(*o*) Mersey Mutual Underwriting Assn. *v.* Poland (1910), 15 Com. Cas. 205.

Sect. 509. that under the liberty to go into dry dock the ship was protected during the transit to and from the dry dock, but it was held that this protection could not be extended to protect her during her stay in the river for a different purpose (*p*). In the Exchequer Chamber Blackburn, J., expressed the opinion that there was the following distinction between an ordinary voyage policy and such a fire policy as this one; while in the case of a voyage policy a deviation destroys the policy, the learned judge thought that there was no reason why the ship should not be taken out of the place to which the policy attached and so cease for a time to be covered, and be then brought back to it, when the risk would again attach (*q*).

Inception and duration of the risk on freight.

510. The object of an insurance on freight is to protect the shipowner from being deprived, by any of the perils insured against, of the benefits he would otherwise derive from the affreightment of his ship or the carriage of his goods or those of another.

Distinction between inception of insurable interest and of the risk.

The duration of the risk on freight is a matter which, as we have already pointed out, is often confounded with the different question whether the assured had at the time of the loss an insurable interest in freight. Whether there be an insurable interest is a matter independent of the policy. If at the time of the loss the assured had no insurable interest, he cannot maintain an action however the policy be worded. If on the other hand he had an insurable interest, the question arises whether the loss occurred within the limits of place or time fixed by the policy (*r*).

(*p*) Pearson *v.* Commercial Union Ass. Co. (1863), 15 C. B. N. S. 304; 33 L. J. C. P. 85; in the Exch. Ch. (1873), L. R. 8 C. P. 548; in the House of Lords (1876), 1 App. Cas. 498.

(*q*) L. R. 8 C. P. 549. Another case on the continuance of the risk in a fire policy is Grant *v.* Ætna Insurance Co. (1862), 15 Moo. P. C. 516. The insurance was for twelve months on a steamship "now lying in Tait's Dock, Montreal, and intended to navigate the St. Lawrence and Lakes." The ship never left the dock and was burnt after being there for eleven months, and the loss was held to be covered.

(*r*) Arnould, in the chapter on insurable interest, confined himself to a statement of general principles, and in the present chapter discussed the question of insurable interest in freight at great length.

Thus, where a policy was effected on freight "at and from any port or ports of loading on the west coast of South America" to the United Kingdom, and the policy also contained a clause saying that the freight was to be covered "from the time of the engagement of the goods," the Court of Appeal held, that notwithstanding the "engagement" clause, the assured could not recover for a loss of freight due to the loss of the ship before she reached her first loading port in South America (*s*).

Sect. 510.

511. When the freight which is the subject of the policy is freight proper, *i.e.*, the price to be paid to the shipowner by the merchant for the carriage of goods in the ship on arrival, Arnould stated that the following rule (as to the commencement of the insurable interest and the attachment of the risk) was established by the cases (*t*):—"Where a cargo has been contracted for and is ready to be shipped on board at the time of the loss, and the ship, being otherwise in a condition to receive the cargo, is only prevented from doing so by the intervention of the perils insured against, the policy on freight attaches, and the underwriters are liable for the loss of the whole freight which would have been earned on the voyage, even though no part of the cargo has ever been shipped at all" (*u*).

Commencement of risk on fraight proper.

It has been submitted, after an examination of the cases on which the learned author relied, that there is an insurable

---

Maclachlan adhered to this arrangement. In this edition, as in the two preceding ones, it has been thought advisable to deal fully with the question of insurable interest in its proper place, and much of the matter which in earlier editions was in this chapter has been transferred to that on insurable interest. See *ante*, §§ 262—279.

(*s*) The Copernicus (C. A.), [1896] P. 237; see also Jones *v.* Neptune Marine Ins. Co. (1872), L. R. 7 Q. B. 702.

(*t*) 2nd ed. p. 524; see also 2nd ed. pp. 288, 289, cited *ante*, § 266.

(*u*) The authorities cited are Montgomery *v.* Eggington (1789), 3 T. R. 362; Truscott *v.* Christie (1820), 2 Brod. & B. 320; Parke *v.* Hebson (*circa* 1820), cited *ibid.* 326; Warre *v.* Miller (1825), 4 B. & Cr. 538; Flint *v.* Flemyng (1830), 1 B. & Ad. 45; Devaux *v.* J'Anson (1839), 5 Bing. N. C. 519.

Sect. 511. interest in freight proper when the assured, having a valid contract for freight, has taken steps towards the earning of the freight (v), and the editors also submitted in the last edition before the Marine Insurance Act, 1906, came into force, that according to the later authorities the risk attached at the same time (x). It has also been suggested that there may perhaps be an insurable interest in freight as soon as a contract under which freight will be earned has been concluded (y).

"At and from" the place of loading.

The question of the attachment of the risk has been settled in accordance with Arnould's statement of the law, by the Marine Insurance Act, 1906, Rule 3 (d) in the First Schedule being as follows:—

> Where freight, other than chartered freight, is payable without special conditions and is insured "at and from" a particular place, the risk attaches *pro ratâ* as the goods or merchandise are shipped; provided that if there be cargo in readiness which belongs to the shipowner, or which some other person has contracted with him to ship, the risk attaches as soon as the ship is ready to receive such cargo (z).

Commencement of risk on freight of shipowner's own goods.

512. The only difference made by this rule between an insurance on freight proper and one on the freight of goods belonging to the shipowner himself is that as the shipowner cannot have a contract for the carriage of the goods, he must

---

(v) *Ante*, §§ 268—271, 278, 279a.

(x) See *ante*, §§ 270, 271.

(y) *Ante*, § 279.

(z) Mr. Arthur Cohen says: "This rule, if interpreted according to the ordinary meaning of the words, overrules certain cases" (he cites Parke v. Hebson, Truscott v. Christie, Warre v. Miller, Devaux v. J'Anson, Flint v. Flemyng, *supra*, note (u)) "which decided that, although the ship be not ready to receive the goods, the policy will, nevertheless, cover the freight in respect of these, if there be a binding contract for the shipment of them. It remains to be seen," he adds, "whether the Courts will give a very strained interpretation to the word 'ready' by holding that the goods are ready to be shipped and the ship ready to receive them, if, but for the perils insured against, the goods would in the ordinary course of things have been shipped on board the vessel": Halsbury's Laws of England, vol. xvii. art. 775.

CHAP. XVII.] DURATION OF THE RISK ON FREIGHT. 673

instead thereof have goods of his own in readiness to be shipped (*a*). Sect. 512.

In Devaux *v.* J'Anson (*b*) the policy was on freight "at and from Calcutta or any port or place on the Coromandel coast." The ship, having been repaired at Coringa, on the Coromandel coast, was about to be floated out of dry dock in order to be loaded in the river there, when she was lost. At that time the cargo, belonging to the shipowner, was lying in warehouse seven miles away, ready to be brought to the ship. It was argued that the shipowner could not recover for a loss of freight, because the ship was not ready to receive the goods and the goods were not ready to be put on board; but the Court held that the risk had already attached. All that they thought necessary to determine with regard to the cargo was "that it must have become the property of the parties insured by a contract made with a view to its being sent on board and actually in a state of readiness, reference being had to the nature and description of the voyage insured, to be put on board when the ship arrives at the place of deposit" (*c*). If readiness to receive the cargo in Rule 3 (d) implies that the ship must actually be in a position to take the cargo on board, this decision is not consistent with the rule (*d*). Devaux *v.* J'Anson.

513. When the interest insured as freight is chartered freight, *i.e.*, a fixed sum stipulated to be paid to the shipowner by the terms of a charter-party for the use of his ship (or part of it) on an entire voyage therein described, the rule as to the attachment of the risk was thus stated by Arnould: Commencement of risk on chartered freight.

(*a*) See *ante*, §§ 268, 279.
(*b*) (1839), 5 Bing. N. C. 519.
(*c*) *Ibid.* p. 539. In Flint *v.* Flemyng (1830), 1 B. & Ad. 45, the assured also claimed for a loss of freight on his own goods; their situation at the time of the loss is not stated in the report.
(*d*) The Court did indeed say that the ship was at the time of the loss quite ready to go to sea, and to receive the cargo on board. Yet she was not then, in fact, able to take the cargo on board, and, as the loss shows, was liable to be prevented from ever reaching her actual loading place. See, however, as to the meaning of "readiness" in relation to a contract of affreightment, Leonis SS. Co., Ltd. *v.* Rank, Ltd., [1908] 1 K. B. 499. See also note (*z*), *supra*.

A.—VOL. I. 43

Sect. 513. "In such cases, as the so-called freight is secured to the shipowner by one entire contract for the whole voyage, it is clear that his inchoate right to such freight accrues from the very inception of the voyage described in the charter-party; and consequently, if commensurately insured, his risk under a policy on such freight commences from the same period" (*e*).

A series of cases, most of which have already been discussed in the chapter on insurable interest, shows clearly that the risk under the policy attaches under these circumstances (*f*).

Foley v. United, &c. Insurance Co. of Sydney.

Thus where a ship was chartered to proceed from Calcutta to Mauritius, and from Mauritius to Akyab, and at Akyab to load a cargo for the United Kingdom, a policy on this freight "at and from Mauritius" was held to attach as soon as the ship arrived at Mauritius; for there was already an inception of the charter-party voyage, and therefore an insurable interest, when the ship sailed from Calcutta (*g*).

Of course, if the insurance be "from" a place only, the policy cannot attach until the ship breaks ground on the voyage insured (*h*).

Rankin v. Potter.

A previous voyage, on which freight is being earned, is frequently in terms incorporated into the chartered voyage. If the policy or freight be intended to cover the freight to be earned on the latter voyage, it will no doubt sometimes be necessary to describe the freight specifically. Thus, in Rankin *v.* Potter (*i*), it was agreed by charter-party that the "Sir William Eyre," then on a voyage from the Clyde to New Zealand, should proceed to New Zealand with a cargo

---

(*e*) 2nd ed. p. 532.

(*f*) Thompson *v.* Taylor (1795), 6 T. R. 478; Atty *v.* Lindo (1805), 1 B. & P. N. R. 236; Horncastle *v.* Suart (1806), 7 East, 400; Mackenzie *v.* Shedden (1810), 2 Camp. 431; Davidson *v.* Willasey (1813), 1 M. & S. 312; Ellis *v.* Lafone (1853), 8 Ex. 546; 22 L. J. Ex. 124; Foley *v.* United Fire and Marine Ins. Co. of Sydney (Exch. Ch.) (1870), L. R. 5 C. P. 155; Rankin *v.* Potter (1873), L. R. 6 H. L. 83. See *ante*, §§ 272—274.

(*g*) Foley *v.* United Fire and Marine Ins. Co. of Sydney (Exch. Ch.) (1870), L. R. 5 C. P. 155.

(*h*) Mar. Ins. Act, 1906, Sched. I. rule 2, *ante*, § 473.

(*i*) (1873), L. R. 6 H. L. 83.

CHAP. XVII.] DURATION OF THE RISK ON FREIGHT.

for owner's benefit, and thence to Calcutta, and there load a cargo for Liverpool for the charterer. The owners of the ship effected a policy on homeward chartered freight " at and from the Clyde to New Zealand," and it was not disputed that there was an insurable interest, and that the risk had attached, during the voyage to New Zealand. It is, however, apprehended that if the policy had been simply on freight, it would have covered the outward and not the homeward freight.

Sect. 513.

The case of Barber *v.* Fleming (*k*) has established that there may be an insurable interest in chartered freight before the inception of the voyage described in terms in the charter-party. The policy was "on freight chartered or otherwise " at and from Bombay to Howland's Island, while there, and thence to the United Kingdom. The ship had been chartered on the 7th of August for a voyage from Howland's Island to the United Kingdom, and was required to be at Howland's Island on the following 1st of June; but the charter-party did not stipulate that she should sail direct. She sailed in ballast from Bombay to Howland's Island and was lost on the voyage thither.

Barber *v.* Fleming.

The Court of Queen's Bench held that the insurable interest in the freight to be earned under the charter-party had commenced, and that the plaintiff could recover (*l*). What the position would have been if the ship had carried a cargo from Bombay to Howland's Island is a question which was raised during the argument and referred to in the judgments; but none of the judges gave a definite opinion thereon.

514. A general rule to be deduced from the decisions, and applicable to all policies on freight, seems to be that the risk attaches as soon as the insurable interest begins, if this be consistent with the description of the voyage in the policy (*m*), provided also in some cases that it may have to

Result.

(*k*) (1869), L. R. 5 Q. B. 59.
(*l*) See *ante*, § 275, where the case is discussed at length.

(*m*) This view seems to underlie the statement of Blackburn, J., in Jones *v.* Neptune Marine Ins. Co.

Sect. 514. appear from the policy, or from the circumstances, that the particular freight was intended to be covered.

The rule laid down by the Marine Insurance Act, 1906, with reference to the attachment of the risk on chartered freight under the ordinary English policy is the following:—

> Where chartered freight is insured "at and from" a particular place, and the ship is at that place in good safety when the contract is concluded, the risk attaches immediately. If she be not there when the contract is concluded, the risk attaches as soon as she arrives there in good safety (*n*).

This rule, it is submitted, must be read subject to Rule 1 in the First Schedule to the Act, which provides that "where the subject-matter is insured 'lost or not lost,' and the loss has occurred before the contract is concluded, the risk attaches unless, at such time, the assured was aware of the loss, and the insurer was not." With this qualification Rule 3 (c) does not conflict with the general rule laid down in the text as the result of the authorities.

Freight of voyage to *terminus a quo* not covered. Bell *v.* Bell.

515. An insurance on freight "at and from" a place does not cover the freight on a voyage terminating at that place, for that freight is not at risk on the voyage described in the policy. Thus when freight was insured at and from Riga to the United Kingdom, and the ship was captured at Riga, it was held that the policy did not cover the freight on the outward voyage to Riga (*o*).

(1872), L. R. 7 Q. B. 706:—"If the freight be in existence, as by the goods being ready to be loaded at the port named, and a peril happens which destroys the ship during the period of the specific voyage over which the policy is intended to apply, then the underwriters are responsible for the loss of freight, although the goods be not put on board; it is enough to prove it to have been in existence, and that it does not rest in mere expectancy and possibility." See also the judgments in Foley *v.* United Fire, &c. Ins. Co. (1870), L. R. 5 C. P. 155. Of course, the risk cannot attach unless the warranty of seaworthiness is satisfied. See *post*, § 686.

(*n*) Mar. Ins. Act, 1906, Sched. I. rule 3 (c).

(*o*) Bell *v.* Bell (1810), 2 Camp 475.

516. In policies on freight, as in all other policies, when the commencement of the risk is made to depend on a certain event, the risk does not attach until the happening of the event.

Sect. 516.
Where commencement of risk depends on a certain event.

A ship was chartered for a voyage from Liverpool to Lagos, and thence with a cargo to the United Kingdom, at a lump sum for the round voyage, and a policy was effected on freight "at and from Lagos," "the insurance to commence on freight from the loading of the goods on board at as above." The ship had arrived at Lagos, and was lost before she had shipped any of her homeward cargo; and it was held that in consequence of the second of the two clauses cited, the first was so modified that the assured could not recover (*p*). If there had been any goods on board at the time of the loss he would have recovered for the freight of those goods (*q*).

Beckett v. West of England Ins. Co.

A policy of reinsurance on chartered freight was effected "lost or not lost, upon freight payable in respect to this present voyage to be performed by the vessel 'Napier,' from Baker's Island to a port of discharge in the United Kingdom; the insurance on the freight beginning from the loading of the vessel." The vessel was wrecked whilst at Baker's Island after she had taken two-thirds of her cargo on board; and the question was, what was the effect of the latter branch of this clause, "beginning from the loading," upon the former describing the insured voyage "from Baker's Island"? The majority of the Court, Mellor and Lush, JJ., held that the loading intended was a complete loading, and that the policy would have attached upon this being completed, although before the vessel sailed from Baker's Island. Blackburn, J., was of the same opinion as to the loading intended being a complete loading, but he was of opinion that the latter part of the clause did not enlarge the effect of the former, and consequently that the policy would not

Jones v. Neptune Marine Ins. Co.

(*p*) Beckett *v.* West of England Ins. Co. (1872), 25 L. T. N. S. 739. See Rigby, L. J.'s, criticism on this decision, [1895] 1 Q. B. 509.

(*q*) Hopper *v.* Wear Marine Ins. Co. (1882), 46 L. T. N. S. 107.

678   DURATION OF THE RISK ON FREIGHT.   [PART I.

Sect. 516.

Where condition as to attachment of risk inapplicable.

Hydarnes SS. Co. v. Indemnity Mutual Mar. Ass. Co.

attach until the vessel sailed on her voyage. By the opinion of the whole Court the assured could not recover (r).

In the following case a clause, which made the risk only attach on the freight of goods loaded at the *terminus a quo*, was rejected as being inapplicable to the voyage insured. The policy was " upon freight of meat at and from Monte Video " to any ports in the River Plate, including the Boca, and thence to the United Kingdom, and was expressly stated to cover any loss occasioned by breaking down of machinery until final sailing of the vessel. By a subsequent clause the insurance was declared to commence " upon the freight and goods or merchandise on board from the loading of the said goods or merchandise on board the said ship or vessel at Monte Video." This clause, except the name Monte Video, was in print. The ship proceeded from Monte Video to the Boca, where a cargo of meat was ready for shipment. At the Boca her refrigerating machinery broke down, so that it became impossible to load the cargo. When the policy was effected both the underwriters and the assured knew that meat was never shipped at Monte Video, where there were no appliances for freezing meat. Under these circumstances the Court of Appeal held that the clause making the commencement of the risk depend on the loading of the meat was inapplicable, and that the policy had attached (s).

The voyage being performed must be that in the policy.

Sellar v. M'Vicar.

517. If the voyage which is being performed at the time of the loss is not covered by the policy, of course the assured cannot recover.

Freight valued at 500*l*. was insured on a voyage " at and from Demerara, Berbice, and any of the Windward and Leeward Islands, to London." By a verbal agreement with a Demerara house, the ship, then in that port, was to carry a cargo of colonial produce for them from Berbice to London, at the current rate of freight, and also take on some bricks

(r) Jones v. Neptune Marine Ins. Co. (1872), L. R. 7 Q. B. 702.

(s) Hydarnes SS. Co. v. Indemnity Mutual Marine Ass. Co., [1895] 1 Q. B. 500.

CHAP. XVII.] DURATION OF THE RISK ON FREIGHT. 679

and planks from Demerara to Berbice on the same terms. The ship was lost while proceeding from Demerara to Berbice with the bricks and planks on board, in virtue of this verbal agreement. The plaintiffs contended that the whole was one entire voyage on which freight was to be earned; but the Court were clearly of opinion that the voyage insured was a voyage at and from Demerara *or* Berbice to London, and that no such voyage had begun at the time of the loss, which took place on a voyage from Demerara to Berbice (*t*).

Sect. 517.

In the following case the contention that an advance of freight was not made in respect of the insured voyage was unsuccessful.

Ellis *v.* Lafone.

By a charter-party made at Monte Video, a vessel was to proceed to the Falkland Island, and thence to Santa Cruz in Patagonia, there to take in a cargo of guano, and to discharge it at a port in Europe; freight at 250*l*. a month, pay for one month to be made when the vessel sailed from the Falkland Islands, the balance at the port of discharge. There was a safe delivery of cargo at the Falklands, and an advance of 250*l*., being one month's freight. She then loaded guano at Santa Cruz and completed the cargo with hides at Monte Video, where a new charter-party, in effect annulling the first, was made, by which the vessel was to proceed to Havre direct with the cargo then on board, freight (at the same rate as by the first charter) to be paid at the port of discharge, after deducting 250*l*. received on account of that charter-party. The vessel sailed and went down at sea a total loss.

In an action by the charterers on a policy, "lost or not lost at and from Monte Video to Havre on 450*l*. freight advanced," it was contended for the underwriters that the plaintiffs could not recover for the advance of 250*l*., on the ground that the sum had been paid in respect of the voyage to the Falkland Islands, and that the money remained no

---

(*t*) Sellar *v.* M'Vicar (1804), 1 B. & P. N. R. 23. The construction put upon the policy may be questionable, but this does not affect the principle of the decision. See Clapham *v.* Cologan (1813), 3 Camp. 382.

Sect. 517. longer at risk after the termination of such voyage. The Court of Exchequer Chamber, however, held the plaintiffs entitled to recover, since that was not a separate sum paid in respect of the voyage to the Falkland Islands, but part of an entire sum payable for the whole voyage insured, which therefore remained at risk till the ship arrived in Havre, her port of discharge in Europe (*u*).

Insurance for part of the voyage.

518. When a ship is going to touch at a port short of that where the cargo is to be landed, the freight may be insured to the intermediate port only. The voyage to that port is not a different voyage from that on which the freight is earned; it is only a part of the larger voyage.

A ship with a cargo for Gothenburg sailed for Portsmouth to call there for convoy. A policy was effected on freight to Portsmouth, and the underwriter was not informed that the ultimate destination of the ship and cargo was Gothenburg. It was held that the assured could recover for a loss which happened before the ship reached Portsmouth (*x*).

Freight of goods loaded at an intermediate port.

519. If freight be insured from one port to another, and the assured, in pursuance of leave granted by the policy, takes goods on board at an intermediate port destined for the *terminus ad quem*, the freight on these goods is covered (*y*). When there is leave to trade at intermediate ports, the freight on any goods taken on board at any of these ports to be carried to any other is no doubt protected; for policies on trading voyages must be liberally construed, and the parties must be taken to have intended to protect such freight.

End of risk on freight.

520. The ordinary policy provides that the insurance on a vessel shall end after she has been moored twenty-four hours in good safety, and on goods when they are safely

---

(*u*) Ellis *v.* Lafone (Exch. Ch.) (1853), 8 Ex. 546; 22 L. J. Ex. 124.

(*x*) Taylor *v.* Wilson (1812), 15 East, 324; overruling Murdock *v.*

Potts (1795), 2 Park, 634; Hall *v.* Brown (1814), 2 Dow, 367.

(*y*) Barclay *v.* Stirling (1816), 5 M. & S. 6.

CHAP. XVII.] DURATION OF THE RISK ON FREIGHT. 681

landed. Though this policy is commonly used for freight insurances, there is no clause determining the end of the risk on freight. Usually the freight is not payable until the goods are delivered. When this is so, it is submitted that, under a voyage policy to the place of discharge, the risk continues as long as the goods remain in the custody of the shipowner exposed to maritime perils, provided there be no unjustifiable delay in discharging them (z).

Sect. 520.

521. Freight is often insured by time policies. So far as the duration of the risk is concerned, the rules relating to time policies on ships are applicable to insurances on freight (a).

Time policy on freight.

In one case it was argued that a loss of freight could not be recovered because the voyage, if there had been no loss, would not have been completed within the time for which the insurance had been effected; for the freight could not be earned during the time covered by the insurance. But this absurd contention was overruled. It was held that as freight can be insured for part of a voyage, so also it can be for a limited period, during which it is at risk (b).

(z) Marshall, 225. Where the freight of a voyage from London to Madeira and Jamaica was agreed to be paid in wine to be put on board at Madeira, the Court of Common Pleas were of opinion that the risk under a policy on freight at and from London to Jamaica endured until the freight wine was safely carried to Jamaica in the ship. Atty v. Lindo (1805), 1 B. & P. N. R. 236.

(a) See *ante*, Chap. XVI.
(b) Michael v. Gillespy (1857), 2 C. B. N. S. 627; 26 L. J. C. P. 306.

PART II.

OF CERTAIN MATTERS THAT RENDER THE CONTRACT
OF INSURANCE VOID OR UNAVAILABLE.

CHAPTER I.

MISREPRESENTATION.

SECT.	SECT.
Misrepresentation and Comment generally 522	Representations of Belief..545—551
Election to avoid the Insurance ....523—526	Communication of Information 552, 553
Representation defined 527, 528	Materiality ....554—557
Distinguished from Warranties ....529—533	What satisfies a Representation ....558—561
Inferred from Silence 534	Whether the Contract is avoided *ab initio* by a Misrepresentation 562, 563
Grounds on which Misrepresentation avoids the Policy.. 535	Construction of Representation ....564—566
Fraudulent Misrepresentations 536, 537	Time to which Representations refer 567, 568
Classification of Representations 538	Withdrawal of Representation 569, 570
Promissory Representations ... 539—544	Effect of Misrepresentation to the first Underwriter ...571—574

522. THE subject of Disclosure and Representations is dealt with in sects. 17 to 21 of the Marine Insurance Act, 1906. Of these, sect. 17 enunciates the general principle, casting a duty on both assured and insurer, and applying both to Disclosure and to Representations. The three following sections are in effect illustrations of sect. 17, and deal with the duty imposed thereby, only so far as it is to be performed by the assured. Of these three sections, the eighteenth and nineteenth relate to Disclosure, and the twentieth to Representations. Sect. 21, like sect. 17, is a general section. *Of misrepresentation and concealment generally.*

In conformity, no doubt, with the law prior to the Act, the seventeenth section declares that: " A contract of marine insurance is a contract based upon the utmost good faith, and, *Marine Insurance is based on good faith.*

Sect. 522. if the utmost good faith be not observed by either party (*a*), the contract may be avoided by the other party" (*b*).

In almost every instance in which a policy of sea assurance is effected, the underwriter must rely solely on the good faith of the assured for supplying him with full and true information of many of those facts on which the character and nature of the risk, and consequently the rate of premium, depend. It is to the assured that all communications respecting the actual state of the property proposed for insurance, such as the time and place at which the goods are to be loaded, or the ship is to sail—the force and equipment of the vessel, her then situation, and progress in her voyage, &c.— are in the first instance addressed: he is thus the natural and sole depositary of much of that information, a full and true communication of which is absolutely essential to the underwriter in order that he may form a right judgment of the nature of the risk and the proper rate of premium.

Hence, on the true principles of equity and justice (*c*), the concealment or misrepresentation by the assured, whether wilful or not, of any facts which were calculated to influence, and did in fact influence, the underwriter (*d*) in taking the risk or fixing the rate of premium will give the latter the right to avoid the policy.

Provisions of Mar. Ins. Act as to representations.

Accordingly it is now expressly enacted by sect. 20 of the Marine Insurance Act, as follows:—

(1) Every material representation made by the assured

(*a*) Lord Mansfield in Carter *v.* Boehm (1766), 1 W. Bl. 594; 3 Burr. 1909, pointed out that the duty lay not only upon the assured, but also upon the underwriter, who, for instance, would not be allowed to retain a premium in respect of a policy made on a ship which he knew at the time to have arrived safely.

(*b*) In Cantiere Meccanico Brindisino *v.* Janson, [1912] 3 K. B. 452, 463, Vaughan Williams, L. J., expressed the view that there might be a duty of disclosure under s. 17, although in the absence of inquiry there might be no such duty under s. 18, *infra*, § 575.

(*c*) As to the principle on which the rule is based, see *infra*, § 535.

(*d*) Arnould's words were (2nd ed. p. 541), "any such facts as might reasonably be supposed to have influenced the underwriter," &c. The text has been altered for reasons which will hereafter be discussed.

CHAP. I.]   MISREPRESENTATION.   687

or his agent to the insurer during the negotiations for   Sect. 522.
the contract, and before the contract is concluded (e),
must be true. If it be untrue the insurer may avoid the
contract.

(2) A representation is material which would influence
the judgment of a prudent insurer in fixing the premium
or determining whether he will take the risk.

(3) A representation may be either a representation
as to a matter of fact, or as to a matter of expectation
or belief.

(4) A representation as to a matter of fact is true, if it
be substantially correct, that is to say, if the difference
between what is represented and what is actually correct
would not be considered material by a prudent insurer.

(5) A representation as to a matter of expectation or
belief is true if it be made in good faith.

(6) A representation may be withdrawn or corrected
before the contract is concluded.

(7) Whether a particular representation be material
or not is, in each case, a question of fact.

523. It is commonly stated, both in the text-books and the   Contract not
cases, that the effect of a material misrepresentation or con-   void, but
cealment is to avoid the insurance. Arnould uses this   voidable by
expression, which is not strictly correct. The party who   innocent
has been guilty of a concealment or misrepresentation   party.
cannot, of course, avail himself of his wrongful act to treat
the contract as void. The other party to the insurance can,
however, elect either to treat the contract as valid or to
repudiate it, in which latter case it is treated as void
ab initio (f).

The question then arises, when the election must be made.   When must
The Marine Insurance Act, 1906, is silent upon this point.   election to
In almost all the cases the fact has been that the concealment   made.
or misrepresentation by the assured was only discovered after
a total loss had become known, or after the voyage insured
had terminated. Under such circumstances the question of

(e) As to these words, see sect. 21; and *post*, §§ 567—569.
(f) Mar. Ins. Act, 1906, ss. 17, 18 (1), *post*, § 575; sect. 20 (1),
ante, § 522. Morrison *v.* Universal Marine Ins. Co. (1872—1873), L. R. 8 Ex. 40, 197.

Sect. 523. election is of no practical importance and has never arisen. When, however, the underwriter becomes aware, before the voyage or period insured has come to an end, that he is entitled to avoid the contract, it may make a great difference to the assured whether the underwriter makes his election at once or delays making it. A prompt election may enable the assured to protect himself by taking out another policy, while a delay may render it impossible for him to effect an insurance at all, or to do so on as favourable terms as before.

It was not finally decided, in the only case in which this question arose, whether the party entitled to elect must do so within a reasonable time, or whether he may repudiate the contract at any time, unless in the meanwhile he has done something to affirm it, or unless the rights of third parties have intervened, or unless the other party to the contract has altered his position under the belief that the contract was a subsisting one.

Morrison *v.* Universal Marine Ins. Co.

524. In that case (*g*) the plaintiff's broker had effected an insurance with the defendants, without disclosing certain material information in his possession. In doing so he acted in good faith, believing that the information was incorrect. The slip was initialed on the 12th October, and on the same day the defendants' assistant underwriter became possessed of the information which had been withheld. On the 14th or 15th the defendants executed and delivered out the policy, without any protest or any notice that they would treat it as void. On the 19th news of the loss of the ship was posted at Lloyd's, and on the 20th the defendants gave notice to the broker that they did not consider the policy binding on them. At the trial, Blackburn, J., directed the jury that when the underwriter discovers that there has been a concealment or misrepresentation he is not entitled to wait until he hears that there has been a loss, and then repudiate the policy. He must make his election, not, indeed, with hot speed, but

---

(*g*) Morrison *v.* Universal Marine Ins. Co. (1872—1873), L. R. 8 Ex. 40, 197.

in a reasonable time (*h*). The learned judge did not express an opinion on the question whether in delivering out the policy the underwriters had done an act which amounted to an election, and the jury found expressly that the defendants had not elected to treat the policy as subsisting. A verdict having been entered for the defendants, the Court of Exchequer (Cleasby, B., dissenting) ordered a new trial on the ground of misdirection. Martin, B., held that the jury should have been told that if the conduct of the defendants in delivering out the policy would induce the plaintiff to suppose that he had a valid policy, they were estopped from denying it. Bramwell, B., considered that delivering out the policy with knowledge of the concealment was *primâ facie* an election, and threw on the defendants the burden of showing circumstances to explain it (*i*).

_{Sect. 524.}

The Court of Exchequer Chamber reversed this judgment (*k*). They accepted the verdict of the jury, that there had been no election in fact to affirm the policy, presumably on the ground urged by the defendants, that by usage the contract is deemed to be complete when the slip is initialed, and that the delivering out of the policy is a mere formal act which the underwriter is in honour bound to perform, even if he intends to dispute its validity, as without the policy no action could be brought. They considered that there was no evidence that the plaintiff had been prejudiced by the defendants not electing earlier to disaffirm the policy, and it was not material to consider whether the plaintiff understood their conduct in delivering out the policy *without a protest* as amounting to an election to affirm it, unless under that belief he altered his position.

525. One question, as we have said, the Exchequer Chamber left undecided, namely, whether the underwriter must make his election in a reasonable time, or whether he may repudiate the contract at any time unless in the meanwhile he has

_{Question of time of election left undecided.}

(*h*) Morrison *v.* Universal Marine Ins. Co. (1872), L. R. 8 Ex. 40, 47. See also per Bramwell, B., *ibid.* p. 55.
(*i*) L. R. 8 Ex. 40.
(*k*) L. R. 8 Ex. 197.

Sect. 525. elected to affirm it, or unless the rights of third parties have intervened, or the other party to the contract has altered his position under the belief that the contract was a subsisting one. The latter position is that maintained by the same Court, in Clough v. London and North-Western Railway Company (*l*), as to the rights of a person who has been induced by fraud to enter into a contract to rescind it. But it is nevertheless there pointed out that, although the party defrauded may keep the question open so long as he does nothing to affirm the contract, yet mere lapse of time without rescinding will furnish evidence that he has determined to affirm the contract, and when the lapse of time is great might be conclusive to that effect.

It was not necessary for the Court of Exchequer Chamber to decide, in Morrison v. Universal Marine Insurance Company, whether Blackburn, J.'s, direction, that the election must be made in a reasonable time, was correct, and the Court expressly refrained from overruling this direction (*m*). The rule laid down in Clough v. London and North-Western Railway Company, and already referred to, was, however, cited in the judgment of the Court; and the opinion of the Court seems, therefore, to have been that the rule should be applied to contracts of marine insurance, whether the representation be fraudulent or innocent (*n*).

Its application to such contracts is, however, not free from difficulty. The Exchequer Chamber said that if, in consequence of the defendants' delay, Morrison had been induced to believe that the defendants waived their right to avoid the contract, and had consequently abstained from effecting an insurance elsewhere, the plaintiff would have been entitled to a verdict; but there was no evidence to that effect. Yet it must be difficult in most cases to determine to what extent the position of an assured has been altered by the delay in rescinding. In this particular case the Exchequer Chamber

---

(*l*) (1871), L. R. 7 Ex. 34.
(*m*) See L. R. 8 Ex. p. 205.

(*n*) Mr. Arthur Cohen adopts this view: Laws of England, vol. xvii. § 794.

CHAP. I.] MISREPRESENTATION. 691

pointed out that the plaintiff had actually attempted, but failed, to effect further insurances, and therefore the delay could have made no difference. But if he had known that he was not protected by the defendants' policy, he might have offered a higher premium. The question whether the assured's position has been altered must often be a speculative one, which cannot be satisfactorily determined.

Sect. 525.

526. When a policy has been avoided for concealment or misrepresentation it may be ordered to be delivered up and cancelled (*o*).

Policy ordered to be cancelled.

527. A representation, in the technical sense which the word bears in the law of insurance, may be stated to be:—

Definition of a representation.

A verbal or written statement made by the assured to the underwriter, at or before the time of the making of the contract, as to the existence of some fact or state of facts calculated to induce an (*p*) underwriter more readily to assume the risk, by diminishing the estimate he would otherwise have formed of it.

Such statement may either be—(1) a positive affirmation by the assured, as of his own knowledge and upon his own responsibility, that the facts represented either do or will exist (*q*); or (2) a mere declaration of his belief or expectation that such facts do or will exist; or (3) a mere communication of information which he has received from others respecting them.

Classification of representations.

The Marine Insurance Act recognizes the first two of these classes of statements, by declaring (sect. 20 (3)) that "a representation may be either a representation as to a matter of fact, or as to a matter of expectation or belief."

(*o*) Rivaz *v.* Gerussi (1880), 6 Q. B. D. 222; Brooking *v.* Maudslay (1888), 38 Ch. D. 636.

(*p*) For "an," Arnould (2nd ed. p. 542) had "the." Arnould here seems to have used "representation" as equivalent to "material representation." The reasons why the editors have substituted "an" for "the" are explained in note (*a*), § 554. A statement which is not a material representation in the technical sense may, nevertheless, if fraudulent, vitiate the contract: see § 536. For statements made in answer to enquiries, see § 555.

(*q*) See *post*, § 542, as to representations of future facts.

44 (2)

Sect. 527. The third class is not specially noticed. It may be regarded as a branch of the first class. For if an assured states that he has received certain information, this is a distinct representation, not indeed as to the accuracy of the information, but of the fact that such information has actually been received. In this work we will call the first class positive representations; and denominate the two other classes respectively representations of belief (*r*) and representations of information (*s*).

Representations may be either oral or written.

528. First, then, a representation is a verbal or written statement made by the assured or his agent to the underwriter at the time of the making of the contract: it may be either oral or in writing, and in point of actual practice generally consists of either verbal communications made, or written instructions shown, by the broker to the underwriter at the time the risk is proposed to him. When made verbally, Lord Mansfield used to urge that every representation should be entered by the broker in his book at the time, and preserved as an evidence of the real terms on which the contract was made (*t*).

Distinction between a representation and a warranty.

529. A representation, to have any effect, must, as we have seen, be made at or before the time of entering into the contract, therefore necessarily before the subscription of the policy. It is never, in terms, inserted in that instrument, though there seems to be no reason why this should not be done, if the parties wish it (*u*). This, in fact, constitutes the main distinction in form between a representation and a warranty, viz., that a representation may be made either orally or in writing, and need not be introduced into the policy; whereas a warranty must always be in writing and inserted in the policy, or incorporated therein by reference (*x*).

(*r*) These are dealt with in §§ 545—551.
(*s*) See § 552.
(*t*) Pawson *v.* Watson (1778), 2 Cowp. 785, 788.
(*u*) See *post*, § 532.
(*x*) Mar. Ins. Act, 1906, s. 35 (2). See also the *dicta* of Lord Mans-

CHAP. I.]   MISREPRESENTATION.   693

No statement not actually written or referred to on the   Sect. 529.
face of the policy will be construed as a warranty: though
the paper on which the statement is written be wrapped up
with the policy, or even wafered to it at the time of subscription, it cannot be more than a representation (*y*).

The same statement, indeed, which when made orally or
in writing distinct from the policy, by the broker to the
underwriter, is construed as a positive representation, would
if written on the face of the policy in almost all cases
amount to a warranty. Thus, where a broker, in effecting a
policy on a ship, showed the underwriter, in order to induce
him to take the risk, written instructions in which it was
stated with reference to the ship, "she mounts twelve guns
and twenty men," this was construed as a positive representation; but had these same words been written on the face of
the policy they would have been held to constitute a
warranty (*z*).

Wherever, therefore, the representation is a positive statement of some fact (*a*) material to the risk, it is only distin-
guishable in form from a warranty by not being written on
the face of the policy.

530. From this distinction in form arises a very important   Difference in
distinction in effect. As a representation is not inserted on   effect between
the face of the instrument, the assured is not tied down to   a warranty
the same rigid and literal compliance with its terms as he is   sentation.
in the case of a warranty. Unless a warranty is true to the
letter and fulfilled with the most scrupulous exactness, the

field in Pawson *v.* Watson (1778), 2 Cowp. 785; M'Dowell *v.* Fraser (1779), 1 Dougl. 260; and of Lord Abinger in Cornfoot *v.* Fowke (1840), 6 M. & W. 378.

(*y*) Pawson *v.* Barnevelt (1778), 1 Dougl. 12, n. 4; Bize *v.* Fletcher (1779), *ibid*. See, however, *post*, § 629, as to clauses wafered or gummed to the policy; and cf. Pearce *v.* Gardner, [1897] 1 Q. B. 688, C. A., as to memoranda satisfying sect. 4 of the Statute of Frauds.

(*z*) Pawson *v.* Watson (1778), 2 Cowp. 785.

(*a*) As to representations of "future facts," or so-called "promissory representations," see *post*, §§ 538—544. They are not expressly recognized by the Mar. Ins. Act, 1906.

Sect. 530. insurer is discharged from liability (*b*), for in such cases there is the breach of an express stipulation which the assured himself has inserted in the instrument as one of its terms. In the case of a representation, on the other hand, the very fact that the assured has declined to insert on the face of the policy the statement which he has yet represented to be true shows that he does not intend to be bound down to this exact and rigorous accuracy, and accordingly a substantial compliance with the terms of a representation is all that is required (*c*).

Thus, to take an illustration from the case already cited, had the words " she mounts twelve guns and twenty men " been written on the face of the policy, this would have been a warranty, and the policy would have been void had the ship carried one gun or one man less than the stipulated number: but as these words were in fact only shown by the broker to the underwriter before subscribing the policy to inform him of the probable risk he would incur, and were not inserted in the policy, they were held to be only a representation; and the policy was not avoided by the ship's carrying a force of men and guns not literally the same with that stated in the representation, but in point of strength, convenience, and for the purpose of resistance, even more favourable to the risk (*d*).

Only a material misrepresentation avoids the policy.

531. It further appears by the definition that a representation is a statement of the existence of some fact or state of facts " calculated to induce an (*e*) underwriter more readily to assume the risk by diminishing the estimate he would otherwise have formed of it": facts, the statement of which may reasonably be presumed likely to have such an influence on the judgment of a prudent underwriter, are called "material facts"; a statement of such facts is called a

(*b*) Mar. Ins. Act, 1906, s. 33 (3).
(*c*) Mar. Ins. Act, 1906, s. 20 (4), *ante*, § 522; Pawson *v.* Watson, *infra*.
(*d*) Pawson *v.* Watson (1778), 2 Cowp. 785; see also Von Tungeln *v.* Dubois (1809), 2 Camp. 151; Nonnen *v.* Kettlewell (1812), 16 East, 176.
(*e*) See note (*p*), § 527.

CHAP. I.] MISREPRESENTATION. 695

material representation (*f*); and it is the falsehood of such a representation only that will, at any rate in the absence of fraud, have the effect of avoiding the policy.

Sect. 531.

And this constitutes a further distinction between a representation and an express warranty. In the case of a warranty all questions of the materiality or immateriality of the fact warranted are entirely excluded; the sole inquiry is whether it be or be not warranted that the fact is or shall be so and so. If it be warranted, then, however unimportant the fact may be to the risk, however little its existence or non-existence may have influenced the judgment of the underwriter as to the rate of premium, the thing warranted must be absolutely true or literally performed, otherwise the policy will be void as from the date of the breach of the warranty. The falsehood of a representation, on the other hand, will produce no effect on the policy unless the fact misrepresented be material.

Hence further distinguished from a warranty.

532. Although as a general rule all positive statements and stipulations relating to the risk or the subjects of insurance will, if inserted in the policy, be construed as express warranties, yet there can be little doubt that if a positive statement of material facts were inserted in the policy with an express stipulation that it should be construed not as a warranty, but as a representation, such express stipulation would prevail over the general rule (*g*).

When statements in the policy can be construed as representations.

It must also be borne in mind that the rule now under consideration is confined to positive representations, and does not extend to statements of belief or information; which latter would in certain cases unquestionably be construed as nothing more than representations, though inserted in writing in the policy.

Thus where the words "ship expected to be loaded between the 13th and 20th of September," were inserted in the policy, this was construed as a representation that the ship had not

(*f*) Mar. Ins. Act, 1906, s. 20 (2), *ante*, § 522.
(*g*) 2 Duer, 645.

Sect. 532. been loaded within the knowledge of the assured before the 13th of September; and as it turned out that he, in fact, knew she had, the policy was held void on this account (*h*).

Cases in which a representation is implied from the language of the policy.

533. The language of the policy may itself be such as to imply a representation, which will thus virtually form a part of the written instrument. Thus where an insurance was effected on ship (*i*) and cargo at and from Genoa to Dublin, "the adventure to begin from the loading to equip for the voyage," Lord Mansfield held that these words plainly implied a representation that Genoa was the port of loading, and as she had loaded not at Genoa but at Leghorn, this being held material, his Lordship considered that the policy was void for misrepresentation and concealment (*k*). So where in an insurance on goods the words "to return five per cent. for convoy and arrival" were inserted in the policy, Lord Eldon was of opinion that these words clearly amounted to a representation that it was probable the vessel would sail with convoy, or at all events that there was a chance she would do so; and as it appeared that the assured knew, when the policy was effected, that the ship had actually sailed without convoy, his Lordship held the misrepresentation fraudulent and the contract void (*l*).

Cases in which representation has been inferred from silence.

534. In one case the Court of Session has held that a representation can be inferred from the silence of the assured. A ship had been transferred by a fictitious sale to the Belgian flag, to avoid inspection as provided by the Merchant Shipping Act, 1873. The assured, when effecting the insurance, did not inform the underwriter, who had on a former occasion insured the ship as British, of the change of flag. The Court

---

(*h*) Stewart *v.* Morrison, Millar on Ins. 59; and see some American decisions to the same effect, cited by Judge Duer, vol. ii. pp. 721—738. See sect. 20, sub-sect. 5, of the Mar. Ins. Act, 1906, *ante*, § 522.

(*i*) The insurance is stated in the report to be on the ship only.

Arnould is, however, probably right in saying that the policy was on ship and cargo.

(*k*) Hodgson *v.* Richardson (1764), 1 W. Bl. 463; 1 Park, Ins. 412. See, as to this case, *post*, § 605.

(*l*) Reid *v.* Harvey (1816), 4 Dow, 97.

held that the policy was void by reason of misrepresentation and concealment, leading the underwriter to believe that the ship was British. It is submitted, however, that the representation made in effecting a previous insurance cannot be considered to have been renewed by implication, and that the decision can only be supported on the ground of concealment (*m*).

Sect. 534.

In Fitzherbert *v.* Mather (*n*), an agent, after posting a letter stating that a ship had sailed, heard that it had been lost. The post had not yet left, but he did not write to report the loss. The Court of King's Bench held that by not doing so he had represented that the ship was safe when the post left. The letter, when it left the hands of the agent, stated his information correctly. The editors submit that his subsequent omission to write was not a misrepresentation, but a concealment of material information.

There may no doubt, however, be cases in which a representation will be inferred from the silence or conduct of a party.

535. Formerly it appears to have been laid down in some cases, and assumed in others, that the ground upon which the misrepresentation of a material fact avoided the policy was actual fraud or a wilful intention on the part of the assured to deceive the underwriter (*o*). This ground, however, has long since been entirely abandoned, and the principle is now firmly established that the misrepresentation from mistake, ignorance, or accident, of any material fact, however innocently made, will avoid the policy quite as much as in cases where such misrepresentation arises from a wilful intention to deceive (*p*).

The ground upon which misrepresentation avoids the policy

(*m*) Hutchinson *v.* Aberdeen Sea Ins. Co. (1876), 3 Ct. of Sess. Cas. (4th Ser.) 682.

(*n*) (1785), 1 T. R. 12.

(*o*) See the *dicta* of Lord Mansfield in Pawson *v.* Watson (1778), 2 Cowp. 785; and Bize *v.* Fletcher (1779), 1 Dougl. 12, n.; the *dictum* of Lord Tenterden in Flinn *v.* Tobin (1829), Moody & Malk. 367; and the remarks of Duer, Lecture on Representation, 112, 113, n. 3.

(*p*) The cases that establish this position are the following: M'Dowell *v.* Fraser (1779), 1 Dougl. 260; Fillis *v.* Brutton (1782), 1 Park,

Sect. 535.

Former English doctrine.

Later still, the doctrine favoured by the English Courts was that in the case supposed, although no pretence existed for alleging actual fraud, yet the policy was to be considered void on the ground of constructive or legal fraud—*i.e.*, such conduct on the part of the assured as, though it does not imply any moral turpitude in himself, yet, from the effect it has in fact of misleading the underwriter, is in legal language said to be fraudulent (*q*).

Judge Duer's doctrine.

This doctrine was questioned by Judge Duer, who contends that the true ground on which the falsity of a material representation avoids the contract, in cases where no actual fraud can be imputed, is that a positive representation on a material point is an essential part of the contract of insurance, though not inserted in the policy (*r*); and this appeared to Arnould to be the sounder view (*s*).

In Blackburn *v.* Vigors, Lord Esher took exception to Duer's theory on the ground that if it be correct "the contract should never be set aside, or treated as void on the ground of concealment (or misrepresentation); the contract should stand and be treated as broken by the assured." Duer's view, said Lord Esher, would raise new complications (*t*). Phillips explains the effect of a misrepresentation or concealment in the contract on the ground of a condition, implied by the fact of entering into the contract, that there is no misrepresentation or concealment, and his proposition was in that case adopted by all the judges in the Court of Appeal and by

Phillips' doctrine.

Ins. 414; Fitzherbert *v.* Mather (1785), 1 T. R. 12; Feise *v.* Parkinson (1812), 4 Taunt. 640; Dennistoun *v.* Lillie (1821), 3 Bligh, 202; per Lord Abinger in Cornfoot *v.* Fowke (1840), 6 M. & W. 378. Per Willes, J.:—"There is no doubt that a material misrepresentation, though perfectly honest at the time, made with the intent that it should be acted on by the insurer, and which has led to the policy being granted, will defeat the policy." Anderson *v.* Pacific Fire & Marine Ins. Co. (1872), L. R. 7 C. P. 65, 68.

(*q*) See the judgment of Lord Abinger in Cornfoot *v.* Fowke (1840), 6 M. & W. 378; and the *dicta* of Baron Parke in Elkin *v.* Jansen (1845), 13 M. & W. 658.

(*r*) 2 Duer, Ins. 648—655, s. xiv.; and 3 Kent, Com. 282.

(*s*) 2nd ed. vol. i. p. 549.

(*t*) Blackburn *v.* Vigors (1886), 17 Q. B. D. 553, 561.

CHAP. I.]   MISREPRESENTATION.   699

Lord Watson in the House of Lords (*u*). It is submitted that this is the proper ground on which to base the rule.

Sect. 535.

536. If the purpose of the representation be fraudulent—that is, to deceive the underwriter by inducing him to believe that which the assured at the time knows to be false, or does not know to be true—the policy, it is said, will be equally avoided whether the false statement be material to the risk or not (*x*).

In cases of fraud a misrepresentation may avoid the policy without being material.

It is submitted that this proposition is subject to the qualification that the fraudulent statement must in fact have influenced the underwriter when he undertook the risk. Speculations as to the materiality of a fraudulent statement made with a view to a particular end cannot be permitted when the end has been attained thereby (*y*), and where the purpose of a falsehood is to induce the underwriter to enter into the contract, there is no doubt, as Arnould says, a presumption that such has been its effect (*z*). But the presumption cannot be conclusive, so as to preclude evidence to the contrary (*a*), and prevent the application of the general principle that a fraud will not avoid a contract unless it has induced one of the parties to enter into the contract (*b*).

537. It is not necessary, in order to avoid the policy on

To avoid the policy, the

(*u*) *Ibid.* 562, 578, 583; 12 App. Cas. 539; 1 Phillips, Ins. s. 537. See also Pickersgill *v.* London & Prov. Mar. & General Ins. Co., Ltd., [1912] 3 K. B. 614.

(*x*) 1 Marshall, Ins. 452; 3 Kent, Com. 283; 1 Duer, Ins. 80, 83, 614; 1 Park, Ins. 405; and Roberts *v.* Fonnereau, there cited; see also Sibbald *v.* Hill (1814), 2 Dow, 268; per Lord Esher, The Bedouin, [1894] P. 1, 12. The Mar. Ins. Act, 1906, has no express reference to this point, but by sect. 91 (2), the rules of the common law continue to apply, save in so far as they are inconsistent with the provisions of the Act.

(*y*) See per Lord Chelmsford, L. C., in Smith *v.* Kay (1859), 7 Cl. & F. 759, cited by Smith, L. J., in Gordon *v.* Street, [1899] 2 Q. B. 646.

(*z*) As to the strength of such a presumption at the present time, when the parties to an action are competent witnesses, see per Lord Blackburn in Smith *v.* Chadwick (1884), 9 App. Cas. 196.

(*a*) 1 Phillips, s. 540.

(*b*) Per Romilly, M. R., Pulsford *v.* Richards (1853), 17 Beav. 87, 96; per Jervis, C. J., Canham *v.* Barry (1855), 15 C. B. 597, 617; and see *post*, § 555.

Sect. 537.
loss need not be connected with the misrepresentation.

the ground of misrepresentation, that the loss should have arisen from a cause connected with the fact or circumstance misrepresented. Thus, if the assured represent that the ship or goods are neutral property, and they are in fact the property of a belligerent, he shall not recover even for a loss occasioned by shipwreck, whether the mis-statement was made through mistake or from design to deceive (*c*).

Where no actual fraud, assured entitled to a return of premium.

If the policy be avoided by a mere misrepresentation without actual fraud, the assured is entitled to a return of premium. If, however, the representation was false within his own knowledge, and made with the intention to deceive, this fraud will disentitle him to a return of premium (*d*).

Positive representations subdivided into affirmative and promissory.

538. Positive representations have been subdivided into— 1. Affirmative; 2. Promissory; the former averring the actual existence of the fact to which they relate, the latter that such fact shall or will thereafter exist (*e*).

Representations, though affirmative in form, may be promissory in effect.

This distinction, however, is often one more of form than substance, as in fact many positive representations, even when in terms affirmative, in effect are promissory. Thus where it is represented that a vessel is neutral, or has a licence to trade, or has a certain armament or a certain kind of cargo, the mere affirmation of these facts as existing at the time is unimportant; it is the implied promise that, as far as depends on the assured, they shall be and continue unchanged throughout the duration of the risk, that alone gives value to the representation.

Thus, to take an instance in point. In the case of Pawson *v.* Watson (*f*) the representation made by the broker in effecting a policy on the ship was in these words:—"She mounts twelve guns and twenty men." Although affirmative in point of form, it is plain that this representation was promissory in its meaning; for when the policy was effected the

---

(*c*) Per Holt, C. J., Skinner, R. 327; 1 Marshall, Ins. 452; 1 Park, Ins. 405.

(*d*) Mar. Ins. Act, 1906, s. 84 (1); *post*, §§ 1247a, 1256.

(*e*) See *post*, §§ 542—544, for a discussion of the doctrine of promissory representations.

(*f*) *Ante*, § 530.

ship, which, as appears by the report, did not sail for a month afterwards, had not a single gun or man on board; so that the representation, unless construed to refer to a future event, was false when made. The whole judgment of Lord Mansfield plainly shows that he took it to be, what undoubtedly it was, not a mere assertion of the actual force of the vessel at the time, but a stipulation that she would sail with the armament described on the voyage insured (*g*). Had the representation just stated been thus expressed:—" She is to (or 'She will') mount twelve guns and twenty men," it would have been an instance of a representation promissory in terms as well as in effect (*h*).

Sect. 538.

539. It is an important question, whether there is any difference between an affirmative representation and a promissory representation, as to the ground on which, if false, they will avoid the policy? In other words, whether the positive misrepresentation of a future fact, material to the risks, will just as much avoid the policy, in the absence of actual fraud, as the positive misrepresentation of a past or existing fact equally material?

Is there any difference between a promissory and an affirmative representation?

It appears from the cases of Flinn *v.* Headlam (*i*) and Flinn *v.* Tobin (*j*), that Lord Tenterden was of opinion that this distinction exists. They were actions on the same policy, and the facts were that, to induce the underwriters to take a risk on a ship about to sail with a cargo of rock salt, the broker represented that the ship would only take

Opinion of Lord Tenterden.

(*g*) See 2 Duer, 766, whose language Arnould adopted almost without a change.

(*h*) See the discussion, *post*, §§ 542—544. Even if the promise, express or implied, be not binding, the representation " She mounts twelve guns " may be considered to mean that this is her usual armament, and that it is expected that she will sail with it on the voyage insured. The representation " She will mount twelve guns " must at any rate be a representation of expectation or belief.

(*i*) (1828), 9 B. & Cr. 693.

(*j*) (1829), 1 Mood. & Malk. 367. Arnould stated that Flinn *v.* Headlam was the later case, but this is a mistake. Flinn *v.* Headlam was tried in 1828, and a rule *nisi* for a new trial, obtained in Michaelmas term of that year, was discharged on the 4th July, 1829. Flinn *v.* Tobin was tried on the 27th July, 1829.

Sect. 539. fifty or sixty tons of rock salt, which would put her in light ballast trim. The ship sailed the day after the policy was signed, with 160 tons of rock salt on board, being a full and very heavy cargo. In the earlier action, Flinn *v.* Headlam, the counsel for the plaintiff contended that if the underwriters meant to insist upon it as part of the contract, that only a certain quantity of rock salt should be carried in the vessel, they should have had it inserted in the policy; and Lord Tenterden advised the jury to find for the defendant if they thought that a material representation was made by the broker as to the rock salt then actually on board, but to find for the plaintiff if they thought that the representation was as to the cargo expected to be shipped, or that the underwriter was not influenced by the representation (*k*). In the later case, Flinn *v.* Tobin, Lord Tenterden directed the jury that the defendant was not entitled to a verdict on the ground of a misrepresentation of the cargo which the ship was to carry, unless it was fraudulent. "The mere fact of a misrepresentation, without fraud," he said, "will not be enough to prevent the plaintiff's recovering; for the contract between the parties is the policy, which is in writing, and cannot be varied by parol."

Distinction between effect of affirmative and promissory representation seems untenable.

540. This distinction, however, even when confined to the sole case of promissory representations, seemed to Arnould to be opposed to the principles on which parol evidence of representation has been admitted in any case, and to be irreconcilable with express authorities of the greatest weight.

The principle on which the false affirmation of the actual or past existence of a material fact avoids the contract in cases where there is no actual fraud, is, that the underwriter only engaged to be liable upon the faith that such fact existed, so that the falsity of the statement is a breach of a condition

---

(*k*) A certificate of seaworthiness was produced to the underwriter, and a verdict for the assured was upheld by the Court of King's Bench on the ground that the jury were right if they thought that the underwriter relied on the certificate (see *infra*, § 555). The correctness of Lord Tenterden's ruling was not challenged.

precedent that the contract should be free from misrepresentation. It is evident that this principle must apply equally to the case in which the assured falsely, though not fraudulently, affirms, in positive terms, that some material fact shall or will hereafter exist; in this case the basis of the underwriter's liability is the future existence of the fact: the falsity of the positive statement, that the fact will exist, is as completely a breach of the condition on which he engaged to be liable, as the falsity of the statement that the fact had existed, or was existing; on principle, therefore, there seems no ground for this distinction, and it is also quite irreconcilable with previous authority (*l*).

Sect. 540.

541. Instead of citing all the cases which show that the doctrine of the Courts has been that representations strictly promissory, although made in good faith, must be substantially complied with in order to sustain the policy, a decision to this effect of the highest English tribunal, presided over by Lord Eldon, may suffice.

Dennistoun *v.* Lillie.

An insurance on ship and goods from Nassau (New Providence) to Clyde (in Scotland) was effected on the 18th June, 1814. On that occasion the broker showed the underwriters a letter, dated the 2nd April, and received by the owners the day before the policy was effected, in which it was stated, "The Brilliant," the ship insured, "will sail on the 1st of May." In point of fact it turned out that the ship had sailed on the 23rd April, and on the 11th of May had been captured by an American privateer. These facts were wholly unknown to the parties by whom the representation was made.

At the trial of the appeal in the House of Lords, it was contended for the plaintiff that the statement of a future event, such as an intended day of sailing, could be no more than an expectation, and therefore could not avoid the policy, unless fraudulent.

(*l*) See Edwards *v.* Footner (1808), 1 Camp. 530; Dennistoun *v.* Lillie (1821), 3 Bligh, 202; see also the American cases to the same effect collected by Duer, 2 Ins. 741 —743, 749—769.

MISREPRESENTATION. [PART II.

Sect. 541.

Lord Eldon, however, held that the policy was avoided by the misrepresentation. "There is a difference," said Lord Eldon, "between the representation of an expectation and the representation of a fact. The former is immaterial, but the latter avoids the policy if the fact misrepresented be material to the risk" (*m*).

This case, then, has been generally regarded as an explicit authority for the position, that a positive promissory representation of a material fact will, if false, avoid the policy though no actual fraud can be alleged.

Edwards v. Footner.

So, where a representation was made some time before the ship sailed, to the effect that she "was to sail" with convoy and a certain armament, so that the representation was both promissory in its terms, and related to an actually future fact, Lord Ellenborough held, that not having been substantially complied with, it avoided the policy, though made without actual fraud (*n*).

Upon the authority of previous cases, then, the distinction assumed by Lord Tenterden appeared to Arnould to be untenable.

Arnould's conclusion.

It was therefore laid down by Arnould (*o*), as the conclusion to be safely derived from all the authorities, that the positive representation of a future fact, material to the risks, will, if false, avoid the policy, though it may not be actually fraudulent.

Promissory representations considered.

542. The view expressed in the text and the reasoning on which it is based have been reproduced from the earlier editions of this work. It is nevertheless desirable to point out that the general law relating to "representations of future facts" has been declared, since this work first appeared, to be different from the law as stated in the text.

General law as to representations of future facts.

The later decisions (none of which, however, relates to marine insurance) are to the effect that what has been called a repre-

(*m*) Dennistoun v. Lillie (1821), 3 Bligh, 202. The proceedings in the Scotch Courts are briefly reported in 1 Shaw's Appeal Cases, 22.

(*n*) Edwards v. Footner (1808), 1 Camp. 530.
(*o*) 2nd ed. p. 557.

CHAP. I.] MISREPRESENTATION. 705

sentation of a future fact (if anything more than an expression of intention or expectation) can only have legal effect as a contract or promise (*p*). "There is a clear difference," says Mellish, L. J., "between a misrepresentation in point of fact, a representation that something exists at that moment which does not exist, and a representation that something will be done in the future. Of course, a representation that something will be done in the future cannot either be true or false at the moment it is made, and although you may call it a representation, if it is anything, it is a contract or promise" (*q*). Regarded as a promise, a representation that something will be done seems to be an express term of the contract in the nature of a warranty, which ought therefore to be in writing, and either included in or incorporated by reference into the policy.

Sect. 542.

543. On the other hand, it will be said that the decision in Dennistoun *v.* Lillie, being one of the House of Lords, has definitely established a different rule with regard to contracts of marine insurance. It may, however, perhaps be argued that Dennistoun *v.* Lillie, which Arnould and Judge Duer both regarded as putting the matter beyond doubt, is not as clear an authority as they considered. The letter, though dated the 2nd of April, was not shown to the underwriters until the 18th of June, nearly two months after the ship had in fact sailed; and it may be possible to contend that inasmuch, as Lord Eldon said, the question was whether the representation was one "of an expectation or a statement as of a past fact" (*r*), he regarded the production of the letter by the broker on the 18th of June as a representation by him of an event which was then past, viz., that the ship had

The English cases as to promissory representations.

(*p*) Jorden *v.* Money (1854), 5 H. L. C. 185; per Lord Selborne, L. C., in Maddison *v.* Alderson (1883), 8 App. Cas. 467, 473; and in Citizens' Bank of Louisiana *v.* First National Bank of New Orleans (1873), L. R. 6 H. L. 352, 360.

(*q*) Beattie *v.* Lord Ebury (1872), L. R. 7 Ch. 777, 804.

(*r*) 3 Bligh, 209. So, on p. 205, it appears that the judge admiral considered the letter as having held forth to the underwriters that the ship remained in harbour till the 1st of May.

A.—VOL. I. 45

Sect. 543. remained in port until the 1st of May. It does not, however, appear from the report that this was the point upon which the underwriters were relying; and the fact that Lord Eldon distinguished the case from Bowden *v.* Vaughan (*s*) (in which case the statement certainly related to a future event), on the ground that in Bowden *v.* Vaughan the policy was effected by the owner of the goods (who had no control over the event), strongly supports the view that his Lordship considered the representation one relating to a future, and not to a past, event.

Apart from Dennistoun *v.* Lillie, there is certainly authority in the English cases in support of the doctrine of promissory representations. Though the term "promissory representation" is not to be found in the reports, it has undoubtedly been decided in this country that a representation relating to a future event over which the assured has control will avoid the policy if it be not substantially satisfied (*t*); and it has also been decided that a representation which in terms relates to an existing fact, may, in effect, be promissory, and require that something shall be done or some state of things exist in the future. Thus, a representation that a ship is of a certain nationality has been held to imply an undertaking that she shall be documented as a ship of that nationality (*u*).

The American cases.

In the United States the validity of a promissory representation was clearly recognized in the earlier cases (*x*). In later cases a different view prevailed (*y*), and there are two cases, the earlier one on a marine policy, the later one on a

---

(*s*) (1809), 10 East, 415.

(*t*) Edwards *v.* Footner (1808), 1 Camp. 530; and see Bowden *v.* Vaughan (1809), 10 East, 415.

(*u*) Steel *v.* Lacy (1810), 3 Taunt. 285; Von Tungeln *v.* Dubois (1809), 2 Camp. 151.

(*x*) See Vanderheuvel *v.* Church (1801), 2 Johns. 127, 173, n.; Murray *v.* Alsop (1802), 3 Johns. Cas. 47; Suckley *v.* Delafield (1804),
2 Caines, 222; Alsop *v.* Coit (1815), 12 Mass. R. 40.

(*y*) See Rice *v.* New England Mar. Ins. Co. (1827), 4 Pick. 439; Allegre *v.* Maryland Ins. Co. (1830), 2 Gill & Johns. R. 136. See also a criticism of the doctrine of promissory representations by Gray, J., in Kimball *v.* Ætna Ins. Co. (1865), 9 Allen (Mass.), 540.

fire policy, which are express decisions that such a representation is nothing more than a statement of intention or expectation, even when relating to something within the control of the assured (z). In the later case the doctrine of promissory representations was vigorously impugned by Chancellor Walworth, in a judgment of great ability, which, however, ignores most of the decisions opposed to his view. More recently, again, the existence of promissory representations has in one case been recognized (a). The whole subject is discussed at great length by Duer, who after an examination of the authorities upholds the validity of promissory representations (b). This view is also shared by Phillips (c), and by Marshall (d), to whom the use of the term "promissory representation" seems to be due.

Sect. 543.

544. Apart from any argument to be derived from the provisions of the Marine Insurance Act, 1906, the result seems to be that, unless Dennistoun v. Lillie is a sufficiently clear authority to establish the doctrine of promissory representations in relation to marine insurance, the question is one which must be considered an open one. On the one hand it may be argued that there is no authority or reason for saying that the law as to representations is not the same with respect to contracts of marine insurance as it is with respect to other contracts; *i.e.*, that no representation other than a representation relating to an existing fact can have any effect on the contract, and that when it is sought to give such effect to any statement relating to the future, it can only be by showing that such statement amounts to a war-

Conclusion.

(z) Bryant v. Ocean Ins. Co. (1839), 22 Pick. 200; Alston v. Mechanics Ins. Co. (1842), 4 Hill, 329.

(a) Lunt v. Boston Marine Ins. Co. (1881), 6 Fed. R. 562; *S. C.*, after second trial (1883), 17 Fed. R. 411.

(b) See 2 Duer, Ins. Lect. xiv. pp. 657 *et seq.*; and notes ii. and vi. thereto, pp. 721, 749. The authorities in the United States are reviewed in the American notes to Barber v. Fletcher, Campbell's Ruling Cases, vol. xiii. pp. 536—539.

(c) 1 Phillips, Ins. s. 553.

(d) Ins. 4th ed. p. 345.

708 MISREPRESENTATION. [PART II.

Sect. 544. ranty, and as such is properly incorporated into the formal contract.

On the other hand it may be said that the general rules of law relating to representations do not necessarily apply to contracts of marine insurance. The law on the latter subject has been developed at common law without reference to the decisions which have been given in relation to other contracts, and it cannot be disputed that in some respects, *e.g.*, the materiality of a misrepresentation, the law as to marine insurance differs widely from the general law. The cases other than Dennistoun *v.* Lillie are of course open to review; but some weight must be given to the fact that for the greater part of a century the rule embodied in them has been recognized by most, if not all, textwriters of authority. From the nature of the contract and the circumstances under which it is effected, the representations made to the underwriter have necessarily a special importance. This may be a reason for upholding the rule that when a representation relates to a future event within the control of the assured, there is an implied condition that the representation shall be substantially satisfied.

The provisions of sect. 20 of the Marine Insurance Act, 1906 (*e*), however, seem to be inconsistent with the doctrine of promissory representations. The classification of representations in the third sub-section, which was apparently intended to be exhaustive, ignores them. For it seems difficult to call a representation of this nature one as to a matter of fact—an expression which is properly applied to existing facts, and not to things which are not facts in the present, but may become so in the future. Moreover, the wording of sub-sect. 4 points to facts, of which the present truth or falsity can be predicated. Nor is a promissory representation, as such, a representation as to a matter of expectation or belief, which satisfies the requirements of the law if made in good faith (*f*). It seems probable,

(*e*) *Ante*, § 522.   (*f*) See § 545.

therefore, that the law as laid down in Jorden *v.* Money (*g*) now applies to contracts of marine insurance, as it does to other contracts, and that the doctrine of promissory representations, whatever foundation there may have been for it before the Act, has ceased to exist since the Act came into force (*h*).

Sect. 544.

545. There is a great distinction to be drawn between such positive promissory representations and those representations of belief or expectation, which we have placed in a distinct class, and come now in the course of the inquiry to consider. The former are positive statements that certain material facts shall or will exist; the latter are merely expressions of an expectation or belief that they either will or do exist. The former, if binding under the existing law, involve a stipulation that unless facts take place substantially corresponding with those specified the underwriter shall not be liable on the policy; the latter imply no stipulation of the kind, and their falsification accordingly can only avoid the policy in cases of actual fraud (*i*). Accordingly it is expressly provided by the Marine Insur-

Distinction between positive promissory representations, and statements of expectation.

(*g*) *Ante,* § 542.

(*h*) This is also the opinion of Mr. Arthur Cohen: Laws of England, vol. xvii. § 808.

(*i*) A view of the nature of a representation as to expectation, belief, or intention, for which there is high judicial authority, is that such a representation is one of fact; that fact relating, however, not to the subject-matter of the expectation, but to the condition of mind of the person making the statement. Thus, if I say " I expect or believe " that a certain state of facts does or will exist, though it is true that I do not make any statement as to the actual or future existence of such facts, I may be said to make an affirmative representation as to the present condition of my mind. See per Bowen, L. J., in Edgington *v.* Fitzmaurice (1885), 29 Ch. D. 459, 483. On this view, it is unnecessary to make a distinction between a representation of an existing fact and one of belief, and the statement that the element of fraud must also be present in order to invalidate a contract on account of a false representation of belief is also superfluous, for it is impossible to make a false representation as to one's own belief without at the same time being conscious that the representation is false. Therefore, when the representation is regarded as one of an existing fact (*i.e.,* the state of a man's mind), it is evident that there must almost of necessity be fraud, when the representation is false.

Sect. 545. ance Act (*j*) that "a representation as to a matter of expectation or belief is true if it be made in good faith."

When false statements of expectation avoid the policy.

A moment's consideration will show that this distinction is well founded. If a man assures me positively that certain events over which he has a control, and without which I should decline entering into the contract with him, shall take place in a given way, and I enter into the contract on the faith of that positive assurance, I may fairly be entitled to contend that such statement must substantially be made good in order to make me liable on such contract. If, however, he merely tells me that he believes or expects that such events will happen in a certain way, and I choose to enter into the contract upon the mere chance of such belief or expectation turning out well founded, I have no right to be released from my contract on its proving fallacious, for its failure was a contingency which I ought to have contemplated on entering into my contract. If, indeed, I can show that, with a design to deceive me, he represented himself as expecting or believing that which he knew at the time to be impossible or untrue, and thereby influenced me, I shall be released from my contract on the ground of this his actual fraud.

Statement made without knowledge whether true or false.

546. The result would appear to be the same if, with the intention to deceive me, he stated his belief or expectation of that with regard to the possibility or truth of which he knows nothing either one way or the other (*k*).

Thus, if with the intention to deceive, the owner of a ship states to the underwriter that he believes the ship to be neutral, knowing nothing on the subject, and having no reason to believe either way, the better opinion would seem to be, that this representation, if false, would avoid the policy (*l*).

(*j*) Sect. 20, sub-sect. (5), *ante*, § 522.

(*k*) Per Maule, J., Evans *v*. Edmonds (1853), 13 C. B. 777, 785; see also Derry *v*. Peek (1889), 14 App. Cas. 337.

(*l*) Lord Mansfield in Pawson *v*. Watson (1778), 2 Cowp. 787, laid down the contrary; but the observations of Maule, J. (*ubi supra*), of Marshall (Ins. 453), and of Duer (2 Ins. 710, 711), seem unanswerable in favour of the other view.

It has this effect, however, only when made with the intention to deceive. Thus, where a broker employed to effect a policy on certain ships engaged in the African trade represented that they were "expected to leave the coast of Africa in November or December," when, in fact, they had all left in May: this, though material to the risk, yet, not having been made fraudulently, was held not to be a representation, but a mere expectation, into the grounds of which the underwriter ought to have inquired before he relied on it (*m*).

Sect. 546.

547. When it is evident from the position of the parties and all the circumstances of the case, that a statement, though in terms a direct and positive assertion, must, in fact, be regarded as a mere expression of expectation or belief, or opinion, it will be so construed.

When positive statement considered only an expression of expectation.

If, for instance, the owner of a ship, meaning to deceive, were to state that he believed, or expected, she would sail long after, or long before, some day on which she had actually sailed, this misrepresentation would, doubtless, be held to avoid the policy; if, however, the owner of goods intended to be embarked on board the same ship were to make a similar statement, as to the time of the ship's sailing, without knowledge either the one way or the other, such statement ought to be looked upon as totally immaterial; for, coming from such a quarter, the underwriter must have received it as the mere expression of an opinion, and if he meant to act upon it, was bound to inquire into the grounds upon which it was founded (*n*). This principle has been extended to cases in which the statement is, on the face of it, a positive promissory representation or explicit engagement for the existence of future facts, where made in the absence of fraud by parties who have no interest in the subject, or control over the event, to which the statement refers.

(*m*) Barber *v.* Fletcher (1779), 1 Dougl. 306. It appears from the report that there was no allegation of actual fraud. See also the remarks made on this case by Bayley, J., in Bridges *v.* Hunter (1813), 1 M. & S. 15.

(*n*) Duer on Representations, 95—97; 2 Duer, Ins. p. 664.

712   MISREPRESENTATION.   [PART II.

Sect. 548.
Cases in illustration.

Bowden v. Vaughan.

548. Thus, where a broker, employed to effect a policy on goods, for a party who had no interest in the ship, represented that "the ship," which was then at Lisbon, "was to sail in a few days," and the ship did not, in fact, sail for a month, Lord Ellenborough and the Court of King's Bench held that this statement, though material to the risks, having been made by the owner of the goods, who had no control over the time of the ship's sailing, must be regarded merely as the expression of a probable expectation, which, as it appeared to have been made *bonâ fide*, could not avoid the policy (*o*).

Hubbard v. Glover.

A broker employed to procure an insurance on a ship, for a homeward voyage "from St. Petersburg or Cronstadt to London," in order to induce the underwriter to take the insurance as a summer risk, told him, on the 13th of June, just before the policy was effected, "the ship had sailed some time (*i.e.*, from London), and must now be at Gottenburg. There is a cargo ready for her (*i.e.*, at Cronstadt), and she is sure to be an early ship." The ship in fact did happen to be at Gottenburg when this statement was made, but at Cronstadt found no cargo ready for her; and in consequence of the delay thus caused, did not begin her voyage from Cronstadt to London till after the winter risk had begun. Lord Ellenborough held that this did not avoid the policy, as the statement must have been understood by the underwriters to mean nothing more than that a cargo had been ordered, and the expression of a probable belief that it would be ready for the ship at Cronstadt, so that she might be expected to be an early ship (*p*).

Statements which from their terms were intended to be only of expectation or belief.

549. This principle of decision applies *à fortiori* where it appears from the terms in which the statement is made that the broker cannot intend it to be taken as a positive assertion

(*o*) Bowden v. Vaughan (1809), 10 East, 415.
(*p*) Hubbard v. Glover (1812), 3 Camp. 313. It is submitted that, with the modern means of communication, a statement that there was a cargo ready would generally not be held to be a mere expression of belief.

of the existence of a fact within his own knowledge. Where a broker, employed to effect an insurance on a ship "at and from Messina to her port or ports of discharge in the Channel," stated to the underwriter, at the time of effecting the policy, "that the ship was then (28th June) either near Messina or at Messina, or on her homeward voyage"; and it turned out in fact that the ship, although she had sailed from London a fortnight before this statement was made, yet had not sailed from Falmouth till two days after it (*i.e.*, on 30th June): Gibbs, C. J., held at the trial, and the Court of Common Pleas confirmed his decision, that this was not a positive representation, but merely the expression of an opinion formed by the broker from knowing the time at which the ship had sailed from London; and therefore, although if he had stated it positively as a fact, it might have bound the assured to a substantial compliance; yet, as he merely stated the ship to be in one of three situations, and did not allege specifically in which, that the very form of the statement showed that it was merely to be taken as a computation, which, though erroneous, could not avoid the policy in the absence of fraud (*q*).

Sect. 549.
Brine *v.* Featherstone.

At the time of effecting a policy on the freight of the "Clarendon" "from Belize to Rendez-vous Point, thence back to Belize, and thence to London," Rendez-vous Point being unknown to either of the parties, the master's letter was shown to the underwriter containing this passage:—"It is considered by the pilot here as a good and safe anchorage, and well sheltered. I have been out and seen the place, and consider it quite safe." It was proved on the trial that Rendez-vous Point was a dangerous place for a vessel to anchor during the hurricane months; but the jury found that the pilot and master considered it was not dangerous.

Anderson *v.* Pacific, &c. Ins. Co.

On a motion for a new trial the Court of Common Pleas

(*q*) Brine *v.* Featherstone (1813), 4 Taunt. 869. In other words, the representation was considered to relate only to the broker's general belief; and it was not shown that he had said he believed anything which he had not in fact believed.

Sect. 549. refused to grant a rule. Willes, J., said: "There is no doubt that a material misrepresentation, though perfectly honest at the time, made with the intent that it should be acted on by the insurer, and which has led to the policy being granted, will defeat the policy." The question, however, continued the learned judge, was whether the passage in question amounted to an absolute statement of fact, or only to a statement of opinion. If the latter, it might be, if the opinion was one which the writer of the letter really did not entertain—a conclusion which the jury would easily have arrived at, if they thought no person could honestly have entertained such a belief—that the assured would be bound. But the jury had found that it was an opinion honestly formed. The learned judge ended by saying that the words did not amount to an absolute statement of a fact, the effect of them being that it was considered by the pilot a safe place, and that from information received from the pilot and from his own inspection, the master also considered it quite safe. Therefore, fraud being out of the question, there was no misrepresentation (*r*).

Positive misstatements, merely wrong inferences from facts truly communicated, will avoid the policy. M'Dowell v. Fraser.

550. If, however, the form of statement be positive (there being nothing in the circumstances to show that it was not so intended), then, although the error may merely consist in a wrong computation from facts truly communicated, the positive nature of the statement will tie the assured down to a substantial compliance, and its falsehood, in fact, will avoid the policy.

Thus a broker, having been informed that a ship was seen in the Delaware five days after she had sailed from New York, understood this to mean, as by the usage of mercantile men it well might, five days after she had sailed from Sandy Hook, which he knew to have been on the 6th of December, and he consequently stated as a positive fact that the ship "was seen safe in the Delaware on the 11th of December";

(*r*) Anderson *v.* Pacific Fire and Marine Ins. Co. (1872), L. R. 7 C. P. 65.

CHAP. I.]   MISREPRESENTATION.   715

this was held to be a representation which must be substantially complied with, although it was shown to be a mere mistake arising from the fact that the party giving the information to the broker meant that he had seen the ship five days after she had sailed, not from Sandy Hook, but from New York quay, which was some days previously (*s*).

Sect. 550.

551. The ground of distinction between these two classes of cases is, that from the one mode of statement the underwriter must necessarily have inferred that the assured did not mean to affirm the fact positively; and from the other he must equally have inferred that he did. In cases of the former kind the underwriter ought not, as a cautious man, to take the risk without inquiring into the grounds of the assured's expectation, belief, or opinion; otherwise the law presumes that he relies and acts exclusively on his own judgment, and he has no right to complain of the consequences of having done so.

Ground of distinction between these cases.

552. A third class (*t*) of representations consists of those in which the assured neither states positively the actual or future existence of a fact, nor his belief or expectation of its existence; but either (1) Qualifies his statement by adding that it is made on the information of others; or (2) Merely submits the information in its whole extent to the underwriters, leaving them to draw their own conclusions from it (*u*).

Statements professedly founded on information.

In these cases the assured is bound, not to any substantial compliance with the statement made, but only to show that such statement corresponded with the information he really received; in other words, he is not answerable for the truth of the facts, but only for the truth with which he has stated the information received.

What compliance therewith necessary.

553. If, however, the information so communicated by the assured to the underwriter proceeds from an agent of the

Responsibility of the assured for informa-

(*s*) M'Dowell *v.* Fraser (1779), 1 Dougl. 260.

(*t*) For the classification of representations, see *ante*, § 527.

(*u*) 2 Duer, Ins. 707.

Sect. 553.
tion derived from his agent.

assured, whose duty it was to give the intelligence (*v*), the assured is just as responsible for the truth of the information as he would be for the truth of a positive representation made by himself of the same facts. The principle here is, that what is known to the agent is impliedly known to the principal (*w*).

The following case illustrates this principle:—

Fitzherbert *v.* Mather.

Thomas, a corn-factor at Hartland (in Devonshire), shipped by order a cargo of oats on the 16th September to a consignee at Portsmouth on account of the assured. The same day he wrote to an agent of the assured at Poole stating that he had that morning shipped the oats, that the ship had sailed immediately, but that he was afraid the wind was coming from the westward and would force her back: he also the same day wrote to the same effect to another agent of the assured in London, adding these words:—"I wish the whole safe to hand. This evening appears stormy." These letters, though written on the 16th, did not by the then course of post leave Hartland till 1 P.M. on the 17th, early on the morning of which day Thomas knew of the loss of the ship, which had been driven back by the wind and wrecked on the night of the 16th off Hartland Pier. He, however, sent no further information to the London agent, who, having on the 20th received the letter which left Hartland on the 17th, and also an order from the assured to procure an insurance, submitted these letters to the underwriters as his instructions, and upon them procured a policy

(*v*) In Blackburn *v.* Vigors (1886), 17 Q. B. D. at p. 563, Lord Esher said that the agent "whose duty it was to give the intelligence" means in this context "the agent who effects the insurance." The editors, however, consider that this passage clearly means, as taken literally it ought to mean, that if the assured submits to the underwriter information received from an agent whose duty it is to keep him informed, he is responsible for any misrepresentation contained in that information. In this sense the rule is analogous to that laid down by the House of Lords in the same case in relation to concealment. See next chapter, "Concealment." Lord Esher, it may be noticed, thought that no agent was under a duty to keep his principal informed as to the matters affecting the subject of the insurance.

(*w*) See Blackburn *v.* Vigors (1887), 12 App. Cas. 531.

to be effected on the oats, "lost or not lost, from Hartland to Portsmouth."

Sect. 553.

The Court held that the policy was void on the ground of misrepresentation. The assured himself was innocent, yet as he had built his information on that of his agent (Thomas), and the agent had been guilty of misrepresentation, the assured himself ought to suffer for it. "This policy," said Lord Mansfield, "was effected by misrepresentation, because the underwriter was warranted on the information of the agent (*i.e.*, Thomas) to take for granted that on the 17th of September, at 12 or 1 o'clock" (the usual post-time at Hartland was about 1 or 2 o'clock), "the ship was safe; for the agent gave an account of the ship being loaded, and said nothing of what had happened to her. Then there was strong ground to believe, on this letter, that she was safe when the post came away" (*x*).

As long as the master is acting as agent for the owner in his general capacity as master, so long it is his legal duty to communicate and truly represent all material facts connected with the ship; and his fraud or neglect in the discharge of that his duty, if it have operated, in fact, to mislead the underwriter, will avoid the contract as much as a concealment or misrepresentation by the assured himself (*y*).

Misrepresentation or concealment by the master.

(*x*) Fitzherbert *v.* Mather (1785), 1 T. R. 12, 15. See per Buller, J., *ibid.* 16:—"According to plaintiff's letter, the insurance was not to be made till Thomas's letter arrived; it was therefore the foundation of the insurance." The editors submit that the agent was guilty not of misrepresentation (for what he wrote was true at the time), but of concealment in not sending news of the loss to supplement his letter. The principle, however, which Arnould rests on this case is not affected by this criticism.

(*y*) Gladstone *v.* King (1813), 1 M. & S. 35. Phillips (vol. i. p. 341, 2nd ed.) cited the American case of Ruggles *v.* General Interest Ins. (1827), 12 Wheaton, S. C. R. 408, as *contra;* but Judge Duer satisfactorily shows that no such doctrine can fairly be deduced from the case cited, 2 Ins. 791—796. Phillips (Ins. s. 549) states his position thus: "A policy made under an essential misunderstanding by both of the parties, into which they are purposely and fraudulently led by a third, whether he be agent of both, or one, or neither, is void." This proposition, however, is criticised by Lord Esher in Blackburn *v.* Vigors, 17 Q. B. D. at p. 564; and see also the same case in the House of Lords (1887), 12 App. Cas. 531.

MISREPRESENTATION. [PART II.

Sect. 554.
What representations are material.
Test of materiality.

554. As we have already seen, when no actual fraud can be imputed a representation, although false, will not avoid the policy unless it be material (z). It becomes important, therefore, to inquire what it is that makes a representation material. Every representation is deemed to be material which is of such a nature as would be likely to induce a prudent underwriter to take the risk, or to take it at a lower premium than he otherwise would. The test of materiality is the probable effect which the statement might naturally and reasonably be expected to produce on the mind of an underwriter (a). Thus the Marine Insurance Act, 1906, provides (b) that "a representation is material which would influence the judgment of a prudent insurer in fixing the premium, or determining whether he will take the risk."

A misrepresentation may be material, though it has no direct bearing on the state or condition of the subject of the proposed insurance. For this rule Arnould cited Sibbald v. Hill (c). In that case a merchant induced an underwriter at Leith to effect insurances at eight guineas per cent. by representing that this was the premium which he had given

---

(z) As to the effect of a fraudulent but immaterial misrepresentation, see ante, § 536; post, § 558.

(a) This is substantially Maclachlan's definition of materiality, which agrees with those of Marshall (1 Ins. 449), of Phillips (1 Ins. ss. 524—526), and of the Marine Insurance Act. Arnould says (2nd ed. vol. i. p. 565): "Every representation is to be deemed material which there is just reason to believe either determined the underwriter to insure, or influenced his estimate of the premium." He continues: "The test of materiality is the probable influence of the statement made on the mind of the underwriter. It is not absolutely necessary that the fact represented should have any direct bearing on the state or condition of the subject of the proposed insurance: it is sufficient that it either in fact did exert, or may reasonably be presumed to have exerted, an influence over the mind of the underwriter in determining him to assume a responsibility he would not otherwise have undertaken." This statement agrees with Judge Duer's view. Mar. Ins. vol. ii. p. 680. The difference between the two definitions is that according to Arnould and Duer a perfectly innocent misrepresentation of a matter which underwriters in general would consider unimportant would avoid the policy, if the particular underwriter could convince the jury that it had in fact influenced his mind. The Mar. Ins. Act, however, leaves no room for any further doubt upon the point.

(b) Sect. 20, sub-sect. 2.

(c) (1814), 2 Dow, 263.

for insurances on the same risk at London, whereas the premiums which he had in fact paid were from fifteen to twenty-five guineas. The House of Lords, on the motion of Lord Eldon, held that the policy was vitiated by the misrepresentation. Sibbald *v.* Hill was clearly a case of fraud (*d*), and may therefore not be a conclusive authority for cases of innocent misrepresentation (*e*). Nevertheless, the correctness of Arnould's statement is confirmed by the definition of materiality in sect. 20 (2) of the Marine Insurance Act, 1906 (*f*), and by the decisions on the question of materiality in relation to concealment (*g*).

Sect. 554.

555. Even where the representation is of material facts, yet it was Arnould's view that if it satisfactorily appears that it did not influence the judgment of the underwriter, its falsity will be held not to avoid the policy. Thus, where the fact stated was "that the vessel would only carry as much rock salt as would put her in ballast trim," but it appeared that a certificate of the ship's fitness to proceed on her voyage with a cargo of rock salt was shown to the underwriters before they signed the policy, Lord Tenterden told the jury to consider whether the underwriter was guided by the certificate or the representation, and the jury, under this direction, having found for the assured, saying they thought the representation was not material, the Court of King's Bench, on motion for a new trial, refused to disturb the verdict (*h*).

A misrepresentation which did not influence the underwriter will not avoid the policy.

(*d*) See, however, the judgment of Brett, L. J., in Rivaz *v.* Gerussi (1880), 6 Q. B. D. at p. 229.
(*e*) See *ante*, § 536.
(*f*) *Ante*, § 522.
(*g*) See *post*, § 589.
(*h*) Flinn *v.* Headlam (1829), 9 B. & Cr. 693. The facts of this case are somewhat inadequately stated in the report, and are partly to be gathered from the report of the case of Flinn *v.* Tobin (an action on the same policy) in M. & M. 367. The jury, in finding that the representation was not material, must have meant that under the circumstances it had not in fact influenced the mind of the underwriter. Taken by itself, it was clearly material in the sense which this word is now recognized to bear in marine insurance law. Phillips (Ins. s. 681) criticises the decision, and is of opinion that the assured cannot be allowed to prove that a material misrepresentation did not influence the underwriter; but his definition of materiality is different

Sect. 555.
When there is a presumption that the underwriter was influenced by a misrepresentation.

Some facts there are which have so plain and direct a bearing on the estimate of the risk that a misrepresentation as to any of them will, in all cases, avoid the policy, unless the assured can show to the satisfaction of the jury that the judgment of the underwriter was not, under the circumstances, influenced by the misrepresentation.

Thus, positive representations of the day on which the ship has sailed (*i*), or on which she was last seen in safety (*k*), of the kind of armament she is fitted out with, the number of men with which she is manned (*l*), her age (*m*), and the nature of the cargo she is to carry (*n*), being all of them statements of facts manifestly material to the risks, and almost necessarily affecting the underwriter's estimate of it, will, if false, avoid the policy, unless the assured can show conclusively that the underwriter was not in fact influenced by them. In the absence of such proof the presumption is the contrary, and against the policy (*o*). In Scotland it has been held that a representation, in effecting a time policy, that a particular voyage was contemplated, was immaterial,

---

from that now established in this country. See Phillips, Ins. s. 524. The editors submit that the rule stated by Arnould is correct, although the evidence in Flinn *v.* Headlam may not have justified its application. The Mar. Ins. Act, however, if the language used in sect. 20, sub-sect. 1, is construed literally, supports Phillips' view; and there is a passage in the judgment of Vaughan Williams, L. J., in Cantiere Meccanico Brindisino *v.* Janson, [1912] 3 K. B. at p. 460, citing an opinion of Scrutton, J., which apparently favours this construction of the Act. But the decision of the case did not turn upon this point, and such a construction involves an anomalous state of the law. For it is clear that, apart from marine insurance, even a fraudulent misrepresentation gives no right to rescind a contract, when it has not influenced the party to whom it was made. See *ante*, § 536. Mr. Arthur Cohen supports the editors' submission: Laws of England, vol. xvii. § 809.

(*i*) Anderson *v.* Thornton (1853), 8 Ex. 425; Fillis *v.* Brutton (1782), 1 Park, Ins. 414; Dennistoun *v.* Lillie (1821), 3 Bligh, 202; Arnot *v.* Stewart (1817), 5 Dow, 274.

(*k*) M'Dowell *v.* Fraser (1779), 1 Dougl. 260.

(*l*) Pawson *v.* Watson (1778), 2 Cowp. 785; Edwards *v.* Footner (1808), 1 Camp. 530.

(*m*) Ionides *v.* Pacific Fire & Marine Ins. Co. (1871), L. R. 6 Q. B. 674; (1872), L. R. 7 Q. B. 517.

(*n*) Flinn *v.* Headlam (1829), 9 B. & Cr. 693.

(*o*) See per Lord Blackburn in Smith *v.* Chadwick (1884), 9 App. Cas. at p. 196.

as under the policy the assured could at will change the destination of the ship (*p*). Sect. 555.

The circumstance that a representation relates to facts which, though material to the risk, the assured is not bound to disclose, as the age, structure or condition of the vessel, and generally all those points which are included in the warranty of seaworthiness (*q*), will not prevent its avoiding the policy, if not substantially true, when it is made in answer to inquiries by the underwriter. Representations made in answer to questions.

According to Phillips, the question of materiality cannot be raised when a representation is made in answer to an inquiry. "A party," he says, "in making a contract has a right to the advantage of his own judgment of what is material; and if, by making specific inquiry, he implies that he considers a fact to be so, the other party is bound to it as such" (*r*). The fact of the inquiry being made is clear evidence that the representation has influenced the mind of the underwriter. Yet when the inquiry relates to a matter which is not material (in the sense in which "material" has been defined), it may be doubted whether an honest, though inaccurate, answer will give him the right to avoid the policy (*s*).

556. Although underwriters at Lloyd's are generally presumed to know the contents of Lloyd's lists (*t*), a positive misrepresentation of a fact material to the risk, the truth as to which may be ascertained by merely referring to Lloyd's lists, will be held to avoid the policy unless distinct proof can be adduced that the underwriter actually did inspect the Misrepresentation of contents of Lloyd's lists.

(*p*) Harvey *v.* Seligman (1883), 10 Ct. of Sess. Cas. (4th ser.) 680.

(*q*) Shoolbred *v.* Nutt (1782), 1 Park, 492; Haywood *v.* Rodgers (1804), 4 East, 590.

(*r*) 1 Phillips, Ins. s. 542. See Kerr *v.* Union Marine Ins. Co. (1904), 130 Fed. R. 415.

(*s*) See per Lord Esher in The Bedouin, [1894] P. 1, 12:—"If he

(*i.e.*, the assured) is asked a question—whether a material fact or not—by the underwriters, he must answer it truly. If he answers it falsely, *with intent to deceive*, though it may not be a material fact, it will vitiate the policy."

(*t*) See *ante*, § 77; *post*, §§ 614 —616.

722 MISREPRESENTATION. [PART II.

Sect. 556.

Rate of premium as a test of materiality.

lists. The presumption is that he relied upon such representation, and not upon the lists (*u*).

Where the facts represented are not thus manifestly material to the risk, a presumption as to the materiality of the representation may be founded on the rate of premium. If the premium is much lower than is required in the absence of such representation, the fair presumption is that the representation induced the underwriter to take the risk at the lower premium; if the premium were higher than, or the same as, usual, the presumption would be the other way (*x*).

Materiality a question for the jury.
Whether evidence of skilled witnesses admissible.

557. "Whether a particular representation be material or not is, in each case, a question of fact" (*y*), a question which falls exclusively within the province of a jury (*z*). Whether the jury, in forming their judgment on this point, are to be left to draw their conclusions simply from the facts, or to be aided by the opinions of witnesses of experience and skill, such as underwriters, insurance brokers, and merchants, is a point on which the authorities are not agreed. This point will be dealt with in the chapter on "Concealment" (*a*).

What amounts to a substantial compliance with a representation.

558. We proceed now to inquire when a representation will be regarded as falsified by fact.

It is provided by the Marine Insurance Act, 1906 (*b*), that " a representation as to a matter of fact is true, if it be substantially correct, that is to say, if the difference between what is represented and what is actually correct would not be considered material by a prudent insurer." Also that " a

---

(*u*) Mackintosh *v.* Marshall (1843), 11 M. & W. 116. There is an opinion not in accord with this decision, attributed to Erle, C. J., in Foley *v.* Tabor (1861), 2 F. & F. 662.

(*x*) See, as to presumptions from the rate of premium, Court *v.* Martineau (1782), 3 Dougl. 161; Bridges *v.* Hunter (1813), 1 M. & S. 18, 20; see also Tate *v.* Hyslop (1885), 15 Q. B. D. 368.

(*y*) Mar. Ins. Act, 1906, s. 20, sub-s. 7, *ante*, § 522.

(*z*) M'Dowell *v.* Fraser (1779), 1 Dougl. 260; Shirley *v.* Wilkinson (1781), 1 Dougl. 306, n.; Willes *v.* Glover (1804), 1 B. & P. N. R. 14; Mackintosh *v.* Marshall (1843), 11 M. & W. 116, 121; Duer on Representations, 78, 196, n. xxii., and the cases there cited.

(*a*) *Post*, § 626.

(*b*) Sect. 20, sub-sects. 4, 5.

representation as to a matter of expectation or belief is true if it be made in good faith" (c).

Sect. 558.

A representation may in general terms be said to be falsified where the facts to which it relates turn out not to correspond with the statements or stipulations it contains.

If the representation be made with the intent to deceive, any want of correspondence between the facts as they occur and the facts as stated, however trivial, or however immaterial to the nature of the risk, will avoid the policy, on the ground of actual fraud (d), unless it be clearly proved that the representation did not influence the underwriter (e).

In case of fraud any variance may avoid the policy.

Thus, to take a case put by Judge Duer: Suppose the owner of a vessel insured "at and from" a foreign port has intelligence of her sailing, and also that a certain number of her crew had died since the commencement of the voyage, if he states truly the fact and time of her sailing, but yet, fearing the effect of the whole truth on the mind of the underwriter, represents the number of deaths to be fewer than he knows to have occurred, then, although the remaining crew may still be abundantly competent to perform the voyage, and the misrepresentation consequently be immaterial to the risk, yet this falsity of statement, being intentional, will avoid the policy (f).

559. In cases, however, where there is no actual fraud, the rule is different. The result of all the cases is that, although a warranty, being in terms written on the face of the policy, will avoid it unless fulfilled to the letter, yet a representation, forming no part of the policy, will, in the absence of actual fraud, be satisfied by a substantial compliance, and will not

In the absence of fraud only a substantial compliance with the representation is required.

(c) See *ante*, §§ 545, 546.

(d) According to Duer, the presumption that the insurer was induced by the falsehood to enter into the contract should prevail in all cases, except where it is apparent that had the truth been known in its whole extent, it could not possibly have varied the terms of the contract; and where the misrepresentation is intentional, such a case can hardly be expected to occur. The underwriter is entitled to the benefit of any uncertainty. 2 Duer, Ins. 692, 693.

(e) See *ante*, § 555.

(f) 2 Duer, Ins. 692.

Sect. 559. be deemed falsified unless departed from in some material point. In the words of Lord Mansfield, "A representation may be equitably and substantially answered, but a warranty must be strictly complied with" (g).

Thus, to take an illustration from a case already more than once referred to, where the representation made as to the ship was, "she mounts twelve guns and twenty men," and it turned out that the ship, in fact, had on board only nine carriage-guns and sixteen men, yet, as she had also on board six swivels and nine boys, and as it was satisfactorily proved that with this force she was stronger than she would have been with twelve carriage-guns and twenty men, Lord Mansfield held that there had been a substantial compliance with the representation, *i.e.*, no such falsification of it as to avoid the policy (h). Had these same words been inserted in the policy as a warranty, the policy would have been avoided by her carrying one man or one gun less than the exact number specified.

So if a ship which is only represented as neutral, and which, in fact, belongs to a neutral state, be documented and navigated according to its laws, condemnation for breach of neutrality will not avoid the policy, though it would be otherwise if she were warranted neutral (i).

A statement that a vessel had been last metalled in 1867 was held to be substantially true, where the bottom had been then overhauled and new metal put on where required, so that the bottom was in as good a state as if it had been entirely re-metalled (k).

Wherever, in fact, there is no intention to deceive, the falsity of the representation, in order to avoid the policy,

(g) De Hahn v. Hartley (1786), 1 T. R. 345.
(h) Pawson v. Watson (1778), 2 Cowp. 785.
(i) Von Tungeln v. Dubois (1809), 2 Camp. 151; see also Nonnen v. Kettlewell (1812), 16 East, 176; where the same point was determined in a case where the assured had represented that his property was neutral, but refused to warrant it as such. See also Christian v. Ditchell (1797), Peake's Additional Cases, 141, as to what will satisfy a representation that ship is to sail with convoy.
(k) Alexander v. Campbell (1872), 41 L. J. Ch. 478.

must produce such an alteration of the risk represented to the underwriter, as to lead to the reasonable conclusion, that, had the truth been known, he would either not have signed the policy at all, or would have asked a higher premium for so doing. If, upon the whole of the evidence, it appears doubtful whether such would be the effect of the non-correspondence of the facts with the statement, the assured is entitled to the benefit of the doubt, and the policy shall stand in force (*l*).

Sect. 559.

560. Under this rule different degrees of strictness in compliance will be required in case of different representations. For instance, positive representations, with regard to the time of the ship's sailing, where that fact is material to the risk, must be complied with almost as literally as express warranties to the same effect. In the case of sailing vessels, the smallest difference is often very material, as in the case mentioned by Lord Ellenborough, of two vessels, "one of which sailed to Nova Scotia and back before the other had made any material progress in her voyage, only from the advantage of having a few hours' start" (*m*).

Representations require more or less strict compliance according to their nature.

Hence, where in an assurance "at and from," the broker's instructions stated the ship to be ready to sail on the 24th of the month, and the broker represented the ship to be in port when in fact she had sailed on the 23rd, this was held such a falsity as to avoid the policy (*n*). So where the representation was that the ship "will sail in the month of October," which by the usage of trade was shown to mean "between the 25th of October and the 1st or 2nd of November," and the ship, in fact, sailed on the 11th of October, this was held fatal to the policy (*o*). So where the broker, proceeding on a false computation founded on a mis-

---

(*l*) Where there is actual fraud, the presumption, according to Duer, is the other way: see *ante*, § 558, note (*d*).

(*m*) In Kirby *v*. Smith (1818), 1 B. & Ald. 672, 674.

(*n*) Fillis *v*. Brutton (1782), 1 Park, Ins. 414; 1 Marshall, Ins. 462, 465.

(*o*) Chaurand *v*. Angerstein (1791), Peake, N. P. 43.

Sect. 560. conception of intelligence truly communicated to him, stated to the underwriter that the ship "was seen safe in the Delaware on the 11th," whereas, in fact, she had been taken on the 9th, this was held such a misrepresentation as to avoid the policy (*p*).

Where, however, it appears reasonable to conclude, from the whole circumstances of the case, that the failure to comply with the strict terms of the representation has not substantially altered the nature of the risk, as described in the policy, such non-compliance will not discharge the underwriter's contract (*q*).

Underwriter signing a policy inconsistent with representation waives compliance therewith.

561. Moreover, if the underwriter subscribe a policy, inconsistent in its terms with those of a representation made to him before doing so, he waives his right to require a substantial compliance with the representation, or to insist on a failure therein as avoiding the policy (*r*).

A representation may be withdrawn before the contract is concluded.

A representation may be withdrawn or corrected at any time before the contract is concluded, either expressly, by a declaration from the assured to the underwriters that he was mistaken or will not be held to a compliance with the representation, or impliedly, by a subsequent qualifying or controlling statement (*s*).

(*p*) M'Dowell *v.* Fraser (1779), 1 Dougl. 260. And see the principle of the above cases further illustrated in that of Arnot *v.* Stewart (1817), 5 Dow, 274.

(*q*) Bize *v.* Fletcher (1779), 1 Dougl. 12, n., 284.

(*r*) *Ibid.*

(*s*) Mar. Ins. Act, 1906, s. 20, sub-s. 6; Carter *v.* Boehm (1766), 3 Burr. 1905; Dawson *v.* Atty (1806), 7 East, 367; Edwards *v.* Footner (1808), 1 Camp. 530. Dawson *v.* Atty, says Maclachlan (Arnould, 6th ed. p. 543), is a remarkable decision, as there was nothing to qualify or cancel the first statement. Lord Ellenborough, however, continued of the same mind when Edwards *v.* Footner was before him, and this case was referred to and approved of by him. In Kerr *v.* Union Marine Ins Co. (1904), 130 Fed. R. 415, the Circuit Court of Appeals held that a representation that a ship had not sailed, made more than a month before the policy was effected, was in the circumstances not only material, but also a continuing representation, and that as it had not been corrected, the policy was avoided.

562. If the representation relates to a fact, the existence of which is to precede the commencement of the risk, its substantial truth when the policy attaches is indispensable; and if then false the policy will be avoided. If, however, the representation promises either expressly or impliedly that certain facts shall continue to exist, as where it states that the vessel is provided with a certain armament, is neutral, &c., and this promissory representation is falsified by facts arising subsequently to the policy having attached (*t*), Judge Duer thinks, by analogy to the doctrine which prevails in the case of warranties (*u*), that this will not relate back so as to avoid the policy *ab initio*, but that the underwriter will be liable for losses that have taken place between the commencement of the risk and the failure to comply with the representation (*x*).

Sect. 562.

Does a representation falsified in all cases avoid the insurance ab initio?

It should seem also that if such breach of a promissory representation be transitory in its nature, it will not exonerate the underwriter from liability for subsequent losses not connected with, or in any degree arising from it (*y*).

Thus, again, to take a case put by Judge Duer: If the master of a vessel represented to be neutral should, on being lawfully detained by a belligerent cruiser, refuse to produce the necessary documents of national character, this, by rendering the ship liable to seizure, would undoubtedly be failure to comply with the implied promissory representation, that the ship should continue neutral throughout the voyage. If the ship on this distinct ground were captured and condemned, the underwriter would, unquestionably, not be liable for the loss; but if she were released, and continued her voyage, and were afterwards lost by the perils of the seas, the better opinion would seem to be, that the assured ought not to be deprived of his indemnity on account of the

---

(*t*) This passage, like the others relating to promissory representations, is preserved subject to the criticism of the doctrine of promissory representations, *ante*, §§ 542–544.

(*u*) See *post*, § 634.
(*x*) 2 Duer, Ins. 696.
(*y*) Duer in suggesting this rule confines it to losses not proceeding from the act or will of the assured. 2 Ins. 697.

Sect. 562. previous failure to comply with the representation of neutrality (*z*).

Promissory representations falsified by an act of the home government, by force or unavoidable accident.

563. There can also be little question that, as in the case of warranties, if promissory representations are falsified after the policy has attached, by an act of the home government (*a*), by irresistible force or unavoidable accident, the validity of the contract will not be affected thereby. Thus, where the government, to which a vessel represented neutral belongs, becomes involved in war after the policy has attached, this, although materially affecting the risks, would not, it seems, avoid the policy (*b*).

So, if it were represented that a vessel should sail with convoy, or a certain armament, and peace be proclaimed before the voyage commenced, it would manifestly be unreasonable to exact the performance of this representation as a condition of the underwriter's liability (*c*).

Construction of representation.

The words are to be taken in their plain and obvious meaning.

564. In the construction of representations, the primary rule is to take the words in their plain and obvious meaning, and in that sense in which it is most reasonable to conclude that they were understood by the underwriter (*d*).

Thus, it has been determined in the United States, in the case of a policy effected at Boston on a New York ship, that a representation on the part of the assured, residing at New York, that she was "coppered," must have been understood by the Boston underwriters to have been used in the sense which it bears in New York (*e*).

All that would reasonably and necessarily be inferred by mercantile men from the language employed will be considered as forming part of the representation.

Ratcliffe v. Shoolbred.

Thus, where the assured, knowing that the ship had sailed from the coast of Africa in the course of the 2nd of October,

---

(*z*) 2 Duer, Ins. 697, 698.
(*a*) See, however, *post*, § 636.
(*b*) 2 Duer, Ins. 699.
(*c*) *Ibid.*
(*d*) See Sibbald *v.* Hill (1814), 2 Dow, 263.
(*e*) Hazard *v.* New England Marine Ins. Co. (1834), 8 Peters, S. C. R. 557; 1 Phillips, Ins. 566.

simply stated to the underwriter "that the ship was on the coast the 2nd of October," this representation was construed as meaning that the last intelligence left the ship on the coast, and that no advice of her actual sailing had been received: and the jury, under the direction of Lord Mansfield, found that the policy was void for misrepresentation and concealment (f).

So, where the owner of a ship, in order to induce the underwriters to take an insurance on her "from Elsinore to Hull," stated to them that the ship "was all well at Elsinore on the 26th of July," Bayley, J., said that "the natural conclusion from this representation would be that she was left there well at that time"; and therefore, as it appeared that she had sailed from Elsinore, to the owner's knowledge, on the 26th of July, six hours before the vessel on board which he himself had left that port, the Court held the policy void for misrepresentation and concealment (g).

Kirby v. Smith.

565. If the language of the representation be designedly ambiguous, the underwriter, if deceived, would be discharged from all liability upon the policy on the ground of fraud.

Words designedly ambiguous.

If in the absence of fraudulent design there be such obvious ambiguity as might have suggested doubts to the underwriter as to the meaning of the representation, and impelled him to seek an explanation from the assured, and if he omit to do so, he will not be permitted to avail himself of the representation not being true in the sense in which he understood it. This rule will especially hold where the form of the statement itself shows that in all probability it was not meant as a positive representation; or where it suggests on the face of it, as by reference to other sources of information, that it is not to be taken as a complete statement of the case (h).

Words obviously ambiguous, without fraud.

Thus, where a policy was effected on a ship "lost or not lost at and from twenty-four hours after her arrival at her

Freeland v. Glover.

(f) Ratcliffe v. Shoolbred (1780), 1 Park, Ins. 413.
(g) Kirby v. Smith (1818), 1 B. & Ald. 672, 675.
(h) Brine v. Featherstone (1813), 4 Taunt. 869; Freeland v. Glover (1806), 7 East, 457.

first place of trade on the coast of Africa, during her stay and trade on the coast, and at and from thence to Liverpool," and the assured had submitted to the underwriters, before the subscription of this policy, a letter from the master containing the latest intelligence as to the then state and condition of the ship, but referring to a former letter from the master on the same subject, which was not exhibited; the Court held that the mention of the former letter, in the second, ought to have put the underwriters upon an inquiry as to the nature of the first communication, and that they were not entitled to complain of the suppression of the first letter as a concealment (*i*).

When representation must be construed with reference to usage.
Chaurand v. Angerstein.

566. The words of a representation, equally with those of the policy itself, must, if technical or of peculiar mercantile import, be construed with reference to the usage of trade. Thus, where it was represented that a ship was to sail "in the month of October," evidence was admitted to show that this, by the usage of trade, meant that she was to sail "between the 20th of October and the 1st or 2nd of November"; and as she actually did sail on the 11th of October, this was held a failure to comply with the representation that avoided the contract (*k*).

Representation refers generally to the time of making the contract.

567. A representation, in order to have any effect upon the policy, must have been made "during the negotiations for the contract, and before the contract is concluded" (*l*). And the contract "is deemed to be concluded when the proposal of the assured is accepted by the insurer, whether the policy be then issued or not; and for the purpose of showing when the proposal was accepted, reference may be made to the slip or covering note or other customary memorandum of the contract, although it be unstamped" (*m*). Every representation is construed to mean that the facts represented are

(*i*) Freeland *v.* Glover (1806), 7 East, 457.
(*k*) Chaurand *v.* Angerstein (1791), Peake, N. P. 43.

(*l*) Mar. Ins. Act, 1906, s. 20, sub-s. 1.

(*m*) *Ibid.* s. 21.

then true, and that no other facts bearing on the representation are then known to the assured.

What has been stated before this time is liable to be qualified or controlled by what passes at such time.

Formerly the practice to consider the contract binding as soon as the slip was initialed was not recognized by the Courts, and the material time, in questions of misrepresentation or concealment, was the time when the policy was subscribed (*n*).

Sect. 567.

Former doctrine. Dawson v. Atty.

568. Among merchants, however, the initialing of the slip was always regarded as the making of the contract, and since the statute 30 Vict. c. 23, the Courts have recognized this course of business (*o*); and accordingly it was held, that after the initialing of the slip any fresh fact coming to the knowledge of the assured need not be communicated to the underwriters, however material it might be (*p*).

Now the initialing of the slip concludes the contract.

So also any misrepresentation made after the agreement for the insurance, as by the signing of a slip, will not avoid the policy, for it did not influence the underwriter in accepting the risk (*q*).

A broker agreed with an insurance company for an open policy for £5,000 on hides by ship or ships, to be declared, and the slip was signed. Hides to the value of £2,455 were shipped on an old French ship called the "Socrate." There was a new Norwegian ship called the "Socrates," and the broker, believing this to be the ship on which the hides were shipped, made a statement to that effect and wrote out a second slip for a policy for £2,455 on hides per the "Socrates," to be issued in respect of the agreed insurance, and in the policy the hides were described as shipped on the "Socrates." It was held that a representation that a ship is new when she is old will vitiate a policy on goods on board of her; for the

Ionides v. Pacific Fire, &c. Ins. Co.

(*n*) See Dawson *v.* Atty (1806), 7 East, 367, and note (*s*) on § 561.
(*o*) *Ante,* § 34.
(*p*) Cory *v.* Patton (1872), L. R. 7 Q. B. 304; (1874), L. R. 9 Q. B. 577; Lishman *v.* Northern Maritime Ins. Co. (1873), L. R. 8 C. P. 216; in the Exch. Ch. (1875), L. R. 10 C. P. 179.

(*q*) Ionides *v.* Pacific Fire & Marine Ins. Co. (1871), L. R. 6 Q. B. 674; in the Exch. Ch. (1872), L. R. 7 Q. B. 517.

Sect. 568. age of the vessel must be material in considering the premium. The Court, however, decided that in the present case the misnomer was of no consequence, as the company had bound themselves to insure hides on board any ship selected by the assured, and the representation was subsequent to the agreement for the insurance (r). It therefore had not influenced the underwriter in making the contract.

Representation may be withdrawn before contract concluded.

569. The assured, it has already been said (s), is at liberty before the contract is concluded to withdraw or qualify any previous representation, by which he does not wish to be bound. It has been held that when the underwriter has, after initialing the slip, become aware that material facts have not been disclosed to him, and has afterwards executed a policy without protest, he is not estopped from setting up the defence of concealment (t). The reason is, that an underwriter who has initialed a slip is in honour bound, according to the practice of underwriters, to execute a stamped policy, if only to enable the assured to sue him. It seems to follow that when a misrepresentation has been corrected after the slip has been initialed, the mere fact that the underwriter has executed a policy is not in itself enough to prevent him from claiming to avoid the contract on the ground of the misrepresentation. It must depend on the circumstances of the particular case whether the underwriter has in fact elected to treat the contract as a binding one, or whether he is estopped from saying that he has not so elected (u).

Effect of issue of policy after correction of misrepresentation.

What diligence necessary in correcting misrepresentation.

570. A representation should be forthwith corrected in case there be reason to suppose that it cannot be sustained as made. Thus, where the agent of the assured, after hearing of the loss of the ship, allowed the post to go with his previous letter uncontradicted, inducing others to suppose that she was safe when the post left, such omission was held

(r) Ionides v. Pacific Fire & Marine Ins. Co., *supra*.

(s) *Ante*, § 561.

(t) Morrison v. Universal Marine Ins. Co. (Exch. Ch.) (1873), L. R. 8 Ex. 197.

(u) See *ante*, §§ 523 *et seq.*

CHAP. I.] MISREPRESENTATION. 733

to amount to a misrepresentation, on the part of the agent, Sect. 570.
which avoided the policy (*x*).

It has been held in the United States, but before the days of the electric telegraph, that although the assured or his agents are bound to act with promptitude and despatch in countermanding an order for insurance founded on false intelligence, they are not bound to resort to extraordinary means of communication for this purpose; they need not send an express unless that be the usual mode (*y*).

571. Where there are several underwriters to the same slip or policy, a representation of a material fact to the underwriter whose name stands first extends to all the rest, so that each, when it proves false, may avail himself of the defence. The ground of this rule is the reasonable presumption that the others subscribed from the confidence reposed by them in the skill and judgment of him whose name stood first, and their belief that he had duly ascertained and weighed all the circumstances material to the risk (*z*). This rule, however, is subject to many limitations. *Misrepresentation to the first underwriter extends to all.*

Limitations on this rule.

It must strictly be confined to intelligence relating to the proposed insurance, with regard to which it is reasonable to suppose that the first underwriter would require information, *(1) It only extends to representations pertinent to an ordinary insurance.*

(*x*) Fitzherbert *v.* Mather (1785), 1 T. R. 12. The editors have already expressed the view that this case is one of concealment rather than of misrepresentation. *Ante*, § 553, note (*x*).

(*y*) See Greene *v.* Merchant Ins. Co. (1830), 10 Pickering, Mass. R. 402; M'Lanahan *v.* Universal Ins. Co. (1828), 1 Peters, S. C. R. 186; 1 Phillips, s. 561. See, however, Proudfoot *v.* Montefiore (1867), L. R. 2 Q. B. 511.

(*z*) The English cases which establish the rule are Pawson *v.* Watson (1778), 2 Cowp. 785; Barber *v.* Fletcher (1779), 1 Dougl. 306; Stackpole *v.* Simon (1779), 2 Park, Ins. 933; Marsden *v.* Reid (1803), 3 East, 572; Feise *v.* Parkinson (1812), 4 Taunt. 640; Forester *v.* Pigou (1813), 1 M. & S. 9, 13; Bell *v.* Carstairs (1810), 2 Camp. 543. The rule has been adversely criticized. The editors have, however, been informed that a broker at Lloyd's, usually tries first to obtain the signature thereto of some underwriter with a high reputation for experience and prudence, and that, if he succeeds, it is easy to obtain further subscriptions. This practice seems to them to afford a strong argument in favour of the rule.

Sect. 571. and without being informed of which, it may be presumed, he would not have accepted the risk. It cannot, therefore, extend to such representations as relate to matters of collateral agreement, which a subsequent underwriter can have no reason to infer, from the terms of the policy, to have been communicated to the first.

Thus, in Pawson v. Watson, Lord Mansfield held, that a representation that " the ship mounts twelve guns and twenty men," being in effect an engagement that the ship should sail with that armament, could not affect subsequent underwriters, to whom it had never been communicated, merely upon proof that it had been made to the underwriter whose name stood first in the policy. "A representation to the first underwriter," says his Lordship, "has nothing whatever to do with that which is the agreement or the terms of the policy; no man who underwrites a policy subscribes, by the act of underwriting, to terms of which he knows nothing, but he reads the agreement and is governed by that: matters of intelligence, such as that a ship is or is not missing, are things in which a man is guided by the name of the first underwriter, who is a good man, which another will therefore give faith and credit to, but not to a collateral agreement which he can know nothing of" (a).

Of course, if the representation to the first underwriter be not of material facts, it cannot avail a subsequent one; and if it was of such a nature that it ought to have put the first underwriter on further inquiry, it will be equally imputed to the negligence of the subsequent underwriter that no such inquiry was made (b).

(2) Formerly the rule was only applicable to the policy.

572. Until the decisions under 30 Vict. c. 23, the applicability of this rule was restricted to the policy, because the slip could not even be given in evidence for any purpose whatever (c); but since the slip may be given in evidence

(a) 2 Cowp. 788.
(b) Barber v. Fletcher (1779), 1 Dougl. 306.

(c) Marsden v. Reid (1803), 3 East, 572. In this case the names of the underwriters appeared in a

whenever it is material (*d*), the rule becomes applicable to either the policy or the slip, and will probably, in consequence of the state of facts, be more frequently applied to the latter than the former.

Sect. 572.

573. A still further limitation of the same rule is, that it only applies where the tendency of the representation is to induce the underwriters to take the risk on lower terms.

(3) The rule includes only representations that lower the terms.

Where the first underwriter was called to prove a representation made to him, the tendency of which would have been to increase the estimate of the risk, Lord Tenterden decided, at Nisi Prius, that this evidence was not admissible as against a subsequent underwriter (*e*).

Even under these limitations the English Courts have regarded the rule with great jealousy, and on many occasions have expressed their dissatisfaction with it. Heath, J., on one occasion said, that "the evidence had been admitted rather on precedent than on reason" (*f*); and Lord Ellenborough—"Whenever the question comes distinctly before the Court, whether a communication to the first underwriter is virtually a notice to all, I shall not scruple to remark that that proposition is to be received with great qualification; it may depend on the time and circumstances under which that communication was made; but on the mere naked unaccompanied fact of one name standing first on the policy, I should not hold that a communication made to him was virtually made to all the subsequent underwriters"; and his Lordship said that the question was one of such magnitude that if it should arise he should direct it to be put on the record for the opinion of all the judges (*g*).

The rule not favoured.

different order on the policy from that on the slip; but the slip was not admissible in evidence, as the law then stood, to show that the underwriter to whom a representation had been made stood first in order on the slip though not on the policy.

(*d*) See Mar. Ins. Act, 1906, s. 89, *ante*, §§ 34 *et seq.*

(*e*) Robertson *v.* Majoribanks (1819), 2 Stark. N. P. 573, 575; 2 Duer, Ins. 779.

(*f*) Brine *v.* Featherstone (1813), 4 Taunt. 869.

(*g*) In Forester *v.* Pigou (1813), 1 M. & S. 13.

MISREPRESENTATION. [PART II.

Sect. 574.

Where the first underwriter is a mere "decoy duck," this avoids the contract.

574. Of course, if the subscription of the first underwriter is obtained under a secret agreement or understanding that it is not to be binding, and for the sole purpose of leading others to insure, the exhibition of the policy or slip thus subscribed is justly regarded as a fraud on the subsequent underwriters, and on that ground avoids the policy (*h*). This rule, it is said, will extend to the case of any prior underwriter, though his name may not be first in the policy (*i*).

(*h*) Whittingham *v.* Thornburgh (1690), 2 Vernon, 206; Wilson *v.* Ducket (1761), 3 Burr. 1361; see also the observations of Lord Eldon in Sibbald *v.* Hill (1814), 2 Dow, 263. The first underwriter in such cases has been called in England, a decoy duck; on the Continent, a dolphin, who leaps from the water that others may follow. 1 Emerigon, c. ii. s. 4, p. 43.

(*i*) 2 Duer, 679.

CHAPTER II.

CONCEALMENT.

SECT.	SECT.
General Principles 575, 576	Facts within the knowledge of
Concealment by Principal 577	the Underwriter ....609—617
by Agent ....578—588	
Test of Materiality ....589—591	Facts disclosure of which is
Concealment of Facts as to	Waived ....618—622
Missing Ship ....592—596	
Concealment of Facts that ag-	Matters of Inference ......623—625
gravate the Risk ....597—608	How Materiality is Proved..626, 627

575. CONCEALMENT, in the law of insurance, is the suppression of, or neglect to communicate, a material fact within the knowledge of one of the parties which the other has not the means of knowing, or is not presumed to know. A material fact is one which is calculated, if communicated to the other of the parties, to induce him either to refrain altogether from the contract or not to enter into it except on more favourable terms (a). Defined in these terms, the principle is equally applicable to the assured and the underwriter.

The contract is one *uberrimæ fidei* (b), and on the plainest principles of equity such a contract which one party has thus been induced to enter upon from his ignorance of the thing concealed shall not be enforced against him by the other who has concealed it. Whether such suppression of the truth arise from fraud (that is, from a wilful intention to deceive for the party's own benefit), or merely from mistake, negligence, or

Definition and general principles.

(a) See *post*, § 589; 1 Marshall, Ins. 463; 1 Phillips, s. 531; and per Tindal, C. J., in Elton v. Larkins (1832), 5 C. & P. 392.

(b) See Mar. Ins. Act, 1906, s. 17, *ante*, § 522.

Sect. 575. accident, the consequences will be the same (*c*). The ground, in short, on which the policy is avoided is that the party has been, in fact, deceived, not that the other party has intended to deceive him.

Principles on which concealment avoids the policy.

As we have seen in the preceding chapter (*d*), it is a condition of this contract, implied by law as a matter of public policy, that the contract is free from misrepresentation or concealment; and if there is a breach of this condition, either by misrepresentation or concealment of a material fact, the contract is voidable. Fraud in its effect goes beyond the condition; for if fraud be present in either form, whether of misrepresentation or concealment, it avoids the policy, although the subject misrepresented or concealed be not a material fact (*e*).

Generally speaking, as the facts lie most within the peculiar knowledge of the assured, it is the underwriter who avails himself of the defence of concealment; yet he, as well as the assured, is bound to disclose all circumstances, peculiarly within his own knowledge, in any degree affecting the risk. Thus, if the underwriter, at the time of subscribing the policy, knew that the ship had arrived safe, the contract will be void as to him, and an action will lie against him to recover back the premium (*f*).

Provisions of the Mar. Ins. Act as to concealment.

The assured's duty as regards Disclosure is particularly enunciated in the eighteenth and nineteenth sections of the Marine Insurance Act, 1906, as follows:—

> Sect. 18.—(1) Subject to the provisions of this section, the assured must disclose to the insurer, before the contract is concluded, every material circumstance which is known to the assured, and the assured is deemed to know

---

(*c*) Carter *v.* Boehm (1766), 3 Burr. 1909; Ratcliffe *v.* Shoolbred (1780), 1 Park, Ins. 413; 1 Marshall, Ins. 464; Shirley *v.* Wilkinson (1786), 1 Dougl. 306, n.; Thompson *v.* Buchanan (1782), 4 Br. P. C. 482; per Willes, J., Anderson *v.* Pacific Fire & Mar. Ins. Co. (1872), L. R. 7 C. P. 65, 68; *per cur.*

Ionides *v.* Pender (1874), L. R. 9 Q. B. 531, 537.

(*d*) *Ante*, § 535.

(*e*) *Ante*, § 536.

(*f*) Per Lord Mansfield in Carter *v.* Boehm (1766), 1 W. Bl. 594; 3 Burr. 1909; *ante*, § 522, note (*a*); see also 3 Benecke, System des Assecuranz, c. x. pp. 90, 91.

every circumstance which, in the ordinary course of business, ought to be known by him. If the assured fails to make such disclosure, the insurer may avoid the contract.

Sect. 575.

(2) Every circumstance is material which would influence the judgment of a prudent insurer in fixing the premium, or determining whether he will take the risk.

(3) In the absence of inquiry the following circumstances need not be disclosed, namely:—

(a) Any circumstance which diminishes the risk;
(b) Any circumstance which is known or presumed to be known to the insurer. The insurer is presumed to know matters of common notoriety or knowledge, and matters which an insurer in the ordinary course of his business, as such, ought to know;
(c) Any circumstance as to which information is waived by the insurer;
(d) Any circumstance which it is superfluous to disclose by reason of any express or implied warranty.

(4) Whether any particular circumstance, which is not disclosed, be material or not is, in each case, a question of fact.

(5) The term "circumstance" includes any communication made to, or information received by, the assured.

Sect. 19. Subject to the provisions of the preceding section as to circumstances which need not be disclosed, where an insurance is effected for the assured by an agent, the agent must disclose to the insurer—

(a) Every material circumstance which is known to himself, and an agent to insure is deemed to know every circumstance which in the ordinary course of business ought to be known by, or to have been communicated to, him; and
(b) Every material circumstance which the assured is bound to disclose, unless it come to his knowledge too late to communicate it to the agent.

576. The duty to disclose ceases to exist as soon as the contract is concluded; and as already stated in respect of Representations (*g*), by the express provision of the Marine

Time of concealment.

(*g*) *Ante*, §§ 522, 567.

Sect. 576. Insurance Act, 1906 (*h*), following the decisions of the Courts, the contract is deemed to be concluded when the proposal of the assured is accepted by the insurer, whether the policy be then issued or not (*i*). Consequently anything coming to the knowledge of either party afterwards, however material it may be, need not be communicated to the other, notwithstanding a policy has not yet been executed in accordance with the slip (*k*).

When policy altered or rectified.

Where a broker was instructed to effect a policy on goods, and by mistake effected one on the ship, and the underwriter afterwards agreed to an alteration of the policy, it was held that the broker was bound to disclose a material fact which had come to his knowledge between the execution of the policy and the rectification of the mistake (*l*). The reason, as Duer points out, is that the underwriter was under no obligation to make the alteration. By doing so he was really making a new and distinct insurance. If on the other hand the alteration does not make a new contract, but merely declares the true meaning of the contract already concluded, this reasoning does not apply, and there is no necessity to disclose the information acquired after the making of the contract (*m*).

In case of re-insurance.

It has been pointed out by Duer, and agrees with what has been said, that the duty of an underwriter who effects a re-insurance to communicate his information relates to the time when he effects the re-insurance, not to the time when the original insurance was made. Therefore he must disclose material information which has come to his knowledge

---

(*h*) Sect. 21.

(*i*) When, however, the policy tendered to the underwriter and executed by him does not correspond with the slip, it is no defence that a fact material to the risk described in the slip, but not to that described in the policy, was not disclosed. British & Foreign Mar. Ins. Co. *v.* Sturge (1897), 77 L. T. 208; 2 Com. Cas. 204.

(*k*) Ionides *v.* Pacific Fire & Mar. Ins. Co. (1871), L. R. 6 Q. B. 674; (1872), 7 Q. B. 517; Cory *v.* Patton (1872), L. R. 7 Q. B. 304; Lishman *v.* Northern Maritime Ins. Co. (1873), L. R. 8 C. P. 216; (1875), 10 C. P. 179.

(*l*) Sawtell *v.* Loudon (1814), 5 Taunt. 359.

(*m*) 2 Duer, 427.

CHAP. II.] CONCEALMENT. 741

between the making of the original contract and the making of the contract of re-insurance (n).

Sect. 576.

577. If an agent, in ignorance of a loss that has happened, effect an insurance for his principal who knew of the loss at the time the contract was concluded, but "too late to communicate it to the agent" (o), the policy will not be avoided by the concealment; if on the other hand the principal, knowing of the loss in time to communicate it to the agent, effected the contract through an agent who was ignorant of it, the non-communication of the fact of loss will of course vitiate the policy (p). For, by the Marine Insurance Act, 1906, "an agent to insure is deemed to know every circumstance which in the ordinary course of business ought to be known by, or to have been communicated to, him" (q).

Policy effected by an agent in ignorance of a material fact known to his principal.

Material facts, brought to the knowledge of the assured after orders given to insure, ought to be forwarded with the utmost degree of reasonable diligence, so as to reach the underwriter before the insurance is actually effected (r). When the principal can communicate by telegraph with his agent, it is no doubt usually his duty to do so in case of a loss (s).

Duty of principal to send information to agent.

If, owing to the fraud, negligence, or mistake of the agent, material information, or an order from his principal countermanding the insurance, do not reach the agent in

---

(n) 2 Duer, 429.
(o) Mar. Ins. Act, 1906, s. 19 (b).
(p) 2 Valin, l. 3, c. 6, art. 40.
(q) Sect. 19 (a). If the final words "communicated to him" include communications which ought to have been made to the agent by third parties, such as his own servants, the result will be that a principal may have to suffer because his agent has not been kept properly informed by such third parties. If so, these words go beyond any decision upon this point. For the construction of the preceding words "ought to be known by him," the authorities afford scarcely any assistance.

(r) Grieve v. Young (1782), Millar, Ins. 65. It has been held in the United States that the diligence required of the principal is not in every case the utmost possible diligence that might be exacted, but a reasonable diligence to be judged of under all the circumstances of the particular case. McLanahan v. Universal Ins. Co. (1828), 1 Peters, 170. See the cases in 1 Phillips, s. 561.

(s) See Proudfoot v. Montefiore (1867), L. R. 2 Q. B. 511.

Sect. 577. time, a policy effected by him in ignorance of the information or of the order will be vitiated. It has been held not to be negligence in an agent to effect a policy in the morning before calling at his office, where news of a loss awaited him (*t*).

When knowledge of agent is imputed to principal.

578. Sect. 18 (1) of the Marine Insurance Act, 1906, declares that "the assured is deemed to know every circumstance which, in the ordinary course of business, ought to be known by him." This statement generalises a principle which has been laid down with reference to matters known to agents of the assured, upon whom he relies for information. There are certain persons employed by shipowners and owners of cargo, such as masters and trading agents, whose duty it is to keep their employers informed of all matters affecting the property which it is sought to insure. If one of these agents has withheld information of a material fact from his principal which he might, in the ordinary course of things, have communicated to the latter at the time when the insurance is effected, the contract can be avoided by the underwriter on account of the non-disclosure of this fact, which, if the agent had done his duty, the principal would have been able to disclose. In such a case it may be said that the knowledge of the agent is the knowledge of the principal (*u*).

Rule laid down in Proudfoot v. Montefiore.

The law on the subject of concealment through the fault of an agent who has taken no part in negotiating the insurance was comprehensively laid down by the Court of Queen's Bench in a judgment (*x*) which, with some qualifications, was adopted by the House of Lords in Blackburn *v.* Vigors. "If an agent," said the Court, "whose duty it is, in the ordinary course of business, to communicate information to his principal as to the state of a ship and cargo, omits to discharge such duty, and the owner, in the absence of infor-

(*t*) Wake *v.* Atty (1812), 4 Taunt. 493.

(*u*) Per Lord Watson and Lord Macnaghten, Blackburn *v.* Vigors (1887), 12 App. Cas. 531, 540, 542.

(*x*) Proudfoot *v.* Montefiore (1867), L. R. 2 Q. B. 511, 521.

mation as to any fact material to be communicated to the underwriter, effects an insurance, such insurance will be void on the ground of concealment or misrepresentation. The insurer is entitled to assume, as the basis of the contract between him and the assured, that the latter will communicate to him every material fact of which the assured has, or in the ordinary course of business ought to have, knowledge; and that the latter will take the necessary measures, by the employment of competent and honest agents, to obtain, through the ordinary channels of intelligence in use in the mercantile world, all due information as to the subject-matter of the insurance. This condition is not complied with where, by the fraud or negligence of the agent, the party proposing the insurance is kept in ignorance of a material fact which ought to have been made known to the underwriter, and through such ignorance fails to disclose it."

Sect. 578.

579. In Blackburn *v.* Vigors the House of Lords held that it is not every agent whose knowledge can be deemed to be the knowledge of his principal. "Some agents," said Lord Halsbury, "so far represent the principal that in all respects their acts and intentions and their knowledge may truly be said to be the acts and intentions and knowledge of the principal. Other agents may have so limited and narrow an authority, both in fact and in the common understanding of their form of employment, that it would be quite inaccurate to say that such an agent's knowledge or intentions are the knowledge or intentions of his principal" (*y*). The agent whose knowledge is deemed to be that of his principal must be one to whom the principal looks for information concerning the property insured (*z*).

Agents whose knowledge is imputed to principal.

The master of a ship and the general agent of a shipowner for the transaction of his shipping business are agents whose knowledge will be deemed to be the knowledge of the ship-

---

(*y*) 12 App. Cas. 537, 538.
(*z*) Per Lord Watson, *ibid.* 541; per Lord Macnaghten, *ibid.* 542.

Sect. 579. owner (a). Similarly, in one case, the consignor and shipper of a cargo, who was directed to send the shipping documents to the agent who effected the insurance (b), and in another case the general representative of the assured at a foreign port (c), have been held to be agents with whose knowledge the owner of cargo is affected. There is an imperfectly reported Scotch case in the House of Lords, in which it seems to have been decided that a policy was vitiated owing to the knowledge of a clerk of the assured that a loss had taken place (d). Whether this be the *ratio decidendi* or not, it is certainly the duty of a clerk to disclose to his employer whatever information he receives in regard to the latter's business, and it is submitted that the employer is responsible for not disclosing a fact which was within the knowledge of his clerk.

Lloyd's agents in foreign ports are not the agents of the individual underwriters at Lloyd's, and therefore the latter are not affected with knowledge of matters known to the former (e).

Insurance broker not under a duty to send information to his principal.

580. An insurance broker who is employed to obtain an insurance on a particular risk is not one of the agents whose duty it is to give information to the principal. Therefore, a policy is not avoided by concealment or by the non-disclosure of facts, unknown to the principal, but within the knowledge of an insurance broker employed by him, but *through whom the policy in question was not made*.

The case in which this was decided was as follows:—

Blackburn v. Vigors.

Blackburn & Co., of Glasgow, the plaintiffs, finding that a ship on which they were insurers was overdue, instructed

(a) Gladstone v. King (1813), 1 M. & S. 35; per Lord Halsbury, 12 App. Cas. 537; per Lord Watson, *ibid.* 540.

(b) Fitzherbert v. Mather (1785), 1 T. R. 12. For the facts of this case, see *ante*, § 553. The decision was approved in Proudfoot v. Montefiore, *infra*, and much discussed in Blackburn v. Vigors

(1886), 17 Q. B. D. 553; (1887), 12 App. Cas. 531.

(c) Proudfoot v. Montefiore (1867), L. R. 2 Q. B. 511.

(d) Stewart v. Dunlop (1785), Park, vol. i. p. 446.

(e) Wilson v. Salamandra Ass. Co. of St. Petersburg (1903), 8 Com. Cas. 129.

Rose, Murison & Co., of the same place, to procure a reinsurance, and the latter applied to their London agents, Rose, Thompson & Co., for that purpose. One hour later on the same day, Murison was informed of facts tending to show that the ship had been lost some days previously. Soon after came the reply from London quoting a higher rate than the limit fixed. Murison showed the plaintiffs the reply, and then, without communicating to them the information as to the loss, telegraphed in the name of the plaintiffs to London, and thus put the plaintiffs in direct communication with their agents in London, through whom re-insurances to the amount of 800*l.* were effected in London the same afternoon; but as rates continued to rise, the plaintiffs closed their communications with Rose, Thompson & Co., and next day through their own brokers, Roxburgh & Co., in London, effected the policy with the defendant Vigors. The ship had, in fact, been lost some days before the plaintiffs tried to re-insure; but they and Roxburgh & Co. both acted in good faith and did not conceal any material fact within their knowledge.

The Court of Appeal decided (Lord Esher dissenting) that the insurance effected by Roxburgh & Co. was void on account of the concealment by Murison (*f*). Lindley, L. J., held that the assured could not take advantage of the ignorance in which they had been improperly kept by someone whose legal, or even whose moral, duty it was to inform them of the facts concealed. Lord Esher declined to follow, or distinguished, the cases on which the majority of the Court relied. He thought that the underwriter cannot be assumed to rely upon the diligence and accuracy of an agent of the assured of whose existence, as in this case, he could not have had a suspicion; further, that there was no agent or servant of a shipowner, still less of an owner of cargo, whose implied duty it is to make an immediate communication of information. Lord Esher, therefore, held that a contract of insurance

(*f*) Blackburn *v.* Vigors (1886), 17 Q. B. D. 553.

Sect. 580. is not vitiated by the concealment of any agent, other than an agent by or through whom the contract was made.

The House of Lords held, as has already been said, that the insurance is not vitiated by the non-disclosure to the underwriter of facts unknown to the assured, but within the knowledge of an agent of his, unless the agent is one to whom the principal looks for information relating to the property insured. They considered that a broker employed to effect an insurance on a particular risk is not an agent whose knowledge can be imputed to his principal, except, of course, in respect of insurances effected by him. He is not employed to gain such knowledge, nor can any insurer suppose that he has knowledge, in the ordinary course of his employment, like the master of a ship or the owner himself, as to the condition or history of the property. Consequently, the House of Lords held that the assured could recover on the policy effected by Roxburgh & Co. (*g*).

Some stress was laid by Lord Halsbury, in Blackburn *v.* Vigors, upon the fact that Murison's agency had terminated when the policy was effected with the defendant. It is submitted that this fact was immaterial. If the agent be one whose duty it is to communicate his information to his principal, the underwriter is entitled to assume that he did, while his agency lasted, fulfil this duty. If the agent has done so, the principal will, in his turn, be able to disclose the information to the underwriter when the policy is effected, and it can make no difference that in the meanwhile the agency has been terminated.

Reason why knowledge of agent imputed to principal.

581. Two reasons have been given in earlier cases for the rule, under which the assured has been affected with the knowledge of an agent who has taken no part in the negotiations for the insurance. One is, that where a loss must fall on one of two innocent parties through the fraud or negligence of a third, it ought to be borne by the party by whom the person guilty of the fraud or negligence has been

(*g*) 12 App. Cas. 531.

CHAP. II.] CONCEALMENT. 747

trusted or employed (*h*). The other is, that if the agent could conceal material information without hazard to the principal, the latter might instruct his agent to remain silent on the subject (*i*). It is true that in such a case the assured would himself be guilty of a fraud which would vitiate the insurance, but the insurer would often be ignorant of the fraud, or not in a position to prove it. The correct way, however, of regarding the question is, no doubt, as was said by Lord Watson, that the underwriter contracts on the basis "that all material facts connected with the property insured, known to the agent employed for that purpose, have been by him communicated in due course to his principal." (*k*).

Sect. 581.

582. In the case of Proudfoot *v.* Montefiore, the plaintiff, in Manchester, employed an agent at Smyrna, who purchased and shipped for him there a cargo of madder, of which he advised the plaintiff on the 12th January. The agent forwarded the shipping documents on the 19th. The ship sailed on the 23rd and went ashore the same day, whereby there was a total loss of the cargo. Next day the agent had intelligence of the loss, and might have telegraphed the casualty to his principal immediately, but refrained on purpose that his principal might insure the cargo. On the 26th, which was the earliest post-day for England, he announced the loss to his principal by letter. Meanwhile, before the arrival of that letter but after the loss had been posted on Lloyd's Lists, the principal effected an insurance on the cargo. It was held, that the policy was void on the ground of the non-disclosure (*l*).

Proudfoot *v.* Montefiore.

583. In the course of their judgment the Court, besides reviewing the English decisions and approving of them, considered the American case of Ruggles *v.* General Interest

Ruggles *v.* General Interest Ins. Co.

(*h*) Fitzherbert *v.* Mather (1785), 1 T. R. 12, 16; Proudfoot *v.* Montefiore (1867), L. R. 2 Q. B. 511, 522. As to the general principle, see Farquharson *v.* King, [1902] A. C. 325.

(*i*) Gladstone *v.* King (1813), 1 M. & S. 35.
(*k*) 12 App. Cas. p. 541.
(*l*) Proudfoot *v.* Montefiore (1867), L. R. 2 Q. B. 511.

Sect. 583. Ins. Co. (*m*), before Story, J., and expressed their disapprobation of the decision, and of the reasoning by which the learned Judge supported it. In that case, on the 9th February the assured, resident at Newport, Rhode Island, effected a policy in Boston on the sloop "Harriet" for six months in the coasting trade of the United States. That vessel had sailed on the 12th January previous, and was totally lost on Cape Hatteras on the 19th of the same month, and between that date and the date of the policy the master had purposely refrained from communicating the loss to her owner in order that he might have time to insure. The learned Judge, in the face of these facts, sustained the validity of the policy, on the ground that the master was not an agent for the purpose of effecting the insurance. This decision was affirmed by the Supreme Court, not only on this ground, but also on another and somewhat curious ground, viz., that by the loss of the vessel the master had ceased to be the agent of the assured (*n*). The latter ground of the decision of the Supreme Court was said by the Court of Queen's Bench, in Proudfoot *v.* Montefiore, to be very unsatisfactory (*o*) and untenable; and the view taken by the Supreme Court of the relation between the captain of a ship and his owners is also criticised by Lord Halsbury, in Blackburn *v.* Vigors (*p*), by Duer (*q*), and by Phillips (*r*).

Exception to rule made in two English cases.

584. There are two English cases which, if correct, created an exception to the general principle as to the effect on an insurance of the non-communication of a material fact. These cases, however, though not overruled, have been adversely criticised, and are of doubtful authority. The exception is, that when an agent whose duty it is to keep his principal informed omits, without fraud, to inform his prin-

(*m*) (1825), 4 Mason, 74.
(*n*) (1827), 12 Wheaton, 408. The principle that the loss put an end to the master's agency was applied in Folsom *v.* Mercantile Mutual Ins. Co. (1871), 8 Blatchford, R. 170; *S. C.*, in the Supreme Court (1873), 18 Wallace, 237.
(*o*) L. R. 2 Q. B. 521.
(*p*) 12 App. Cas. 538.
(*q*) 2 Duer, 423.
(*r*) 1 Phillips, s. 549.

cipal of an occurrence causing an average loss, and thereby prevents the principal from disclosing the occurrence, the insurance is not entirely avoided. The only consequence is, that the underwriter is not liable for the average loss.

In Gladstone v. King (s), the vessel had been driven on the rocks in Manchineal Harbour, Jamaica, and got off again, seemingly without injury; and the master, with no fraudulent intent, omitted to mention it in a letter to his owner; but on arriving home the vessel was examined and found to have sustained damage from the rocks to the extent of 15 per cent. Lord Ellenborough and the rest of the Court held, that a policy effected by the owner after the receipt of the master's letter was not void, but that the partial loss, the only claim in the action, was an implied exception out of the policy. "If this principle be new," said his Lordship, " it is consistent with justice and convenience." The effect of it in respect of the assured was, that he neither recovered his loss nor, as the policy was held to be valid, got back his premiums.

In the later case (t) before the Queen's Bench Division, the ship whilst lying off Mazagan, in an open roadstead, the usual place of loading, had been driven out to sea by a hurricane from her anchorage, with loss of her anchor and chain; but no mention of this had been made by the master in a letter written to his owner a week after it had happened, and consequently no mention was made of it by the owner to the underwriter at the time of effecting the policy. This was the last letter the owner had from the master, and the ship after leaving Mazagan was never again heard of. The Court, as to the total loss, sent the case to a second trial on a question of concealment by the owner himself, which will come under notice separately; but as to this partial loss of the anchor and chain, Lush and Blackburn, JJ., held, following Gladstone v. King, that, in the absence of fraud on the part of the master in suppressing all mention of it, the loss

(s) (1813), 1 M. & S. 35.
(t) Stribley v. Imperial Mar. Ins. Co. (1876), 1 Q. B. D. 507.

Sect. 584. was not recoverable under the policy, though the policy was not thereby rendered void. Quain, J., declined to give an opinion on the point, and the Court refused to enter the verdict for the defendant, even as to the partial loss, as it might be the subject of further investigation at the new trial.

Criticism of these decisions.

585. A grave objection to these two decisions is, that the ultimate effects of any mishap must in many cases be a matter of speculation. For this reason it is not just to the underwriter merely to exempt him from liability for the damage caused directly by the occurrence. The facts of Gladstone *v.* King itself show the danger of the rule which Lord Ellenborough laid down. For in that case the ship had sustained serious damage without those on board being aware of it, and although the voyage was safely accomplished, the risk was certainly increased by the accident. Lord Ellenborough said: "No mischief will ensue from holding in this case that the antecedent damage was an implied exception out of the policy." Yet this was purely an *ex post facto* argument, and the test whether a matter is material to be disclosed is certainly not whether it has or has not *in fact* been the cause of loss to the underwriter.

It is not impossible to imagine a partial loss which will not affect the risk. If, for instance, a lost anchor be replaced, as Lush, J., assumed, in Stribley *v.* Imperial Marine Insurance Co., had been done (*u*), the loss of the anchor is in itself no concern of the underwriter when he is not liable for the loss. But when, as must usually have happened, the loss of the anchor is caused by bad weather it is material that the underwriter should know that the ship had been subject to weather bad enough to cause the loss of an anchor. In fact, it can so rarely happen that information about an occurrence which has caused a partial loss is not material to the risk, that it would have been wiser not to make in favour of the assured the dangerous exception to the general principle which Gladstone *v.* King established.

(*u*) (1876), 1 Q. B. D. 514.

Gladstone v. King was, however, said by the Court of Queen's Bench, in Proudfoot v. Montefiore, to have been well decided; but that expression of opinion was accompanied by language wholly subversive of the decision so approved of, in so far as that decision sustained the validity of the policy notwithstanding the concealment of a material fact (x).

Lord Esher expressed the opinion, in Blackburn v. Vigors, that Gladstone v. King was wrongly decided (y). He, however, took this view on the wide ground that the assured was not responsible for concealment on the part of any agent, except one through whom the contract was made; and his criticism is deprived of most of its force by the fact that the House of Lords laid down a contrary rule. Still Lord Halsbury's judgment shows that he also did not approve of Gladstone v. King (z), and Lord Watson said: "I have a difficulty in comprehending the principle upon which the Court, in Gladstone v. King and Stribley v. Imperial Marine Insurance Co., held that the innocent non-communication of a material fact by an agent who was the *alter ego* of the ship-owner merely created an exception from the policy. In both these cases the Court appears to me to have undertaken the somewhat perilous task of settling the terms of the contract which the insurer would have made for himself if the fact had been communicated to him" (a).

The editors submitted before the Marine Insurance Act, 1906, was passed that the decision in the two cases in question cannot be supported. Their view is confirmed by the fact that the Act does not mention the exception to the duty of disclosure, for which these cases are an authority.

But even if these cases be good law, an occurrence which has caused a partial loss may nevertheless be material to be disclosed; for, independently of the partial loss, the occurrence may have some effect on the risk. This point was quite

---

(x) See the passage from the judgment of the Court cited *ante*, § 578.

(y) 17 Q. B. D. 567, 568.

(z) Blackburn v. Vigors (1887), 12 App. Cas. 536.

(a) 12 App. Cas. 540.

Sect. 585. overlooked by the Court in Gladstone *v.* King, but not in Stribley *v.* Imperial Marine Insurance Co. For Blackburn, J. (though holding that the loss of the anchor was excepted from the policy), and Quain, J., both said that the jury should have been asked whether the loss was a fact material to be communicated (*b*).

When the agent must telegraph.

586. In the case of the loss of the subject of the insurance, an agent whose duty it is to keep his principal informed is, no doubt, bound to send him information of the loss by telegraph, when this is practicable (*c*). It cannot, however, be supposed that it is the agent's duty to send information by telegraph of every occurrence which, if known to his principal, ought to be disclosed by the latter. It is submitted that it must be a question of fact in each case whether the agent has used such means of communication as were reasonable under the circumstances (*d*).

Concealment by the agent who effects the insurance.

587. In Blackburn *v.* Vigors, the House of Lords were careful to point out that their decision, that an insurance broker is not an agent whose knowledge can be imputed to his principal, had no reference to an insurance effected by the particular broker. "Where the employment of the agent is such," said Lord Halsbury, "that in respect of the particular matter in question he really does represent the principal, the formula that the knowledge of the agent is his knowledge is, I think, correct." And his Lordship further remarked: "The reason why, if he (the broker) had effected the insurance, his knowledge, unless he communicated it would have been fatal to the policy, is because his agency was to effect an insurance, and the authority to make the contract drew with it all the necessary powers and responsibilities which are involved in such an employment (*e*). Thus an insurance broker or other agent who effects a policy

(*b*) 1 Q. B. D. 512, 514.
(*c*) Proudfoot *v.* Montefiore (1867), L. R. 2 Q. B. 511.
(*d*) See *ante*, § 577.

(*e*) 12 App. Cas. pp. 538, 539; see also per Lord Watson, *ibid.* p. 541; per Lord Macnaghten, p. 542.

CHAP. II.] CONCEALMENT. 753

is bound to communicate to the underwriter all the material facts within his knowledge, from whatever source he may have obtained his information " (*f*). And now the Marine Insurance Act, 1906, expressly provides that where an insurance is effected by an agent, the latter must disclose to the insurer "every material circumstance which is known to himself" (*g*).

Sect. 587.

588. Sometimes an agent employed to effect an insurance, instead of dealing direct with the underwriter, acts through an intermediate agent. Whenever two or more agents have been employed in the transaction on behalf of the assured, the concealment of a material fact within the knowledge of any agent *through whose agency, whether mediately or directly, the insurance has been effected* vitiates the policy. This was decided in a case on another policy effected for the plaintiff in Blackburn *v.* Vigors on the same risk (*h*).

Concealment by an agent through whom the insurance is effected.

Blackburn, in Glasgow (as has been mentioned in connection with Blackburn *v.* Vigors) instructed Murison & Co., a firm of insurance brokers there, to re-insure a ship which was overdue. Thereupon Murison & Co. telegraphed to their London agents to effect the re-insurance. Soon afterwards Murison & Co. received information, of which their principals were ignorant, tending to show that the ship was lost. They did not disclose the information, but put their principals into communication with their London agents, who ultimately effected the re-insurance through another firm of London brokers. The jury found that there was no new negotiation commenced, but that the policy was effected in pursuance of the original agency. On these findings a Divisional Court held that the concealment avoided the policy. "It is the negotiation," they said, "that is tainted,

(*f*) *Ibid.;* Blackburn *v.* Haslam (1888), 21 Q. B. D. 144; see also Lynch *v.* Dunsford (1811), 14 East, 494.

(*g*) Sect. 19 (a), *ante*, § 575; the section proceeds to declare what such an agent is deemed to know. As to this, see *ante*, § 577.

(*h*) Blackburn *v.* Haslam, *supra.* See also Republic of Bolivia *v.* Indemnity Mutual Mar. Ass. Co. (1908), 14 Com. Cas. 156, 166.

A.—VOL. I. 48

Sect. 588. and the contract is void because it is founded upon the negotiation; and through however many hands the offer of an insurance may pass, if there be a concealment by the assured or his agent, the policy is avoided " (*i*). The distinction between this case and Blackburn *v.* Vigors lies in the fact that the policy sued on in Blackburn *v.* Vigors was effected by an independent firm of brokers, who received their instructions direct from Blackburn. If the latter had opened a new and independent negotiation with Murison's London agents by giving a fresh order for the policy, it seems to follow from Blackburn *v.* Vigors that the concealment by Murison would not have affected the policy (*k*).

Material facts defined.

589. The duty on the part of the assured to disclose material facts is not limited to facts which have a direct bearing on the extent of the risks or dangers to which the subject of the insurance will be exposed. All facts are material which would affect the mind of a rational underwriter, governing himself by the principles on which underwriters in practice act, as to either of the following points: 1st, whether he will take the risk at all; 2nd, at what premium he will take it (*l*).

Rivaz v. Gerussi.

A series of four open policies on fruit and produce from Greece and the Ionian Islands to Liverpool or London " by

---

(*i*) 21 Q. B. D. 153. The fact was one which within the meaning of sect. 19 (a) of the Marine Insurance Act ought to have been communicated to the agent who actually effected the insurance.

(*k*) 21 Q. B. D. 150.

(*l*) Ionides *v.* Pender (1874), L. R. 9 Q. B. 531; Rivaz *v.* Gerussi (1880), 6 Q. B. D. 222; Thames & Mersey Mar. Ins. Co., Ltd. *v.* "Gunford" Ship Co., Ltd., [1911] A. C. 529; Mar. Ins. Act, 1906, s. 18, sub-s. 2, *ante*, § 575. See also § 554, *ante*. In Glasgow Ass. Corpn. *v.* Symondson (1911), 16 Com. Cas. at p. 119, Scrutton, J., is reported to have said: "The material facts are as to the subject-matter, the ship, and the perils to which the ship is exposed." He, however, apparently agreed that other circumstances might in a particular case be proved by evidence to be material. The learned judge cannot have intended in all cases to limit "material facts" in any such way as the words which we have quoted, if taken by themselves, would suggest. Any such limitation appears to be inconsistent with the express words of sect. 18 (2) of the Mar. Ins. Act, 1906.

ship or ships" was effected at several successive dates in the year 1875, the one to follow and succeed the other of them *seriatim*. At the time of effecting the later two of these policies respectively, declarations of shipments had been made on the earlier two of the four policies, but they remained unexhausted to a large amount in consequence of the shipments having been declared very much under their real value. It was after the safe arrival of the respective cargoes and to enable the assured to place other cargoes under protection of the policies already exhausted by previous shipments, that these declarations under value were made. In this state of facts there was a total loss of a large shipment of produce sunk in the Thames, which was declared on the apparently unexhausted policies, and on the policies which had been effected to follow. The jury, having regard to the effect of what seemed to be the unexhausted state of the earlier policies in inducing the underwriters to subscribe the later policies, found that the declarations under value were a material fact which had been fraudulently concealed at the time of negotiating the two later policies; and the Court of Appeal sustained their finding, and held that the underwriters were entitled to have the later policies set aside and cancelled (*m*).

Sect. 589.

Similarly, excessive valuation may be a circumstance material to be communicated.

Excessive valuation.

Part of a cargo insured to Vladivostock consisted of

Ionides v. Pender.

(*m*) Rivaz *v.* Gerussi, *supra*. In effect the fact which the jury found to be material seems to be, that the assured had under similar policies been guilty of dishonest practices in fraud of the underwriter, the inference being that he would resort to similar practices under the later policies. In the United States it has been held that an assured is not bound to say anything about his own character. He is "not bound nor could it be expected that he should speak evil of himself." New York Bowery Co. *v.* New York Fire Ins. Co. (1837), 17 Wend. N. Y. R. 359; approved by the Supreme Court in Sun Mutual Ins. Co. *v.* Ocean Ins. Co. (1882), 107 U. S. (17 Otto), 485. But see Gordon *v.* Street, [1899] 2 Q. B. 641, where a jury found that a money-lender, notorious for his oppressive practices, had been guilty of fraudulent concealment in contracting under an assumed name, and the verdict was upheld by the Court of Appeal.

Sect. 589. 222 casks of whisky, the cost, charges and insurance of which amounted to 973*l*., but which were valued for insurance at 2,800*l*. It was in evidence that excessive valuation, to such an extent as here, was considered by underwriters to be a speculative risk, which one class of underwriters would not take at all, and another class would take only if a sufficient premium were offered; that 25 per cent. added was not unusual; and that in one case 30 per cent. added had been taken by the former class; but that beyond this it became a speculative risk. The excuse offered by the assured was that the excess represented expected profits at Vladivostock, which was not at the time of shipment within the geographical range of the Russian Custom House, but was to be shortly brought within that line, when a heavy duty would be imposed; and that a paper was shown to the English underwriter, containing these words, but in German: "On spirits with anticipated profits, however high or low." The underwriter saw the German words, but did not understand them. The jury could not satisfy themselves whether the valuations were fraudulent or not, but found that they were excessive and that it was material for the underwriter to know that they were excessive. On these findings the verdict was entered for the defendant underwriter, which the Court refused to disturb (*n*).

Insurances based on excessive valuations may tempt the assured to resort to foul play to bring about a loss; or they may have a tendency to make him less careful than he otherwise would be in selecting the ship or the master, or in safeguarding the adventure, and also a tendency to diminish the efforts which, in case of disaster, he ought to make to minimize the loss as far as possible. These considerations are the foundation of the rule that excessive valuations must be disclosed (*o*). Cases, however, occur rarely in which the

(*n*) Ionides *v.* Pender (1874), L. R. 9 Q. B. 531; see also Herring *v.* Janson (1895), 1 Com. Cas. 177; Gooding *v.* White (1913), 29 T. L. R. 312.

(*o*) See the passage in the judgment of the Court in Ionides *v.* Pender (1874), L. R. 9 Q. B. at pp. 538, 539.

CHAP. II.] CONCEALMENT. 757

insurers seek to avoid a policy on a ship on the ground that Sect. 589.
there was no disclosure of the fact that the valuation therein
was excessive (*p*), because the insurers usually have ample
information about the vessel, which enables them to form a
fairly accurate estimate of her value.

Yet, even though in a particular case there be no duty to The Gunford.
make any disclosure with regard to the valuation of the
subject-matter insured, there may be other contracts of
insurance which place the assured or his servants who have
the management of the property in the position of making
a profit out of its destruction. When such is the position,
the House of Lords held in the recent case of the "Gunford,"
that the existence of the other insurances must be disclosed (*q*).
The action was brought on two policies on hull, and at the
date of the policies the vessel was worth about 9,000*l*. to
sell, and the freight at risk was about 4,800*l*. (*r*). The
following were the insurances effected on behalf of the owners
(a limited company) to cover their interest in the adventure:

Hull, valued at 18,500*l*.	£19,000
Freight, valued at 5,500*l*.	5,500
Disbursements by "p.p.i." policy	4,600
Total	£29,100

The payments on account of which it was sought to justify
the insurance of disbursements were made for the purpose of
earning the freight and covered by the insurance of the gross
freight, or were for repairs, outfit and premiums ordinarily
included in insurances on ship.

(*p*) Herring *v.* Janson was such a case; but the insurance was on a foreign yacht, and the jury found for the assured.

(*q*) Thames & Mersey Mar. Ins. Co. *v.* "Gunford" Ship Co., [1911] A. C. 529. See also Pickersgill *v.* London & Prov. Ins. Co., [1912] 3 K. B. 614.

(*r*) Lord Loreburn, L. C., said that one-half of the freight had been paid in advance and was not at risk. This was a mistake. The voyage insured by the freight policies was from Rotterdam to Hamburg, and while there and thence to Santa Rosalia. The advance freight was paid at Hamburg, and the whole freight was at risk during the voyage from Rotterdam to Hamburg.

Sect. 589.

All the business of the ship (including the employment of her officers and the effecting of insurances) was transacted by the manager of the company, who had taken out on his own behalf insurances by "p.p.i." policies on disbursements to the amount of 6,500*l*. The disbursements which he purported to insure were moneys owing to him by the company, in respect of which he had no insurable interest. The underwriters made no objection to the valuations of the ship and freight (*s*), but they pleaded non-disclosure of the existence of the insurances on disbursements effected on behalf of the company and of the manager. The House of Lords, reversing the decision of the Court of Session, held that both sets of disbursement policies ought to have been disclosed, although (1) they were insurances on other subject-matters than those covered by the policies on which the action was brought, (2) they were mere "honour" policies, involving no legal liability to pay, (3) the insurances for 6,500*l*. were effected by the manager of the company on his own behalf.

When the duty of disclosure attaches.

Events subsequent to the making of the contract do not affect the question of materiality.

590. The duty attaches at the time of effecting the insurance, and cannot depend on subsequent events (*t*), for the effect of a concealment in avoiding the policy is to be determined not by its eventual relation to the nature of the risk, but with reference to its immediate influence on the judgment of the underwriter. Consequently, although the intelligence concealed may turn out to be wholly unfounded, or the loss to arise from a cause totally unconnected with the fact concealed, the policy will be nevertheless avoided. It will be noticed that the Marine Insurance Act, 1906, states that the "circumstances" which must be disclosed include "any com-

---

(*s*) For the remarks of Lord Shaw and Lord Robson about the valuation of a ship as part of the going concern of a business, see *ante*, § 343. When the cost of the freight insurance is taken into consideration, the freight was only over-insured to a small extent.

(*t*) See the *dicta* of Mansfield, C. J., in Lynch *v*. Hamilton (1810), 3 Taunt. 44; and of Lord Ellenborough in Lynch *v*. Dunsford (1811), *S. C.* in error, 14 East, 497; and of the Court in Stribley *v*. Imperial Mar. Ins. Co. (1876), 1 Q. B. D. 507.

munication made to, or information received by, the assured," without any qualification as to the truth of the communication or information (*u*).

<small>Sect. 590.</small>

The agent of the assured, before effecting the policy, held a letter from the captain of another ship, stating that he had been in company with the ship insured and lost sight of her all at once at twelve o'clock at night, that she had been reported leaky the day before by her captain, and that a hard gale had ensued the next day. It was held that this intelligence ought to have been communicated to the underwriter, and that the policy was avoided by its suppression. Yet in point of fact the inference suggested by the intelligence turned out to be unfounded, and the ship was lost, not by perils of the sea, but by capture, and that a week after the period to which the letter referred (*x*).

<small>Seaman *v.* Fonnereau.</small>

A policy was effected on goods on board "ship or ships" from the Canary Islands to London, by an agent of the assured, who, at the time, knew that a portion of the goods to be insured were on board the "President" and also that the "President" had been reported at Lloyd's as at sea, deep and leaky. He did not inform the underwriter that the "President" was one of the ships on which part of the goods insured had been loaded, so that the underwriter had no means of applying the intelligence at Lloyd's to the risk. Under these circumstances the Court of Common Pleas held, and the Court of King's Bench confirmed their decision, that the suppression of this fact by the assured avoided the policy, although it turned out that the intelligence at Lloyd's was unfounded, the "President" never having been deep or leaky on any part of the voyage insured, and having been lost, not by perils of the seas at all, but by capture, which occurred three weeks after the period referred to in Lloyd's intelligence (*y*).

<small>Lynch *v.* Hamilton.</small>

(*u*) Sect. 18, sub-s. 5, *ante*, § 575. See *post*, § 602.

(*x*) Seaman *v.* Fonnereau (1743), 2 Str. 1183.

(*y*) Lynch *v.* Hamilton (1810), 3 Taunt. 37; Lynch *v.* Dunsford (1811), 14 East, 494, *S. C.* in error.

Sect. 591. Result of the authorities.	591. The result therefore is, that every concealment of a material circumstance whether by design or mistake, avoids the policy; and that it has this effect, although the intelligence suppressed should ultimately turn out to be untrue, or the loss to have arisen from a cause quite different from that which the intelligence, if communicated, might have given reason to apprehend.
Practical rule for brokers.	The practical rule for policy brokers and other agents, therefore, is to disclose to the underwriter all they know respecting the proposed adventure, and not to exercise their own judgment as to the materiality of any part of the information they possess; for if they do not disclose the whole, and what is kept back appears to the jury to be material, the policy will be avoided, though the concealment was without any intention of fraud, and arose merely from an error of judgment (z).
Fraud.	If fraud enter into the contract, it makes no difference whether the thing concealed be material or not (a).
Minute disclosure unnecessary.	A minute disclosure of every material circumstance is not required. The assured complies with the rule if he discloses sufficient to call the attention of the underwriter to the matter in such a way that, if the latter desires further information, he can ask for it (b).
Materiality of concealment a question of fact.	The question whether the circumstance concealed is material is in each case one of fact, and essentially one for the jury (c).
Time of sailing or being last heard of.	592. The time of the ship's sailing, or the time of her being last heard of, are facts which, one or other, must enter into and form part of every conceivable case. But whether in any particular case, this or that, as it happens to be, is a material fact to be disclosed on occasion of proposing to insure, is often a question of critical and perplexing difficulty. The criterion of the materiality of any fact has been already

---

(z) See *per cur.* in Shirley *v.* Wilkinson (1781), 1 Dougl. 306, n.
(a) *Ante*, § 536.
(b) Asfar *v.* Blundell (C. A.), [1896] 1 Q. B. 123, 129; Cantiere Meccanico Brindisino *v.* Janson, [1912] 3 K. B. 452.
(c) See *post*, § 626; Mar. Ins. Act, 1906, s. 18, sub-s. 4.

stated. Beyond this, it seems that nothing more definite can be laid down. What seemed to be a more definite rule, laid down by so high an authority as Tindal, C. J., must now be considered as set aside.

That learned judge, in Elton *v.* Larkins (*d*), said: "The law clearly is, that a party is not bound to communicate the time of sailing of a ship, unless at the time of effecting the policy the ship is what is called a missing ship. If the underwriter inquires and a false answer is given, that will vitiate the policy; but it is not generally necessary *à priori* that the assured should communicate the time of sailing."

The following case, however, shows clearly that circumstances may make it necessary to disclose the time of sailing or when the ship was last heard of:—

A policy on ship "at and from Mazagan" was effected by the plaintiff on the 24th of February, who, at the time of effecting it, made no mention of a letter received by him on the 24th of January, from the master of the ship, dated the 9th of January, and stating that he had had a fine passage out, that he had commenced loading, but had very bad weather and did not know when he would finish; he would write again. The master never did write again; and the ship after sailing from Mazagan was never again heard of. The main question put to the jury by Grove, J., following the above authority of Tindal, C. J., was, whether the ship was, at the time of effecting the policy, an overdue ship? The jury found in the negative, and gave a verdict for the plaintiff. But the defendant moved for a new trial on the ground of misdirection. The Court, Blackburn, J., presiding, held that the proper question had not been put to the jury, and said that the proper question was, whether the contents of the master's letter, the dates at which it had been written and received, and the time that had elapsed since anything had been heard of the vessel, were not facts which might properly have influenced the underwriter as to the accepting

Stribley v. Imperial Mar. Ins. Co.

(*d*) Elton *v.* Larkins (1831), 5 C. & P. 392.

Sect. 592.   of the risks. "I think," said Blackburn, J., "the test is whether a fair and reasonable underwriter, looking at this letter and the circumstances under which it was received, would say, 'I think this is a speculative risk, which I will either decline to take, or if I do take it, it shall be at a greater premium than is usual'" (e).

Cases in which news of the ship has been held material.
Ratcliffe v. Shoolbred.

593. The following are some of the cases in which the concealment of the time of the ship's sailing, or of circumstances relating to the time when she was likely to sail, has been held fatal to the policy. A shipowner, on the 22nd of February, having information that his ship had sailed from the coast of Africa on the 2nd of October, directed his broker, "as the ship had been rather long, and he did not think it prudent to run so large a risk at so critical a time," to effect an insurance on her "at and from the coast of Africa to the West Indies," adding, "We expect to hear of her soon," and ordering the broker to communicate to the underwriters "that the ship was on the coast on the 2nd of October," but saying nothing of her having sailed on that day. Lord Mansfield directed the jury that the plaintiff having concealed a material part of the information he received, it was a fraud, and the underwriters were not liable (f).

M'Andrew v. Bell.

So where the assured on the 24th of November received a letter from Lisbon, written on the 8th of November, informing him that the ship was then ready to sail from that port, but he did not effect an insurance on her until the 2nd of December, after the arrival from Lisbon of another vessel which had sailed at the same time as the ship insured, and then without communicating to the underwriters the letter he had previously received: Lord Kenyon held that the keeping back this letter avoided the policy, considering, upon the whole evidence, that the plaintiff did not intend to insure till he believed the ship to be missing (g).

(e) Stribley v. Imperial Marine Ins. Co. (1876), 1 Q. B. D. 507.

(f) Ratcliffe v. Shoolbred (1780), 1 Marshall, Ins. 466; 1 Park, Ins. 413.

(g) M'Andrew v. Bell (1795), 1 Esp. 373.

All ships sailing to the Baltic, before the abolition of the Sound dues, used to touch at Elsinore to pay these dues, and were entered in a list called the Sound List; the voyage from Liverpool to Elsinore could then be performed in from fourteen to eighteen days, and the list be brought to England in ten or twelve; so that in thirty days at the most it could be known here whether a ship sailing from Liverpool had or had not touched at Elsinore. Hence, where an insurance was effected on the 23rd of October on a ship from Liverpool to the Baltic, and it appeared that the ship had sailed from Liverpool on the 7th of September, or more than six weeks (forty-six days) before the policy was effected, and no news had been heard of her down to that time, Lord Kenyon told the jury that the plaintiffs, at the time they procured the policy to be effected, must have suspected the ship to be a missing ship, and ought, therefore, to have communicated to the underwriter the time of her sailing (*h*).

Sect. 593.
Webster *v.* Foster.

In this case also his Lordship remarked as a suspicious circumstance, that, though the plaintiffs were in London at the date of the policy, and could have effected it there, they had chosen to get it effected at Hull. It also appeared that the underwriters inquired of the broker the time of the ship's sailing, and that he told them he knew nothing about it, having received no information from the plaintiff on the subject.

The voyage from Berderygge to London was often performed in four or five days, and when the weather was not favourable, in about ten days. On the 13th of December the consignees in London received from the shipper of the goods in Berderygge a letter dated the 30th of November, saying: "I think the captain will sail to-morrow; but should he not be arrived in your port, be so kind as to make the insurance as low as you possibly can on my account." The consignees accordingly effected an insurance on the goods "from Berderygge to London" the day after receiving this letter, and without communicating it to the underwriters.

Willes *v.* Glover.

(*h*) Webster *v.* Foster (1795), 1 Esp. 407.

Sect. 593. It turned out that the ship did not in fact sail till the 24th of December, yet the Court held the suppression of the letter to be a fatal concealment, and though the jury had found for the plaintiff on the ground that the concealment was not material, they sent the case down for a new trial, in which a verdict was given for the defendant (*i*). It appeared, moreover, to the Court from the terms of the shipper's letter that, in his opinion, a high premium would probably be exacted if the ship had not arrived before his letter; the letter, therefore, seemed to them material to be communicated to the underwriters with a view to the premium (*k*).

Bridges v. Hunter.

An insurance was effected, on the 12th of November, on wines by the "Stag," "at and from Oporto to Liverpool," "to return four guineas per cent. for convoy and arrival." Twelve days before effecting this insurance the plaintiff had received two letters, written from Oporto: one dated the 11th of October, stating, "We are loading the wines on board the 'Stag,' Captain Wheatley, who pretends to sail after tomorrow"; the other dated the 13th of October, enclosing the bills of lading, which were filled up with the words, "With convoy." Neither of these letters was communicated to the underwriters. The "Stag," it appeared, did sail from Oporto on the 13th of October, but, failing to come up with convoy, put into Lisbon. The convoy with which she ought to have sailed arrived in London without her on the 30th of October, and on the 1st of November a list of the ships that had sailed with it was entered at Lloyd's, in which the name of the "Stag" was not included. The underwriters contended that if these two letters had been communicated, they would, on reference to the convoy list at Lloyd's,

---

(*i*) Willes *v.* Glover (1804), 1 B. & P. N. R. 14.

(*k*) *Ibid.* 16. Maclachlan submitted, on the high authority of Maule, J., in Mackintosh *v.* Marshall (1843), 11 M. & W. 119, that the only illegal suppression was of the date of the expected sailing, and that if that date had been communicated the letter, containing besides only an expression of opinion or of apprehension founded on nothing that was unknown to the underwriter, need not have been shown. Arnould, 6th ed. p. 565, n.

have ascertained that the ship was a missing ship. Lord Sect. 593.
Ellenborough told the jury that the question was, whether a
disclosure of these letters would probably have varied the
judgment of the underwriter, so as to have induced him either
to decline subscribing the policy or to demand a higher premium; that if such might have been the consequence of a
disclosure of them, they were material letters to be communicated. The jury, notwithstanding, found a verdict for the
plaintiff; but the Court, thinking they had come to a wrong
conclusion on the facts, granted a new trial (*l*).

594. In the three following cases the facts concealed were Cases in which news of the ship was held immaterial.
held to be immaterial on the question whether the ship was a
missing ship. In connection with them it must be remembered that the materiality of the facts concealed is a question
for the jury, and that in a more recent case it has been held
that the question whether the facts showed that the ship was
overdue is not the only one to be considered (*m*).

The non-communication of a letter, showing that a vessel Foley *v.* Moline.
was out only nine days on the voyage from Youghal to
Weymouth, which usually took eight or ten days, was held
not such a concealment as would avoid the policy (*n*).

A policy was effected at Whitehaven on the 8th January Littledale *v.* Dixon.
upon the "Cumberland," "at and from Barbadoes to Liverpool," in consequence of a letter of orders from a Liverpool
broker, in which he said: "The 'Cumberland,' we expect, will
have taken her departure from Barbadoes on the 26th of
November; the 'Barton' sailed on the 24th, and arrived at
Liverpool last Sunday (the 5th January), but she is coppered,
and a remarkably fast vessel." This letter was shown to the
underwriters at the time of effecting the policy; but it was
not communicated that the "Agreeable," also coppered and
remarkably fast, which had left Barbadoes on the 29th November, had also arrived at Liverpool on the 5th of January.

(*l*) Bridges *v.* Hunter (1813), 1 M. & S. 15.
(*m*) Stribley *v.* Imperial Marine Ins. Co. (1876), 1 Q. B. D. 507.
(*n*) Foley *v.* Moline (1814), 5 Taunt. 430.

Sect. 594. The "Cumberland" was not coppered, was full built, and a slow sailer, and was not considered a missing ship at the time the letter of orders was written. Evidence was also given that knowledge of the arrival of the "Barton" and "Agreeable" could not have varied the premium. Upon these facts the jury found for the plaintiff, and the Court of Common Pleas refused to disturb their verdict (*o*).

Elton v. Larkins.

An insurance was effected on the "Fanny," "at and from Cadiz to London," on the 29th of December, at which time the plaintiff held a letter from the captain, stating that she was to sail on the 22nd of November. This letter the plaintiff did not communicate. It was in this case that Tindal, C. J., laid down the doctrine already cited, which is no longer the doctrine of the English Courts (*p*), and accordingly put it to the jury as the main question, whether the "Fanny," having been out thirty-seven days from Cadiz to London at the time of effecting the policy, could fairly be called a missing ship; and the jury having found for the plaintiff, the Court refused to disturb their verdict (*q*). In a more recent case, facts tending to show that the ship had been out forty-one days on a voyage from Seville to London, were held material (*r*).

Facts which tend to show that the ship is missing.

595. Besides the time of the ship's sailing, all facts must be fully and fairly communicated, which would lead a reasonable underwriter to infer that the ship was a missing ship when the policy was effected.

Rickards v. Murdock.

A merchant at Sydney consigned goods to England by the "Cumberland" (which had sailed from Sydney about the end of April, and was to sail from Van Diemen's Land about the last week in May), and sent an order to insure this risk by the "Australia" (which sailed from Sydney on the 20th of May),

---

(*o*) Littledale *v.* Dixon (1805), 1 B. & P. N. R. 151. Marshall thinks this case wrongly decided; Duer, however, adduces cogent reasons for upholding its authority. 2 Ins. 544, 545. It may safely be said that the Court of Appeal also would uphold the verdict.

(*p*) *Ante,* § 592.

(*q*) Elton *v.* Larkins (1831), 5 C. & P. 86, 385; (1832), 8 Bing. 198.

(*r*) Elkin *v.* Jansen (1845), 13 M. & W. 655.

directing his London correspondents to wait thirty days after the arrival of the "Australia" before effecting the insurance on the "Cumberland," in order to give the latter ship every chance of arriving. This order by the "Australia" was retained for thirty-six days, and then, as the "Cumberland" had not arrived, and two ships had in the meantime come in, which had left Sydney after the "Australia," they procured an insurance, informing the underwriters of the time the "Cumberland" had sailed from Sydney, and was expected to sail from Van Diemen's Land, but not stating when, or by what ship, the order to insure had arrived, nor how long and why they were to wait before effecting the policy. The jury having found this a material concealment, the Court refused to disturb their verdict, being unanimous that the time when the order to insure was received, and the delay which had been interposed before insuring, were facts which ought to have been communicated to the underwriters (*s*).

Sect. 595.

Two ships, the "Fruiter" and the "King George," sailed from Malaga for London; the first on the 9th of October, the second on the 10th. They were frequently in sight of each other till the 21st of October, when the "Fruiter," off Oporto, parted company with the "King George" in a gale. The "Fruiter" arrived in London on the 30th of October, and with knowledge of these facts, the plaintiff, on the 3rd of November, effected a policy on the "King George" "at and from Malaga to London," informing the underwriter of the timt at which the two ships had sailed from Malaga, but not that the "Fruiter" had seen the "King George" off Oporto on the 21st. The "King George" had in point of fact been lost in the chops of the Channel on the 25th of October.

Westbury v. Aberdein.

(*s*) Rickards *v.* Murdock (1830), 10 B. & Cr. 527; see *S. C.* at N. P., Danson & Ll. 221; and Ll. & Wels. 132.

Sed quære as to the part of the letter which required the delay, and stated the reason. No one can doubt its having an effect—a most prejudicial effect; but it is not on that ground, surely, a proper subject of discovery, since it would be the occasion of blind prejudice, and therefore an impediment to the exercise of sound judgment. See *post*, § 596, that a direction not to insure until a reasonable risk has been run need not be disclosed.

Sect. 595. Lord Abinger told the jury that the fact of the "Fruiter" having seen the "King George" off Oporto was not material to be communicated, and they found for the plaintiff. The Court, however, granted a new trial, holding that the question of the materiality of these facts ought to go to the jury (*t*).

Elkin *v.* Jansen.

When the master abroad draws a bill on his owners at home for the disbursements of the ship, that is a fact from which the completion of the ship's loading, and consequently the probable time of her sailing, may be inferred. Consequently such a bill drawn at Seville on the 11th of January, which was sent thence on the 17th, and arrived at London on the 31st, was held to be material as to those dates, considering the average duration of the voyage from Seville to London, where the policy on the ship was effected on the 21st of February (*u*).

Kirby *v.* Smith.

The ship "Ocean" sailed from Elsinore for Hull in rough weather on the 26th of July; six hours after, her owner sailed from Elsinore for Hull in another ship. This was a voyage sometimes of four or five days, but of the average duration of eight to ten. Owing to tempestuous weather the owner of the "Ocean" did not arrive at Hull till the 9th of August, or fourteen days after leaving Elsinore, when, finding that the "Ocean" had not arrived, he immediately caused his broker to effect an insurance on her "at and from Elsinore to Hull, from the 26th July inclusive;" the broker at the time of effecting this policy did not communicate any more of these facts than that the "Ocean" was "all well at Elsinore on the 26th of July." The Court held that this was a concealment fatal to the policy (*x*).

Mackintosh *v.* Marshall.

A Liverpool merchant, on whose account a quantity of train oil was to be shipped at St. John's, Newfoundland, on board the "Elizabeth," wrote on the 27th of January to his brokers in London to effect an insurance, telling them "that he had advices from St. John's, of the 27th of December, of

---

(*t*) Westbury *v.* Aberdein (1837), 2 M. & W. 267.

(*u*) Elkin *v.* Jansen (1845), 13 M. & W. 655.

(*x*) Kirby *v.* Smith (1818), 1 B. & Ald. 672.

the train oil being shipped for him on board the 'Elizabeth,' Sect. 595.
to sail the end of the month." The real facts were: 1st. That
he had received no advices of that date from St. John's, but
had been merely told that intelligence from St. John's down
to the 27th had come to hand, which made no mention of the
sailing of the "Elizabeth"; and 2nd. That before giving the
order to insure, he had received two letters from St. John's,
both dated the 24th of December, but the second not sent
till the 30th, in the first of which his correspondents stated
that the "Elizabeth" was to sail on the 25th, that she was a
new vessel, that he could endeavour to save the insurance by
giving three or four days, according to the state of the
weather in England; and in the second they said, "You can
allow her from sixteen to twenty days; you can run a reasonable risk to save the insurance, but all will depend on the
state of the weather." The insurance having been effected
on the 27th January solely on the letter of instructions sent
to the broker, the Court were clearly of opinion that these
facts showed both a positive mis-statement and a material
concealment, either of them sufficient to avoid the policy (y).

596. In this case, the counsel for the underwriter, besides the objection arising from the non-communication of the letters, and the admission of improper evidence, contended that the underwriter ought, at all events, to have been informed that the assured was endeavouring to save the insurance. Maule, J., however, who tried the case, told the jury that the direction not to insure till a reasonable risk had been run, was not, in his opinion, a circumstance which the broker was bound to communicate. In moving for a new trial, the counsel for the underwriters contended that this was

Non-disclosure of the fact that the assured wishes to save the insurance.

(y) Mackintosh v. Marshall (1843), 11 M. & W. 116. The jury at the trial had found for the plaintiff, partly on the ground that the underwriter must be presumed to have consulted Lloyd's Lists, from which he might have inferred the true time of the "Elizabeth's" sailing; and one main ground on which the Court granted the new trial was that this presumption did not arise, as the underwriter must be taken to have relied on the misrepresentation. This part of the case is noticed *post*, § 615.

A.—VOL. I. 49

Sect. 596. a mis-direction; but the Court, on making the rule absolute, did not particularly allude to this branch of the alleged mis-direction, but rested their judgment almost entirely on the improper admission of Lloyd's lists under the peculiar circumstances of the case.

On the question, therefore, whether circumstances which show that the assured was endeavouring to save the insurance by delaying to insure, ought to be communicated to the underwriter, no general rule can be laid down, but that the necessity of communicating this circumstance, like any other, must depend on the influence it might have in leading the underwriter to infer that the ship was out of time when he was asked to insure upon her.

There can be no doubt that, in all cases where it might reasonably be supposed likely to have this effect, the direction to delay the insurance ought to be communicated. Wherever, in fact, it appears that the intention of the assured was not to effect the policy till there was reason to suspect that the ship was a missing ship, the facts tending to show this ought to be communicated (*z*).

Concealment of the national character of the subject insured, and of other facts that aggravate the risk.

597. In time of war, any circumstance within the knowledge of the assured and not equally within the knowledge of the underwriter, which affects the national character of the subject insured, and exposes it to capture or detention, must be disclosed to the underwriters (*a*).

Yet if the materiality of the fact be due to circumstances not within the knowledge of the assured or his means of information, he will not be bound to communicate it.

Mayne *v.* Walter.

Thus a ship, warranted Portuguese, was taken by a French

(*z*) See the *dictum* of Lord Kenyon in M'Andrew *v.* Bell (1795), 1 Esp. 373; see, however, Bell *v.* Bell (1810), 2 Camp. 475, 479, *post*, § 623, that facts only, and not apprehensions, need to be disclosed.

(*a*) If, however, capture or detention be not risks insured against, it appears to the editors that the national character of the thing insured is not necessarily material to the risk. It may, however, be material in a particular case on the ground that a detention may prolong the voyage, and thereby increase the risk.

privateer, and condemned because she had an English super-   Sect. 597.
cargo on board, on the ground of a recent French ordinance
declaring all neutral ships liable to capture where the supercargo was the subject of a state at war with France; Lord
Mansfield held that as neither the assured nor the underwriters appeared to have known anything of this ordinance,
the former was not guilty of a material concealment in not
disclosing the fact of the supercargo being English (*b*).

His Lordship, however, was of opinion that, though this
ordinance was contrary to the law of nations, yet if the
assured knew it there would have been a material concealment,
in not disclosing the fact of his not having complied with it;
and if, on the other hand, the underwriters had known of it,
they ought to have inquired who was to be supercargo (*c*).

In a recent case it was held by Bigham, J., that the   Regulations
assured was not obliged to disclose to the underwriter an   not enforced.
edict of the Persian Government prohibiting the importation
of arms into Persia, when the trade had, in spite of the
nominal prohibition, been openly carried on for years, the
Persian Government exacting duties on the arms im-
ported (*d*).

598. In the absence of inquiry, it is not necessary to dis-   Matters
close any circumstance which is known or presumed to be   which the
known to the insurer. The insurer is presumed to know   is presumed
matters of common notoriety or knowledge, and matters   to know.
which an insurer in the ordinary course of his business, as
such, ought to know (*e*). Thus an insurer is presumed to
know that it is impossible to make a floating dry-dock as seaworthy as an ordinary ocean-going craft, and is put on

---

(*b*) Mayne *v.* Walter (1782), 1 Park, Ins. 431; 1 Marshall, Ins. 402, 471.

(*c*) 1 Marshall, Ins. 402, 471; see also Barzillay *v.* Lewis (1782), 1 Marshall, Ins. 402; 404; and Marshall *v.* Union Ins. Co. (1809),

2 Wash. C. C. R. 357; 1 Phillips, s. 624.

(*d*) Fracis *v.* Sea Ins. Co. (1898), 3 Com. Cas. 229.

(*e*) Mar. Ins. Act, 1906, s. 18, sub-s. 3 (b), *ante*, § 575. See *post*, § 609.

Sect. 598.

Private information of new regulations.

Facts which may expose the property to capture.

inquiry, if he admits seaworthiness, as to the means adopted to strengthen it (*f*).

A knowledge of the political state of the world, of the allegiance of particular countries, of their standing mercantile regulations, of the risk and embarrassment affecting the course of trade contemplated by the insurance, must all necessarily be imputed to the underwriter, and therefore need not be disclosed by the assured; but it has been held in the United States, and apparently on very good grounds, that the new or shifting regulations of foreign states, by which the property is exposed to seizure, if privately known to the assured, ought to be disclosed by him, for they cannot be presumed to have been necessarily within the knowledge of the underwriter (*g*).

All facts lying peculiarly within the knowledge of the assured, which may expose the property to risk of capture, ought to be disclosed to the underwriters (*h*).

Thus, it has been held in the United States, that not disclosing that the property insured belongs to a house established and doing business in a belligerent state, will be a material concealment, and defeat a policy made in a neutral country "for whom it may concern" (*i*); so the omission to disclose that enemy's property embarked in a neutral ship was covered as the property of a neutral, was there also held to be a material concealment vitiating the policy (*k*). As by the Declaration of Paris, enemy's goods on board a

---

(*f*) Cantiere Meocanico Brindisino, [1912] 2 K. B. 112; 3 K. B. 452 (C. A.).

(*g*) Hoyt *v.* Gilman (1811), 8 Mass. R. 336; Blagge *v.* New York Ins. Co. (1804), 1 Caines, 549; 1 Phillips, ss. 595, 596, 597; see also 2 Duer, 516, 561.

(*h*) When an insurance is effected in a belligerent country, has the underwriter any right to assume that the property insured does not belong to a subject of his own sovereign? If he wish only to insure neutral property, should he not protect himself by having a warranty of neutrality inserted in the policy?

(*i*) Banduy *v.* Union Ins. Co. (1809), 2 Wash. C. C. R. 391, cited 1 Phillips, s. 224. See, however, Buck *v.* Chesapeake Ins. Co. (1828), 1 Peters, S. C. R. 151; 1 Phillips, s. 625.

(*k*) Stocker *v.* Merrimack Fire & Marine Ins. Co. (1810), 6 Mass. R. 220, cited 1 Phillips, s. 629.

CHAP. II.] CONCEALMENT. 773

neutral ship (except contraband) are not liable to capture, there seems to be no reason now why, during a war in which the belligerents have adhered to the Declaration, the national character of goods carried under a neutral flag should be declared; for the risk is no greater when the goods belong to a belligerent than when they belong to a neutral (*l*).

Sect. 598.

The "Georgia" had been in the service of the Confederate States of America as a cruiser during 1863-4, and was afterwards laid up and dismantled in Liverpool, and there purchased at public auction by the plaintiff, who converted her into a merchant vessel. When, in July, 1864, he proposed her to the defendant for insurance, it was as "The 'Georgia,' ss., chartered on a voyage from Liverpool to Lisbon and the Portuguese Settlements on the West Coast of Africa and back." She was captured on her voyage by a war steamer of the United States. It was held that the plaintiff ought to have communicated the fact that she had been the Confederate cruiser, and consequently that by reason of this suppression the policy was void (*m*).

Bates *v.* Hewitt.

Goods, the property of the Bolivian Government, were insured against capture for a voyage up the Amazon to Bolivian territory. It was a matter of common knowledge that the frontier region was in a disturbed state, but the agents of the Government, who gave orders for the insurance, had also private information that an expedition was being fitted out by insurgents to intercept the goods. Pickford, J., held that the non-disclosure of this information was fatal to the policy (*n*).

Republic of Bolivia *v.* Indemnity, &c. Ass. Co.

A ship and goods, the property of an American subject, were insured "from London to certain ports in America against all risks, American capture and seizure included"; on arrival, the ship was seized by the American government (for a breach of their Non-importation Act), on account of

Campbell *v.* Innes.

(*l*) See, as to contraband goods, *post*, § 613.
(*m*) Bates *v.* Hewitt (1867), L. R. 2 Q. B. 595. See further, as to this case, *post*, § 609.
(*n*) Republic of Bolivia *v.* Indemnity Mutual Mar. Ass. Co. (1908), 14 Com. Cas. 156, 166.

Sect. 598.   a war with Britain, which had broken out before, but was not known till after, the policy was effected. The fact that the assured was an American subject was not stated on the face of the policy, nor disclosed by the broker to the underwriter. Lord Tenterden and the Court of King's Bench held that the suppression vitiated the policy, because the fact, if disclosed, might have made a material difference to the risk; for, if the property had been British owned, they said, the owner would have done all in his power to prevent the risk from occurring, but if American owned, he might lend himself to the purposes of his own government, and assist them in obtaining possession of the property insured (*o*).

Sailing without convoy.
Sawtell *v.* Loudon.

599. Unless a ship was within the exception of the Convoy Acts, her sailing without convoy, during the operation of those Acts, was held a material circumstance to be disclosed to the underwriters. A broker having proposed an insurance on the "Sophia," from Bristol to Port Mahon, &c., with liberty to seek, join and exchange convoy in the English and Irish Channels, the underwriter stated that a ship called the "Sophia," of Bristol, was reported at Lloyd's as being then at sea without convoy; the broker was afterwards informed by his employer that this was the same ship. The letter containing this statement was not communicated, and the Court held that, as the ship in question was not within any of the exceptions of the Convoy Act, the concealment was fatal to the policy (*p*).

Long *v.* Duff.   If the ship was foreign built, and therefore not within the scope of the Convoy Act, the fact of her having sailed without convoy need not have been communicated, nor yet

---

(*o*) Campbell *v.* Innes (1821), 4 B. & Ald. 423. Although the war did not break out until July, 1812, differences had arisen some time previously between the British and United States Governments, and, as Maclachlan points out (Arnould, 6th ed. p. 573), the fact that American seizure was included as one of the risks in the policy shows that the war was feared and anticipated when it was effected. The point that the insurance was void as being on enemy's property was not taken.

(*p*) Sawtell *v.* Loudon (1814), 1 Marshall, R. 99; 5 Taunt. 359.

the fact that she was foreign built, or otherwise excepted from the operation of the Act; for it is the duty of the underwriter to obtain such information for himself (*q*). *Sect. 599.*

Where an insurance was effected on goods, to return five per cent. for convoy and arrival, the non-communication of the fact that the vessel was to be a running ship (*i.e.*, that she was sailing without convoy) was held fatal to the policy (*r*). *Reid v. Harvey.*

600. The "circumstances" which must be disclosed to the underwriter include, as is stated in sect. 18 (5) of the Marine Insurance Act, 1906 (*s*), "any communication made to, or information received by, the assured." *Information received by the assured.*

Thus, all material information communicated to the assured with regard to the state of the ship, or dangers to which she is exposed, in the course of the voyage, ought to be disclosed to the underwriter, and not only certain intelligence, but even doubtful rumours, if not too remote. If information concern matters preceding the commencement of the voyage, which would be covered by the warranty of seaworthiness, Lord Mansfield and Lord Ellenborough were of opinion that it is unnecessary to disclose it (*t*); under a time policy it may be otherwise (*u*). *The state of the ship on the voyage, and dangers to which she is exposed.*

One who had a doubtful account of a ship like his own being captured caused his ship to be insured, without communicating to the underwriter what he had heard, and the insurance was held to be void (*x*). So also where the owner of a ship hears a doubtful report of a shipwreck which he has reason to think may relate to his own ship, he must disclose it on effecting an insurance (*y*). *Da Costa v. Scandaret.*

A policy was effected on the 24th of March on a privateer, *Durrell v. Bederley.*

(*q*) Long *v.* Duff, and Long *v.* Bolton (1800), 2 B. & P. 209.
(*r*) Reid *v.* Harvey (1816), 4 Dow, 97.
(*s*) *Ante,* § 575.
(*t*) Shoolbred *v.* Nutt (1782), 1 Park, Ins. 493; 1 Marshall, Ins. 474; Haywood *v.* Rodgers (1804), 4 East, 590. See *post,* § 619.
(*u*) Russell *v.* Thornton (1859), 4 H. & N. 788; 29 L. J. Ex. 9; in error, 30 L. J. Ex. 69.
(*x*) Da Costa *v.* Scandaret (1723), 2 P. Wms. 179.
(*y*) Nicholson *v.* Power (1869), 20 L. T. N. S. 580.

Sect. 600. which had sailed from Jersey on the 6th, and reports in Jersey that some French frigates were about the coast, and had made a capture on the 7th of March, continued to prevail until the plaintiff sent the orders on which the insurance was effected, yet he had not said a word about them in his letter: this was held to be a material concealment which vitiated the policy (*z*). So where the plaintiff concealed from the underwriters the fact that he had received a letter from the Cape of Good Hope, stating that there were then two or three French privateers in those seas, he was nonsuited on the ground of that concealment (*a*).

Beckwaite v. Nalgrove.

Information which the assured does not believe.

601. Though the assured be satisfied that a report or rumour is incorrect, and therefore, acting in good faith, do not disclose his intelligence, the concealment is none the less fatal, if the mere report be such as would influence an underwriter. It is not for the assured to judge whether the news be true or false.

Morrison v. Universal Mar. Ins. Co.

The plaintiff in Liverpool, on the 8th October, wrote to his broker in London to insure 5,000*l*. on the ship "Cambria," and a similar sum on her freight. On the evening of that day his eye met a paragraph in the *Liverpool Mercury*, which caused him to telegraph to his broker on the 10th thus: "Since writing on Saturday, paragraph in *Mercury*: 'Cambria qy., Cameo, from New Orleans, aground on North Breaker.' To-day's *Mercury* says: 'The vessel on the North Breaker reported yesterday as the Cambria is stated to be the Cameo from New Orleans.' Can you find out at Lloyd's? Let me know before acting." The "Cameo" had also gone to New Orleans, and the broker made inquiries that satisfied him that the ship aground was the "Cameo"; and on the 12th he effected a policy on freight with the defendants, without mentioning what had appeared in the public newspapers or in Lloyd's list, in which the above announcement had first

---

(*z*) Durrell *v.* Bederley (1816), Holt, N. P. 283. The privateer, it appeared, had actually been captured by the French on the 7th of March, about thirty miles from Jersey.

(*a*) Beckwaite *v.* Nalgrove, cited 3 Taunt. 41.

appeared on the 8th. It turned out to be, in fact, the "Cambria," and the concealment was held fatal to the policy (*b*).

602. Even though the report eventually prove to be totally false and unfounded, its communication, as we have already seen (*c*), is not on that account less indispensable, if it would materially have influenced the judgment of an underwriter in assuming the risk (*d*).

Information which proves eventually to be false.

"Loose rumours, indeed, which have gathered together, no one knows how, need not be communicated" (*e*); and intelligence may be so general, and its application to the subject insured so doubtful and remote, that the assured need not communicate it, though it may possibly turn out to have related to the subject insured (*f*). For the sake, however, of caution, a full disclosure of rumours is advisable.

Loose rumours and news of doubtful application.

603. Whether the assured in a retrospective policy is bound to disclose the state of weather subsequently to the ship's sailing may be regarded as very doubtful; at all events, it may be laid down that he can only be obliged to do so in cases where the ship has sailed from a foreign port, and he has private information of some violent storm at or near that port within so short a period after her sailing that she has probably been exposed to it. If the ship has sailed from a home port, the underwriter is as well informed as the assured of the state of the weather; and unless the storm was of considerable violence, it would not be likely to affect his estimate of the risk (*g*).

The weather subsequent to the ship's sailing.

604. The nature of the cargo shipped or intended to be shipped may be most material to be communicated. For

Nature of the cargo.

(*b*) Morrison *v.* Universal Marine Ins. Co. (1872), L. R. 8 Ex. 40, 197.
(*c*) *Ante*, § 590.
(*d*) Seaman *v.* Fonnereau (1741), 2 Str. 1183; Lynch *v.* Hamilton (1810), 3 Taunt. 37; *S. C.*, in error, Lynch *v.* Dunsford (1811), 14 East, 494.
(*e*) Per Gibbs, C. J., in Durrell *v.* Bederley (1816), Holt, N. P.
283, 285. Yet see Leigh *v.* Adams (1871), 25 L. T. N. S. 566.
(*f*) 1 Phillips, Ins. s. 610; Ruggles *v.* General Int. Ins. Co. (1825), 4 Mass. R. 74; *S. C.*, in error (1827), 12 Wheaton, 408.
(*g*) See the two American cases, Ely *v.* Hallett (1804), 2 Caine, R. 57; and Fiske *v.* New England Ins. Co. (1834), 15 Pick. R. 310, cited 1 Phillips, s. 577. The ground of

Sect. 604. without exactly rendering the ship unseaworthy, a cargo may be of a nature less desirable for safety than another, owing to the dead weight in proportion to bulk, or its tendency to shift, its unwieldiness for stowage, or its gaseous or other dangerous chemical or inflammable qualities, and the like (*gg*).

The true port of loading.

605. **The port of loading may be material.** Goods were insured "at and from Genoa to Dublin, the adventure to begin from the loading to equip for the voyage," but the goods were loaded actually at Leghorn and not at Genoa, which was an intermediate port into which the ship was obliged to put and wait five months for convoy, and the non-communication of this fact was held to be a material concealment (*h*).

Harrower v. Hutchinson.

When it was known that the ship was to load at a place called Laguna de los Padres, a mere anchorage in an open

decision in Ely *v.* Hallett was, that the assured's knowledge was precise and specific, his communication vague and general: he knew there had been a violent storm at the port; he only communicated that there had been "blowing weather and severe storms on the coast." Even thus the case is *inter apices juris*. See the comments of Duer, vol. ii. pp. 399—401. The editors submit that the distinction between home and foreign ports has lost most of its cogency, now that there is telegraphic communication with all parts of the world, and that the assured need only disclose his private information, when it is such as an underwriter's ordinary means of information will not enable him to acquire. They fail to see why such information need not be disclosed, when the ship has sailed from a home port.

(*gg*) For the effect as regards non-disclosure of a clause providing that the assured should be held covered at an extra premium in case of any incorrect description of the goods, see Hewitt *v.* Wilson (1914), 30 Times L. R. 609.

(*h*) Hodgson *v.* Richardson (1764), 1 W. Bl. 463. Arnould states, on the authority of this case, the unqualified rule that the true port of loading must be disclosed. Goods shipped before arrival at the *terminus a quo* are not generally covered by a policy in the ordinary form. (*Ante*, § 448.) The question of disclosure of the true port of loading does not therefore arise. Where the policy is framed to cover goods loaded before the commencement of the risk, the editors submit that generally speaking the actual port of loading is immaterial. The fact, however, of such a delay as took place at Genoa may well be material, on the ground stated by the Court, viz., that damage might have happened during the ship's stay at Genoa. In the report, it may be pointed out, the insurance is stated to be on the ship, but there can be little doubt that this is a mistake.

roadstead, which was unknown to underwriters as a port of loading for Europe, and the risk when express mention of that place was made had been already refused, a policy on the same risk, without further description of it than "at and from the port of Buenos Ayres and port or ports of loading in the province of Buenos Ayres," was held by the Exchequer Chamber to be void on the ground of concealment (*i*). So also where, under a licence to call at any places, it had been arranged to take cargo at an unknown and dangerous port, Mathew, J., held that this fact should have been disclosed (*k*).

Sect. 605.

Laing v. Union Mar. Ins. Co.

606. If it be intended that the ship shall take a course, which, though within the limits of the policy, may not be the best under the circumstances of the voyage insured, this intention should be disclosed to the underwriter: hence, as the customary course of the voyage for a ship insured from London to Jamaica was to leave the captain at liberty to take which of three tracks he pleased in sailing past St. Domingo; where he was limited by his instructions to take only one of those three tracks, it was held that the failure to communicate this fact to the underwriters vitiated the policy (*l*).

Intention to depart from usage. *Middlewood v. Blakes.*

If a ship is to be employed on a service of peculiar danger, and this cannot be inferred from the terms of the policy, it ought to be communicated to the underwriter; as where the intention is to employ her in the foreign smuggling trade (*m*).

Any service of danger.

Neglect by the captain of a ship, aware of her having sustained an accident which might be the cause of serious damage, to inform his owners of it before they effect the policy, will at least prevent them from recovering for a loss

Accident to ship.

(*i*) *Harrower v. Hutchinson* (1870), L. R. 5 Q. B. 584; reversing the judgment below, L. R. 4 Q. B. 523.

(*k*) *Laing v. Union Marine Ins. Co.* (1895), 1 Com. Cas. 11.

(*l*) *Middlewood v. Blakes* (1797), 7 T. R. 162; *ante,* § 389. See the observations of Duer on this case, vol. ii. pp. 494, 495.

(*m*) 1 Emerigon, 172. And see his opinion in 2 Valin, Tit. des Ass. l. 3, t. 6, art. 49.

Sect. 606. resulting from the accident, the knowledge of which he has thus been the means of concealing from the underwriters (*n*).

Name of ship under a floating policy.

607. It has never been decided that when goods are insured by a floating policy and the assured knows by what ship they will be carried, he must disclose its name; and on principle it would seem that the insurer, by underwriting such a policy, waives this information as to the ship, and is willing to take a risk by any seaworthy ship (*o*). When, however, the assured knows that the goods will or may be shipped by a vessel concerning which there is intelligence material to the risk, he must when insuring disclose the name of the ship instead of waiting to declare the shipment at the usual time (*p*).

An anonymous letter was received at Lloyd's stating that the owners of the "Candida" intended to lose her on her next voyage. A., accustomed to open floating policies, on which he declared shipments from abroad as he heard of them, received intelligence of a shipment for him to be made by the "Candida." He was aware of the contents of the letter, but considered them unworthy of credit. Under these circumstances he opened a fresh policy believing that he should be able to declare the shipment on the policy already open. He was disappointed of this expectation by advices of other vessels coming to hand before advice as to the "Candida," and when such advice did come forward he was obliged to declare her on the fresh policy. The Court of

---

(*n*) Gladstone *v.* King (1813), 1 M. & S. 35; Stribley *v.* Imperial Marine Ins. Co. (1876), 1 Q. B. D. 507. See, however, *ante*, § 584.

(*o*) See per Mansfield, C. J., Lynch *v.* Hamilton (1810), 3 Taunt. 37, 39; Knight *v.* Cotesworth (1883), 1 Cab. & E. 48, in which case a usage at Lloyd's to disclose the name of a ship by which the goods are expected to come was set up, but negatived by the jury. As to non-disclosure of the captain's past record, see Thames & Mersey Co. *v.* "Gunford" Ship Co., [1911] A. C. 529.

(*p*) Lynch *v.* Hamilton (1810), 3 Taunt. 37; Lynch *v.* Dunsford, in error (1811), 14 East, 494; Leigh *v.* Adams (1871), 25 L. T. N. S. 566. See, as to disclosure on opening a cover, Republic of Bolivia *v.* Indemnity Mut. Mar. Ins. Co. (1908), Pickford, J., 14 Com. Cas. 156.

CHAP. II.] CONCEALMENT. 781

Queen's Bench held that the concealment was material, and that he was not entitled to recover (*q*). The Court did not in terms hold the policy to be void. The question of the validity of subsequent declarations in respect of goods coming forward by other vessels was not raised; but it seems to follow logically that the policy was vitiated *in toto*, and not only so far as the declaration on the "Candida" was concerned.

Sect. 607.

A broker is not bound to disclose the name of the person on whose behalf he effects the insurance (*r*).

Name of assured.

608. When the assured has entered into a contract which makes the risk of ultimate loss to the underwriter greater than the usual one, this fact ought to be disclosed (*s*).

Contract which may aggravate the risk.

The Thames lightermen, finding that the law of common carriers bore hard upon them when it gave insurers recourse against them for losses not the consequence of negligence, formed an association for the purpose of doing the lighterage on the terms of being subject for loss only in case of negligence, called "no recourse terms." Underwriters thereupon refused to subscribe policies containing craft risks, except on a higher scale of premium, wherever the "no recourse terms" had been adopted by the assured. Policies on goods containing the craft risk were effected for the plaintiffs with the defendant, after they had agreed with a particular lighterman that he should lighter all their goods on the "no recourse terms." This was not made known to the defendant, and therefore the policies were underwritten for a lower premium than would have been demanded for

Lighterage on the "no recourse terms."

(*q*) Leigh *v.* Adams (1871), 25 L. T. N. S. 566.

(*r*) Glasgow Ass. Corpn. *v.* Symondson (1911), 16 Com. Cas. 109.

(*s*) Tate *v.* Hyslop (1885), 15 Q. B. D. 368; see also Asfar *v.* Blundell, [1896] 1 Q. B. 123. In Property Insurance Co. *v.* National Protector Insurance Co. (1913), 18 Com. Cas. 119, Scrutton, J., considered that this principle was applicable to a reinsurance, "subject to the same clauses and conditions as the original policy," where the original contract of insurance contained an unusual clause enlarging the liability of the original underwriter.

Sect. 608.

craft risk coupled with "no recourse terms." A loss having occurred under these policies in the course of the lighterage, this action was brought. The Court of Appeal considered that it had not been proved that the practice to employ lightermen on the less onerous terms was general, and held that there had been concealment of a material fact which a fair and reasonable underwriter would have taken into account in fixing the terms on which he would accept the risk, and therefore vitiated the policies (*t*).

Cancellation clause.

Lord Coleridge held, in The Mercantile Steamship Company *v.* Tyser (*u*), that where a charter-party contained a clause giving the charterer an option to cancel the contract if the ship did not arrive on a certain date, the assured on freight was bound to disclose the existence of the clause. The reason given by the learned Chief Justice was, that there was no general usage (the policy was made in 1875) to insert this cancelling clause in charter-parties, and that it enormously increases the risk. It is submitted, however, that the insertion of a power to cancel cannot increase the risk, and that for this reason the fact that the contract contains this term is not material. Lord Coleridge's own decision and that of the House of Lords in a later case (*x*) show that where, in consequence of perils insured against, a ship does not arrive at the stipulated date and the power to cancel is exercised, the underwriter is not liable. The freight has been lost, not by any of the perils insured against, but by the exercise of the option.

If, however, a charter-party contained a stipulation that if the ship did not arrive in port on a given day the contract should be at an end, without the exercise of any power to

---

(*t*) Tate *v.* Hyslop (1885), 15 Q. B. D. 368.

(*u*) (1880), 7 Q. B. D. 73.

(*x*) Inman Steamship Co. *v.* Bischoff (1882), 7 App. Cas. 670. See, however, Lord Selborne's *dictum, ibid.* p. 676; and see *post,* §§ 785—788. It may be that Lord Coleridge meant that if he was wrong in holding that the exercise of the option did not cause a loss by a peril insured against, the policy would be void for concealment; but this is certainly not what he is reported to have said.

CHAP. II.] CONCEALMENT. 783

cancel, it would seem that this fact is material to the risk   Sect. 608.
in a policy on freight. For if, in consequence of a peril
insured against, the ship did not arrive on that day, there
would be a loss of freight caused directly by such a peril (*y*).

It must, however, be remembered that when the insertion
of a particular term in a mercantile contract has become very
general, the underwriter will be deemed to have knowledge
of it, and thenceforth there will be no obligation on the part
of the assured to give information of its insertion (*z*). Therefore it may cease after some time to be the duty of the
assured to give information as to the terms of a contract,
the non-disclosure of which would at one time have been fatal
to the insurance.

609. By sect. 18 (3) of the Marine Insurance Act, 1906,—   Matters that
                                                                                               need not
In the absence of inquiry the following circumstances be disclosed.
need not be disclosed, namely:—

(a) Any circumstance which diminishes the risk;
(b) Any circumstance which is known or presumed to be known to the insurer. The insurer is presumed to know matters of common notoriety or knowledge, and matters which an insurer in the ordinary course of his business, as such, ought to know;
(c) Any circumstance as to which information is waived by the insurer;
(d) Any circumstance which it is superfluous to disclose by reason of any express or implied warranty.

"The assured," said Lord Mansfield, "need not mention
what the underwriter knows, what way soever he came by
that knowledge; or what he ought to know; or takes upon
himself the knowledge of; or waives being informed of; or
what lessens the risk agreed and understood to be run; or
general topics of speculation; or every cause which may

(*y*) The Alps, [1893] P. 109; The Bedouin, [1894] P. 1; see also Inman Steamship Co. *v.* Bischoff (1882), 7 App. Cas. 670, 682, 690; Scottish Shire Line, Ltd. *v.* London & Prov. Mar. Ins. Co., Ltd., [1912] 3 K. B. 51.

(*z*) See *post*, § 611; Mar. Ins. Act, 1906, s. 18, sub-s. 3 (b), *infra*.

Sect. 609. occasion natural perils, as the difficulty of the voyage, kind of seasons, probability of hurricanes, earthquakes, &c.; or every cause which may occasion political perils, from the rupture of states, from war, and the various operations of it, upon the probability of safety from the continuance and return of peace, or from the imbecility of the enemy " (*a*).

Material facts not present to the underwriter's mind.

The assured cannot, however, excuse his omission to communicate a material fact on the ground that the fact had previously come to the knowledge of the underwriter, unless at the time when the contract was made the fact was present to the underwriter's mind.

Bates v. Hewitt.

In the case of the "Georgia," the policy was effected in 1864 on a vessel which had been a Confederate cruiser in the years 1863 and 1864, and which afterwards was dismantled and sold to the plaintiff. The "Georgia" had been notorious to the British public at the time she was cruising, and after she had been laid up in Liverpool had been the subject of comment in the London newspapers and in the House of Commons, as appeared by the published debates. The defendant, one of Lloyd's underwriters in London, had been cognizant of all this; but at the time that the risk was proposed to him nothing revived his recollection of these things, and it did not occur to him that this was or might be the Confederate cruiser. It was a fact that at the time of the risk being proposed there was no "Georgia," s.s. in Lloyd's Lists. Under these circumstances the jury found that the defendant was not aware that the "Georgia" he was underwriting was the Confederate cruiser, but that at that time he had abundant means from his previous knowledge, coupled with the particulars supplied by the plaintiff, of identifying the ship. The Court held that the previous knowledge possessed by the defendant of the material fact omitted from the particulars of the risk did not release the plaintiff from the obligation to communicate it (*b*).

(*a*) Carter *v.* Boehm (1766), 3 Burr. 1909.
(*b*) Bates *v.* Hewitt (1867), L. R. 2 Q. B. 595.

| CHAP. II.] | CONCEALMENT. | 785 |

It has also been held in the Supreme Court of the United States that the assured cannot excuse his omission to disclose material facts by showing that they were actually known to the underwriter, unless the knowledge of the latter was as full and particular as his own (c).

Sect. 609. Facts of which the underwriter's knowledge is not so complete as the assured's.

610. On the principle that the assured need not disclose what the underwriter ought to know, it has been decided in several cases that facts comprised in the general usages of trade need not be communicated to the underwriter; e.g., the usage of the Newfoundland trade for ships arriving on the coast either to be employed for some time in fishing on the Banks (called banking), or to make intermediate voyages in the American seas, before beginning to take in their homeward cargo (d); or the established custom during the great French war for a ship insured "at and from London or Ramsgate to Nantes, with liberty to touch at Ostend," to sail direct to Nantes, with false clearances for Ostend, and false bills of lading purporting to be made at Ostend and expressing that the goods were shipped there (e). But to dispense with communication of anything done according to usage, such usage must be general and universally known to all engaged in the trade (f).

Usages of trade.

611. Where it is the general and well-known practice to put a certain clause in a particular kind of mercantile contract, the underwriter is presumed to know that the

Usual clauses in mercantile contracts.

(c) Sun Mutual Ins. Co. v. Ocean Ins. Co. (1882), 107 U. S. 485, citing 2 Duer, 399.

(d) Vallance v. Dewar (1809), 1 Camp. 503; Ougier v. Jennings (1800), ibid. 505, n.; Kingston v. Knibbs (1808), 1 Camp. 508, n. For further illustrations of the same principle, see Moxon v. Atkins (1812), 3 Camp. 200; Da Costa v. Edmunds (1815), 4 Camp. 142; Stewart v. Bell (1821), 5 B. & Ald. 238; and the cases decided on the East India trade, as Salvador v. Hopkins (1765), 3 Burr. 1707; Gregory v. Christie (1784), 3 Dougl. 419; Grant v. Paxton (1809), 1 Taunt. 463; 1 Marshall, Ins. 259; 2 Chitty, 319.

(e) Planché v. Fletcher (1779), 1 Dougl. 251. See Barnewall v. Church (1803), 1 Caines, 217; 1 Phillips, s. 598.

(f) Tennant v. Henderson (1813), 1 Dow, 324.

Sect. 611. contract contains the clause, and therefore the assured is not bound to give information about its insertion, though the clause may tend to increase the risk.

In time charters it is now the universal practice to insert the so-called "twenty-four hours" clause, which provides that payment of hire shall cease when the ship has, from certain causes, become inefficient for twenty-four hours, until she is able to resume the voyage. And when the "twenty-four hours" clause is put into immediate operation by a peril insured against, the underwriter on freight is liable for the loss. An underwriter of a policy on chartered freight knew, from the form of the slip, that it was intended to insure a time freight. The Court of Appeal held that, considering that the "twenty-four hours" clause is practically universal in time charters, the assured was not bound to disclose the fact that the charter-party contained this clause (*g*).

In a subsequent case, where a policy was effected by charterers on "profit on charter," and it was a material fact that the freight payable by the charterers was a lump freight, the Court of Appeal held that the assured was not bound specifically to disclose this fact. A clause for payment of a lump sum for freight, they said, is a usual clause in charter-parties, and the obligation specifically to disclose the contents of a charter-party extends only to unusual clauses, the insertion of which the underwriters could not reasonably have anticipated (*h*). So also it has been held in the United States that underwriters are now presumed to have knowledge of cancellation clauses in charter-parties (*i*).

Similarly, it was held by Bigham, J., that an underwriter who re-insures a time risk need not disclose the fact that the original policy contains a continuation clause (*k*).

(*g*) The Bedouin, [1894] P. 1; see also Salvador *v.* Hopkins (1765), 3 Burr. 1707, where it was held that the underwriter need not be told that a charter-party of the East India Company contained a clause entitling the company to keep the ship out in India for a year, there being a general usage of the East India trade to this effect.

(*h*) Asfar *v.* Blundell, [1896] 1 Q. B. 123.

(*i*) Ruger *v.* Firemen's Fund Ins. Co. (1898), 90 Fed. R. 310.

(*k*) Charlesworth *v.* Faber (1900), 5 Com. Cas. 408.

612. Every underwriter is presumed to be as well acquainted as the assured with the general and established restrictions on commercial freedom imposed by different states for the sake of revenue or fancied protection to their interests (*l*); but if a prohibition be of recent date, or only occasional in its nature, the assured, supposing him to have private means of information, ought to communicate the fact to the underwriter: if he be himself ignorant of it, of course the rule will not apply (*m*).

<small>Sect. 612. General trade and revenue laws.</small>

613. It has been held in the United States that, under an insurance on " all lawful goods," it is not necessary to disclose that they are contraband of war, or that such constitute a part of the cargo (*n*). So, in this country, where an American neutral, who had effected an insurance on goods on board an American ship, did not inform the British underwriters that enemy's property, not included in the goods insured, was also on board the same ship, no objection was made to his right of recovery (*o*).

<small>Where part of the cargo is contraband or enemy's property.</small>

(*l*) Lever *v.* Fletcher (1780), 1 Park, Ins. 507.

(*m*) See Mayne *v.* Walter (1782), 1 Park, Ins. 431; 1 Marshall, Ins. 478; and the American cases, 1 Phillips, ss. 595 *et seq.*

(*n*) Juhel *v.* Rhinelander (1800—1802), 2 Johnson's Cases, 120, 487; and Seton *v.* Low (1799), 1 Johnson's Cases, 1, cited 1 Phillips, s. 628. Generally speaking, as contraband goods, and other goods on board, the property of the same owner, are liable to condemnation, and the ship to be carried into port for inquiry, the nature of the goods ought, it would seem, to be declared. This is the opinion of Phillips (vol. i. s. 624). The owner of part of the cargo cannot, however, necessarily be expected to know that there are contraband goods on board belonging to other persons.

(*o*) Barker *v.* Blakes (1808), 9 East, 283. The editors venture to point out that the question of concealment was not raised in this case. Indeed, the assured may not have known that enemy's goods would also be carried. Before the Declaration of Paris the fact of enemy's goods being on board would have subjected the ship and cargo to delay and detention, as the ship might have been carried into port for the condemnation of the goods. It may, however, be said that the underwriter had no right to assume that a neutral shipowner would not, in the ordinary way of trade, carry belligerent-owned goods.

Sect. 614.
Contents of Lloyd's Lists.

614. As to the contents of Lloyd's Lists (which are now incorporated in the *Shipping Gazette*), whether the underwriter, being a member of Lloyd's or a subscriber, and as such receiving or having access to these Lists daily, is to be affected with knowledge thereof, irrespective of its being actual knowledge, so as to be bound thereby in law, is a question concerning which the cases are conflicting. In the earlier cases the juries were directed that the assured need not disclose matters of fact which had been published in Lloyd's Lists. For instance, upon an insurance on the "Lusitania" from Brazil to Lisbon being proposed, it was stated that the ship was out fifty-seven days; but the fact that another vessel which had sailed at the same time had arrived at Lisbon ten days before the date of the orders to insure might have been learned from Lloyd's List, and was not stated. Burroughs, J., there held that the policy was not vitiated, on the ground that "what the underwriter by fair inquiry and due diligence may learn from the ordinary sources of information need not be disclosed" (*p*). A similar opinion is attributed to Erle, C. J., at Nisi Prius, in the following terms: "Actual knowledge is not essential; if the insurer knew he had the means of knowing the fact, then it was within his knowledge. If, for example, he knew that he could learn the exact cargo at Lloyd's, and chose not to ascertain it, knowing or believing it would include iron, it was within his knowledge" (*q*). To the same effect seems to be an opinion expressed by Lord Abinger, *in banc* (*r*).

In the last-mentioned case objection was taken before the Court to the admission in evidence, on the trial, by Maule, J., of Lloyd's Lists, and the learned judge was sustained in thinking them evidence. So far there seems to be no ground for doubt, the same point having been frequently ruled as to

---

(*p*) Friere *v.* Woodhouse (1817), 1 Holt, N. P. 572. So, upon the first trial of Elton *v.* Larkins (1831), 5 C. & P. 86; *S. C.* (1832), *ibid.* 385; 8 Bing. 198.

(*q*) Foley *v.* Tabor (1861), 2 F. & F. 662. And cf. Gandy *v.* Adelaide Ins. Co. (1871), L. R. 6 Q. B. 746.

(*r*) Mackintosh *v.* Marshall (1843), 11 M. & W. 116.

CHAP. II.] CONCEALMENT. 789

the admissibility in evidence of a newspaper which the party against whom it is adduced is proved to take in regularly. It is upon the next point that the difference of opinion exists, namely, the use to be made of it when admitted in evidence, unless the particular entry in it can by evidence be traced to his knowledge.

In Nicholson *v.* Power it was not necessary to consider the point, because, although the same entry had first appeared in Lloyd's Lists which afterwards appeared in the *Shipping Gazette,* and of which no mention was made to the underwriter, the assured had peculiar information from his captain that enabled him to fix the entry as applying to his own ship, and to none other (*s*).

In Morrison *v.* Universal Marine Insurance Co. (*t*), the defendants were subscribers to Lloyd's, and the entry found in the *Liverpool Mercury* newspaper had first appeared in Lloyd's Lists, where, however, their underwriter did not discover it until after he had initialed the slip; and as the broker, admitting his own knowledge of the entry, had taken upon himself to suppress all mention of it, this concealment defeated the policy. Upon the point here under consideration, Bramwell, B., said: "It is impossible to say that there is any rule of law or any principle or authority which affects the underwriter with knowledge of what is contained in Lloyd's Lists. No doubt some knowledge may be assumed in the underwriter—what, I will not attempt to define or describe; though I agree with what was thrown out by my brother Cleasby in the course of the argument, that the matters he must take knowledge of are matters of general knowledge, not matters relating to any particular ship. But to hold that the underwriter is bound to carry in his head all that is contained in Lloyd's Lists relating to a ship in which he has no interest, rather than to hold the owner of the ship

Sect. 614.

Morrison *v.* Universal Mar. Ins. Co.

(*s*) Nicholson *v.* Power (1869), 20 L. T. N. S. 580. See, however, the remarks of Cockburn, C. J., *ibid*. See *post*, § 616.

(*t*) Morrison *v.* Universal Mar. Ins. Co. (1872), L. R. 8 Ex. 40; on appeal (1873), *ibid*. 197; *ante*, § 601.

CONCEALMENT. [PART II.

Sect. 614. bound to disclose it, would be to put a difficult and useless burden on the underwriter, while the opposite view puts no difficulty at all in the way of the owner."

This view of the law thus expressed by Bramwell, B., was concurred in by the other members of the Court of Exchequer; and Blackburn, J., presiding in the Court of Exchequer Chamber upon the same case, expressed his concurrence in this with the Court below (*u*).

Summary. It may be gathered from this last case and the case of Bates *v.* Hewitt (*x*) that there is no presumption of knowledge of particular facts concerning particular ships on the part of the underwriter merely on the ground that such facts have appeared in Lloyd's Lists or a newspaper.

Underwriter relying on representation and not consulting Lloyd's Lists.
615. The sole ground upon which Lloyd's Lists are admissible in evidence against the underwriter upon a question of concealment is that he is presumed to have consulted them with reference to the risk proposed before assuming it; if, therefore, there has been any false representation made to the underwriter as to the nature of the risk, and the underwriter acted solely in reliance on that representation without in fact consulting the lists, the presumption that he knows their contents of course falls to the ground. If in such case there have also been the concealment of a material fact, this will avoid the policy, although the fact concealed might have been learnt from the lists (*y*).

Private information connected with intelligence in Lloyd's Lists.
616. If the intelligence conveyed in Lloyd's Lists can only be connected with the risk proposed by means of information which the assured is privately possessed of, he will be bound to disclose such information if he is aware of its connection with such intelligence and the latter makes it material, and his failure to do so will vitiate the policy; for, although in such case the mere fact as it stands in Lloyd's Lists is

---

(*u*) Morrison *v.* Universal Mar. Ins. Co. (1873), L. R. 8 Ex. 197.
(*x*) (1867), L. R. 2 Q. B. 595.

(*y*) Mackintosh *v.* Marshall (1843), 11 M. & W. 116.

CHAP. II.] CONCEALMENT. 791

presumed to be known to the underwriter, yet its connection with the risk could only be known to him through the information which the assured has privately received and withholds (*z*).

Sect. 616.

617. It has been a question a good deal canvassed in the United States how far maritime intelligence inserted in the public papers, and open to all the world, need be stated. The conclusion upon the whole appears to be that such articles of intelligence need not be stated, unless they apply peculiarly to the case of the assured, or unless he is privately in possession of information which enables him to infer, with more certainty than the rest of the public, that the intelligence in the journals is in fact material to the risk (*a*). Mere items of ordinary shipping intelligence in the public papers, equally open to both parties and too general to lead to any particular application to the risk insured, need not be communicated (*b*).

General maritime intelligence. Decisions in the United States.

Where the facts in question are comprised under the head of marine intelligence in papers actually and habitually taken in and filed at the office where the insurance is effected, it seems a fair general presumption that the insurers " have examined with some care the items of marine intelligence which are expressly designed speedily to diffuse information on a subject so immediately interesting to them, especially in relation to vessels belonging to their own port " (*c*). This is, however, at the highest only a *primâ facie* presumption; no case in the United States has carried it beyond this; and in New York and Massachusetts the law, we are told by Judge

---

(*z*) Lynch *v.* Dunsford (1811), 14 East, 494; Nicholson *v.* Power (1869), 20 L. T. N. S. 580; see also Bates *v.* Hewitt (1867), L. R. 2 Q. B. 595.

(*a*) See the cases cited in the last note. See also Republic of Bolivia *v.* Indemnity Mutual Mar. Ass. Co., *ante*, § 598.

(*b*) 3 Kent, Com. 285; 1 Phillips, s. 606; 2 Duer, 480, 481; and see the case of Ruggles *v.* General Int. Ins. Co. (1825), 4 Mason, 74; cited 1 Phillips, s. 610; and Alsop *v.* Com. Ins. Co. (1833), 1 Sumner, R. 451; 1 Phillips, *ibid*.

(*c*) Per Shaw, C. J., in Greene *v.* Merchants' Ins. Co. (1830), 10 Pick. Mass. R. 402; 1 Phillips, s. 606; 2 Duer, 481.

Sect. 617. Duer, may be regarded as settled, that in such cases the defence of a concealment is only to be met by direct or circumstantial proof of actual knowledge on the part of the underwriter (*d*).

In one of the cases cited in illustration of this position, the defence set up was that a letter of the plaintiff's alleged to contain material information had been withheld; the answer was, that the same information had appeared in substance in a New York *Gazette* that had been received at the office of the defendants, and was on the file there when the application for the insurance was made. The Judge told the jury that if they thought the newspaper contained all the information the letter did, and was actually seen by the president of the Insurance Company before he subscribed the policy, and that part of it which contained the information read by him, then the omission to communicate the letter was immaterial. The jury found for the plaintiff. On application for a new trial the Court upheld the direction of the Judge (*e*).

Inference from rate of premium.

Where, from the rate of premium or other circumstances, the fair probability appears to be that the insurer, though subscribing to and regularly taking in the *Gazette*, could not, before completing the insurance, have read the paragraph conveying the information complained of as withheld, the *primâ facie* presumption is repelled, and the defence of concealment unanswered. Thus, an insurance was effected at New York on a sloop from Washington, North Carolina, to Charleston, South Carolina. The premium was at the ordinary rate. The sloop had been in fact lost on Ocracocke Bar, North Carolina, nine days before the policy was effected. The day before effecting the insurance the plaintiff had read a paragraph in a New York mercantile gazette, stating that information had been received " that a New York sloop, bound from Washington, North Carolina, to Charleston, South Carolina, had been stranded, Thursday

(*d*) 2 Duer, 481, 482. cited 2 Duer, 481, and 1 Phillips,
(*e*) Greene *v.* Merchants' Ins. s. 606.
Co. (1830), 10 Pick. Mass. R. 402,

week, on Ocracocke Bar." He did not disclose this fact. The Insurance Company subscribed to and regularly received the *Gazette* in question. It was contended that they must, therefore, be held to be as well acquainted with its contents as the plaintiff. The Judge, however, held that the plaintiff ought to have disclosed the fact, and that the concealment was material and avoided the policy. Judge Duer adds: " The rate of premium was doubtless considered by the Judge as such conclusive proof of the ignorance of the underwriter that it superseded the necessity of submitting the question to the jury. The verdict was in conformity with the charge of the Judge and no attempt was made to disturb it. In New York the propriety of the decision has never been questioned " (*f*).

Sect. 617.

618. Another principle laid down by Lord Mansfield in the celebrated judgment already cited and embodied in sect. 18 (3) (c) of the Marine Insurance Act, 1906, is that nothing need be disclosed to the underwriter which he himself waives being informed of. Thus, to take the illustration given by his Lordship in the same case:—" If the insurance be on a private ship of war, from port to port, the underwriter needs not to be told of the secret enterprise it is destined upon, for from the nature of the contract he waives this information " (*g*).

Nothing need be disclosed which the underwriter impliedly waives being informed of.

In case of privateer.

Upon the same principle, an insurance on a ship for a

Need of repairs.

(*f*) Dickenson *v.* The Comm. Ins. Co. of New York, Anthon's N. P. R. 92; 2 Duer, 480, n. (*a*). Phillips, in his statement of the case, adds a fact that makes the decision still stronger, viz., that on account of the intelligence another office had in the earlier part of the same day refused the risk. 1 Phillips, s. 606. For the inference from the payment of an unusually heavy premium, see Court *v.* Martineau (1782), 3 Dougl. 161; *post*, § 622.

(*g*) Carter *v.* Boehm (1766), 3 Burr. 1909. In Property Insurance Co. *v.* National Protector Insurance Co. (1913), 18 Com. Cas. 119, Scrutton, J., held that the words "without notice" in a re-insurance policy containing the following clause: "subject without notice to the same clauses and conditions, &c.," relieved the reassured from disclosing the existence of an unusual clause in the original policy.

Sect. 618. homeward voyage, "at and from" a foreign port, implies that in all probability repairs will be required before she can sail on her homeward voyage; the fact, therefore, that she requires to be detained there for repairs beyond the time of her loading need not be communicated to the underwriter, who, if he wishes for particular information on the point, ought to ask for it (*h*).

Date of sailing in retrospective policy.

So, where a ship is insured "at and from" a particular place, "lost or not lost," it is not necessary to disclose that she has in fact sailed before the policy is effected; for if the underwriters want to be satisfied as to this point, they ought to inquire into it (*i*).

Delay before ship reaches terminus a quo.

An insurance "at and from" a port by no means implies that the ship is already at the port in question, and consequently information that she is not then there is not required. But as it is implied in such a policy that the vessel will be there within a reasonable time, the assured ought to communicate any information possessed by him that this reasonable time is likely to be exceeded, otherwise the insurer may avoid the policy (*j*). Yet if such delay in excess be excused by a general usage, such usage is one of those things that the underwriter is bound to know, and therefore need not be mentioned in the particular case (*k*).

Strengthening floating dock, where seaworthiness admitted.

Where the owners of a floating dock insured it against loss on a voyage by sea by a policy containing the words, "seaworthiness admitted," it was held by the Court of Appeal that it was not necessary for the owners to disclose that it required special strengthening for the voyage, on the ground that the underwriters were under the circumstances

---

(*h*) Beckwith v. Sydehotham (1807), 1 Camp. 116. As a justifiable delay after the risk has attached, however prolonged, does not put an end to the insurance, it is submitted that the assured must, when the policy is retrospective, disclose any extraordinary delay which has taken place since the beginning of the risk. See Hodgson v. Richardson (1764), 1 W. Bl. 463.

(*i*) Fort v. Lee (1811), 3 Taunt. 381.

(*j*) Mar. Ins. Act, 1906, s. 42. See *ante*, §§ 479, 480.

(*k*) Per Tindal, C. J., in Mount v. Larkins (1831), 8 Bing. 108, 121.

put on inquiry as to its construction, and should have asked for further information if they required it (*l*). *Sect. 618.*

The form of Lloyd's policy shows that when an agent effects an insurance in his own name (*m*), the insurer waives information as to the identity of the assured (*n*). *Identity of assured.*

619. On the same principle it is that, as there is in every voyage policy an implied warranty of seaworthiness, the assured need not proffer any disclosure as to the ship's unseaworthiness when she sailed. The underwriter waives his right to a spontaneous disclosure of facts, which, whether disclosed or not, will exempt him from his liability, as being a breach of this implied warranty. Hence, in an action on a policy " at and from Madeira to Charleston," it was held that the captain's letters from Madeira to the owner, stating that the ship had been very leaky on her voyage thither, need not be communicated (*o*). *Unseaworthiness.*

Shoolbred v. Nutt.

So where the owners of a ship insured " at and from Trinidad to London," &c., without communicating the captain's letter, stating that he had been obliged to have a survey on the ship at Trinidad " on account of her bad character," or the survey which accompanied the letter and gave the ship a good character: it was held, that the non-disclosure of this letter and survey to the underwriters did not vacate the policy; though it appeared in evidence, that such circumstance, if known, would have enhanced the premium (*p*). *Haywood v. Rodgers.*

In a time policy there is no warranty of seaworthiness; and, therefore, material facts relating to the condition of the ship when the policy attaches must be disclosed (*q*).

(*l*) Cantiere Meccanico Brindisino *v.* Janson, [1912] 3 K. B. 452, affirming Scrutton, J., [1912] 2 K. B. 112.

(*m*) See *ante*, § 11.

(*n*) Glasgow Ass. Corpn. *v.* Symondson (1911), 16 Com. Cas. 109, 120.

(*o*) Shoolbred *v.* Nutt (1782), 1 Marshall, Ins. 474; 1 Park, Ins. 493.

(*p*) Haywood *v.* Rodgers (1804), 4 East, 590; see also Beckwith *v.* Sydebotham (1807), 1 Camp. 116.

(*q*) Russell *v.* Thornton (1859), 29 L. J. Ex. 9. See Gandy *v.* Adelaide Ins. Co., *post*, § 625. The rule is, of course, the same where

Sect. 619. A time policy on a ship to run from the 21st of January was effected on the 19th. The assured then knew that the ship had been ashore on the 2nd of January, and had sprung a leak and been forced to go into port for repairs. The Court of Exchequer held that the non-communication of these facts avoided the policy (*r*).

The general rule is that no circumstance need be disclosed which it is superfluous to disclose by reason of any express or implied warranty (*s*).

Where the underwriter calls for information.

620. If, indeed, the underwriter, even though the policy be on a voyage, particularly calls for information on the subject, then the assured must disclose truly all that he knows in the respect required (*t*).

The principles upon which this doctrine rests are thus clearly and admirably stated in Lord Ellenborough's judgment in the case of Haywood *v.* Rodgers:—" It certainly," said his Lordship, " would have some weight in guiding the judgment of an underwriter, to know how old the ship was; where she was built, whether originally British or foreign; what was the form of her construction, whether clinker built or not, whether copper bottomed or not; what repairs she had received, and when, and in what docks those repairs were done to her, and how lately before the voyage insured; and if the voyage were, as this was, a voyage home, what accidents the ship had met with in her outward voyage. All

seaworthiness is admitted in a voyage policy. See Cantiere Meccanico Brindisino *v.* Janson, *ubi supra.*

(*r*) Russell *v.* Thornton, *supra.* In delivering the judgment of the Court, Bramwell, B., said (p. 13) that even if there had been a warranty of seaworthiness the facts ought to have been disclosed, as the ship, though made seaworthy, might never be as good a ship as before the calamity. This *dictum* does not agree with the authorities already cited. The logical consequence, if it were good law, would be that in all insurances all bygone calamities to the ship ought to be disclosed. See, as to this, *post,* § 621.

(*s*) Mar. Ins. Act, 1906, s. 18, sub-s. 3 (d), *ante,* § 609.

(*t*) So, according to the Mar. Ins. Act, 1906, s. 18, sub-s. 3, *ante,* § 609, it is only "in the absence of inquiry" that the circumstances there enumerated need not be disclosed.

this may be very proper and convenient for an underwriter to be informed of, before he takes upon him the risk, and all this may be asked of the assured; and if he should withhold, on being asked for it, any material part of such required information, his policy could not be sustained for a moment; for such a suppression would be a fraudulent concealment of material facts, which has always been considered as avoiding the policy. But the question is, Is it the duty of the assured, in the first instance, and as a condition precedent on his part, to inform the underwriter of all these circumstances to the extent of his, the assured's, own actual knowledge on the subject?" His Lordship answers this question in the negative, upon the grounds:—1st. That the underwriter is exempted from the effect of these circumstances, as far as they render the ship not a proper object of insurance; for if the ship be not seaworthy at the commencement of the risk, he never incurred any responsibility. 2nd. From the almost absolute impossibility for the assured to state (without any specific inquiry) everything which the underwriter might have deemed material to the question, whether he should underwrite at all, and, if so, at what premium (u).

Sect. 620.

621. On the same principle, the assured on perishable goods is not bound to make any disclosure as to whether they were in a damaged condition; because, if they be put on board in such a state as to produce spontaneous combustion and are thereby consumed, the assured can make no claim in respect of the loss which he has himself occasioned (x).

Condition of perishable goods.

Upon the same principle it has been decided that the assured need not, unasked, disclose all the bygone calamities that have befallen the ship, or produce his whole portfolio of letters; it is enough, in the first instance, if he communicates

Bygone casualties to the ship.

(u) Haywood v. Rodgers (1804), 4 East, 590, 597, 598. The decisions in the United States follow the law as thus laid down. See Walden v. New York Firemen's Ins. Co. (1815), 12 Johns. R. 128; De Wolf v. New York Firemen's Ins. Co. (1822), 20 Johns. R. 214; 3 Kent, Com. 281; 2 Duer, 523; 2 Parsons, 178.

(x) Boyd v. Dubois (1811), 3 Camp. 133.

Sect. 621. fully and truly all material facts relative to the state the ship was in at the time the last intelligence left her; and it is for the underwriters to require further information if they wish it, especially where the letter laid before them expressly refers to a prior communication as to the state of the ship in the earlier part of the same voyage (*y*).

Inference from high rate of premium.

622. The payment of a very high premium may be evidence that the underwriter accepted the risk as an unusually hazardous one and waived the disclosure of a particular matter.

Court v. Martineau.

A Liverpool merchant directed his London broker to effect insurance on a prize ship, informing him by letter that should the ship arrive, he (the merchant) would send up an express to communicate the fact. The broker delayed insuring to give time for the arrival of the express, and, none having arrived, effected an insurance at 50 guineas per cent. without saying anything about the non-arrival of the express. It was held that, under the circumstances of the case, and especially the enormous amount of premium, this was not a fatal concealment; the underwriter ought to have inquired (*z*).

Apprehensions.

623. Although it be fatal to represent untruthfully that previous underwriters have taken the proposed risk at the same or a lower premium than that offered (*a*), yet the assured is not bound to disclose the estimate formed by other underwriters of the risk, that they have declined it, or what their apprehensions or opinions were respecting it (*b*). Nor

---

(*y*) Freeland *v.* Glover (1806), 7 East, 457.

(*z*) Court *v.* Martineau (1782), 3 Dougl. 161; Cantiere Meccanico Brindisino *v.* Janson, [1912] 3 K. B. at p. 466. See Duer, vol. ii. pp. 568, 569.

(*a*) Sibbald *v.* Hill (1814), 2 Dow, 263.

(*b*) Lebon *v.* Straits Ins. Co. (1894) (C. A.), 10 Times L. R. 517; Glasgow Ass. Corpn. *v.* Symondson (1911), 16 Com. Cas. 109. The same has been held in the United States. Ruggles *v.* General Int. Ins. Co. (1825), 4 Mason, 74; Clason *v.* Smith (1812), 3 Wash. Circ. R. 156; 1 Phillips, s. 578.

need he communicate the fears and apprehensions of foreign correspondents, or even the state of his own mind as to matters of mere opinion (*c*): it is enough to state the facts on which such apprehensions are founded (*d*).

Sect. 623.

The assured on a policy on a ship " at and from Riga," &c., at the time of effecting the policy were in possession of a letter from their correspondents in that place, stating that a great sensation had been produced there by an order of the Russian Government to send the papers of all vessels arriving at Riga to St. Petersburg, and that the ship on which the policy was effected must share the same fate with the rest; this letter was not shown to the underwriters, but the broker stated, as a fact, that the ship's papers had been sent to St. Petersburg for examination. Lord Ellenborough held that it was enough that the broker had communicated the fact of the ship's papers being sent to St. Petersburg for examination (*e*).

Bell *v.* Bell.

624. "The assured," says Lord Mansfield, "need not disclose what lessens the risk agreed and understood to be run " (*f*).

What lessens the risk.

Thus, to take the instances furnished by his Lordship: " If the underwriter insures for three years, he needs not to be told any circumstances to show it may be over in two; so if he insures a voyage, with liberty of deviation, he needs not to be told what tends to show there will be no deviation " (*g*).

625. Where a fact is a matter of inference, and the materials for informing the judgment of the underwriter are common to both parties, the assured is not bound to make any communication on the subject (*h*).

Matters of inference.

(*c*) Cantiere Meccanico Brindisino *v.* Janson, [1912] 3 K. B. 452; see the judgment of Buckley, L. J., at p. 471.
(*d*) Bell *v.* Bell (1810), 2 Camp. 479.
(*e*) Bell *v.* Bell (1810), 2 Camp. 475.

(*f*) See Mar. Ins. Act, 1906, s. 18, sub-s. 3 (a), *ante*, § 609.
(*g*) Carter *v.* Boehm (1766), 3 Burr. 1909.
(*h*) Per Cockburn, C. J., Bates *v.* Hewitt (1867), L. R. 2 Q. B. 595, 605; Gandy *v.* Adelaide Ins. Co. (1871), L. R. 6 Q. B. 746.

Sect. 625.   By the rules of Lloyd's Register, a ship classed in it A 1 for seven years is required, in order to retain that class, to undergo a half-time survey in the fourth year. If the survey is satisfactory she retains her class, and the letters "H. T.," with the date of the survey, are placed opposite the entry of her name in the register. The plaintiff, the owner of a vessel classed A 1, informed Lloyd's surveyor, when her half-time survey was due, that he would not continue her in Lloyd's Register. Shortly afterwards he effected an insurance on her for a year with the defendant, who at the time referred to the register and, finding her classed A 1, took the risk at the rate for a ship so classed. Nineteen days afterwards, the ship was struck off the register, and subsequently she was lost. The Court of Queen's Bench held, Cockburn, C. J., dissenting, that the plaintiff was not bound to disclose the fact that he had resolved not to let the ship undergo the survey; for the underwriter ought to have seen from the entry in the register that the time for the survey had passed, and that no survey had been held. The Chief Justice refused to apply the rule which he had laid down in Bates v. Hewitt, on the ground that the fact which was not disclosed was a matter of positive knowledge to the plaintiff, and only of possible inference from imperfect materials to the underwriter. (It was in evidence that the period for the half-time survey was not always strictly observed.)

The jury found that the fact that the plaintiff had resolved not to continue the ship on the list was not material. The majority of the Court declined to say that this finding was wrong. Cockburn, C. J., however, thought that this fact was material. The refusal to submit to the survey, he said, led fairly to the inference that the owner was conscious that the condition of the vessel had so far deteriorated, that the result of the survey would be unfavourable. Applied to a time policy, as this was, the opinion of the Chief Justice, it is submitted, has great force (*i*).

(*i*) Gandy *v.* Adelaide Ins. Co. (1871), L. R. 6 Q. B. 746.

626. "Whether any particular circumstance, which is not disclosed, be material or not is, in each case, a question of fact" (*k*).

Sect. 626.
Materiality a question of fact.

Therefore the materiality of the facts concealed is a question mainly for the jury, whose finding thereon is not lightly disturbed, unless, indeed, it is clearly against the weight of evidence, or the result of erroneous direction by the Judge presiding at the trial (*l*).

Materiality of concealment, how proved.

Whether the jury, in forming their judgment upon the materiality of the fact concealed, may be assisted by the evidence of skilled witnesses, such as brokers, underwriters, &c., called to give their opinion whether the fact, in their judgment, was one which, if communicated to a prudent underwriter, would be likely materially to influence him in his estimate of the risk, is a question that has been very much canvassed in this country, and on which the authorities are indecisive.

Evidence of skilled witnesses.

Lord Mansfield (*m*), Sir Vicary Gibbs (*n*), and Lord Denman (*o*) have maintained that the evidence is inadmissible; on the other hand, Lord Kenyon (*p*), Holroyd, J. (*q*), Lord Tenterden (*r*), and Tindal, C. J. (*s*), have all held this evi-

Authorities against its admissibility.
Authorities in its favour.

(*k*) Mar. Ins. Act, 1906, s. 18 (4).
(*l*) See Willes *v.* Glover (1804), 1 B. & P. N. R. 14; Littledale *v.* Dixon (1805), *ibid.* 151; Bridges *v.* Hunter (1813), 1 M. & S. 15; Elton *v.* Larkins (1831), 8 Bing. 198; Westbury *v.* Aberdein (1837), 2 M. & W. 267; Mackintosh *v.* Marshall (1843), 11 M. & W. 116; Gandy *v.* Adelaide Ins. Co. (1871), L. R. 6 Q. B. 746.

(*m*) In Carter *v.* Boehm (1766), 3 Burr. 1909. Judge Duer points out that this was a case of a very unusual insurance, not against any marine risk, but against the capture by enemies of a fort in the East Indies. The previous experience of a broker could furnish him with no light or data to guide his judgment on the question proposed to be asked. 2 Duer, 783.

(*n*) At N. P., in Durrell *v.* Bederley (1816), 1 Holt, 283.

(*o*) In Campbell *v.* Rickards (1833), 5 B. & Ad. 840.

(*p*) Chaurand *v.* Angerstein (1791), Peake, N. P. 43.

(*q*) Berthon *v.* Loughman (1817), 2 Stark. 229.

(*r*) Rickards *v.* Murdock (1830), 10 B. & Cr. 527.

(*s*) Chapman *v.* Walton (1833), 10 Bing. 57. In this case the opinion of brokers was given in evidence, not on a question of materiality, but on the question what alterations a skilful broker would have made in the policy. The principle involved is, however,

Sect. 626. dence admissible; and it was also admitted without objection in two reported cases which came respectively before Sir James Mansfield (*t*) and Lord Ellenborough (*u*), in the former of which it had a material influence on the judgment, both of the Court and jury.

Law in the United States on this point.
In the United States the leading authorities, including Chancellor Kent (*x*), Story, J. (*y*), and Judge Duer (*z*), are all in favour of the admissibility of this evidence.

Conclusion.
The arguments in favour of the admission of this evidence far outweighed, in Arnould's opinion, those which have been urged against it.

Since the learned author wrote, the evidence of underwriters and brokers on such questions has been frequently resorted to without objection (*a*); and it is now settled practice to admit their evidence.

Onus et modus probandi.
627. The burthen of proof of concealment lies on him who pleads it. In the days when parties to the cause could not be examined as witnesses, it was held that, whenever it was proved to the satisfaction of the jury that the assured, before the policy was effected, was in possession of facts which would probably have induced the underwriter to decline the risk or ask a higher premium than that at which the policy was actually effected, there was a fair presumption that the facts were not communicated (*b*). In the present state of the

---

the same. See also Elton *v.* Larkins (1832), 5 C. & P. 392, tried the year before the decision of Chapman *v.* Walton and Campbell *v.* Rickards.

(*t*) Littledale *v.* Dixon (1805), 1 B. & P. N. R. 151.

(*u*) Haywood *v.* Rodgers (1804), 4 East, 590.

(*x*) 3 Kent, Com. 284, n. (*b*).

(*y*) Per Story, J., in M'Lanahan *v.* Universal Ins. Co. (1828), 1 Peters, S. C. R. 188, cited 2 Duer, 786.

(*z*) 2 Duer, Ins. 783—789. The matter is fully discussed, and the authorities reviewed in the notes to Carter *v.* Boehm, in Smith's Leading Cases, vol. i. See, also, *ante*, §§ 158—160.

(*a*) See, *e.g.*, Ionides *v.* Pender (1874), L. R. 9 Q. B. 531; Herring *v.* Janson (1895), 1 Com. Cas. 177; Thames & Mersey Mar. Ins. Co. *v.* "Gunford" Ship Co., [1911] A. C. 529; Scottish Shire Line, Ltd. *v.* London & Prov. Co., [1912] 3 K. B. at p. 70.

(*b*) See Robertson *v.* Marjoribanks (1819), 2 Stark. 575; and Elkin *v.* Janson (1845), 13 M. & W. 655. Duer considers that the

law it would not be safe for the underwriter defending, if the policy was effected with him personally, to rely on evidence to this effect and refrain from giving evidence in person under this plea. It must, moreover, be proved on his behalf—1, that the facts were known to the plaintiff before the conclusion of the contract (c); and, 2, that these facts were of such a nature that, if communicated, it is unreasonable to suppose that the underwriter would have taken the risk, at all events, on the same terms (d).

good sense of the matter is not to require further proof from the underwriter. 2 Duer, 685, 686.

(c) Mar. Ins. Act, 1906, ss. 18, 21.

(d) Per Blackburn, J., in Ionides v. Pender (1874), L. R. 9 Q. B. 531; and in Stribley v. Imperial Mar. Ins. Co. (1876), 1 Q. B. D. 507; 2 Duer, Ins. 685, 686.

END OF VOL. I.

AUGUST, 1916.

A

SELECTION

OF

RECENT LAW WORKS

PUBLISHED BY

STEVENS & SONS, LIMITED,

119 & 120, CHANCERY LANE, LONDON.

---

* A Discount of **20 per cent.** off all new Books (except where marked *net*) for Cash with Order. (Carriage or Postage extra.)

Complete Catalogue of Law Works post free.

A B C GUIDE TO THE PRACTICE OF THE SUPREME COURT, 1916. *Net,* 5s.
"Of great service to the profession."—*Solicitors' Journal.*

ACCOUNTS.—Hodsoll's Practical Accounts for Executors and Trustees. 1914. *Net,* 10s. 6d.
"Invaluable to law and accountancy students, solicitors and others."—*Law Times.*

ADVOCACY.—Harris' Hints on Advocacy.—Fourteenth Edition. 1911. 7s. 6d.
"Deserves to be carefully read by the young barrister whose career is yet before him."—*Law Magazine.*

AGRICULTURAL LAW.—Spencer's Agricultural Holding Acts. Fifth Edition. With Notes. 1911 to 1915. 8s.
"A thoroughly practical and useful treatise."—*Saturday Review.*

ANNUAL COUNTY COURTS PRACTICE, 1916. (India paper edition 3s. 6d. extra.) 1l. 5s.
"It admirably fulfils the essential requisites of a practice book."—*Law Times.*

ANNUAL PRACTICE, 1916. (India paper edition 3s. 6d. extra.) *Net,* 1l. 5s.
"A book which every practising English lawyer <u>must</u> have."—*Law Quarterly Review.*

ANNUAL STATUTES, 1915. 15s.

BANKING.—Hart's Law of Banking.—Third Edition. 1914. 1*l*. 12*s*.

"The best all-round work on banking law which is in existence."—*Financial News*.

BANKRUPTCY.—Aggs' Handbook on Bankruptcy. 1915. Net, 4*s*.

Lawrance's Deeds of Arrangement, with Precedents. Eighth Edition. By SYDNEY E. WILLIAMS. 1914. 7*s*. 6*d*.

"Concise, practical, and reliable."—*Law Times*.

Williams' Law and Practice in Bankruptcy.—Eleventh Edition. By E. W. HANSELL and M. E. HANSELL. 1915. 1*l*. 10*s*.

"The leading text-book on bankruptcy."—*Law Journal*.

CARRIERS.—Disney's Law of Carriage by Railway.—Fourth Edition. 1915. 7*s*. 6*d*.

"Can be cordially recommended to the lawyer."—*Law Times*.

CHANCERY.—Daniell's Chancery Practice.—Eighth Edition. By SYDNEY E. WILLIAMS and F. GUTHRIE-SMITH. 2 vols. 1914. 5*l*. 5*s*.

Daniell's Chancery Forms and Precedents.—Sixth Edition. By R. WHITE, F. E. W. NICHOLS and H. G. GARRETT. 1914. 2*l*. 10*s*.

"The two volumes on Practice and the one volume of Forms constitute together a most valuable work on the practice of the Chancery Division."—*Law Quarterly Review*.

COMPANY LAW.—Palmer's Company Law. A Practical Handbook for Lawyers and Business Men. Tenth Edition. 1916. 15*s*.

"Palmer's 'Company Law' is one of the most useful and convenient text-books on the practitioner's bookshelf."—*Law Times*.

Palmer's Company Precedents.—Eleventh Edition.
Part I. General Forms. 1912. 2*l*.
Part II. Winding-up Forms and Practice. 1912. 1*l*. 14*s*.
Part III. Debentures and Debenture Stock. 1912. 1*l*. 6*s*.

"Palmer's works on Company Law are all beyond criticism."—*Law Magazine*.

COMPANY LAW—*continued.*

Palmer's Private Companies.—Twenty-ninth Edition. 1915. Net, 1s.

Palmer's Shareholders', Directors', and Voluntary Liquidators' Legal Companion.—Twenty-ninth Edition. 1915. Net, 2s. 6d.

CONSTITUTIONAL LAW.—Ridges' Constitutional Law of England.—Second Edition. 1915. 15s.

"It enables the student to obtain a completer view of the whole field than is obtainable from any other book with which we are acquainted."—*Law Notes.*

CONTRACTS.—Addison's Law of Contracts.—Eleventh Edition. By W. E. GORDON and J. RITCHIE. 1911. 2l. 2s.

"Among all the works on Contracts, there is none more useful to the practitioner than Addison."—*Law Times.*

Leake's Principles of the Law of Contracts.—Sixth Edition. By A. E. RANDALL. 1911. 1l. 12s.

"A full and reliable guide to the principles of the English Law of Contract."—*Law Journal.*

Pollock's Principles of Contract.—Eighth Edition. 1911. 1l. 8s.

"There is no book on the English Law of Contract which deals so lucidly and yet so comprehensively as this."—*Law Journal.*

CONVEYANCING.—Prideaux's Forms and Precedents in Conveyancing.—Twenty-first Edition. By B. L. CHERRY and R. BEDDINGTON. 2 vols. 1913. 4l. 4s.

"'Prideaux' is the best work on Conveyancing."—*Law Journal.*

Wolstenholme's Conveyancing and Settled Land Acts.—Tenth Edition. By B. L. CHERRY, A. E. RUSSELL and C. V. RAWLENCE. 1913. 1l. 5s.

"The work is valuable not only as an accurate statement of the present law, but as the most reliable guide on matters of detail intended to be covered by the new legislation."—*Law Journal.*

COPYHOLD ENFRANCHISEMENT.—Lloyd's Practice in Enfranchisements under the Copyhold Act, 1894. 1913. 5s.

"The book is well arranged and well written, and the subject is so clearly dealt with as to be easily understood."—*Law Notes.*

CRIMINAL LAW.—Archbold on Indictments.—With Forms. By H. D. ROOME. 1916. 10s. 6d.

Russell's Treatise on Crimes and Misdemeanors.—Seventh Edition. By W. F. CRAIES and L. W. KERSHAW. 3 vols. 1909. 4l. 10s.

*** May be had in 2 vols. bound in buckram, price 4l. 14s. 6d.

"Indispensable in every Court of criminal justice here and in our colonies."—*The Times.*

DEATH DUTIES.—Webster-Brown's Finance Acts.—Third Edition. 1915. 12s. 6d.

"Contains much practical advice which will be of substantial assistance to practitioners."—*The Times.*

DICTIONARY.—Wharton's Law Lexicon.—Twelfth Edition. By E. A. WURTZBURG. 1916. 2l. 2s.

"The most useful of legal works."—*Law Journal.*

The Pocket Law Lexicon.—Fourth Edition. 1905. 6s. 6d.

"A wonderful little legal Dictionary."—*Law Students' Journal.*

DIGEST.—Mews' Quinquennial Digest, 1911-1915. By JOHN MEWS. 1916. 2l. 10s.

DIVORCE.—Browne and Watts' Law and Practice in Divorce and Matrimonial Causes.—Eighth Edition. By J. H. WATTS. 1913. 1l. 8s.

"The practitioner's standard work on divorce practice."—*Law Quarterly Review.*

EASEMENTS.—Goddard's Treatise on the Law of Easements.—Seventh Edition. 1910. 1l. 5s.

"Nowhere has the subject been treated so exhaustively."—*Law Times.*

Innes' Digest of the Law of Easements.—Eighth Edition. 1911. 7s. 6d.

"The student will find in it everything that he wants, while the practitioner will be glad to have so safe and comprehensive a guide."—*Law Journal.*

EQUITY.—Seton's Forms of Judgments and Orders. With Practical Notes. Seventh Edition. By A. R. INGPEN, K.C., F. T. BLOXAM and H. G. GARRETT. 3 vols. 1912. 6l.

"A most valuable and indispensable work."—*Law Journal.*

Smith's Practical Exposition of the Principles of Equity.—Fifth Edition. 1914. 21s.

"Useful to both practitioner and student alike."—*Law Students' Journal.*

EVIDENCE.—Tregarthen's Law of Hearsay Evidence.—
1915. Net, 5s.
"An elaborate and detailed account of a very imperfectly understood topic."—*Law Quarterly Review.*

EXECUTORS.—Ingpen's Treatise on the Law relating to Executors and Administrators.—Second Edition. 1914. Net, 1l. 5s.
"The book may be recommended, with confidence, as accurate, practical, and learned."—*Law Quarterly Review.*

FORMS.—Bowstead's Collection of Forms and Precedents other than Conveyancing, Company, Local Government and Practice Forms.—2 vols. 1914. Net, 2l. 10s.
"An indispensable adjunct to every practising lawyer's library."—*Law Journal.*

Chitty's Forms of Civil Proceedings in the King's Bench Division.—Fourteenth Edition. By T. W. CHITTY, E. H. CHAPMAN and P. CLARK. 1912. 2l. 2s.
"An indispensable adjunct to every working lawyer's library."—*Law Journal.*

Daniell's Chancery Forms and Precedents.—Sixth Edition. By R. WHITE, F. E. W. NICHOLS and H. G. GARRETT. 1914. 2l. 10s.
"The standard work on Chancery Procedure."—*Law Quarterly Review.*

HIRE-PURCHASE SYSTEM.—Russell's Practical Manual of Hire-Trade Law.—Fifth Edition. 1914. 7s. 6d.
"The book is full of practical suggestions."—*Solicitors' Journal.*

INSURANCE.—Arnould on the Law of Marine Insurance and Average.—Ninth Edition. By E. L. DE HART and R. I. SIMEY. 2 vols. 1914. 3l. 10s.
"Arnould's 'Marine Insurance' is recognised throughout the British Empire and the United States as a standard work of almost judicial authority."—*Law Journal.*

Stone's Insurance and Workmen's Compensation Cases.—2 vols. 1914. Net, 2l. 2s.
"A very valuable compendium of the case law of insurance."—*Solicitors' Journal.*

INTERNATIONAL LAW.—Cheng's Rules of Private International Law Determining Capacity to Contract. 1916. 7s. 6d.

Wheaton's Elements of International Law.—Fifth English Edition. By COLEMAN PHILLIPSON, LL.D. With an Introduction by the Right Hon. Sir FREDERICK POLLOCK, Bart., D.C.L., LL.D. 1916. 1l. 15s.
"Wheaton stands too high for criticism."—*Law Times.*

LAND VALUES.—Napier's New Land Taxes and their Practical Application.—Second Edition. 1912. 18s.
"Napier's explanatory summary of the new taxation and his notes on the sections are admirable."—*Law Quarterly Review.*

LANDLORD AND TENANT.—Woodfall's Law of Landlord and Tenant.—Nineteenth Edition. By W. Hanbury Aggs. 1912. 1l. 18s.
"Woodfall is really indispensable to the practising lawyer, of whatever degree he may be."—*Law Journal.*

LEADING CASES.—Caporn's Selected Cases on the Law of Contracts.—Second Edition. 1914. 15s.

Petrides' Student's Cases, illustrative of all branches of the Law. 1910. 10s. 6d.
"The cases appear to be well chosen and correctly stated."—*Solicitors' Journal.*

Randall's Selection of Leading Cases in Equity.—1912. 9s.
"One of the foremost, if not the best, of Equity case books."—*Law Students' Journal.*

Shirley's Selection of Leading Cases in the Common Law.—Ninth Edition. By R. Watson. 1913. 16s.
"The selection is very large, though all are distinctly 'Leading Cases,' and the notes are by no means the least meritorious part of the work."—*Law Journal.*

LEGAL HISTORY.—Deans' Student's Legal History.—Third Edition. 1913. 7s. 6d.
"There is no better short introduction to the study of the law."—*Law Notes.*

LIBEL AND SLANDER.—Ball's Law of Libel as affecting Newspapers and Journalists.—1912. 6s.
"A well-arranged and well-executed work."—*Law Journal.*

Odgers' Digest of the Law of Libel and Slander.—Fifth Edition. 1911. 1l. 15s.
"Should be found on the shelves of every practitioner."—*Law Students' Journal.*

LUNACY.—Heywood and Massey's Lunacy Practice.—Fourth Edition. 1911. 1l. 10s.
"A complete treatise on lunacy practice."—*Solicitors' Journal.*

MAGISTRATES' PRACTICE, 1916.—By C. M. Atkinson, Stipendiary Magistrate for Leeds. 20s.

MENTAL DEFICIENCY.—Davey's Law relating to the Mentally Defective.—Second Edition. 1914. 10s.
"This admirably arranged and handy book."—*Law Journal.*

MORTGAGE.—Coote's Treatise on the Law of Mortgages.—Eighth Edition. By SYDNEY E. WILLIAMS. 2 vols. 1912. 3*l*. 3*s*.

"It is essentially a practitioner's book, and we pronounce it 'one of the best.'"—*Law Notes.*

NATIONAL INSURANCE.—Watts on National Insurance.—1913. 12*s*. 6*d*.

"Mr. Watts has studied this complicated Act with great care, and produced a very elaborate and complete edition."—*Law Magazine.*

NOTARY.—Brooke on the Office and Practice of a Notary.—Seventh Edition. By J. CRANSTOUN. 1913. 1*l*. 5*s*.

"The book is an eminently practical one, and contains a very complete collection of notarial precedents."—*Law Journal.*

PARTNERSHIP.—Pollock's Digest of the Law of Partnership.—Tenth Edition. 1915. 10*s*.

PLEADING.—Bullen and Leake's Precedents of Pleadings.—Seventh Edition. By W. BLAKE ODGERS, K.C., and WALTER BLAKE ODGERS. 1915. 2*l*. 2*s*.

"The standard work on modern pleading."—*Law Journal.*

Eustace's Practical Hints on Pleading.—1907. 5*s*.

"Especially useful to young solicitors and students of both branches of the legal profession."—*Law Times.*

Odgers' Principles of Pleading and Practice.—Seventh Edition. 1912. 12*s*. 6*d*.

"The safest possible guide in all matters affecting pleading and practice."—*Law Journal.*

POOR LAW SETTLEMENT.—Davey's Poor Law Settlement and Removal.—Second Edition. 1913. 15*s*.

"The law of the subject is most industriously and lucidly set out."—*The Spectator.*

POWERS.—Farwell's Concise Treatise on Powers.—Third Edition. By C. J. W. FARWELL and F. K. ARCHER. 1916. 1*l*. 15*s*.

RATES AND RATING.—Davey's Law of Rating.—1913. 1*l*. 10*s*.

"A complete and exhaustive treatise on the subject, beyond doubt the most comprehensive which has yet appeared."—*Law Journal.*

RECEIVERS AND MANAGERS.—Riviere's Law relating to Receivers and Managers.—1912. 9*s*.

"A reliable guide to an intricate subject, and should be of great service to practitioners."—*Law Journal.*

TORTS.—Addison's Law of Torts.—Eighth Edition. By W. E. GORDON and W. H. GRIFFITH. 1906.   1*l*. 18*s*.

"Essentially the practitioner's text-book."—*Law Journal.*

Pollock's Law of Torts.—Tenth Edition. 1916.   26*s*.

"Concise, logically arranged, and accurate."—*Law Times.*

*** An Analysis of the above for Students.—Second Edition. By J. K. MANNOOCH. 1916.   5*s*.

TRADE UNIONS.—Greenwood's Law relating to Trade Unions.—1911.   10*s*.

"An admirably clear exposition of the law."—*Law Quarterly Review.*

A SUPPLEMENT to above, including the Trade Union Act, 1913. 1913.   Net, 3*s*. 6*d*.

The two works together, net, 10s.

TRUSTS AND TRUSTEES.—Godefroi on the Law of Trusts and Trustees.—Fourth Edition. By SYDNEY E. WILLIAMS. 1915.   1*l*. 10*s*.

"An eminently practical and useful work."—*Law Times.*

WAR.—Chartres' Munitions of War Acts.—An Analysis, with Notes. 1916.   Net, 5*s*.

Higgins' Armed Merchant Ships.—1914.   Net, 1*s*. 6*d*.

Page's War and Alien Enemies.—The Law affecting their Personal and Trading Rights; and herein of Contraband of War and the Capture of Prizes at Sea. Second Edition. 1915.   Net, 6*s*. 6*d*.

Scott's Trading with the Enemy.—The Effect of War on Contracts. Second Edition. 1914.   Net, 2*s*. 6*d*.

Stringer's Practice of the High Court under the Courts (Emergency Powers) Act, 1914, &c.. 1915. Net, 3*s*. 6*d*.

WILLS.—Theobald's Concise Treatise on the Law of Wills.—Seventh Edition. 1908.   1*l*. 15*s*.

"Indispensable to the conveyancing practitioner."—*Law Times.*

WORKMEN'S COMPENSATION.—Knowles' Law relating to Compensation for Injuries to Workmen.—Third Edition. 1912.   15*s*.

"Its merits entitle it to rank with the best of the treatises on the subject."—*Law Quarterly Review.*

Workmen's Compensation Reports.—A complete Series of Reports of Cases on the subject of Workmen's Compensation. With Annotated Index.

Subscription for 1916, 15s. net (postage 1s. extra).

STEVENS & SONS, Ltd., 119 & 120, Chancery Lane, London.